PUBLII VIRGILII MARONIS

OPERA

OR

THE WORKS OF VIRGIL.

WITH COPIOUS NOTES,

MYTHOLOGICAL, BIOGRAPHICAL, HISTORICAL, GEOGRAPHICAL, PHILOSOPHICAL, ASTRONOMICAL, CRITICAL, AND EXPLANATORY, IN ENGLISH;

COMPILED FROM THE BEST COMMENTATORS, WITH MANY THAT ARE NEW.

TOGETHER WITH

AN ORDO OF THE MOST INTRICATE PARTS OF THE TEXT

UPON THE SAME PAGE WITH THE TEXT.

DESIGNED FOR THE USE OF

STUDENTS IN THE COLLEGES, ACADEMIES, AND OTHER SEMINARIES, IN THE UNITED STATES.

SPECIALLY CALCULATED TO LIGHTEN THE LABOUR OF THE TEACHER, AND TO LEAD THE STUDENT INTO A KNOWLEDGE OF THE POET.

TO WHICH IS ADDED

A Table of Reference.

BY THE REV. J. G. COOPER, A. M.

NEW YORK:
SHELDON AND COMPANY, PUBLISHERS,
498 AND 500 BROADWAY.
1868.

MANUFACTURED BY
CASE, LOCKWOOD & CO.,
Printers, Electrotypers and Bookbinders
HARTFORD, CONN.

RECOMMENDATIONS.

NEW-YORK, July 6, 1815.

An edition of the Works of Virgil, upon the plan adopted by the Rev. J. G. Cooper, I think preferable to those usually put into the hands of boys. His notes and explanations, so far as I have examined them, are both copious and judicious. Believing that classical literature will be promoted thereby, I do cheerfully recommend the work.

WILLIAM HARRIS, D. D.
President of Columbia College.

In the above opinion expressed by Dr. Harris, we do fully and cordially unite

JOHN BOWDEN, D. D.
Professor of Rhetoric, &c. &c. Columbia College.
Rev. EDMUND D. BARRY,
Principal of the Ep. Academy, New-York.
JOHN BORLAND, A. M.
Teacher of a Select Classical School, New-York.
TILLOTSON BRUNSON, D. D.
Principal of the Ep. Academy, Cheshire, Connecticut.

BALTIMORE, Oct. 20, 1825.

In the above opinion expressed by Dr. Harris, we do fully and cordially unite.

W. E. WYATT, D. D.
Associate Min. of St. Paul's Parish.
Rev. JOHN ALLEN, A. M.
Professor of Math. in the University of Maryland, and author of an edition of the Elements of Euclid, &c. &c.

NEW-YORK, April, 1827.

In the above opinion expressed by Dr. Harris, I do fully and cordially agree.

JAMES RENWICK,
Professor of Nat. Philosophy and Chemistry in Col. College.

PHILADELPHIA, June, 1827.

In the above opinion expressed by Dr. Harris, I do fully and cordially agree.

JAMES ROSS, L. L. D.
Author of a Latin Grammar, &c. &c.

LEXINGTON, Ky. April 1, 1825.

Having recently examined the Rev. J. G. Cooper's proposed edition of the Works of Virgil, I have no hesitation in giving my opinion, that the plan which he has pursued is excellent, and the execution highly creditable to his talents and scholarship. Such a work will greatly facilitate the study of the poet, on the part of the youthful learner. It will give him a correct idea of the meaning of the author in the more difficult passages; and by its copious notes upon ancient history, and mythology, will enable him to relish beauties that are now rarely perceived in the early course of classical instruction. I have no doubt but that its appearance will be welcomed by the intelligent and discerning, as a publication admirably adapted to enlist the feelings, and stimulate the application of youth, in the elementary schools of our country.

GEORGE T. CHAPMAN, D. D.
Professor of History, &c. &c. in Transylvania University, Ky.

BALTIMORE, Oct. 20, 1825.

The edition of the Works of Virgil proposed to be published by the Rev. J G. Cooper, appears to me, as far as a very partial examination of it has enabled me to judge, to be a work of merit, both as to the plan and execution. And I am persuaded, that its adoption into our Colleges and Seminaries of learning will greatly facilitate the acquisition of a correct knowledge of that elegant and distinguished poet.

JAMES KEMP, D. D.
Bishop of the Prot. Epis. Church in the state of Maryland.

So far as I have had opportunity to examine the manuscript of the Rev. J. G. Cooper for a new edition of the Works of Virgil, I highly approve of the plan, and think it well calculated to facilitate the study of the poet. It appears to be a leading object with Mr. Cooper, to lighten the burden of the student, by elucidating the difficult passages of the author, and by leading the youthful mind into a relish of his beauties and excellencies.

The substitution of an *Ordo* of the most intricate passages in the room of a general interpretation of the text, I consider a material advantage. While it removes the difficulties in the collocation of the words, it leads the student more directly to the text, and tends to fix his attention more closely upon the language of the poet. On the whole, I consider the work deserving of public patronage· and I wish him every encouragement in his endeavours to promote the interests of classical literature.

FRANCIS E. GODDARD, A. M
President of the Southern College, Bowling-Green, Ky.

November 6, 1823.

LOUISVILLE, Ky. December 20, 1823.

Having been favoured with the perusal of notes upon the Works of Virgil, compiled by the Rev. J. G. Cooper, together with an *Ordo* of the more intricate parts of the text, I am fully persuaded they are well calculated to assist the younger classical students to read and understand the poet, especially in the more difficult passages; to enlarge the mind in the Geography of the country, and to explain the mythology of the age in which he wrote.

The criticisms on the text are generally correct, and display an intimate acquaintance with the syntax of the Latin language: and I do not hesitate to say, that in my opinion, the work would be very useful in the Academies and Seminaries of the United States.

GIDEON BLACKBURN, D. D

CAMBRIDGE, MASS. May 10, 1815.

AN edition of the Works of Virgil, upon the plan adopted by the Rev. J. G Cooper, will. I am persuaded, be found useful in instruction It provides for a portion of that assistance in the interpretation of the poet, for which resort is frequently and injudiciously had to translations; while it is, at the same time, exempt from any of the disadvantages attending such a mode of studying this author.

JOHN T. KIRKLAND, D. D.
President of Harvard University.

HINGHAM, MASS. May 8, 1815.

From a partial examination of the manuscript copy of the Works of Virgil, with English notes, &c. by the Rev. J. G. Cooper, it appears to have been prepared with much labour and care. I have no doubt that a work of this kind would be of essential advantage to classical students, especially to those who have not made considerable progress in the Latin language, previous to their commencing the study of the poet.

DANIEL KIMBALL, A. M.
Principal of Derby Academy.

I fully assent to the opinion expressed above by Mr. Kimball, as to the value and usefulness of an edition of Virgil, upon the plan proposed by the Rev. Mr. Cooper.

HENRY WARE, D. D.
Professor of Divinity in Harv. University.

THE edition of the Works of Virgil, prepared by the Rev. J. G. Cooper, appears to be well calculated to facilitate a knowledge of the poet. To those who may wish to study the poet, without the aid of an instructor; and to instructors themselves, who have not enjoyed a correctly-classical education, it will be eminently useful.

JOHN S. J. GARDINER, D. D.

BOSTON, May, 1815.

At the request of the Rev. J. G. Cooper, I have cursorily examined a printed specimen of his proposed edition of the Works of Virgil; and am of opinion, that, if the whole should be executed in the manner of this sample, it will be deserving of patronage.

J. L. KINGSLEY,
Professor of the Latin Language.

YALE COLLEGE, April 14, 1827.

ELLWOOD SEMINARY, (near Philadelphia,) Dec. 9, 1826.

I have perused the specimen of your proposed edition of the Works of Virgil, which, I think, will deserve a reception into every classical Academy.

JAMES TATHAM.

Rev. J. G. COOPER.

From a specimen of the proposed edition of the Works of Virgil, by the Rev. J. G. Cooper, I am induced to believe the publication will be an aid to the cause of our literature, by going into use among the younger students.

HECTOR HUMPHREYS,
Professor of ancient Languages, Washington College.

HARTFORD, April 14, 1827

I highly approve of the plan adopted by the editor, having for many years believed such an edition of Virgil a great *desideratum* in our schools.

THOMAS DUGDALE, jr.
Teacher of Latin and Greek, in Friends' Academy, Philadelphia.

WASHINGTON CITY, Dec. 1825.

SIR—I am highly pleased with your edition of Virgil. I think the English notes will be of infinite advantage to the scholar, and very interesting to the teacher. I am anxious to have a sufficient number of copies to supply my school, as I am determined to use no other for the future.

Yours, respectfully,
A. R. PLUMLEY.

Rev. J. G. COOPER.

BOSTON, May 9th, 1815.

SIR—So far as I can judge of the plan on which you propose to publish an edition of Virgil, from the few pages of manuscript submitted to my inspection, I think it calculated to facilitate the progress of the learner; and peculiarly adapted to the younger class of pupils, who are with difficulty made to understand the notes in the original, when hurried, as they frequently are, into this author.

BENJAMIN A. GOULD,
Principal of the public Grammar School.

I cheerfully concur in approving the plan of Mr. Cooper's proposed edition of the Works of Virgil.

FRANCIS FELLOWS,
Associate Principal of the Mount Pleasant Classical Institution, (near Amherst,) Mass.

April, 1827.

We, the subscribers, do approve of the plan adopted by the Rev J. G Cooper for a *new edition* of the Works of Virgil: and, when published, we do hereby recommend his work to those classical students, who may attend our respective Seminaries.

Rev. WM. RAFFERTY, D. D.
Principal of St. John's College, Maryland.
EDWARD SPARKS, M. D.
Professor of Languages in St. John's College, Md.
Rev. SAM'L. K. JENNINGS, M. D.
Principal of the Asbury College, Baltimore.
MICHAEL POWER, A. M.
Professor of Languages, Asbury College Baltimore.
Rev. TIMOTHY CLOWES, L. L. D.
Principal of Washington College, Maryland.
Rev. HENRY L DAVIS, D. D.
Principal of Wilmington College, Delaware.
Rev. FREDERIC BEASELY, D. D.
Provost of the University of Pennsylvania.
J. G. THOMSON, A. M.
Professor of Languages of the University of Penn.
B. CONSTANT,
Principal of the Literary, Scientific and Military Lyceum, Germantown, Penn
JOHN BORLAND,
Professor of Classical Literature in the Collegiate School, New-York.
Rev. E. D. BARRY, D. D.
Principal of a Classical Academy, New-York.
A. PARTRIDGE,
Superintendant of the American Literary, Scientific and Military Academy, Middletown, Conn
E. B. WILLISTON,
Professor of the Greek and Latin languages in the A. L. S. and Military Academy, Middletown, Conn
Rev. JOSEPH SPENCER,
Professor of Languages in Dickinson College, Pennsylvania
Rev. JAMES WILTBANK,
Principal of the Grammar School of the University of Pennsylvania.
Rev. SAMUEL B. WYLIE, D. D.
Principal of a Classical Academy, Philadelphia.
GEORGE HALENBAKE,
Principal of a Classical and Mathematical Academy, Philadelphia.
JOHN ANDERSON,
Principal of a Classical Academy, Philadelphia.
C. FELLT,
Principal of a Classical Academy, Philadelphia.
W. J. BIRKEY,
Principal of a Classical Academy, Philadelphia.
HENRY HOOD,
Principal of a Classical Academy, Philadelphia
B. J. SCHIPPER,
Principal of a Classical Academy, Philadelphia.

We, the subscribers, do approve of the plan adopted by the Rev. J. G. Cooper for a *new edition* of the Works of Virgil; and, when published, we do hereby recommend his work to those classical students, who may attend our respective Seminaries.

Rev. WM. BALLANTINE,
Principal of a Classical Academy, Philadelphia.
WM. MANN, A. M.
Principal of a Classical Academy, Philadelphia.
J. P. ESPY,
Principal of a Classical Academy, Philadelphia.
DAVID PATTERSON,
Principal of a Classical Academy, New-York.
WM SHERWOOD,
Principal of a Classical Academy, New-York.
W. H. BOGART, A. B.
Principal of a Classical Academy, New-York.
JOSEPH PERRY, A. M.
Principal of a Classical Academy, New-York.
GOULD BROWN,
Principal of a Classical Academy, New-York.
JACOB T. BERGEN,
Principal of a Classical Academy, New-York
JAMES ANDERSON,
Classical Teacher in the La Fayette Seminary, N. York
J. SLOCOMB,
Principal of a Classical Academy, New-York.
SAMUEL U. BERRIAN,
Classical Teacher, New-York.
W. LORD,
Associate Principal of a Classical Academy, Baltimore.
A. ROGERS,
Principal of a Select Classical Academy, Baltimore.
JAMES STEEN,
Principal of the Wentworth Academy, Baltimore.
JOHN PRENTISS,
Princioal of a Classical Academy, Baltimore.
Rev. J. G. ROBERTSON,
Principal of a select Classical Academy, Baltimore.
JAMES GOULD,
Principal of a Classical Academy, Baltimore.
ELIJAH GARFIELD,
Teacher of Languages, Middletown, Conn.
ELIJAH P. BARROWS, Jr.
Preceptor of the Hartford Grammar School, Conn.
JOHN M. KEAGY, M. D.
Principal of the Harrisburg Academy, Penn.
BARNABAS BATES,
Principal of a Classical Academy, New-York.
THOMAS P. HAGGERTY,
Principal of a Classical Academy, Georgetown, D. C.

To Professors and Teachers of Classical Literature in the Colleges, Academies, and other Seminaries in the United States:

Gentlemen,

The very favorable opinion that many of you have expressed, of the plan and execution of this *Edition of the works of Virgil*, claims my respectful acknowledgments.

Every attempt to facilitate the acquisition of classical literature will, I am persuaded, meet your approbation; I shall, therefore, offer no apology for adding this new edition to the many others, already before the public.

Soon after I commenced the instruction of youth, I became sensible of the impropriety of the use of the editions of Virgil, then in our schools. Those of Ruæus and Davidson were generally, if not exclusively, read; both equally objectionable, the former by affording too little aid to the student in the illustration of the text, the latter by affording him too much. It was at this early period that I formed the plan of the present edition. Except the two last books of the Æneid, it was finished in the year 1815, as you will perceive by the date of several of the recommendations. Since which time, they have been completed, and the whole carefully revised and greatly improved. This delay in the publication gave me a further opportunity to become acquainted with the wants of students, especially in the early course of study, and to collect the opinions of teachers upon this subject. That opinion has uniformly been in favor of my plan; which takes a middle course between the opposite extremes of affording too little, and too much assistance to the student.

The partial *ordo* is designed to assist him in the more intricate parts of the text; and where recourse otherwise must be had to the teacher. The notes and explanations are copious. They embrace whatever was deemed necessary to elucidate the poet, and to lead the youthful mind to relish his beauties. Some of the more difficult passages I have translated; and, in general, where a word is used out of its common acceptation, I have given its sense and meaning in that particular place: and where commentators are not agreed upon the meaning of a word or phrase, I have given their respective opinions. In the text, I have adopted the reading of Heyne, except in a few instances, where the common reading appeared preferable.

To the Bucolics, Georgics, and Æneid, I have given, in the first instance, a general introduction; and to each Eclogue, and book of the Georgics and Æneid, a summary or particular introduction: so that the student, knowing beforehand the subject, and anticipating the beauties and excellences of the poet, will proceed with ease and pleasure, and in a manner catch his spirit. To each I have added a number of questions, to be asked by the teacher, and answered by the pupil. They may be increased or modified at discretion. This method of instruction, by question and answer, will be found useful. It serves to excite inquiry and attention on the part of the student, and affords the teacher a ready method of discovering the degree of knowledge which he has obtained of the subject. In this particular, I acknowledge my obligation to several eminent teachers, who suggested the improvement.

The commentators, to whom I am principally indebted, are Heyne, Ruæus, Dr. Trapp, Davidson, and Valpy. But it will be seen, in the course of the work, that I have not been confined to these alone. Wherever I found any thing useful, tending either to elucidate the poet, or to interest the student, I have taken it.

Throughout the whole, it has been a principal object with me, to render the poet intelligible, and to elucidate those passages which are obscure and intricate. To the whole is added, a table of reference to the notes, where any particular article is considered or passage explained.

To you, gentlemen, I present it, with the humble trust that it will be found to answer the purposes for which it was designed, namely, to lighten the labor of the teacher, and to facilitate the acquisition of a knowledge of the poet.

J. G. COOPER.

NEW YORK. Oct. 1827.

THE LIFE OF VIRGIL.

Publius Virgilius Maro was born at a village called Andes, about three miles from the city of Mantua, on the 15th day of October, in the year of Rome 684, and 70 years before the Christian era. Pompey the Great and Marcus Licinius Crassus were consuls.

His parents were in humble circumstances. His father cultivated a small farm for the maintenance of his family. His mother, whose name was Maia, was related to Quintilius Varus, who rose to be proconsul of Syria, and afterwards was appointed to the command of the Roman army in Germany.

The first seven years of his life were passed under his paternal roof: after which he was removed to Cremona, a town situated upon the banks of the Po, and not far from Mantua. While here, he distinguished himself in those studies suited to his age, and gave presage of his future eminence. In this pleasant retreat he passed ten years, till he assumed the *Toga virilis*, which, among the Romans, was at the age of 17. At an early period he showed himself to be a favorite of the Muses, and manifested a genius that one day was to rival the author of the Iliad. At this time Pompey and Crassus were in their second consulship.

From Cremona he removed to Mediolanum, a town not far distant, and soon after to Naples. Here he devoted his time to the study of the Greek language, of which he soon became master. By this means he was enabled to read the Greek poets in the original, to enter fully into their spirit, and to discover their beauties and excellencies. This proved of essential service to him in his future labors. With a mind thus stored with literature, and a taste formed by the best models, he entered upon the study of medicine, mathematics, and philosophy. These last, more especially, were his pleasure and delight, as he has intimated in several parts of his works.

He studied the Epicurean philosophy, then in much repute, under one Syro, an eminent teacher. He afterwards composed his Sixth Eclogue, with a view to compliment his preceptor, and to express a grateful remembrance of his instructions. Varus was a pupil with him at the same time. Here they contracted a friendship for each other, which continued during the remainder of their lives. Having finished his studies at Naples, which occupied several years, it is said, he visited Rome; but it is more probable that he returned to Mantua, and retired to his paternal inheritance. Here he acquired that practical information which so eminently qualified him for writing the Georgics.

A person of Virgil's extensive attainments, and above all, of his poetic genius, could not long remain in obscurity. His fame reached the ears of Pollio, who was no less distinguished for his love of literature, and of the muse, than for his military achievements. He was a particular friend of Antony, and under him commanded the troops in Cis-Alpine Gaul; in which Mantua was situated. Here he became acquainted with Virgil, who was introduced to him either by Varus or Gallus; both of whom our poet has mentioned in his Eclogues, in the most affectionate terms.

After the battle of Philippi, which proved fatal to the republican party, Augustus divided the lands in the neighborhood of Mantua among his veteran troops, to whom he was indebted for that victory. Virgil was involved in the common calamity. This circumstance, in all human appearance to be lamented, and which to others proved a heavy calamity, to our poet was the commencement of an illustrious career, and the harbinger of an immortal day.

Pollio, who entertained a sincere friendship for Virgil, and was well qualified to form a correct estimate of his talents and acquirements, becoming acquainted with his case, recommended him to Mæcenas, who was then at Rome, and held the highest place of honor and confidence with his prince. The friend of Pollio found also a friend in Mæcenas. He laid his case before Augustus, and by his influence with his prince, obtained the restoration of his estate. Virgil, at this time, probably was about 29 years of age. He immediately returned with the edict of the emperor for the restoration of his farm, which had fallen into the hands of one Areus, a centurion; but he was resisted and ill-treated by the new possessor, and forced to swim over the Mincius to save his life. This cruel treatment is the subject of the ninth Eclogue.

He went a second time to Rome upon the subject. But it is probable he never after resided upon his estate. A wider field now opened before him; and he made the seat of the empire the place of his residence. Here his acquaintance and friendship were sought by the most distinguished men; and the favorite of the Muses became also the favorite of Augustus.

With a view to compliment his prince, and to express the happy state of the empire under his administration, it is said, he composed the following distich, which, in a private manner, he affixed to the gate of the palace:

> Nocte pluit tota, redeunt spectacula mane:
> Divisum imperium cum Jove Cæsar habet.

Augustus was highly pleased with the compliment paid to him, and the delicate manner in which it was expressed; and he desired to find out the author. Virgil's modesty and diffidence prevented him from making an avowal. At length, one Bathyllus, a poet of inferior merit, had the hardihood to claim to be the author. The emperor richly rewarded him. This greatly mortified our poet, who wrote the same lines upon the gate of the palace, with the following one under them:

> Hos ego versiculos feci, tulit alter honores:

together with the beginning of another line in these words,

> Sic vos non vobis,

repeated three times. Augustus wished to find the author; and as the surest way of doing it, demanded that the lines should be finished. Several attempts were made without effect. Bathyllus was not able to do it; which led to a suspicion of his imposture. At last Virgil finished them, and thus avowed himself the author of the previous distich. The lines are as follow:

> Sic vos non vobis nidificatis aves;
> Sic vos non vobis vellera fertis oves;
> Sic vos non vobis mellificatis apes:
> Sic vos non vobis fertis aratra boves.

This detected the impostor, and covered him with ridicule and contempt.

About this time, at the suggestion of Pollio, Virgil commenced writing his Eclogues; which occupied him three years. The first was written to express his gratitude to his prince for the restoration of his lands. This he did in so delicate and modest a manner, that it raised him greatly in the estimation of his friends and countrymen: and the poet conferred a greater favor upon Augustus, by immortalizing this act of his beneficence, than he did by restoring to him his lands. The others were written upon various occasions, and for various purposes.

The Eclogues were extremely popular. So well were they received, that they were several times repeated upon the stage. Cicero, upon hearing them, was so much pleased, that he did not hesitate to say of the author: *Magnæ spes altera Romæ*, which words the poet afterwards introduced into the twelfth book of the Æneid, applied to Iülus. Virgil may be considered the first who introduced pastorals among the Romans. It is a fact worthy of notice, that he was the introducer, and at the same time the perfector, of this kind of writing. All succeeding poets have taken him as their model, and found the surest way to success to be, to copy his beauties. It is true, he was much indebted to Theocritus, who was the first pastoral writer of eminence among the Greeks. but he followed him with judgment, and improved upon him so much in correctness of taste, in purity of thought, and delicacy of expression, that we lose sight of the original. So much was he esteemed, that all classes of persons crowded to see him, whenever he appeared in public; and on entering the theatre, the people rose up to do him reverence, no less than to Augustus himself.

During the civil wars, agriculture had been much neglected: and so general had the distress become on that account, that serious apprehensions were entertained for the peace of Italy. All classes of people began to murmur, and to cast the blame upon Augustus, and his administration. In this state of things, it occurred to Mæcenas, that the most effectual method of averting the impending evils, and of restoring peace to the people, and confidence in the administration, was to revive the agricultural interests of the country. For this purpose, he desired Virgil to write a treatise upon agriculture. He well knew no person was better qualified for a work of this kind. He possessed an extensive knowledge of the subject, a correct taste, and could enliven it with the charms of poetic numbers; and he already possessed the confidence and affections of his countrymen.

After a short respite, he entered upon the work. That he might be less interrupted in its prosecution, he retired from Rome to Naples, a city more tranquil, and, at the same time, more healthy. In this pleasant retreat, removed from the bustle of the capital, the intrigue of courts, and the jarring interests of politics, he composed the Georgics—a poem, the most perfect and finished of any composition in the Latin language. He spent seven years in the work. The public expectation was raised high; but it was far surpassed: and Virgil conferred a greater blessing upon his country, than if, in the field, he had obtained the most splendid victory over its enemies.

The Georgics were every where well received, and Italy soon assumed a flourishing appearance. The people found themselves in the enjoyment of peace, plenty, and domestic happiness. The poet dedicated the work to his friend Mæcenas, a statesman distinguished equally for his love of literature and science, the correctness of his politics, and the wisdom of his councils.

Virgil was now forty years of age. At this time, he found himself in the possession of a large estate, chiefly from the liberality of his prince. His fame was coextensive with the empire, and the lovers of the muse courted his society. Among the particular friends of Virgil, may be reckoned Horace, a distinguished poet of that age, and a friend equally of Pollio and Mæcenas. Between these two favorites of the Muses there subsisted, during their lives, the most cordial friendship. How sincerely they esteemed each other, we may learn from an ode which Horace afterwards composed upon the occasion of Virgil's setting sail for Greece, on account of his health.

Having completed the Georgics, our poet soon commenced the Æneid an epic or heroic poem. This is the noblest species of poetic composition requiring a correct judgment, a lively imagination, and an universal knowledge. Virgil possessed them all in a high degree. It is supposed that he had the subject in contemplation for several years previous, and that he alludes to it in the sixth Eclogue in these words:

> Cùm canerem reges et prælia, Cynthius aurem
> Vellit et admonuit: Pastorem, Tityre, pingues
> Pascere oportet oves, deductum dicere carmen.

He probably had something of the kind in view; but whether it was, what the Æneid afterwards proved to be, is uncertain.

The subject of the poem is the removal of a colony of Trojans from Asia Minor, under the conduct of Æneas, and their settlement in Italy. The Iliad and Odyssey undoubtedly suggested to Virgil the idea of the Æneid; and without the former we should not have had the latter.

It has been supposed by some, that the Æneid was designed merely as a encomium upon Augustus, who was now raised to the highest temporal power. But if this had been his only object, the poet might have saved much time and labor, by composing short pieces, or brief panegyrics upon his prince, as Horace did on several occasions. It is true, Virgil was very fond of complimenting the Cæsars, and in several parts of his works, he has done it in the most extravagant manner.

The Æneid was undoubtedly designed for the benefit and instruction of the Roman people generally, who were now happily enjoying the blessings of peace, after having suffered, for a series of years, all the calamities of civil war. The poet wished these blessings to be perpetuated. He, therefore, endeavors to dissuade his countrymen from further attempts to restore the republic, and advises them to submit to the authority of a man who derived his origin from the gods, and under his auspices, to cultivate harmony, and the arts of civilized life. This is the moral of the poem, and an object worthy of the patriotism and benevolence of the poet.

Virgil wrote with a wonderful degree of exactness. Every thing which he mentions is founded upon historical truth; and the voyage and adventures of his hero are given with geographical precision. He has also given us a full and perfect account of the religious rites and ceremonies of the age. The whole so artfully blended with the subject, and so skilfully interwoven into it, as to become an essential part of the poem. And while he is delighting the fancy with the harmony of his numbers, he informs the understanding, and enlarges, the bounds of our knowledge.

As soon as it was known that Virgil had commenced the Æneid, the public expectation was raised very high; and so great was the general enthusiasm on the occasion, that Sextius Propertius did not hesitate to say:

> Cedite, Romani scriptores, cedite Graii;
> Nescio quid majus nascitùr Iliade.

His delicate health caused considerable interruption in his labors; and he found himself under the necessity of travelling, to sustain his feeble constitution He visited Sicily, and several parts of Italy; but Naples was his favorite place of residence.

He spent seven years in composing the first six books of the Æneid. Augustus wished to hear what he had written, and desired him to recite them to him. The poet complied with the request of his prince; and for this purpose, selected the second, fourth, and sixth books. Into this last, he had incorporated, with an ingenious hand, the funeral rites of Marcellus, who died a short time before, and whom Augustus designed for his successor in the empire. He was a very promising youth, the darling of his mother, Octavia, and the favorite of the people. When the poet came to this part, Octavia, who was present, was so much affected, that she fainted away: and Augustus was so highly pleased with the compliment paid to his nephew, that he ordered ten *sestertia* to be given for every line of the eulogium. This amounted to a very large sum. The verse 165, had been left in an unfinished state, and in the heat of fancy, occasioned by the recital, it is said, the poet added the words, *Martemque accendere cantu*, which complete the measure.

In four years afterwards, he finished the remaining six books, so that the poet spent eleven years in writing the Æneid. At this time, he was in the fifty-first year of his age, and his health considerably impaired. He had revised the Eclogues and the Georgics, and continued to improve them till the year before his death, as appears from some passages, particularly the closing verses of the last Georgic. Augustus was on the banks of the Euphrates, in the year of Rome 734. At this time Virgil was fifty years of age, and the Georgics had been published ten years.

It was the intention of Virgil to revise the Æneid also, before it was published. And for this end he visited the classic soil of Greece, where he purposed to devote three years to the poem: and, this being done, to turn his attention to philosophy. This, from his earliest years, had been his darling study, as he informs us in the latter part of the second Georgic; and he wished to spend the remaining years of his life in contemplating the works of nature, and in elevating his mind to its divine Author.

But soon after his arrival, his health became so delicate, and his strength so much exhausted, that he was obliged to relinquish it; and Augustus being on his return from Asia, Virgil thought proper to accompany him. At Megara, a town not far from Athens, he became seriously indisposed, and apprehensions were entertained of his recovery. He hastened his return to Italy, but continued to decline, and a few days after his arrival at Brundusium, a town in the eastern part of Italy, he expired, on the 22d day of September, being nearly 51 years of age. He died with that composure and resignation, which became so good and virtuous a man. He wished to be interred at Naples, the favorite place of his residence; and Augustus ordered his body to be removed thither, according to his desire; where it was buried with every testimony of respect and esteem. Just before his death, he wrote the following lines, as his epitaph:

> Mantua me genuit: Calabri rapuere: tenet nunc
> Parthenope: Cecini pascua, rura, duces.

This was inscribed upon his tomb; and it is characteristic of the modesty of that great poet and distinguished philosopher. It is said his tomb is to be seen at the present day on the road from Naples to Puteoli, about two miles from the former place.

Virgil left a will. By it, he directed the Æneid to be burned, as being imperfect and unfinished. But this was countermanded by Augustus, at whose desire, it is said, it was undertaken; and we are indebted to him for the preservation of one of the greatest efforts of human genius. The manuscript was put into the hands of Varus, Tucca, and Plotius, all friends of Virgil, and poets of some distinction, with direction to expunge whatever they deemed improper:

but to make no additions themselves. To this circumstance it is probably owing that we find so many imperfect lines in the Æneid.

Virgil died in the possession of a large estate, the half of which he bequeathed to Valerius Proculus, his half-brother, on his mother's side. Of the rest, he gave half to Augustus, and the remainder to Mæcenas, Tucca, Varus, and Plotius.

Virgil was tall and of a brown complexion, extremely temperate and regular in his habits. His constitution was feeble, and his health often delicate. He was much afflicted with a pain in his head and stomach; and often with the spitting of blood. He was extremely modest, and even bashful to a fault, attended with a hesitation in his speech. Like other great men he had his enemies and detractors: but their aspersions only served to increase his fame, and add new lustre to it.

Virgil has been emphatically styled the prince of Latin poets; and it has not been decided whether the palm should be awarded to the Roman or Grecian poet. It is true, Virgil was much indebted to Homer, who may be considered the master; but the pupil had the happy talent of making every thing that passed through his hands, *his own.*

The condition of these two great favorites of the Muses was very different in their lives. Homer, as his name implies, was blind; and so humble was his birth and parentage, that the place of his nativity has not been ascertained He wrote the Iliad and Odyssey in detached pieces, and recited them in the various cities of Greece, to obtain a subsistence. Virgil wrote under the auspices of one of the greatest of princes, and nothing was wanting that could contribute to his ease and comfort. His friends were the best and the greatest men of the age. He was honored in his life, and lamented in his death. Homer left no friend to point the traveller to his monument; and nearly four centuries rolled away, before his countrymen sufficiently appreciated his merits, to collect his scattered productions, and rescue them from oblivion. The world is indebted to Pisistratus, an Athenian, for the preservation of these inimitable poems; which are, and will ever be, the delight, and, at the same time, the wonder and admiration of civilized man.

INTRODUCTION TO THE BUCOLICS.

Of the several kinds of poetry, none is more generally admired than the pastoral. Its subjects, the variegated scenes of the country, the innocent employment of shepherds and shepherdesses, possess charms which never fail to please and interest our minds. But this species of poetry is difficult in execution; which may be the reason that there have been so few, who excelled in it.

If the poet were to make his shepherd talk like a courtier, a philosopher, or a statesman, we should immediately perceive the impropriety; or were he to make him utter low and vulgar sentiments, we should turn from him with disgust. The medium is the true course. To maintain this, however, at all times, is no easy matter.

Theocritus was the only pastoral writer of eminence among the Greeks, and Virgil among the Romans. The former denominated his pastorals *Idyllia*, the latter *Eclogæ*. Virgil, however, cannot so properly be called an original pastoral writer, as an imitator of Theocritus. Many of his finest touches are taken from the Grecian. He imitated him, however, with judgment, and in some respects improved upon him, particularly in preserving the true character of pastoral simplicity; in which the other on many occasions failed.

The word *Bucolica* is of Greek derivation, and signifies pastoral songs, or the songs of shepherds. Virgil denominated his Bucolica, *Eclogæ;* which is also from a Greek word signifying *to choose* or *select out of*. The Eclogues are, then, a selection of choice pieces, such as he thought worthy of publication.

He began this part of his works in the twenty-ninth year of his age, and in the year of Rome 713; and finished it in the space of three years. The Eclogues were so well received by his countrymen, that they were pronounced publicly on the stage. After hearing one of them, Cicero, it is said, did not hesitate to say of him: *Magnæ spes altera Romæ.*

It appears to have been the design of Virgil in writing his pastorals, to celebrate the praises of Augustus, and of some other of his friends at Rome, particularly Mæcenas and Pollio.

QUESTIONS.

What are the subjects of pastoral poetry?

Does this kind of poetry possess any peculiar charms?

Is it difficult in execution?

Who among the Greeks was the first pastoral poet of eminence?

What did he call his pastorals?

What did Virgil denominate his?

In what light are we to consider Virgil, as a pastoral poet?

At what age did he begin this part of his works?

In what year of Rome?

How many years did he spend in writing the Eclogues?

Were they well received by his countrymen?

What was probably the reason of his writing the Eclogues?

P. VIRGILII MARONIS

BUCOLICA.

ECLOGA PRIMA.

MELIBŒUS, TITYRUS.

At the termination of the civil war, which placed Augustus securely on the Imperial throne, to reward his soldiers for their services, he gave them the lands lying about Mantua and Cremona, dispossessing the former owners. Among the unfortunate sufferers was Virgil himself; who, however, by the interest of Mæcenas with the Emperor, received his lands again.

In the character of Tityrus, the poet sets forth his own good fortune; and in that of Melibœus, the calamity of his Mantuan neighbors. This is the subject of the pastoral. The scene is laid in a beautiful landscape. A shepherd, with his flock feeding around him, is lying at ease under a wide-spreading beech-tree: the sun is approaching the horizon: shadows are falling from the mountains: the air is tranquil and serene: the smoke is ascending from the neighboring villages. This scenery a painter could copy.

Mel. TITYRE, tu patulæ recubans sub tegmine fagi,
Sylvestrem tenui Musam meditaris avenâ:
Nos patriæ fines, et dulcia linquimus arva;
Nos patriam fugimus: tu, Tityre, lentus in umbrâ
Formosam resonare doces Amaryllida sylvas.
Tit. O Melibœe, Deus nobis hæc otia fecit.
Namque erit ille mihi semper Deus: illius aram
Sæpe tener nostris ab ovilibus imbuet agnus.
Ille meas errare boves, ut cernis, et ipsum
Ludere, quæ vellem, calamo permisit agresti.
Mel. Non equidem invideo: miror magis: undique [totis
Usque adeò turbatur agris. En ipse capellas
Protenùs æger ago: hanc etiam vix, Tityre, duco:
Hìc inter densas corylos modò namque gemellos,

8. Sæpe tener agnus ab nostris

9. Ille permisit meas boves errare, et me ipsum ludere carmina, quæ

14. Namque modò connixa gemellos, spem gregis, ah! reliquit eos hìc inter densas corylos, in nuda silice.

NOTES.

1. *Fagi:* gen. of *Fagus*, the beech-tree. It is glandiferous.

2. *Sylvestrem musam.* A pastoral song. *Avena:* properly oats. By Met. the straw; and hence an *oaten*, or *oat-straw pipe*. *Meditaris:* you practice or exercise.

3. *Arva.* neu. plu. properly cultivated fields: from the verb *aro*.

4. *Tu lentus:* thou at ease in the shade, dost teach the woods, &c. *Amaryllida*, a Greek acc. of Amaryllis. See 31. infra.

6. *Deus.* A god, namely Augustus, who had reinstated him in his possessions; and whom the Romans had deified. *Hæc otia:* this rest or ease. *Otium* is opposed to *labor* in significa ion.

9. *Errare.* To feed at large.

10. *Calamo agresti:* upon a rural reed. Musical instruments were at first made of oat, or wheat straw; then of reeds and box-wood; afterwards of the leg bones of the crane; of the horns of animals, &c. Hence they are called *avena*, *stipula; calamus*, *arundo*, *cicuta*, *fistula; buxus*, *tibia*, *cornua*, &c.

12. *Turbatur usque adeò totis*, &c. Lit. *It is disturbed so much in the whole country all around.* There is so much commotion in the whole country, I wonder that you should enjoy such peace and quiet.

14. *Corylos:* hazles—*Gemellus:* twins.

Spem gregis, ah! silice in nudâ connixa reliquit.
Sæpe malum hoc nobis, si mens non læva fuisset,

17. Memini quercus tactas de cœlo sæpe prædicere

De cœlo tactas memini prædicere quercus:
Sæpe sinistra cavâ prædixit ab ilice cornix.
Sed tamen, ille Deus qui sit, da, Tityre, nobis.

20. Ego stultus putavi urbem, quam dicunt Romam *esse* similem huic nostræ *Mantuæ*,

TIT. Urbem, quam dicunt Romam, Melibœe, putavi
Stultus ego huic nostræ similem, quò sæpe solemus
Pastores ovium teneros depellere fœtus.
Sic canibus catulus similes, sic matribus hœdos
Nôram: sic parvis componere magna solebam.

25. Hæc *Roma* extulit

Verùm hæc tantùm alias inter caput extulit urbes,
Quantùm lenta solent inter viburna cupressi.
MEL. Et quæ tanta fuit Romam tibi causa videndi?
TIT. Libertas: quæ sera, tamen respexit inertem;
Candidior postquam tondenti barba cadebat:
Respexit tamen, et longo pòst tempore venit,
Postquam nos Amaryllis habet, Galatea reliquit.
Namque (fatebor enim) dum me Galatea tenebat,

NOTES.

16. *Hoc malum nobis.* There seem to be required here, to make the sense complete, the words: *and I might have understood it; si mens*, &c. *If my mind had not been foolish.*

18. *Sinistra cornix: the ill-boding crow.* The Romans were very superstitious. They considered every thing as ominous. The flight of some kinds of birds, the croaking of others, the darting of a meteor, a peal of thunder, were signs of good or bad luck. Those that appeared on their left hand, for the most part, they considered unlucky. Hence *sinister* and *lævus* came to signify *unlucky, ill-boding*, &c. And those that appeared on their right hand, they considered to be lucky. Hence, *dexter* came to signify *fortunate, lucky*, &c. The best reason that can be given, why they used *sinister* and *lævus*, sometimes in a good, at other times in a bad sense, is, that they occasionally interpreted the omens after the manner of the Greeks, who considered those that appeared in the eastern part of the heavens to be lucky; and turning their faces to the north, as their custom was, they would be seen on the right hand. The Romans, on the contrary, turned their faces to the south in observing the omens; and consequently, their left hand would be toward the east, corresponding to the right hand of the Greeks. *Ilice:* the holm-oak.

19. *Qui sit Deus: who may be that God* of yours–of whom you speak? *Da nobis:* tell me. *Nobis:* in the sense of *mihi.*

20. *Romam.* Rome, a city of Italy, situated on the river Tiber, founded by Romulus 753 years before Christ. Mantua was a city of the Cis-Alpine Gaul, now Lombardy, situated on the eastern bank of the river Mincius, which falls into the Po.

22. *Fœtus.* This word signifies the *young* of any thing or kind, whether animate or inanimate. We have introduced it into our language without any variation. *Teneros fœtus ovium*, simply, *our lambs.*

23. *Sic canibus*, &c. This passage Servius thus explains: I thought before that Rome resembled Mantua and other cities, as I knew whelps and kids resemble their dams or mothers, differing only in size. In this I was mistaken: I find it to be of a different species from other cities, as the cypress differs from the shrub.

24. *Componere:* in the sense of *comparare.*

25. *Extulit caput: hath raised its head.* A figurative expression, but extremely beautiful.

26 *Viburna*, plu. of *viburnum*, a species of shrub. Some take it for *a withy*, others for the *wild-vine.*

28. *Libertas.* Virgil here speaks of himself as being an old man, having a hoary beard, and as having been a slave. Neither of which was the case. But it was not necessary for him to describe himself in all his circumstances. That would have been too plain, and would have taken from the beauty of the pastoral. *Inertem:* indolent—inactive. *Sera: late* in life.

29. *Candidior barba:* my gray, or hoary beard. The comp. is here plainly to be taken in the sense of the pos. *Tondenti:* to me shaving it.

31. *Amaryllis—Galatea.* Some think these are to be taken allegorically; the former for Rome, the latter for Mantua. But this is not necessary; nor will it be easy to support the allegory throughout. It is better to take them literally, for the names of the poet's mistresses. Servius thinks nothing in the Bucolics is to be taken allegorically. Dr. Trapp thinks Virgil insinuates that his old mistress Galatea was in favor of Brutus, and his new one Amaryllis in favor of Augustus; and by changing mistresses, he de-

Nec spes libertatis erat, nec cura peculî :
Quamvis multa meis exiret victima septis,
Pinguis et ingratæ premeretur caseus urbi,
Non unquam gravis ære domum mihi dextra redibat.
MEL. Mirabar, quid mœsta Deos, Amarylli, vocares,
Cui pendere suâ patereris in arbore poma.
Tityrus hinc aberat. Ipsæ te, Tityre, pinus,
Ipsi te fontes, ipsa hæc arbusta vocabant.
TIT. Quid facerem ? neque servitio me exire licebat,
Nec tam præsentes alibi cognoscere divos.
Hìc illum vidi juvenem, Melibœe, quotannis
Bis senos cui nostra dies altaria fumant.
Hìc mihi responsum primus dedit ille petenti :
Pascite, ut antè, boves, pueri : submittite tauros.
MEL. Fortunate senex ! ergo tua rura manebunt :
Et tibi magna satìs : quamvis lapis omnia nudus,
Limosoque palus obducat pascua junco
Non insueta graves tentabunt pabula fœtas,
Nec mala vicini pecoris contagia lædent.
Fortunate senex ! hìc inter flumina nota,
Et fontes sacros, frigus captabis opacum.
Hinc tibi, quæ semper vicino ab limite sepes
Hyblæis apibus florem depasta salicti,

37. Mirabar, quid tu mœsta, Amarylli, vocares Deos *ei* cui patereris

54. Hinc sepes, quæ *dividit tuum agrum* ab vicino limite, semper depasta *quoad* florem salicti Hyblæis apibus, sæpe suadebit tibi inire somnum levi susurro *apum.*

NOTES.

licately hints at his changing political sides, and in consequence thereof leaving Mantua, and going to Rome.

From the circumstance of Augustus depriving the Mantuans of their lands, we may infer that they were generally in favor of the Republic, and Virgil might have been of that party, till all hope of liberty was lost, and prudence dictated a change of politics. *Galatea reliquit*, is for *reliqui Galateam*, by Euphemismus. After he had left Galatea, and transferred his affections to Amaryllis, he obtained liberty and property : that is, after he had changed political sides.

33. *Pecult.* By apocope for *Peculii.* This word properly denotes the property of a slave—that which his master suffers him to possess, and call his own. In this sense, it is peculiarly proper, as Virgil here speaks of himself as having been in that humiliating condition.

35. *Urbi.* The city Mantua.

36. *Non unquam*, &c. Never did my right hand return home heavy with money. —*Mihi :* in the sense of *mea.*

40. *Arbusta :* the groves themselves, &c. There is a great beauty in the personification of inanimate things ; or attributing to them the actions of real life. The *Arbusta* were large pieces of ground set with elms or other trees, commonly at the distance of about 40 feet, to leave room for corn to grow between them. They were sometimes pruned, and served for stages to the vine. The verb *vocabant* is to be repeated with each of the nominatives preceding, and to govern the pronoun *te.*

42. *Præsentes :* propitious or favorable.—*Alibi :* in any other place—*any where else.* —*Cognoscere :* to experience, or find.

43. *Hic. Here*, at Rome.—*Juvinem :* Octavius, who was then about twenty-two years of age ; afterward by a decree of the senate called *Augustus.*—*Cui nostra :* for whom our altars smoke,—in honor of, &c.

46. *Pueri.* Swains. The word *puer* properly signifies a boy, in opposition to a girl—also a male slave or waiter.

49. *Obducat omnia pascua*, &c. Ruæus understands this not of Virgil's own lands, but of the lands of his neighbors. Dr. Trapp very justly rejects this interpretation. The poet is felicitating himself on his good fortune under the character of an old man. And, though his farm was covered over partly with rocks and stones, and partly with a marsh ; yet no unusual or improper pasture should injure his (*graves fœtas*) pregnant ewes; nor any noxious contagion of a neighboring flock should infect or hurt them. —*Fœta :* the female of any kind big with young—a breeder.

52. *Inter flumina nota.* The Mincius and Po.

55. *Sæpes depasta florem*, &c. This construction frequently occurs among the poets, and is in imitation of the Greeks; who sometimes placed the noun or pronoun in the acc. case, omitting the governing prep. *Fed upon as to, or with respect to, its flower of willow*, &c.—*Hyblæis :* an adj. from Hy.

Sæpe levi somnum suadebit inire susurro.
Hinc altâ sub rupe canet frondator ad auras.
Nec tamen interea raucæ, tua cura, palumbes,
Nec gemere aëriâ cessabit turtur ab ulmo.
Tit. Antè leves ergo pascentur in æthere cervi,
Et freta destituent nudos in litore pisces:
Antè, pererratis amborum finibus, exul
Aut Ararim Parthus bibet, aut Germania Tigrim,
Quàm nostro illius labatur pectore vultus.
Mel. At nos hinc alii sitientes ibimus Afros,
Pars Scythiam, et rapidum Cretæ veniemus Oaxem,
Et penitùs toto divisos orbe Britannos.
En unquam patrios longo pòst tempore fines,

65. At nos *expulsi* hinc, alii *nostrum* ibimus *ad* sitientes Afros, pars *nostrûm* veniemus *ad* Scythiam,

68. En unquam mirabor videns patrios

NOTES.

bla, a town and mountain in Sicily, famous for honey.—*Vicino limite:* from the neighboring field. *Hinc: on the one hand.* It is opposed to the *Hinc* in line 57. infra; which is to be rendered: *on the other hand.*

57. *Ad auras:* to the air—aloud, so as to pierce the air.

60. *Antè.* The ante in this line is merely expletive; the sense is complete without it.

61. *Destituent:* in the sense of *relinquent.*

62. *Antè, pererratis,* &c. Parthus, by Synec. for the Parthians collectively. They were a people descended from the Scythians, and possessed that part of Asia, which is bounded on the west by Media, on the north by the Caspian sea, on the east by Bactriana, and on the south by the deserts of Carmania. In process of time, they became very powerful, and were the most formidable enemies of the Persians: and from their frequent conquests over that people, are sometimes confounded with them. *Germania.* An extensive country in Europe, put, by meton. for the inhabitants of that country. *Ararim.* A river of France arising from mount *Vogesus* (hodie *Vauge*) and running in a southern direction, falls into the Rhodanus at Lyons, and along with it, into the Mediterranean. It is famous for the bridge built over it by Julius Cæsar. Its present name is the *Soane. Tigrim.* This is a very rapid river of Asia, rising in Armenia, and taking a southerly direction, passing by Mesopotamia and Assyria, unites with the Euphrates, and with it falls into the *Sinus Persicus.* The *Araris* is not in Germany properly so called. But it is well known that the Germans extended their conquests beyond that river, and effected settlements among the Sequani, and other nations of Gaul. Nor is the Tigris in Parthia proper. But the Parthians extended their conquests as far west as the Euphrates. Not far from this river they vanquished Crassus, the Roman general. The meaning of this passage, which hath so much divided the opinions of commentators, appears to be this: that these two nations, the Germans and the Parthians, shall exchange countries with each other (*finibus amborum pererratis*) sooner than (*ante quam*) the image of that youth should be effaced from his breast. But the former could never be; therefore, the latter would remain. *Pererratis,* in the sense of *permutatis.*

65. *Sitientes:* thirsting or parched. This epithet is peculiarly proper for the inhabitants of Africa, the greater part of which lies between the tropics.

66. *Scythiam.* The Scythians were a brave and warlike people, leading a wandering life. They extended their conquests over a very considerable part of Europe and Asia. Hence the term Scythia came to be used indefinitely, to denote any part or the whole of the northern parts of Europe and Asia. *Oaxis:* a river of Crete; a large island in the Mediterranean. It is celebrated for having been the birth-place of Jupiter, and for its having once had a hundred cities. *Veniemus,* in the sense of *ibimus.*

68. *En unquam.* Alas! shall I ever wonder, beholding, &c. Germanus, Ruæus and Davidson connect *aliquot aristas* with *mea regna.* But Dr. Trapp takes *post aliquot aristas* to mean *after some years;* and construes *mea regna* with *culmen tuguri.* It is true, *aristæ* may be taken for years. But *aliquot aristas* does not very well answer to the *longo tempore pòst,* mentioned just before. And if it did, it would be only a useless repetition. But connect *aliquot aristas* with *mea regna,* as in the ordo; any impropriety of this kind is removed; and we have a beautiful representation of Melibœus's possessions; which consisted in a few acres of land, lying adjacent to his cottage, the roof of which just rose above the corn that was planted around it, and might not improperly be said to be concealed among it, or behind it. *Tuguri,* by apocope, for *tugurii. Congestum cespiti:* covered over with turf

Pauperis et tugurî congestum cespite culmen,
Post aliquot, mea regna, videns mirabor aristas?
Impius hæc tam culta novalia miles habebit?
Barbarus has segetes? En quo discordia cives
Perduxit miseros! en queis consevimus agros!
Insere nunc, Melibœe, pyros, pone ordine vites:
Ite meæ, felix quondam pecus, ite capellæ.
Non ego vos posthac, viridi projectus in antro,
Dumosâ pendere procul de rupe videbo.
Carmina nulla canam: non, me pascente, capellæ
Florentem cytisum et salices carpetis amaras.
TIT. Hìc tamen hanc mecum poteris requiescere noc-
Fronde super viridi. Sunt nobis mitia poma, [tem
Castaneæ molles, et pressi copia lactis.
Et jam summa procul villarum culmina fumant,
Majoresque cadunt altis de montibus umbræ.

fines longo tempore post, et culmen pauperis tuguri, congestum cespite, *stans* post aliquot aristas, *tota* mea regna.

76. Ego posthac projectus in viridi antro, non videbo vos procul pendere

NOTES.

71. *Novalia:* fallow-ground.

72. *Quò:* whither—to what state of misery. *Perduxit:* hath reduced, or brought.

74. *Insere nunc*, &c. Melibœus says this ironically to himself, being vexed that he had labored, and had improved his lands, to be now possessed by a cruel soldier.

82. *Copia pressi lactis:* a plenty of curds and cheese. *Molles*, may here mean *ripe*, or soft and smooth, in opposition to the *hirsutæ*, or rough.

QUESTIONS.

What is the subject of this pastoral?

To reward his troops, what did Augustus do?

Who is represented under the character of Tityrus?

Who under that of Melibœus?

Where is the scene of the pastoral laid?

What is the time of the day?

What is the state of the atmosphere?

To what is *otium* opposed?

Were the Romans a superstitious people?

ECLOGA SECUNDA.

ALEXIS.

THE subject of this charming pastoral is the passion of the shepherd Corydon for the beautiful youth Alexis. The shepherd complains of the cruelty of the boy in slighting his overtures; and withal advises him not to trust too much to his complexion and beauty. He endeavors to prevail on him to visit the country, where he promises to entertain him with music, nuts, apples, and flowers. But when he finds nothing will avail, he resolves to seek another lover. By Corydon some understand Virgil himself, and by Alexis a beautiful slave, belonging to his friend and patron, Mæcenas. In several parts of this pastoral, the poet is indebted to Theocritus. The scene is laid in Sicily.

FORMOSUM pastor Corydon ardebat Alexim,
Delicias domini: nec, quid speraret, habebat.

NOTES.

1. *Ardebat:* he greatly loved—he burned for. This word very forcibly marks the degree of his passion.

2. *Delicias:* the darling—the delight of his master. It is placed in apposition with *Alexim*. It is used only in the plural.

3. Inter densas fagos *habentes* umbrosa cacumina.

Tantùm inter densas, umbrosa cacumina, fagos
Assiduè veniebat : ibi hæc incondita solus
Montibus et sylvis studio jactabat inani.
O crudelis Alexi, nihil mea carmina curas :
Nil nostri miserere : mori me denique coges.
Nunc etiam pecudes umbras et frigora captant ;
Nunc virides etiam occultant spineta lacertos :

10. Thestylis contundit allia serpyllumque, olentes herbas, messoribus fessis rapido æstu. At, dum lustro tua vestigia, arbusta

Thestylis et rapido fessis messoribus æstu
Allia serpyllumque herbas contundit olentes.
At mecum raucis, tua dum vestigia lustro,
Sole sub ardenti resonant arbusta cicadis.
  Nonne fuit satius tristes Amaryllidis iras,
Atque superba pati fastidia ? nonne Menalcan ?
Quamvis ille niger, quamvis tu candidus esses.
O formose puer, nimium ne crede colori :
Alba ligustra cadunt, vaccinia nigra leguntur.
Despectus tibi sum, nec qui sim quæris, Alexi.
Quàm dives pecoris nivei, quàm lactis abundans.
Mille meæ Siculis errant in montibus agnæ :

23. Canto *carmina*, quæ Dircæus Amphion solitus *est cantare*,

Lac mihi non æstate novum, non frigore defit.
Canto, quæ solitus, si quando armenta vocabat,

NOTES

4. *Ibi solus jactabat*, &c. *There alone he poured forth these indigested* complaints. *Jactabat:* he threw them away—they were of no avail to him, because they were unheeded by Alexis.

5. *Inani studio:* with unavailing pleasure, or fondness. He speaks the language of a lover. The beauty and accomplishments of the boy had taken possession of his affections. He dwells upon them with rapture and delight. But all this is vain and unavailing. The boy regards him not. He then breaks forth: *O crudelis Alexi, nihil mea carmina curas*, &c.

7. *Nil.* This word is often used in the sense of *non*, as a simple negative. So also is *nihil.*

9. *Lacertos:* lizards. *Spinetum:* a place where thorns and prickly shrubs grow: here put for the thorns themselves, by meton.

10. *Thestylis.* The name of a servant; taken from Theocritus.

11. *Allia:* plu. of *allium*, an herb called garlic. *Serpyllum:* wild-thyme, or running-betony; an odoriferous herb.

13. *Cicadis.* The cicada is an insect of the species of the grasshopper, making a very hoarse and disagreeable noise, particularly in the heat of the day. *Satius:* in the sense of *melius.*

15. *Menalcan.* A Greek acc. of Menalcas. See Ecl. 3. *Fastidia:* plu. of *fastidium:* disdain—haughtiness. *Pati:* to bear—endure.

18. *Ligustra:* plu. of *Ligustrum:* a *privet* or *with-bind*, a species of shrub or plant bearing very white flowers; taken for the flowers themselves, by meton. *Vaccinia:* *the blackberries* or *bilberries.* Some take them for the *Hyacinth* of Theocritus, whom Virgil here imitates. The meaning of the poet is this: as the privets, though white and fair, (*cadunt,*) lie neglected because they are useless; and the blackberry is gathered and saved for its usefulness: so, *Alexis*, shall you, though fair and beautiful to the sight be neglected for your pride; while Menalcas, though black and swarthy, shall be loved for his good disposition, and his conciliating temper.

21. *Siculis.* The mountains of Sicily are mentioned, either because they are famed for excellent pastures, or because the scene of the pastoral is laid in that country.

22. *Æstate:* in summer. *Frigore:* in winter.

23. *Siquando:* the same as *quando.* When he called his herds. It was usual with shepherds to walk before their sheep, and call them.

24. *Amphion.* A celebrated musician, said to have been the son of Jupiter and Antiope, and born on mount Cythera. He was king of Thebes, and is said to have built the walls of that city by the music of his lyre. We are to understand by this, perhaps, his persuading, by his eloquence, a barbarous people to unite, and build a city for their common safety. His mother was wife to Lycus, king of Thebes, and put away by him for the sake of *Dirce*, whom he married. *Dircæus:* an adj. either from *Dirce* his step-mother, or from a fountain of that name in Beotia. *Aracyntho* · a town and mountain

Amphion Dircæus in Actæo Aracyntho.
Nec sum adeò informis: nuper me in litore vidi,
Cùm placidum ventis staret mare: non ego Daphnim,
Judice te, metuam, si nunquam fallat imago.
O tantùm libeat mecum tibi sordida rura,
Atque humiles habitare casas, et figere cervos,
Hœdorumque gregem viridi compellere hibisco!
Mecum unà in sylvis imitabere Pana canendo.
Pan primus calamos cerâ conjungere plures
Instituit: Pan curat oves, oviumque magistros.
Nec te pœniteat calamo trivisse labellum.
Hæc eadem ut sciret, quid non faciebat Amyntas?
Est mihi disparibus septem compacta cicutis
Fistula, Damœtas dono mihi quam dedit olim:
Et dixit moriens: Te nunc habet ista secundum.
Dixit Damœtas: invidit stultus Amyntas.
Præterea duo, nec tutâ mihi valle reperti,
Capreoli, sparsis etiam nunc pellibus albo,
Bina die siccant ovis ubera: quos tibi servo.
Jampridem à me illos abducere Thestylis orat:
Et faciet: quoniam sordent tibi munera nostra.
Huc ades, ô formose puer. Tibi lilia plenis

38. Nunc ista *fistula* habet te secundum *dominum*.

40. Duo capreoli reperti mihi, nec tutâ valle, siccant bina ubera ovis *in* die, pellibus etiam nunc sparsis albo.

NOTES.

in Beotia. But why it should be called *Actæus*, there is a difference of opinion. Servius thinks it is so called from a Greek word which signifies the *shore*. Probus derives it from *Actæon*, who, hunting near this mountain, was torn in pieces by his dogs, for having discovered Diana bathing herself. Mr. Davidson places the mountain in the confines of Attica and Beotia; and thinks it is so called from *Acta* or *Acte*, the country about Attica. Ruæus interprets *Actæo* by *maritimo*.

26. *Daphnim.* A beautiful shepherd. See in Ecl. 5. *Placidum:* in the sense of *tranquillum*.

27. *Imago.* His image reflected from the water. *Nunquam:* in the sense of *non*.

28. *O tantùm libeat tibi:* O that it would please you to inhabit with me, &c. These are sweet lines. *Sordida rura.* Most commentators join *tibi* to *sordida*, disdained or despised by thee. But there is no need of this refinement. *Sordida* is a very proper epithet for cottages and country villages, which in general are indifferent in themselves, and poorly furnished, when compared with the splendor and luxury of cities. Or, we may suppose the poet to speak in the character of a lover, who thinks nothing good enough for the object of his affections. *Rus* is opposed to *urbs*.

30. *Viridi hibisco.* Ruæus takes these words to be in the dative case, and understands by them: *to green* or *verdant pasture; ad virentem hibiscum*, says he: taking the *hibiscum* for a kind of plant. But this interpretation is attended with difficulty. Dr. Trapp takes it for a large plant or little tree, out of which wands were made. He observes, Virgil no where mentions it as food for cattle. *Compellere*, &c.: to drive them with a green switch.

31. *Pana.* Pan, the god of shepherds and hunters, is said to have been the son of Mercury and the nymph Dryope. He was educated in Arcadia; and wrapped in the skin of a goat, he was carried up to heaven by Jupiter, where all the gods ridiculed his appearance. He chiefly resided in Arcadia. He is said to have invented the pipe with seven reeds. He was worshipped in Arcadia, and is said to have given out oracles on mount Lycæus. His festivals, called by the Greeks *Lycæ*, were introduced into Italy by Evander, and established at Rome under the name of *Lupercalia*, and celebrated the 15th of February. He was the chief of the Satyrs.

34. *Trivisse labellum:* to have worn the lip. From the verb *tero*.

36. *Cicutis.* Cicuta, an herb much like the Hemlock. Hence used for any hollow reed: hence also, by Meton. for a *pipe*. *Fistula:* a pipe connected together with seven unequal reeds, &c. These were put together with wax, as mentioned 32 supra.

41. *Duo Capreoli:* two young goats. *Capreoli:* a diminitive noun, from *capra* or *caper*. These were undoubtedly wild kids, taken from their dams, which he esteemed very much; and not those lost by him, and recovered again. Servius says: kids have

Ecce ferunt Nymphæ calathis: tibi candida Naïs
Pallentes violas et summa papavera carpens,
Narcissum et florem jungit benè olentis anethi:
Tum casiâ, atque aliis intexens suavibus herbis,
Mollia luteolâ pingit vaccinia calthâ.
Ipse ego cana legam tenerâ lanugine mala,
Castaneasque nuces, mea quas Amaryllis amabat.
Addam cerea pruna: et honos erit huic quoque pomo:
Et vos, ô lauri, carpam, et te, proxima myrte:
Sic positæ quoniam suaves miscetis odores.
Rusticus es, Corydon; nec munera curat Alexis:
Nec si muneribus certes, concedat Iolas.
Eheu, quid volui misero mihi? floribus Austrum
Perditus, et liquidis immisi fontibus apros.

55. Quoniam *vos* positæ sic miscetis

58. Quid *ego* volui mihi misero? Perditus immisi austrum floribus, et apros.

NOTES.

at first white spots, which afterwards change, and lose their beauty. If it be so, this circumstance will explain the words, *sparsis etiam nunc pellibus albo:* which also denotes that they were young.

46. *Ecce ferunt: behold the nymphs bring for you lilies in full baskets*, &c. The following lines are extremely beautiful. Mr. Warton observes, they contain the sweetest garland ever offered by a lover. The agitation and doubts of a lover's mind are finely set forth: *nec munera curat Alexis*, &c. At length he seems to come to himself, and to reflect upon the state of his affairs: *vitis semiputata est*, &c. *Nymphæ.* They were a kind of female Divinities supposed to exist for a very great length of time; but not to be altogether immortal. They were divided into two general classes—Nymphs of the land, and Nymphs of the water. Each of these classes was divided into several others. The former into *Dryades—Hamadryades—Oreades—Napææ—Limoniades*, &c. The latter into *Oceanides—Nereïdes—Naïades* or *Naides—Potamides—Limniades*, &c. All of which are of Greek derivation.

The nymphs were further distinguished by an epithet taken from the place of their residence. Thus the Nymphs of Sicily are called *Sicelides*—those of *Corycus*, *Corycíades* or *Corycides*, &c.

Echo is said to have been formerly a nymph; but falling in love with a beautiful youth called *Narcissus*, who refused her addresses, at which she was so much grieved that she pined away, till every part of her was consumed but her voice, that continued to haunt the woods and fountains, which she once frequented. *Narcissus*, stopping to repose himself by the side of a fountain, where he chanced to see his image reflected in the water, became enamoured with it: taking it for a nymph, he endeavored to approach it; but all his attempts being unavailing, he was so much disappointed that he killed himself. His blood was changed into a flower, which bears his name.

47. *Summa papavera carpens:* gathering the heads of poppies. *Papaver* and *Anethus* were two beautiful youths; who, according to Servius, were changed, the former into the flower, which we call the *poppy;* the latter into the herb, which we call *anise* or *dill. Benè olentis:* sweet-smelling.

50. *Pingit mollia*, &c. She adorns or sets off the soft hyacinths with saffron-colored marygold. *Vaccinium*, here is plainly the Hyacinthus of Theocritus, whom Virgil here copies; so say Turnebus, Salmasius, and Ruæus.

51. *Mala.* Malum signifies several kinds of fruit, such as apples, peaches, quinces, &c. The last is here meant, as appears from the *cana tenera lanugine:* white with soft down, or fur. Mr. Dryden renders *mala*, peaches.

53. *Cerea:* of waxen-color.

54. *Myrte.* The Romans used crowns or garlands of laurel in their most splendid triumphs: and those of myrtle, in the *ovatio*, which was on horseback, and considered the lesser triumph, or triumph of less honor and dignity than that in which the conqueror rode in a chariot. The myrtle tree was sacred to Venus, and the laurel to Apollo. *Proxima: next* in honor to the laurel.

56. *Rusticus:* in the sense of *stultus.*

57. *Iolas.* The owner or master of Alexis.

58. *Eheu, quid volui*, &c. Lit. *what have I done to myself, a miserable* man? *Alas! ruined, I have let in the south winds*, &c. These expressions are proverbial, and applicable to those who wish for things that prove ruinous to them. Dr. Trapp explains the passage thus: By my folly in indulging this extravagant passion, I have ruined my peace and quiet, and permitted my affairs to go to decay, which were before well managed, flourishing, and prosperous. *Volui.* Ruæus interprets it by *feci.*

Quem fugis, ah, demens! habitârunt dî quoque sylvas,
Dardaniusque Paris. Pallas, quas condidit arces,
Ipsa colat: nobis placeant ante omnia sylvæ.
Torva leæna lupum sequitur: lupus ipse capellam:
Florentem cytisum sequitur lasciva capella:
Te Corydon, ô Alexi: trahit sua quemque voluptas.
Aspice, aratra jugo referunt suspensa juvenci,
Et sol crescentes decedens duplicat umbras.
Me tamen urit amor: quis enim modus adsit amori?
Ah, Corydon, Corydon, quæ te dementia cepit!
Semiputata tibi frondosâ vitis in ulmo est.
Quin tu aliquid saltem potius, quorum indiget usus,
Viminibus mollique paras detexere junco?
Invenies alium, si te hic fastidit Alexim.

71. Quin potius tu paras detexere saltem aliquid *eorum*, quorum usus indiget viminibus.

NOTES.

60. *Demens:* O foolish boy, whom do you flee? *Demens*, compounded of *de* and *mens*.

61. *Paris.* See nom. prop. under *Paris. Dardanius*, an adj. of *Dardanus*, one of the founders of Troy. *Pallas*, the same as Minerva. See Geor. I. 18.

62. *Colat:* in the sense of *incolat*.

65. *Sua voluptas trahit quemque:* his own pleasure draws every one—every one is drawn by his own pleasure.

66. *Referunt.* After the labor of the day, they drew home the plough inverted, so that the share would glide easily over the ground, and hang, as it were, lightly upon the yoke.

71. *Quin tu*, &c. Why do you not rather prepare to make (weave) at least some of those things which need requires, of osiers and pliant rushes? The verb *indigeo* governs the genitive. *Usus:* need, or necessity.

QUESTIONS.

What is the subject of this pastoral?

Who is represented under the character of Corydon?

Who under that of Alexis?

Where is the scene laid?

Who was Amphion? What is said of him?

Who was Pan? What is said of him?

What were his festivals called by the Greeks? What by the Romans?

B whom were they introduced into Italy?

When were they celebrated?

Who were the Nymphs? Into how many classes may they be divided?

Was each of these classes subdivided into other classes?

Can you mention some of those subdivisions?

Who was Echo said to have been?

From what language are the names of the Nymphs derived?

ECLOGA TERTIA.

MENALCAS, DAMŒTAS, PALÆMON.

THE subject of this pastoral is a trial of skill in music between the shepherds Menalcas and Damœtas; who after rallying each other a while, resolve to try a song in the presence of their neighbor Palæmon, whom they constitute judge of their performances. Having heard each of them attentively, he declared he was unable to decide so weighty a controversy; but pronounced each one to be deserving of the pledge.

This beautiful pastoral is in imitation of the fifth and eighth of the Idylls of Theocritus. It is conjectured that under the character of Damœtas, we are to understand Virgil; and under that of Menalcas, some rival poet at Rome.

1. Cujum pecus *est istud?* an *est pecus* Melibœi? non: verùm *est pecus* Ægonis.

8. Novimus et qui *corruperint* te et *in* quo sacello, hircis tuentibus transversà, sed

10. Tum, credo, *illæ riserunt*, cum vidêre me incidere arbustum

16. Audent *facere* talia.

MEN. DIC mihi, Damœta, cujum pecus? an Melibœi?
DA. Non, verùm Ægonis: nuper mihi tradidit Ægon.
ME. Infelix, ô, semper, oves, pecus! ipse Neæram
Dum fovet, ac, ne me sibi præferat illa, veretur,
Hic alienus oves custos bis mulget in horâ:
Et succus pecori, et lac subducitur agnis.
DA. Parciùs ista viris tamen objicienda memento.
Novimus et qui te, transversà tuentibus hircis,
Et quo, sed faciles Nymphæ risêre, sacello.
ME. Tum, credo, cùm me arbustum vidêre Myconis,
Atque malâ vites incidere falce novellas.
DA. Aut hìc ad veteres fagos, cùm Daphnidis arcum
Fregisti et calamos: quæ tu, perverse Menalca,
Et cùm vidisti puero donata, dolebas;
Et, si non aliquà nocuisses, mortuus esses.
ME. Quid domini facient, audent cùm talia fures?

NOTES.

1. *Cujum:* an adj. agreeing with *pecus:* in the sense of *cujus.*

2. *Ægon.* The name of a shepherd, the rival of Menalcas in the love of *Neæra.* It is derived from a Greek word signifying a goat.

3. *O oves, infelix pecus.* The sheep are called unhappy, because their master Ægon, while in love with *Neæra*, had given up all care of them; and because they had fallen into the hands of a hireling, who treated them so inhumanly.

5. *Alienus.* An alien, or hireling shepherd—*custos.*

6. *Succus:* may mean the same with *lac* mentioned just after. By milking the dams, the natural food (*lac*) of the young would be taken from them, and they suffered to starve. Or *succus* may mean nourishment in general. It being taken away or diminished to the dams, the milk would be diminished or taken away proportionably from their young. This was a heavy charge brought against Damœtas. He highly resented it.

8. *Transversà:* crosswise—asquint. An adv. from the adj. of the neu. plu. in imitation of the Greeks.

9. *Sacello:* any place consecrated to the worship of God—a cave or grotto; as in the present case.

10. *Arbustum:* properly, a place planted with trees for vines to grow up by. By meton. the trees themselves. See Ecl. I. 40. *Novellas:* new, or young.

13. *Quæ tu*, &c. *Which* (bow and arrows) *when you saw given to the boy, you both grieved, and would have died, if you had not, in some way, injured him.*

16. *Fures:* slaves. They were sometimes so called, because notorious for stealing.

Non ego te vidi Damonis, pessime, caprum
Excipere insidiis, multùm latrante lyciscâ?
Et cùm clamarem; "Quò nunc se proripit ille?
Tityre, coge pecus:" tu post carecta latebas.
Da. An mihi cantando victus non redderet ille,
Quem mea carminibus meruisset fistula, caprum?
Si nescis, meus ille caper fuit; et mihi Damon
Ipse fatebatur, sed reddere posse negabat.
Me. Cantando tu illum? aut unquam tibi fistula cerâ
Juncta fuit? non tu in triviis, indocte, solebas
Stridenti miserum stipulâ disperdere carmen?
Da. Vis ergò inter nos, quid possit uterque, vicissim
Experiamur? ego hanc vitulam (ne fortè recuses,
Bis venit ad mulctram, binos alit ubere fœtus)
Depono: tu dic, mecum quo pignore certes.
Me. De grege non ausim quicquam deponere tecum;
Est mihi namque domi pater, est injusta noverca:
Bisque die numerant ambo pecus; alter et hœdos.
Verùm, id quod multò tute ipse fatebere majus,
Insanire libet quoniam tibi, pocula ponam
Fagina, cœlatum divini opus Alcimedontis:
Lenta quibus torno facili superaddita vitis
Diffusos hederâ vestit pallente corymbos.
In medio duo signa, Conon: et quis fuit alter,

25. Tu vicisti illum cantando?

35. Verum, quoniam libet tibi insanire, ponam id quod tute ipse fatebere *esse* multò majus *pignus*, *nempe*, *duo* fagina pocula, cœlatum opus

NOTES.

18. *Lycisca.* A mongrel dog—an animal half dog and half wolf.

20. *Post carecta:* behind the sedges. See Ecl. I. 68.

21. *An non victus cantando: vanquished in singing, should he not return to me the goat which*, &c.

26. *Triviis. Trivium*, a place in which three ways met. So *Bivium* and *Quadrivium*, places in which two and four ways met. *Disperdere miserum carmen: to murder a sorry*, or wretched *tune, on a squeaking straw*-pipe.

30. *Ubere:* the udder. By meton. for the milk contained in it. *Fœtus:* calves.

31. *Quo pignore:* with what pledge or bet. Tell me what pledge you will put against my heifer.

34. *Ambo numerant: they both count the flock twice in a day; and one counts the kids. Pecus* is properly a *flock* or *herd* of neat-cattle, as here. *Alter*, properly is one of two —*unus*, one of many.

36. *Insanire: to be beside yourself*—to play the fool; by contending with me, who am so much more skilful than you. *Pocula fagina:* beechen bowls—made of the beech-wood

37. *Alcimedontis.* The name of a very skilful and ingenious carver. Mr. Martin thinks he was some intimate friend of Virgil, who wished to transmit his name to posterity. History is silent respecting him.

38. *Lenta vitis quibus: around which a limber vine, superadded by the easy carving instrument, covers over* (mantles) *the diffused* (loosely hanging) *clusters with pale ivy.*—These lines are somewhat intricate, and have divided the opinions of commentators. Ruæus takes *quibus* in the abl. and interprets *facili torno* by *ope facilis torni.* Dr Trapp and some others take *facili torno* in the dat. and understand by it the wood after it is smoothed and polished in the turner's lathe, by meton. Davidson, on the other hand, takes *quibus* for the dat. and *facili torno* for the abl. but then he takes these last for the *ingenious carver*, or *easy skilful workman*, which he might do by meton. The sense I have given is the most natural and easy. The meaning of the poet is this: That each of these bowls was engraved or carved with vine and ivy boughs, so curiously interwoven, that the ivy-berries were shaded or mantled with the limber or pliant vine.

40. *Conon.* The name of a famous mathematician and astronomer of *Samos*, a cotemporary and friend of Archimedes. *Signa:* figures. *Et quis fuit alter?* This is a very pleasant turn. There is something agreeable in this picture of pastoral simplicity. He had mentioned the name of one, but had forgotten the name of the other. He turns to himself and asks: *quis fuit alter?* but the name not recurring to him, he goes on to describe him by his works. It was he,

Descripsit radio totum qui gentibus orbem?
Tempora quæ messor, quæ curvus arator haberet?
Necdum illis labra admovi, sed condita servo.
  Da. Et nobis idem Alcimedon duo pocula fecit,
Et molli circùm est ansas amplexus acantho:
Orpheaque in medio posuit, sylvasque sequentes.
Necdum illis labra admovi, sed condita servo.
Si ad vitulam spectes, nihil est quòd pocula laudes.
  Me. Nunquam hodie effugies: veniam quocunque vocâris
Audiat hæc tantùm vel qui venit: ecce, Palæmon:
Efficiam posthac ne quemquam voce lacessas.
  Da. Quin age, si quid habes; in me mora non erit ulla:
Nec quemquam fugio: tantùm, vicine Palæmon,

NOTES.

who, &c. It is supposed that *Aratus* or *Archimedes* is meant. The former wrote in Greek a treatise concerning the situation and motions of the heavenly bodies: which was translated into Latin. The latter was a famous mathematician and astronomer of Syracuse, in Sicily. By the help of his burning-glasses and engines, he nobly defended that city when besieged by the Romans under Marcellus. After a siege of three years, however, it was taken by stratagem. Archimedes was slain by a soldier, while in the act of demonstrating a proposition.

45. *Amplexus est ansas:* he encircled handles around with soft acanthus. The parts of the verb are here separated for the sake of the verse, by Tmesis. *Acantho:* a plant called *Bear's-foot.*

46. *Orphea:* acc. of Greek ending.—Orpheus was a most ancient and excellent poet, the son of Œagrus, king of Thrace. But according to fable, he was the son of Apollo and Caliope, one of the Muses. He received a lyre from Apollo, some say from Mercury, upon which he performed in such a masterly manner, that the rivers ceased to flow—the savage beasts forgot their ferocity—and the lofty oaks bowed their heads and listened to his song. He was beloved by all the nymphs. Eurydice alone could make an impression on his mind. He married her; but their happiness was short. For Aristæus fell in love with her; and fleeing from him, a serpent lying in the way wounded her in the foot, of which she died. Orpheus was so much afflicted at the loss, that he resolved to recover her, or perish in the attempt. For this purpose, he descended to Hell, and gained admittance to Pluto, who was so charmed with his music, that he consented to restore to him his wife, upon the condition that he would forbear to look behind him till he passed the bounds of his empire. The condition was accepted; but as they were very near the region of light, the unhappy lover turned his eyes to behold his long-lost Eurydice. He saw her, but she immediately vanished away. He attempted to follow her, but was refused. The only consolation he could find, was in the sound of his lyre in groves and mountains apart from society. The Thracian women, whom by his neglect and coldness he had offended, set upon him, while they were celebrating the orgies of Bacchus, and having torn his body in pieces, they threw his head into the river Hebrus, which continued to articulate Eurydice! Eurydice! as it was carried down the stream into the Ægean sea. After his death, some say, he received divine honors. His lyre was transferred to the heavens, and made a constellation. *Sequentes:* obedient to his lyre.

47. *Condita:* laid up safe: a part. from *condo*, agreeing with *pocula.*

49. *Nunquam effugies hodie:* you shall by no means avoid the trial this day. Damœtas had proposed to stake a heifer which Menalcas said he could not do through fear of his father and step-mother; but proposed to pledge his bowls. Damœtas insisted upon the heifer, and so seemed to avoid the contest, because the conditions could not be accepted by Menalcas. At length, however, confident of victory, and laying aside his fear, he says: *Veniam quocunque vocâris:* I will come to any conditions you shall propose. Accordingly the bowls are laid aside, and a heifer is the prize.

50. *Tantum vel qui venit,* &c. Only (I have nothing more to say) even let him who comes yonder, hear these things. Menalcas was so sure of victory, that he was willing to submit to the decision of any third person; and accordingly seeing some person at a distance, says: even let him, who is coming there, be the judge of our controversy, whoever he may be. Upon his near approach, discovering who he was, he says, behold, it is Palæmon our neighbor. *Voce:* in the sense of *cantu.*

51. *Efficiam:* I will cause.

53. *Fugio:* in the sense of *recuso.*

Sensibus hæc imis, res est non parva, reponas.
Pal. Dicite: quando quidem in molli consedimus herba:
Et nunc omnis ager, nunc omnis parturit arbos:
Nunc frondent sylvæ, nunc formosissimus annus.
Incipe, Damœta: tu deinde sequêre, Menalca.
Alternis dicetis: amant alterna Camenæ.
Da. Ab Jove principium, Musæ; Jovis omnia plena:
Ille colit terras; illi mea carmina curæ.
Me. Et me Phœbus amat: Phœbo sua semper apud me
Munera sunt, lauri, et suavè rubens hyacinthus.
Da. Malo me Galatea petit, lasciva puella:
Et fugit ad salices, et se cupit antè videri.
Me. At mihi sese offert ultro, meus ignis, Amyntas
Notior ut jam sit canibus non Delia nostris.
Da. Parta meæ Veneri sunt munera: namque notavi
Ipse locum, aëriæ quo congessere palumbes.
Me. Quod potui, puero sylvestri ex arbore lecta
Aurea mala decem misi: cras altera mittam.
Da. O quoties, et quæ nobis Galatea locuta est!
Partem aliquam, venti, divûm referatis ad aures.
Me. Quid prodest, quòd me ipse animo non spernis, Amynta,
Si, dum tu sectaris apros, ego retia servo?
Da. Phyllida mitte mihi, meus est natalis, Iola.
Cùm faciam vitulâ pro frugibus, ipse venito.
Me. Phyllida amo ante alias: nam me discedere flevit:

60. O musæ, principium *omnium est* ab Jove:

62. Sunt Phœbo semper apud me sua munera, *nempe*, lauri

71. Quod *solum* potui *facere*

72. Et quæ *dulcia verba*

NOTES.

54. *Imis sensibus:* your deepest attention, or thoughts. *Res:* the controversy.

59. *Alternis:* in alternate verses. This is called *carmen amœbœum.* It consists not solely in the dialogue; but requires that what the first says shall be replied to by the other upon the same or similar subject. *Carmina:* *verses*, is understood. *Camœnæ:* the Muses. It was formerly written *Carmenæ* and *Casmenæ.* Theme, *carmen.*

60. *Musæ.* They were nine in number, the daughters of Jupiter and Mnemosyne. They were supposed to preside over the arts and sciences. They were born in *Pieria* in Macedonia, and were said to reside on mount Helicon and mount Parnassus, the former in Beotia, the latter in Phocis.—Their names are: *Calliope*, *Clio*, *Erato*, *Thalia*, *Melpomene*, *Terpsichore*, *Euterpe*, *Polyhymnia*, and *Urania.*

61. *Ille colit:* he regards the earth he regards my verses.

62. *Phœbus.* The same as *Apollo* and *Sol;* the son of Jupiter and Latona. The laurel and hyacinth were sacred to him. Hence they are called *sua munera*, his own gifts. See Ecl. IV. 10.

66. *Ignis:* properly a fire or flame. By meton. love—also the object of love; as in the present case.

67. *Ut jam Delia non:* so that Delia now is not better known, &c. *Diana* is sometimes called *Delia* from *Delos*, the place of her birth. She was the goddess of hunting, and protectress of Dogs. Ruæus and Dr. Trapp understand by *Delia*, not *Diana*, but a servant of Menalcas by that name.

68. *Meæ veneri:* for my love—the dear object of my affections.

69. *Congessere:* in the sense of *nidificaverunt.*

71. *Aurea:* yellow—ripe.

72. *Venti, referatis:* bear some part of them, O winds, &c. Either because her words were so sweet that they would delight even the ears of the gods: or that the gods might be witnesses to her promises.

74. *Quid prodest*, &c. Damœtas had been just before expressing his joy at the conversation which he had with his mistress. Menalcas now endeavors to go beyond him in sentiments of tenderness and affection; and intimates that he cannot have any enjoyment while Amyntas is absent; nay, unless he share with him his dangers.

75. *Retia:* plu. of *rete:* toils, or snares set to take any prey.

76. *Phillida:* a Greek acc. of Phillis. She was the slave of Iolas, and mistress both to Damœtas and Menalcas.

77. *Faciam vitulâ:* that is, *faciam sacra ex vitula:* I will make the sacrifice of a heifer for the fruits.

Et, "longum, formose, vale, vale," inquit, Iola.
DA. Triste lupus stabulis; maturis frugibus imbres;
Arboribus venti; nobis Amaryllidis iræ.
ME. Dulce satis humor; depulsis arbutus hœdis,
Lenta salix fœto pecori: mihi solus Amyntas.
DA. Pollio amat nostram, quamvis est rustica, Musam

86. Pascito taurum *illi*, qui jam

Pierides, vitulam lectori pascite vestro.
ME. Pollio et ipse facit nova carmina; pascite taurum,
Jam cornu petat, et pedibus qui spargat arenam.

88. Veniat quoque quò gaudet *eum te pervenisse.*

DA. Qui te, Pollio, amat; veniat quò te quoque gaudet:
Mella fluant illi, ferat et rubus asper amomum.
ME. Qui Bavium non odit, amet tua carmina, Mævi:
Atque idem jungat vulpes, et mulgeat hircos.

92. O pueri, qui legitis flores et fraga nascentia humi, fugite

DA. Qui legitis flores, et humi nascentia fraga,
Frigidus, ô pueri! fugite hinc, latet anguis in herbâ.
ME. Parcite, oves, nimiùm procedere: non benè ripæ
Creditur: ipse aries etiam nunc vellera siccat.
DA. Tityre, pascentes à flumine reice capellas:
Ipse, ubi tempus erit, omnes in fonte lavabo.
ME. Cogite oves pueri: si lac præceperit æstus,
Ut nuper, frustrà pressabimus ubera palmis.
DA. Eheu, quàm pingui macer est mihi taurus in arvo!
Idem amor exitium pecori est, pecorisque magistro.

102. Neque est amor certè causa his *meis ovibus, cur sint tam macræ.*

ME. His certè neque amor causa est: vix ossibus hærent.
Nescio quis teneros oculus mihi fascinat agnos.

NOTES.

79. *Longum, formose,* &c. These are not the words of Phillis, addressed to Iolas, but of Menalcas; and first addressed to Menalcas by Phillis. They made a deep impression on his mind—they stole his affections. O beautiful youth, said she, farewell —farewell, a long time. *Stabulis:* sheepfolds. By meton. the sheep. *Triste* is to be supplied with each member of the sentence following, as also the verb *est.*

82. *Arbutus:* the strawberry tree, so called from the resemblance of its fruit to a strawberry. *Depulsis:* the words *à lacte* are understood.

82. *Satis.* The dat. plu. a substantive from the part. pass. of the verb *sero,* I sow. It signifies any thing sown or planted–standing corn. *Depulsis hœdis:* to the weaned kids. *Dulcis* is to be supplied in each member of the sentence; as also the verb *est.*

85. *Pierides.* The Muses are so called from *Pieria,* the place of their birth. See 60. supra.

86. *Pollio.* A noble Roman, the friend and patron of Virgil. See next Ecl. *Nova:* good—excellent.

88. *Veniat quò gaudet,* &c. May he also arrive at those honors to which it delighteth him that thou hast arrived. Pollio was invested with the consulate in the year of Rome 714, and in the following year he received a triumph. He was also a poet and historian; and considered among the most learned men of his time. See Ecl. IV. 12.

89. *Amomum.* An aromatic fruit of great value. The Assyrian was considered the best. *Rubus:* the blackberry bush.

90. *Qui Bavium non odit.* Bavius and Mœvius were two contemptible poets, and very inimical to Virgil and Horace. These two lines are wonderfully satirical. Let the same persons yoke oxen and milk he-goats. But this would be a useless, as well as a ridiculous employment.

93. *Frigidus:* deadly, by meton. or cold; descriptive of the nature of the snake.

95. *Creditur.* It is not easy to translate impersonal verbs always literally. They frequently occur in sentences, when such a version would be very awkward English. This is the case here. Menalcas is cautioning his sheep not to proceed too far; and adds as a reason for so doing, that it is *not well to trust to the bank.* To give force to this caution, he mentions the case of the ram that had just recovered of a fall from it into the river, and was then drying his fleece.

96. *Reice.* Imp. of the verb *reicio,* by syncope for *rejicio:* drive back.

98. *Præceperit:* if the heat should dry up the milk—should take it before us, then in vain, &c.

103. *Quis oculus:* what evil eye bewitches my tender lambs. *Mihi:* in the sense of *meos.*

DA. Dic quibus in terris, et eris mihi magnus Apollo,
Tres pateat cœli spatium non ampliùs ulnas.
ME. Dic quibus in terris inscripti nomina regum
Nascantur flores et Phyllida solus habeto.
PA. Non nostrum inter vos tantas componere lites.
Et vitulâ tu dignus, et hic: et quisquis amores
Aut metuet dulces, aut experietur amaros.
Claudite jam rivos, pueri: sat prata biberunt.

109. Et tu *es* dignus vitulâ, et hic.

110. Quisquis aut metuet dulces amores, aut experietur amaros *amores*.

NOTES.

105. *Spatium cœli pateat.* Damœtas here proposes a very intricate riddle. Various have been the conjectures to solve it. It is most generally thought that the place intended is the bottom of a well, from whence the space of the heavens appears no broader than its mouth, which in the general may be taken for three ells.

107. *Flores nascantur inscripti.* Without solving the riddle of Damœtas, Menalcas proposes this one, and it is an equal match for his. The solution of it is all conjecture. It is generally supposed that the hyacinth is the flower alluded to. *Nomina inscripti:* inscribed as to the names of kings—or with the names of kings. See Ecl. I. 55.

108. *Non nostrum:* it is not in my power to settle, &c. *Est* is to be supplied. Palæmon declares his inability to determine the controversy between them; but pronounces them both worthy of the prize.

110. *Metuet dulces:* shall fear successful love—shall fear that it would not be lasting. *Experietur amaros:* shall experience disappointed love—love not returned or reciprocated.

111. *Claudite.* This is a beautiful line: shut up your streams, O swains, the meads have drunk enough. It is a metaphor taken from rivers refreshing the meadows through which they pass; to music and poetry, delighting the ear, the fancy, and the judgment. It implies that it was time to cease their song; they had given sufficient proofs of their skill in music.

QUESTIONS.

What is the subject of this pastoral?

Does Virgil here imitate Theocritus?

Who is to be understood under the character of Damœtas? Who under that of Menalcas? Who under that of Palæmon?

Who was Conon? Who was Archimedes?

What did he do against the Romans?

What became of him afterwards?

Who was Orpheus? Whom did he marry?

What did he do to recover his lost Eurydice?

What became of him at last?

In what consists the *carmen amœbœum?*

Who were the Muses? How many were they in number? What were their names?

Who was Diana? Where was she born? Over what did she preside

ECLOGA QUARTA.

POLLIO.

Virgil's design in this pastoral is to celebrate the birth of a son of Pollio, as appears from verse 17; on which account he dedicated it to that noble Roman. But it is evident that he ascribes to the son of his friend, what cannot be attributed, with any propriety to a being merely human. On examination, it will be found that there are several expressions and passages, which remarkably correspond with the prophecies and predictions of the Messiah, contained in the scriptures of the Old Testament; and particularly with those of the prophet Isaiah. That the poet was inspired is not pretended. We are assured, on the most credible testimony, that about this time there was a general expectation of the Messiah's appearance. This was partly from the dispersion of the Jews over the Roman empire, who carried with them their scriptures; and partly from the Sibylline oracles then much in repute. What, therefore, was generally said, and was the common opinion concerning the Messiah, the poet applies to the son of Pollio. It was not fulfilled in him. For he died on the ninth day after his birth. It was, however, actually fulfilled in about forty years afterwards, when the Savior appeared. Some suppose that the poet hath in view Marcellus, the son of Octavia, the sister of Augustus, whose birth corresponds with the consulship of Pollio. Augustus adopted him, and designed him for his successor in the empire. This is the same Marcellus whom Virgil highly compliments in the sixth book of the Æneid. He died soon after he arrived at manhood.

SICELIDES Musæ, paulò majora canamus.
Non omnes arbusta juvant, humilesque myricæ.
Si canimus sylvas, sylvæ sint consule dignæ.
Ultima Cumæi venit jam carminis ætas:

NOTES.

1. *Sicelides:* an adj. from *Silicia*, the island of Sicily, the country of Theocritus, the father of pastoral poetry. Hence *Sicelides Musæ*, pastoral muses.

2. *Arbusta—myricæ.* Trees and shrubs seem to be put here for pastoral subjects, or the style and manner in which they are sung, by meton. *Myricæ:* a shrub called the *tamarisk.* The poet here proposes to write in a style different from the usual style of pastoral; for that does not please every ear. A more elevated strain he will now attempt.

3. *Sylvas:* the woods. By meton. pastoral or rural subjects. If we sing of pastoral subjects, those subjects should be worthy of a consul's ear.

4. *Ultima ætas:* the last age of the sibylline prophecy hath now arrived—the last age, which was the subject, &c. I would here observe that *the last days—the latter days*, or *times*, are common expressions in the scriptures to denote the age of the Gospel, which is the last dispensation of grace. *Cumæi:* an adj. from *Cumæ*, a city of Campania, in Italy, famous for having been the residence of a sibyl. There were several others of the same name; but the most distinguished were, a city of *Æolis*, in Asia Minor, and a city of *Eubœa*, an island in the Ægean sea: *hodie, Negropont.* The residence of this sibyl was a cave or vault dug into a rock. Justin Martyr informs us, that he visited the spot, and was shown a kind of chapel in the rock, into which the inhabitants told him (as they received it from their forefathers) she retired whenever she gave out her oracles. He also mentioned several other particulars. Onuphrius tells us, that the cave or residence of the sibyl remained in the same state Justin Martyr described it, until 1539, when it was entirely destroyed by an earthquake which shook all Campania. See Prideaux's Con. Part 2. Lib. 9. The sibyls were women said to have been endued with the spirit of prophecy, and to have foretold the destinies of states and kingdoms. They lived at different periods of time, and in different countries. They took the name of *Sibyllæ*, or Sibyls, from the first, who was thus endued, her name being *Sibylla.* Varro enu-

Magnus ab integro sæclorum nascitur ordo.
Jam redit et Virgo, redeunt Saturnia regna:
Jam nova progenies cœlo demittitur alto.
Tu modò nascenti puero, quo ferrea primùm
Desinet, ac toto surget gens aurea mundo,
Casta, fave, Lucina: tuus jam regnat Apollo.

8. Tu modò, casta Lucina, fave nascenti puero, *sub* quo ferrea *gens* primum desinet, ac aurea gens surget toto mundo.

NOTES.

merates ten: The *Delphica*, *Erythræa*, *Cumæa*, *Samia*, *Cumana*, *Hellespontica*, *Libyca*, *Persica*, *Phrygia*, and the *Tiburtina*. Of these, the one most noted was the *Cumæan*. She seems to have been the same that the Greeks called *Erythræa*. from the circumstance of her being born at *Erythræ* in Ionia, of the Lesser Asia; from whence she removed to *Cumæ*, in Italy. *Carminis:* in the sense of *vaticinii*.

5. *Magnus ordo.* Some suppose that the poet here hath reference to the great Platonic year; of which Claudius says, Ch. 1 of the sphere: *Omnia, quæcunque in mundo sunt, eodem ordine esse reditura, quò nunc cernuntur.* This would embrace the period of 25,920 of our years; when the equinoxes will have made the circuit of the ecliptic, and the same stars, which describe the equator, tropics, and polar circles, by the diurnal motion of the earth, will describe them over again. Ruæus, however, is of a different opinion, and very justly understands by *magnus*, great and illustrious; implying that the period of which the poet spake as then commencing, should be distinguished by great and illustrious characters. *Sæclorum*, by syncope for *sæculorum*. *Sæculum* properly signifies the period of a hundred years. It is also used to denote an indefinite period, as in the present instance.

6. *Virgo.* The poet here means *Astræa*, the goddess of justice, the daughter of Jupiter and Themis. See nom. prop. under *Astræa*. *Saturnia regna:* the reign of Saturn. According to fable, Saturn was the son of *Cœlus* and *Terra*, or *Vesta*. Cœlus confined in Tartarus all his sons, except Saturn; who with the assistance of his mother, banished his father, and set his brothers at liberty. He succeeded to the kingdom by the consent of his brother Titan, on the condition that he should raise no male offspring. He accordingly devoured his sons as soon as they were born. But when Jupiter was born, his wife Rhea, or Ops, unwilling to see all her sons perish, concealed him; giving to her husband a stone in room of the child, which he devoured, without discovering the cheat. In the same way she preserved Neptune and Pluto.

Titan being informed that his brother had broken the terms of their contract, made war upon him, and made both him and his wife prisoners; they were, however, soon set at liberty by Jupiter. But Saturn did not long remain mindful of this favor. He conspired against him to dethrone him, and possess the empire himself. Upon this, Jupiter banished him from heaven. He came to Italy, which was afterwards called *Latium*, from the circumstance of its being the place of his concealment; from the verb *lateo*. Janus, who was then king, received him with hospitality, and made him partner in his kingdom. Saturn employed his time in civilizing his subjects, teaching them agriculture, and the several arts and sciences. His reign was so mild, so beneficent and virtuous, that it came to be denominated the *Golden Age*, to intimate the happiness and tranquillity which then were enjoyed. The *Silver Age* succeeded, when men began to degenerate, and their peace to be disturbed by feuds and animosities. The *Brazen Age* followed, when avarice and licentiousness took possession of the heart. To this succeeded the *Iron Age*, when the world became sunk into a general and total depravity. These four ages are much spoken of by the poets, but particularly the first. By this time men had become so wicked and degenerate, that they were all destroyed by a deluge, which took place in the reign of Deucalion, king of Thessaly. He and his wife Pyrrha were the only survivors.

8. *Fave nascenti puero:* favor, or be propitious to the infant boy. *Nascens* does not refer here so much to his birth, as to his infant years. As *Lucina* had safely brought the child into the world, it is the desire of the poet that she should continue her attention and regard to him during the dangers of infancy.

9. *Gens:* in the sense of *ætas*.

10. *Casta Lucina.* Lucina was the goddess supposed to preside over child-bearing, and called *Lucina* from *lux*, because through her means children were brought to see the light. This office was attributed both to *Juno* and *Diana;* the latter of whom is the one here meant, as appears from *Tuus jam regnat Apollo:* now thy Apollo reigns.—This hath led some into a singularity. By Apollo they would understand Augustus, and by Lucina his sister Octavia. Virgil was fond of complimenting his prince, but there can be no necessity of such an interpretation here. Ruæus understands it of *Apollo* himself, who may be said to reign,

11. Adeò hoc decus ævi inibit, te, te consule, O Pollio.

Teque adeò decus hoc ævi, te consule, inibit,
Pollio : et incipient magni procedere menses
Te duce, si qua manent sceleris vestigia nostri,
Irrita perpetuâ solvent formidine terras.
Ille Deûm vitam accipiet, Divisque videbit
Permixtos heroas, et ipse videbitur illis :
Pacatumque reget patriis virtutibus orbem.

NOTES.

because it is now manifest that his predictions are true. Apollo was the god, under whose influence the *Sibyls* were, when they prophesied, or gave out their oracles.

Apollo was the son of Jupiter and Latona, and brother of Diana. Juno, in order to vent her rage against Latona, sent the serpent *Python*, to vex and torment her. She was unable to find a place where she could be delivered of her children in peace, till Neptune, taking pity on her, raised the island Delos, where she was safely delivered of Apollo and Diana at a birth. As soon as he was born, Apollo slew the serpent *Python*, from which circumstance he is sometimes called *Pythius*. He was accounted the god of medicine, music, poetry, and eloquence, all of which, it is said, he invented. His son Æsculapius being killed by Jupiter for raising the dead, he in turn slew the Cyclops, who had made the thunderbolt that slew him. Jupiter being much enraged at this piece of conduct, banished him from heaven, and deprived him of his dignity. He came to Admetus, king of Thessaly, and hired himself as a shepherd, in which employment he served nine years. Hence he is sometimes called the god of shepherds. Apollo was amorous, and had many children. His worship was very general. At *Delphi*, *Delos*, *Claros*, *Tenedos*, *Patara*, &c. he had celebrated oracles. He had several names: *Pythius*, already mentioned; *Delius*, from the island *Delos*, where he was born; *Cynthius*, from *Cynthus*, the name of a mountain on the same island; *Pæan*, from a Greek word which signifies to strike, or wound, in allusion to his killing the Python ; *Delphicus*, from *Delphi*, in Phocis, where he had his most famous temple and oracle; *Clarus*, &c. He was called *Phœbus*, or *Sol*, in heaven. There were several among the ancients, who went under the name of *Apollo*. Cicero mentions three, besides the son of Jupiter and Latona.

11. *Hoc decus ævi:* this glory of the age, i. e. this glorious age, shall commence in your consulship.

12. *Magni menses.* Servius and Pomponius think we are to understand the months of July and August, because they bore the names of *Julius* and *Augustus*. But we are undoubtedly to understand the *magni menses* here, in the same manner and sense as *magnus ordo sæclorum*, verse 5, supra *Pollio.* A very distinguished Roman. He arrived to the highest honors that the people could bestow. He was appointed *Præfectus* of *Hispania Ulterior* by Julius Cæsar. On some occasion or other, being in Cis-alpine Gaul, he became acquainted with Virgil, for whom he conceived a very high regard, and recommended him to Mæcenas, who was then at Rome. A way was thus opened to our poet for the recovery of his lands. In the year of Rome, 714, Pollio was appointed consul, and in the following year he triumphed over the *Partheni*, a people of Illyricum, who adhered to the party of Brutus and Cassius. He wrote the history of the civil wars, and was both a poet and orator. He died in the eightieth year of his age, and in the year of Rome, 757.

13. *Siqua vestigia*, &c. The poet here alludes, most probably, to the perjury of Laomedon, king of Troy; to which the Trojans attributed their misfortunes and calamities. See Geor. I. 502; or to the civil wars which were carried on between Cæsar and Pompey. Or lastly, to the death of Julius Cæsar, who was slain by Brutus in the senate house; which was the cause of a second civil war, between Brutus and Cassius on the one part, and Octavius and Anthony on the other. It terminated in the ruin of the Republic, and in the establishment of the Empire.

14. *Irrita:* being effaced, or done away will free the earth, &c. *Irrita*, of *in* negativum, and *ratus;* agreeing with *vestigia.*

15. *Ille accipiet vitam:* he shall partake the life of the gods, &c. Here is an allusion to the Golden Age, when, the poets say, the gods had familiar intercourse with men, and dwelt on the earth. That happy period was again about to return.

17. *Reget*, &c. He shall rule the peaceful world by his father's virtues. Meaning that the child should arrive at the highest honors of the state, that is, should be a consul. Or, he shall rule the world, reduced to peace by his father's virtues. Pollio and Mæcenas effected a reconciliation between Octavius and Anthony, which gave hope of a lasting peace. *Orbem* here means the Roman Empire; which, in the height of its greatness, comprehended the greater par of the world that was then known.

At tibi prima, puer, nullo munuscula cultu,
Errantes hederas passim cum baccare tellus,
Mixtaque ridenti colocasia fundet acantho.
Ipsæ lacte domum referent distenta capellæ
Ubera : nec magnos metuent armenta leones.
Ipsa tibi blandos fundent cunabula flores :
Occidet et serpens, et fallax herba veneni
Occidet : Assyrium vulgò nascetur amomum.
At simul heroum laudes, et facta parentis
Jam legere, et quæ sit poteris cognoscere virtus :
Molli paulatim flavescet campus aristâ,
Incultisque rubens pendebit sentibus uva,
Et duræ quercus sudabunt roscida mella :
Pauca tamen suberunt priscæ vestigia fraudis,
Quæ tentare Thetim ratibus, quæ cingere muris
Oppida, quæ jubeant telluri infindere sulcos.
Alter erit tum Tiphys, et altera quæ vehat Argo
Delectos heroas : erunt etiam altera bella,
Atque iterum ad Trojam magnus mittetur Achilles.
Hinc, ubi jam firmata virum te fecerit ætas,
Cedet et ipse mari vector : nec nautica pinus

18. At tellus fundet prima munuscula tibi, O puer, nullo cultu, *nempe*, errantes hederas passim cum baccare, colocasia que mixta ridenti acantho.

26. At simul jam poteris legere laudes heroum, et facta parentis et

32. Quæ jubeant *homines* tentare Thetim ratibus; quæ *jubeant illos* cingere oppida muris; *et* quæ *jubeant illos* infindere sulcos telluri

NOTES.

19. *Baccare. Baccar*, a sweet herb called by some *ladies-glove;* by others, *clown-spikenard. Colocasia:* Egyptian beans. *Acantho:* the herb called *bear's-foot.* It has a long and broad leaf.

23. *Cunabula ipsa:* the cradle itself—the very cradle. *Blandos:* in the sense of *jucundos.*

24. *Serpens occidet:* the serpent shall die. This is a very remarkable passage. The Messiah was promised *to bruise the head of the serpent*, Gen. Ch. iii. 15th verse. *Fallax herba veneni:* the deceiving herb of poison shall die—every herb whose poisonous quality is not known. For if it were known, no person would meddle with it, and consequently none would be deceived. *Amomum.* See Ecl. iii. 89.

28. *Molli:* ripe. For the fields do not grow yellow till the approach of harvest. *Arista:* corn—an ear of corn.

29. *Sentibus:* thorn-bushes.

31. *Tamen pauca*, &c. We may here observe the several gradations of the Golden Age. With the birth of the child it commenced: *Cunabula fundent flores.* During the years of his youth, the earth is to bring forth abundantly. There is to be no want of any thing: *Campus flavescet*, &c. All vestiges of former crimes, however, were not done away. Some traces of the Iron Age were to be visible in the conduct and actions of men : *Quæ jubeant*, &c. But when he has arrived to years of full maturity, then the earth is to produce all things spontaneously *Omnis tellus feret omnia:* and the Golden Age is to appear in all its felicity and glory. *Fraudis:* in the sense of *sceleris.*

32. *Thetim.* Thetis, a goddess of the sea, the daughter of *Nereus* and *Doris.* Jupiter fell in love with her, and determined to marry her; but being informed by Prometheus of a decree of the fates, that she should bear a son who should be greater than his father, he desisted from his purpose. Whereupon Peleus, king of Thessaly took her to wife, and of her begat Achilles. *Thetis*, be meton. is put for the sea in this place.

34. *Tiphys.* The name of the pilot of the ship *Argo.* It was so called, either from *Argus*, the architect; or from *Argivi*, Greeks, whom it carried. It was built at *Pegasæ*, a promontory and town of Thessaly. Hence sometimes called *navis Pegasæa.*

35. *Delectos heroas:* chosen heroes.—These were noble Greeks, chiefly of Thessaly. They were about fifty in number, and went to *Colchis* in the ship *Argo*, to bring away the golden fleece, which was guarded by a dragon, and bulls breathing fire. Jason commanded the expedition. *Castor, Pollux, Hercules, Theseus, Orpheus, Zetes*, and *Calaïs* accompanied him. The crew collectively was called *Argonautæ.* See nom. prop. under Jason.

36. *Achilles—Trojam—Argo—Tiphys.* These are here put for any hero, any city any ship, any pilot.

36. *Nec nautica pinus, &c.* Nor shall the naval pine exchange commodities—carry on traffic. *Pinus* is here put for a ship made of that tree, by meton. *Vector:* the mariner. *Cedet:* shall leave, or abandon.

Mutabit merces: omnis feret omnia tellus.
Non rastros patietur humus, non vinea falcem :
Robustus quoque jam tauris juga solvet arator.
Nec varios discet mentiri lana colores :
Ipse sed in pratis aries jam suavè rubenti
Murice, jam croceo mutabit vellera luto :
Sponte suâ sandyx pascentes vestiet agnos.
Talia sæcla suis dixerunt, currite, fusis
Concordes stabili fatorum numine Parcæ.
Aggredere, ô, magnos, aderit jam tempus, honores,
Clara Deûm soboles, magnum Jovis incrementum!
Aspice convexo nutantem pondere mundum,
Terrasque, tractusque maris, cœlumque profundum
Aspice venturo lætentur ut omnia sæclo.
O mihi tam longæ maneat pars ultima vitæ,
Spiritûs et, quantùm sat erit tua dicere facta!
Non me carminibus vincet, nec Thracius Orpheus,
Nec Linus : huic mater quamvis, atque huic pater adsit,
Orphei Calliopea, Lino formosus Apollo.
Pan etiam Arcadiâ mecum si judice certet,
Pan etiam Arcadiâ dicat se judice victum.
Incipe, parve puer, risu cognoscere matrem :

43. Sed aries ipse in pratis mutabit vellera jam suavè rubenti murice, jam

46. Parcæ concordes stabili numine fatorum dixerunt suis fusis, O talia sæcla, currite. O clara soboles Deûm, magnum incrementum Jovis, aggredere magnos honores

53. O ultima pars tam longæ vitæ maneat mihi, et *tantùm* spiritûs, quantùm

NOTES.

42 *Lana discet*, &c. Nor shall the wool learn to counterfeit various colors.

44. *Murice.* Murex, a sea-fish of the shell kind. It is said to have been of great use among the ancients for dying purple. Hence, by meton. put for the purple color itself. *Croceo:* an adj. from *crocum*, or *crocus*, saffron. *Luto:* the *Lutum* was an herb used in dying yellow. Hence the color itself, by meton. Modern botanists describe it under the name of *luteola*, wild-woad, and dyer's weed. It is used in coloring both wool and silk. *Mutabit:* shall tinge, or dye.

45. *Sandyx:* the scarlet color—vermilion.

46. *Fusis:* to their spindles.

47. *Parcæ.* They were the daughters of Erebus and Nox, and said to be three in number: *Clotho*, *Lachesis*, and *Atropos.* They were supposed to preside over the birth, life, and death of mankind. The first was represented as presiding over the moment of birth, and holding a distaff in her hand; the second, as spinning out the events and actions of human life; the last as cutting the thread of it with a pair of scissors. They were considered powerful goddesses, and were worshipped with great solemnity. *Stabili numine:* in the fixed purpose or decree. *Clara.* Some copies have *cara.*—*Magnum incrementum:* great son of Jove.

48. *Aggredere.* Ruæus says *accede.*

50. *Aspice mundum:* see the world with its globous mass or load, nodding (reeling to and fro) both the land, &c. Dr. Trapp takes *convexo pondere* in the sense of *convexi ponderis*, and connects it with *mundum*, and not with *nutantem*, as is commonly done. For he observes, that it is impossible for the earth to reel to and fro or nod, with its own weight or load. He chooses, therefore, to understand it of the load of its guilt and misery: *mole malorum, vitiorumque;* but rejoicing at the happy change about to be introduced, which is expressed in the next line: *omnia lætentur sæclo futuro.* Some explain the words, *aspice mundum*, &c., look with compassion upon a world, *nutantem mole malorum vitiorumque:* laboring and oppressed with a load of guilt and misery. *Ut:* in the sense of *quomodo.*

55. *Non vincet. Non* appears to be used in the sense of *nullus.* No one shall excel me in singing, neither Thracian, &c.

56. *Linus.* He was the son of Apollo and Terpsichore, one of the muses. He was an excellent musician, and the preceptor of Orpheus and Hercules. He is said to have been killed by the latter, by a stroke of his lyre, because he laughed at his singing. *Quamvis mater Calliopea adsit*, &c. Although the mother Calliopea should assist this Orpheus; and fair Apollo, the father, should assist this Linus. *Orphei:* a Greek dat. of *Orpheus.*

59. *Arcadiâ judice:* Arcadia being judge. Arcadia was an inland country of the Peloponnesus, famous for its excellent pastures. The whole of it was sacred to Pan. See Ecl. ii. 31.

60. *Risu cognoscere*, &c. Begin, sweet boy, to know thy mother by her smiles.

Matri longa decem tulerunt fastidia menses.
Incipe, parve puer, cui non risere parentes,
Nec Deus hunc mensâ, Dea nec dignata cubili est.

63. Nec Deus *dignatus est* hunc mensâ

NOTES.

This is the sense which Ruæus and some others give to *risu.* But Dr. Trapp takes it otherwise, applying it to the boy. Begin to know and acknowledge thy mother by smiling on her; as a kind of recompense for the pains she endured for thy sake.

61. *Fastidia:* qualms, as of a woman with child. *Longa:* tedious—without intermission. *Decem menses:* ten months brought to your mother, &c.

62. *Cui parentes non risere,* &c. It is plain the poet here intends a threat of some kind to the child. But upon the nature or extent of the threat, commentators are not agreed. It is generally thought that reference is here made to verse 15, where the babe was promised divine honors: *ille accipiet vitam Deorum;* and lest he should fail of it, the poet urges him to smile upon his parents, that in turn they might smile upon him. For, on whom his parents have not smiled, him hath a god neither honoured with his table, nor a goddess with her bed. Thus Dr. Trapp.

QUESTIONS.

What is the subject of this pastoral?

In what light has it been considered by some?

Are there any passages in it which have a resemblance to the prophecies of our Saviour, as contained in the scriptures?

Was the poet divinely inspired?

About this time was there a general expectation of the Messiah's appearance?

How was this occasioned?

At what age did the son of Pollio die?

How many years before the birth of Christ?

Do some suppose the poet celebrates the birth of Marcellus?

Who was this Marcellus? To what age did he live?

Who were the Sibyls? How many does Varro mention? Of these, which was the most distinguished?

Where did she reside?

What does Justin Martyr say of her residence?

Who was Saturn? What is said of him:

Whence did *Latium* derive its name?

How did Saturn employ his time after his banishment to Italy?

How many ages do the poets mention before the deluge in the reign of Deucalion?

Describe those ages?

Who was Apollo? What is said of him?

For what was he banished from heaven? What did he then do?

Where were his most celebrated oracles? What were his names?

Who was Pollio? To what honors did he arrive?

Was it through his means that Virgil recovered his land? In what way?

To what age did he live?

Who were the Parcæ? How many in number? What was their supposed office?

ECLOGA QUINTA.

MENALCAS, MOPSUS.

The subject of this excellent pastoral is the death of some eminent person under the character of Daphnis. But concerning the person intended, there have been various conjectures. It is most probable the poet had in view Julius Cæsar, who was killed in the senate-house by Brutus, and afterwards enrolled among the Roman deities. By Menalcas, we are to understand Virgil; and by Mopsus, some poet of reputation, who probably had been Virgil's pupil.

Ruæus thinks it was written when some games or sacrifices were performed in honor of Cæsar. The scene is beautiful, and adapted to the subject. The shepherds sit on the verdant grass in the awful gloom of a grotto, overhung with wild vines. The pastoral is properly divided into two parts—the Lamentation at his death, and his Deification, or Apotheosis.

1. *O* Mopse, quoniam *nos* convenimus *unà*, ambo boni; tu *bonus* inflare leves calamos, ego *bonus* dicere versus; cur non consedimus hìc inter ulmos mixtas corylis?

5. Sub *imus* umbras incertas motantibus,

6. Aspice ut sylvestris labrusca sparsit

9. Idem *Amyntas* certet

Me. CUR non, Mopse, boni quoniam convenimus ambo,
Tu calamos inflare leves, ego dicere versus,
Hìc corylis mixtas inter consedimus ulmos?
Mo. Tu major: tibi me est æquum parere, Menalca:
Sive sub incertas Zephyris motantibus umbras,
Sive antro potiùs succedimus: aspice, ut antrum
Sylvestris raris sparsit labrusca racemis.
Me. Montibus in nostris solus tibi certet Amyntas.
Mo. Quid si idem certet Phœbum superare canendo?
Me. Incipe, Mopse, prior, si quos aut Phyllidis ignes,
Aut Alconis habes laudes, aut jurgia Codri.

NOTES.

1. *Boni:* skilful—expert. An adj. agreeing with *nos*, understood.

4. *Major.* Thou art the older: or it may mean, my superior, in singing.

5. *Umbras:* shades. By meton. put for the trees causing them. *Incertas:* waving—moving to and fro.

7. *Sylvestris labrusca.* Simply, the wild vine. *Raris racemis:* with thin bunches of grapes—its bunches scattered here and there.

10. *Si habes aut quos ignes:* if you have either any loves of Phyllis, or &c. She was the daughter of Lycurgus, king of Thrace, and fell in love with Demophoon, the son of Theseus, king of Athens, on his return from the Trojan war. He went home to settle some business, and tarrying longer than the time appointed for their nuptials, Phyllis, imagining herself neglected, hung herself, and was changed into a leafless almond-tree. Demophoon afterwards returned and on his embracing the tree, it put forth leaves. *Ignis:* by meton love; also the object loved.

11. *Alconis.* Gen. of *Alcon*, a celebrated archer of Crete. He aimed an arrow so truly at a serpent, entwined around the body of his son, that he killed him without injuring the child. *Jurgia Codri:* the strife or contentions of *Codrus.* He was the son of Menander, and the last king of Athens. In a war with the Lacedemonians, it was given out by an oracle that victory should be on that side, whose king was slain. In the mean time the enemy had given strict charge not to hurt the Athenian king. Being informed of this, as well as what the oracle had given out, Codrus put on the habit of a peasant, went among the enemy, raised a quarrel, and suffered himself to be slain. As soon as this was known, the Lacedemonians were panic struck, and the Athenians obtained a complete victory. This noble sacrifice of himself for the good of his country, so endeared his name to them, that they considered no person worthy to succeed him.

Incipe : pascentes servabit Tityrus hœdos.
Mo. Immò hæc, in viridi nuper quæ cortice fagi
Carmina descripsi, et modulans alterna notavi,
Experiar : tu deinde jubeto certet Amyntas.
Me. Lenta salix quantùm pallenti cedit olivæ,
Puniceis humilis quantùm saliunca rosetis :
Judicio nostro tantùm tibi cedit Amyntas.
Mo. Sed tu desine plura, puer : successimus antro.
Extinctum Nymphæ crudeli funere Daphnim
Flebant : vos coryli testes et flumina Nymphis :
Cùm, complexa sui corpus miserabile nati,
Atque Deos atque astra vocat crudelia mater.
Non ulli pastos illis egêre diebus
Frigida, Daphni, boves ad flumina : nulla neque amnem
Libavit quadrupes, nec graminis attigit herbam.
Daphni, tuum Pœnos etiam ingemuisse leones
Interitum, montesque feri sylvæque loquuntur.
Daphnis et Armenias curru subjungere tigres
Instituit : Daphnis thiasos inducere Baccho,
Et foliis lentas intexere mollibus hastas.
Vitis ut arboribus decori est, ut vitibus uvæ,

13. Immò experiar hæc carmina, quæ nuper descripsi

15. Jubeto *ut* Amyntas certet *mecum*

19. Desine *loqui* plura *verba*

21. Vos, O coryli et flumina *fuistis* testes nymphis;

25. O Daphni, non ulli *pastores* egere pastos boves

28. Ferique montes, sylvæque loquuntur, etiam Pœnos leones

30. Daphnis *instituit* inducere

NOTES.

15. *Modulans alterna notavi:* tuning, or singing them alternate, I wrote them down. *Experiar:* I will try—attempt. *Carmina:* verses.

17. *Saliunca:* the herb lavender. *Puniceis rosetis:* to red rose-beds: or by meton. the red rose. *Puniceus*, sometimes written *Phœniceus*, an adj. from *Phœnicia*, a country lying along the eastern shore of the Mediterranean, including Tyre and Sidon, famous for its purple or red color. The same word is used for an inhabitant of Carthage, because that city was founded by a colony from Tyre, or Phœnicia.

20. *Daphnim extinctum:* Daphnis slain, or cut off by a cruel death. This circumstance applies very well to the case of Julius Cæsar, who was slain unexpectedly, receiving no less than twenty-three wounds with the dagger.

22. *Cùm mater complexa*: when the mother embracing, &c. Cerdanus understands by *mater* the wife of Cæsar, who a little before his death dreamed her husband was stabbed in his breast. Ruæus understands Rome, and Dr. Martyn Venus. *Vocat*, &c. She calls the gods and stars cruel—she blames the gods and cruel stars. *Vocat*, Dr. Trapp takes for *vocabat*, where the sense evidently determines it.

25 *Amnem:* in the sense of *aquam.*

26. *Nulla quadrupes.* Ruæus thinks the poet hath in his view a passage in Suetonius. Speaking of the prodigies which preceded the death of Cæsar, he says: *Proximis diebus equorum greges, quos in trajiciendo Rubicone flumine consecrârat, ac vagos et sine custode dimiserat, comperit pertinacissimè pabulo abstinere, ubertimque flere.* In this case, by *quadrupes*, we are to understand *equus*, a horse. *Libavit:* drank—tasted.

27. *Pœnos leones:* African lions. *Pœnos:* in the sense of *Punicos, vel Africanos.* Carthage was the principal city of Africa.—Hence by synec. it may be put for Africa in general. Being founded by a colony from *Phœnicia*, its inhabitants were called *Pœni*, as well as *Carthaginienses.* These lions are mentioned, either because they were the most savage, or because Africa abounded in lions, and other savage beasts.

28. *Interitum:* in the sense of *mortem. Feri:* wild—uncultivated.

29. *Armenias:* an adj. from *Armenia*, an extensive country of Asia, abounding in tigers. *Curru*, for *currui*, the dat. case. Nouns of the fourth declension sometimes formed the gen. in *uis*, and when the gen. was contracted into *ûs*, the dat. was sometimes contracted into *u.* Many instances of this contraction we find in Virgil and other writers.

30. *Thiasos.* Thiasus, a kind of dance. The word is of Greek origin.

31. *Intexere lentas hastas*, &c. To wreath, or entwine limber spears, &c. Ruæus interprets *intexere*, by *induere.*

32. *Ut vitis est decori arboribus:* as the vine is for an ornament to the trees, as the grapes, &c. The words *sunt decori* are to be supplied.

Ut gregibus tauri, segetes ut pinguibus arvis;

34. *Sic* tu *eras* omne decus tuis

Tu decus omne tuis: postquam te fata tulerunt,
Ipsa Pales agros, atque ipse reliquit Apollo.

36 *In* sulcis, quibus mandavimus grandia hordea, sæpe

Grandia sæpe quibus mandavimus hordea sulcis.
Infelix lolium, et steriles nascuntur avenæ.
Pro molli violâ, pro purpureo narcisso,
Carduus et spinis surgit paliurus acutis.
Spargite humum foliis; inducite fontibus umbras,
Pastores: mandat fieri sibi talia Daphnis.
Et tumulum facite, et tumulo superaddite carmen:

43. Ego Daphnis *jacio hic* in sylvis, notus hinc

Daphnis ego in sylvis, hinc usque ad sidera notus;
Formosi pecoris custos, formosior ipse.
Me. Tale tuum carmen nobis, divine poëta,
Quale sopor fessis in gramine; quale per æstum
Dulcis aquæ saliente sitim restinguere rivo.
Nec calamis solùm æquiparas, sed voce magistrum.
Fortunate puer, tu nunc eris alter ab illo:

50. Tamen nos dicemus hæc nostra *carmina*

Nos tamen hæc quocunque modo tibi nostra vicissim
Dicemus; Daphninque tuum tollemus ad astra;
Daphnin ad astra feremus: amavit nos quoque Daphnis.
Mo. An quicquam nobis tali sit munere majus?
Et puer ipse fuit cantari dignus, et ista
Jampridem Stimicon laudavit carmina nobis.
Me. Candidus insuetum miratur limen Olympi,
Sub pedibusque videt nubes et sidera Daphnis

58. Ergo alacris voluptas tenet sylvas

Ergò alacris sylvas et cætera rura voluptas,
Panaque, pastoresque tenet, Dryadasque puellas

NOTES.

34. *Tu omne decus tuis:* so thou wast all the ornament to thy friends. *Tuis:* to thy fellow swains. Virgil represents Daphnis, whoever he be, as a swain and shepherd.

35. *Pales.* See Geor. iii. 1. *Apollo.* He is considered here under the character of the god of shepherds. See Ecl. iv. 10.

36. *Hordea:* barley, here put for any kind of grain; the *species* for the *genus.*

37. *Infelix lolium:* the hurtful cockle.

38. *Narcisso:* the flower *Narcissus*, of which there are two kinds, the white and the purple. See Ecl. ii. 46.

39. *Carduus:* the thistle. *Paliurus:* a species of thorn. It abounds in Italy.

42. *Carmen:* an epitapn, or inscription.

45. *Tale tuum carmen.* The elegance and sweetness of this and the two following lines are not to be equalled, unless by the answer, which Mopsus returns in verse 82, et sequens. *Est* is to be supplied.

47. *Restinguere,* &c. To allay thirst in a purling rivulet of sweet water in the summer heat. This is a most beautiful comparison. Nothing could give a livelier idea of the charms of his music, and the melody of his song.

48. *Magistrum:* the master. It appears from this, that Mopsus had been a pupil of Menalcas, and much esteemed by him.

49. *Alter ab illo:* the next from him—the next in fame after him.

50. *Quocunque modo:* in some manner or other—as well as I can.

52. *Daphnis,* &c. As we are to understand Virgil under the character of Menalcas, it is urged that Daphnis cannot be Julius Cæsar, because Virgil was little known in his time. But Ruæus explains it of the Mantuans in general, who, with the other inhabitants of Cis-alpine Gaul, were cherished and protected by Cæsar.

53. *An quicquam sit:* can there be any thing more acceptable (*majus*) to me than such an employment?

54. *Puer ipse.* Servius infers from this that Daphnis cannot be Julius Cæsar, since he was 56 years old when he was killed. Ruæus understands it of his being lately enrolled among the gods. But this is an unnecessary refinement, and the objection of Servius will be of no weight, when it is considered that Virgil speaks of *Daphnis* under the character of a shepherd, or swain. See 43 and 44, supra; and *puer* is the word generally used to denote either.

56. *Candidus:* white—clothed in white. This is an emblem of divinity; white being the color assigned to the celestial gods, as black is to the infernal gods. *Insuetum:* a

Nec lupus insidias pecori, nec retia cervis
Ulla dolum meditantur: amat bonus otia Daphnis.
Ipsi lætitiâ voces ad sidera jactant
Intonsi montes: ipsæ jam carmina rupes;
Ipsa sonant arbusta: Deus, Deus ille, Menalca.
Sis bonus, ô felixque tuis! en quatuor aras:
Ecce duas tibi, Daphni, duoque altaria Phœbo.
Pocula bina novo spumantia lacte quotannis,
Craterasque duos statuam tibi pinguis olivi.
Et multo imprimis hilarans convivia Baccho,
Ante focum, si frigus erit; si messis, in umbrâ,

60. Lupus *meditatur*

63. Jam rupes ipsæ sonant carmina; *jam* arbusta ipsa *sonant hoc*: O Menalca, ille *est* Deus, *ille est* Deus.

65. En *aspice* quatuor aras: ecce *aspice* duas *aras* tibi

67. Statuam bina pocula spumantia novo lacte, duosque

NOTES.

part. of *insuesco*, unaccustomed, referring to his being but lately deified. *Lymen Olympi:* the threshold of heaven. There were several mountains by the name of Olympus. The most distinguished, however, was one in Thessaly, near the confines of Macedonia; the top of which arose above the clouds. Hence the poets feigned it to be heaven, the seat of the gods.

60. *Insidias:* plots. This word hath no singular. *Retia:* neu. plu. toils—snares. *Meditantur:* devise, or prepare.

61. *Amat otia*, &c. This expression seems to allude to the clemency of Cæsar toward his enemies, for which he is much celebrated by Cicero and others.

62. *Jactant:* in the sense of *emittunt.*

63. *Intonsi:* uncultivated—wild.

64. *Deus ille.* Divine honors were decreed to Julius Cæsar by the Triumviri, in the year of Rome 712, Lepidus and Plancus being consuls. From this time, Octavius began to be called the son of a god.

65. *Aras. Ara* was an altar dedicated both to the gods above, and to those below. *Altare* was a high altar, and dedicated to the gods above exclusively. *Felix:* propitious—kind.

68. *Crateras:* acc. plu. of *crater*, a large cup, or bowl. This word is purely Greek. *Statuam:* in the sense of *offeram.*

69. *Hilarans convivia*, &c. Cheering or making merry the feasts with much wine. Bacchus, the god of wine, was the son of Jupiter and Semele. He was educated, according to some, in the island of *Naxus*, one of the Cyclades, under the care of the nymphs Philia, Coronis, and Clyda; and while asleep was carried off by some mariners, all of whom he changed into dolphins, except the pilot, who showed him some tenderness and regard. Bacchus is celebrated as a warrior. He marched into India at the head of a large army composed of men and women, all inspired with a divine fury, and armed with the *thyrsus*, *cymbal*, &c. His conquests were easy—the people submitting wherever he came, without resistance. Pentheus, king of Thebes, refused to acknowledge his divinity, and forbade his subjects to pay adoration to him; and even ordered Bacchus himself to be seized and cast into prison. But the doors opened of their own accord, as if refusing to contain him a prisoner. Whereupon the king became enraged, and ordered the whole band of Bacchanals to be destroyed. But this was not carried into effect. Pentheus became desirous to see the celebration of the Orgies, or feasts of Bacchus. For this purpose, he concealed himself on mount Citheron, whence he could see all their ceremonies. But being discovered, the Bacchanals fell upon him. His mother was the first who attacked him, and was followed by her two sisters, *Ino* and *Autone*, who immediately tore him in pieces. See Ovid Met. Lib. 3.

Midas, king of Phrygia, had entertained Silenus, the preceptor of Bacchus; who desired him to ask any thing he might please, and it should be granted him.—Whereupon he asked that whatever he might touch should be converted into gold. This was granted. But he was soon convinced of his imprudent choice; for his food became gold in his mouth, and he was on the point of perishing with hunger, when he besought Bacchus to take back his gift; he readily did so, and directed him to wash in the river *Pactolus*, whose sands were converted into gold.

The festivals of Bacchus, called *Orgia*, *Bacchanalia*, or *Dyonisia*, were introduced into Greece by Danaus and his daughters, from Egypt. The panther was sacred to him, because in his expedition to India, he was covered with the skin of that animal. The fir-tree, the yew-tree, the fig-tree, the ivy, and the vine, were all sacred to him. Bacchus had several names: *Liber*, *Bromius*, *Lyæus*, *Evan*, *Thryonæus*, *Iacchus*, &c. He is represented as drawn in a chariot by a tiger and a lion, accompanied by Pan, Silenus, and the other satyrs. *Bacchus*, by meton. is frequently put for *wine*, as in the present case.

71. **Arvisia** vina *quæ sunt.*

79. Ut Agricolæ facient vota quotannis Baccho Cererique, sic *facient ea tibi*

81. Quæ, quæ dona reddam

82. Nam neque sibilus venientis Austri *juvat* me tantùm; nec litora percussa fluctu tam juvant *me;* nec flumina quæ decurrunt inter saxosas valles, *tam juvant me.*

Vina novum fundam calathis Arvisia nectar.
Cantabunt mihi Damœtas, et Lyctius Ægon:
Saltantes Satyros imitabitur Alphesibœus.
Hæc tibi semper erunt; et cùm solennia vota
Reddemus Nymphis, et cùm lustrabimus agros.
Dum juga montis aper, fluvios dum piscis amabit,
Dumque thymo pascentur apes, dum rore cicadæ,
Semper honos, nomenque tuum, laudesque manebunt.
Ut Baccho Cererique, tibi sic vota quotannis
Agricolæ facient: damnabis tu quoque votis.
Mo. Quæ tibi, quæ tali reddam pro carmine dona?
Nam neque me tantùm venientis sibilus Austri,
Nec percussa juvant fluctu tam litora, nec quæ
Saxosas inter decurrunt flumina valles.

NOTES.

71. *Arvisia vina:* Chian wine. *Arvisia:* an adj. from *Arvisus*, a promontory of the island Chios, in the Archipelago, famous for its good wine. *Novum nectar:* nectar was properly any kind of pleasant wine, or other liquor. Hence the poets feigned it to be the drink of the gods. *Novum:* good—excellent. The wine here offered was to be as good as nectar—good or excellent nectar. See Ecl. iii. 66.

72. *Lyctius:* an adj. from *Lyctus*, a city of Crete.

73. *Saltantes Satyros:* leaping or wonton satyrs. The *Satyri* were demi-gods of the country, the origin of whom is not well known. They were of a hideous form, and generally distinguished themselves by their riotous and wanton demeanor in the orgies of Bacchus, which they generally attended. The Romans called them indiscriminately *Fauni*, *Panes*, and *Sylvani*. *Alphesibœus.* See Ecl. 8.

75. *Lustrabimus.* *Lustro* may here be taken in the sense of *circumeo*, to go around or encompass; or of *purgo*, to cleanse or purify by sacrifice; or it may comprehend both. For it is agreed by all, that the poet hath a reference to what is called the *sacrificium ambervale*, spoken of Geor. i. 345, which see. *Circumimus campos cum hostia*, says Ruæus. *Reddemus:* in the sense of *solvemus.*

79. *Cereri.* *Ceres* was the goddess of husbandry, the daughter of Saturn and Ops, and mother of Proserpine by Jupiter, whom Pluto carried off while she was gathering flowers in the plains of *Enna*, in Sicily. The loss was grievous to Ceres, who sought her both day and night; when at length she found her veil near the fountain of Cyane. She could obtain no information of her daughter, till the nymph Arethusa told her that she was carried off by Pluto. Upon this, she immediately ascended to heaven, and demanded of Jupiter the restoration of her darling child. He endeavored to reconcile her to Pluto as a son-in-law; but to no purpose. At length he consented that she should be restored, provided she had eaten nothing in the dominions of the ravisher. Ceres repaired immediately to the infernal regions, and found she had eaten the seeds of a pomegranate, found in the Elysian fields. Her return, therefore, was impossible: but Jupiter consented that she might pass six months of the year with her mother on earth, and the remainder with Pluto.

During all this time, the cultivation of the earth had been neglected. To repair the loss which mankind sustained by her absence, Ceres went to Attica and instructed *Triptolemus*, the son of Celeus, in all that pertained to agriculture.

Ceres is supposed to be the same as the Egyptian *Isis*, and her worship to have been brought into Greece by Erechtheus about 1426 years before Christ. She is supposed to be the same as *Tellus*, *Cybele*, *Berecynthia*, &c. The Romans paid her great veneration, and her festivals were generally celebrated for eight days in the month of April. *Ceres*, by meton. is often put for bread grain, &c.

80. *Damnabis tu*, &c. Thou shalt also bind them to their vows—thou shalt grant the requests of those, who ask. The propriety of this mode of expression will appear, when it is considered that the person who asked any thing of a God, virtually, if not directly, promised or vowed something in return; and if his requests were granted, then he became condemned, and judicially bound to the performance of his promise or vow. And the god, when he granted any petition or request, was said to condemn, or bind the promiser to pay his vows.

82. *Sibilus:* the whistling of the rising south wind.

ME. Hâc te nos fragili donabimus antè cicutâ.
Hæc nos, Formosum Corydon ardebat Alexim:
Hæc eadem docuit, Cujum pecus? an Melibœi?
Mo. At tu sume pedum, quod, me cùm sæpe rogaret,
Non tulit Antigenes (et erat tum dignus amari)
Formosum paribus nodis atque ære, Menalca.

86. Hæc eadem *cicuta* docuit nos,

88. Sume pedum formosum paribus nodis atque ære, quod Antigenes non tulit, cùm sæpe rogaret me, et

NOTES.

85. *Nos donabimus:* I will present thee with this, &c. *Cicuta:* properly a pipe made of the stalk of the hemlock. See Ecl. I. 10.

86. *Hæc eadem docuit:* this same pipe taught me: *formosum Corydon*, &c. i. e. with this same pipe I sang the second Eclogue. *Hæc docuit:* this same taught me: *Cujum pecus?* i. e. with this same pipe I sang the third Eclogue.

88. *Sume pedum:* take this crook, as a testimony of my regard.

90. *Formosum:* beautified with equal knobs and brass—with knobs at equal distances: or uniform, in regard to size.

QUESTIONS.

What is the subject of this pastoral?

Who probably is meant by Daphnis?

Who is to be understood under the character of Menalcas? Who under that of Mopsus?

When does Ruæus suppose it to have been written?

Where is the scene laid?

Into how many parts is the pastoral divided?

Who was Alcon? and what is said of him?

Who was Codrus? and what is said of him?

Who was Bacchus? What is said of him? What were his festivals called?

By whom were they introduced into Greece? and from what country?

What were his votaries called?

What were some of the names of Bacchus?

How is he represented as drawn?

What is the word Bacchus frequently used for?

Who were the Satyri? How did they distinguish themselves?

Who was Ceres? What is said of her?

Is she supposed to be the same with the Egyptian *Isis?*

By whom was her worship introduced into Greece? and at what time?

When were her festivals celebrated?

ECLOGA SEXTA.

SILENUS.

The subject of this fine pastoral is Silenus. He had promised the swains Chromis and Mnasilus a song; but had put it off from time to time. Wearied with the delay, they surprised him asleep in his grotto, just recovering from his intoxication. His garlands lay at some distance from him: with these they bind him fast; and in this condition they demand of him the fulfilment of his promise. At this moment, Ægle, one of the nymphs, joins them. Upon which he begins, and explains to them the origin of the world upon the principles of the Epicurean philosophy; and concludes with several interesting fables by way of episode.

It is generally supposed this pastoral was designed as a compliment to *Syro* the Epicurean, who taught Virgil the principles of that philosophy. By Silenus we are to understand Syro, and by the swains *Chromis* and *Mnasilus*, his two pupils, Virgil and Varus

PRIMA Syracosio dignata est ludere versu
2. Nostra Thalia prima dignata est
Nostra, nec erubuit sylvas habitare, Thalia.
Cùm canerem reges et prælia, Cynthius aurem
Vellit, et admonuit: Pastorem, Tityre, pingues
Pascere oportet oves, deductum dicere carmen.
6. Namque, *O Vare*, supererunt tibi *alii poetæ* qui cupiant
Nunc ego (namque super tibi erunt, qui dicere laudes,
Vare, tuas cupiant, et tristia condere bella)
Agrestem tenui meditabor arundine Musam.
Non injussa cano: si quis tamen hæc quoque, si quis

NOTES.

1. *Syracosio versu:* in pastoral verse. *Syracosio:* an adj. from *Syracusæ*, the birth place of Theocritus, the first pastoral poet of eminence; the chief city of Sicily, and famous for its defence against the Romans under Marcellus.

2. *Thalia.* One of the Muses. See Ecl. iii. 60. *Nec erubuit*, &c. Nor did she blush to inhabit the woods. This verb here is both expressive and beautiful; the perf. of *erubesco.* Thalia was supposed to preside over comedy and pastoral poetry. Virgil was the first pastoral writer among the Romans; which explains the words, *nostra Thalia prima:* my muse first deigned, &c.

3. *Cum canerem*, &c. Virgil is said to have begun a work upon the affairs of *Alba Longa*, but afterwards relinquished it, and commenced the Bucolics. *Cynthius:* a name of Apollo. See Ecl. iv. 10. *Vellit:* pinched my ear; a proverbial expression, implying admonition.

5. *Deductum:* a part. of *deduco*, humble, or slender. A metaphor taken from wool spun out till it is made fine or slender.

6. *Supererunt:* in the sense of *erunt alii poetæ.* The parts of the verb are separated by Tmesis.

7. *Vare.* It is generally thought that the poet here means *Quintilius Varus*, who arose to the highest honors under Augustus. He was consul in the year of Rome 741; after which he was præfect of Syria eight years. Having returned home, he was sent into Germany with three legions, which he lost, being drawn into an ambush. This mortified him so much, that he killed himself. This happened in the year 762. *Condere:* to write--record.

9. *Non injussa cano:* I do not sing things forbidden by Apollo. He permits me to sing of pastoral subjects, but not of kings and battles. *Si quis tamen*, &c. The *tamen* does not refer to the words, *non injussa cano*, but to the third and fourth lines, where Apollo forbids him to write in the lofty style of heroic poetry. The meaning seems to be this: though he forbid me to describe your actions in heroic verse, he permits me to do it in the humble style of pastoral. And if any should be taken, *captus amore*, with the love of this kind of writing, and should read these pastorals, he shall here find them. *Hæc:* these things—these my Bucolics. *Quoque:* in the sense of *etiam.*

Captus amore leget; te nostræ, Vare, myricæ,
Te nemus omne canet: nec Phœbo gratior ulla est,
Quàm sibi quæ Vari præscripsit pagina nomen.
Pergite, Pierides. Chromis et Mnasilus in antro
Silenum pueri somno vidêre jacentem,
Inflatum hesterno venas, ut semper, Iaccho.
Serta procul tantùm capiti delapsa jacebant:
Et gravis attritâ pendebat cantharus ansâ.
Aggressi (nam sæpe senex spe carminis ambo
Luserat) injiciunt ipsis ex vincula sertis.
Addit se sociam, timidisque supervenit Ægle
Ægle Naïadum pulcherrima: jamque videnti
Sanguineis frontem moris et tempora pingit.
Ille dolum ridens: Quò vincula nectitis? inquit.
Solvite me, pueri: satìs est potuisse videri.
Carmina, quæ vultis, cognoscite: carmina vobis,
Huic aliud mercedis erit: simul incipit ipse.
Tum verò in numerum Faunosque ferasque videres
Ludere, tum rigidas motare cacumina quercus.
Nec tantùm Phœbo gaudet Parnassia rupes,
Nec tantùm Rhodope mirantur et Ismarus Orphea
Namque canebat utì magnum per inane coacta

10. Nostræ myricæ *canent* **te, O Vare, omne nemus canet te: nec est ulla pagina gratior Phœbo, quàm** *illa* **quæ**

14. Pueri Chromis et Mnasilus vidêre

15. Ut semper *est mos illi*

24. Satis est *me* **potuisse videri** *sic vobis.*

25. *Sunt* **carmina vobis: huic** *Ægle* **erit aliud mercedis.**

NOTES.

10. *Nostræ myricæ:* in the sense of *nostra Bucolica.* The *omne nemus* in the following line probably means every elevated composition, such as epic or heroic. We are led to this interpretation from the declaration of the poet in the sixth line, that there would be other poets, who would celebrate the praises of Varus in heroic verse, though he himself would prefer to do it in the humbler style of pastoral.

14. *Silenum.* Silenus was one of the rural deities, the god of mysteries and knowledge, and the foster-father of Bacchus. He is said, by some, to have been the son of Pan; others say, the son of Mercury. Malea, in the island of Lesbos, is the supposed place of his nativity. He is represented as a fat and merry old man, riding on an ass, crowned with flowers, always intoxicated.

15. *Inflatum,* &c. Swollen as to his veins, with his yesterday's wine. See Ecl. i. 55. *Iaccho:* a name of Bacchus; here put, by meton. for *wine.* It is derived from a Greek word signifying a shout or confused noise. It was given to him on account of the riot and vociferation of his inebriated followers. See Ecl. v. 69.

16. *Serta:* plu. of *sertum,* a garland, or wreath of flowers. To be crowned with a garland, was an indication of drunkenness. Silenus had all the signs of being in such a state. He was lying down—he was sleeping; but his garlands were not on his head; *tantùm delapsa:* they had only fallen off—they were neither broken nor bruised.

18. *Aggressi,* &c. The swains, seizing, put on him cords of these very garlands—they bind him with cords made of them.

20. *Ægle.* The name of a nymph, derived from a Greek word signifying splendor, or brightness. *Naïadum.* See Ecl. ii. 46. *Videnti:* to him just opening his eyes. *Timidis:* to the trembling swains.

22. *Moris.* Morus was the fruit of the mulberry-tree. It is here called *sanguineus,* red, or bloody. It is said to have been originally white; but assumed the red or purple color, in memory of the two lovers, *Pyramus* and *Thisbe,* who slew themselves under a mulberry-tree. See Ovid. Met. Lib. 4.

23. *Quò:* why—for what purpose.

25. *Cognoscite:* in the sense of *audite.*

26. *Aliud mercedis.* The same as *alia merces:* another reward.

27. *Ludere in numerum:* to dance, or leap about in regular time, or measure. Their motions exactly corresponded to the notes or measure of the verse. *Faunos* The Fauni were demi-gods of the country, to whom the first fruits of all things were generally offered. See Ecl. v. 73.

29. *Parnassia rupes.* The mountain Parnassus in Phocis; a country in *Grecia Propria,* much celebrated by the poets, and sacred to the Muses. Here Apollo had a famous temple.

30. *Rhodope—Ismarus.* Two mountains, or rather ranges of mountains, in Thrace the country of *Orpheus.*

31. *Namque canebat,* &c. For he sung how the seeds, both of the earth and of the air

Semina terrarumque, animæque, marisque fuissent,
Et liquidi simul ignis : ut his exordia primis
Omnia, et ipse tener mundi concreverit orbis.
Tum durare solum, et discludere Nerea ponto
Cœperit, et rerum paulatim sumere formas.
Jamque novum ut terræ stupeant lucescere solem,
Altiùs utque cadant submotis nubibus imbres :
Incipiant sylvæ cùm primùm surgere, cùmque
Rara per ignotos errent animalia montes.
Hinc lapides Pyrrhæ jactos, Saturnia regna,
Caucaseasque refert volucres, furtumque Promethei.

33. Ut *ex* his primis omnia *susceperunt*

35. Tum *canebat quomodo* solum cœperit

37. Jamque *canebat* ut terræ stupeant

38. Utque imbres cadant *è* nubibus submotis altiùs *à terra.*

NOTES.

and of the sea, &c. Silenus here relates the origin of the world, according to the system of Epicurus, who taught that incorporeal space, and corporeal atoms, were the first principles, or elements, of all things. The former he denomenated *Inane*, the latter *Plenum*. The *Inane* or *Vacuum*, he considered space, every way indefinitely extended. By the *Plenum*, he understood the atoms or minute particles of matter moving in every direction through the *Inane*, which Virgil here calls the *semina*, because it was thought by their fortuitous concurrence arose what we call the four elements, earth, air, water, and fire. Epicurus held many other erroneous notions, particularly concerning the nature of God. He was an Athenian, and born about 340 years before the Christian era. He had many followers.

32. *Animæ :* in the sense of *aëris*. Without air, there could be no animal existence.

33. *Liquidi ignis :* of pure fire. *His primis :* of these first principles or elements (*earth*, *air*, *water*, and *fire*) all things sprang or had a beginning. The Epicureans maintained that, though their atoms and incorporeal space were the first principles or elements of earth, air, water, and fire, yet these last were the principles or elements of all other things, or out of which all other things sprang. *Omnia exordia :* all things received or took a beginning. The verb *susceperunt*, or some other of the like import, is plainly understood, and to be supplied. *Ut :* how.

35. *Nerea :* acc. sing of *Nereus*, a god of the sea, the son of Oceanus and Terra. He married Doris, by whom he had fifty daughters who were called *Nereïdes*. He possessed the gift of prophecy, and is said to have informed Paris of the fatal consequences of his carrying off Helen, the wife of Menelaus. It was by the direction and assistance of *Nereus*, that Hercules obtained the golden apples of the Hesperides. The word *Nereus* often put, by meton. for the sea, as in this place. *Solum*, &c. Then he sang how the land began to grow hard and to separate the waters from itself, and confine them to their channel. Ruæus says, *Dispellere aquas a se in mare.*

38. *Utque.* Some copies have *atque*, but *utque* is the easier.

40. *Rara :* few in number, or thinly dispersed.

41. *Hinc refert lapides*, &c. After that he relates the thrown stones of Pyrrha, &c. Pyrrha was the daughter of Epimetheus, and wife of Deucalion, the son of Prometheus, and king of Thessaly. The poets say, that some time during his reign the inhabitants of the earth were destroyed by a universal deluge, except himself and his wife Pyrrha. They were preserved in a small ship, and carried by the waters to mount Parnassus, which was the only place not overwhelmed. Here they consulted the oracle of *Themis* concerning the restoration of the human race; when they were informed, to cast behind them the bones of their great mother; by which they understood stones. They immediately obeyed the command of the oracle, and those thrown by Deucalion became men, and those by Pyrrha, women. See Ovid. Met. Lib. 1. *Saturnia regna :* the reign of Saturn, or the Golden age. See Ecl. iv. 6.

42. *Furtum Promethei :* the theft of Prometheus. The poets say that he stole fire from heaven, with which he animated a man of clay, made by himself. At this, Jupiter was so much enraged, that he ordered Mercury to chain him to a rock on mount Caucasus. He did so, and placed a vulture to prey upon his liver; which, however, grew as fast as it was consumed. Hence *Caucaseas volucres :* the vultures of Caucasus. This is a very celebrated mountain, or rather range of mountains, lying between the Euxine and Caspian seas. *Promethei :* the word Prometheus is of Greek origin, and properly signifies foresight, or an anxious care or solicitude. This is a key to the story. It conveys a strong idea of the troubles men create to themselves, by taking too much care and thought for the morrow.

His adjungit, Hylan nautæ quo fonte relictum
Clamâssent: ut litus, Hyla, Hyla, omne sonaret.
Et fortunatam, si nunquam armenta fuissent,
Pasiphaën nivei solatur amore juvenci.
Ah, virgo infelix, quæ te dementia cepit?
Prœtides implêrunt falsis mugitibus agros:
At non tam turpes pecudum tamen ulla secuta est
Concubitus; quamvis collo timuisset aratrum,
Et sæpe in levi quæsîsset cornua fronte.
Ah, virgo infelix, tu nunc in montibus erras!
Ille, latus niveum molli fultus hyacintho,
Ilice sub nigrâ pallentes ruminat herbas,
Aut aliquam in magno sequitur grege. Claudite, Nymphæ,
Dictææ Nymphæ, nemorum jam claudite saltus:
Si quà fortè ferant oculis sese obvia nostris
Errabunda bovis vestigia. Forsitan illum,
Aut herbâ captum viridi, aut armenta secutum,
Perducant aliquæ stabula ad Gortynia vaccæ.
Tum canit Hesperidum miratam mala puellam:
Tum Phaëthontiadas musco circumdat amaræ

46. Et solatur Pasiphaën amore nivei juvenci, fortunatam, si

49. At tamen non ulla earum secuta est tam turpes

53. Ille *taurus* fultus *quoad* niveum latus molli hyacintho, ruminat

55. Aut aliquam *vaccam*

58. Forsitan aliquæ vaccæ perducant illum, aut captum viridi herbâ, aut secutum armenta ad

NOTES.

43. *Hylan.* Hylas was the companion of Hercules in the Argonautic expedition, and much beloved by him. Having gone on shore to obtain water, by some means or other, he was lost. The poets say he was carried off by the nymphs. Hercules and his companions were much grieved at the loss of the boy, and went along the shores, when they found he was missing, calling him by name, *Hyla, Hyla. Clamâssent:* in the sense of *vocavissent.* See Ecl. iv. 35.

46. *Pasiphaën:* a Greek acc. the daughter of the sun, and wife of Minos, king of Crete. See Æn. vi. 24.

47. *Virgo.* The poet here calls *Pasiphaë* a virgin, though she was the mother of *Phædra, Ariadne,* and *Androgeus.* The ancients sometimes called any woman in early life a virgin.

48. *Prœtides:* the daughters of *Prœtus,* king of the Argives, who vied with Juno in beauty. The goddess, by way of punishment, caused them to imagine they were changed into heifers. Their lowings, *mugitus,* are here called false, because they were not in reality heifers. *Secuta est:* in the sense of *quæsivit.*

50. *Quamvis timuisset:* although each one had feared the plough upon her neck—the yoke from which the plough was hung or suspended.

53. *Fultus:* supported—resting or reclining.

56. *Dictææ:* an adj. from *Dicte,* a mountain of Crete. Silenus turns again to the story of Pasiphaë, whom he here introduces as speaking, and calling upon the nymphs to shut up the openings of the groves. Perhaps some where or other the wandering steps of my bull may present themselves to my eyes. *Obvia:* an adj. from *obvius,* agreeing with *vestigia.* The sense is complete without it. *Saltus,* is properly a lawn, or opening in a grove or park, where cattle have room to sport and play; from the verb *salio.*

59. *Captum:* delighted with, desirous of, the green pastures. Ruæus says, *cupidum.*

60. *Gortynia:* an adj. from *Gortyna,* a city of Crete, famed for its excellent pastures.

61. *Tum canit puellam,* &c. Then he sings the damsel admiring the apples of the Hesperides. This was Atalanta, the daughter of *Schœneus,* king of the island of Scyrus, in the Ægean sea. She consented to marry the man who should outrun her, but if he were beaten, he should lose his life. Several had lost their lives. At length she was beaten by Hippomenes, the grandson of Neptune or Mars. At the suggestion of Venus, Hippomenes cast three apples, taken from the garden of the Hesperides, on the ground, one at a time, when she was gaining upon him; which so captivated the virgin, that she stopped to pick them up; and by this means he obtained the beauteous prize. *Hesperidum.* The Hesperides were three in number, *Ægle, Arethusa,* and *Hesperethusa,* the daughters of Hesperus, the brother of Atlas. They resided in Mauritania, in Africa, where it is said they had gardens, in which were trees that bore golden apples. These gardens were watched by a dragon that never slept. Hercules slew him, and stole the apples. See Æn. iv. 484.

62. *Tum circumdat,* &c. Then he encloses the sisters of *Phaëthon* in the moss of bitter bark—he sings them transformed into pop-

64. Tum canit ut una sororum duxerit Gallum errantem ad flumina Permessi

67. Ut Linus pastor ornatus *quoad* crines floribus, atque amaro apio dixerit hæc illi divino carmine: *O Galle*, Musæ dant hos calamos tibi; en accipe *eos*, quos *illæ dederant*

74. Aut *ut narraverit* Scyllam *filiam* Nisi, *aut eam* quam fama secuta est succinctam *quoad*

Corticis, atque solo proceras erigit alnos.
Tum canit errantem Permessi ad flumina Gallum
Aonas in montes ut duxerit una sororum:
Utque viro Phœbi chorus assurrexerit omnis;
Ut Linus hæc illi divino carmine pastor,
Floribus atque apio crines ornatus amaro,
Dixerit: Hos tibi dant calamos, en accipe, Musæ,
Ascræo quos antè seni: quibus ille solebat
Cantando rigidas deducere montibus ornos.
His tibi Grynæi nemoris dicatur origo:
Ne quis sit lucus, quo se plùs jactet Apollo.
Quid loquar aut Scyllam Nisi, aut quam fama secuta est,
Candida succinctam latrantibus inguina monstris,

NOTES.

lar or alder trees. *Phaëthontiadas:* These were the sisters of *Phaëthon*, or *Phaëton*, and daughters of the sun. They were sometimes called *Heliades*. Their names were *Phaëthusa*, *Lampetie*, and *Lampethusa*. *Phaëton* imprudently desired of his father the management of his chariot for one day. Phœbus refused for a long time. But, at last, overcome by his importunity, he consented. He was, however, soon convinced of his rashness; for the horses, perceiving an unusual driver, became impatient of the reins; and when they had passed the meridian in their course, and began to descend, he was no longer able to restrain them, and the youth was thrown headlong from the car into the Eridanus, or Po. His sisters grieved immoderately at this misfortune of their brother; and were changed, some say, into poplar trees, others say, into alder trees. See Ovid. Met. Lib. 2.

63. *Circumdat.* Ruæus says, *cingit. Proceras:* stately.

64. *Permessi.* Permessus, a river of Beotia, rising at the foot of mount Helicon. *Gallum.* See Ecl. 10.

65. *In Aonas montes:* to the Beotian mountains, *Helicon* and *Citheron*, famous for being the seat of the Muses. Beotia was originally called *Aonia*, from *Aon*, the son of Neptune, who reigned in that country.

66. *Omnis chorus.* Here Virgil pays Gallus a very high compliment as a poet; and he does it in the most delicate manner. They rose up in his presence, to do him honor: *assurrexerit viro.*

67. *Linus.* See Ecl. iv. 56. *Carmine:* in the sense of *versibus.*

70. *Ascræo seni:* to the Ascrean sage—Hesiod; who was a native of Ascra, a town of Beotia not far from Helicon. He was a celebrated poet.

71. *Quibus ille*, &c. It is said of Orpheus, that the lofty oaks bowed their heads, and listened to the charms of his music. The same effects are ascribed here to the music of Hesiod. It is the highest compliment that possibly could be paid him.

72. *Grynæi:* an adj. from *Grynium*, a city of Æolis, where Apollo had a temple, built of white marble, and a grove. Here was a famous oracle.

74. *Scyllam.* There were two by the name of Scylla: one the daughter of Nisus, king of the Megarenses, who, falling in love with Minos, king of Crete, as he lay siege to Megara, betrayed her father to his enemy. For which deed, it is said, she was changed into a lark; while he was changed into a hawk. See nom. prop. under *Nisus.*

The other was the daughter of Phorcus. Some there are, who think Virgil here confounds the two, attributing to the former what properly belongs to the latter. But there will be no need of this, if we only supply the word *eam*, or *illam.*

The story of Scylla, the daughter of Phorcus, is briefly this: Glaucus, the sea god, fell in love with her, but she refused his addresses. In order to render her more favorable to him, he applied to the sorceress Circe; who, as soon as she saw him, became enamoured with him herself; and instead of affording him any assistance, endeavored to divert his affections from Scylla, and fix them on herself, but without any effect. For the sake of revenge, Circe poured the juice of some noxious herbs into a fountain, where Scylla used to bathe her self. And as soon as she entered it, to her great surprise, she found the parts below her waist changed into frightful monsters, like dogs, that were continually barking or making a growling noise. The rest of her body assumed an equally hideous form. This sudden and unexpected metamorphosis, filled her with such horror, that she threw herself into that part of the sea, which divides Sicily from Italy, where she became a rock, or rather a ledge of rocks. See Æn. iii. 420. *Secuta est:* reported. *Loquar:* in the sense of *dicam.*

Dulichias vexâsse rates, et gurgite in alto
Ah! timidos nautas canibus lacerâsse marinis?
Aut ut mutatos Terei narraverit artus?
Quas illi Philomela dapes, quæ dona parârit?
Quo cursu deserta petiverit, et quibus antè
Infelix sua tecta supervolitaverit alis?
Omnia quæ, Phœbo quondam meditante, beatus
Audiit Eurotas, jussitque ediscere lauros,
Ille canit: pulsæ referunt ad sidera valles;
Cogere donec oves stabulis, numerumque referre
Jussit, et invito processit Vesper Olympo.

candida inguina latrantibus monstris, vexâsse

78. Mutatos *in upupam.*

80. Et quibus alis infelix *Tereus* supervolitaverit tecta sua antè.

82. Ille *Silenus* canit omnia, quæ beatus Eurotas audiit, Phœbo quondam meditante

84. Valles pulsæ *cantu* referunt *eum* ad sidera: donec Vesper jussit *pastores* cogere oves

NOTES.

76. *Dulichias:* an adj. from *Dulichium,* an island in the Ionian sea, forming a part of the kingdom of Ulysses. *Dulichias rates:* the ships of Ulysses.

78. *Terei:* gen. of *Tereus,* a king of Thrace, who married Procne, or Progne, daughter of Pandion, king of Athens. She had a sister by the name of Philomela, whom she tenderly loved. Finding herself unhappy in being separated from her, she desired her husband to go and bring her to Thrace. Accordingly he went to Athens; but as soon as he saw her, he was enamoured with her, and resolved to gratify his passion. This he did, and afterwards cut out her tongue, to prevent her from disclosing the barbarous deed. He left her in confinement; and having taken every precaution to prevent its coming to light, he returned to his wife, and informed her that Philomela had died on the way. Not long after, however, she found otherwise. Philomela, during her captivity, described on a piece of tapestry her misfortunes and sufferings, and privately conveyed it to her sister, who hastened to her release. Here they concerted measures how to be revenged on Tereus. It was agreed that Progne should kill her son Itys, and serve him up for his father. In the midst of his meal, he called for his son, when his wife told him that he was then feasting on his flesh. At this moment, Philomela appeared, and threw the head of Itys on the table before him. At this moment he drew his sword, and was going to punish them both, when he was changed into a *upupa,* a bird called by some the *hoopoë,* by others, the *lapwing;* Philomela, into the *nightingale;* Progne, into the *swallow;* and Itys, into the *pheasant.* See Ovid. Met. Lib. 6.

80. *Cursu:* in the sense of *celeritate. Deserta:* the deserts: *loca,* is to be understood: desert places.

81. *Tecta sua antè:* his palace his own before his transformation—but his own no longer. *Tectum,* is any covered place that is inhabited; from the verb *tego.*

82. *Phœbo quondam meditante:* Apollo, formerly singing. The poet here alludes to the fable of Apollo's being in love with the beautiful youth Hyacinthus, the son of Lacon; and in that state wandering along the banks of the Eurotas, singing upon his harp.

83. *Eurotas.* A very celebrated river of the Peloponnesus: its banks abounded in the laurel. In its course, it forms nearly a semicircle, passing by the ancient city Lacedæmon, and falls into the *Sinus Laconicus.*

84. *Valles pulsæ,* &c. The vallies struck with the song, waft it back to the stars—bear it to the stars.

85. *Referre:* to count over their number to see that none be missing.

86. *Vesper.* The same as the planet Venus. When it precedes or goes before the sun, it is called Lucifer, and sometimes Phosphorus, from the Greek; but when it goes behind him, Vesper, or Hesperus, the evening star. It is also taken for the evening, particularly that part denominated the twilight. *Processit invito Olympo:* marches along the unwilling heaven. The word *invitus,* beautifully represents the struggle between the light and darkness in the time of twilight. The day is loth, or unwilling to yield; or, it may refer to its regret at being deprived of so charming a song as that of Silenus.

QUESTIONS.

What probably was the design of this pastoral?

Who is intended under the character of Silenus? Who was Syro?

Whom are we to understand by the swains Chromis and Mnasilus?

Where is the scene laid?

What is said of Silenus?

Does Virgil give the principles of the Epicurean philosophy?

What were those principles?

Who was Epicurus?

Who was Nereus? Of whom was he the father?
What is the word Nereus sometimes taken for?
By what figure is it so taken?
Who was Deucalion? What is said to have taken place in his reign?
Who was his wife?
What were they directed to do in order to re-people the earth?
What do you understand by the words *Saturnia regna?*
Who was Prometheus? What is said of him?
What is the proper meaning of *saltus?*
Who was Atalanta? What is said of her?
Who were the Hesperides? What were their names?
Who was Phaëton? What rash act did he attempt?
What became of him?
What were the names of his sisters?
What became of them?
Who was Hesiod? Where was he born?
How many were there of the name of Scylla?
Describe, or give an account of each?
Who was Tereus?
What is said of him?
Into what was he transformed?
What was the name of his wife? Into what was she transformed? &c.

ECLOGA SEPTIMA.

MELIBŒUS, CORYDON, THYRSIS.

This pastoral contains a trial of skill in song between the shepherds Corydon and Thyrsis. It is much of the nature of the fourth, and is an imitation of the eighth of the Idylls of Theocritus. It is conjectured that by Corydon and Thyrsis we are to understand Gallus and Pollio; of whom our poet speaks on several occasions in the most honorable terms. The scene is laid on the pleasant banks of the river Mincius. Melibœus is thought to be Virgil himself, and Daphnis some mutual friend of theirs. They both listen attentively to their song; which being ended, they give the palm to Corydon.

Mel. FORTE sub argutâ consederat ilice Daphnis,
Compulerantque greges Corydon et Thyrsis in unum:
Thyrsis oves, Corydon distentas lacte capellas.
Ambo florentes ætatibus, Arcades ambo:
Et cantare pares, et respondere parati.
Hìc mihi, dum teneras defendo à frigore myrtos,
Vir gregis ipse caper deerraverat: atque ego Daphnim
Aspicio: ille ubi me contrà videt; Ocyùs, inquit,

3. Thyrsis *compulerat* oves, Corydon *compulerat* capellas

6. Hìc caper ipse vir gregis deerraverat mihi, dum

NOTES.

1. *Arguta:* whispering. The word very aptly expresses the rustling noise made by the wind among the leaves: to which reference is here had.

2. *Corydon:* this is derived from a Greek word signifying a lark. *Thyrsis:* from a Greek word signifying a spear bound with vine, in honor of Bacchus. *In unum:* into one place, *locum* being understood.

3. *Capellas distentas lacte:* his goats distended with milk—having their udders distended.

4. *Ambo Arcades.* Not indeed that they were both natives of Arcadia; but they are so called, because that country was famous for its pastures and flocks; and in a manner sacred to shepherds. They were both in the prime of life: *florentes ætatibus.*

5. *Pares cantare:* equal at singing. *Par* is properly equal in match to contend for victory.

7. *Daphnim:* from a Greek word signifying a laurel. *Vir:* in the sense of *dux.*

8. *Contrà.* This is here used adverbially, *in turn;* or over against him. The word may be taken in either sense. The former seems preferable in this place.

9. *Ades:* in the sense of *veni. Melibœe:* from a Greek word signifying a shepherd: or one who has the care of flocks.

Huc ades, ô Melibœe; caper tibi salvus et hœdi;
Et si quid cessare potes, requiesce sub umbrâ.
Huc ipsi potum venient per prata juvenci:
Hìc viridis tenerâ prætexit arundine ripas
Mincius, èque sacrâ resonant examina quercu.
Quid facerem? neque ego Alcippen, nec Phyllida habe-
Depulsos à lacte domi, quæ clauderet agnos · [bam,
Et certamen erat, Corydon cum Thyrside, magnum.
Posthabui tamen illorum mea seria ludo.
Alternis igitur contendere versibus ambo
Cœpêre: alternos Musæ meminisse volebant.
Hos Corydon, illos referebat in ordine Thyrsis.
Cor. Nymphæ, noster amor, Libethrides, aut mihi car-
Quale meo Codro, concedite: proxima Phœbi [men,
Versibus ille facit: aut si non possumus omnes,
Hìc arguta sacrâ pendebit fistula pinu.
Th. Pastores, hederâ crescentem ornate poëtam,
Arcades, invidiâ rumpantur ut ilia Codro.
Aut si ultrà placitum laudârit, baccare frontem
Cingite, ne vâti noceat mala lingua futuro.
Cor. Setosi caput hoc apri tibi, Delia, parvus
Et ramosa Mycon vivacis cornua cervi.
Si proprium hoc fuerit, levi de marmore tota

9. Caper *est* salvus tibi, et hœdi *quoque sunt salvi*

12. Hìc viridis Mincius prætexit

16. Corydon *certabat* cum Thyrside

19. Volebant *me* meminisse alternos *versus*

20. Corydon *referebat* hos

21. Aut concedite *tale* carmen mihi, quale *concessistis*

23. *Nos* omnes non possumus *facere id*

27. Cingite *meam* frontem

29. O Delia, parvus Mycon *offert* tibi hoc caput.

NOTES.

10. *Quid: temporis* is understood, governed by *quid:* any time—a little time.

11. *Potum:* to drink: a sup. in *um*, of the verb *poto*, put after the verb *venient.*

12. *Prætexit:* in the sense of *tegit.*

13. *Mincius:* a small river rising out of the lake *Benacus*, and falling into the Po. *Hodie, Menzo.*

14. *Alcippen—Phyllida:* the names of two servants; both derived from the Greek.

15. *Depulsos à lacte:* taken away from the milk: weaned. *Domi:* at home.

17. *Posthabui*, &c. I postponed my serious business to their song: to listen to their song. *Ludo:* in the sense of *cantui.*

19. *Musæ volebant:* the meaning is, the Muses would have them sing alternate verses.

20. *Referebat:* in the sense of *cantabat.*

21. *Libethrides:* an adj. from *Libethra*, a fountain in *Beotia;* others say in *Magnesia*, over which they presided. Hence they are called *Libethrian nymphs. Noster amor:* my delight, or love.

22. *Concedite:* grant such a song to me as ye granted to my Codrus: inspire such a song, &c. Codrus was a poet cotemporary with Virgil, as we learn from Servius, and of superior merit. *Proxima:* next in excellence to the verses of Apollo. *Carmina* is understood.

23. *Facit:* in the sense of *componit.*

24. *Sacra pinu:* the pine-tree was sacred to *Cybele*, the mother of the gods, on account of the transmutation of her darling *Atys* into that tree. It was a custom, when any one lay down his art or profession, to hang up and consecrate the instruments which he had used, to the god who presided over that art.

25. *Hederâ.* Poets were crowned sometimes with ivy, at other times, with laurel. These both were evergreens, and designed to denote a lasting fame. *Ornate:* in the sense of *coronate.* By *poetam* we are to understand Thyrsis himself.

26. *Ilia Codro:* the sides to Codrus; the same as *Ilia Codri.* This construction is frequent with Virgil: the dat. in the sense of the gen.

27. *Ultra placitum:* beyond my pleasure, or desire. Immoderate praise was thought by the *ancients* to have in it something of the nature of fascination; and to avert its malignant influence, they wore a garland of *baccar*, or lady's-glove, as a counter charm. The pron. *me* is understood.

29. *Delia:* A name of Diana, from *Delos*, the place of her birth. *Setosi:* bristly.

30. *Mycon.* The swain Mycon is supposed to be Corydon's friend, and to promise these things to Diana in his name.

31. *Si hoc fuerit proprium.* If this (success which you granted me in hurting) shall be lasting, you shall stand entire in polished marble: I will make you a full-length statue of polished, &c. It was usual to make only the head and neck of a marble statue. Here Corydon promises Diana an entire statue, provided she continued to prosper his pursuits.

32. *Tu* stabis tota de levi marmore evincta *quoad* suras

33. O Priape, sat est te expectare quotannis *à me*

42. Algâ projecta *ad litus*

44. Si *sit vobis* quis pudor

Puniceo stabis suras evincta cothurno.
TH. Sinum lactis, et hæc te liba, Priape, quotannis
Expectare sat est: custos es pauperis horti.
Nunc te marmoreum pro tempore fecimus: at tu,
Si fœtura gregem suppleverit, aureus esto.
COR. Nerine Galatea, thymo mihi dulcior Hyblæ,
Candidior cycnis, hederâ formosior albâ:
Cùm primùm pasti repetent præsepia tauri,
Si qua tui Corydonis habet te cura, venito.
TH. Immò ego Sardois videar tibi amarior herbis,
Horridior rusco, projectâ vilior algâ;
Si mihi non hæc lux toto jam longior anno est.
Ite domum pasti, si quis pudor, ite juvenci.
COR. Muscosi fontes, et somno mollior herba,
Et quæ vos rarâ viridis tegit arbutus umbrâ,
Solstitium pecori defendite: jam venit æstas

NOTES.

32. *Puniceo:* in the sense of *purpureo.* See Ecl. 5. 17. *Cothurno.* The *cothurnus* was a kind of high-heeled shoe or boot worn when hunting and on the stage, by both sexes. See Geor. 2. 9.

33. *Priape:* Priapus was the tutelar god of gardens, lakes, &c. He was the son of Venus, by Mercury or Bacchus. The place of his birth was Lampsacus, near the Hellespont, where he was chiefly worshipped. He was usually represented with a human face and the ears of a goat. He held a stick in his hand to drive away birds, a club to drive away thieves, and a scythe to prune the trees. *Sinum:* in the sense of *vas;* a kind of vessel swelling out in the middle like a pitcher.

35. *Pro tempore:* according to the time; in proportion to my present ability. Thyrsis promises him now a marble statue, and if his flocks increase so that he can afford it, he will make him a golden one.

36. *Suppleverit:* shall enlarge—multiply.

37. *Nerine:* an adj. from *Nereus,* a god of the sea. The poet does not here mean that this Galatea was actually the daughter of Nereus; but he merely intends it as a compliment, intimating that she possessed equal charms with her namesake. *Hyblæ.* Hybla was a mountain in Sicily, abounding in *Thyme,* and celebrated for its bees, and excellent honey—*sweeter than the thyme of Hybla, fairer than the swans, more beautiful than the white ivy.* These comparisons are extremely chaste and delicate.

39. *Cùm primùm:* in the sense of *ut primùm.*—*Cura:* regard.

41. *Sardois herbis.* The herb here spoken of is supposed to be the *Holly-bush,* of sharp and prickly leaves, and of a very bitter taste. It is called *Sardinian,* from the island Sardinia, where it grew in great abundance. It is said to have caused a convulsive laughter with grinning. Hence *Sardinicus risus,* a forced laughter; some take it for the *Crow-foot.*

42. *Horridior rusco:* rougher than the *butcher's broom.* This is a prickly shrub or plant.—*Vilior:* more vile, or worthless.—*Alga.* This was a kind of weed or grass, which grew in great abundance about the island of Crete. When torn from the rocks where it grew, by the violence of the waves, tost about the sea, and then cast upon the shore, it became quite useless: it lost its color, and presented to the eye an unseemly appearance.

43. *Lux:* in the sense of *dies.*

44. *Pasti:* in the sense of *saturati.*

45. *Muscosi fontes:* ye cool (mossy) fountains. The epithet *muscosi* is expressive of coolness, because moss will seldom grow where there is any considerable degree of heat. It grows the best on the banks of rivers that face the north. Also on the north side of trees.—*Herba mollior,* &c. This charming expression is taken from Theocritus. Ruæus says, *dulcis ad somnum,* which is not the meaning of the poet. The expression, *softer than sleep,* is extremely delicate.

46. *Viridis arbutus,* &c. This is a singular construction. The nom. here seems to be used in the place of the *voc.* By using the nom. it placed the relative *quæ* in the third person, and consequently the verb; whereas they should be in the second person sing. *O viridis arbute, quæ tegis vos rara umbrâ.* The *vos* refers to the fountains and grass mentioned above.

47. *Solstitium.* This word properly signifies that point in the ecliptic, which coincides with the tropics, or is 23° 28′ from the equator, measured on an arc of the meridian: and the sun being in this point on a particular day in June and December, the word is taken by Synec. for either *summer* or *winter.* Again by meton. for *heat* or *cold,* according as the sun is either in the

Torrida jam læto turgent in palmite gemmæ.
TH. Hìc focus, et tædæ pingues: hìc plurimus ignis
Semper, et assiduâ postes fuligine nigri.
Hìc tantùm Boreæ curamus frigora, quantùm
Aut numerum lupus, aut torrentia flumina ripas.
COR. Stant et juniperi, et castaneæ hirsutæ:
Strata jacent passim sua quâque sub arbore poma:
Omnia nunc rident: at si formosus Alexis
Montibus his abeat, videas et flumina sicca.
TH. Aret ager; vitio moriens sitit aëris herba:
Liber pampineas invidit collibus umbras.
Phyllidis adventu nostræ nemus omne virebit:
Jupiter et læto descendet plurimus imbri.
COR. Populus Alcidæ gratissima, vitis Iaccho:
Formosæ myrtus Veneri, sua laurea Phœbo.
Phyllis amat corylos: illas dum Phyllis amabit,
Nec myrtus vincet corylos, nec laurea Phœbi.
TH. Fraxinus in sylvis pulcherrima, pinus in hortis,

49. Hìc *est* focus, et *hìc sunt*

52. Quantùm aut lupus *curat* numerum *ovium*, aut torrentia flumina *curant* ripas

53. *Hìc* stant et juniperi

59. *Sed* omne nemus virebit.

NOTES.

sign of *Cancer* or *Capricorn.* It is the solstice of *Cancer*, or the summer solstice, which is here meant. *Defendite:* in the sense of *avertite.*

48. *Palmite:* the shoot or branch of the vine—*Gemmæ:* the buds, or first appearances of the young shoots of trees or shrubs. *Læto:* fruitful—fertile.

49. *Pingues tædæ:* fat pines; or, we may take *tædæ* in a wider sense, implying any fuel, or combustible matter.

50. *Fuligine:* in the sense of *fumo.* The cottages of the poor seldom had a chimney. The fire was made directly under an aperture in the roof to discharge the smoke. We may well suppose the interior of the house to be *blackened* by that vapor.

51. *Hìc tantùm curamus.* The meaning is: we care nothing for the cold of Boreas. Boreas is the Greek word for the north wind. The poets say he was the son of *Astræus* and *Aurora;* or, according to others, of the river Strymon, in Macedonia. He was king of Thrace, and carried away by force *Orythia*, the daughter of Erictheus, king of Athens, by whom he had two sons, *Zetes* and *Calaïs.* He was worshipped as a god.

53. *Juniperi.* The juniperus was a tree, having sharp and narrow leaves, and bearing a small, round, and odoriferous fruit. Servius understands *juniperi* and *castaneæ* to be the trees which are loaded with their respective fruit. Mr. Davidson takes them for the fruit itself, and considers *stant* in opposition to *strata jacent:* the former stand or hang ripening on the boughs, the latter in rich profusion cover the ground under their respective trees. *Hirsutæ:* rough—prickly, in opposition to those that were smooth, mentioned Ecl. i. 82: or it may only mean that they were yet in the shell. See Ecl. x. 76.

54. *Poma jacent*, &c. Much hath been said upon the reading of this line. Some read it thus; *Poma jacent strata passim, quæque sub sua arbore:* apples lie scattered all around, every one under its own tree. Others read it thus: *sua poma jacent strata passim, sub quâque arbore:* their own apples lie scattered all around under every or each tree. This last, Dr. Trapp is fully persuaded is the correct reading. Heyne reads, *quâque.*

56. *Videas et*, &c. You would even see the rivers dry. The word *et* here is emphatical.

57. *Vitio aëris:* by the infection of the air; or, the excessive heat of the air. *Sitit:* is parched.

58. *Liber.* A name of Bacchus. See Ecl. v. 69. *Invidit:* hath refused the shadows of the vine to our hills. The meaning is: the vine does not flourish upon our hills.

60. *Jupiter:* the air—condensed vapor. *Læto imbri:* in fertilizing showers.

61. *Alcidæ:* Hercules, called also *Alcides*, from *Alcæus*, his grand-father. The *populus* was sacred to him. It is said he wore a crown of white poplar leaves when he descended to the infernal regions.

62. *Myrtus.* The myrtle tree was sacred to Venus, on account of the delicacy of its odor, or because it flourishes best on the margin of the sea, out of the foam of which she is said to have sprung.

61. *Iaccho:* a name of Bacchus. The vine was sacred to him, because, it is said, he was the inventor of wine; or at least taught men the cultivation of the vine.

62. *Laurea.* The laurel tree was sacred to Apollo, on account of his beloved *Daphne*, who was changed into a laurel; therefore it is called *sua*, his own.

65. *Fraxinus:* the ash-tree.

Populus in fluviis, abies in montibus altis:
Sæpiùs at si me, Lycida formose, revisas;
Fraxinus in sylvis cedat tibi, pinus in hortis.
  Me. Hæc memini, et victum frustrà contendere Thyrsin.
Ex illo Corydon, Corydon est tempore nobis.

NOTES.

70. *Ex illo tempore*: from that time, Corydon, Corydon is the one for me. Heyne observes, this line is unworthy of Virgil. It is in imitation of Theocritus, Idyl. viii. 92. but far inferior to the original.

QUESTIONS.

What is the subject of this pastoral?
Whom are we to understand by Corydon and Thyrsis? Whom by Melibœus and Daphnis?
Where is the scene laid?
Who comes off conqueror?
Is this pastoral imitated from Theocritus?
Who was Priapus? and what is said of him?
Who was Boreas? For what did the Greeks take the word?
For what is the word Jupiter sometimes taken?
What do you understand by the word solstitium?
For what is it used figuratively?

ECLOGA OCTAVA.

PHARMACEUTRIA.

DAMON, ALPHESIBŒUS.

This pastoral consists of two parts: the first is taken chiefly from the third Idyl of Theocritus: the latter from the second Idyl. The shepherd Damon bewails the loss of his mistress, Nisa, and is much grieved at the success of Mopsus, who had succeeded in obtaining her for a wife. Alphesibœus relates the charms, or incantations of some enchantress, who endeavored, by magic arts, to make Daphnis in love with her. *Pharmaceutria*, the title of this Eclogue, is the same with the Latin *Venefica*, and signifies a *sorceress*. This Eclogue was written in the year of Rome 715, when L. Marcus Censorinus, and C. Calvisius Sabinus, were consuls. It is not certain to whom it was inscribed, whether to Augustus or Pollio; most commentators are in favor of the latter.

1. Dicemus musam pastorum Damonis et Alphesibœi, quos certantes Juvenca immemor herbarum mirata

PASTORUM Musam, Damonis et Alphesibœi,
Immemor herbarum quos est mirata juvenca,
Certantes, quorum stupefactæ carmine lynces,
Et mutata suos requiêrunt flumina cursus:

NOTES.

1. *Musam:* in the sense of *carmen.*

4. *Mutata flumina,* &c. This line may be read in two ways. The first and easiest is given in the ordo; the other is, *mutata flumina requièrunt suos cursus.* In this case, *requiesco* must be taken actively, and *mutata*, in the sense of *turbata*, as Ruæus interprets it. But Virgil never uses that verb in an active sense in any part of his works, and as he is fond of imitating the Greeks it is better to suppose that he follows them in the present instance, than that he deviates here from his uniform practice in the use of the verb. Beside, if we take *requiesco* actively, we must take *mutata* out of its usual acceptation.

Damonis Musam dicemus et Alphesibœi.
Tu mihi, seu magni superas jam saxa Timavi;
Sive oram Illyrici legis æquoris: en erit unquam
Ille dies, mihi cùm liceat tua dicere facta!
En erit, ut liceat totum mihi ferre per orbem
Sola Sophocleo tua carmina digna cothurno!
A te principium: tibi desinet: accipe jussis
Carmina cœpta tuis, atque hanc sine tempora circùm
Inter victrices hederam tibi serpere lauros.[a]
Frigida vix cœlo noctis decesserat umbra,
Cùm ros in tenerâ pecori gratissimus herbâ est:
Incumbens tereti Damon sic cœpit olivæ.
Da. Nascere, præque diem veniens age, Lucifer, almum:
Conjugis indigno Nisæ deceptus amore
Dum queror, et divos (quanquam nil testibus illis
Profeci) extremâ moriens tamen alloquor horâ.

est; quorum carmine lynces stupefactæ *sunt;* et flumina mutata *quoad* suos cursus requièrunt *dicemus, inquam,* musam

6. Tu, O *Pollio, fave* mihi, seu

8. En *ille dies* erit, cùm liceat mihi

11. Principium *meorum laborum erat* à te: *meus labor* desinet tibi

12. Sine hanc hederam serpere

17. O Lucifer, nascere, præveniensque age almum diem: dum *ego* deceptus indigno amore

NOTES.

5. *Dicemus:* in the sense of *narrabimus.*

6. *Tu mihi,* &c. It is generally thought that the poet addresses himself to Pollio, who, about this time, returned to Rome in triumph, having overcome the *Partheni,* a people of *Illyricum.* The verb *fave,* or *adsis,* must be supplied, to make the sense complete. Ellipses of this kind are frequent, particularly among the poets. *Timavi.* See Æn. i. 244.

7. *Sive legis,* &c. Whether you coast along the shore of the Illyrian sea. Illyricum was a very extensive country lying on the right of the Adriatic sea, or gulf of Venice, including the ancient *Liburnia* and *Dalmatia.* *Æquoris.* *Æquor* properly signifies any plain or level surface, whether land or water. *Erit:* in the sense of *aderit.*

10. *Cothurno.* The cothurnus was properly a high-heeled shoe, worn by the tragedians to make them appear taller; by meton. put for tragedy, or the tragic style. *Sophocleo:* an adj. from *Sophocles,* an Athenian, the prince of tragic poetry. He was cotemporary with Pericles. *Tua carmina sola,* &c. Your verses alone worthy of the buskin—worthy of being introduced upon the stage. The *cothurnus* is here called Sophoclean, because Sophocles introduced it upon the stage. Pollio was not only a statesman, but a poet, and a distinguished writer of tragedy. See Ecl. iv. 12.

11. *Principium,* &c. This line is elliptical. The ellipsis is supplied in the ordo: the beginning of my labors was from thee; my labors shall end with thee. From this circumstance, some have been led to think that the poet alludes to Augustus, and not to Pollio. He wrote his first Eclogue, it is true, to compliment the generosity of his prince, and the Æneid to flatter his vanity. But we are to remember, it was through the interest and friendship of Pollio, that he recovered his lands, and so had an occasion given him for writing; and further, that poets promise many things, which they do not perform.

12. *Sine hanc,* &c. Permit this ivy to creep around thy temples amidst thy victorious laurels—permit me to crown thee with ivy, while others crown thee with laurel. This is a very delicate verse. The poet here entreats his patron to permit his ivy to entwine about his temples among his victorious laurels; in other words, to accept these his verses, in the midst of his victories. The poetic crown was originally made of ivy exclusively, afterwards, sometimes it was made of laurel: but the triumphal crown was always made of laurel. *Victrices lauros:* alluding to the triumph with which he was honored for his victory over the *Partheni.*

16. *Tereti olivæ:* leaning against a tapering olive, Damon thus began.

17. *Præveniens.* The parts of the verb are separated for the sake of the verse, by Tmesis. This figure is frequent among the poets. *Lucifer:* the morning star, or Venus. It is called Lucifer when going before the sun; Hesperus, when following after him. There is a fitness and propriety in Damon's calling upon the star, or planet Venus to arise, as if to listen to his complaint, since it was a love affair. *Age:* in the sense of *advehe.*

18. *Conjugis.* *Conjux* here is a betrothed or expected wife. *Indigno amore:* may mean immoderate love; or a love ill-requited—a love of which Nisa was unworthy.

20. *Profeci:* I have gained, or profited nothing. *Illis testibus.* It would seem that Nisa had pledged her faith to Damon, and called the gods to witness it; yet she violated her promises.

Incipe Mænalios mecum, mea tibia, versus.
Mænalus argutumque nemus pinosque loquentes
Semper habet: semper pastorum ille audit amores,
Panaque, qui primus calamos non passus inertes.
Incipe Mænalios mecum, mea tibia, versus.
Mopso Nisa datur: quid non speremus amantes?
Jungentur jam gryphes equis; ævoque sequenti
Cum canibus timidi venient ad pocula damæ.
Mopse, novas incide faces; tibi ducitur uxor.
Sparge, marite, nuces; tibi deserit Hesperus Oetam
Incipe Mænalios mecum, mea tibia, versus.
O digno conjuncta viro! dum despicis omnes,
Dumque tibi est odio mea fistula; dumque capellæ,
Hirsutumque supercilium, prolixaque barba:
Nec curare Deûm credis mortalia quemquam.
Incipe Mænalios mecum, mea tibia, versus.
Sepibus in nostris parvam te roscida mala,
(Dux ego vester eram) vidi cum matre legentem
Alter ab undecimo tum me jam ceperat annus:
Jam fragiles poteram à terrâ contingere ramos.

23. Ille *mons Mænalus*
24. Passus *est* calamos *esse*
32. O *Nisa* conjuncta digno viro; dum despicis omnes *alios*
34. Prolixaque *mea* barba *sunt tibi odio.*
38. Vidi te *adhuc* parvam legentem rocida mala

NOTES.

21. *Mænalios versus:* Mænalean, or pastoral verses—such as used to be sung on mount Mænalus in Arcadia. It was sacred to Pan. By reason of its pleasant groves, and whispering pines, it was much frequented by shepherds, where they sang their loves. The poet personifies the mountain, and makes it listen to the songs of shepherds.

22 *Loquentes:* whispering—tuneful.

24. *Qui primus:* who first, &c. See Ecl. ii. 31. *Inertes:* in the sense of *inutiles.*

27. *Gryphes:* griffons. They were fabulous animals, having the body of a lion, and the wings and beak of an eagle.

28. *Damæ timidi:* the timid deer. *Ad pocula:* in the sense of *ad aquam,* vel *potum;* by meton.

29. *Incide faces.* It was a custom among the Romans to lead the bride to the house of her husband with lighted torches before her. These torches were pieces of pine, or some unctuous wood, which were cut to a point, that they might be lighted the easier. It was usual to have five of these torches. Hence *ducere uxorem,* came to signify, to marry a wife; it is said of the husband: *nubere viro,* to marry a husband; this is said of the wife.

30. *Sparge nuces:* scatter nuts. It was a custom among the Romans at nuptials, for the husband to throw nuts, &c. upon the floor, that the boys and the rest of the company might divert themselves in gathering them. *Hesperus deserit Oetam tib:* the evening star is leaving Oeta for you. Oeta was a mountain, or rather range of mountains, of great height, in Thessaly. The inhabitants of Attica and Beotia being to the eastward, would observe the stars retiring or settling behind it. Hence, as it respected them, the expression is the same as saying, the evening star is setting, and consequently the evening somewhat advanced; which would not be an unpleasant circumstance to the new-married couple.

34. *Hirsutum supercilium:* my rough, or shaggy eyebrows. There could be no ground of complaint against *Nisa* for not loving these, and his long beard. These surely possess no charms. But as Dr. Trapp observes, the ground of his complaint lay in this: that her cruelty and scorn had so disheartened him, as to render him negligent of his outward appearance.

35. *Mortalia:* things done by mortals. This line is both beautiful and pathetic.

37. *In nostris sepibus:* in our enclosures—gardens, fields. This and the four following lines are extremely delicate, and show the hand of a master. The circumstances here enumerated, the age of the young shepherd, his being just able to reach the boughs, his officiousness in helping the girl and her mother gather the fruit, and his falling in love with her at the same time, are so well chosen, and happily expressed, that we may consider this passage as one of those happy and delicate touches which characterize the writings of Virgil. *Roscida.* By this we are to understand, Heyne observes, that the apples were wet with the dew of the morning. This will determine the time of the day, when they took their walk into the orchard.

39. *Alter annus,* &c. Lit. another year after the eleventh had just then taken me—I had just entered my twelfth year.

Ut vidi, ut perii, ut me malus abstulit error!
Incipe Mænalios mecum, mea tibia, versus
Nunc scio quid sit amor. Duris in cotibus illum
Ismarus, aut Rhodope, aut extremi Garamantes,
Nec generis nostri puerum, nec sanguinis edunt.
Incipe Mænalios mecum, mea tibia, versus.
Sævus amor docuit natorum sanguine matrem
Commaculare manus: crudelis tu quoque, mater:
Crudelis mater magis, an puer improbus ille?
Improbus ille puer, crudelis tu quoque mater.
Incipe Mænalios mecum, mea tibia, versus.
Nunc et oves ultrò fugiat lupus, aurea duræ
Mala ferant quercus, narcisso floreat alnus,
Pinguia corticibus sudent electra myricæ.
Certent et cycnis ululæ: sit Tityrus Orpheus:
Orpheus in sylvis; inter delphinas Arion.
Incipe Mænalios mecum, mea tibia, versus.
Omnia vel medium fiant mare: vivite sylvæ.
Præceps aërii speculâ de montis in undas
Deferar: extremum hoc munus morientis habeto.

45. Edunt illum *in* **duris cotibus, puerum nec nostri generis, nec** *nostri* sanguinis

48. Tu, *O* mater ***eras*** quoque crudelis: *eras ne* mater magis crudelis, an ille puer *magis* improbus! ille puer *erat* improbus; *sed* tu, *O* mater, quoque *eras* crudelis.

60. Habeto *tu* **hoc extremum** munus *tui* **morientis** *amatoris*

NOTES.

41. *Ut vidi, ut*, &c. How I gazed, how I languished, how a fatal delusion carried me away! Nothing can exceed this line in tenderness of expression. The *me malus abstulit error*, represents him as snatched from himself, deprived of his reason and judgment, and lost in wonder and admiration, while he surveyed her beauteous form, and attractive charms. It also conveys to us a just idea of the nature of love, which is often delusive, deceptive, and unsuccessful, as was the particular case of Damon. *Error:* in the sense of *insania*, vel *amor*, says Heyne. *Malus:* fatal—unhappy.

44. *Ismarus*, &c. Ismarus and Rhodope were two very wild and rocky mountains in Thrace. *Garamantes*. These were a savage people inhabiting the interior parts of Africa. Hence they are here called *extremi*.

45. *Edunt:* plainly for *ederunt*, by Enallage; and that in the sense of *produxerunt* or *genuerunt*.

47. *Matrem*. Medea, the daughter of Ætes, king of Colchis, a famous sorceress. She fell in love with Jason, one of the Argonauts, and by her directions and assistance, he obtained the golden fleece. She married him, and returned with him to Thessaly. He afterwards repudiated her, and married *Creüsa*, the daughter of the king of Corinth. In revenge for which, she slew the children, whom she bore him, before his eyes. See Ovid. Met. 7. *Docuit:* in the sense of *impulit*.

48. *Commaculare:* in the sense of *polluere*.

50. *Improbus:* wicked—impious.

52. *Nunc lupus ultrò*, &c. Now may the wolf of his own accord flee from the sheep; the hard oaks, &c. As if he had said: now the natural course of things may be changed. The most unlikely and unnatural things may take place, since a woman is found capable of such unfeeling and cruel conduct.

53. *Alnus:* the alder-tree. *Narcisso:* the flower *daffodil*. See Ecl. ii. 46.

54. *Myricæ:* shrubs—tamarisks. The word is sometimes taken for pastoral poetry. *Sudent:* in the sense of *stillent*. *Electra pinguia:* rich amber.

55. *Tityrus sit Orpheus*, &c. May Tityrus become an Orpheus;—Orpheus in the woods, and an Orion among the dolphins. *Orion* was a famous lyric poet of Lesbos, who, on his return home from Italy with great wealth, was cast into the sea by the sailors for the sake of his money. A dolphin that had been charmed with his music, it is said, took him on his back, and carried him safe to *Tænarus*, a town on the southern promontory of the Peloponnesus. For *Orpheus*, see Ecl. iii. 46.

58. *Omnia vel medium*, &c. Let all things become even the middle of the sea—the deep sea. Since I must perish, let all the world be drowned. *Vivite:* elegantly put for *valete*.

59. *Specula:* the top, or summit. It properly signifies any eminence which commands a prospect of the country around it. *Aërii montis*. This may allude to the famous rock in Arcadia, called the lover's leap; from which, those, who threw themselves into the sea, were cured of their love.

60. *Deferar*. This appears to be used in the sense of the Greek middle voice, which generally hath a reflex signification: I will throw myself.

Desine Mænalios, jam desine, tibia, versus.
Hæc Damon: vos, quæ responderit Alphesibœus,
Dicite, Pierides: non omnia possumus omnes.
Alp. Effer aquam, et molli cinge hæc altaria vittâ:
Verbenasque adole pingues, et mascula thura,
Conjugis ut magicis sanos avertere sacris
Experiar sensus. Nihil hìc nisi carmina desunt.
Ducite ab urbe domum, mea carmina, ducite Daphnim.
Carmina vel cœlo possunt deducere Lunam:
Carminibus Circe socios mutavit Ulyssei:
Frigidus in pratis cantando rumpitur anguis.
Ducite ab urbe domum, mea carmina, ducite Daphnim
Terna tibi hæc primùm triplici diversa colore
Licia circumdo, terque hæc altaria circùm
Effigiem duco. Numero Deus impare gaudet.
Ducite ab urbe domum, mea carmina, ducite Daphnim
Necte tribus nodis ternos, Amarylli, colores;
Necte, Amarylli, modò: et Veneris, dic, vincula necto.
Ducite ab urbe domum, mea carmina, ducite Daphnim.
Limus ut hic durescit, et hæc ut cera liquescit,
Uno eodemque igni: sic nostro Daphnis amore.
Sparge molam, et fragiles incende bitumine lauros.

62. Damon *dixit* hæc: vos, Pierides, dicite *ea*, quæ

63. *Nos* omnes non possumus *facere* omnia

73. Primùm circumdo hæc terna licia tibi, diversa

78. Necte *eos* modò: et

81. Sic Daphnis *emolliatur* nostro

83. Ego *uro* hanc

NOTES.

63. *Pierides:* the Muses. They were so called from *Pieria*, where, it is said, they were born. See Ecl. iii. 60.

64. *Effer aquam.* Here Alphesibœus personates some enchantress, who by charms and magic rites endeavors to make Daphnis in love with her. The words are supposed to be addressed to her servant maid Amaryllis, mentioned verse 78, infra.

65. *Verbenas.* A species of plant or herb called *vervain*, much used in magic operations. It is sometimes taken for all kinds of herbs used in such rites. *Mascula.* By this we are to understand the strongest and best kind of frankincense.

66. *Ut experiar:* that I may try to turn away the sound mind of my spouse: i. e. throw him into a violent passion for me, causing him to lose his reason and judgment. *Conjux*, here means an intended or pected husband. By it we are to understand Daphnis, who it seems had left her for some other mistress. *Sacris:* rites, or ceremonies.

67. *Carmina:* charms—a solemn form of words; to which the ancients attributed great efficacy.

70. *Circe.* The name of a famous sorceress. See Æn. vii. 10.

71. *Cantando:* ger. in *do*, of the verb *canto*. Ruæus says: *dum incantatur:* while the incantations or magic rites are performing.

73. *Triplici colore:* with triple color. The ancients had a great veneration for the number three. This was thought the most perfect of all numbers, having regard to the beginning, the middle, and the end. *Diversa:* diversified—various.

74. *Circumdo:* in the sense of *circumligo.*

78. *Veneris:* in the sense of *amoris.* *Modò:* in the sense of *nunc.*

80. *Ut hic Limus*, &c. The sorceress made two images or figures, one of mud (*limus*) to represent herself; the other of wax (*cera*) to represent Daphnis. The former would naturally harden, and the other melt in the same fire. It was the received opinion that as the image melted and consumed, so did the person it represented melt and dissolve into love, losing all his cruelty and hardness of heart toward his mistress; while she, who was represented by the other figure, would grow harder, and more indifferent to the object of her love.

82. *Sparge molam:* break, or scatter the salt-cake. The *mola* was a kind of cake much used in sacrifices. It was made of the flour of grain that grew the same year, highly seasoned with salt. It was placed upon the forehead of the victim, and upon the fire. *Incende:* burn the crackling laurels with bitumen. The laurels were burnt to consume the flesh of Daphnis, on whose account these rites were performed. The cake was crumbled upon his image, or upon the victims in sacrifices. Such was the nature of these ridiculous rites.

83. *Malus Daphnis:* cruel Daphnis burns me; I burn this laurel upon Daphnis—upon his image. By burning the effigy of a per-

Daphnis me malus urit, ego hanc in Daphnide laurum.
Ducite ab urbe domum, mea carmina, ducite Daphnim.
Talis amor Daphnim, qualis, cùm fessa juvencum
Per nemora, atque altos quærendo bucula lucos,
Propter aquæ rivum viridi procumbit in ulvâ
Perdita, nec seræ meminit decedere nocti:
Talis amor teneat: nec sit mihi cura mederi.
Ducite ab urbe domum, mea carmina, ducite Daphnim.
Has olim exuvias mihi perfidus ille reliquit,
Pignora chara sui: quæ nunc ego limine in ipso,
Terra, tibi mando: debent hæc pignora Daphnim.
Ducite ab urbe domum, mea carmina, ducite Daphnim.
Has herbas, atque hæc Ponto mihi lecta venena
Ipse dedit Mœris, nascuntur plurima Ponto.
His ego sæpe lupum fieri, et se condere sylvis
Mœrin, sæpe animas imis excire sepulchris,
Atque satas aliò vidi traducere messes.
Ducite ab urbe domum, mea carmina, ducite Daphnim.
Fer cineres, Amarylli, foras: rivoque fluenti,
Transque caput jace: ne respexeris. His ego Daphnim
Aggrediar nihil ille Deos, nil carmina curat.
Ducite ab urbe domum, mea carmina, ducite Daphnim
Aspice: corripuit tremulis altaria flammis.

85. *Utinam* talis amor *occupet* Daphnim, qualis, cùm bucula fessa quærendo juvencum per nemora, atque altos lucos, procumbit

89. Teneat *Daphnim*

95. Mœris ipse dedit has herbas

96. *Enim* plurima *venena* nascuntur *in* Ponto. Ego *vidi* Mœrin *ipsum* sæpe fieri lupum his *venenis*, et condere se sylvis; vidi *illum* sæpe excire

NOTES.

son magically, it was thought that they burnt the person himself; or that some how or other, he was affected in a similar manner.

85. *Juvencum:* the bull. *Talis.* Here is an ellipsis of the words, *occupat juvencam*, or some other of the like import, to make the sense complete.

87. *Ulva:* a kind of sedge, or meadow-grass. Some copies have *herba.*

88. *Perdita:* wretched—desperate; without hope of finding the object of her search. *Nec seræ nocti*, &c. She is so intent upon the object of her love, that she thinks of nothing else—she thinks not of returning home, even though it be late at night. *Decedere seræ nocti:* to yield or give place to the late night.

89. *Mederi:* to cure him.

91. *Ille perfidus*, &c. That perfidious (shepherd) formerly left these clothes with me, as the dear pledges of himself. It appears hence that Daphnis had pledged his love to her, but afterward violated his word. This justifies the use of the word *conjux*, as applied to him, verse 66.

92. *In ipso limine:* in the very threshold, or entrance. Servius thinks we are to understand the entrance of the temple of Vesta; others, of Daphnis' own house. But it is better to understand it of her own house, for it appears that here she performed her magic rites.

93. *Mando:* in the sense of *committo*. *Hæc pignora:* these pledges owe Daphnis to me. The clothes that a person once wore, or any thing that belonged to him, were thought to be very efficacious in enchantments. Accordingly she lays much stress upon them; she is sure they will bring him home to her. One part of these magic rites was to bury the clothes of the lover under the threshold, to constrain him to return.

95. *Ponto.* Pontus, an extensive country in Asia Minor, bordering upon the Euxine sea. It abounded in poisonous herbs. Mithridates, king of Pontus, rendered his country notorious by the long and bloody wars which he maintained against the Romans. He was, however, at last overcome by Pompey the Great. *Venena:* magic plants. Those of a poisonous quality were considered the most efficacious, and were particularly sought for, and required in all enchantments.

101. *Fer cineres.* The most powerful, and usually the last efforts of the enchanter, were to throw the ashes of the magical sacrifice over the head backward into running water. Servius says, this was done that the gods might catch the ashes without being seen, as they were unwilling to show themselves, unless on extraordinary occasions.

102. *Ne respexeris:* in the sense of *ne respice.*

103. *Aggrediar his*, &c. With these ashes I will assail Daphnis. *Nihil* and *nil* are often used as simple negatives, in the sense of *non:* he does not regard the gods, &c. In other words, he does not regard his solemn promises made in the presence of the gods; he regards not my charms.

105. *Aspice.* This and the following line

106. **Bonum** *omen*

Sponte suâ, dum ferre moror, cinis ipse : bonum sit
Nescio quid certè est : et Hylax in limine latrat.
Credimus ? an, qui amant, ipsi sibi somnia fingunt ?

109. *O mea* carmina

Parcite, ab urbe venit, jam parcite, carmina, Daphnis.

NOTES.

to *cinis ipse*, were spoken by Amaryllis, as appears from *dum ferre moror :* while I delay to carry them. If we attribute the words to the enchantress, we must suppose her to do what she commands to be done. But beholding the ashes kindle the altar into a trembling flame of its own accord, in a transport, she exclaims : may it be a good omen. The ancients considered the sudden blazing of fire to be a good omen.

107. *Nescio quid*, &c. As if she had said : some body is coming ; I know not certainly who it is. *Hylax.* The name of a dog ; from a Greek word signifying *to bark*.

108. *Credimus ? an qui*, &c. Do I believe it ? or, do those who love form dreams to themselves ? Yes, it is he. Cease, now cease, my charms, Daphnis comes from the city.

QUESTIONS.

How is this pastoral to be divided ?
What is the subject of it ?
What is the meaning of the word *Pharmaceutria*, the title of the Eclogue ?
When was this Eclogue written ?
Who were consuls ?
To whom was it probably dedicated ?
Why do you suppose it to be dedicated to Pollio rather than to Augustus ?
When is the planet Venus called Lucifer ?
When Hesperus ?
Can you mention any line that has been noticed by commentators as extremely tender ?
Who was Medea ?
What is said of her ?
Why are the Muses sometimes called *Pierides* ?

ECLOGA NONA.

LYCIDAS, MŒRIS.

When Augustus divided the lands about Mantua among his soldiers, the estate of Virgil fell to Arius, a centurion. When he went to re-enter upon his estate, after it had been restored to him, he met with much severe treatment from the new possessor, and on one occasion, was near being killed. He saved his life by swimming over the river Mincius. In consequence of which, he returned to Rome to acquaint the Emperor of the matter. He left his steward, who is here called Mœris, behind, and directed him to treat his new landlord with civility and respect. Mœris is going to him with a present of some kids, and meets Lycidas, who is supposed to be some Mantuan shepherd. Upon their meeting the pastoral opens. The scene is the road to the town. The evening is coming on : the air is tranquil and serene. The pastoral contains a complaint of Virgil's hard treatment under the character of Menalcas ; a compliment to his friend Varus, and another to Julius Cæsar, and consequently to Augustus ; together with several scraps of poetry artfully interwoven with the subject. The whole pastoral is elegant and beautiful.

1. *O* Mœri, quò *tui* pedes *ducunt* te ? an *ducunt te* in urbem, quò via ducit ?

Lyc. Quò te, Mœri, pedes ? an, quò via ducit, in urbem ?
Mœ. O Lycida, vivi pervenimus ; advena nostri
(Quod nunquam veriti sumus) ut possessor agelli

NOTES.

2. *Vivi pervenimus :* we living have come to that condition—or have lived to see the day, that, &c. *Advena :* a noun of common gender, here used as an adj. It may signify *intruding—usurping*, as well as *foreign* : in the present case, it includes the idea of all of them.

Diceret: Hæc mea sunt; veteres migrate coloni.
Nunc victi, tristes, quoniam fors omnia versat,
Hos illi (quod nec benè vertat) mittimus hœdos.
LY. Certè equidem audieram, quâ se subducere colles
Incipiunt, mollique jugum demittere clivo,
Usque ad aquam et veteris jam fracta cacumina fagi,
Omnia carminibus vestrum servâsse Menalcan.
MŒ. Audieras, et fama fuit: sed carmina tantùm
Nostra valent, Lycida, tela inter Martia, quantùm
Chaonias dicunt, aquilâ veniente, columbas,
Quòd nisi me quâcumque novas incidere lites
Antè sinistra cavâ monuisset ab ilice cornix;
Nec tuus hic Mœris, nec viveret ipse Menalcas.
LY. Heu! cadit in quemquam tantum scelus? heu tua [nobis
Penè simul tecum solatia rapta, Menalca!
Quis caneret Nymphas? quis humum florentibus herbis
Spargeret? aut viridi fontes induceret umbrâ?
Vel quæ sublegi tacitus tibi carmina nuper,
Cùm te ad delicias ferres Amaryllida nostras?
"Tityre, dum redeo, brevis est via, pasce capellas:
"Et potum pastas age, Tityre, et inter agendum
'Occursare capro, cornu ferit ille, caveto."
MŒ. Immò hæc, quæ Varo, necdum perfecta, canebat.
"Vare, tuum nomen (superet modò Mantua nobis,

2. *Nos* vivi pervenimus *eò miseriæ*, ut advena possessor

4. Hæc *arva* sunt mea; *vos*, O veteres coloni,

7. Certè equidem audieram vestrum *Dominum* Menalcan servâsse *sibi* omnia *arva suis* carminibus *ab eo loco*, quà colles incipiunt subducere se

11. Audieras *illud*, et *talis* fuit fama

13. Columbas *valere*

14. Quòd nisi sinistra cornix monuisset me antè ab ilice cava incidere

18. Heu tua solatia rapta *sunt* penè nobis simul tecum

21. Vel *quis caneret* carmina, quæ tacitus

23. *Quorum versuum hoc est fragmentum:* O Tityre, pasce

26. Immo *potius quis caneret* hæc *carmina*, quæ *ille Menalcas*

NOTES.

3. *Agelli:* a noun diminutive from *ager:* *a little farm.*

5. *Fors:* in the sense of *fortuna.*

6. *Quod nec benè vertat:* which (present of the kids,) I wish may not turn out well to him. The usual mode of congratulation upon receiving a favor was: *Benè vertat,* I wish you joy—may it turn out well to you. *nec benè vertat,* therefore, was a kind of imprecation: *may it prove a mischief to you.*

7. *Subducere se:* to decline—to fall.

8. *Demittere jugum:* to lower their ridge, or top, by an easy descent. Here we have a description of the farm of Virgil. It was bounded on one side by a sloping hill; in other parts of its limits, were the broken top of an old beech-tree, a marsh, and the river *Mincius.*

9. *Ad aquam:* perhaps the river Mincius.

13. *Aquilâ veniente:* the eagle coming upon them—pursuing them. Here we have a beautiful circumlocution, expressing the inutility of his verses, and the charms of poetry, amidst martial arms. *Chaonias:* an adj. from *Chaonia,* a part of Epirus, where was the city *Dodona,* and a grove of the same name, famous for its oracular oaks. *Columbas:* two doves endued with a prophetic spirit are said to have resided among these oaks. Afterward one of them is said to have flown to the temple of Apollo at *Delphi,* and the other to the temple of Jupiter Ammon in Africa. They are here put for *doves* in general.

14. *Incidere novas lites,* &c. To break off my new disputes in any way whatever. *Lis,* is properly an action or case at law.

15. *Sinistra:* ill-boding. See Ecl. 1. 18.

16. *Hic tuus Mœris.* It appears from this that the life of Virgil, who is here called Menalcas, and that of Mœris, had been in danger from the new landlord.

17. *Heu, tantum scelus,* &c. Alas! that so great wickedness should fall upon any one. Or the words may be rendered thus; Alas! that so great wickedness should come into any one's mind:—that any one should conceive the idea of perpetrating the horrid deed of murder. This is the usual sense given to the words.

18. *Heu, tua solatia,* &c. Alas, Menalcas, your delight (the delight of your song,) was almost snatched from us with yourself: and if you had been quite slain, in that case, *who would have sung the nymphs,* &c. Heyne observes that by *solatia* we are to understand the song, *carmina,* or verses of Menalcas.

21. *Sublegi:* I purloined from you. Ruæus says, *surripui.*

22. *Nostras delicias:* for *nostram amicam.* *Deliciæ* is used only in the plural; *delight—darling:* here *a mistress.*

24. *Age pastas:* drive them full fed to drink. *Potum:* sup. in *um,* to drink—take water. *Inter agendum:* in driving them—while driving them, beware, &c.

26. *Varo:* to Varus. See Ecl. 6. 7

"Mantua, væ miseræ nimiùm vicina Cremonæ!)
"Cantantes sublime ferent ad sidera cycni."
Ly. Sic tua Cyrneas fugiant examina taxos,
Sic cytiso pastæ distentent ubera vaccæ.
Incipe, si quid habes: et me fecere poëtam
Pierides: sunt et mihi carmina: me quoque dicunt
Vatem pastores, sed non ego credulus illis.
Nam neque adhuc Varo videor, nec dicere Cinnâ
Digna, sed argutos inter strepere anser olores.
Mœ. Id quidem ago, et tacitus, Lycida, mecum ipse voluto,
Si valeam meminisse: neque est ignobile carmen.
"Huc ades, ô Galatea: quis est nam ludus in undis?
"Hìc ver purpureum; varios hìc flumina circùm
"Fundit humus flores: hìc candida populus antro
"Imminet, et lentæ texunt umbracula vites.
"Huc ades; insani feriant sine litora fluctus."
Ly. Quid, quæ te purâ solum sub nocte canentem
Audieram? numeros memini, si verba tenerem.
Mœ. "Daphni, quid antiquos signorum suspicis ortus?
Ecce, Dionæi processit Cæsaris astrum.

27. *Quorum hoc est fragmentum:* O Vare, cantantes cycni ferent tuum nomen

34. Ego *sum* non credulus illis.

35. Nam adhuc videor *mihi* dicere *carmina* digna neque

38. *Nunc recordor fragmentum ejus:* ades huc, O Galatea:

43. Sine *ut* insani

44. Quæ *carmina* audieram te solum canentem sub pura nocte

NOTES.

28. *Cremonæ.* Cremona was a city on the western bank of the river Po, not far from Mantua. Its inhabitants were involved in the same misfortune with those of Mantua, in having their property and lands taken from them by Augustus. Hence the epithet *miseræ.*

29. *Cycni:* properly swans. By meton. poets. The meaning of this fragment is, that if Mantua should be preserved from the calamity which had befallen Cremona, through the influence of Varus, the Mantuan poets would celebrate his praises and raise his name to the stars. By *Cantantes cycni,* says Heyne, we are to understand the *Mantuan poets.*

30. *Cyrneas;* an adj. from *Cyrnus,* an island in the Mediterranean sea. *Hodie Corsica.* This island abounded in the yew-tree: hence the epithet Cyrnean. The honey made of this tree was of a bitter quality, and universally considered bad. For this reason Lycidas wished the swarms of his friend to shun those trees. *Examina:* swarms of bees.

32. *Poetam:* a poet. *Vatem:* a poet, or prophet. These words are frequently used as synonymous, but they are not strictly so.

35. *Cinnâ.* Cornelius Cinna, the grandson of Pompey the Great. He became a favorite of Augustus.

36. *Digna:* things worthy of: or it may agree with *carmina,* understood; verses worthy of the attention of Varus and Cinna; or worthy to celebrate their actions. *strepere anser:* to gabble as a goose among tuneful swans—to make inharmonious sounds, &c.

37. *Ago:* in the sense of *facio.* *Tacitus ipse voluto:* I am thinking silently with myself, if I can recollect it. *Voluto:* I am revolving it in my mind.

39. *Quisnam ludus:* what sport is there in the waves? The parts of the word are separated by Tmesis. Nothing can be more beautiful than the whole of this fragment. It is in imitation of the eleventh Idyl of Theocritus.

40. *Purpureum:* blooming—gay. *Est* is to be supplied.

41. *Fundit:* in the sense of *producit.*

42. *Texunt:* in the sense of *efficiunt.* *Umbracula:* a dim. noun from *umbra,* a little, or pleasant shade.

43. *Insani:* raging—stormy.

44. *Quid:* in the sense of *cur.*

45. *Mimini numeros:* I recollect the tune; if I knew the words, I would sing them. These last, or some other of the like import, are evidently implied. Or else we must take *si* in the sense of *Utimam;* I wish—O that.

46. *Suspicis:* in the sense of *miraris.*

47. *Astrum.* This word properly signifies a constellation of stars. The poet uses it here for a single star, thereby giving the greater dignity to the star of Cæsar. Virgil makes Iülus the son of Æneas, the founder of the Julian family. Iülus was the grandson of Venus, who according to some was the daughter of *Dione,* a nymph of the sea, by Jupiter. Hence the epithet *Dionæan.* About the time of Julius Cæsar's death, it is said a remarkable comet appeared, which the Romans considered to be the soul of Cæsar received up to heaven. The poet calls it the star of Cæsar, agreeable to the vulgar notion. This comet, according to Dr Halley, appeared the third time in

"Astrum, quo segetes gauderent frugibus, et quo
"Duceret apricis in collibus uva colorem.
"Insere, Daphni, piros, carpent tua poma nepotes."
Omnia fert ætas, animum quoque. Sæpe ego longos
Cantando puerum memini me condere soles.
Nunc oblita mihi tot carmina: vox quoque Mœrim
Jam fugit ipsa: lupi Mœrim vidêre priores.
Sed tamen ista satìs referet tibi sæpe Menalcas.
  Ly. Causando nostros in longum ducis amores:
Et nunc omne tibi stratum silet æquor, et omnes
(Aspice) ventosi ceciderunt murmuris auræ.
Hinc adeò media est nobis via: namque sepulchrum
Incipit apparere Bianoris: hìc, ubi densas
Agricolæ stringunt frondes; hìc, Mœri, canamus:
Hic hœdos depone, tamen veniemus in urbem:
Aut si, nox pluviam ne colligat antè, veremur:
Cantantes licet usque (minùs via lædet) eamus.
Cantantes ut eamus, ego hoc te fasce levabo.
  Mœ. Desine plura, puer: et quod nunc instat, agamus.
Carmina tum meliùs, cùm venerit ipse, canemus.

51. Ego memini me puerum sæpe condere

55. **Ista *carmina* tibi sæpe satìs**

56. Longum *tempus*

62. Tamen veniemus *opportunè*

63. Antè *quàm pervenerimus ad eam*, licet *nobis ut* eamus usque cantantes.

66. Desine *loqui* plura *verba*

67. Cùm *Menalcas* ipse

NOTES.

1680. In its nearest approach to the sun, its tail was about 60 degrees long. *Processit;* moves along—hath begun its course.

48. *Quo segetes*, &c. Under which (by the influence of which) the fields shall rejoice with corn. Or, the crops shall abound in grain; taking *segetes* for the stalks or springing corn. *Gauderent*, by enallage for *gaudebunt*. *Sata abundabunt frumento*, says Ruæus.

49. *Uva duceret colorem:* shall take color—grow ripe. *Duceret:* for *ducet*, by enallage.

50. *Insere piros:* plant or graft your pear-trees. The star of Cæsar shall extend its influence to them. They will grow and flourish; and if you should not live to reap the fruit of your labor yourself, be assured your offspring will. *Piros* may be put for fruit trees in general: the *species* for the *genus*.

51. *Ætas:* in the sense of *tempus*. *Animum:* in the sense of *memoriam*.

52. *Condere longos Soles:* to pass or spend long days in singing. *Sol* is often taken for the day, as *Luna* is for the night. See Æn. 2. 255.

54. *Lupi priores:* the wolves first have seen Mœris. He hath lost his voice—he cannot sing. Alluding to a superstitious notion that if a wolf saw a man the first, he would lose his voice.

55. *Referet:* in the sense of *recitabit*.

56. *Causando:* by framing excuses. From the verb *causor*. *Ducis:* you put off—defer. *Amores:* pleasure—entertainment.

57 *Omne stratum æquor*, &c. The whole level surface of the water, is still for you. *Stratum:* smooth—level. To consider *stratum* as expressing the tranquillity of the water is mere tautology: that is sufficiently expressed by *silet*. *Æquor* any plain or level surface, whether land or water; here, probably, the river *Mincius*. *Omnes auræ*, &c. Every breeze of whispering wind hath ceased. *Ventosi murmuris:* in the sense of *murmurantis venti*.

59. *Adeò:* only—surely.

60. *Sepulchrum Bianoris:* the tomb of Bianor. He was said to be the son of the river Tiber and the nymph *Manto*. He founded, or rather enlarged Mantua, and called it after the name of his mother. See Æn. 10. 198. His tomb was placed by the side of the way.

61. *Stringunt:* prune, or lop off the thick boughs.

62. *Urbem*. The city Mantua. *Depone hœdos:* lay down your kids. He was probably carrying them upon his shoulders. Let us stay here awhile and amuse ourselves in singing: we shall, nevertheless, arrive in town in good time.

64. *Usque:* all the way—all the time. *Lædet:* in the sense of *fatigabit*.

65. *Levabo te*, &c. I will ease you of this burden—load: to wit, the kids, which he was carrying to town for his new landlord. See verse 6, supra.

66. *Puer:* swain. It is applied to shepherds in general.

67. *Cùm ipse*, &c. It is probable that Virgil composed this Eclogue when he was at Rome.

QUESTIONS.

To whom did the estate of Virgil fall in the distribution of the Mantuan lands? Did he receive any hard treatment from *Arius?* How did he save his life? What was the name of his steward? Who is *Lycidas* supposed to be? When does the pastoral open? Where is the scene laid? What is the time of the day? What is the subject of this pastoral? What is the character of it?

What is the distinction between *poeta*, and *Vates?*

What remarkable appearance was observed in the heavens about the time of Julius Cæsar's death?

What does the poet call it?

When did it appear the third time?

Who was Bianor? What did he do?

ECLOGA DECIMA.

GALLUS.

The subject of this fine pastoral is the love of Gallus for Lycoris, who refused his addresses, and gave her affections to an officer. This Gallus was a particular friend of Virgil, and was an excellent poet. He raised himself from a humble station to great favor with Augustus, who appointed him governor of Egypt after the death of Anthony and Cleopatra.

The scene of the pastoral is laid in Arcadia, whither the poet supposes his friend to have retired in the height of his passion. Here all the rural deities assemble around him, inquire the cause of his grief, and endeavor to moderate it. This Eclogue is not surpassed by any of the preceding, except the fourth, in beauty and grandeur. Here, too, Virgil imitates Theocritus, particularly in his first Idyl. By Lycoris is meant Cytheris, a most beautiful woman, and celebrated actress.

EXTREMUM hunc, Arethusa, mihi concede laborem.
2. Pauca carmina sunt dicenda — Pauca meo Gallo, sed quæ legat ipsa Lycoris,
Carmina sunt dicenda: neget quis carmina Gallo?
Sic tibi, cùm fluctus subter labêre Sicanos,
Doris amara suam non intermisceat undam.
Incipe, sollicitos Galli dicamus amores,

NOTES.

1. *Arethusa.* A nymph of great beauty, the daughter of Nereus and Doris. Also, a fountain on the island *Ortygia*, in the bay of *Syracuse*, upon which stood a part of the city. Syracuse was famous for its being the birth place of Theocritus and Archimedes; and for its valiant defence against the Roman fleet and army under Marcellus. It was taken after a siege of three years. *Concede*, &c. Grant me this last work—favor me in the execution of this my last pastoral essay. The reason that the poet invoked this nymph is, that she was the goddess of a fountain of that name, in the place where Theocritus was born, and where pastoral poetry was much cultivated.

4. *Tibi:* with thee—with thy water.

5. *Amara Doris.* Doris, a nymph of the sea, the daughter of Oceanus and Tethys, and married to her brother *Nereus*, of whom he begat the nymphs called *Nereïdes;* here put by meton. for the sea, whose water is salt and of an unpleasant taste; which the poet prays may not be mingled with the sweet and pleasant waters of the fountain Arethusa, in its passage under the Sicilian sea. See Æn. iii. 694 and 6. Alpheus, a river of the Peloponnesus, is said to have been in love with the nymph Arethusa, who, flying from him, was turned by Diana into a fountain. She made her escape under the sea, to the island Ortygia, where she rose up. But Alpheus pursuing her by the same way, arose up in the same fountain, mingling his waters with hers. *Undam:* in the sense of *aquam.*

6. *Galli.* There were several persons by the name of *Gallus.* The one here meant is *Publius Cornelius Gallus.* He raised himself by his extraordinary merit to great favor with Augustus, who appointed him

Dum tenera attondent simæ virgulta capellæ.
Non canimus surdis, respondent omnia sylvæ.
Quæ nemora, aut qui vos saltus habuere, puellæ
Naiades, indigno cùm Gallus amore periret?
Nam neque Parnassi vobis juga, nam neque Pindi
Ulla moram fecere, neque Aonia Aganippe.
Illum etiam lauri, illum etiam flevêre myricæ.
Pinifer illum etiam solâ sub rupe jacentem
Mænalus, et gelidi fleverunt saxa Lycæi.
Stant et oves circùm, nostrî nec pœnitet illas.
Nec te pœniteat pecoris, divine poëta.
Et formosus oves ad flumina pavit Adonis.
Venit et upilio, tardi venêre bubulci:
Uvidus hybernâ venit de glande Menalcas.
Omnes, unde amor iste, rogant, tibi? Venit Apollo.
Galle, quid insanis? inquit: tua cura Lycoris,
Perque nives alium, perque horrida castra secuta est.
Venit et agresti capitis Sylvanus honore,

11. Nam neque ulla juga Parnassi, nam neque *ulla juga* Pindi, neque *fons*, Aonia Aganippe, fecere *ullam* moram vobis. Etiam lauri *fleverunt* illum

21. Unde *est* iste amor tibi, *O Galle*

NOTES.

governor of Egypt after the death of Antony and Cleopatra. His prince, however, for some cause or other, conceiving a violent enmity against him, sent him into banishment; which sentence was ratified by the senate. This cruel and undeserved treatment had such an effect upon his mind, that he killed himself. After his death, Augustus lamented his own severity and that of the senate toward so worthy a man. Gallus was a great friend of Virgil, and highly esteemed by Pollio and Cicero. He was a poet as well as statesman and soldier. It is said he wrote four book of elegies to *Cytheris*, whom Virgil calls *Lycoris*. He also translated some part of the works of *Euphorion*, a poet of *Chalcis*.

7. *Simæ:* flat-nosed.

8. *Respondent:* will answer—will echo back our song.

9. *Habuere vos:* in the sense of *detinuerunt vos*. *Nemora:* properly signifies a grove or wood thinly set with trees, where flocks may feed and graze; derived from the Greek. *Saltus:* properly a thick wood, where bushes and fallen trees do not permit animals to pass without leaping; from *salio*. *Habuere vos:* detained you from coming to console Gallus in his grief. *Puellæ:* in the sense of *nymphæ*.

11. *Juga:* in the sense of *cacumina*. *Parnassi.* Parnassus was a mountain, or rather range of mountains in Phocis, sacred to the Muses. *Pindi.* Pindus was a range of mountains in the confines of Epirus and Macedonia, also sacred to the Muses. *Aganippe* was the name of a fountain issuing from mount Helicon in Beotia, and flowing into the river Permessus. It is called *Aonian*, from *Aon*, the son of Neptune, who reigned in Beotia.

15. *Mænalus.* A mountain in Arcadia, celebrated for its pines. *Lycæi.* Lycæus, a mountain of the same country, noted for its rocks and snows; hence the epithet *gelidi*. The whole of this passage is very fine. It contains a reproof to the nymphs for not assisting in alleviating the grief of Gallus.

16. *Stant et oves*, &c. His flocks too stand around him—nor are they ashamed of him—nor do they disregard his grief. Gallus is represented under the character of a swain, feeding his sheep on the mountains of Arcadia. *Nostri:* our friend—Gallus.

18. *Adonis.* He was the son of Cinyras, king of the island of Cyprus, by his daughter *Myrrha*. He was so beautiful, that Venus ranked him among her favorites, and honored him with her bed. When hunting, he received a wound from a boar, of which he died, and was greatly lamented by her.

19. *Venit et upilio:* the shepherd too came, and the slow moving herdsmen came. *Upilio*, for *opilio*, by metaphasmus. *Opilio*, probably from *oves*, by changing the *v* into *p*. The word *et* is often used to express emphasis, and has the force of *etiam* or *quoque*, as in the present case. When it has its correspondent *et* in the following member of the sentence, it is usually translated by the word *both*, and the following *et* by *and*. The conj. *que*, when it has its correspondent *que*, is rendered in the same way.

20. *Uvidus de:* wet from gathering the winter mast.

21. *Apollo.* He came, the first of the gods; because he was the god of poetry.

22. *Tua cura:* for *tua amica*.

24. *Sylvanus.* He was the god of the woods, and said to be the son of Mars. He always bore on his head a branch of cypress Like Pan, he was represented as half man

Florentes ferulas et grandia lilia quassans.
Pan Deus Arcadiæ venit, quem vidimus ipsi
Sanguineis ebuli baccis minioque rubentem.
Ecquis erit modus? inquit: amor non talia curat
Nec lacrymis crudelis amor, nec gramina rivis,
Nec cytiso saturantur apes, nec fronde capellæ.
Tristis at ille: Tamen cantabitis, Arcades, inquit,
Montibus hæc vestris: soli cantare periti
Arcades. O mihi tum quàm molliter ossa quiescant,
Vestra meos olim si fistula dicat amores!
Atque utinam ex vobis unus, vestrique fuissem
Aut custos gregis, aut maturæ vinitor uvæ!
Certè sive mihi Phyllis, sive esset Amyntas,
Seu quicumque furor (quid tum, si fuscus Amyntas?
Et nigræ violæ sunt, et vaccinia nigra.)
Mecum inter salices lentâ sub vite jaceret.
Serta mihi Phyllis legeret, cantaret Amyntas.
Hìc gelidi fontes, hìc mollia prata, Lycori:
Hìc nemus: hìc ipso tecum consumerer ævo
Nunc insanus amor duri me Martis in armis

26. Quem *nos* ipsi vidimus

29. Crudelis amor nec *saturatur* lacrymis

31. At ille tristis inquit: tamen, O Arcades, *vos*

35. Utinam fuissem unus ex vobis

37. Certe sive Phillis, sive Amyntas, seu quicumque esset mihi furor, jaceret

42. Hìc, O Lycori, *sunt* gelidi

44. Insanus amor detinet me in armis duri Martis inter

NOTES.

and half goat. He fell in love with *Cyparissus*, the favorite of Apollo, who was changed into a tree of that name. *Agresti honore capitis:* with the rustic honor of his head—with a garland of leaves upon his head. *Honore:* in the sense of *corona.*

25. *Florentes ferulas:* blooming fennel. There are two kinds of *ferula*, or fennel, the small, or common, and the large, or giant fennel. This last grows to the height of six or seven feet. The stalks are thick, and filled with a fungous pith, which is used in Sicily for the same purpose as tinder is with us, to kindle fire. From this circumstance, the poets feigned that Prometheus stole the heavenly fire and brought it to earth in a stalk of ferula. Some derive the name from *ferendo*, because its stalk was used as a walking-stick; others derive it from *feriendo*, because it was used by school-masters to strike their pupils with on the hand. Hence the modern instrument, or *ferula*, which is used for the same purpose, though very different from the ancient one, and capable of giving much greater pain.

27. *Rubentem:* stained with the red berries of alder, and with vermilion. *Ebuli. Ebulum* is the plant called dwarf elder. It grows about three feet high, and bears red berries. In England it has obtained the name of dane-wort; because it was fabled to have sprung from the blood of the Danes, at the time of their massacre. It is chiefly found in church-yards. *Minio.* Minium is the native *cinnabar.* It was the vermilion of the ancients; it is our present red-lead.

28. *Modus:* in the sense of *finis.*

29. *Rivis:* with streams, or rills of water.

30. *Saturantur:* are satisfied.

31. *Arcades.* This address of Gallus to the Arcadians is tender and pathetic, especially that part of it where he wishes he had been only a humble shepherd like them.

32. *Hæc:* these my misfortunes.

33. *O quàm molliter:* O how softly then my bones, &c.; alluding to a superstitious notion of the ancients that the bodies of the dead might be oppressed by the weight of the earth cast upon them. Accordingly they crumbled it fine, and cast it lightly into the grave, using the words, *sit tibi terra levis:* may the earth be light upon thee.

34. *Olim:* hereafter. This word refers to future as well as to past time. *Mihi:* in the sense of *mea*, agreeing with *ossa.*

36. *Vinitor:* a vine-dresser. It seems to be used here in the sense of *vindemiator*, a gatherer of grapes—a vintager.

38. *Furor.* This word properly signifies any inordinate passion, such as love, anger, rage, fury, and the like; by meton. the object of such passion—the person loved.—*Fuscus:* black. The verb *sit* is to be supplied.

39. *Vaccinia:* whortle-berries, or bil-berries. Mr. Martyn takes the word for the flower of the hyacinth.

41. *Serta:* garlands of flowers.

43. *Consumerer*, &c. I could spend my very life here with you in this pleasant retreat, gazing upon the beauty of your person. Ruæus says: *traducerem omnem ætatem tecum.* But *consumerer* may be used in the sense of the Greek middle voice. Virgil was fond of the Greek idiom.

44. *Nunc insanus amor*, &c. The meaning of this passage appears to be: in this

Tela inter media atque adversos detinet hostes.
Tu procul à patriâ (nec sit mihi credere) tantùm
Alpinas, ah dura, nives, et frigora Rheni
Me sinè sola vides. Ah te ne frigora lædant!
Ah tibi ne teneras glacies secet aspera plantas!
Ibo, et Chalcidico quæ-sunt mihi condita versu
Carmina pastoris Siculi modulabor avenâ.
Certum est in sylvis, inter spelæa ferarum,
Malle pati, tenerisque meos incidere amores
Arboribus: crescent illæ, crescetis amores.
Intereà mixtis lustrabo Mænala Nymphis,
Aut acres venabor apros: non me ulla vetabunt
Frigora Parthenios canibus circumdare saltus.

46. Tu, ah dura *femina!* procul à patria (*utinam* sit mihi nec credere *id*) vides tantùm Alpinas nives, et frigora Rheni, sola sinè me.

50. Et modulabor avenâ Siculi pastoris *Theocriti*, carmina, quæ

54. Illæ *arbores* crescent: *vos, O mi* amores

NOTES.

pleasant place, if you had consented, we might have both lived happy and secure. But now, on account of your cruelty, we are both unhappy and miserable. Through despair, I expose myself to the dangers and hazards of war; and in the mean time your love of a soldier hurries you to distant countries, over the snows of the Alps, &c. Gallus here supposes *Cytheris* to accompany her lover, and to undergo the fatigues and hardships incident to a military life. *Me.* This passage would be much easier, if we could read *te* in the room of *me.* The sense naturally leads to such reading; but we have no authority for making the substitution. *Martis.* Mars was esteemed the god of war. He was the son of Jupiter and Juno, as some say; others say, of Juno alone. His education was intrusted to *Priapus*, who taught him all the manly exercises. In the Trojan war, he took a very active part, and was always at hand to assist the favorites of Venus. His amours with that goddess have been much celebrated by the poets. Vulcan, her husband, being informed of their intrigue, made a net of such exquisite workmanship, that it could not be perceived. In this net he caught the two lovers, and exposed them to the ridicule of the gods. He kept them in this situation for a considerable time, till Neptune prevailed upon him to set them at liberty. The worship of Mars was not very general among the Greeks, but among the Romans he received the most unbounded honors. His most famous temple was built by Augustus, after the battle of Phillippi, and dedicated to *Mars Ultor.* His priests were called *Salii*, and were first instituted by Numa. Their chief office was to keep the sacred *ancyle*, or shield, which was supposed to have fallen from heaven. Mars was sometimes called *Gradivus*, *Mavors*, and *Quirinus;* by meton. put for war in general —a battle—a fight, &c.

45. *Adversos:* in the sense of *infestos.*

46 *Tantùm.* only—nothing beside.

57. *Alpinas:* an adj. from *Alpes*, a very high range of mountains separating Italy from France, Switzerland, and Germany, and covered with almost perpetual snow. *Rheni:* the river Rhine. It rises in the mountains of Switzerland, and runs a northerly course, forming the boundary between France and Germany, and falls into the German sea near the Hague. Its length is near six hundred miles. *Dura:* in the sense of *crudelis.* *Sola:* Lycoris was alone, as respected Gallus.

49. *Plantas:* in the sense of *pedes.* *Aspera:* sharp. The whole of this address to his mistress is extremely tender and pathetic.

50. *Quæ condita sunt*, &c. Which were composed by me in elegiac verse. *Chalcidico:* an adj. from *Chalcis*, a city of Eubœa, (*hodie*, *Negropont*,) the birth-place of Euphorion, an elegiac poet; some of whose verses, it is said, Gallus turned into Latin verse. To this, Ruæus thinks, the poet refers. However this may be, it cannot be made from the words without straining them. They simply imply that Gallus wrote some verses or poems in the same kind of verse, or measure, in which Euphorion wrote.

51. *Modulabor:* in the sense of *canam.*

52. *Certum est*, &c. It is certain—I am resolved, that I had rather suffer in the woods any dangers and hardships than follow after Lycoris. These, or words of the like import, seem to be necessary to make the sense complete. *Spelæa:* dens, or haunts of wild beasts; from the Greek.

53. *Incidere:* to cut, or inscribe.

55. *Mænala:* neu. plu. a mountain in Arcadia. In the sing. *Mænalus.* *Lustrabo:* in the sense of *circumibo.* *Mixtis nymphis.* The meaning is, that he was in company with the nymphs; or that they, in confused and irregular order, pursued their course.

56. *Acres:* fierce—dangerous. *Vetabunt.* in the sense of *prohibebunt.*

57. *Parthenios.* Parthenius was a moun-

Jam mihi per rupes videor lucosque sonantes
Ire: libet Partho torquere Cydonia cornu
Spicula: tanquam hæc sint nostri medicina furoris,
Aut Deus ille malis hominum mitescere discat.
Jam neque Hamadryades rursùm, nec carmina nobis
Ipsa placent: ipsæ rursùm concedite sylvæ.
Non illum nostri possunt mutare labores;
Nec si frigoribus mediis Hebrumque bibamus,
Sithoniasque nives hyemis subeamus aquosæ:
Nec si, cùm moriens altâ liber aret in ulmo,
Æthiopum versemus oves sub sidere Cancri
Omnia vincit amor; et nos cedamus amori.
Hæc sat erit, Divæ, vestrum cecinisse poëtam,
Dum sedet, et gracili fiscellam texit hibisco,
Pierides: vos hæc facietis maxima Gallo:
Gallo, cujus amor tantùm mihi crescit in horas,
Quantùm vere novo viridis se subjicit alnus.
Surgamus: solet esse gravis cantantibus umbra:

60. Tanquam hæc *omnia* sint

61. Aut *tanquam* ille Deus *Cupido*

64. Illum *Deum Cupidinem; nec equidem*, si

67. Nec *equidem*, si versemus oves Æthiopum, sub sidere cancri, cùm

70. *O* Divæ Pierides, sat erit vestrum poetam cecinisse hæc *carmina*

72. Facietis hæc *fieri*

NOTES.

tain in Arcadia, where virgins used to hunt; from a Greek word signifying a virgin. It is here used as an adj. *Circumdare:* in the sense of *cingere.*

58. *Sonantes:* echoing—resounding.

59. *Cydonia:* an adj. from *Cydon*, a city of Crete, the arrows of which were held in great estimation. *Partho cornu:* a Parthian bow. The Parthians were a people famed for their skill in handling the bow, which they made of horn. Hence *cornu:* a bow. *Libet:* in the sense of *juvat.*

60. *Medicina furoris:* a remedy for our love. *Tanquam:* as if.

61. *Malis:* in the sense of *miseriis.*

62. *Hamadryades:* nymphs of the woods and trees. Their fate was supposed to be connected with that of particular trees, with which they lived and died. It is derived from the Greek. See Ecl. ii. 46.

63. *Rursum concedite:* again, ye woods, farewell. *Concedite*, is here elegantly put for *valete.* I wish *you* may grow and flourish, though *I* languish and die.

65. *Hebrum.* The Hebrus is the largest river of Thrace, rising out of mount Rhodope, near its junction with mount *Hæmus*, and taking a southerly course, falls into the Ægean sea: *hodie, Marisa.* The ancient Thrace forms a province of the Turkish empire, by the name *Romania. Frigoribus:* in the sense of *hyeme.*

66. *Sithonias:* an adj. from *Sithonia*, a part of Thrace, bordering upon the Euxine sea. *Subeamus:* endure—undergo.

67. *Moriens liber* the withering bark, or rind.

68. *Versemus:* feed, or tend upon; in the sense of *pasceremus. Æthiopum:* gen. plu. of *Æthiops*, an inhabitant of Æthiopia, an extensive country in Africa, lying principally within the torrid zone. Here it is put for the inhabitants of any country lying in a hot climate. *Cancri.* Cancer is one of the twelve signs of the Zodiac. The sun enters it about the twenty-first day of June, causing our longest day.

69. *Amor vincit*, &c. The poet here hath finely represented the various resolutions and passions of a lover. Gallus having tried various expedients to divert his affections, and finding nothing sufficiently enticing to him, to accomplish that end, finally abandons the vain pursuit with this reflection: *Love conquers all things—let us yield to love.*

71. *Texit:* formed—made. *Hibisco:* in the sense of *vimine.*

72. *Maxima:* most acceptable—most precious.

73. *In horas* hourly—every hour

74. *Subjicit se:* shoots itself up—springs up.

75. *Umbra solet*, &c. The shade of the evening is wont to be injurious to singers. *Umbra* here must mean the shade or dusk of the evening, which, on account of the falling dew, is reckoned an unhealthy part of the day. That the word is to be taken in this sense, appears from the circumstance mentioned in the following line. *Hesperus venit:* the evening star is approaching. *Cantantibus;* some read *cunctantibus:* to those delaying, or loitering.

Juniperi gravis umbra: nocent et frugibus umbræ.
Ite domum saturæ, venit Hesperus, ite capellæ.

77. *Vos, O meæ* saturæ capellæ, ite, ite domum

NOTES.

76. *Umbra juniperi:* the shade of the juniper tree is injurious: not so in fact; it is both pleasant and healthy. It is odoriferous in itself, and is often burned, to absorb the noxious part of the atmosphere, and to prevent infection. Poets often take liberties that are not allowable in prose writers. They may follow the common received opinions of things, however incorrect, without justly incurring censure. This we may be sure Virgil did in the present instance. It might have been the current opinion that the juniper tree changed its qualities as the evening came on; or, we may understand it thus: so noxious is the evening air, that even the juniper tree will not secure from its effects.

77. *Saturæ:* full-fed—sufficiently fed; implying that time enough had been spent in pastoral writing.

QUESTIONS.

What is the subject of this pastoral?
Who was Gallus?
Where is the scene of the pastoral laid?
What took place after his arrival in Arcadia?
What is the character of this pastoral?
Whom does Virgil imitate?
Who was Lycoris?
Who was Arethusa?
Was there any fountain of that name?
Where was it situated?
For what was Syracuse famous?
Why did the poet invoke the nymph Arethusa?
What is said of the river Alpheus?
Where was the mountain Parnassus?
Where was Pindus?
Where were the mountains Mænalus and Lycæus?
What is said of them?
Who was Mars?
What is said of him?
By whom was the most celebrated temple of Mars built?
What were his priests called?
What was their chief office?
What were the names of Mars?
For what is the word *Mars* put for by meton.?
Where is the river Hebrus?
Where does it rise and empty its waters?
Where is Æthiopia situated?

INTRODUCTION TO THE GEORGICS.

The civil wars, that had distracted the Roman empire, had nearly desolated Italy. The land lay neglected, and the inhabitants were reduced to great distress for want of the necessaries of life. In this state of things, they cast the blame upon Augustus, and murmured against his administration. To remedy the existing evils, and to avert heavier calamities, it became necessary to revive agriculture; which for many years had been almost wholly neglected, the people being taken from their lands to supply the armies. It occurred to Mæcenas that a treatise upon that subject would be highly useful to the inhabitants of Italy; he therefore engaged Virgil, who had just finished his Eclogues, to undertake the work. It had the desired effect. For, after the publication of the Georgics, Italy began to assume a new and flourishing appearance, and the people found themselves in plenty, and in the enjoyment of peace and content.

Virgil spent about seven years in this part of his works. His correct taste, his chaste style, and above all, his extensive knowledge, duly qualified him for a work of this kind. The Georgics, like the Eclogues, were every where well received.

The rules for the improvement of husbandry, and the advice given to the farmer upon the several subjects connected with it, were not only suited to the climate of Italy, but have been esteemed valuable in every country where "due honor has been paid to the plough," down to the present time.

The word *Georgica* is from the Greek. Its original word properly signifies the cultivation or tillage of the earth. In the Georgics, Virgil imitated Hesiod, who wrote a treatise upon this subject, entitled, *Opera et Dies*, but he far excelled him in every respect. He began this part of his works in the year of Rome 717, being then about thirty-two years of age, and dedicated it to Mæcenas, his friend and patron, at whose request he wrote it.

The Georgics are divided into four books. The first treats of the various soils, and the proper method of managing each. The second treats of the various ways of propagating fruit trees, and particularly the vine. The third treats of the several kinds of grass, and the proper method of raising horses, cattle, sheep, and goats. The fourth treats of the proper management of bees.

With the main subject, the poet hath interwoven several very interesting fables and episodes, which contribute to our pleasure, and relieve the mind under the dryness of precept.

QUESTIONS.

What was the state of Italy, when Virgil began his Georgics?

At whose request did he write them?

To whom did he dedicate them?

What is the meaning of the word *Georgica*, or Georgics?

From what language is the word derived?

What effect had the Georgics upon the state of Italy?

How long was Virgil in writing them?

In what year of Rome did he begin them?

Were they well received by his countrymen

Was Virgil well qualified to write upon the subject of agriculture?

Whom did he imitate?

What is the comparative merit of each work?

Do the Georgics contain valuable rules and directions to the agriculturist in all countries?

Into how many books are they divided?

What is the subject of each book? &c.

P. VIRGILII MARONIS

GEORGICA.

LIBER PRIMUS.

This Book opens with the plan of the whole work: and in the four first lines informs us of the subject of each book. The poet then proceeds to invoke the gods, that were thought to have any concern in the affairs of tillage or husbandry; and particularly, he compliments Augustus with divinity. After which, he goes on to show the different kinds of tillage proper for the different soils. He traces out the origin of agriculture. He describes the various implements proper for that use. He notices the prognostics of the weather. And concludes, by relating the prodigies which happened about the time of Julius Cæsar's death; and by invoking the gods for the safety of Augustus, his prince.

The whole is embellished with a variety of other matter, so judiciously blended with the subject, that, besides preventing languor and fatigue under the dryness of precept, it contributes to our pleasure and delight.

QUID faciat lætas segetes; quo sidere terram
Vertere, Mæcenas, ulmisque adjungere vites,
Conveniat: quæ cura boum; qui cultus habendo
Sit pecori; atque apibus quanta experientia parcis;
Hinc canere incipiam. Vos, ô clarissima mundi
Lumina, labentem cœlo quæ ducitis annum:
Liber et alma Ceres, vestro si munere tellus
Chaoniam pingui glandem mutavit aristâ,
Poculaque inventis Acheloïa miscuit uvis:

2. O Mæcenas, incipiam canere hinc, quid faciat lætas segetes, quo sidere conveniat vertere terram

3. Quæ *sit* cura boum; qui

7. O Liber, et alma Ceres, si

NOTES.

1. *Lætas:* in the sense of *copiosas* vel *fertiles.*

3. *Qui cultus*, &c. What management is necessary for raising cattle. It is plain that *necessarius*, *aptus*, or some word of the like import, is to be supplied, agreeing with *cultus*. *Habendo* may be a future part. pass. or a gerund in *do*, of the dat. case.

4. *Quanta experientia*, &c. How great care, or attention, is necessary to rear the frugal bees. Or, it may mean; how great experience, foresight, and regular management, in their affairs, there may be to the frugal bees. When sentences are very elliptical, it is sometimes difficult to fall upon the meaning of the author.

6. *Lumina.* We are here to understand, I apprehend, the sun and moon, as they govern the seasons; rather than Ceres and Bacchus, as some imagine.

7. *Liber et alma Ceres.* Ruæus considers these as the *Clarissima Lumina mundi* in the preceding line. But the reason which he gives for so doing appears insufficient. *Alma:* an adj. *cherishing—nourishing.* In this sense it is a very appropriate epithet of *Ceres*, as being the goddess of husbandry. It also signifies, *pure—holy*, &c.

8. *Chaoniam glandem: Chaonian acorns*, or *mast:* here put for *mast* in general; the *species* for the *genus*. *Chaoniam:* an adj. from *Chaonia*, a part of Epirus, in which was the famous grove *Dodona*, that abounded in mast-trees.

9. *Acheloïa pocula:* draughts of pure water. *Pocula*, properly the cups, here put by

10. Et vos, O Fauni, præsentia numina agrestûm; O Faunique Dryadesque puellæ, ferte pedem simul:

14. Et, *tu O Aristæe,* cultor nemorum, cui ter centum nivei juvenci

16. *Tu* ipse, O Tegeæe Pan, custos ovium, linquens patrium nemus,

Et vos, agrestûm præsentia numina, Fauni,
Ferte simul Faunique pedem Dryadesque puellæ;
Munera vestra cano. Tuque ô, cui prima frementem
Fudit equum magno tellus percussa tridenti,
Neptune: et cultor nemorum, cui pinguia Cææ
Ter centum nivei tondent dumeta juvenci:
Ipse nemus linquens patrium, saltusque Lycæi,
Pan ovium custos, tua si tibi Mænala curæ,
Adsis, ô Tegeæe, favens: oleæque Minerva

NOTES.

meton. for the water itself. *Acheloïa:* an adj. from Achelous, a river of Ætolia, supposed by the ancients to have been the first that arose out of the earth: hence put, frequently, for water in general. Ceres, it is said, taught men husbandry, and Bacchus, the cultivation of the vine: to which the words *vestro munere* allude. At the first, men lived upon the spontaneous productions of the earth.

10. *Præsentia:* in the sense of *propitia.*

11. *Dryades.* Nymphs or goddesses of the woods, from a Greek word signifying an oak. See Ecl. ii. 46

14. *Neptune.* Neptune, god of the sea, and father of fountains and rivers. He was the son of Saturn and Ops, and brother of Jupiter and Pluto. In the division of the world with his brothers, he obtained the empire of the sea. He is said to have married Amphitrite, the daughter of *Nereus* or *Oceanus.* He is said to have been the first who tamed the horse. Hence the poets feign, that when a dispute arose between him and Minerva, respecting the name to be given to the city Athens, it was referred to the gods for their decision; who declared it should be called by the name of the party that should confer on mankind the greatest benefit; whereupon Neptune struck the earth with his trident and produced the horse, a warlike animal; and Minerva with her spear produced the olive, the emblem of peace: upon which the case was given in her favor. *Neptunus,* by meton. is often put for the sea. *Cultor nemorum.* The person here meant is *Aristæus,* the reputed son of Apollo and the nymph Cyrene, the daughter of *Peneus,* the god of the river *Peneus* in Thessaly. After his son *Actæon* was torn to pieces by dogs for looking upon *Diana,* as she was bathing, *Aristæus* left Thebes, and took up his residence in the island *Cæa,* one of the Cyclades. He is said to have been the first, who taught mankind the cultivation of bees. See Geor. iv. 317.

17. *Si tua Mænala,* &c. The meaning is: if you have a regard for Mænalus, Lycæus, and the rest of your mountains in Arcadia, come and be propitious to my undertaking. These mountains were sacred to Pan.

18. *Tegææe:* an adj. from *Tegea,* a city of Arcadia, sacred to Pan. *Minerva.* Goddess of wisdom and the liberal arts. She is said to have been produced from the brain of Jupiter full grown, and immediately admitted into the assembly of the gods; where she distinguished herself by her wise counsel. Her power was very great. She could hurl the thunderbolts of Jupiter, prolong the lives of men, and bestow the gift of prophecy. *Arachne,* the daughter of Idmon, a Lydian, challenged the goddess to a trial of skill in embroidery. She represented on her piece the amours of Jupiter in a masterly manner. She was, however, outdone, and having hung herself through chagrin, was changed into a spider by the victorious goddess. Minerva took a very active part in support of the Greeks at the siege of Troy, and protected her favorite Ulysses in all his dangers. Her worship was universally established. She had magnificent temples dedicated to her in most countries. *Sais, Rhodes,* and *Athens,* were her favorite places. She was variously represented according to the characters in which she appeared; but most generally with a helmet on her head, and a large plume waving in the air; with one hand holding a spear; with the other a shield, having the head of Medusa upon it. This shield was called the *Ægis.* When she is represented as the goddess of the liberal arts, she is covered with a veil called the *Peplum.* She had a very celebrated statue called the *Palladium,* said to have been about three cubits in height, and represented her sitting, and holding in her right hand a pipe, and in her left a distaff and a spindle. It is said to have fallen from heaven near the tent of *Ilus,* as he was building the citadel of Troy, on the preservation of which, the safety of that city depended. It was carried off by Ulysses and Diomede, who privately found a way into the temple. It is said, however, that the true palladium was not taken away, but only a statue of similar shape; and that Æneas carried the true one with him to Italy. The olive-tree, the cock, the owl, and the dragon, were sacred to her. She had various names, and as various offices and functions attributed to her. She was called *Athena,* from the city of Athens, of which she was the tutelar goddess: *Pallas,* from a giant of that name whom she slew;

Inventrix, uncique puer monstrator aratri:
Et teneram ab radice ferens, Sylvane, cupressum:
Dîque, Deæque omnes, studium quibus arva tueri,
Quique novas alitis non ullo semine fruges,
Quique satis largum cœlo demittitis imbrem.
Tuque adeò, quem mox quæ sint habitura Deorum
Concilia, incertum est, urbesne invisere, Cæsar,
Terrarumque velis curam: et te maximus orbis
Auctorem frugum, tempestatumque potentem
Accipiat, cingens maternâ tempora myrto:
An deus immensi venias maris, ac tua nautæ
Numina sola colant: tibi serviat ultima Thule,
Teque sibi generum Tethys emat omnibus undis.
Anne novum tardis sidus te mensibus áddas,
Quà locus Erigonen inter Chelasque sequentes
Panditur: ipse tibi jam brachia contrahit ardens

saltusque Lycæi, si tua Mænala *sint* tibi curæ, adsis favens: *Tu* quoque O Minerva, inventrix

21. O omnes Dique Deæque, quibus *est* studium

24. Tuque adeò O Cæsar, quem, incertum est, quæ concilia Deorum habitura sint mox: ne velis invisere urbes, et *suscipere* curam terrarum:

NOTES.

or rather, from a Greek word signifying *to vibrate*, because as goddess of war, she brandished a spear in her right hand: *Parthenos*, because she preserved her chastity: *Tritona*, because she was worshipped near a lake of that name in Africa: *Glaucopia*, because she had blue eyes: *Agorea*, because she presided over markets: *Hippia*, because she taught mankind to manage the horse: *Stratia*, and *Area*, because of her martial character.

19. *Puer.* Triptolemus the son of Celeus, king of *Elusina*, a city of Attica. He is said to have taught the Greeks agriculture, having himself been previously instructed by Ceres. See Ecl. v. 79.

20. *Sylvane.* One of those demi-gods that go under the general name of satyrs. He is said to have been passionately fond of the boy *Cyparissus*, who having, through mistake, killed a deer, of which he was very fond, pined away and died. He was changed into the Cypress tree. See Ecl. 5. 73.

21. *Studium:* in the sense of *cura.*

22. *Non ullo semine.* Some read *nonnullo semine.* But the former appears to be the better; and it is supported by several ancient manuscripts, as Pierus informs us. *Nonullo semine:* from no seed, that is, such as spring up spontaneously. Heyne, after Heinsius, reads *non ullo semine.*

24. *Adeò:* in the sense of *præcipuè.*

25. *Urbes.* The common reading is *urbis;* but as all interpreters agree that it is for *urbes*, the acc. plu. I have ventured so to write it. The nom. and acc. plu. of the third declensions sometimes ended in *eis*, which was contracted into *is;* as, *omneis*, contracted *omnis*—*urbeis*, contracted *urbis.* But there is no reason that it should be retained in preference to the regular termination Valpy reads *urbes.*

26. *Maximus:* the sup. in the sense of the pos.: the great world.

27. *Potentem:* the ruler—one who has power over: *rectorem*, says Ruæus. It has here the force and efficacy of a substantive. *Tempestatum:* in the sense of *temporum.*

28. *Materna myrto.* The myrtle tree was sacred to Venus, the mother of Æneas, from whom, according to Virgil, Cæsar descended.

30. *Thule.* One of the Shetland islands on the north of Scotland, the farthest land westward known to the ancients. The poet, therefore, calls it *ultima. Colant:* in the sense of *adorent*, vel *precentur.*

31. *Tethys.* The daughter of *Cœlus* and *Terra*, and wife of *Oceanus.* She was mother of the nymphs *Oceanides;* elegantly put; by meton. for the sea itself.

32. *Anne addas*, &c. Or whether you would add yourself a new constellation to the slow summer months. The months are called slow, because the days in the summer are the longest, and so their motion appears the slower; or rather, to speak philosophically, because the earth moves slower in her orbit, during the summer months.

33. *Erigonen.* Erigone, the daughter of Icarus, who, on account of the murder of her father, hung herself for grief; but was translated to heaven, and made the constellation *Virgo. Sequentes Chelas:* the following claws—the claws following the sign *Virgo.* The *Chelæ* were the claws or arms of *Scorpio*, extending over, and occupying the sign of *Libra.* The ancients at first divided the Ecliptic into eleven parts, leaving out the sign *Libra*, and giving to *Scorpio* a space of the Zodiac equal to 60°. By reducing it to an equality with the rest of the signs, a space of 30° remained for *Cæsar*, if he chose to occupy it.

34. *Ardens:* impatient—greatly desirous of thy coming; rather than arde burning, &c. as it is sometimes rendered.

Scorpius, et cœli justâ plus parte reliquit.

36. Quicquid *Numen* eris, da

Quicquid eris (nam te nec sperent Tartara regem,
Nec tibi regnandi veniat tam dira cupido:
Quamvis Elysios miretur Græcia campos,
Nec repetita sequi curet Proserpina matrem)
Da facilem cursum, atque audacibus annue cœptis:

41. Tuque miseratus agrestes ignaros viæ, mecum ingredere

Ignarosque viæ mecum miseratus agrestes
Ingredere, et votis jam nunc assuesce vocari.
Vere novo, gelidus canis cùm montibus humor
Liquitur, et Zephyro putris se gleba resolvit;
Depresso incipiat jam tum mihi taurus aratro
Ingemere, et sulco attritus splendescere vomer.
Illa seges demum votis respondet avari
Agricolæ, bis quæ solem, bis frigora sensit:
Illius immensæ ruperunt horrea messes.
At priùs ignotum ferro quàm scindimus æquor,
Ventos et varium cœli prædiscere morem

52. Cura sit *nobis* prædiscere

Cura sit, ac patrios cultusque habitusque locorum:
Et quid quæque ferat regio, et quid quæque recuset.
Hìc segetes, illìc veniunt feliciùs uvæ:
Arborei fœtus alibi, atque injussa virescunt
Gramina. Nonne vides, croceos ut Tmolus odores,
India mittit ebur, molles sua thura Sabæi?

58. At nudi Chalybes *mittunt ad nos* ferrum

At Chalybes nudi ferrum, virosaque Pontus

NOTES.

39. *Proserpina.* See Ecl. v. 79.

42. *Ingredere:* enter upon your office of a god, and even now accustom yourself to be invoked by vows.

43. *Gelidus humor:* here, ice or snow. *Humor* is properly any kind of moisture or liquor. *Novo vere.* The poet advises the husbandman to begin his ploughing in the early part of the spring, as soon as the snow melts from the mountains, and the earth be sufficiently softened, that he may be in due season with the work of the year.

45. *Depresso aratro:* in the plough put, or laid, deep in the earth. Or the words may be put absolutely: the plough being put deep in the earth.

48. *Quæ bis sensit,* &c. Which feels twice the summer, and twice the winter; that is, lies fallow for two years together, or without tillage. *Seges:* in the sense of *terra,* vel *ager,* says Heyne.

49. *Ruperunt.* The sense seems to require the present; accordingly Ruæus hath interpreted it by *rumpunt:* his immense harvests burst his barns—his barns are not capable of containing his crops.

50. *Æquor:* properly any plain or level surface, whether land or water. Here used in the sense of *ager* or *campus. Ignotum: cujus natura ignota est nobis.*

51. *Prædiscere ventos,* &c. To learn before hand the winds and the various qualities of the weather—to observe, to what winds the fields are most exposed, and whether the climate be moist or dry, cold or hot. *Morem cœli: naturam vel temperiem aëris,* says Heyne.

52. *Patrios cultus:* the culture of our fathers. This is the sense of Davidson and Heyne. *Colendi rationem probatam usu majorum,* says the latter. Ruæus says: *Propriam culturam. Habitus locorum:* the habits of the places—the habit or peculiar nature of the various soils. Land, by being tilled in a certain way, acquires an aptitude to produce some kinds of grain better than others. This is what is meant here.

54. *Feliciùs:* more luxuriantly.

55. *Arborei fœtus:* nurseries, or young trees. *Fœtus* signifies the young of any kind, animate or inanimate. *Injussa:* not sown—spontaneously.

56. *Tmolus.* A mountain in Phrygia, in the confines of Lydia, famous for its saffron: hence the epithet *croceos.*

57. *Molles Sabæi:* the effeminate Sabeans. These were a people inhabiting Arabia Felix, which abounded in frankincense.

58. *Chalybes nudi:* the naked Chalybes send us iron, and Pontus, &c. The Chalybes were a people of Spain, according to Justin; but of Pontus, according to Strabo, said to have wrought naked, on account of the heat of their furnaces, or forges. Hence *Chalybs* came to signify the best kind of iron and steel. *Pontus.* See Ecl. viii. 95

Castorea, Eliadum palmas Epirus equarum ?
Continuò has leges æternaque fœdera certis
Imposuit natura locis, quo tempore primùm
Deucalion vacuum lapides jactavit in orbem :
Unde homines nati, durum genus. Ergò age, terræ
Pingue solum primis extemplò à mensibus anni
Fortes invertant tauri : glebasque jacentes
Pulverulenta coquat maturis solibus æstas.
At si non fuerit tellus fœcunda, sub ipsum
Arcturum tenui sat erit suspendere sulco :
Illìc officiant lætis ne frugibus herbæ ;
Hìc, sterilem exiguus ne deserat humor arenam.
Alternis idem tonsas cessare novales,
Et segnem patiere situ durescere campum.
Aut ibi flava seres mutato sidere farra ;
Unde priùs lætum siliquâ quassante legumen,
Aut tenues fœtus viciæ, tristisque lupini
Sustuleris fragiles calamos, sylvamque sonantem.
Urit enim lini campum seges, urit avenæ :
Urunt Lethæo perfusa papavera somno.

64. Extemplò à primis mensibus anni fortes tauri

71. *Tu* idem patiere tonsas novales cessare alternis *annis*, et

74. Unde priùs sustuleris lætum legumen quassante siliquâ, aut tenues fœtus viciæ, fragilesque

77. *Seges* avenæ urit *eum*.

NOTES.

59. *Virosa castorea:* strong-scented castor. According to Pliny, the castor was contained in the testicles of the beaver. But the moderns have found that the castor is contained in certain odoriferous glands about the groin, and in both sexes. *Epirus palmas*, &c. Epirus (produces) the victors of the Olympic mares—produces those mares that obtain the palm of victory in the Olympic races. *Palmas equarum ;* Ruæus says *equas victrices in Olympico cursu.* Epirus, once a powerful kingdom, is bounded by the Ionian sea on the south and west, and by Thessalia, Macedonia, and Achaia on the north and east, famous for its excellent horses. *Elidum:* an adj. gen. plu. from *Elis*, or *Elea*, a maritime country of the Peloponnesus, the chief cities of which were *Elis*, on the river *Peneus*, and *Olympia*, on the river *Alpheus*, famous for the games there celebrated in honor of Jupiter. They were instituted 1458 years before Christ, and celebrated every fifth year.

60. *Fœdera:* in the sense of *conditiones.*

62. *Deucalion.* See Ecl. vi. 41.

63. *Nati :* in the sense of *orti sunt.*

66. *Solibus:* Sol, properly the sun, by meton. heat. *Maturis:* in the sense of *vehementibus*, vel *ardentibus. Coquat: emoliat et rarefaciat*, says Heyne.

68. *Sub ipsum Arcturum:* about the rising of Arcturus. This is a star of the first magnitude in the constellation Bootes, near the tail of the great Bear. The poet recommends, if the soil be rich, to turn it up with a deep furrow early, that it may lie and bake through the heat of the summer; but if the land be of a thin soil, and light, it will be sufficient to turn it up with a thin furrow, and some time in the fall, about the rising of Arcturus. In the former case, (*illìc*) that the grass and weeds may not injure the springing crop; in the latter case (*hìc*) that the scanty moisture may not leave the barren land.

71. *Tonsas novales*, &c. You should suffer your reaped fallow grounds to rest every other year. *Novalis terra*, is properly new ground, or ground newly broken up. Hence it came to signify fallow ground, because by resting it is recruited, and, as it were, renewed.

72. *Situ:* with a sword. *Situs* here means the grass, weeds, &c. which overspread the ground, and bind it down into what is commonly called a sword. *Campum segnem:* your field lying idle.

73. *Sidere mutato:* the year being changed. Some copies read *semine mutato. Sidus*, in the sense of *annus*, is frequently used by Virgil.

74. *Lætum:* in the sense of *fertile* vel *copiosum. Siliqua:* in the rattling pod, or shell.

75. *Tristis:* bitter. *Tenues fœtus*, Ruæus interprets by *parva grana.*

76. *Sylvam.* This word is frequently used for a thick luxurious crop or growth of any thing.

78. *Papavera perfusa:* poppies impregnated with oblivious sleep, or possessing the quality of causing sleep. *Lethæo :* an adj. from *Lethe*, a word of Greek origin, implying forgetfulness or oblivion. The poets feigned it to be one of the rivers of hell, the water of which the dead were said to drink after they had been in the regions below some time. It was represented as

79. Labor *erit* facilis alternis *annis:*
80. Tantùm ne pudeat *te* saturare sola

91. Seu *ille calor* magis durat *terram*, et
92. Ne tenues pluviæ *penetrent altiùs;* acriorve potentia
95. Adeò *ille* juvat arva multùm, qui frangit
97. Et *ille multùm juvat arva*, qui perrumpit terga, quæ suscitat *in primo* procisso æquore, aratro verso rursus in obliquum:

Sed tamen alternis facilis labor: arida tantùm
Ne saturare fimo pingui pudeat sola; neve
Effœtos cinerem immundum jactare per agros.
Sic quoque mutatis requiescunt fœtibus arva:
Nec nulla intereà est inaratæ gratia terræ.
Sæpe etiam steriles incendere profuit agros,
Atque levem stipulam crepitantibus urere flammis
Sive inde occultas vires et pabula terræ
Pinguia concipiunt; sive illis omne per ignem
Excoquitur vitium, atque exudat inutilis humor:
Seu plures calor ille vias, et cæca relaxat
Spiramenta, novas veniat quà succus in herbas:
Seu durat magis, et venas astringit hiantes:
Ne tenues pluviæ, rapidive potentia solis
Acrior, aut Boreæ penetrabile frigus adurat.
Multùm adeò, rastris glebas qui frangit inertes,
Vimineasque trahit crates, juvat arva; neque illum
Flava Ceres alto nequicquam spectat Olympo:
Et qui, procisso quæ suscitat æquore, terga
Rursus in obliquum verso perrumpit aratro:
Exercetque frequens tellurem, atque imperat arvis
    Humida solstitia atque hyemes orate serenas,

NOTES.

having the power of causing them to forget whatever they had done, seen, or heard before. A river in Africa of that name, which flowed under ground for some distance, and then rose to its surface, is supposed to have given rise to this extravagant fable.

79. *Labor facilis.* The meaning appears to be this: that the above mentioned crops may be sown every other year, notwithstanding their injurious qualities, provided the land be well manured.

80. *Arida sola:* dry or thirsty soils.

81. *Effœtos:* worn out—exhausted.

82. *Fœtibus:* in the sense of *segetibus*.

83. *Nec nulla gratia est inaratæ terræ:* nor, in the mean time is there no gratitude in the land untilled—left fallow every other year.

The whole of this section contains a number of excellent precepts and instructions for the husbandman. In the first place, he advises the farmer to let his land rest every other year; or, if he cannot do that with convenience, then to change the crops, and to sow wheat after the several kinds which he mentions, but not to sow flax, oats, or poppies: for these burn and impoverish the land. He says, notwithstanding this, they may be sown in turn, provided care be taken to recruit and enrich the land by manure. The poet concludes by observing, that if the ground be left fallow, as he at first advised, instead of being sown with any of those grains, it would not be ungrateful—it would abundantly repay the farmer for this indulgence.

86. *Sive inde*, &c. The poet here gives four reasons for the farmer's firing his lands. 1. That they might hence receive an increase of nutriment. 2. That the noxious moisture might be dried up to them. 3. That the close and dense soil might be loosened. And 4. That the loose soil might be rendered closer. This he founds upon the principle of those philosophers who taught that fire was the universal element.

88. *Vitium:* the bad quality.

90. *Spiramenta cæca:* secret avenues, or passages, by which moisture is drawn into the new plants.

93. *Penetrabile:* in the sense of *penetrans*, penetrating—searching. *Rapidi:* in the sense of *ardentis*.

97. *Et qui*, &c. The poet recommends to the farmer to harrow his ground well, before he commit the seed to it; but if it be hard and obstinate, and lie up in ridges, (*terga*) so that it will not yield to the harrow, then it will be profitable to plough it again crosswise. *Proscisso æquore:* in breaking up his field. *Suscitat:* raises up—makes.

99. *Exercet*, &c. He exercises his land frequently, and commands his fields. This is a metaphor taken from a general training or exercising his troops giving them commands, and dispensing discipline among them.

100. *Solstitia:* summers.

Agricolæ hyberno lætissima pulvere farra,
Lætus ager: nullo tantùm se Mysia cultu
Jactat, et ipsa suas mirantur Gargara messes.
Quid dicam, jacto qui semine cominùs arva
Insequitur, cumulosque ruit malè pinguis arenæ?
Deinde satis fluvium inducit, rivosque sequentes?
Et cùm exustus ager morientibus æstuat herbis,
Ecce, supercilio clivosi tramitis undam
Elicit: illa cadens raucum per levia murmur
Saxa ciet, scatebrisque arentia temperat arva.
Quid, qui, ne gravidis procumbat culmus aristis,
Luxuriem segetum tenerâ depascit in herbâ,
Cùm primùm sulcos æquant sata? quique paludis
Collectum humorem bibulâ deducit arena?
Præsertim incertis si mensibus amnis abundans
Exit, et obducto latè tenet omnia limo,
Unde cavæ tepido sudant humore lacunæ.
Nec tamen (hæc cùm sint hominumque, boumque labores
Versando terram experti) nihil improbus anser,
Strymoniæque grues, et amaris intuba fibris
Officiunt, aut umbra nocet. Pater ipse colendi

101. Farra *sunt* lætissima hyberno pulvere: ager *est* lætus

104. Quid dicam *de eo*, qui

111. Quid *dicam de illo*, qui, ne culmus procumbat gravidis aristis, depascit

113. Quique deducit humorem collectum *instar* paludis bibulâ arenâ

121. Colendi *terram*

NOTES.

101. *Farra:* in the sense of *segetes.*

102. *Mysia.* There were two countries of this name: the one in Europe, and bounded on the north by the Danube; the other in Asia Minor, near the Propontis and Hellespont. The latter is here meant. Mysia delights herself so much in no cultivation, as in moist summers and dry winters—no culture renders her so fruitful, as to have moist, &c.

103. *Gargara:* neu. plu. A part of mount Ida, the country near which was much famed for its fertility.

104. *Quid dicam,* &c. What shall I say of him, who, the seed being sown, closely plies his fields, and breaks down the clods or ridges (*cumulos*) of his barren soil? For *malè pinguis;* Ruæus says, *malè compactæ;* and Valpy, *too rich* and *adhesive.* *Ruit:* in the sense of *frangit.*

106. *Sequentes rivos:* in the sense of *fluentes rivulos.*

108. *Ecce, elicit aquam,* &c. Lo! he leads down a stream of water from the brow of a hilly tract. *Æstuat:* is parched, or burned.

110. *Scatebris:* with its streams, or rills. *Temperat:* Ruæus says, *humectat.*

114. *Quique deducit.* The probable meaning of this passage is: that the husbandman, for the purpose of watering his fields in the dry season, should form reservoirs or ponds, by collecting into them the water that fell in the rainy season. He had already advised the plan of bringing water from the higher grounds upon his fields. But where that could not be done, he advises to substitute the reservoir or pond, as the only alternative. This appears to be the opinion of Heyne. *Humorem:* in the sense of *aquam.*

115. *Incertis mensibus:* in the variable months—those months when the weather is most changeable.

118. *Nec tamen,* &c. Though the farmer be never so careful in the culture of his land, the poet reminds him not to stop there. After the crop is put into the ground, it still requires his attention. For the foul or greedy goose, the Thracian cranes, the succory, or endive, as also the shade, injure it. The two negatives, *nec—nihil,* amount to an affirmative.

120. *Strymoniæ:* an adj. from *Strymon,* a river in the confines of Macedonia and Thrace, where cranes abounded.

121. *Pater ipse voluit:* father Jupiter himself willed that the way of cultivating the earth should not be easy. He was fabled to have been the son of Saturn and Ops; and called the father of gods, and king of men. Saturn, who received the kingdom of the world from his brother Titan, on the condition of his raising no male offspring, devoured his sons as soon as they were born; but his mother, regretting that so fair a child should be destroyed, concealed him from his father, as she also did Neptune and Pluto, and intrusted him to the care of the *Corybantes,* or *Curetes,* who educated him on mount *Ida,* in Crete. As soon as he came to mature years, he made war against the Titans, who had made his father a prisoner. He was victorious and set him at liberty. But growing jealous of his son's power, he conspired against him; whereupon Jupiter expelled him from his kingdom, and he fled

Haud facilem esse viam voluit, primusque per artem
Movit agros, curis acuens mortalia corda:
Nec torpere gravi passus sua regna veterno.
Ante Jovem nulli subigebant arva coloni:
Nec signare quidem, aut partiri limite campum
Fas erat: in medium quærebant: ipsaque tellus
Omnia liberiùs, nullo poscente, ferebat.
Ille malum virus serpentibus addidit atris,
Prædarique lupos jussit, pontumque moveri,
Mellaque decussit foliis, ignemque removit,
Et passim rivis currentia vina repressit:
Ut varias usus meditando extunderet artes
Paulatim, et sulcis frumenti quæreret herbam,
Et silicis venis abstrusum excuderet ignem.
Tunc alnos primùm fluvii sensêre cavatas:
Navita tum stellis numeros et nomina fecit,
Pleïadas, Hyadas, claramque Lycaonis Arcton.
Tum laqueis captare feras, et fallere visco,
Inventum; et magnos canibus circumdare saltus.
Atque alius latum fundâ jam verberat amnem

138. *Appellans eas* Pleiadas

NOTES.

for safety to Italy, where Janus was king. After this, Jupiter divided the empire of the world with his two brothers, reserving to himself the empire of heaven and earth. The Giants, the offspring of the earth, to avenge the death of the Titans, whom Jupiter slew, rebelled against him. Piling mountains, one upon another, they hoped to scale heaven itself, and attack Jupiter in person. He, however, completely vanquished them, and inflicted on them the severest punishment for their crimes. He married his sister *Juno*, who was very jealous of him, and sometimes very troublesome. His power was the most extensive of any of the gods. His worship was general, and surpassed that of any of the gods in dignity and solemnity. He had several celebrated oracles, but that at *Dodona*, in Epirus, and at *Ammon*, in Lybia, perhaps took the lead. He had several names, chiefly derived from the places where he was worshipped, and from his offices and functions. He was called *Hospitalis*, because he was the protector of strangers; *Optimus*, because he was the best; *Maximus*, because he was the greatest; *Olympius*, because he was worshipped at Olympia, &c. *Jupiter*, is sometimes put for the air, or weather.

123. *Movit:* in the sense of *coluit*.

124. *Gravi veterno. Veternus*, or *veternum*, is a disease causing a stupor both of mind and body, something like the lethargy. *Torpere gravi veterno*, is highly metaphorical. *Veterno:* in the sense of *otio*, vel *desidia*, says Ruæus.

131. *Removit ignem:* he removed fire from the sight of men, and concealed it in the veins of the flint. Prometheus is said to have stolen it from heaven, because it was found necessary to man. *Decussit:* he shook off the honey from the leaves, i. e. he caused the honey to cease.

133. *Ut usus extunderet:* that experience, by observation, might find out the various arts by degrees.

134. *Sulcis:* by agriculture—by the plough.

136. *Cavatas alnos:* simply, boats; because, at first, they were made of the alder-tree.

138. *Pleïadas:* acc. plu. of Greek termination. They are seven stars in the neck of Taurus, and are called *Pleïades*, from a Greek word signifying, to sail; because by their rising, they indicated the proper time to put to sea. They were sometimes called *Atlantides*, from *Atlas*, a king of Mauritania, whose daughters they were fabled to be, by the nymph *Pleïone*. The Romans sometimes called them *Vergiliæ*. Their names were, *Electra*, *Alcynoë*, *Celæno*, *Sterope*, *Taygeta*, *Maia*, and *Merope*. *Hyadas*. These are seven stars in the front of Taurus, so called from a Greek word signifying, to rain. They were fabled to have been the daughters of *Atlas* and *Æthra*. Refusing consolation for the death of their brother *Hyas*, who was slain by a lion, Jupiter, taking pity on them, changed them into as many stars. Their names are *Ambrosia*, *Eudoxa*, *Pasithoë*, *Cirone*, *Plexauris*, *Pytho*, and *Syche*. *Arcton*. A constellation near the north pole, called the *Ursa Major*. Lycäon was a king of Arcadia, whose daughter Calisto, out of jealousy, was transformed by Juno into a bear; and Jupiter, for his regard to her, translated her in that form to heaven, and made her the constellation *Arcton*.

Alta petens, pelagoque alius trahit humida lina.
Tum ferri rigor, atque argutæ lamina serræ;
(Nam primi cuneis scindebant fissile lignum)
Tum variæ venêre artes. Labor omnia vincit
Improbus, et duris urgens in rebus egestas.
  Prima Ceres ferro mortales vertere terram
Instituit: cùm jam glandes atque arbuta sacræ
Deficerent sylvæ, et victum Dodona negaret
Mox et frumentis labor additus; ut mala culmos
Esset rubigo, segnisque horreret in arvis
Carduus: intereunt segetes, subit aspera sylva,
Lappæque, tribulique: interque nitentia culta
Infelix lolium et steriles dominantur avenæ.
Quòd nisi et assiduis terram insectabere rastris,
Et sonitu terrebis aves, et ruris opaci
Falce premes umbras, votisque vocaveris imbrem:
Heu, magnum alterius frustrà spectabis acervum,
Concussâque famem in sylvis solabere quercu.
  Dicendum, et quæ sint duris agrestibus arma:
Queis sinè, nec potuere seri, nec surgere messes.
Vomis, et inflexi primùm grave robur aratri,
Tardaque Eleusinæ matris volventia plaustra,
Tribulaque, traheæque, et iniquo pondere rastri:
Virgea præterea Celei vilisque supellex,
Arbuteæ crates, et mystica vannus Iacchi.

144. Primi *homines*

160. **Dicendum** *est nobis*, **et quæ**

162. **Primùm vomis, et** grave

NOTES.

142. *Petens alta:* seeking the deep parts of the sea, or river. *Altum*, when it is used for the sea, properly signifies the channel, or the deepest part of it; while *pelagus* properly signifies that part of the sea near the land.

143. *Tum rigor ferri:* then the hardening of iron, and the blade of the grating saw, were invented.

145. *Improbus labor:* constant, persevering labor overcomes all difficulties. *Duris rebus:* in poverty. *Egestas:* in the sense of *necessitas*. *Venêre:* in the sense of *inventæ sunt*.

148. *Arbuta:* the fruit of the arbute tree. *Dodona:* a famous grove in Epirus, abounding in mast trees. See Ecl. ix. 13.

150. *Labor:* in the sense of *morbus*, disease. *Mala rubigo esset:* that the noxious mildew should consume the stalks. *Esset*, for *ederet*.

152. *Segnis carduus:* the useless thistle wave, or look rough. *Sylva.* See 76, supra.

153. *Lappæ:* burrs, a species of herb. *Tribuli:* the brambles—land-caltrops. *Infelix:* noxious—injurious.

154. *Dominantur:* bear rule—have the ascendency.

157. *Premes umbras:* you should trim off the limbs (of the trees) of a shaded field, &c. *Umbras:* in the sense of *ramos*, by meton.

159. *Solabere famem*, &c. The poet assures the farmer that, unless he follow the directions just given, he will behold the abundant crops of his neighbor, while his will fail him, and he be under the necessity of allaying the craving of nature upon nothing better than acorns.

160. *Arma:* implements, tools, &c. necessary to the farmer. *Et:* in the sense of *quoque*.

163. *Tarda volventia:* the slow-moving wagons of mother Ceres. *Elusinæ:* an adj. from *Eleusis*, a city of Attica, where she was worshipped. *Inflexi:* in the sense of *curvi*.

164. *Tribula.* This was a kind of sledge or carriage, used among the ancients to thresh their corn with. It was pointed with iron, and drawn over the grain by oxen. *Trahea.* This was an instrument something like the *tribulum*, and made use of for the same purpose; a sledge.

164. *Iniquo:* Ruæus says, *magno*.

165. *Vilis virgeaque supellex:* the cheap or common wicker-baskets. *Celei:* Celeus was the father of Triptolemus, whom Ceres, it is said, instructed in the art of tillage and husbandry. See Ecl. v. 79.

166. *Arbuteæ crates:* hurdles of the arbute tree. *Vannus:* a sieve, or winnowing machine. It is called *mystica*, mystic, because used in the mysteries of Bacchus. *Iacchi:* *Iacchus*, a name of Bacchus.

Omnia quæ multò antè memor provisa repones
Si te digna manet divini gloria ruris.
Continuò in sylvis magnâ vi flexa domatur
In burim, et curvi formam accipit ulmus aratri.
Huic à stirpe pedes temo protentus in octo,
Binæ aures, duplici aptantur dentalia dorso.
Cæditur et tilia antè jugo levis, altaque fagus,
Stivaque, quæ currus à tergo torqueat imos;
Et suspensa focis explorat robora fumus.
Possum multa tibi veterum præcepta referre,
Ni refugis, tenuesque piget cognoscere curas.
Area cum primis ingenti æquanda cylindro,
Et vertenda manu, et cretâ solidanda tenaci:
Ne subeant herbæ, neu pulvere victa fatiscat:
Tum variæ illudunt pestes. Sæpe exiguus mus
Sub terris posuitque domos, atque horrea fecit:
Aut oculis capti fodêre cubilia talpæ.
Inventusque cavis bufo, et quæ plurima terræ
Monstra ferunt: populatque ingentem farris acervum
Curculio, atque inopi metuens formica senectæ.
Contemplator item, cùm se nux plurima sylvis

169. Continuò in sylvis flexa ulmus domatur magna vi in burim, et accipit

171. Huic *buri* temo protentus à stirpe in octo pedes *aptatur;* binæ aures, *et* dentalia *cum* duplici dorso aptantur.

178. Cum primis *rebus* area *est* æquanda ingenti

184. Bufo inventus *est* cavis, et plurima monstra, quæ

NOTES.

167. *Omnia quæ memor:* all which things, being provided long before hand, you should be mindful to lay up.

168. *Divini ruris.* The country is here called divine, either on account of its innocence and happiness, or because it was originally the habitation of the gods. *Gloria:* reward. Ruæus says, *laus;* for *divini*, he says, *beati.*

171. *Stirpe:* from the back part, or bottom.

172. *Binæ aures:* two mould or earth boards, one on each side of the *temo*, or beam. The poet here mentions the several parts of the plough. The *buris*, or *bura*, was the part which the ploughman held in his left hand—the plough tail. The *dentale*, the chip, or part of the plough to which the *vomer*, or share, is fastened. *Duplici dorso:* with a double back. Some understand *duplex* in the sense of *latus;* but there is no need of this. The plough, which the poet is describing, is altogether of a singular kind to us. It had two mould-boards; two chips or share-beams we might supposed it to have had, one on each side of the *temo*, or main beam, which, being joined together, might not improperly be said to form a double back. *Stiva:* the handle, which the ploughman holds in his right hand.

173. *Et levis tilia.* *Tilia*, the linden, or lime-tree. It is a light wood, and therefore more suitable for the plough.

174. *Quæ torqueat:* which may turn the lowest wheels from behind—may turn the extreme or hinder part of the plough. The plough here described we may suppose run upon wheels, which is the reason of the poet's calling it *currus*, a carriage. Ruæus says: *quibusdam in regionibus aratrum instruitur rotis;* but commentators are by no means agreed as to the form and construction of this plough of the poet.

175. *Fumus explorat.* Wood seasoned in the way here mentioned will be less liable to crack or split, than if seasoned in the usual way, in the sun and open air.

180. *Victa pulvere:* overcome with dryness, should crack. *Pulvere.* Ruæus says: *siccitate, quæ creat pulverem.*

181. *Tum:* in the sense of *prætereà.*

183. *Talpæ capti oculis.* *Talpa*, the mole, a small animal, supposed to have no eyes, and living chiefly under the ground.

184. *Bufo:* the toad. *Monstrum*, properly signifies any thing contrary to the ordinary course of nature; also, any mischievous animal, whether man or brute; which is the meaning here.

186. *Curculio:* the weavel; a mischievous animal among grain.

187. *Contemplator item*, &c. Observe in like manner when the nut-tree in the woods clothes itself abundantly with blooms. Of the nut-tree, there are several kinds. The one here meant is supposed to be the *Amygdala*, or almond-tree, because its flowers or blossoms were supposed to be an indication of the fertility of the year. *Plurima:* an adj. sup. agreeing with *nux* This construction frequently occurs, and is more elegantly translated by its corresponding adverb.

Induet in florem, et ramos curvabit olentes:
Si superant fœtus, pariter frumenta sequentur,
Magnaque cum magno veniet tritura calore.
At si luxuriâ foliorum exuberat umbra,
Nequicquam pingues paleâ teret area culmos.
Semina vidi equidem multos medicare serentes,
Et nitro priùs et nigrâ perfundere amurcâ,
Grandior ut fœtus siliquis fallacibus esset.
Et quamvis igni exiguo properata maderent,
Vidi lecta diu, et multo spectata labore,
Degenerare tamen; ni vis humana quotannis
Maxima quæque manu legeret: sic omnia fatis
In pejus ruere, ac retrò sublapsa referri.
Non aliter quàm qui adverso vix flumine lembum
Remigiis subigit: si brachia fortè remisit,
Atque illum in præceps prono rapit alveus amni.
Præterea tam sunt Arcturi sidera nobis,
Hœdorumque dies servandi, et lucidus anguis;
Quàm quibus in patriam ventosa per æquora vectis
Pontus et ostriferi fauces tentantur Abydi.
Libra die somnique pares ubi fecerit horas,

194. Equidem **vidi** multos serentes medicare semina, et priùs *quàm serent*, perfundere *ea* nitro et nigra amurca, ut

196. Quamvis *semina* properata exiguo igni maderent; tamen vidi *ea* lecta diu, et spectata multo labore, degenerare; ni

199. Sic *vidi* omnia fatis ruere in pejus, ac sublapsa referri retrò.

202. Si forte remisit brachia, *ruit et sublapsus refertur retrò*, atque alveus rapit illum in præceps prono amni.

206. Quàm *iis* vectis per ventosa æquora in *suam* patriam, quibus Pontus et ostriferi fauces Abydi

NOTES.

189. *Fœtus:* in the sense of *flores.*

190. *Magno calore.* Calor here seems to mean the sweat and heat of the laborer or thresher, rather than the heat of the summer.

191. *At si umbra:* but if the boughs abound in a luxuriancy of leaves, in vain, &c. The meaning seems to be this: that if the blossoms upon the tree shall exceed the leaves, then you may expect a plentiful crop. But if, on the contrary, the leaves be the most numerous, you may expect a scanty crop—a crop rich only in husks and chaff. *Umbra:* in the sense of *rami.*

193. *Serentes:* part. of the verb, *sero*, taken as a substantive: Sowers. The poet here gives the husbandman to understand that the greatest care is to be taken in selecting his seeds; that it is sometimes useful to impregnate them with other qualities to prevent them from degenerating; and sometimes to soak and steep them over a slow fire, in order to hasten their sprouting and coming forward. And although care be taken in the selection, they will be found nevertheless to degenerate: and all that remains for him to do, is, to select every year with his own hand the fairest and best seeds; and in this way only he may keep his crops from degenerating to any great extent. This advice is worthy the attention of every farmer.

194. *Perfundere:* this may either mean to sprinkle them (*semina*) over with, or put them into. Ruæus says, *spargere.*

195. *Fallacibus.* The pods or ears are called fallacious, because they are sometimes large, when there is very little in them. *Fœtus:* the grain or produce.

198. *Humana vis:* human care. In the sense of *homines.* Unless men should select with the hand, &c. Ruæus says, *hominum industria.*

201. *Adverso flumine:* against the current.

203. *Atque.* Ruæus, on the authority of Gellius, takes *atque* in the sense of *statim.* Davidson and Heyne take it in its usual signification as a conjunction, supposing an ellipsis of the words: *ille ruit ac sublapsus refertur retrò.* And carries him headlong down the stream. *Alveus:* properly the channel or bed of a river; here, the river in general: the current, or *impetus* of the water; by meton.

205. *Hœdi.* Two stars in the shoulder of *Auriga*, a constellation in the heavens. *Lucidus Anguis:* a constellation called *Draco.* The poet here intimates that it is the duty of the farmer to observe the stars, and the various signs of the weather; and that he will find it as useful to him in the course of his business, as it is to the mariner.

207. *Fauces Abydi.* The Hellespont or straits, which separate Europe from Asia: called *ostriferi*, because abounding in Oysters. *Abydus:* a city on the Asiatic shore, over against *Sestus. Tentantur:* in the sense of *navigantur.*

208. *Die:* for *Diei.* The gen. of the fifth declension was sometimes thus written. *Somni*, is elegantly put for *noctis. Ubi Libra fecerit. Libra* is one of the signs of the zodiac, which the sun enters the 23d of September; at which time he is on the equator, and makes the days and nights equal.

Et medium luci atque umbris jam dividit orbem :
Exercete, viri, tauros, serite hordea campis,
Usque sub extremum brumæ intractabilis imbrem.
Necnon et lini segetem et Cereale papaver
Tempus humo tegere, et jamdudum incumbere rastris,
Dum siccâ tellure licet, dum nubila pendent.
Vere fabis satio : tum te quoque, Medica, putres
Accipiunt sulci ; et milio venit annua cura :
Candidus auratis aperit cùm cornibus annum
Taurus, et averso cedens canis occidit astro.
At si triticeam in messem robustaque farra
Exercebis humum, solisque instabis aristis :
Antè tibi Eoæ Atlantides abscondantur,
Gnossiaque ardentis decedat stella coronæ ;
Debita quàm sulcis committas semina, quàmque
Invitæ properes anni spem credere terræ.
Multi ante occasum Maiæ cœpêre : sed illos
Expectata seges vanis elusit aristis.
Si verò viciamque seres, vilemque faselum,

213. Tempus *est* tegere et segetem lini et Cereale papaver humo

214. Dum licet *tibi facere id*, tellure siccâ, et dum

215. Satio fabis *est in vere*: tum

225. Multi cœpere *serere* ante

NOTES.

211. *Brumæ:* properly the shortest day of winter, or the winter solstice: this is its meaning here. By synec. it is sometimes put for the whole winter. The meaning is, that the farmer may extend his sowing as late as the winter solstice, which is about the 21st of December. *Intractabilis:* in the sense of *duræ*, vel *asperæ*.

212. *Cereale:* an adj. from *Ceres*. The poppy was so called, most probably, because it was consecrated to her. Her statues were generally adorned with it. *Necnon:* in the sense of *quoque*.

213. *Incumbere rastris:* to ply the harrows. The poet is speaking of sowing, or committing to the earth the several crops: which could not be done till after the ploughing. Besides it requires dry weather to use the harrow: to which reference is made in the following line. But the plough may be used in wet weather. Heyne reads *aratris*. But he informs us that Heinsius, Pierius, and others read *rastris*, which the sense seems to require.

214. *Pendent:* in the sense of *suspensa sunt*.

215. *Medica*. A species of grass, or plant, brought into Greece by the Medes in the time of the Persian wars. Hence called *medica*, now *lucerne*. It made the best provender for cattle, and when sown, it is said to last in the ground thirty years.

216. *Milio*. The milium wâs a species of grass, or plant, which required to be sown every year. Hence *annua cura*. Now called *millet*.

218. *Cum candidus Taurus*. *Taurus* is a sign of the ecliptic. The sun enters it about the 21st of April. The year was commonly thought to be opened by *Aries*, or the month of March: but Virgil dissents from the received opinion, and assigns it to *Taurus*, or the month of April; because, as the etymology of the word implies, all nature seems to be released from the fetters of winter, and vegetation opens and shoots forth. *Canis cedens*, &c. The dog giving way to the retrograde sign, sets. Sirius (commonly called *the dog star*) is a star in the mouth of the *great dog*, a constellation in the heavens. *Averso Astro*. Astrum here is the constellation or sign *Argo*, which immediately follows the dog, and sets after him. It rises with its stern foremost, and in that manner goes through the heavens, contrary to the ordinary motion of a ship. The epithet *averso*, inverted, or turned about, is very proper.

221. *Eoæ Atlantides*. The morning Pleïades; that is, when they set in the morning, or go below the horizon about the rising of the sun. This is called their cosmical setting. See 138. supra.

222. *Coronæ*. The *Corona* is a constellation in the heavens called *Ariadne's Crown*. *Gnossia:* an adj. from *Gnossus*, a town in the island of *Crete*, where *Minos* reigned, whose daughter *Ariadne* was carried off by Theseus, and left in the island *Naxus*, where she married *Bacchus*. At the time of their nuptials, among the other presents she received from the gods, was a *Corona* or crown from *Venus;* which Bacchus translated to the heavens. *Ardentis:* in the sense of *splendentis*.

225. *Maiæ*. The name of one of the *Pleïades*, by synec. put for the whole of them.

227. *Viciam*. The *vicia* is a species of pulse called the *vetch*. *Faselum:* the faselus was a kind of pulse, common and

Nec Pelusiacæ curam aspernabere lentis;
Haud obscura cadens mittet tibi signa Bootes:
Incipe, et ad medias sementem extende pruinas.
 Idcirco certis dimensum partibus orbem
Per duodena regit mundi Sol aureus astra.
Quinque tenent cœlum zonæ: quarum una corusco
Semper Sole rubens, et torrida semper ab igni:
Quam circùm extremæ dextrâ lævâque trahuntur,
Cœruleâ glacie concretæ atque imbribus atris.
Has inter mediamque, duæ mortalibus ægris
Munere concessæ Divûm, et via secta per ambas,
Obliquus quà se signorum verteret ordo.
Mundus ut ad Scythiam Riphæasque arduus arces
Consurgit; premitur Libyæ devexus in Austros.
Hic vertex nobis semper sublimis; at illum
Sub pedibus Styx atra videt, Manesque profundi.
Maximus hìc flexu sinuoso elabitur anguis
Circùm, perque duas in morem fluminis Arctos:
Arctos, Oceani metuentes æquore tingi.

231. Idcirco aureus Sol regit orbem dimensum certis partibus per duodena astra mundi.

234. Quarum una *zona est* semper rubens

235. Circùm quam *duæ* extremæ *zonæ* trahuntur dextrâ lævâque, concretæ

237. Inter has *duas*, mediamque *zonam*, duæ *aliæ* concessæ *sunt* ægris mortalibus munere Divûm; et via secta *est* per ambas, quâ

244. Hìc (*ad sublimem polum*) Maximus anguis elabitur circùm *polum* sinuoso flexu, *extendens* que

NOTES.

cheap, which is the meaning of *vilis*, in this place.

228. *Lentis.* The *lens* was a kind of pulse, which abounded in Egypt, and particularly at *Pelusium*, a town situated near the eastern mouth of the Nile. Hence the adj. *Pelusiacæ.*

229. *Bootes cadens:* the Bootes setting will give, &c. *Bootes*, a star in the constellation of the same name, near the north pole. It sets acronically, or with the sun, about the beginning of November; and cosmically, or at the time of his rising, about the beginning of March. The former is here meant. *Mittet:* in the sense of *dabit.*

232. *Duodena astra.* Astronomers divide the ecliptic, or the circle in which the sun appears to move, into 12 equal parts, called signs, and each of these signs into 30 equal parts called degrees. A space 8 degrees in breadth on each side of this circle is called the zodiac, because it contains the 12 constellations, which take the names of certain animals: as *Aries*, *Taurus*, &c. It also contains the orbits of the planets.

233. *Quinque zonæ.* Geographers divide the surface of the earth into five grand portions called zones: one of which they denominate the torrid or burning; two the temperate; and two the frozen zones. The torrid is that portion of the earth's surface included between the tropics of Cancer and Capricorn. In every part of which the sun is vertical twice in every year. The ancients supposed it to be uninhabitable on account of its great heat. Those parts of the earth's surface that lie between the two tropics and polar circles, are denominated the temperate zones. The two frozen zones embrace those parts between the polar circles and the poles.

235. *Trahuntur:* are extended—stretched out.

239. *Obliquus ordo:* the ecliptic. It is called *obliquus*, because it makes an angle with the equator. The quantity of the angle is 23° 28′.

240. *Scythiam:* a vast country lying toward the arctic circle. See Ecl. i. 66. *Riphæas arces:* the Riphæan mountains. An extensive range stretching along the north of Europe, and covered with perpetual snow. *Ut:* as. *In austros:* simply, to the south.

242. *Hic vertex.* The poles are two imaginary points in the heavens directly in a line with the axis of the earth. On the equator these points are in the horizon. In all places on the north of the equator, the north pole is visible; while the south pole will be depressed below the horizon. *Illum:* the south pole.

244. *Maximus anguis.* The dragon, (*Draco*,) the keeper of the garden of the Hesperides, after he was killed by Hercules, was translated to heaven, and made a constellation near the north pole. With his tail he touches *Ursa major*, and with the flexure of his body embraces *Ursa minor:* the greater and lesser bears: here called *Arctos.* This will be seen by looking upon a celestial globe.

246. *Arctos metuentes:* fearing to be touched in the waters of the ocean. The elevation of the pole at any given place is always equal to the latitude of that place. Consequently all those stars that are nearer the pole than the distance any place is from the equator in degrees, will not set below the horizon at that place, but continue to revolve about the pole. This is the case with the two constellations here mentioned, in the latitude of Italy.

247. Illic, (*ad australem polum*) ut perhibent *homines*, aut

Illìc, ut perhibent, aut intempesta silet nox
Semper, et obtentâ densantur nocte tenebræ ;
Aut redit à nobis Aurora, diemque reducit ;
Nosque ubi primus equis oriens afflavit anhelis,
Illìc sera rubens accendit lumina Vesper.
Hinc tempestates dubio prædicere cœlo
Possumus ; hinc messisque diem, tempusque serendi ;
Et quando infidum remis impellere marmor
Conveniat ; quando armatas deducere classes,
Aut tempestivam sylvis evertere pinum.
  Nec frustrà signorum obitus speculamur et ortus,
Temporibusque parem diversis quatuor annum.

259. Si quando frigidus imber continet agricolam *domi, tunc tempus* datur maturare multa, quæ mox forent properanda, cœlo sereno:

Frigidus agricolam si quando continet imber :
Multa, forent quæ mox cœlo properanda sereno,
Maturare datur : durum procudit arator
Vomeris obtusi dentem ; cavat arbore lintres :
Aut pecori signum, aut numeros impressit acervis.
Exacuunt alii vallos, furcasque bicornes,
Atque Amerina parant lentæ retinacula viti.
Nunc facilis rubeâ texatur fiscina virgâ :
Nunc torrete igni fruges, nunc frangite saxo
Quippe etiam festis quædam exercere diebus
Fas et jura sinunt : rivos deducere nulla
Religio vetuit, segeti prætendere sepem,
Insidias avibus moliri, incendere vepres,
Balantûmque gregem fluvio mersare salubri.

NOTES.

248. *Densantur:* is thickened—rendered still more dark, night being extended, or lengthened out. At the poles there are six months day, and six months night, alternately.

249. *Aurora:* Aurora returns to them, from us. She was goddess of the morning, the daughter of *Titan* and *Terra.* She fell in love with *Tithonus*, the son of Laomedon, king of Troy, by whom she had *Memnon*, who came to assist Priam against the Greeks, and was slain by Achilles. She obtained for her lover immortality; but forgot, at the same time, to ask for perpetual youth and beauty. At last he grew old and infirm; and requested her to remove him from the world; but as that could not be done, she is said to have changed him into a grasshopper: which, as often as it grows old, renews its age. By meton. elegantly put for the morning.

250. *Oriens:* in the sense of *Sol.*

255. *Deducere:* to launch the armed fleets. *Marmor:* in the sense of *mare.*

256. *Tempestivam:* seasonable—denoting the time proper for cutting the pine. *Evertere:* in the sense of *cædere.*

261. *Maturare:* to do in season—or, at leisure.

262. *Dentem:* the edge of his dull or blunt share. *Lintres.* These were vessels dug out of the solid body of trees—troughs—bowls, &c.

263. *Signum:* in the sense of *notas. Acervis.* Acervus is a heap or pile of any thing—a heap of grain. Here, probably, it is taken for the sacks or bags that contained the grain.

265. *Amerina retinacula:* osier strings, to fasten the limber vine. *Amerina:* an adj. from *Ameria*, a town in *Umbria*, a spacious country in Italy, where osiers abounded.

266. *Rubea virgâ:* with the osier or wicker twig. *Rubea:* an adj. probably from *Rubi*, a town of Campania, near which the *virga*, or wicker abounded. Dr. Trapp understands it in this sense, and as a reason for so doing, he observes that *rubeus*, from *rubus*, the bramble, is no where found. Heyne is of the same opinion.

267. *Torrete:* dry. *Fruges:* grain—corn.

269. *Fas et Jura sinunt exercere*, &c. There is a difference of signification between *fas* and *jus*. The former implies a divine law, or what may be done, or is permitted to be done, by the laws of God. The latter a natural right—or a law founded in reason—common law. *Deducere rivos:* to drain the water from his fields.

272. *Balantûm:* gen. plu. of the pres. part. of *balo*, here used as a substantive—sheep.

Sæpe oleo tardi costas agitator aselli,
Vilibus aut onerat pomis: lapidemque revertens
Incusum, aut atræ massam picis, urbe reportat.
Ipsa dies alios alio dedit ordine Luna
Felices operum. Quintam fuge: pallidus Orcus,
Eumenidesque satæ: tum partu Terra nefando
Cœumque, Iapetumque creat, sævumque Typhœa,
Et conjuratos cœlum rescindere fratres.
Ter sunt conati imponere Pelio Ossam
Scilicet, atque Ossæ frondosum involvere Olympum:
Ter Pater extructos disjecit fulmine montes.
Septima post decimam felix, et ponere vitem,
Et prensos domitare boves, et licia telæ
Addere: nona fugæ melior, contraria furtis.
Multa adeò gelidâ meliùs se nocte dedêre:
Aut cùm Sole novo terras irrorat Eoüs.
Nocte leves stipulæ meliùs, nocte arida prata
Tondentur: noctes lentus non deficit humor.
Et quidam seros hyberni ad luminis ignes
Pervigilat, ferroque faces inspicat acuto.
Intereà longum cantu solata laborem
Arguto conjux percurrit pectine telas:
Aut dulcis musti Vulcano decoquit humorem,
Et foliis undam tepidi despumat aheni.

274. Revertens **domum** *ex* urbe, reportat

277. Pallidus **Orcus** *satus est*, Eumenidesque satæ *sunt*, *illo die.*

284. Septima **dies post** decimam *est* felix, et ponere

286. Nona *dies est* melior fugæ, *sed*

294. Conjux solata longum laborem cantu percurrit

NOTES.

274. *Lapidem incusum:* a furrowed or indented stone, for the purpose of grinding corn; something like our mill-stone.

276. *Alios dies:* other days. *Alio ordine:* in a different order from those above mentioned. The ancients superstitiously thought some days of the month to be lucky, and others unlucky.

278. *Eumenides:* the furies. They were said to have sprung from the blood of a wound, which Cœlus received from his brother Saturn. Some say they were the daughters of Acheron and Nox, or of Pluto and Proserpine. They were three in number: *Tisiphone*, *Megæra*, and *Alecto.* They were supposed to be the ministers of vengeance to the gods, and to be constantly employed in punishing the wicked in hell. They were sometimes called *Furiæ* and *Erinnyes.* They were worshipped; but the people dared not to mention their names, or even to fix their eyes upon their temple. They were represented holding a burning torch in one hand, and a whip of scorpions in the other hand.

278. *Creat:* in the sense of *edidit*, vel *produxit.*

279. *Cœumque*, &c. These are the names of three giants, who attempted to scale heaven and dethrone the gods. They were the sons of Titan and Terra. Those here named were the principal ones. *Conjuratos fratres.* These included the whole fraternity, that were engaged in the enterprise.

281. *Pelio.* The mountains here mentioned were very high mountains in Thessaly, near the *Sinus Thermaicus.* The latter is sometimes taken for heaven.

286. *Fugæ:* in the sense of *itineri;* and, *contraria*, in the sense of *adversa*, vel *sinistra.*

288. *Eoüs:* the morning star; by meton. the morning. *Novo sole:* in the sense of *die incipiente*, vel *oriente.*

289. *Stipulæ:* in the sense of *aristæ*, says Ruæus. Mowing in general is best effected when the dew is upon the grass.

292. *Inspicat:* he forms matches with a sharp knife. Any instrument made of iron may be called *ferrum.*

295. *Decoquit:* she boils away the liquor of sweet must, and skims, &c. *Mustum* is sweet or new made wine. The juice of the grape, when boiled down one third part, formed what was called *sapa*, and when one half, it formed the *defrutum. Vulcanus* was the son of Jupiter and Juno. On account of his deformity, he was cast down from heaven upon the island of Lemnos, where he taught the inhabitants the smith trade, and married Venus. The Cyclops were his workmen and assistants. He was the god of fire; hence *Vulcanus*, by meton. often is put for fire itself, as in the present instance. He was sometimes called *Mulciber*, *Ignipotens*, and *Pandamator.*

296. *Undam.* By this we are to understand the liquor in the boiling kettle. *Terit*

At rubicunda Ceres medio succiditur æstu,
Et medio tostas æstu terit area fruges.
Nudus ara, sere nudus: hyems ignava colono.
Frigoribus parto agricolæ plerumque fruuntur,
Mutuaque inter se læti convivia curant:
Invitat genialis hyems, curasque resolvit.
Ceu pressæ cùm jam portum tetigêre carinæ,
Puppibus et læti nautæ imposuêre coronas.
Sed tamen et quernas glandes tum stringere tempus,
Et lauri baccas, oleamque, cruentaque myrta:
Tunc gruibus pedicas, et retia ponere cervis,
Auritosque sequi lepores; tum figere damas
Stupea torquentem Balearis verbera fundæ,
Cùm nix alta jacet, glaciem cùm flumina trudunt.
Quid tempestates autumni et sidera dicam?
Atque, ubi jam breviorque dies, et mollior æstas,
Quæ vigilanda viris? vel cùm ruit imbriferum ver:
Spicea jam campis cùm messis inhorruit, et cùm
Frumenta in viridi stipulâ lactentia turgent?
Sæpe ego, cùm flavis messorem induceret arvis
Agricola, et fragili jam stringeret hordea culmo,
Omnia ventorum concurrere prælia vidi,
Quæ gravidam latè segetem ab radicibus imis
Sublimè expulsam eruerent; ita turbine nigro
Ferret hyems culmumque levem, stipulasque volantes.
Sæpe etiam immensum cœlo venit agmen aquarum,

307. Tunc *tempus est quoque* ponere

308. Tum *est tempus venatorem* figere damas torquentem stupea verbera Balearis fundæ, cùm

318. Ego sæpe vidi omnia prælia ventorum concurrere, quæ eruerent

NOTES.

threshes, or beats out. *Fruges tostas:* the dry, or ripe grain.

297. *Medio æstu:* in the middle of the day. *Ceres:* for *seges*, the grain, or harvest. *Rubicunda:* in the sense of *flava*.

299. *Nudus ara*, &c. The poet's meaning here is, that the farmer should be industrious, and turn the summer to the best account; for the winter is a season of rest and festivity, when he may enjoy the fruit of his labors.

300. *Parto:* what he had gotten during the summer. *Rebus per æstatem comparatis*, says Ruæus.

301. *Curant:* in the sense of *parant*.

304. *Ceu pressæ carinæ:* may either mean laden ships, or weather-beaten ships. *Carina* is properly, the keel; by synec. the whole ship.

305. *Stringere:* in the sense of *colligere*.

309. *Balearis fundæ:* the Balerian sling. The islands Majorca, Minorca, and Uvica, on the coast of Spain, were called by the ancients *Balearides;* the inhabitants of which were famous for the use of the sling. *Stupea verbera:* the hempen strings.

312. *Æstas:* in the sense of *calor*, vel *æstus*. The verb *est* is to be supplied. *Vigilanda: curanda*, vel *providenda*, says Heyne. *Viris:* for *agricolis*.

313. *Ruit:* hastens to a close. Ruæus says *desinit*, and Servius, *præcipitatur*.

315. *Lactentia:* milky—filling with milk.

318. *Omnia prælia ventorum:* all the powers of the winds in fierce contest engage. Ruæus says: *pugnas omnium ventorum misceri*. This comparison of the wind with the wind, and of growing corn with chaff, has been censured by some critics; but the passage is probably to be understood as representing the growing corn uprooted by the tempest, and whirled aloft (*sublimè*) as easily as light straw is by an ordinary whirlwind. Martyn, Heyne, and Vossius, concur, says Valpy, in this interpretation.

320. *Expulsam:* in the sense of *dissipatam*. *Nigro turbine:* in a black whirlwind; a whirlwind bringing with it clouds and darkness, and imbruing a storm. *Hyems* in the sense of *tempestas*.

322. *Immensum agmen*, &c. Nothing can surpass, in grandeur and sublimity, the description which we here have of a sudden storm, of its rise, and effect. An immense band or army of vapors march along the heavens; the clouds, impregnated deeply with vapor, collect together from the sea; and, forming themselves into globous wreaths, brew a deep and threatening storm. They then burst, and discharge such a deluge of water, that the whole heaven seems dissolved, and pouring upon the fields. The floods sweep away the fertile (*læta*) crops, the labors of man and beast; the ditches

Et fœdam glomerant tempestatem imbribus atris
Collectæ ex alto nubes: ruit arduus æther,
Et pluviâ ingenti sata læta, boumque labores
Diluit: implentur fossæ, et cava flumina crescunt
Cum sonitu, fervetque fretis spirantibus æquor.
Ipse pater, mediâ nimborum in nocte, coruscâ
Fulmina molitur dextrâ. quo maxima motu
Terra tremit: fugêre feræ, et mortalia corda
Per gentes humilis stravit pavor: ille flagranti
Aut Atho, aut Rhodopen, aut alta Ceraunia telo
Dejicit: ingeminant Austri, et densissimus imber:
Nunc nemora ingenti vento, nunc litora plangunt.
  Hoc metuens, cœli menses et sidera serva:
Frigida Saturni sese quò stella receptet:
Quos ignis cœli Cyllenius erret in orbes.
Imprimìs venerare Deos, atque annua magnæ
Sacra refer Cereri, lætis operatus in herbis,
Extremæ sub casum hyemis, jam vere sereno.
Tunc agni pingues, et tunc mollissima vina:
Tunc somni dulces, densæque in montibus umbræ.
Cuncta tibi Cererem pubes agrestis adoret:
Cui tu lacte favos, et miti dilue Baccho,

341 Tunc agni *sunt*

NOTES.

are filled; the winding rivers swell, and the sea roars in its foaming friths.

327. *Fretis. Fretum* is properly a strait, or arm of the sea. *Spirans*, as here used, is beautiful and expressive. The figure is taken from water boiling, which seems to breathe (*spirare*) by emitting a steam or vapor, and is all in commotion.

329. *Molitur:* in the sense of *vibrat*, vel *jacit. Quo motu.* By this we are to understand probably the act of vibrating or hurling the thunder-bolt—the thunder itself. What the ancients supposed to be the bolt, was nothing more than the lightning—the electric matter, passing from one cloud, or part of the atmosphere, to another, that was differently electrified, and thus became visible.

330. *Feræ fugere:* the wild beasts have fled. There is a peculiar force in the use of the perfect tense here. The beasts of the forest fear, and they are gone, and are out of sight in a moment, seeking their wonted retreats.

332. *Atho:* a Greek acc. A mountain in Macedonia, which overlooked the Ægean sea. *Rhodopen.* A mountain, or rather range of mountains in Thrace. *Ceraunia:* acc. plu. neu. mountains in Epirus. They were so called from a Greek word signifying thunder, because, from their height, they were much exposed to it.

333. *Imber densissimus.* Ruæus says: *pluvia est copiosissima.*

336. *Quò frigida stella:* to what part of heaven the cold star of Saturn betakes itself. Saturn is called cold most probably from the circumstance of its great distance from the sun, and the small degree of heat it receives from him. On the other hand, the planet Mercury is called *ignis*, on account of its nearness to the sun, and the degree of heat it probably receives from him. *Cyllenius.* A name of the god Mercury. He was the son of Jupiter and Maia, the god of eloquence, and messenger of the gods. He had a winged cap called *Petasus*, and winged feet called *Talaria.* The invention of the lyre, and its seven strings, is attributed to him; which he gave to Apollo, and received in return the celebrated *Caduceus*, which was a rod or wand encircled with serpents, and said to possess extraordinary virtues and qualities. It was his business to conduct the *manes* of the dead to the infernal regions. He presided over orators, merchants, and thieves. The worship of Mercury was established in Greece, Egypt, and Italy. He was called *Cyllenius*, from a mountain in Arcadia of that name, where he is said to have been born; *Caduceator*, *Triplex*, *Delius*, &c. According to Cicero, there were four others to whom the name of Mercury was given. Of these, was a famous philosopher of Egypt, whom they called *Hermes Trismigistus. Cyllenius ignis:* the planet Mercury.

337. *Erret:* in the sense of *moveat. Orbes:* planets.

344. *Cui tu dilue favos:* for whom d thou mingle honey with milk and sweet wine. *Favos:* the comb; by meton. the honey contained in it.

Terque novas circùm felix eat hostia fruges,

346. Quam *hostiam* omnis chorus, et *tui* socii

Omnis quam chorus et socii comitentur ovantes;
Et Cererem clamore vocent in tecta: neque antè
Falcem maturis quisquam supponat aristis,
Quàm Cereri, tortâ redimitus tempora quercu,
Det motus incompositos, et carmina dicat.
  Atque hæc ut certis possimus discere signis,
Ætusque, pluviasque, et agentes frigora ventos;
Ipse pater statuit, quid menstrua Luna moneret,
Quo signo caderent Austri, quid sæpe videntes
Agricolæ propiùs stabulis armenta tenerent.
Continuò, ventis surgentibus, aut freta ponti
Incipiunt agitata tumescere, et aridus altis
Montibus audiri fragor; aut resonantia longè
Litora misceri, et nemorum increbrescere murmur.
Jam sibi tum curvis malè temperat unda carinis:
Cùm medio celeres revolant ex æquore mergi,
Clamoremque ferunt ad litora, cùmque marinæ

363. Sicco *litore*

364. Ardeaque deserit notas paludes, atque volat supra altam nubem.

In sicco ludunt fulicæ; notasque paludes
Deserit, atque altam supra volat ardea nubem.
Sæpe etiam stellas, vento impendente, videbis
Præcipites cœlo labi; noctisque per umbram
Flammarum longos à tergo albescere tractus;
Sæpe levem paleam et frondes volitare caducas;
Aut summâ nantes in aquâ colludere plumas.
At Boreæ de parte trucis cùm fulminat, et cùm
Eurique Zephyrique tonat domus; omnia plenis
Rura natant fossis; atque omnis navita ponto

NOTES.

345. *Felix hostia.* The poet here alludes to the *sacrificium ambervale*, so called, because the victim was led three times around the field; *ab ambire arva.*

346. *Omnis chorus et socii:* the same as *omnis chorus sociorum.*

349. *Redimitus tempora:* bound as to his temples with a wreath of oak. The poet enjoins upon the farmer to make two offerings to *Ceres:* the first of honey and wine, at the beginning of spring: *dilue favos*, &c. The other of a victim at the beginning of harvest: *ter felix hostia*, &c.

350. *Incompositos motus:* the irregular or unmethodical dance; such as is performed by rustics. *Cereri:* nempe, *in honorem Cereris.*

351. *Hæc:* nempe, *æstusque, pluviasque.*

353. *Moneret:* in the sense of *indicaret.*

354. *Signo:* in the sense of *indicio. Quod indicium esset venti mox cessuri*, says Heyne. *Austri:* here put for any boisterous wind: the *species* for the *genus.*

356. *Freta ponti:* simply, for *pontus*, vel *mare. Fretum*, properly a strait, or narrow part of the sea.

358. *Aridus fragor:* a dry cracking sound, such as is made among dry trees when they break.

360. *Jam tum unda malè temperat:* then the waves scarcely restrain themselves from (swallowing up) the bending ships. *Malè:* in the sense of *difficilè.*

361. *Mergi:* a species of sea-fowl, generally taken to be the cormorant: from the verb *mergo.*

363. *Fulicæ:* a species of sea-fowl much like the common duck; a coot, or moor-hen

364. *Ardea:* a bird, swift on the wing, and soaring high. From which circumstance called *ardea, quasi pro ardua;* a heron.

365. *Sæpe videbis stellas:* you will also often see stars, &c. The poet speaks in conformity to the vulgar notion. No star moves from its station. Those appearances to which the poet alludes are of an electric nature—meteors. They are sometimes seen to dart across the heavens, and through the darkness of the night, appear to draw after them a train (*tractus*) of light or flame. *Impendente:* threatening--being near at hand.

371. *Domus Eurique*, &c. That part of the heavens from which these winds blow, the poet calls their house or habitation. The expression is highly poetical. Here the poet mentions twelve signs or prognostics of rain.

Humida vela legit. Nunquam imprudentibus imber
Obfuit. Aut illum surgentem vallibus imis
Aëriæ fugêre grues; aut bucula cœlum
Suspiciens, patulis captavit naribus auras.
Aut arguta lacus circumvolitavit hirundo:
Et veterem in limo ranæ cecinêre querelam.
Sæpius et tectis penetralibus extulit ova
Angustum formica terens iter; et bibit ingens
Arcus; et è pastu decedens agmine magno
Corvorum increpuit densis exercitus alis.
Jam varias pelagi volucres, et quæ Asia circùm
Dulcibus in stagnis rimantur prata Caystri,
Certatim largos humeris infundere rores;
Nunc caput objectare fretis, nunc currere in undas,
Et studio incassùm videas gestire lavandi.
Tum cornix plenâ pluviam vocat improba voce,
Et sola in siccâ secum spatiatur arenâ.
Nec nocturna quidem carpentes pensa puellæ
Nescivere hyemem: testâ cùm ardente viderent
Scintillare oleum, et putres concrescere fungos.
Nec minùs ex imbri soles, et aperta serena
Prospicere, et certis poteris cognoscere signis.
Nam neque tum stellis acies obtusa videtur,
Nec fratris radiis obnoxia surgere Luna:

376. Suspiciens ad cœlum

383. Jam videas varias volucres pelagi, et *eas*, quæ rimantur circum Asia prata in dulcibus stagnis Caystri, certatim infundere largos rores humeris

393. Nec minus ex imbri poteris prospicere, et, certis signis, cognoscere *sudos* soles, et aperta *et* serena *cœla*.

NOTES.

373. *Imprudentibus*, &c. Never hath a shower hurt any person unforwarned: that is, a shower always gives such certain signs of its approach, that any who will attend to them, may avoid receiving injury from it. Heyne informs us, that the Medicean, and some other copies, read *prudentibus;* he, however, prefers the usual reading, *imprudentibus*. *Prudentibus* is the easier.

374. *Illum surgentem*, &c. This sentence is capable of two constructions: 1. The cranes may flee the shower, rising out of the valleys; which is the sense Ruæus gives. 2. Davidson takes it to mean that the cranes flee into the valleys, to avoid the rising storm. This is also the opinion of Valpy.

378. *Et ranæ cecinere*, &c. This alludes to the fable of the transformation of the Lycians into frogs for reproaching *Latona*, of which hard treatment, when they croak, they are said to complain. See Ovid. Met. Lib. 6.

380. *Ingens arcus:* the spacious bow hath drunk; alluding to a vulgar notion that the rainbow drank the water that supplied the clouds.

383. *Asia:* an adj. from *Asius*, a lake and town between the river *Caystrus* and the mountain *Tmolus*, in the confines of Lydia and Phrygia Major. *Caystrus* falls into the Ægean sea, not far from the once famous city of Ephesus. On its banks the swan abounded. *Rimantur:* in the sense of *frequentant.*

385. *Infundere largos:* to throw eagerly much water upon their backs. *Rores:* in the sense of *aquam.*

387. *Studio lavandi:* through a desire of washing themselves in vain. *Incassùm* may be understood in three senses. 1. Because nothing can add to the whiteness of the swan, the fowl here spoken of. 2. Because they need take no pains to wash themselves, for the impending rain will do it without their labor. 3. Because, according to Servius, water will not wet their feathers.

390. *Carpentes:* carding their nightly tasks of wool.

392. *Fungos:* the clots or spungy substance that gathers round the wick of the lamp or candle. *Scintillare:* to sputter or snap in the burning shell.

393. *Nec minùs.* Having mentioned the signs of a storm, the poet now enumerates those of fair weather. He makes them in number nine. *Ex imbri:* after a shower. *Soles:* days.

395. *Acies stellis:* Ruæus says, *lux stellarum. Videtur:* in the sense of *apparet.*

396. *Luna surgere obnoxia:* nor will the moon seem to rise beholden (or indebted) to the beams of her brother. The moon will rise so clear and bright that she will seem to shine by her own inherent light, and not by reflecting the rays of the sun. *Sol* and *Luna* in heaven, the same as Apollo and Diana on earth, were said to have been the children of Latona. See Ecl. iv. 10.

Tenuia nec lanæ per cœlum vellera ferri.
Non tepidum ad solem pennas in litore pandunt
Dilectæ Thetidi Halcyones: non ore solutos
Immundi meminere sues jactare maniplos.
At nebulæ magìs ima petunt, campoque recumbunt;
Solis et occasum servans de culmine summo
Nequicquam seros exercet noctua cantus.
Apparet liquido sublimis in aëre Nisus,
Et pro purpureo pœnas dat Scylla capillo.
Quâcunque illa levem fugiens secat æthera pennis,
Ecce inimicus, atrox, magno stridore per auras,
Insequitur Nisus: quà se fert Nisus ad auras,
Illa levem fugiens raptim secat æthera pennis
Tum liquidas corvi presso ter gutture voces
Aut quater ingeminant: et sæpe cubilibus altis,
Nescio quâ præter solitum dulcedine læti,
Inter se foliis strepitant: juvat imbribus actis
Progeniem parvam, dulcesque revisere nidos.
Haud equidem credo, quia sit divinitùs illis
Ingenium, aut rerum fato prudentia major:
Verùm, ubi tempestas et cœli mobilis humor
Mutavere vias: et Jupiter humidus Austris
Densat, erant quæ rara modò; et, quæ densa, relaxat:
Vertuntur species animorum, et pectora motus
Nunc alios, alios, dum nubila ventus agebat,

401. **Ima** *loca*

410. Tum corvi ter aut quater ingeminant liquidas

412. Læti, nescio quâ dulcedine, præter solitum *morem* strepitant

415. Haud equidem credo *hoc fieri ita*, quia

419. Densat *ea*, quæ modò erant rara, et relaxat *ea*, quæ *priùs erant* densa

421. Concipiunt nunc

NOTES.

397. *Tenuia vellera:* thin white clouds, like fleeces of wool.

399. *Halcyones.* Ceyx, king of *Trachinia*, going to consult the oracle of Apollo at *Clarus*, was shipwrecked in the Ægean sea. His wife, *Halcyone*, seeing his dead body floating near the shore, flung herself upon it in a transport of her passion. *Thetis*, out of compassion to the lovers, transformed them into the birds called king-fishers: hence *dilectæ Thetidi.* It is said the sea is calm a certain number of days about the winter solstice, that they may more conveniently bring forth their young. Hence those days were sometimes called *Halcyon* days.

400. *Maniplos:* bundles of straw—straw in general.

403. *Noctua servans:* the owl observing the setting of the sun, &c. The meaning of the expression seems to be this: that as the hooting of the owl in general is a sign of foul weather, yet when these signs of fair weather occur, she hoots in vain, she will be disregarded; or, if any regard her prognostics, they will find themselves disappointed. The owl is the only bird that sings exclusively in the night; hence, *seros cantus exercet.*

404. *Nisus:* the falcon, or hawk. *Scylla:* the lark. See Ecl. vi. 74; also nom. prop. under *Nisus.*

405. *Scylla dat pœnas.* Scylla is punished for the purple lock. *Dare—reddere—penaere—solvere pœnas*, vel *supplicium*, to be punished. These are phrases. In like manner: *afficere pœnâ* vel *suppliciô—capere—sumere—petere pœnas*, vel *supplicium*, to punish.

410. *Presso guttere:* with their throats compressed. This would render the sounds more clear and shrill.

416. *Ingenium:* discernment, or mental capacity. *Major prudentia fato*, &c. *A greater knowledge or foresight in the course and order of things*, than men have. This passage, as it is commonly rendered, is unintelligible. To take *fato* in the ablative, governed by *major*, Dr. Trapp observes, is complete nonsense; and yet this is the opinion of Heyne, and Valpy who follows him: and it is very little better to take it for the agent or means by which this greater knowledge was obtained. It is perfectly easy as rendered above. Ruæus says: *rerum prudentia, quæ potentior est fato;* which is with difficulty understood.

417. *Mobilis humor:* the moving vapor of heaven. *Vias* is here used in the sense of *modus*, or *qualitates*. *Tempestas:* the weather—temperature of the weather.

418. *Jupiter humidus:* the air moistened by the south winds. *Jupiter* is here put poetically for the air; which passing over the sea that lay to the south of Italy, became moist, or impregnated with vapor.

420. *Motus:* motions—affections.

Concipiunt: hinc ille avium concentus in agris,
Et lætæ pecudes, et ovantes gutture corvi.
Si verò Solem ad rapidum Lunasque sequentes
Ordine respicies; nunquam te crastina fallet
Hora, neque insidiis noctis capiere serenæ.
Luna, revertentes cùm primùm colligit ignes,
Si nigrum obscuro comprenderit aëra cornu;
Maximus agricolis pelagoque parabitur imber.
At, si virgineum suffuderit ore ruborem,
Ventus erit: vento semper rubet aurea Phœbe.
Sin ortu in quarto (namque is certissimus auctor)
Pura, neque obtusis per cœlum cornibus ibit;
Totus et ille dies, et qui nascentur ab illo
Exactum ad mensem, pluviâ ventisque carebunt:
Votaque servati solvent in litore nautæ
Glauco, et Panopeæ, et Inoö Melicertæ.
Sol quoque, et exoriens, et cùm se condit in undas,
Signa dabit: Solem certissima signa sequuntur,
Et quæ manè refert, et quæ surgentibus astris.
Ille ubi nascentem maculis variaverit ortum,
Conditus in nubem medioque refugerit orbe;
Suspecti tibi sint imbres: namque urget ab alto

alios motus, *et nunc* alios dum

422. Hinc *oritur* ille concentus avium in agris, et *hinc* pecudes *sunt*

432. Sin *illa fuerit* pura in quarto ortu, neque ibit per cœlum

436. Servati *à tempestate*

440. Et quæ refert manè, et quæ *refert*

NOTES.

425. *Crastina hora:* simply, to-morrow.

427. *Colligit revertentes ignes:* when first the moon collects the reflected, or returning rays, (*ignes;*) if she embrace, &c. The poet here mentions three prognostics of the weather from the moon. 1. If the new moon be obscured by dusky air, (*nigrum aëra,*) look for rain. 2. If she be red, look for wind. 3. If, on the fourth day, she be bright, expect the remainder of the month to be fair weather; whence the common saying: *pallida Luna pluit; rubicunda flat; alba serenat.*

432. *Auctor:* sign—prognostic.

437. *Glauco.* Glaucus was a fisherman of *Anthedon*, in Beotia, by some said to have been the son of Neptune and the nymph Naïs. As he was fishing, he observed the fish that he caught, as he laid them on the grass, to receive fresh vigor, and immediately to escape from him by leaping into the sea. From this circumstance, he imagined there must be some extraordinary virtue in the grass; whereupon he tasted it, and found himself suddenly moved with a desire to live in the watery element; and leaping into the sea, he was made a sea-god by *Oceanus* and *Tethys. Panopeæ:* a nymph of the sea, the daughter of *Nereus* and *Doris. Melicertæ.* Melicerta, or Melicertes, was the son of *Ino*, the daughter of *Cadmus*, and wife of *Athamas*, king of Thebes; who fleeing from her husband, who had slain her son *Learchus*, leaped into the sea with *Melicerta* in her arms, both of whom were changed into sea-gods, and worshipped *Inoo:* an adj. from *Ino*, agreeing with *Melicertæ.* Melicertes was sometimes called *Palæmon.* See Æn. v. 823.

440. *Astris surgentibus.* When the stars appear in the evening at the approach of darkness, in the language of poetry, they are said to rise: so when they disappear at the approach of day, they are said to set.

442. *Medio refugerit orbe.* Most commentators take *orbis* here for the face or disc of the sun; and understand by the words *medio refugerit orbe*, when he shall disappear with half his orb or disc, the other half remaining visible. Ruæus says: *latuerit mediâ sui parte.* Valpy says, "When the rising sun appears bordered by clouds, the centre alone remaining visible." Davidson translates the whole passage thus: "When he (the sun) shall chequer his new-born face with spots, hidden in a cloud, and coyly shun the sight with half his orb." Servius seems to understand the words to imply that the centre of the sun retired, as it were, from view, by appearing hollow like the cavity of the hand, while the edge was concealed in a cloud. I know not that philosophers have noticed any such appearances of the sun; I am sure they must be very rare. Besides, this half concealment of the sun does not come up to the obvious meaning of *conditus in nubem*, which certainly means that he was wholly concealed from sight. By taking *medio orbe*, for, *in the middle of his course*, or diurnal revolution, which may very well be done, the passage will be rendered intelligible and easy. Thus: when the sun, in his ascent above the horizon, shall have passed behind fleecy clouds, and

Aboribusque satisque Notus, pecorique sinister.
Aut ubi sub lucem densa inter nubila sese
Diversi erumpent radii, aut ubi pallida surget
Tithoni croceum linquens Aurora cubile ;
Heu, malè tum mites defendet pampinus uvas,
Tam multa in tectis crepitans salit horrida grando

450. Magis profuerit meminisse hoc, etiam cùm jam *sol* decedet, Olympo emenso:

Hoc, etiam emenso cùm jam decedet Olympo,
Profuerit meminisse magis : nam sæpe videmus
Ipsius in vultu varios errare colores.

453. Cæruleus *sol*

Cœruleus pluviam denunciat, igneus Euros
Sin maculæ incipient rutilo immiscerier igni ;
Omnia tunc pariter vento nimbisque videbis
Fervere. Non illâ quisquam me nocte per altum
Ire, neque à terra moneat convellere funem.

458. At si orbis *solis* erit lucidus, cum

At si, cùm referetque diem, condetque relatum,
Lucidus orbis erit, frustrà terrebere nimbis;
Et claro sylvas cernes Aquilone moveri.

461. Denique Sol dabit signa tibi, quid serus vesper

Denique, quid Vesper serus vehat, unde serenas
Ventus agat nubes, quid cogitet humidus Auster,
Sol tibi signa dabit: Solem quis dicere falsum
Audeat ? ille etiam cæcos instare tumultus
Sæpe monet, fraudemque, et operta tumescere bella.
Ille etiam extincto miseratus Cæsare Romàm ;
Cùm caput obscurâ nitidum ferrugine texit,
Impiaque æternam timuerunt sæcula noctem.
Tempore quanquam illo tellus quoque, et æquora ponti,
Obscœnique canes, importunæque volucres,
Signa dabant. Quotiès Cyclopum effervere in agros
Vidimus undantem ruptis fornacibus Ætnam,
Flammarumque globos, liquefactaque volvere saxa ?
Armorum sonitum toto Germania cœlo
Audiit ; insolitis tremuerunt motibus Alpes.

NOTES.

be sometimes concealed by them from sight; and when he shall have approached the meridian, and finished half his course, he shall be wholly concealed from sight by the increased and condensed vapor in the atmosphere, then rain is to be expected. *Imbres :* in the sense of *pluvia.*

444. *Sinister :* injurious—hurtful.

452. *In vultu :* in the sense of *per vultum.*

454. *Immiscerier :* by Paragoge, for *immisceri*, to be mingled with sparkling light. *Igni : lumine*, says Ruæus.

456. *Fervere.* This verb forcibly expresses the violence of the storm. All things are confusion and wild disorder. *Turbari*, says Ruæus.

462. *Cogitet :* in the sense of *præparet. Serenas :* in the sense of *siccas.*

467. *Obscura ferrugine :* with a dark red color—a color resembling blood.

468. *Sæcula.* Sæculum is properly an age; by meton. the inhabitants or men of that age. *Impia sæcula* : the same as *impii homines.*

470. *Obscœni canes :* foul dogs—dogs of bad omen—howling frightfully. The ancients considered any thing of this kind inauspicious. *Importunæ :* inauspicious. *Cujus cantus erat mali ominis.*

471. *Quoties vidimus :* how often have we seen Ætna rising in waves, its furnaces being burst, &c. *Undantem*, expresses very forcibly the violence and agitation of the flames pent up in the mountain, rising by turns against its sides, which, no longer able to resist the shock, open a passage; when, in an instant, it covers the adjacent country with lava. The Cyclops were the servants of Vulcan, and said to be the sons of *Cœlus* and *Terra.* They were so called from their having but one eye, which was in the middle of their forehead. Their business was to assist Vulcan in forming the thunder-bolts of Jupiter, and the arms of the gods, and celebrated heroes. Their forges were under Ætna. The most noted of them were *Brontes*, *Steropes*, and *Pyracmon.* When Ulysses visited Sicily, *Polyphemus*, say the

Vox quoque per lucos vulgò exaudita silentes
Ingens; et simulacra modis pallentia miris
Visa sub obscurum noctis· pecudesque locutæ,
Infandum! sistunt amnes, terræque dehiscunt:
Et mœstum illacrymat templis ebur, æraque sudant.
Proluit insano contorquens vortice sylvas
Fluviorum rex Eridanus, camposque per omnes
Cum stabulis armenta tulit: nec tempore eodem
Tristibus aut extis fibræ apparere minaces,
Aut puteis manare cruor cessavit; et altè
Per noctem resonare, lupis ululantibus, urbes.
Non aliàs cœlo ceciderunt plura sereno
Fulgura, nec diri toties arsere cometæ.
Ergò inter sese paribus concurrere telis
Romanas acies iterum vidêre Philippi;
Nec fuit indignum Superis, bis sanguine nostro
Emathiam et latos Hæmi pinguescere campos.

481. **Eridanus proluit sylvas, contorquens** ***eas*** **insano.**

484. Fibræ nec *cessaverunt* aut apparere minaces *in* tristibus extis; aut cruor cessavit manare *è* puteis; et urbes *non cessaverunt* resonare altè per noctem, lupis ululantibus.

491. Nec *visum* fuit

NOTES.

poets, was their king. Diodorus informs us that the Cyclops were the first inhabitants of Sicily, of a gigantic stature, and of a fierce and savage nature. They dwelt chiefly about mount Ætna.

477. *Simulacra:* spectres, or ghosts, pale in a wonderful manner, were seen, &c.

478. *Obscurum:* an adj. of the neu. taken as a sub. in the sense of *obscuritatem.* Ruæus interprets it by *crepusculum.*

480. *Mœstum ebur:* the mournful ivory (ivory statues) wept. *Æra:* brass—statues made of brass.

481. *Insano vortice:* with its rapid current—eddies.

482. *Eridanus:* the river Po. It is here called the king of rivers, because the largest in Italy. It rises in Piedmont, and running an easterly course, after receiving a number of tributary streams, falls into the Gulf of Venice by several mouths.

483. *Tristibus extis.* One mode of consulting the omens, was an examination of the entrails of the victim. If any defect or singularity appeared, it was thought to be portentous. *Tristibus:* ominous—baleful.

485. *Altè.* Heyne reads *altæ*, agreeing with *urbes.*

488. *Cometæ.* Plutarch informs us that a very bright comet appeared at Rome for several days about the time of Cæsar's death. To this the poet refers in Ecl. ix. 47. Suetonius says: *Ludis, quos primo consecratos ei hæres Augustus edebat, stella crinita per septem dies continuos fulsit, exoriens circa undecimam horam: creditumque est animum esse Cæsaris in cœlum recepti.*

489. *Ergò:* therefore—on account of the death of Cæsar, which was the cause of the civil war.

490. *Philippi iterum:* Philippi hath seen the Roman armies again, &c. It is agreed that Virgil here alludes to the two famous battles, one fought between Cæsar and Pompey; the other, between Brutus and Cassius on one side, and Augustus and Anthony on the other. But history informs us that the former was fought on the plains of *Pharsalia*, in Thessaly, the latter at *Philippi*, in the confines of Thrace, more than two hundred miles distant. To explain this apparent inconsistency, there have been many attempts. The most probable solution is, that the poet does not mean that both these battles were fought on the same spot. This would contradict history. He would not commit such a blunder. We are told that the city *Thebæ Thessalicæ*, or *Phthoticæ*, which was in sight of Pharsalia, was called also *Philippi.* And though historians, for sake of distinction, called the one *Philippi*, and the other *Pharsalia*, the poet might, without any impropriety, call them both by the common name of *Philippi.* Ruæus has one conjecture which may be deserving of notice: that the adverb *iterùm* may refer, not to Philippi, but to the Roman armies: *Philippi* saw the Roman armies *again* engage for the empire of the world, though not for the first time. They had engaged for a similar purpose before on the plains of Pharsalia. This appears to solve the difficulty.

492. *Emathiam—Latos campos Hæmi.* Here is an apparent difficulty. Hæmus is a mountain in Thrace; and neither of the battles was fought in *Emathia* or *Macedonia*, properly so called. But the language of poetry does not always conform to historical or geographical exactness. We are told that the ancient *Emathia* was considered by the poets to extend as far east as the river Nessus, including a considerable part of Thrace beyond *Philippi;* and to the south comprehending all Thessaly, and consequently *Pharsalia*, or the Pharsalian

Scilicet et tempus veniet, cùm finibus illis
Agricola, incurvo terram molitus aratro,
Exesa inveniet scabrâ rubigine pila:
Aut gravibus rastris galeas pulsabit inanes,
Grandiaque effossis mirabitur ossa sepulchris.
Dii patrii Indigetes, et Romule, Vestaque mater,
Quæ Tuscum Tiberim et Romana palatia servas,
Hunc saltem everso juvenem succurrere sæclo
Ne prohibete: satìs jampridem sanguine nostro
Laomedonteæ luimus perjuria Trojæ.
Jampridem nobis cœli te regia, Cæsar,
Invidet, atque hominum queritur curare triumphos.
505 *Sunt* tot bella — Quippe ubi fas versum atque nefas, tot bella per orbem,
Tam multæ scelerum facies: non ullus aratro 506
507. Colonis abductis *ad malitiam* — Dignus honos; squalent abductis arva colonis,
Et curvæ rigidum falces conflantur in ensem.

NOTES.

Philippi. Taken in this extent, the poet would be consistent. Emathia could be wet twice with Roman blood. Again Hæmus is not so much a single mountain as a range of mountains, branching out in various directions, and in various parts assuming different names. Casting our eye on a map of that country, we find the range commencing at the Euxine sea, and taking a south-westerly direction till it enters Macedonia, then turning northerly till it reaches the 43° of N. lat. when it takes a southern direction, passing into Thessaly; and consequently its extensive plains might be fattened by the blood, shed in both those battles.

494. *Molitus:* in the sense of *vertens.* *Scabra:* in the sense of *corrosa.*

498. *Dii patrii, Indigetes.* The Romans divided their deities into three classes. The first embraced the supreme or select gods, who were honored with the highest adoration, and considered eminent above the rest. Of these, twelve were called *Consentes*, because on particular occasions they were admitted to the council of Jupiter. Six of these were male and six female: *Jupiter*, *Apollo*, *Mercury*, *Mars*, *Neptune*, and *Vulcan*: *Juno*, *Diana*, *Minerva*, *Venus*, *Vesta*, and *Ceres*. These were sometimes called *Dii Majores.* The second class comprehended those of inferior power, and was very numerous. It embraced all the deified heroes, such as *Romulus*, *Hercules*, *Perseus*, &c. and all that in any manner had obtained divine honors. These were sometimes called the *Dii Minores.* The third class was without number. It embraced all the sylvan deities: all the nymphs; the penates; the genii; the virtues, &c. *Indigetes:* properly deified heroes. Some derive the word from *Indigetare*, to call by name; because it was customary to address them by their name. Others derive it from *degere*, because they had been men, and dwelt on the earth: or because they were now dwelling among the gods. Others again, and perhaps with more propriety, derive it from *Indegere;* because being translated to heaven, they stood in need of nothing. *Mater Vesta.* There were two by the name of *Vesta*, one the mother of Saturn, the other his daughter; but commonly confounded together. The latter presided over the perpetual fire. It is said that Æneas brought her along with his household gods into Italy, and introduced her worship. Her mysteries were transmitted to the Albans, and from them introduced among the Romans by Numa. He instituted a college of virgins, who kept alive the perpetual fire as the safety, or *palladium* of the state.

500. *Hunc Juvenem:* meaning Octavius, afterward called Augustus Cæsar. *Everso sæclo:* the ruined or falling age.

502. *Satis luimus jampridem:* we have long ago atoned sufficiently for the perjury of Trojan Laomedon, with our blood. Laomedon was the father of Priam, and king of Troy. During his reign, the poets tell us, the walls of Troy were built by Neptune and Apollo, for a certain price; but when the work was done, he refused to pay them. On which account, they became hostile to the Trojans, and exerted all their power against them in the war with the Greeks. The Romans, pretending to descend from them, the poet supposes were punished for this injustice of their ancestor. The story, perhaps, may be explained by supposing Laomedon to have employed the money, which had been designed for religious purposes, to this use.

505. *Ubi:* where—(that is,) here among men. *Fas atque nefas versum:* right and wrong are confounded.

507. *Squalent:* lie neglected—are overgrown with weeds.

Hinc movet Euphrates, illinc Germania bellum:
Vicinæ ruptis inter se legibus urbes
Arma ferunt: sævit toto Mars impius orbe
Ut, cùm carceribus sese effudêre quadrigæ,
Addunt se in spatia: et frustrà retinacula tendens,
Fertur equis auriga, neque audit currus habenas.

NOTES.

509. *Euphrates.* A noble river of Asia, rising in the mountains of Armenia, fertilizing *Mesopotamia*, as the Nile does Egypt, and uniting with the Tigris in its course, falls into the Persian gulf. It is here put, by a figure of speech, for the nations of the east, particularly the Parthians, who were very troublesome to the Romans.

510. *Legibus:* in the sense of *fœderibus.*

511. *Impius:* cruel—merciless; a suitable epithet of *Mars.*

512. *Ut, cum quadrigæ.* This is a noble simile. The uncontrolled licentiousness of the age is likened to the rapidity and violence of ungovernable horses in the chariot race, when they mock both the driver and the reins. *Quadrigæ:* four horses harnessed together; also, a chariot drawn by four horses, by meton. Of *Quatuor* and *ago*, because four were driven together: or contracted of *Quadrijugus*, four yoked together. *Carceribus.* Carcer was the mark, or starting place, in races. *Spatia:* the race ground, or course. *Effudêre.* Ruæus says, *eruperunt.*

513. *Addunt:* in the sense of *immittunt*, says Heyne. Some copies leave out the *se*. Others read *in spatio.* Ruæus, in his interpretation, omits the words *addunt se*, and connects *in spatia* with the preceding verb. They are not necessary to make the sense complete.

514. *Currus:* a chariot: by meton. the horses in the chariot. *Neque audit habenas:* nor do they regard, or obey the reins.

QUESTIONS.

How does this book open?
What does the poet proceed to do?
What does he do in the next place?
To whom does he ascribe the origin of agriculture?
What signs or prognostics of the weather does he mention?
How does he conclude the book?
Are there any fables introduced by way of episode? What are they?
Why are Bacchus and Ceres invoked next after the heavenly bodies?
Who was Neptune? and what is said of him?
Who is said to have been the first who taught mankind the propagation of bees?
Who was Aristæus?
Who was Minerva? and what is said of her?
What power did she possess?
How is she represented under her different characters?
What celebrated statue had she?
What are some of her names?
Who is said to have first taught the Greeks agriculture?
What is probably meant by *Ultima Thule*?
Was the Ecliptic at first divided into 12 signs? How was it divided?
Where were the Olympic games celebrated? In what year before Christ were they instituted?
How often were they celebrated? and in honor of what god?
What precepts does the poet give about ploughing land?
What does he give about planting, and changing crops?
Who was Jupiter?
To whom was his education intrusted?
Where was he educated?
What are some of his names?
Who were the Giants? and what is said of them?
What are the Pleïades?
What other names have they?
What are the Hyades?
What are their names?
Who was Aurora?
What is said of her?
What were the Furies?
What were their names?
What was their office?
Who was Vulcan? What is said of him?
What were some of his names?
What is the word *Vulcanus* often used for?
By what figure is it so used?
Who were the Cyclops?
Where does the poet represent them as residing?
Why are they called *Cyclops*?
Who was Mercury?
What is said of him?
What was his office?
How is he represented?
Of what was he the inventor?
What were some of his names?
Who was Glaucus? What is said of him?

Into how many classes were the Roman deities divided? Of these, how many were called *Consentes?*
Why were they so called?
What were their names?
What were these sometimes called?
What did the second class contain?
What were these sometimes called?
What did the third class contain?
Were they very numerous?
Who were the *Indigetes?*
From what is the word probably derived?
Who was Vesta?
How many were there of that name?
What was her office?
Who introduced her worship into Italy?
By whom were her mysteries introduced among the Romans?

LIBER SECUNDUS.

THE subject of this book is the cultivation of the several kinds of trees. The poet describes with much judgment the soils proper for each: and after giving a variety of excellent precepts for the management of the vine, the olive, &c. he digresses into the praises of Italy; and concludes with a panegyric upon a country life.

1. Hactenus *cecini* cultus

8. Tingeque mecum nudata crura novo musto, cothurnis direptis.

15. Æsculusque maxima nemorum, quæ frondet Jovi, atque quercus, *quæ* habitæ *sunt*

HACTENUS arvorum cultus, et sidera cœli:
Nunc te, Bacche, canam, necnon sylvestria tecum
Virgulta, et prolem tardè crescentis olivæ.
Huc, pater ô Lenæe: tuis hìc omnia plena
Muneribus; tibi pampineo gravidus autumno
Floret ager, spumat plenis vindemia labris.
Huc, pater ô Lenæe, veni: nudataque musto
Tinge novo mecum direptis crura cothurnis.
  Principio arboribus varia est natura creandis.
Namque aliæ, nullis hominum cogentibus, ipsæ
Sponte suâ veniunt, camposque et flumina latè
Curva tenent: ut molle siler, lentæque genistæ,
Populus, et glaucâ canentia fronde salicta.
Pars autem posito surgunt de semine: ut altæ
Castaneæ, nemorumque Jovi quæ maxima frondet
Æsculus, atque habitæ Graiis oracula quercus.

NOTES.

2. *Necnon:* also. Two negatives have the force of an affirmative in Latin and English.

3. *Virgulta:* shrubs, or underbrush; here put for trees in general. *Tardè crescentis olivæ.* The olive is of a very slow growth. Some say it is a hundred years in growing.

4. *Lenæe:* Lenæus, a name of Bacchus, from a Greek word signifying a vine-press. *Adsis*, is to be supplied, or some word of the same import.

5. *Ager gravidus:* the field heavy with the produce of the vine. *Autumno:* the season for gathering grapes and other productions of the earth, put, by meton. for the grapes themselves. *Floret:* in the sense of *maturescit.* The fields do not bloom in autumn, but with propriety they may be said to ripen. *Pampineo autumno:* the produce of the vine—grapes.

9. *Cothurnis.* The cothurnus was a kind of high-heeled shoe, worn by Bacchus. Reference is here made to the custom of treading out the grapes with their feet. The cothurnus was used by tragedians to make them appear taller; hence put for tragedy itself—also for the tragic style. *Natura:* in the sense of *ratio*, vel *modus.*

12. *Siler:* an osier, or small withy. *Genistæ:* the broom. *Populus:* the poplar tree, of which there are three kinds.

13. *Salicta:* willow-grounds; by meton, the willows.

16. *Æsculus:* a species of oak, sacred to Jupiter. The *Æsculus* was a mast-tree, and abounded in *Dodona*, in Epirus, where there were oaks said to have given out oracles; to which here is an allusion.

Pullulat ab radice aliis densissima sylva:
Ut cerasis, ulmisque: etiam Parnassia laurus
Parva sub ingenti matris se subjicit umbrâ.
Hos natura modos primùm dedit: his genus omne
Sylvarum, fruticumque viret, nemorumque sacrorum.
Sunt alii, quos ipse viâ sibi repperit usus.
Hic plantas tenero abscindens de corpore matrum
Deposuit sulcis: hic stirpes obruit arvo,
Quadrifidasque sudes, et acuto robore vallos:
Sylvarumque aliæ pressos propaginis arcus
Expectant, et viva suâ plantaria terrâ.
Nil radicis egent aliæ: summumque putator
Haud dubitat terræ referens mandare cacumen.
Quin et caudicibus sectis, mirabile dictu,
Truditur è sicco radix oleagina ligno.
Et sæpe alterius ramos impunè videmus
Vertere in alterius, mutatamque insita mala
Ferre pyrum, et prunis lapidosa rubescere corna.
Quare agite, ô, proprios generatim discite cultus,
Agricolæ, fructusque feros mollite colendo.
Neu segnes jaceant terræ: juvat Ismara Baccho
Conserere, atque oleâ magnum vestire Taburnum.

20. **Natura primum** dedit hos *tres* modos *pro ducendi arbores*: *in* his *viis*.

NOTES.

17. *Sylva:* here means the suckers, that shoot up under, and near the trunk of the parent tree.

18. *Cerasis:* to the cherry-trees. *Laurus.* This tree is called *Parnassian*, because it abounded on mount Parnassus. It was sacred to Apollo.

19. *Subjicit se:* shoots itself up.

21. *Sylvarum fruticumque:* trees and shrubs.

22. *Viâ:* by practice, or experience. *Sunt alii:* there are other methods of producing trees, which, &c. The poet proceeds to enumerate the methods of raising the several kinds of trees, which he reduces to seven. 1. By planting the shoot or scion. 2. By burying the stump or stock in the earth. 3. By burying the stake or trunk split at the bottom. 4. By the layer. 5. By planting in the earth a bough or twig taken from the top of the tree. 6. By planting the trunk or stalk of the tree, deprived of its root and branches. This succeeds very well with the olive-tree. 7. By grafting or transferring a branch or scion of one tree into another.

23. *Plantas:* the shoots or scions from the body of the mother tree.

24. *Obruit stirpes:* another buries the stocks in the ground, and stakes split in four parts at the lower end, and poles, the wood being sharpened into a point.

26. *Aliæ sylvarum:* other trees of the wood—simply, other trees. Ruæus says, *aliæ arbores*. *Propaginis.* The *propago* was the layer, or branch of the parent tree, bent down and fastened in the ground, until it took root, firm enough to support itself; and was then severed from it. This was about the third year. *Arcus:* the arches, or curved figures of the layers, or branches so bent down.

27. *Viva plantaria:* living shoots to be put in their own earth—not cut off as in other cases, but suffered to grow to the parent tree for a time. *Defodi*, or a word of the like import, is understood.

29. *Referens mandare:* to commit the topmost shoot to the earth whence it sprang. *Summum cacumen:* the highest shoot, or branch. *Referens mandare*, simply for *mandare*, says Heyne.

30. *Caudicibus:* Caudex, is properly the body of the tree distinguished from the root, as *truncus* is the body distinguished from the top or head.

32. *Impunè:* without injury. *Alterius*; in the sense of *unius*. *Arboris* is understood.

33. *Vertere:* for *verti*, the active for the passive, by enallage: or, *vertere se in ramos alterius arboris*.

34. *Corna lapidosa:* the corneil trees, which naturally produce a stony hard fruit, by being grafted, will produce the plum—will redden with plums.

37. *Neu segnes terræ jaceant.* Dr. Trapp renders these words: let not your lands lie idle. *Ne terræ sint inutiles*, says Ruæus. But the connexion is better preserved by rendering it: let not your barren lands lie neglected or unimproved. *Ismara* neu. plu. a mountain in Thrace. *Taburnus*: a mountain in Campania, fertile in olives.

Tuque ades, inceptumque unà decurre laborem;
O decus, ô famæ meritò pars maxima nostræ,
Mæcenas, pelagoque volans da vela patenti.
Non ego cuncta meis amplecti versibus opto:
Non, mihi si linguæ centum sint, oraque centum,
Ferrea vox: ades, et primi lege litoris oram.
In manibus terræ: non hìc te carmine ficto,
Atque per ambages et longa exorsa tenebo.
  Sponte suâ quæ se tollunt in luminis auras,
Infœcunda quidem, sed læta et fortia surgunt.
Quippe solo natura subest. Tamen hæc quoque si quis
Inserat, aut scrobibus mandet mutata subactis,
Exuerint sylvestrem animum: cultuque frequenti,
In quascunque voces artes; haud tarda sequentur.
Necnon et sterilis quæ stirpibus exit ab imis,
Hoc faciet, vacuos si sit digesta per agros:
Nunc altæ frondes et rami matris opacant,
Crescentique adimunt fœtus, uruntque ferentem.
  Jam, quæ seminibus jactis se sustulit, arbos
Tarda venit, seris factura nepotibus umbram:
Pomaque degenerant, succos oblita priores:
Et turpes avibus prædam fert uva racemos.
Scilicet omnibus est labor impendendus, et omnes
Cogendæ in sulcum, ac multâ mercede domandæ.
Sed truncis oleæ meliùs, propagine vites
Respondent, solido Paphiæ de robore myrtus,
Plantis et duræ coryli nascuntur, et ingens

39. Tuque, Mæcenas, ades, decurreque inceptum laborem unà *mecum: tu*, O decus, O meritò maxima pars nostræ famæ

43. *Non possem amplecti ea*, si sint mihi

47. *Arbores* quæ tollunt se suâ sponte

53. Et *illa arbor* quæ exit sterilis

63. Sed oleæ respondent meliùs *de* truncis; vites *de* propagine, *et* myrtus

NOTES.

The object of the poet is to persuade the farmer not to neglect his rugged and barren lands, and suffer them to lie useless; for, by culture, he may render them profitable to him. He adduces the case of Ismarus and Taburnus, which, though naturally rugged and barren, had become, by cultivation and proper attention, very productive. *Baccho* is here put for the vine.

39. *Decurre.* Here we have a beautiful allegory, drawn from the sailing of a ship. The verb *decurro* signifies to sail before the wind—to sail with a prosperous gale. *Laborem:* the work or task, viz. the *Georgics*, which he begun at the request of Mæcenas.

41. *Da volans*, &c. And flying, spread the sails to the opening sea—accompany me through this great work, which spreads before me like an open sea, expanding on every side. Some copies have *volens*.

45. *Ficto carmine:* in the sense of *fabuloso poëmate.*

46. *Ambages et longa exorsa:* preambles, and tedious introductions.

50. *Scrobibus subactis:* in trenches prepared for the purpose. *Mutata:* transplanted—removed from their native soil.

52. *In quascunque artes*, &c.: in the sense of *in quocunque modo*, vel *via tractes.* In whatever mode you may require, says Valpy.

56. *Adimunt fœtus:* and take away the fruit from it growing up, and starve it while bearing. The poet's meaning appears to be this: that the sucker, which springs up from the root of the parent tree, will be fruitful and productive, if transplanted into open ground, and arranged in proper rows. For while it remains, the leaves and boughs of the parent tree will overshadow it, and prevent it from bearing fruit as it grows up: or, if it should bear fruit, it will be pinched and small, by being deprived of the rays of the sun and proper nourishment.

57. *Jam:* here is used in the sense of *porrò*, or *præterea.*

60. *Uva:* the grape; by meton. for the vine. *Prædam:* as a prey for birds—only fit for birds.

62. *Multa mercede:* with much labor, or expense.

63. *Oleæ respondent*, &c. The olive is raised or propagated better from the stump; the vine from the layer; the myrtle from the solid wood; the hazle, the ash, the poplar, and the oak, from the scion, or young shoot.

64. *Paphiæ:* Venus, so called from *Paphos*, a city of Cyprus, where she was particularly worshipped. The myrtle was sacred to her. *Respondent:* in the sense of *proveniunt*, vel *oriuntur.*

Fraxinus, Herculeæque arbos umbrosa coronæ,
Chaoniique patris glandes; etiam ardua palma
Nascitur, et casus abies visura marinos.
Inseritur verò ex fœtu nucis arbutus horrida,
Et steriles platani malos gessere valentes:
Castaneæ fagus, ornusque incanuit albo
Flore pyri; glandemque sues fregêre sub ulmis.
Nec modus inserere atque oculos imponere simplex
Nam quà se medio trudunt de cortice gemmæ,
Et tenues rumpunt tunicas, angustus in ipso
Fit nodo sinus: huc alienâ ex arbore germen
Includunt, udoque docent inolescere libro.
Aut rursum enodes trunci resecantur, et altè
Finditur in solidum cuneis via: deinde feraces
Plantæ immittuntur. Nec longum tempus, et ingens
Exiit ad cœlum ramis felicibus arbos,
Miraturque novas frondes, et non sua poma.
Præltereà genus haud unum, nec fortibus ulmis,
Nec salici, lotoque, nec Idæis cyparissis:
Nec pingues unam in faciem nascuntur olivæ,
Orchades, et radii, et amarâ pausia baccâ:
Pomaque, et Alcinoï sylvæ: nec surculus idem
Crustumiis, Syriisque pyris, gravibusque volemis.

71. Fagus incanuit *flore* castaneæ, ornusque *incanuit* albo flore pyri

79 In solidum *lignum*

NOTES.

66. *Umbrosa arbos:* the poplar-tree. It was sacred to Hercules. He wore a crown made of the leaves of this tree, to the infernal regions.

67. *Glandes:* properly acorns; by meton. the oaks that bore them. *Chaonii patris:* Jupiter; so called because he had a temple, and was splendidly worshipped at Dodona, a town of Chaonia in Epirus. The oak was sacred to him.

68. *Visura.* This is said of the fir-tree, because ships were built of its timber. *Marinos casus:* in the sense of *periculæ maris.*

69. *Arbutus inseritur:* the arbute or strawberry-tree is grafted with the shoot or scion of the nut-tree.

70. *Platani.* The plane tree affords a large and pleasant shade, but bears no fruit. It is therefore called *sterilis.* However, says the poet, even this has been made to bear apples by being grafted.

73. *Imponere oculos:* to inoculate. *Oculus* is the bud which is enclosed or put in the bark of the tree to be inoculated. *Inserere:* to ingraft. *Nec modus,* &c. Neither is the method of ingrafting and inoculating one and the same—they are different processes.

76. *Sinus angustus:* a small slit or gash, made in the bark of the tree, (where the bud was putting forth,) for the purpose of receiving the graft.

77. *Docent:* they teach it to grow up, or incorporate itself with the moist bark. *Liber* is the inward part of the bark of the tree; *Cortex,* the whole bark, or rind.

78. *Aut rursum.* Having described the process of inoculation, the poet gives us that of ingrafting. *Truncus:* the body of the tree, properly after the top and branches are cut off. This is split, and the graft put into the fissure. He seems to prefer this mode of cultivating trees, inasmuch as they soon come to maturity. *Nec longum tempus* (says he,) *et ingens arbos:* it is not a long time, and the mighty tree, *exiit,* hath shot up to the skies. There is a peculiar elegancy in the use of the perfect tense here.

80. *Plantæ:* grafts, or scions of fruit-bearing trees.

82. *Poma non sua:* that is, *poma non sui generis.*

84. *Idæis Cyparissis:* to the Idæan Cypresses. There were two mountains by the name of Ida, the one in Phrygia, the other in Crete; the latter is here meant.

86. *Orchades.* The poet here mentions three species of olives: the *orchades,* a round olive, a word derived from the Greek; the *radii,* an oblong olive; the *pausia,* an olive of a bitter taste, so called from *pavio,* says Columella, because its chief use was for oil; to obtain which, it was brayed or beaten.

87. *Sylvæ Alcinoï:* the orchards of Alcinoüs, king of the Phæaceans. They were celebrated by the poets.

88. *Crustumiis:* to the Crustumean pears. so called from *Crustumium,* a town in Tuscany, whose pears were much esteemed; they were of a reddish cast. *Syriis pyris.* These were so called, because they were brought from Syria. They were also called

95. *Sunt* purpureæ, preciæque *uvæ*
99. *Est* Argitis minor *uva*, cui
102. Et, *te*, *O* bumaste, *cum tuis* tumidis racemis. Sed neque est numerus, quàm multæ species *sunt*, nec quæ
105. Quem *numerum* qui velit scire, idem velit discere quàm multæ arenæ Libyci æquoris turbentur

Non eadem arboribus pendet vindemia nostris,
Quam Methymnæo capit de palmite Lesbos.
Sunt Thasiæ vites, sunt et Mareotides albæ:
Pinguibus hæ terris habiles, levioribus illæ.
Et passo Psythia utilior, tenuisque lageos
Tentatura pedes olim, vincturaque linguam.
Purpureæ, preciæque: et quo te carmine dicam
Rhætica? nec cellis ideò contende Falernis.
Sunt et Ammineæ vites, firmissima vina.
Tmolus et assurgit quibus, et rex ipse Phanæus;
Argitisque minor, cui non certaverit ulla,
Aut tantùm fluere, aut totidem durare per annos.
Non ego te, Dîs et mensis accepta secundis,
Transierim, Rhodia; et tumidis, bumaste, racemis.
Sed neque, quàm multæ species, nec nomina quæ sint,
Est numerus: neque enim numero comprendere refert.
Quem qui scire velit, Libyci velit æquoris idem
Discere, quàm multæ Zephyro turbentur arenæ;

NOTES.

Tarentina, and were of a blackish cast. Some think them to be the Bergamot pear. *Volemis:* to the Volemian pears. These were so called from the circumstance of their filling the palm of the hand; from *vola.* The *surculus*, or shoot, of all these was different.

89. *Arboribus:* in the sense of *vitibus.*

90. *Methymnæo:* an adj. from *Methymna*, a city of Lesbos, an island in the Ægean sea, famous for its vines.

91. *Thasiæ:* an adj. from *Thasus*, an island in the Ægean sea. *Mareotides:* an adj. probably from *Mareotis*, a lake near Alexandria, in Egypt. Some take it from a place of the same name in Lybia, in the confines of Egypt. These latter (*hæ*) required a rich soil; the former (*illæ*) a light soil.

93. *Psythia:* an adj. agreeing with *vitis*, understood. Its derivation is uncertain. It is probably from the name of some town in Greece, where that species of vine flourished. *Utilior passo:* better for *passum*, or sweet wine. This was made of raisins or dried grapes; from the word *patior: quòd solem aut ignem patitur. Lageos.* This was a species of grape, deriving its name from a Greek word signifying a hare, because it resembled the color of that animal. *Tenuis:* subtle or penetrating. *Quòd facilè ebrietatem inducit*, says Servius.

95. *Purpureæ, preciæque.* These are both adjectives, and agree with *vites*, or more probably with *uvæ*, understood. *Preciæ:* early ripened—ripened before other grapes.

96. *Rhætica:* a grape, so called from *Rhetia*, a country bordering upon Italy on the west. *Cellis Falernis:* with the Falernian wine. *Cellis:* the cellars; by meton. for the wine in them. *Falernis:* an adj. from *Falernus*, a mountain in Campania, celebrated for its good wines.

97. *Ammineæ vites.* There are various conjectures concerning this vine, but nothing certainly known. It produced excellent wine—*firmissima vina*, strong, and of good body.

98. *Quibus et Tmolus:* to which both Tmolus, and Phanæus himself, the king of vine-bearing mountains, rise up in sign of respect—they yield the pre-eminence to the Amminean vine. *Assurgit*, as here used, is highly metaphorical. It conveys to our minds the idea of one mountain rising up to another in token of respect, and yielding to it precedency. *Tmolus:* a mountain in Lydia, famous for its wines. *Phanæus:* another mountain in the island Chios, in the Ægean sea, celebrated for its wines.

99. *Argitis:* a species of the grape, probably derived from a Greek word signifying *white*, or from *Argos*, a city of the Peloponnesus.

100. *Tantùm fluere:* to yield so much juice.

101. *Mensis et Dis secundis.* The first table or course was composed of meats. The second of fruits, and what we generally call *desserts.* At this second table or course there were libations made to certain gods. *Secundis* is generally connected with *Dis.* It is, however, better to connect it with *mensis:* it will then be: the Rhodian wine is acceptable to the second table or course, and to the gods that were then invoked—acceptable, or fit for libations.

102. *Rhodia:* an adj. from *Rhodus*, a famous island in the Mediterranean sea. *Bumaste:* the bumastus was a species of grape, whose clusters were swollen out, like the udder of a cow. It is derived from the Greek.

103. *Quàm:* in the sense of *tam.*

Aut, ubi navigiis violentior incidit Eurus.
Nôsse, quot Ionii veniant ad litora fluctus.
Nec verò terræ ferre omnes omnia possunt.
Fluminibus salices, crassisque paludibus alni
Nascuntur, steriles saxosis montibus orni,
Litora myrtetis lætissima: denique apertos
Bacchus amat colles, Aquilonem et frigora taxi.
Aspice et extremis domitum cultoribus orbem,
Eoasque domos Arabum, pictosque Gelonos.
Divisæ arboribus patriæ. Sola India nigrum
Fert ebenum, solis est thurea virga Sabæis.
Quid tibi odorato referam sudantia ligno
Balsamaque, et baccas semper frondentis acanthi?
Quid nemora Æthiopum molli canentia lanâ?
Velleraque ut foliis depectant tenuia Seres?
Aut quos Oceano propior gerit India lucos,
Extremi sinus orbis? ubi aëra vincere summum
Arboris haud ullæ jactu potuere sagittæ:

120. Quid *referam tibi* nemora

NOTES.

110. *Salices nascuntur:* the willows by the side of rivers—the alders by stagnant pools—the barren wild ashes on the stony mountains, spring up, and flourish.

112. *Myrtetis:* in groves of myrtle. *Lætissima:* in the sense of *feracissima.*

113. *Bacchus:* here put for *vites*, by meton. *Taxi:* the yew trees. The verb *amant* is to be supplied.

114. *Aspice orbem.* The meaning is, that the remotest parts of the world were reduced to a state of cultivation by their respective inhabitants, both the east (*Eoas domos Arabum*) and the north, the country of the *Geloni.* The inhabitants, by meton. put for the country. They painted themselves that they might be more terrible to their enemies. This explains the word *pictos.*

115. *Gelonos:* the Geloni were a people inhabiting the northern parts of Europe.

116. *Patriæ divisæ:* countries are distinguished by their trees. *Patria*, one's native country—*Regio*, any country.

117. *Thurea virga:* the frankincense tree.

118. *Referam:* in the sense of *dicam*, vel *describam.*

119. *Balsama:* plu. of *balsamum*, a plant of a very delicious fragrance. Its juice is obtained by cutting the branches in the summer months, from which incisions the juice flows. *Acanthi.* There were two kinds of Acanthus; one the herb commonly called *brank-ursin*, or bear's-foot; the other an Egyptian tree, always green, and abounding in berries.

120. *Molli lanâ:* with soft cotton. *Æthiopum:* gen. plu. of *Æthiops:* an inhabitant of *Æthiopia*, an extensive country in Africa, abounding in the cotton tree. *Ut:* in the sense of *quomodo.*

121. *Seres:* a people of India, who furnished the rest of the world with silk. It was a common received opinion that they collected it from the leaves of trees. To this the poet refers in the words, *depectant*, &c. they comb off the fine fleeces from the leaves.

123. *Extremi sinus orbis.* It is somewhat difficult to fix the meaning of *sinus*, in this place. If it could be read *sinui*, in the dat. to agree with *oceano*, it would be easy. But it is usually read in the nom. It must therefore mean the same as *India*, in the preceding line. But how it can be applied with any propriety, to express a tract of country, doth not appear. If we take *sinus* for the gen. connected with *extremi*, the difficulty will be removed, in a good degree, and *orbis* for the nom. Now *orbis* sometimes means no more than a single country, or any division or part of the earth. If we take it thus, the passage may be rendered: Or, why need I mention the groves which India, nearer the ocean, the country of (bordering upon) the farthest bay, produces? Valpy says: the extreme convexity of the globe. Heyne: *interior remotiorque terra extremæ orbis partis.* Ruæus: *recessus ultimi mundi.* The *sinus* I take for the bay of Bengal, called by the ancients the *Sinus Gangeticus.* The parts of India beyond the Ganges were very little known to them; *extremi*, therefore, may e very well applied to them. *Summum aëra:* the highest air—the air surrounding the topmost branches. This is evidently an extravagant hyperbole, notwithstanding the declaration of Pliny, as to the height of the trees. *Vincere:* in the sense of *superare.*

126. *Media.* A country of Asia, bounded on the north by the Caspian sea, on the

Et gens illa quidem sumptis non tarda pharetris
Media fert tristes succos, tardumque saporem
Felicis mali: quo non præsentius ullum
(Pocula si quando sævæ infecêre novercæ,
Miscueruntque herbas, et non innoxia verba)
Auxilium venit, ac membris agit atra venena.

131. Ipsa arbor *est* ingens, simillimaque lauro *quoad* faciem

Ipsa ingens arbos, faciemque simillima lauro;
Et, si non alium latè jactaret odorem,
Laurus erat: folia haud ullis labentia ventis:
Flos apprimà tenax: animas et olentia Medi
Ora fovent illo, et senibus medicantur anhelis.
Sed neque Medorum sylvæ, ditissima terra,
Nec pulcher Ganges, atque auro turbidus Hermus,
Laudibus Italiæ certent: non Bactra, neque Indi,
Totaque thuriferis Panchaïa pinguis arenis.
Hæc loca non tauri spirantes naribus ignem
Invertêre, satis immanis dentibus hydri:
Nec galeis densisque virûm seges horruit hastis:
Sed gravidæ fruges, et Bacchi Massicus humor
Implevere: tenent oleæque, armentaque læta.
Hinc bellator equus campo sese arduus infert:
Hinc albi, Clitumne, greges, et maxima taurus

NOTES.

west by Armenia, on the east by Hyrcania and Parthia, and on the south by Persia proper. Under Cyrus the great, it became a constituent part of the Persian monarchy.

127. *Mali:* the citron. Its rind is bitter, and its seeds are covered with a bitter skin: hence *tristes succos*, bitter juices; and *tardum saporem*, a taste remaining long on the palate. It is called *Felix*, happy, on account of its many virtues, and qualities; some of which are mentioned. *Non tarda:* ~~in the sense of *strenua vel fortis*.~~

128. *Infecere:* have poisoned. *Pocula:* by meton. the wine. *Præsentiùs:* more certain—more efficacious. Some copies have *præstantiùs*.

129. *Non innoxia verba:* in the sense of *noxias incantationes*.

134. *Apprimà:* an adj. neu. plu. taken as an adverb, in imitation of the Greeks. The same as *apprimè*. *Animas et olentia ora*, &c. With this (fruit, *malo*) the Medes correct their breath, and (cleanse) their stinking mouths. ~~See Æn. viii. 410.~~ Ruæus says; *Corrigunt halitum suum et graveolentia ora.*

137. *Ganges.* One of the finest rivers in the world. It rises in the kingdom of Thibet, and taking a south-easterly direction, after a course of about 2000 miles, falls into the gulf or bay of Bengal; having in its course received a number of tributary treams, eleven of which, it is said, are as large as the Rhine. It is considered by the inhabitants upon its banks, as a god. *Hermus;* a river of Lydia, famous for its golden sands. It received in its course the celebrated *Pactolus;* and with it, fell into the *Sinus Phocaicus*.

138. *Bactra:* neu. plu. the principal city of the *Bactrii*. By synec. put for their whole country, which was called *Bactriana*, and was bounded by *Parthia* on the west, *India* on the east, and by the river *Oxus* on the north.

139. *Panchaïa:* a country of *Arabia Felix*. *Pinguis:* rich, in frankincense-bearing soil.

140. *Hæc loca:* these places bulls breathing fire have not turned, &c. This alludes to the fable of Jason, who, with a company of men, went to Colchis to get the golden fleece. Here were bulls breathing fire bound to a plough. Upon their turning the earth, it was sown with dragon's teeth, which immediately sprang up, *seges virûm*, into men armed and prepared for combat, to supply the place of those that had been slain. The dragon that guarded the fleece being slain, Jason obtained the prize. This was the famous Argonautic expedition. See Ovid, Met. vii. It is supposed that this was only a commercial expedition, which proved very lucrative.

143. *Massicus:* a mountain in Campania, fertile in the vine; here used as an adj. *Massicus humor Bacchi:* Massic wine. *Humor Bacchi:* the liquor of Bacchus, i. e. wine.

146. *Clitumne:* Clitumnus a river of Umbria in Italy, famous for the flocks of white

Victima, sæpe tuo perfusi flumine sacro,
Romanos ad templa Deûm duxere triumphos.
Hic ver assiduum, atque alienis mensibus æstas.
Bis gravidæ pecudes, bis pomis utilis arbos.
At rabidæ tigres absunt, et sæva leonum
Semina: nec miseros fallunt aconita legentes:
Nec rapit immensos orbes per humum, neque tanto
Squameus in spiram tractu se colligit anguis.
Adde tot egregias urbes, operumque laborem;
Tot congesta manu præruptis oppida saxis;
Fluminaque antiquos subter labentia muros.
An mare, quod suprà, memorem, quodque alluit infrà?
Anne lacus tantos? te, Lari maxime; teque
Fluctibus et fremitu assurgens, Benace, marino?
An memorem portus, Lucrinoque addita claustra,
Atque indignatum magnis stridoribus æquor;
Julia quà ponto longê sonat unda refuso,

153. Nec squameus anguis rapit immensos orbes per humum, neque colligit se in spiram *cum* tanto tractu *hic*, *quàm quibusdam aliis regionibus.*

158. An memorem mare, quod alluit *Italiam* suprà, quodque *alluit eam* infra? Anne *memorem* tantos lacus, te, *O* maxime Lari, teque, *O*, Benace,

162. Æquor indignatum *circa illa claustra* magnis

NOTES.

sheep that fed on its banks. The victims were washed in it, to make them the whiter. White victims alone were offered to Jove on triumphal days. To this the poet alludes.

149. *Æstas alienis mensibus:* summer in other months—in months not its own. *Assiduum:* in the sense of *perpetuum.*

150. *Bis pecudes,* &c. The meaning is, that the flocks bring forth twice in a year, and the trees produce two crops of fruit. *Pecudes;* here must mean sheep and other minor animals. It could not be said of cattle or horses. The poet, in many instances, in praising his country, exceeds the bounds of credibility. *Utilis:* in the sense of *fertilis,* says Heyne.

152. *Aconita:* wolf's bane. It is taken here for any noxious or poisonous plant, or herb. According to *Solinus,* it takes its name from *Acon,* a port in *Pontus,* a country notorious for poisonous plants. Others take it from a Greek word signifying a stone, because it grew principally on stony grounds. *Semina:* in the sense of *proles.*

155. *Laborem operum:* the labor, or work of artificers. *Operum* appears to be used in the sense of *Opificum,* or *Operariorum.* Heyne takes *laborem operum,* simply for *opera,* vel *ædificia.*

156. *Tot oppida.* Many of the cities of Italy were built upon high and elevated grounds. To this the words *præruptis saxis* allude. *Congesta* in the sense of *extructa.*

157. *Subter:* Heyne takes this in the sense of *præter:* making the sense to be, that the rivers flowed or passed by the walls of cities. He observes that many of the cities of Italy were built upon the margin of rivers: which seems to warrant that sense of the word.

158. *An Mare,* &c. Italy is washed by the Adriatic sea, on the north-east, and by the Tuscan sea on the south. The former was sometimes called *Mare superum,* and the latter *Mare inferum;* hence the *suprà* applied to the one, and *infrà,* to the other.

159. *Maxime Lari:* Larius, a large lake at the foot of the Alps. It communicates with the *Po,* by the river *Addua. Hodie, Lago di Coma.*

160. *Benace:* Benācus, a large lake, communicating with the *Po,* by the river Mincius. Its present name is *Lago di Garda. Assurgens:* swelling with the waves, and roaring of a sea.

161. *Lucrino—Avernis.* Lucrinus and Avernus were two lakes in Campania. Here Augustus made a haven, which he called the Julian port. This was done by uniting them by a canal, and connecting them with the sea. *Portum Julium apud Baias, immisso in Lucrinum et Avernum Lacum mari, efficit,* says *Suetonius. Addita claustra.* It would seem from this, that *Lucrinus* was originally a bay, and probably connected with the sea, by a narrow strait, but afterward, either by some operation of the water, or artificially, was separated from it, forming a lake. This was the opinion of Strabo, who informs us that Lucrinus was originally a bay; but had been separated from the sea, ever since the days of Hercules, by a mound or bank of sand; that this was occasionally broken over by the waves of the sea, but was repaired and made secure against all encroachments of that element, by Agrippa, for the purpose of making it a safe and convenient station for the Roman fleet.

162. *Indignatum:* the same as *indignans:* roaring—raging.

163. *Julia aqua.* Heyne seems to understand this in the sense of *Julius portus,* the

165. Hæc eadem *Italia* ostendit *in* venis rivos
167. Hæc *Italia* extulit acre genus virûm, *nempe.*
169. Hæc *Italia* extulit
177. Locus *est dicendi de* ingeniis
180. Ubi *sunt* tenuis argilla, et calculus

Tyrrhenusque fretis immittitur æstus Avernis?
Hæc eadem argenti rivos, ærisque metalla
Ostendit venis, atque auro plurima fluxit.
Hæc genus acre virûm, Marsos, pubemque Sabellam,
Assuetumque malo Ligurem, Volscosque verutos
Extulit: hæc Decios, Marios, magnosque Camillos,
Scipiadas duros bello; et te, maxime Cæsar,
Qui nunc extremis Asiæ jam victor in oris
Imbellem avertis Romanis arcibus Indum.
Sálve, magna parens frugum, Saturnia tellus,
Magna virûm: tibi res antiquæ laudis et artis
Ingredior, sanctos ausus recludere fontes:
Ascræumque cano Romana per oppida carmen
Nunc locus arvorum ingeniis: quæ robora cuique,
Quis color, et quæ sit rebus natura ferendis
Difficiles primùm terræ, collesque maligni,
Tenŭis ubi argilla, et dumosis calculus arvis,
Palladiâ gaudent sylvâ vivacis olivæ.
Indicio est tractu surgens oleaster eodem

NOTES.

harbor that had been made by excluding the sea—the water in the harbor. Lucrinus was not entirely separated from the sea. It was connected with it by a strait, or narrow channel, for the ingress and egress of the fleet, and for the admission of the water of the sea.

164. *Fretis Avernis:* the canal which connected *Avernus* with *Lucrinus*, is here called *fretum*, a strait. *Æstus:* in the sense of *mare*.

165. *Metalla æris:* simply, brass. *Fluxit:* in the sense of *abundavit*.

167. *Marsos.* The Marsi were a people of Italy lying to the south of the Appenines, and to the east and north of the *Æqui* and *Volsci*. They originated, according to some, from a son of the sorceress Circe: others say, from *Marsia*, a king of Lydia. Their principal city was *Marrubium*, or *Marruvium*, not far from the *Lacus Fucinus*. *Pubem Sabellam:* the *Sabelli* were a very ancient people of Italy, originally including the *Samnites*, the *Sabines*, and the *Ausoneans*.

168. *Ligurem:* the Ligurean accustomed to fatigue or toil. The *Ligures* were a people inhabiting that part of Italy, which lies at the head of the *Mare Ligusticum*, or sea of Genoa. The *Volsci* were a very warlike people. They inhabited that part of Italy, through which the river Liris passes, and were bounded on the west by the *Rutuli* and *Latini*, on the east by *Aurunci* and *Campani*, and on the north by the *Æqui* and *Hernici*. *Verutos*, armed with darts: from *veru* a kind of dart.

169. *Decios:* these were three Romans, who sacrificed their lives for their country. *Marios:* the *Marii*, of whom Caius Marius was the most celebrated. Though of humble birth, he rose to the highest honors. He triumphed over Jugurtha, king of Numidia, and over the *Cimbri*. He died in his seventh consulship. *Camillos.* The most celebrated of the *Camilli* was *Marcus Furius Camillus*. He triumphed over the *Vientes*. He rescued Rome from the Gauls. He was called a second Romulus, and died at the age of eighty years. See Æn. vi. 825. *Scipiadas.* See Æn. vi. 843. *Duros:* invincible—capable of enduring the fatigues of war.

173. *Saturnia tellus.* Italy is so called because here Saturn found a safe retreat after his expulsion from heaven. He reigned here conjointly with Janus. *Res:* a subject. *Tibi:* for thee—for thy advantage.

174. *Virûm:* in the sense of *heroüm*. *Laudis antiquæ, et artis.* *Laudatas et excultas ab antiquis*, says Ruæus.

176. *Ascræum carmen:* an Ascrean strain, or verse; that is, in imitation of Hesiod, who was a native of *Ascra*, a village in Beotia, not far from mount Helicon. It is said, he wrote a treatise upon agriculture.

177. *Ingeniis:* the nature or quality of the lands. *Robora*, plu. of *robur*, strength or ability to produce. The poet proceeds to point out the several methods of distinguishing the various soils. He makes ten such methods.

179. *Maligni:* thin—poor, with reference to the quality of the soil. *Difficiles:* rough.

181. *Palladia sylvâ:* Minerva's grove *Palladia:* an adj. from *Pallas*, a name of Minerva, to whom the olive was sacred.

182. *Oleaster nascens plurimus:* the wild olive, springing up thick and luxuriant in the same tract, is for a sign.

Plurimus, et strati baccis sylvestribus agri.
At quæ pinguis humus, dulcique uligine læta,
Quique frequens herbis, et fertilis ubere campus,
Qualem sæpe cavâ montis convalle solemus
Despicere: huc summis liquuntur rupibus amnes,
Felicemque trahunt limum: quique editus Austro,
Et filicem curvis invisam pascit aratris:
Hic tibi prævalidas olim multoque fluentes
Sufficiet Baccho vites: hic fertilis uvæ,
Hic laticis; qualem pateris libamus et auro,
Inflavit cùm pinguis ebur Tyrrhenus ad aras,
Lancibus et pandis fumantia reddimus exta.
Sin armenta magis studium, vitulosque tueri,
Aut fœtus ovium, aut urentes culta capellas:
Saltus et saturi petito longinqua Tarenti,
Et qualem infelix amisit Mantua campum,
Pascentem niveos herboso flumine cycnos.
Non liquidi gregibus fontes, non gramina desunt:
Et quantùm longis carpent armenta diebus,
Exiguâ tantùm gelidus ros nocte reponet.
Nigra ferè, et presso pinguis sub vomere, terra,
Et cui putre solum (namque hoc imitamur arando)
Optima frumentis; non ullo ex æquore cernes
Plura domum tardis decedere plaustra juvencis:
Aut unde iratus sylvam devexit arator,
Et nemora evertit multos ignava per annos,
Antiquasque domos avium cum stirpibus imis
Eruit: illæ altum nidis petiere relictis:
At rudis enituit impulso vomere campus.

184. At humus, quæ *est* pinguis, lætaque dulci uligine, campusque, qui *est* frequens herbis, et fertilis ubere

188. *Campus*que, qui *est* editus Austro, et pascit

190. Hic *campus* sufficiet tibi

191. Hic *campus erit* fertilis uvæ, hic *idem erit fertilis talis* laticis; qualem

195. Sin studium *sit tibi* magis tueri armenta

198. Et *talem* campum, qualem

201. Quantùm *herbarum* armenta

203. Terra ferè nigra, et pinguis sub presso vomere; et cui *est*

207. Aut *illa terra est optima frumentis*, unde

210. Altum *aërem*

NOTES.

183. *Strati:* covered with.

184. *Læta:* in the sense of *abundans. Uligine:* the natural moisture of the earth.

187. *Liquuntur:* in the sense of *defluunt.*

188. *Felicem:* fertilizing, or enriching.

189. *Filicem:* the fern or brake, whose roots, by their contexture, are very troublesome to the plough. *Invisam:* hated.

191. *Sufficiet:* in the sense of *producet.*

192. *Pateris et auro:* by Hendiadis, for *aureis pateris:* in golden bowls.

193. *Tyrrhenus;* an inhabitant of Etruria or Tuscany, an extensive country in Italy, whose ancient inhabitants were famous for indulging their appetite; hence the epithet *pinguis:* fat or corpulent. *Reddimus:* we offer to the gods the warm entrails, &c. *Ebur:* properly ivory—any thing made of ivory. Here, an ivory pipe.

195. *Tueri:* in the sense of *alere*, vel *nutrire.*

196. *Urentes:* nipping—destroying. *Culta:* an adj. from *cultus.* This denotes any thing that is dressed, taken care of, or managed in any way by culture. Here it means young trees—nurseries.

197. *Tarenti:* Tarentum, a town in Calabria, in the eastern part of Italy; which justifies the epithet *longinqua:* remote fields. *Arva* is understood.

198. *Mantua infelix amisit:* such as unhappy Mantua hath lost. The poet alludes to the circumstance of Augustus' depriving the Mantuans of their lands, and bestowing them upon his soldiers, as a reward for their services. *Infelix*, here, is peculiarly appropriate. Mantua was situated upon the river Mincius, which abounded in grass and reeds. *Flumine:* perhaps, in the sense of *ripa*, vel *litore.*

200. *Liquidi:* in the sense of *puri. Desunt:* Heyne reads *deerunt*, in the future.

204. *Imitamur hoc*, &c. The design of ploughing land being to loosen its texture, and to render it soft and mellow; by doing this, we imitate, says the poet, a soil which is naturally so. He observes, that a dark mould, and one that looks fat and greasy, as it is broken up with the share, and is, at the same time, rotten or mellow, is the best for grain: *non ex ullo æquore cernes*, &c. The same too may be said, he observes, of land newly cleared: *unde iratus*, &c. *Iratus*, angry, on account of the barrenness of the wood. *Ignava:* barren—useless.

205. *Æquore:* in the sense of *agro*, vel *campo.*

211. *Rudis campus:* but the new (before uncultivated) field hath shone under the deep laid share. For *enituit*, Dr. Trapp would read *enitet*, the pres.

Nam jejuna quidem clivosi glarea ruris
Vix humiles apibus casias roremque ministrat:

214. Chelydris *vix ministrant eas quoque*

Et tophus scaber, et nigris exesa chelydris
Crèta: negant alios æquè serpentibus agros
Dulcem ferre cibum, et curvas præbere latebras.

217. *Illa terra* quæ exhalat

Quæ tenuem exhalat nebulam, fumosque volucres,
Et bibit humorem, et, cùm vult, ex se ipsa remittit,
Quæque suo viridi semper se gramine vestit,
Nec scabie et salsâ lædit rubigine ferrum;

221. Illa *terra* intexet

Illa tibi lætis intexet vitibus ulmos:
Illa ferax oleæ est: illam experiêre colendo
Et facilem pecori, et patientem vomeris unci.
Talem dives arat Capua, et vicina Vesevo
Ora jugo, et vacuis Clanius non æquus Acerris.

226. Nunc dicam quomodo possis cognoscere *unam* quamque *terram*, *si* requiras, *an* sit rara

229. Densa *terra favet* Cereri magis

Nunc, quo quamque modo possis cognoscere, dicam.
Rara sit, an supra morem sit densa, requiras:
(Altera frumentis quoniam favet, altera Baccho:
Densa, magis Cereri; rarissima quæque, Lyæo)
Antè locum capies oculis; altèque jubebis
In solido puteum demitti, omnemque repones
Rursus humum, et pedibus summas æquabis arenas.

233. Si *arenæ* deerunt *ad replendum locum*, uber erit rarum, aptiusque

Si deerunt, rarum, pecorique et vitibus almis
Aptius, uber erit: sin in sua posse negabunt
Ire loca, et scrobibus superabit terra repletis,
Spissus ager; glebas cunctantes crassaque terga
Expecta, et validis terram proscinde juvencis.
Salsa autem tellus, et quæ perhibetur amara,
Frugibus infelix: ea nec mansuescit arando,
Nec Baccho genus, aut pomis sua nomina servat:

NOTES.

212. *Nam jejuna glarea.* Having mentioned the land best for grain, the poet here observes, that the land in which the dry gravel, *jejuna glarea;* or the rough rottenstone, *scaber tophus;* or the chalk stone, *creta,* abounds, will scarcely produce the herb *casia,* and consequently is unfit for grain: besides, it is the haunt of noxious reptiles and vermin. *Rorem:* in the sense of *flores,* says Heyne: *quibus ros solet inesse.*

215. *Tophus scaber,* &c. Heyne takes *tophus scaber* and *creta exera* as nominatives to *negant.*

220. *Scabie, rubigine:* with scurf—with rust. *Ferrum:* the plough-share.

221. *Intexet:* will entwine—embrace. *Implicabit,* says Ruæus.

223. *Facilem pecori:* to be good for pasture, and patient of the bending plough—will bear frequent tillage.

224. *Capua:* a city of Campania, surrounded by a fertile country. Its inhabitants were celebrated for their wealth and luxury. It took its name from *Capys,* a companion of Æneas; but Strabo derives it from *caput,* because it was the chief city in that part of Italy.

225. *Ora:* in the sense of *regio. Jugo Vesevo:* the mountain Vesuvius, in Campania, near Naples, well known as a volcano. *Acerris:* Acerræ was an ancient city of Campania, which the river *Clanius,* by its frequent inundations, almost depopulated. Hence the propriety of *non æquus,* not just, or kind—destructive.

227. *Rara. Rarus,* loose, light, is the opposite of *spissus;* and in the present case, of *densus.*

228. *Baccho—Lyæo.* These both by meton. are here put for the vine.

230. *Antè:* in the sense of *primùm.*

231. *Demitti:* in the sense of *defodi. Puteum:* in the sense of *foveam. In solido:* in the solid ground.

234. *Uber:* in the sense of *solum,* vel *humus.*

236. *Expecta cunctantes:* expect hard clods, and large tough ridges.

239. *Ea nec mansuescit:* that land neither mellows by ploughing, nor preserves its kind to the vine, nor their own names to the fruit. The vine and fruit degenerate, and lose their original flavor and qualities when planted in such a soil. *Infelix:* in the sense of *inapta,* vel *infecunda.*

Tale dabit specimen. Tu spisso vimine qualos,
Colaque prelorum fumosis deripe tectis.
Huc ager ille malus, dulcesque à fontibus undæ
Ad plenum calcentur: aqua eluctabitur omnis
Scilicet, et grandes ibunt per vimina guttæ.
At sapor indicium faciet manifestus; et ora
Tristia tentantûm sensu torquebit amaror.
Pinguis item quæ sit tellus, hoc denique pacto
Discimus; haud unquam manibus jactata fatiscit;
Sed picis in morem ad digitos lentescit habendo.
Humida majores herbas alit, ipsaque justo
Lætior: ah nimiùm ne sit mihi fertilis illa,
Neu se prævalidam primis ostendat aristis!
Quæ gravis est, ipso tacitam se pondere prodit;
Quæque levis. Promptum est oculis prædiscere nigram,
Et quisquis color. At sceleratum exquirere frigus
Difficile est: piceæ tantùm, taxique nocentes
Interdum, aut hederæ pandunt vestigia nigræ.
His animadversis, terram multò antè memento
Excoquere, et magnos scrobibus concidere montes,
Antè, supinatas Aquiloni ostendere glebas,
Quàm lætum infodias vitis genus: optima putri
Arva solo: id venti curant, gelidæque pruinæ,
Et labefacta movens robustus jugera fossor.
At si quos haud ulla viros vigilantia fugit:
Antè locum similem exquirunt, ubi prima paretur
Arboribus seges, et quo mox digesta feratur;

251. Humida *terra alit* majores herbas, ipsa *quæ est* lætior justo.

254. *Terra, quæ est* gravis, quæque *est* levis, prodit se tacitam

256. Et quisquis color *sit unicuique terræ.*

262. Optima arva *sunt* è putri solo

266. Exquirunt locum similem *illi*, ubi prima seges

NOTES.

242. *Deripe:* in the sense of *cape*, vel *sume*. *Qualos:* baskets made of thick wicker.

243. *Huc:* hither—into the basket. *Malus ager:* the earth of bad quality. *Undæ:* in the sense of *aqua*.

244. *Eluctabitur:* in the sense of *effluet*, vel *elabitur*.

246. *Sapor:* the taste or relish, denoting the quality of any thing. It differs from *sensus*, which here means the sensation or effect produced on the mouth by the act of tasting. *Indicium:* a discovery of the quality of the land.

247. *Tentantûm:* in the sense of *gustantium*. *Tristia:* in the sense of *salsa*, vel *amara*.

249. *Jactata:* in the sense of *versata*.

250. *Habendo:* by handling.

251. *Justo:* than just—above due measure. The abl. after the comparative.

253. *Aristis:* *arista* here means the blade or stalk of the grain.

254. *Tacitam:* in the sense of *tacitè*.

255. *Promptum:* in the sense of *facile*.

256. *Sceleratum:* in the sense of *noxium*, vel *perniciosum*.

260 *Excoquere terram:* to drain, or dry your land. *Concidere*. Davidson, on the authority of Pierius, reads *circumdare*. *Excoquere:* to dry—bake. The poet here advises to let the land lie exposed both to the heat of the sun during the summer, and to the north wind during winter; that is, for a whole year. The *antè* in the following line appears entirely expletive. Some have proposed to read in room of it, *atque*, which would be preferable, if there were authority for the change. Heyne seems to approve of *atque*.

261. *Ostendere:* in the sense of *exponere*. *Supinatas:* turned toward, or lying exposed to.

264. *Labefacta jugera:* his loosened acres—mellowing under the instruments of husbandry. *Curant:* in the sense of *efficient:* will render the ground soft and mellow.

265. *Si quos:* some men.

267. *Seges:* a nursery, or place where trees are first planted or reared, till they be of sufficient size to be transplanted. In this passage, the meaning appears to be, that those who would have good orchards, should pay a particular attention to the soil, where they intend to plant the trees, and select a soil of the like kind for the nursery; from which (*ex quo*) afterward the trees are to be taken and transplanted; lest when so transplanted, they should not readily unite with the earth. Not only so, they should

Mutatam ignorent subitò ne semina matrem.
Quin etiam cœli regionem in cortice signant;

270. Ut restituant unamquamque eò modo, quo quæque steterit, quà parte

Ut, quo quæque modo steterit, quâ parte calores
Austrinos tulerit, quæ terga obverterit axi,
Restituant. Adeò in teneris consuescere multum est.
Collibus, an plano melius sit ponere vites,
Quære priùs. Si pinguis agros metabere campi,
Densa sere. In denso non segnior ubere Bacchus

276. Sin eligas solum acclive tumulis

Sin tumulis acclive solum, collesque supinos,
Indulge ordinibus: nec seciùs omnis in unguem
Arboribus positis secto via limite quadret.
Ut sæpe ingenti bello, cùm longa cohortes
Explicuit legio, et campo stetit agmen aperto,
Directæque acies, ac latè fluctuat omnis
Ære renidenti tellus, necdum horrida miscent
Prælia, sed dubius mediis Mars errat in armis.

284. Omnia intervalla viarum sint dimensa

Omnia sint paribus numeris dimensa viarum:
Non animum modò utì pascat prospectus inanem,
Sed quia non aliter vires dabit omnibus æquas
Terra, neque in vacuum poterunt se extendere rami.
Forsitan et scrobibus quæ sint fastigia quæras.
Ausim vel tenui vitem committere sulco.
Altiùs ac penitùs terræ defigitur arbos:

NOTES.

carefully observe what particular side stood toward the several parts of heaven, that they might be placed, every one in the same manner—on what side they sustained the summer heat, and on what side the winter cold. *Seges:* in the sense of *seminarium*, says Heyne. *Digesta:* arranged in rows. *Feratur:* in the sense of *transferatur.*

268. *Semina:* young plants, or trees. *Matrem:* the ground into which they are transplanted.

271. *Axi:* in the sense of *septentrioni.*

272. *Consuescere in teneris:* to be accustomed in their tender age avails so much—has so much influence over them. Some copies have *à teneris. Annis* is understood.

274. *Metabere:* if you shall lay out for planting. Ruæus interprets it by *eligas.*

275. *Densa:* for *densè*, an adv. *Bacchus non segnior:* the vine will not be less fruitful in a thick and rich soil. Some take *in denso* simply for *densè*, and render it thus: the vine will not be less fruitful in a rich soil, if planted thickly. In this case, *ubere* is taken for richness or fertility of soil. This appears to be the opinion of Heyne. Ruæus connects *denso* with *ubere.* In this case, *denso* must be taken in the sense of *pingui*, vel *spisso;* and *ubere* in the sense of *solo.*

276. *Supinos:* sloping—descending gradually.

277. *Indulge ordinibus:* indulge in your rows—plant your vines farther apart. *Nec seciùs:* also—likewise; *porrò*, says Heyne.

278. *Omnis via*, &c. Every space, or avenue, should square exactly, the trees being placed in a path or line cut across—every space should exactly form a square, the rows of trees being planted at equal distances, and at right angles to each other *In unguem:* exactly—to a tittle.

281. *Acies directæ:* the lines are formed—the battalions are marshalled. *Acies:* an army in order of battle; *agmen:* in order of march; *exercitus:* in order of exercise. *Fluctuat:* in the sense of *coruscat.*

282. *Renidenti ære:* with gleaming brass, *Ære:* in the sense of *æreis armis.*

283. *Dubius:* doubtful—uncertain—not knowing on which side of the embattled armies the victory will fall.

284. *Omnia sint*, &c. All the spaces should be measured out in equal proportions. Davidson supposes *intervalla*, or a word of the like import, to agree with *omnia*, and to govern *viarum.* Ruæus connects *viarum* with *numeris*, and supposes it to be governed by that word. But to take *omnia viarum* in the sense of *omnes viæ*, is more simple: and of this construction we have many examples in Virgil. *Opaca locorum:* dark places. Æn. ii. 725. *Opaca viarum:* dark ways, or passages. Æn. vi. 633.

288. *Fastigia:* in the sense of *profunditas. Scrobibus:* to the trenches—holes.

290. *Altiùs.* The common reading is *altiùs;* but Heyne, Heinsius, and some others, have *altior.*

Æsculus imprimìs, quæ quantùm vertice ad auras
Æthereas, tantùm radice in Tartara tendit.
Ergò non hyemes illam, non flabra, neque imbres
Convellunt: immota manet, multosque per annos,
Multa virûm volvens durando sæcula vincit.
Tum fortes latè ramos et brachia tendens
Huc illuc, media ipsa ingentem sustinet umbram.
Neve tibi ad Solem vergant vineta cadentem:
Neve inter vites corylum sere: neve flagella
Summa pete, aut summas defringe ex arbore plantas,
(Tantus amor terræ:) neu ferro læde retuso
Semina: neve oleæ sylvestres insere truncos.
Nam sæpe incautis pastoribus excidit ignis,
Qui furtim pingui primùm sub cortice tectus
Robora comprendit, frondesque elapsus in altas
Ingentem cœlo sonitum dedit: inde secutus
Per ramos victor, perque alta cacumina regnat,
Et totum involvit flammis nemus, et ruit atram
Ad cœlum piceâ crassus, caligine nubem:
Præsertim si tempestas à vertice sylvis
Incubuit, glomeratque ferens incendia ventus.
Hoc ubi; non à stirpe valent, cæsæque reverti
Possunt, atque imâ similes revirescere terrâ;
Infelix superat foliis oleaster amaris.
Nec tibi tam prudens quisquam persuadeat auctor
Tellurem Boreâ rigidam spirante movere.
Rura gelu tum claudit hyems, nec semine jacto

297. **Ipsa media** *inter suos ramos* **sustinet**

312. **Ubi hoc** *accidit, tum vites* **non valent** *reverti* **à stirpe**

NOTES.

292. *Tartara tendit: Tartarus*, mas. in the sing. neu. in the plu. one of the regions of hell. Here, as the poets say, the wicked and impious are punished. Ixion, Tityus, Tantalus, Sysyphus, and the Danaïdes, were sentenced to this place. The poet advises to commit the vine to a light furrow, just below the surface of the earth; but to put the tree, and especially the *Æsculus*, deep in the earth, that they may take root better and more firmly. The vine properly belongs neither to the species of the tree, nor to that of the shrub; but is between both: *tertium quiddam, quod nec arborem, nec fruticem propriè dixerim*, says Columella. See Æn. iv. 445.

294. *Multos per annos.* Heyne reads, *multos nepotes.* He observes that Heinsius, and some others, read the same. *Per annos*, is the general reading, and appears to be the easiest. If *nepotes* be read, it must be taken in the sense of *ætates*, vel *æva;* but that is expressed in the following line, by the words, *multa sæcula virûm.*

295. *Vincit:* in the sense of *superat.*

299. *Neve pete summa.* neither seek the topmost shoots, nor break off the topmost scions from the tree.

The advice which the poet gives, is: that in propagating trees, whether by grafting, or otherwise, you should not take the topmost shoots of the tree, but those that are nearer the root; for they will grow and flourish better, having more strength in them, and having already contracted a fondness for the earth—*tantus amor terræ. Semina:* in the sense of *surculos*, vel *plantas.*

300. *Defringe.* Heyne reads *destringe.*

302. *Neve insĕre*, &c. Nor plant the trunks of the wild olive among your vines. *Inter vites*, is understood.

306. *Secutus:* increasing more and more, it reigns victorious.

308. *Ruit:* in the sense of *emittit*, vel *erigit. Nemus:* in the sense of *vinetum.*

310. *A vertice:* from on high; or, according to Servius, from the north. *Desuper*, vel *de cœlo*, says Heyne; *à septentrione*, says Ruæus.

312. *Ubi hoc:* when this happens—when your vineyards are burnt, your vines cannot shoot forth again from the root; nor, if they be cut, can they do it, and spring up such as they were before. They will be entirely destroyed, and nothing but the barren wild olive will survive and remain. *Reverti:* in the sense of *renasci.*

317. *Rura:* in the sense of *arva. Semine jacto:* in the sense of *surculo defosso.*

Concretam patitur radicem affigere terræ.
Optima vinetis satio est, cùm vere rubenti
Candida venit avis longis invisa colubris:
Prima vel autumni sub frigora, cùm rapidus Sol
Nondum hyemem contingit equis, jam præterit æstas.

323. Adeò ver *est utile* frondi nemorum, ver *est*

Ver adeò frondi nemorum, ver utile sylvis;
Vere tument terræ, et genitalia semina poscunt.
Tum pater omnipotens fœcundis imbribus æther
Conjugis in gremium lætæ descendit, et omnes
Magnus alit, magno commixtus corpore, fœtus
Avia tum resonant avibus virgulta canoris,
Et Venerem certis repetunt armenta diebus.
Parturit almus ager: Zephyrique tepentibus auris

331. Omnibus *arvis*

Laxant arva sinus: superat tener omnibus humor·
Inque novos soles audent se germina tutò
Credere: nec metuit surgentes pampinus Austros,
Aut actum cœlo magnis Aquilonibus imbrem:
Sed trudit gemmas, et frondes explicat omnes.

336. Non crediderim alios dies illuxisse *in* prima origine crescentis mundi, habuisseve alium tenorem: illud *tempus* erat ver

Non alios primâ crescentis origine mundi
Illuxisse dies, aliumve habuisse tenorem
Crediderim: ver illud erat, ver magnus agebat
Orbis, et hybernis parcebant flatibus Euri;
Cùm primùm lucem pecudes hausere, virûmque
Ferrea progenies duris caput extulit arvis,
Immissæque feræ sylvis, et sidera cœlo.
Nec res hunc teneræ possent perferre laborem,

NOTES.

319. *Rubenti:* blooming—blushing; in the sense of *purpureo.*

320. *Candida avis:* the Ciconia, or stork. So esteemed was this bird on account of its destroying serpents and noxious reptiles, that in Thessaly, Pliny informs us, it was a capital crime for any person to kill one; hence, *invisa longis colubris.*

325. *Tum omnipotens pater:* then almighty father Æther descends into the bosom of his joyous spouse in fructifying showers, and great himself, mingling with her great body, nourishes all her offspring.

These lines are extremely beautiful, as well as this whole description of spring. The Æther, or air, by the poets, is frequently called Jupiter, on account, perhaps, of its great utility, and its necessity to life and vegetation; and because of the intimate connexion between the surrounding air and the earth, the poet represents the latter as Juno, calling it the spouse of Jove.

328. *Avia virgulta:* the sequestered woods, or thickets. *Avius* is evidently compounded of the Greek *alpha*, negativum, and *via*, a way. We meet with several instances of the like composition in the Latin language: as *demens*, of *de* and *mens*, *amens*, &c.

331. *Arva laxant*, &c. The fields open their bosom to the warm breezes of the zephyrs. This is extremely beautiful, and highly poetical.

332. *Germina.* The usual reading is *gramina.* Heyne reads *germina.* Burmanus, Martyn, Vossius, and some others, do the same. It is evidently the better.

340. *Cum primùm*, &c. This is an allusion to the deluge, which, the poets say, happened in the reign of Deucalion, king of Thessaly, of which he and his wife Pyrrha were the only survivors. Being grieved at the general destruction of men, they were directed by an oracle to cast behind them the bones of their great mother, which they understood to be stones, and they should instantly spring up into men. See Ec. vi. 41.

341. *Duris arvis:* stony fields. *Ferrea* because they sprang up all armed and equipped for war.

343. *Res teneræ.* It is not certain whether the poet here speaks of spring at the creation of the world, or returns to his description of spring in general. In the former case, *res teneræ* will be the tender and infant creation; in the latter, the tender productions of nature. Dr. Trapp takes it in this latter case, and understands by *teneræ*, frail, an epithet, says he, which was, and ever will be, proper for all sublunary things. Ruæus seems to take it in the for-

Si non tanta quies iret, frigusque caloremque
Inter; et exciperet cœli indulgentia terras.
Quod superest; quæcumque premes virgulta per agros,
Sparge fimo pingui, et multâ memor occule terrâ:
Aut lapidem bibulum, aut squalentes infode conchas.
Inter enim labentur aquæ, tenuisque subibit
Halitus, atque animos tollent sata; jamque reperti,
Qui saxo super atque ingentis pondere testæ
Urgerent: hoc effusos munimen ad imbres;
Hoc, ubi hiulca siti findit canis æstifer arva.
Seminibus positis, superest deducere terram
Sæpiùs ad capita, et duros jactare bidentes;
Aut presso exercere solum sub vomere, et ipsa
Flectere luctantes inter vineta juvencos:
Tum leves calamos, et rasæ hastilia virgæ,
Fraxineasque aptare sudes, furcasque bicornes:
Viribus eniti quarum, et contemnere ventos
Assuescant, summasque sequi tabulata per ulmos.
Ac, dum prima novis adolescit frondibus ætas,
Parcendum teneris: et dum se lætus ad auras
Palmes agit, laxis per purum immissus habenis,
Ipsa aciê nondum falcis tentanda; sed uncis
Carpendæ manibus frondes, interque legendæ.
Inde ubi jam validis amplexæ stirpibus ulmos

348. Infode circum et bibulum lapidem aut squalentes conchas: enim inter *eas*

350. Reperti *sunt homines*, qui urgerent *illa* super saxo, atque

352. Hoc *est* munimen ad effusos imbres: hoc *est munimen*, ubi æstifer canis findit

358. *Superest* tum aptare *vitibus*

363. Parcendum *est tibi* teneris *vitibus*, dum prima

365. Ipsa *vitis* nondum tentanda acie falcis

NOTES.

mer sense. *Mundus adhuc tener*, says he. Heyne follows the opinion of Dr. Trapp, and by *teneræ res* understands the young and tender vegetation in general. Davidson is of the same opinion. *Hunc laborem:* this suffering, viz. the extremes of heat and cold.

345. *Exciperet:* in the sense of *excepisset.* So *iret* in the preceding line, for *ivisset. Exciperet:* had favored—visited.

346. *Premes:* in the sense of *plantabis. Virgulta:* in the sense of *surculos.*

348. *Infode bibulum lapidem:* bury around them the spongy stone, and rough shells.

349. *Tenuis halitus*, &c. This is said probably from an opinion, that a circulation of air about the root was necessary to the growth of the plant or scion. *Sata:* in the sense of *surculi. Animos:* in the sense of *vires.*

352. *Effusos imbres:* excessive, or immoderate rains.

353. *Æstifer canis:* the sultry dog. This is a star in the mouth of the great dog, a constellation in the heavens. It is said to have a considerable influence, while in conjunction with the sun, upon the heat of the weather. This space of time is usually denominated the dog-days. The name of the star is *Sirius.*

355. *Capita:* here plainly means the roots; which are so called, either because by them they draw nourishment from the earth as by a mouth; or because, by propagating the vine by the layer, the top was placed into the ground, which consequently became the root. Ruæus says, *radices. Bidentes: Bidens* was a kind of rake or hoe, having two teeth or forks—a grubbing hoe; compounded of *bis* and *dens. Seminibus positis:* in the sense of *surculis defossis*, vel *plantatis.*

358. *Hastilia:* poles pointed like spears. *Rasæ virgæ:* of peeled wood—the bark taken off to render them more smooth. *Virgi. decorticatis*, says Ruæus.

359. *Bicornes furcas:* two-pronged forks. *Bicornis*, of *bis* and *cornu.*

360. *Quarum viribus:* by whose support they may accustom themselves to rise, or mount up.

361. *Tabulata.* These were branches of elms extended at proper distances, to sustain the vine and enable it to spread. We have no word in English answering to it.

364. *Immissus laxis habenis:* rushing forth with loosened reins. This is a metaphor taken from the horses in the race. *Agit;* in the sense of *erigit.*

365. *Acie falcis.* This is the reading of Heyne, Valpy, and some others. *Acies*, in the nom. is the common reading. The vine is not to be attempted with the pruning-knife, but the leaves are to be plucked and carefully culled by the bending hand, *interlegendæ.*

367. *Validis stirpibus:* with strong wreaths—stems. *String :* thin—trim off.

Exierint ; tum stringe comas, tum brachia tonde :
Antè reformidant ferrum : tum denique dura
Exerce imperia, et ramos compesce fluentes.
Texendæ sepes etiam, et pecus omne tenendum,
Præcipuè dum frons tenera, imprudensque laborum :
Cui, super indignas hyemes, Solemque potentem,
Sylvestres uri assiduè capreæque sequaces
Illudunt : pascuntur oves, avidæque juvencæ.
Frigora nec tantùm canâ concreta pruinâ,
Aut gravis incumbens scopulis arentibus æstas ;
Quantùm illi nocuere greges, durique venenum
Dentis, et admorso signata in stirpe cicatrix.
Non aliam ob culpam Baccho caper omnibus aris
Cæditur, et veteres ineunt proscenia ludi ;
Præmiaque ingeniis pagos et compita circùm,
Thesidæ posuere : atque inter pocula læti
Mollibus in pratis unctos saliere per utres.
Necnon Ausonii, Trojâ gens missa, coloni
Versibus incomptis ludunt, risuque soluto :
Oraque corticibus sumunt horrenda cavatis.
Et te, Bacche, vocant per carmina læta, tibique
Oscilla ex altâ suspendunt mollia pinu.

371. Sepes texendæ *est circùm vites*, et omne pecus tenendum *est ab illis* :

376. Nec frigora concreta cana pruinâ, aut gravis æstas incumbens arentibus scopulis, nocuere *vitibus* tantùm, quantùm illi greges

NOTES.

370. *Exerce dura imperia:* exercise rigid sway—rule them imperiously. *Fluentes:* superfluous—wide-spreading.

372. *Imprudens laborum:* unused—unaccustomed to hardships.

373. *Indignas:* in the sense of *duras*, vel *sævas*. *Super:* in the sense of *præter*.

375. *Illudunt:* in the sense of *nocent*.

377. *Gravis æstas:* excessive heat.

381. *Proscenia.* The Roman theatre was of a semi-circular form, and divided into four parts. The *porticus*, or gallery. Here were the seats for the common people, in the form of a wedge, and were called *Cunei*. The *Orchestra* was the inner part, or centre of the theatre. Here the senators and equites sat, and the dancers and musicians performed. The *Proscenium* was the space between the *Orchestra* and *Scena*, more elevated than the former, but lower than the latter. Here the actors performed. The *Scena* was that part over against the spectators. The *Postscenium* was the place behind the *Scena*, or curtain, where the actors retired. The amphitheatre was built in a circular form, with nothing to obstruct the view from any part. Seats were all around it, and in the middle was a large open space or area, where the gladiators and wild beasts used to fight.

382. *Ingeniis:* to genius, or wit. The common reading is *ingentes*, an epithet entirely useless. Davidson, on the authority of Pierius, reads *ingeniis*. He says he found it so in the most ancient manuscripts. It is also the reading of Heyne and Burmannus.

383. *Theseidæ:* the Athenians, so called from *Theseus*, one of their kings, the son of Ægeus and Æthra. He taught them to live in cities, and contributed much to their civilization. Tragedy is said to have originated among the Athenians. Thespis, one of their poets, hath the honor of inventing it. It is said he performed in a kind of cart.

384. *Unctos utres.* The *utres* were bags of goat skins filled with wind, and besmeared with oil. At the feasts of Bacchus, it was the custom to leap upon them with one foot, and being slippery, often caused the leaper or dancer to fall, which always excited mirth and laughter in the by-standers.

385. *Coloni.* *Colonus* signifies both a tiller of the earth, and any inhabitant of a country. In this last sense it seems to be used here, denoting the Romans generally. They were originally a colony of Trojans, led into Italy by Æneas. Hence the propriety of their being called *gens missa Trojâ*. *Ausonii:* an adj. from *Ausonia*, the original name of Italy: in the sense of *Romani*, vel *Itali*.

386. *Soluto:* in the sense of *immodico*.

387. *Ora:* in the sense of *larvas*, masks.

389. *Oscilla.* These most probably were small earthen images of Bacchus, hung upon the branches of trees, where they swung, and were turned about by the wind. They were supposed to confer fertility to the vine, in whatever direction they chanced to turn their faces. *Mollia:* moveable, because they turned easily, and obeyed every breeze; or perhaps, effeminate, because Bacchus was

Hinc omnis largo pubescit vinea fœtu:
Complentur vallesque cavæ saltusque profundi,
Et quòcumque Deus circùm caput egit honestum.

392. Et *locus*, quocumque Deus circumagit

Ergò ritè suum Baccho dicemus honorem
Carminibus patriis, lancesque et liba feremus;
Et ductus cornu stabit sacer hircus ad aram:
Pinguiaque in verubus torrêbimus exta colurnis
Est etiam ille labor curandis vitibus alter,
Cui nunquam exhausti satìs est; namque omne quotannis
Terque quaterque solum scindendum, glebaque versis
Æternùm frangenda bidentibus, omne levandum
Fronde nemus. Redit agricolis labor actus in orbem,
Atque in se sua per vestigia volvitur annus.
Et jam olim seras posuit cùm vinea frondes,
Frigidus et sylvis Aquilo decussit honorem;
Jam tum acer curas venientem extendit in annum
Rusticus, et curvo Saturni dente relictam
Persequitur vitem attondens, fingitque putando.
Primus humum fodito, primus devecta cremato
Sarmenta, et vallos primus sub tecta referto:
Postremus metito. Bis vitibus ingruit umbra:
Bis segetem densis obducunt sentibus herbæ:
Durus uterque labor. Laudato ingentia rura,
Exiguum colito. Necnon etiam aspera rusci
Vimina per sylvam, et ripis fluvialis arundo

413. Aspera vimina rusci *cæduntur* per sylvam, et fluvialis arundo cæditur ripis

NOTES.

always represented as youthful and debauched. *Mobilia*, says Heyne.

390. *Fœtu:* in the sense of *proventu*, says Heyne.

393. *Honorem:* in the sense of *laudes*.

396. *Colurnis verubus:* hazle-spits. The hazle seems here to be mentioned, as the instrument on which the sacrifice was to be roasted, because it was injurious to the vine. The goat was sacred to Bacchus, and usually offered to him. See 380, supra.

397. *Est etiam ille alter:* there is also another labor. *Curandis:* in the sense of *colendis*. The dat. is here plainly used in the sense of the gen. But this construction is common with the poets.

398. *Satis exhausti:* enough of pains taken. *Exhaustum*, though properly a part. of the verb *exhaurio*, is here used as a substantive, governed by the adv. *satis*.

400. *Æternùm:* in the sense of *assiduè*. *Bidentibus:* the same with *ligonibus*. *Nemus:* in the sense of *vinea*, vel *vinetum*.

401. *Actus in orbem:* that is, *perpetuus*, vel *continuus:* because there is no end or termination in a circle.

402. *Annus:* in the sense of *annuus labor*, vel *annua opera*. The same labor or work is to be done every year, and it returns in the same order and course.

404. *Decussit honorem:* hath shaken from the trees their beauty and foliage.

406. *Curvo dente:* with the crooked knife of Saturn. The scythe, or pruning-hook, was the badge of Saturn. *Relictam:* deprived of its fruit and foliage, like a forlorn mother bereaved of her children. Nothing can surpass this in force and beauty. *Dente:* in the sense of *falce*.

408. *Primus.* The poet here advises the vintager to be the first to perform every piece of business belonging to his vineyard; such as digging and mellowing the ground, carrying home and burning the useless branches (*sarmenta*) of the vine, and carrying home and securing from the weather the stakes and poles (*vallos*) that supported the vine; but to be the last to gather his grapes, as they would grow better by remaining on the vine, and having a longer time to ripen.

410. *Bis umbra*, &c. The vine requires to be cleared of its superfluous leaves twice in the season, and twice to be cleared of weeds and grass. This circumstance will explain the words of the poet.

411. *Sentibus:* with weeds—briars.

412. *Laudato.* The poet here means: you may admire a large farm, but be sure to till a small one: or, you may praise a large one in the possession of another, but you should prefer a small one yourself, because you will find it in the end more profitable.

413. *Rusci:* the shrub called the butcher's broom.

416 Vites vinctæ *ulmis* jam *reponunt falcem*

422. *Radices* hæserunt arvis, *verticesque earum* tulerunt auras. Tellus ipsa, cum recluditur unco dente, sufficit humorem satis *oleis:* et *sufficiet* gravidas fruges cùm *recluditur* vomere:

432. *E quibus* nocturni ignes

439. Juvat videre arva non obnoxia rastris, non ulli curæ hominum.

Cæditur; incultique exercet cura salicti.
Jam vinctæ vites, jam falcem arbusta reponunt,
Jam canit extremos effœtus vinitor antes:
Sollicitanda tamen tellus, pulvisque movendus:
Et jam maturis metuendus Jupiter uvis.
Contrà, non ulla est oleis cultura: neque illæ
Procurvam expectant falcem, rastrosque tenaces;
Cùm semel hæserunt arvis, aurasque tulerunt.
Ipsa satis tellus, cùm dente recluditur unco,
Sufficit humorem, et gravidas cùm vomere fruges.
Hoc pinguem et placitam paci nutritor olivam.
Poma quoque, ut primùm truncos sensere valentes,
Et vires habuere suas, ad sidera raptim
Vi propriâ nituntur, opisque haud indiga nostræ.
Nec minùs intereà fœtu nemus omne gravescit,
Sanguineisque inculta rubent aviaria baccis.
Tondentur cytisi: tædas sylva alta ministrat,
Pascunturque ignes nocturni, et lumina fundunt.
Et dubitant homines serere, atque impendere curam?
Quid majora sequar? salices, humilesque genistæ,
Aut illæ pecori frondem, aut pastoribus umbram
Sufficiunt; sepemque satis, et pabula melli.
Et juvat undantem buxo spectare Cytorum,
Naryciæque picis lucos: juvat arva videre,
Non rastris, hominum non ulli obnoxia curæ.

NOTES.

415. *Salicti:* willow-ground. The pron. *te*, is to be supplied after *exercet*.

416. *Reponunt.* In the language of poetry, the vines are said to lay aside the pruning knife, when they no longer stand in need of its being applied to them. This takes place when they have sufficiently embraced or entwined around the elms, and other trees planted in the vineyard for the purpose of supporting them. *Vinctæ:* in the sense of *ligatæ*, says Ruæus. *Arbusta:* in the sense of *vineta*. See Ecl. i. 40.

417. *Effœtus vinitor:* the wearied vintager sings his last rows—that he hath gotten to his last rows. *Pervenit ad extremos ordines* (*antes*) *vitium*, says Heyne.

419. *Jupiter:* the air, or weather.

423. *Unco dente.* *Dens* is any instrument of one tine or fork for opening the earth about the roots of trees or plants, or for loosening the ground in any way. The meaning of the poet is: that the earth of itself, if opened and kept loose with this instrument, will afford sufficient moisture to the olives (*satis*) lately planted; but if opened and kept loose with the plough, it will render the olive more thrifty, and cause it to bear a fruit full, large, and good. Ploughing the land, says Mr. Martyn, is always considered to increase the produce of the olive. This circumstance fully explains the poet's meaning; which Ruæus, and Dr. Trapp after him, evidently mistook, considering it as an hyperbole, denoting that the fruit would be almost coeval with the ploughing. *Statim cum ipso vomere*, says Ruæus.

425. *Hôc:* with this—the plough. Or *ob hoc*, according to Servius, on account of this facility in propagating. *Placitam paci;* delighting in peace.

426. *Poma:* the fruits: by meton. put for the trees that bore them.

429. *Omne nemus:* Heyne says, *omne genus arborum*.

431. *Cytisi tondentur.* This may mean either browsed upon by cattle, or cut and prepared for their use. The *cytisus* was a shrub much esteemed for its property of causing cattle to give excellent milk. *Tædas:* torches—materials for making torches.

433. *Serere:* to plant them.

434. *Salices:* the willows. *Genistæ:* the brooms. *Sequar majora:* in the sense of *commemorem majores arbores*.

436. *Pabula melli:* materials for honey—flowers for the bees.

437. *Cytorum:* Cytorus, a mountain in Paphlagonia, in the neighborhood of the Euxine sea, abounding in the box-tree.

438. *Naryciæ:* an adj. from *Naryx*, or *Narycia*, a city in that part of Italy called *Magna Græcia*. It abounded in trees of the pitch and resinous kind.

439. *Non obnoxia:* not requiring—not exposed to. Ruæus says, *non egentia*.

Ipsa Caucaseo steriles in vertice sylvæ,
Quas animosi Euri assiduè franguntque feruntque,
Dant alios aliæ fœtus; dant utile lignum
Navigiis pinos, domibus cedrosque cupressosque.
Hinc radios trivere rotis, hinc tympana plaustris
Agricolæ, et pandas ratibus posuere carinas.
Viminibus salices fœcundæ, frondibus ulmi:
At myrtus validis hastilibus, et bona bello
Cornus; Ityræos taxi torquentur in arcus.
Nec tiliæ leves, aut torno rasile buxum,
Non formam accipiunt, ferroque cavantur acuto.
Necnon et torrentem undam levis innatat alnus
Missa Pado; necnon et apes examina condunt
Corticibusque cavis, vitiosæque ilicis alveo.
Quid memorandum æquè Baccheïa dona tulerunt?
Bacchus et ad culpam causas dedit: ille furentes
Centauros leto domuit, Rhœtumque, Pholumque,
Et magno Hylæum Lapithis cratere minantem.
  O fortunatos nimiùm, sua si bona nôrint,
Agricolas! quibus ipsa, procul discordibus armis,
Fundit humo facilem victum justissima tellus.
Si non ingentem foribus domus alta superbis
Manè salutantûm totis vomit ædibus undam;
Nec varios inhiant pulchrâ testudine postes,
Illusasque auro vestes, Ephyreïaque æra;
Alba neque Assyrio fucatur lana veneno,
Nec casiâ liquidi corrumpitur usus olivi:

442. Dant alios fœtus: aliæ dant pinos, lignum utile navigiis, *aliæ dant* cedrosque cupressosque, *lignum utile* domibus:

447. Myrtus *est bona* validis hastilibus,

449. Necnon leves

454. Quid Baccheia dona tulerunt æquè memorandum?

461. Si *apud illos* alta domus *cum* superbis foribus non vomit ingentem undam *hominum* salutantûm manè *è* totis ædibus; nec *illi* inhiant

NOTES.

440. *Caucaseo:* an adj. from *Caucasus*, a mountain, or rather range of mountains, extending from the Euxine to the Caspian sea.

444. *Tympana:* the naves or felloes of the wheel, in which the (*radii*) spokes are fastened. Some take the *tympanum* to be a solid wheel, or one without spokes. *Trivêre:* in the sense of *fecerunt*, vel *tornaverunt*.

447. *Bello:* for war—the implements or weapons of war. *Ad alia arma*, says Ruæus.

448. *Ityræos:* an adj. from *Ityræi*, a people of Parthia, according to Servius; but others say of Syria, famous for shooting the bow. *Cornus:* the corneil-tree, or wild cherry-tree. *Taxi:* the yew-trees. *Buxum:* the box-tree, or box-wood. Pierius found, in some ancient manuscripts, *curvantur* for *torquentur*. Ruæus says, *flectuntur*.

451. *Alnus:* the alder-tree, of which boats were at first made. They were dug out of the solid wood. *Pado:* the Po, the largest river in Italy, put for any river.

453. *Alveo:* cavity.

454. *Memorandum:* in the sense of *dignum laude*, or simply, *laudandum*.

456. *Centauros—Lapithis.* These were people of Thessaly, the former inhabiting mount Pelion, the latter mount Pindus. The poet here mentions the principal or chief of the Centaurs only.

459. *Discordibus armis:* not wars, for that would not be strictly true. They rage in the country, as well as city; but rather factions, quarrels, and civil commotions, which are more frequent in cities and populous towns, than in the country.

460. *Facilem:* easy procured. *Justissima:* the earth may be considered most just, because it returns what is committed to it, with a liberal reward. *Fundit:* in the sense of *producit*.

461. *Si non*, &c. It was a custom among the Romans, for clients and dependants to come early in the morning to salute their patrons. *Undam:* in the sense of *multitudinem*.

463. *Varios:* in the sense of *variatos*.

464. *Illusas auro:* embroidered with gold. *Ephyreïa:* an adj. from *Ephyra*, the original name of Corinth. Ruæus says, *Corinthia*.

465. *Assyrio veneno:* with the Syrian, or purple color. The invention of the purple, and the method of dying that color are attributed to the Syrians, or Phœnicians. Phœnicia was a part of that region of Asia, called Syria; sometimes Assyria, Cœlosyria, and Leucosyria. Syria and Assyria were frequently confounded.

466. *Casiâ:* the bark of a tree, or shrub, in India, used as a spice—bastard cinna-

467. At *apud illos* secura quies

At secura quies, et nescia fallere vita,
Dives opum variarum; at latis otia fundis,
Speluncæ, vivique lacus; at frigida Tempe,
Mugitusque boum, mollesque sub arbore somni

471. Illic *sunt* saltus

Non absunt. Illic saltus, ac lustra ferarum,
Et patiens operum parvoque assueta juventus,
Sacra Deûm, santique patres. Extrema per illos
Justitia excedens terris vestigia fecit.
Me verò primùm dulces ante omnia Musæ,

476. Perculsus ingenti amore *earum*

Quarum sacra fero, ingenti perculsus amore,
Accipiant; cœlique vias et sidera monstrent,
Defectus Solis varios, Lunæque labores:
Unde tremor terris: quâ vi maria alta tumescant
Objicibus ruptis, rursusque in seipsa residant:
Quid tantùm Oceano properent se tingere Soles
Hyberni: vel quæ tardis mora noctibus obstet.
Sin, has ne possim naturæ accedere partes,
Frigidus obstiterit circùm præcordia sanguis;
Rura mihi et rigui placeant in vallibus amnes,

NOTES.

mon. The ancients used it to flavor their oil. *Liquidi:* in the sense of *puri.*

467. *Vita nescia fellere:* a life knowing not to deceive—a life of substantial happiness, in opposition to that of cities and courts, which is showy, false, and deceitful.

468. *Latis:* some copies have *lætis.* Heyne takes it in the sense of *apertis* vel *patentibus.*

469. *Tempe:* neu. plu. A most pleasant vale in Thessaly, surrounded by the mountains Ossa, Pelion, and Olympus. The river *Peneus* flows through it. The poet here means any pleasant vale, putting the *species* for the *genus.* *Vivi lacus:* in the sense of *perennis aqua.* *Frigida Tempe,* for *umbrosæ valles.*

474. *Justitia:* the goddess *Astræa.* See Ecl. iv. 6.

475. *Verò primùm ante:* but, in the first place, above all things, may the sweet muses accept of me, whose sacred ensigns, &c. Though the poet praises the country life so much, he prefers the charms of poetry, and the noble entertainments of science, particularly philosophy and astronomy. The muses presided not only over poetry, but also over the sciences and liberal arts. The poets called themselves the priests of the muses. Hence the propriety of *quarum sacra fero.*

477. *Vias et sidera cœli:* in the sense of *cursus siderum in cœlo.*

479. *Unde tremor terris:* whence earthquakes arise: by what power the deep seas swell. *Objicibus ruptis:* its barriers being broken down. The poet is speaking of the ebbing and flowing of the tide. He hath in his view the swelling of a mighty stream. It rises with the mountain torrent. It rushes against the opposing mounds. Here it is stopped in its course for a time; but gathering strength from its accumulated waters, it bursts the barriers, sweeping every thing in its course. *Vis:* here, not simply violence or force, but the moving or efficient cause of the rising of the waters. The true cause of the ebbing and flowing of the tide was not known, till the immortal Sir Isaac Newton placed it beyond doubt. He demonstrated it to be the attraction of the heavenly bodies, particularly of the moon.

481. *Quid tantùm,* &c. The poet here speaks of winter and summer. What may be the reason, why the winter days are so quick in ending; and what delay may put off, or retard the approach of the summer nights. What may be the reason that the days in summer are so long. *Tingere:* in the sense of *occidere.*

484. *Sin frigidus sanguis:* but if cold blood around my heart should hinder, that I could not, &c. *Secundum Physicos, qui dicunt stultos homines esse frigidioris sanguinis, prudentes calidi. Unde et senes, in quibus jam friget; et pueri, in quibus necdum calet, minus sapiunt;* says Servius. *Præcordia:* properly a membrane surrounding the heart, and separating it from the lungs. It is taken often for the heart itself, as in the present instance.

485. *Rigui:* in the sense of *fluentes.* The meaning of the poet appears to be: that if he had not capacity for the higher subjects of philosophy and astronomy, he would retire into the country, and there pass his time, unheeded and unknown, amidst rural delights.

Flumina amem sylvasque inglorius. O ubi campi,
Sperchiusque, et virginibus bacchata Lacænis
Taygeta! ô qui me gelidis in vallibus Hæmi
Sistat, et ingenti ramorum protegat umbrâ!
Felix, qui potuit rerum cognoscere causas,
Atque metus omnes et inexorabile fatum
Subjecit pedibus, strepitumque Acherontis avari!
Fortunatus et ille, Deos qui novit agrestes,
Panaque, Sylvanumque senem, Nymphasque sorores!
Illum non populi fasces, non purpura regum
Flexit, et infidos agitans discordia fratres;
Aut conjurato descendens Dacus ab Istro:
Non res Romanæ, perituraque regna: neque ille,
Aut doluit miserans inopem, aut invidit habenti.
Quos rami fructus, quos ipsa volentia rura
Sponte tulere suâ, carpsit; nec ferrea jura,
Insanumque forum, aut populi tabularia vidit.
Sollicitant alii remis freta cæca, ruuntque
In ferrum, penetrant aulas et limina regum.

486. O *si essem*, ubi *sunt* campi, *fluvius*que Sperchius, et Taygeta.
487. O *sit aliquis*, qui sistat me
490. *Ille est* felix, qui potuit

NOTES.

486. *O, ubi—O qui*, &c. These, as Mr. Davidson justly observes, are not questions, as Ruæus and Dr. Trapp both take them; but exclamations, which in all languages are usually elliptical. *Campi: Tempe*, those pleasant fields of Thessaly are undoubtedly intended. *Sperchius:* a river of Thessaly, rising at the foot of mount *Pindus*, and falls into the *Sinus Maliacus*.

488. *Taygeta:* neu. pleu. a mountain of Laconia, famous for hunting, and the celebration of the *orgies* of Bacchus: hence, *Viginibus bacchata Lacænis;* frequented by the Laconian or Spartan virgins. *Hæmi.* See Geor. i. 49.

492. *Acherontis:* Acheron, a fabulous river of hell. It seems here to be put for death. In that sense the epithet *avari* is very proper. *Strepitum*, &c. will then mean the noise or tumultuous dread generally occasioned through the fear of death. Or, it may mean, the noise, tumult, and bustle of the infernal regions generally. In this last case, *Acherontis* will mean hell, or the infernal regions, by synec.

494. *Pana.* See Ecl. ii. 31. *Nymphas sorores.* See Ecl. ii. 46. *Sylvanum.* See Ecl. x. 24.

495. *Non fasces populi:* not the honors of the people, nor the purple, &c. The Roman magistrates were chosen by the people, in the *Comitia*. The *fasces*, properly, was a bundle of birchen rods. The dictator had 24 of these rods—the consuls 12—the provincial prætors 6—the city prætors 2; which were carried before them by persons, who were called lictors. *Fasces* is frequently put for the power and authority of the magistrate, by meton. *Flexit:* in the sense of *movet.*

497. *Dacus.* The *Dacii* were a people inhabiting the north of the Danube, or Ister, very troublesome to the Romans. *Istro conjurato:* the conspiring, or leagued Danube. The name of the river put for the people living near it, by meton. The Danube is one of the largest rivers in Europe. It rises in Germany, and taking an easterly course, it falls into the Euxine sea by six mouths, at a distance of about 1600 miles from its source.

498. *Res Romanæ:* the Roman republic. It is opposed to *regna peritura.* The former they vainly imagined would always endure; while kingdoms would fall, and their names be forgotten. *Flexerunt illum*, is understood.

499. *Doluit miserans*, &c. The poet could not mean that his countryman possessed a stoical apathy, which rendered him insensible to the wants, and deaf to the calls of the poor; but that in the country, there were not those objects of poverty and wretchedness to excite his grief and compassion; or at least, few of them in comparison to the number in cities. In this very circumstance, we see a high commendation of a country life.

501. *Ferrea jura:* the same as *duras leges.*

502. *Insanum:* noisy—tumultuous, or, perhaps, litigious. *Tabularia.* The *tabularium* was a place at Rome, in which the public records were kept, and the accounts of the public money received, and paid out. It answers to our treasury office. *Cæca:* in the sense of *ignota.*

504. *Penetrant*, &c. *Insinuant se principibus, ut intimi fiant*, says Servius.

Hic petit excidiis urbem miserosque Penates,
Ut gemmâ bibat, et Sarrano indormiat ostro:
Condit opes alius, defossoque incubat auro:
Hic stupet attonitus rostris: hunc plausus hiantem
Per cuneos (geminatur enim) plebisque patrumque
Corripuit; gaudent perfusi sanguine fratrum,
Exilioque domos et dulcia limina mutant,
Atque alio patriam quærunt sub Sole jacentem.
Agricola incurvo terram dimovit aratro:
Hinc anni labor: hinc patriam, parvosque nepotes
Sustinet: hinc armenta boum, meritosque juvencos
Nec requies; quin, aut pomis exuberet annus,
Aut fœtu pecorum, aut Cerealis mergite culmi:
Proventuque oneret sulcos, atque horrea vincat.
Venit hyems; teritur Sicyonia bacca trapetis:
Glande sues læti redeunt: dant arbuta sylvæ:
Et varios ponit fœtus autumnus; et altè
Mitis in apricis coquitur vindemia saxis.
Intereà dulces pendent circùm oscula nati:
Casta pudicitiam servat domus: ubera vaccæ
Lactea demittunt: pinguesque in gramine læto
Inter se adversis luctantur cornibus hœdi

510. *Alii* gaudent perfusi

514. Hinc *est* labor anni: hinc *agricola* sustinet

516. Nec requies *est anno;* quin

523. Dulces nati pendent circùm oscula *parentum:*

NOTES.

505. *Penates.* These were the household gods; and were thought to preside over houses and domestic affairs. Their statues or images were usually made of wax, ivory, silver, or earth, and generally placed in the innermost part of the house: hence that place was called *Penetrale:* and they were called sometimes, from that circumstance, *Penetrales.* They were worshipped with wine, incense, fruits, and sometimes with the sacrifice of a lamb. *Penates*, by meton. is used for one's country, habitation, house, or dwelling: and sometimes for the family, or inhabitants, as in the present instance. See Æn. ii. 717.

506. *Sarrano ostro:* upon Tyrian purple. *Sarrano*, an adj. from *Sarra*, the ancient name of Tyre. *Gemma:* a cup made, or set with gems.

508. *Rostris.* The *Rostrum* was the place of common pleas, at Rome, so called, as Livy informs us, from this circumstance: The *Antiates*, a maritime people of *Latium*, being overcome by the Romans; to perpetuate the memory of the victory, they placed the beaks of their ships (*rostra*) around the *suggestum*, or place of pleading, by way of ornament. *Hic stupet:* this one stands amazed, being astonished at the courts of justice. *Plausus patrumque plebisque*, &c. It appears that the orders of patricians and plebeians expressed their approbation by turns. If we suppose the patricians, who occupied the *Orchestra*, or the part of the theatre near the stage, to be the first; this will give a reason for the words, *enim geminatur per cuneos:* for it is redoubled, or repeated along the *cunei.* These were seats in the back part of the theatre, appropriated to the common people, or plebeians. See 381. supra. *Hunc:* in the sense of *alium.* *Geminatur.* Heyne reads *Geminatus*, agreeing with *plausus;* without a parenthesis.

512. *Sub alio sole:* under another sun—in another clime. This is beautiful, and highly poetical.

516. *Nec requies:* there is no rest: but the year abounds either, &c. This passage is extremely beautiful and poetical. The poet represents the year as laboring without intermission, in bringing forth her productions. Ruæus refers the whole of this fine passage to the husbandman: *Nec cessat agricola donec annus abundet*, &c. says he. But he gives no reason for his taking *quin* in the sense of *donec.*

517. *Mergite Cerealis culmi:* with bundles or sheaves of grain.

519. *Sicyonia:* an adj. from *Sicyon*, a city of Achaia, not far from the isthmus of Corinth, abounding in olive trees. *Bacca:* the olive.

520. *Arbuta:* properly the fruit of the arbute tree. Here, perhaps, taken for wild fruit in general. *Læti:* in the sense of *saturati.*

521. *Ponit fœtus:* in the sense of *dat*, vel *reddit fructus.*

524. *Casta domus:* the virtuous family preserves, &c. By being trained to industry and good order, they are not in danger of losing their virtue, or character.

Ipse dies agitat festos: fususque per herbam,
Ignis ubi in medio, et socii cratera coronant,
Te libans, Lenæe, vocat: pecorisque magistris
Velocis jaculi certamina ponit in ulmo,
Corporaque agresti nudat prædura palæstrâ.
Hanc olim veteres vitam coluere Sabini,
Hanc Remus et frater: sic fortis Etruria crevit,
Scilicet et rerum facta est pulcherrima Roma,
Septemque una sibi muro circumdedit arces.
Antè etiam sceptrum Dictæi regis, et antè
Impia quàm cæsis gens est epulata juvencis;
Aureus hanc vitam in terris Saturnus agebat.
Necdum etiam audierant inflari classica, necdum
Impositos duris crepitare incudibus enses.
Sed nos immensum spatiis confecimus æquor,
Et jam tempus equûm fumantia solvere colla.

528. Ubi *est* ignis

533. Remus et frater *ejus Romulus coluerunt* hanc:

535. Unaque circumdedit septem

539. Necdum etiam *homines*

542. Tempus *est* solvere *à jugo*

NOTES.

527. *Agitat:* in the sense of *celebrat. Fusus:* in the sense of *stratus.*

528. *Coronant:* they fill up to the brim.

531. *Palæstra:* this may mean either the exercise itself, or the place of exercise.

532. *Sabini.* An ancient people of Italy, whose young women were seized by the Romans, at certain shows or exhibitions, to which they had been invited. Upon this, the Sabines made war upon them to avenge the atrocious deed. A treaty of amity, however, was concluded between the two parties; and in the event they became one people. *Coluere:* they religiously observed, or practised.

533. *Etruria:* the same as *Tuscia*, Tuscany, a country in Italy, separated from *Latium* by the Tyber.

534. *Scilicet et*, &c. What is here said of Rome was literally true in the time of Virgil. It was then in all its glory, and was truly the wonder of the world: *Rerum: res* hath a variety of significations. Here it evidently means the world, or the whole earth.

535. *Una circumdedit.* The walls of Rome embraced seven hills, when that city was in the height of its glory. Their names were: *Palatinus*, *Cœlius*, *Capitolinus*, *Aventinus*, *Esquilinus*, *Quirinalis*, and *Viminalis.*

536. *Antè sceptrum:* before the reign of the Dictean king. Jupiter is so called from *Dicte*, a place in the island of Crete, where it is said, he was nourished and brought up by the Corybantes or Curetes.

Before the reign of Jove, and before the impious race of men fed upon bullocks slain, golden Saturn led this life upon the earth. This is a beautiful allusion to the golden age. See Ecl. iv. 6. *Agebat:* in the sense of *ducebat.*

537. *Gens:* in the sense of *genus hominum*, says Heyne.

541. *Sed nos.* This is an allegory taken from the chariot race. By *confecimus æquor immensum spatiis*, the poet may mean that he had run over a plain not measured by stages; or one which did not lie within the limits or bounds of his proposed race or course. In this sense, divested of the figure, it will be: I have now finished my digression into the praises of a country life, it is time to lay aside my pen. Ruæus interprets *spatiis* by *longitudine*, and understands by *æquor immensum spatiis*, a plain immeasurable in length.

Each course of chariots in the race was called *spatium.* This was repeated seven times. Hence *spatia*, the plural, came to signify the race ground. *Cum septimo spatio palmæ appropinquant.*

The starting place was called *carcer*, and the turning place *meta.*

QUESTIONS.

What is the subject of this book?

What does the poet do in the first place?

How many methods does he mention for the propagation of trees?

What is the difference between grafting and inoculation?

For what is the *propago* or layer the best?

After the several kinds of trees, and the methods of producing them, what does the poet consider in the next place?

How many kinds of soil does he make?

Where does the Ganges rise?

What is its length?

What is it considered to be, by the inhabitants upon its banks?

Where does it empty?

What did the ancients call the bay?

What city now stands near the mouth of this river?

Of what country was *Hemus* a river?

What river did it receive in its course?
What was the *Pactolus* celebrated for?
Where did these rivers empty?
What was the Argonautic expedition?
Why was it so called?
Who commanded that expedition?
Where was Colchis?
What was the object of that expedition?
How is this fable to be understood?
How many accompanied Jason?
What direction does the poet give for planting trees?
How should the rows be arranged?
Among what people did scenic representations originate?
Why were the Athenians called *Theseidæ?*
Who may be considered the inventor of tragedy?
What did he make use of as a stage?
What was the form of the Roman theatre?
Into how many parts was it divided?
What was the form of the amphitheatre?
What was the original name of Italy?
Why were the Romans sometimes called *Ausones?*
What do you understand by the word *fasces?*
How many of these rods were carried before the Roman magistrates?
By whom were they carried?
For what is the word *fasces* used by meton.?
Who were the *Dacii?*
Where did they inhabit?
Where does the river *Ister* rise?
What course does it run?
Where does it empty?
What is its length?
Who were the *Penates?*
How were they represented?
Where were their statues placed?
What were they sometimes called from that circumstance?
For what is the word taken by meton.?
Why was the place of common please, at Rome, called *Rostrum?*
What was the word *Rostrum* properly?
Who were the *Sabines?*
Did the Romans offer any violence to their young women?
What was the event of the affair?
How many hills did the walls of Rome encompass?
What were they called?
How many courses were there in the ch' riot race?
How does the book end?

LIBER TERTIUS.

THE subject of this book is the raising of cattle. The poet begins with an invocation of some of the rural deities, and a compliment to Augustus. After which, he addresses himself to his friend Mæcenas. He then proceeds to give rules for the breeding and management of horses, oxen, sheep, and goats. And, by way of episode and embellishment, he gives us a description of a chariot race, of a battle of bulls, of the force of love, and of a Scythian winter. He enumerates the diseases incident to cattle, and prescribes their remedies: and concludes by giving an account of a fatal murrain, which once raged among the Alps.

1. Et te, O pastor, memorande ab Amphryso: *Canemus* vos, O Sylvæ
4. Omnia cætera car-

TE quoque, magna Pales, et te, memorande, canemus,
Pastor ab Amphryso: vos, sylvæ, amnesque Lycæi
Cætera, quæ vacuas tenuissent carmina mentes,
Omnia jam vulgata. Quis aut Eurysthea durum,

NOTES.

1. *Pales.* The goddess of shepherds, and of feeding cattle. She was worshipped with milk. Her feasts were called *Palilia*, and were celebrated on the 12th of the calends of May.

2. *Amphryso.* A river of Thessaly, where Apollo fed the flocks of Admetus, when he was driven from heaven for having killed the Cyclops. See Ecl. iv. 10. *Sylvæ, et amnes Lycæi:* the groves and streams of Arcadia. *Lycæus:* a mountain in Arcadia, evidently taken for the whole country, by synec.

3. *Carmina:* by meton. the argument, or subjects of song. Heyne reads *carmine*, connecting it with *vacuas.* In this case, it is to be taken in its usual sense. *Tenuissent:* in the sense of *delectavissent.* Ruæus says, *omnia argumenta.*

4. *Eurysthea.* Eurystheus, was king of *Mycenæ.* Instigated by Juno, he imposed upon Hercules, who had been given up to

Aut illaudati nescit Busiridis aras?
Cui non dictus Hylas puer, et Latonia Delos,
Hippodameque, humeroque Pelops insignis eburno,
Acer equis? Tentanda via est, quâ me quoque possim
Tollere humo, victorque virûm volitare per ora.
Primus ego in patriam mecum (modò vita supersit)
Aonio rediens deducam vertice Musas:
Primus Idumæas referam tibi, Mantua, palmas:
Et viridi in campo templum de marmore ponam
Propter aquam, tardis ingens ubi flexibus errat
Mincius, et tenerâ prætexit arundine ripas.
In medio mihi Cæsar erit, templumque tenebit.
Illi victor ego, et Tyrio conspectus in ostro,
Centum quadrijugos agitabo ad flumina currus.
Cuncta mihi, Alpheum linquens lucosque Molorchi,

mina, quæ tenuissent vacuas mentes, jam vulgata *sunt*.

NOTES.

him at the command of an oracle, the severest labors: they were twelve in number, and go under the name of the twelve labors of Hercules.

5. *Busiridis.* Busiris, a king of Egypt, who sacrificed to his gods the strangers who visited him. He was slain by Hercules. *Illaudati:* impious—infamous. This kind of negatives express, generally, more than the mere want of a good quality. They imply the possession of a contrary one. *Detestati*, says Heyne.

6. *Hylas.* See Ecl. vi. 43. *Latonia:* an adj. from *Latona*, the daughter of *Cœus*, one of the Titans, and mother of Apollo and Diana, whom she brought forth at a birth on the island *Delos:* hence called Latonian Delos.

7. *Hippodame.* She was the daughter of Œnomaus, king of *Elis*, and *Pisæ*. who having learned from an oracle that he was to be slain by his son-in-law; in order to avoid it, he proposed to the suitors of his daughter, a chariot race, upon this condition, that the one who got the victory should have his daughter; but if vanquished should be slain. After thirteen had lost their lives, Pelops won the beauteous prize, by bribing Myrtillus, the charioteer of Œnomaus, to place the chariot upon a frail or brittle axle. It broke during the race, and Œnomaus was so much bruised by the fall, that he died of his wounds. Thus the oracle was fulfilled. *Pelops* was the son of *Tantalus*, king of Phrygia; who, as the fable goes, invited the gods to a banquet, and having a mind to try their divinity, dressed his own son, and set before them. All abstained from so horrid a repast except *Ceres*, who took a piece of the child's shoulder. Jupiter afterwards restored him to life, and gave him an ivory one in its room. Hence *insignis eburno humero:* famed for his ivory shoulder. For this horrid deed, Tantalus, after death was doomed to perpetual hunger and thirst; and compelled to abstain from both meat and drink, which were placed before him, by way of aggravation.

8. *Acer equis.* This may allude to his victory over Œnomaus; or it may mean no more than that he was skilled in the management of horses; which is the sense of Ruæus.

11. *Aonio vertice:* from the Aonian mount, *Helicon*. This was a mountain in *Beotia*, originally called *Aonia*, sacred to the muses.

12. *Primus referam:* I, the first, will bring to thee, O Mantua, Idumæan palms—noble palms. The palm-tree abounded in Idumæa, a country of Syria; so called from Edom, a son of Esau, who settled there. Virgil was not the first who introduced the Greek poetry into Italy; and, therefore, to do away, or prevent any objection, he mentions Mantua, the place of his birth. He was, however, the first who brought it to any degree of perfection.

13. *Ponam Templum.* The poet appears to mean, that he will not only imitate the Greeks, but he will surpass them; and in honor of his victory, he will build a temple, and institute games. Through the whole, under color of honoring himself, he very artfully compliments Augustus, his prince and patron. *Ponam:* in the sense of *extruam*.

14. *Errat:* meanders—winds.

18. *Centum.* I will drive a hundred four-horse chariots along the river. The poet takes the definite number 100 for an indefinite number; or he alludes to the Circensian games, when in one day there were twenty-five races of four chariots each, making the exact number here mentioned. These were in imitation of the Olympic games, and were on the margin of a river. *Illi:* for him—in honor of Cæsar.

19. *Cuncta Græcia.* The meaning is, that all Greece would leave their own games

Cursibus et crudo decernet Græcia cæstu.
Ipse, caput tonsæ foliis ornatus olivæ,
Dona feram. Jam nunc solemnes ducere pompas
Ad delubra juvat, cæsosque videre juvencos:
Vel scena ut versis discedat frontibus, utque
Purpurea intexti tollant aulæa Britanni.
In foribus pugnam ex auro solidoque elephanto
Gangaridûm faciam, victorisque arma Quirini:
Atque hìc undantem bello, magnùmque fluentem
Nilum, ac navali surgentes ære columnas.
Addam urbes Asiæ domitas, pulsumque Niphaten,
Fidentemque fugâ Parthum versisque sagittis;
Et duo rapta manû diverso ex hoste trophæa,

24. Vel *videre* ut scena discedat,

28. Atque hìc *sculpam* Nilum undantem bello

NOTES.

and come to these, as far excelling in grandeur and magnificence. *Alpheum:* a river of Elis, in the Peloponnesus, near the city Olympia. Hence the games there celebrated were called Olympic. The river here, by meton. is put for the games themselves. They were instituted by Hercules, in honor of Jupiter, as near as their date can be ascertained, in the summer of the year of the world, 3228, and before Christ, 776. They were celebrated every fifth year; or after an entire revolution of four years; which was denominated an *Olympiad.* This formed a very important era in the history of Greece.

Lucos Molorchi: the groves of Molorchus: by meton. the *Nemæa certamina,* or Nemean games. These were instituted in honor of Hercules, on account of his killing the lion in the *Sylva Nemæa,* near *Cleonæ,* a city of the Peloponnesus. *Molorchus* was the name of the shepherd who entertained the hero, and at whose request he slew the Nemæan lion. Besides these, there were other games called *Pythia,* instituted in honor of Apollo, on account of his killing the serpent *Python.* Hence he derived the name *Pæan,* from a Greek word signifying to pierce or wound. There were also games called *Isthmia.* These were instituted by Theseus, king of Athens, in honor of Neptune. They derived their name from the circumstance of their being celebrated on the *Isthmus* of Corinth. *Mihi:* for me—in honor of me.

20. *Crudo:* because the *cæstus,* or gauntlet, was made of raw hide: or simply, cruel —bloody. See Æn. v. 379.

22. *Pompas.* These were images of the gods carried in procession before the people at the Circensian games—the procession itself. *Feram dona:* in the sense of *proponam præmia.*

24. *Ut:* in the sense of *quomodo. Scena:* that part of the stage where the actors were —the curtain, or hanging, behind which they retired from the audience. It was raised up when the actors were upon the stage, and let down when they retired from it. It appears to mean the same thing with *aulæa* in the following line. See Geor. ii. 381.

25. *Intexti.* The Britons (the victories of Julius Cæsar over them) supposed to be painted on, or interwoven in, the curtains; which, by a figure of speech, they might be said to hold, or lift up.

27. *Gangaridûm.* The Gangaridæ were a people of India, near the Ganges. *Quirini.* This is one of the many reasons we have for believing that Virgil continued to revise the Georgics until his death. It was debated in the senate, whether Octavius should be complimented with the name of Augustus, or Romulus, who was also called Quirinus. But this debate did not take place till three years after the publication of the Georgics; and was seven years before his victory over the *Gangaridæ.* The poet must, therefore, have added this line at least ten years after the first publication, or in the year of Rome, 734.

27. *Faciam:* in the sense of *sculpam.*

28. *Magnùm:* Ruæus takes it in the sense of *longè. Copiosè,* says Heyne. *Undantem:* swelling and waving with war, as it did with its waters. This is a metaphor, beautiful and grand. The poet here alludes to the victory obtained by Augustus over Anthony and Cleopatra, and the capture of Alexandria, the principal city of Egypt, near the mouth of the Nile. It was built by Alexander the Great. All Egypt soon followed the fate of Alexandria, its capital.

29. *Navali ære:* with naval brass. Augustus is said to have made four columns out of the brazen beaks of the ships, taken from Cleopatra and Anthony; to which the poet here seems to allude.

30. *Niphaten:* Niphates, a mountain of Armenia, taken for the inhabitants of that country: by meton. *Armenios fugatos,* says Ruæus.

32. *Duo trophæa.* Probably those two victories obtained by Augustus over Antho-

Bisque triumphatas utroque ab litore gentes
Stabunt et Parii lapides, spirantia signa,
Assaraci proles, demissæque ab Jove gentis
Nomina; Trosque parens, et Trojæ Cynthius auctor.
Invidia infelix furias amnemque severum
Cocyti metuet, tortosque Ixionis angues,
Immanemque rotam, et non exsuperabile saxum.
Intereà Dryadum sylvas saltusque sequamur
Intactos, tua, Mæcenas, haud mollia jussa.
Te sine nil altum mens inchoat: en age, segnes
Rumpe moras: vocat ingenti clamore Cithæron,
Taygetique canes, domitrixque Epidaurus equorum:

36. Trosque **parens** *Assaraci*

40. Sylvasque, saltusque intactos *ab aliis scriptoribus.*

NOTES.

ny, the one at Actium, in Epirus, on the northern shore of the Mediterranean, the other at Alexandria, in Egypt, on the southern. Hence the propriety of *utroque litore. Rapta manu:* obtained by valor, or by his own hand—where he commanded in person. *Diverso hoste*, and *triumphatas gentes*, mean the same; and probably we are to understand the Asiatic and African troops that composed the army of Anthony in these two battles. This is the opinion of Ruæus. Some understand the passage as referring to the *Gandaridæ*, a people of Asia, and to the *Britanni*, situated in Europe, in different quarters of the world. But Augustus did not conquer the Britons.

34. *Parii lapides:* Parian marble. *Parii:* an adj. from *Paros*, one of the *Cyclades*, famous for its shining marble. *Spirantia signa:* figures, or statues to the life. They shall be of such exquisite sculpture, that one could scarcely distinguish them from real life—they should almost breathe.

35. *Proles Assaraci:* the offspring of Assaracus, and the names of the family, &c. The poet here, as in other places, compliments the Cæsars with divine descent. According to him, it may be thus traced: Dardanus was the son of Jupiter and Electra; Erichthonius, the son of Dardanus; Tros, the son of Erichthonius; Ilus and Assaracus, sons of Tros; Ilus begat Laomedon, the father of Priam, and Assaracus begat Capys, the father of Anchises; of Anchises and Venus sprang Æneas, the father of Ascanius, or Iulus; the father of the Julian family.

36. *Cynthius:* Apollo. He was born on the island Delos, where was a mountain by the name of Cynthus; hence he was called *Cynthius.* He and Neptune, it is said, built the walls of Troy in the reign of Laomedon. See Ecl. iv. 10, and Geor. i. 502.

37. *Infelix.* This epithet is added to envy, because it is the principal source of unhappiness to men.

38. *Cocyti:* Cocytus, a fabulous river of hell, flowing out of Styx. *Ixionis:* Ixion, the father of the Centaurs. For making an attempt upon Juno, he was cast down to hell, and bound with twenty snakes to a wheel, which kept constantly turning, as a punishment for his crime. The poets say, that Jupiter substituted a cloud in the form of Juno, and of it he begat the Centaurs. Upon his return to the earth, he boasted of his amour with the queen of the gods, and was punished for it by Jupiter in this exemplary manner. The truth is, the Centaurs were a people of Thessaly. They dwelt in a city by the name of *Nephele.* That being the Greek word for a cloud, gave rise to the story of their being the offspring of a cloud. They were the first who broke and tamed the horse. Ixion was their king. The poet here intimates in a very delicate manner the unhappy end of those who envied Augustus the glory due to his illustrious deeds; who dared refuse to submit to his authority; and who meditated a renewal of the civil wars.

39. *Saxum.* Sisyphus, a notorious robber, was slain by Theseus, king of Athens, and for his punishment, he was sentenced to hell; there to roll a stone to the top of a hill, which always rolled back before he could reach it. This made his labor perpetual. *Non exsuperabile:* not to be gotten to the top of the hill.

41. *Tua haud mollia jussa:* thy difficult commands.

Virgil, at the request of Mæcenas, wrote the Georgics; to which circumstance he here alludes—a subject new, and which had not been handled or treated of by any preceding writer. *Sequamur:* we will enter upon.

43. *Cithæron:* a mountain in Beotia, abounding in pasture, and herds of cattle. *Taygeti:* Taygetus, a mountain in Laconia, famous for hunting. *Epidaurus.* There were several places by that name. The one here intended, is probably in Argolis, on the eastern shore of the Peloponnesus, near the *Sinus Saronicus*, that part being celebrated for its horses. The meaning is, that he shall now treat of those animals that abounded in the above mentioned places

Et vox assensu nemorum ingeminata remugit.
Mox tamen ardentes accingar dicere pugnas
Cæsaris, et nomen famâ tot ferre per annos,
Tithoni primâ quot abest ab origine Cæsar.
Seu quis, Olympiacæ miratus præmia palmæ,
Pascit equos, seu quis fortes ad aratra juvencos;
Corpora præcipuè matrum legat. Optima torvæ
Forma bovis, cui turpe caput, cui plurima cervix,
Et crurum tenùs à mento palearia pendent.
Tum longo nullus lateri modus: omnia magna;
Pes etiam, et camuris hirtæ sub cornibus aures.
Nec mihi displiceat maculis insignis et albo:
Aut juga detrectans, interdumque aspera cornu,
Et faciem tauro proprior: quæque ardua tota,
Et gradiens imâ verrit vestigia caudâ.
Ætas Lucinam justosque pati Hymenæos
Desinit ante decem, post quatuor incipit annos:
Cætera nec fœturæ habilis; nec fortis aratris.
Intereà, superat gregibus dum læta juventus,
Solve mares: mitte in Venerem pecuaria primus,
Atque aliam ex aliâ generando suffice prolem.
Optima quæque dies miseris mortalibus ævi
Prima fugit: subeunt morbi, tristisque senectus:
Et labor, et duræ rapit inclementia mortis.
Semper erunt, quarum mutari corpora malis.

52. Forma torvæ bovis *est* optima, cui *est* turpe caput, cui *est* plurima cervix, et *cui* palearia pendent à mento tenùs crurum.

54. Omnia *membra sunt* magna:

56. Nec *vacca* insignis maculis et albo displiceat mihi:

58. Et *est* propior tauro *quoad* faciem: quæque *est* tota

62. Cætera *ætas earum est* nec habilis fœturæ, nec *est* fortis aratris.

69. Erunt semper *aliquæ pecudes*, quarum corpora, *tu* malis mutari. Enim semper refice *armenta;* ac, ne pòst requiras *ea* amissa, anteveni-

NOTES.

45. *Vox Assensu*, &c. The meaning is, that the groves unite in inviting him, and echo back the call.

46. *Ardentes:* in the sense of *illustres. Accingar:* in the sense of the Greek middle voice: I will prepare myself. The poet here seems to intimate his purpose of writing the *Æneid;* which was chiefly designed to flatter Augustus and the Roman people.

48. *Tithoni.* Tithonus was either the son or brother of Laomedon, and greatly beloved by Aurora. From his time down to Augustus, were one thousand years, according to the best accounts. But to extend his fame only for that length of time, would not come up to the design of the poet, whose wish was to perpetuate his fame to the latest posterity. According to Servius and Eustathius, *Tithonus* may here be taken for the sun, in the same sense that *Titan* is; they both being derived from the same Greek verb. This would fully come up to the views of the poet in immortalizing his prince. The sun having existed from the beginning of time, may be considered a *quædam eternitas;* or the poet may assume the definite number, 1000 years, for an indefinite period. See Æn. iv. 585.

51. *Legat:* in the sense of *eligat.*

52. *Turpe:* large—disproportionate. *Bovis:* in the sense of *vaccæ.*

56. *Maculis— et albo:* the same as *albis maculis*, by Hendiadis. *Aspera:* pushing, or butting.

60. *Lucinam:* the goddess of child-bearing, so called *à luce*, *quam infantibus dabat:* by meton. child-bearing itself—the bringing forth of young in general. *Hymenæos:* Hymen or Hymenæus, was the son of Bacchus and Venus; the god of marriage: by meton. marriage itself—also the intercourse of the sexes, as in the present instance. The meaning of the poet is, that the proper time for cattle to breed, ends before the tenth, and begins after the fourth year of their age.

63. *Intereà:* in the mean time—between the years of four and ten, let loose the males among your herds. *Superat:* abounds—is vigorous.

64. *Pecuaria:* properly pasture grounds: by meton. the cattle fed upon them. Here, the females; the *boves*, vel *vaccæ.*

65. *Suffice:* raise up one stock after another. *Ævi:* in the sense of *vitæ.*

68. *Inclementia:* rigor—severity.

69. *Semper erunt.* This, and the two following lines, Dr. Trapp thinks to be an interpolation. He says, the sense of the whole three lines is extremely jejune and flat. What occasion of admonishing the farmer to continue the succession of his cattle? The thing had just been expressed before. Let it be further considered, what a different face it puts upon the whole, if these lines are left out. Having concluded the article of the propagation of kine, with that fine reflection upon the imperfect state

Semper enim refice: ac, ne pòst amissa requiras,
Anteveni, et sobolem armento sortire quotannis.
Necnon et pecori est idem delectus equino.
Tu modò, quos in spem statues submittere gentis,
Præcipuum jam inde à teneris impende laborem
Continuò pecoris generosi pullus in arvis
Altiùs ingreditur, et mollia crura reponit:
Primus et ire viam, et fluvios tentare minaces
Audet, et ignoto sese committere ponti:
Nec vanos horret strepitus. Illi ardua cervix,
Argutumque caput, brevis alvus, obesaque terga;
Luxuriatque toris animosum pectus: honesti
Spadices, glaucique; color deterrimus albis,
Et gilvo: tum, si qua sonum procul arma dedêre,
Stare loco nescit, micat auribus, et tremit artus;
Collectumque fremens volvit sub naribus ignem.
Densa juba, et dextro jactata recumbit in armo.
At duplex agitur per lumbos spina: cavatque
Tellurem, et solido graviter sonat ungula cornu.
Talis Amyclæi domitus Pollucis habenis
Cyllarus, et, quorum Graii meminere poëtæ,
Martis equi bijuges, et magni currus Achilles.
Talis et ipse jubam cervice effudit equinâ
Conjugis adventu pernix Saturnus, et altum
Pelion hinnitu fugiens implevit acuto.
Hunc quoque, ubi aut morbo gravis, aut jam segnior
Deficit, abde domo, nec turpi ignosce senectæ. [annis

74. Impende præcipuum laborem *illis* jam inde à teneris *annis*, quos,

79. *Est* illi ardua

82. Spadices, glaucique *sunt* honesti *colores*

84. Tremit *per* artus

90. Et *tales erant* bijuges equi Martis, et currus magni Achilles quorum

NOTES.

of mortality, he immediately passes on to the propagation of horses. And what further confirms him in this opinion, is, the use of the verbs *antevenio* and *sortior*. The former, says he, is no where else used by Virgil; and the latter never, in the sense it is used here: for *substituo*.

71. *Sobolem:* a succession—issue.

73. *Submittere:* in the sense of *seponere*.

75. *Pullus generosi:* a colt of generous breed—of noble blood. *Continuò:* from the first—as soon as foaled.

76. *Reponit mollia crura:* he moves his pliant, or nimble legs. *Reponit* implies both the alternate movements of his feet, and the quickness and frequency of them.

81. *Luxuriat toris:* his courageous breast abounds (swells out) in muscles.

82. *Spadices, glauci:* the bright bay, and dappled-gray, are good colors; the worst color is the white and dun. It is very difficult, as Dr. Trapp observes, to ascertain the names of colors in a foreign and dead language. Besides, one nation may prefer this color, and another may prefer that. He takes *albus* for a dull, dirty white, and to be distinguished from *candidus;* because, *anteire nives candore*, Virgil makes the mark of a fine horse. See Æn. xii. 84.

84. *Fremens.* The common reading is *premens;* but several ancient copies have *fremens*, as Heyne informs us. That learned editor reads, *fremens*. *Ignem:* in the sense of *calorem*, vel *ardentes anhelitus*. Of the horses of Diomede, *Lucretius* says: *ignem naribus spiraverunt*.

87. *Duplex:* round—large. In a lean horse, as the spine or back-bone rises up sharp; so in a fat horse, there is a kind of hollow or gutter running through the middle of the back, and seeming to divide it into two parts. In this sense, *duplex spina* may be a double spine. *Agitur:* passes along, or extends.

87. *Lumbos:* in the sense of *dorsum*, vel *tergum*.

89. *Talis Cyllarus:* such was Cyllarus, broke by the reins, &c. *Amyclæi:* an adj. from *Amyclæ*, a city of Laconia, not far from Lacedæmon, where Castor and Pollux were born. Hence they are sometimes called *Lacedæmonii*, as well as *Amyclæi*. Cyllarus was the name of the horse.

91. *Currus:* in the sense of *equi*, by meton.

92. *Et talis pernix Saturnus ipse:* and such swift Saturn himself spread his mane. Saturn, as the poets say, was in love with Philyra, the daughter of Oceanus. During their amours, on a certain occasion, Rhea, his wife, came upon them. To prevent a discovery, Saturn transformed himself into

97. Senior *equus est* frigidus

102. Quis dolor *sit* cuique victo, quæ gloria *sit cuique* palmæ

105. Spes juvenum arrectæ *sunt*.

111. *Equi* humescunt spumis flatuque *eorum* sequentûm

116. Dorso *equorum*

117. Et *equum* glomerare

118. Magistri *utriusque artis* æquè exquirunt *equum* juvenemque, calidumque animis

120. *Non exquirunt senem equum* quamvis

122. Ipsa origine *equi* Neptuni.

123. Tempus *admissuræ*; et

124. Distendere *equum* denso pingui, quem

Frigidus in Venerem senior, frustràque laborem
Ingratum trahit: et, si quando ad prælia ventum est,
Ut quondam in stipulis magnus sinè viribus ignis,
Incassùm furit. Ergò animos ævumque notabis
Præcipuè: hinc alias artes, prolemque parentum
Et quis cuique dolor victo, quæ gloria palmæ.
Nonne vides? cùm præcipiti certamine campum
Corripuere, ruuntque effusi carcere currus;
Cùm spes arrectæ juvenum, exultantiaque haurit
Corda pavor pulsans: illi instant verbere torto,
Et proni dant lora: volat vi fervidus axis:
Jamque humiles, jamque elati sublimè videntur
Aëra per vacuum ferri, atque assurgere in auras.
Nec mora, nec requies. At fulvæ nimbus arenæ
Tollitur: humescunt spumis flatuque sequentûm:
Tantus amor laudum, tantæ est victoria curæ.
  Primus Erichthonius currus et quatuor ausus
Jungere equos, rapidisque rotis insistere victor.
Fræna Pelethronii Lapithæ, gyrosque dedêre,
Impositi dorso; atque equitem docuere sub armis
Insultare solo, et gressus glomerare superbos.
Æquus uterque labor: æquè juvenemque magistri
Exquirunt, calidumque animis, et cursibus acrem:
Quamvis sæpe fugâ versos ille egerit hostes,
Et patriam Epirum referat, fortesque Mycenas;
Neptunique ipsâ deducat origine gentem.
  His animadversis, instant sub tempus; et omnes
Impendunt curas denso distendere pingui,
Quem legêre ducem et pecori dixere maritum;

NOTES.

a horse, and fled to Pelion, a mountain of Thessaly, filling it with his shrill neighings. Philyra bore to him Chiron, one of the Centaurs.

96. *Ignosce senectæ nec turpi:* spare his old age, not inglorious. This is the sense usually given to the words, and implies that the old horse should be treated with kindness and humanity, now in his old age, in consequence of his former glorious deeds. *Abde hunc domo:* in the sense of *include hunc stabulis.*

101. *Hinc alias artes:* after that (you should observe) his other qualities. *Artes* here evidently means the qualities, properties, or endowments of the horse. *Prolem:* the stock, breed, or ancestry.

102. *Palmæ:* to the victor, or conqueror. The palm of victory, by meton. put for the victor, or conqueror.

104. *Effusi:* starting—springing. In races, *carcer* was the mark, or starting place. *Exultantia:* beating—palpitating.

107. *Vi:* with the rapid motion of the wheel.

114. *Rapidis rotis.* This is the common reading. But Heinsius and Heyne read *rapidus* in the nom. agreeing with *victor*. *Rotis:* properly the wheels; by meton. the chariot borne upon them.

115. *Lapithæ:* a people of Thessaly, near mount Pelion. *Pelethronii:* an adj. from *Pelethronium*, one of their cities. The meaning of the poet appears to be this: that Erichthonius invented the use of the chariot and horses, and that the *Lapithæ* afterward improved upon the use of the horse by managing him with the bridle, and turning him about with the reins at their will. *Dedêre:* in the sense of *invenerunt.*

116. *Equitem.* Ruæus takes this in the sense of *equum*. Heyne observes that the old grammarians understood it in the same sense. But Davidson refers the whole to the rider. It appears that the last clause of the following line should be applied to the horse rather than to the rider. *Eques:* properly, the rider; by meton. the horse.

118. *Uterque labor æquus:* each labor, or art, is equal; the management of horses in the chariot, and the management of them with the bridle.

121. *Epirum—Mycenas.* Epirus and Mycenæ were both famous for their excellent horses. *Referat:* have, claim, or boast.

124. *Pingui:* in the sense of *pinguedine.*

125. *Maritum:* in the sense of *admissarium.*

Pubentesque secant herbas, fluviosque ministrant,
Farraque: ne blando nequeat superesse labori,
Invalidique patrum referant jejunia nati.
Ipsa autem macie tenuant armenta volentes.
Atque ubi concubitus primos jam nota voluptas
Sollicitat; frondesque negant, et fontibus arcent:
Sæpe etiam cursu quatiunt, et Sole fatigant;
Cùm graviter tunsis gemit area frugibus, et cùm
Surgentem ad Zephyrum paleæ jactantur inanes.
Hoc faciunt, nimio ne luxu obtusior usus
Sit genitali arvo, et sulcos oblimet inertes:
Sed rapiat sitiens Venerem, interiùsque recondat.
  Rursus, cura patrum cadere, et succedere matrum
Incipit, exactis gravidæ cùm mensibus errant.
Non illas gravibus quisquam juga ducere plaustris,
Non saltu superare viam sit passus, et acri
Carpere prata fugâ, fluviosque innare rapaces.
Saltibus in vacuis pascant, et plena secundùm
Flumina: muscus ubi, et viridissima gramine ripa,
Speluncæque tegant, et saxea procubet umbra.
  Est lucos Silari circa, ilicibusque virentem
Plurimus Alburnum volitans, cui nomen asilo
Romanum est, œstron Graii vertêre vocantes:
Asper, acerba sonans: quo tota exterrita sylvis
Diffugiunt armenta, furit mugitibus æther
Concussus, sylvæque, et sicci ripa Tanagri.
Hoc quondam monstro horribiles exercuit iras
Inachiæ Juno pestem meditata juvencæ.

137. Sed *ut ilia pars* sitiens

138. Et *cura* matrum *incipit* succedere

140. Non quisquam passus sit illas

144. Ubi *sit* muscus, et ripa

NOTES.

127. *Superesse:* to accomplish—be sufficient for. *Fluvios:* in the sense of *aquam copiosam.*

128. *Nati:* the colts. *Referant:* in the sense of *ferant.*

129. *Volentes:* willing—on purpose, or with design. *Armenta* here is evidently taken for *equas*, the mares.

131. *Frondes:* in the sense of *pabulum*, vel *victum*. *Quatiunt:* in the sense of *agitant.*

135. *Ne usus genitali arvo sit obtusior nemio luxu.* These words Ruæus interprets thus: *Ne trajectus (via) genitalis partis sit strictior ob nimiam pinguitudinem.*

136. *Oblimet:* in the sense of *claudat.*

137. *Venerem:* the object of their desire—the *semen masculinum.*

142. *Acri fugâ:* in the sense of *celeri cursu.* *Rapaces:* in the sense of *rapidos.*

143. *Saltibus.* *Saltus* is properly an opening, or vacant space, in a grove, or park. It is, however, sometimes used in the sense of *nemus* and *lucus;* from the verb *salio.* Ruæus says *spatiis apertis.*

145. *Saxea umbra:* a rocky shade may fall on them—a rocky clift may project over them, under which they may be sheltered from the sun and rains.

146. *Circa lucos Silari, Alburnumque.* Silarus, a river of Italy, in Lucania: *hodie Selo*, *Alburnum:* Alburnus, a mountain in Italy, abounding in the holm-oak: *hodie Alborno;* out of which issues the river Tanagrus, small, and nearly dry in summer. *Plurimus volitans:* around the groves, &c. there are many flies, to which *asylus* is the Roman name, but the Greeks called it *œstron.* This construction is very peculiar; the idiom we cannot introduce into our language. *Plurimus volitans* we must take in the sense of *plurimi volitantes. Cui nomen asylo.* This is evidently the same as *cui asylus est Romano nomini:* perhaps by antiptosis. Asylus is what we commonly call the gad-fly, or breeze. It is the same as the *tabanus*, or *tabanum.* The sting of this insect causes great pain to the animal that is wounded by it.

148. *Vocantes vertêre:* simply, *vocaverunt*, vel *reddiderunt.*

149. *Acerbà:* an adj. neu. plu. taken as an adverb in imitation of the Greeks; the same as *acerbè.* *Asper.* This may have reference to the sharpness of its bite or sting. *Sonans:* making a sharp or shrill noise.

150. *Furit:* in the sense of *resonat.*

153. *Inachiæ juvencæ.* Io, the daughter of Inachus, king of the Argives, (or of a

154. Hunc *asilum*

Hunc quoque (nam mediis fervoribus acrior instat)
Arcebis gravido pecori; armentaque pasces,
Sole recèns orto, aut noctem ducentibus astris.
Post partum, cura in vitulos traducitur omnis:
Continuòque notas et nomina gentis inurunt:

159. Et *notant eos*, quos malint aut submittere pecori

Et quos, aut pecori malint submittere habendo,
Aut aris servare sacros, aut scindere terram,
Et campum horrentem fractis invertere glebis.
Cætera pascuntur virides armenta per herbas.
Tu, quos ad studium atque usum formabis agrestem,

164. Jam tu hortare vitulos, quos formabis ad studium

Jam vitulos hortare, viamque insiste domandi;
Dum faciles animi juvenum, dum mobilis ætas.
Ac primùm laxos tenui de vimine circlos
Cervici subnecte: dehinc, ubi libera colla
Servitio assuêrint; ipsis è torquibus aptos
Junge pares, et coge gradum conferre, juvencos.
Atque illis jam sæpe rotæ ducantur inanes
Per terram, et summo vestigia pulvere signent.
Pòst valido nitens sub pondere faginus axis
Instrepat, et junctos temo trahat æreus orbes.

174. Intereà carpes manu non tantùm gramina indomitæ pubi

Intereà pubi indomitæ non gramina tantùm,
Nec vescas salicum frondes, ulvamque palustrem;
Sed frumenta manu carpes sata: nec tibi fœtæ,
More patrum, nivea implebunt mulctralia vaccæ;
Sed tota in dulces consument ubera natos.

179. Sin *tuum* studium *sit* magìs ad bellum, ferocesque

Sin ad bella magìs studium, turmasque feroces,

NOTES.

river god of that name,) whom Jupiter transformed into a heifer, when he was likely to be surprised by Juno in his amour with her. But discovering the trick, the goddess sent *Asilus* to torment her. Upon which she fled to Egypt; where Jupiter, taking pity on her, restored her to her proper shape. After which, she was married to king Osiris; and, after her death, was worshipped as a goddess under the name of Isis.

154. *Mediis fervoribus:* for *media die.*

158. *Inurunt:* in the sense of *imprimunt.*

159. *Submittere:* to set apart for breeders —for propagating your stock or herd.

161. *Horrentem:* in the sense of *asperum.*

162. *Cætera armenta.* The poet's meaning is plainly this: that those calves that are designed for breeding, for sacrifice, or for the plough, are to be particularly designated, and taken care of; while it is sufficient for the rest of the herd to feed at large, without any such care or attention; and with regard to those designed for the plough, they should be trained up from the first, and be accustomed to the yoke, while they are docile and tractable.

164. *Hortare:* imp. of *hortor:* teach, or train up. *Ad studium:* for labor. *Mobilis:* in the sense of *docilis.*

166. *Circlos:* by syn. for *circulos:* bind loose collars about their necks.

169. *Junge pares,* &c. The poet directs the farmer to begin with his steers at an early age; and first to hang collars lightly about their necks. Afterwards, join two of equal size by a cord connecting these collars; and in this state make them walk and keep pace together; and after they have become accustomed to this discipline, then make them draw empty wheels along the ground—wheels without any carriage upon them.

172. *Valido:* in the sense of *magno. Orbes:* for *rotas,* wheels.

174. *Pubi indomitæ:* for your steers unbroken—not entirely subdued to the yoke.

175. *Ulvam.* The *ulva* was a kind of grass, which grew in marshy grounds. We have no particular name for it in our language. *Nec:* in the sense of *et.*

176. *Frumenta sata:* planted, or sown corn.

The poet would have the farmer to understand, that the care of his steers is so important, that he should not only gather for them grass, and the tender leaves of the willow, and the marshy *ulva;* but even the growing corn. He should consider nothing too costly for them.

177. *Fœtæ vaccæ:* your suckling cows. *Fœtæ:* having young. The word also signifies, being with young.

Aut Alphea rotis prælabi flumina Pisæ,
Et Jovis in luco currus agitare volantes;
Primus equi labor est, animos atque arma videre
Bellantûm, lituosque pati, tractuque gementem
Ferre rotam, et stabulo frænos audire sonantes.
Tum magìs atque magìs blandis gaudere magistri
Laudibus, et plausæ sonitum cervicis amare.
Atque hæc jam primò depulsus ab ubere matris
Audiat, inque vicem det mollibus ora capistris
Invalidus, etiamque tremens, etiam inscius ævi.
At, tribus exactis, ubi quarta accesserit æstas,
Carpere mox gyrum incipiat, gradibusque sonare
Compositis: sinuetque alterna volumina crurum,
Sitque laboranti similis: tum cursibus auras
Provocet: ac per aperta volans, ceu liber habenis,
Æquora, vix summâ vestigia ponat arenâ.
Qualis hyperboreis Aquilo cùm densus ab oris
Incubuit, Scythiæque hyemes atque arida differt
Nubila: tum segetes altæ campique natantes
Lenibus horrescunt flabris, summæque sonorem
Dant sylvæ, longique urgent ad litora fluctus:
Ille volat, simul arva fugâ, simul æquora verrens
Hic, vel ad Elei metas et maxima campi
Sudabit spatia, et spumas aget ore cruentas;
Belgica vel molli meliùs feret esseda collo.
Tum demum crassâ magnum farragine corpus

187. **Audiat hæc jam primò depulsus ab ubere**

201. **Ille *ventus* volat**

NOTES.

180. *Prælabi rotis.* The poet here alludes to the chariot races at the Olympic games, celebrated upon the banks of the river Alpheus.

183. *Lituos:* the clarion, or curved horn; put, by meton. for the sound of that instrument.

Gementem tractu: in the sense of *stridentem dum trahitur*, says Heyne.

186. *Sonitum plausæ cervicis:* the sound of the patted neck.

This refers to the custom of stroking, or gently patting the horse on the neck, to inspire him with courage.

188. *Inque vicem:* by Tmesis, for *invicem que:* and now and then—occasionally.

Audiat. This is the common reading. But Heyne, after Heinsius, reads *audeat*, of the verb *audeo*.

189. *Inscius ævi:* ignorant, or inexperienced, on account of his age—not conscious of strength—knowing his weakness. Servius says: *nondum habens ab annis fiduciam.* Davidson says: *propter imbecilitatem ævi.* It is a Greek construction.

191. *Sonare compositis gradibus:* to prance in regular steps.

Sinuetque: and let him bend the alternate joints of his legs—or alternately the joints of his legs.

Carpere: in the sense of *describere.*

193. *Similis laboranti.* The meaning of the poet appears to be this: After the horse hath commenced his fourth year, let him begin to amble, and prance, and exercise, however laborious and fatiguing it may be to him. Or rather: let not his exercise in reality be laborious and fatiguing, on account of his age; but let him resemble, or be like to one laboring only, lest he be dispirited from experience of his weakness. But when he is properly trained by exercise, his courage increased, and his confidence in himself confirmed, then let him labor—let him challenge the winds in his course.

194. *Provocet.* This is the common reading. Heyne reads *tum vocet.*

Æquora: in the sense of *campos.*

197. *Incubuit:* rushes forth. Ruæus says, *imminet.*

198. *Natantes:* in the sense of *undantes.*

182. *Animos:* courage. *Contentiones*, says Ruæus.

202. *Hic, vel ad metas:* this horse, either at the goals of Elis, &c.

204. *Esseda.* The essedum was a kind of vehicle, or carriage, adapted both for travelling or war. It was used by the ancient Gauls and Britons. *Molli:* tractable. in opposition to reluctant.

205. *Crassa farragine:* with rich or fattening marsh. The *farrago* was a mixture of wheat bran and barley meal, according to Servius.

206. *Illis* domitis *jugo:*

Crescere jam domitis sinito: namque ante domandum.
Ingentes tollent animos; prensique negabunt
Verbera lenta pati, et duris parere lupatis.
   Sed non ulla magìs vires industria firmat,
Quàm Venerem et cæci stimulos avertere amoris;
Sive boum, sive est cui gratior usus equorum.
Atque ideò tauros procul atque in sola relegant
Pascua, post montem oppositum, et trans flumina lata:
Aut intus clausos satura ad præsepia servant.
Carpit enim vires paulatim, uritque videndo
Fœmina: nec nemorum patitur meminisse, nec herbæ

217. Illa quidem *facit hoc* dulcibus illecebris, et sæpe subigit

Dulcibus illa quidem illecebris, et sæpe superbos
Cornibus inter se subigit decernere amantes.
Pascitur in magnâ sylvâ formosa juvenca:
Illi alternantes multâ vi prælia miscent
Vulneribus crebris: lavit ater corpora sanguis,

222. Obnixos *adversarios*

Versaque in obnixos urgentur cornua vasto
Cum gemitu: reboant sylvæque et magnus Olympus.

224. Nec *est* mos *duos* bellantes

Nec mos bellantes unà stabulare: sed alter
Victus abit, longèque ignotis exulat oris;

226. Plagas *factas cornibus* superbi victoris, tum *eos* amores, quos

Multa gemens ignominiam, plagasque superbi
Victoris, tum quos amisit inultus amores:
Et stabula aspectans regnis excessit avitis.

229. Et inter dura saxa jacet

Ergò omni curâ vires exercet, et inter
Dura jacet pernox instrato saxa cubili;
Frondibus hirsutis et carice pastus acutâ:
Et tentat sese, atque irasci in cornua discit,
Arboris obnixus trunco: ventosque lacessit
Ictibus, et sparsâ ad pugnam proludit arenâ.
Pòst, ubi collectum robur, viresque refectæ,
Signa movet, præcepsque oblitum fertur in hostem:

NOTES.

206. *Namque.* The poet advises the farmer not to pamper or fatten his horses before they are broken, and rendered tractable. If he do, they will be mettlesome and high minded, (*tollunt ingentes animos,*) they will show a stout and surly temper, and when caught, will refuse to bear the limber whip, and to obey the hard bits. *Ante domandum:* before breaking. The gerund in *dum* is of the nature of a substantive noun. Ruæus says, *antequàm domentur.*

209. *Industria:* in the sense of *cura.*

211. *Usus:* in the sense of *cultus.*

214. *Satura:* in the sense of *plena.*

216. *Fœmina:* the female—the heifer.

220. *Alternantes:* in the sense of *vicissim.*

222. *Cornua versa in obnixos:* and their horns turned against the contending foes, are struck, &c.

Cum vasto gemitu. This seems not to refer to the rage and violence of the antagonists, so much as to the groans and bellowings of the conquered party, or to the occasional groans of each, produced by the repeated strokes given and received.

224. *Bellantes:* a part. of the verb *bello,* used in the sense of *adversarios.*

Stabulare: in the sense of *habitare.*

226. *Multa:* in the sense of *multùm.*

228. *Avitis regnis:* from his hereditary realms—from those fields in which he was born, and in which he bore rule.

Aspicens: in the sense of *respiciens.*

230. *Instrato cubili.* Dr. Trapp, and Davidson understand this to be a naked or unstrowed bed. Ruæus takes *instrato* in the sense of *strato,* strowed or made. The prep. *in* sometimes in composition adds to the signification of the primitive word; at other times, changes it to an opposite sense.

Carice acutâ: sharp sedge.

235. *Refectæ.* This is the reading of Heyne, after Heinsius. But *receptæ* is the common reading.

236. *Movet signa:* he moves his standards. A metaphor taken from the movement of an army.

Fluctus ut, in medio cœpit cùm albescere ponto,
Longiùs ex altoque sinum trahit: utque volutus
Ad terras, immanè sonat per saxa, nec ipso
Monte minor procumbit: at ima exæstuat unda
Vorticibus, nigramque altè subjectat arenam.
  Omne adeò genus in terris hominumque ferarumque,
Et genus æquoreum, pecudes, pictæque volucres,
In furias ignemque ruunt: amor omnibus idem.
Tempore non alio catulorum oblita leæna
Sævior erravit campis: nec funera vulgò
Tam multa informes ursi stragemque dedêre
Per sylvas: tum sævus aper, tum pessima tigris:
Heu! malè tum Libyæ solis erratur in agris.
Nonne vides, ut tota tremor pertentet equorum
Corpora, si tantùm notas odor attulit auras!
Ac neque eos jam fræna virûm, neque verbera sæva,
Non scopuli, rupesque cavæ, atque objecta retardant
Flumina, correptos undâ torquentia montes.
Ipse ruit, dentesque Sabellicus exacuit sus,
Et pede prosubigit terram, fricat arbore costas,
Atque hinc atque illinc humeros ad vulnera durat.
Quid juvenis, magnum cui versat in ossibus ignem
Durus amor? nempe abruptis turbata procellis
Nocte natat cæcâ serus freta: quem super ingens
Porta tonat cœli, et scopulis illisa reclamant
Æquora: nec miseri possunt revocare parentes,
Nec moritura super crudeli funere virgo.

258. Quid juvenis *facit*, cui durus

NOTES.

238. *Trahit sinum:* and draws a billowy train, far from the deep.

Utque. Davidson reads *atque*, and thinks it to be the correct reading, as being easier. Some other copies have *atque.*

The whole of this description of the battle of the bulls, as well as what precedes it, of the power of love, is among Virgil's master-pieces, and is admired by all critics. Nor less admired is what follows. The variety of objects, the force of the illustrations, the propriety of the arrangement, and the beauty and grandeur of the descriptions, are obvious to every reader.

241. *Subjectat:* in the sense of *erigit.*

244. *Ruunt in furias ignemque:* rush into a passion, and flame of this kind.

Furia, the same as *furor*, denotes any inordinate passion or affection of the mind, such as love, anger, &c. from the verb *furo. Ignem* is much more expressive than *amorem.* Besides the simple idea of love, it implies the consuming and destructive effects of that passion upon the subjects of it.

248. *Pessima:* most fell—or savage.

249. *Libyæ.* Libya, a part of Africa, taken for the whole of it, by synec. This is mentioned, because it abounded in the most savage beasts. *Malè erratur:* it is dangerous to wander.

251. *Odor attulit notas auras.* This is, by *Commutatio*, for, *aura attulit notum odorem. Equæ* vel *fœminæ* is understood

254. *Aquâ:* in the sense of *vi aquarum. Objecta:* Ruæus says, *interjecta.*

255. *Sabellicus sus ipse:* The Sabelline boar rushes forth, &c. *Sabellicus:* an adj. from *Sabelli*, or *Sabini*, a people of Italy, whose country abounded in forests, and haunts of wild beasts.

258. *Quid juvenis.* The poet here alludes to the story of Leander and Hero.

Leander was an inhabitant of Abydus, on the Asian shore of the Hellespont, and passionately in love with Hero, a beautiful maid, and priestess of Venus, who resided at Sestus, on the European shore, and opposite to Abydus. He used to swim the strait to visit his fair mistress. On a certain occasion, passing over in a storm, he was drowned. His dead body was driven to the European shore, and espied by Hero; who, in a transport of passion, threw herself upon the corpse of her lover, and perished also.

259. *Abruptis:* violent—sudden.

261. *Reclamant:* in the sense of *resonant.*

263. *Nec virgo moritura.* This alludes to the case of Hero, above mentioned. *Super:* in, or by.

265. Quid cervi *faciunt, et* quæ prælia *illi* imbelles dant?

277. Non ad tuos ortus, O Eure; neque *ad ortus* Solis; *neque* in Boream, Caurumque, aut *ad eam partem*, unde

283. Miscuerunt herbas *cum eo*

285. Dum *nos* capti amore *describendi*

286. Hoc *est* satis

Quid Lynces Bacchi variæ, et genus acre luporum,
Atque canum? quid, quæ imbelles dant prælia cervi?
Scilicet ante omnes furor est insignis equarum:
Et mentem Venus ipsa dedit, quo tempore Glauci
Potniades malis membra absumpsêre quadrigæ.
Illas ducit amor trans Gargara, transque sonantem
Ascanium: superant montes, et flumina tranant:
Continuòque avidis ubi subdita flamma medullis,
Vere magìs (quia vere calor redit ossibus) illæ
Ore omnes versæ in Zephyrum, stant rupibus altis,
Exceptantque leves auras: et sæpe sinè ullis
Conjugiis, vento gravidæ, mirabile dictu!
Saxa per et scopulos et depressas convalles
Diffugiunt: non, Eure, tuos, neque Solis, ad ortus,
In Boream, Caurumque, aut inde nigerrimus Auster
Nascitur, et pluvio contristat frigore cœlum.
Hinc demum, Hippomanes, vero quod nomine dicunt
Pastores, lentum distillat ab inguine virus:
Hippomanes, quod sæpe malæ legêre novercæ,
Miscueruntque herbas, et non innoxia verba.
Sed fugit intereà, fugit irreparabile tempus,
Singula dum capti circumvectamur amore.
Hoc satìs armentis: superat pars altera curæ,
Lanigeros agitare greges, hirtasque capellas.
Hìc labor: hinc laudem fortes sperate coloni.
Nec sum animi dubius, verbis ea vincere magnum

NOTES.

264. *Lynces.* The Lynx is an animal, some say, of the species of the wolf and deer; others say, only spotted like a deer, or panther, very quick sighted, and swift of foot. The Lynces, as well as tigers, were bound to the car of Bacchus. Hence *Lynces Bacchi. Dant:* in the sense of *gerunt.*

267. *Mentem:* disposition—passion. *Indolem*, says Heyne.

268. *Potniades:* an adj. from *Potnia*, a town in Beotia, the native place of Glaucus: who, it is said, withheld the horse from his mares; which so enraged them, that, by way of revenge, at the instigation of Venus, they tore him in pieces.

Potniades quadrigæ. The Potnian mares. See Geor. i. 437.

269. *Gargara:* neu. plu. a part of mount Ida, in Troas: here put for any mountain. *Ascanium.* Ascanius, a river in Bithynia, in Asia: here put for any river.

275. *Gravidæ vento.* This account of the mares becoming pregnant by the wind, is wholly fabulous; although mentioned by *Salinus*, *Columella*, and *Varro*, as Ruæus observes.

277. *Non Eure*, &c. Some understand the passage thus: not to thy rising, O east, nor the rising of the sun; but to the north, &c. Ruæus, thus: they fled not to the east, nor to the north, nor to the part whence the black south wind arises. And he gives, as his reason: *Quòd maxima pars scriptorum videtur tribuere hanc vim (impregnandi equas) uni Zephyro.* Heyne understands it in the first sense: *sed in Boream*, &c.

278. *Caurum:* the north-west wind.

279. *Contristat:* blackens. Ruæus takes *pluvio frigore* in the sense of *pluvia tempestate.* So does Heyne. *Frigus*, it is plain, is not here to be taken in its usual sense. For the south wind is not cold; on the contrary, it is hot, and generally brings with it heavy rains. It seems here to be used in the sense of *nimbus;* a cloud impregnated with vapor and rain.

280. *Hippomanes.* The Hippomanes was of two kinds. The one a tough clammy substance, *lentum virus*, which fell from the mare, when she wanted the horse. This is the kind here meant. The other was a bunch, said to be on the forehead of the newly foaled colt. See Æn. iv. 516.

Hinc demum: from hence at length. After the conception, above mentioned, at length, *lentum virus distillat.* Heyne reads: *Hìc demum.*

283. *Non innoxia:* in the sense of *malefica*, says Ruæus.

287. *Agitare:* to treat of fleecy flocks.

Quàm sit, et angustis hunc addere rebus honorem.
Sed me Parnassi deserta per ardua dulcis
Raptat amor: juvat ire jugis, quà nulla priorum
Castaliam molli divertitur orbita clivo.
Nunc, veneranda Pales, magno nunc ore sonandum.
Incipiens, stabulis edico in mollibus herbam
Carpere oves, dum mox frondosa reducitur æstas:
Et multâ duram stipulâ filicumque maniplis
Sternere subter humum, glacies ne frigida lædat
Molle pecus, scabiemque ferat, turpesque podagras.
Pòst, hinc digressus, jubeo frondentia capris
Arbuta sufficere, et fluvios præbere recentes;
Et stabula à ventis hyberno opponere Soli
Ad medium conversa diem: cùm frigidus olim
Jam cadit, extremoque irrorat Aquarius anno.
Hæ quoque non curâ nobis leviore tuendæ,
Nec minor usus erit: quamvis Milesia magno
Vellera mutentur, Tyrios incocta rubores.
Densior hinc soboles, hinc largi copia lactis.
Quàm magìs exhausto spumaverit ubere mulctra;
Læta magìs pressis manabunt flumina mammis.
Nec minùs intereà barbas incanaque menta
Cinyphii tondent hirci, setasque comantes,

292. Quà nulla orbita priorum *poëtarum*

294. Nunc sonandum *est nobis*

298. Subter *ipsis ovibus*

300. Jubeo *agricolam* sufficere

305. Hæ *capræ* tuendæ *sunt* nobis non leviore curâ *quàm oves*

306. Milesia vellera incocta *quoad* Tyrios rubores mutentur magno *pretio*.

310. *Tantò* magìs læta flumina *lactis*

312. Intereà *pastores* tondent barbas, incanaque

NOTES.

290. *Quam magnum:* how great, or difficult.

According to Heyne, *vincere ea verbis*, may mean, to reduce, or bring those things into poetic numbers: *Exprimere hæc commodè poëtica oratione*, says he. Ruæus says, *superare ista argumenta sermonis dignitate.*

Angustis: in the sense of *parvis* vel *humilibus.*

291. *Parnassi.* Parnassus was a mountain in Phocis, at the foot of which was the fountain *Castalia*, sacred to the muses. See Ecl. vi. 29.

292. *Quà nulla orbita priorum.* This is a most happy circumlocution, to denote a subject entirely new, and which had never been treated of by any one before him.

294. *Magno ore:* in a high and lofty strain, in order to add dignity to the subject; which, in importance, was inferior to what he had just before been treating of. *Pales:* see note 1, supra.

297. *Maniplis filicum:* with bundles of the fern.

299. *Ferat scabiem:* should bring on the scab, and foul gout.

The *podagra* was a disease of the feet, as its name implies.

Columella mentions two diseases, that affect the feet of sheep. One, when there is a galling, and filth in the parting of the hoof: the other, when there is a tubercle, or swelling, in the same place, with a hair in the middle and a worm under it.

300. *Frondentia arbuta:* in the sense of *frondes arbuti.*

301. *Fluvios:* in the sense of *aquam.*

Sufficere: in the sense of *dare.*

304. *Cum frigidus Aquarius:* when cold Aquarius at length sets, and sheds his dew in the end of the year.

Aquarius is a sign of the Ecliptic, into which the sun enters about the 22d of January. Also the same as *Ganymedes*, the son of Tros, king of Troy, whom Jupiter, in the form of an eagle, carried up to heaven, and made his cup-bearer. Hence he is usually represented with a pitcher pouring out water. The poet here seems to consider the year as beginning with the month of March, or *Aries.*

306. *Milesia:* Milesian wool. *Milesia* an adj. from *Milesus*, a city in the confines of Ionia and Caria, famous for its wool.

308. *Hinc densior:* from hence (from the goats) is a more numerous breed than from the sheep—from them too a greater quantity of milk.

Copia largi lactis: for *larga copia lactis.* This is not, properly speaking, by any figure of speech, but by what is commonly called *poetica licentia.*

309. *Ubere exhausto:* their udders being drained.

Quàm magis: in the sense of *quantò magis.*

312. *Cinyphii:* an adj. from *Cinyps*, a river of Africa, near the Garamantes, where the goat was the most shaggy

314. Verò *capræ* pascuntur

317. Ducuntque suos *fœtus secum*

322. Cùm læta æstas *instat*, Zephyris vocantibus, mittes utrumque gregem *ovium et caprarum*

333. Sicubi nemus nigrum crebris ilicibus accubet

335. Tum *jube pastores* dare *illis* tenues

Usum in castrorum et miseris velamina nautis.
Pascuntur verò sylvas, et summa Lycæi,
Horrentesque rubos, et amantes ardua dumos.
Atque ipsæ memores redeunt in tecta, suosque
Ducunt, et gravido superant vix ubere limen.
Ergò omni studio glaciem ventosque nivales,
Quò minùs est illis curæ mortalis egestas,
Avertes: victumque feres et virgea lætus
Pabula: nec totâ claudes fœnilia brumâ.
At verò, Zephyris cùm læta vocantibus æstas,
In saltus utrumque gregem atque in pascua mittes
Luciferi primo cum sidere, frigida rura
Carpamus: dum manè novum, dum gramina canent,
Et ros in tenerâ pecori gratissimus herbâ est.
Inde, ubi quarta sitim cœli collegerit hora,
Et cantu querulæ rumpent arbusta cicadæ;
Ad puteos, aut alta greges ad stagna jubeto
Currentem ilignis potare canalibus undam:
Æstibus at mediis umbrosam exquirere vallem,
Sicubi magna Jovis antiquo robore quercus
Ingentes tendat ramos; aut sicubi nigrum
Ilicibus crebris sacrâ nemus accubet umbrâ.
Tum tenues dare rursus aquas, et pascere rursus
Solis ad occasum: cùm frigidus aëra Vesper
Temperat, et saltus reficit jam roscida Luna,
Litoraque halcyonen resonant et acanthida dumi.

NOTES.

314. *Sylvas:* in the sense of *arbores*, vel *per sylvas*, &c.

Summa: in the sense of *cacumina.*

Lycæi: Lycæus was a mountain in Arcadia, sacred to Pan.

315. *Ardua:* high grounds. *Loca* is understood.

316. *Suos:* their young—the kids.

320 *Virgea pabula:* osier food—tender twigs, or browse.

324. *Cum primo*, &c. The meaning is, when the planet Venus first rises, going before the sun, for then it is called *Lucifer*, the farmer should drive his flocks to pasture; and early in the morning, when the grass is moist and tender, let them feed. *Sidere:* in the sense of *ortu.*

Carpamus frigida rura. Servius interprets these words thus: *Cogamus capras carpere frigida rura:* hoc est, *educamus greges ad carpenda*, &c.

327. *Cœli.* Davidson connects *cœli* with *sitim.* Ruæus and some others take it in the sense of *dies*, and connect it with *quarta hora.* Either preserves the sense and spirit of the poet.

He begins the day at the rising of the sun, otherwise by the fourth hour, the sun could not have caused thirst to man or beast. This would correspond with our ten o'clock, on those days when the sun is upon the equator, but on every other day in the year, it would vary from it.

The Jews, and some other nations, began their day at the rising of the sun. They divided the time of his being above the horizon into 12 equal parts, and the time of his being below it into 12 other equal parts, making 24 portions of each diurnal revolution. But this would make the hours of very different lengths in the different parts of the year. Some nations, on the other hand, began the day at the setting of the sun, and divided it in the same manner. Modern nations generally begin the day at midnight. The nautical day begins at noon, or when the sun is upon the meridian.

328. *Rumpent:* weary, or rend the groves. *Cantu:* in the sense of *stridore.*

330. *Ilignis canalibus:* in oaken troughs *Ilignis:* an adj. from *Ilex:* the holm-oak.

331. *Æstibus:* in the sense of *die.*

334. *Accubet sacrâ umbrâ:* hangs down, or bends, with its sacred boughs. *Umbra*, in the sense of *ramis*, by meton. Ruæus says: *Explicat sacram umbram.*

338. *Litora resonant:* the shores resound the king-fisher, and the bushes, the goldfinch—with the music of the king-fisher, and that of the goldfinch.

Acanthida: a Greek acc. of *Acanthus.* See Geor. i. 399.

Quid tibi pastores Libyæ, quid pascua versu
Prosequar, et raris habitata mapalia tectis?
Sæpe diem noctemque, et totum ex ordine mensem
Pascitur, itque pecus longa in deserta sinè ullis
Hospitiis: tantum campi jacet. Omnia secum
Armentarius Afer agit, tectumque, laremque,
Armaque, Amyclæumque canem, Cressamque pharetram.
Non secùs ac patriis acer Romanus in armis
Injusto sub fasce viam cùm carpit, et hostem
Ante expectatum positis stat in agmine castris.
At non, quà Scythiæ gentes, Mæoticaque unda,
Turbidus et torquens flaventes Ister arenas:
Quàque redit medium Rhodope porrecta sub axem.

340. Quid prosequar tibi versu pastores Libyæ, quid

342. Sæpe pecus pascitur

349. At non *est sic*, quà *sunt* Scythiæ gentes

NOTES.

340. *Prosequar:* in the sense of *dicam.* Sallust describes these *Mapalia,* (or *Magalia,*) thus: *Edificia Numidarum, quæ mapilia illi vocant, oblonga incurvis lateribus tecta sunt; quasi navium carinæ.* Heyne says of them: *Sparsa passim per agros, non in vicos collecta.* Ruæus takes *habitata* in the sense of *constantes. Paucis casis constantes,* says he.

341. *Ex ordine:* in succession—one after another without intermission.

343. *Hospitiis:* retreat—shelter.

344. *Larem.* The *Lares* were domestic gods like the *Penates.* There is some uncertainty with regard to their origin. At the first, their office was confined to houses and domestic affairs. Afterward, however, their power and influence were very much extended. We find the *Lares Urbani,* that presided over cities; *Lares Rustici,* that presided over the country; *Lares Compitales,* that presided over cross-ways; *Lares Marini,* that presided over the sea; *Lares Viales,* that presided over roads, &c. Some say there were only two that were properly called *Lares,* and these the sons of Mercury and the nymph Lara, or Larunda. It is more probable, however, that they were the *Manes* of parents, who being buried within the walls, or at the entrance of the house they inhabited, were thought to have a care of the things pertaining to it, and through the superstition of the age, received divine honors. They were worshipped under the form of a dog: or, as some say, only covered with the skin of that animal, because he is a trusty guard to the house.

Lares, by meton. is often put for one's house, habitation, or family. *Agit:* in the sense of *fert.*

345. *Amyclæum:* an adj. from *Amyclæ,* a city of Laconia, famous for its dogs and hunting, and for its being the reputed place of the nativity of Castor and Pollux.

Cressam: an adj. from *Creta,* a well known island in the Mediterranean, whose inhabitants were famous in the art of shooting. *Arma:* utensils.

346. *Non secùs:* no otherwise than the brave Roman in the arms of his country, when he marches out under his unequal load, and stands in battle array against the expected enemy.

This passage hath somewhat divided commentators. Vegetius, quoting it in his art of war, hath *hostem* instead of *hosti: ante hostem expectatum.* This certainly is the best and easiest reading. But *hosti* is the usual reading. *Ante expectatum* is usually taken in the sense of *antequam expectetur,* on the authority of verse 206, where *ante domandum* is plainly for *ante dometur.* But the two cases are not exactly similar; the latter being a gerund, and the former a participle adjective. On the whole, I prefer *hostem,* as being the easiest.

But there is another reason, which hath some weight. Let it be asked, why the Roman should march forth, pitch his camp, and stand in battle array, while an enemy is not looked for, or expected? But taking *expectatum,* with Vegetius, to agree with *hostem,* the difficulty will be removed.

Ante expectatum hostem: before, or against the expected foe—in the way to meet him. *Ante* signifies before, with respect to place, to time, and to dignity.

Heyne informs us that the Medicean, and some other copies have *hostem,* but he retains the usual reading.

347. *Sub injusto fasce.* The Roman soldier carried his shield, sword, helmet, &c. and also provisions sufficient for half a month: in weight about 60 pounds. *Fasce:* in the sense of *onere.*

349. *Mæotica unda.* This is the *Palus Mæotis,* or the sea of Azof, lying to the north of the Euxine, but connected with it by the straits of Caffa. The ancients called all those nations lying toward the north of Europe and Asia, *Scythians.*

350. *Ister:* the Danube.

351. *Rhodope.* A range of mountains rising in Thrace, and extending to the east

Illìc clausa tenent stabulis armenta: neque ullæ
Aut herbæ campo apparent, aut arbore frondes:
Sed jacet aggeribus niveis informis, et alto
Terra gelu latè, septemque assurgit in ulnas.
Semper hyems, semper spirantes frigora Cauri.
Tum Sol pallentes haud unquam discutit umbras.
Nec cùm invectus equis altum petit æthera; nec cùm
Præcipitem Oceani rubro lavit æquore currum.
Concrescunt subitæ currenti in flumine crustæ:
Undaque jam tergo ferratos sustinet orbes,
Puppibus illa priùs patulis, nunc hospita plaustris:
Æraque dissiliunt vulgò, vestesque rigescunt
Indutæ, cæduntque securibus humida vina,
Et totæ solidam in glaciem vertêre lacunæ,
Stiriaque impexis induruit horrida barbis.
Intereà toto non seciùs aëre ningit:
Intereunt pecudes: stant circumfusa pruinis
Corpora magna boum: confertoque agmine cervi
Torpent mole novâ, et summis vix cornibus extant.
Hos non immissis canibus, non cassibus ullis,
Puniceæve agitant pavidos formidine pennæ:
Sed frustrà oppositum trudentes pectore montem
Cominùs obtruncant ferro, graviterque rudentes
Cædunt, et magno læti clamore reportant.
Ipsi in defossis specubus secura sub altâ
Otia agunt terrâ: congestaque robora, totasque
Advolvêre focis ulmos, ignique dedêre.
Hìc noctem ludo ducunt, et pocula læti
Fermento atque acidis imitantur vitea sorbis.
Talis Hyperboreo septem subjecta trioni

354. Terra jacet informis niveis aggeribus, et alto gelu latè

356. *Illic* semper *est* hyems

364. Cædunt vina *priùs* humida

371. *Incolæ* non agitant hos pavidos

373. Sed cominùs obtruncant *eos* ferro frustrà trudentes pectore oppositum montem *nivis*

376. *Incolæ* ipsi agunt secura otia

NOTES.

and south till it meets mount Hemus; after which it turns, and stretches toward the north.

354. *Informis:* deformed—disfigured by the mounds of snow.

355. *Septem ulnas:* this is about ten and a half feet of our measure.

357. *Discutit:* in the sense of *dissipat.*

359. *Lavit:* washes his descending car in the red surface of the ocean.

The ocean is here called red, on account of the reflection of the sun's rays from its surface, when near the horizon.

361. *Ferratos orbes:* wheels bound with iron.

362. *Illa priùs hospita:* that (the water in the rivers) before friendly to the broad ships—now to wagons.

Hospita: hospitable—kind; receiving them as a guest, and treating them with kindness.

364. *Humida:* in the sense of *liquida. Priùs liquida*, says Ruæus.

So intense is the cold in high northern latitudes, that the spirit of wine has been frozen in the thermometer.

371. *Non agitant hos:* they do not pursue them, &c.

The *formido* was a line or cord, to which plumes of various colors were fastened, for the purpose of terrifying wild beasts. It was so extended or stretched in their usual haunts, or paths, as to lead or direct them insensibly into the net. *Puniceæ:* red-crimson.

379. *Læti imitantur:* joyous, they imitate the draughts of wine with their beer and acid cider.

Fermento: any fermented liquor.

Acidis sorbis: the acid sorb-apples, or service-berries; by meton. for the liquo made of them, usually rendered cider.

380. *Vitea pocula:* wine. This is highly poetical.

381. *Septem—trioni.* The parts of the word are separated by Tmesis.

The *Septemtrio* is a constellation near the north pole, called the greater bear, in which are seven stars, sometimes called the plough, because they are supposed to lie in that shape; also the parts of the world

Gens effræna virûm Riphæo tunditur Euro
Et pecudum fulvis velantur corpora setis.
Si tibi lanicium curæ: primùm aspera sylva,
Lappæque tribulique absint: fuge pabula læta:
Continuòque greges villis lege mollibus albos.
Illum autem, quamvis aries sit candidus ipse,
Nigra subest udo tantùm cui lingua palato,
Rejice, ne maculis infuscet vellera pullis
Nascentûm; plenoque alium circumspice campo.
Munere sic niveo lanæ, si credere dignum est,
Pan Deus Arcadiæ captam te, Luna, fefellit,
In nemora alta vocans: nec tu aspernata vocantem.
At cui lactis amor, cytisum, lotosque frequentes
Ipse manu, salsasque ferat præsepibus herbas.
Hinc et amant fluvios magìs, et magìs ubera tendunt,
Et salis occultum referunt in lacte saporem.
Multi jam excretos prohibent à matribus hœdos,
Primaque ferratis præfigunt ora capistris.
Quod surgente die mulsêre, horisque diurnis,
Nocte premunt: quod jam tenebris, et sole cadente,
Sub lucem exportans calathis adit oppida pastor,
Aut parco sale contingunt, hyemique reponunt.
Nec tibi cura canum fuerit postrema: sed unà
Veloces Spartæ catulos, acremque Molossum
Pasce sero pingui: nunquam, custodibus illis,
Nocturnum stabulis furem, incursusque luporum,
Aut impacatos à tergo horrebis Iberos.
Sæpe etiam cursu timidos agitabis onagros:
Et canibus leporem, canibus venabere damas.
Sæpe volutabris pulsos sylvestribus apros
Latratu turbabis agens: montesque per altos
Ingentem clamore premes ad retia cervum.

387. Autem, quamvis aries ipse sit candidus, rejice illum, cui tantùm nigra

393. Nec tu aspernata *es eum*

400. Quod *lactis* mulsere die

401. Quod *lactis* mulsere tenebris

NOTES.

lying under that constellation; also simply, the north. *Subjecta:* lying—placed.

384. *Lanicium:* the woollen trade, or manufacture.

Lappæque, tribulique: both burrs, and thistles.

386. *Greges:* in the sense of *oves.*

390. *Nascentûm:* a part of *nascor*, used as a sub.: of the lambs.

391. *Niveo munere.* The poet hath reference here to the fable of Pan's being in love with Luna. By changing himself into a snow-white ram, he deceived her; and decoying her into the woods, deflowered her. Probus, however, relates the story differently. He says, Pan being in love with Luna, offered her the choice of any of his flock; and choosing the whitest, she was deceived, because they were the worst.

396. *Tendunt:* in the sense of *distendunt.*

398. *Excretos:* grown large—or sufficiently grown to take care of themselves; of *ex* and *cresco.*

399. *Prima ora præfigunt ferratis capistris:* by Hypallage for, *præfigunt ferrata capistra primis oribus:* they prefix to the end of their mouths iron muzzles. These were in such a form as to prick the dam, if she offered to let them suck; but not to prevent them from eating grass.

402. *Exportans calathis:* carrying it in baskets, he goes, &c.—carrying it made into butter, curds, and cheese.

405. *Spartæ:* the most famous city of the Peloponnesus, and celebrated for its excellent dogs.

Molossum: a dog, so called from *Molossia*, a country of Epirus, so called from *Molossus*; the son of Pyrrhus, king of Epirus, and Andromache, the widow of Hector. See Æn. ii. 292.

408. *Iberos:* the Spaniards, so called from the *Iberus*, (*Hodie*, *Ebro*,) a river of Spain. They were so notorious for their robberies, that they became a proverb. The poet here uses their name for robbers in general.

Disce et odoratam stabulis accendere cedrum,
Galbaneoque agitare graves nidore chelydros.
Sæpe sub immotis præsepibus, aut mala tactu
Vipera delituit, cœlumque exterrita fugit;
Aut tecto assuetus coluber succedere et umbræ,
Pestis acerba boum, pecorique aspergere virus,
Fovit humum. Cape saxa manu, cape robora, pastor,
Tollentemque minas, et sibila colla tumentem,
Dejice: jamque fugâ timidum caput abdidit altè,
Cùm medii nexus, extremæque agmina caudæ,
Solvuntur, tardosque trahit sinus ultimus orbes.
Est etiam ille malus Calabris in saltibus anguis,
Squamea convolvens sublato pectore terga,
427. Maculosus *quoad* longam — Atque notis longam maculosus grandibus alvum:
Qui, dum amnes ulli rumpuntur fontibus, et dum
428. Qui *serpens* colit stagna — Vere madent udo terræ, ac pluvialibus Austris,
Stagna colit; ripisque habitans, hìc piscibus atram
Improbus ingluviem, ranisque loquacibus explet.
Postquam exhausta palus, terræque ardore dehiscunt,
433. In siccum *campum* — Exilit in siccum; et flammantia lumina torquens,
Sævit agris, asperque siti, atque exterritus æstu.
Ne mihi tum molles sub dio carpere somnos,
Neu dorso nemoris libeat jacuisse per herbas,
Cùm positis novus exuviis, nitidusque juventâ,
Volvitur, aut catulos tectis aut ova relinquens,
Arduus ad Solem, et linguis micat ore trisulcis.
Morborum quoque te causas et signa docebo.

NOTES.

415. *Galbaneo:* an adj. from *galbanum,* a gum, or liquor, at the smell of which serpents flee.

Chelydros: Chelydrus is properly a water tortoise—a land or water snake: *qui modò in paludibus, modò in arboribus latet.*

417. *Vipera:* a species of serpent, very poisonous; so called from the circumstance of its bringing forth its young alive.

Cœlum: for *lucem. Mala:* noxious—poisonous.

418. *Coluber:* a species of snake, which Mr. Martyn takes for the same that Pliny calls *boas,* from the circumstance of its feeding on cow's milk, which it draws from the teat. If this be the case, we see the propriety of the poet's calling the serpent, *acerba pestis boum:* the direful pest of cattle.

420. *Fovit terram:* hugs the ground.

423. *Medii nexus:* the middle joints.

Agminaque extremæ caudæ: the movements, or windings of the end of his tail.

Agmen is properly an army of men on the march; it is also said of a serpent: *Quia corporis pars pòst partem succedit, atque agitur instar exercitûs agminatim procedentis,* says Ruæus.

424 *Ultimus sinus:* the extreme joints or folds of his tail draw the slow wreaths or spires along. Ruæus says, *extrema curvatura.*

425. *Calabris:* an adj. from *Calabria,* the south-eastern part of Italy.

It is agreed that the snake here spoken of is the *chersydrus.* These serpents abounded in that part of Italy. They were amphibious. Their name is of Greek origin.

The poet here gives a very lively description of that destructive reptile.

428. *Rumpuntur:* in the sense of *erumpunt,* vel *rumpunt se.*

430. *Improbus implet:* greedy, he fills his filthy maw with fish, &c.

432. *Exhausta:* exhausted—dried up. Valpy reads *exusta,* but mentions no authority. *Exhausta* is the common reading.

435. *Tum ne libeat mihi:* then may it not please me to take, &c.

436. *Dorso.* Some render *dorso,* on the back, referring it to the posture of lying. But there is no necessity of this, if we suppose the grove to be on an eminence, or hill —on the side or edge of a grove.

437. *Positis exuviis:* his skin being put off. The snake, it is well known, changes his skin every year. *Exuit à capite primùm,* says Pliny.

438. *Tectis:* his habitation—den.

439. *Micat ore:* he vibrates with his three forked tongue in his mouth; that is, his three forked tongue vibrates in his mouth.

Turpis oves tentat scabies, ubi frigidus imber
Altiùs ad vivum persedit, et horrida cano
Bruma gelu: vel cùm tonsis illotus adhæsit
Sudor, et hirsuti secuerunt corpora vepres.
Dulcibus idcirco fluviis pecus omne magistri
Perfundunt, udisque aries in gurgite villis
Mersatur, missusque secundo defluit amni:
Aut tonsum tristi contingunt corpus amurcâ,
Et spumas miscent argenti, vivaque sulphura,
Idæasque pices, et pingues unguine ceras,
Scillamque, helleborosque graves, nigrumque bitumen.
Non tamen ulla magis præsens fortuna laborum est,
Quàm si quis ferro potuit rescindere summum
Ulceris os: alitur vitium, vivitque tegendo:
Dum medicas adhibere manus ad vulnera pastor
Abnegat, et meliora Deos sedet omina poscens
Quin etiam ima dolor balantûm lapsus ad ossa
Cùm furit, atque artus depascitur arida febris;
Profuit incensos æstus avertere, et inter
Ima ferire pedis salientem sanguine venam,
Bisaltæ quo more solent, acerque Gelonus,
Cùm fugit in Rhodopen, atque in deserta Getarum,
Et lac concretum cum sanguine potat equino.
  Quam procul, aut molli succedere sæpiùs umbræ
Videris, aut summas carpentem ignaviùs herbas,
Extremamque sequi, aut medio procumbere campo
Pascentem, et seræ solam decedere nocti;
Continuò culpam ferro compesce, priusquàm

443. Bruma horrida cano gelu

461. *Eodem* more, quo Bisaltæ solent *ferire venam*

464. Quam *ovem* videris procul, aut succedere sæpiùs molli umbræ

466. Extremamque sequi *cæteras*

NOTES.

443. *Tonsis:* to the shorn sheep. *Ovibus* is understood.

445. *Magistri:* in the sense of *pastores.*

446. *Gurgite:* in the sense of *fluvio.*

448. *Tristi:* bitter.

Contingunt: in the sense of *ungunt.*

449. *Spumas argenti:* litharge. Some understand quicksilver; but it is not certain whether the ancients called that, *spuma argenti.*

450. *Idæas pices:* the pitch is here called Idæan, from mount Ida, in Troas, whose pitch was the best.

451. *Scillam:* the squill, or sea onion; it is a bulbous root, like an onion, but much larger.

Helleboros. There are two kinds of hellebore, the white and the black. The former, says Mr. Martyn, is serviceable in diseases of the skin, if it be externally applied; but it will not do to be taken internally, as the black kind will. Hence he thinks, Virgil here means the white, by his using the epithet *gravis*, strong-scented.

452. *Fortuna laborum:* remedy of their disease, or sufferings. *Præsens:* speedy—efficacious.

454. *Summum os ulceris:* the highest part, or head of the sore. *Vitium:* the malady, or disease. *Tegendo:* by being concealed.

456. *Meliora omina:* better success—or luck.

Verbs of asking, teaching, &c. govern two accusatives, one of the person, the other of the thing.

457. *Lapsus:* penetrating.

460. *Inter ima pedis:* in the sense of *inter imas ungulas pedis:* between the divisions or parts of the hoof. *Ferire:* to open a vein.

461. *Bisaltæ:* a people of Macedonia.

Geloni: a people of Scythia, who painted their bodies, to be more terrible to their enemies.

462. *Getarum:* the Getæ were a people of Thrace, inhabiting *Mœsia interior*, not far from the mouth of the *Ister.*

463. *Concretum:* thickened.

467. *Decedere seræ nocti:* to yield or give place to the late night. She was the last to leave the pasture grounds, and then compelled only by the darkness of the night. She yielded to the darkness, and went home.

468. *Culpam.* By this we are to understand the diseased sheep, and not simply the affected part, as Ruæus and some others understand it. The poet advises, as soon as you discover, by the signs above mentioned

Dira per incautum serpant contagia vulgus.
Non tam creber, agens hyemem, ruit æquore turbo;
Quàm multæ pecudum pestes: nec singula morbi
Corpora corripiunt; sed tota æstiva repentè,
Spemque, gregemque simul, cunctamque ab origine gentem.
Tum sciat, aërias Alpes et Norica si quis
Castella in tumulis, et Iapidis arva Timavi,
Nunc quoque pòst tantò videat, desertaque regna
Pastorum, et longè saltus latèque vacantes.
  Hìc quondam morbo cœli miseranda coorta est
Tempestas, totoque autumni incanduit æstu,
Et genus omne neci pecudum dedit, omne ferarum,
Corrupitque lacus, infecit pabula tabo.
Nec via mortis erat simplex: sed ubi ignea venis
Omnibus acta sitis miseros adduxerat artus;
Rursus abundabat fluidus liquor; omniaque in se
Ossa minutatim morbo collapsa trahebat.
Sæpe in honore Deûm medio stans hostia ad aram,
Lanea dum niveâ circumdatur infula vittâ,
Inter cunctantes cecidit moribunda ministros.
Aut si quam ferro mactaverat antè sacerdos;
Inde neque impositis ardent altaria fibris,
Nec responsa potest consultus reddere vates:
Ac vix suppositi tinguntur sanguine cultri,
Summaque jejunâ sanie infuscatur arena.
Hinc lætis vituli vulgò moriuntur in herbis,
Et dulces animas plena ad præsepia reddunt.
Hinc canibus blandis rabies venit; et quatit ægros
Tussis anhela sues, ac faucibus angit obesis.
Labitur infelix studiorum, atque immemor herbæ

471. Quàm pestes pecudum *sunt* multæ

474. Tum *ille* sciat *hoc esse verum*, siquis *etiam* nunc quoque tantò pòst videat aërias Alpes, et Norica castella in tumulis, et arva Iapidis Timavi, desertaque regna pastorum, et saltus

489. Aut si sacerdos mactaverat quam *hostium* ferro, antè-*quàm ceciderat*, inde

492. Suppositi *visceribus* vix tinguntur

498. Victor equus, infelix, *et* immemor studiorum, atque herbæ, labitur

NOTES.

that any one of your sheep is diseased, to take away the faulty animal: kill it forthwith, that the contagion may not spread among the unwary flock. This is the sense of Davidson and Valpy.

474. *Norica:* an adj. from *Noricum*, a country of Germany, in the neighborhood of the Alps, but beyond them with regard to Italy.

Timavi: Timavus, a small river in the Venetian territory, called *Iapidis* (*Iapidian*) from *Iapides*, an ancient people, who inhabited that part of it, through which the *Timavus* flowed.

476. *Regna:* possessions.

479. *Miseranda tempestas:* a direful pestilence arose.

Æstu: heat. *Incanduit:* raged during the whole heat of autumn.

481. *Tabo:* with a poisonous quality.

Lacus: in the sense of *aquam*.

482. *Nec via mortis:* nor was the manner of their death simple and common. It was complicated, and attended with affecting circumstances.

483. *Sitis:* properly thirst. By meton. the fever causing it. *Ignea sitis:* the raging fever.

485. *Trahebat omnia:* and drew all the bones, wasted, or consumed, little by little, by the disease, into itself. *Convertebat in se*, says Ruæus.

487. *Infula.* This was a broad wreath, or band, made of wool, and bound about the temples of the victim; but not covering the whole head: from it hung the *vitta*, or fillet.

490. *Fibris:* the flesh.

492. *Suppositi:* applied to the carcass, or flesh.

493. *Jejuna sanie:* with the meagre gore. In these diseases, the blood was wasted, or converted into a thin meagre fluid, which the poet calls *fluidus liquor.* This pervaded the body so thoroughly, that it even converted the marrow, and life of the bones, into itself.

496. *Rabies:* madness.

497. *Anhela tussis:* a wheezing cough shakes the diseased swine.

Obesis: a disease something like the quinsy.

498. *Studiorum:* of his exercises—those races in which he bore off the palm of victory.

Victor equus, fontesque avertitur, et pede terram
Crebra ferit: demissæ aures: incertus ibidem
Sudor; et ille quidem morituris frigidus: aret
Pellis, et ad tactum tractanti dura resistit.
Hæc ante exitium primis dant signa diebus:
Sin in processu cœpit crudescere morbus,
Tum verò ardentes oculi, atque attractus ab alto
Spiritus interdum gemitu gravis: imaque longo
Ilia singultu tendunt: it naribus ater
Sanguis, et obsessas fauces premit aspera lingua.
Profuit inserto latices infundere cornu
Lenæos: ea visa salus morientibus una.
Mox erat hoc ipsum exitio: furiisque refecti
Ardebant: ipsique suos, jam morte sub ægrâ,
(Dî meliora piis, erroremque hostibus illum)
Discissos nudis laniabant dentibus artus.
  Ecce autem duro fumans sub vomere taurus
Concidit, et mixtum spumis vomit ore cruorem,
Extremosque ciet gemitus: it tristis arator,
Mœrentem abjungens fraternâ morte juvencum,
Atque opere in medio defixa relinquit aratra.
Non umbræ altorum nemorum, non mollia possunt
Prata movere animum, non, qui per saxa volutus
Purior electro campum petit, amnis: at ima
Solvuntur latera, atque oculos stupor urget inertes,
Ad terramque fluit devexo pondere cervix.
Quid labor, aut benefacta juvant? quid vomere terras
Invertisse graves? atqui non Massica Bacchi
Munera, non illis epulæ nocuere repôstæ:
Frondibus et victu pascuntur simplicis herbæ:
Pocula sunt fontes liquidi, atque exercita cursu
Flumina: nec somnos abrumpit cura salubres.
  Tempore non alio, dicunt, regionibus illis,
Quæsitas ad sacra boves Junonis, et uris

501. Et ille *sudor* quidem *erat* frigidus *iis* morituris

504. In processu *temporis*

509. *Primò* profuit.

511. *Illi* refecti *illo vino*

512. Ipsique jam sub ægra morte, laniabant suos artus discissos

525. Quid *eorum* labor, aut benefacta *homini* juvant *eos?* Quid *juvat eos* invertisse graves terras vomere?

NOTES.

Infelix: Unhappy—miserable, after all his noble deeds. This is the sense of Ruæus.

500. *Incertus:* uncertain—the cause of which was unknown: or, various—fluctuating—coming on, and going off, by turns.

Crebrà: here used adverbially; a Grecism.

506. *Spiritus attractus:* their breath, drawn from the bottom of the breast, is sometimes heavy (interrupted) with a groan.

Singultu: a sob, or sobbing.

508. *Obsessas:* swollen—obstructed.

510. *Lenæos latices:* simply, wine.

Cornu inserto: a horn put down their throat, through which the wine was poured.

513. *Dii meliora,* &c. May the gods grant better things to the pious, and that madness, or destruction to our enemies.

The verb *reddant,* or another of the like import, is understood.

523. *Ima latera:* their flanks are lank, or flabby. *Flaccescunt,* says Heyne.

Stupor: a stupor, or death-like appearance, rests upon their heavy eyes.

525. *Juvant:* Ruæus says, *prosunt.*

526. *Massica:* the Massic gifts of Bacchus—wine.

Massica: an adj. from *Massicus,* a mountain in Campania, famous for its rich wines.

530. *Nec cura,* &c. Nor does care interrupt their healthful slumbers.

The whole account of this fatal murrain is one of Virgil's finest pieces. But from the 515th line, *Ecce autem,* &c. it is extremely tender, and inimitable in beauty; and particularly the last six lines. They were so much admired by Scaliger, that he declares, he had rather have been the author of them, than to have had the favor of Crœsus, or Cyrus.

532. *Quæsitas:* sought after—wanted.

533. Currus *ejus* ductos *fuisse* ad

534. Ergò *agricolæ* ægre rimantur

549. Magistri *medicinæ* cessere *mederi.*

552. Antè *se*

558. Donec *Agricolæ* discant tegere *illa* humo

561. Nec possunt quidem tondere vellera, peresa

Imparibus ductos alta ad donaria currus.
Ergò ægrè rastris terram rimantur, et ipsis
Unguibus infodiunt fruges, montesque per altos
Contentâ cervice trahunt stridentia plaustra.
Non lupus insidias explorat ovilia circùm,
Nec gregibus nocturnus obambulat: acrior illum
Cura domat. Timidi damæ, cervique fugaces
Nunc interque canes, et circùm tecta vagantur.
Jam maris immensi prolem, et genus omne natantûm,
Litore in extremo, ceu naufraga corpora, fluctus
Proluit: insolitæ fugiunt in flumina phocæ.
Interit et curvis frustrà defensa latebris
Vipera, et attoniti, squamis astantibus, hydri.
Ipsis est aër avibus non æquus, et illæ
Præcipites altâ vitam sub nube relinquunt.
Prætereà, nec jam mutari pabula refert,
Quæsitæque nocent artes: cessêre magistri,
Phillyrides Chiron, Amythaoniusque Melampus.
Sævit et in lucem Stygiis emissa tenebris
Pallida Tisiphone: morbos agit antè metumque,
Inque dies avidum surgens caput altiùs effert.
Balatu pecorum, et crebris mugitibus, amnes,
Arentesque sonant ripæ, collesque supini.
Jamque catervatim dat stragem, atque aggerat ipsis
In stabulis turpi dilapsa cadavera tabo:
Donec humo tegere, ac foveis abscondere discant.
Nam neque erat coriis usus: nec viscera quisquam
Aut undis abolere potest, aut vincere flammâ.
Nec tondere quidem morbo illuvieque peresa
Vellera, nec telas possunt attingere putres.

NOTES.

533. *Uris imparibus:* by buffaloes, unequally matched. *Ductos:* drawn. *Rimantur:* break up, or till.

536. *Contenta cervicè:* with their strained neck, they draw, &c.

537. *Explorat:* meditates, or designs. *Meditatur*, says Ruæus.

541. *Jam fluctus:* now the waves wash up the race of the boundless, &c.

Such was the extent, and degree of the infection of the air, that it reached even to the scaly tribes. But Aristotle observes, that infectious diseases never reach to, or invade, fishes.

Natantûm: a pres. part. of the verb *nato*, taken as a sub. of fishes.

543. *Insolitæ;* unusual—contrary to their custom.

550. *Chiron.* He was the son of Saturn and Phillyra. It is said he taught Æsculapius in physic, Hercules in astronomy, and Achilles in music.

Melampus: the son of Amythaon and Doripe. They were both famous physicians: here used for the masters of medicine in general.

551. *Stygiis:* an adj. from *Styx*, a river of Arcadia, whose water was so cold and poisonous, that it proved fatal to all who drank it. This, together with the circumstance of its disappearing under the earth, led the poets to feign it to be a river of hell, around which, they say, it flowed nine times. It was held in such veneration by the gods, that they usually swore by it; and if they violated their oath at any time, they were to be deprived of their divinity for 100 years.

553. *In dies:* daily—every day.

555. *Supini colles:* sloping hills.

556. *Jamque dat:* and now she (Tisiphone) deals destruction by herds, &c.

557. *Dilapsa:* wasted, or consumed.

559. *Nec quisquam:* nor could any one cleanse it with water, or purify it by fire—conquer, or overcome the infection by fire.

Viscera: the flesh in general; all that is under the skin.

560. *Undis:* in the sense of *aqua.*

562. *Putres telas:* the putrid, or infectious cloth—the cloth made of the filthy and corrupted wool.

Telas: the web, put by synec. for the whole cloth.

Verùm etiam invisos si quis tentârat amictus;
Ardentes papulæ, atque immundus olentia sudor
Membra sequebatur; nec longo deinde moranti
Tempore, contactos artus sacer ignis edebat

565. Deinde sacer ignis edebat contactos artus *illi* moranti *dimittere eos amictus à se*, nec longo tempore.

NOTES.

564. *Ardentes papulæ:* red, fiery pimples, or blains.

565. *Sequebatur:* spread over the noisome body.

566. *Sacer ignis:* the erysipelas, or St. Anthony's fire. It consumed those parts of the body with which the garments (*amictus*) came in contact.

The meaning of these last six lines appears to be this: That the people were forced at length to abstain from shearing the infected fleeces; or touching the wool; or ever wearing any garments, when made of it: because those, who had done so, had been great sufferers thereby.

QUESTIONS.

What is the subject of this book?
How does the poet commence?
Why does he first invoke Pales?
How was she worshipped?
What were her festivals called?
After finishing the main subject, does he add any thing by way of episode?
What number of episodes has he added?
What are the subjects of these episodes?
What is the general character of them?
May they be reckoned among the finest parts of the Georgics?
How does the book conclude?
Who was Hippodame?
What is said of Œnomaus?
Who was his daughter?
Who was Pelops?
And what is said of his father?
In what year of the world were the Olympic games instituted?
How often were they celebrated?
Did they form an important era in the Grecian history?
What other games were there in Greece?
In honor of whom were the Nemean games instituted?
And to commemorate what event?
In honor of whom were the Pythian games instituted?
And to commemorate what event?
Who instituted the Isthmean games?
Where were they celebrated?
And in honor of whom?
Who was Tithonus?
How long did he live before Augustus?
In what sense do Servius and Eustathius consider the word *Tithonus*, as used by the poet in reference to Augustus?
Who were the Lapithæ?
What are they said to have done?
What was the name of their principal city?
Can you mention any nation that began the day at the rising of the sun?
How did they divide the day?
How did they divide the night?
What effect would this have upon the length of their hours?
When do modern nations begin the day?
When does the nautical day commence?
Who, probably, were the *Lares*?
Over what did they preside?
For what is the word *Lares* taken by meton.?
What was the usual weight which the Roman soldier carried on his march?
Of what did it consist?
What were all those nations called by the Romans that inhabited the northern part of Europe and Asia?
Was there any particular part of this book much admired by Scaliger?
What part was that?

LIBER QUARTUS.

THIS Book treats of the culture of bees. After proposing the subject, the poet shows the proper stations for placing their hives; and having noticed some particulars respecting the management of the swarms, &c. he digresses into a noble description of a battle between two discordant kings. He then proceeds to consider their different kinds and qualities, the nature and form of their government, and the diseases, which often rage among them—together with the proper remedies for each; and concludes with the story of Aristæus' recovery of his bees, after his swarms were lost, and of Orpheus' descent into hell after his wife Eurydice. This episode runs through 277 lines, and is one of the finest pieces of heathen poetry.

PROTINUS aërii mellis cœlestia dona
Exequar: hanc etiam, Mæcenas, aspice partem
Admiranda tibi levium spectacula rerum,
Magnanimosque duces, totiusque ordine gentis
Mores, et studia, et populos, et prælia dicam.
In tenui labor; at tenuis non gloria: si quem
Numina læva sinunt, auditque vocatus Apollo.
Principio, sedes apibus statioque petenda,
Quò neque sit ventis aditus (nam pabula venti
Ferre domum prohibent) neque oves hœdique petulci
Floribus insultent; aut errans bucula campo
Decutiat rorem, et surgentes atterat herbas.
Absint et picti squalentia terga lacerti
Pinguibus à stabulis; meropesque, aliæque volucres,

2. Hanc partem *Georgicorum*. Dicam spectacula levium rerum admiranda tibi

6. *Ille est* labor in tenui *re*

7. Si læva Numina sinunt quem *scriptorem exequi id*

10. Prohibent *apes* ferre domum

13. Picti *quoad* squalentia

NOTES.

1. *Aërii:* an adj. from *aër*. Honey is here called aërial, because it was thought to come from the dew, which fell from the air upon the flowers, whence the bees collected it. For the same reason the poet uses the epithet *cœlestia*.

2. *Exequar:* in the sense of *describam*.

6. *Tenui:* on a low subject. *Re* is understood. The consideration of bees may be considered low, or inferior to the subjects treated of in the preceding books. If, however, the farmer attend properly to them, he will find them very profitable; and their government and polity will afford to the philosopher and politician much useful instruction. This is what we are to understand by the words, *at gloria non tenuis*.

7. *Læva numina*. *Lævus* is used both in a good and a bad sense. Ruæus interprets it by *adversa*. By the deities, here called adverse, or inauspicious, we are probably to understand the infernal deities, Pluto, the Furies, &c. who were thought to be opposed to the welfare of men. Valpy understands by *læva*, propitious, or favorable. Heyne seems to be of the same opinion. Gellius and Wakefield take it with Ruæus, to mean adverse. When words are indefinite, or are used in opposite senses, we can hardly expect unanimity among commentators. If the adverse deities should not interfere to prevent him, and Apollo should come to his aid, the poet promises to execute a work, worthy of his friend and patron, even upon the humble subject of the bee.

8. *Principio:* in the sense of *primò*. *Sedes*. The poet proceeds to mention the proper places for the hives, and the form and fashion of constructing them.

11. *Insultent:* bruise—frisk about upon the flowers.

13. *Picti:* in the sense of *maculosi*.

14. *Meropes*. These were a species of bird that fed upon bees; hence called the bee-eater. They were about the size of our blackbird, but of various colors.

Et manibus Procne pectus signata cruentis.
Omnia nam latè vastant, ipsasque volantes
Ore ferunt, dulcem nidis immitibus escam.
At liquidi fontes, et stagna virentia musco
Adsint, et tenuis, fugiens per gramina, rivus :
Palmaque vestibulum, aut ingens oleaster inumbret
Ut, cùm prima novi ducent examina reges
Vere suo, ludetque favis emissa juventus ;
Vicina invitet decedere ripa calori,
Obviaque hospitiis teneat frondentibus arbos.
  In medium, seu stabit iners, seu profluet humor,
Transversas salices et grandia conjice saxa :
Pontibus ut crebris possint consistere, et alas
Pandere ad æstivum Solem ; si fortè morantes
Sparserit, aut præceps Neptuno immerserit Eurus,
Hæc circùm casiæ virides et olentia latè
Serpylla, et graviter spirantis copia thymbræ
Floreat : irriguumque bibant violaria fontem.
  Ipsa autem, seu corticibus tibi suta cavatis,
Seu lento fuerint alvearia vimine texta,
Angustos habeant aditus ; nam frigore mella
Cogit hyems, eademque calor liquefacta remittit :
Utraque vis apibus pariter metuenda : neque illæ
Nequicquam in tectis certatim tenuia cerâ
Spiramenta linunt, fucoque et floribus oras

15. Procne signata *quoad* pectus cruentis manibus, *absint ab iis.*

16. Ipsasque *apes*

25. Conjice salices transversas et granida saxa in medium *humorem*, seu

27. Consistere *in iis tanquam* pontibus

30. Circùm hæc *loca* virides

33. Autem alvearia ipsa, seu suta *sint* tibi *e* cavatis corticibus, seu

37. Neque illæ nequicquam linunt tenuia spiramenta in tectis cerâ

NOTES.

15. *Procne.* By *Procne*, or *Progne*, is here meant the swallow which has some red feathers on its breast. For the story of *Procne*, see Ecl. vi. 78.

17. *Dulcem escam:* as a sweet morsel for their merciless young. *Nidis:* the nests; by meton. for the young ones in them.

18. *Liquidi:* in the sense of *puri.* *Virentia musco:* either the banks of these ponds, or pools skirted with green moss, or the surface of them covered with it.

19. *Fugiens:* in the sense of *fluens.*

21. *Nova examina:* the new swarms.

22. *Emissa:* in the sense of *egressa.* The spring abounds in flowers more than any season of the year; honey is collected in greater abundance, and the bees are then most diligent. In this sense, the spring may emphatically be called theirs: *suo vere*, their own spring.

24. *Obvia:* in the sense of *adversa:* opposite, or in front of them. *Teneat* in the sense of *accipiat.*

25. *Humor:* in the sense of *aqua.*

26. *Conjice*, &c. These willows and rocks were to be cast into the water, whether running or stagnant, that the bees might rest upon them: if, by any means, they fell into it, that they might creep upon them, expand their wings to the warm sun, and dry themselves.

29. *Neptuno:* in the sense of *aquâ.* See Geor. i. 14

30. *Casiæ.* Some take the *casia* to be the same with the rosemary; but Columella, speaking of the plants that should grow about an apiary, mentions casia and rosemary as two different plants.

31. *Serpylla.* There were two kinds of this plant; one of the gardens, and the other wild. It is a strong-scented herb, and resembles thyme. It is proper to be planted near bees, and is usually called wild-thyme. *Thymbræ:* the herb savory. *Spirantis:* in the sense of *olentis.* It was a strong-scented herb.

32. *Violaria:* beds of violets—places sown or planted with the violet.

33. *Suta:* in the sense of *compacta.* *Corticibus.* The bark of the cork-tree is called *cortex*, by way of eminence.

34. *Lento vimine:* of limber osier, or wicker.

36. *Cogit:* thickens. *Remittit:* in the sense of *reddit.*

37. *Vis:* force—violence; the excess of heat or cold.

38. *Tectis:* in their hives. *Certatim:* in the sense of *diligenter.*

39. *Fuco.* *Fucus* was properly a kind of marine weed, resembling lettuce. It was anciently used in dying; used also by women as a kind of paint for the face. Hence all kinds of daubing obtained the name of *fucus:* not with the flowers (*floribus*) themselves, but rather with the substance ex-

Explent: collectumque hæc ipsa ad munera gluten
Et visco et Phrygiæ servant pice lentius Idæ.
Sæpe etiam effossis (si vera est fama) latebris
Sub terrâ fovêre larem; penitùsque repertæ
Pumicibusque cavis, exesæque arboris antro.
Tu tamen et levi rimosa cubilia limo
Unge fovens circùm, et raras superinjice frondes
Neu propiùs tectis taxum sine, neve rubentes
Ure foco cancros: altæ neu crede paludi:
Aut ubi odor cœni gravis, aut ubi concava pulsu
Saxa sonant, vocisque offensa resultat imago.
Quod superest, ubi pulsam hyemem Sol aureus egit
Sub terras, cœlumque æstivâ luce reclusit;
Illæ continuò saltus sylvasque peragrant,
Purpureosque metunt flores, et flumina libant
Summa leves. Hinc nescio quâ dulcedine lætæ,
Progeniem nidosque fovent: hinc arte recentes
Excudunt ceras, et mella tenacia fingunt.
Hinc ubi jam emissum caveis ad sidera cœli
Nare per æstatem liquidam suspexeris agmen,

45. Tamen tu et circùm unge rimosa cubilia levi limo.

48. Neu crede *alvearia*

49. Gravis odor cœni *est*, aut

55. Hinc *illæ* lætæ, nescio qua dulcedine

NOTES.

tracted from them, by meton. *Oras:* the margin, or edge, of their hives. Valpy takes *fuco et floribus*, by Hendiadis, for *fuco floreo*.

40. *Ad hæc ipsa munera:* in the sense of *ad hos ipsos usus.*

41. *Lentius:* an adj. of the com. deg. (of *lentus*) agreeing with *gluten:* tougher than, &c.

43. *Sæpe etiam fovêre:* they have even cherished their families in caverns dug under the earth. Several manuscripts have *fodêre*, but *fovêre* is the best. Ruæus has *fodêre*. He interprets the passage thus: *aperuerunt sibi domum sub terra.* But it is not necessary to suppose that the bees dug these caves or cells for themselves, any more than that they prepared their cells in the pumice stone, or cavities in the trees, for their reception. Davidson, Heyne, and Heinsius, read *fovêre*. *Larem.* See Geor. iii. 344. *Penitus:* in the sense of *profundè.*

45. *Cubilia:* in the sense of *alvearia. Unge:* smear, or plaster all around. *Fovens:* cherishing—keeping them warm.

48. *Cancros.* Crabs and lobsters, it is well known, in boiling, pass from a dark or brown, to a red color. Hence the epithet *rubentes*. *Altæ paludi.* The poet advises not to place the hives near marshy or fenny places, which afford no stones or bridges, on which the bees may rest, if occasion should require.

49. *Gravis:* stinking. *Pulsu:* by the stroke of the voice.

50. *Imago vocis:* the image of the voice being struck, rebounds; i. e. where an echo is heard. This is always the case when the pulses or waves of air, put in motion by some stroke or concussion, meet with an obstacle, and are reflected, or turned back, so as to make an impression on the ear. This the poet calls the image of the voice.

51. *Quod superest.* The poet now proceeds to speak of the food, the swarming, and the battles of the bees; and to give directions how to appease the fury of their contests, and bring them back to the hive.

52. *Sub terras:* under the earth—to the southern pole. This is a beautiful circumlocution to express the return of summer. The seasons are opposite, on the opposite sides of the equator, beyond the tropics. When it is summer on the north, it is winter on the south, and *vice versâ*. This is occasioned by the motion of the earth in its orbit, making an angle with the equator of 23° 28′.

54. *Purpureos.* The poet frequently uses purple for any gay color. *Metunt:* in the sense of *carpunt.*

55. *Leves libant:* and lightly taste or sip. *Dulcedine:* in the sense of *delectatione.*

56. *Fovent:* cherish—grow fond of. *Nidos:* either the apartments formed in the hive for the purpose of depositing their young, or simply, the hives themselves.

57. *Excudunt:* they form the fresh or new made wax. This is a metaphor taken from the smith, who is said (*excudere*) to strike, or hammer out the instrument of iron which he forms. The bees are here compared in their labors to the Cyclops, laboring at the anvil.

59. *Suspexeris agmen emissum:* when now you shall see the swarm issuing from the hives, &c. *Nare:* in the sense of *volare.*

Obscuramque trahi vento mirabere nubem,
Contemplator: aquas dulces et frondea semper
Tecta petunt: huc tu jussos asperge sapores,
Trita melisphylla, et cerinthæ ignobile gramen
Tinnitusque cie, et Matris quate cymbala circùm.
Ipsæ consident medicatis sedibus: ipsæ
Intima more suo sese in cunabula condent.
  Sin autem ad pugnam exierint (nam sæpe duobus
Regibus incessit magno discordia motu)
Continuòque animos vulgi, et trepidantia bello
Corda licet longè præsciscere: namque morantes
Martius ille æris rauci canor increpat, et vox
Auditur fractos sonitus imitata tubarum.
Tum trepidæ inter se coëunt, pennisque coruscant,
Spiculaque exacuunt rostris, aptantque lacertos,
Et circa regem atque ipsa ad prætoria densæ
Miscentur, magnisque vocant, clamoribus hostem.
Ergò, ubi ver nactæ sudum, camposque patentes,
Erumpunt portis: concurritur: æthere in alto
Fit sonitus: magnum mixtæ glomerantur in orbem,
Præcipitesque cadunt: non densior aëre grando,
Nec de concussâ tantum pluit ilice glandis.
Ipsi per medias acies, insignibus alis,
Ingentes animos angusto in pectore versant:
Usque adeò obnixi non cedere, dum gravis, aut hos,

61. **Frondea tecta,** *ubi considant:*

64. Matris ***Cybeles***

69. Continuò licet *tibi* longè *priùs* præsciscere

74. Lacertos *ad pugnam*

77. Nactæ *sunt* ver sudum, *aërios*que campos patentes

82. ***Reges*** ipsi ***volantes*** per medias

NOTES.

60. *Trahi:* in the sense of *ferri.* *Obscuram:* a dark cloud of bees.

63. *Melisphylla:* balm-gentle. It is an herb, of which bees are very fond. It is thought to be the same that was sometimes called *apiastrum* by the Romans. *Cerinthæ:* the honey-suckle. The poet calls it *ignobile gramen,* because it was common. It abounds in a sweet juice, like honey.

64. *Cie tinnitus:* make, or excite a ringing. The effect of the sound of brass upon the swarm is very great. It is the most effectual means to stop them in their flight, and collect them into the hive. Some have attributed this to fear, others to pleasure. But more probably it confounds the sound of their queen, or leader; and being without command or direction, they fall or settle upon the first place they meet. *Matris:* Cybele was the mother of the gods—the same as Rhea, or Ops. At her sacrifices, cymbals were always used.

65. *Medicatis sedibus:* prepared seats, or places for them to light upon.

66. *Cunabula:* in the sense of *recessus,* vel *alvearia.*

68. *Incessit:* hath seized—invaded. Nothing can be more lively or animated than this description of a battle of bees. We here find the ardor of the warrior, the sound of the trumpet, the glittering of armour, the shouts of the soldiers, the bravery of the leaders, and all the rage and madness of battle.

69. *Trepidantia:* eager—anxious.—

70. *Præscisere:* in the sense of *præsentire.*

71. *Canor:* in the sense of *strepitus,* vel *sonitus.* *Morantes:* those that are behind. *Increpat:* rouses—urges on.

73. *Trepidæ:* eager—hurrying. *Pennis:* in the sense of *alis.*

75. *Ipsa prætoria.* In the Roman camp, the tent of the commanding officer was called *Prætorium;* hence, by meton. put for the cells of the royal bees. *Densæ miscentur:* they are crowded thick.

77. *Sudum ver:* a clear spring day. Ruæus says, *serenum tempus.* *Campos patentes.* the fields of air open—unobstructed by wind or clouds.

78. *Concurritur:* in the sense of *concurrunt.*

79. *Glomerantur.* This verb hath a reflex signification here, like the middle voice of the Greeks: they form themselves into a great circle. *Mixtæ:* in the sense of *commistæ.*

81. *Pluit:* in the sense of *cadit.* It is to be joined with *grando,* in the preceding line.

82. *Insignibus alis:* with distinguished wings—distinguished from the rest by their wings.

83. *Versant:* in the sense of *exercent,* vel *manifestant.*

84. *Obnixi usque adeò:* determined all the time not to yield, until the mighty conqueror hath forced one side or the other, &c.

89. Dede eum neci, qui visus *fuerit* deterior
90. Sine *ut* melior regnet in aulâ vacua *ab hoste.*
92. Genera *apum*: hic *est*
99. Corpora lita *sunt*
106. Nec *est* magnus labor prohibere *eos*

Aut hos, versa fugâ victor dare terga subegit.
Hi motus animorum, atque hæc certamina tanta
Pulveris exigui jactu compressa quiescent.
Verùm ubi ductores acie revocaveris ambos:
Deterior qui visus, eum, ne prodigus obsit,
Dede neci: melior vacuâ sine regnet in aulâ.
Alter erit maculis auro squalentibus ardens:
(Nam duo sunt genera) hic melior, insignis et ore,
Et rutilis clarus squamis: ille horridus alter
Desidiâ, latamque trahens inglorius alvum.
Ut binæ regum facies, ita corpora plebis.
Namque aliæ turpes horrent, ceu pulvere ab alto
Cùm venit, et terram sicco spuit ore, viator
Aridus: elucent aliæ, et fulgore coruscant,
Ardentes auro, et paribus lita corpora guttis.
Hæc potior soboles: hinc cœli tempore certo
Dulcia mella premes; nec, tantùm dulcia, quantùm
Et liquida, et durum Bacchi domitura saporem.
At cùm incerta volant cœloque examina ludunt,
Contemnuntque favos, et frigida tecta relinquunt,
Instabiles animos ludo prohibebis inani.
Nec magnus prohibere labor: tu regibus alas
Eripe: non illis quisquam cunctantibus altum
Ire iter, aut castris audebit vellere signa.

NOTES.

85. *Aut hos.* The meaning is: till one side or the other of the combatants should yield. The repetition of the *aut hos*, from the end of the preceding line, gives additional energy. The figure is called *Anadiplosis.*

87. *Compressa:* in the sense of *repressa.* It agrees with *certamina.*

89. *Ne prodigus obsit:* lest the prodigal should be an injury to the rest, either by consuming their food himself, or by setting an example of sloth and gluttony.

90. *Aula:* in the sense of *alveari.*

91. *Alter erit ardens*, &c. The poet here mentions the different kinds of bees. There are more particularly two: the red, which are the smaller ones, and the dark, or various, which are the larger. The red ones are the best. *Squalentibus:* a part. of the verb *squaleo*, (from *squama*:) it signifies any thing resembling the scales of fish, or serpents, in roughness or shape. It also signifies any thing filthy or unseemly, in any respect whatever. *Ardens:* shining with spots rough with gold—resembling the form of scales, and glittering like gold. Ruæus interprets it by *asperis.*

92. *Ore:* in the sense of *forma.*

95. *Facies:* in the sense of *formæ.* The verb *sunt* is to be supplied. *Plebis.* This is the reading of Heyne, and of Valpy after him. The common reading is *gentis.*

96. *Namque aliæ:* for the one look foul, or dirty, as when, &c. *Terram:* in the sense of *pulverem.*

97. *Coruscant:* sparkle with brightness—gleaming with gold; and their bodies are covered over with equal spots—spots, equal in size and proportion.

100. *Soboles:* in the sense of *genus.* Also *cœli:* in the sense of *anni.* *Hinc:* from these bees.

102. *Liquida:* in the sense of *pura.*

103. *At cùm volant.* Here the poet prescribes the means of preventing the bees from deserting their hives.

104. *Favos.* Virgil uses no less than eleven different words to express the hive: *cunabula*, *cubilia*, *stabula*, *præsepia*, *caveæ*, *tecta*, *alveare*, *favus*, *domus*, *sedes*, and *ædes.* For this diversity of style, he is remarkable. By this means he avoided a disagreeable repetition. *Frigida.* This Servius explains by empty, or inactive, in opposition to what is afterward said of their activity: *opus fervet.*

105. *Prohibebis:* in the sense of *revocabis.*

107. *Altum iter:* an aërial journey.

108. *Aut vellere signa:* or to move the standards—to decamp. It was a phrase among the Romans. When they pitched their camp, they stuck their ensigns, or standards, into the ground before the *prætorium*, or general's tent; and pulled them up again when they decamped: so the bees. The metaphor is beautiful.

Invitent croceis halantes floribus horti:
Et custos furum atque avium, cum falce saligna,
Hellespontiaci servet tutela Priapi.
Ipse thymum pinosque ferens de montibus altis,
Tecta serat latè circùm, cui talia curæ:
Ipse labore manum duro terat; ipse feraces
Figat humo plantas, et amicos irriget imbres.
Atque equidem, extremo ni jam sub fine laborum
Vela traham, et terris festinem advertere proram,
Forsitan et pingues hortos quæ cura colendi
Ornaret, canerem, biferique rosaria Pæsti:
Quoque modo potis gauderent intyba rivis,
Et virides apio ripæ; tortusque per herbam
Cresceret in ventrem cucumis: nec sera comantem
Narcissum, aut flexi tacuissem vimen acanthi,
Pallentesque hederas, et amantes litora myrtos.
Namque sub Œbaliæ memini me turribus altis,
Quà niger humectat flaventia culta Galesus,
Corycium vidisse senem: cui pauca relicti

112. Ipse, cui talia *sunt* curæ, ferens

121. **Quomodoque cucumis tortus per herbam cresceret**

125. **Namque memini me vidisse**

NOTES.

109. *Croceis floribus.* Saffron flowers appear to be put here for odorous flowers in general. *Halantes:* in the sense of *spirantes.*

111. *Priapi.* Priapus was fabled to have been the son of Bacchus and Venus. He was worshipped principally at Lampsacus, a city of Mysia Minor, near the Hellespont. Hence the epithet *Hellespontiacus.*

The statue of Priapus was usually placed in gardens to protect them from thieves, and to fray away birds. Hence he is called, *custos furum atque avium.* The meaning appears to be: that the bees should be invited by such gardens as deserve to be under the protection of Priapus. *Custos:* in the sense of *abactrix.* See Ecl. vii. 33.

112. *Thymum.* This is not our common thyme, but the *thymus capitatus,* which grows in great plenty on the mountains in Greece. The Attic honey was considered the best, on account of the excellence of this thyme, which is found in abundance near Athens.

114. *Duro labore:* with the hard labor of transferring them from the mountains, and planting them around the hives.

115. *Irriget:* he should sprinkle, or pour the friendly water upon them—he should be careful to water these plants when thus transplanted, that they might flourish the more, and afford more abundant food for the bees.

116. *Atque equidem:* and indeed, unless I were furling my sails, now in the conclusion of my labors, &c. These are fine lines, and lead us to wish that the poet had enlarged upon the subject of gardening. *Traham vela.* This is a metaphor taken from sailing. On the approach to land, they take in, or furl their sails.

118. *Pingues hortos.* Some gardens among the ancients were much celebrated, especially those of the Hesperides, of Adonis, of Alcinoüs, &c.

119. *Pæsti.* Pæstum was a town of Lucania, where the rose bloomed twice in a year; in September and May. Hence the epithet *bifer.*

120. *Intyba:* plu. endive, or succory. *Potis rivis:* in refreshing streams.

121. *Apio:* with parsley. This herb was called *apium,* from *apes,* because the bees were fond of it. Some take it for smallage or celery.

122. *Cucumis tortus:* the cucumber, creeping along the grass, swells. This is a concise, but beautiful description. *Sera:* an adj. neu. plu. used as an adv. in imitation of the Greeks: in the sense of *serò.*

123. *Narcissum:* the narcissus of the ancients is the herb we now call daffodil. *Comantem:* in the sense of *florentem. Acanthi:* Acanthus, the herb bears-foot.

125. *Œbaliæ.* This was the city of Tarentum in the eastern part of Italy, so called from *Phalantus,* a native of *Œbalia,* or Laconia, who rebuilt it. It was once inhabited by the Lacedemonians.

126. *Galesus:* a river in Calabria, falling into the gulf of Tarentum. It is called *niger,* either, on account of the depth of its waters, or of its banks being shaded by trees. *Flaventia:* yellow with ripening grain. *Arva* is understood.

127. *Corycium.* Either the name of the old man, or an adj. taken from the place of his nativity. *Corycus* was the name of a

Jugera ruris erant; nec fertilis illa juvencis,
Nec pecori opportuna seges, nec commoda Baccho

130. Tamen hic premens rarum

Hic rarum tamen in dumis olus, albaque circùm
Lilia, verbenasque premens, vescumque papaver,
Regum æquabat opes animis: seràque revertens
Nocte domum, dapibus mensas onerabat inemptis.

134. *Ille erat* primus carpere

Primus vere rosam, atque autumno carpere poma
Et cùm tristis hyems etiam nunc frigore saxa
Rumperet, et glacie cursus frænaret aquarum;
Ille comam mollis jam tondebat hyacinthi
Æstatem increpitans seram, Zephyrosque morantes

139. Ergò idem *senex erat* primus abundare

141. *Erant* illi tiliæ, atque

Ergò apibus fœtis idem atque examine multo
Primus abundare, et spumantia cogere pressis
Mella favis: illi tiliæ, atque uberrima pinus:
Quotque in flore novo pomis se fertilis arbos
Induerat, totidem autumno matura tenebat.
Ille etiam seras in versum distulit ulmos,
Eduramque pyrum, et spinos jam pruna ferentes,
Jamque ministrantem platanum potantibus umbras.

148. Atque relinquo *talia* commemoranda aliis *scriptoribus* pòst me

Verùm hæc ipse equidem, spatiis exclusus iniquis,
Prætereo, atque aliis pòst commemoranda relinquo
Nunc age, naturas, apibus quas Jupiter ipse

NOTES.

mountain, and city of Cilicia in Asia Minor. Pompey made war upon the Cilicians; some of whom he brought and planted in Calabria near Tarentum. The old man here mentioned, might have been one of them. *Relicti:* barren—neglected, not worth tilling. Dr. Trapp renders it hereditary; left him by his ancestors.

128. *Nec illa seges fertilis:* nor was that land fit for ploughing, nor suitable for pasture, nor proper for the vine. *Fertilis:* in the sense of *apta*, or *commoda.*

129. *Seges.* This word most commonly signifies the crop after it is sown and coming forward to maturity. Here it means the soil or land itself.

130. *Albaque lilia circùm:* the white lilies were most celebrated, and the best known among the ancients.

131. *Verbenas:* the herb *vervain.* It was highly esteemed by the Romans. *Premens:* in the sense of *plantans. Vescum papaver:* the white poppy, called *vescum*, esculent, or eatable; because its seeds were roasted by the ancients, and eaten with honey.

137. *Comam:* in the sense of *frondes.*—*Hyacinthi.* This is the reading of Heyne and Vossius, and of several ancient manuscripts. It appears to be approved of by Valpy, although he adopts the common reading, *acanthi.* Heyne leaves out *tum*, which is also retained by some editors.

139. *Ergò idem primus.* Having mentioned the advantage, which a diligent cultivation of his fields brought to the old Corycian, particularly in the culture of bees, he returned to his main subject. He was the first to abound, &c. *Fœtis:* in the sense of *fœcundis.*

141. *Favis:* the comb—those cells which contain the honey. *Tiliæ:* the linden, or lime-tree.

142. *Quotque pomis*, &c. The meaning is, that as many blossoms as his fertile trees put forth in the spring, so much fruit they had in autumn. There were no false blooms, neither did they fail to bring all to maturity. *Poma* is to be supplied with *matura.* The word properly means apples, but it is used for all kind of fruit: as in the present case.

144. *Distulit ulmos:* he planted (transplanted) his elms in rows. *Seras.* Ruæus says, *tardè crescentes*, slow growing. But the poet may mean, far grown, or sufficiently grown to be fit for transplanting; as he observes with respect to the other trees here mentioned. This is the opinion of Davidson and Valpy.

145. *Spinos.* Spinus, is the sloe tree. These were sufficiently grown to produce fruit; and the plane tree, to afford a considerable shade, before he transplanted them.

147. *Iniquis spatiis:* narrow bounds—insufficient room.

149. *Nunc age.* The poet now proceeds to treat of the polity of the bees—the method of depositing their honey—the regular management of their affairs—their obedience to their sovereign, &c.

Addidit, expediam: pro quâ mercede, canoros
Curetum sonitus crepitantiaque æra secutæ,
Dictæo cœli regem pavêre sub antro.
Solæ communes natos, consortia tecta
Urbis habent, magnisque agitant sub legibus ævum;
Et patriam solæ, et certos novêre penates.
Venturæque hyemis memores, æstate laborem
Experiuntur, et in medium quæsita reponunt.
Namque aliæ victu invigilant, et fœdere pacto
Exercentur agris: pars intra septa domorum
Narcissi lachrymam, et lentum de cortice gluten,
Prima favis ponunt fundamina: deinde tenaces
Suspendunt ceras: aliæ, spem gentis, adultos
Educunt fœtus: aliæ purissima mella
Stipant, et liquido distendunt nectare cellas.
Sunt, quibus ad portas cecidit custodia sorti;
Inque vicem speculantur aquas et nubila cœli,
Aut onera accipiunt venientûm, aut, agmine facto,
Ignavum fucos pecus à præsepibus arcent.
Fervet opus, redolentque thymo fragrantia mella.
Ac veluti lentis Cyclopes fulmina massis
Cùm properant: alii taurinis follibus auras

150. Pro qua *tanquam* mercede, *illæ* secutæ canoros sonitus

153. *Hæ* solæ *omnium animalium* habent

161. *Tanquam* prima fundamina favis

165. Sunt *aliæ*, quibus custodia

166. *Quæque* invicem

NOTES.

150. *Expediam:* in the sense of *describam. Pro quâ mercede.* According to fable, Saturn intending to devour his infant son Jupiter, he was concealed by his mother among the *Curetes*, or *Corybantes*, her priests, the sound of whose brazen armour and cymbals, as they revelled, prevented his cries from betraying him to his father. It is said that *Melissus* was then king of Crete, whose daughters, *Melissæ* nourished Jupiter with the milk of a goat and honey. Hence arose the story of his being nourished by a goat called *Amalthea* and bees, *Melissæ* being the Greek name for bees. For which reason, the goat was translated to the heavens, and his horns given to the nymphs, with this quality added to them, that whatever they should ask for, should flow from them plenteously: and for the service, which the bees rendered on this occasion, they were endowed by Jupiter with an extraordinary degree of sagacity and wisdom, as a reward.

152. *Dictæo:* an adj. from *Dicte*, a city and mountain in Crete. On this mountain, it is said, Jupiter was brought up.

153. *Consortia:* in the sense of *communia.*

154. *Agitant:* in the sense of *ducunt.* The poet here speaks of the bees as living in a regular, and well organized society.

155. *Certos penates:* in the sense of *fixas domos.*

157. *Experiuntur:* they practise or use.

158. *Victu:* for *victui.* See Ecl. 5, 29. *Invigilant:* watch over—have the care of providing. *Pacto fœdere:* in the sense of *certa lege.*

159. *Exercentur:* in the sense of *laborant Septa:* the enclosures of their hives.

160. *Narcissi.* The flower of Narcissus or daffodil, forms a kind of cup in the middle, which is supposed to contain the tear of the youth *Narcissus*, who pined away with the love of himself. See Ecl. ii. 48.

163. *Educunt adultos fœtus:* they nourish or tend upon their young, till they are full grown: or, they lead forth their full grown young. Servius prefers the former sense: as also Ruæus.

164. *Liquido:* in the sense of *puro. Nectare:* nectar here, evidently, is to be taken for honey—the purest, and most refined part of it.

166. *Aquas:* in the sense of *pluviam.*

168. *Fucos:* the drones, a lazy herd. These are bees that make no honey. They have no stings, and they do not assist the others in their labors. *Præsepibus.* See note, verse 104. supra.

169. *Opus fervet:* the work glows—it goes on briskly.

170. *Cùm properant Cyclopes.* The Cyclops are said to have forged the thunderbolts of Jove. To this the poet alludes. This comparison of the bees in their labors, with those workmen of Jupiter in their shops, has been censured by some. *Properant:* in the sense of *fabricantur.*

172. *Alii accipiunt:* simply: some blow the bull-hide bellows. *Lacu:* in the trough of water.

Accipiunt, redduntque: alii stridentia tingunt
Æra lacu: gemit impositis incudibus Ætna:
Illi inter sese magnâ vi brachia tollunt
In numerum, versantque tenaci forcipe ferrum.
Non aliter, si parva licet componere magnis,
Cecropias innatus apes amor urget habendi,
Munere quamque suo. Grandævis oppida curæ,
Et munire favos, et Dædala fingere tecta.
At fessæ multâ referunt se nocte minores,
Crura thymo plenæ: pascuntur et arbuta passim,
Et glaucas salices, casiamque, crocumque rubentem,
Et pinguem tiliam, et ferrugineos hyacinthos.
Omnibus una quies operum, labor omnibus unus.
Manè ruunt portis, nusquam mora: rursus easdem
Vesper ubi è pastu tandem decedere campis
Admonuit, tum tecta petunt, tum corpora curant.
Fit sonitus, mussantque oras et limina circùm.
Pòst, ubi jam thalamis se composuere, siletur
In noctem, fessosque sopor suus occupat artus.
  Nec verò à stabulis, pluviâ impendente, recedunt
Longiùs, aut credunt cœlo, adventantibus Euris:
Sed circùm tutæ sub mœnibus urbis aquantur,
Excursusque breves tentant: et sæpe lapillos,
Ut cymbæ instabiles, fluctu jactante, saburram,
Tollunt: his sese per inania nubila librant.
  Illum adeò placuisse apibus mirabere morem;
Quòd nec concubitu indulgent, nec corpora segnes

177. Habendi *mella*

178. Oppida *sunt* curæ grandævis

181. Plenæ *quoad* crura thymo

184. *Est* omnibus una quies

185. Rursus, ubi vesper admonuit easdem *apes esse tempus* tandem decedere

193. Tutæ *ab pluvia et vento*

194. Et sæpe tollunt lapillos, ut instabiles cymbæ *tollunt* saburram, fluctu jactante *eas*: his *lapillis*

NOTES.

175. *In numerum:* they raise their arms in regular order, making a sort of harmony with the strokes of their hammers.

Jamblicus informs us that the sound of the smith's hammer led Pythagoras to invent the monochord, an instrument for measuring the quantities, and proportions of sounds geometrically.

177. *Cecropias:* Attic, or Athenian bees, so called from Cecrops, the first king of Athens. The Attic honey was much celebrated.

178. *Quamque suo munere:* each one in his own office—department.

179. *Dædala:* an adj. from Dædalus, a very ingenious artificer of Athens. The word, as here used, signifies any thing artificial, or curiously and ingeniously wrought.

180. *Minores:* in the sense of *juniores.*

181. *Plenæ crura.* The hairiness of the legs of the bee is favorable to the retention of the juices, which they collect from the flowers.

182 *Rubentem:* yellow, or of a golden hue. Ruæus says, *rufum.*

183. *Ferrugineos:* purple—dark red.

184. *Operum:* in the sense of *ab opere. Una:* one and the same rest.

188. *Oras:* this Ruæus interprets by *vestibulum. Mussant:* they buzz—they make a buzzing noise.

189. *Thalamis:* in the sense of *cellis.*

190. *Suus:* in the sense of *proprius.* Ruæus says, *conveniens.*

191. *Stabulis.* See note, verse 104. supra.

192. *Euris.* Eurus, the east wind, here put for wind in general: the *species* for the *genus.*

193. *Aquantur.* This verb appears to be used in the sense of the middle voice of the Greeks: they water themselves. This manner of expression is common with the poet. Ruæus says, *hauriunt aquas.*

195. *Saburram:* ballast. This is some ponderous substance, as sand, gravel, iron, &c. that light vessels usually take on board to render them steady.

198. *Nec indulgent,* &c. This account of the production of bees here given by the poet, is justly exploded. It is found that no animal is produced without the concurrence of the sexes. However as this method was the general received one among the ancients, the poet might very well adopt it, whatever his own opinion might have been upon the subject. Pliny says of the bees: *Foetus quonam modo progenerarent, magna inter eruditos, et subtilis quæstio fuit: Apum enim coitus visus est nusquam.* This, however, modern philosophers have solved in a satisfactory manner. They have found that the laboring bees are of neither sex; that the

In Venerem solvunt, aut fœtus nixibus edunt.
Verùm ipsæ è foliis natos et suavibus herbis
Ore legunt: ipsæ regem, parvosque Quirites
Sufficiunt: aulasque et cerea regna refingunt.
Sæpe etiam duris errando in cotibus alas
Attrivêre, ultròque animam sub fasce dedêre:
Tantus amor florum, et generandi gloria mellis.
Ergò ipsas quamvis angusti terminus ævi
Excipiat (neque enim plùs septima ducitur æstas)
At genus immortale manet, multosque per annos
Stat fortuna domûs, et avi numerantur avorum.
Prætereà regem non sic Ægyptus, et ingens
Lydia, nec populi Parthorum, aut Medus Hydaspes,
Observant. Rege incolumi, mens omnibus una est;
Amisso, rupere fidem: constructaque mella
Diripuere ipsæ, et crates solvêre favorum.
Ille operum custos; illum admirantur; et omnes
Circumstant fremitu denso, stipantque frequentes;
Et sæpe attollunt humeris, et corpora bello
Objectant. pulchramque petunt per vulnera mortem.
His quidam signis, atque hæc exempla secuti,
Esse apibus partem divinæ mentis, et haustus
Æthereos dixere: Deum namque ire per omnes
Terrasque, tractusque maris, cœlumque profundum.
Hinc pecudes, armenta, viros, genus omne ferarum,

205. *Est illis* tantus amor florum. et *tanta*

207. Enim neque plus *quàm* septima æstas ducitur *ab illis*

213. *Rege* amisso

215. Ille *est* custos

217. *Sua* corpora bello *pro illo*

219. Quidam *homines inducti* his signis, atque secuti hæc exempla *prudentiæ apum* dixere

221. Namque *dixere* Deum

223. Hinc *dixere* pecudes

NOTES.

drones alone have the male organ of generation, and that the monarch is of the female sex. She is wholly employed in the increase of her family, laying several thousand eggs every summer, in each of which is hatched a small white worm, which in due time, changes itself into a drone or bee.—*Concubitu:* for *Concubitui.* See Ecl. v. 29.

199. *Nec solvunt:* nor do they debilitate their bodies in lust. *Segnes:* in the sense of *inertes vel inutiles. Edunt:* in the sense of *parturiunt. Nixibus:* by labor, or travail.

200. *Foliis:* from the leaves of flowers.

201. *Parvos Quirites:* they raise up a king, and little subjects. The bees are here called *Quirites*, by meton. taken from the Romans, who were sometimes called *Quirites* from Romulus, who was also called *Quirinus.*—See Æn. 1. 274.

204. *Dedêre:* in the sense of *amiserunt.*

207. *Septima Æstas.* Aristotle informs us that bees live six, and sometimes seven years; but if the swarm subsists nine or ten years, it is considered fortunate.

208. *At*, in the sense of *tamen.*

210. *Ægyptus.* The name of the country put, by meton. for the inhabitants. The Ægyptians were very great admirers of their monarchs, many of whom they deified.

211. *Lydia:* a country of Asia Minor proverbial for its wealth, and the grandeur of its kings. *Populi Parthorum:* simply, the Parthians. They are said to have been so submissive to their king, as to kiss his feet, and to touch the ground with their lips, when they approached him. *Hydaspes:* the name of a river put, by meton. for the inhabitants of the country, through which it flowed.

There have been various opinions and conjectures with a view to reconcile the poet with matters of fact. Hydaspes is a river of India, and falling into the Indus, forms one of its branches. How it could be called Median, with any propriety, does not appear. There might have been a small river by that name, rising in Media, to which the poet alludes. Mr. Davidson thinks the river Choaspes, which rises in Media, and passes through the province of Susiana, near Susa, one of the capitals of the Persian empire, is intended. However this be, poets do not always confine themselves to historical or geographical precision.

212. *Observant:* in the sense of *venerantur.*

213. *Fidem:* in the sense of *societatem.*

214. *Crates:* the structure or fabric.

215. *Custos:* in the sense of *præses.*

216. *Denso fremitu:* with loud buzzing or humming.

220. *Haustus:* in the sense of *spiritus.*

Quemque sibi tenues nascentem arcessere vitas.
Scilicet huc reddi deinde, ac resoluta referri
Omnia: nec morti esse locum; sed viva volare
Sideris in numerum, atque alto succedere cœlo
  Si quando sedem augustam, servataque mella
Thesauris relines, priùs haustu sparsus aquarum,
Ora fove, fumosque manu prætende sequaces.
Bis gravidos cogunt fœtus, duo tempora messis.
Taygete simul os terris ostendit honestum
Pleias, et Oceani spretos pede reppulit amnes:
Aut eadem sidus fugiens ubi piscis aquosi,

225. Deinde *dixere* omnia resoluta scilicet reddi, ac referri huc

226. Sed *omnia* viva volare, *quæque* in numerum

231. *Sunt* duo tempora messis: *unum* simul Pleias Taygete

234. Aut ubi eadem *Pleïas*

NOTES.

224. *Quemque nascentem:* that every one, at his birth, derives tender life to himself, from him. *Hinc:* from hence—from God.

225. *Scilicet:* in the sense of *certè. Huc:* hither—to God. *Resoluta:* in the sense of *dissoluta.*

226. *Nec locum,* &c. Virgil here gives the opinions of those philosophers, who rejected the doctrine of a *vacuum,* and atoms. They maintained that the universe was animated: that God was omnipresent: that all animals received existence from him: that after death they are all returned, and carried back to him: that there is no room for extinction (*morti*) or loss of existence: that all, *volare viva,* fly alive into the order of his star, and take their station in high heaven. In other words, all transmigrate into other beings in a perpetual round. This notion was held by many distinguished philosophers of the heathen world. But it was far from the truth. All irrational animals perish at their death. Man alone is immortal. When unassisted reason is employed upon the subject of a future state of existence, it discovers its own weakness. The researches of philosophy serve only to bewilder the mind. All correct information upon that subject must come through the medium of divine revelation. Pythagoras and his followers strenuously maintained this doctrine. The Epicurians maintained the doctrine of a *vacuum,* and the atomic theory.

228. *Si quando,* &c. The poet now proceeds to mention the proper seasons for opening the hives. He gives directions how to proceed in the business, and notices the passionate temper of the bees upon such occasions.

Augustam. This is the reading of the best editions, and is supported by ancient manuscripts. Ruæus, Davidson, Valpy, and some others, have *angustam.* But if the poet intended to inform us that the hive was small, he might have saved himself the pains. Besides, *augustam* is, by no means, an improper epithet. It is exactly in the spirit of poetry. It is well known that the bee-hive is a most exquisite piece of architecure, whether we regard the form of the comb, the materials of which it is composed, or the manner of the workmanship. Virgil emphatically calls their hives, *Dædala tecta.* Verse 179. supra. Heyne reads *augustam.*

229. *Thesauris:* in the sense of *favis.*

Priùs haustu, &c. Commentators do not agree upon this passage; and it must be confessed a difficult one. Davidson follows Servius, who takes *sparsus* for *spargens:* making the meaning to be: First hold in your mouth draughts of water, spouting it upon them. Dr. Trapp rejects *sparsus* for *spargens,* and thinks *sparsus* should be retained; thus: *Fove ore haustus aquarum,* take water in your mouth; then by an ellipsis of the words; *projice in modum pluviæ,* spout it upon them in the manner of rain, which you cannot do without being wet yourself, *sparsus.* Heinsius, Ruæus, Heyne, and some others read: *Priùs haustu aquarum ora fove.* This, however, is not without objections. If we could read *haustum* or *haustus* for *haustu,* the passage would be easier; then *ore* would be preferable to *ora.* But whatever difficulties may attend the construction, the meaning is obvious. Heyne takes *Fove ora haustu aquarum,* in the sense of, *tene vel contine aquam haustam ore.*

Davidson reads *haustus,* and *ore.*

230. *Fumos:* it is customary, at the present day, to drive or force the bees from the hive with smoke.

231. *Gravidos fœtus:* in the sense of *plenos favos.* The comb is properly the *fœtus* or production of the bees. *Messis:* gathering or taking the honey: here called the harvest.

232. *Taygete:* one of the Pleïades, here put for the whole, by synec. This, and the three following lines, is a beautiful circumlocution to express the rising and setting of these stars; the former is in the latter part of April, the latter about the end of October, or the beginning of November. See Geor. 1. 138.

233. *Amnes:* in the sense of *aquas.*

234. *Sidus aquosi piscis:* the constellation of the rainy fish. The *Pisces* here cannot be meant: for the sun does not enter that sign till some time in February. Probably the

Tristior hybernas cœlo descendit in undas.
Illis ira modum supra est, læsæque venenum
Morsibus inspirant, et spicula cæca relinquunt
Affixæ venis, animasque in vulnere ponunt.
Sin duram metues hyemem, parcesque futuro,
Contusosque animos et res miserabere fractas;
At suffire thymo, cerasque recidere inanes
Quis dubitet? nam sæpe favos ignotus adedit
Stellio, lucifugis congesta cubilia blattis:
Immunisque sedens aliena ad pabula fucus,
Aut asper crabro imparibus se immiscuit armis
Aut dirum tineæ genus, aut invisa Minervæ
In foribus laxos suspendit aranea casses.
Quò magìs exhaustæ fuerint; hôc acriùs omnes
Incumbent generis lapsi sarcire ruinas,
Complebuntque foros, et floribus horrea texent.
Si verò (quoniam casus apibus quoque nostros
Vita tulit) tristi languebunt corpora morbo;
Quod jam non dubiis poteris cognoscere signis:
Continuò est ægris alius color: horrida vultum

239. Futuro *pabulo, nempe, melli*

243. Cubilia *sunt* congesta

245. Se *cum apibus*

NOTES.

Dolphin may be intended, as that constellation rises soon after the setting of the *Pleïades.*

236. *Læsæ:* in the sense of *offensæ.*

237. *Cæca:* in the sense of *occulta: morsibus:* stings. *Inspirant:* they infuse.

238. *Affixæ:* having affixed themselves.

240. *Parces futuro:* you should spare their future nourishment, and pity their drooping spirits, and afflicted state.

Commentators have embarrassed the sense of this passage. The meaning is plainly this: If you are afraid of a hard winter, and that the bees will not be able to sustain the cold, unless they be well fed, you should spare their honey, their future nourishment, and take none of it from them.

241. *At quis dubitet,* &c. However you may be disposed to follow my direction in leaving the honey untouched, there is one thing that should not be neglected in any case; and that is, to fumigate the hives, and to cut away the superfluous wax.

243. *Stellio.* This is a small spotted lizard, called also an eft or swift. It creeps into holes and corners; hence the poet calls it *ignotus. Congesta:* in the sense of *plena. Blattis.* The *blatta* is an insect something like a beetle. Some take it to be the cockroach. They are called *lucifugis,* because they do not appear in the day time.

244. *Fucus immunis.* The Drones are the male bees. They have neither stings, nor those elastic teeth which the laboring bees have for the purpose of collecting honey. Their only business seems to be, to have intercourse with the queen: they may be said to be her husbands: they are several hundred in number in each hive. After they have performed their office, they soon die. Their way of living is very different from the rest: they are exempt from labor, and enjoy a most luxurious fare, being fed with the best of the honey: *Immunis sedens ad aliena pabula,* may very properly be said of them.

245. *Crabro:* the hornet, a well known insect. It is larger and stronger than the bee. Hence it is said to engage them with *imparibus armis.*

246. *Tineæ:* the moth; an insect very injurious to clothes. The common reading is *durum:* Heyne, Valpy, and some others, read *dirum.*

247. *Aranea invisa.* Arachne, daughter of Idmon, a Lydian, is said to have vied with Minerva in the arts of spinning and weaving. She performed her work to admiration; but being outdone, she hung herself through grief; whereupon the goddess, out of pity, changed her into the spider. Some say she represented on her work several of the crimes of the gods, which so displeased the goddess, that she, in a rage, destroyed it. Hence *invisa Minervæ.* See Ovid Met. Lib. 5.

248. *Quò magìs.* The poet here observes, the more you drain the honey from the bees, the more industrious they will be to repair the loss. By being too full fed, they become idle, and consequently less profitable. He then proceeds to consider the diseases incident to them, and the remedies proper for each.

250. *Horrea:* in the sense of *favos. Texent:* they will form, or make.

252. *Vita:* the state, or condition of life.

255: Corpora *earum* carentûm luce

Deformat macies; tum corpora luce carentûm
Exportant tectis, et tristia funera ducunt:
Aut illæ pedibus connexæ ad limina pendent,
Aut intus clausis cunctantur in ædibus omnes:
Ignavæque fame, et contracto frigore pigræ.
Tum sonus auditur gravior, tractimque susurrant:
Frigidus ut quondam sylvis immurmurat Auster,
Ut mare sollicitum stridet refluentibus undis,
Æstuat ut clausis rapidus fornacibus ignis.

264. **Suadebo** *te* incendere

Hìc jam galbaneos suadebo incendere odores,
Mellaque arundineis inferre canalibus, ultrò
Hortantem, et fessas ad pabula nota vocantem.
Proderit et tunsum gallæ admiscere saporem,
Arentesque rosas, aut igni pinguia multo
Defruta, vel psythiâ passos de vite racemos,
Cecropiumque thymum, et graveolentia centaurea.
Est etiam flos in pratis, cui nomen amello
Fecere agricolæ, facilis quærentibus herba.
Namque uno ingentem tollit de cespite sylvam,

NOTES.

255. *Luce:* in the sense of *vita.*

256. *Ducunt.* Pliny observes, that the bees accompany the bodies of their dead after the manner of a funeral procession.

257. *Illæ connexæ:* clung together by their feet, they hang, &c.

259. *Contracto.* Ruæus takes this in the sense of *contrahente.* He says: *Frigore contrahente membra.* But it may be taken in its usual acceptation, without any impropriety: for the bees may be said to contract, or take cold; and this the poet mentions as one of their diseases.

260. *Tractim:* in a drawling manner—one after another.

262. *Sollicitum:* in the sense of *turbatum.*

263. *Rapidus:* intense—excessive. *Æstuat:* roars.

264. *Galbaneos:* an adj. from *galbanum,* a strong-scented gum, the smell of which is said to drive away serpents. It is made of the juice of the plant called *ferula.*

The poet here directs the bee-master, when his bees show these symptoms, to burn galbanum around the hives, which will expel the vermin, if any there are; to introduce honey into the hives through reeds, to make up the deficiency of their food, and to use every means to allure them to partake of it. But in many cases, this would be insufficient. He must add to this honey certain medicinal substances, as remedies of their diseases.

266. *Fessas:* in the sense of *languidas,* and agreeing with *apes,* understood. *Saporem:* juice.

267. *Gallæ:* the nut-gall. This possesses very powerful astringent qualities. It was very proper, therefore, to recommend the use of it, to check the looseness to which the bees are subject in the spring, occasioned, says Columella, by their feeding greedily upon spurge after their winter penury.

269. *Defruta.* *Defrutum* was a mixture made of new wine, boiled away one half, or one third, into which several sorts of sweet herbs or spices were put. *Pinguia:* rich; implying that it should be boiled away, and made thick, and enriched by spices. *Passos racemos:* properly, bunches of grapes hung up to dry in the sun—raisins. Hence by meton. put for the wine made of such grapes—raisin wine. See Geor. ii. 93.

270. *Cecropium:* Attic, or Athenian; from *Cecrops,* one of the first kings of Athens. *Centaurea:* plu. the herb centaury. There are two kinds of centaury, the greater and the less. They have no other similitude than the bitterness of their taste. It is said to have derived its name from Chiron, one of the Centaurs, whom it cured of a wound received by an arrow from Hercules.

271. *Amello.* Mella, or Mela, a river of Cis-alpine Gaul, on the banks of which the flower here spoken of abounded. Hence, according to Servius, it was called *Amellus.* Mr. Martyn thinks it the same with the *purple Indian star-wort,* or *Aster Atticus.* *Cui nomen amello.* This construction frequently occurs in Virgil, and is taken from the Greeks. It is to be taken in the sense of *cui amellus nomini:* so, *cui nomen Iülo,* in the sense of *cui Iülus nomini:* also, *cui nomen asilo.* See Geor. iii. 147.

272. *Facilis:* easy to be found by those who seek for it.

273. *Cespite.* *Cespes,* here must mean the root of the plant. *Sylvam:* in the sense

Aureus ipse. sed in foliis, quæ plurima circùm
Funduntur, violæ sublucet purpura nigræ.
Sæpe Deûm nexis ornatæ torquibus aræ.
Asper in ore sapor: tonsis in vallibus illum
Pastores, et curva legunt prope flumina Mellæ.
Hujus odorato radices incoque Baccho,
Pabulaque in foribus plenis appone canistris.
  Sed si quem proles subitò defecerit omnis,
Nec, genus unde novæ stirpis revocetur, habebit:
Tempus, et Arcadii memoranda inventa magistri
Pandere, quoque modo cæsis jam sæpe juvencis
Insincerus apes tulerit cruor. Altiùs omnem
Expediam primâ repetens ab origine, famam.
Nam quà Pellæi gens fortunata Canopi
Accolit effuso stagnantem flumine Nilum,
Et circum pictis vehitur sua rura phaselis;
Quàque pharetratæ vicinia Persidis urget,
Et viridem Ægyptum nigrâ fœcundat arenâ
Et diversa ruens septem discurrit in ora,
Usque coloratis amnis devexus ab Indis;
Omnis in hâc certam regio jacit arte salutem.

277. Sapor *ejus est* **asper in ore**

280. Apponeque pabula *apibus* **plenis canistris in foribus** *alvearis.*

283. Tempus *est* **pandere**

290. Quàque amnis devexus usque ab coloratis Indis urget

NOTES.

of *copiam caulium. Fecēre:* in the sense of *dederunt.*

275. *Nigræ:* deep colored. *Funduntur:* sprout, or shoot up.

276. *Nexis:* made, or formed of this *amellus.*

279. *Incoque:* boil, or simmer.

281. *Sed si quem,* &c. The poet now proseeds to give an account of the method practised by Aristæus for the recovery of his bees, after all his swarms were lost. *Omnis proles:* the whole stock, or race.

285. *Insincerus:* in the sense of *putridus. Altiùs:* in the sense of *longè.* It is to be connected with *repetens.*

286. *Expediam:* in the sense of *narrabo.*

287. *Gens fortunata:* the Egyptians. They are here called happy, or fortunate, on account of the fertility of their country, which is occasioned by the annual inundation of the river Nile. *Canopi.* Canopus was a city of Egypt, near Alexandria, founded by Alexander the Great, who was born at Pella, in Macedonia. Hence the city Canopus is called *Pellæus.* The city, by meton. for the inhabitants; who may be put, by synec. for all the Egyptians.

288. *Stagnantem:* in the sense of *inundantem. Agros* is understood.

289. *Vehitur circùm.* During the continuance of the inundation, the inhabitants pass from one part of the country to another in boats, or small barges; here called *phaseli. Vehitur* agrees with *gens.*

290. *Urget vicinia.* The Nile did not touch, or border upon the neighborhood of Persia, properly so called. But we are informed by Xenophon, that the Persian empire under Cyrus extended as far west as Egypt. The Nile may therefore be said to press upon the borders of Persia, since the Persians extended their dominions as far as Egypt; which justifies the expression of the poet. *Vicinia:* plu. of *vicinium.* The Persians were famous for their skill in archery; hence *pharetratæ Persidis.*

293. *Amnis:* the river Nile. It rises in Abyssinia, in the mountains of the Moon, in about the lat. 11° N. and runs in a northerly direction; and, after receiving a number of tributary streams, it falls into the Mediterranean sea in seven different channels, or mouths, in lat. 32 N. forming the *Delta* of Lower Egypt. The inundation of the Nile occasions the fertility of Egypt. Its waters bring with them the richness, or wash of the upper country, and here deposit it. This the poet calls, *nigra arena.* The rise of the Nile is occasioned by the rain that falls at a certain season of the year in the mountains of Abyssinia. The proper height to which the water should rise in Egypt is 16 cubits, or 24 feet. If it fall short of that, a famine is expected; if it exceed it, an injury is sustained. By means of canals, the water is carried to every part of the country. For an excellent description of the Nile, see Rollin's An. His. Vol. 1. *Indis.* Any country that lay in a hot climate, the ancients denominated *India,* and its inhabitants *Indi. Coloratis:* tawny—sun-burnt. *Devexus:* flowing down from

294. *Arte:* in the sense of *invento*

Exiguus primùm, atque ipsos contractus ad usus
Eligitur locus: hunc angustique imbrice tecti
Parietibusque premunt arctis; et quatuor addunt
Quatuor à ventis obliquâ luce fenestras.
Tum vitulus, bimâ curvans jam cornua fronte,
Quæritur: huic geminæ nares, et spiritus oris
Multa reluctanti obstruitur; plagisque perempto
Tunsa per integram solvuntur viscera pellem
Sic positum in clauso linquunt: et ramea costis
Subjiciunt fragmenta, thymum, casiasque recentes.
Hoc geritur, Zephyris primùm impellentibus undas,
Antè novis rubeant quàm prata coloribus, antè
Garrula quàm tignis nidum suspendat hirundo.
Intereà teneris tepefactus in ossibus humor
Æstuat: et visenda modis animalia miris,
Trunca pedum primò, mox et stridentia pennis
Miscentur, tenuemque magìs, magìs aëra carpunt·
Donec, ut æstivis effusus nubibus imber,
Erupêre: aut, ut nervo pulsante sagittæ,
Prima leves ineunt si quando prælia Parthi.
Quis Deus hanc, Musæ, quis nobis extudit artem?
Unde nova ingressus hominum experientia cepit?
Pastor Aristæus, fugiens Peneïa Tempe,
Amissis, ut fama, apibus morboque fameque,

300. Geminæ nares obstruuntur

301. Visceraque tunsa plagis per integram pellem solvuntur *huic* perempto.

303. Sic linquunt *vitulum* positum in clauso *loco*

306. Coloribus *florum*

312. Donec erupêre *tam densè*, ut

313. Aut *tam densè*, ut sagittæ

NOTES.

296. *Hunc premunt:* they contract this (still more) by a narrow roof and confined walls —walls close together. *Imbrex* is properly the gutter-tile of the roof, to carry off the water. Hence it may be taken for the roof itself. *Imbrice angusti tecti:* with the covering of a narrow roof.

297. *Parietibus: parietes*, properly the walls of a house: *muri*, the walls of a city. *Premunt:* in the sense of *contrahunt.*

299. *Bima:* in the sense of *bienni.*

301. *Multa:* in the sense of *multùm*, in imitation of the Greeks.

302. *Viscera tunsa*, &c. The meaning is: that the entrails of the animal, as he lay dead, being beaten with blows, are broken in pieces, the hide remaining entire. *Viscera*, is properly the whole animal within the hide, as well the flesh as the entrails. *Perempto:* in the sense of *interfecto.*

305. *Geritur:* in the sense of *agitur. Zephyris.* The zephyrs begin to blow, in that climate, early in the month of February, according to Pliny. *Impellentibus:* in the sense of *agitantibus.*

307. *Antequàm hirundo.* The time of the swallow's coming is said by Columella, to be in the latter part of February, in that climate; with us it is much later.

309. *Æstuat:* ferments. *Trunca:* destitute of—wanting. *Miscentur:* mingle—swarm. *Carpunt:* in the sense of *tentant.*

312 *Erupêre:* in the sense of *evolaverunt. Nervo pulsante* (flew) from the whizzing string. *Nervo:* the string or cord of the bow. The Parthians were expert archers, and usually commenced the fight by a flight of arrows.

314. *Si quando:* in the sense of *quando*

315. *Extudit:* in the sense of *invenit.*

316. *Ingressus:* acc. plu. in the sense of *originem.*

317. *Aristæus.* He is said to have been the son of Apollo and the nymph Cyrene, the daughter of the river god Peneus, and born in the deserts of Lybia. He married the daughter of Cadmus, by the name of *Antonoë*, by whom he had *Acteon.* Being enamoured with Eurydice, the wife of Orpheus, he pursued her into the fields, where a snake, laying in the grass unobserved, bit her; of which wound she died. Whereupon, the gods were angry, and, by way of punishment, destroyed his bees. In this calamity, he applied to his mother, who directed him to apply to the river god Proteus. He directed him to appease the manes of Eurydice by the sacrifice of four bulls, and four heifers. It is said that he travelled over various countries, teaching men the cultivation of the olive, and the use of bees. He visited Arcadia; hence he is called *Arcadius magister apum.* He received divine honors, and was worshipped as a demi-god. *Tempe:* neu. plu. a pleasant valley of Thessaly, through which the river Peneus flows. Hence the epithet *Penean.*

Tristis ad extremi sacrum caput astitit amnis,
Multa querens: atque hâc affatus voce parentem:
Mater Cyrene, mater, quæ gurgitis hujus
Ima tenes: quid me præclarâ stirpe Deorum
(Si modò, quem perhibes, pater est Thymbræus Apollo)
Invisum fatis genuisti? aut quò tibi nostri
Pulsus amor? quid me cœlum sperare jubebas?
En etiam hunc ipsum vitæ mortalis honorem,
Quem mihi vix frugum et pecudum custodia solers
Omnia tentanti extuderat, te matre, relinquo!
Quin age, et ipsa manu felices erue sylvas,
Fer stabulis inimicum ignem, atque interfice messes:
Ure sata, et validam in vites molire bipennem:
Tanta meæ si te ceperunt tædia laudis.
At mater sonitum thalamo sub fluminis alti
Sensit: eam circùm Milesia vellera Nymphæ
Carpebant, hyali saturo fucata colore:
Drymoque, Xanthoque, Ligeaque, Phyllodoceque,
Cæsariem effusæ nitidam per candida colla;
Nesæe, Spioque, Thaliaque, Cymodoceque,
Cydippeque, et flava Lycorias; altera virgo,
Altera tum primos Lucinæ experta labores;
Clioque, et Beroë soror, Oceanitides ambæ,
Ambæ auro, pictis incinctæ pellibus ambæ;
Atque Ephyre, atque Opis, et Asia Deïopeia;
Et tandem positis velox Arethusa sagittis.
Inter quas curam Clymene narrabat inanem

322. Tenes ima *loca* hujus gurgitis: quid genuisti me invisum fatis *è* præclara stirpe Deorum; si modò Thymbræus Apollo, quem perhibes *meum patrem*, est *meus* pater: aut quò *est tuus* amor nostri pulsus tibi

326. En, te matre, etiam relinquo hunc ipsum honorem

329. *Tu* ipsa erue *meas* felices

337. Effusæ *quoad* nitidam

339. Altera *adhuc* virgo; alter tum

342. Ambæ incinctæ auro, ambæ *incinctæ* pictis

NOTES.

319. ***Ad sacrum caput:*** at the sacred source of the remote river. Aristæus resided in the vale of Tempe. After the loss of his bees, he retired to the source of the river Peneus, in mount Pindus, where his mother had her residence. After her amour with Apollo, it is said that god conveyed her to Africa, where she resided during the period of her gestation and delivery. Her son was brought up by the *Seasons*, and fed upon *ambrosia*.

321. *Gurgitis:* in the sense of *fontis*.

323. *Modò:* in the sense of *certè*. *Thymbræus:* a name of Apollo, from *Thymbra*, a town of Troas, where he had a magnificent temple. *Perhibes:* in the sense of *dicis*, vel *vocas*.

327. *Custodia:* in the sense of *cura*.

328. *Relinquo:* in the sense of *amitto*. *Extuderat:* had provided, or procured.

329. *Felices:* in the sense of *fœcundas*.

331. *Molire:* in the sense of *immitte*.

332. *Tædia:* in the sense of *negligentia*.

334. *Milesia:* an adj. from *Miletus*, a city in the confines of Ionia and Caria. Its wool was held in great estimation among the Romans.

335. *Carpebant:* in the sense of *nebant*. *Fucata:* dyed with a rich sea-green color. *Hyali:* gen. of *hyalus:* glass; also a glassy, or sea-green color; from a Greek word signifying glass.

336. *Drymo.* The names of the nymphs here mentioned are taken from Homer and Hesiod, and are all of Greek derivation.

337. *Effusæ:* in the sense of *diffusæ:* their hair hung loose, and flowing over their snow-white necks.

340. *Experta:* in the sense of *passa*. *Lucinæ:* child-bearing. The name of the goddess of child-bearing; by meton. taken for child-bearing itself. It is an epithet both of Juno and Diana.

341. *Oceanitides:* daughters of the ocean. See Ecl. ii. 46.

343. *Deïopeia.* This nymph is called *Asian*, because she was of the Asian fen: *Asia appellatur quia ex Asia palude.*

344. *Arethusa.* She had been at first a huntress, and one of Diana's train; but afterward changed by her into a fountain nymph. Hence the propriety of *sagittis positis.*

345. *Inter quas:* among whom Clymene was relating, &c. Venus, the wife of Vulcan, was taken in adultery with Mars. Her husband cast a net over them, as they were in each other's embrace, and in this situation they were exposed to the laughter of all the gods. The poet calls Vulcan's care

347. Vulcani *de custodienda Venere*
348. *Nymphæ* captæ *sunt*

Vulcani, Martisque dolos, et dulcia furta,
Aque Chao densos Divûm numerabat amores.
Carmine quo captæ, dum fusis mollia pensa
Devolvunt, iterum maternas impulit aures
Luctus Aristæi, vitreisque sedilibus omnes
Obstupêre: sed ante alias Arethusa sorores
Prospiciens, summâ flavum caput extulit undâ.

353. Et procul *dixit:* O soror Cyrene

Et procul: O, gemitu non frustrà exterrita tanto,
Cyrene soror; ipse tibi, tua maxima cura,
Tristis, Aristæus, Penei genitoris ad undam
Stat lachrymans, et te crudelem nomine dicit

357. Mater perculsa *quoad* mentem nova formidine ait huic: age, duc, duc *illum* ad nos: fas *est* illi

Huic perculsa novâ mentem formidine mater,
Duc, age, duc ad nos: fas illi limina Divûm
Tangere, ait. Simul alta jubet discedere latè
Flumina, quà juvenis gressus inferret: at illum
Curvata in montis faciem circumstetit unda,
Accepitque sinu vasto, misitque sub amnem.
Jamque domum mirans genitricis et humida regna,
Speluncisque lacus clausos, lucosque sonantes,
Ibat: et, ingenti motu stupefactus aquarum,
Omnia sub magnâ labentia flumina terrâ
Spectabat diversa locis, Phasimque, Lycumque,
Et caput, unde altus primùm se erumpit Enipeus,

371. Et *unde* Eridanus auratus *quoad* gemina cornua

Unde pater Tyberinus, et unde Aniena fluenta,
Saxosùmque sonans Hypanis, Mysusque Caïcus,
Et gemina auratus taurino cornua, vultu

NOTES.

inanem, vain, because it had no effect to reclaim his wife, or because it served only to propagate his own disgrace: or rather, because he was unable, with all his care and watchfulness, to prevent her from defiling his bed. Venus was a wanton dame.

346. *Dulcia furta.* This alludes to the amour of Mars with Venus: stolen embraces—sweet thefts.

347. *Chao:* from the origin of the world; or from Chaos, who, according to fable, was the first of the gods. *Densos:* in the sense of *frequentes*, vel *multos*.

348. *Mollia pensa:* the soft yarn. *Carmine:* song, story, or subject.

351. *Antè:* before her other sisters.

353. *Non frustrà:* not in vain alarmed: you are alarmed, and not without reason.

355. *Undam:* in the sense of *fontem*.—*Peneus*, the river god, was the father of Cyrene.

360. *Inferret gressus:* might introduce his foot-steps—might march along: a phrase. *Flumina:* in the sense of *aquas*.

361. *Curvata:* rolled or heaped up in the form of a mountain.

362. *Misit:* in the sense of *admisit. Eum* is understood.

364. *Speluncis.* There were two opinions among the ancients respecting the origin of rivers. Aristotle considered the sea to be the source: but Plato, whom Virgil here follows, was of the opinion, that there was under the earth, a general receptacle or reservoir of water, from which the rivers were all fed. This they called *barathrum*. By *lacus clausos*, &c. the poet means this general reservoir of water.

367. *Diversa.* remote—widely separated. *Phasim:* Phasis, a noble river of Colchis, rising in the mountains of Armenia, falls into the Euxine sea. It is famous for the expedition of the Argonauts, who entered it after a long and perilous voyage. *Lycum: Lycus*, the name of several rivers. It is not certain, which one the poet here intends.

368. *Caput:* the source, whence, &c. Enipeus is a river of Thessaly, watering the plains of Pharsalia, and falling into the river Peneus.

369. *Tyberinus:* the river Tyber in Italy. It is called by way of eminence *pater*. It falls into the Tuscan sea. *Aniena:* an adj. from *Anio*, the name of a small river in Italy.

370. *Hypanis:* a river of the ancient Sarmatia, uniting with the Borysthenes or Neiper, and with it, flows into the Euxine sea *Hodie, Bog. Saxosùm:* an adj. of the neu. gen. used adverbially—among the rocks. *Caïcus:* a river of *Mysia major* in the Lesser Asia. It falls into the Ægean sea, nearly opposite to Mitylene on the Island of Lesbos. Hence the epithet *Mysus.*

Eridanus, quo non alius per pinguia culta
In mare purpureum violentior influit amnis.
Postquam est in thalami pendentia pumice tecta
Perventum, et nati fletus cognovit inanes
Cyrene: manibus liquidos dant ordine fontes
Germanæ, tonsisque ferunt mantilia villis
Pars epulis onerant mensas, et plena reponunt
Pocula; Panchæis adolescunt ignibus aræ.
Et mater: Cape Mæonii carchesia Bacchi:
Oceano libemus, ait. Simul ipsa precatur
Oceanumque patrem rerum, Nymphasque sorores,
Centum quæ sylvas, centum quæ flumina servant.
Ter liquido ardentem perfudit nectare Vestam:
Ter flamma ad summum tecti subjecta reluxit.
Omine quo firmans animum, sic incipit ipsa:
Est in Carpathio Neptuni gurgite vates,

372. Quo *amne* non alius amnis influit violentior per

374. Postquam perventum est in tecta thalami

380. Et mater ait: Cape

NOTES.

372. *Eridanus:* the river Po. This is the largest river of Italy.

There is a seeming difficulty in reconciling what is here said of this river with matter of fact. We are told the Po is not a rapid river. It flows the greater part of its course through a level and highly cultivated country This taken into consideration, no other river perhaps, under the same circumstances, flows with greater rapidity. We are not to understand the poet as speaking absolutely, but comparatively. It falls into the Adriatic sea, or gulf of Venice.

Taurino vultu. The form of a bull is often, by the poets, given to rivers, from their roaring and rapid course: the noise which they make, bearing some resemblance to the bellowing of that animal. They are also called *cornuti*, or horned, from the double banks or channels, into which they divide themselves: or perhaps from the circumstance of their being sometimes formed by the union of two streams or smaller rivers. As for example, the river Ohio is formed by the union of the rivers Alleghany and Monongahela.

Hercules is said to have broken off one of the horns of *Achelöus.* It is thus explained. That hero reduced the river to one channel or stream. The dried part or broken horn of the river was converted into fruitful fields and gardens. This gave rise to the fable of the cornucopiæ, or horn of plenty. This was given to the nymphs, and by them presented to the Goddess of Plenty. The verb *erumpit* is to be supplied with each of the preceding nominatives.

374. *Pendentia:* vaulted, or arched with pumice stone. Ruæus says; *structa impendente pumice. Perventum est:* imp. verb, used in the sense of *pervenit.*

375. *Inanes: vain,* says Servius, because they were excited by a calamity easy to be removed.

376. *Dant:* in the sense of *ferunt. Liquidos fontes:* in the sense of *puras aquas.* This water was brought for the use of Aristæus; *manibus* may therefore refer to his hands—for washing his hands: or it may refer to the hands of the nymphs who brought it—in their hands.

377. *Mantilia:* towels. It would seem they were made of some shaggy or nappy cloth, which was sometimes shorn for the greater smoothness and delicacy. Our napkins were probably of the same sort formerly, the word seeming to be derived from *nap. Tonsis villis:* the shag or nap being cut off.

379. *Panchæis:* an adj. from *Panchæa,* a region of Arabia, abounding in frankincense. *Aræ:* the altars burn with Arabian frankincense.

380. *Carchesia.* The *carchèsium* was a large oblong bowl or goblet, flatted about the middle, having handles reaching quite to the bottom. *Mæonii:* an adj. from *Mæonia,* the ancient name of Lydia in Asia Minor. It abounded in vines. *Bacchi:* for *vini.*

383. *Servant:* in the sense of *præsident.*

384. *Perfundit:* she sprinkled—wet. *Ardentem Vestam:* the flaming fire: See Æn. 1. 292. *Nectare:* for *vino.* Nectar was properly the best and purest wine, such as they assigned to the use of the gods.

385. *Subjecta.* This Ruæus takes in the sense of *supposita;* with what propriety, however, does not appear. The meaning plainly is: that when the wine was poured upon the fire, a flame arose, or blazed, and shone bright, as high as the roof of the house. *Subjicio,* from which *subjecta* is derived, signifies to rise, or mount up. See Ecl. x. 74, and Æn. xii. 288. It is here used in the sense of *surgens.*

387. *Carpathio:* an adj. from *Carpathus,* an island in the Mediterranean sea, between

393. Quæ sint *præsentia*, quæ fuerint *præterita*, et

400. Circùm hæc *vincula*

401. Ego ipsa ducam te in secreta senis, quò

402. Gratior pecori *quàm herba*

405 *Illum* correptum

413. Qualem videris *illum*

Cœruleus Proteus, magnum qui piscibus æquor,
Et juncto bipedum curru metitur equorum.
Hic nunc Emathiæ portus, patriamque revisit
Pallenen ; hunc et nymphæ veneramur, et ipse
Grandævus Nereus : novit namque omnia vates,
Quæ sint, quæ fuerint, quæ mox ventura trahantur.
Quippe ita Neptuno visum est : immania cujus
Armenta, et turpes pascit sub gurgite phocas.
Hic tibi, nate, priùs vinclis capiendus, ut omnem
Expediat morbi causam, eventusque secundet.
Nam sinè vi non ulla dabit præcepta, neque illum
Orando flectes: vim duram et vincula capto
Tende: doli circùm hæc demum frangentur inanes.
Ipsa ego te, medios cùm Sol accenderit æstus,
Cùm sitiunt herbæ, et pecori jam gratior umbra est,
In secreta senis ducam, quò fessus ab undis
Se recipit ; facilè ut somno aggrediare jacentem.
Verùm ubi correptum manibus, vinclisque tenebis ;
Tum variæ eludent species, atque ora ferarum.
Fiet enim subitò sus horridus, atraque tigris,
Squamosusque draco, et fulvâ cervice leæna.
Aut acrem flammæ sonitum dabit, atque ita vinclis
Excidet, aut in aquas tenues dilapsus abibit.
Sed quantò ille magìs formas se vertet in omnes ;
Tantò, nate, magìs contende tenacia vincla :
Donec talis erit, mutato corpore, qualem
Videris, incepto tegeret cùm lumina somno

NOTES.

Rhodes and Crete, whence the neighboring sea was called *Carpathian.* It is now called *Scarpanto. Neptuni:* Neptunus, the god of the sea, by meton. put here for the sea itself, according to Ruæus. That commentator takes *gurgite* in the sense of *sinu;* but it is better to take it in the sense of *mari*, and *Neptuni* in its usual acceptation. *Vates Neptuni:* the prophet of Neptune. For Proteus, it is said, received from that god the gift of prophecy.

388. *Proteus:* a sea-god. According to fable, he was the son of Oceanus and Tethys, and received the gift of prophecy from Neptune. He was very difficult of access, and when consulted, he frequently eluded the answers by transforming himself into various shapes, and so making his escape. Homer makes him an Egyptian, and Herodotus, a king of Egypt. Sir Isaac Newton, finding him cotemporary with Amenophis, or Memnon, conjectures he was only a viceroy to that prince, and governed some part of Lower Egypt in his absence.

Proteus is represented as drawn in a car by marine horses; that is, their fore part resembling the horse, their hinder a fish. They would consequently have only two feet, and those before. Hence *bipedum equorum.*

389. *Metitur:* he measures, or rides over. *Juncto:* yoked, or harnessed; alluding to his marine horses, that were harnessed in his car.

391. *Pallenen:* Pallene, a peninsula of Macedonia, whose original name was *Emathia.*

393. *Trahantur.* There is a great propriety in the use of this word, according to the heathen notion of fate. Future events are said to be drawn, (*trahi,*) because, in that series, or chain of causes and effects, they so follow that one may be said to draw the other.

395. *Turpes:* in the sense of *immanes.*

399. *Flectes:* in the sense of *vinces.*

400. *Tende:* apply rigid force and chains to him, when seized. *Doli:* tricks—stratagems.

406. *Ora:* in the sense of *formæ. Eludent. Illudent* is the common reading. Pierius found in the Roman manuscript *ludent;* in the Lombard, Medicean, and most of the ancient manuscripts, *eludent* which is the reading of Heyne.

408. *Draco:* a serpent, or snake.

410. *Excidet:* will escape. *Dilapsus* dissolved into water, &c.

412. *Contende:* in the sense of *constringe.*

414. *Tegeret:* in the sense of *clauderet*

Hæc ait: et liquidum ambrosiæ diffudit odorem,
Quo totum nati corpus perduxit; at illi
Dulcis compositis spiravit crinibus aura,
Atque habilis membris venit vigor. Est specus ingens
Exesi latere in montis; quò plurima vento
Cogitur, inque sinus scindit sese unda reductos;
Deprensis olim statio tutissima nautis.
Intus se vasti Proteus tegit objice saxi.
Hìc juvenem in latebris aversum à lumine Nympha
Collocat: ipsa procul nebulis obscura resistit.
Jam rapidus torrens sitientes Sirius Indos
Ardebat cœlo, et medium Sol igneus orbem
Hauserat: arebant herbæ, et cava flumina siccis
Faucibus ad limum radii tepefacta coquebant:
Cùm Proteus consueta petens è fluctibus antra
Ibat: eum vasti circùm gens humida ponti
Exultans, rorem latè dispergit amarum.
Sternunt se somno diversæ in litore phocæ.
Ipse (velut stabuli custos in montibus olim,
Vesper ubi è pastu vitulos ad tecta reducit,
Auditisque lupos acuunt balatibus agni)
Considit scopulo medius, numerumque recenset.
Cujus Aristæo quoniam est oblata facultas:
Vix defessa senem passus componere membra,
Cum clamore ruit magno, manicisque jacentem
Occupat. Ille suæ contrà non immemor artis,
Omnia transformat sese in miracula rerum,
Ignemque, horribilemque feram, fluviumque liquentem.

419. Quò plurima unda cogitur.

423. Nympha *Cyrene* collocat juvenem *Aristæum*

427. Et radii *Solis* coquebant cava flumina tepefacta faucibus siccis *usque* ad

437. Quoniam facultas *capiendi* cujus oblata est Aristæo; vix

439. Ruit *in eum* cum

NOTES.

omno incepto: at the beginning of his sleep.

415. *Ambrosiæ. Ambrosia* was the food of the gods, and *nectar* their drink. But the two are often confounded, as here, *liquidus odor* is said of *ambrosia. Liquidum odorem:* a pure fragrancy, or perfume.

416. *Perduxit:* in the sense of *perunxit.* Pierius found *perfudit* in the Roman MS.

417. *Aura:* in the sense of *odor. Illi:* the dat. in the sense of *illius.* This use of the dat. case is frequent with Virgil. *Compositis:* in the sense of *unctis.*

419. *Exesi:* in the sense of *excavati.*

421. *Olim:* in the sense of *aliquando. Deprensis:* caught, or overtaken in a storm.

423. *Aversum:* in the sense of *remotum.*

424. *Resistit:* in the sense of *remanet. Obscura:* in the sense of *occulta.*

425. *Sirius:* a star of the first magnitude in the mouth of the dog. It rises about the time the sun enters the sign Leo, which takes place in the latter part of July, causing what we call the dog-days. *Torrens:* pres. part. in the sense of *comburens. Indos.* This word is here used for the inhabitants of any warm climate. Such countries are subject to long and excessive droughts: hence the propriety of the epithet *sitientes.*

426. *Igneus Sol:* the fiery sun had completed (drawn out) half his course. This is a circumlocution to denote the middle of the day. *Hauserat:* in the sense of *cucurrerat.*

428. *Coquebant:* in the sense of *siccabant. Faucibus:* in the sense of *alveis.*

431. *Amarum:* the bitter spray. The sea-water is bitter as well as salt.

432. *Diversæ:* dispersed, or scattered along the shore.

433. *Stabuli:* in the sense of *armenti*, by meton.

435. *Auditis.* Some read *auditi*, to agree with *agni:* but the sense leads to *auditis:* the bleating of the lambs being heard. Mr. Davidson observes, that *auditis* is found in the Roman, Medicean, and Cambridge manuscripts. Heyne reads *auditis.*

437. *Facultas:* an opportunity was presented.

439. *Manicis:* in the sense of *vinculis.* Some manuscripts read *vinculis.*

441. *Miracula:* in the sense of *prodigia*, wonderful shapes, says Valpy.

442. *Liquentem:* in the sense of *fluentem.*

Verùm ubi nulla fugam reperit fallacia, victus
In sese redit, atque hominis tandem ore locutus:
Nam quis te, juvenum confidentissime, nostras
Jussit adire domos? quidve hinc petis? inquit. At ille,
Scis, Proteu, scis ipse: neque est te fallere cuiquam.
Sed tu desine velle. Deûm præcepta secuti
Venimus huc, lapsis quæsitum oracula rebus.
Tantum effatus. Ad hæc vates vi denique multâ
Ardentes oculos intorsit lumine glauco:
Et, graviter frendens, sic fatis ora resolvit:
Non te nullius exercent numinis iræ;
Magna luis commissa: tibi has miserabilis Orpheus
Haudquaquam ob meritum pœnas (ni fata resistant)
Suscitat, et raptâ graviter pro conjuge sævit.
Illa quidem, dum te fugeret per flumina præceps,
Immanem ante pedes hydrum, moritura puella,
Servantem ripas altâ non vidit in herbâ.
At chorus æqualis Dryadum clamore supremos
Implêrunt montes: flêrunt Rhodopeïæ arces,
Altaque Pangæa, et Rhesi Mavortia tellus,
Atque Getæ, atque Hebrus, atque Actias Orithyia.
Ipse, cavâ solans ægrum testudine amorem,
Te, dulcis conjux, te solo in litore secum,
Te veniente die, te decedente canebat.
Tænarias etiam fauces, alta ostia Ditis,

446. At ille *Aristæus respondit: O* Proteu, scis, *tu* ipse

448 Velle *fallere me*

450. Effatus *est hoc* tantum

457. Illa puella quidem moritura, dum præceps per flumina fugeret te, non vidit, ante pedes in alta herba, immanem

464. Ipse Orpheus solans ægrum amorem cava testudine, canebat te, *O* dulcis conjux; *canebat* te secum in solo litore: *canebat* te, die veniente; *canebat* te, die decedente,

NOTES.

443. *Fugam:* escape. *Fallacia:* wiles—tricks—stratagems.

447. *Neque est cuique:* nor is it in the power of any one to deceive you.

449. *Quæsitum:* to seek divine counsel in my ruined state—my adverse circumstances. A supine in *um*, put after *venimus*.

451. *Ardentes:* in the sense of *coruscantes.* It is to be connected with *lumine glauco.*

452. *Sic resolvit.* The poet now proceeds to the answer of Proteus, in which he tells Aristæus that the cause of his disaster was the injury offered to Eurydice, the wife of Orpheus. The whole story is told in so beautiful a manner, that it does not seem unworthy of the mouth of a god.

453. *Non nullius numinis.* Davidson renders this: of no mean deity. But the ordinary sense and meaning of the words are to be preferred: of some deity. The two negatives express affirmatively. Besides the punishment of Aristæus was procured by Orpheus and the nymphs, who were inferior deities Ruæus and Heyne say *alicujus Dei. Exercent:* in the sense of *persequuntur.*

454. *Commissa:* in the sense of *scelera. Miserabilis,* &c. Unhappy Orpheus procures this punishment for thee, by no means proportionate to thy deserts, (and would procure greater,) if the fates did not oppose. This appears to be the plain meaning of the passage. It would be a useless labor to enumerate the various opinions of commentators upon it. Dr. Trapp observes, the parenthesis, *ni fata resistant,* is the most difficult passage in Virgil's works. To make any sense of it, we must supply the words: and would procure greater punishment. *Ob:* equal—proportionate to.

Orpheus was the son of Œagrus, king of Thrace, and Calliope, one of the Muses. He was distinguished for his skill in music and poetry. He was one of the Argonauts. It is said there are some hymns of his extant; but there is reason to believe they are spurious. See Ecl. iii. 46.

456. *Sævit:* and grieves immoderately for.

461. *Arces:* the Rhodopean mountains. See Geor. iii. 351.

462. *Pangæa:* neu. plu. sing. *Pangæus*, a mountain in Thrace, in the confines of Macedonia. *Rhesi.* See Æn. I. 469.

463. *Getæ.* See Geor. iii. 462. *Orithyia.* See Ecl. vii. 51.

464. *Testudine.* The lyre was called *testudo,* because anciently it was made of tortoise shell. It is said that Mercury finding a dead tortoise on the banks of the river Nile, made a lyre of it; whence he is called, *parens curvæ lyræ.*

467. *Ingressus Tænarias.* *Tænarus*, a promontory of the Peloponnesus, separating the *Sinus Messenicus* from the *Sinus.*

Et caligantem nigrâ formidine lucum
Ingressus, Manesque adiit, regemque tremendum,
Nesciaque humanis precibus mansuescere corda.
At cantu commotæ Erebi de sedibus imis
Umbræ ibant tenues, simulacraque luce carentûm:
Quàm multa in sylvis avium se millia condunt,
Vesper ubi, aut hybernus agit de montibus imber
Matres, atque viri, defunctaque corpora vitâ
Magnanimûm heroum, pueri, innuptæque puellæ,
Impositique rogis juvenes ante ora parentum
Quos circum limus niger, et deformis arundo
Cocyti, tardâque palus inamabilis undâ
Alligat, et novies Styx interfusa coërcet.
Quin ipsæ stupuere domus, atque intima leti
Tartara, cæruleosque implexæ crinibus angues
Eumenides; tenuitque inhians tria Cerberus ora;
Atque Ixionii cantu rota constitit orbis.
Jamque pedem referens, casus evaserat omnes;
Redditaque Eurydice superas veniebat ad auras,

471. Cantu *Orphei* tenues

482. Eumenides implexæ *quoad* cæruleos angues crinibus

NOTES.

Laconicus, fabled to be the entrance of the infernal regions. Here Orpheus made his descent to hell after his Eurydice. *Ostia:* the doors, or gates of Pluto.

470. *Corda nescia:* and hearts knowing not (incapable of) to relent at human prayers.

472. *Simulacra:* the shades or forms of those wanting life. *Luce:* in the sense of *vita.*

475. *Corpora:* and bodies of gallant heroes deprived of life. *Corpora* is here used to denote the airy vehicle, or form, which the ancients assigned to departed spirits. This is the meaning here.

479. *Cocyti.* Cocytus, a river of Italy, of no great magnitude, feigned by the poets to be a river of hell. Its banks abounded in reeds. *Inamabilis:* in the sense of *odiosa;* and *undâ* for *aquâ.*

430. *Circum alligat:* surrounds—confines. The parts of the verb are frequently separated by Tmesis, for the sake of the verse. *Styx.* A fabulous river of hell, around which, the poets say, it flowed nine times. It may therefore be said to restrain the shades, and prevent them from returning to the upper regions. See Geor. iii. 551. *Interfusa:* flowing between them and the upper regions of light.

482. *Tartara:* properly the lowest part of hell—the place in which the impious are punished, according to the poets. *Intima:* in the sense of *profundissima. Letum,* or *Lethum,* seems here to be used for the place, or regions of the dead in general.

483. *Eumenides.* The furies were three in number, and represented with their hair entwined with serpents, to render them more dreadful. See Geor. i. 278. *Cerberus:* a huge dog with three heads, the door-keeper of Pluto.

484. *Cantu.* Most copies have *vento.* But it is extremely difficult to make any sense of that. Davidson reads *cantu,* and informs us that Pierius found *cantu* in several ancient MSS. This makes the sense easy, and the passage intelligible.

Commentators have shown a good deal of ingenuity in attempting to render this passage intelligible with *vento.* Ruæus says: *Orbis rotæ Ixioniæ quievit flante vento contrario.* Valpy: that the wind relaxed, by which the wheel was carried round: or it stood to the wind.

Heyne hath a long note upon it. He thinks *vento* should be taken in the abl. The wind, by which the wheel was carried round, subsiding, the wheel ceased to revolve: *Vento,quo aliàs circum agibatur rota, subsidente, subsideret motus rotæ.* Or, by *ventus,* may be understood the air or wind, occasioned by the revolution of the wheel: or lastly, says he, *rota orbis* may be taken simply for the wheel: *rota substitit vento:* the impulse of the wind ceasing, *venti impulsu cessante,* the wheel stopped.

The fable represents all the infernal regions charmed with the music of Orpheus The furies, the depths of Tartarus, Cerberus with his triple mouth, the wheel of Ixion, all stopped to listen to it. *Ixionii:* an adj. from *Ixion,* agreeing with *orbis.* Ixion was sentenced to be bound to a wheel, that kept perpetually in motion. *Rota orbis:* the rotation, or revolution of the wheel. or simply for *rota.* See Geor. iii. 38.

486. *Veniebat:* was just coming to the upper regions of light.

Ponè sequens; namque hanc dederat Proserpina legem
Cùm subita incautum dementia cepit amantem,
Ignoscenda quidem, scirent si ignoscere Manes.
Restitit, Eurydicenque suam jam luce sub ipsâ,
Immemor, heu! victusque animi, respexit: ibi omnis
Effusus labor; atque immitis rupta tyranni
Fœdera: terque fragor stagnis auditus Avernis.
Illa, quis et me, inquit, miseram, et te perdidit Orpheu?
Quis tantus furor? en iterum crudelia retrò
Fata vocant, conditque natantia lumina somnus!
Jamque vale: feror ingenti circumdata nocte,
Invalidasque tibi tendens, heu! non tua, palmas.
Dixit: et ex oculis subitò, ceu fumus in auras
Commixtus tenues, fugit diversa: neque illum
Prensantem nequicquam umbras, et multa volentem
Dicere, prætereà vidit: nec portitor Orci
Ampliùs objectam passus transire paludem.
Quid faceret? quò se, raptâ bis conjuge, ferret?
Quo fletu Manes, quâ numina voce moveret?
Illa quidem Stygiâ nabat jam frigida cymbâ.
Septem illum totos perhibent ex ordine menses
Rupe sub aëriâ, deserti ad Strymonis undam
Flevisse et gelidis hæc evolvisse sub antris,

489. *Dementia* quidem ignoscenda, si Manes

492. Rupta *sunt*

494. Illa *Eurydice* inquit: quis perdidit et me miseram, et te, *O Orpheu!* quis tantus furor *est hic?*

498. Non *ampliùs* tua *conjux*. Dixit: et fugit diversa ex oculis *Orphei*

503 [illegible] et *Orpheum*

507. Perhibent illum per septem totos menses ex ordine flevisse sub aëria rupe, ad

NOTES.

487. *Legem:* condition.

488. *Subita dementia:* a sudden frenzy, which put the lover off his guard; or caused him to forget the condition upon which his Eurydice was suffered to return.

489. *Ignoscenda quidem:* pardonable indeed, if, &c. Orpheus looked back to behold his loved Eurydice. This was the fatal error, and not to be blamed in a lover. Even Eurydice herself did not blame him, for it proceeded from love to her. Ovid says: *Jamque iterum moriens non est de conjuge quicquam questa suo: quid enim sese quereretur amatam?* *Manes*, here, is put for the infernal gods.

490. *Sub ipsa luce:* in the very region of light.

491. *Victus animi:* not master of his affections. *Effusus:* in the sense of *perditus est.*

493. *Fœdera:* the terms, or conditions. *Avernis:* sing. *Avernus;* plu. *Averna:* a lake of Campania, in Italy, by the poets placed in the infernal regions; also, by meton. put for the regions themselves. *Fragor.* Servius takes *fragor* to mean the joy and exultation of the shades at the return of Eurydice among them: a shout—a certain dismal and hollow sound.

495. *Furor:* force, or violence. It is plain that *furor* is not to be taken here in its usual sense. It is probable that it refers to the force or power which prevented her from following her husband, which she must have felt previous to her second death, or return to the shades. This is the opinion of Vossius

496. *Condit:* in the sense of *claudit.*

497. *Feror circumdata:* I am carried away, encompassed by thick darkness, and stretching, &c.

500. *Diversa:* in the sense of, *in diversam partem.* It agrees with *illa.*

502. *Prætereà:* in the sense of *posteà.* *Portitor Orci:* Charon. He was fabled to be the son of Erebus and Nox. It was his business to ferry the souls of the deceased over the rivers Styx and Acheron, to the place of the dead. Hence he is called *portitor orci.* The fable of Charon and his boat seems to have originated from the Egyptians, who had a custom of carrying their dead across a lake to a place, where sentence was to be passed upon them; and according to their good or bad actions in life, they were honored with a splendid burial, or left unnoticed in the open air. *Orci:* *Orcus* here signifies the regions of the dead in general—hell.

503. *Objectam paludem:* the intervening river—Styx. Orpheus had already re-crossed the Styx, and was approaching the regions of light, when Eurydice was taken from him, and hurried back to the shades. The infernal river, therefore, lay between him and the regions of the dead, to which Eurydice was carried a second time in the Stygian boat.

506. *Illa:* she—Eurydice, lifeless, was crossing, &c.

508. *Strymonis:* gen. of *Strymon*, a river of Macedonia, on the borders of Thrace.

509. *Hæc:* these misfortunes of his.

Mulcentem tigres, et agentem carmine quercus.
Qualis populeâ mœrens Philomela sub umbrâ
Amissos queritur fœtus, quos durus arator
Observans nido implumes, detraxit: at illa
Flet noctem, ramoque sedens miserabile carmen
Integrat, et mœstis latè loca questibus implet.
Nulla Venus, nullique animum flexere hymenæi.
Solus Hyperboreas glacies, Tanaïmque nivalem,
Arvaque Riphæis nunquam viduata pruinis
Lustrabat, raptam Eurydicen, atque irrita Ditis
Dona querens: spreto Ciconum quo munere matres,
Inter sacra Deûm, nocturnique orgia Bacchi,
Discerptum latos juvenem sparsere per agros.
Tum quoque marmoreâ caput à cervice revulsum,
Gurgite cùm medio portans Œagrius Hebrus
Volveret, Eurydicen, vox ipsa et frigida lingua,
Ah miseram Eurydicen! animâ fugiente, vocabat:
Eurydicen toto referebant flumine ripæ.
  Hæc Proteus: et se jactu dedit æquor in altum;
Quàque dedit, spumantem undam sub vertice torsit.

514. Flet *per* noctem

516. Animum *Orphei*

519. Raptam *à se*

520. Quo *nuptiali* munere spreto, matres Ciconum

523. Tum quoque cùm Œagrius Hebrus volveret *ejus* caput revulsum à marmoreâ cervice, portans *id* medio gurgite, *ejus* vox ipsa, et frigida lingua, vocabat

NOTES.

510. *Agentem:* in the sense of *ducentem.*

511. *Philomela:* the nightingale. See Ecl. vi. 78. This is a most exquisite simile, not more generally admired than beautifully conceived. To heighten the picture, the birds are not only *implumes,* without feathers, but they are taken from the nest; not only so, they are drawn from it by the hands of a cruel, hard-hearted ploughman. In reading it, an emphasis should be placed upon *durus* and *detraxit.* It may be observed that the poplar shade is very judiciously selected by the poet to heighten the image; because the leaves of the poplar tree, trembling with the least breath of air, make a kind of melancholy rustling. See Ecl. vi. 78.

512. *Queritur:* laments her lost young.

514. *Miserabile carmen:* mournful song. *Integrat:* in the sense of *renovat.*

516. *Venus:* love—person loved.

517. *Tanaïm:* Tanaïs, a large river of Europe. It flows through the ancient Scythia, and falls into the *Palus Mæotis,* or sea of Azoff, forming a part of the boundary line between Europe and Asia. *Hodie, the Don.*

518. *Viduata:* free from—destitute of. *Riphæis.* See Geor. i. 240.

520. *Dona irrita.* This alludes to the condition, on which Pluto consented to the return of Eurydice to life. The event proved the favor to be a useless, and unavailing one to him. *Querens:* lamenting—bemoaning. *Ciconum.* The Cicones were a people of Thrace near mount Ismarus, where the feasts of Bacchus were celebrated. *Quo munere spreto.* The Thracian women, as the fable goes, were much in love with Orpheus. None, however, was able to make any impression upon his mind except Eurydice. After her death, they renewed their suit, which was rejected. To this circumstance the words, *quo munere spreto,* may refer: which (whose) offer being despised. They may, however, refer to his total indifference to all female charms, and his disregard of marriage. In this sense, Mr. Davidson takes them. It is said, verse 516, supra.: *Nulla Venus, et nulli Hymenæi flexere animum.* See Ecl. iii. 46. Heyne reads *spretæ,* but the sense determines in favor of *spreto.* This disregard and indifference of Orpheus to the charms of the Thracian women, so enraged them, that during their revellings at a feast of Bacchus, they set upon him, tore him in pieces, and strowed his limbs over the Thracian fields.

521. *Nocturni.* The orgies of Bacchus were usually celebrated in the night; hence the epithet *nocturnus,* applied to Bacchus.

523. *Marmorea:* in the sense of *candida.*

524. *Œagrius:* an adj. from *Œagrus,* a king of Thrace, and father of Orpheus. *Gurgite:* in the sense of *fluvio,* vel *alveo Hebrus.* It is the principal river of Thrace With its tributary streams, it waters a considerable extent of country. It falls into the head of the Archipelago. Into this river the furious Bacchanals cast the head of Orpheus, which, as it floated down the current, continued to repeat the name of Eurydice.

527. *Referebant:* repeated—echoed.

528. *Dedit:* in the sense of *immisit.*

529. *Torsit spumantem:* he threw the foaming water over his head. Dr. Trapp observes, that although this episode be admirable in itself, it is obvious to observe that

530. At Cyrene non *dedit se in altum mare*. namque affata *est* timentem *filium* ultrò *dicens*.

532. Hæc *est* omnis causa morbi *apibus tuis*

538. *Primùm* delige quatuor

540. *Earum* cervice intactâ *jugo*

541. His *victimis* constitue

545. *Tanquam* inferias Orphei

548. *Est* haud mora *illi*

554. Hìc verò aspiciunt monstrum subitum, ac mirabile dictu, *nempe*, apes stridere *in* toto utero

557. Immensasque nubes *earum*

At non Cyrene: namque ultrò affata timentem:
Nate, licet tristes animo deponere curas.
Hæc omnis morbi causa: hinc miserabile Nymphæ,
Cum quibus illa chòros lucis agitabat in altis,
Exitium misêre apibus. Tu munera supplex
Tende, petens pacem, et faciles venerare Napæas.
Namque dabunt veniam votis, irasque remittent.
Sed, modus orandi qui sit, priùs ordine dicam
Quatuor eximios præstanti corpore tauros,
Qui tibi nunc viridis depascunt summa Lycæi,
Delige, et intactâ totidem cervice juvencas.
Quatuor his aras alta ad delubra Dearum
Constitue, et sacrum jugulis demitte cruorem,
Corporaque ipsa boum frondoso desere luco.
Pòst, ubi nona suos aurora ostenderit ortus,
Inferias Orphei, lethæa papavera mittes,
Placatam Eurydicen vitulâ venerabere cæsâ,
Et nigram mactabis ovem, lucumque revises.
Haud mora: continuò matris præcepta facessit·
Ad delubra venit, monstratas excitat aras,
Quatuor eximios præstanti corpore tauros
Ducit, et intactâ totidem cervice juvencas.
Pòst, ubi nona suos aurora induxerat ortus,
Inferias Orphei mittit, lucumque revisit.
Hìc verò subitum, ac dictu mirabile monstrum
Aspiciunt; liquefacta boum per viscera toto
Stridere apes utero, et ruptis effervere costis,
Immensasque trahi nubes; jamque arbore summâ

NOTES.

it is introduced a little inartificially. For it is not to be supposed that Proteus, having been made a prisoner, and speaking by constraint, would tell this long story to entertain Aristæus, who had thus offered violence to him. It would have been enough for him, to inform Aristæus that his misfortunes were occasioned by the death of Eurydice, without relating all the circumstances consequent upon it. But it may be said, this relation is more to the point than is usually imagined. These circumstances greatly aggravate the guilt of Aristæus, and so it was proper enough, if not necessary, to relate them. However the case may be, I would not, says he, lose this episode to be the author of all the best criticisms that were ever written upon it. *Sub vertice:* in the sense of *super verticem.*

532. *Hinc:* hence, for the cause or reasons, which Proteus had just mentioned.

533. *Illa:* Eurydice. *Agitabat:* in the sense of *ducebat.*

535. *Tende:* in the sense of *offer. Napææs:* Nymphs of the groves, from a Greek word, signifying a grove. *Faciles:* easy to be appeased.

539. *Summa viridis:* the tops of verdant *Lycæus.* This was a mountain in Arcadia, where it is said, Aristæus sometimes resided. *Eximios:* in the sense of *insignes.*

541. *Dearum:* the Nymphs. See Ecl. ii. 46.

542. *Demitte:* let out the sacred blood from their throats.

543. *Desere:* in the sense of *relinque.*

545. *Mittes:* you shall offer Lethæan poppies, as a sacrifice to Orpheus: i. e. to appease the Manes of Orpheus. *Inferiæ.* properly were offerings, or sacrifices to the gods below for the dead—to the Manes. The poppy was usually offered in sacrifice on such occasions, because its property is to cause sleep, or forgetfulness: sleep being a lively emblem of death. *Lethæa:* an adj. from *Lethum:* of Greek origin.

549. *Excitat:* in the sense of *erigit.—Monstratas:* in the sense of *præscriptas.*

550. *Præstanti:* in the sense of *pulchro.* The prep. *è* is understood.

553. *Mittit:* in the sense of *offert.*

554. *Monstrum:* in the sense of *prodigium.*

555. *Liquefacta:* in the sense of *putrefacta.*

556. *Stridere:* to hum or buzz—*effervere* in the sense of *erumpere.*

557. *Trahi:* to be borne along.

Confluere, et lentis uvam demittere ramis.
Hæc super arvorum cultu pecorumque canebam,
Et super arboribus: Cæsar dum magnus ad altum
Fulminat Euphratem bello, victorque volentes
Per populos dat jura, viamque affectat Olympo.
Illo Virgilium me tempore dulcis alebat
Parthenope, studiis florentem ignobilis otî:
Carmina qui lusi pastorum: audaxque juventâ,
Tityre, te patulæ cecini sub tegmine fagi.

563. Illo tempore dulcis Parthenope alebat me

NOTES.

558. *Confluere:* to collect together—to swarm. *Demittere:* to hang from the flexile boughs, like a bunch of grapes. *Dependere in modum uvæ*, says Ruæus.

562. *Affectat viam:* he prepares his way to heaven. By the splendor of his actions, he lays the foundation for divine honors. These he afterward received by a decree of the Senate. From this passage, it is inferred, that Virgil continued the care of the Georgics as long as he lived; for the time here mentioned was only the year before his death. At that time, in the year of Rome 734, Augustus was at the head of the Roman army on the banks of the Euphrates, and forced *Phraates*, king of the Parthians, to restore the Eagles, which they had taken from Crassus, the Roman consul, in a former war. The neighboring nations, and even the Indians, awed by the splendor of his actions, made a voluntary submission to him.

564. *Parthenope:* the city Naples. It was founded by the *Chalsidenses*, and by them called *Parthenope*, from the circumstance of their finding the tomb of one of the *Sirenes*, of that name; who, because she was unable to allure Ulysses on shore with her music, killed herself. They how ever demolished it afterward, because it proved an injury to *Cumæ*, which they built in the neighborhood. They re-built it at the command of an oracle, and called it *Neapolis*, or the New City. *Studiis:* flourishing in the studies of inglorious ease. *Otium*, very properly denotes the peaceful, and retired life of a philosopher: which the poet modestly calls inglorious, (*ignobilis*) in comparison of a public life. Every other occupation besides war and public affairs, received from the Romans, the name of *Otium*. Or, *ignobilis* may here mean private, retired, without noise and show. This is the sense in which Dr. Trapp understands it. Ruæus says, *privati otii*. *Otium* is properly opposed to *labor*, in signification. *Oti:* by apocope for *otii*.

565. *Lusi:* in the sense of *cecini*. *Audax:* in the sense of *confidens*. Virgil was about twenty-nineyears of age when he began his Eclogues, and finished them when he was about thirty-three. Mr. Wharton imagines these four last lines are spurious. He thinks the book naturally concludes with the words: *Viamque affectat Olympo.* For, says he, nothing can be a more complete and sublime conclusion, than this compliment to Augustus.

QUESTIONS.

What is the subject of this book?

Why does the poet call honey *aërial?*

What places are proper for placing the hives?

What direction is given for recalling the swarms, when flying away?

Is this practised by bee-masters at the present day?

What is the character of the poet's description of a battle between two discordant swarms?

The poet represents the leaders under the appellation of kings: Is that strictly correct?

To which of the sexes do they belong?

How many different words does the poet use for the hive?

What are they?

Was Virgil remarkable for this diversity of style?

Is the bee a very sagacious animal?

Whence did they receive, according to the poets, this extraordinary sagacity?

What was this in consideration of?

How is this fable interpreted?

Why was the goat transferred to heaven, and made a constellation?

To whom were his horns given?

What property was added to these?

Was the opinion of the ancients concerning the production of the bee, incorrect?

Is that opinion now exploded?

How many kinds of bees are there in the hive?

Of what sex are the *Drones?*

There is only one female bee in the hive, and what is she called?

What is her employment?

Of what sex are the laboring bees?

Is the bee-hive a piece of exquisite workmanship?

What does the poet emphatically call the hives?

Where was the city Canopus situated?

By whom was it built?

Why is it called *Pellæan?*

Why does the poet call the Egyptians, *Gens fortunata?*

Where does the Nile take its rise?

What is the cause of its overflowing?

What course does it run?

By how many mouths does it empty?

What does it form towards its mouth?

How is the water of the Nile conducted to the different parts of Egypt?

How high must it rise for that purpose?

If it fall short of that, what is expected?

What did the Romans call any people living in a hot climate?

In what sense may the Nile be said to have pressed upon the borders of Persia?

Who was Aristæus?

What is the character of this episode respecting him?

Is the production of the bee, as here related, fabulous?

Who was Proteus?

What property did he possess in an eminent degree?

Where is he said to have had his place of residence?

Whom does Herodotus make him?

Whom does Sir Isaac Newton consider him?

With whom was he contemporary?

How is Proteus represented as drawn?

How many opinions were there among the ancients of the origin of rivers?

What were they?

By what distinguished philosophers were these different opinions maintained?

Which opinion does Virgil follow?

What was this grand reservoir or receptacle called?

Why were the epithets *Taurinus* and *Cornutus* sometimes given to rivers?

What is said of the river Acheloüs?

Whence arose the fable of the *cornucopiæ?*

Who was Orpheus?

What is said of the music of his lyre?

What effect had it upon the shades below?

What effect had it upon Pluto himself?

Why did he descend to the realms of Pluto?

What was the issue of it?

What was the probable origin of the fable of Charon and his boat?

What does Dr. Trapp observe concerning this episode of Aristæus?

Is there reason to believe that Virgil continued to revise his Georgics as long as he lived?

What is that reason?

INTRODUCTION TO THE ÆNEID.

The Æneid is a heroic, or epic poem. It takes its name from Æneas, the son of Anchises and Venus. By his father, he was allied to the royal family of Troy. He was also the son-in-law of Priam; whose daughter, Creüsa, he had married. Æneas is the hero of the poem. Its subject is his removal into Italy with a colony of Trojans, and their settlement in that country.

Virgil was forty years of age when he commenced the Æneid. He had just finished the *Georgics:* and Augustus, now thirty-three years old, had undisturbed possession of the Roman empire. And nothing appeared to interrupt the universal repose, so desirable after the long civil wars that had desolated the fairest portions of it. It was at this moment, when the minds of the Roman people were turned from the desolating scenes of war to the milder arts of peace, that the poet conceived the plan of writing the Æneid, a poem second only to the Iliad, for the entertainment and instruction of his countrymen. There are some, who think the principal object of the poet was to flatter the pride and vanity of the Roman people, and especially Augustus, who was now raised to the highest temporal power.

This part of his works is by far the noblest, though not the most perfect and finished. It was his intention to have revised it before he published it to the world; but he died leaving it incomplete, as appears by several imperfect lines found in different parts of it. He bequeathed the whole to Augustus, who put the manuscript into the hands of Tucca and Varus for publication, with an injunction not to alter, in any way, the manuscript, nor to fill up the imperfect lines.

In the first six books, Virgil imitates the Odyssey of Homer; in the last six, he follows the Iliad; and it is probable that we should not have had the Æneid, if we had not, at the same time, the Odyssey and the Iliad also. Homer may be considered the master, Virgil the pupil; but it must, at the same time, be acknowledged, that the Roman excelled the Grecian in many instances, particularly in propriety and judgment.

Paris, the son of Priam, an accomplished prince, visited the court of Menelaus, by whom he was received with the greatest cordiality. Here he became enraptured with the beautiful Helen, the wife of his host, and conceived the base purpose of taking her with him to Troy. Taking advantage of the absence of her husband, he put his plan into execution. This atrocious deed excited a general indignation through the states of Greece; and, after sending an embassy to Troy upon the subject, to no purpose, it was determined, as the last resort, to declare war against Priam, and with the united forces of the Grecian princes, to avenge the perfidious act.

After a siege of ten years, the city was taken by stratagem, and rased to the ground. Æneas, in the fatal night, after performing prodigies of valor, retired some distance from the city, bearing his aged father upon his shoulders, and leading his little son by the hand. He was followed by great numbers of his countrymen, who had escaped the flames and the sword. At *Antandros*, a small town in the neighborhood of Troy, he built him a fleet of twenty ships, and having furnished himself with all things necessary for his enterprise, set sail in search of a new settlement. He visited Thrace. Here he founded a city which he called *Ænos*. He abandoned his undertaking at the direction of the ghost of his friend. Thence he sailed to Crete, the land of *Teucer*, one of the founders of the Trojan race. Here he attempted a settlement, but through the unhealthiness of the climate, was compelled to relinquish it, after losing a great number of his companions. In the midst of his distress, he is informed in a vision, that Italy, the birth place of Dardanus, was the land destined to him by the gods. Upon this information he left Crete; and, after various fortunes by sea and land, he arrived in Italy in about seven years after his departure from his native land. He was kindly received by Latinus, king of *Latium*, who proposed to bestow upon him his daughter *Lavinia*, the heiress of his kingdom. Turnus, king of the *Rutuli*, a brave and valiant prince, had long sought her in marriage. He opposed her connexion with Æneas. This occasioned a bloody war, in which most of the Italian princes were engaged, on one side or the other. It ended in the death of Turnus, which closes the Æneid.

Æneas afterwards married Lavinia, and succeeded Latinus in his kingdom. He built a city, which he called *Lavinium*, in honor of his wife. This he made the seat of his government. He was succeeded by Ascanius, or Iülus, who reigned thirty years, when he built *Alba longa*, to which he removed with his court. Here the government was administered by a line of Trojan princes for three hundred years, till Romulus arose, who founded the city of Rome. After Romulus, the royal line was broken, and the government transferred to Numa Pompilius, a Sabine.

The three first books are not arranged in the order of time. The second book, which relates the downfall of Troy, and is the basis of the poem, is the first in time. The third, which relates the voyage of Æneas, till after his departure from Sicily for Italy, follows. The first, which relates the dispersion of his fleet, and his arrival in Africa, with his kind reception by Dido, succeeds the third. The rest are all in the order of time. But this change, so far from being a defect in the poem, is an advantage, and shows the judgment of the poet. He was enabled thereby to make his hero relate the downfall of his country, and the various fortunes of his long and eventful voyage.

The poet hath contrived to introduce into his poem the outlines of the Roman history, and a number of interesting episodes, which add to the whole beauty and entertainment.

For further particulars, see the introduction to the several books.

QUESTIONS.

What kind of poem is the Æneid?
Who is the hero of it?
What is its subject?
What was the age of Virgil, when he began the Æneid?
How long was he engaged in it?
Who was then at the head of the Roman empire?
What was the state of that empire?
What probably was the principal object of the poet in writing the Æneid?
Do some suppose a different object?
In what light may the Æneid be considered, in regard to the Iliad?
Did Virgil live to perfect the Æneid?
To whom did he bequeath it?
Under whose inspection was it published?
What gave rise to the Trojan war?
How long was the city besieged?
What was the issue of the siege?
What did Æneas do in the fatal night?
From what place did he set sail?

How many ships had he?

What place did he first visit?

What city did he found there?

To what place did he next sail?

Why did he go to Crete?

What befel him there?

From Crete, to what place did he direct his course?

How many years elapsed before he arrived in Italy?

Why was he directed to go to Italy?

How was he received by Latinus?

What prince opposed his connexion with Lavinia, the daughter of Latinus?

What was the consequence?

What was the issue of the war?

What did he do afterwards?

Did he build a city?

What did he call it?

Who succeeded him in the government

What city did Ascanius afterwards build?

How long did it continue to be the seat of the government?

Do the books of the Ænied follow each other in the order of time?

What books are not placed in this order?

Did this afford the poet any advantage?

P. VIRGILII MARONIS

ÆNEIS.

LIBER PRIMUS.

THIS Book is considered one of the finest and the most perfect of the Æneid. Its subject, and the cause of Juno's resentment being premised, it opens seven years after the embarkation of Æneas. He had now arrived in the Tuscan sea, and was in sight of Italy; when Juno, to avenge herself upon the Trojans, repaired to Æolus, and by fair promises, prevailed upon him to let loose his winds. They rush forth in every direction, and cause a violent tempest; which dispersed the Trojan fleet. It sunk one ship, and drove several others on the shore. Neptune assuages the tumult of the waves, and causes a calm. Having severely rebuked the winds for invading his dominions without his permission, he assists in getting off the ships.

After this, Æneas directs his course southward, and arrives on the coast of Africa. Venus complains to Jupiter of the hardship of her son, and prays that an end may be put to his sufferings. Whereupon, he sends Mercury to procure him a kind reception among the Carthaginians. In the mean time, Æneas walks abroad to make some discoveries of the country, accompanied by Achates. Venus, in the form and attire of a virgin huntress, presents herself to him. Upon his inquiry, she informs him to what country he had arrived, what were the inhabitants, their manners, and customs. She also gives him a brief account of Dido, and of the settlement of the country; and, veiled in a cloud, she conducts him to the city. Passing through the crowd unseen, he goes to the temple. Here he finds his companions, whom he expected to be lost. Here he sees Dido, and is struck with her majesty and grace. By a device of Venus, she conceives a passion for him; which, in the end, proves her ruin.

The poet hath introduced several interesting episodes; particularly the description of Carthage, the representation of the Trojan battles, the song of Iopas, &c. The book concludes, leaving Dido inquiring concerning Priam, and the Trojan heroes; concerning Achilles and Diomede; concerning the Trojan disasters, the stratagems of the Greeks, and the voyage of Æneas. These form the subject of the two following books.

ARMA, virumque cano, Trojæ qui primus ab oris
Italiam, fato profugus, Lavinaque venit
Litora: multùm ille et terris jactatus et alto,

1. Qui profugus fato, primus venit ab oris Trojæ *in* Italiam

NOTES.

1. *Virum:* Æneas, the hero of the poem. *Vir*, properly signifies a man, as distinguished from a woman; also, the male of any species or kind, as distinguished from the female. *Trojæ:* Troy, once a famous city of Phrygia Minor, in the Lesser Asia; so called from *Tros*, one of its kings. It was sometimes called *Ilium*, *Ilios*, or *Ilion*, from *Ilus*, the son of Tros; *Dardania*, from *Dardanus*, the grand-father of Tros. Having killed his brother Janus, he fled from Italy to Phrygia, and founded this city in conjunction with *Teucer*, whose daughter he married. It was also called *Teucria*, from Teucer.

2. *Profugus fato:* driven—impelled by fate. Æneas left his country at the direction of the gods; and under their conduct, he came to Italy, and settled in Latium This circumstance the poet turns to the honor of Æneas and the Romans, whom he makes to descend from him. *Lavina:* an

5. Et passus est multa quoque

8. O Musa, memora mihi causas earum rerum

12. Quam Tyrii coloni tenuere, Carthago nomine, contra Italiam, Tiberinaque ostia longè

Vi Superûm, sævæ memorem Junonis ob iram.
Multa quoque et bello passus, dum conderet urbem,
Inferretque Deos Latio: genus unde Latinum,
Albanique patres, atque altæ mœnia Romæ.
Musa, mihi causas memora: quo numine læso,
Quidve dolens regina Deûm tot volvere casus
Insignem pietate virum, tot adire labores,
Impulerit. Tantæne animis cœlestibus iræ?
Urbs antiqua fuit, Tyrii tenuere coloni,
Carthago, Italiam contra, Tiberinaque longè

NOTES.

adj. from *Lavinium*, a city built by Æneas; so called from *Lavinia*, the daughter of Latinus, whom he married. It was situated about eight miles from the shore, in lat. 41° 40′ north, and long. 13° 10′ east from London.

4. *Ob memorem iram:* on account of the lasting resentment of cruel Juno. Juno was the daughter of Saturn and Ops, and the sister and wife of Jupiter. She was born, some say at Argos, but others say at Samos. She was jealous of her husband, and implacable in all her resentments. She was enraged against Paris, the son of Priam, because he adjudged the prize of beauty, which was a golden apple, to Venus, rather than to herself. From that moment, she became a bitter enemy to the whole Trojan race, and even to Venus herself. Not content with the subversion of the kingdom of Priam, she used her endeavor to destroy the few, who escaped the sword and the flames.

Juno had sumptuous temples dedicated to her in various places. Among the chief may be reckoned her temples at Argos, Samos, and Carthage. The hawk, the goose, and the peacock were sacred to her. Various names were given her, chiefly on account of her offices, and the places where she was worshipped; some of which are the following: Saturnia, Olympia, Samia, Argiva, Lacedæmonia, Lucina, Pronuba, Sospita, and Ophegena.

6. *Unde Latinum genus:* hence (arose) the Latin race.

Here is some difficulty. The Latins could not spring from Æneas; for he found them in Italy on his arrival. Some refer the word *unde* to *Latium*, taking the meaning to be: from which country sprung the Latin race. Servius would explain it thus: Æneas, having overcome all opposition, and being seated on the throne of Latinus, instead of changing the Latin name, as he might have done, in right of his conquest, incorporated his Trojans along with his subjects under the general name of Latins, so that he might not improperly be called the founder of the Latin race.

7. *Albanique patres.* Ascanius, who succeeded his father, left Lavinium, and having built Alba Longa, made it the seat of his government. This city gave birth to Romulus, who founded the city Rome. The Albans may therefore be called the fathers of the Romans. *Albani* may be either an adj. or a sub.

8. *Quo numine læso:* what god being injured—what god had he injured. *Quid:* in the sense of *cur*. *Dolens:* in the sense of *offensa*. Ruæus interprets *læso* by *violato*.

9. *Volvere casus:* to struggle with misfortunes as with a load. Ruæus takes this in the sense of *volvi casibus;* but it is much more poetical to take the verb in the active voice. *Volvere* imports labor and difficulty, like a person rolling a great weight, or a river bearing down before it all opposition. *Volvere casus* then represents Æneas resolutely going forward, and rising superior to all difficulties and dangers; but *volvi casibus* would show him overcome and vanquished by misfortunes. But this is not the design of the poet.

10. *Adire.* This verb properly signifies, to brave dangers—to look an enemy in the face—to undertake any thing resolutely. *Labores*, probably refers to the wars and hardships which Æneas underwent after his arrival in Italy; while *casus* may refer to the toils, dangers, and misfortunes which he passed through on his way thither. *Impulerit:* forced, or doomed.

12. *Tyrii:* an adj. from *Tyrus*, a city in Phœnicia, on the shore of the Mediterranean. *Hodie*, *Sur.*

From this city, a colony removed to Africa under Xorus and Carchedon, and settled at Utica: afterwards Dido followed with her wealth, and a great number of her countrymen, and founded, or, as some say, fortified Carthage. See Æn. iv. 1. *Tyrii coloni:* a Tyrian colony. *Tenuere:* inhabited—held.

13. *Tiberina:* an adj. from *Tiber*, the name of a river of Italy. It rises in the Appenines, and running in a south-easterly direction, falls into the Mediterranean sea. A few miles above its mouth, Rome was afterwards built. It is the second river in size in Italy.

Ostia, dives opum, studiisque asperrima belli:
Quam Juno fertur terris magìs omnibus unam
Posthabitâ coluisse Samo. Hìc illius arma,
Hìc currus fuit: hoc regnum Dea gentibus esse,
Si quà fata sinant, jam tum tenditque fovetque.
Progeniem sed enim Trojano à sanguine duci
Audîerat, Tyrias olim quæ verteret arces.
Hinc populum latè regem, belloque superbum,
Venturum excidio Libyæ: sic volvere Parcas.
Id metuens, veterisque memor Saturnia belli,
Prima quod ad Trojam pro charis gesserat Argis.
Necdum etiam causæ irarum, sævique dolores
Exciderant animo. Manet altâ mente repôstum
Judicium Paridis, spretæque injuria formæ,
Et genus invisum, et rapti Ganymedis honores.
His accensa super, jactatos æquore toto

21. *Audîerat* populum regem latè, et superbum bello, venturum *esse* hinc excidio Libyæ: *audîerat* Parcas volvere sic. Saturnia metuens id, memorque

29. Arcebat longè à Latio Troas, relliquias Danaûm, atque immitis Achillei, jactatos toto æquore: actique fatis errabant

NOTES.

14. *Dives opum:* abounding in wealth. *Opes* properly signifies power acquired by wealth. *Asperima*, &c. *Dedita studiis belli*, says Heyne. Carthage was situated in Africa, near where Tunis now stands. The Carthaginians were a very commercial people. They planted colonies in various parts of Europe, and widely extended their conquests. For a long time, they disputed with the Romans the empire of the world. They were brave, and much devoted to the study of the arts of war. See Æn. iv. 1.

15. *Quam unam Juno:* which one city, Juno is reported to have loved more than all lands. *Samo posthabita:* Samos being less esteemed, or set by. Samos is an island in the Icarian sea, over against Ephesus. Here Juno was brought up and married to Jupiter. Here she had a most splendid temple.

17. *Dea jam tum regnum:* the goddess even then both intended and cherished (the hope that) it would become the ruler over the nations—would be the capital of the world. Ruæus interprets *Hoc regnum gentibus*, by *illa imperat populis.* Heyne takes the words in the sense of *caput imperii terrarum.*—*Currus.* Juno had two kinds of chariots, one in which she was wafted through the air by peacocks, the other for war, drawn by horses of celestial breed. These last are here meant.

20. *Olim:* hereafter.

21. *Populum*, &c. (She had heard) that a people of extensive sway, and renowned in war, should come hence to the destruction of Lybia. *Regem* is plainly in the sense of *regentem*, vel *dominantem.* Ruæus interprets *excidio Lybiæ*, by, *per cladem Lybiæ*, implying by the destruction of Carthage, the chief city of Africa, Rome would become powerful and renowned in war. The sense I have given is evidently in the spirit of the poet, and the best. *Hinc:* hence—from Trojan blood.

22. *Parcas:* the fates. See Ecl. iv. 47.

23. *Metuens id.* In the long and bloody war which the Greeks carried on against Troy, Juno took a very active part, and exerted all her power in favor of the Greeks, and she feared she should be again involved in a similar contest with the Trojan race, in favor of her beloved Carthage. The *id* refers to the whole preceding sentence. *Argis.* Argos was one of the chief cities of Greece. Here Juno had a particular residence: put, by synec. for Greece in general.

24. *Prima:* an adj. agreeing with *Saturnia.* It appears to be used here in the sense of *princeps*, the chief or principal in the business.

25. *Dolores:* grief—resentment. Ruæus says, *indignatio. Sævi:* cruel—unrelenting.

27. *Judicium Paridis:* the judgment, or decision of Paris. See verse 4, supra, and nom. prop. under Paris. *Repôstum:* by syn. for *repositum. Formæ:* beauty. *Injuria:* affront.

28. *Genus invisum.* In addition to the decision of Paris, Juno hated the Trojans on account of Dardanus, one of the founders of their race. He was the son of Jupiter and Electra, the daughter of Atlas. All her husband's illegitimate children were the objects of her bitter resentment. *Honores rapti Ganymedis:* the honors of (conferred upon) stolen Ganymede. The office of cup-bearer to the gods was taken from Hebe, the daughter of Juno, and conferred upon Ganymede, a beautiful youth, the son of Tros, king of Troy. He was taken up to heaven by Jupiter in the form of an eagle, when he was upon mount Ida. This was another cause of her resentment.

29. *Accensa super his:* inflamed at these things; namely, the amour of her husband with Electra, the honors conferred upon Ganymede, and the decision of Paris in favor of Venus. The fear of the future

33. Condere Romanam gentem, erat *opus* tantæ molis

35. Vix *Trojani* læti dabant vela

37. *Volvebat* hæc secum: Me-ne victam

Troas, relliquias Danaûm atque immitis Achillei,
Arcebat longè Latio: multosque per annos
Errabant, acti fatis, maria omnia circùm.
Tantæ molis erat Romanam condere gentem.
  Vix è conspectu Siculæ telluris in altum
Vela dabant læti, et spumas salis ære ruebant;
Cùm Juno, æternum servans sub pectore vulnus,
Hæc secum: Mene incepto desistere victam,
Nec posse Italia Teucrorum avertere regem?
Quippe vetor fatis. Pallasne exurere classem
Argivûm, atque ipsos potuit submergere ponto,
Unius ob noxam, et furias Ajacis Oïlei?

NOTES.

destruction of her favorite Carthage, and the recollection of her past war, in which she had encountered so many difficulties, do not appear the only cause of her procedure. They contributed, no doubt, with the other particulars just mentioned, to increase the flame in her breast.

30. *Achillei:* gen. of Achilles. He was the son of Peleus, king of Thessaly, and Thetis, a goddess of the sea. While he was an infant, his mother dipped him all over in the river Styx, to render him invulnerable, except the heel by which she held him. He was concealed among the daughters of Lycomedes, king of the island of *Scyros*, in female apparel, that he might not go to the siege of Troy. While there, he deflowered *Deïdamia*, one of the princesses, who bore him Pyrrhus. He was, however, discovered by Ulysses, and afterward went to Troy. He slew Hector in single combat, and drew his dead body, behind his chariot, seven times around the walls of Troy, in revenge for his friend Patroclus, whom Hector had slain in battle. And he was himself slain by Paris, with an arrow, which pierced his heel, while he was in the temple of Thymbrian Apollo. He is sometimes called *Pelides*, from *Peleus* his father: also *Æacides*, from his grand-father *Æacus.* He is represented to have been of a cruel and vindictive temper, but at the same time, very brave.

33. *Molis:* magnitude—labor—difficulty.

34. *Siculæ:* an adj. from *Sicilia.* Sicily is the largest island in the Mediterranean, lying to the south of Italy, and separated from it by the straits of Messina.

35. *Ære:* with the brazen prow. The beaks of their ships were of brass, or overlaid with brass.—*Dabant:* spread.

36. *Vulnus æturnum:* a lasting resentment. The same as *memorem iram*, verse iv. *supra.* *Servans:* feeding, cherishing.

37. *Me-ne victam:* shall I overcome, desist from my purpose, nor be able, &c.—*Me victam:* the acc. after the verb *volvebat*, or some other of the like import, understood. *Ne*, when joined to a verb, is generally interrogative, as in the present case. When it does not ask a question, it either is a negative particle, or expresses some circumstance or condition of an action.

38. *Teucrorum.* The Trojans were sometimes called *Teucri*, from *Teucer*, one of their founders. See note 1. supra. By *Regem Teucrorum* we are to understand Æneas. It seems now to be the purpose of Juno to prevent the settlement of the Trojans in Italy; and by that means, counteract the purposes of the gods concerning their future grandeur and power; to destroy them utterly, if it be possible, and disperse them over the deep. To this end, she applies to Æolus to raise a tempest on the sea, as the most likely way to effect her object.

40. *Argivûm:* for *Argivorum*, by syn. properly the citizens of *Argos:* but by *synec.* put for the Greeks in general, or any part of them. Here it means the *Locrians*, who, with Ajax, their king, returning home from Troy, were shipwrecked. Ajax was struck by Pallas with a thunderbolt for having ravished Cassandra, the daughter of Priam, in the temple of Pallas. But Homer gives us a different account. He says, that Ajax was drowned by Neptune, for having impiously boasted that he would escape the dangers of the sea, even against the will of the gods.

The Greeks are sometimes called *Danai*, from *Danaus*, one of their kings. He led a colony from Egypt into Greece; and, for his services and talents, was held in high estimation through all the Grecian states.

41. *Ajacis Oïlei.* There were two persons at the siege of Troy, by the name of Ajax. The one here meant was the son of Oïleus, king of the Locrians. He went with forty ships against Troy. The other was the son of Talemon king of Salamis, an island in the *Sinus Saronicus*, between Attica, and the Morea, or Peloponnesus. It is said he fell upon his own sword, because the armour of Achilles was adjudged to Ulysses rather than to himself. *Noxam et furias.* These both refer to the crime committed by him upon Cassandra. He offered violence to her during the sack of Troy.

Ipsa, Jovis rapidum jaculata è nubibus ignem,
Disjecitque rates, evertitque æquora ventis:
Illum expirantem transfixo pectore flammas
Turbine corripuit, scopuloque infixit acuto.
Ast ego, quæ Divûm incedo regina, Jovisque
Et soror et conjux, unâ cum gente tot annos
Bella gero: et quisquam numen Junonis adoret
Prætereà, aut supplex aris imponat honorem?
  Talia flammato secum Dea corde volutans,
Nimborum in patriam, loca fœta furentibus Austris,
Æoliam venit. Hìc vasto rex Æolus antro
Luctantes ventos, tempestatesque sonoras
Imperio premit, ac vinclis et carcere frænat.
Illi indignantes magno cum murmure montis
Circùm claustra fremunt. Celsâ sedet Æolus arce,
Sceptra tenens; mollitque animos, et temperat iras.
Ni faciat, maria ac terras cœlumque profundum
Quippe ferant rapidi secum, verrantque per auras.
Sed pater omnipotens speluncis abdidit atris,
Hoc metuens: molemque et montes insuper altos
Imposuit; regemque dedit, qui fœdere certo
Et premere, et laxas sciret dare jussus habenas.
Ad quem tum Juno supplex his vocibus usa est:
Æole, (namque tibi Divûm pater atque hominum rex
Et mulcere dedit fluctus, et tollere vento,)

45. Turbine corripuit illum expirantem flammas

52. Hìc rex Æolus in vasto antro premit imperio luctantes

58. Quippe, ni faciat *id*, *illi* rapidi ferant secum maria

62. Qui jussus sciret et premere *eos* certo fœdere, et dare *illis* laxas habenas

NOTES.

42. *Ipsa jaculata.* Beside Jove, several of the Gods and Goddesses could hurl the thunder of heaven. Here Pallas is said to do it, to burn the ships of Ajax, to drown their crews, and to pierce his breast with a stream of lightning.

46. *Quæ incedo:* I who walk the Queen of the Gods, and both the sister and wife of Jove, carry on war, &c.

Servius observes that the verb *incedo* signifies to walk with dignity, and in state: *Cum dignitate aliqua ambulare:* and is properly applied to persons of rank, and distinguished characters.

49. *Prætereà:* beside—in addition to the reasons already given. If I shall show myself unable to effect my purpose, and satiate my revenge—if I shall let them alone: who will adore, &c.—*Honorem*, in the sense of *victimam.*

The whole of this speech of Juno is animated, full of pride and haughtiness. If Pallas, a goddess of inferior honor, dignity, and power, could destroy the fleet of Ajax, drown his followers, and kill their leader; surely I, who am both the sister and wife of Jove, am able to destroy these few fugitive Trojans, and their king.

51. *Austris furentibus:* places pregnant with furious winds. *Auster* properly signifies the south wind; but it frequently is put for wind in general: the *species* for the *genus.*

52. *In Æoliam venit:* she came into *Æolia*, the country of storms.

The Æolian islands are seven in number, situated between Italy and Sicily on the west. They were sometimes called *Vulcaniæ*, and *Hephæstiades*. The chief of which are *Lipara*, *Hiera*, and *Strongyle*. Here Æolus the son of Hippotas reigned. He is said to have invented sails, and to have been a great astronomer, and observer of the winds.—Hence the poets make him the god of the winds. Homer tells us that he gave to Ulysses all the winds, that could impede his course to Ithaca, confined in a bag; but that his companions, out of curiosity, untied it, and let out all the adverse winds.

54. *Frænat:* he curbs or governs. This is a metaphor taken from the rider, who manages his steed. *Imperio:* power, authority.

61. *Molem et altos montes:* for *molem altorum montium*, by hendiadis: the weight of lofty mountains. This mode of expression is frequent with Virgil.—*Insuper* in the sense of *præterea.*

63. *Premere:* in the sense of *cohibere.*—*Jussus:* commanded by Jove. Here again is a metaphor taken from the rider: *Dare laxas habenas:* to give loose reins—to let the horse go at full speed.—*Fœdere:* law—rule.

Gens inimica mihi Tyrrhenum navigat æquor,
Ilium in Italiam portans, victosque Penates.
Incute vim ventis, submersasque obrue puppes·
Aut age diversas, et disjice corpora ponto.
Sunt mihi bis septem præstanti corpore Nymphæ:
Quarum, quæ formâ pulcherrima, Deïopeiam
Connubio jungam stabili, propriamque dicabo:
Omnes ut tecum meritis pro talibus annos
Exigat, et pulchrâ faciat te prole parentem.
  Æolus hæc contrà: Tuus, ô regina, quid optes,
Explorare labor: mihi jussa capessere fas est.
Tu mihi, quodcunque, hoc regni, tu sceptra, Jovemque
Concilias: tu das epulis accumbere Divûm,
Nimborumque facis tempestatumque potentem.
  Hæc ubi dicta, cavum conversâ cuspide montem
Impulit in latus; ac venti, velut agmine facto,
Quà data porta, ruunt, et terras turbine perflant.
Incubuere mari, totumque à sedibus imis
Unà Eurusque Notusque ruunt, creberque procellis
Africus, et vastos volvunt ad litora fluctus.
Insequitur clamorque virûm, stridorque rudentum.
Eripiunt subitò nubes cœlumque, diemque,
Teucrorum ex oculis: ponto nox incubat atra.
Intonuere poli, et crebris micat ignibus æther:
Præsentemque viris intentant omnia mortem.
  Extemplò Æneæ solvuntur frigore membra.
Ingemit, et duplices tendens ad sidera palmas,
Talia voce refert: O terque quaterque beati,

70. Aut age *eas in* diversas *partes*, et

72. Quarum jungam *tibi* stabili connubio Deïopeiam, quæ *est* pulcherrima *earum omnium* forma, dicaboque *eam* propriam; ut exigat omnes annos

76. Contrà Æolus *respondit* hæc: O regina, tuus labor *est*

78. Tu concilias mihi hoc regni, quodcunque *est:* tu *concilias*

81. Ubi hæc dicta *sunt*, impulit cavum montem in latus

84. Incubuere mari Eurusque notusque Africusque creber procellis, unàque ruunt totum *mare*

NOTES.

67. *Tyrrhenum mare.* That part of the Mediterranean between the islands of Corsica, Sardinia, and Sicily, was called the Tuscan Sea.

68. *Ilium:* Troy; by meton. for the Trojans—those that survived the catastrophe of the city. See note 1. supra.—*Penates:* see Geor. 2. 505.

69. *Incute vim:* add force to your winds, and overwhelm their ships sunk in the sea.

71. *Præstanti:* in the sense of *pulchro.*

73. *Dicabo propriam:* I will consecrate her (to be) your own—your peculiar property. This passage is in imitation of Homer. Iliad 14. 301.

77. *Labor:* concern—business.—*Fas est,* in the sense of *æquum est.*

78. *Tu concilias,* &c. The meaning of the passage appears to be: I owe to thy favor and kind offices the empire of the winds, and the power and authority of a king, which thou didst obtain of Jove for me. Through thy favor also, I sit at the table of the gods. Both duty and gratitude, therefore, impel me to comply with your request, to do thy commands.—*Regni: gen. sing.* governed by *hoc.* It is best translated as if it were of the same case with *hoc. Concilias hoc regni,* &c. You procure for me this power, whatever it be. Servius thinks no more is meant by Æolus' receiving his kingdom and sceptre from Juno, than that " the winds are, air put into motion; which is sometimes called Juno."

80. *Potentem:* the present part. used as a substantive: ruler of storms and tempests.

82. *Agmine facto:* in a formed battalion—or a battalion being formed.—*Impulit:* he struck.

84. *Incubuere:* the perf. in the sense of the pres. *they rest upon.*

87. *Rudentum:* in the sense of *funium.*

90. *Poli.* Polus is properly that part of the heavens, called the pole. By *synec.* put for the whole heavens. *Poli:* the heavens thundered.—*Ignibus:* lightning.—*Æther:* in the sense of *aër.*

92. *Solvuntur:* shudder—are unnerved. *Duplices:* in the sense of *ambas.*

93. *Ingemuit:* he groaned. Not indeed at the fear of death absolutely considered, but at the prospect of dying an inglorious death among the waves.

94. *Refert:* he says, or pronounces such like words. O *terque, quaterque beati:* Simply: O thrice happy they, to whom it happened to die before the faces, &c. This mode of expression denotes the highest state of felicity. Or, if we suppose it an apo-

Queis ante ora patrum, Trojæ sub mœnibus altis,
Contigit oppetere! ô Danaûm fortissime gentis
Tydide, mene Iliacis occumbere campis
Non potuisse? tuaque animam hanc effundere dextrâ?
Sævus ubi Æacidæ telo jacet Hector, ubi ingens
Sarpedon: ubi tot Simoïs correpta sub undis
Scuta virûm, galeasque, et fortia corpora volvit.
Talia jactanti stridens Aquilone procella
Velum adversa ferit, fluctusque ad sidera tollit.
Franguntur remi: tum prora avertit, et undis
Dat latus: insequitur cumulo præruptus aquæ mons.
Hi summo in fluctu pendent: his unda dehiscens
Terram inter fluctus aperit: furit æstus arenis.
Tres Notus abreptas in saxa latentia torquet;
Saxa, vocant Itali, mediis quæ in fluctibus Aras,
Dorsum immane mari summo. Tres Eurus ab alto
In brevia et syrtes urget, miserabile visu;

96. O Tydide, fortissime gentis Danaûm, menè non potuisse occumbere Iliacis

100. Ubi Simoïs volvit sub undis tot scuta galeasque, et fortia corpora virûm

102. Procella stridens *ab* aquilone, adversa *illi* jactanti talia, ferit velum

103. Notus torquet tres *naves* abreptas in latentia saxa, *illa* saxa, quæ in mediis fluctibus, Itali vocant aras; *quorum* immane dorsum *est in* summo mari. Eurus urget tres *naves* ab alto

NOTES.

strophe to those, who fell on the plains of Troy, fighting for their country, we may render it: O thrice happy ye, to whom, &c. This last is the more animated and poetical. The former is the sense of Ruæus.

97. *Tydide.* Diomede, the son of Tydeus, king of Ætolia. He was wounded by Æneas in a combat. *Me-ne potuisse:* the acc. after the verb *refert*, or some other of the same import, understood: why could I not have fallen on the Trojan plains? &c.

98. *Effundere:* in the sense of *amittere.*—*Jacet:* lies slain.

99. *Sævus Hector:* valiant Hector. He was the son of Priam and Hecuba, and the bravest of all the Trojans. He was at last slain by Achilles, and his dead body drawn behind his chariot around the walls of Troy, and the tomb of *Patroclus*, whom Hector had slain some time before. It was afterwards ransomed by Priam at a great price, and honorably buried. *Æacidæ:* Achilles. See note 30. supra.

100. *Sarpedon.* He was the king of Lycia, and came to the assistance of Priam.—He was slain by Patroclus. It is said that he was the son of Jupiter by Laodamia.

Simoïs: a river in Troas, rising out of Mount Ida, and flowing into the Scamander, and with it into the Hellespont, near the promontory of Sigeum. *Correpta:* carried—hurried down its current. *Virûm*, by syn. for *virorum:* of heroes. The poet here alludes to the bloody battle fought on the banks of this river, between the Greeks and Trojans, related by Homer; in which the latter suffered a signal defeat.

102. *Procella:* properly, a storm at sea. *Hyems*, a cold storm in the winter. *Nimbus*, a storm of rain with black angry clouds and wind; a squall. *Imber*, a gentle shower of rain. They are, however, not always used with this discrimination. *Jactanti:* in the sense of *dicenti.*

103. *Adversa:* an adj. agreeing with *procella.* As Æneas was steering toward Italy, a north wind would be in his face, or against him.

105. *Insequitur.* Nothing can exceed this picture of a rolling billow. It follows (*sequitur*) rolling along, constantly on the increase, (*cumulo*) till it becomes a broken and rugged mountain of water: *præruptus mons aquæ.*

107. *Aperit terram.* So high did the waves roll, that between them the sand or bottom of the sea appeared visible. This may not appear incredible, when it is considered that they were near shore, and on shallows. *Dehiscens:* opening. Ruæus interprets *unda*, by *mare.* *Æstus:* the tide, or current.

108. *Saxa.* These rocks are generally supposed to be the *Ægates*, three Islands not far from the western promontory of Sicily, where the Romans and Carthaginians made a treaty, which ended the first Punic war. They received the name of *altars*, from the oaths that were then made by the contracting parties. There is a difficulty in this interpretation. For it is said their huge back was in the surface of the water, and in the preceding line they are called *latentia saxa.* *Abreptas:* driven—forced.

111. *Brevia et Syrtes:* shoals and quicksands. Syrtis is properly a large bank of sand made by the action of the water.—There were two of these banks, or *Syrtes* on the coast of Africa, called the *Syrtis Major*, and the *Syrtis Minor:* the former lay to the east of Carthage, at a considerable distance; the latter nearly opposite. *Urget:* in the sense of *impellit.* *Miserabile:* shocking—distressing. *Visu*, is either the supine in *u*,

Illiditque vadis, atque aggere cingit arenæ.
Unam, quæ Lycios fidumque vehebat Orontem.
Ipsius ante oculos ingens à vertice pontus
In puppim ferit: excutitur pronusque magister
Volvitur in caput: ast illam ter fluctus ibidem
Torquet agens circùm, et rapidus vorat æquore vortex
Apparent rari nantes in gurgite vasto:
Arma virûm, tabulæque et Troïa gaza per undas
Jam validam Ilionei navem, jam fortis Achatæ;
Et quâ vectus Abas, et quâ grandævus Alethes,
Vicit hyems: laxis laterum compagibus omnes
Accipiunt inimicum imbrem, rimisque fatiscunt.
  Intereà magno misceri murmure pontum,
Emissamque hyemem sensit Neptunus, et imis
Stagna refusa vadis: graviter commotus, et alto
Prospiciens, summâ placidum caput extulit undâ
Disjectam Æneæ toto videt æquore classem,
Fluctibus oppressos Troas, cœlique ruinâ.
Nec latuere doli fratrem Junonis, et iræ.
Eurum ad se Zephyrumque vocat: dehinc talia fatur
Tantane vos generis tenuit fiducia vestri?
Jam cœlum terramque, meo sinè numine, venti,

114. Ingens pontus, ante oculos *Æneæ* ipsius, ferit à vertice unam *navem* in puppim, quæ vehebat

116. Ast circùmagens fluctus torquet illam *navem* ter ibidem

118. *Homines* apparent rari nantes in vasto gurgite. *Apparent quoque* arma

120. Hyems vicit jam validam navem Ilionei; jam *navem* fortis Achatæ; et *navem, in* quâ Abas vectus *est*, et *navem, in* quâ

125. Neptunus sensit pontum

126. Stagna refusa *esse, ex*

129. *Et* Troas oppressos *esse* fluctibus

133. Jam audetis, *O*

NOTES.

to be seen; or, for *visui*, the dat. of *visus*, to the sight. See Ecl. 5. 29.

112. *Vadis:* against the bottom. *Vadum* is properly a shallow part of the sea; or a part of a river that may be forded. *Aggere:* a bank of sand.

113. *Lycios.* The Lycians were a people of Asia Minor, who came to assist Priam. After the death of Sarpedon their king, they chose to accompany Æneas. *Orontes* took the command of them.

114. *Pontus:* here put for a wave of the sea, by synec. It was so great that it seemed as if the whole ocean was breaking upon the ship. *A vertice.* Some understand by this, the head or prow of the ship. The common acceptation of the word is the best: *from above.* It was so high that it appeared to fall down upon the ship.

115. *Pronus.* I take this to denote the posture of the helmsman, *bending* or *stooping* forward, in order to stand more firmly. The helmsman (*magister*) is thrown from his feet, and tumbled headlong into the sea.

117. *Circumagens fluctus:* the whirling water.

118. *Rari:* scattered here and there.—*Gurgite:* in the sense of *mari.*

119. *Gaza:* this word, signifies all kinds of valuable furniture, as well as treasures of gold and silver.

122. *Compagibus:* the seams or streaks of the sides being loosened, they all let in the hostile water. *Imber*, though properly a shower of rain, is here used for *water* in general. *Hyems*, in the sense of *tempestas.* *Fatiscunt rimis:* gape open in cracks, or leaks.

126. *Stagna:* plu. of *stagnum*, the bottom or deep part of the sea. *Alto: altum*, the deep, or open sea—out of sight of land.—*Fretum*, a strait, or narrow sea. *Pelagus* the sea near the land. But they are not always used with this discrimination.

127. *Placidum.* This must refer either to Neptune's natural character—to his mildness in regard to the Trojans, or to the effect, which his countenance had upon the raging sea. For he was greatly moved, *graviter commotus*, at the winds, for invading his realms without his permission.

129. *Ruina cœli:* with the ruin of heaven. These words strongly denote the violence of the tempest—the floods of rain—the thunderings and lightnings: all which seemed to threaten the destruction of the world.

130. *Doli Junonis:* the wiles of Juno, and her anger, did not lie concealed from her brother—had not escaped the knowledge of her brother. Neptune and Juno were children of Saturn and Ops. See Geor. i. 14.

132. *Tanta-ne fiducia:* hath so great confidence of your race possessed you? The winds were the offspring of Aurora and Astræus, one of the Titans. Neptune here intimates, that if they imitated the rebellion of the Giants, their ancestors, they must expect to share in their punishment; or, at least, they could not expect to escape with impunity.

133. *Numine:* in the sense of *auctoritate* vel *voluntate.* *Moles:* in the sense of *fluctus*

Miscere, et tantas audetis tollere moles?
Quos ego—Sed motos præstat componere fluctus.
Pòst mihi non simili pœnâ commissa luetis.
Maturate fugam, regique hæc dicite vestro:
Non illi imperium pelagi, sævumque tridentem,
Sed mihi sorte datum: tenet ille immania saxa,
Vestras, Eure, domos: illâ se jactet in aulâ
Æolus, et clauso ventorum carcere regnet.
  Sic ait: et dicto citiùs tumida æquora placat,
Collectasque fugat nubes, Solemque reducit.
Cymothoë simul, et Triton adnixus, acuto
Detrudunt naves scopulo: levat ipse tridenti,
Et vastas aperit syrtes, et temperat æquor;
Atque rotis summas levibus perlabitur undas.
Ac, veluti magno in populo cùm sæpe coorta est
Seditio, sævitque animis ignobile vulgus;
Jamque faces et saxa volant; furor arma ministrat:
Tum, pietate gravem ac meritis si fortè virum quem
Conspexere, silent, arrectisque auribus adstant.
Ille regit dictis animos, et pectora mulcet.
Sic cunctus pelagi cecidit fragor; æquora postquàm
Prospiciens genitor, cœloque invectus aperto,
Flectit equos, curruque volans dat lora secundo.
  Defessi Æneadæ, quæ proxima litora cursu
Contendùnt petere, et Libyæ vertuntur ad oras.

Venti, miscere cœlum terramque

138. Imperium pelagi, sævumque tridentem non datum *esse* illi, sed mihi

151. Tum, si fortè conspexere quem virum gravem pietate et meritis, silent

153. Ille *vir* regit animos

158. Contendunt petere litora, quæ *sunt* proxima *in* cursu

NOTES.

135. *Quos ego.* Here *puniam*, or some word of the like import, is understood: whom I will punish, or chastise. But it is better to still the raging waves, before I do it.

136. *Pòst non luetis mihi:* hereafter ye shall not atone to me for your offences with a like punishment. Neptune here intimates it to be a matter of clemency in him in permitting them to escape; but they must beware; the next time they thus presume, he shall chastise them in an exemplary manner.

138. *Imperium pelagi.* In the division of the world between the sons of Saturn, the sea fell to Neptune, the heavens and the earth to Jupiter, and the regions below to Pluto. *Sævum:* in the sense of *potentem.*

139. *Tenet immania:* let him possess those wild and uncultivated rocks, thy habitations, O east wind. *Immania saxa* are the realms of Æolus, mentioned verse 52, supra.

140. *Jactet se:* boast, or glory. *Aula:* in the sense of *regia.*

142. *Citiùs dicto:* sooner than said. The comp. *citiùs* governs *dicto*, in the abl. *Placat:* calms.

144. *Cymothoë:* a nymph of the sea, the daughter of Nereus and Doris. *Triton:* the son of Amphitrite. His upper part was like a man, and his lower part like a fish. He was very powerful among the sea-gods, and could calm and embroil the sea at his pleasure. Many of the marine gods were called Tritons, but the name is properly applicable to those only that were half man and half fish. *Levat:* assists—lightens.

148. *Ac veluti cùm:* as when in a great crowd, a tumult often rises, and the ignoble throng rages in their minds, &c.

This comparison is extremely beautiful, as well as just. Nothing can be more proper to represent the disorder and havoc of a violent hurricane, than the rage and the desolation occasioned by an incensed mob. The suddenness, with which the noisy waves subside, and sink into a calm, as soon as Neptune surveys them, is finely marked by the awe and silence, with which the seditious multitude is immediately struck, at the sight of a man of superior merit and authority.

150. *Arma:* in the sense of *tela.* *Gravem:* in the sense of *insignem.* *Arrectis:* with listening, or attentive ears.

155. *Cœlo.* Cœlum here means simply, the air. He was wafted in the open air, just above the surface of the ocean. *Fragor:* the raging, or tumult.

156. *Curru:* the dat. for *currui.* See Ecl. v. 29. *Secundo:* light—easy-moving.

157. *Æneadœ:* the Trojans; so called from Æneas, their leader. *Contendunt:* they strive to reach, or get to the nearest shore.

Est in secessu longo locus: insula portum
Efficit objectu laterum: quibus omnis ab alto
Frangitur, inque sinus scindit sese unda reductos.
Hinc atque hinc vastæ rupes, geminique minantur
In cœlum scopuli: quorum sub vertice latè
Æquora tuta silent: tum sylvis scena coruscis
Desuper, horrentique atrum nemus imminet umbrâ.
Fronte sub adversâ scopulis pendentibus antrum:
Intus aquæ dulces, vivoque sedilia saxo;
Nympharum domus: hìc fessas non vincula naves
Ulla tenent; unco non alligat anchora morsu.
Huc septem Æneas collectis navibus omni
Ex numero subit: ac magno telluris amore
Egressi, optatâ potiuntur Troës arenâ,
Et sale tabentes artus in litore ponunt.
Ac primùm silici scintillam excudit Achates
Suscepitque ignem foliis, atque arida circùm
Nutrimenta dedit, rapuitque in fomite flammam.
Tum Cererem corruptam undis, Cerealiaque arma
Expediunt fessi rerum: frugesque receptas
Et torrere parant flammis, et frangere saxo.
Æneas scopulum intereà conscendit, et omnem
Prospectum latè pelago petit, Anthea si quà
Jactatum vento videat, Phrygiasque biremes,
Aut Capyn, aut celsis in puppibus arma Caïci.

160. Quibus *lateribus* omnis unda *veniens* ab alto frangitur, scindit que sese

166. *Est* antrum *in* pendentibus scopulis

167. Intus *sunt* dulces aquæ, sediliaque *è* vivo saxo: *videtur* domus

175. Circumdedit arida

177. Tum fessi rerum expediunt Cererem

NOTES.

159. *Longo secessu:* in a long or dark recess. This description of the port and harbor is beautiful in itself, and seasonably introduced to relieve the reader, and compose his mind, after having dwelt upon the former images of horror and distress.

160. *Objectu:* in the sense of *opposítu.*

162. *Rupes:* properly, a precipice, or broken rock. *Scopulus*, a high, sharp rock. *Saxum*, any rock, or stone. *Minantur:* reach, or extend to heaven.

164. *Scena sylvis:* an arbor formed of waving trees, and a grove dark with its awful shade, hangs over it from above. Ruæus interprets *scena* by *umbraculum.*

166. *Sub adversa fronte.* This cave was right in front, or opposite to them, as they entered the harbor, and approached the shore. *Pendentibus:* its roof was arched with rocks. Ruæus says *suspensis*, for *pendentibus.*

169. *Non ulla vincula tenent.* The meaning is: the harbor was so safe and secure, that ships needed neither cables nor anchors. *Morsu:* the fluke.

170. *Huc Æneas:* here Æneas entered with seven ships, collected, &c. He left Troas with twenty ships. One he had just lost, and the rest were scattered in the storm, but were not lost.

173. *Artus tabentes sale* their limbs drenched with salt water—dripping with salt water.

176. *Arida nutrimenta:* dry fuel. *Ignem:* the spark struck from the flint. *Rapuit:* he quickly kindled a flame among the fuel.

177. *Cererem corruptam:* their grain damaged by the water—wet. For *Ceres*, see Ecl. v. 79. *Arma:* properly, the instruments or tools of any art or profession. *Cerealia arma*, therefore, will be the instruments or utensils used in breaking corn, and preparing it for eating.

178. *Fessi rerum:* weary of their misfortunes—their toils—their dangers. *Fruges receptas:* the grain saved. The same with *Cererem*, just mentioned.

179. *Parant torrere.* Ruæus takes *torrere* in the sense of *coquere;* and in that case it follows *frangere*, which must be connected with *fruges receptas:* they prepare to break the corn, and to bake it into bread. But *torrere* may be taken for the act of drying the corn that had been wet, and partially damaged by the water; which must precede its being broken, or prepared for making bread. *Expediunt:* they unlade, or fetch it out of their ships.

181. *Anthea:* a Greek acc. of Antheus.

182. *Biremes:* biremis is properly a galley of two banks of oars. See Æn. v. 119.

183. *Arma Caïci:* the arms of Caïcus; that is, Caïcus himself.

Navem in conspectu nullam; tres litore cervos
Prospicit errantes: hos tota armenta sequuntur
A tergo, et longum per valles pascitur agmen.
Constitit hic, arcûmque manu celeresque sagittas
Corripuit, fidus quæ tela gerebat Achates.
Ductoresque ipsos primùm, capita alta ferentes
Cornibus arboreis, sternit: tum vulgus, et omnem
Miscet agens telis nemora inter frondea turbam.
Nec priùs absistit, quàm septem ingentia victor
Corpora fundat humi, et numerum cum navibus æquet.
Hinc portum petit, et socios partitur in omnes.
Vina, bonus quæ deinde cadis onerârat Acestes
Litore Trinacrio, dederatque abeuntibus heros,
Dividit, et dictis mœrentia pectora mulcet:
O socii, (neque enim ignari sumus antè malorum)
O passi graviora: dabit Deus his quoque finem.
Vos et Scyllæam rabiem, penitusque sonantes
Accêstis scopulos; vos et Cyclopea saxa
Experti: revocate animos, mœstumque timorem
Mittite: forsan et hæc olim meminisse juvabit.
Per varios casus, per tot discrimina rerum,
Tendimus in Latium; sedes ubi fata quietas
Ostendunt: illìc fas regna resurgere Trojæ.
Durate, et vosmet rebus servate secundis.
Talia voce refert: curisque ingentibus æger,
Spem vultu simulat, premit altum corde dolorem.
Illi se prædæ accingunt dapibusque futuris.

185. **Hos *tres* *ductore* à tergo**

195. **Deinde dividit vina, quæ bonus Acestes onerârat in cadis Trinacrio litore, herosque dederat *illis* abeuntibus**

199. **O *vos* passi graviora**

202. **Vos expert *estis***

NOTES.

186. *A tergo.* This might seem mere tautology, but it is consistent with the purest Latin. Cicero says: *Adolescens cursu à tergo insequens.* *Longum agmen:* the long, or extended herd.

189. *Ferentes alta:* bearing their lofty heads with branching horns. The poet finely describes the leaders. They move with a degree of majesty, having their heads erect, and their horns branching out like trees. *Gerebat:* in the sense of *ferebat.*

191. *Agens telis vulgus:* pursuing with his weapons the herd and the rest of the throng, among the leafy groves, he disperses them—he puts them into confusion by breaking their ranks. The word *misceo,* as here used, is beautiful and expressive. *Omnem turbam:* in the sense of *reliquam multitudinem.*

194. *Partitur:* he divides them among all his companions. He had killed seven huge deer, so that there was one for the crew of each ship.

195. *Acestes.* See Æn. v. 35. *Onerârat:* had put in casks, and given them.

196. *Trinacrio:* an adj. from *Trinacria,* a name of Sicily, derived from its triangular form. Its three promontories are: *Pachynum,* on the south; *Lilybæus,* on the west; and *Pelorus,* on the north.

198. *Antè malorum:* of past evils, or distresses. Ruæus takes *antè* here in the sense of *præteritorum.* Or perhaps, *malorum quæ fuerunt antè.*

200. *Vos accêstis:* ye have approached both the rage of Scylla, and the rocks roaring within. See Ecl. vi. 74, and Æn. iii. 420. Opposite the rock of Scylla is Charybdis, a dangerous whirlpool; which, taken together, render the passage of the straits between Sicily and Italy very hazardous. Hence arose the proverb: *Incidit in Scyllam, qui vult vitare Charybdem.* This Charybdis, as fable says, was a voracious old woman, who stole the oxen of Hercules. For which, being struck by the thunder of Jove, she was turned into this whirlpool. *Accêstis:* by syn. for *accessistis.*

203. *Olim:* hereafter. *Discrimina:* in the sense of *pericula.*

207. *Secundis rebus:* preserve yourselves for prosperity. *Durate:* persevere.

208. *Æger ingentibus:* oppressed with heavy cares, (full of anxious solicitude for his friends,) he dissembles hope on his countenance, but represses, &c. *Refert:* in the sense of *dicit.*

210. *Accingunt se:* they prepare themselves for. *Tergora:* the skins or hides of the slain deer.

Tergora diripiunt costis, et viscera nudant:
Pars in frusta secant, verubusque trementia figunt
Litore ahena locant alii, flammasque ministrant.
Tum victu revocant vires: fusique per herbam,
Implentur veteris Bacchi, pinguisque ferinæ.
Postquàm exempta fames epulis, mensæque remotæ,
Amissos longo socios sermone requirunt,
Spemque metumque inter dubii: seu vivere credant,
Sive extrema pati, nec jam exaudire vocatos
Præcipuè pius Æneas, nunc acris Orontei,
Nunc Amyci casum gemit, et crudelia secum
Fata Lyci, fortemque Gyan, fortemque Cloanthum.
Et jam finis erat: cùm Jupiter æthere summo
Despiciens mare velivolum, terrasque jacentes,
Litoraque, et latos populos; sic vertice cœli
Constitit, et Libyæ defixit lumina regnis.
Atque illum tales jactantem pectore curas,
Tristior, et lachrymis oculos suffusa nitentes,
Alloquitur Venus: O, qui res hominumque Deûmque

212. Figunt *frusta adhuc* trementia verubus

216. Exempta *est*

218. Seu credant *eos*

220. Æneas gemit secum nunc casum acris Orontei; nunc *casum* Amyci

227. Atque Venus tristior, et suffusa *quoad* nitentes oculos alloquitur illum jactantem

229. O *tu*, qui regis res hominumque

NOTES.

211. *Viscera:* neu. plu. of *viscus*, or *viscum*. It properly signifies all the parts of the animal within the skin. Here it means *the flesh*.

212. *Pars secant:* a part cut into pieces. Nouns of multitude may have verbs in the singular or plural.

213. *Ahena:* neu. plu. brazen dishes or vessels. An adj. taken as a substantive.—*Ministrant flammas:* tend the fires.

215. *Implentur.* This is in imitation of the Greeks, with whom verbs of *filling* govern the genitive. *Bacchi:* in the sense of *vini*.

217. *Requirunt:* they inquire after their lost companions—converse about them.

219. *Pati extrema:* to suffer death—death being the last of all earthly things.—*Pati:* the present in the sense of the perf. *Vocatos nec jam:* being invoked, should not now hear. This alludes to a custom among the Romans, of calling the dead three times by name: which was the last ceremony in funeral obsequies. After which, the friends pronounced the word *Vale*, three times, as they departed from the tomb. The same was observed of those, who perished by shipwreck, or otherwise, when their bodies could not be found.

220. *Æneas gemit*· Æneas laments now the fate of brave Orontes, now, &c. The most exalted and heroic minds are the most susceptible of humanity and compassion.—Virgil therefore says: *Præcipuè pius Æneas gemit.* But at the same time, he conducts his grief with prudence, and carefully avoids whatever would tend to discourage the rest; and therefore it is said, that he grieves privately, *secum*, keeping his sorrow and grief in his own bosom; and showing to his companions an example of magnanimous fortitude only, which rises superior to dangers and misfortunes.

224. *Velivolum:* navigable. *Jacentes terras:* the earth may be said to be lying (*jacens*) still, dead and at rest, in opposition to the sea, which is always in motion. The poet considers here the sails of a ship under the notion of wings, by which it flies over the sea, as a bird moves through the air.—Ruæus takes *jacentes* in the sense of *humiles:* low—lying low. *Populos:* in the sense of *gentes*.

225. *Vertice:* the pinnacle of heaven: the zenith, or point over our heads.

226. *Defixit oculos.* Dr. Trapp observes, that nothing to him breathes the soul of poetry, particularly Virgil's, more than this delightful passage, in which the majesty of Jupiter, and the beautiful grief of Venus are so finely contrasted. She still remembers, in all the abruptness of extreme sorrow, that she is addressing the almighty Thunderer, and yet maintains all the sweetness of female complaint, and tender expostulation. *Jactantem:* in the sense of *volventem*.

228. *Suffusa oculos:* wet, as to her shining eyes, with tears. See Ecl. i. 55. Female beauty never appears so engaging, and makes so deep an impression upon the beholder, as when *suffused with tears*, and manifesting a degree of anxious solicitude. The poet therefore introduces Venus in that situation, making suit to her father. The speech is of the chastest kind, and cannot fail to charm the reader.

229. *Venus.* The goddess of beauty and love. She is said to have sprung from the foam of the sea, near the island of Cyprus

Æternis regis imperiis, et fulmine terres,
Quid meus Æneas in te committere tantum,
Quid Troës potuere? quibus tot funera passis,
Cunctus ob Italiam terrarum clauditur orbis?
Certè hinc Romanos olim, volventibus annis,
Hinc fore ductores, revocato à sanguine Teucri,
Qui mare, qui terras omni ditione tenerent,
Pollicitus: quæ te, genitor, sententia vertit?
Hoc equidem occasum Trojæ tristesque ruinas
Solabar, fatis contraria fata rependens.

230. Terres ***mundum*** fulmine: quid tantum ***scelus potuit*** meus Æneas committere in te!

234. Certè pollicitus ***es*** Romanos ***orituros esse*** hinc olim, annis volventibus, fore ductores hinc à revocato sanguine Teucri, qui tenerent

238. Equidem hoc *promisso* solabar occa-

NOTES.

or according to Hesiod, near the island of Cythera. She was taken up to Heaven, when all the Gods were struck with her beauty, and became jealous of her superior attractions. Jupiter attempted, in vain, to gain her affection; and as a punishment to her, for the refusal, bestowed her upon his deformed son Vulcan. She, however, had many intrigues with Mars, Mercury, and Bacchus. Her partiality for Adonis, induced her to leave Olympus. She also had an affection, it is said, for Anchises, and for his sake, often visited the Groves of Mount Ida. By him she had Æneas.

Venus possessed a mysterious girdle or *cestus*, which gave to any, however ugly and deformed, beauty, elegance, and grace. Her worship was universally established. The rose, the myrtle, and the apple, were sacred to her. The dove, the swan, and the sparrow, were her favorite birds.

She had various names, derived chiefly from the places where she was worshipped; or from some property or quality she was thought to possess. Some of which, are the following: *Cypria*, from the island Cyprus: *Paphia*, from Paphos: *Cytherea*, from the island Cythera; in each of which places she had splendid temples. She was also called *Telepegema*, because she presided over marriage: *Verticordia*, because she turned the hearts of women to chastity: *Etaira*, because she was the patroness of courtezans: *Acidalia*, from Acidalus, a fountain in Beotia: *Basilea*, because she was the queen of love: *Myrtea*, because the myrtle was sacred to her: *Libertina*, on account of her inclinations to licentious amours: *Pontea*, *Marina*, *Lemnesia*, and *Pelagea*, because she sprung from the sea. The word *Venus* is often taken for beauty and love; also for the object of love—the person loved. It is used sometimes for any sensual passion, or lust—the intercourse of the sexes. *Imperiis:* in the sense of *potentia*.

233. *Quibus passis:* against whom, suffering so many deaths, the whole world, &c.

234. *Hinc:* hence—from the Trojans. *Ductores:* probably, as Heyne observes, we are to understand JuliusCæsar, and Octavius.

235. *Revocato*, &c. Commentators are divided in opinion, on these words. Corradus takes *sanguine Teucri*, for the Trojans, the offspring of *Teucer;* and *revocato*, in the sense of *restituto*. Ruæus rejects this in part. By *sanguine Teucri*, he understands the Trojans; and by *revocato*, their return into Italy, whence Dardanus, the founder of their race, originated. The blood of Teucer, and that of Dardanus, were united in the Trojans, their descendants. *Revocato:* recalled—called back to take possession of the land of their ancestor.

236. *Ditione:* sway—authority. *Tenerent:* in the sense of *regerent*. *Sententia:* in the sense of *consilium*.

238. *Hoc quidem:* with this promise, I was mitigating the fall, and sad catastrophe of Troy:—I was consoling myself, at, &c.

239. *Fatis rependens contraria:* to these fates balancing, (or placing) fates contrary, or of an opposite nature. *Fatum*, as here used, may mean, either the purposes of the gods concerning the Trojans, or simply, their fortune or destiny. Their city had been rased, and a numerous train of ills had befallen them. These, we are to understand by *fatis*. By *fata contraria*, it is plain, we are to understand prosperity, or a state of things different from their former one. Or, if *fata* be taken for the purposes of the gods toward them, the interpretation will be the same.

The downfall of Troy was a very afflicting circumstance to Venus. She strove hard to prevent it. And after the event, she consoled herself with the consideration, that Troy was destined to rise again—that their race was to be restored to the land of Dardanus, and there become the rulers of the world. This lightened her sorrow, and assuaged her grief. Here, perhaps, it may be asked, if she knew that the future glory of the Trojan race had been decreed and fixed by fate; why does she appear to express so much anxiety and solicitude upon that subject? It may be said, that the opposition which Juno made to it, might make her doubt, and her mind waver. For, Jupiter alone had a perfect insight into futurity, and

sum, tristesque ruinas Trojæ

242. Antenor elapsus mediis Achivis potuit tutus penetrare

250. Nos, quibus *tu* annuis arcem cœli, navibus, *O* infandum! amissis prodimur *periculis* ob iram Junonis unius

253. *Est-ne* hic honos *nostræ* pietatis? sic

Nunc eadem fortuna viros tot casibus actos
Insequitur: quem das finem, rex magne, laborum?
Antenor potuit, mediis elapsus Achivis,
Illyricos penetrare sinus, atque intima tutus
Regna Liburnorum et fontem superare Timavi:
Unde per ora novem vasto cum murmure montis
It mare proruptum, et pelago premit arva sonanti.
Hìc tamen ille urbem Patavî sedesque locavit
Teucrorum, et genti nomen dedit, armaque fixit
Troïa: nunc placidâ compôstus pace quiescit.
Nos, tua progenies, cœli quibus annuis arcem,
Navibus, infandum! amissis, unius ob iram
Prodimur, atque Italis longè disjungimur oris.
Hic pietatis honos? Sic nos in sceptra reponis!
Olli subridens hominum sator atque Deorum,
Vultu, quo cœlum tempestatesque serenat,
Oscula libavit natæ: dehinc talia fatur:

NOTES.

the rest of the gods, knew no more than he was pleased to reveal to them. See Æn. iii. 251.

It is said, by some, that Virgil makes even Jupiter subject to fate or destiny. But from several passages, it will appear, that his notion of fate was truly philosophical. He makes fate to be nothing more than the decrees, purposes, or counsels of Heaven, pronounced by the mouth of Jove; as the etymology of the word implies. He often calls destiny *Fata deorum*, which can mean nothing else than the Divine decrees, or counsels. And, if he give to fate the epithets, *inexpugnabile* and *inexorabile*, he must mean that the laws and order of nature are fixed and unchangeable, as being the result of Infinite wisdom and foresight, and having their foundation in the *Divine mind*, which is subject to none of those changes that affect feeble and erring mortals.

242. *Antenor.* He was a noble Trojan. After the sack of Troy, he led a colony of Trojans, and *Henetes*, a people who came to assist Priam, and lost their king, in quest of a settlement. After various toils and disasters, he arrived at the head of the Adriatic, and having expelled the *Euganes*, a people inhabiting between the Alps and the sea, he took possession of their country. He built a city called *Antenorea*, after his own name. Some say he built *Patavium*, now Padua. The whole nation was called *Veneti.*

243. *Illyricos:* an adj. from Illyricum, an extensive country on the borders of the Adriatic, over against Italy, including the ancient *Liburnia* and *Dalmatia*. *Penetrare:* in the sense of *intrare.*

244. *Superare fontem Timavi:* to pass beyond the fountain of Timavus. We are told by Servius, on the authority of Varro, that the Timavus was a large river, and the neighboring people gave to it the name of sea. It was formed, says he, by the confluence of nine streams, issuing from a mountain. It is, however, at the present, a small and inconsiderable stream, falling into the Adriatic, near *Istria.*

245. *Unde:* whence—from the fountain. The *novem ora*, I take to mean the nine streams which formed the river, and not so many channels, through which it fell into the sea. *Os* signifies the fountain, or head of a river, as well as its mouth.

246. *It:* it pours along. *Proruptum:* rough—swollen. *Premit:* overflows—deluges. Thompson has finely imitated, in his "Winter," this description of the Timavus.

249. *Compôstus:* by syn. for *compositus.* settled. *Fixit:* in the sense of *suspendit.* *Nos.* Here Venus speaks in the person of Æneas to show how nearly she had his interest at heart. *Annuis:* in the sense of *promittis.* Thou hast promised that after death he should be received among the gods—should be deified. *Arcem cœli:* the court or palace of heaven.

251. *Infandum.* This word is thrown in like an interposing sigh, when she comes to the most moving part of her complaint; and the artful pauses in this and the two following lines, together with the abrupt manner in which the speech breaks off, show her quite overpowered by the tide of her grief. *Unius:* of one, to wit, Juno. *Prodimur:* we are given up to destruction—we are doomed to toils, misfortunes, and dangers. through the resentment and influence of Juno.

253. *Honos:* reward—recompense.

254. *Olli:* for *illi*, by antithesis. *Sator:* in the sense of *pater.*

256. *Libavit:* he kissed the lips of his

Parce metu, Cytherea: manent immota tuorum
Fata tibi: cernes urbem et promissa Lavinî
Mœnia, sublimemque feres ad sidera cœli
Magnanimum Æneam, neque me sententia vertit.
Hic (tibi fabor enim, quando hæc te cura remordet;
Longiùs et volvens fatorum arcana movebo)
Bellum ingens geret Italiâ, populosque feroces
Contundet, moresque viris et mœnia ponet:
Tertia dum Latio regnantem viderit æstas,
Ternaque transîerint Rutulis hyberna subactis.
At puer Ascanius, cui nunc cognomen Iülo
Additur (Ilus erat, dum res stetit Ilia regno)
Triginta magnos, volvendis mensibus, orbes
Imperio explebit, regnumque ab sede Lavinî
Transferet, et longam multâ vi muniet Albam.
Hìc jam tercentum totos regnabitur annos
Gente sub Hectoreâ; donec regina sacerdos
Marte gravis, geminam partu dabit Ilia prolem.

261. **Hic geret ingens bellum** *in* **Italiâ**

267. **At puer Ascanius,** cui nunc cognomen Iülo additur, **explebit** imperio triginta **magnos orbes,** mensibus

273. **Donec Ilia, regina** sacerdos, **gravis** Marte dabit

NOTES.

daughter. The name *Venus* was given to several. The one here meant, is the daughter of Jupiter and Dione, but is often confounded with her, who sprung from the froth of the sea. See 229. supra.

257. *Metu:* for *metui.* See Ecl. v. 29. *Cytherea:* Venus.

261. *Fabor:* in the sense of *dicam.*

262. *Movebo arcana:* I will unfold the secrets of the fates, tracing (*volvens*) them down to a great distance of time. *Remordet:* troubles you.

264. *Contundet:* in the sense of *domabit. Mores:* in the sense of *leges.*

265. *Dum tertia ætas:* until the third year shall see him, &c. The meaning is, that three years were to be spent in the wars with Turnus and the Rutuli; at the expiration of which, having subdued his enemies, Æneas should commence his government in Latium. *Dum:* in the sense of *donec.*

266. *Terna hyberna:* three winters shall have passed, the *Rutuli* being conquered.

267. *Cui nunc cognomen:* to whom now the sir-name of Iülus is added. This circumstance is thrown in to show the origin of the Julian family, and the occasion of changing the name of *Ilus,* to *Iülus* or *Julius.* The poet designs this as a compliment to the Cæsars. Iülus succeeded his father in the government, and reigned thirty years at *Lavinium.* He built *Alba Longa,* and made it the seat of his government. The throne was filled for three hundred years by a succession of Trojan princes, down to the time of Romulus. He founded Rome, and changed the seat of government from *Alba Longa* to the new city. At his death, the line of succession was changed, and *Numa Pompilius,* a wise and virtuous prince of the Sabines, filled the throne.

268. *Ilia res:* the Trojan state. *Ilia:* an adj. from *Ilium,* a name of Troy. See 1. supra.

269. *Orbes:* in the sense of *annos.*

270. *Imperio:* government—reign. *Lavinî:* by apocope for *Lavinii.* See 2. supra. *Vi:* labor—strength.

273. *Hectorea gente:* under a Trojan line. After the building of Rome, Alba continued for a considerable time an independent government, and was a rival of the new city. It was finally destroyed by the Romans, and its inhabitants transferred to Rome.

274. *Ilia:* a daughter of Numitor, king of Alba Longa. She is called *regina,* on account of her royal descent. She was one of the vestal virgins, and for that reason called *sacerdos,* or priestess. Being pregnant (*gravis*) by Mars, as it is said, she brought forth twins, Romulus and Remus.

Amulius, having expelled his brother Numitor, commanded one Faustus, a shepherd, to expose the children to wild beasts, that they might perish. Instead of which, he took them home, where they were nourished by his wife, whose name was *Lupa.* This gave rise to the story of their being brought up by a wolf, *lupa* being the name of that animal.

The children grew up, and when they became acquainted with the conduct of their uncle, they collected a band of men, attacked him in his palace, slew him, and restored Numitor to the throne. Afterwards, it is said, each of the brothers began to build a city. Remus leaped over the walls of the city founded by Romulus; whereupon, being angry, he slew him. He called the city *Rome,* after his own name. *Romulus* was sometimes called *Quirinus,* from *Quiri,* a Sabine word, which signifies a spear. *Geminam prolem:* simply, twins.

275. Inde Romulus lætus fulvo tegmine nutricis lupæ excipiet gentem

277 Dicet *incolas* Romanos

288. *Ille erit* Julius, nomen

Inde lupæ fulvo nutricis tegmine lætus
Romulus excipiet gentem, et Mavortia condet
Mœnia, Romanosque suo de nomine dicet.
His ego nec metas rerum, nec tempora pono:
Imperium sine fine dedi. Quin aspera Juno,
Quæ mare nunc terrasque metu cœlumque fatigat,
Consilia in melius referet, mecumque fovebit
Romanos rerum dominos, gentemque togatam.
Sic placitum. Veniet, lustris labentibus, ætas,
Cùm domus Assaraci Phthiam clarasque Mycenas
Servitio premet, ac victis dominabitur Argis.
Nascetur pulchrâ Trojanus origine Cæsar,
Imperium Oceano, famam qui terminet astris,
Julius, à magno demissum nomen Iülo.
Hunc tu olim cœlo, spoliis Orientis onustum,
Accipies secura: vocabitur hic quoque votis.
Aspera tum positis mitescent sæcula bellis.
Cana Fides, et Vesta, Remo cum fratre Quirinus,

NOTES.

276. *Mavortia:* an adj. from *Mavors*, a name of Mars: warlike—martial. *Mœnia:* in the sense of *urbem*.

278. *Nec pono metas:* I place (prescribe) to them neither bounds nor duration of dominion. The Romans had a belief that their empire would always continue, while other governments would be unstable and fluctuating.

280. *Metu:* through fear that the Trojans would rise to power, and become dangerous to her dear Carthage and Argos. *Fatigat:* in the sense of *commovet*.

281. *In melius.* This is taken adverbially: for the better. *Referret:* shall change.

282. *Gentem togatam:* the nation of the gown. The *toga*, or gown, was the distinguishing badge of the Romans, as the *pallium* was that of the Greeks. *Rerum. Res* signifies power—rule—dominion. In the present case it signifies, the world.

283. *Sic placitum:* thus it pleases me—this is my pleasure—it is my decree. The verb *est* is to be supplied. *Ætas venit:* the time shall come, years having passed away, when, &c. *Lustrum:* properly the period of four years. It is often put for time in general. *Ætas:* in the sense of *tempus*, and *lustris:* for *annis*.

284. *Domus Assaraci.* By this we are to understand the Romans. Assaracus was the son of Tros, and brother of Ilus. He was the father of Capys, and Capys the father of Anchises, the father of Æneas, from whom the Romans descended. *Phthiam.* This was a city of Thessaly, the royal seat of Achilles. *Mycenas—Argis.* These were cities of the Peloponnesus, over which Agamemnon reigned, put, by synec. for Greece in general. This prophecy was fulfilled under the Roman generals Mummius, who conquered Achaia; and Paulus Æmilius, who subdued Macedonia and Thessaly. *Argis:* in the sing. *Argos*, neu.; in the plu. *Argi*, mas. It was situated about two miles from the sea, on the *Sinus Argolicus.* It was founded by Inachus, 1856 years before Christ. Its inhabitants were called *Argolici* and *Argivi:* by synec. put for the Greeks in general. *Premet:* shall subject to servitude—shall subdue.

286. *Pulchra:* in the sense of *illustris:* Cæsar, a Trojan of illustrious origin.

288. *Nomen demissum:* a name derived from, &c.

289. *Tu secura:* you, sure, shall receive him hereafter. Cæsar was honored with four triumphs on four successive days. To this, refer the words: *Onustum spoliis orientis.* Cæsar received divine honors by a decree of the senate.

291. *Aspera sæcula.* Here is an allusion to the golden age; or, at least, to the universal peace which took place in the reign of Augustus, when the temple of Janus was shut. *Mitescent:* shall grow mild—soften. *Aspera:* in the sense of *dura*.

292. *Cana fides.* The meaning is, that the fidelity of former times should return—that men should devote more of their time to the service of the gods—that there should be no more civil wars, in which brother should be armed against brother. The epithet *cana* alludes to the figure of faith, which was represented with hoary locks, to denote that it was the peculiar virtue of former times—the golden age. By the word *Vesta*, Servius says, we are to understand religion. Vesta was the daughter of Saturn and Ops, the goddess of fire, and patroness of the vestal virgins. Æneas was the first who introduced her mysteries into Italy

Jura dabunt · diræ ferro et compagibus arctis
Claudentur belli portæ: Furor impius intus
Sæva sedens super arma, et centum vinctus ahenis
Post tergum nodis, fremet horridus ore cruento.
Hæc ait: et Maiâ genitum demittit ab alto;
Ut terræ, utque novæ pateant Carthaginis arces
Hospitio Teucris: ne fati nescia Dido
Finibus arceret. Volat ille per aëra magnum
Remigio alarum, ac Libyæ citus adstitit oris:
Et jam jussa facit: ponuntque ferocia Pœni
Corda, volente Deo: imprimis Regina quietum
Accipit in Teucros animum mentemque benignam.
At pius Æneas, per noctem plurima volvens,
Ut primùm lux alma data est, exire, locosque
Explorare novos; quas vento accesserit oras,
Qui teneant (nam inculta videt) hominesne, feræne,
Quærere constituit, sociisque exacta referre.
Classem in convexo nemorum, sub rupe cavatâ,
Arboribus clausam circùm atque horrentibus umbris,
Occulit: ipse uno graditur comitatus Achate,
Bina manu lato crispans hastilia ferro.
Cui mater mediâ sese tulit obvia sylvâ,
Virginis os habitumque gerens, et virginis arma
Spartanæ: vel qualis equos Threïssa fatigat

295. Et vinctus post tergum *cum* centum ahenis nodis, fremet

305. Volvens *animo*

306. Constituit exire, explorareque novos locos, *et* quærere *ad* quas oras accesserit vento; qui teneant *eas*, homines-ne, feræ-ne (nam videt *loca* inculta) referreque exacta sociis. Occulit classem

314. Cui mater obvia tulit se mediâ sylva, gerens os, habitumque

316. Vel *erat talis* qualis Threïssa

NOTES.

The *Palladium* of Troy was supposed to be preserved in her temple; where a fire was continually kept burning by certain virgins, who dedicated themselves to her service. There was another goddess of the same name, but generally confounded with *Ceres*, *Cybelle*, *Tellus*, &c. The word *Vesta* is frequently used for fire, by meton.

293. *Arctis compagibus:* with close joints—bound fast with bars of iron.

294. *Portæ.* The gates, or doors of the temple of Janus were open in time of war, and shut in time of peace. This happened only three times during a period of seven hundred years, so constantly engaged were the Romans in the work of death! *Impius furor.* This, Turnebus thinks, alludes to the image of warlike rage drawn by Apelles, and dedicated by Augustus in the Forum. But Germanus thinks it alludes to the statue of Mars, which the Spartans had in their city, bound in this manner, in chains of brass. *Nodis:* in the sense of *catenis.*

297. *Genitum Maiâ:* the son of Maia. Mercury was the son of Jupiter, and Maia, the daughter of Atlas. See Geor. i. 336.

298. *Arces.* This appears to be used in the sense of *urbs:* that the country and city of New Carthage might open in hospitality to the Trojans—might receive them kindly, and treat them with hospitality.

301. *Remigio alarum:* by the motion of his wings. *Utens alis quasi remis*, says Ruæus. The motion of his wings is beautifully expressed; it was like the motion of oars in propelling a boat forward.

302. *Pœni.* The Carthaginians were sometimes called *Pœni*, or *Phœni*, from *Phœnicia*, the country from which they came. *Corda:* in the sense of *animos.*

304. *Quietum animum:* a friendly mind, and a benevolent disposition, or temper.

306. *Data est:* in the sense of *orta est.*

309. *Exacta:* neu. plu. the particulars of his discovery.

310. *In convexo.* The place where Æneas moored his fleet, lay in a circular form, nearly surrounded by a grove. Here they could be in safety, without fear of discovery. The words *convexus* and *concavus* are sometimes used for each other, which seems to be the case here; the former properly signifying the exterior of a round surface; the latter the interior. *Horrentibus:* deep—thick shades. *Uno:* in the sense of *solo.* See Æn. iv. 451.

313. *Crispans:* in the sense of *quassans.* *Lato ferro:* of a broad barb, or point.

316. *Spartanæ.* The Spartan virgins were trained to all kinds of manly exercises, such as running, wrestling, throwing the quoit and javelin, riding and hunting, which is the reason that the poet attires Venus in their habit, or dress. *Os:* in the sense of *vultum.*

321. Ac *illa* prior inquit: Heus, juvenes, monstrate, si vidistis fortè quam mearum sororum errantem hìc, succinctam pharetrâ

327. Mortalis vultus haud *est* tibi, nec *tua* vox

330. Quæcunque *es*, sis felix

Harpalyce, volucremque fugâ prævertitur Eurum.
Namque humeris de more habilem suspenderat arcum
Venatrix, dederatque comam diffundere ventis;
Nuda genu, nodoque sinus collecta fluentes.
Ac prior, Heus, inquit, juvenes, monstrate, mearum
Vidistis si quam hìc errantem fortè sororum,
Succinctam pharetrâ et maculosæ tegmine lyncis,
Aut spumantis apri cursum clamore prementem.
  Sic Venus: at Veneris contrà sic filius orsus:
Nulla tuarum audita mihi, neque visa sororum,
O, quam te memorem, Virgo? namque haud tibi vultus
Mortalis, nec vox hominem sonat. O Dea certè:
An Phœbi soror, an Nympharum sanguinis una?
Sis felix, nostrumque leves quæcunque laborem:
Et quo sub cœlo tandem, quibus orbis in oris
Jactemur, doceas: ignari hominumque locorumque
Erramus, vento huc et vastis fluctibus acti.
Multa tibi ante aras nostrâ cadet hostia dextrâ.
  Tum Venus: haud equidem tali me dignor honore.
Virginibus Tyriis mos est gestare pharetram,
Purpureoque altè suras vincire cothurno.
Punica regna vides, Tyrios, et Agenoris urbem:
Sed fines Libyci, genus intractabile bello

NOTES.

317. *Harpalyce:* a celebrated Amazon, said to have rescued her father, who had been taken in battle by the *Getæ.* The comparison here is simply between the habits of Venus, and those of Harpalyce. *Eurum.* Many copies read *Hebrum;* but there appears a manifest incongruity in it. It can hardly be supposed, that the poet, describing the swiftness of her speed, should say that she could outride the course of a river, however rapid it might be. In that there could be no difficulty. Besides, the epithet *volucrem,* is not very applicable to a river. *Eurum* is certainly the best reading; it is the language of poetry, while *Hebrum* is not. *Fuga:* in the sense of *cursu.*

320. *Nuda genu,* &c. This is a Grecism: *naked* as to her *knee,* and *collected* as to her *flowing robe in a knot.* See Ecl. i. 55. The meaning is, that she had her knee naked, and her flowing robe collected in a knot. *Sinus:* the folds of a garment; also the garment itself, by synec. *Nodo: nodus* is properly any thing that binds or ties.—Hence, a girdle, or belt—a knot, &c.

321. *Quam:* in the sense of *aliquam.*

323. *Tegmine.* It was a custom among the ancients for hunters to wear the skin of some one of the animals, they had killed. *Prementem:* pursuing.

325. *Orsus:* part. of the verb *ordior:* he began. The verb *est* is understood.

327. *Quam te memorem?* whom shall I call you?

328. *Nec vox sonat:* nor does your voice sound (like) a human being—it does not indicate you to be mortal. *Homo,* is properly either a man or woman—a human being.

329. *An soror Phœbi:* art thou the sister of Phœbus, or one of the blood of the nymphs? See Ecl. iv. 10. The verb *es* is to be supplied.

330. *Felix:* kind—propitious. *Oris:* in the sense of *regione.* *Orbis:* of the world, or earth.

334. *Multa hostia:* many a victim shall fall for you before the altars.

335. *Haud me dignor:* I do not consider myself worthy, &c.

338. *Urbem Agenoris:* Carthage, founded by Dido, a descendant of Agenor. *Punica regna:* the kingdom, or realm of Carthage. It is distinguished from the city, which is called *Urbs Agenoris.* *Punica:* an adj. from *Pœni,* or *Phœni.*

339. *Fines Libyci:* the country is Africa. *Libyci:* an adj. from *Libya,* agreeing with *fines.* Libya was properly that part of Africa bordering upon Egypt on the west; but is frequently used for any part of Africa, or Africa in general. *Genus intractabile:* a race fierce in war. The Carthaginians extended their conquests with unexampled rapidity, and were the only people that appeared to dispute the empire of the world with the Romans. Their misfortunes, and final ruin, were owing more, perhaps, to party spirit and civil cabals, than to the arms of the Romans. See Rol. An. His. Art. Carthage.

Imperium Dido Tyriâ regit urbe profecta,
Germanum fugiens: longa est injuria, longæ
Ambages: sed summa sequar fastigia rerum.
Huic conjux Sichæus erat, ditissimus agri
Phœnicum, et magno miseræ dilectus amore:
Cui pater intactam dederat, primisque jugârat
Ominibus: sed regna Tyri germanus habebat
Pygmalion, scelere ante alios immanior omnes.
Quos inter medius venit furor: ille Sichæum,
Impius ante aras, atque auri cæcus amore,
Clam ferro incautum superat, securus amorum
Germanæ: factumque diu celavit; et ægram,
Multa malus simulans, vanâ spe lusit amantem.
Ipsa sed in somnis inhumati venit imago
Conjugis, ora modis attollens pallida miris:
Crudeles aras, trajectaque pectora ferro
Nudavit, cæcumque domûs scelus omne retexit.
Tum celerare fugam, patriâque excedere suadet:
Auxiliumque viæ veteres tellure recludit
Thesauros, ignotum argenti pondus et auri.
His commota, fugam Dido sociosque parabat.
Conveniunt, quibus aut odium crudele tyranni,
Aut metus acer erat: naves, quæ fortè paratæ,
Corripiunt, onerantque auro: portantur avari
Pygmalionis opes pelago: dux fœmina facti.

344. Dilectus magno amore miseræ *Didonis*

345. Dederat *eam* intactam

349. Ille impius atque cæcus amore auri, clam superat Sichæum ferro ante aras incautum

352. *Ille* malus simulans multa lusit ægram amantem

358. Recluditque veteres thesauros, *depositos in* tellure *tanquam* auxilium viæ, ignotum pondus

361. *Omnes* conveniunt, quibus erat, aut crudele

NOTES.

340. *Dido:* the name of a Tyrian princess, implying beautiful, or well-beloved. See Æn. iv. 1. *Regit imperium:* manages the government.

342. *Ambages longæ:* the circumstances are long and tedious. *Sequar summa fastigia rerum:* I will mention only the chief heads of the business—I will trace only the outlines of the affair. Ruæus takes *sequar* in the sense of *perstringam.*

345. *Primis ominibus:* with the first omens. This alludes to a custom among the Romans of consulting the omens in all the important concerns of life, before they entered upon them, to see if they would prove successful or not. *Jugârat:* by syn. for *jugaverat.* *Cui:* to whom, to wit, Sichæus. *Intactam: adhuc virginem,* says Ruæus.

347. *Immanior scelere ante:* great in wickedness above all others. The comp. is here used in the sense of the pos.

348. *Sichæum.* He was the priest of Hercules, an office in dignity next to royalty. It appears that Pygmalion came upon Sichæus unexpectedly, while he was officiating at the altar, and slew him. This circumstance greatly adds to the atrocity of the deed. *Furor:* in the sense of *odium.* *Inter quos:* between Sichæus and Pygmalion.

350. *Securus.* regardless of the love of his sister. *Superat* in the sense of *interficit.*

352. *Ægram amantem:* the afflicted, or disconsolate lover. *Lusit:* deceived—deluded.

353. *Inhumati.* According to their system of religion, the shades of those, who were unburied, must wander a hundred years, before they could be at rest. The circumstance of Pygmalion's leaving the body of Sichæus unburied, in this view, greatly heightens the enormity of the crime first committed. *Imago:* in the sense of *umbra.*

354. *Conjugis. Conjux* is either a husband or a wife; here the former. *Pallida:* pale in a wonderful manner. *Os:* in the sense of *vultum.*

356. *Nudavit:* laid bare the cruel altars, at which he was slain. *Retexit:* disclosed—brought to light.

358. *Recludit:* shows, or opens to her, &c. Justin tells us that Sichæus, for fear of the king, buried his money in the earth, fearing to keep it in his house; but no one knew the place of its deposit during his life.

362. *Paratæ.* Tyre, being a great commercial city, in the ordinary course of business, many ships might be prepared and ready for sea. The verb *sunt* is to be supplied.

364. *Opes avari,* &c. Either the wealth of Sichæus, which Pygmalion now imagined his own; or along with her husband's

Devenêre locos, ubi nunc ingentia cernes
Mœnia, surgentemque novæ Carthaginis arcem.
Mercatique solum, facti de nomine Byrsam,
Taurino quantum possent circumdare tergo.
Sed vos qui tandem? quibus aut venistis ab oris?
Quòve tenetis iter? Quærenti talibus ille
Suspirans, imoque trahens à pectore vocem:
O Dea, si primâ repetens ab origine pergam,
Et vacet annales nostrorum audire laborum;
Antè diem clauso componet vesper Olympo.
Nos, Trojâ antiquâ, si vestras fortè per aures
Trojæ nomen iit, diversa per æquora vectos,
Forte suâ Libycis tempestas appulit oris.
Sum pius Æneas, raptos qui ex hoste Penates
Classe veho mecum, famâ super æthera notus.
Italiam quæro patriam; et genus ab Jove summo.
Bis denis Phrygium conscendi navibus æquor,
Matre Deâ monstrante viam, data fata secutus:
Vix septem convulsæ undis Euroque supersunt.
Ipse ignotus, egens, Libyæ deserta peragro,
Europâ atque Asiâ pulsus. Nec plura querentem
Passa Venus: medio sic interfata dolore est.

365. *Illi* devenêre *ad* locos, ubi

367. Mercati *sunt* solum, *dictum* Byrsam de nomine facti, *tantum spatii*, quantum possent

369. Sed tandem, qui *estis* vos?

370. Ille suspirans, trahensque vocem à pectore imo *respondet ei* quærenti *in* talibus *verbis.*

375. Tempestas suâ forte appulit Libycis oris nos vectos per diversa æquora *ab* antiqua Trojâ, si

380. *Meum* genus *est* ab

385. Nec Venus passa *est eum* querentem plura

NOTES.

money, Dido took the treasure of her brother, and fled with it to Africa.

367. *Mercati solum*, &c. This passage hath been differently interpreted. Donatus explains it, of the money being made of bull's leather, with which she purchased the ground (*solum*) for the city. Others say, that she cut the hide into very small strings, and by connecting them together, surrounded twenty-two *stadia*, or furlongs. Neither of these appears to be the true solution. The language of the Phœnicians was a dialect of the Hebrew, in which language the word *Bosra* means a fortification, or fortified place. The Greeks, mistaking this meaning of the word, or overlooking it, supposed, from the similarity of the words, that it was the same with their *Byrsa*, which means a bull's hide. Virgil followed the common received opinion. *Mercati:* they bought the ground, which they called *Byrsa*, from the name of the deed, &c. This story of the bull's hide, Mr. Rollin observes, is now generally exploded. It appears, however, that Dido was to pay the Africans an annual tribute, as a quit rent, for the land which she purchased. This the Carthaginians afterward refused to do, which was the cause of the first war in which they were engaged. See Æn. iv. 1.

373. *Et vacet:* and there should be leisure to you to hear, &c.

374. *Annales:* in the sense of *historiam. Componet:* the evening star shall shut up the day, before I shall have done my story. This is an allusion to the opinion that night shut or sealed up the gate of heaven, and the day opened it. *Clauso Olympo:* heaven being closed. Olympus is a mountain in Thessaly. The ancients supposed its top touched the heavens: from which circumstance, the poets placed upon it the court of heaven. It is about a mile and a half high. Olympus is often put for heaven.

376. *Iit:* hath reached, or come to.

377. *Suâ forte.* Ruæus says, *solito casu. Sua vi*, says Minelius.

378. *Penates:* properly, household gods. See Geor. ii. 505. In the sack of Troy, Æneas saved his *Penates* from the hands of the Greeks, and took them as companions of his adventures. See Æn. ii. 717. *Æthera:* a Greek acc. in the sense of *cœlum.*

380. *Quæro Italiam:* I seek Italy, my country: my descent (*genus*) is from Jove supreme. Dardanus was an Italian, and one of the founders of the Trojan race. He was the son of Jove.

381. *Bis denis navibus:* with twenty ships. *Æquor:* in the sense of *mare:* properly, any level surface, whether land or water.

382. *Secutus fata data:* following the decrees of the gods made in my favor—obeying the decrees, &c.

383. *Convulsæ:* in the sense of *concussæ*, agreeing with *naves*, understood. *Euro:* the east wind, put for wind in general; the *species* for the *genus.*

384. *Ignotus:* a stranger.

386. *Interfata est:* she thus interrupted him in the midst of his grief: she could bear the piteous story no longer.

Quisquis es haud credo, invisus cœlestibus auras
Vitales carpis, Tyriam qui adveneris urbem.
Perge modò, atque hinc te Reginæ ad limina perfer.
Namque tibi reduces socios classemque relatam
Nuntio, et in tutum, versis Aquilonibus, actam:
Ni frustrà augurium vani docuere parentes.
Aspice bis senos lætantes agmine cycnos,
Æthereâ quos lapsa plagâ Jovis ales aperto
Turbabat cœlo: nunc terras ordine longo
Aut capere, aut captas jam despectare videntur
Ut reduces illi ludunt stridentibus alis,
Et cœtu cinxere polum, cantusque dedêre:
Haud aliter puppesque tuæ, pubesque tuorum
Aut portum tenet, aut pleno subit ostia velo.
Perge modò, et, quà te ducit via, dirige gressum
Dixit: et avertens roseâ cervice refulsit,
Ambrosiæque comæ divinum vertice odorem
Spiravere; pedes vestis defluxit ad imos,
Et vera incessu patuit Dea. Ille, ubi matrem
Agnovit, tali fugientem est voce secutus:
Quid natum toties crudelis tu quoque falsis
Ludis imaginibus? cur dextræ jungere dextram
Non datur, ac veras audire et reddere voces?
Talibus incusat, gressumque ad mœnia tendit.
At Venus obscuro gradientes aëre sepsit,
Et multo nebulæ circùm Dea fudit amictu

387. Quisquis es, haud credo, *ut tu* carpis vitales auras, invisus cœlestibus, qui

390. Nuntio tibi socios *esse* reduces, classemque relatam *esse*, et actam in tutum *locum*

394. Quos ales Jovis lapsa *ex* æthereâ plagâ turbabat

407. Quid tu quoque, O crudelis *mater*, toties ludis natum falsis

410. Ille incusat *eam* talibus verbis

NOTES.

387. *Cœlestibus:* in the sense of *superis.*

388. *Carpis:* you breathe the vital air, &c.

390. *Reduces:* returned safe—brought back.

392. *Ni parentes vani:* unless my parents vainly taught me divination in vain—to no purpose. Unless through a love of vanity and ostentation, they taught, &c. Heyne observes, that a person may be called *vanus*, who promises what he cannot perform, or professes a false or useless doctrine. *Actam:* in the sense of *provectam.*

394. *Ales Jovis:* the bird of Jove—the eagle. *Ætherea plagâ:* from the etherial region. *Agmine:* in a flock. *Turbati:* pursued—chased.

396. *Nunc videntur:* now they seem to choose the ground where to alight, in a long train: or to look down upon it chosen and selected. By alighting, they would be out of danger from their pursuer.

397. *Reduces:* in the sense of *tuti. Stridentibus:* flapping—making a whizzing noise.

398. *Dedēre:* in the sense of *emiserunt. Pubes tuorum:* the same in sense with *tui socii. Cinxere polum:* and have made a circle in the heavens in company. *Polus*, is properly the pole; but by synec. is often put for the whole heaven, or any part thereof. Fowls in a flock usually fly around, making one or more circles in the air before they alight. By doing this, they descend with more ease and safety.

403. *Ambrosæ:* an adj. from *ambrosia*, the food of the gods, according to the poets; perfumed with ambrosia. *Vertice:* in the sense of *capite. Spiravere:* in the sense of *emiserunt.*

405. *Patuit vera Dea.* The poet here mentions four characteristics of divinity: her rosy-colored neck—her ambrosial locks—her long flowing robe, (which she had gathered up in a knot to prevent discovery,) and her gait, or motion. It was the opinion of the ancients that their divinities did not move upon the ground, but glided along the surface with a regular motion. By these signs, Æneas knew her to be Venus, whom he had hitherto taken for a Lybian virgin. *Voce:* in the sense of *verbis.*

408. *Ludis:* in the sense of *decipis Imaginibus:* forms—figures. *Veras:* true—real—not dissembled.

411. *Gradientes: eos* is understood. The poet here hath in his view that passage of the Odyssey, where Pallas spreads a veil of air around Ulysses, and renders him invisible.

412. *Circumfudit.* The parts of the verb are separated by Tmesis, for the sake of the verse: she surrounded them with the thick garment of a cloud, that no one &c.

Cernere ne quis eos, neu quis contingere posset,
Molirive moram, aut veniendi poscere causas.
Ipsa Paphum sublimis abit, sedesque revisit

416. Ubi *est* templum illi

Læta suas; ubi templum illi, centumque Sabæo
Thure calent aræ, sertisque recentibus halant.
Corripuere viam intereà, quà semita monstrat
Jamque ascendebant collem, qui plurimus urbi
Imminet, adversasque aspectat desuper arces.
Miratur molem Æneas, magalia quondam:
Miratur portas, strepitumque et strata viarum.

423. Pars *instat* ducere

Instant ardentes Tyrii: pars ducere muros,
Molirique arcem, et manibus subvolvere saxa:
Pars optare locum tecto, et concludere sulco.
Jura magistratusque legunt, sanctumque senatum
Hìc portus alii effodiunt; hìc alta theatris
Fundamenta locant alii, immanesque columnas

429. Exciduntque immanes columnas è rupibus, *quæ sint* alta

430. *Eorum* labor *est talis*, qualis exercet apes

Rupibus excidunt, scenis decora alta futuris.
Qualis apes æstate novâ per florea rura
Exercet sub sole labor, cùm gentis adultos
Educunt fœtus, aut cùm liquentia mella
Stipant, et dulci distendunt nectare cellas;
Aut onera accipiunt venientûm, aut, agmine facto,
Ignavum, fucos, pecus à præsepibus arcent.
Fervet opus, redolentque thymo fragrantia mella

NOTES.

414. *Moliri*: to cause—make.

415. *Paphum:* a city of Cyprus, an island in the north-eastern part of the Mediterranean sea, dedicated to Venus. Verbs of motion to a place have the acc. after them.

416. *Sabœo thure:* with Arabian frankincense. *Sabœo:* an adj. from *Saba*, a country of Arabia Felix, abounding in frankincense. *Illi:* for her—in honor of her.

417. *Halant:* emit odour from fresh garlands—wreaths of flowers. *Calent:* burn—are hot.

419. *Collem.* This hill was probably near the city, from the top of which the whole city appeared in full view. It seems that it rose above the walls, so that you looked down upon it from above. *Imminet:* impends—overlooks. *Plurimus:* in the sense of *valdè*, or *maximè*. *Arces:* in the sense of *turres*.

421. *Miratur molem:* he wonders at the magnitude of the city, where there were once only cottages.

422. *Strata viarum:* the paved work of the streets—causeways.

423. *Ardentes.* An adj. or part. closely connected with a verb is more elegantly translated by its corresponding adverb. *Tyrii ardentes instant:* the Tyrians eagerly push on the work. The *ardentes* strongly marks their zeal and activity. *Ducere:* in the sense of *extendere*.

424. *Moliri:* to erect—build.

425. *Pars optare:* a part (*instat*, pushes on) to select the ground for building houses, and to mark it out by a furrow—to arrange and lay off the streets and squares of the city.

426. *Legunt:* in the sense of *eligunt*. *Jura:* by meton. the courts of justice—the place where justice is administered. They choose the place for the courts of justice, &c.

427. *Theatris:* for the theatres—buildings for public exhibitions.

429. *Excidunt:* they cut, or hew.

430. *Nova æstate:* in the beginning of summer.

431. *Sub sole:* for *per diem*, says Heyne. *Educunt:* lead out. *Liquentia:* in the sense of *pura*. This fine comparison of the industry of the Carthaginians in erecting the buildings of their city, and other works of improvement, to the zeal and assiduity of the bees in collecting honey, and arranging the business of the hive, is taken from Homer, who compares the movements of the Grecian troops from their ships and tents, to the issuing of bees from their hives.

433. *Stipant:* they lay up their pure honey. *Cellas:* the comb.

435. *Arcent:* they drive from the hives the drones, an idle herd. These are the male bees. See Geor. iv. 200. *Agmine facto:* a battalion being formed.

436. *Opus fervet:* the work goes briskly on. It is a metaphor taken from the boiling of water.

O fortunati, quorum jam mœnia surgunt!
Æneas ait: et fastigia suspicit urbis.
Infert se septus nebulâ, mirabile dictu,
Per medios, miscetque viris: neque cernitur ulli.
Lucus in urbe fuit mediâ, lætissimus umbrâ;
Quo primùm jactati undis et turbine Pœni
Effodêre loco signum, quod regia Juno
Monstrârat, caput acris equi: sic nam fore bello
Egregiam, et facilem victu per sæcula gentem
Hìc templum Junoni ingens Sidonia Dido
Condebat, donis opulentum et numine Divæ:
Ærea cui gradibus surgebant limina, nexæque
Ære trabes: foribus cardo stridebat ahenis.
Hoc primùm in luco nova res oblata timorem
Leniit: hìc primùm Æneas sperare salutem
Ausus, et afflictis meliùs confidere rebus.
Namque, sub ingenti lustrat dum singula templo,
Reginam opperiens; dum, quæ fortuna sit urbi,
Artificumque manus inter se operumque laborem
Miratur; videt Iliacas ex ordine pugnas,
Bellaque jam famâ totum vulgata per orbem;
Atridas, Priamumque et sævum ambobus Achillem.
Constitit, et lachrymans: Quis jam locus, inquit, Achate,

442. Quo loco Pœn jactati undis, et turbine primùm effodêre signum, *nempe* caput acris equi

444. Nam sic *monstravit* gentem fore egregiam bello, et facilem victu per secula

NOTES.

445. *Nam sic fore:* for thus (by this sign) she showed that the nation should be illustrious in war, and victorious through ages —easy to conquer through ages. Ruæus interprets *facilem victu*, by *aptam vivere æterna famâ*, deriving *victu* from *vivo*, I live. Others, with more propriety, derive it from *vinco*, I conquer; making the meaning to be: easy to conquer through ages—victorious. The supine in *u* hath both an active and passive signification; but most frequently the latter. The former is the meaning in this place.

446. *Sidonia:* an adj. from *Sidon*, a famous city of Phœnicia, not far to the north of Tyre, subject to the same government. *Hodie, Sayd.*

447. *Numine Divæ:* with the presence of the goddess. By this we are probably to understand some rich statue of the goddess, that was set up in the temple.

448. *Cui ærea limina:* to which the brazen threshold rose in steps, &c.—whose brazen threshold, &c. *Cui:* in the sense of *cujus:* this is common with Virgil.

449. *Trabes:* these most probably were the door posts, which were framed or fastened together with brass.

452. *Confidere:* in the sense of *sperare*, says Ruæus. *Cœpit nunc habere magis fiducium suæ fortunæ, benè de ea sperare*, says Heyne.

453. *Singula. Singuli* properly means *all*, taken one by one. *Omnis* signifies *all*, collectively or individually. *Cunctus, all* by parts, and *universus*, the *whole*.

454. *Opperiens:* waiting for the queen. *Dum miratur:* while he wonders at the fortune of the city; and at the skill of the artists, and the difficulty of the work, (*inter se*,) by turns. Ruæus refers the *inter se* to the hands of the workmen, agreeing with one another, *manus artificum*. In this case the sense will be: he contemplates the skill displayed in the workmanship and the magnitude of the work by turns—he compares them together. But La Cerda observes, that by *manus artificum*, the skill of the artists, we are probably to understand the paintings of the Trojan battles, and the other events of that war, which Æneas saw on his entering the temple, and which ornamented its walls: while *operum laborem*, may refer to the temple itself—the magnitude, and difficulty of rearing such a magnificent edifice. *Fortuna:* this Ruæus interprets by *felicitas*. *Manus:* properly the hand: by meton. art, skill.

456. *Videt Iliacas pugnas.* Dr. Trapp, observes, there never was a finer picture of a picture than this. Virgil in a few verses, selects the most striking, and beautiful scenes in the Iliad, proper for the painter.

458. *Atridas:* acc. plu. of *Atridæ*, the sons of Atreus, Agamemnon, and Menelaus.—Against the former, Achilles had a quarrel on account of the beautiful *Brisseïs*, a captive. He withdrew with his troops, and refused to take any part with the Greeks,

Quæ regio in terris nostri non plena laboris.
En Priamus: sunt hìc etiam sua præmia laudi:
Sunt lachrymæ rerum, et mentem mortalia tangunt
Solve metus: feret hæc aliquam tibi fama salutem.
Sic ait: atque animum picturâ pascit inani,
Multa gemens, largoque humectat flumine vultum.
Namque videbat, utì bellantes Pergama circum
Hâc fugerent Graii, premeret Trojana juventus;
Hâc Phryges, instaret curru cristatus Achilles.
Nec procul hinc Rhesi niveis tentoria velis
Agnoscit lachrymans: primo quæ prodita somno
Tydides multâ vastabat cæde cruentus:
Ardentesque avertit equos in castra, priusquàm
Pabula gustâssent Trojæ, Xanthumque bibissent.
Parte aliâ fugiens amissis Troïlus armis,
Infelix puer, atque impar congressus Achilli,
Fertur equis, curruque hæret resupinus inani,
Lora tenens tamen: huic cervixque comæque trahuntur
Per terram, et versâ pulvis inscribitur hastâ.
Intereà ad templum non æquæ Palladis ibant
Crinibus Iliades passis, peplumque ferebant
Suppliciter tristes, et tunsæ pectora palmis.

467. Utì bellantes Graii fugerent hàc circum Pergama, *dum* Trojana juventus premeret *eos;* hàc Phryges *fugerent,* *dum* cristatus Achilles instaret *iis è* curru.

472. Castra *Græcorum* priùsquàm

481. Tunsæ *quoad* pectora palmis

NOTES.

till after the death of Patroclus, whom Hector slew in battle. Some copies have *Atriden,* which appears to be the more correct; for we have no account that Achilles had any disagreement with *Menelaus.* The *ambobus* refers to Agamemnon and Priam. Achilles afterwards slew Hector, and ignominiously treated his dead body. He refused to restore it to Priam, till he received a large sum of money as a ransom.

460. *Nostri labores:* our sufferings, calamities.

461. *Laudi:* in the sense here of *virtuti.*

462. *Lachrymæ rerum:* tears for our afflictions—compassion for our calamities or sufferings. *Mortalia:* an adj. neu. plu. taken as a sub. *human calamities.*

465. *Largo flumine:* a large flood of tears.

466. *Pergama:* neu. plu. In the sing. *Pergamus,* properly the citadel of Troy, built on the highest ground, whence the whole city could be seen. Here, and in many other places, put for the city itself; by synec. *Bellantes:* valiant—warlike.

468. *Cristatus:* plumed--wearing a plume. *Instaret:* in the sense of *premeret.*

469. *Rhesi.* Rhesus, king of Thrace, and reputed son of Mars. When he came to assist the Trojans, it was reported, as a decree of the gods, that if his horses should drink of the water of the river Xanthus, or taste the grass of Troy, the city should not be taken. On his arrival, he encamped on the shore, when he was betrayed by one Dolon to Diomede, and Ulysses, who slew him on the first night of his arrival, and carried off his horses to the Grecian camp.

470. *Quæ prodita:* which being betrayed in the first night, &c. *Somno:* in the sense of *nocte.* See Æn. 11. 242.

472. *Ardentes:* in the sense of *acres.*

473. *Xanthum:* a river of Troas, rising out of mount Ida, and flowing into the Hellespont. It is the same with the Scamander.

474. *Troïlus.* A son of Priam. Virgil calls him *puer,* probably on account of his age. He was slain by Achilles.

475. *Impar congressus Achilli:* an unequal match for Achilles:—or meeting Achilles, an unequal match is drawn, &c. *Resupinus:* on his back, he hangs from his empty chariot.

478. *Hasta versâ.* The dust is not marked with the spear of Troïlus; but with the spear of Achilles, which had pierced has body; and as he lay on his back, might be said to be inverted; its point being downward. *Huic:* in the sense of *hujus.*

479. *Non æquæ Palladis:* of Pallas, unkind—offended on account of the decision of Paris, in the contest of beauty between her, Juno, and Venus.

480. *Iliades:* the Trojan matrons with dishevelled hair, went, &c. Homer informs us (Iliad. 6. 302.) that after the great slaughter of the Trojans, Hecuba and the Trojan matrons went in solemn procession, with every external sign of sorrow, to the temple of Pallas, carrying the richest presents, in hope to render her favorable to

Diva solo fixos oculos aversa tenebat.
Ter circum Iliacos raptaverat Hectora muros,
Exanimumque auro corpus vendebat Achilles.
  Tum verò ingentem gemitum dat pectore ab imo,
Ut spolia, ut currus, utque ipsum corpus amici,
Tendentemque manus Priamum conspexit inermes.
Se quoque principibus permixtum agnovit Achivis,
Eoasque acies, et nigri Memnonis arma.
Ducit Amazonidum lunatis agmina peltis
Penthesilea furens, mediisque in millibus ardet,
Aurea subnectens exertæ cingula mammæ,
Bellatrix, audetque viris concurrere virgo.
  Hæc dum Dardanio Æneæ miranda videntur,
Dum stupet, obtutuque hæret defixus in uno :
Regina ad templum, formâ pulcherrima Dido,
Incessit, magnâ juvenum stipante catervâ.
Qualis in Eurotæ ripis, aut per juga Cynthi
Exercet Diana choros, quam mille secutæ
Hinc atque hinc glomerantur Oreades : illa pharetram
Fert humero, gradiensque Deas supereminet omnes :
Latonæ tacitum pertentant gaudia pectus.

493. Virgoque subnectens aurea cingula exertæ mammæ, *utpote* bellatrix, audet

NOTES.

their cause. *Peplum:* this was the richest of vestments, embroidered by the Sidonian women in the most costly manner, and brought by Paris from Sidon. This they carried to the goddess, hoping she would be moved by it to regard their sufferings. *Passis:* a part. of the verb *pandor*, spread, or hanging loose.

482. *Aversa:* in the sense of *offensa.*

483. *Achilles raptaverat.* See Æn. 2, 542.

486. *Ut spolia conspexit:* as he beheld the spoils; as he beheld the chariot, &c. The verb *conspexit* is to be repeated with each nom. as is plain, from the repetition of the *ut.* This verse is of the same tender nature with Ecl. viii. 41. *Ut vidi*, &c. It plainly shows the skill of the poet. Any other would have used the conjunction *et* or *que.* But by the repetion of the *ut*, he shows Æneas tracing these several affecting objects, and every now and then fetching a deep sigh. *Corpus amici:* the body of Hector, we are to understand.

487. *Inermes:* unarmed—suppliant. Of *n*, negativum, and *arma.*

489. *Memnonis.* Memnon the son of Aurora and Tithonus, the son of Laomedon, king of Troy. He came to the assistance of the Trojans with many troops from India and Ethiopia. He was slain by Achilles. *Nigri:* swarthy—alluding to his color. *Eoas acies:* eastern troops.

491. *Penthesilea.* She was queen of the Amazons, who came to the aid of the Trojans after the death of Hector. Her troops were armed with bucklers in the form of a crescent, or half-moon. *Agmina lunatis peltis:* her troops (armed) with crescent shields. She was slain by Achilles; some say by his son Neoptolemus. *Furens:* eager—courageous.

493. *Bellatrix virgo:* the warlike virgin, binding a golden girdle under her naked breast, dares, &c. It was a custom of the Amazons to cut or scar one of their breasts that it might be no hindrance to their shooting or darting of the javelin; the other they bound with a girdle. The word *Amazon* is compounded of the Greek *alpha* negativum, and a word which signifies a *breast*; implying that they had only one breast. See nom. prop. under *Amazon.*

494. *Miranda:* wonderful—worthy of admiration. It is to be taken with the verb *videntur.* *Obtutu:* posture. *Hæret:* in the sense of *stat.*

497. *Incessit:* approached. See 46. supra.

498. *Qualis Diana exercet:* as Diana leads the dance on the banks of Eurotas, or over the tops of Cynthus, whom a thousand mountain nymphs surround, &c. *Eurotas*, a river of *Laconia*, near Sparta, a country famous for hunting. *Cynthi:* Cynthus was a mountain in the island of Delos, the birth place of *Diana.* *Glomerantur:* in the sense of *glomerant.* See Ecl. iv. 10.

500. *Oreades:* mountain nymphs; from a Greek word which signifies a mountain. See Ecl. ii. 46.

502. *Latonæ.* Latona, the mother of Diana and Apollo. Joy pervaded her silent breast at the sight of the grace and dignity of her daughter.

Talis erat Dido, talem se læta ferebat
Per medios, instans operi regnisque futuris.
Tum foribus Divæ, mediâ testudine templi,
Septa armis solioque altè subnixa, resedit.
Jura dabat legesque viris, operumque laborem
Partibus æquabat justis, aut sorte trahebat:
Cùm subitò Æneas, concursu accedere magno
Anthea Sergestumque videt, fortemque Cloanthum,
Teucrorumque alios: ater quos æquore turbo
Dispulerat penitùsque alias avexerat oras.
Obstupuit simul ipse, simul perculsus Achates
514. *Ambo* avidi ardebant
Lætitiâque metuque; avidi conjungere dextras
Ardebant: sed res animos incognita turbat.
Dissimulant, et nube cavâ speculantur amicti,
517. Quæ fortuna *sit* viris
Quæ fortuna viris, classem quo litore linquant,
518. *Ob* quid veniant; nam *homines*
Quid veniant: cunctis nam lecti navibus ibant
Orantes veniam, et templum clamore petebant.
520. Introgressi *sunt*, et copia fandi coram *regina* data *est illis*
Postquàm introgressi, et coràm data copia fandi,
Maximus Ilioneus placido sic pectore cœpit:
O regina, novam cui condere Jupiter urbem,
Justitiâque dedit gentes frænare superbas:
524. *Nos* miseri Troes, vecti *per*
Troes te miseri, ventis maria omnia vecti,
Oramus: prohibe infandos à navibus ignes;
Parce pio generi, et propiùs res aspice nostras
Non nos aut ferro Libycos populare Penates
Venimus, aut raptas ad litora vertere prædas.
Non ea vis animo, nec tanta superbia victis.

NOTES.

503. *Talis erat Dido:* such was Dido. The comparison here between Diana and Dido is taken from the Odyssey. Probus considered the passage to be copied unhappily by Virgil. The comparison, according to Scaliger lies in these particulars: *Quemadmodum Diana in montibus, ita Dido in urbe: illa inter nymphas, hæc inter matronas: illa instans venatoribus, hæc urbi.*

505. *Foribus Divæ.* In the interior part of the temples, there was a place separated from the rest by a wall, or vail, called the *Adytum* or *Penetrale.* Here the poet supposes Juno to have had an image or statue, or some symbol of her presence. The door or gate that led to it he therefore calls the *door of the goddess. Mediâ testudine:* under the middle of the arch, or canopy. *Subnixa altè:* raised high on a throne, she sat down. *Foribus:* fores, properly folding doors—opening on both sides. It has no singular.

506. *Septa armis:* surrounded by her guards. *Armis,* by meton. for the men bearing them.

507. *Dabat jura:* dispensed justice. *Jus,* properly a natural law, or right: *Lex,* a written or statute law: *fas,* a divine law.

509. *Concursu:* a crowd. *Multitudine,* says Ruæus.

511. *Avidi:* eager. See 423. supra. *Ardebant:* in the sense of *cupiebant.*

512. *Avexerat:* had carried to other shores far remote.

516. *Speculantur:* they conjecture what is the fortune of their friends; on what coast they had left their fleet; for what purpose they came thither. For men chosen, &c.

519. *Veniam:* peace—favor. *Clamore:* with a cry, lamenting the hardness of their fortune.

521. *Maximus:* the chief, or principal speaker. *Placido pectore:* from his composed breast. A composed breast, or mind regulates the voice and speech. *Copia:* leave—liberty.

523. *Frænare:* to restrain proud nations with justice—with laws. By *superbas gentes* we may understand the Numidians, and other warlike nations of Africa, her neighbors. For *superbas,* Ruæus says, *feroces.*

525. *Prohibe:* avert—turn away. *Infandos:* direful—cruel.

527. *Libycos Penates:* the African territory, or settlements: or, simply, the African gods.

528. *Vertere* in the sense of *abducere. Raptas prædas:* the plundered, or seized booty.

529. *Vis:* in the sense of *violentia.* The verb *est* is understood.

Est locus, Hesperiam Graii cognomine dicunt;
Terra antiqua, potens armis atque ubere glebæ:
Œnotrii coluere viri; nunc fama, minores
Italiam dixisse, ducis de nomine, gentem.
Huc cursus fuit.
Cùm subitò assurgens fluctu nimbosus Orion
In vada cæca tulit, penitùsque procacibus Austris
Perque undas, superante salo, perque invia saxa
Dispulit: huc pauci vestris adnavimus oris.
Quod genus hoc hominum? quæve hunc tam barbara [morem
Permittit patria? hospitio prohibemur arenæ:
Bella cient, primâque vetant consistere terrâ.
Si genus humanum et mortalia temnitis arma;
At sperate Deos memores fandi atque nefandi.
Rex erat Æneas nobis, quo justior alter
Nec pietate fuit, nec bello major et armis·
Quem si fata virum servant, si vescitur aurâ

532 Nunc fama *est* minores

536. Procacibusque Austris dispulit *nos* penitùs perque undas, perque invia

539. Quod genus hominum *est* hoc? quæve patria tam barbara permittit

543. Sperate Deos *esse* memores

544. Quo nec fuit alter justior *in* pietate, nec major bello

NOTES.

530. *Hesperiam.* Italy hath been called by various names: *Hesperia*, (which was the name also sometimes given to Spain,) from *Hesperus* the brother of Atlas, king of Mauritania, in Africa; or from *Hesperus*, the name of the star *Venus*, when it goes behind the sun, and signifies, a *setting*, or the *west*. From which circumstance, the Greeks to the eastward of those countries called Italy *Magna Hesperia*, and Spain, *Hesperia Minor*: *Œnotria*, from *Œnotrus*, a king of the Sabines, or from a son of Lycaon, king of Arcadia, of that name: *Ausonia*, from the *Ausones*, an ancient people of that country; and lastly, *Italia*, from *Italus*, a king of Sicily; or, as some say, from a Greek word signifying *cattle*, because they abounded there. *Dicunt:* in the sense of *vocant*.

531. *Ubere:* richness—fertility. *Cognomine:* in the sense of *nomine*.

532. *Œnotrii viri:* simply, the Œnotrians inhabited it. *Minores:* their descendants.

535. *Orion:* a constellation in the heavens. It rises with the sun in the month of July, and was supposed to have an influence upon the weather; hence the epithet *nimbosus*. It will appear hence, that the time of Æneas' arrival at Carthage, was some time in that month. He remained there till the latter part of the following winter, when he set sail for Italy, where he arrived, as Sagrais supposes, some time in the spring. *Fluctu:* in the sense of *mari*.

536. *Austris procacibus:* by violent winds. *Auster* is here put for wind in general, and not for the south wind, which would have driven him from Africa. *Tulit:* carried, or drove. *Cæca:* in the sense of *latentia*.

537. *Salo:* in the sense of *mari*. For *procacibus*, Heyne says *vehementibus*.

540. *Prohibemur:* we are prohibited from the enjoyment of the shore

543. *At sperate:* but expect that the gods are mindful of right and wrong. *Fandi atque nefandi:* gerunds in *di*, of the verb *for;* in the sense of *fas* and *nefas:* for what is right and just may be spoken; but what is unjust, we may not speak.

The meaning of the passage is: if ye despise the human race, and fear not the just punishment from men, which this savage and barbarous conduct deserves, know that the gods are mindful of right and wrong, and will not fail to reward or punish accordingly. *Mortalia arma:* Ruæus says, *vindictam hominum*, the vengeance of men.

544. *Quô justior alter*, &c. Here we have a summary of Æneas' character, *piety* and *valor*. The first comprehends devotion to the gods, and all the moral virtues. It shows him a tender son, an affectionate father, and husband. He bore his father upon his shoulders, and led his little son through the flames of Troy to a place of safety. And having lost his wife in the general confusion of that fatal night, he ventured into the midst of enemies in search of her: nor did he cease, till her ghost appeared to him, and bade him to desist: and on all occasions, Ascanius appears the darling of his soul. Æneas was also a patriot, and firmly attached to the interests of his country. In valor and prowess in war, he appears on all occasions the real hero. Homer represents him second only to Hector. He was the first to resist Achilles on his return after the death of Patroclus. He did not engage him, but he manifested a calm and determined courage. We see then how justly he is characterized by, *nec bello major et armis*. But his piety and moral virtues have ennobled his character more than all his deeds of valor.

546. *Vescitur:* in the sense of *spirat*,

Æthereâ, neque adhuc crudelibus occubat umbris;
Non metus, officio nec te certâsse priorem
Pœniteat. Sunt et Siculis regionibus urbes,
Armaque, Trojanoque à sanguine clarus Acestes.
Quassatam ventis liceat subducere classem,
Et sylvis aptare trabes, et stringere remos.
Si datur Italiam, sociis et rege recepto,
Tendere, ut Italiam læti Latiumque petamus:
Sin absumpta salus, et te, pater optime Teucrûm,
Pontus habet Libyæ, nec spes jam restat Iüli,
Ut freta Sicaniæ saltem sedesque paratas,
Unde huc advecti, regemque petamus Acesten.
Talibus Ilioneus: cuncti simul ore fremebant
Dardanidæ.
Tum breviter Dido, vultum demissa, profatur:
Solvite corde metum, Teucri, secludite curas.
Res dura, et regni novitas me talia cogunt
Moliri, et latè fines custode tueri.
Quis genus Æneadûm, quis Trojæ nesciat urbem?
Virtutesque, virosque, et tanti incendia belli?
Non obtusa adeò gestamus pectora Pœni:
Nec tam aversus equos Tyriâ Sol jungit ab urbe.
Seu vos Hesperiam magnam, Saturniaque arva,
Sive Erycis fines, regemque optatis Acesten;
Auxilio tutos dimittam, opibusque juvabo.
Vultis et his mecum pariter considere regnis?
Urbem quam statuo, vestra est; subducite naves
Tros Tyriusque mihi nullo discrimine agetur.

548. Non *sit* metus *nobis*, nec pœniteat te priorem certâsse *cum illo* officio

551. Liceat *nobis* subducere *ad terram* classem quassatam

554. Ut læti petamus Italiam Latiumque, si datur *nobis* tendere *cursum ad* Italiam, sociis, et

555. Sin salus absumpta *est*, et pontus Libyæ habet te, O optime

557. Ut saltem petamus freta Sicaniæ paratasque sedes, unde advecti *sumus* huc

560. Ilioneus *orabat* talibus *verbis*.

561. Demissa *quoad* vultum

569. Seu vos optatis magnam

NOTES.

Occubat: lies dead—yields up his life to the cruel shades.

549. *Et:* in the sense of *etiam*, or *quoque*.

550. *Acestes.* See Æn. v. 30.

552. *Et aptare:* and to fit (procure) spars in the wood, to supply the place of those that had been broken, or lost in the violence of the storm and waves. *Stringere remos:* to cut our oars—to cut timber, of which to make oars.

557. *Freta. Fretum* is properly a narrow sea, or strait: here used for the sea in general. *Ut.* Most copies have *at*, but the former is preferable. *Advecti:* in the sense of *pulsi*.

560. *Fremebant ore:* they applauded with their mouth—they expressed their approbation of his speech. *Dardanidæ:* the Trojans; so called from *Dardanus*. They were also called *Teucri*, from *Teucer*, both founders of Troy. See 1, supra.

563. *Dura res:* the difficult state of my affairs. *Moliri:* in the sense of *facere*.

565. *Genus Æneadûm:* the ancestry of the Trojans—the stock from which they sprung. *Æneadæ:* the Trojans; from *Æneas*, their leader.

566. *Virtutes:* illustrious actions. *Viros:* heroes.

567. *Pœni gestamus:* we Carthaginians do not carry with us hearts so insensible, as to disregard the sufferings of our fellow men.

568. *Nec tam aversus:* nor does the sun so far from the Tyrian city join his steeds to his chariot.

This is an allusion to an opinion of the ancients, that the inhabitants of cold climates are less susceptible of the tender and humane feelings, than those of warm climates.

569. *Saturnia arva:* the lands of Saturn—Italy. See Ecl. iv. 6. *Magnam:* powerful, or great; to distinguish it from Spain, which was sometimes called *Hesperia Minor*.

570. *Fines Erycis:* the coast of Eryx—Sicily, where Eryx reigned. See Æn. v. 24.

571. *Opibus.* This refers to the assistance which Dido would afford them by *her wealth*. *Pariter:* on equal terms, or conditions. *Et:* in the sense of *etiam*.

573. *Urbem quam: urbem*, for *urbs*, by antiptosis. Some take the words thus: *quam urbem statuo:* which city I build; it is yours.

574. *Agetur:* shall be treated. *Discrimine* difference—distinction.

Atque utinam rex ipse Noto compulsus eodem
Afforet Æneas! Equidem per litora certos
Dimittam, et Libyæ lustrare extrema jubebo;
Si quibus ejectus sylvis aut urbibus errat
His animum arrecti dictis, et fortis Achates,
Et pater Æneas, jamdudum erumpere nubem
Ardebant: prior Ænean compellat Achates:
Nate Deâ, quæ nunc animo sententia surgit?
Omnia tuta vides, classem, sociosque receptos.
Unus abest, medio in fluctu quem vidimus ipsi
Submersum: dictis respondent cætera matris.
Vix ea fatus erat, cùm circumfusa repentè
Scindit se nubes, et in æthera purgat apertum.
Restitit Æneas, clarâque in luce refulsit,
Os, humerosque Deo similis: namque ipsa decoram
Cæsariem nato genitrix, lumenque juventæ
Purpureum, et lætos oculis afflârat honores.
Quale manus addunt ebori decus, aut ubi flavo
Argentum Pariusve lapis circumdatur auro.
Tum sic reginam alloquitur, cunctisque repentè
Improvisus ait: Coràm, quem quæritis, adsum
Troïus Æneas, Libycis ereptus ab undis.
O sola infandos Trojæ miserata labores!
Quæ nos, relliquias Danaûm, terræque marisque
Omnibus exhaustos jam casibus, omnium egenos,
Urbe, domo socias. Grates persolvere dignas
Non opis est nostræ, Dido: nec quicquid ubique est
Gentis Dardaniæ, magnum quæ sparsa per orbem:
Dî tibi (si qua pios respectant numina, si quid
Usquam justitiæ est, et mens sibi conscia recti,)

575. Utinam Æneas ipse, *vester* rex, afforet, compulsus eodem noto.

578. Si *fortè ille* ejectus errat *in* quibus sylvis, aut urbibus.

589. Similis Deo, *quoad* os, humerosque

595. *Ego* Troïus Æneas adsum coram *vobis*, quem quæritis

597. O *tu* sola miserata *es*

598. Quæ socias nos *in vestra* urbe, *et* domo, relliquias Danaûm, exhaustos jam omnibus

601. Nec *est opis* Dardaniæ gentis, ubique quicquid *ejus* est, quæ sparsa *est* per magnum

NOTES.

576. *Certos:* in the sense of *fidos.* The word *homines* is understood.

577. *Extrema:* the farthest, or extreme parts of Africa.

579. *Arrecti animum:* animated—encouraged in mind. A Grecism.

584. *Unus abest:* one is wanting. This was *Orontes,* mentioned verse 113, supra. His ship and crew were lost.

585. *Cætera respondent:* the rest answer to, &c. See 390, supra, et seq.

587. *Purgat in apertum:* it clears up (dissolves) into pure air. *Circumfusa nubes:* the surrounding cloud—the cloud that hitherto had encompassed them. Here Virgil imitates Homer, Odys. vii. 143.

589. *Namque genitrix:* for his mother had breathed upon her son graceful locks, and the bright bloom of youth, and a sparkling lustre to his eyes. *Honores:* grace—beauty.

592. *Quale decus:* such beauty art gives, &c. *Manus:* by meton. the skill of the workman.

593. *Parius lapis:* the Parian marble. Parus, an island in the Ægean sea, famous for its white marble. *Circumdatur:* encompassed—enchased.

597. *Labores:* disasters—calamities.

599. *Exhaustos:* worn out—having undergone. *Socias:* in the sense of *recipis.*

601. *Non est nostræ opis:* it is not in our power to render you, O Dido, suitable thanks, nor is it (in the power) of the Trojan nation, wherever any of it is, which, &c.

603. *Dî tibi ferant:* may the gods grant you suitable rewards. *Siqua numina:* if there be any powers above that regard, &c. These words are not designed to express any doubt in the mind of the speaker upon the subject. They put an acknowledged truth in the form of a supposition, the more to strengthen the conclusion. You shall be rewarded, as sure as there are any gods above—as sure as there is any justice among men, and any mind conscious to itself of virtue and worth. Ruæus concludes the parenthesis at the verb *est.* The meaning will then be: may the gods and your own mind, conscious of its own rectitude, reward you. Others extend it to embrace *recti.* Heyne has no parenthesis *Pios*

Præmia digna ferant. Quæ te tam læta tulerunt
Sæcula? qui tanti talem genuere parentes?
In freta dum fluvii current, dum montibus umbræ
Lustrabunt convexa, polus dum sidera pascet;
Semper honos, nomenque tuum, laudesque manebunt
Quæ me cunque vocant terræ. Sic fatus, amicum
Ilionea petit dextrâ, lævâque Serestum;
Pòst, alios, fortemque Gyan, fortemque Cloanthum.
  Obstupuit primò aspectu Sidonia Dido,
Casu deinde viri tanto; et sic ore locuta est:
Quis te, nate Deâ, per tanta pericula casus
Insequitur? quæ vis immanibus applicat oris?
Tu-ne ille Æneas, quem Dardanio Anchisæ
Alma Venus Phrygii genuit Simoëntis ad undam?
Atque equidem Teucrum memini Sidona venire,
Finibus expulsum patriis, nova regna petentem
Auxilio Beli. Genitor tum Belus opimam
Vastabat Cyprum, et victor ditione tenebat.
Tempore jam ex illo casus mihi cognitus urbis
Trojanæ, nomenque tuum, regesque Pelasgi.
Ipse hostis Teucros insigni laude ferebat,

610. Quæcunque terræ vocant me

612. Pòst, *petit* alios, fortemque

617. Tu-ne *es* ille Æneas, quem Alma Venus genuit Dardanio

623. Casus Trojanæ urbis *est* cognitus mihi

625. *Teucer* ipse *quamvis* hostis ferebat Teucros

NOTES.

This word signifies virtuous men in general; especially the kind, beneficent, and generous.

605. *Læta:* in the sense of *felicia. Sæcula:* in the sense of *tempora.*

607. *Dum umbræ:* while the clouds shall move around, or encompass the mountains. Ruæus says, *umbræ arborum:* the shades of trees. But with what propriety the shades of trees can be said to move round, or encompass the mountains, doth not appear. It certainly is not the meaning of the poet. It is well known that the tops of high mountains rise above the clouds; and the region, or elevation of the clouds will be a greater or less distance below the summit, according to the height of the mountain, and the density of the atmosphere. *Convexa:* properly the exterior of any round, or circular body. It may then very properly denote the top, or curved surface of a mountain; also its sides. *Montibus:* in the sense of *montium. Convexa montibus:* the tops of the mountains. The dat. among the poets, is often used in the sense of the gen.

608. *Dum polus:* while the heaven feeds (sustains) the stars—while there are any stars in the heavens. *Polus,* properly the pole; by synec. the whole heavens.

611. *Ilionea:* a Greek acc. of *Ilioneus.* He was a Trojan, the son of Phorbas. The penult syllable is naturally short, but it is made long for the sake of the verse. Nothing is known of *Serestes, Gyas,* and *Cloanthus,* further than Virgil informs us.

614. *Casu:* calamity—misfortune. *Deinde:* in the next place. It has reference to *primò,* in the preceding line.

615. *Quis casus:* what fortune. *Quæ vis:* what power drives you, &c.

618. *Genuit:* in the sense of *peperit.*

619. *Memini quidem.* This Teucer was the son of Telamon, king of the island of Salamis, and Hesione, daughter of Laomedon, king of Troy. On his return from the Trojan war, he was banished by his father, for not preventing the death of his brother Ajax, who slew himself, because the arms of Achilles were adjudged to Ulysses rather than to him. This unnatural treatment of his father, led him to disclaim all relationship to him, and to reckon his lineage from his mother. The poet, by concealing this circumstance, hath made it reflect much honor upon the Trojans.

621. *Belus.* See Æn. iv. 1.

622. *Cyprum:* an island in the Mediterranean sea, sacred to Venus. Here, it is said, she was born, and had a splendid temple. Hence she was sometimes called the *Cyprian Goddess. Opimam:* rich—fertile. Belus had been at war with the inhabitants of the island, and at that time it was subject to him.

624. *Pelasgi.* These were a people of Thessaly so called from *Pelasgus,* a son of Lycaon, king of Arcadia, from whom they were descended. They were frequently taken for the Greeks in general. Here, and in some other places, used as an adj.

625. *Ferebat Teucros:* he extolled the Trojans with distinguished praise.

Seque ortum antiquâ Teucrorum à stirpe volebat.
Quare agite, ô tectis, juvenes, succedite nostris!
Me quoque per multos similis fortuna labores
Jactatam, hâc demum voluit consistere terrâ.
Non ignara mali, miseris succurrere disco.
Sic memorat, simul Ænean in regia ducit
Tecta, simul Divûm templis indicit honorem.
Nec minùs intereà sociis ad litora mittit
Viginti tauros, magnorum horrentia centum
Terga suum, pingues centum cum matribus agnos
Munera, lætitiamque Dei.
At domus interior regali splendida luxu
Instruitur, mediisque parant convivia tectis.
Arte laboratæ vestes, ostroque superbo:
Ingens argentum mensis, cœlataque in auro
Fortia facta patrum, series longissima rerum
Per tot ducta viros antiquæ ab origine gentis.
Æneas (neque enim patrius consistere mentem
Passus amor) rapidum ad naves præmittit Achaten,
Ascanio ferat hæc, ipsumque ad mœnia ducat.
Omnis in Ascanio chari stat cura parentis.
Munera prætereà, Iliacis erepta ruinis,
Ferre jubet, pallam signis auroque rigentem,

628. **Similis fortuna** voluit me quoque jactatam per multos labores consistere

633. Mittit munera sociis ad litora, *nempe* viginti tauros, centum

639. *Hic sunt* vestes laboratæ arte

645. *Ut* ferat hæc Ascanio, ducatque

647. Jubet *Ascanium* ferre *secum* munera erepta *ex* Iliacis ruinis, *nempe* pallam

NOTES.

626. *Volebatque se:* and he wished (it to be considered) that he sprang from the ancient stock of the Trojans. He sprang from that stock by Hesione, the daughter of Laomedon, who was the fifth from Teucer and Dardanus, the founders of Troy. See Geor. iii. 35. For *volebat*, Ruæus says *aiebat.*

628. *Labores:* in the sense of *casus.*

630. *Mali.* This is a fine verse. The sentiment is worthy of the most distinguished character. *Memorat:* in the sense of *loquitur.*

632. *Indicit honorem:* she orders an offering (to be made) in the temples. It was an ancient custom to offer libations to Jove, as being the god of hospitality, upon the arrival of strangers. Servius thinks the words, *indicit honorem*, mean, that she orders contributions to be made in honor of the gods; but this is questionable. He observes that the ancients, from their poverty, were obliged to make collections from the people, for their sacrifices: they also applied to that use the property of convicts and malefactors. Hence *supplicia*, punishments, came to signify prayers, supplications, and thanksgivings. So also *sacer* came to signify both holy, and accursed.

633. *Nec minùs:* in the sense of *quoque*, or *nec non.*

634. *Centum horrentia terga:* a hundred bristly backs of huge swine; simply, a hundred large swine. *Terga:* the backs, by synec put for the whole bodies, or carcasses.

636. *Lætitiam Dei:* the joy of the god (*Bacchus*—wine.) This is a beautiful circumlocution. The opinions of commentators upon this passage are various. The sense, however, is easy. The queen sent them presents (*munera*) of twenty bulls, a hundred swine, and wine to cheer their hearts.

637. *Interior domus:* the inner part of the palace, itself splendid, was furnished with royal magnificence.

639. *Superbo:* rich—costly. *Laboratæ:* finely wrought.

640. *Ingens argentum:* much silver (was) upon the tables, and the mighty deeds of her ancestors carved in gold, a very long series of history, traced down through so many heroes from the origin of their ancient family. *Ingens argentum:* by this we are to understand a great quantity of plate, and silver vessels of various descriptions, on which were carved the noble actions of her ancestors.

644. *Præmittit:* in the sense of *mittit*, the compound for the simple word. Or reference may be had to the entertainment which Dido had ordered upon the occasion. He sends Achates before supper, to bear the news to Ascanius, and to bring him to the city. He suffers no time to be lost, before he communicates to his son the tidings of their kind reception. Servius takes *Præmittit rapidum*, for *mittit prærapidum*. *Rapidum:* in the sense of *celerem.*

648. *Rigentem signis auroque:* stiff with

Et circumtextum croceo velamen acantho:
Ornatus Argivæ Helenæ quos illa Mycenis,
Pergama cùm peteret, inconcessosque Hymenæos,
Extulerat: matris Ledæ mirabile donum.
Præterea sceptrum, Ilione quod gesserat olim
Maxima natarum Priami, colloque monile
Baccatum, et duplicem gemmis auroque coronam
Hæc celerans, iter ad naves tendebat Achates.
At Cytherea novas artes, nova pectore versat
Consilia. ut faciem mutatus et ora Cupido
Pro dulci Ascanio veniat, donisque furentem
Incendat reginam, atque ossibus implicet ignem.
Quippe domum timet ambiguam, Tyriosque bilingues.
Urit atrox Juno, et sub noctem cura recursat.
Ergò his aligerum dictis affatur Amorem:
Nate, meæ vires, mea magna potentia; solus,
Nate, patris summi qui tela Typhoëa temnis:
Ad te confugio, et supplex tua numina posco.
Frater ut Æneas pelago tuus omnia circum
Litora jactetur, odiis Junonis iniquæ,
Nota tibi: et nostro doluisti sæpe dolore.

650. Quos illa extulerat è Mycenis, cùm peteret

653. Præterea *jubet eum ferre* sceptrum, quod Ilione maxima

656. Achates celerans *ferre* hæc

658. Ut Cupido mutatus *quoad* faciem, et ora veniat pro

664. O nate, meæ vires, mea magna potentia; O nate, qui solus temnis

667. *Hæc* nota *sunt* tibi, ut tuus frater Æneas jactetur pelago

NOTES.

figures, and with gold—with golden figures, by Hendiadis. *Velamen circumtextum:* a vail woven round.

650. *Ornatus Argivæ:* the ornaments of Grecian Helen. According to the poets, Helen was the daughter of Jupiter, and Leda, the wife of Tyndarus, king of Laconia. She produced two eggs: from one of them sprung Pollux and Hellen; from the other, Castor and Clytemnestra. Horace says that Castor and Pollux were from the same egg. Helen married Menelaus, the brother of Agamemnon, king of Mycenæ and Argos. Having become son-in-law to Tyndarus, he succeeded to the throne of Laconia, after the death of Castor and Pollux. Helen is called *Argiva*, either on account of her relationship to the royal family of *Argos*, or because the Greeks in general were sometimes called *Argivi*. *Mycenis. Mycenæ* and *Argos*, the two principal cities of Greece, are sometimes put for Greece in general, by synec. See also nom. prop. under *Helen*.

651. *Pergama:* Troy. See 466, supra. *Inconcessos Hymenæos:* unlawful match—marriage.

653. *Ilione:* the eldest (*maxima natarum*) of the daughters of Priam. She was married to Polymnestor, king of Thrace, and was invested with royal dignity.

654. *Baccatumque monile:* a pearled collar for the neck—a necklace set with pearl. *Coronam duplicem:* a crown double with gems and gold—set with a double row of golden gems; by Hend.

657. *Cytherea:* Venus; so called from *Cythera*, an island in the Peloponnesus, sacred to that goddess.

659. *Furentem reginam:* the loving queen. The queen already in love with Æneas. Cupid was a celebrated deity, the god of love, from the verb *cupio*. The one here spoken of was the son of Jupiter and Venus, and consequently was half brother to Æneas. There were two others of the same name among the ancients. *Furentem:* in the sense of *amantem*. *Furens* signifies, being transported with an inordinate passion, whether of love, or anger.

660. *Implicet:* should apply the fire (of love) to her bones--should entwine it around them.

661. *Ambiguam domum:* the equivocating race, and double-tongued Tyrians. *Bilingues*, either alludes to their speaking both the Phœnician and Libyan languages, or to their notorious perfidy. *Punica fides* was proverbial for deceit and perfidy. *Domum:* in the sense of *gentem*.

662. *Urit:* troubles her.

663. *Amorem:* Cupid. He is represented as a winged infant, naked, and armed with a bow and quiver full of arrows.

665. *Typhoëa:* an adj. from *Typhoëus*, one of the giants that made war against the gods. Jupiter struck him with a thunderbolt, and laid him under mount Ætna. *Typhoëa arma:* the thunder-bolts of Jove. These words very forcibly express the irresistible power of love.

666. *Numina:* in the sense of *opem*, vel *auxilium*.

668. *Iniquæ:* in the sense of *iratæ*, vel *infensæ*. See 4 and 27, supra.

Hunc Phœnissa tenet Dido, blandisque moratur
Vocibus: et vereor, quò se Junonia vertant
Hospitia: haud tanto cessabit cardine rerum.
Quocircà capere antè dolis et cingere flammâ
Reginam meditor: ne quo se numine mutet;
Sed magno Æneæ mecum teneatur amore.
Quà facere id possis, nostram nunc accipe mentem.
Regius, accitu chari genitoris, ad urbem
Sidoniam puer ire parat, mea maxima cura,
Dona ferens pelago et flammis restantia Trojæ.
Hunc ego sopitum somno, super alta Cythera,
Aut super Idalium, sacratâ sede recondam.
Ne quà scire dolos, mediusve occurrere possit.
Tu faciem illius, noctem non ampliùs unam,
Falle dolo: et notos pueri puer indue vultus,
Ut, cùm te gremio accipiet lætissima Dido,
Regales inter mensas laticemque Lyæum,
Cùm dabit amplexus, atque oscula dulcia figet;
Occultum inspires ignem, fallasque veneno.
Paret Amor dictis charæ genitricis, et alas
Exuit, et gressu gaudens incedit Iüli.
At Venus Ascanio placidam per membra quietem
Irrigat: et fotum gremio Dea tollit in altos
Idaliæ lucos, ubi mollis amaracus illum

677. Regius puer, mea maxima cura, parat ire ad

684. *Tu* puer indue notos vultus pueri, ut, cùm Dido

688. Fallasque *eam* veneno *amoris*

692. Et Dea tollit *eum* fotum in altos

NOTES.

670. *Phœnissa:* Dido. She is here called a *Phœnician*, or woman of *Phœnicia.* This was a country extending along the eastern shore of the Mediterranean, including Tyre and Sidon. The Phœnicians were among the earliest navigators, and are said to have been the inventors of letters. *Blandis:* kind—smooth words. *Tenet:* in the sense of *detinet.*

671. *Quò Junonia.* The hospitality and friendship which Æneas received at Carthage, are here called *Junonian;* either because Juno may be considered the goddess, as well as Jupiter the god, of hospitality; or because she was the special guardian and protectress of Carthage. Venus fears lest this hospitality of Juno may turn to the destruction of Æneas and his friends.

672. *Tanto cardine rerum:* in so great a crisis, or juncture of affairs.

674. *Meditor antecapere:* I contemplate to take possession of the queen beforehand by stratagem, and to besiege her with the flame of love. This is a metaphor taken from the manner of blocking up a town, by planting fires around the walls to prevent any from making their escape. *Ne mutet:* lest Dido should change herself through the influence of any god—should change her mind through the influence of Juno.

676. *Accipe:* hear my opinion.

678. *Sidoniam:* an adj. from *Sidon*, a city of Phœnicia, belonging to Tyre. Dido and the Carthaginians were a colony from Tyre. Hence *Sidonia* vel *Tyria urbs*, for Carthage.

679. *Restantia:* in the sense of *servata.*

680. *Recondam hunc:* I will conceal him in a sacred place, laid in sleep, &c. *Cythera:* neu. plu. an island lying southward of the Peloponnesus, sacred to Venus. *Idalium*, or *Idalia:* a town and grove in the island of Cyprus, sacred to Venus. Hence she is sometimes called *Idalæa.*

682. *Nequâ possit:* lest by some means he could know the deceit, or intervene, to prevent the success of the plan.

684. *Falle dolo:* counterfeit, through artifice, his appearance for one night, and no more.

686. *Lyæum laticem:* simply, wine.—Lyæus, a name of Bacchus, derived from the Greek. *Mensas:* in the sense of *epulas*, vel *dapes*, by meton.

687. *Figet:* and she shall give you sweet kisses—shall press your sweet lips. *Inspires:* in the sense of *insinues. Fallas veneno.* Heyne takes these words in the sense of; *per fraudem instilles venenum.*

692. *Irrigat placidam:* diffuses a placid rest through, &c. *Fotum gremio:* pressed to her bosom.

693. *Amaracus:* the herb marjoram. It was said to be baneful to serpents, and therefore a very proper bed for Ascanius. It abounded in Cyprus. *Mollis:* in the sense of *dulcis*

Floribus et dulci aspirans complectitur umbrâ.
Jamque ibat dicto parens, et dona Cupido
Regia portabat Tyriis, duce lætus Achate.
Cùm venit, aulæis jam se Regina superbis
Aureâ composuit spondâ, mediamque locavit.
Jam Pater Æneas, et jam Trojana juventus
Conveniunt, stratoque super discumbitur ostro.
Dant famuli manibus lymphas, Cereremque canistris
Expediunt, tonsisque ferunt mantilia villis
Quinquaginta intus famulæ, quibus ordine longo
Cura penum struere, et flammis adolere Penates:
Centum aliæ, totidemque pares ætate ministri,
Qui dapibus mensas onerent, et pocula ponant.
Necnon et Tyrii per limina læta frequentes
Convenêre, toris jussi discumbere pictis.
Mirantur dona Æneæ, mirantur Iülum,
Flagrantesque Dei vultus, simulataque verba;
Pallamque et pictum croceo velamen acantho.
Præcipuè infelix, pesti devota futuræ,
Expleri mentem nequit, ardescitque tuendo

703. Intus *erant* quinquaginta famulæ, quibus *erat* cura struere penum longo ordine, et

705. *Erant* centum aliæ *famulæ*, totidemque ministri

712. Præcipuè infelix Phœnissa devota futuræ pesti nequit

NOTES.

694. *Aspirans:* sending forth a sweet smell—odoriferous.

695. *Cupido parens dicto:* Cupid obeying the command, &c. As Cupid personates Ascanius, he may be said to obey the commands of Æneas, delivered by Achates. This is the sense given to the words by Ruæus. Davidson refers them to Venus.

697. *Regina jam composuit.* The couches were calculated for three persons each. The middle couch was considered the most honorable, and of the seats, the middle one of the middle couch. Here Dido sat down. *Locavitque mediam:* and placed herself in the middle, between Æneas and Cupid, supposed to be Ascanius.

It was usual to have three of these couches at table. Hence *triclinium* came to signify a dining room. *Aulæis* may mean the rich tapestry and curtains that were suspended over the couch on which Dido sat; or the rich coverings of the couch itself. This appears to be the opinion of Ruæus: *In aurea sponda, et magnificis tapetibus,* says he.

700. *Discumbitur:* a verb imp. they sit down upon a couch richly ornamented with purple. Ruæus says, *in purpureis lectis. Ostrum:* the purple color itself, taken as an adj.

702. *Mantilia tonsis:* towels of soft nap—smooth and soft towels; the prep. *è* or *ex* being understood. Or, *tonsis villis* may be put absolutely: the shag, or nap being cut off, would render them smooth. It was a custom to wash before meals; hence, *dant lymphas manibus. Lymphas:* in the sense of *aquam.*

703. *Famulæ.* These were female servants. They are distinguished from the male servants, who are called *ministri.*

704. *Penum:* properly all kinds of provisions and stores. Here the word is taken in a more limited sense. *Adòlere Penates flammis:* to worship the Penates by fire—to burn incense to the Penates. See Geor. ii. 505.

The business of the female servants seems to have been to cook and dress the provisions, and to arrange the several dishes before they were brought upon the table. The other servants spread the table, brought forward the several dishes when prepared, and waited upon the guests at supper.—*Struere penum: instruere et adornare edulia ac cibos,* says Heyne.

705. *Pares ætate:* equal in age—of equal age. *Pocula:* by meton. for wine.

707. *Nec non:* also—in like manner *Frequentes:* in crowds—in great numbers.

708. *Pictis toris:* upon ornamented couches.

709. *Iülum:* Cupid, who came in the form of Iülus, or Ascanius.

710. *Flagrantes:* fresh—glowing *Simulata:* in the sense of *ficta.*

711. *Pictum:* Ruæus says, *intextum.* It is to be taken after *velamen.* When any circumstance depends upon the adj. it is to be taken after the noun.

712. *Devota futuræ:* devoted to future love. It was the plan of Venus all along, that Dido should fall in love with Æneas; she may therefore be said to have been devoted to it. *Pestis* very strongly marks the nature and destructive effects of love, when indulged beyond due bounds.

713. *Expleri:* the pass. in the sense of

Phœnissa: et pariter puero donisque movetur.
Ille, ubi complexu Æneæ colloque pependit,
Et magnum falsi implevit genitoris amorem,
Reginam petit: hæc oculis, hæc pectore toto
Hæret; et interdum gremio fovet, inscia Dido,
Insideat quantus miseræ Deus: at memor ille
Matris Acidaliæ, paulatim abolere Sichæum
Incipit, et vivo tentat prævertere amore
Jampridem resides animos desuetaque corda.
Postquàm prima quies epulis, mensæque remotæ;
Crateras magnos statuunt, et vina coronant.
Fit strepitus tectis, vocemque per ampla volutant
Atria: dependent lychni laquearibus aureis
Incensi: et noctem flammis funalia vincunt.
Hìc Regina gravem gemmis auroque poposcit,
Implevitque mero, pateram; quam Belus, et omnes
A Belo soliti. Tum facta silentia tectis:
Jupiter, (hospitibus nam te dare jura loquuntur)
Hunc lætum Tyriisque diem Trojâque profectis
Esse velis, nostrosque hujus meminisse minores.
Adsit lætitiæ Bacchus dator, et bona Juno:

717. Hæc hæret *in eum cum* oculis, hæc *hæret in eum cum* toto pectore

718. Interdum Dido fovet *eum* gremio, inscia

719. Memor *mandatorum* matris

721. Prævertere vivo amore *Æneæ* resides animos *reginæ*

724. *Ministri* statuunt

728. Regina poposcit pateram gravem

729. Quam Belus, et omnes à Belo soliti *sunt implere*

731. Tum silentia facta *sunt* totis tectis, *Dido inquit:* O Jupiter, (nam *homines* loquuntur te dare jura hospitibus) velis hunc diem esse lætum Tyriisque *iis*que profectis à Trojà

NOTES.

the act. *explere*. Or *expleri quoad mentem*, a Grecism: to be satisfied as to her mind —to satisfy her mind. *Ardescitque:* and she is inflamed with love, while she gazes upon him.

715. *Falsi genitoris:* his pretended, or fictitious father.

717. *Hæc hæret:* she sticks upon him with her eyes—she sticks upon him with her whole heart. This very strongly marks the steadfast attention, with which Dido observed, and gazed upon him.

718. *Fovet:* she hugs him to her bosom.

719. *Insideat:* lies in wait for her, unhappy (ill-fated) woman. This word very forcibly expresses the insidious designs of Cupid.

720. *Acidaliæ.* Venus, so called from a fountain of that name in Beotia, dedicated to the Graces, the daughters of Venus and Bacchus. *Abolere Sichæum:* to obliterate or efface from her mind the memory of Sichæus. He had been the husband of Dido; to whom she had sworn inviolable constancy.

721. *Prævertere:* he endeavors to preoccupy her languid affections, with an ardent love for Æneas, and her heart long since unaccustomed to love: lest Juno should inspire her with hatred toward him, and his friends. *Vivo amore.* Some commentators understood by these words: *a love for a living object*, in opposition to one that is dead, as was Sichæus. Ruæus takes *vivo* in the sense of *vehementi;* and *prævertere*, in the sense of *præoccupare.* Heyne has this remark *Quod occupamus, in eo simul prævertimus alios* (we prevent others) *ne occupent.*

723. *Mensæ:* the tables, by *meton.* the food upon them. *Postquàm prima:* when the first rest was to the feast—when the first course or service was ended. It was customary among the Romans to divide the feast into two courses, and sometimes into three. Hence we find: *prima mensa*, and *secunda mensa.*

724. *Coronant vina.* By this we are to understand that they filled the bowls or goblets to the brim. Some understand by it their dressing or adorning of the bowls with garlands; which was a custom among the Romans on certain occasions. *Volutant:* in the sense of *mittunt.*

726. *Incensi lychni:* lighted lamps hung from the golden ceilings.

727. *Noctem:* the darkness. *Funalia:* torches lighted. *Flammis:* in the sense of *luce.*

728. *Gemmis auroque* in the sense of *aureis gemmis*, by Hend.

729. *Belus.* This cannot be the father of Dido, but some one of her ancestors; perhaps the founder of her family. For otherwise there can be no propriety in the words: *omnes à Belo:* all after Belus. *Mero:* properly *new wine.* Here wine in general.

733. *Minores:* descendents. *Bona:* propitious—kind.

736. *Libavit.* This libation or offering consisted in pouring some drops of wine upon the table at feasts, or upon the altar at sacrifices, as an acknowledgment of the bounty of the gods. *Laticum:* gen. plu. of *latex*, in the sense of *vini*

Et vos, ô cœtum, Tyrii, celebrate faventes.
Dixit: et in mensam laticum libavit honorem:
Primaque libato, summo tenùs attigit ore.
Tum Bitiæ dedit increpitans: ille impiger hausit
Spumantem pateram, et pleno se proluit auro:
Pòst alii proceres. Citharâ crinitus Iopas
Personat auratâ, docuit quæ maximus Atlas
Hic canit errantem Lunam, Solisque labores:
Unde hominum genus, et pecudes: unde imber, et ignes
Arcturum, pluviasque Hyadas, geminosque Triones:
Quid tantùm Oceano properent se tingere soles
Hyberni, vel quæ tardis mora noctibus obstet.
Ingeminant plausum Tyrii, Troësque sequuntur.
Necnon et vario noctem sermone trahebat
Infelix Dido, longumque bibebat amorem;
Multa super Priamo rogitans, super Hectore multa
Nunc, quibus Auroræ venisset filius armis:
Nunc, quales Diomedis equi: nunc, quantus Achilles.
Immò age, et à primâ, dic, hospes, origine nobis
Insidias, inquit, Danaûm, casusque tuorum,
Erroresque tuos: nam te jam septima portat
Omnibus errantem terris et fluctibus æstas.

737 *Eoque* libato, *illa* prima attigit *reliquum vini*

740. Pòst alii proceres *hauserunt*

743. Unde genus hominum *ortum est*, et

744. *Canit* Arcturum

748. Vario sermone *cum Ænea*

751. Quibus armis filius Auroræ venisset *ad Trojam:* nunc quales *essent* equi Diomedis

753. Age, O hospes, et dic nobis à prima origine, insidias

755. Nam jam septima æstas portat te errantem omnibus terris.

NOTES.

737. *Attigit:* she just touched it with her lips. *Tenùs:* in the sense of *tantummodò*. The Roman ladies were not permitted to drink wine except at religious ceremonies. Dido, therefore, takes it, but she does not drink deep. She touches it with her lips: she just tastes it, and no more. *Summo ore:* the extremity of her mouth—her lips. *Hausit:* in the sense of *potavit*. Betias drank off the bowl with so much haste and eagerness, that he wet himself (*proluit se*,) by spilling some of the wine, which ran down his chin and clothes. *Auro:* properly *gold*. Hence by meton. any thing made of gold. Here the golden bowl out of which he drank.

741. *Atlas.* See Æn. 4. 247.

742. *Labores solis:* eclipses of the sun. *Personat:* he sings—plays upon his lyre. *Ignes:* lightning.

744. *Arcturum:* a star in the constellation Bootes, near the tail of the Great Bear. *Hyadas:* these were seven stars in the front of the Bull. See Geor. 1. 138. *Geminos Triones.* These were two Northern signs; formerly called, sometimes, *the greater and less Plough*, because the stars were thought to be in the form of a team of oxen, before a plough. *Pluvias:* in the sense of *imbriferas.*

745. *Quid hyberni soles:* why the winter suns hasten so much to touch themselves in the ocean, or what delay retards the slow nights. Simply: why the winter days are so short, and those of summer so long.

The summer nights may be said to be slow in their coming on, because of the length of the day. They seem to be tardy and reluctant, as if unwilling to arrive.

This song of Iopas is imitated from the Odyssey of Homer. Virgil, however, has surpassed his master. The subject of Homer's song is the actions of Ulysses. But this of Virgil is of the sublimest kind, comprehending the most profound subjects of philosophy.

749. *Infelix Dido:* unhappy Dido drew out the night in various conversation, and drank large draughts of love. Virgil, says Davidson, is always very happy in setting objects in contrast to one another. Here the anxious situation of Dido's lovesick mind is seen in a fine light in opposition to the general mirth. While Tyrians and Trojans give loose to joy, and are making the roofs resound with their repeated acclamations, Æneas alone engages Dido's thoughts and attention. She relishes neither the pleasures of the feast, nor of the song; and can listen to no music, but the charms of his voice. *Bibebat quasi longo haustu*, says Heyne.

750. *Filius Auroræ.* Memnon. See 489 supra. *Super:* about or concerning.

753. *Dic:* by Apocope for *dice*, in the sense of *narra.*

755. *Septima æstas:* the seventh summer. The meaning seems to be: the seventh summer now brings you hither, after you have wandered on every land, and on every sea. *Fluctibus:* in the sense of *maribus.*

QUESTIONS.

What is the character of this book?

When does it open?

Where was Æneas at that time?

What prevented him from proceeding to Italy?

Who caused the storm?

At whose instigation was it raised?

What damage did the fleet of Æneas sustain?

Who assuaged the storm?

Did he render the Trojans any other assistance?

Where did Æneas then direct his course?

After his arrival, how was he received?

Who conducted him to Carthage, and gave him an account of the country?

Having entered the city, to what place does he go first?

Whom does he see there?

What effect had the appearance of Dido upon him?

Are there any episodes in this book?

How many can you mention?

Who were the founders of Troy?

What are its several names?

And from whom derived?

Who was *Dardanus?*

Of what country was he a native?

Of what country was *Teucer* a native?

After Æneas arrived in Italy, whom did he marry?

What city did he build?

What did he call it?

Where was it situated?

Who was Juno?

What is said of her?

What are some of her names?

What were the causes of her resentment against the Trojans?

Where was Carthage situated?

Who was the Guardian Goddess of that city?

What was the prize of beauty?

To whom was it adjudged?

By whom was it adjudged?

Where did Æolus reside?

How do you understand the fable of his being the god of the winds?

In the division of the world between the sons of Saturn, to whom did the empire of the sea fall?

What is Neptune represented as bearing in his hand?

What is the difference between *procella*, *hyems*, *nimbus*, and *imber?*

Are they sometimes used indiscriminately for each other?

Why was Sicily called *Trinacria?*

What are the names of its promontories?

Is the passage between Sicily and Italy dangerous?

What is the cause of it?

Can you explain the fables of *Sylla* and *Charybdis?*

Who was Venus?

What is said of her?

What are some of her names?

For what is the word taken, by meton.?

What part did she take in the affairs of the Trojans?

Does the poet represent her as making any speech in their favor, after their arrival in Africa?

What is the character of that speech?

What does Dr. Trapp say of it?

Who was Antenor?

What did he do?

What city did he build?

Who succeeded Æneas in the government?

What city did Ascanius build?

How long was this city the seat of government?

Who was the mother of Romulus?

Whose daughter was she?

How were Romulus and his brother Remus brought up?

What is the fabulous account?

What is the more probable account?

What was their mode of life?

What did Romulus do as soon as he came to years of maturity?

Where did Romulus found his city?

What was the end of Remus?

What gave rise to the quarrel between the brothers?

What other name had Romulus?

From what is it derived?

Who were the Amazons?

From what is the name derived?

Are they supposed to have been altogether a fabulous people?

Who was their queen in the time of the Trojan war?

What were the several names of Italy?

From what were they derived?

Who were the *Pelasgi* properly?

For whom is the word sometimes used?

What was *Pergama* properly?

For what was the word used by synec.?

What is the last episode in this book?

What are the subjects of that song?

From whom is it imitated?

What are the subjects of Homer's song?

How does this book conclude?

LIBER SECUNDUS.

Dido having desired Æneas to relate to her the sufferings of his countrymen, he proceeds to the mournful subject. He informs her that the city was taken after a siege of ten years, through the treachery of Sinon, and the stratagem of a wooden horse: that it was his determination not to survive the ruins of his country, till otherwise advised by Hector's ghost, and the appearance of his mother Venus: that he then conceived the plan of leaving his country, and seeking a settlement in another land. He then informs her of his carrying his aged father upon his shoulders, while his little son followed by his side, and his wife Creüsa at some distance behind: that when he came to the place of general rendezvous, he found a great concourse of people ready to engage in any enterprise: that here he misses his wife, and, frantic with despair, he resolved to rescue her, at the peril of his life. For this purpose he returned to the city; but, in the adventure, her ghost appeared to him, quieted his mind, and informed him of the land destined to him by fate. He also relates the particulars of his own adventures in that fatal night, when the powerful kingdom of Priam fell to the ground. This book may justly be considered the most interesting one of the whole Æneid; and was one of the six which the poet himself read in the presence of Augustus and Octavia.

CONTICUERE omnes, intentique ora tenebant.
Inde toro pater Æneas sic orsus ab alto:
Infandum, Regina, jubes renovare dolorem:
4. *Narrando* ut Danai — Trojanas ut opes, et lamentabile regnum
Eruerint Danai; quæque ipse miserrima vidi,
7. Aut *quis* miles Myrmidounm — Et quorum pars magna fui. Quis talia fando,
Myrmidonum, Dolopumve, aut duri miles Ulyssei,

NOTES.

2. *Toro:* the couch on which he sat at supper. *Orsus:* began. From the verb *ordior. Est* is to be supplied.

3. *Ut:* in the sense of *quomodo. Opes:* in the sense of *potentiam. Lamentabile:* in the sense of *plorandum.*

5. *Danai:* the Greeks, so called from *Danaus,* one of their kings. *Quæque miserrima ipse:* both what things (scenes) the most pitiable I myself saw, and those of which I was a principal part.

7. *Myrmidonum.* The Myrmidons were the troops of Achilles. *Dolopum.* The Dolopians were the troops of Phenix; or, as some say, of Pyrrhus, the son of Achilles. *Ulyssei.* Ulysses was the son of *Laërtes,* and Anticlea, king of the islands of *Ithaca* and *Dulachium.* He married Penelope, the daughter of Icarus, a virtuous and amiable woman, with whom he lived for a time in great happiness and domestic enjoyment.

After the rape of Helen by Paris, he was summoned by the other princes of Greece, to the war that had been resolved upon against Troy. Unwilling to leave his kingdom and beloved wife, he pretended to be insane: and yoking an ox and an horse together, he went ploughing the shore, which he sowed with salt. But he was detected by Pelamides, a wise and eminent statesman, in this manner. He took his son Telemachus, then a child, and laid him before the plough of his father, who turned it aside to save his son. He was obliged to go to Troy, where he distinguished himself both by his valor, his prudence, and his sagacity. By his means, Achilles was discovered among the daughters of Lycomedes, king of the island of Scyros, under whose guardianship his mother had placed him; and Philoctetes was obliged to leave Lemnos, and take with him the arrows of Hercules; without which it was said Troy could not be taken.

He performed many daring achievements, and executed many hazardous enterprises. After the death of Achilles, he was rewarded with the arms of that hero. On his return home, he was exposed to many dangers, hardships, and misfortunes, during the space of ten years. After an absence of twenty years, he arrived in his kingdom, to the great joy of his constant wife. He is said to have been slain by Telegonus, a son of his by the sorceress Circe.

During his absence, his wife had many suitors, whom she put off by telling them

Temperet à lachrymis? et jam nox humida cœlo
Præcipitat, suadentque cadentia sidera somnos
Sed, si tantus amor casus cognoscere nostros,
Et breviter Trojæ supremum audire laborem;
Quanquam animus meminisse horret, luctuque refugit,
Incipiam. Fracti bello, fatisque repulsi
Ductores Danaûm, tot jam labentibus annis,
Instar montis equum, divinâ Pallidis arte,
Ædificant: sectâque intexunt abiete costas.
Votum pro reditu simulant: ea fama vagatur.
Huc delecta virûm sortiti corpora furtim
Includunt cæco lateri: penitùsque cavernas
Ingentes, uterumque armato milite complent.
Est in conspectu Tenedos, notissima famâ
Insula, dives opum, Priami dum regna manebant:

10. Si tantus amor *sit tibi*

17. Simulant *equum esse* votum pro reditu *domum*

18. *Illi* sortiti delecta

NOTES.

that she could not comply with their wishes, until she had finished a piece of work which was then in her loom; but which she was careful not to do: for she undid in the night what she did in the day. By this device she continued faithful to her husband.

The return of Ulysses to his native land, and the adventures of Telemachus in search of his father, form the basis of the Odyssey.

9. *Cadentia sidera.* In the language of poetry, the stars may be said to set, when they disappear at the approach of day; and they are said to rise, when they become visible, at the approach of night. From this, we are to understand that it was near morning, when Æneas entered upon the mournful subject. *Suadent:* invite to sleep.

11. *Laborem:* struggle. Heyne says, *cladem, ipsum excidium urbis.*

12. *Horret:* shudders at, or dreads, the recollection. *Refugit luctu.* The verb here is in the perfect tense. As soon as his mind was turned to the mournful subject, it shrunk back, and revolted from it. This change of tense is an elegance: it marks the quickness of the impression upon his mind. The verb *refugio* forms the third person of the present and perfect of the indicative, *refugit.* The penult of the former is short, of the latter long, as in the present case. Some read *Luctumque refugit:* declines the mournful task; which is the same sentiment.

13. *Repulsi.* The Greeks are here said to be repulsed by the fates, because it was decreed that Troy could not be taken till the expiration of ten years, from the commencement of the siege. *Fracti:* disheartened.

15. *Instar montis.* It hath been objected that this story of the horse has not probability enough to support it; that, besides the hardiness of the enterprise, it is not to be supposed that the Trojans would receive within their walls so enormous and suspicious an engine with so implicit credulity. But the poet, as Mons. Segrais observes, has finely contrived the matter, so as to render it not only plausible, but in a manner necessary and unavoidable.

The Trojans, having heard the story of Sinon, and seeing so strong a confirmation of the truth of it in the terrible disasters that befel Laocoon and his sons, had every reason to believe the machine was an offering sacred to Minerva, and that all who offered violence to it should feel the vengeance of heaven, as Laocoon and his sons had done; and therefore they could not act otherwise than the poet supposes them to have done, consistently with their religion, and system of belief. As to the hardiness of the undertaking on the part of the Greeks, M. Segrais observes, that modern history furnishes examples of equally hardy enterprises, undertaken and executed with success. He instances the Hollanders, forty of whom ventured to conceal themselves in a vessel, seemingly laden with turf, and underwent those examinations which are usually made for contraband goods, and having landed, retook the town of Breda from the Spaniards.

16. *Intexunt:* they line or cover the ribs. *Costas.* These were the timbers that gave form and figure to the horse—the frame. *Sectâ abiete:* with sawn fir—with planks or boards of fir.

17 *Fama:* in the sense of *rumor.*

18. *Sortiti delecta corpora:* having chosen a select body of men, they privately shut them up, &c. *Sortiti:* properly, having chosen by lot.

19. *Penitùs:* in its inmost recesses.

21. *Tenedos:* an island lying opposite Troy, not far from the promontory of *Sigæum*, and about forty stadia from the main land.

24. *Ductores Danaûm* provecti
25. Nos rati *sumus eos* abiisse.
30. Hìc *erat* locus
31. Pars *nostrum* stupet
34. Sive *faciebat id* dolo, seu
35. Capys, et *illi* quorum menti *erat* melior sententia, jubent aut præcipitare
40. Ibi Laocoon primus ante omnes decurrit
42. Et procul *exclamat:* quæ tanta insania *est vobis*
44. *An est* Ulysses sic notus *vobis*

Nunc tantùm sinus, et statio malefida carinis :
Huc se provecti deserto in litore condunt.
Nos abiisse rati, et vento petiisse Mycenas.
Ergò omnis longo solvit se Teucria luctu :
Panduntur portæ : juvat ire, et Dorica castra,
Desertosque videre locos, litusque relictum.
Hìc Dolopum manus, hìc sævus tendebat Achilles
Classibus hìc locus : hìc acies certare solebant.
Pars stupet innuptæ donum exitiale Minervæ,
Et molem mirantur equi : primusque Thymœtes
Duci intra muros hortatur, et arce locari ;
Sive dolo, seu jam Trojæ sic fata ferebant.
At Capys, et quorum melior sententia menti,
Aut pelago Danaûm insidias suspectaque dona,
Præcipitare jubent, subjectisve urere flammis
Aut terebrare cavas uteri et tentare latebras.
Scinditur incertum studia in contraria vulgus.
Primus ibi ante omnes, magnâ comitante catervâ,
Laocoon ardens summâ decurrit ab arce :
Et procul : O miseri, quæ tanta insania, cives ?
Creditis avectos hostes ? aut ulla putatis
Dona carere dolis Danaûm ? sic notus Ulysses ?
Aut hoc inclusi ligno occultantur Achivi :
Aut hæc in nostros fabricata est machina muros,

NOTES.

23. *Malefida:* unsafe for ships. *Carinis:* the keels: by synec. the whole ships.

26. *Omnis Teucria:* all Troy: the name of the place put, by meton. for the inhabitants. See Æn. i. 1.

27. *Dorica:* an adj. from *Doris*, a country of Greece, situated between Ætolia, Phocis, and Thessaly ; by synec. for Greece in general.

29. *Tendebat:* pitched his camp. Ruæus says, *habebat tentoria. Manus Dolopum:* simply, the Dolopians.

30. *Acies:* is properly an army drawn up in order of battle: *agmen*, an army in order of march, from *ago: exercitus*, an army in order of exercise, from *exerceo*. But they are often used indiscriminately.

32. *Thymœtes.* It is said he married the sister of Hecuba, the wife of Priam, by whom he had a son, born on the same day with Paris. Priam being informed by an oracle that on that day a child was born, who should be the cause of the destruction of Troy, interpreted it against the son of Thymœtes, and caused him to be put to death. On this account, it is supposed, that he entertained a grudge against Priam, and acted the part of a traitor to his country. He was one of Priam's counsellors.

33. *Duci:* the inf. pass. of *ducor*. *Equum* is understood before it.

34. *Fata:* destiny—fate. *Ferebant:* in the sense of *velebant*.

35. *At Capys:* but Capys, and others, to whose mind there was a better judgment, advised, &c.

Capys accompanied Æneas on his voyage, and was one of his chief men. He afterwards founded *Capua*, in Italy, which was a long time a rival of Rome, in wealth and splendor.

37. *Subjectis-ve.* The common reading is *subjectisque*. The former is to be preferred. Valpy reads *subjectis-ve.*

38. *Terebrare:* to lay open and examine the hollow recesses of the womb.

39. *Incertum:* fickle—inconstant. *Contraria studia:* into different sentiments, or opinions. Some were in favor of the measure proposed, others were against it.

40. *Ante.* Ruæus interprets this by *coram*, in the presence of all. Davidson thinks it implies that Laocoon was the first, or principal (*primus*) person among those who opposed the admission of the horse into the city. Heyne thinks we are to understand that Laocoon ran before—outran the rest. *Ante*, signifies, before, with respect to time, place, and degree. Laocoon, some say, was the brother of Anchises; others say, he was the son of Priam, and priest of Apollo.

41. *Ardens:* eager. Ruæus says *celer*.

43. *Avectos:* in the sense of *profectos*. The verb *esse* is understood.

Inspectura domos, venturaque desuper urbi;
Aut aliquis latet error: equo ne credite, Teucri.
Quicquid id est, timeo Danaos et dona ferentes
Sic fatus, validis ingentem viribus hastam
In latus, inque feri curvam compagibus alvum
Contorsit: stetit illa tremens, uteroque recusso
Insonuere cavæ gemitumque dedêre cavernæ.
Et, si fata Deûm, si mens non læva fuisset,
Impulerat ferro Argolicas fœdare latebras:
Trojaque, nunc stares, Priamique arx alta, maneres!
Ecce manus juvenem intereà post terga revinctum
Pastores magno ad regem clamore trahebant
Dardanidæ: qui se ignotum venientibus ultrò,
Hoc ipsum ut strueret, Trojamque aperiret Achivis,
Obtulerat fidens animi, atque in utrumque paratus,
Seu versare dolos, seu certæ occumbere morti.
Undique visendi studio Trojana juventus
Circumfusa ruit, certantque illudere capto.
Accipe nunc Danaûm insidias; et crimine ab uno
Disce omnes.
Namque, ut conspectu in medio turbatus, inermis
Constitit, atque oculis Phrygia agmina circumspexit:
Heu, quæ nunc tellus, inquit, quæ me æquora possunt
Accipere! aut quid jam misero mihi denique restat!
Cui neque apud Danaos usquam locus; insuper ipsi

50. Sic fatus, validis viribus contorsit ingentem

54. Si fata Deûm *non fuissent adversa*

55. *Ille* impulerat *nos* fœdare

57. Ecce, intereà Dardanidæ pastores magno clamore trahebant ad regem juvenem revinctum *quoad* manus post terga; qui ultrò obtulerat se ignotum *illis*

63. Visendi *illius*

67. Ut *Sinon* constitit

NOTES.

47. *Inspectura:* about to overlook our houses, and to come down upon the city. It was higher than the walls and houses, and might, with propriety, be said to overlook them, and to come down upon the city —to make an attack upon it.

48. *Error:* guile, deceit, or trick. It properly signifies whatever is opposed to truth.

49. *Et:* in the sense of *etiam:* I fear the Greeks even offering presents. There is a peculiar emphasis to be placed upon the *et* in this instance.

51. *Feri:* the horse. *Ferus* does not always signify a wild beast, or beast of prey: it signifies a tame or domesticated animal also. He struck that part of the horse, where the timbers or ribs arose from their horizontal to a perpendicular position *Curvam compagibus:* bending out in seams or joints. *Juncturis*, says Ruæus. *Recusso:* in the sense of *repercusso.*

53. *Gemitum.* This groan probably was made by the Greeks within, who now began to be alarmed at their situation.

54. *Fata:* decrees, or purposes of the gods.

55. *Argolicas:* an adj. from *Argos*, a city of Greece, situated in the Peloponnesus; by sync. sometimes put for Greece in general. *Latebras:* hiding places—recesses. *Trojaque*, &c. This is a happy apostrophe: had we taken his advice—had our minds not been stupid and infatuated; now O Troy, thou wouldst be standing, and thou, lofty citadel of Priam, wouldst be remaining! *Fœdare:* in the sense of *excindere.*

59. *Dardanidæ:* the Trojans; so called from *Dardanus*, one of their founders. It is here used as an adj.

60. *Strueret:* in the sense of *efficeret.*

61. *Fidens animi:* bold—daring of soul. and prepared for either event; to carry into execution his purpose, (*versare dolos;*) or, in case of discovery, to yield to certain death. He threw himself a stranger, and unknown, in the way of these shepherds, on purpose that they might take him, and bring him before Priam and the Trojan chiefs, the better to effect his purpose, to persuade them to admit the horse within their city.

64. *Circumfusa:* surrounding him—encompassing him on every side: a part. from *circumfundor.* *Capto:* in the sense of *captivo.*

65. *Accipe:* in the sense of *audi.* *Ab uno crimine:* from one criminal person, (namely, Sinon,) learn the character of all the Greeks. This appears to be the sense in which Heyne takes the words. Valpy says: "From this instance of deceit and treachery," &c. Davidson: "From one crime, take a specimen of the whole nation." *Crimen:* properly a crime; by meton. a criminal, or villanous person.

66. *In medio conspectu:* in the midst of the gazing crowd.

73. Quo gemitu *nostri* animi *sunt* conversi, et.
74. *Eum* fari, *ex* quo sanguine cretus *sit;* memoret, quid ferat, quæ-ve
78. Me *cretum esse* de Argolica
79. Hoc *est* primum: nec, si improba fortuna finxit Sinonem
83. Quem* insontem Pelasgi demisere neci sub falsa proditione, infando
85. *At* nunc lugent *eum*
87. *Meus* pater pauper misit me comitem illi, et
88. Dum *Palamides* stabat

Dardanidæ infensi pœnas cum sanguine poscunt.
Quo gemitu conversi animi, compressus et omnis
Impetus: hortamur fari, quo sanguine cretus;
Quidve ferat, memoret, quæ sit fiducia capto.
Ille hæc, depositâ tandem formidine, fatur:
Cuncta equidem tibi, Rex, fuerint quæcunque, fatebor,
Vera, inquit: neque me Argolicâ de gente negabo;
Hoc primum: nec si miserum fortuna Sinonem
Finxit, vanum etiam mendacemque improba finget.
Fando aliquid si fortè tuas pervenit ad aures
Belidæ nomen Palamedis, et inclyta famâ
Gloria: quem falsâ sub proditione Pelasgi.
Insontem, infando indicio, quia bella vetabat,
Demisere neci; nunc cassum lumine lugent:
Illi me comitem, et consanguinitate propinquum,
Pauper in arma pater primis huc misit ab annis.
Dum stabat regno incolumis, regnumque vigebat
Consiliis, et nos aliquod nomenque decusque

NOTES.

74. *Impetus:* fury—violence. *Compressus:* restrained. The verb *est* is understood.

75. *Memoret:* in the sense of *dicat. Quid ferat:* what message or news he brought, or what confidence there might be placed in him, a captive. This is the sense usually given to the words; but Valpy gives them another turn: "What he might have to relate in his own defence, and what ground he had for hoping for mercy, now he was a prisoner."

77. *Cuncta vera:* the whole truth—all things true. Heyne and Valpy read, *quodcunque fuerit*, for *quæcunque*, &c.

80. *Vanum:* in the sense of *fallacem. Finxit:* hath made, or rendered. *Improba:* in the sense of *adversa.*

81. *Si fortè, fando aliquid:* if by chance, by common report, the name of, &c. *Fando aliquid:* the same as *dum aliquid dicitur. Narratione aliorum*, says Heyne.

82. *Belidæ Palamedis.* Palamedes was the son of Nauplius king of Eubœa, an island in the Ægean sea, and descended from *Belus*, a king of Africa, by *Amymone*, the daughter of Danaus. Ulysses, to avoid going to the Trojan war, pretended to be insane; but the deception was discovered by Palamedes. See note 7, supra. This, Ulysses never forgave, and finally he wrought his ruin, by accusing him of holding a correspondence with Priam. To support this charge, he forged letters from Priam to Palamedes, which he pretended to have intercepted. He also conveyed gold to his tent, pretending it was sent from Priam as a bribe. Upon which Palamedes was accused of treason, and stoned to death.

The whole of Sinon's speech is artful, and calculated to impose upon his audience, being made up, partly of truth, and partly of falsehood. What he says of himself is downright falsehood; what he says of Palamedes is in substance true. His death might have been known to the Trojans by common report, (*fando aliquid*,) though the circumstances of it might not have been. By relating them, therefore, he could not fail of becoming interesting, of gaining a favorable reception, and of preparing the way for the accomplishment of his purpose.

83. *Sub falsa proditione:* under a false accusation of treachery—treason. This alludes to the letters, which Ulysses forged, mentioned above. *Pelasgi.* See Æn. i. 624.

84. *Infando indicio.* This alludes to the gold, which Ulysses conveyed to his tent, and pretended to have been sent him by Priam. This was adduced in evidence against him: we may therefore render *infando indicio:* upon an iniquitous evidence. *Quia vetabat bella.* This was false: so far from Palamedes being opposed to the war against Troy, that he was among the first to promote it.

85. *Cassum lumine:* deprived of the light of life. *Demisere:* they condemned to death.

86. *Illi me comitem.* Here, too, Sinon speaks falsely. So far from his being a relation of *Palamedes*, he was the relation of Ulysses, whose mother was the sister of Æsinus, the father of Sinon.

87. *Ab primis annis:* not from his infancy, but from the first years of his bearing arms, which among the Romans was at the age of seventeen. *Arma:* by meton. war.

88. *Regno. Regnum* may either mean the kingdom of Eubœa, where his father reigned; or the confederate power and council of the Grecian states, that had leagued together for the destruction of Troy.

Gessimus: invidiâ postquam pellacis Ulyssei
(Haud ignota loquor) superis concessit ab oris;
Afflictus vitam in tenebris luctuque trahebam,
Et casum insontis mecum indignabar amici.
Nec tacui demens: et me, fors si qua tulisset,
Si patrios unquam remeâssem victor ad Argos,
Promisi ultorem, et verbis odia aspera movi.
Hinc mihi prima mali labes: hinc semper Ulysses
Criminibus terrere novis: hinc spargere voces
In vulgum ambiguas, et quærere conscius arma.
Nec requievit enim, donec Calchante ministro—
Sed quid ego hæc autem nequicquam ingrata revolvo?
Quidve moror? si omnes uno ordine habetis Archivos,
Idque audire sat est; jamdudum sumite pœnas.
Hoc Ithacus velit, et magno mercentur Atridæ.
Tum verò ardemus scitari, et quærere causas,
Ignari scelerum tantorum artisque Pelasgæ.
Prosequitur pavitans, et ficto pectore fatur:
Sæpe fugam Danai Trojâ cupiere relictâ

92. *Ego* afflictus trahebam vitam

94. Et promisi *me fore* ultorem, si qua fors tulisset, si unquam

97. Hinc Ulysses *sævit* semper

104. Magno *pretio*. Tum verò *nos* ignari tantorum

NOTES.

90. *Gessimus aliquod:* I also bore some reputation and honor. *Et:* in the sense of *etiam*. *Nos:* for *ego*.

91. *Ab superis oris:* from the upper regions—this upper world. *Concessit:* in the sense of *decessit*.

93. *Indignabar:* I grieved, or repined at the death of my innocent friend.

94. *Demens nec tacui:* I, a fool, did not hold my peace. *Demens*, compounded of *de* and *mens*. *Si qua fors:* if any opportunity or chance should present. *Tulisset:* in the sense of *obtulisset*.

95. *Remeâssem:* in the sense of *rediissem*.

97. *Hinc mihi prima:* hence the first source of misfortune to me. *Labes*, properly signifies a stain, or blemish. An allusion is here made to the first appearance of a plague or contagious disease breaking out upon the surface of the body in spots. Sinon's declaration that he would avenge the death of Palamedes roused the bitter resentment of Ulysses; and from that time, (*hinc*,) he began to plot his destruction. *Labes:* in the sense of *origo*, vel *causa*. *Fuit* is understood.

98. *Novis criminibus:* with new charges or accusations. *Voces:* in the sense of *verba*, vel *sermones*.

99. *Conscius:* conscious, (of his crime—that he was guilty of the death of Palamedes,) he began to seek the means of destroying me also. *Arma:* the means or implements by which any thing is done. Valpy says: the means of defence against Sinon.

100. *Calchante ministro:* Calchas being his assistant—being employed. Calchas was a famous soothsayer in the Grecian camp, and nothing of any moment was done without his being consulted. This sudden pause and transition are very artfully contrived, and show the great judgment of the poet in the management of his subject. *Requievit:* in the sense of *cessavit*. *Enim:* in the sense of *equidem*.

101. *Autem:* here is an expletive; or used in the sense of *verè*, vel *equidem*. *Revolvo:* in the sense of *narro*. *Nequicquam:* in vain—to no purpose: because the relation of those unpleasant topics would not save his life. *Habetis:* if ye regard or consider. *Uno ordine:* on one footing—in the same state, or condition of enemies.

103. *Jamdudum*. This is to be taken in the sense of *jam*. Or we must suppose, as Dr. Trapp observes, something to be understood. *Sumite pœnas jamdudum debetas*, or the like.

104. *Ithacus*. Ulysses is so called from *Ithaca*, a barren and rocky island in the Ionian sea, where he was born, and where his father *Laërtes* reigned. Sinon gives this appellation to him by way of contempt. *Atridæ:* Agamemnon and Menelaus, the sons of Atreus. Their religion required that a devoted victim that had escaped from the altar, should be put to death wherever found: and Sinon having been destined as a victim to the gods, to procure favorable winds for their return, nothing could afford the Greeks in general, and the leaders in particular greater joy, than to hear that the Trojans had put him to death. *Hoc velit:* this, Ulysses wishes, and the sons of Atreus will purchase it at a great price.

106. *Artis:* in the sense of *fraudis* *Pelasgæ:* Grecian See Æn. i. 624

Moliri, et longo fessi discedere bello.
Fecissentque utinam. Sæpe illos aspera ponti
Interclusit hyems, et terruit Auster euntes.
Præcipuè, cùm jam hic trabibus contextus acernis
Staret equus, toto sonuerunt æthere nimbi.
Suspensi Eurypylum scitatum oracula Phœbi
Mittimus: isque adytis hæc tristia dicta reportat
Sanguine placâstis ventos, et virgine cæsâ,
Cùm primùm Iliacas, Danai, venistis ad oras:
Sanguine quærendi reditus, animâque litandum
Argolicâ. Vulgi quæ vox ut venit ad aures,
Obstupuere animi, gelidusque per ima cucurrit
Ossa tremor; cui fata parent, quem poscat Apollo
Hìc Ithacus vatem magno Calchanta tumultu
Protrahit in medios: quæ sint ea numina Divûm,
Flagitat: et mihi jam multi crudele canebant
Artificis scelus, et taciti ventura videbant.
Bis quinos silet ille dies, tectusque recusat
Prodere voce suâ quemquam, aut opponere morti.
Vix tandem magnis Ithaci clamoribus actus,
Compositò rumpit vocem, et me destinat aræ.

110. Aspera hyems ponti interclusit, et Auster terruit illos euntes.

116. O Danai, *vos* placâstis

118. Reditus *sunt* quærendi

119. Ut quæ vox venit

121. *Omnes sunt soliciti noscere*, cui fata parent *mortem*

NOTES.

109. *Moliri fugam:* in the sense of *efficere fugam.*

110. *Aspera hyems:* a violent storm at sea.

112. *Contextus:* framed, or built of maple timber. Some part of the horse might have been built of maple, others of fir and pine: so that the poet may be consistent in what he says of this same machine, verse 15: *Intexunt costas sectâ abiete;* and also in verse 258, infra, where he calls it, *pinea claustra.*

113. *Sonuerunt:* raged—roared. *Nimbi: turbines,* says Heyne. See Æn. i. 102.

114. *Suspensi:* in suspense we send Eurypulus. Homer informs us that he was a famous augur, and brought with him forty ships to the Trojan war. *Scitatum:* to consult; a sup. in *um,* from the verb *scitor,* put after *mittimus,* a verb of motion.

115. *Adytis.* Adytum was the most secret, as well as the most sacred place of the temple, and where the images of the gods were placed—the shrine from which the responses were delivered. It is governed by the preposition *à* or *ab,* understood.

116. *Placâstis ventos:* ye appeased the winds with blood, and a virgin slain, when, &c.

The Greeks, on their way to the siege of Troy, came to *Aulis,* a port of Beotia, where Diana, incensed against Agamemnon for killing one of her favorite deer, withheld the wind. Upon which Calchas was sent to consult the oracle upon the subject. He brought back the answer that *Iphigenia,* the daughter of Agamemnon, must be sacrificed to appease the anger of the goddess. When the virgin was brought to the altar, he informed them that Diana was satisfied with that act of submission; but demanded that the virgin should be transported to *Tauris,* and there serve her in capacity of priestess. *The virgin was slain* in intention, and saved only by the interposition of the goddess. This warrants the expression of the poet, *Virgine cæsa.*

118. *Litandum:* a ger. in *dum* of the verb *lito:* an atonement must be made with the life of a Greek. Ruæus interprets it by *sacrificandum.* But it implies more than simply to offer sacrifice; it includes the idea of expiation, or atonement. The gerund in *dum* has a peculiar signification. While it has the form of a noun, it retains the nature of the verb; and implies the *necessity, duty, or obligation, to do, or perform an action.*

123. *Numina Divûm:* the will, purpose, or response of the gods. *Numen,* from the verb *nuo:* I express my will by a nod.

124. *Et jam:* and now many foretold to me the atrocious design, or plot, of the villanous man.

125. *Taciti:* not silent; for that would contradict what is said just before: but quiet, content, well satisfied. *Ventura:* in the sense of *res venturas.* The best reason why *canere* came to signify *to prophesy,* or *to foretell,* is, that the responses of oracles were at first delivered, and written in verse.

126. *Tectus:* in the sense of *occultatus.*

127. *Prodere:* in the sense of *designare. Opponere:* in the sense of *damnare.*

128. *Tandem vix actus:* at length, with difficulty forced or compelled, &c.

129. *Rumpit vocem:* he opens his mouth.

Assensere omnes: et, quæ sibi quisque timebat,
Unius in miseri exitium conversa tulere.
Jamque dies infanda aderat: mihi sacra parari,
Et salsæ fruges, et circum tempora vittæ.
Eripui, fateor, leto me, et vincula rupi:
Limosoque lacu per noctem obscurus in ulvâ
Delitui, dum vela darent, si fortè dedissent.
Nec mihi jam patriam antiquam spes ulla videndi,
Nec dulces natos exoptatumque parentem:
Quos illi fors ad pœnas ob nostra reposcent
Effugia, et culpam hanc miserorum morte piabunt.
Quòd te, per Superos et conscia numina veri;
Per, si qua est, quæ restat adhuc mortalibus usquam,
Intemerata fides, oro; miserere laborum
Tantorum; miserere animi non digna ferentis.
His lachrymis vitam damus, et miserescimus ultrò.
Ipse viro primus manicas atque arcta levari
Vincla jubet Priamus; dictisque ita fatur amicis:
Quisquis es, amissos hinc jam obliviscere Graios.
Noster eris: mihique hæc edissere vera roganti:
Quò molem hanc immanis equi statuêre? quis auctor?
Quidve petunt? quæ relligio? aut quæ machina belli?
Dixerat. Ille, dolis instructus et arte Pelasgâ,
Sustulit exutas vinclis ad sidera palmas:

131. **Conversa** *esse* **in** exitium

132. **Sacra** ***cœperunt*** parari

141. **Quòd oro te, per** Superos, et numina conscia veri; per *fidem*, si qua est intemerata fides, quæ

146. **Priamus ipse primus jubet**

151. **Quæ religio** *est in eo*

NOTES.

130. *Et, tulere quæ:* they permitted (were content to have) what every one feared to himself, to be turned to the destruction of one unhappy being. *Tulere conversa:* simply for *converterunt*, says Heyne.

133. *Salsæ fruges:* the salted cakes. This cake was made of bran, or meal, mixed with salt, and called *mola*. They sprinkled it upon the head of the victim, the fire of the altar, and upon the sacrificing knife. The ceremony was called *immolatio:* hence the verb *immolare* came to signify, *to sacrifice* in general. *Vittæ:* these were fillets of white wool, with which the temples of the victim, and also the priest, and statues of the gods, were bound.

134. *Rupi vincula.* The victims were loose and unbound when they were brought forward to the altar. But even so, it is not probable that Sinon could have made his escape from the guards and spectators, that would accompany him. By *rupi vincula*, we may understand that he broke the prison in which he was confined against the day of sacrifice, and made his escape. Any thing that binds, holds, or restrains another, may be called *vinculum*. *Eripui:* rescued or delivered.

135. *Delituique obscurus:* and I lay concealed or hid. *Lacu.* Lacus here means *a fen*, or marshy ground. *Ulva:* weeds, or rushes.

137. *Antiquam:* dear country; or *antiquam* may be used in the sense of *veterem*, or *pristinam.*

138. *Natos:* in the sense of *liberos. Exoptatum:* dear—greatly beloved.

139. *Quos illi fors:* whom they, perhaps, will demand for punishment on account of my escape; and will expiate this fault of mine by the death of those innocents.

Here the poet alludes to an ancient law among the Romans, which subjected children to suffer for some particular crimes, committed against the state by their parents.

143. *Intemerata:* inviolable—pure—holy. *Laborum:* sufferings.

144. *Animi:* animus, the soul, is here used by meton. for *the man*, viz. *Sinon.*—Pity me bearing such undeserved, or unmerited treatment. *Non digna:* in the sense of *indigna.*

146. *Manicas:* hand-cuffs. *Arcta vincla:* tight cords.

149. *Edissere:* declare—speak. *Vera:* plu. of *verum*, truth.

150. *Quò statuere:* for what purpose did they erect this mass of a huge horse? Who was the author of it? The following interrogatories, as Mr. Davidson observes, are elliptical. They are thus supplied: *Quid petunt?* What do they intend? Is it to fulfil some duty of religion? If it be so, *quæ religio?* What duty or motive of religion led to it? Or is it an engine of war? If so, *quæ machina belli?* What engine of war is it?

153. *Exutas vinclis:* free from cords—fetters

154. Ait: Testor vos, O æterni ignes,
155. *Testor* vos, O aræ, infandique
158. Fas *est mihi* odisse
160. Modò tu, O Troja, maneas *fidelis* promissis *tuis*,
164. Sed enim ex quo *tempore* impius
168. Ausique *sunt* contingere
169. Ex illo *tempore* spes Danaûm sublapsa *cœpit* fluere
170. *Eorum* vires fractæ *sunt*, *et*
172. Vix simulacrum *fuit* positum in castris, *cùm* coruscæ

Vos, æterni ignes, et non violabile vestrum
Testor numen, ait; vos, aræ, ensesque nefandi,
Quos fugi; vittæque Deûm, quas hostia gessi:
Fas mihi Graiorum sacrata resolvere jura;
Fas odisse viros, atque omnia ferre sub auras,
Si qua tegunt: teneor patriæ nec legibus ullis.
Tu modò promissis maneas, servataque serves
Troja fidem: si vera feram, si magna rependam
Omnis spes Danaûm, et cœpti fiducia belli,
Palladis auxiliis semper stetit. Impius ex quo
Tydides sed enim scelerumque inventor Ulysses,
Fatale aggressi sacrato avellere templo
Palladium, cæsis summæ custodibus arcis,
Corripuere sacram effigiem; manibusque cruentis
Virgineas ausi Divæ contingere vittas:
Ex illo fluere, ac retrò sublapsa referri
Spes Danaûm; fractæ vires, aversa Deæ mens.
Nec dubiis ea signa dedit Tritonia monstris.
Vix positum castris simulacrum; arsere coruscæ

NOTES.

154. *Testor vos:* ye eternal fires, I call you, and your inviolable divinity, to witness.

Some think this is an allusion to the fire of the altar. But Servius, with more propriety, thinks the sun, moon, and other heavenly luminaries are meant: which the ancients thought to be globes of fire, to shine with their own proper lustre; and to be inhabited by divinities. The fire of the altar could hardly be called *eternal*, unless there be an allusion to the fire of *Vesta*.

155. *Nefandi enses:* ye horrid instruments of death, which I escaped. I take *enses* here for the implements used in offering the sacrifice, such as the axe, knife, &c.

156. *Vittæque Deûm:* and ye fillets of the gods, which as a victim I wore.

In order to excite their compassion the more, and to show the horrid apprehensions he had of the act, he speaks as if he had actually been brought to the altar, and as if that had been actually put in execution, which had only been intended against him.

157. *Sacrata jura:* sacred obligations. *Jus* properly signifies a natural right, law, duty, or obligation. It differs from *fas*, which properly signifies a divine right, law, &c. Any thing that the laws of God permit may be called *fas*.

158. *Sub auras:* into light.

159. *Siqua tegunt:* if any lie hid. *Nec ullis legibus*, &c. He is no longer bound by any ties of his country. He is at liberty to break or dissolve his allegiance, and place himself under the protection of the Trojans. Their barbarous treatment had cancelled all his obligations to them: the *aræ* on which he was to have been slain—the *enses nefandi*, by which he was to have been slain—the *vittæ*, with which he was to have been bound, were so many witnesses that he was now under no obligations to regard the interests of the Greeks, who had withdrawn all protection from him.

161. *Si feram vera:* if I relate the truth, if I repay thee largely—great things.

164. *Enim:* in the sense of *equidem.*

166. *Fatale Palladium.* The Palladium was a statue of Pallas with a small shield and spear. It was said to have fallen from heaven near the tent of *Ilus*, when he was building the citadel of Troy. Some say it was made of the bones of *Pelops*. All, however, agree that it was a pledge of the safety of Troy.

Ulysses and Diomede entered the temple where it stood, and carried it away to the Grecian camp, having slain the guards. It is called *fatale*, because, on the safe keeping of it, the preservation of Troy depended.

169. *Ex illo:* from that time, the hope of the Greeks, tottering, began to slip, and to be carried backward.

This is a metaphor taken from a person standing on a slippery place, and with difficulty maintaining his position. The least movement of his body destroys his equilibrium. At first he totters, and reels to and fro in order to recover himself. Unable to do it, he is borne away, and hurried along with accelerated motion.

171. *Tritonia.* This was a name of Pallas or Minerva, taken from a lake in Africa, called *Tritona*, where she is said to have been born: or, at least, where she first made her appearance on earth. *Monstris:* prodigies—indications of her anger.

172. *Coruscæ flammæ:* sparkling flames flashed from her steady eyes. The signs

Luminibus flammæ arrectis, salsusque per artus
Sudor iit, terque ipsa solò, mirabile dictu!
Emicuit, parmamque ferens hastamque trementem.
Extemplò tentanda fugâ canit æquora Calchas: 176
Nec posse Argolicis exscindi Pergama telis,
Omina ni repetant Argis, numenque reducant,
Quod pelago et curvis secum advexere carinis.
Et nunc quòd patrias vento petiere Mycenas; 180
Arma Deosque parant comites, pelagoque remenso,
Improvisi aderunt: ita digerit omina Calchas.
Hanc pro Palladio moniti, pro numine læso,
Effigiem statuêre, nefas quæ triste piaret;
Hanc tamen immensam Calchas attollere molem 185
Roboribus textis, cœloque educere jussit:
Ne recipi portis, aut duci in mœnia possit;
Neu populum antiquâ sub relligione tueri.
Nam si vestra manus violâsset dona Minervæ; 189
Tum magnum exitium (quod Dî priùs omen in ipsum
Convertant) Priami imperio Phrygibusque futurum:
Sin manibus vestris vestram ascendisset in urbem,
Ultrò Asiam magno Pelopeia ad mœnia bello
Venturam, et nostros ea fata manere nepotes.
Talibus insidiis, perjurique arte Sinonis, 195
Credita res: captique dolis, lachrymisque coactis,

176. **Æquora** tentanda *esse*

183. *Illi* moniti statuêre hanc effigiem *equi*, quæ

185. Tamen Calchas jussit *eos* attollere

189. Nam *dicebat*, si vestra

193. *Dicebat* Asiam ultrò venturam *esse*

196. *Nos*-que, quos neque Tydides, nec Larissæus Achilles *domuit*; *nos*, quos decem anni non domuere; *quos* mille carinæ non *domuere*, capti *sunt* dolis

NOTES.

here mentioned are truly ominous; and sufficient to have excited in the minds of the Greeks fear and alarm.

174. *Ipsa:* the goddess—the image of the goddess. *Emicuit:* in the sense of *salivit.*

175. *Parmam—hastam:* the shield and brandished spear. These were the arms by which the Palladium was distinguished.

176. *Canit:* in the sense of *declarat. Cano* is properly applied to oracles and predictions. It implies that Calchas spoke by inspiration, and declared it to be the will of the gods, *that the sea,* &c. *Exscindi:* be rased—destroyed.

178. *Ni repetant:* unless they should repeat the omens at Argos, and bring back the goddess, which, &c.

This, Servius observes, alludes to a custom of the Romans, when they were unsuccessful in war, to return home, and again consult the omens: or, if they were too far for that purpose, they used to appropriate a part of the enemy's territory, and call it Rome, where they renewed the omens. *Numen:* the *Palladium*—the image or symbol of Pallas' divinity; which Sinon would make the Trojans believe had been carried to Argos: and in the mean time, until they should return, as an atonement or offering to the offended goddess (*numine læso,*) the Greeks had built, and consecrated to her, this horse.

181. *Arma:* troops—forces, by meton. *Omina.* Some copies have *omnia. Digerit:* interprets—explains.

184. *Quæ piaret:* which might expiate the horrid crime of carrying off the Palladium from her temple.

186. *Roboribus textis:* with compacted or joined timber. Robur properly signifies the heart of the oak. Hence it may signify timber in general, and all wooden materials, as planks, boards, &c. *Immensam:* very high. *Molem:* for *equum.*

188. *Neu tueri:* nor defend the people under their ancient religion—under the religious patronage and protection of their ancient guardian goddess, Pallas, or Minerva.

190. *In ipsum:* which omen may the gods rather turn upon him, to wit, Calchas. It would be more emphatical, if it were *in ipsos,* meaning upon the Greeks. Some copies have *in ipsos.*

193. *Asiam.* Asia Minor, or Natolia, in which Troy was situated. It is put, by meton. for the inhabitants. *Ultrò.* Servius explains this by *statim.* But the usual acceptation of the word is easier, and more emphatic. *Pelopeia mœnia:* the city Argos, where Pelops reigned: by syncc. put for Greece in general. See Geor. iii. 7.

194. *Ea fata:* the same fate or destiny.

195. *Insidiis:* in the sense of *fraudibus.*

196. *Coactis lachrymis:* by his feigned or forced tears. Some copies read *coacti,* in

Quos neque Tydides, nec Larissæus Achilles,
Non anni domuere decem, non mille carinæ.

199. Hìc aliud majus *prodigium* multòque magìs tremendum

Hìc aliud majus miseris multòque tremendum
Objicitur magìs, atque improvida pectora turbat.
Laocoon, ductus Neptuno sorte sacerdos,
Solennes taurum ingentem mactabat ad aras.
Ecce autem gemini à Tenedo tranquilla per alta

204. Gemini angues *venientes* à Tenedo per tranquilla alta

(Horresco referens) immensis orbibus angues
Incumbunt pelago, pariterque ad litora tendunt:
Pectora quorum inter fluctus arrecta, jubæque
Sanguineæ exsuperant undas: pars cætera pontum
Ponè legit, sinuatque immensa volumine terga.
Fit sonitus spumante salo: jamque arva tenebant,

210. Suffecti *quoad* ardentes

Ardentesque oculos suffecti sanguine et igni,
Sibila lambebant linguis vibrantibus ora.
Diffugimus visu exsangues: illi agmine certo
Laocoonta petunt: et primùm parva duorum
Corpora natorum serpens amplexus uterque

NOTES.

the nom. agreeing with *nos*, meaning the Trojans. But this is not so easy and natural; nor does it so well agree with the subject. The poet uniformly represents Sinon as an impostor, a cheat, and all his words and tears feigned and dissembled. Servius strongly insists upon *coactis*. Valpy reads *coacti*. Heyne, *coactis*.

197. *Larissæus:* an adj. from *Larissa*, a town of Thessaly, near *Phthia*, the place where Achilles was born.

198. *Mille carinæ.* Homer makes 1186 ships in all, that went in the Trojan expedition. *Carina*, the keel, put, by synec. for the whole ship. The poets often use a definite number for an indefinite, particularly if the number be very large.

199. *Hìc aliud:* here another greater prodigy, and one much more to be dreaded, is presented to our sight, nobis *miseris*.

200. *Improvida:* improvident—not expecting any thing of the kind. *Pectora:* in the sense of *animos*.

201. *Laocoon.* The priest of Neptune having been put to death, because, by his prayers and sacrifices, he did not prevent the arrival of the Greeks, Laocoon was chosen by lot to sacrifice to that god upon the departure of their enemies. He was the priest of *Apollo Thymbræus*. Some say he was the brother of Anchises; others that he was the son of Priam.

Hyginus, who relates the story, says the crime for which Laocoon was thus severely punished, was his having married, and had children, contrary to the orders of Apollo: and that the Trojans construed this calamity, which befel him, as an act of vengeance of the gods for his having violated the offering of Minerva. Virgil, therefore, judiciously introduces this event, not only as it is a fine embellishment of his poem; but also as it gives the greater probability to the episode of the wooden horse, and accounts for the credulity of the Trojans.

202. *Solennes aras:* the appointed altars.

503. *Tenedo.* Tenedos is here mentioned to signify, as Servius says, that the ships were to come from hence to the destruction of Troy. *Per tranquilla alta:* over the smooth or calm sea. This circumstance is mentioned, because it would afford the Trojans an opportunity the better to view the whole progress of the serpents, to hear their dreadful hissings, and every lash they gave the waves: it adds much terror to the hideous spectacle.

204. *Referens:* in the sense of *narrans*. *Orbibus:* in the sense of *spiris*.

205. *Incumbunt:* with their immense folds they rest (swim) upon the sea; and equally (abreast, head and head) stretch to the shore.

208. *Sinuat:* winds their huge backs in folds. Their necks down to their breast, were raised above the water; the other part of them swept the sea behind. *Jubæ:* necks—crests. *Salo:* in the sense of *mari*. *Arva:* in the sense of *litus*.

210. *Suffecti ardentesque:* spotted as to their glaring eyes with blood and fire, they licked their hissing mouths. *Vibrantibus:* in the sense of *motantibus*. Naturalists observe that no animal moves its tongue with so much velocity as the serpent.

212. *Certo agmine:* in the sense of *recto cursu*. *Agmen* here denotes the spiral motion of a serpent, shooting forward, fold after fold, in regular order, like a body of men marching in military array.

214. *Uterque serpens:* each serpent embracing, twines around the bodies of his two sons, and mangles their wretched limbs with their teeth.

Implicat, et miseros morsu depascitur artus.
Pòst, ipsum auxilio subeuntem ac tela ferentem
Corripiunt, spirisque ligant ingentibus: et jam
Bis medium amplexi, bis collo squamea circùm
Terga dati, superant capite et cervicibus altis.
Ille simul manibus tendit divellere nodos,
Perfusus sanie vittas atroque veneno:
Clamores simul horrendos ad sidera tollit:
Quales mugitus, fugit cùm saucius aram
Taurus, et incertam excussit cervice securim.
At gemini lapsu delubra ad summa dracones
Effugiunt, sævæque petunt Tritonidis arcem:
Sub pedibusque Deæ, clypeique sub orbe teguntur.
Tum verò tremefacta novus per pectora cunctis
Insinuat pavor: et scelus expendisse merentem
Laocoonta ferunt; sacrum qui cuspide robur
Læserit, et tergo sceleratam intorserit hastam.
Ducendum ad sedes simulacrum, orandaque Divæ
Numina conclamant.
 Dividimus muros, et mœnia pandimus urbis.
Accingunt omnes operi: pedibusque rotarum
Subjiciunt lapsus, et stupea vincula collo

216. Pòst, corripiunt ipsum subeuntem auxilio *natorum*

223. *Tales* **.** magitus, quales **taurus** *tollit*, cum **saucius**

229. Insinuat *se novus* **cunctis**

NOTES.

Dr. Trapp renders *depacitur*, devours; but there is no necessity of this; for it often signifies no more than to mangle, prey upon, waste, or consume away. Beside, we can hardly suppose that the serpents *devoured* or *eat up* the bodies of his sons, and then laid hold upon the father, to satiate their hunger.

There was a statue in the palace of Vespasian, representing this story, (as mentioned by Pliny,) which showed Laocoon entwined by the serpents, and his sons dead on the ground. It is probable that Virgil took this description from that statue.

215. *Morsu:* teeth—fangs.

218. *Bis amplexi.* The serpents embrace him twice about the middle; then rising upward, they bind their scaly backs twice about his neck; and holding him in that situation, elevate their heads and bloody crests above the head of their unhappy victim. *Circumdati.* The parts of a compound verb are sometimes separated by Tmesis, for the sake of the verse. This word is either to be taken actively, in the sense of *circumdantes*, and governing *squamea terga;* or we must take the expression as a Grecism. See Ecl. i. 55.

220. *Tendit:* in the sense of *conatur. Nodos:* the folds of the serpent.

221. *Perfusus:* smeared, or stained, as to his fillets.

224. *Incertam securim:* the erring blow—he axe struck with an erring blow.

225. *Delubra. Delubrum* was properly the place before the temple, or near the altar, where they washed before they entered, or before they performed sacrifice. It is derived from *deluo.* Varro, however, thinks it was the shrine or place where the image of the god was placed. It is often used for the temple itself, by synec. *Lapsu:* by a gentle easy motion. *Dracones:* in the sense of *serpentes.*

226. *Arcem:* the shrine of stern Minerva. *Tritonis*, a name of that goddess.

230. *Ferunt:* they declare that Laocoon justly suffered for his crime—that it was a just punishment inflicted upon him for doing violence to the sacred offering of Minerva. By this their doubt was removed, and they resolved to admit the fatal machine within the city.

231. *Tergo:* in the sense of *lateri.*

232. *Simulacrum.* Virgil had an admirable talent at varying his style. He hath found out no less than twelve names for this horse, all equally significant: *Lignum, Machina, Monstrum, Dolum, Pinea Claustra, Donum, Moles, Effigies Equi, Equus, Sacrum Robur, Simulacrum,* and *Cavum Robur. Ad sedès:* to the proper place—the hill, or eminence, on which the temple of Minerva stood. *Numina:* in the sense of *divinitatem.*

234. *Mœnia:* properly, the fortifications or bulwarks of a city, from *munio. Murus:* the wall that surrounds it. They are, however, used indiscriminately for a city, frequently. *Accingunt:* apply themselves to the work.

236. *Lapsus rotarum:* they place wheels (or rollers) under its feet, and fasten hempen cords to its neck. *Lapsus rotarum:* simply for *rotas.*

239. Circùm canunt sacra *carmina*
240. Illa *machina* subit
244 Immemores *prodigii*
246. Tunc etiam Cassandra, jussu Dei *Apollinis* non unquam credita Teucris,
248. Nos miseri *Trojani*, quibus

Intendunt: scandit fatalis machina muros,
Fœta armis: pueri circùm innuptæque puellæ
Sacra canunt, funemque manu contingere gaudent
Illa subit, mediæque minans illabitur urbi.
O patria, ô Divûm domus, Ilium, et inclyta bello,
Mœnia Dardanidûm! quater ipso in limine portæ
Substitit, atque utero sonitum quater arma dedêre
Instamus tamen immemores, cæcique furore,
Et monstrum infelix sacratâ sistimus arce.
Tunc etiam fatis aperit Cassandra futuris
Ora, Dei jussu non unquam credita Teucris.
Nos delubra Deûm miseri, quibus ultimus esset
Ille dies, festâ velamus fronde per urbem.
Vertitur intereà cœlum, et ruit Oceano nox,
Involvens umbrâ magnâ terramque polumque,
Myrmidonumque dolos. Fusi per mœnia Teucri
Conticuere: sopor fessos complectitur artus.

NOTES.

237. *Scandit muros:* it ascends, or mounts over the ruins of our walls. They had been demolished to admit it, and afford it entrance.

239. *Funem:* the ropes that had been fastened to the neck and other parts of the horse, by which they moved it forward.

241. *Ilium, domus Divûm:* Ilium, the habitation of the gods; either because its walls had been built by Apollo and Neptune; or, on account of the numerous temples and consecrated places with which it abounded.

242. *Dardanidûm:* the same as *Trojanorum*, vel *Trojæ*.

243. *Substitit quater*, &c. Some are of opinion that this stumbling, or stopping of the horse in the very threshold, alludes to a notion that prevailed of its being a bad omen for one to stumble on the threshold, especially when going out to war; as it is said to have happened to Protesilaus, the first of the Greeks, who was killed on the plains of Troy. The malignity of this omen was thought to proceed from the Furies, who had their seats on the threshold.

244. *Immemores.* Servius thinks that Virgil here alludes to the custom of the Romans in devoting their enemies and the places to which they laid siege. In the form of words which they used upon the occasion, they poured forth these imprecations against them: *Eique populo civitatique metum, formidinem, oblivionem injiciatis, Dii.* According to him, *immemores* will imply that the Trojans were abandoned by the gods, and given up to stupidity and infatuation. *Furore:* with zeal—infatuation. *Furor* signifies any inordinate passion whatever, as love, hatred, anger, zeal, &c. *Immemores:* heedless—unmindful.

245. *Infelix:* in the sense of *perniciosum*, vel *fatale.*

246. *Cassandra.* She was the daughter of Priam and Hecuba, and endued with the spirit of prophecy by Apollo, upon her promising to grant him her love; which, however, she afterwards refused to do. Not being able to withdraw from her the gift he had bestowed, he rendered it of no avail, by destroying her credibility, and making all her predictions to be considered as false. *Jussu Dei:* by the command of the god Apollo. *Ora:* for *os;* the plu. for the sing. *Fatis futuris:* to our approaching destruction.

249. *Velamus delubra.* It was their custom, not only on festival days, but at all times of public rejoicing, to adorn, or dress the temples of the gods with the branches of laurel, olive, ivy, &c.

250. *Vertitur cœlum:* the heavens are turned around. By the diurnal rotation of the earth, the heavens appear to revolve about it once in twenty-four hours. The heavens as well as the earth are divided into two hemispheres, the upper and the lower, by the horizon. The diurnal hemisphere rises with the sun, and sets with him in the west, below the horizon. At the same time the nocturnal hemisphere rises in the east. This tends to explain *nox ruit Oceano:* night rushes from the ocean, or rises from the ocean.

251. *Terramque.* There is a great beauty in thus singling out the stratagems of the Greeks, as the object of chief attention, among all the things in heaven and earth, which that night concealed.

252. *Fusi:* stretched upon their beds, expecting no danger, and taking needful repose. *Mœnia:* in the sense of *urbem.*

Et jam Argiva phalanx instructis navibus ibat
A Tenedo, tacitæ per amica silentia Lunæ,
Litora nota petens: flammas cùm regia puppis
Extulerat; fatisque Deûm defensus iniquis,
Inclusos utero Danaos et pinea furtim
Laxat claustra Sinon: illos patefactus ad auras
Reddit equus, lætique cavo se robore promunt
Tisandrus Sthenelusque duces, et dirus Ulysses,
Demissum lapsi per funem; Athamasque, Thoasque,
Pelidesque Neoptolemus, primusque Machaon,
Et Menelaus, et ipse doli fabricatór Epeüs.
Invadunt urbem somno vinoque sepultam:
Cæduntur vigiles: portisque patentibus omnes
Accipiunt socios, atque agmina conscia jungunt.
Tempus erat, quo prima quies mortalibus ægris
Incipit, et dono Divûm gratissima serpit.
In somnis ecce ante oculos mœstissimus Hector
Visus adesse mihi, largosque effundere fletus:
Raptatus bigis, ut quondam, aterque cruento

258. Furtim laxat pinea claustra, et Danaos inclusos utero *equi*

268. Erat tempus *noctis*, quo

270. Ecce Hector mœstissimus visus *est* adesse mihi ante oculos in somnis

NOTES.

254. *Phalanx* properly a body of men, consisting of eight thousand, placed in a square; here used for troops in general. *Instructis navibus:* in their furnished ships

255. *Tacitæ Lunæ.* Commentators have variously interpreted these words. Some have understood by them that the moon was then new and shone with feeble light, and the darkness in consequence was favorable to the Greeks, by preventing discovery. Valpy understands by them the absence of the moon during the first part of the night. The Grecian army, says he, may have chosen the decrease of the moon, when she does not rise till near midnight. This darkness was favorable or friendly to them. But we are told by Scaliger and others, that Troy was taken about the full moon, when she shines the brightest. This led Ruæus to understand by the silence of the moon, the middle of the night, when all things are silent and still. But *Luna* may, by meton. be taken for *nox*, as *Sol* is often put for *dies*. This will render it more intelligible: the friendly silence of the still (or calm) night. This is the opinion of Heyne.

256. *Cùm regia puppis:* when the royal ship erected a light, then Sinon protected by, &c. We are to understand that Helen or Sinon first gave the signal to Agamemnon that they were ready, by showing a lighted torch from the citadel, and he returned it to them, by setting up a light upon the stern of his ship.

257. *Fatis:* will, or purposes of the gods. *Iniquis:* in the sense of *adversis*, vel *infestis*. *Nobis* is understood.

259. *Furtim laxat Danaos:* he opens privately the piny doors, and (lets out) the Greeks shut up in the womb. Here we may observe that Virgil uses the verb *laxat* with both the nouns *claustra* and *Danaos*, when in strict propriety, it can be applied to one only. This is a freedom which our language will not always admit; but it frequently occurs in the Latin and Greek writers. See Æn. vii. 431.

260. *Reddit:* in the sense of *effundit.*

262. *Lapsi per funem.* After they were let out, they slid down by a rope, secured at the top of the horse, and reaching to the ground.

263. *Pelides:* Pyrrhus, the son of Achilles, and grandson of *Peleus*, king of Thessaly. He was also called *Neoptolemus.* See 469. seq. *Primus.* By this we are to understand that he was the first who descended the rope; and not the first, or chief among these leaders.

263. *Doli:* for *equi.*

265. *Sepultam somno, vinoque.* This is a very expressive metaphor, representing the inhabitants of the city so deeply in sleep, and so silent and still, that it would almost seem as if their beds had been their graves. This greatly moves our pity toward the Trojans, and our indignation against Sinon and the treacherous Greeks. *Accipiunt:* in the sense of *admittunt. Portis patentibus* may be put absolutely.

267. *Conscia:* friendly; or conscious, because they were acquainted with the plan of attack.

268. *Ægris:* in the sense of *fessis.*

269. *Dono:* by the favor, or indulgence. *Serpit:* creeps, or spreads over them. This is extremely significant. *Illis*, vel *iis*, is to be supplied.

272. *Bigis*. *Bigæ*, propely a chariot

Pulvere, perque pedes trajectus lora tumentes
Hei mihi, qualis erat! quantùm mutatus ab illo
Hectore, qui redit exuvias indutus Achillis,
Vel Danaûm Phrygios jaculatus puppibus ignes!
Squalentem barbam, et concretos sanguine crines,
Vulneraque illa gerens, quæ circum plurima muros
Accepit patrios: ultrò flens ipse videbar
Compellare virum, et mœstas expromere voces.
O lux Dardaniæ! spes ô fidissima Teucrûm!
Quæ tantæ tenuêre moræ? quibus Hector ab oris
Expectate, venis? ut te post multa tuorum
Funera, post varios hominumque urbisque labores,
Defessi aspicimus? quæ causa indigna serenos
Fœdavit vultus? aut cur hæc vulnera cerno?
Ille nihil: nec me quærentem vana moratur;
Sed graviter gemitus imo de pectore ducens:
Heu! fuge, nate Deâ, teque his, ait, eripe flammis
Hostis habet muros; ruit alto à culmine Troja:
Sat patriæ Priamoque datum: si Pergama dextrâ
Defendi possent, etiam hâc defensa fuissent.
Sacra, suosque tibi commendat Troja Penates:
Hos cape fatorum comites: his mœnia quære,
Magna pererrato statues quæ denique ponto.
Sic ait, et manibus vittas, Vestamque potentem,
Æternumque adytis effert penetralibus ignem.

273. Trajectus *quoad* lora per tumentes

275. Indutus *quoad* exuvias

276. Vel *qui* jaculatus *est*

277. *Nunc* gerens squalentem barbam, et crines

281. *O* Hector expectate, ab quibus oris, venis! Ut *nos* defessi aspicimus te, post

287. Ille *respondit* nihil *ad hæc:*

288. Graviter ducens gemitus de imo pectore, ait: Heu! fuge

291. *Ulla* dextrâ, fuissent defensa etiam hâc *mea dextrâ.*

294. Quære mœnia his, quæ statues magna, ponto denique pererrato,

NOTES.

drawn by two horses. Here it means the chariot of Achilles, behind which Hector's dead body was drawn around the walls of Troy several times. See Æn. i. 99.

273. *Trajectus-que per tumentes:* pierced through his swelling feet with thongs. It agrees with Hector, mentioned above.

274. *Qualis erat!* how he looked! how much changed from that Hector, &c.

275. *Indutus exuvias:* clad in the spoils of Achilles. When Achilles left the Greeks in disgust, his friend Patroclus requested of him the favor of wearing his armour, with a view of striking the greater terror to the Trojans. He was slain by Hector, and stripped of his armour. See Ecl. i. 55.

280. *Expromere:* to utter these sorrowful words. This word is very appropriate here; it shows him laboring to bring out his words and give them utterance, like a person drawing a heavy load.

281. *Lux:* in the sense of *salus*.

282. *Tantæ:* in the sense of *longæ*. The pron. *te* is understood.

283. *Expectate:* earnestly desired, or longed for. *Ut defessi:* how gladly do we, worn out, (with toil and fatigue,) see thee, after the many deaths of thy friends, &c. By *labores hominum*, perhaps we are to understand the disasters of their allies, and by *labores urbis*, the disasters of his countrymen. *Urbis:* the city; by meton. put for the inhabitants.

286. *Fœdavit:* hath disfigured thy serene countenance.

287. *Moratur:* nor did he, by answering these questions, detain me, &c.

291. *Sat datum:* enough has been done for our country, and for Priam. *Sat* here performs the office of a noun. *Pergama:* properly the fort and fortifications of Troy, but frequently used and taken for the whole city, as in the present case, by synec.

293. *Penates.* Macrobius, in his *Saturnalia*, explains the *Penates* to be those gods by whom we breathe, and to whom we owe the faculties of our minds and bodies, i. e. *Jupiter*, *Juno*, and *Minerva*. To these he adds *Vesta:* on which account the consuls, and other magistrates, when they entered upon their offices, used to pay divine honors to the *Penates*, and *Vesta*. This seems to be confirmed by the passage before us, where *Vesta* is delivered to the care of Æneas, as well as the *Penates*. These gods, he observes, were styled the *great gods*. They were also styled *powerful:* on which account Virgil here styles *Vesta*, the *powerful goddess: Vestam potentem.*

Dionysius Halycarnassus informs us, that the symbols of these *Penates* at Rome were two wooden statues of young men, in a sitting posture, with javelins in their hands.

294. *Mœnia:* in the sense of *urbem*. *Fatorum:* of thy fortunes.

297. *Æternum ignem.* The sacred fire was

Diverso intereà miscentur mœnia luctu:
Et magìs atque magìs (quanquam secreta parentis
Anchisæ domus, arboribusque obtecta recessit)
Clarescunt sonitus, armorumque ingruit horror.
Excutior somno, et summi fastigia tecti
Ascensu supero, atque arrectis auribus adsto.
In segetem veluti cùm flamma furentibus Austris
Incidit; aut rapidus montano flumine torrens
Sternit agros, sternit sata læta boumque labores,
Præcipitesque trahit sylvas: stupet inscius alto
Accipiens sonitum saxi de vertice pastor.
Tum verò manifesta fides, Danaûmque patescunt
Insidiæ; jam Deïphobi dedit ampla ruinam,
Vulcano superante, domus: jam proximus ardet
Ucalegon: Sigea igni freta lata relucent.
Exoritur clamorque virûm, clangorque tubarum.
Arma amens capio, nec sat rationis in armis:

298. Et sonitus clarescunt magìs atque magìs

309. Fides *verborum Hectoris fuit* manifesta

314. Nec *erat* sat rationis *mihi* in armis. Sed animi ardent glomerare

NOTES.

kept burning all the year. It was brought by Æneas into Italy, where Numa Pompilius re-established the order of the Vestal Virgins; whose office was to preserve this fire in the temple of Vesta. It was suffered to die away on the last day of the year, and was rekindled again on the first day of March from the beams of the sun. The origin of this religious custom seems to have been derived from the Persians, who were famous for worshipping the sun, and the fire, as an emblem of that luminary. This everlasting fire was not only preserved in the temple of Vesta, but also in private houses, and in the palaces of the great; where was an altar to *Jupiter Hercæus*, on which fire was kept perpetually burning. Some suppose that this was the fire which Priam had consecrated on the altar, at which he was slain. *Adytis.* Adytum properly was the most sacred part of the temple—the place where the images and statues of the gods were—the shrine. This was commonly the interior or middle of the temple. Hence the propriety of *adytis penetralibus.* It is often taken for the temple itself by synec.

298. *Diverso:* in the sense of *vario.*

299. *Secreta:* private, separated from others—by itself: it agrees with *domus. Fuit* is understood.

300. *Obtecta:* surrounded (covered) by trees, was retired from noise and bustle.

301. *Sonitus clarescunt:* the sounds are heard more and more clearly: and the din or clashing of arms increases.

303. *Ascensu:* by climbing up, I ascend to the summit of the palace. By this we are to understand the watch tower, which was usually built on the ridge, or highest part of the house, that it might afford them a more extensive prospect. *Arrectis auribus:* with listening ears. It is a metaphor taken from those animals that prick up their ears at every sound which gives them alarm.

304. *Velut cùm flamma,* &c. This fine simile is taken from Homer, Iliad ii. 455 *Austris:* for *ventis.*

305. *Torrens rapidus:* a torrent rapid with a mountain flood prostrates the fields, prostrates, &c. *Auctus colluvie aquarum è montibus,* says Heyne.

306. *Sata:* properly crops of corn; from *sero. Læta:* in the sense of *copiosa,* or *fertilia.*

308. *Accipiens:* in the sense of *audiens. Inscius:* ignorant of the cause of the sound.

309. *Fides:* the truth of Hector's words was now manifest.

310. *Deïphobi.* Deïphobus was the son of Priam and Hecuba. After Paris was slain by Pyrrhus, he married Helen, by whose treachery he fell a sacrifice to the resentment of the Greeks, among the first of his countrymen. See Æn. vi. 494, et seq.

311. *Vulcano:* in the sense of *igne.* The god of fire, by meton. put for fire itself.

312. *Ucalegon.* He was one of Priam's counsellors: here put, by meton. for the house of Ucalegon. His house burns the next. *Lata Sigea freta:* the broad Sigean straits shine with the light of the flames. *Sigea:* an adj. from *Sigeum,* a promontory of Troas. *Fretum* is properly a narrow sea or strait: it here means that part of the Ægean sea lying between *Tenedos* and *Troas.*

313. *Exoritur clamorque,* &c. This is one of the finest lines that ever imaged the sense in the sound. The words and syllables are rough, hoarse, and sonorous; and so artfully put together as to strike the ear like the thrilling notes of the trumpet which they describe. *Clangor:* in the sense of *sonus.*

314. *Amens:* compounded of the Greek

317. Succurrit *mihi in mentem* pulchrum *esse*

320. Ipse trahit sacra, victosque

322. *In* quo loco *est* summa res

331. *Tot* millia, quot nunquam venêre *è* magnis

Sed glomerare manum bello, et concurrere in arcem
Cum sociis ardent animi: furor iraque mentem
Præcipitant; pulchrumque mori succurrit in armis.
  Ecce autem, telis Pantheus elapsus Achivûm,
Pantheus Otriades, arcis Phœbique sacerdos,
Sacra manu, victosque Deos, parvumque nepotem
Ipse trahit: cursuque amens ad limina tendit:
Quo res summa loco, Pantheu? quam prendimus arcem?
Vix ea fatus eram gemitu cùm talia reddit:
Venit summa dies et ineluctabile tempus
Dardaniæ: fuimus Troës, fuit Ilium, et ingens
Gloria Teucrorum: ferus omnia Jupiter Argos
Transtulit: incensâ Danai dominantur in urbe
Arduus armatos mediis in mœnibus adstans
Fundit equus, victorque Sinon incendia miscet
Insultans: portis alii bipatentibus adsunt,
Millia quot magnis nunquam venêre Mycenis.

NOTES.

alpha privitivum, and *mens*. It properly signifies, deprived of reason—destitute of presence of mind, from any cause whatever.

315. *Glomerare:* in the sense of *colligere*.

316. *Animi ardent:* my mind burns to collect, &c. The plural here has plainly the sense of the singular *animus*.

319. *Pantheus:* he was the son of Otreus. Servius informs us, that on the overthrow of Troy by Hercules, and the death of Laomedon, Priam sent the son of Antenor to consult the oracle of *Delphi*, whether he should build up Troy again upon the same foundations. Pantheus was then priest of the Delphic Apollo, a youth of exquisite beauty; and Antenor was so well pleased with him, that he carried him off by force to Troy. To make some amends for this injury, Priam made him priest of Apollo. However this may be, he was a person of great note and authority among the Trojans. *Sacerdos arcis Phœbique:* priest of the tower and of Apollo: (that is) of the citadel or tower, where Apollo was worshipped, together with Pallas or Minerva, to whom it was sacred.

320. *Sacra:* sacred utensils. Here again Virgil applies one verb to two or more nouns, when in strictness it can be applied to one only. *Trahit* is applicable enough to a child who can hardly walk, and must be half dragged along; but it cannot so well be applied to things that are carried in the hand.

321. *Limina.* Some copies have *Litora.* But Servius, Donatus, Heyne, and others, read *limina*, which is manifestly to be preferred. *Litora* appears inconsistent with the case. Beside, it reflects much honor upon Æneas, that both Hector and Pantheus should bring the sacred things of Troy to him for safe-keeping. It is a chief object with the poet to aggrandize his hero.

322. *Summa res:* the commonwealth—the common interests of his country; which was the *summa res* of Æneas, his chief, his highest concern; and will always be nearest the heart of every good patriot. Virgil, to show the haste and impatience of Æneas, makes him throw out these short questions abruptly, without any previous introduction. *Loco:* state, or condition. *Reddit:* in the sense of *respondet*.

324. *Ineluctabile tempus.* Ruæus takes these words in the sense of *inevitabilis ruina Trojæ. Summa:* in the sense of *suprema vel ultima*.

325. *Fuimus Troes, fuit Ilium:* we Trojans are no more; Ilium, and the great glory of the Trojans, hath fallen.

It was a custom among the Romans, when they would intimate a person to be dead, to say *fuit*, or *vixit*, to shun sounds that were shocking, and accounted of bad omen. Beside, there is a greater degree of elegance in expressing the death of a person, or the overthrow of a city, thus, indirectly, by *fuit, stetit, vixit*, &c. than in plain words. The one is the language of poetry, the other of prose. This seems to be an imitation of Euripides in his *Troades*, where Andromache and Hecuba thus alternately complain: once we were happy—! Hecuba: now our happiness is gone—Troy is no more.

329. *Miscet:* in the sense of *spargit*.

330. *Bipatentibus:* in the sense of *apertis*. Doors or gates that open both ways, or on both sides, may be called *bipatentes*. *Adsunt:* in the sense of *intrant*.

331. *Mycenis.* Mycenæ and Argos were the chief cities of Greece; and frequently put for Greece in general. They were situated in the Peloponnesus. *Hodie, Morea*

Obsedère alii telis angusta viarum
Oppositi: stat ferri acies mucrone corusco
Stricta, parata neci: vix primi prælia tentant
Portarum vigiles, et cæco Marte resistunt.
Talibus Otriadæ dictis, et numine Divûm
In flammas et in arma feror: quò tristis Erinnys,
Quò fremitus vocat, et sublatus ad æthera clamor.
Addunt se socios Ripheus, et maximus annis
Iphitus, oblati per lunam, Hypanisque, Dymasque;
Et lateri agglomerant nostro: juvenisque Chorœbus
Mygdonides: illis ad Trojam fortè diebus
Venerat, insano Cassandræ incensus amore;
Et gener auxilium Priamo Phrygibusque ferebat:
Infelix, qui non sponsæ præcepta furentis
Audîerat.
Quos ubi confertos audere in prælia vidi,
Incipio super his: Juvenes, fortissima frustrà
Pectora, si vobis audentem extrema cupido est
Certa sequi; quæ sit rebus fortuna, videtis.
Excessêre omnes adytis arisque relictis
Dî, quibus imperium hoc steterat: succurritis urbi
Incensæ: moriamur, et in media arma ruamus.

339. **Ripheus, et Iphitus maximus annis, Hypanisque, Dymasque oblati per Lunam addunt se socios *mihi***

345. **Infelix *juvenis!* qui non**

349. **Si certa cupido est vobis sequi *me* audentem extrema; *vos* videtis, quæ fortuna sit *nostris***

NOTES.

332. *Angusta viarum:* the narrow places, or passages of the streets. *Loca* seems to be understood. It is used in the sense of *angustas vias.*

Cæco Marte: in the blind (doubtful) encounter. It is so called on account of the darkness of the night; or because it was sudden and unexpected, and resistance could not, therefore, be made with any prospect of success. *Marte:* in the sense of *pugna* vel *certamine.*

336. *Numine:* impulse, or will of the gods.

337. *Erinnys:* this is a common name of the three furies. See Geor. i. 278. *In arma:* in the sense of *in pugnas.*

339. *Maximus annis.* Some read *armis:* but the former appears to be the true reading from verse 435, seq. Heyne has *armis.*

340. *Oblati:* meeting me by the light of the moon.

341. *Agglomerant:* in the sense of *adhærent.*

343. *Insano:* in the sense of *magno*, or *vehementi.* Virgil has here applied to *Chorœbus*, what Homer says of *Othryoneus.*

He was passionately in love with Cassandra, the daughter of Priam, and hoped to become his son-in-law: with that view he came to his assistance. He was the son of Mygdon.

345. *Furentis: furens* here means inspired—prophetic. *Sponsa:* properly a woman promised, or betrothed in marriage; from the verb *spondeo:* also a young married woman.

347. *Audere in prælia:* to have courage for fight—to be ready to engage. *Quos.* in the sense of *illos.*

348. *Super his:* upon these things. Having observed them collected together, and prepared for fight, he then begins. Or, *super his* may be in the sense of *ad hæc*, to these things—to their readiness and courage for fight, he begins. Servius takes them differently. *I begin in these* words, *the more* to animate them. In this case, *super* must be for *insuper;* in the former, a prep. Davidson follows Servius. Heyne has *post hæc—inde.*

248. *Juvenes, pectora:* there is a great confusion, and neglect of order and method, in this speech, to mark the hurry and disorder of Æneas' mind. O youths, souls most valiant! *Frustra:* in vain; because they could not save their country.

349. *Certa cupido:* a fixed, determined resolution. *Audentem:* in the sense of *tentantem. Cupido:* in the sense of *animus.*

351. *Omnes Dî, quibus:* all the gods, by whom this empire stood, have departed from, &c. It was a prevailing opinion that a city, or place, could not be taken, while its tutelary divinities remained in it. It was the practice, therefore, of the besiegers to invite, or call them away. For this reason the Romans took care to conceal the Latin name of the god under whose protection Rome was; and the priests were not allowed to call the Roman gods by their names, lest, if they were known, an enemy might solicit and entice them away. To this cus-

Una salus victis, nullam sperare salutem.
Sic animis juvenum furor additus. Inde lupi ceu
Raptores, atrâ in nebulâ, quos improba ventris
Exegit cæcos rabies, catulique relicti
Faucibus expectant siccis: per tela, per hostes
Vadimus haud dubiam in mortem, mediæque tenemus
Urbis iter: nox atra cavâ circumvolat umbrâ.
Quis cladem illius noctis, quis funera fando
Explicet? aut possit lachrymis æquare labores?
Urbs antiqua ruit, multos dominata per annos.
Plurima perque vias sternuntur inertia passim
Corpora, perque domos, et relligiosa Deorum
Limina. Nec soli pœnas dant sanguine Teucri:
Quondam etiam victis redit in præcordia virtus,
Victoresque cadunt Danai: crudelis ubique
Luctus, ubique pavor, et plurima mortis imago.
Primus se Danaûm, magnâ comitante catervâ,
Androgeos offert nobis, socia agmina credens,
Inscius; atque ultrò verbis compellat amicis:
Festinate, viri: nam quæ tam sera moratur:
Segnities? alii rapiunt incensa feruntque

357. Quos improba rabies ventris exegit *ex antris* cæcos *periculo*, *quos*-que catuli relicti *in antris*

359. *Sic nos* vadimus per tela

365. Domos *hominum*, et *per*

368. Ubique *est* crudelis

370. Androgeos primus Danaûm offert se nobis, magna caterva comitante *eum*, credens *nostra* agmina *esse* socia

NOTES.

tom the poet may here allude; or rather to the poetical fiction, that when Troy was like to be taken, the gods were seen carrying away their statues from the temples.

354. *Una salus:* the only safety to the vanquished, is, to hope for no safety. This is the same argument which the brave Leonidas used to animate his men to sell their lives as dear as possible. *Una:* in the sense of *sola.*

355. *Inde ceu lupi:* after that, as ravenous wolves in a dark night, which excessive hunger hath driven out blind to danger, &c. *Improba rabies ventris:* excessive greediness of the belly—pressing hunger. *Raptores:* in the sense of *rapaces*, ravenous, rapacious. Dr. Trapp objects to the justness of this simile; but the comparison does not lie in the action, but in the manner of performing it. As hungry rapacious wolves are forced from their retreats precipitately into danger, without fear or dread, so we rush desperately on our foes, looking death and danger in the face. The poet mentions another circumstance. *Catuli relicti:* their whelps, left behind, wait with parched jaws. By which he intended to represent those animals in their fiercest and most ravenous state; and, therefore, the more proper to denote the fierceness and rage of men driven to despair. *In atra nebula:* in the dark night; because in the night, or dark weather, they are the fiercest and least mindful of danger.

359. *Vadimus:* we march to certain death, and take the way through the middle of the city. This circumstance is mentioned to show their courage and intrepidity. Afterward he is afraid of the enemy, when, he has in charge his aged father, his wife, and infant son; and endeavors to shun them by tracing out the by-paths and unfrequented lanes.

361. *Fando:* in the sense of *verbis.*

362. *Labores:* disasters—toils.

365. *Inertia corpora.* By these bodies, it is most probable, we are to understand the feeble and helpless part of the inhabitants—old men, women, and children; and all who did not take up arms in defence of their country: they were slain (*sternuntur*) every where, in their own houses, in the streets, and in the temples whither they had fled for protection. They are called *inertia* in opposition to those who dared to make resistance, and nobly die. This is much better than to take *corpora* in the sense of *cadavera*, as is usually done; for then the epithet *inertia* would be quite useless and superfluous.

366. *Relligiosa limina:* the sacred temples of the ods. *Limen*, the threshold, by synec. put for the temple. *Dant pœnas sanguine;* simply, suffer punishment with their blood—by shedding their blood.

367. *Præcordia:* in the sense of *corda*, vel *pectora.*

369. *Plurima imago:* very many forms of death. This mode of expression is common with Virgil, and is conformable to the Latin idiom. So *multa virtus—multusque honos.* Æn. iv. 3. Such expressions, however, convey an idea of plurality rather than of unity; and, in our language, require to be rendered in the plural number.

271. *Socia:* friendly. Androgeos took them to be of the party of the Greeks.

374. *Nam quæ segnities:* what sloth so

Pergama: vos celsis nunc primùm à navibus itis?
Dixit: et extemplò (neque enim responsa dabantur
Fida satis) sensit medios delapsus in hostes.
Obstupuit, retròque pedem cum voce repressit.
Improvisum aspris veluti qui sentibus anguem
Pressit humi nitens, trepidusque repentè refugit
Attollentem iras, et cœrula colla tumentem.
Haud secùs Androgeos visu tremefactus abibat.
Irruimus, densis et circumfundimur armis:
Ignarosque loci passim et formidine captos
Sternimus: aspirat primo fortuna labori.
Atque hìc exultans successu animisque Chorœbus,
O socii, quà prima, inquit, fortuna salutis
Monstrat iter, quàque ostendit se dextra, sequamur.
Mutemus clypeos, Danaûmque insignia nobis
Aptemus: dolus, an virtus, quis in hoste requirat?
Arma dabunt ipsi. Sic fatus, deinde comantem
Androgei galeam, clypeique insigne decorum
Induitur: laterique Argivum accommodat ensem.
Hoc Ripheus, hoc ipse Dymas, omnisque juventus
Læta facit: spoliis se quisque recentibus armat.
Vadimus immixti Danais, haud numine nostro:
Multaque per cæcam congressi prælia noctem

379. Veluti *homo* qui nitens humi pressit anquem improvisum *ex* aspris sentibus

381. Refugit *eum* attollentem

387. O socii, qua fortuna prima monstrat *nobis* iter salutis, quàque dextra ostendit se,

390. Quis requirat in hoste, *an sit* dolus, *an* virtus. Ipsi *occisi*

394. Ripheus *facit* hoc, Dymas ipse *facit* hoc

NOTES.

late detains you. *Rapiunt:* in the sense of *vastant.* *Ferunt:* in the sense of *evertunt.*

376. *Extemplò sensit:* he instantly perceived that he had fallen into the midst of enemies. *Delapsus:* in the sense of *delapsum esse.* A Grecism.

377. *Fida:* in the sense of *amica.* *Neque:* in the sense of *non.*

378. *Repressit pedem:* he retreated back with his words. As soon as he perceived his mistake, he retreated back.

379. *Aspris:* by syncope for *asperis.* This simile is taken from Homer, Iliad iii. verse 33. But Virgil is very happy in the application, and has improved upon the original, by the addition of several circumstances that heighten the comparison, and give it more force and likeness.

380. *Nitens humi:* walking on the ground, steps upon a snake unseen, &c.

382. *Haud secùs:* no otherwise—just so.

383. *Circumfundimur:* this verb here has an active signification: we encompass them with our weapons close joined. Or, it may have the sense of *miscemur*, as Ruæus interprets it.

384. *Captos formidine.* Mr. Davidson observes: by this we are to understand that they were so under the power of fear, as not to be able to exert themselves—enchained, arrested, or nonplussed by fear; and so enslaved to it, that they could obey nothing but its impulse. Ruæus interprets it by *percitos metu.*

385. *Aspirat.* in the sense of *favet.* *Labori:* in the sense of *conatui.*

386. *Animis:* courage—boldness.

388. *Dextra:* in the sense of *propitia.*

389. *Insignia Danaûm:* the armour of the Greeks. This seems to allude to the figures, or images, engraven upon their bucklers—those of the Greeks having the figure of Neptune, and those of the Trojans the figure of Minerva. Putting on the Grecian figures, was the same thing as putting on their armour.

Zenobius tells us, that *Corœbus* was noted for stupidity: as an instance, he mentions that he used to amuse himself on the sea shore by counting the waves as they dashed against it. He came to the assistance of Priam just before the city was taken; and now he shows his stupidity and want of foresight in suggesting a plan, rash in its nature, and which in the event proved fatal to him and his associates.

390. *Requirat:* ask—demand.

393. *Induitur comantem:* he puts on the waving helmet of Androgeos. *Induitur* is plainly to be taken actively, in the sense of *induit.* *Comantem:* waving with a hairy crest. The crests of their helmets were made of the hair of beasts. *Decorum insigne clypei:* the beautiful, or comely figure of his shield; i. e. his beautiful shield—his shield richly ornamented.

396. *Haud nostro numine:* not with our god. This is an allusion to their having put off their own armour, on which was engraven the figure of Minerva, their guardian goddess and protectress, and put on the

Conserimus, multos Danaûm demittimus Orco.
Diffugiunt alii ad naves, et litora cursu
Fida petunt: pars ingentem formidine turpi
Scandunt rursus equum, et notâ conduntur in alvo.
Heu, nihil invitis fas quenquam fidere Divis!
Ecce trahebatur passis Priameïa virgo
Crinibus à templo Cassandra adytisque Minervæ,
Ad cœlum tendens ardentia lumina frustrà,
Lumina, nam teneras arcebant vincula palmas.
Non tulit hanc speciem furiatâ mente Chorœbus,
Et sese medium injecit moriturus in agmen.
Consequimur cuncti, et densis incurrimus armis.
Hic primùm ex alto delubri culmine telis
Nostrorum obruimur, oriturque miserrima cædes,
Armorum facie, et Graiarum errore jubarum.
Tum Danai gemitu, atque ereptæ virginis irâ,
Undique collecti invadunt: acerrimus Ajax,
Et gemini Atridæ, Dolopumque exercitus omnis.
Adversi rupto ceu quondam turbine venti
Confligunt, Zephyrusque, Notusque, et lætus Eois
Eurus equis: stridunt sylvæ, sævitque tridenti
Spumeus atque imo Nereus ciet æquora fundo.
Illi etiam, si quos obscurâ nocte per umbram

400. Pars *præ* turpi formidine

403. Ecce Cassandra Priameïa Virgo passis crinibus

406. Lumina, *inquam:* nam,

412. *Ex* facie *nostrorum* armorum

413. Danai *commoti* gemitu, atque irâ virginis ereptæ *ex suis manibus*

416. Ceu adversi venti, Zephyrusque, Notusque, et Eurus lætus Eois equis, quondam confligunt, turbine rupto

NOTES.

Grecian armour, with the figure of Neptune, the inveterate enemy of the Trojans. *Immixti Danais.* It is one characteristic of the valiant, that they mingle with the ranks of the enemy. Homer says of Diomede, that he so mingled with the Trojans, that a spectator would have, sometimes, been at a loss to know whether he belonged to the Trojans, or to the Greeks.

398. *Conserimus multa prælia:* we wage many a fight. *Orco:* in the sense of *ad inferos.*

402. *Nihil fas:* it is not right that any one should have confidence, (trust in any thing) the gods being against him. *Nihil* and *nil* are often used simply in the sense of *non.* The verb *est* is understood.

404. *Crinibus passis:* with loose or dishevelled hair. *Passis,* from the verb *pandor,* to be loose or spread open.

405. *Tendens:* raising her glaring eyes to heaven in vain. *Frustra:* in vain, either because the gods were inexorable, or because she could not move the compassion of the Greeks. This is a most moving representation of the beautiful prophetess and princess in distress. No wonder that it roused the indignation of this valiant band, and brought them to her rescue. They avenged the horrid deed upon their enemies.

407. *Speciem:* sight—spectacle. This sight Chorœbus could not bear.

409. *Incurrimus:* we rush upon them to the rescue of Cassandra. *Densis armis:* with close weapons—in close array. Heyne understands it of their rushing upon the close or compacted body of the Greeks. *Irruimus in densum agmen hostium,* says he.

412. *Facie armorum:* from the appearance of their armour, the Trojans took them to be Greeks. *Jubarum:* crests or plumes.

413. *Gemitu:* in the sense of *dolore.* The Greeks (moved) with grief and resentment, on account of the virgin rescued from their hands, being collected together from all quarters, attack us. *Gemitus* here is plainly used in a wider sense than usual. Both Ruæus and Heyne take it in the sense of *dolor.*

414. *Ajax.* He was the son of Oïleus. He ravished Cassandra in the temple of Minerva, for which he was afterward severely punished by that goddess. See Æn. i. 41. Ajax, the son of Telamon, had some time before killed himself, for his failure in the contest for the armour of Achilles.

415. *Gemini Atridæ:* the two sons of Atreus, Agamemnon and Menelaus.

416. *Ceu adversi venti:* as when opposite winds, &c. This simile is in imitation of Homer, Iliad 9. In comparing the two, Scaliger found the preference so much due to Virgil, that he reckons him the master, and Homer the scholar. *Confligunt:* in the sense of *certant.*

419. *Nereus:* a marine god. The trident was assigned to him by the poets, as well as to Neptune. See Ecl. vi. 35.

420. *Si quos fudimus:* if we have routed any by stratagem through the shades in the

Fudimus insidiis, totâque agitavimus urbe,
Apparent primi clypeos mentitaque tela
Agnoscunt, atque ora sono discordia signant.
Ilicèt obruimur numero, primusque Chorœbus
Penelei dextrâ divæ armipotentis ad aram
Procumbit: cadit et Ripheus, justissimus unus,
Qui fuit in Teucris, et servantissimus æqui;
Dîs aliter visum. Pereunt Hypanisque, Dymasque,
Confixi à sociis: nec te tua plurima, Pantheu,
Labentem pietas, nec Apollinis infula texit.
Iliaci cineres, et flamma extrema meorum,
Testor, in occasu vestro, nec tela, nec ullas
Vitavisse vices Danaûm: et, si fata fuissent
Ut caderem, meruisse manu. Divellimur inde,
Iphitus et Pelias mecum: quorum Iphitus ævo
Jam gravior, Pelias et vulnere tardus Ulyssei.
Protinùs ad sedes Priami clamore vocati.
Hìc verò ingentem pugnam, ceu cætera nusquam
Bella forent, nulli totâ morerentur in urbe:
Sic Martem indomitum, Danaosque ad tecta ruentes

422. Illi etiam apparent; primique

427. Qui fuit unus justissimus, et

432. Testor *vos*, *me* vitavisse nec tela, nec ullas vices Danaûm

438. Hic vero *cernimus* ingentem pugnam, ceu

NOTES.

dusky night, &c. they also appear. *Mentita tela:* false or fictitious armour. It purported that those who wore it were Greeks; but in *truth* were Trojans.

423. *Signant ora:* they observe our words differing in sound from theirs. We speak not their language, and, therefore, they know there must be some deception in the business. Some understand by *sono*, the Grecian watch-word. *Ora:* in the sense of *verba*, by meton.

424. *Ilicèt obruimur:* instantly we are overpowered by numbers. The word *ilicèt* was anciently used in the sense of *actum est:* all is over. It was an expression used by the judge, who, when he thought fit to put an end to business, ordered the crier to pronounce *ilicèt*, i. e. *ire licet:* all may go—the business is over.

425. *Armipotentis Divæ:* the warlike goddess—Pallas. See Geor. i. 18. *Peneleï:* Peneleus was one of the five generals of the Beotians who came to the Trojan war.

428. *Visum aliter Dîs.* Having mentioned that his friend was the most just, and most observant of justice among the Trojans, Æneas certainly could not mean that it seemed otherwise to the gods. Something it is evident must be understood. Now, the mention of this excellent man, would naturally suggest the reflection that he deserved a better end: he ought not to have fallen with the rest; but he checks himself: *Dîs aliter visum:* it seemed otherwise to the gods. Commentators have been much divided in opinion upon these words. But in this view they are plain and intelligible. The verb *est* is understood.

429. *Nec tua plurima pietas:* nor did thy great piety, nor the fillets of Apollo, protect thee from falling.

431. *Iliaci cineres:* ye Trojan ashes, and the last flames of my country, I call you to witness, that, &c. *Vices.* By this Servius understands *pugnæ*, fights; because they fought by courses. Scaliger takes it to mean wounds and deadly blows, *vulnera et cædes;* because wounds in fighting are mutually given and received. Donatus considers it an allusion to the gladiators; the verb *vito*, joined with it, being a term used in fencing to parry off a thrust, in opposition to *peto*, to aim one. For *vices*, Ruæus says *pericula*. Heyne says *casus pugnæ*.

433. *Fuissent:* in the sense of *sinuissent.*

434. *Meruisse manu:* that I merited it by this right hand, i. e. by fighting. There is something noble in this sentiment. It considers death as a prize or reward, which the valiant win by their merit or valor. This agrees with his former reflection: *pulchrum que mori succurrit in armis. Divellimur inde Iphitus, et:* we are torn away from thence. He speaks of it as a great affliction; and, as it were, accuses his fate that denied him the honor of so glorious a death.

435. *Gravior ævo:* Iphitus was now oppressed or enfeebled with age; and Pelias disabled by a wound which he had received from Ulysses. *Ævo:* for *annis.*

437. *Protinùs:* immediately—in haste *Vocati:* *sumus* is understood.

438. *Ceu:* in the sense of *quasi.* It is understood before *nulli. Bella:* in the sense of *pugnæ.*

440 *Martem indomitum:* Mars, furious, ungoverned. *Mars*, the god of war, put for

Cernimus, obsessumque actâ testudine limen.
Hærent parietibus scalæ, postesque sub ipsos
443. *Danai* nituntur — Nituntur gradibus; clypeosque ad tela sinistris
Protecti objiciunt, prensant fastigia dextris.
Dardanidæ contrà turres ac tecta domorum
446. His telis parant defendere se — Culmina convellunt: his se, quando ultima cernunt,
Extremâ jam in morte parant defendere telis;
Auratasque trabes, veterum decora alta parentum,
Devolvunt: alii strictis mucronibus imas
Obsedêre fores: has servant agmine denso.
451. *Nostri* animi *sunt* instaurati — Instaurati animi, regis succurrere tectis,
Auxilioque levare viros, vimque addere victis.
  Limen erat, cæcæque fores, et pervius usus
455. Dum regna *Priami* — Tectorum inter se Priami, postesque relicti
A tergo: infelix quà se, dum regna manebant,

NOTES.

war, or fighting in general. *Ad tecta:* to the palace.

441. *Testudine actâ:* the testudo being formed. The *testudo* was a figure into which the soldiers formed themselves in attacking towns and other fortified places. The first rank stood upright, the next behind them stooped lower and lower by degrees, till the last rank kneeled down: all holding their targets or shields over their heads in their left hands. By these means they were secure from the missive weapons of the enemy from the walls and towers. To carry on an attack in this way was called, *agere testudinem:* to form the testudo, or target defence. *Limen:* the passage which led up to the palace—the place before the door.

442. *Parietibus. Paries* is properly the wall of a house—*murus*, the wall of a city.

443. *Nituntur gradibus sub*, &c. By *gradibus*, here, we may either understand the steps that led up to the palace, or the steps of the scaling ladders by which they mounted up, or pressed to get up, to the roof, the foot of these ladders being placed at the very door-posts. Mr. Davidson understands the passage in this last sense. The former, however, is the easier: which is the sense of Ruæus. *Ad ipsas portas*, says he. The Greeks ascend (*nituntur*) by the steps up to the very doors. *Postes*, properly the frame of the door, put, frequently, for the door itself, by meton.

444. *Protecti sinistris:* protected by their left hands, (by the shields which they supported on their left arm,) they oppose their shields, &c. *Fastigia:* the roof, or the eaves or edge of the roof.

445. *Tecta culmina domorum:* the covered tops of their houses. Here *tecta* is a participial adjective, from the verb *tego*. Its neuter, *tectum*, properly signifies the roof or covering of any building. Hence by synec. the building itself—a house, a palace.

447. *In extrema morte:* in the last catastrophe. *Suprema ruinâ*, says Ruæus.

448. *Devolvunt auratas trabes:* they tumble down upon their enemies the gilded rafters, the stately decorations of their ancestors. In this passage, the poet has drawn a lively picture of men in despair. Some copies have *decora illa parentum;* which has a peculiar emphasis.

449. *Alii obsedêre.* These, I take to be Trojan guards, who had taken possession of the lower doors, to prevent the entrance of the Greeks. Others understand the Greeks themselves, who had besieged the doors. *Mucronibus. Mucro* is properly the point of the sword; by synec. put for the whole sword.

450. *Denso agmine:* in a close, or compact body. *Animi:* courage.

452. *Levare:* in the sense of *juvare. Victis:* to those despairing—fighting without any hope of victory. *Vim:* force—vigor In the sing. it is a triptot; in the plu. regular.

453. *Pervius usus tectorum:* lit. a thoroughfare (free communication) between the palaces of Priam with each other, and a gate left free (unobserved by the enemy) from behind, where unhappy Andromache, &c.

It appears that Priam had two palaces near each other, with a communication between them; in one of which Hector and Andromache resided, while he and Hecuba resided in the other. *Limen:* an entrance *Cæcæ:* private—secret. Through this private, or back door, Æneas entered the palace, and ascended by the usual passage up to the watch-tower.

454. *Postes:* in the sense of *porta.*

455. *Quà infelix Andromache.* The mention of her using this secret passage of the palace, gives a dignity to the circumstance, which in itself is low

Sæpiùs Andromache ferre incomitata solebat
Ad soceros, et avo puerum Astyanacta trahebat.
Evado ad summi fastigia culminis, unde
Tela manu miseri jactabant irrita Teucri.
Turrim in præcipiti stantem, summisque sub astra
Eductam tectis, unde omnis Troja videri,
Et Danaûm solitæ naves, et Achaïca castra;
Aggressi ferro circùm, quà summa labantes
Juncturas tabulata dabant, convellimus altis
Sedibus, impulimusque. Ea lapsa repentè ruinam
Cum sonitu trahit, et Danaûm super agmina latè
Incidit: ast alii subeunt: nec saxa, nec ullum
Telorum intereà cessat genus.
Vestibùlum ante ipsum primoque in limine Pyrrhus
Exultat, telis et luce coruscus ahenâ.
Qualis ubi in lucem coluber, mala gramina pastus,
Frigida sub terrâ tumidum quem bruma tegebat;

458. *Hâc via* evado

460. *Nos* circùm aggressi ferro turrim

461. Unde omnis Troja *solita est* videri, et naves Danaûm solitæ *sunt videri*

468. Cessat *jactari* e Danais

471. *Talis*, qualis coluber *est*, ubi *serpit* in lucem, pastus mala gramina, quem tumidum frigida bruma tegebat sub terra; nunc,

NOTES.

457. *Soceros:* her parents-in-law—Priam and Hecuba. *Astyanacta:* a Greek acc. of *Astyanax*. Some say he was carried off by Ulysses, others say by Menelaus, in the absence of Pyrrhus, and thrown over a precipice, to evade the prophecy, which imported that, if he lived, he would avenge his parents and country. The name is of Greek origin, and signifies, a king of a city.

458. *Evado ad fastigia:* I ascend to the top of the highest roof. The word *evado* marks the danger of the enterprise, and the hazard he ran of being intercepted by the enemy.

It is probable that by *fastigia* here, we are to understand the battlements, or watch-tower, which had been built upon the highest part of the palace. We may suppose the palace to have been of different heights, or to have consisted of several buildings, differing in height, and connected together so as to form one mass, each of them with its respective roof; hence the propriety of the expressions: *summi tecti—summi culminis*, &c.

460. *In præcipiti:* in a dangerous place —in a projecting situation.

461. *Summis tectis:* with its highest roof, or simply, with its top. It is plain that *tectum* here means the roof, or ridge of the tower.

463. *Ferro. Ferrum* properly signifies iron. Hence any instrument made of iron —any edged tool; such as swords, axes, &c. With these instruments they cut the tower loose, where the topmost story gave weak joints. Mr. Davidson observes, it is somewhat difficult to determine the meaning of *summa* in this place; because the poet speaks as if the whole tower had been torn from its place, and not one story of it only. He therefore thinks we may understand by the *summa tabulata*, the highest story of the palace, on which the tower stood, and to which it was fastened: or perhaps the highest story, or part of the tower only, was overthrown. *Labantes:* in the sense of *infirmas*.

464. *Dabant:* in the sense of *habebant*.

469. *Ante ipsum:* before the very entrance, or vestibule. The *vestibulum* properly was the court yard or space before the door of the house. By *primo limine*, we may understand the outer gate; perhaps the one that gave admittance into the *vestibulum*.

470. *Coruscus ahenâ luce:* gleaming in arms, and brazen light; the brass of his armour reflected the light.

Pyrrhus. He was the son of Achilles and Deïdamia, so called from the color of his skin, which was red. He was sometimes called *Neoptolemus*, from two Greek words, which together signify a *new war*. He inherited much of the spirit and temper of his father. He slew Priam while holding the altar, to which he had fled for refuge; and sacrificed his daughter Polyxena at the tomb of his father. After the destruction of Troy, he carried off Andromache, whom he married; at least he had a son by her, named *Molossus*. He afterwards married her to Helenus, the son of Priam, upon his falling in love with Hermione, the daughter of Menelaus and Helen.

Pyrrhus was slain in the temple of Apollo, at Delphi, by Orestes, to whom Hermione had been promised. He was also called *Pelides*, from *Peleus*, his grandfather.

471. *Pastus mala:* having fed upon poisonous herbs. It is said that serpents, when they lie in wait for either man or beast, eat poisonous herbs and roots, to make their bite more fatal.

472. *Bruma:* properly the shortest day of winter—the winter solstice; hence by

Nunc positis novus exuviis, nitidusque juventâ,
Lubrica convolvit, sublato pectore, terga
Arduus ad Solem, et linguis micat ore trisulcis.
Unà ingens Periphas, et equorum agitator Achillis
Armiger Automedon; unà omnis Scyria pubes
Succedunt tecto, et flammas ad culmina jactant.
Ipse inter primos, correptâ dura bipenni,
Limina perrumpit, postesque à cardine vellit
Æratos; jamque excisâ trabe firma cavavit
Robora, et ingentem lato dedit ore fenestram.
Apparet domus intus, et atria longa patescunt:
Apparent Priami et veterum penetralia regum:
Armatosque vident stantes in limine primo.
At domus interior gemitu miseroque tumultu
Miscetur: penitùsque cavæ plangoribus ædes
Fœmineis ululant: ferit aurea sidera clamor.
Tum pavidæ tectis matres ingentibus errant:
Amplexæque tenent postes, atque oscula figunt.
Instat vi patriâ Pyrrhus; nec claustra, neque ipsi
Custodes sufferre valent: labat ariete crebro

475. Unà *cum Pyrrho* ingens Periphas, et Automedon Armiger *Pyrrhi, quondam* agitator equorum Achillis, unà *etiam* omnis

479. *Pyrrhus* ipse inter primos

485. *Danai* vident armatos *custodes* stantes

490. Figunt oscula *illis*

NOTES.

synec. the whole winter. *Tumidum:* swollen, or bloated with poison.

473. *Novus exuviis:* now, renewed, his skin being cast off, and sleek with youth, he rolls, &c. It is well known that the snake changes, or creeps out of his skin, in the spring of the year. Aristotle informs us that they begin at the head, and having divested themselves of their old garment, they appear renewed in youth and beauty. This is effected in about the space of twenty-four hours.

475. *Arduus ad solem:* raised or elevated to the sun; in order to receive his heat, especially in the spring, when his warm beams are the most cherishing. *Trisulcis.* The poets represent serpents as having three-forked tongues, probably on account of the volubility of their tongues, in which they are said to exceed all other animals. *Micat:* in the sense of *vibrat.*

477. *Scyria:* an adj. from *Scyros*, one of the Cyclades. Achilles was placed here in the habit of a woman, under the care of Lycomedes, king of the island, where he defiled his daughter Deïdamia, who brought him Pyrrhus. Some say Lycomedes gave him his daughter in marriage. *Pubes:* in the sense of *juventus.*

478. *Succedunt tecto:* come up to the palace, so that they could reach the roof with the flames. They advance up to a proper distance, to throw flames upon the roof.

481. *Cavavit firma robora:* and now hath he pierced, or cut through the firm wood, &c. This change of tense is very expressive and beautiful. It marks the violence of Pyrrhus, and the rapidity of his progress. By *trabe* here, we may understand the bar, or crosspiece, or other impediments, on the inside of the door, to secure it. By *limina*, we may understand the impediments or defences on the outside of the door; and by *postes*, the door itself, by meton. The *perrumpit dura limina*, and the *vellit postes à cardine*, show Pyrrhus breaking through all obstructions, and tearing down the doors; and *cavavit* being in the perf. tense, marks the ease and rapidity with which the effect was produced. *Dedit:* in the sense of *fecit.*

484. *Penetralia. Penetrale* properly signifies the interior or private apartments of a house, as here—that part of the temple where the images stood—the place whence the responses of the oracles were given—the shrine. Ruæus says, *recessus.*

487. *Cavæ ædes:* the rooms with concave arches, or ceilings. *Ululant:* in the sense of *resonant. Plangoribus:* shrieks, or lamentations. These rooms, or apartments of the females, were in the middle, or interior part of the palace. This is expressed by *penitùs.*

490. *Amplexæ tenent,* &c. This is an allusion to a superstitious opinion among the Romans, that the door-posts, gates, &c. possessed a kind of divinity. These, therefore, the poet represents as being seized and embraced by the Trojan matrons, who hoped by these means to recommend themselves to the protection of the deities that were supposed to preside over them. *Figunt oscula:* fix their lips to them—kiss them.

489. *Ingentibus tectis:* in the spacious apartments—halls.

492. *Sufferre:* in the sense of *impedire. Crebro ariete:* with the frequent strokes of the ram. This was an engine used in the

Janua, et emoti procumbunt cardine postes.
Fit via vi: rumpunt aditus, primosque trucidant
Immissi Danai, et latè loca milite complent.
Non sic, aggeribus ruptis cùm spumeus amnis
Exiit, oppositasque evicit gurgite moles,
Fertur in arva furens cumulo, camposque per omnes
Cum stabulis armenta trahit. Vidi ipse furentem
Cæde Neoptolemum, geminosque in limine Atridas:
Vidi Hecubam, centumque nurus, Priamumque per aras
Sanguine fœdantem, quos ipse sacraverat, ignes.
Quinquaginta illi thalami, spes tanta nepotum,
Barbarico postes auro spoliisque superbi,
Procubuere: tenent Danai, quà deficit ignis.
Forsitan et, Priami fuerint quæ fata, requiras.
Urbis ubi captæ casum, convulsaque vidit
Limina tectorum, et medium in penetralibus hostem;
Arma diu senior desueta trementibus ævo

495. Danai rumpunt aditus, immissique

496. Amnis, cùm exiit spumeus, aggeribus ruptis, evicitque oppositas moles gurgite, non fertur in arva sic furens

498. Cumulo *aquarum*

505. Danai tenent *locum*, quà

509. Senior nequicquam circumdat arma diu desueta humeris trementibus ævo, et

NOTES.

attack of towns and fortified places, to make a breach in the walls. It was a long beam or piece of timber, one end of which was prepared with iron, somewhat resembling in form the head of a ram, whence it took its name. This was suspended in the middle by the help of ropes, to another beam, extended across two posts, and thrown forward by the besiegers with great violence against the wall.

493. *Postes:* the door, or gate, by meton.

494. *Rumpunt aditus:* they force a passage, or entrance.

496. *Non sic fertur:* a river, when it hath rushed forth foaming, its barriers being burst, and hath overcome the opposing mounds with its whirling current, is not borne into the fields so furious with its flood, &c. The poet here gives us a very lively idea of the rage of the Greeks. It exceeded that of a river pent up; at length, bursting its barriers, overflowing the adjacent country, and spreading desolation and destruction every where in its course. *Cumulo: auctu aquarum*, says Ruæus.

501. *Hecubam.* She was the wife of Priam, and daughter of *Cisseüs*, king of Thrace. She was carried into slavery by the Greeks. *Centum nurus.* Homer informs us that Priam had only fifty sons, Iliad vi. He could not therefore have a hundred daughters-in-law, unless we suppose each one to have had two wives. This might have been the case; but there is no mention made of it. To explain this difficulty, some take the definite number *centum*, for an indefinite one. Others, among whom is Ruæus, take *nurus* for an attendant, or waiter, understanding by *centum nurus*, the hundred servants, or waiters of Hecuba. But there is no impropriety in supposing that the sons of Priam, imitating the example of their father, had more than one wife each; who, in the whole, might make the exact number of a hundred. This last is the best, or most probable explanation.

502. *Fœdantem:* defiling with his blood the fires which, &c. In the open court of his palace, Priam had an altar consecrated to *Jupiter Hercæus*, or the Protector: on this altar, we are told that hallowed fire was kept perpetually burning.

503. *Illi thalami:* those fifty bed-chambers, the so great hope of posterity. These were the separate rooms where his sons lodged with their wives. Homer tells us that Priam had twelve daughters, who, with their husbands, lodged over against his sons. He had therefore sixty-two children by his several wives, nineteen of whom Hecuba bore him. The rest he had by his other wives. All these bed-chambers were in Priam's palace.

504. *Superbi barbarico auro:* decorated with foreign gold and spoils. The Romans frequently called *Phrygia*, Barbary. Some therefore understand by *barbarico auro*, Phrygian gold. It is better to understand it of the gold, which had been taken from their vanquished enemies; more especially since *spoliis* immediately follows it. *Superbi:* in the sense of *ornati*, or *decorati*. *Postes:* in the sense of *portæ:* doors.

505. *Danai tenent*, &c. The Greeks are here beautifully represented more cruel than the flames. The fire abated, and fell from its rage: but the more merciless Greeks press on till all is destroyed.

507. *Casum:* in the sense of *ruinam*.

508. *Limina tectorum convulsa:* the door of his palace torn down—broken through. *Penetralibus:* in the inner or private apartments of his palace.

Circumdat nequicquam humeris, et inutile ferrum
Cingitur, ac densos fertur moriturus in hostes.
Ædibus in mediis, nudoque sub ætheris axe
Ingens ara fuit, juxtàque veterrima laurus,
Incumbens aræ, atque umbrâ complexa Penates.
Hìc Hecuba et natæ nequicquam altaria circùm,
Præcipites, atrâ ceu tempestate columbæ,
Condensæ, et Divûm amplexæ simulacra tenebant.
Ipsum autem sumptis Priamum juvenilibus armis
Ut vidit: Quæ mens tam dira, miserrime conjux,
Impulit his cingi telis? aut quò ruis? inquit.
Non tali auxilio, nec defensoribus istis
Tempus eget: non, si ipse meus nunc afforet Hector
Huc tandem concede: hæc ara tuebitur omnes;
Aut moriere simul. Sic ore effata, recepit
Ad sese, et sacrâ longævum in sede locavit.
Ecce autem elapsus Pyrrhi de cæde Polites,
Unus natorum Priami, per tela, per hostes
Porticibus longis fugit, et vacua atria lustrat
Saucius: illum ardens infesto vulnere Pyrrhus
Insequitur, jam jamque manu tenet, et premit hastâ.
Ut tandem ante oculos evasit et ora parentum,
Concidit, ac multo vitam cum sanguine fudit.
Hìc Priamus, quanquam in mediâ jam morte tenetur,
Non tamen abstinuit, nec voci, iræque pepercit:
At, tibi pro scelere, exclamat, pro talibus ausis,
Dî (si qua est cœlo pietas, quæ talia curet)

515. Condensæ *sunt* circum altaria præcipites, ceu columbæ *volant ab* atra tempestate, et amplexæ

518. Autem *Hecuba*, ut vidit Priamum ipsum, juvenilibus armis sumptis, inquit:

520. Impulit *te* cingi

524. Aut *tu* moriere simul *nobiscum*.

531. Tandem, ut evasit ante oculos et ora parentum

NOTES.

510. *Circumdat:* in the sense of *induit*. *Cingitur:* in the sense of *cingit*.

512. *Sub nudo axe:* under the naked (open) canopy of heaven. *Axis*, properly the pole, by synec. the whole heaven or sky. This altar was situated in the middle, or centre of the palace—*mediis ædibus*. On this altar, Priam had consecrated the perpetual fire. Here he was slain. If we suppose the palace of such form and dimensions as to admit a large space or area in the centre, exposed to the open air above, there will be no difficulty in understanding this passage.

514. *Complexa Penates:* embracing the Penates with its shade. La Cerda would understand by *Penates*, the palace, or house, as the word sometimes signifies; because this was not the place of the *Penates*, or household gods. But others think the statues of the *Penates* were placed here, on the same altar with that of *Jupiter Hercæus*.

515. *Natæ:* in the sense of *filiæ*, vel *nurus*.

516. *Præcipites:* quick—in haste.

517. *Condensæ circùm:* crowded around the altars. *Simulacra:* in the sense of *statuas*.

519. *Miserrime:* in the sense of *infelicissime*, the voc. *Conjux* is either a husband or wife; from the verb *conjungo*. *Mens:* thought—purpose.

522. *Ipse meus Hector:* if my Hector himself were now here, he could be of no avail.

523. *Concede:* betake yourself hither now, in this last extremity. This altar will protect us all. Altars and other consecrated places were looked upon as sanctuaries and places of refuge: to which it was usual to flee for safety.

525. *Longævum:* in the sense of *senem*.

526. *De cæde Pyrrhi:* not from the death of Pyrrhus; but from death by the hand of Pyrrhus.

528. *Longis porticibus:* in the long passages. Mr. Davidson renders the words, the long galleries. *Lustrat:* in the sense of *pererrat*.

529. *Investo vulnere:* with the hostile weapon. *Vulnus* is here used by meton. for the wounding instrument—the weapon that inflicts the wound.

530. *Jam jamque:* almost seizes him with his hand, and presses upon him with his spear.

531. *Evasit:* in the sense of *pervenit*.

534. *Abstinuit:* in the sense of *conticuit*.

535. *Pro scelere, pro:* for such wickedness, for such audacious deeds, may the gods make you suitable returns, &c. *Pro-*

Persolvant grates dignas, et præmia reddant
Debita: qui nati coràm me cernere letum
Fecisti, et patrios fœdâsti funere vultus.
At non ille, satum quo te mentiris, Achilles
Talis in hoste fuit Priamo; sed jura fidemque
Supplicis erubuit; corpusque exsangue sepulchro
Reddidit Hectoreum, meque in mea regna remisit.
Sic fatus senior, telumque imbelle sinè ictu
Conjecit: rauco quod protinùs ære repulsum,
Et summo clypei nequicquam umbone pependit.
Cui Pyrrhus: Referes ergo hæc, et nuntius ibis
Pelidæ genitori: illi mea tristia facta,
Degeneremque Neoptolemum narrare memento.
Nunc morere. Hæc dicens, altaria ad ipsa trementem
Traxit, et in multo lapsantem sanguine nati:
Implicuitque comam lævâ; dextrâque coruscum
Extulit, ac lateri capulo tenus abdidit, ensem.
Hæc finis Priami fatorum: hic exitus illum

539. Funere *ejus filii*

540. *A* quo mentiris te satum *esse*

545. Quod repulsum *est* protinùs

547. Cui Pyrrhus *respondit*

549. Memento narrare illi mea tristia facta, Neoptolemum *esse*

553. Ac abdidit *eum* lateri *Priami* tenùs capulo

NOTES.

sometimes signifies, in proportion to—corresponding to. In the present case it is also emphatic. *Ausis. Ausum* is properly a part. of the verb *audeo;* used as a sub.

538. *Qui fecisti me coràm,* &c. Priam does not complain of his killing his son; but for the barbarity in making him to be the witness of so shocking a sight—for slaying him before his eyes.

539. *Fœdâsti patrios:* hast defiled a father's face with the dead body of his son. *Funus,* says Servius, is a carcass or dead body, warm and newly slain. When carried out to receive funeral rites, it is called *Exsequiæ;* the ashes of it, when burned, are called *Reliquiæ;* and the interment of it is called *sepulchrum.*

540. *At Achilles ille, quo:* but Achilles himself, by whom, you falsely say, you was begotten, was not such toward Priam, his enemy.

This is a severe sarcasm; as if he had said: you claim descent from Achilles, but your actions give you the lie; no man of humanity could beget such a son. *Satum:* in the sense of *genitum.*

542. *Erubuit jura:* he blushed at the laws of nations, and the faith due to a suppliant—he had regard to the laws, &c. The word *erubuit* is extremely beautiful and expressive.

After the death of Hector, Achilles bound his dead body to his chariot, and drew it round the tomb of Patroclus, whom Hector had slain, and around the walls of Troy, for several days in succession. At this piteous sight, Priam was induced to go to Achilles, and beg the body, that it might receive the rites of sepulture; who, after much entreaty, and many rich presents given him, restored the body on the twelfth day after it was slain. Virgil, however, forbears to mention these circumstances, and attributes the restoration of Hector's corpse to the generosity, justice, and sense of honor, of Achilles, in order to set the character of Pyrrhus in a more forcible light.

Achilles had it in his power to have detained the aged monarch, or to have put him to death; but he blushed (*erubuit*) at the thought of violating the laws of nations, which forbid all violence to the person of a king; which require the forms of burial to be allowed to the dead, and the laws of humanity to be observed even to an enemy, when disarmed: those laws he observed, and that faith (*fidem*) which is due to a suppliant, whose person has always been held sacred by the laws of hospitality

544. *Ictu:* in the sense of *impetu.*

545. *Repulsum:* it was so repelled, that it fell short of wounding him. It, however, pierced the boss of his buckler, and hung there harmless, having produced no effect.

546. *Umbone.* Umbo was the middle part of the shield. This rose or projected forward from the plane of the shield, in a curved or circular form. By *summo umbone,* we are to understand the farthest point of projection; which was also the centre of the shield. Here the spear of Priam stuck. It is sometimes taken for the whole shield, by synec.

547. *Ibis nuntius:* you shall go a messenger to my father Achilles, whom you so much praise, and tell him that his son has degenerated from the virtues of his father.

548. *Tristia:* foul—horrid. Ruæus says *indigna.*

554. *Fatorum:* in the sense of *vitæ.* This was the end of the life of Priam. *Hic exi*

Sorte tulit, Trojam incensam et prolapsa videntem
Pergama, tot quondam populis terrisque superbum
Regnatorem Asiæ: jacet ingens litore truncus,
Avulsumque humeris caput, et sinè nomine corpus
At me tum primùm sævus circumstetit horror:

560. Subiit *mihi in mentem*

Obstupui: subiit chari genitoris imago,
Ut regem æquævum crudeli vulnere vidi
Vitam exhalantem: subiit deserta Creüsa,
Et direpta domus, et parvi casus Iüli.
Respicio, et, quæ sit me circùm copia, lustro.
Deseruere omnes defessi, et corpora saltu

566. Dedêre *ea* ægra ignibus

Ad terram misêre, aut ignibus ægra dedêre.
Jamque adeò super unus eram, cùm limina Vestæ

NOTES.

tus tulit: this death carried him off (*sorte*) by divine appointment. This is a singular idiom. The several circumstances here mentioned in the death of Priam, aggravate the cruelty of the action, and set forth the ferocious temper of Pyrrhus. He drew him (*traxit,*) trembling with age and decay of nature, to the very altar where he had fled for safety; and slipping (*lapsantem*) in the blood of his son; the sight of which was worse than death: then he twisted his hair with his left hand, and, with his right hand, drew his glittering sword from its scabbard, and plunged it into his body up to the hilt. Here we have a lively picture of a man lost to all sense of humanity, and capable of perpetrating the most atrocious deeds. It shows, also, the pen of a master. A painter could copy it.

556. *Pergama:* neu. plu. properly the fort of Troy. It is frequently taken for the city itself, by synec. Here it is used in its appropriate sense and meaning, as distinguished from the city.

555. *Videntem:* it agrees with *illum.*

557. *Superbum regnatorem:* the proud ruler over so many nations and countries of Asia. Priam is said to have once reigned over *Phrygia Major* and *Minor:* which included the greater part of Asia Minor, or Natolia. Ruæus interprets the words thus: *Regem Asiæ, clarum propter tot gentes, et tot regiones. Jacet ingens truncus:* he lies a large trunk upon the shore. Some think the poet had here in his view, the circumstances of the death of Pompey, whose head his assassins cut off, and threw his body on the shore. Others say that Priam was not slain at the altar; but drawn by Pyrrhus to the tomb of his father, which was on the promontory of Sigæum, and there slain to appease his *Manes.* He may have been slain at the altar, and his dead body afterward cast upon the shore. This supposition will make the poet consistent and intelligible. *Regnatorem* put in apposition with *illum.*

558. *Corpus sinè nomine:* a body without a name. The head being the index of the person, that being cut off, there is no means left to come at the name, or to distinguish the person. Or, *sinè nomine* may mean, without honor—despicable.

561. *Ut:* in the sense of *cùm.*

562. *Creüsa.* The daughter of Priam and Hecuba, and wife of Æneas. She perished in the sack of Troy. *Direpta:* plundered

563. *Casus:* in the sense of *periculum.*

565. *Saltu:* by a leap or spring.

566. *Ægra:* faint—worn out with fatigue, so that they could fight no longer.

567. *Jamque adeò:* and so I was now remaining alone, when I behold Helen, &c. The parts of the verb *supersum* are here separated, for the sake of the verse, by Tmesis.

Some critics have doubted the genuineness of this passage concerning Helen down to the 588th line inclusive. The reasons assigned are three. First: What is here said of her fearing the resentment of Menelaus, contradicts what he says of her, (lib. vi. 525.) having sought to make peace with him by betraying Deïphobus. Secondly That Virgil here outrages the character of his hero, by making him entertain a thought of killing a woman, and perpetrating the deed in the temple of Vesta. Thirdly: That Virgil cannot be supposed so unacquainted with the history of Helen, as not to know that she left Troy long before it was taken.

In answer to the first objection, it may be said that, though she endeavored to ingratiate herself with Menelaus, by betraying Deïphobus to him, it does not follow that he was entirely reconciled to her. And we are told by Euripides that he carried off Helen as a captive along with the Trojan women, with a view to have her put to death by the Greeks whose sons had fallen in the war. To the second objection, it may be replied, that Æneas did not put her to death; and even if he had, the deed might have been palliated, in a good degree, by a consideration of the circumstances of the case. In the hurry and confusion of min-

Servantem, et tacitam secretâ in sede latentem
Tyndarida aspicio: dant clara incendia lucem
Erranti, passimque oculos per cuncta ferenti.
Illa, sibi infestos eversa ob Pergama Teucros,
Et pœnas Danaûm, et deserti conjugis iras
Permetuens, Trojæ et patriæ communis Erinnys,
Abdiderat sese, atque aris invisa sedebat.
Exarsere ignes animo: subit ira cadentem
Ulcisci patriam, et sceleratas sumere pœnas.
Scilicet hæc Spartam incolumis patriasque Mycenas
Aspiciet? partoque ibit regina triumpho?
Conjugiumque, domumque, patres, natosque videbit,
Iliadum turbâ et Phrygiis comitata ministris?
Occiderit ferro Priamus? Troja arserit igni?
Dardanium toties sudârit sanguine litus?
Non ita: namque etsi nullum memorabile nomen
Fœmineâ in pœnâ est, nec habet victoria laudem;
Extinxisse nefas tamen, et sumpsisse merentis

570. *Mihi* **erranti, ferentique oculos**

571. Illa, **communis** Erinnys Trojæ et *ejus* patriæ, permetuens Teucros infestos sibi ob eversa Pergama, et

577. Hæc-*ne* scilicet, *inquiebam*, incolumis aspiciet Spartam

583. Non ita ***erit*** **namque**

NOTES.

gled passions with which his mind must then have been racked, who could have blamed him if he had avenged his own and his country's sufferings upon her, who was justly chargeable with the guilt of so many thousand deaths, and the utter desolation of a whole innocent people—a once flourishing and powerful kingdom? But when, instead of giving way to the first emotions of a just resentment, he checks himself, deliberates upon the merits of the action, and is at length prevented from doing it by the interposition of his goddess mother; or, in other words, by the force of superior judgment, there is no reason even for the severest critics to censure his conduct. Lastly: Herodotus informs us that he learned from some Egyptian priests, who had received the same from Menelaus himself, that the Trojans had sent Helen to Egypt before the Greeks redemanded her. Of this fact, the historian appears to have been fully convinced. But whether Virgil was acquainted with this piece of his history or not, it is sufficient that he had poetical tradition on his side; and that he is supported by the authority of Homer and Euripides. A moment's attention to the style and manner of expression in these lines, will convince any one that they are no interpolation. *Unus:* in the sense of *solus.*

568. *Servantem limina Vestæ;* the verb *servare* signifies to look after any thing with anxiety, and solicitude; with a jealous eye, and watchful of every danger. *Limina:* in the sense of *templum.*

569. *Tyndarida:* acc. of *Tyndaris,* a name of Helen, the daughter of Jupiter and Leda; so called, because *Tyndarus,* king of Sparta, married Leda, her mother.

572. *Deserti conjugis:* her deserted, or abandoned husband, Menelaus.

573. *Permetuens:* dreading—greatly fearing. The *per* in composition increases the signification of the simple word. Helen proved fatal both to Greece and Troy; to the former, in the loss of so many heroes; to the latter, in being the cause of its ruin. She is therefore styled the *common* fury. *Erinnys,* a name common to the three furies. See Geor. i. 278.

574. *Invisa:* hated—an odious sight; rather than unseen, as Ruæus has it.

575. *Ignes exarsere:* flames flashed in my mind. *Ira subit:* my resentment rose to avenge my falling country.

576. *Sumere sceleratas pœnas:* to take severe punishment. Or, perhaps, to take punishment of such a cursed woman. The same as, *sumere pœnas de scelerata fœmina.* Ruæus says, *pœnas sceleris.* Heyne, *pœna sumptas à scelerata.*

577. *Mycenas:* Mycenæ was not the place of her own nativity, but of Menelaus, her husband. She was born at Sparta. *Scilicet hæc:* shall she, indeed, in safety behold, &c. These are all animated interrogatories and show the mind of Æneas hurrying from object to object, and agitated with a tide of passions. At last he concludes it must not be. She must suffer the punishment due to her crimes.

578. *Parto triumpho:* having obtained a triumph—a triumph being obtained.

580. *Comitata turbâ:* accompanied by a train of Trojan matrons, and Phrygian servants, shall she see her former marriage bed, &c. *Iliadum:* gen. plu. of *Ilias,* a Trojan woman. *Conjugium: pristinum conjugem,* says Heyne. *Patres:* for *parentes.*

582. *Dardanium:* an adj. the same as *Trojanum.*

583. *Nomen:* glory—renown.

585. *Tamen laudabor:* nevertheless, I shal

Laudabor pœnas; animumque explêsse juvabit
Ultricis flammæ, et cineres satiâsse meorum.
Talia jactabam, et furiatâ mente ferebar,
Cùm mihi se, non antè oculis tam clara, videndam
Obtulit, et purâ per noctem in luce refulsit
Alma parens, confessa Deam; qualisque videri
Cœlicolis et quanta solet; dextrâque prehensum
Continuit, roseoque hæc insuper addidit ore:
Nate, quis indomitas tantus dolor excitat iras?
Quid furis? aut quònam nostri tibi cura recessit?
Non priùs aspicies, ubi fessum ætate parentem
Liqueris Anchisen? superet conjuxne Creüsa,
Ascaniusque puer? quos omnes undique Graiæ
Circùm errant acies: et, ni mea cura resistat,
Jam flammæ tulerint, inimicus et hauserit ensis.
Non tibi Tyndaridis facies invisa Lacænæ,
Culpatusve Paris: Divûm inclementia, Divûm,
Has evertit opes, sternitque à culmine Trojam.
Aspice: namque omnem, quæ nunc obducta tuenti
Mortales hebetat visus tibi, et humida circùm
Caligat, nubem eripiam: tu ne qua parentis

587. Meorum *civium.*

589. Cùm alma parens, non *visa* tam clara *meis* oculis antè, obtulit se videndam mihi, et refulsit per noctem

592. Continuit *me* prehensum dextrâ

596. Non aspicies priùs, ubi liqueris parentem Anchisen, fessum

598. Circùm quos, omnes Graiæ acies errant undique

600. Tulerint *eos*, et inimicus ensis hauserit *eorum sanguinem.*

602. *Sed* inclementia Divûm, Divûm, *inquam*, evertit

604. Namque eripiam omnem nubem, quæ nunc obducta hebetat

NOTES

be praised for having put an end to the monster of wickedness, and taken vengeance of one so justly deserving it. *Nefas*, very forcibly expresses the enormity of her crimes: she was wickedness itself.

We are told that Helen was first ravished by Theseus. Afterward she married Menelaus, whom she left for Paris. She also committed incest with her son-in-law Orythus, the son of Paris and Œnone. It is also said that she had an amour with Achilles. She may truly be called (*nefas*) *a monster of wickedness*. *Merentis:* part. of *Mereor*, agreeing with *ejus* understood: of her deserving or meriting it.

586. *Juvabit:* it will delight me to have satisfied my desire of burning or ardent revenge. *Flammæ* may here be used in the sense of *flammeæ* vel *ardentis*. *Animum:* in the sense of *desiderium*. *Animus* may signify any affection of the mind; especially in the plural. For *ultricis flammæ*, Ruæus says, *ardentis ultionis*. Heyne says, *flammâ sive irâ ultrice* (*hoc est*) *ultione*.

589. *Clara:* manifest—clear: attended with evident marks of Divinity.

591. *Confessa Deam:* manifesting the goddess. *Qualisque, et quanta:* such, and as illustrious as she used to be seen, &c. Venus was the most proper deity to interpose in behalf of Helen, whom she had long protected, and had conferred on Paris, as a reward for his adjudging the prize of beauty to her, rather than to Juno or Minerva. See Æn. i. 27. This interposition of Venus was very seasonable in another respect; to check the ardor of his soul, to divert him from his present object, and to direct his regard to his own—to his aged father, his infant son, and his beloved wife, who otherwise might have fallen victims to the fury of the Greeks.

593. *Addidit hæc:* she added these words.

595. *Tibi:* in the sense of *tua:* thy care—regard. *Quònam:* the compound in the sense of the simple *quò*.

597. *Superet:* in the sense of *superest*.

600. *Tulerint:* would have carried them off—consumed them.

601. *Lacænæ Tyndaridis:* of Spartan Helen. See 569. supra. *Invisa tibi:* hateful or odious to you.

602. *Divûm inclementia.* This reading is much more emphatic than *verùm inclementia Divûm*, as in the common editions: and it is supported by the authority of ancient manuscripts: it is the reading of Heyne and Valpy. Homer makes Priam exculpate Helen, and lay the blame of the destruction of his country to the gods themselves. Iliad iii. 164.

603. *Has opes:* in the sense of *hanc potentiam*. *Opes*, is, properly, power acquired by wealth.

604. *Quæ nunc obducta:* which now spread before you, looking earnestly, blunts your mortal sight, &c. This passage Milton appears to have had in view, where the angel prepares Adam for beholding the future vision of his posterity, and their history; which he is going to set before him. See Paradise Lost, lib. xi. verse 411. *Humida:* moist—impregnated with vapor so as to increase the darkness.

Jussa time, neu præceptis parere recusa
Hìc, ubi disjectas moles, avulsaque saxis
Saxa vides, mixtoque undantem pulvere fumum;
Neptunus muros, magnoque emota tridenti
Fundamenta quatit, totamque à sedibus urbem
Eruit. Hìc Juno Scæas sævissima portas
Prima tenet, sociumque furens à navibus agmen
Ferro accincta vocat.
Jam summas arces Tritonia, respice, Pallas
Insedit, nimbo effulgens et Gorgone sævâ.
Ipse Pater Danais animos viresque secundas
Sufficit: ipse Deos in Dardana suscitat arma.
Eripe, nate, fugam, finemque impone labori.
Nusquam abero, et tutum patrio te limine sistam
Dixerat: et spissis noctis se condidit umbris.
Apparent diræ facies, inimicaque Trojæ
Numina magna Deûm.
Tum verò omne mihi visum considere in ignes

mortales visus tibi tuenti

608. Hìc, ubi vides moles disjectas, saxaque avulsa saxis, fumumque undantem mixto pulvere, Neptunus quatit muros *Trojæ*, fundamentaque emota magno tridenti

624. Omne Ilium visum *est* mihi

NOTES.

610. *Hìc Neptunus quatit:* here Neptune shakes the walls, &c. Neptune took an active part against the Trojans, having become their enemy on account of the perfidy of Laomedon. See Geor. i. 502. This fable is explained by supposing that Laomedon employed the money which had been destined for the service of that god, in building the walls of Troy. *Emota:* in the sense of *evulsa.*

612. *Hìc Juno:* here Juno, most fierce, occupies the Scæan gate in front, &c. It is most probable that *prima*, here, has reference to the place of her standing, before, or in front of the gate. It may, however, mean that Juno was the *first*, or *chief*, in urging on the Greeks in the work of destruction. We are told the gates of Troy were six in number: the gate of Antenor; the gate of Dardanus; the Ilian; the Catumbrian; the Trojan; and the Scæan. Through this gate the Trojan horse is said to have entered. On which account, it is probable, the poet placed Juno at this gate, clad in armour, and calling upon her Greeks.

615. *Pallas.* She is sometimes called Tritona: hence the adj. *Tritonia.* See 171. supra.

616. *Effulgens nimbo:* resplendent with a cloud. By *nimbo*, in this place, Servius understands a lucid circle, resembling a diadem about the head, to distinguish the gods from mortals. *Gorgone:* the three daughters of Phorcus and Ceto, *Medusa*, *Euryale*, and *Stenyo*, were called *Gorgones*, Gorgons, or terrible sisters. The name is of Greek derivation, and signifies fierceness. It is said they had but one eye, which served them all by turns. They had great wings: their heads were attired with vipers instead of hair their teeth were tusks like those of a boar: they were armed with sharp and crooked claws.

Medusa having been ravished in the temple of Minerva by Neptune, the goddess gave her serpents the quality of transforming men into stones at the sight of them. Perseus cut off her head by the aid of Minerva's buckler, which, being so finely polished, that it reflected the image of the Gorgon's head, secured him from the fatal influence of her eye. This head Minerva afterward wore upon her shield or buckler, to render her more awful and tremendous. See Lexicon, sub *Ægide.*

617. *Pater ipse:* the father himself gives courage and successful strength to the Greeks. Juno and Minerva opposed the Trojans from selfish motives, because they had been slighted by Paris; but Jove was an enemy to them, because their cause was unjust, in detaining Helen against the laws of nations, when properly demanded.

620. *Abero:* in the sense of *relinquam.*

622. *Diræ facies:* horrid images appear the images of desolation, death, and despair.

623. *Magna numina Deûm.* The Romans divided the gods into two classes: the *Dii majorum*, and the *Dii minorum gentium.* In the first were ranked *Jupiter*, *Neptune*, *Minerva*, and *Juno.* The three last, in an especial manner, are represented as hostile to Troy; and Jove, on this occasion, is opposed to them also. The *magna numina Deûm* may simply mean the great gods; or rather, the great powers of the gods, hostile to Troy. The overthrow of Troy is all along represented to have been effected, not so much by the power of the Greeks, as by the power of the gods. I am now persuaded of the inutility of making any further resistance, since it evidently appears that the great powers of the gods are against us.

Ilium, et ex imo verti Neptunia Troja.
Ac veluti summis antiquam in montibus ornum
Cùm ferro accisam crebrisque bipennibus instant
Eruere agricolæ certatim; illa usque minatur,
Et tremefacta comam concusso vertice nutat:
Vulneribus donec paulatim evicta, supremùm
Congemuit, traxitque jugis avulsa ruinam.
Descendo, ac, ducente Deo, flammam inter et hostes
Expedior: dant tela locum, flammæque recedunt
Ast ubi jam patriæ perventum ad limina sedis,
Antiquasque domos: genitor, quem tollere in altos
Optabam primùm montes, primùmque petebam,
Abnegat excisâ vitam producere Trojâ,
Exiliumque pati. Vos ô, quibus integer ævi
Sanguis, ait, solidæque suo stant robore vires;
Vos agitate fugam.
Me si cœlicolæ voluissent ducere vitam,
Has mihi servâssent sedes: satìs una supèrque
Vidimus excidia, et captæ superavimus urbi.
Sic, ô, sic positum affati discedite corpus.

625. Ac veluti cùm agricolæ certatim instant eruere antiquam ornum in summis montibus, accisam ferro

628. Illa usque minatur *ruinam*, et tremefacta *quoad* comam

636. *Quem*que primùm petebam, abnegat *se posse* producere vitam, Trojâ excisâ

638. Ait: O vos, quibus *est* sanguis integer ævi; *quibus*que vires stant solidæ suo robore

642. *Est* satìs supèrque vidimus una excidia, et

644. O *vos*, affati *meum* corpus, sic, sic positum, discedite.

NOTES.

626. *Ac veluti*, &c. This simile is taken from Homer, Iliad xvi. 481, who applies it to the death of Sarpedon; but the copy exceeds the original.

627. *Bipennibus.* The axe is here used for the stroke, or blow of the axe, by meton. *Accisam:* in the sense of *circumcisam.*

628. *Usque:* in the sense of *diu.*

629. *Nutat comam.* It is usual with Virgil to consider a tree in analogy to a human body, and to call the extended limbs, or branches, *brachia*, arms; and the leaves, *comam*, hair, or locks. This diversifies his style, and renders it pleasant.

630. *Vulneribus.* in the sense of *ictibus.* This is beautifully figurative. The allusion to the human body is still kept up.

631. *Avulsa jugis:* torn from the sides of the mountains.

632. *Deo ducente. Deus* is either a god or goddess. Here it means Venus. Under her conduct, Æneas made his way through the dangers that beset him, to the house of his father.

633. *Expedior. Habeo liberum iter*, says Heyne.

634. *Ast ubi perventum.* The imp. verb *perventum est* is used for the personal verb *perveni.* This mode of expression is very common among the poets. Our language will not admit of it, and we are under the necessity of rendering such impersonals by the personals of the correspondent verb, as in the present case: *perventum est:* I came, or had come.

637. *Abnegat:* refuses to prolong his life. We learn from Varro that the Greeks having given permission to Æneas to carry off what was dearest to him, he took his father upon his shoulders. The Greeks, struck with this eminent example of filial tenderness and affection, gave him a second option, when he carried off his gods. Upon this, they were induced to grant him full liberty to take along with him his whole family and all his effects.

638. *Integer ævi:* unimpaired, or entire, on account of age. *Causâ*, or some word of the like import, is probably to be understood, to govern the gen. O ye, whose blood is not chilled and wasted by age, and who are yet in the full vigor of youth, do ye attempt your flight. The repetition of the *vos* is emphatical. For *robore*, Ruæus says *firmitate.*

642. *Satìs supèrque:* it is enough, and more, that I have seen one destruction of my country, and survived the captured city. This is an allusion to the siege and capture of Troy by Hercules, in the reign of Laomedon, a fact mentioned by historians as well as by poets. And Virgil says of Anchises, that he had been twice saved from the ruins of Troy. Æn. iii. 476.

644. *Sic, O, sic affati:* O ye, having addressed my body, thus, thus laid out, depart. There is a peculiar emphasis in the repetition of the word *sic.* Anchises considers himself as already dead, and his body laid out in burial: *corpus positum*, placed on the funeral pile: at which time it was usual for the friends of the deceased to take a solemn farewell, by repeating the word *vale* three times. The repetition of the *sic* shows his determined purpose of dying and his earnest desire of being left to pursue his resolution. It is used in the same way in the fourth book, where Dido, bent

Ipse manu mortem inveniam: miserebitur hostis,
Exuviasque petet: facilis jactura sepulchri est
Jampridem invisus Divis et inutilis annos
Demoror, ex quo me Divûm pater atque hominum rex
Fulminis afflavit ventis, et contigit igni.
 Talia perstabat memorans, fixusque manebat.
Nos contrà effusi lachrymis, conjuxque Creüsa,
Ascaniusque, omnisque domus, ne vertere secum
Cuncta pater, fatoque urgenti incumbere vellet.
Abnegat, inceptoque et sedibus hæret in îsdem.
 Rursus in arma feror, mortemque miserrimus opto.
Nam quod consilium, aut quæ jam fortuna dabatur?
Mene efferre pedem, genitor, te posse relicto
Sperâsti? tantumque nefas patrio excidit ore?
Si nihil ex tantâ Superis placet urbe relinqui;
Et sedet hoc animo, perituræque addere Trojæ
Teque tuosque juvat: patet isti janua leto.

647. Inutilis *hominibus*

648. Ex *tempore*. quo pater

652. *Precamur*, ne pater vellet vertere cuncta secum

656. Nam quod *aliud* consilium, aut quæ *alia* fortuna jam

657. O genitor, sperâsti-ne me posse efferre pedem, te relicto

NOTES.

on death, is just going to plunge the dagger into her bosom. She breaks forth into this abrupt exclamation: *Sic, sic juvat ire sub umbras.*

645. *Manu.* Servius understands by *manu*, the hand of the enemy; but it is easier to understand it of his own hand. Ruæus says, *propriâ manu. Hostis:* the enemy will take pity on me. This strongly marks the anguish of his soul. He was so weary of life, that he would consider it a favor in the enemy to put an end to it.

646. *Jactura:* the loss of burial is easy—the deprivation of burial rites is a matter of no concern to me.

648. *Demoror annos:* I linger out my years. *Traho vitam*, says Ruæus.

649. *Afflavit me:* blasted me with the winds of his thunder, and struck me with his lightning. The ancients supposed the winds were the efficient cause of thunder.

It is said that this calamity was inflicted upon Anchises for divulging his amour with Venus. Some say he was struck blind: others, with more propriety, say that he was blasted in his limbs. *Memorans:* in the sense of *dicens.*

651. *Nos effusi:* on the other hand, we, bathed in tears, (beseech) my father that he would not destroy all with himself, and press upon the calamity (*fato*) already weighing us down—that he would not, by the afflicting circumstance of his own death, increase the calamity already pressing us down with its own weight. *Ne vellet accelerare perniciem instantem*, says Heyne.

Dr. Trapp would read *occumbere*, or rather *succumbere*, if there were authority for it. As it is, he thinks it a metaphor taken from the falling on a sword. Mr Davidson takes it to be a metaphor drawn from one's leaning or lying with all his weight upon a load, which presses another down, so as to add to the pressure, and to render it more insupportable. Æneas and his family were already grievously oppressed and weighed down by the public calamity, (*fato urgenti*, the fate that lay so heavy upon them,) and therefore pray Anchises not to increase the burden, by the additional weight of his personal sufferings and death. Ruæus interprets *incumbere urgenti fato*, by: *addere vim fato prementi nos.*

654. *Sedibus:* in the sense of *loco.*

655. *Miserrimus:* most miserable—distracted—in despair.

656. *Nam quod*, &c. The meaning of this line appears to be: for what other course could I take, what else could I do, than arm myself, and seek to renew the conflict? Anchises had positively refused to survive the fall of his country: Æneas could not leave him behind: nothing remained for him to do, but to sell his life as dear as possible. For *dabatur*, Ruæus says *offerebatur.*

657. *Efferre pedem:* to depart. *Sperâstine:* didst thou expect that I could depart, O father, without thee?

658. *Nefas:* impiety.

659. *Superis. Superi* are properly the gods above, as distinguished from those below.

660. *Et hoc sedet:* and this be fixed in thy mind, and it pleases thee to add thyself, &c. Ruæus understands this of the gods just mentioned; but Davidson and others refer it to Anchises. This appears the more correct and natural; for Anchises is left perfectly free to act, either to stay behind, or to depart, and to form his plans deliberately *Si hoc fixum est in eorum mente, et delectat eos*, &c. says Ruæus.

661. *Janua isti leto:* the door to that death is open. The *isti* refers to what An-

Jamque aderit multo Priami de sanguine Pyrrhus,
Natum ante ora patris, patrem qui obtruncat ad aras
Hoc erat, alma parens, quòd me, per tela, per ignes,
Eripis ? ut mediis hostem in penetralibus, utque
Ascaniumque, patremque meum, juxtàque Creüsam,
Alterum in alterius mactatos sanguine cernam ?
Arma, viri, ferte arma : vocat lux ultima victos.
Reddite me Danais, sinite instaurata revisam
Prælia : nunquam omnes hodie moriemur inulti.
Hìc ferro accingor rursus : clypeoque sinistram
Insertabam aptans, meque extra tecta ferebam.
Ecce autem complexa pedes in limine conjux
Hærebat, parvumque patri tendebat Iülum.
Si periturus abis, et nos rape in omnia tecum :
Sin aliquam expertus sumptis spem ponis in armis,
Hanc primùm tutare domum. Cui parvus Iülus,
Cui pater, et conjux quondàm tua dicta, relinquor ?
Talia vociferans, gemitu tectum omne replebat :
Cùm subitum dictuque oritur mirabile monstrum.
Namque manus inter mœstorumque ora parentum,

664. Erat-*ne ob* hoc

665. Ut cernam hostem in mediis penetralibus, utque *cernam* Ascaniumque

669. Sinite *ut* revisam

673. Conjux *Creüsa* complexa *meos* pedes in limine *domûs*

675. In omnia *pericula*

677. Cui parvus Iülus *relinquitur;* cui *tuus* pater; et *cui ego* relinquor, quondam dicta tua conjux?

NOTES.

chises had said, verse 645, supra, of his finding death by his own hand, or that the enemy would take pity on him, and kill him. Æneas here tells him the door to that death is open, and easy to come at; for he immediately adds: *Jamque Pyrrhus:* Pyrrhus will soon be here from the slaughter of Priam. Servius takes *isti* for *istic*, but without sufficient reason. *Iste*, properly, is *that* of yours, *hic*, *this* of mine.

663. *Qui obtruncat:* who butchers the son, &c. This alludes to his killing Polites in the presence of his father, and after that atrocious deed, killing the aged monarch, dragged to the altars.

664. *Hoc erat:* was it for this, dear parent, that, &c. Ruæus says: *Hæc-cine erat causa, cùr.*

665. *Eripis:* in the sense of *servavisti. Penetralibus:* in the sense of *domo*, vel *tecto.* See 484, supra.

667. *Mactatos:* butchered the one in the blood of the other. This part. refers to the three preceding nouns.

668. *Lux:* in the sense of *dies.*

670. *Prælia instaurata:* the fight renewed. *Nunquam:* in the sense of *non.*

672. *Insertabam:* I put my left hand to my shield, fitting it—I fixed my shield upon my left arm. The *clypeus* was a shield of an oval form, not so large as the *scutum.* It was usually made of the skins of beasts, and interwoven in such a manner, as to be impenetrable to the missive weapons of the enemy. They carried it upon the left arm.

674. *Tendebatque parvum*, &c. The poet here appears to have had in his view that affecting scene between Hector and Andromache, in the sixth book of the Iliad, where the circumstances are nearly the same. Andromache expostulates with Hector, as Creüsa does with Æneas, and in like manner pleads her future forlorn condition, and that of her child, in case he should abandon them: and to add force to her entreaties, she puts *Astyanax* into his arms, as Creüsa here does *Iülus* into the arms of Æneas.

675. *Et:* in the sense of *quoque. Rape:* in the sense of *cape*, vel *trahe.*

676. *Expertus:* having experience in the art of war—being skilled in war. *Ponis* you place any, &c.

677. *Tutare:* in the sense of *defende.*

678. *Quondam:* once called your wife. This is a very tender expostulation.

680. *Subitum monstrum.* This unexpected prodigy, or miracle, is extremely well timed. Had Anchises finally persisted in his resolution, it must have put an end to the poem, by involving Æneas and all his family in one common ruin. He had been urged by all human arguments in the strongest manner, without any avail; what then remained for the poet, but to have recourse to the interposition of the gods, to save his hero in this extremity. This was completely successful. Anchises is convinced of his duty to yield to the present necessity, and to save his life by flight. *Oritur:* in the sense of *apparet.*

681. *Inter manus oraque:* between the hands and face of his mournful parents—while they were holding him in their arms behold, &c.

Ecce levis summo de vertice visus Iüli
Fundere lumen apex, tactuque innoxia molli
Lambere flamma comas, et circum tempora pasci
Nos pavidi trepidare metu, crinemque flagrantem
Excutere, et sanctos restinguere fontibus ignes.
At pater Anchises oculos ad sidera lætus
Extulit, et cœlo palmas cum voce tetendit:
Jupiter omnipotens, precibus si flecteris ullis,
Aspice nos: hoc tantùm: et, si pietate meremur,
Da deinde auxilium, pater, atque hæc omina firma.
Vix ea fatus erat senior, subitoque fragore
Intonuit lævum, et de cœlo lapsa per umbras
Stella facem ducens multâ cum luce cucurrit.
Illam, summa super labentem culmina tecti,
Cernimus Idæâ claram se condere sylvâ,
Signantemque vias: tum longo limite sulcus
Dat lucem, et latè circùm loca sulfure fumant.

682. Levis apex visus *est* fundere lumen de summo vertice Iülii flammaque innoxia *visa est* lambere *ejus* comas molli tactu

685. Nos pavidi metu *cœpimus* trepidare

690. *Petimus* tantùm hoc: et, si meremur *aliquid* pietate, O Pater, da

695. Cernimus illam, labentem super summa culmina tecti, condere se

NOTES.

682. *Levis apex:* the waving tuft, or plume. *Apex* properly signifies the top, or eminence of any thing. Hence it may mean the top of one's hat, cap, or bonnet, as in Æn. viii. 664. *Vertice:* in the sense of *capite*.

683. *Fundere:* in the sense of *emittere*. *Innoxia:* inoffensive—not hurting him. *Tactu*. This is the reading of Heyne and Davidson. But Ruæus and Valpy read *tractu*. *Molli:* gentle—easy. Heyne has *mollis*, agreeing with *flamma*. Most copies have *molli*.

684. *Lambere:* to glide along his hair—gently touch it.

685. *Nos pavidi:* we, trembling for fear, (begin) to bustle about, to shake his flaming hair, and to extinguish the sacred fire with water. *Fontibus:* in the sense of *aqua*.

689. *Si flecteris:* if thou art moved.

691. *Firma hæc omina:* confirm this omen. The Romans deemed one omen not sufficient, unless it were followed or confirmed by a second. Hence *secundus* and *secundo* came to signify prosperous, and to prosper.

693. *Lævum intonuit:* the left thundered with a sudden peal.

Both the Greeks and Romans considered those omens, that were presented in the eastern part of heaven, to be prosperous or lucky. But the former, in observing the omens, turned their faces to the north, which brought the east on their right hand. The Romans, on the contrary, turned their faces to the south, which brought the east on their left hand. This was therefore a lucky omen. It seconded, or confirmed the former, that is, the lambent flame on the head of Iülus. See Ecl. i. 18. *Lævum*. an adj. of the neu. gender, used as a sub. the same with *læva pars cœli*.

694. *Stella lapsa*, &c. Servius applies the several parts of this prodigy as figurative of the events that were to happen to Æneas and his followers. The star is said, *condere se Idæa sylva*, to fall or hide itself upon mount Ida, to indicate that the Trojans were to resort to that mountain: *cum multa luce*, with much light, to figure their future glory and dignity: *signantem vias*, the sparkles of fire left behind, intimate the dispersion of his followers, and that they should fix their residence in various parts: *longo limite sulcus*, marks Æneas' many wanderings, and the length of his voyage: lastly, by the smoke and sulphur, he understands the death of Anchises. The stars do not move from their stations; they are fixed, and remain in the same part of the heavens. Meteors are of common occurrence, and are supposed to consist of electric matter, which in passing from one part of the atmosphere to another, becomes visible. In the language of the vulgar and ignorant, such an appearance is called the shooting of a star. Virgil conforms to this mode of expression. He calls the meteor a star. *Facem:* a train.

695. *Labentem*. Ruæus takes this in the sense of *cadentem:* falling behind the roof of the house. But it may be taken in its usual acceptation, gliding, or passing over the roof: for it appears that the meteor was near, since it filled the air about them with its sulphurous smell.

697. *Sulcus:* a trail—indented track.—The meteor drew after it a trail of light, as it passed through the heavens. It appeared to mark its way or path, which it left luminous behind it.

Hìc verò victus genitor se tollit ad auras,
Affaturque Deos, et sanctum sidus adorat:
Jam jam nulla mora est: sequor, et, quâ ducitis, adsum
Dî patrii, servate domum, servate nepotem.
Vestrum hoc augurium, vestroque in numine Troja est.
Cedo equidem, nec, nate, tibi comes ire recuso.
  Dixerat ille: et jam per mœnia clarior ignis
Auditur, propiusque æstus incendia volvunt.
Ergò age, chare pater, cervici imponere nostræ:
Ipse subibo humeris: nec me labor iste gravabit.
Quò res cunque cadent, unum et commune periclum,
Una salus ambobus erit: mihi parvus Iülus
Sit comes, et longè servet vestigia conjux.
Vos, famuli, quæ dicam, animis advertite vestris.
Est urbe egressis tumulus, templumque vetustum
Desertæ Cereris; juxtàque antiqua cupressus,
Relligione patrum multos servata per annos.
Hanc ex diverso sedem veniemus in unam.

709 Quòcunque res cadent, periclum *erit* unum, et commune *nobis* ambobus, salus erit una *et eadem nobis*

712. Tumulus est *iis* egressis urbe

716. *Nos omnes* veniemus ex diverso

NOTES.

699. *Ad auras:* upright—or towards heaven.

702. *Patrii Dii.* By these we are to understand the guardian gods of Anchises' family; those that his ancestors worshipped; who presided over parental and filial affection. *Domum:* in the sense of *familiam.*

703. *Hoc augurium est:* this omen is yours: Troy is under your protection. This is plainly the meaning of *numine* in this place. Ruæus says, *potestate.*

706. *Incendia:* in the sense of *flammæ. Æstus:* heat.

707. *Imponere:* 2d person of the imp. be thou placed, i. e. place yourself upon my neck: I will bear you upon my shoulders. *Subibo humeris: portabo te humeris,* says Ruæus. *Labor:* in the sense of *pondus.*

710. *Mihi parvus Iülus.* Donatus reads, *mihi solus Iülus:* let Iülus only be a companion to me. This avoids the too frequent repetition of *parvus Iülus,* and at the same time shows the prudent caution of Æneas, to secure their flight; since the fewer went together, they would be the less liable to be discovered. Pierius approves this reading.

711. *Conjux servet:* let my wife observe my steps at a distance—let her stay behind, yet so as to have me in view, that she may not lose her way. The reason for his giving this direction was perhaps to prevent discovery, and to diminish the danger of escape by being divided into parties. This reason justifies Æneas. It was proper for the poet to mention this circumstance, to give probability to the account of her being lost. Servius takes *longè* in the sense of *valdè.* The meaning then will be: let my wife carefully observe my steps. The usual acceptation of *longè* is the better. The loss of Creüsa is a fine device of the poet. It gave him an opportunity of finishing the catastrophe of Troy from the mouth of Æneas. As soon as he found his wife was missing, he resolves to return in search of her. He carefully retraces his footsteps, visits his own house, which was now in flames, and searches for her in the most frequented parts of the city. In the course of his search, he sees the spoils collected together in the temple of Juno, and the Grecian guards standing around. Unable to find her in any of these places, he calls her by name, and makes the streets resound with *Creüsa.* Her ghost met him, solaced his mind, unfolded to him the purposes of the gods, and encouraged him to look for more prosperous times. She tells him that in the land destined him by fate, a royal bride awaited him.

712. *Advertite:* turn with your minds to those things which I shall say. This is equivalent to, *advertite vestros animos ad ea, quæ dicam.*

714. *Desertæ Cereris.* This epithet of *deserted,* is added to Ceres, on account of her being deprived of her daughter Proserpine by Pluto; or on account of the state of her worship, which was then neglected, her priest having been slain. Ruæus understands it as referring to her temple: an ancient temple of Ceres deserted. He interprets *desertæ* by, *desertum,* agreeing with *templum.* See Ecl. v. 79.

715. *Relligione:* by the religious veneration of our ancestors. *Servata* agrees with *antiqua cupressus. Juxtà:* near—near by.

716 *Ex diverso:* the same as *ex diversis viis. Sedem:* in the sense of *locum.*

Tu, genitor, cape sacra manu, patriosque Penates.
Me, bello è tanto digressum et cæde recenti,
Attrectare nefas; donec me flumine vivo
Abluero.
Hæc fatus, latos humeros subjectaque colla
Veste super, fulvique insternor pelle leonis,
Succedoque oneri: dextræ se parvus Iülus
Implicuit, sequiturque patrem non passibus æquis.
Ponè subit conjux. Ferimur per opaca locorum:
Et me, quem dudum non ulla injecta movebant
Tela, neque adverso glomerati ex agmine Graii,
Nunc omnes terrent auræ, sonus excitat omnis
Suspensum, et pariter comitique onerique timentem.
Jamque propinquabam portis, omnemque videbar
Evasisse viam; subitò cùm creber ad aures

718. Nefas *esset* me digressum

722. Fatus hæc, insternor super latos humeros, subjectaque colla

726. Et nunc omnes auræ terrent, omnis sonus excitat me, *et reddit me* suspensum, et pariter timentem comitique, onerique; *me, inquam,* quem dudum non ulla injecta tela, neque Graii

NOTES.

717. *Sacra:* the holy, or sacred utensils; such as were used in offering sacrifices, and in other ceremonies of religious worship: neu. plu. of *sacer*, used as a sub. Heyne thinks *sacra* here, and in verse 293, supra, means the images of the gods; thus making it the same with *Penates.* The reader must judge for himself. His words are: *Sacra et Penates possunt pro eadem re haberi: et sic de Deorum simulacris, etiam de Penatibus ipsis.*

Penates. This word is derived probably from *penus*, which signifies all kinds of food or provisions for the use of man. The *Penates* were usually worshipped in the interior part of the house. Their number is not known, nor is it certain what gods were so denominated. Some reckon *Jupiter*, *Juno*, and *Minerva*, among the *Penates;* others, *Neptune* and *Apollo;* others again, *Cœlus* and *Terra:* and Arnobius reckons the *Dii Consentes*, or *Complices*, among their number. There were three orders of the *Dii Penates.* Those that presided over kingdoms and provinces, were called solely *Penates:* those that presided over cities only, were called *Dii Patrii*, domestic gods, or gods of the country: those that presided over particular houses and families, were called *Parvi Penates.*

It is not certain under what shape or figure they were worshipped. Some suppose it was under the figure of a young man sitting and holding a spear. It is said that Dardanus introduced them from *Samothracia* into Troy, and that Æneas took them with him into Italy. See Geor. ii. 505.

719. *Nefas me:* it is unlawful for me, having come, &c. In like manner, Homer makes Hector say he was afraid of performing religious worship to Jupiter, while his hands were polluted with blood, Iliad vi. 334. It was the custom of the Greeks and Romans, and most other nations, to wash their hands, and sometimes their whole bodies in water, before they performed acts of religion, especially if they had been polluted with bloodshed. On such occasions they were obliged to use pure water, like that of fountains or running water. Hence Æneas says: *Donec abluero me vivo flumine:* until I shall have washed myself in pure or living water. *Flumine:* in the sense of *aqua. Bello:* in the sense of *pugnâ.*

722. *Insternor super:* I am covered upon my broad shoulders and bended neck with a garment, &c.—I cover myself, &c. This use of the verb answers to the middle voice of the Greeks. So *imponere:* be thou placed—place thyself; verse 707, supra. *Subjecta:* in the sense of *submissa.*

723. *Succedo oneri.* The meaning is: I take my father upon my shoulders—I place myself under the load.

725. *Opaca locorum:* the same as *opaca loca.* Or the word *spatia* may be understood, connected with *opaca*, and governing *locorum.*

727. *Glomerati ex adverso:* collected together in hostile array. Here we have a very beautiful image of our hero's pious and filial affection. With unshaken fortitude he faced the greatest dangers, when his own person only was exposed: now every appearance of danger strikes him with terror, on account of his dear charge. *Adverso:* in the sense of *hostili.*

729. *Suspensum:* in the sense of *solicitum.*

730. *Videbar*, &c. Ruæus interprets the following words by, *excessisse ex omnibus viis;* which appears entirely inadmissible. The meaning is: that he seemed to have escaped all the danger of the way; when, to his surprise, a frequent sound of feet suddenly struck his ears.

731. *Viam.* This is the common reading. Heyne, at the suggestion of Markland, reads *vicem*, in the sense of *periculum;* which is preferable, if we had sufficient authority for the substitution.

Visus adesse pedum sonitus: genitorque per umbram
Prospiciens, Nate, exclamat, fuge, nate: propinquant
Ardentes clypeos atque æra micantia cerno.
Hìc mihi nescio quod trepido malè numen amicum
Confusam eripuit mentem. Namque avia cursu
Dum sequor, et notâ excedo regione viarum:
Heu! misero conjux fatone erepta Creüsa
Substitit, erravitne viâ, seu lassa resedit,
Incertum: nec pòst oculis est reddita nostris.
Nec priùs amissam respexi, animumve reflexi,
Quàm tumulum antiquæ Cereris, sedemque sacratam
Venimus: hìc demum, collectis omnibus, una
Defuit; et comites, natumque, virumque fefellit.
Quem non incusavi amens hominumque Deorumque?
Aut quid in eversâ vidi crudelius urbe?
Ascanium, Anchisenque patrem, Teucrosque Penates,
Commendo sociis, et curvâ valle recondo.
Ipse urbem repeto, et cingor fulgentibus armis.
Stat casus renovare omnes, omnemque reverti
Per Trojam, et rursus caput objectare periclis.
Principio, muros, obscuraque limina portæ,
Quà gressum extuleram, repeto: et vestigia retrò
Observata sequor per noctem, et lumine lustro.
Horror ubique animos, simul ipsa silentia terrent.
Inde domum, si fortè pedem, si fortè tulisset,

733. *Hostes* propinquant

735. Hìc malè amicum numen, necio quod *numen*, eripuit mihi trepido

738. Conjux Creüsa substitit; incertum *est*, erepta-ne misero fato, erravit-ne viâ, seu

741. Nec respexi, reflexive animum, *eam esse* amissam, priùsquàm venimus *ad*

743. *Uxor* una defuit

748. Recondo *eos, in*

750. Stat *sententia* renovare omnes

755. Ubique *est* horror; simul ipsa silentia *noctis* terrent animos. Inde refero me domum, *ut viderem*, si fortè, si fortè *Creüsa* tulisset pedem *huc.*

NOTES.

732. *Umbram:* in the sense of *tenebras.*

734. *Cerno:* I see their glittering shields and gleaming brass. *Æra:* brazen armour.

735. *Malè:* in the sense of *non. Malè amicum:* in the sense of *inimicum* vel *infestum.*

736. *Confusam mentem.* His mind was confused, and in a state of perturbation, for fear that something might befall him in his retreat. He had retained his presence of mind so far as to make good his escape in the best possible manner. Now, on a sudden, he loses all recollection; he forgets himself; he knows not what he does: he is deprived of that presence of mind which he had hitherto retained, by some *unfriendly deity.* In consequence of this he left the plain road, taking the by-paths: nor did he recollect to look back to see if his wife was following him.

Avia: an adj. agreeing with *loca* understood; out of the way: from the ordinary or common way. Of *a*, privativum, and *via.*

737. *Nota regione viarum:* simply, from the known or beaten way.

738. *Misero fato.* Some render *misero*, with *mihi* understood. But *miser* signifies that which makes miserable, as well as simply, miserable. In this sense it may be connected with *fato:* distressing fate. When thus construed, it hath a peculiar force. Both Ruæus and Heyne say, *misero mihi.*

4 *Reflexi animum:* turned back my mind—reflected. Heyne reads *ve.* The common reading is *que.*

742. *Tumulum.* The hill, or eminence, on which the temple of Ceres was situated. See 714. supra.

745. *Quem hominumque:* whom both of men and gods did I not blame? *Amens:* distracted in mind—deprived of my reason: of *a*, privativum, and *mens.*

747. *Teucros:* in the sense of *Trojanos.*

750. *Stat. Sententia*, or some word of the like import, is understood: my purpose is fixed: *I am resolved.* While the mind is in doubt and uncertainty, it reels to and fro from one thing to another, *fluctuat, vacillat:* but when it is determined and resolved, then it stands still; it is at rest. *Casus:* in the sense of *pericula. Reverti:* in the sense of *redire.*

752. *Limina:* threshold—entrance.

753. *Extuleram gressum:* where I had come out. A phrase.

754. *Lumine. Lumen* properly signifies light: it also signifies an eye. In this last sense, Ruæus takes it, and interprets it by *oculis.* It is perhaps better to understand it of the light occasioned by the conflagration of Troy. In this case, *sequor*, &c. may be rendered: I follow back my footsteps observed in the darkness, and search them out by the light of the flames. Davidson agrees with Ruæus.

756. *Si fortè, si fortè:* if by chance, if by

Me refero. Irruerant Danai, et tectum omne tenebant.
Ilicèt ignis edax summa ad fastigia vento
Volvitur; exsuperant flammæ; furit æstus ad auras.
Procedo ad Priami sedes, arcemque reviso.
Et jam porticibus vacuis, Junonis asylo,
Custodes lecti Phœnix et dirus Ulysses
Prædam asservabant: huc undique Troïa gaza
Incensis erepta adytis, mensæque Deorum,
Crateresque auro solidi, captivaque vestis
Congeritur. Pueri et pavidæ longo ordine matres
Stant circùm.
Ausus quinetiam voces jactare per umbram
Implevi clamore vias: mœstusque Creüsam
Nequicquam ingeminans, iterumque iterumque vocavi.
Quærenti, et tectis urbis sinè fine furenti,
Infelix simulacrum, atque ipsius umbra Creüsæ
Visa mihi ante oculos, et notâ major imago.
Obstupui, steteruntque comæ, et vox faucibus hæsit.
Tum sic affari, et curas his demere dictis:
Quid tantùm insano juvat indulgere dolori,
O dulcis conjux? non hæc sinè numine Divûm
Eveniunt: nec te comitem asportare Creüsam

765. Solidi *ex* auro

771. Infelix simulacrum, atque umbra Creüsæ ipsius, et imago major notâ visa *est* mihi ante oculos, quærenti *eam*, et furenti

775. Tum *illa cœpit* sic affari *me*

778. Nec fas *est*, aut ille regnator superi

NOTES.

chance, she had returned thither. *Tulisset pedem:* had returned, or gone thither. The repetition of the *si fortè*, is emphatical.

760. *Procedo.* Creüsa was the daughter of Priam, by Hecuba; which, perhaps, is the reason of his going to his palace in search of her.

761. *Asylo:* in the sense of *templo. Porticibus:* in the passages or aisles.

763. *Gaza.* This word signifies all kinds of rich furniture—wealth—property. It is of Persian origin. *Erepta*, is connected with it.

764. *Mensæ Deorum.* These were the tripods of the gods, which served for delivering the oracles, or for bearing the sacred vessels. *Adytis:* in the sense of *templis.*

763. *Undique.* This word may imply, that the things here mentioned were collected from all parts of the town, and thrown in this place (*huc*,) or that they were piled up here all around--in every part of the building.

770. *Ingeminans:* repeating her name in vain—in vain, because she did not answer him. *Mœstus*, agrees with *ego*, understood. *Furenti:* for *currenti.*

772. *Infelix simulacrum:* the unhappy apparition—unhappy, not on her own account, for she was blessed and at rest; but because she was the source of sorrow and unhappiness to her husband. *Umbra.* The introduction of Creüsa's ghost is extremely well timed. No other expedient could be found to stop the further search of Æneas for his wife, and permit him to return to his friends in their expedition. It shows the judgment of the poet.

773. *Imago major notâ:* her image larger than life—than when alive. Spectres and apparitions are usually represented of a large size; fear having a tendency to enlarge objects that are presented to the imagination. The darkness of the night has a tendency to enlarge the appearance of objects seen obscurely and imperfectly.

This episode of Creüsa's death is introduced, not merely for the importance of the event, but because it answered several important purposes of the poet. It gave him an opportunity of more fully illustrating the piety of Æneas, by showing him once more exposed to all the dangers of the war in search of his wife; and, in consequence of that, leads us back with his hero to visit Troy smoking in its ruins, and makes us acquainted with several affecting circumstances, without which the narration would not have been complete. And then it makes way for the appearance of her ghost, that affords comfort to Æneas in his distress, by predicting his future felicity; and relieves the mind of the reader from the horrors of war and desolation, by turning him to the prospect of that peace and tranquillity which Æneas was to enjoy in Italy; and of that undisturbed rest, and happy liberty, of which herself was now possessed in the other world.

776. *Insano dolori:* immoderate grief. *Numine:* in the sense of *voluntate.*

Olympi sinit te asportare hinc Creüsam, comitem tibi

780. Longa exilia futura sunt

784. Parta sunt tibi

787. Ego quæ sum Dardanis, et

790. Deseruit me lachrymantem, et volentem dicere

792. Ibi conatus sum ter circumdare

Fas, aut ille sinit superi regnator Olympi.
Longa tibi exilia, et vastum maris æquor arandum.
Ad terram Hesperiam venies, ubi Lydius arva
Inter opima virûm leni fluit agmine Tybris.
Illìc res lætæ, regnumque, et regia conjux
Parta tibi: lachrymas dilectæ pelle Creüsæ.
Non ego Myrmidonum sedes Dolopumve superbas
Aspiciam, aut Graiis servitum matribus ibo,
Dardanis, et Divæ Veneris nurus.
Sed me magna Deûm genitrix his detinet oris
Jamque vale, et nati serva communis amorem.
Hæc ubi dicta dedit, lachrymantem et multa volentem
Dicere deseruit, tenuesque recessit in auras.
Ter conatus ibi collo dare brachia circùm:
Ter frustrà comprensa manus effugit imago,
Par levibus ventis, volucrique simillima somno.
  Sic demum socios, consumptâ nocte, reviso.
Atque hìc ingentem comitum affluxisse novorum
Invenio admirans numerum; matresque, virosque,
Collectam exilio pubem, miserabile vulgus.

NOTES.

779. *Superi Olympi:* of high heaven.

780. *Exilia:* in the sense of *itinera.* It implies that Æneas should be for a long time destitute of any country, or fixed habitation. *Æquor:* properly any level surface, whether land or water. It is often used in the sense of *mare. Arandum:* in the sense of *navigandum.*

781. *Ad:* Heyne reads *et.* Some copies have *ut:* that you may arrive or come, &c. In this case there must not be a full point after *arandum.* The usual reading is *ad.*

782. *Lydius Tybris:* the Tuscan Tyber flows, with its gentle stream, between lands rich in heroes.

The Tyber is here called *Lydian,* or Tuscan. It separated Tuscany from *Latium.* The former having been settled by a colony of *Lydians* under *Tyrrhenus,* the son of *Atys,* king of Lydia, in Asia Minor. He called the inhabitants *Tyrrheni,* after his own name. *Agmine:* in the sense of *cursu* vel *flumine. Virûm. Vir,* properly signifies a man, as opposed to a woman—a hero. Also, the male of any kind or species of animals. *Arva:* properly cultivated lands, from the verb *aro.*

783. *Res lætæ:* prosperity. The same as *res secundæ.* Æneas, after his arrival in Italy, and the death of Turnus, married *Lavinia,* the daughter of *Latinus,* king of *Latium,* and succeeded him in his kingdom.

Æneas, in relating this prophecy to Dido, plainly informs her that he was destined by fate for *Lavinia;* and, by so doing, pleads the necessity of his leaving Carthage. Dido, therefore, betrays herself by an indiscreet passion, and is not betrayed by any perfidy of Æneas. See lib. iv. passim.

784. *Dilectæ Creüsæ:* for, or on account of your beloved Creüsa.

786. *Servitum:* to serve in the capacity of a servant. The sup. in *um,* of the verb *servio,* put after *ibo.*

787. *Dardanis.* Creüsa was the daughter of Priam, and consequently descended in a direct line from *Dardanus,* the founder of the Trojan race: at least one of the founders of it. See Æn. i. 1. *Nurus:* the daughter-in-law. Æneas was the son of Venus and Anchises, which made *Creüsa* the daughter-in-law to *Venus.*

788. *Genitrix:* Cybele. She is said to have been the mother of all the gods.

789. *Serva:* retain, or keep. *Nati:* Ascanius, who was the son of Creüsa and Æneas.

792. *Circumdare.* The parts of the verb are separated, for the sake of the verse, by Tmesis.

793. *Comprensa:* a part. agreeing with *imago. Manus:* acc. plu. Her image, seized in vain three times, escaped his hands.

794. *Par:* in the sense of *similis. Somno:* a dream.

796. *Hìc admirans invenio,* &c. The poet, by this circumstance, signifies how greatly Æneas was beloved by the Trojans, and the weight and importance of his character. It appears that this multitude, by resorting to Æneas, and putting themselves under his protection, chose him their king; which appellation is given him throughout the Æneid. *Affluxisse:* in the sense of *advenisse.*

797. *Miserabile vulgus:* a pitiable multitude. They assembled, from all quarters, prepared in mind and fortune to follow me, to whatsoever countries I might wish to lead

Undique convenere, animis opibusque parati,
In quascunque velim pelago deducere terras.
Jamque jugis summæ surgebat Lucifer Idæ,
Ducebatque diem: Danaique obsessa tenebant
Limina portarum: nec spes opis ulla dabatur
Cessi, et sublato montem genitore petivi.

799. *Illi* convenere undique, parati animis opibusque *sequi me*

NOTES.

them over the sea. *Pubem:* in the sense of *juventutem.*

801. *Jugis summæ Idæ.* Mount Ida lay to the east of Troy, and, consequently, *Lucifer, Venus,* or the Morning Star, as it is called when going before the sun, appeared to those at Troy to rise from the top (*jugis*) of that mountain. *Summæ:* in the sense of *altæ.*

803. *Opis.* Ruæus interprets this by *auxilii;* but it may mean wealth—property: and by the expression we may understand, that there was now no hope of obtaining any more of their wealth or property, the city being completely in the possession of the Greeks.

804. *Cessi:* I yielded to my fate. Dr. Trapp renders it, *I retired;* but it is much better to understand it as an expression of the piety and resignation of Æneas, especially if we consider what immediately precedes: *nec spes opis ulla dabatur. Genitore sublato.* This instance of filial piety is highly pleasing. A modern commander would never have submitted to the task of bearing such a load; but would have assigned it to a servant, or imposed it upon a soldier. Ruæus says, *ferens patrem.*

QUESTIONS.

What is the subject of this book?

What is its character, when compared with the rest?

How long did the siege of Troy continue?

How was it taken at the last?

To whom was this horse designed as a present?

In return for what?

What was the Palladium?

By whom was it taken from the temple of Minerva?

After building the horse, what did the Greeks do?

How far was Tenedos from Troas?

Did they pretend that they were about to return home, and relinquish the siege?

Did this obtain belief among the Trojans?

What was the real object of the Greeks in building this horse?

Who acted a very distinguished part in this business?

What is the character of Sinon?

Who opposed the admission of this horse within the walls?

What prodigy happened just at this time, which overcame all doubts in the minds of the Trojans?

Who was Laocoon?

To what office had he been appointed by lot?

What was the design of offering sacrifice to Neptune at this time?

What did this horse contain?

How did it enter into the city?

Where was it placed?

How many names has the poet invented for this engine of destruction?

What time was the assault made upon the city?

What office did Sinon perform upon this occasion?

Did the Grecian troops return from Tenedos, and join their friends?

How were they received into the city?

In what state were the Trojans at this time?

Were they aware of any such treachery?

Finding the city in the hands of the enemy, what course did Æneas pursue?

What were some of his actions?

Where were his last efforts made to avenge his country?

What became of Priam?

What were the last actions of the aged monarch?

What particularly roused his indignation against Pyrrhus?

By whom was Priam slain?

What was the manner of it?

What were the circumstances of it?

Where was Æneas during these transactions?

What did he do, after he beheld the death of Priam?

Under whose conduct did he pass in safety through his enemies?

Did Æneas receive direction to leave the city, and to seek his safety in flight?

How did he receive it? From whom?

What was the determination of his father Anchises?

What effect had his refusal upon the mind of Æneas?

What did his wife Creüsa do upon this occasion?

How was the determination of Anchises, not to survive the capture of the city, changed?

What were the prodigies that effected that change?

To what place did he retire?

How did he convey his father?

How his son Ascanius?

What direction did he give his wife Creusa?

Did he arrive in safety to the place appointed?

What became of his wife?

What did he do in consequence of her loss?

What effect had her loss upon him at the first?

How was his mind quieted?

What directions did her apparition give him?

After his return to the place of rendezvous, did he find great numbers there collected?

Did they consider him their leader and king?

Were they prepared and willing to undertake any enterprise, he might think proper

---

LIBER TERTIUS.

Æneas, having finished the sack of Troy, proceeds to relate to Dido the particulars of his voyage. Having built a fleet of twenty ships near Antandros, he set sail in the spring, probably, of the year following the capture of Troy. He landed on the shores of Thrace, and there commenced the building of a city, which he called, after his own name, *Ænos*, and the inhabitants, *Æneadæ*. He was, however, soon interrupted in the prosecution of his work, by the shade of Polydorus, the son of Priam. He had been barbarously put to death by Polymnestor, king of Thrace, his brother-in-law, and buried in this place. It directed him to leave the polluted land, and to seek another clime for his intended city.

Having performed the funeral rites to Polydorus, he set sail, directing his course to the south; and soon arrived on the coast of Delos, one of the Cyclades. Here he was hospitably received by Anius, king of the island, and priest of Apollo. He was directed by the oracle to seek the land of his ancestors; there he should found a city, which should bear rule over all nations. This information was joyfully received. Whereupon, they concluded that Crete, the birth-place of Teucer, was the land to which the oracle directed them.

Leaving Delos, in a short time they arrive on the shores of Crete. They hail it with joy as the termination of their wanderings. Here Æneas lays the foundation of a city which he called *Pergama*, and was preparing to enter upon the business of agriculture, when a sudden plague arose, which put an end to his prospects, and carried off many of his companions. In this juncture, it was agreed that he should go back to Delos, to obtain further instructions. In the mean time, in a vision, he was informed that Crete was not the land destined to him, and that the oracle of Apollo intended he should seek Italy, the land of Dardanus. This quieted his mind; and Anchises acknowledged that both Teucer and Dardanus were the founders of their race, and that he had been mistaken in reckoning their descent in the line of Teucer.

Æneas, without delay, leaves Crete; and in a few days arrived on the coast of the *Strophades*, in the Ionian sea, on the west of the Peloponnesus. Here he landed with his fleet, and found these islands in the possession of the Harpies. Celæno, one of them, informed him, that, before he should found a city, they should be reduced to the necessity of consuming their tables. This was the first intimation which he had received of want and suffering, in the land destined to him. It sunk deep into his mind.

Leaving these islands, he directed his course westward, and soon arrived on the coast of Epirus. He landed at *Actium*, and celebrated the Trojan games.

From Actium, he proceeded to that part of Epirus called Chaonia. On his entering the harbor, he heard that Helenus, the son of Priam, sat upon the throne of Pyrrhus, and that Andromache had become his wife. Desirous of hearing the truth of this report, he proceeds direct to *Buthrotus*, the seat of government. Here, to his great joy, he finds his friends, and remained with them for some time. Helenus, at their departure, loads them with presents. Andromache gives to Ascanius alone, who was the exact picture of her son Astyanax.

From Epirus, Æneas passes over the Ionian sea, and arrives at the promontory *Iapygium.* Thence he sails down the coast of *Magna Græcia*, and the eastern shore of Sicily, to the promontory *Pachynum;* thence along the southern shore to the port of *Drepanum*, where he lost his father Anchises; which concludes the book.

This book contains the annals of seven years, and is replete with geographical and historical information. Nor is it wanting in fine specimens of poetry, and in interesting incidents. The joy of Æneas at finding Helenus and Andromache on the throne of Epirus—their happy meeting—their tender and affectionate parting—the description of Scylla and Charybdis, and the episode of the Cyclops, are all worthy of the poet.
In this book, Virgil in a particular manner follows the Odyssey of Homer.

POSTQUAM res Asiæ Priamique evertere gentem
Immeritam visum Superis, ceciditque superbum
Ilium, et omnis humo fumat Neptunia Troja:
Diversa exilia, et desertas quærere terras,
Auguriis agimur Divûm: classemque sub ipsa
Antandro, et Phrygiæ molimur montibus Idæ:
Incerti quò fata ferant, ubi sistere detur;
Contrahimusque viros. Vix prima inceperat æstas,
Et pater Anchises dare fatis vela jubebat.

1. Postquam visum *est* Superis evertere res Asiæ

7 Ferant *nos* ubi detur *nobis* sistere *pedem*

NOTES.

1. *Res Asiæ:* the power of Asia.

2. *Immeritam:* undeserving such a calamity. The ruin of their country was owing to the crimes of Paris and Laomedon. See Geor. i. 502, and Æn. i. *Visum Superis:* it pleased, or seemed good to the gods. This was a common mode of expression, when events were not prosperous. The verb *est* is to be supplied with *visum.*

3. *Neptunia.* Troy is here called *Neptunean,* because Neptune, with Apollo, it is said, built its walls in the reign of Laomedon. Homer and Virgil ascribe the building of the walls to Neptune alone. Ruæus takes *Ilium* to mean the citadel of Troy, and distinguishes it from the whole town, which is here expressed by, *omnis Troja.* Homer uses *Ilios,* and Ovid, *Ilion. Fumat.* The present here is much more expressive than the past tense would have been: smokes to the ground.

4. *Diversa:* in the sense of *remota,* or *longinqua.* Although the Trojans, under different leaders, as Æneas, Helenus, and Antenor, settled in different regions, yet *diversa exilia* plainly refers to Æneas and his followers only, who were all appointed to go in quest of the same settlement. *Desertas terras:* unoccupied—uncultivated lands; where they might settle in peace. Or, we may suppose Æneas to speak the language of his heart at that time. Having the dismal idea of the destruction of his country fresh in his mind, and the uncertain prospect of a settlement in some unknown land, (*incerti quò fata ferant, ubi sistere detur,*) it was natural for him to have uncomfortable apprehensions of the country to which he was going; to call it an exile, or place of banishment, a land of solitude and desertion. Some read *diversas,* for *desertas.*

5. *Auguriis Divûm:* by the intimations, or prodigies of the gods. This refers to the several prophetic intimations given to him of his future fate by the ghost of Hector—by the lambent flame on the head of Ascanius—and by the interview which he had with the ghost of Creüsa. *Ominibus Deorum,* says Ruæus.

6. *Antandro.* Antandros was a city of the lesser Phrygia, at the foot of mount Ida, and a convenient place to build and equip a fleet. *Molimur:* in the sense of *fabricamus*

7. *Incerti quò.* We may be somewhat surprised to hear Æneas express any doubt as to his course and intended settlement. He had been distinctly informed by the ghost of his wife, that Italy was the place destined for him in the counsels of the gods: he could not therefore have given full credence to the account; or the dangers and difficulties of the undertaking might have filled his mind with anxious and distrustful apprehensions: or perhaps it is a passage, which the author would have corrected, if he had lived to revise his work.

8. *Prima æstas.* Scaliger thinks that Troy was taken about the full moon, and near the end of spring, and that Æneas set out the beginning of summer. But it is evident that it would require a greater length of time to build a fleet, and make other preparations for his long voyage. If he be correct in the time of the capture of Troy, the *prima æstas,* with more propriety, will mean the beginning of the summer of the following year. This better agrees with history. Dionysius of Halicarnassus, informs us that he collected an army and fortified himself on mount Ida; but not thinking it prudent to engage the enemy, he capitulated on honorable terms; one of which was, that he should be allowed to depart from Troas with his followers without molestation, after a certain time, which he employed in building and equipping a fleet.

9. *Fatis: quò fata vellent,* says Ruæus *Propter jussa et monita Deorum,* says Heyne Some copies have *ventis.*

Litora tum patriæ lachrymans, portusque relinquo,
Et campos, ubi Troja fuit: feror exul in altum,
Cum sociis, natoque, Penatibus, et magnis Dîs.
Terra procul vastis colitur Mavortia campis,
Thraces arant, acri quondam regnata Lycurgo:
Hospitium antiquum Trojæ, sociique Penates,
Dum fortuna fuit. Feror huc, et litore curvo
Mœnia prima loco, fatis ingressus iniquis:
Æneadasque meo nomen de nomine fingo.
Sacra Dionææ matri, Divisque ferebam
Auspicibus cœptorum operum: superoque nitentem
Cœlicolûm regi mactabam in litore taurum.
Fortè fuit juxtà tumulus, quo cornea summo

14. *Quam* Thraces arant

15. *Fuit* antiquum hospitium Trojæ, *cujus*que Penates *erant* socii *nostris*, dum fortuna fuit *nobis*

22. Quo summo *erant* cornea virgulta, et myrtus horrida densis

NOTES.

10. *Lachrymans.* The shedding of tears is an indication of compassion and humanity. It is not inconsistent with true fortitude and greatness of mind, and no way unbecoming a hero. But there is no necessity of understanding it here, and in various other passages where it occurs, as if Æneas actually shed tears. Ruæus takes it in the sense of *lugens*, grieving at the idea of leaving his native country, and at the prospect of the dangers which were before him.

12. *Magnis Dîs.* The great gods were Jupiter, Juno, Mars, Pallas, Mercury, and Apollo; sometimes called the *Dii majorum gentium.* The *Penates* were domestic gods, without any particular name. The images of all these gods Æneas took with him into Italy, and introduced their worship, as we are told, into *Latium*, after he was settled in that kingdom. Some take the *Magnis Dîs* to be the same with the *Penatibus.* See Geor. ii. 505. and Æn. ii. 717.

13. *Mavortia terra:* a martial land.—Thrace is so called, because said to be the birthplace of Mars. This was a very extensive country, bounded on the east by the Euxine sea, south by the Propontis, Hellespont, and Ægean sea, and on the West by Macedonia. *Colitur:* in the sense of *habitatur. Procul.* This word sometimes signifies near, in view, as if *pro oculis*, as in Ecl. vi. 16. In this sense it may be taken here; for Thrace was only a short distance from the port where Æneas set sail. But it may have reference to Carthage, the place where he then was; and then it may be taken in its usual acceptation.

14. *Acri Lycurgo:* warlike Lycurgus. He was the son of Dryas. Being offended at Bacchus, it is said, he banished him and his votaries from his kingdom; and ordered all the vines to be destroyed in his dominions. For which impiety the god deprived him of his sight. *Regnata*, refers to *terra:* governed, or ruled.

15. *Hospitium* an ancient retreat of Troy, and its gods were our friends, while fortune was with us There had been a long and friendly alliance between the two countries, by virtue of which the Thracians gave a hospitable reception to all strangers from Troy; and the Trojans, in turn, repaid the kindness by civilities to the Thracians. This hospitality was sometimes between whole nations, between one city and another, and sometimes between particular families. Polymnestor, king of Thrace, married *Ilione*, the daughter of Priam. By these means the two nations became related in their respective heads: and their gods might be said to be allied, confederate, and friends, in consequence of it.

17. *Prima mœnia:* I place my first walls. The city which Æneas first founded, we are told, he called *Ænos.* It was not far from the mouth of the Hebrus, on the shore of the Ægean sea. The tomb of Polydorus was near this place. *Ingressus:* having entered upon the business with fates unkind—against the will and purposes of the gods, who directed him to the land of Dardanus.

18. *Fingo Æneadas:* I call the inhabitants *Æneadæ*, a name derived from my name. *Fingo:* in the sense of *voco.*

19. *Dionææ:* an adj. from *Dione*, the mother of Venus. *Matri:* to his mother, Venus. *Sacra:* in the sense of *sacrificia.* And *ferebam:* in the sense of *offerebam.*

20. *Auspicibus:* the favorers or patrons of our work begun. It is put in apposition with *Divis.*

21. *Mactabam:* I was sacrificing a shining bull to the high king of the gods. Servius tells us that a bull was one of those animals forbidden to be offered in sacrifice to Jove; and thinks Virgil, designedly, makes Æneas offer here an unlawful sacrifice, in order to introduce the inauspicious omen that followed. But *La Cerda* assures us, upon the best authority, that it was usual to sacrifice bulls to Jupiter, as well as to the other gods. *Nitentem.* Ruæus says, *pinguem:* and Heyne, *candidum.*

22. *Tumulus:* a rising ground, or hillock. *Quo summo:* on whose top. *Cornea:* as

Virgulta, et densis hastilibus horrida myrtus.
Accessi, viridemque ab humo convellere sylvam
Conatus, ramis tegerem ut frondentibus aras:
Horrendum et dictu video mirabile monstrum.
Nam, quæ prima solo, ruptis radicibus, arbos
Vellitur, huic atro liquuntur sanguine guttæ,
Et terram tabo maculant. Mihi frigidus horror
Membra quatit, gelidusque coit formidine sanguis
Rursus et alterius lentum convellere vimen
Insequor, et causas penitùs tentare latentes:
Ater et alterius sequitur de cortice sanguis.
Multa movens animo, Nymphas venerabar agrestes,
Gradivumque patrem, Geticis qui præsidet arvis,
Ritè secundarent visus, omenque levarent.
Tertia sed postquam majore hastilia nixu
Aggredior, genibusque adversæ obluctor arenæ:
Eloquar, an sileam? gemitus lachrymabilis imo
Auditur tumulo, et vox reddita fertur ad aures:
Quid miserum, Ænea, laceras? jam parce sepulto,
Parce pias scelerare manus: non me tibi Troja
Externum tulit: haud cruor hic de stipite manat.

24. Accessi *ad locum*, conatusque *sum* convellere

27. Quæ arbos prima vellitur solo, huic guttæ *ex* atro

30. Coit circum cor.

31. Alterius *arboris*, et penitùs tentare latentes causas *earum rerum;* et ater

36. *Ut* ritè secundarent visus, levarentque *malum* omen

41. Quid, *O* Ænea, laceras *me* miserum? jam parce *mihi*

43. De stipite *arboris sed de meo corpore*

NOTES.

adj. of the corneil tree. *Densis hastilibus.* The long and tapering branches of a tree may not improperly be called *hastilia*, spears. There is a peculiar propriety in the use of the word here, as being the spears with which the body of Polydorus had been transfixed; and had sprung up into a thick body of trees or shrubs. *Horrida:* awful. Ruæus says, *aspera.*

24. *Sylvam:* in the sense, here, of *ramos* vel *ramum.*

26. *Monstrum:* in the sense of *prodigium.*

27. *Arbos:* a shrub, bush, or small tree. *Solo:* from the earth.

28. *Huic:* in the sense of *ex hâc. Liquuntur:* in the sense of *defluunt. Atro sanguine:* in the sense of *atri sanguinis.* The prep. *e* or *ex* is understood.

29. *Horror:* in the sense of *tremor. Mihi:* in the sense of *mea.*

30. *Sanguis gelidus:* my blood, chilled through fear, collects together—ceases to flow in its regular course.

32. *Insequor:* I proceed to tear up. *Vimen lentum:* a limber, or pliant shoot or shrub.

34. *Venerabar Nymphas.* These rustic nymphs, to whom Æneas here prays, were probably the *Hamadryades*, whose destiny was connected with that of some particular trees, with which they lived and died. Æneas might consider this horrid omen, as an indication of their displeasure, for his ffering to violate those pledges of their existence. *Movens:* in the sense of *volvens.*

35. *Gradivum patrem:* Mars. We are told that *Gradivus* was an epithet, or name, of Mars in time of war, as *Quirinus* was in time of peace. Its derivation is uncertain. *Geticis:* an adj. from *Getæ*, a people bordering upon the *Ister*, or Danube; here put for *Thracian*, on account of the vicinity of the two countries: or, because Thrace was thought to extend, indefinitely, to the North.

36. *Secundarent.* Two omens were required for confirmation: if the first happened to be unlucky, and the second prosperous, the latter destroyed the former, and was termed *omen secundum;* and hence *secundo*, to prosper. Æneas, therefore, wished to have the omen repeated, that the bad or unlucky import of it might be removed, or taken away. *Visus:* vision, acc. plu. *Levarent:* in the sense of *averterent.*

37. *Tertia hastilia:* a third shrub or tree. *Nixu:* in the sense of *vi.*

38. *Aggredior:* I attempt, or try to pull up, &c. He exerted himself to eradicate it, with his knees upon the ground, that he might have the greater purchase, or power. *Adversæ:* opposite, right against his knees.

40. *Reddita:* in the sense of *emissa ex eo.*

42. *Parce scelerare:* forbear to pollute your pious hands. It was the law of the Twelve Tables, and, indeed, it is the voice of humanity, that no injury be done to the dead: *defuncti injuriâ ne afficiantur.* The ghost of Polydorus, therefore, calls out to Æneas: *parce jam sepulto:* let me alone: leave me, at least, to my rest in the grave.

43. *Externum non.* Polydorus was the son of Priam, and the brother of *Creüsa*, the wife of Æneas. He was therefore not a stranger or foreigner, in the truest sense of the word, to Æneas. Cicero makes him the

Heu! fuge crudeles terras, fuge litus avarum,
Nam Polydorus ego: hìc confixum ferrea texit
Telorum seges, et jaculis increvit acutis.
Tum verò ancipiti mentem formidine pressus
Obstupui, steteruntque comæ, et vox faucibus hæsit.
Hunc Polydorum auri quondam cum pondere magno
Infelix Priamus furtim mandârat alendum
Threïcio regi; cùm jam diffideret armis
Dardaniæ, cingique urbem obsidione videret.
Ille, ut opes fractæ Teucrûm, et fortuna recessit,
Res Agamemnonias victriciaque arma secutus,
Fas omne abrumpit, Polydorum obtruncat, et auro
Vi potitur. Quid non mortalia pectora cogis,
Auri sacra fames! Postquam pavor ossa reliquit,
Delectos populi ad proceres, primùmque parentem,
Monstra Deûm refero; et, quæ sit sententia, posco.
Omnibus idem animus, sceleratâ excedere terrâ,
Linquere pollutum hospitium, et dare classibus Austros
Ergò instauramus Polydoro funus, et ingens
Aggeritur tumulo tellus: stant manibus aræ,
Cœruleis mœstæ vittis atrâque cupresso:

45. Ferrea seges telorum texit *me* confixum hìc

47. Pressus *quoad* mentem ancipiti

49. Quondam infelix Priamus furtim mandârat hunc Polydorum Threïcio regi alendum, cum magno pondere auri

53. Ille, *nempe Polymnestor*, ut opes Teucrûm fractæ *sunt*

59. Quæ sit *eorum* sententia *de iis*.

60. *Est* idem nimus omnibus excedere

NOTES.

son of *Ilione*, the daughter of Priam, and wife of Polymnestor, king of Thrace. *Tulit:* produced, or bore. *Stipite:* the body, or trunk.

45. *Ferrea seges.* To understand this passage, we may suppose that these darts were thrown in upon the body of Polydorus as he lay in the grave; which they pierced: and, taking root in that place, sprang up, and grew in the form of sharp pointed javelins, forming a shade over the tomb. Heyne says: *excreverunt in arbores unde jacula petuntur.*

46. *Increvit acutis:* grew up into sharp javelins: into trees like sharp javelins.

47. *Pressus:* in the sense of *percussus. Ancipiti: dubia*, says Ruæus.

50. *Mandârat:* in the sense of *miserat.*

51. *Diffideret:* in the sense of *desperaret. Dardaniæ:* in the sense of *Trojæ.* See Æn. i. 1.

53. *Opes Teucrûm:* the power of the Trojans was broken. *Ut:* in the sense of *quando.*

54. *Res Agamemnonias:* embracing (*secutus*) the Grecian cause, and their victorious arms, he breaks every sacred obligation. Agamemnon was captain general of the Grecian forces in the expedition against Troy. His interest, therefore, is the general interest of the Greeks. *Fas:* properly a divine, or sacred law. By the murder of Polydorus, he broke through the ties of consanguinity, hospitality, and friendship; which are considered of a sacred nature.

57. *Sacra fames auri:* O cursed desire of gold, what dost thou not force the hearts of men to perpetrate! The word *sacer* signifies, usually, sacred, holy: here, accursed, execrable. The word *facere* or *perpetrare*, is to be supplied. Heyne says, *ad quid:* to what, &c.

59. *Monstra Deûm:* the prodigies of the gods. *Primùm:* in the sense of *præcipuè* Heyne says, *primo loco*

61. *Hospitium:* in the sense of *locum Dare austros classibus:* to give the winds to the fleet. In the sense of *dare vela ventis. Auster*, is here taken for the wind in general: the *species* for the *genus.* The south wind would have been against him, going from Thrace to *Delos.*

62. *Instauramus funus:* we perform the funeral rites to Polydorus. He had not been buried with the usual solemnities, a matter which the ancients considered of great moment. These rites were called *justa.* Without them, they thought the soul wandered 100 years without any rest. Virgil here gives a full account of the funeral rites performed by the Romans, at the interment of the dead.

63. *Ingens tellus:* a huge pile of earth is thrown up for the tomb. *Aræ stant manibus.* It appears that two altars were consecrated to the *Manes.* See 305, infra, also, Ecl. v. 66. By *manibus* here, we are to understand the soul or spirit of Polydorus.

64. *Mœstæ:* mournful—dressed in mourning. These fillets were of a deep purple or violet color—a color between blue and black Ruæus says, *tristes.*

Et circùm Iliades crinem de more solutæ.
Inferimus tepido spumantia cymbia lacte,
Sanguinis et sacri pateras: animamque sepulchro
Condimus, et magnâ supremùm voce ciemus.
Inde ubi prima fides pelago, placataque venti
Dant maria, et lenis crepitans vocat Auster in altum;
Deducunt socii naves, et litora complent.
Provehimur portu, terræque urbesque recedunt.
Sacra mari colitur medio gratissima tellus
Nereïdum matri et Neptuno Ægæo:
Quam pius Arcitenens oras et litora circum
Errantem, Mycone celsâ Gyaroque revinxit;

65. Iliades, solutæ *quoad* crinem de more, *stant* circùm

69. Prima fides *est* pelago.

72. Recedunt *à nostro aspectu*

73. Gratissima tellus sacra matri Nereidum, et Ægæo:

75. Quam errantem *anteà* circum oras, et litora

NOTES.

65. *Solutæ crinem:* loose as to their hair —having their hair loose or dishevelled. See Ecl. i. 55.

66. *Inferimus cymbia:* we offer bowls foaming with warm milk, and goblets of the consecrated blood. From the verb *infero*, is formed *inferiæ*, sacrifices for the dead, which consisted in pouring into or upon the grave, milk and the blood of a victim slain, as here mentioned.

67. *Condimus animam:* we place, or bury the soul in the grave. Ruæus says, *claudimus animam.*

It was a prevailing opinion among the Romans and Greeks, that the soul could not rest without burial; for this reason, they were so anxious about funeral rites. Hence *conditorium* came to signify a burial-place. *Et supremùm:* and lastly, we call upon him with a loud voice. This they did, to call the soul to its place of its rest, and to take the last farewell, by pronouncing the word *vale*, three times. *Ciemus:* in the sense of *conclamamus.* See Æn. i. 219.

69. *Fides:* confidence—security. *Placata:* in the sense of *quieta*, vel *tranquilla.* It agrees with *maria.*

70. *Auster:* properly the south wind; here taken for wind in general. *Crepitans:* murmuring—rustling—blowing gently.

73. *Gratissima tellus.* The island Delos is meant, the birth-place of Apollo and Diana. *Matri Nereïdum:* to Doris, the wife of Nereus, and mother of fifty sea-nymphs, called *Nereïdes. Colitur:* in the sense of *incolitur*, vel *habitatur.*

74. *Ægæo.* That part of the Mediterranean sea, lying between Asia on the east, and the Morea, Attica, and Thessaly on the west, was called the Ægean sea; from *Ægeus*, the father of Theseus, who threw himself into it, and was drowned, expecting that his son, who had undertaken to fight the *Minotaur*, was slain.

The fable is this: it was agreed between the father and son, that if he subdued the monster, and returned victorious, he should hang out a white flag, or have white sails: but if he should fail in the attempt, the ship should return with black sails.

Theseus, on his return, forgot to hang out the white flag, through grief for his beloved Ariadne, whom Bacchus had ravished from him. The father, who was expecting him with impatience, as soon as he, from the top of a high rock, saw the ship in mourning, threw himself into the sea, supposing his son to have been slain. Ægeus was king of Athens.

The islands in the southern part of this sea were called *Sporades*, from a Greek word which signifies, to scatter, or sow; because they lay as if scattered or sown, without order or regularity. The islands farther north were called *Cyclades*, from a Greek word signifying a circle, because they lay around Delos in the form of a circle. *Hodie*, the *Archipelago.*

Neptune is here called *Ægean*, because he was supposed to have his residence in the Ægean sea.

75. *Arcitenens.* This was an epithet of Apollo; also a name of Apollo, as in this place; compounded of *arcus* and *teneo.* He is here called *pius*, because, it is said, that as soon as he was born, he slew the serpent *Python*, which Juno sent to persecute his mother Latona. Pierius would read *priùs*, instead of *pius*, connecting it with *errantem.* He assures us that it is found in several ancient copies.

Delos is a small island in the Ægean sea in lat. 37° 30′ north, having Mycone on the north-east, Gyarus and Naxus on the east and south, and Rhena on the west.

The fable is this: Juno being angry at her husband for loving Latona, resolved she should have no place to bring forth in peace. Jupiter directed her to Delos, which was then a floating or wandering island, as a place of safe retreat. Apollo, after his birth, fixed and rendered it immoveable, for the residence of his mother. Its original name was *Ortygia.* This was changed into the name *Delos*, which, in the Greek, signifies apparent, or brought to view, it having been

Immotamque coli dedit, et contemnere ventos.
Huc feror: hæc fessos tuto placidissima portu
Accipit. Egressi veneramur Apollinis urbem.
Rex Anius, rex idem hominum Phœbique sacerdos,
Vittis et sacrâ redimitus tempora lauro
Occurrit, veterem Anchisen agnoscit amicum.
Jungimus hospitio dextras, et tecta subimus.
Templa Dei saxo venerabar structa vetusto;
Da propriam, Thymbræe, domum, da mœnia fessis,
Et genus, et mansuram urbem: serva altera Trojæ
Pergama, relliquias Danaûm atque immitis Achillei.
Quem sequimur? quòve ire jubes? ubi ponere sedes?
Da, pater, augurium, atque animis illabere nostris.
Vix ea fatus eram: tremere omnia visa repentè,
Liminaque, laurusque Dei: totusque moveri
Mons circùm, et mugire adytis cortina reclusis.
Submissi petimus terram, et vox fertur ad aures:
Dardanidæ duri, quæ vos à stirpe parentum

78. Hæc placidissima *insula* accipit *nos*

79. Egressi *navibus* veneramur

82. Occurrit *nobis*

85. *Et sic dixi:* O Thymbræe *Apollo*, da *nobis* fessis propriam domum

88. Quòve jubes *nos* ire? ubi *jubes nos* ponere *nostras* sedes?

90. Repentè omnia visa *sunt* tremere

91. Totusque mons *visus est* moveri

94. Eadem tellus, quæ tulit vos à prima stirpe

NOTES.

hidden before under the waves. This part of the fable some explain, by saying that Apollo here gave out his oracles plain and intelligible, but in every other place, in terms dark and obscure. See Ecl. iv. 10.

77. *Deditque:* and rendered it fixed to be inhabited, and to condemn the winds. This alludes to the story of its having been a wandering island, and driven about by the winds, till fixed by Apollo for the residence of his mother. Hence it became sacred to her.

80. *Idem rex hominum.* It was a custom among many nations to unite in the same person the offices of king and priest. Anius was both king, and priest of Apollo.

81. *Redimitus:* bound as to his temples with fillets, and the sacred laurel. The laurel was sacred to Apollo. Hence the propriety of his priest being bound with it: and the propriety of the epithet *sacra.*

83. *Subimus tecta:* we come under his roof—we enter his palace. But *tecta* here may mean the temple mentioned below: the word *tectum* properly signifying any covered building. Or *tecta* may be taken for the buildings of the city in general. The meaning then will be; *we enter the city.*

84. *Structa vetusto saxo:* built of ancient stone, or rock. Macrobius informs us that, when the temple at *Delphi*, and the temples built to Apollo in other places, were destroyed in any way whatever, his temple at *Delos* continued to stand unimpaired; and consequently retained its ancient or original stone. Whatever ravages the island had suffered, the sanctity of the temple preserved it from violation. *Venerabar:* I worshipped—I offered prayers. It is said that the altar of Apollo at *Delos* was never stained with the blood of victims; but only honored with prayers, and other simple rites of ancient worship.

85. *Thymbrææ.* Thymbræus was an epithet of Apollo, derived, as we are told by Strabo, from *Thymbra*, a place near Troy, where he had a famous temple. *Propriam:* fixed, lasting.

86. *Genus:* offspring—posterity. Ruæus says, *familias. Mansuram:* permanent, to remain.

87. *Pergama:* neu. plu. properly the fort or citadel of Troy; often used for the whole city. *Altera Pergama.* Simply, the other Troy—the city which Æneas prayed Apollo to grant to him, and his followers, the remains of the Greeks, and of cruel Achilles.

89. *Augurium:* a sign, or omen.

91. *Laurus.* Either the laurel, with which the image of the god was crowned; or rather the laurel tree, which was placed at the entrance of the temple. It was an opinion among the ancients that the gods gave signs of their approach, by causing the earth to move and shake. To this the poet here alludes. The laurel was sacred to Apollo.

92. *Cortina.* The covering of the tripod, whence the priest delivered responses. Hence by meton. the oracle itself. *Adytis.* The sanctuary, or inner part of the temple, where the Oracle was. *Reclusis:* in the sense of *apertis. Mons.* This was mount *Cynthus*, on which the temple was built: whence Apollo was sometimes called *Cynthius*, and Diana, *Cynthia. Mugire:* in the sense of *sonare.*

94. *Dardanidæ:* the same as *Trojani.* Servius observes that the Trojans might

Prima tulit, tellus eadem vos ubere læto
Accipiet reduces: antiquam exquirite matrem
Hic domus Æneæ cunctis dominabitur oris,
Et nati natorum, et qui nascentur ab illis.
Hæc Phœbus: mixtoque ingens exorta tumultu
Lætitia; et cuncti, quæ sint ea mœnia, quærunt,
Quò Phœbus vocet errantes, jubeatque reverti.
Tum genitor, veterum volvens monumenta virorum,
Audite, ô proceres, ait, et spes discite vestras.
Creta Jovis magni medio jacet insula ponto,
Mons Idæus ubi, et gentis cunabula nostræ.
Centum urbes habitant magnas, uberrima regna
Maximus unde pater, si ritè audita recordor,
Teucrus Rhœteas primùm est advectus in oras,

99. Ingensque lætitia exorta *est cum* mixto
101. *Nos* errantes
105. Ubi *est* Idæus mons
106. *Incolæ* habitant centum
107. Unde Teucrus *noster* maximus pater primùm

NOTES.

have understood from this declaration of the Oracle, that Italy was designed them, whence Dardanus came; and not *Crete*, which was the birthplace of *Teucer*. *Stirpe:* in the sense of *origine.*

95. *Læto ubere:* in its joyous bosom: or perhaps, in its fertile soil. *Uber:* signifies the richness or fertility of the soil. Ruæus says, *fertili sinu.*

96. *Reduces:* brought back, or returning in safety. *Matrem.* It is supposed that the poet had in view the circumstance of Brutus, and the Tarquins, who went to *Delphi* to consult the Oracle of Apollo, concerning the succession to the kingdom. They received for answer, that the empire should be his, who first kissed his great mother. Brutus, on leaving the ship, feigned a fall, and kissed the ground, which he considered as the great parent of all. He received the government, after the expulsion of the Tarquins, being chosen Consul. He was slain by *Aruns*, one of the Tarquins, soon after he entered upon his office.

97. *Domus Æneæ:* here the family of Æneas shall bear rule over all lands, &c. These two lines are taken from the Iliad. Lib. 20. 306. It is there said, however, that Æneas should reign over the Trojans. Hence some have inferred that he remained in Troas, and that the whole account of the origin of the Romans is a mere fiction, a compliment only to Augustus. But Dionysius of Halicarnassus understands it of his reigning over the Trojans in Italy. And in this he is followed by Eustathius in his commentary upon this passage of the Iliad. It may be observed that Virgil does not say, *Trojanis dominabitur*, which answers to the Greek of Homer; but *cunctis dominabitur oris.* This circumstance hath led some to alter the Greek text so as to conform to the Roman.

101. *Reverti:* in the sense of *procedere. Quò:* in the sense of *ad quæ loca.*

102. *Monumenta:* records, or memorials. These were of various kinds; not only writings, but paintings, columns, tombs, and statues. Ruæus says, *historias. Volvens:* in the sense of *recogitans*, vel *revolvens in mente.*

104. *Creta.* A large island in the Mediterranean, lying between the Archipelago on the north, and the Lybian sea on the south: *Hodie, Candia.* It was called *Creta*, from *Cres*, who is said to have reigned there after Jupiter. It is also sometimes called *Crete. Teucer*, from whom the Trojans were sometimes called *Teucri*, and Troy, *Teucria*, was a native of this island. He was the son of *Scamander;* and, in the time of a famine, led a colony to *Troas*, and settled at *Rhœteum*, a promontory on the shore of the Hellespont. He was most probably the founder of the Trojans: whence Anchises calls him *Maximus pater.* They were, however, very fond of deriving their descent from *Dardanus*, who fled from Italy to Troas, and became the son-in-law to Teucer. By marrying his daughter, he obtained a share in the kingdom, and at his death succeeded him in the government. Crete is here called the island of great Jove; because it was the place of his birth and education. See Georg. 1. 121.

105. *Cunabula:* neu. plur. the cradle or nursing place of your race. Ruæus says, *origo. Idæus:* an adj. from Ida, a mountain in Crete.

106. *Habitant:* in the sense of *occupant. Uberrima regna:* most fertile realms. This answers to *læto ubere*, mentioned, 95, supra, and tended to mislead Anchises.

107. *Audita:* reports—traditions.

108. *Rhœteas oras:* the coast of Rhœteum. *Rhœteum* was a promontory of Troas, where Teucer landed with his colony from Crete. He introduced the worship of Cybele, the mother of the gods, and gave to the mountains of Phrygia the name of *Ida*, from mount Ida in Crete. He also changed the name of *Xanthus* into that of Scamander, after the name of his father. Hence Homer says that the river was called *Xan-*

Optavitque locum regno: nondum Ilium et arces
Pergameæ steterant; habitabant vallibus imis.
Hinc mater cultrix Cybele, Corybantiaque æra,
Idæumque nemus: hinc fida silentia sacris,
Et juncti currum dominæ subiere leones.
Ergò agite, et, Divûm ducunt quà jussa, sequamur
Placemus ventos, et Gnossia regna petamus.
Nec longo distant cursu: modò Jupiter adsit,
Tertia lux classem Cretæis sistet in oris.

111. Hinc *veni.* mater Cybele

112. Hinc *venerunt* fida silentia

116. *Illa* distant longo cursu

NOTES.

thus by the gods, but *Scamander* by men—the former being its original, and more honorable name.

109. *Optavit:* in the sense of *elegit.* Strabo agrees with Virgil in making Teucer the first who reigned in Troy. Dardanus arrived not long after, married his daughter *Batea*, and succeeded him in the government.

110. *Pergameæ:* in the sense of *Trojanæ.*

111. *Cybele.* The same with Rhea or Ops, and wife of Saturn. She is so called probably from Cybelus, a mountain in Phrygia, where she was worshipped. She is taken sometimes for the earth; and in that sense is the common parent of all its inhabitants. Her priests were called *Corybantes*, *Curetes*, and *Idæi Dactyli.* Among other things in her worship, they used to *beat* brazen cymbals together. The origin of this practice was to prevent the cries of the child Jupiter from being heard by his father. Cybele is here called *Cultrix*, most probably because she was worshipped in a mountain of Phrygia: whence it might be said that she inhabited it, and, as it were, became the *protectress* of that country. This is the sense Ruæus gives. He says, *protectrix loci.* *Æra:* brazen cymbals. Any thing made of brass may be called *æs*, or *æra.*

Heyne reads *Cybelæ*, the gen. of *Cybela*, sometimes written *Cybelus*, the name of a mountain in Phrygia. *Mater Deûm*, says he, *quæ colit, inhabitat Cybelen, montem Phrygiæ:* taking *cultrix* in the sense of *quæ colit* vel *inhabitat.* After the arrival of *Teucer* from Crete, he probably changed the name of the mountain *Cybela* or *Cybelus*, calling it *Ida*, after the *Cretan Ida.*

This goddess had several names: *Cybele*, from the mountain already named, where it is said she was first worshipped by sacrifices: *Ops*, from a word implying help, because she brings help or assistance to every production of nature: *Rhea*, from a Greek word signifying *to flow*, because her benefits flow without ceasing: *Dindymene*, from the mountain *Dindymus* in Phrygia: *Berecynthia*, from *Berecynthus*, a castle in the same country. See Æn. vi. 784. She was also called *Bona Dea*, and *Mater Deorum.* See Ecl. iv. 6. and Geor. i. 121.

Corybantia: an adj. from *Corybantes*, the priests of *Cybele*, derived from the Greek. During her worship, they made a confused noise with timbrels, pipes, and cymbals. They danced, tossed their heads, and struck their foreheads against each other, appearing like mad men.

They were sometimes called *Curetes*, from a Greek word which signifies a virgin, because they wore a long robe like young virgins. They were also called *Dactyli*, from a Greek word signifying a finger, because they were ten in number, there being so many fingers on both hands. The epithet *Idæi* is here added, because they chiefly resided on mount *Ida.*

Cybele is represented sitting on a car with a robe of divers colors, and holding a key in her hand, to denote that she unlocks and distributes in summer those treasures, that the winter had hid and concealed. She wears a turreted crown on her head, and is drawn by a pair of harnessed lions. The box and the pine tree were sacred to her: the former, because pipes were made of that wood, and used in her worship; the latter for the sake of the boy *Atys*, whom she loved, and made president of her rites, or ceremonies: but afterwards changed him into the pine tree. Her sacrifices were performed in private, and men were excluded from participation. Silence was especially enjoined in her mysteries. This will explain *fida silentia sacris*, in the following line.

112. *Hinc fida:* hence the faithful secrecy in her sacred rites. The mysteries of Cybele, as well as those of Ceres, were carefully concealed from the common people. Her chariot was drawn by harnessed lions, *juncti leones*, to denote that maternal affection, figured by Cybele, or the earth, the common parent of all, triumphs over the most ferocious and savage natures. *Subiere:* in the sense of *traxerunt.* *Dominæ.* This is an epithet of Cybele, as being the mother of the gods.

115. *Gnossia:* an adj. from Gnossus, the principal city of Crete, put by synec. for the whole island.

116. *Nec distant:* nor are the realms of Crete *a long way distant.* *Modò:* provided that—in case that.

117. *Lux:* in the sense of *dies.*

Sic fatus, meritos aris mactavit honores:
Taurum Neptuno; taurum tibi, pulcher Apollo;
Nigram Hyemi pecudem, Zephyris felicibus albam.
Fama volat, pulsum regnis cessisse paternis
Idomenea ducem, desertaque litora Cretæ,
Hoste vacare domos, sedesque adstare relictas.
Linquimus Ortygiæ portus, pelagoque volamus:
Bacchatamque jugis Naxon, viridemque Donysam,
Olearon, niveamque Paron, sparsasque per æquor
Cycladas, et crebris legimus freta consita terris.
Nauticus exoritur vario certamine clamor.
Hortantur socii, Cretam proavosque petamus.
Prosequitur surgens à puppi ventus euntes:
Et tandem antiquis Curetum allabimur oris.
Ergò avidus muros optatæ molior urbis,
Pergameamque voco: et lætam cognomine gentem
Hortor amare focos, arcemque attollere tectis.
Jamque ferè sicco subductæ litore puppes:

119. *Mactavit* taurum Neptuno; taurum tibi, O pulcher

121. Fama volat ducem Idomenea, pulsum cessisse paternis regnis, litoraque Cretæ *esse* deserta, *et* domos vacare *nostro* hoste

125. Legimusque Naxon bacchatam jugis, viridemque Donysam

130. *Nos* euntes

133. Vocoque *urbem* Pergameam

135. Puppes subductæ *sunt è mari* in sicco litore

NOTES.

118. *Mactavit:* he offered—sacrificed. *Honores:* in the sense of *victimas.* And *meritos:* in the sense of *dignos.*

120. *Hyemi.* By *hyemi* we are here to understand the *stormy winds.* They were considered as a kind of divinities, and were accordingly worshipped in order to avert their fury. *Pecudem:* in the sense of *ovem. Felicibus:* in the sense of *propitiis.*

122. *Idomenea:* an acc. of Greek ending. Idomeneus was the son of Deucalion, and grand-son of Minos, king of Crete. He was one of the leaders in the war against Troy. On his return, being overtaken in a storm, he made a vow to the gods to sacrifice to them whatsoever he should first meet, if they would save him. This happened to be his own son. The father, however, performed his vow. A plague soon arising in his country, and his subjects considering him to have been the cause of it by this inhuman deed, rose against him, and expelled him from his kingdom. *Litora deserta:* the shores to be deserted—left without a guard, or defence.

123. *Sedes relictas adstare:* that the country being abandoned, lies open to us. *Sedes:* in the sense of *regiones.*

124. *Ortygiæ.* The ancient name of Delos was *Ortygia,* from a Greek word signifying a quail: those fowls having abounded in that island.

125. *Bacchatam:* frequented in its mountains by the priests of Bacchus—whose mountains resounded with the tumultuous rantings of the Bacchanals. *Viridem Donysam.* This island was famous for its *green* marble, as *Paros* was for its *pure white* marble. See 75 supra.

127. *Cycladas sparsas.* These were a bcr of Islands. so called from a Greek ignifying *a circle,* because they lay in that form around Delos. *Freta consita:* the straits set with many islands—the straits and narrow passes formed by the numerous islands, which diversified the sea.

127. *Legimus:* we coast along the shore—we sail near.

128. *Certamine:* in the sense of *æmulatione. Nauticus clamor:* a shout of the sailors.

130. *Surgens à puppi.* This wind blew from the north: their course lay to the southward, and consequently it would be at their stern.

131. *Allabimur:* we arrive at the ancient shores of the *Curetes.* These were the ministers of Cybele, and thought by some to be the same with the *Corybantes* and *Idæi Dactyli.* Of *ad* and *labor.* See 111, supra. The *Curetes* are said to have been the original inhabitants of Crete; from whom the island probably took its name.

132. *Molior:* in the sense of *extruo.*

133. *Pergameam.* Pliny mentions *Pergamus,* among the cities of Crete. Homer calls it, the hundred-city island. It is said to have had a hundred cities. *Gentem lætam:* my people delighted with the name. *Gentem,* in the sense of *populum,* vel *socios.*

134. *Amare focos:* to love their homes—to keep close at home, and not wander abroad, until they should discover the disposition of the inhabitants towards them. This agrees with the following injunction: *attollere arcem tectis,* to raise a tower on their houses in case of an attack, the better to defend themselves.

Servius thinks Æneas here intends to recommend to his people to cultivate the study of religion. It is an unnecessary refinement. *Focos:* properly the fire-places, or hearth, by synec. put for the whole house, in this place: also sometimes for the fire on the hearth, by meton.

136. Juventus operata *est* connubiis
137. Tabida, miserandaque lues, tractu cœli corrupto, venit *eorum* membris, arboribusque satisque, et annus *est* letifer
141. Sirius *cœpit* exurere
143. Pater hortatur *me* ire rursus ad oraculum
145. *Et quærere* quem finem
150. Visi *sunt* adstare ante oculos *mei* jacentis insomnis
153. Tum sic *visi sunt* affari *me*, et
154. Apollo canit hìc *idem*. quod dicturus est tibi delato *ad*
156. Nos secuti *sumus* te, tuaque
158. *Nos* iidem tollemus
159. Imperium *orbis tuæ* urbi

Connubiis arvisque novis operata juventus:
Jura domosque dabam: subitò cùm tabida membris,
Corrupto cœli tractu, miserandaque venit
Arboribusque satisque lues, et letifer annus.
Linquebant dulces animas, aut ægra trahebant
Corpora: tum steriles exurere Sirius agros.
Arebant herbæ, et victum seges ægra negabat.
Rursus ad orâclum Ortygiæ Phœbumque remenso
Hortatur pater ire mari, veniamque precari:
Quem fessis finem rebus ferat; unde laborum
Tentare auxilium jubeat; quò vertere cursus.
Nox erat, et terris animalia somnus habebat.
Effigies sacræ Divûm, Phrygiique Penates,
Quos mecum à Trojâ mediisque ex ignibus urbis
Extuleram, visi ante oculos adstare jacentis
Insomnis, multo manifesti lumine: quà se
Plena per insertas fundebat Luna fenestras.
Tum sic affari, et curas his demere dictis:
Quod tibi delato Ortygiam dicturus Apollo est,
Hìc canit: et tua nos en ultrò ad limina mittit.
Nos te, Dardaniâ incensâ, tuaque arma secuti;
Nos tumidum sub te permensi classibus æquor;
Iidem venturos tollemus in astra nepotes,
Imperiumque urbi dabimus. Tu mœnia magnis
Magna para, longumque fugæ ne linque laborem.

NOTES.

136. *Juventus operata:* the youth had sacrificed for their nuptials, and new lands. They were prepared for contracting marriages, and for commencing the business of agriculture.

It was a custom among the Romans to offer sacrifices before they entered upon marriage, or any important business of life. To this, the poet alludes. *Sacrificabant pro felici successu conjugiorum, et agrorum.*

137. *Dabam:* in the sense of *distribuebam.* *Jura:* justice among my people. *Domos:* either the houses that had been abandoned by the inhabitants; or the places where they should build houses for themselves.

139. *Tabida miserandaque:* a wasting and pitiable disease came upon their limbs, &c. This disease, or plague, was occasioned by the infection of the air. *Cœli:* in the sense of *aëris.* *Tractu:* a space, tract, or region, *Satis.* *Sata*, properly, crops—any thing planted and growing; from the verb *sero.* Here, in the sense of *segetes.*

140. *Animas:* lives. *Anima* properly signifies the animal life; *animus*, the soul. Dr. Trapp thinks the expression an odd one, and proposes to change *linquebant* to *reddebant* Ruæus says, *amittebant.* The difficulty is removed by rendering *dulces animas*, sweet, or dear lives.

141. *Sirius:* the dog-star; a pestilential constellation, rising about the end of July, when the heat of the sun is most intense. It is sometimes called *canicula.*

142. *Ægra seges:* the diseased, or sickly crop—corn.

144. *Precari veniam:* to supplicate his favor, or assistance.

145. *Fessis rebus:* to our afflicted state, or condition. *Ferat:* in the sense of *ponat.* *Laborum:* distress—sufferings. *Tentare:* in the sense of *quærere.*

146. *Auxilium laborum:* relief in our sufferings.

148. *Effigies:* forms, or figures. Ruæus says *statuæ.* *Penates.* See Æn. ii. 717.

151. *Insomnis:* awake; an adj. agreeing with *mei jacentis.* Most editors separate the word into *in* and *somnis*, in my sleep. This is evidently incorrect: for if he had been asleep, the light of the moon would have been unnecessary. Besides, verse 173 infra, he declares it was no delusion of the fancy in sleep. *Manifesti:* in the sense of *conspicui.*

152. *Insertas fenestras:* windows inserted, or made in the side of the house. *Fenestras, quæ sunt in pariete*, says Heyne. *Fundebat se:* in the sense of *mittebat se;* simply, shone.

154. *Delato:* carried back, or returned to Delos. *Canit:* declares, or reveals.

160. *Para magna:* prepare a great city *Populis*, or some word of the like import, is

Mutandæ sedes: non hæc tibi litora suasit
Delius, aut Cretæ jussit considere, Apollo.
Est locus, Hesperiam Graii cognomine dicunt;
Terra antiqua, potens armis atque ubere glebæ.
Œnotrii coluere viri: nunc fama, minores
Italiam dixisse, ducis de nomine, gentem.
Hæ nobis propriæ sedes: hinc Dardanus ortus,
Iasiusque, pater; genus à quo principe nostrum.
Surge, age, et hæc lætus longævo dicta parenti
Haud dubitanda refer. Corytum, terrasque require
Ausonias: Dictæa negat tibi Jupiter arva.
Talibus attonitus visis ac voce Deorum,
(Nec sopor illud erat; sed coràm agnoscere vultus,
Velatasque comas, præsentiaque ora videbar:

165. Nunc fama *est* **minores dixisse gentem**

167. Hinc Iasius ortus *est*, paterque Dardanus, à quo principe nostrum genus *deductum est.*

173. Sed videbar *mihi* agnoscere vultus coràm *me*, velatasque

NOTES.

to be understood, with which *magnis* is to agree: for your powerful people. *Magnis nepotibus*, says Heyne. Ruæus hath *nobis magnis:* for us the great gods. *Longum laborem fugæ:* the same as *laborem longæ fugæ:* the labor, or fatigue of the long voyage.

161. *Sedes:* in the sense of *regio.* The verb *sunt* is to be supplied. *Non suasit hæc:* Delian Apollo does not advise, or recommend these shores to thee.

162. *Cretæ:* at Crete. The place where is put in the gen. The same with, *in Creta. Delius:* a name, and epithet of Apollo; from *Delos*, the place of his birth.

163. *Est locus.* This passage had been recited to Dido by Ilioneus, Æn. i. 530. As they were the words of the oracle, it would have been disrespectful and improper to alter them in the least: besides, Dido would be more confirmed in the truth of Æneas' relation, when she found two witnesses delivering their testimony in the same words. *Locus:* in the sense of *regio.*

165. *Œnotrii:* an adj. from *Œnotria*, a name given to that part of Italy, afterwards called *Lucania.* It took its name from *Œnotrus*, the son of Lycaon, who settled here with a colony of Arcadians. The Œnotrians spread so widely, that all Italy was sometimes called *Œnotria. Œnotrii viri:* simply, the Œnotrians.

167. *Propriæ nobis:* destined, or allotted to us by the gods. The verb *sunt* is to be supplied. Mr. Davidson takes *propriæ* in the sense of *perpetuæ.* Ruæus says, *addictæ.*

167. *Hinc:* hence Iäsius sprang, and father Dardanus; from which prince our race is derived. *Principe* here is a sub. a prince—a chief—a founder. The construction is easier and more natural by connecting *pater* with *Dardanus.* In this instance I have ventured to depart from the common ordo. Iäsius and Dardanus were sons of Electra, the daughter of Atlas, king of Mauritania in Africa; who married Coritus, king of Tuscany. It is said, however, that Jove had an amour with her, and begat Dardanus. Upon the death of their father Coritus, a quarrel arose between the two brothers, which ended in the death of Iäsius. Upon which Dardanus fled first to Samothracia, and afterwards to Phrygia, where he married the daughter of Teucer, and, in connexion with him, founded the Trojan race.

170. *Corytum:* a city and mountain in Tuscany, so called from *Corytus*, the supposed father of Dardanus, and king of that country. The name is derived from a Greek word which signifies a helmet. Both the city and mountain are now called *Cortona. Require.* Heinsius, and after him Heyne, reads *requirat.* But *require* is the common reading, and is the easier.

171. *Ausonias:* an adj. from *Ausonia*, a name of Italy; from *Auson*, or *Ausonius*, as Servius informs us. *Dictæa arva:* the Cretan territory, or lands. Crete is called *Dictæan*, from *Dicte*, a mountain on that island, where Jupiter was educated; put, by synec. for the whole island.

172. *Talibus visis:* at such a vision, or sight.

173. *Nec sopor erat*, &c. Dr. Trapp, and some other commentators, imagine a difficulty occurs here. To solve it, they make a difference between *sopor* and *somnus.* But this difficulty arises entirely from their taking *insomnis* to mean, in sleep, and not taking it as an adj. See verse 151, supra.

174. *Velatas comas:* the heads of the images, or statues, were generally adorned with fillets and flowers. *Ora præsentia* their forms present before me. We see how much pains the poet takes to make us believe that it was no dream—no mere fancy. He mentions a variety of circumstances, all of which go to show that Æneas was awake, and not in sleep.

Tum gelidus toto manabat corpore sudor)
Corripio è stratis corpus, tendoque supinas
Ad cœlum cum voce manus, et munera libo
Intemerata focis. Perfecto lætus honore
Anchisen facio certum, remque ordine pando.
Agnovit prolem ambiguam, geminosque parentes,
Seque novo veterum deceptum errore locorum.
Tum memorat: Nate, Iliacis exercite fatis,
Sola mihi tales casus Cassandra canebat.
Nunc repeto hæc generi portendere debita nostro,
Et sæpe Hesperiam, sæpe Itala regna vocare.
Sed quis ad Hesperiæ venturos litora Teucros
Crederet? aut quem tum vates Cassandra moveret?
Cedamus Phœbo, et moniti meliora sequamur.
Sic ait: et cuncti dictis paremus ovantes.
Hanc quoque deserimus sedem, paucisque relictis
Vela damus, vastumque cavâ trabe currimus æquor.
    Postquam altum tenuere rates, nec jam ampliùs ullæ
Apparent terræ, cœlum undique, et undique pontus;
Tum mihi cœruleus supra caput adstitit imber,
Noctem hyememque ferens; et inhorruit unda tenebris

179. Certum *de his rebus*

181. Seque deceptum *esse* novo

184. Nunc repeto *eam* portendere hæc *loca* debita *esse* nostro generi; et *eam* sæpe vocare

188. Moniti *nos* sequamur meliora *consilia*.

193. *Sed* undique cœlum *apparet*, et

NOTES.

176. *Corripio:* I snatch my body from my bed. *Supinas:* palm upward; agreeing with *manus*.

177. *Libo intemerata:* I pour pure offerings on the fire. This private offering consisted of pure wine and incense, and was usually poured upon the fire in honor of the *Lares*.

178. *Honore perfecto:* the offering being made, or completed.

179. *Rem:* in the sense of *prodigium*.

180. *Geminos parentes:* the double founders. The Trojans reckoned both Teucer and Dardanus the founders of their race; the former from Crete, the latter from Italy. This *ambiguam prolem*, ambiguous, or double descent, led Anchises to mistake the oracle of Apollo. *Agnovit:* he owned—acknowledged.

181. *Novo errore.* It is not easy, perhaps, to fix the meaning of this line. Pierius informs us that some copies have *parentum* instead of *locorum*, which mends it much: through the recent mistake of our ancient founders. If *locorum* be read, it will be: through the recent mistake of the places of their birth.

Apollo had directed them to seek the land of their ancestors, promising that it should receive them in its fertile bosom. This Anchises had interpreted of the land of Crete, the birth-place of Teucer. It appears, then, that this mistake lay in reckoning their descent from him, and not from Dardanus, whose country had been Italy. This mistake in computing he calls *novus*, a recent, or new one because they usually deduced their descent from Dardanus. See verse 94, et seq.

182. *Exercite:* exercised, or tried, in the disasters of Troy.

183. *Canebat:* in the sense of *prædicabat*. *Cassandra.* The daughter of Priam, endued by Apollo with the gift of prophecy; but no body believed her predictions. See Æn. ii. 246.

184. *Repeto:* I remember—I call to mind. *Portendere:* in the sense of *prædicere*. *Vocare:* mentioned—spake of by name.

188. *Moniti meliora:* being advised, let us follow better counsels. This is the sense of Ruæus and Dr. Trapp. Mr. Davidson renders them: being better advised, let us follow (the gods); taking *meliora* as a Grecism. *Cedamus:* in the sense of *obediamus*.

189. *Ovantes:* in the sense of *læti*.

190. *Sedem:* in the sense of *terram*. *Deserimus:* in the sense of *relinquimus*.

191. *Cava trabe:* in the sense of *cavis navibus*. *Currimus:* we sail upon the vast sea. *Trabe*, by synec. put for the whole ship.

192. *Altum:* properly, the deep, or open sea. *Rates:* in the sense of *naves*.

194. *Imber:* properly, a shower of rain; by meton. the cloud containing, or bearing along the rain, as in the present instance. *Cœruleus*, is what we may properly call leaden-colored. Clouds, that threaten thunder and rain, are often tinged with a deep blue, intermingled with black. This is the kind of cloud here meant.

195. *Hyemem:* in the sense of *tempesta-*

Continuò venti volvunt mare, magnaque surgunt
Æquora: dispersi jactamur gurgite vasto.
Involvêre diem nimbi, et nox humida cœlum
Abstulit: ingeminant abruptis nubibus ignes.
Excutimur cursu, et cæcis erramus in undis.
Ipse diem noctemque negat discernere cœlo,
Nec meminisse viæ mediâ Palinurus in undâ.
Tres adeò incertos cæcâ caligine soles
Erramus pelago, totidem sinè sidere noctes
Quarto terra die primùm se attollere tandem
Visa, aperire procul montes, ac volvere fumum.
Vela cadunt; remis insurgimus: haud mora, nautæ
Adnixi torquent spumas, et cœrula verrunt.
Servatum ex undis Strophadum me litora primùm
Accipiunt. Strophades Graio stant nomine dictæ
Insulæ Ionio in magno: quas dira Celæno,
Harpyiæque colunt aliæ: Phineïa postquam

198 **Abstulit cœlum** ***à nobis***

201. **Negat** ***se posse*** **discernere**

205. **Terra visa** ***est*** **tandem attollere se,** ***et***

207. Haud mora ***est***

208. Verrunt cœrula ***maria***

210. **Insulæ, dictæ Strophades Graio nomine, stant in**

NOTES.

tem, vel *procellam*. *Unda:* in the sense of *mare*. *Inhorruit:* looked terrific with the darkness.

197. *Æquora:* in the sense of *fluctus*.

198. *Involvêre:* wrapped up the day—obscured. *Nimbi:* in the sense of *nubes*. So also *imber*, in verse 194, supra. So impervious was this cloud to the rays of the sun, that it became dark as night—it converted the day into night. Darkness, or night, being the absence or want of the light of the sun. *Humida:* in the sense of *imbrifera*. *Cœlum:* for *lucem*.

199. *Ignes:* lightnings, in quick succession, flash from the broken clouds. Some copies have *abrupti*, agreeing with *ignes;* which would be preferable, if it could be supported by sufficient authority.

200. *Excutimur:* in the sense of *dejicimur*. *Cæcis:* dark—unknown sea.

201. *Palinurus ipse:* Palinurus himself denies that he can distinguish the day and night, (the day from the night, on account of the darkness,) in the heavens. *Meminisse:* in the sense of *cognoscere*. He was the pilot of Æneas' ship, and represented as the most skilful mariner in the fleet.

203. *Adeò erramus:* thus we wander over the sea for three doubtful days in thick darkness. Or, *incertos* may mean, uncertain—undistinguished; because they could be scarcely distinguished from night, on account of the thick darkness. This is the sense put upon the words by Ruæus and others. *Ambiguas propter tenebras obscuras*, says that commentator. *Soles:* in the sense of *dies*.

206. *Volvere:* in the sense of *emittere*, or *erigere*.

207. *Insurgimus remis:* we rise upon our oars—we ply them briskly.

208. *Adnixi:* part. of the verb *adnitor:* exerting themselves—laboring with all their strength, they toss the foam, and sweep the azure deep.

209. *Litora Strophadum:* the shores of the Strophades. These were two small islands, lying on the west of the Peloponnesus, near the *Sinus Cyparissæus*. Here Æneas with his fleet landed.

211. *Magno Ionio*. That part of the Mediterranean, lying between Greece on the east, and Sicily and Italy on the west, was called the Ionian sea. *Mari* is to be supplied.

212. *Harpyiæ aliæ*. The Harpies were commonly reckoned three in number: *Iris*, *Aëllo*, and *Ocypeta*. Virgil here calls one of them *Celæno*. They are said to have been the daughters of Neptune and Terra, (according to Hesiod, of Thaumus and Electra,) and are therefore supposed to inhabit the islands principally. They had the faces of women, but the bodies of vultures. Their feet and fingers were armed with claws. They emitted an infectious smell, and poisoned whatever they touched. They were called *Harpyiæ*, from the circumstance of their rapacity and voracious nature. Servius thinks they were called *Harpyiæ* on earth, *Furiæ* in hell, and *Diræ* in heaven. *Phineia:* an adj. from *Phineus*, a king of Arcadia or Thrace, who put out the eyes of his two sons, at the instigation of his wife, their step-mother. For this unnatural conduct, Jove deprived him of sight, and sent the Harpyiæ to torment them; which they did, till Calais and Zetes, the sons of Boreas and Orithyia, expelled them from his kingdom, in return for the favors which they had received of him on their way to Colchis, after the golden fleece. They pursued these monsters as far as these islands; when, being admonished by Jove to pursue

213. Phineïa domus clausa *est illis*

Clausa domus, mensasque metu liquêre priores
Tristius haud illis monstrum, nec sævior ulla
Pestis et ira Deûm Stygiis sese extulit undis.

216. Vultus *earum* volucrum *sunt* Virginei; *est iilis* fœdissima proluvies

Virginei volucrum vultus, fœdissima ventris
Proluvies, uncæque manus, et pallida semper
Ora fame.
Huc ubi delati portus intravimus; ecce
Læta boum passim campis armenta videmus,

221. Caprigenumque pecus *errans* per herbas *cum* nullo custode. Irruimus *in ea* ferro

Caprigenumque pecus, nullo custode, per herbas.
Irruimus ferro, et Divos ipsumque vocamus
In partem prædamque Jovem: tunc litore curvo
Extruimusque toros, dapibusque epulamur opimis.
At subitæ horrifico lapsu de montibus adsunt
Harpyiæ, et magnis quatiunt clangoribus alas:
Diripiuntque dapes, contactuque omnia fœdant

228. Tum dira vox *crat illis* inter

Immundo: tum vox tetrum dira inter odorem.
Rursùm in secessu longo, sub rupe cavatâ,

230. *Nos* circum clausi arboribus

Arboribus clausi circùm atque horrentibus umbris,
Instruimus mensas, arisque reponimus ignem.
Rursùm ex diverso cœli, cæcisque latebris,
Turba sonans prædam pedibus circumvolat uncis,
Polluit ore dapes. Sociis tunc, arma capessant,

236. Faciunt haud secùs ac jussi *sunt*

Edico, et dirâ bellum cum gente gerendum.
Haud secùs ac jussi faciunt, tectosque per herbam

NOTES.

them no farther, they returned. Hence they were called *Strophades*, from a Greek word implying a return. Their former name was *Plotæ*. Here the *Harpyiæ* took up their residence. This serves to explain the words, *postquam Phineïa domus:* after they were expelled from the palace of Phineus.

214. *Haud tristius:* there is not a monster more fell than they; nor any more cruel pest and scourge (*ira*) of the gods, &c. *Est*, is understood.

215. *Stygiis undis:* from the waters of Styx. This was a fabulous river of Hell, around which, the poets say, it flowed nine times. The gods held its waters in great veneration. If they swore by it, the oath was inviolable. It is said to have derived its name from the nymph *Styx*, who assisted Jupiter in the war against the giants. See Geor. iii. 551.

217. *Proluvies ventris:* a most offensive efflux of the belly. *Ora semper pallida:* and their faces always pale through hunger.

220. *Læta:* in the sense of *pinguia*, agreeing with *armenta*.

223. *In partem prædamque:* for *in partem prædæ*, by hendiadis. It was a custom among the Romans when they went out to war, or to the chase, to vow to consecrate a part of the spoils, or booty, to the gods. *Vocamus:* we invoke the gods, and Jove himself, to a share of the booty.

224. *Toros:* tables—couches. *Opimis dapibus:* upon the rich, or delicious meat. See 231, infra.

225. *Lapsu:* motion. *Adsunt:* in the sense of *adveniunt*, vel *advolant*.

226. *Magnis clangoribus:* with a mighty noise. Some copies have *plangoribus*, as Pierius informs us.

227. *Diripiunt:* in the sense of *rapiunt*.

230. *Horrentibus:* in the sense of *densis*. *Secessu longo:* in a long retreat—in a remote place.

231. *Instruimus mensas:* we spread our tables.

232. *Ex diverso cœli:* from a different quarter of the sky, and from their secret retreats. The word *tractu* is to be supplied with *diverso:* in the sense of *diversa parte cœli*. The Mythologists make the harpies only three in number. Virgil however speaks of them as being numerous, calling them *turba* and *gens*, so that they no sooner left one part of the Island than they were troubled with them in another. But the poets do not always conform to historical or fabulous tradition, farther than suits their design.

233. *Prædam.* This I take for their meat, or flesh in general; while *dapes* means that portion of it dressed, and prepared for eating. *Polluit:* spoils—or defiles with the mouth. *Sonans*, flapping their wings—whizzing.

235. *Edico:* in the sense of *jubeo*.

236. *Faciunt haud:* they do no other-

Disponunt enses, et scuta latentia condunt.
Ergò, ubi delapsæ sonitum per curva dedêre
Litora; dat signum speculâ Misenus ab altâ
Ære cavo: invadunt socii, et nova prælia tentant,
Obscœnas pelagi ferro fœdare volucres.
Sed neque vim plumis ullam, nec vulnera tergo
Accipiunt: celerique fugâ sub sidera lapsæ,
Semesam prædam et vestigia fœda relinquunt.
Una in præcelsâ consedit rupe Celæno,
Infelix vates, rumpitque hanc pectore vocem:
Bellum etiam pro cæde boum stratisque juvencis,
Laomedontiadæ, bellumne inferre paratis?
Et patrio insontes Harpyias pellere regno?
Accipite ergò animis atque hæc mea figite dicta:
Quæ Phœbo pater omnipotens, mihi Phœbus Apollo
Prædixit, vobis furiarum ego maxima pando.
Italiam cursu petitis, ventisque vocatis
Ibitis Italiam, portusque intrare licebit.
Sed non antè datam cingetis mœnibus urbem,
Quàm vos dira fames, nostræque injuria cædis,
Ambesas subigat malis absumere mensas.

238. Ubi *Harpyiæ* delapsæ

245. Celæno una *ex iis*, infelix vates, consedit in

248. Paratis-ne inferre bellum *nobis*, etiam bellum, *inquam*, pro cæde boum

251. Ego maxima furiarum pando vobis *ea*, quæ Omnipotens pater *prædixit* Phœbo, *et* Phœbus Apollo prædixit mihi.

255. Cingetis urbem datam *vobis* mœnibus antèquam dira fames

NOTES.

wise than they are commanded—they do just as they are commanded.

237. *Condunt:* they hide their shields, concealed among the grass. *Latentia:* in the sense of *occulta.* *Delapsæ:* in the sense of *advolantes.*

239. *Specula.* This was an elevated spot, or place, commanding a wide prospect. It is derived from the old verb *specio.* Hence the verb *speculor.* *Signum:* the signal for the attack.

240. *Tentant nova:* and try a new kind of fight. *Ære:* trumpet: see 111. supra.

242. *Vim:* in the sense of *ictum.* The epithet *obscœnas* is added to these birds, either because they were of bad omen; or were filthy, and to be abhorred on account of their nastiness. *Fœdare:* the primary meaning of this word is, *to mangle—to cut in pieces—to make havoc of.* Hence the propriety of its being connected with *ferro.*

243. *Lapsæ:* flying—shooting away.

244. *Semesam:* half eaten. Of *semi,* and *esam,* of the verb *edo.*

246. *Infelix.* As *felix* sometimes signifies propitious, favorable, auspicious; so *infelix* oftentimes signifies *ill-boding, inauspicious,* as here: ill-boding prophetess. *Hanc vocem:* the same as *hæc verba.*

247. *Pro cæde:* for (in return for) the slaughter of our cattle, and bullocks slain. In addition to the crime of killing our herds and taking our property; do you prepare to wage war against us, and to drive *us* from our paternal realms, who have done you no injury or harm, and are in every respect innocent.

In calling them the *sons of Laomedon,* Celæno reproaches them as being impious, unjust and faithless, like that prince, who did not keep his promises even with the gods. See Geor. i. 502.

248. *Laomedontiadæ:* a patronymic noun from *Laomedon,* the father of Priam, and king of Troy. The same with *Trojani.*

249. *Patrio regno:* from our paternal kingdom. This is said, because Neptune, their father, had the empire of the sea, and the islands.

250. *Accipite:* hear—attend to.

252. *Maxima furiarum.* Servius infers from this passage that the *Harpies* and the *Furies* were the same. *Pando:* in the sense of *explico.*

255. *Datam:* in the sense of *concessam,* vel *prædictam.*

256. *Dira fames:* direful hunger, and the injury (done to) of our race, forces you to consume your gnawed trenchers. *Malis:* in the sense of *dentibus.* *Injuria nostræ cædis.* This injury consisted in killing their cattle; and in making an attack upon them.

257. *Absumere mensas,* &c. The sense of this prediction is seen from its accomplishment in the seventh book, verse 116. The story is not merely a poetical invention; it was a historical tradition. Dionysius and Strabo say that Æneas had received a response from an Oracle, foretelling that before he came to a settlement in Italy, he should be reduced to the necessity of eating his trenchers, *mensas.* Varro says he received it from the Oracle of *Dodona* in Ep[illegible]

260. *Eorum* animi cecidere: nec jam ampliùs jubent exposcere pacem armis, sed votis

265. *Inquit:* O Dî, prohibete *has* minas *à nobis*

274. Nimbosa cacumina montis Leucatæ *aperiuntur conspectui*

Dixit: et in sylvam pennis ablata refugit.
At sociis subitâ gelidus formidine sanguis
Diriguit: cecidere animi: nec jam ampliùs armis,
Sed votis precibusque jubent exposcere pacem,
Sive Deæ, seu sint diræ obscœnæque volucres
  At pater Anchises, passis de litore palmis,
Numina magna vocat, meritosque indicit honores:
Dî, prohibete minas; Dî, talem avertite casum,
Et placidi servate pios. Tum litore funem
Diripere, excussosque jubet laxare rudentes.
  Tendunt vela Noti: ferimur spumantibus undis,
Quà cursum ventusque gubernatorque vocabant.
Jam medio apparet fluctu nemorosa Zacynthos,
Dulichiumque, Sameque, et Neritos ardua saxis.
Effugimus scopulos Ithacæ, Laërtia regna,
Et terram altricem sævi exsecramur Ulyssei.
Mox et Leucatæ nimbosa cacumina montis,

NOTES.

rus. Virgil puts it in the mouth of the *Harpyiæ*, as being both suitable to their nature, and more apt to raise surprise, when coming from them. This prophecy received its fulfilment in the following manner. Having arrived in Italy, and being destitute of dishes, they were forced to eat their meat or flesh upon large oval cakes, made of flour, which they used for bread. And after they had eaten their flesh, *they consumed their cakes* also; which they had used in the room of plates.

258. *Pennis:* in the sense of *alis. Ablata:* in the sense of *sublata.*

259. *Sanguis gelidus:* the blood chilled through sudden fear, grew thick, &c. Their blood ceased to flow in its ordinary course; the heart being unable to propel it to the extremities with its usual force.

263. *Palmis passis de litore:* in the sense of *palmis extensis de litore.*

264. *Magna numina:* the great gods. See Geor. i. 498. *Indicit:* and appoints proper sacrifices or offerings.

265. *Prohibete:* in the sense of *avertite. Casus:* calamity—misfortune.

266 *Placidi:* in the sense of *placati*, vel *benigni. Funem:* the cable.

267. *Diripere:* in the sense of *avellere.* Some copies have *deripere:* which is the reading of Heyne.

Rudentes: in the sense of *funes.* By these we are probably to understand those ropes, by the help of which the sails were hoisted and spread—the main sheets. They had already weighed anchor: they now let off the sheets—they extended the sails, and the wind fills them. *Excussos.* Heyne takes this in the sense of *evolutos.*

270. *Zacynthos.* An island in the Ionian sea, on the west of the Peloponnesus: *Hodie, Zante.* The south wind was necessary in sailing from the *Strophades* to this place. *Fluctu:* in the sense of *mari.*

271. *Dulichium.* This island lies in the mouth of the *Sinus Corinthiacus*, and is one of the *Echinades. Hodie, Dolicha. Same* vel *Samos: hodie, Cephalonia.* These islands formed a part of the kingdom of Ulysses.

272. *Ithacæ. Ithaca* was a very barren and rocky island, between *Cephalonia* and *Dulichium*, the birth-place of Ulysses. Hence he is called *Ithacus.* On this island was a barren and rocky mountain, called *Neritos.* The word is sometimes applied to the whole island. *Scopulos Ithacæ.* This is said by way of irony and contempt, in allusion to its rocks and barrenness. He adds, *Laërtia regna*, the realms of *Laërtes.* He was king of that island, and the father of Ulysses.

273. *Execramur terram:* we execrate the land, the nurse (birth-place) of cruel Ulysses. These words express very forcibly his detestation of so great an enemy to the Trojans.

274. *Leucatæ montis:* the cloudy summit of the mountain Lucates. *Leucas, Leucates* vel *Leucate*, an island lying very near the coast of *Acarnania*, in Epirus. *Hodie, St. Maura.* It is said to have once been connected with the main land. It took its name from a famous white mountain, or rock, called *Leucate*, (from a Greek word, signifying *white*,) lying at the southern extremity of the island. It was supposed to have the virtue of curing despairing lovers, who were wont to cast themselves from it into the sea. Among those who made the experiment of its virtues, was the celebrated poetess *Sappho*, who fell in love with *Phaon*, a beautiful youth of *Lesbos.*

According to Strabo, Apollo had a temple on this rock, or mountain, from which a human victim was cast yearly into the sea, as a sacrifice to that god. On account

Et formidatus nautis aperitur Apollo.
Hunc petimus fessi, et parvæ succedimus urbi.
Anchora de prorâ jacitur; stant litore puppes
Ergò insperatâ tandem tellure potiti,
Lustramurque Jovi, votisque incendimus aras.
Actiaque Iliacis celebramus litora ludis.
Exercent patrias oleo labente palæstras
Nudati socii: juvat evasisse tot urbes
Argolicas, mediosque fugam tenuisse per hostes.
Intereà magnum Sol circumvolvitur annum,
Et glacialis hyems Aquilonibus asperat undas.
Ære cavo clypeum, magni gestamen Abantis,
Postibus adversis figo, et rem carmine signo
Æneas hæc de Danais victoribus arma.

286. Figo **adversis** postibus *templi* clypeum *è* cavo ære, gestamen magni Abantis, et signo rem *hoc* carmine: Æneas *suspendit* hæc arma *capta*

NOTES.

of this; or on account of the roughness of the coast, he is called *Apollo formidatus nautis:* Apollo dreaded by sailors. The name of the god, put by meton. for the temple. *Nimbosa:* some copies have *umbrosa.*

276. *Hunc.* This may refer to mount *Leucatæ*, mentioned before. Or we may suppose, with more probability, that Æneas continued his course hence to the *Sinus Ambracius*, where there was the small city *Ambracia*, (afterwards enlarged by Augustus, and called *Nicopolis*, in allusion to his victory,) and another temple of Apollo. If we make this supposition, the *hunc* may refer to this latter temple, or to the god to whom it was dedicated. Near this place Augustus afterwards obtained a complete victory over the combined forces of Anthony and Cleopatra, queen of Egypt. To this victory the poet alludes, with a view to compliment his prince. Here he landed, and performed those games, which Augustus afterwards instituted, in commemoration of his victory; and celebrated every fifth year.

277. *Puppes:* in the sense of *naves.* Or it may imply that the sterns of his ships lay aground, while the prows were afloat. This is the opinion of Dr. Trapp.

278. *Insperata:* greatly desired, or longed for. The prep. *in*, in composition, often increases the signification of the simple word, as well as changes it to a contrary sense. The former I take to be the case here; the same as *valdè sperata.* For after the many dangers and perils of his voyage, what could be more desirable, than to find a place where he could land in safety, and enjoy the hospitality of the shore?

279. *Lustramur Jovi:* in the sense of *sacrificamus Jovi. Incendimus aras votis.* Ruæus says, *cumulamus aras victimis. Votum*, by met. the thing vowed—the victim.

280. *Actia litora.* The poet here plainly alludes to the famous games which Augustus instituted on the promontory of Epirus, in commemoration of his victory over Anthony and Cleopatra, in the year of Rome 723. These were celebrated every fifth year. Hence, some have conjectured, that four years had now elapsed since Æneas left Troy. Virgil would make his prince believe that Æneas landed on this shore, and instituted these very games.

281. *Exercent patrias:* they practise their country's exercises with the slippery oil. The *palæstra* was an exercise, in which the persons were naked; and, that they might free themselve the easier from the hands of their antagonists, they used to besmear their bodies and arms with oil. It is also applied to all kinds of games or exercises, such as wrestling, leaping, &c. Also the place where these exercises are performed.

283. *Fugam:* in the sense of *cursum*, vel *iter.*

284. *Magnum annum:* the sun completes (rolls round) a great year: a solar year of 12 months, as distinguished from a lunar year, which consists of 12 lunations, or 354 days. *Circumvolvitur*, is plainly in the sense of *circumvolvit.*

285. *Hyems asperat:* the icy winter roughens. *Undas:* in the sense of *mare.*

286. *Gestamen.* This word signifies any covering—any thing worn or carried by a person; from the verb *gesto. Abantis.* It is probable that *Abas* was one of those Greeks, whom Æneas and his party slew in the night of the sack of Troy, stript of their armour, and exchanged for their own. *Gestamen*, is put in apposition with *clypeum.*

287. *Adversis postibus:* the fronting door posts of the temple. *Figo:* in the sense of *suspendo. Signo rem carmine:* I declare the transaction by this verse—inscription. *Rem:* in the sense of *factum*

289. Tum jubeo *socios* linquere

298. Pectus incensum *est* miro

301. Tum fortè Andromache libabat cineri *Hectoris* solemnes dapes, et tristia dona, ante urbem in luco ad undam falsi Simoentis, vocabatque Manes ad Hectoreum tumulum, quem inanem sacraverat è viridi cespite, et geminas aras, causam lachrymis.

Linquere tum portus jubeo, et considere transtris.
Certatim socii feriunt mare, et æquora verrunt.
Protinùs aërias Phæacum abscondimus arces,
Litoraque Epiri legimus, portuque subimus
Chaonio, et celsam Buthroti ascendimus urbem.
Hìc incredibilis rerum fama occupat aures,
Priamiden Helenum Graias regnare per urbes,
Conjugio Æacidæ Pyrrhi sceptrisque potitum,
Et patrio Andromachen iterum cessisse marito.
Obstupui: miroque incensum pectus amore
Compellare virum, et casus cognoscere tantos
Progredior portu, classes et litora linquens.
Solemnes tum fortè dapes et tristia dona,
Ante urbem, in luco, falsi Simoëntis ad undam,
Libabat cineri Andromache, Manesque vocabat
Hectoreum ad tumulum, viridi quem cespite inanem,

NOTES.

289. *Transtris:* upon the benches or thwarts. They extended across the vessels from side to side: the rowers sat upon them.

290. *Certatim:* eagerly—striving to outdo one another. *Æquora:* the surface of the sea, which they sweep with their oars. *Æquor:* properly any plain or level surface, whether land or water. It is here used in its appropriate sense.

291. *Phæacum:* of the Phæacians—so called from *Phæacia*, an island lying to the west of the promontory of Actium. *Hodie, Corfu.* It was famous for its orchards. Here Homer placed the gardens of Alcinoüs, who was king of the island. *Abscondimus:* we hide the aërial towers, &c. we lose sight of them.

292. *Legimus Epiri:* we coast along the shores of Epirus. This was once a flourishing kingdom, bounded on the east by Achaia and Thessaly; on the north by Macedonia; and on the south and west by the Ionian sea. It was divided into four principal parts; *Ætolia, Acarnania, Thesprotia,* and *Chaonia.* In the last of which was the city *Buthrotus* or *Buthrotum.* It was built upon a hill. Hence the epithet *celsam.* For *ascendimus,* Heinsius, and Heyne after him, read *accedimus.*

294. *Incredibilis fama rerum:* an incredible report of things. It was an incredible revolution of fortune indeed, that a son of Priam should reign in Epirus, and should be married to Andromache, the widow of his brother, after she had been the wife of Pyrrhus, that very son of Achilles, who slew the venerable Priam in the most cruel manner. Yet these things are not the mere invention of the poet. Justin informs us, that after the taking of Troy, Pyrrhus was reconciled to Helenus, shared with him his kingdom, and gave him Andromache in marriage.

295. *Priamiden:* the son of Priam—a patronymic noun.

296. *Æacidæ Pyrrhi:* of Pyrrhus, a descendent of *Æacus.* He was king of Thessaly, and father of *Peleus. Æacides* was a name both of *Achilles* and *Pyrrhus. Conjugio:* in the sense of *uxore. Sceptris:* in the sense of *regno.*

297. *Andromachen cessisse:* that Andromache again had fallen to a husband of her own country. She was a Theban princess by birth; but by marrying Hector, Troy became her country. *Patrio marito:* in the sense of *Trojano marito.*

298. *Miro:* in the sense of *magno,* vel *vehementi. Amore:* desire.

299. *Tantos casus:* so great events—such a wonderful change of fortune.

301. *Tum fortè libabat:* then by chance Andromache was offering the yearly feast, and mournful gifts to the ashes of Hector, &c. Among other funeral ceremonies, was the custom of pouring into, or upon the grave, blood and milk; because it was thought that the (*animæ*) souls delighted and fed upon these, and particularly upon the blood. These constituted the feast and mournful gifts, which Andromache repeated yearly to the ashes or shade of Hector. See verse 66, supra.

302. *Falsi Simoëntis:* fictitious Simois. This was a small river of Epirus, to which Helenus and Andromache gave the name of *Simoïs,* after a river of that name in Troas. It was not the real Simoïs. *Undam:* in the sense of *aquam.*

304. *Inanem:* empty—not the real tomb of Hector; but one in memory of him. Such a one was called *tumulus vacuus,* vel *inanis.* These tombs, or cenotaphs were

Et geminas, causam lachrymis, sacraverat aras.
Ut me conspexit venientem, et Troïa circùm
Arma amens vidit; magnis exterrita monstris,
Diriguit visu in medio: calor ossa reliquit:
Labitur; et longo vix tandem tempore fatur:
Verane te facies, verus mihi nuntius affers,
Nate Deâ? vivisne? aut, si lux alma recessit,
Hector ubi est? Dixit: lachrymasque effudit, et omnem
Implevit clamore locum. Vix pauca furenti
Subjicio, et raris turbatus vocibus hisco:
Vivo equidem, vitamque extrema per omnia duco.
Ne dubita, nam vera vides.
Heu! quis te casus dejectam conjuge tanto
Excipit? aut quæ digna satìs fortuna revisit?
Hectoris Andromache, Pyrrhin' connubia servas?

309. Et tandem vix fatur longo tempore post
311. Recessit *à te*

319. *O* Andromache, *quondam uxor* Hectoris, servas-ne connubia Pyrrhi?

NOTES.

honorary merely, and erected to persons buried in another place; or to those who received no burial, and whose relics could not be found. The same religious regard was paid to these *tumuli inanes et honorarii*, as to real tombs. *Viridi cespite:* she made (consecrated) this tomb of green turf.

305. *Geminas aras.* Some will have it, that one altar was for Hector, and the other for Astyanax, her son, whom the Greeks threw headlong from the tower of Troy. Others, however, think she erected (consecrated) both to Hector, it being customary to erect two altars to the *Manes*, especially of Heroes, who were considered inferior deities. See verse 63, supra. *Causam:* the cause, or incentive to her tears. They brought more forcibly to her mind the recollection of her husband, and renewed her former grief.

307. *Amens:* amazed. It agrees with *illa* understood. *Exterrita monstris:* astonished at the mighty prodigy, she fainted in the midst of the sight.

Any thing that happens, or is contrary to the ordinary course of things, may be called *monstrum.* The sight of her countrymen was so unexpected, so improbable, and so far from the ordinary course of events, that it might well enough be called *magnum monstrum.*

308. *Diriguit:* in the sense of *defecit.*

309. *Labitur:* she falls.

310. *Vera-ne facies:* do you, a real form, a true messenger, present yourself to me? —are you really Æneas, or are you his image only?—are the things which I behold true and real, or are they mere phantoms? *Lux:* in the sense of *vita.*

313. *Furenti:* to her grieving, or sorrowing. *Furens* properly signifies, being transported with any inordinate passion or affection, as love, sorrow, anger, &c.—grieving immoderately Ruæus says, *mœrenti.*

314. *Subjicio:* in the sense of *respondeo. Hisco:* I open my mouth in broken, disconnected words. They were few in number, and interrupted by sighs and tears.

315. *Per omnia extrema:* through all perils and distress. *Extrema*, here, is a sub. Ruæus says, *per omnes miserias.*

316. *Vera:* true things—realities.

317. *Quis casus:* what event hath befallen thee, deprived of so great a husband? *Conjuge*, here, plainly means Hector, her former husband. Ruæus interprets *excipit te*, by, *successit tibi;* and *dejectam*, by *privatam.*

319. *Servas connubia*, &c. These words of Æneas would carry with them a severe reproach, if Andromache had been the mistress of her own fortune. Catrou observes, that this slavery rendered her connexion with Pyrrhus excusable; yet she is confused upon the occasion, casts her eyes upon the ground, and replies with a low voice, not answering his question directly, but breaking out into a passionate exclamation: *O felix*, &c. The sense which Ruæus gives to the passage is plainly incorrect. He interprets the words thus: *O Andromache, tenes-ne conjugem Hectoris, an Pyrrhi:* which will be: Andromache, are you wedded to Hector, or to Pyrrhus? which is manifestly absurd, especially after what Æneas had said just before; *dejectam tanto conjuge*, meaning that she was brought low by being deprived of so great a husband. The construction is as in the ordo: is Hector's Andromache wedded to Pyrrhus? which is not so much a question, as an exclamation of surprise. That *Hectoris Andromache* is to be construed in this way, appears from Justin, who gives them the same honorable designation, Lib. xvii. cap. 3. He there says, that Pyrrhus gave the kingdom of Epirus to Helenus, the son of Priam; and also gave him (*Andromachen Hectoris*) Hector's An-

321. O Priameïa virgo, una felix, ante alias *virgines*, jussa mori ad nostilem

325. Nos vectæ per diversa æquora, patriâ incensâ, enixæ servitio, tulimus fastus Achilleæ stirpis

330. Ast Orestes, inflammatus magno amore conjugis ereptæ *à se*, et agitatus furiis scelerum, excipit illum, *nempe*, *Pyrrhum*,

Dejecit vultum, et demissâ voce locuta est
O felix una ante alias Priameïa virgo,
Hostilem ad tumulum Trojæ sub mœnibus altis,
Jussa mori: quæ sortitus non pertulit ullos,
Nec victoris heri tetigit captiva cubile!
Nos patriâ incensâ diversa per æquora vectæ,
Stirpis Achilleæ fastus, juvenemque superbum
Servitio enixæ tulimus: qui deinde secutus
Ledæam Hermionem, Lacedæmoniosque Hymenæos,
Me famulam famuloque Heleno transmisit habendam
Ast illum, ereptæ magno inflammatus amore
Conjugis, et scelerum furiis agitatus, Orestes

NOTES.

dromache, who had been his wife. *Servas.* This is the usual reading: but Heyne observes that some copies have *servat.* This renders the passage somewhat easier: does Hector's Andromache preserve the marriage of Pyrrhus?—Is she joined in marriage with Pyrrhus?

320. *Demissa voce:* in a low voice.

321. *Priameïa virgo:* Polyxena, the daughter of Priam and Hecuba. Achilles fell in love with her; and being invited to Troy by Priam for the purpose of celebrating their nuptials, while in the temple of Apollo, where the marriage was to have been performed, he was killed by Paris with an arrow. Achilles, with his last breath, conjured his son Pyrrhus to revenge his death upon Priam's family, and to immolate Polyxena at his tomb, whenever Troy should be taken. This accordingly he did. Quinctilian quotes this passage as an instance of Virgil's talent at the pathetic. In order, says he, to show the extremity of Andromache's misery, he makes her even envy the fate of Polyxena, who, in the eyes of all the world besides, was most wretched and miserable. How wretched then must Andromache's condition have been, if, when compared to her, even Polyxena was happy! Instit. Lib. vi. cap. 3. *Una:* in the sense of *sola.*

323. *Quæ non pertulit:* who hath not borne any lots. The Grecian princes, after the capture of Troy, cast lots among themselves for the captives.

324. *Nec captiva:* nor as a captive, hath touched the bed of a victorious lord. This is the calamity from which Andromache declares Polyxena happy, in being delivered by death.

325. *Nos vectæ:* in the sense of *ego vecta.*

326. *Fastus:* acc. plu. pride—haughtiness. *Stirpis Achilleæ:* Pyrrhus, the offspring of Achilles. Some read *fastum.*

327. *Enixæ:* a part. of the verb *enitor*, agreeing with *nos vectæ*, above. It signifies to labor and toil with our hands in general; also the pain and labor of bearing children. In this last sense, perhaps, we are to take it here. For it is said, she bore a son to Pyrrhus, called *Molossus*, who gave his name to a part of Epirus. Some, however, understand it of labor and toil in general: laboring in servitude. Ruæus says, *parientes in captivitate:* bringing forth children in captivity.

328. *Hermionem.* Hermione was the daughter of Menelaus, king of Sparta or Lacedæmon, and Helen, the daughter of Jupiter and Leda; hence the adj. *Ledæam*, Ledæan. She was betrothed by Tyndarus to her cousin Orestes, in the absence of her father, who, it seems, had promised her to Pyrrhus, while he was at Troy. After his return, he went to Sparta, and carried off his spouse. This so enraged Orestes, that he followed Pyrrhus to Delphi, where he went to consult the oracle of Apollo concerning his future race, and there slew him. *Hymenæos:* marriage—match: also nuptials

329. *Transmisit:* in the sense of *dedit*, vel *tradidit.* *Habendam:* to be had—possessed—enjoyed.

331. *Conjugis:* namely, Hermione. *Agitatus furiis:* hurried on by the furies of his crimes. Orestes, it is said, slew his mother Clytemnestra, for assisting Ægistus in procuring the death of his father Agamemnon. After which he is said to have been haunted and tormented by the furies, (the remorse and stings of a guilty conscience,) for imbruing his hands in his mother's blood. It is said he was acquitted by the court of the *Areopagus* at Athens; and, after the death of Pyrrhus, he married Hermione, and added the kingdom of Sparta to his own hereditary dominions.

The furies were three in number, *Alecto, Tisiphone*, and *Megæra.* After they ceased to torment Orestes, they received the name of *Eumenides*, which implies benevolence and compassion. He built a temple to them, and offered them sacrifices. They were represented as holding a burning torch in one hand, and a whip in the other. The stings and remorses of conscience were the

Excipit incautum patriasque obtruncat ad aras.
Morte Neoptolemi, regnorum reddita cessit
Pars Heleno; qui Chaonios cognomine campos,
Chaoniamque omnem Trojano à Chaone dixit:
Pergamaque, Iliacamque jugis hanc addidit arcem.
Sed tibi qui cursum venti, quæ fata, dedêre?
Aut quis te ignarum nostris Deus appulit oris?
Quid puer Ascanius? superatne, et vescitur aurâ?
Quem tibi jam Troja—
Ecqua jam puero est amissæ cura parentis?
Ecquid in antiquam virtutem animosque viriles,
Et pater Æneas, et avunculus excitat Hector?
  Talia fundebat lachrymans, longosque ciebat
Incassùm fletus; cùm sese à mœnibus heros
Priamides multis Helenus comitantibus affert,
Agnoscitque suos, lætusque ad limina ducit;
Et multùm lachrymas verba inter singula fundit.
Procedo, et parvam Trojam, simulataque magnis
Pergama, et arentem Xanthi cognomine rivum,
Agnosco: Scææque amplector limina portæ

334. Pars regnorum reddita cessit Heleno: qui dixit campos Chaonios cognomine, omnemque *illam regionem* Chaoniam.

339. Quid puer Ascanius *agit?*

345. Cùm heros Helenus Priamides affert sese à mœnibus, multis comitantibus *eum*

349. Et agnosco parvam Trojam, Pergamaque *parva* simulata magnis

350. *Dictum* cognomine Xanthi

NOTES.

furies of Orestes, which the poet calls the *Furiæ scelerum*, the furies of his crimes. It is probable that he pictured to his imagination this notion of his being haunted by the furies, armed with all those terrors, with which they were represented by the poets. Suetonius says of Nero: *Sæpe confessus exagitari se maternâ specie, verberibus furiarum, ac tædis ardentibus.*

332. *Excipit:* surprised—caught. *Ad patrias aras:* at his country's altars. The temple of Apollo at Delphi was nearly in the centre of Greece, the country of Pyrrhus. In this sense Ruæus and Turnebus understand the expression. Others take the words to mean: at his father's altars; because Achilles was slain at the altar of *Thrymbæan Apollo*, at Troy; and he, at the altar of Apollo at *Delphi.*

333. *Reddita:* in the sense of *data. Cessit:* fell to Helenus.

335. *Dixit:* in the sense of *vocavit*, vel *nominavit. Chaone.* Chaon was the son of Priam, and consequently the brother of Helenus, who slew him, while hunting, accidentally: and in memory of him, he called his kingdom *Chaonia.*

336. *Jugis:* in the sense of *monte. Addidit:* in the sense of *condidit.*

338. *Appulit:* in the sense of *duxit*, vel *direxit. Ignarum:* Ruæus says, *inscium.*

339. *Superat:* in the sense of *superest. Vescitur:* in the sense of *spirat.*

340. *Quem tibi*, &c. This, and some other imperfect lines in the Æneid, is a proof that Virgil did not put the finishing stroke to this part of his works. It was his intention, if he had lived, to revise it. To complete the sense of the line, something must be supplied. Some have added: *peperit fumante Creüsa.* But at the time of the sack of Troy, Ascanius was several years old, and able to accompany his father. Æn. ii. 724. Others have added: *obsessâ est enixa Creüsa:* whom Creüsa bore you, Troy already being besieged—during the siege of Troy. This probably is the sense, but it has not the poetic spirit of Virgil.

341. *Cura:* in the sense of *dolor*, vel *solicitudo.*

342. *Ecquid.* This word is used here merely as an interrogative, in the sense of *an*, vel *num.*

Dr. Trapp, in his translation of the Æneid, makes a number of excellent remarks upon this interesting interview between Æneas and Andromache. He concludes by saying: "That man surely can have no idea of friendship, nor of human nature itself, who is not sensibly touched with this whole passage; which to me is the most affecting in all the Æneid." *Animos:* courage. *Antiquam virtutem:* in the sense of *virtutem majorum. Excitat* is to be connected with each nominative case. *Eum*, vel *illum*, is understood after the verb.

344. *Fundebat:* in the sense of *dicebat. Ciebat:* in the sense of *excitabat*, vel *movebat. Longos:* in the sense of *multos.* Heinsius reads *largos.*

348. *Multùm:* an adv. in the sense of *copiosè*, vel *abundè;* or rather in the sense of *multas*, agreeing with *lachrymas.*

349. *Simulata:* resembling—looking like.

350. *Arentem:* in the sense of *parvum.* It was small, and perhaps, at some seasons of the year, dry.

351. *Amplector*, &c. It was a custom, when persons were going from home, or re-

Necnon et Teucri sociâ simul urbe fruuntur.
Illos porticibus rex accipiebat in amplis.
Aulaï in medio libabant pocula Bacchi,
Impositis auro dapibus, paterasque tenebant.
Jamque dies, alterque dies processit; et auræ
Vela vocant, tumidoque inflatur carbasus Austro.
His vatem aggredior dictis, ac talia quæso:
Trojugena, interpres Divûm, qui numina Phœbi,
Qui tripodas, Clarii lauros, qui sidera sentis,
Et volucrum linguas, et præpetis omina pennæ,
Fare, age (namque omnem cursum mihi prospera dixit
Relligio; et cuncti suaserunt numine Divi
Italiam petere, et terras tentare repôstas:
Sola novum dictuque nefas Harpyia Celæno
Prodigium canit, et tristes denuntiat iras,
Obscœnamque famem) quæ prima pericula vito?

356. Jamque *unus* dies, alterque

360. Qui sentis numina Phœbi, qui *sentis* tripodas, *et* lauros Clarii *Apollinis*, qui *sentis*

365. Harpyia Celæno sola canit novum prodigium

NOTES.

turning, to embrace the pillars and threshold of their houses.

354. *Aulaï:* for *aulæ.* The gen. of the first declension was sometimes formed in *ai.* See Grammar. *Bacchi:* Bacchus, the god of wine, by meton. put for wine itself. *Libabant pocula.* It was customary at entertainments, after the first table or course, to introduce wine, with a libation to the gods; which consisted in pouring a few drops upon the altar, or upon the table. *Libabant:* in the sense of *bibebant.*

355. *Impositis auro:* served up in gold—in golden dishes.

357. *Tumido Austro:* by the rising wind. *Auster* here is put for wind in general. *Carbasus:* the canvass, of which the sails were made.

358. *Aggredior:* I address the prophet Helenus.

360. *Qui sentis numina:* who knowest the will of Phœbus. The verb *sentis* is to be supplied with each accusative following. The poet here enumerates five ways of divination. First, by the immediate inspiration of the gods—*sentis numina Phœbi.* Second, by sitting upon the Tripod. Third, by burning laurel. Fourth, by contemplating the stars. Fifth, by the observation of birds.

360. *Tripodas.* The tripod was a kind of three footed stool, upon which the priestess of Apollo sat, when she delivered the oracles. *Clarii. Clarius* was an epithet of Apollo, from *Claros,* a city of Greece, where he had a celebrated temple. One way of divination was, to burn a branch of the laurel tree. If it made a crackling noise, it was a good omen; but if not, it was considered a bad one.

361. *Linguas volucrum.* The omens were taken from birds in two ways; from the sounds they uttered, and the manner of their flight. The former was called *augurium;* the observation of which constituted the art of the *augures:* the latter was called *auspicium;* the observation of which constituted the art of the *auspices.*

Omina præpetis pennæ: the omens of the swift wing—widely extended wings. The augurs were certain persons, who pretended to foretell future events, principally from the noise of certain birds. Romulus created *three;* Servius Tullius added *another,* and Sylla appointed six additional ones. So that the number in his time was ten. They generally sat upon some tower, or high place, the better to make their observations.

362. *Prospera relligio:* favorable or propitious auspices and predictions have directed (*dixit*) my whole course. *Numine:* in the sense of *auctoritate.* Some take this for *omnis relligio dixit mihi prosperum cursum:* by *hypallage.* Here *relligio* is to be taken for the responses and predictions of the oracles, and the various intimations which he had received: all which declared that he should arrive safe in Italy. Ruæus says, *ceremoniæ propitiæ.*

364. *Repôstas:* by syn. for *repositas.* It may mean *remote,* or *at a distance:* also reserved, laid up in store. In this sense Ruæus takes it here. In either case it will be true, as it respects the land of Italy, whither he was going. *Tentare:* to search out—to find: in the sense of *petere.*

365. *Nefas dictu:* horrible to be told. *Nefas* here is taken as an adj. indeclinable: the same as *nefandum.*

366. *Canit:* in the sense of *prædicit.*

367. *Obscœnam:* in the sense of *rabidam* vel *vehementem.* *Quæ pericula prima vito?* What dangers first do I shun?—what are the first, or chief dangers, which I have to avoid?

Quidve sequens, tantos possim superare labores?
Hìc Helenus, cæsis primùm de more juvencis,
Exorat pacem Divûm, vittasque resolvit
Sacrati capitis, meque ad tua limina, Phœbe,
Ipse manu multo suspensum numine ducit:
Atque hæc deinde canit divino ex ore sacerdos:
Nate Deâ; nam te majoribus ire per altum
Auspiciis manifesta fides: sic fata Deûm rex
Sortitur, volvitque vices: is vertitur ordo.
Pauca tibi è multis, quò tutior hospita lustres
Æquora, et Ausonio possis considere portu,
Expediam dictis: prohibent nam cætera Parcæ

371. Ipseque manû ad tua limina, *O* Phœbe, suspensum multo numine

274. Manifesta fides *est mihi* te ire

377. Expediam dictis pauca tibi, è multis, quò *tu* tutior lustres hospita æquora

NOTES.

368. *Quid sequens:* following what counsel, can I surmount, &c.

370. *Resolvit vittas:* the priest in performing sacrifice, had his head bound about with fillets: now he is about to prophesy, he unbinds, and takes them from his head. *Pacem:* favor—grace.

372. *Suspensum:* in the sense of *solicitum*, vel *trepidantem. Multo numine:* at thy awful majesty—thy mighty power. Ruæus says, *ob magnam reverentiam Dei.*

Some copies have *suspensus*, which means that *Helenus* was full of anxiety, perturbation, and awe, from the power or influence of the god. But *suspensum* is the better reading, referring to Æneas, who had good reason to be in awful suspense and anxiety about his future fortune, which the god was about to declare to him by the mouth of Helenus.

373. *Canit:* in the sense of *eloquitur.*

374. *Majoribus auspiciis:* may mean, *with the greater auspices*, signs, or manifestations. Among the various omens or signs, which were thought to give insight into futurity, some were considered more important than others. Of these were visions, appearances in the heavens, &c. which all along had accompanied Æneas. But *auspicium* signifies any event or fortune. If this be the meaning here, which most probably is the case, then *majoribus auspiciis* will be, for greater or more important events—for better fortune—for more prosperous days. This is the opinion of Heyne.

375. *Sic rex Deûm:* thus the king of the gods dispenses his decrees, and fixes (*volvit*, rolls) the series of events: this order (or course of things) is fixed.

It is plain the poet hath here in view the fabulous story of the *Parcæ*, who were thought to preside over the events of human life; and to order, or fix, whatever befell to every individual from his birth to the close of his life. The first was represented as holding the distaff; the second as drawing out, or turning off (*volvere*,) and fixing the course of events; the third as cutting the thread. See Ecl. iv. 46.

376. *Sortitur.* This alludes to the custom of consulting the oracle, which was sometimes done by casting or drawing lots: *ordinat*, says Heyne.

377. *Hospita:* an adj. intervening. Ruæus interprets it by, *quæ excipient te:* which shall receive you.

It is plain that the seas over which he was to pass, were those that *intervened*, or lay between Epirus, and that part of Italy to which he was bound. These would be the *Ionian sea*, lying between Epirus and the extremity of the peninsula; that part of the Mediterranean lying to the east and south of Sicily; and the *Tuscan sea*, lying between Sicily, Italy, and the islands of Sardinia and Corsica. *Lustres:* in the sense of *naviges.* Valpy takes *hospita*, in the sense of *ignota:* to which he was a stranger.

379. *Parcæ prohibent:* the fates forbid that you should know the rest. Pierius observes, that in most of the ancient copies there is a full stop after *scire;* Servius approves of it, and it appears the best. The sense is easier, and we avoid any inconsistency. If we make both the verbs, *prohibent* and *vetat*, refer to Helenus, there will be an inconsistency. For, would Juno forbid him to declare what he did not know himself? Besides, he had just said that he would only inform him of a few of the events that were to befall him; which certainly implies that he knew the rest, but was restrained by heaven from communicating them to him. Some of these events it was not proper for him to know; because the accomplishment depended on his own free will. Others Juno prevented him from revealing, that he might be the more perplexed with doubts and uncertainty; and the more surprised and unprovided against the calamity when it came. Of this kind is the interpretation of Celæno's prophecy, which Helenus appears to have understood: for he forbids him to be much concerned about it, for the gods would find a way to extricate him from it: verse 394. infra.

Another particular is the death of Anchises Æneas does not question the fore-

381. Principio, longa via invia longis terris procul dividit Italiam *à te*, quam tu, *O ignare vir*, jam rere *esse* propinquam, parasque invadere vicinos portus.

386. Infernique lacus *transeundi sunt*, insulaque Ææœ Circœ *adeunda est*, antè quàm *tu* possis

389. Cùm ingens sus, inventa tibi sollicito ad undam secreti fluminis sub litoreis ilicibus, enixa fœtus triginta capitum, jacebat solo re-

Scire: Helenum farique vetat Saturnia Juno.
Principio, Italiam, quam tu jam rere propinquam,
Vicinosque, ignare, paras invadere portus,
Longa procul longis via dividit invia terris.
Antè et Trinacriâ lentandus remus in undâ,
Et salis Ausonii lustrandum navibus æquor,
Infernique lacus, Ææeque insula Circæ,
Quàm tutâ possis urbem componere terrâ.
Signa tibi dicam: tu condita mente teneto.
Cùm tibi sollicito secreti ad fluminis undam
Litoreis ingens inventa sub ilicibus sus,
Triginta capitum fœtus enixa jacebit,
Alba, solo recubans, albi circum ubera nati;
Is locus urbis erit; requies ea certa laborum.
Nec tu mensarum morsus horresce futuros.
Fata viam invenient, aderitque vocatus Apollo.

NOTES.

knowledge of Helenus concerning that event: he only complains that he did not reveal it to him: verse 712. infra. *Expediam:* in the sense of *explicabo*.

381. *Rere:* in the sense of *putas*.

382. *Invadere:* to take possession of—to enter.

383. *Longa via invia:* a long voyage, interrupted by extensive lands, separates Italy at a distance from you, which, &c. *Invia:* in the sense of *perdifficilis*. Æneas' voyage was much lengthened by his being obliged to sail round the southern part of Sicily; the islands that lay in his course, and other lands, rendered it long, difficult, and dangerous; and much interrupted and turned from a direct course.

384. *Trinacriâ:* a name of Sicily, (used here as an adj.) taken from its triangular form. Its three promontories were *Pelorus*, *Pachynus*, and *Lilybeum*. *Remus lentandus:* the oar must be bent in the Sicilian sea. This implies that they were to labor hard at the oar. The verb *est* is to be supplied.

385. *Æquor Ausonii salis:* the surface of the Italian (Tuscan) sea is to be sailed over. *Salis:* gen. of *sal:* by meton. put for the *sea*. *Æquor* is here used in its proper sense and meaning.

386. *Inferni lacus:* the infernal lakes must be passed, and the island of Ææan Circe must be approached, before that (*antè quàm*) you can, &c. Helenus here intimates to Æneas his descent to hell, which is the subject of the 6th book.

Circe was a celebrated sorceress, the daughter of the sun, and the nymph Perse. She is here called *Ææan*, from *Æa*, an island and city of Colchis, not far from the river Phasis. She married a king of *Sarmatia*, whom she poisoned. After which she fled into Italy, to a mountain and promontory, which, from her, was called Circe's Mount. *Hodie, Circello.*

387. *Componere:* in the sense of *condere*. *Tuta terra:* in a safe land. This, perhaps, is said in allusion to his being obliged to abandon the settlements he had made in Thrace and in Crete. In Italy he should find a sure and permanent residence.

388. *Condita:* in the sense of *reposita:* it agrees with *ea*, understood.

389. *Tibi sollicito—inventa:* found by you solicitous—anxious—musing. The dat. is frequently used by the poets in the sense of the abl.; also, in the sense of the gen. *Ad undam fluminis.* The river Tiber is here meant.

390. *Sub litoreis:* under the holm-trees shading the river—growing on the banks of the river.

391. *Enixa fœtus:* having brought forth a litter of thirty head.

392. *Recubans:* this I take in the sense of *prostratus*, flat (at full length) on her side, in reference to the manner of her lying; that being the position of the female when she gives suck to her young. *Jacebit solo recubans, alba:* shall lie on the ground flat on her side; herself white, and her pigs white around her teats. In this ordo of construction, *recubans* conveys an additional idea to that already communicated by the verb *jacebit*, and is very significant. In the usual *ordo* it is mere tautology. This circumstance of finding a white sow, with thirty pigs, was founded on ancient historical tradition. *Alba*, a city built by Ascanius, and made the seat of his government, took its name from this omen of the white sow and her pigs, as Varro informs us.

394. *Morsus:* the eating, or consumption of your tables.

395. *Aderit:* in the sense of *adjuvabit*.

Has autem terras, Italique hanc litoris oram,
Proxima quæ nostri perfunditur æquoris æstu,
Effuge: cuncta malis habitantur mœnia Graiis
Hîc et Narycii posuerunt mœnia Locri,
Et Salentinos obsedit milite campos
Lyctius Idomeneus: hìc illa ducis Melibœi
Parva Philoctetæ subnixa Petilia muro.
Quin, ubi transmissæ steterint trans æquora classes,
Et positis aris jam vota in litore solves;
Purpureo velare comas adopertus amictu:
Ne qua inter sanctos ignes in honore Deorum
Hostilis facies occurrat, et omina turbet.
Hunc socii morem sacrorum, hunc ipse teneto:
Häc casti maneant in relligione nepotes.
Ast, ubi digressum Siculæ te admoverit oræ
Ventus, et angusti rarescent claustra Pelori;
Læva tibi tellus et longo læva petantur

cubans, ipsa alba; *et* nati albi

401. Hîc *est* illa parva Petilia subnixa muro Philoctetæ

406. Ne qua hostilis facies occurrat inter sanctos ignes

408. Socii *tenento* hunc morem sacrorum, *tu* ipse teneto hunc

410. Te digressum *hinc* Siculæ oræ

NOTES.

396. *Effuge has terras.* Helenus means the lands of Calabria, Apulia, and all the lower part of the peninsula of Italy, which was called *Magna Græcia:* the whole of which lies not far from *Chaonia*, in Epirus. After the Trojan war, many of the Greeks were forced on this coast, and formed settlements in various places. Hence this part of the peninsula of Italy took the name of *Magna Græcia.* It now constitutes a considerable part of the kingdom of *Naples.* It was washed on the east by the Ionian sea, which Helenus here calls *nostri æquoris*, because the same sea washed the shores of Epirus.

398. *Malis:* in the sense of *hostilibus.*

399. *Narycii Locri.* The Locrians originally were a people of Phocis, in Achaia. They followed *Ajax*, the son of *Oïleus*, to the Trojan war: and, after the capture of that city, a colony of them settled in this part of Italy, most probably under the conduct of Evanthes; Ajax having perished on his return home. There they built a city called *Narycia* or *Narycium*, probably after the name of *Naryx*, the city of Ajax.

401. *Idomeneus.* He was called *Lyctius*, from Lyctus, a city of Crete. Being expelled from his dominions, he came to Italy, and planted a colony on the promontory of *Salentum*, then in possession of the *Salentini.* This peninsula, which extends almost to the coast of Epirus, was formerly called *Messapia*, and *Iäpygia; hodie*, *Terra d'Otranto:* and its extremity, the cape of St. Mary, or *St. Mary de Lucca.* Idomeneus either subdued the *Salentini;* or, which is more probable, expelled them from their country. See verse 122. supra. *Obsedit:* in the sense of *occupat.*

402. *Philoctetæ.* Philoctetes was the son of Pæas, king of Melibœa, a city of Thessaly, near the foot of mount Ossa. He set fire to the funeral pile of Hercules, at the request of that hero, and received in return his bow and arrows, that had been dipped in the poisonous blood of the *Hydra Lernæa.* He set out for Troy with the other Greeks, but was abandoned by them in the island of Lemnos, on account of a wound which he had received from a serpent. But it being predicted, that Troy could not be taken without these arrows, the chiefs were obliged to send for him. On his return from Troy, hearing that the Melibœans had revolted, he went to Italy, and founded the city *Petilia*, or as some say, only fortified it. *Subnixa:* in the sense of *defensa.*

404. *Solves:* you shall pay, or discharge.

405. *Velare adopertus:* be thou veiled—covered as to your hair, with a purple veil. Simply, cover your head with a purple veil. From this circumstance, it is said, the Romans derived the custom of veiling or covering the head in sacrifice, and other acts of worship. *Velare.* Heyne takes this actively, the verb *memento* being understood: remember to veil your locks, covering them, &c

406. *Honore.* Ruæus says, *cultu.*

409. *Casti:* in the sense of *pii.* *Relligione:* rites—ceremonies.

410. *Admoverit:* in the sense of *appulerit*, vel *attulerit.*

411. *Claustra:* the straits of narrow Pelorus shall widen—grow wider. Pelorus is the northern promontory of Sicily: *hodie*, *Capo di Faro.* It is separated from Italy by the straits of Messina. As Æneas approached, the shores would appear to separate and grow wider.

412. *Læva Tellus.* Helenus advises Æneas, as soon as he had approached Sicily so near that the straits of Pelorus should appear to view, and plainly to grow wider, it

414. *Homines* ferunt hæc loca, quondam convulsa vi, et vastâ ruinâ

419. Angustoque æstu interluit arva, et urbes diductas, *quasque suo* litore

426. Prima facies *est* hominis, et *illa est* virgo *cum* pulchro pectore, tenùs pube: postrema *pars est* pristis *cum* immani corpore, commissa *quoad* caudas Delphinûm utero luporum

429. Præstat *te* cessantem lustrare metas

Æquora circuitu: dextrum fuge litus et undas.
Hæc loca, vi quondam et vastâ convulsa ruinâ,
(Tantùm ævi longinqua valet mutare vetustas)
Dissiluisse ferunt: cùm protinùs utraque tellus
Una foret, venit medio vi pontus, et undis
Hesperium Siculo latus abscidit, arvaque et urbes
Litore diductas angusto interluit æstu.
Dextrum Scylla latus, lævum implacata Charybdis
Obsidet: atque imo barathri ter gurgite vastos
Sorbet in abruptum fluctus, rursusque sub auras
Erigit alternos, et sidera verberat undâ.
At Scyllam cæcis cohibet spelunca latebris,
Ora exsertantem, et naves in saxa trahentem.
Prima hominis facies, et pulchro pectore virgo
Pube tenùs: postrema immani corpore pristis,
Delphinûm caudas utero commissa luporum.
Præstat Trinacrii metas lustrare Pachyni
Cessantem, longos et circumflectere cursus,
Quàm semel informem vasto vidisse sub antro

NOTES.

would then be time to alter his course to the left, and coast down the eastern shore of Sicily, rather than venture through the strait, the passage of which was attended with many difficulties and dangers to those who were not acquainted with it.

415. *Longinqua vetustas ævi:* in the sense of *longa duratio temporis potest mutare res tantùm. Ferunt:* they report.

416. *Cùm utraque tellus:* when each land was entirely one—united and formed one contiguous tract. It is supposed that Sicily at first was united to Italy, and rent or torn from it by some convulsion of nature; and there is some ground for such a supposition. Virgil here gives us a full account of the tradition.

417. *Pontus:* in the sense of *fretum.*

418. *Abscidit:* in the sense of *separavit.* It separated the Italian shore from the Sicilian.

419. *Angusto æstu:* with a narrow strait or current, flows between, &c. meaning the straits of Pelorus, now Messina, which separate Sicily from Italy. *Diductas:* in the sense of *disjunctas.*

420. *Scylla—Charybdis. Scylla,* is a rock lying in the straits of Messina on the Italian side. *Charybdis,* a dangerous whirlpool opposite to *Scylla,* on the Sicilian side. These rendered the passage of the straits very dangerous. They were represented by the poets as hideous monsters.

Scylla was the daughter of Phorcus, whom Circe is said to have transformed into this monster, because she was her rival. Charybdis is said to have been a rapacious prostitute, who, having stolen the oxen of Hercules, was thunderstruck by Jupiter, and thrown into the sea, where she was changed into this devouring whirlpool. See Ecl. vi. 74. *Implacata:* insatiable—greedy. Ruæus says, *immanis. Obsidet:* in the sense of *occupat.*

421. *Atque imo gurgite:* and thrice she swallows the vast waves precipitately into the deep gulf of her maw, and again raises them alternate on high, and strikes the stars. Charybdis is represented as a hungry and voracious monster. *In abruptum,* may be taken adverbially, denoting the rapidity and quickness with which she absorbs the water. Taken as a sub. it conveys no additional idea: it is merely expletive.

425. *Exsertantem:* in the sense of *pandentem.* It agrees with *Scyllam.* She is here represented as a most hideous monster; her upper part down to her waist resembling a human being, while her parts below were a huge *Pristis,* whose belly resembled that of a wolf, with the tail of a dolphin.

426. *Hominis:* gen. of *homo.* It is here used in the sense of *humana. Homo* properly signifies a man or woman—the human kind. *Prima facies:* in the sense of *superior pars.*

428. *Commissa:* in the sense of *conjuncta.* It is a part. adj. agreeing with *pristis.* This is a fish of the whale kind, said to be of great length. Pliny mentions one of them in the Indian sea, to have been two hundred cubits in length.

429. *Lustrare:* in the sense of *circumnavigare. Pachyni.* Pachynum is the southern promontory of Sicily. *Trinacrii:* an adj. from *Trinacria,* a name of Sicily, from its triangular figure, or form. *Hodie, Capo Passaro.*

430. *Cessantem:* delaying.

Scyllam, et cœruleis canibus resonantia saxa.
Præterea, si qua est Heleno prudentia, vati
Si qua fides, animum si veris implet Apollo;
Unum illud tibi, nate Deâ, præque omnibus unum
Prædicam, et repetens iterumque iterumque monebo.
Junonis magnæ primùm prece numen adora:
Junoni cane vota libens, dominamque potentem
Supplicibus supera donis: sic denique victor
Trinacriâ fines Italos mittêre relictâ.
Huc ubi delatus Cumæam accesseris urbem,
Divinosque lacus, et Averna sonantia sylvis,
Insanam vatem aspicies, quæ rupe sub imâ
Fata canit, foliisque notas et nomina mandat.
Quæcunque in foliis descripsit carmina virgo,
Digerit in numerum, atque antro seclusa relinquit:
Illa manent immota locis, neque ab ordine cedunt.
Verùm eadem verso tenuis cùm cardine ventus
Impulit, et teneras turbavit janua frondes;
Nunquam deinde cavo volitantia prendere saxo,
Nec revocare situs, aut jungere carmina curat.
Inconsulti abeunt, sedemque odêre Sibyllæ.
Hìc tibi ne qua moræ fuerint dispendia tanti,
Quamvis increpitent socii, et vi cursus in altum
Vela vocet, possisque sinus implere secundos;

434. Si qua fides *est habenda ei* vati; si Apollo

435. Prædicam tibi unum, unumque præ omnibus, et repetens illud iterumque iterumque monebo *te*

441. Ubi *tu* delatus huc accesseris

448. Verùm cùm tenuis ventus impulit eadem

450. Curat prendere *folia* volitantia cavo saxo, nec

NOTES.

432. *Saxa:* and the rocks resounded with sea-green dogs. This interprets that part of the fable respecting the lower part of the monster resembling dogs, or wolves. The waves, dashing against the rocks in the lower part, caused a hoarse growling noise, which resembled that of a dog, or the howling of a wolf. See Ecl. vi. 74, and Æn. I. 200. Virgil took this description from the Odyssey of Homer, Lib. xii.

433. *Prudentia:* in the sense of *scientia.*

436. *Monebo:* in the sense of *inculcabo. Numen:* Ruæus says, *divinitatem.*

438. *Cane:* offer vows to Juno. Ruæus says, *fer*, vel *ferto. Dominam:* in the sense of *reginam.*

441. *Cumæam:* an adj. from *Cumæ*, a city of Campania, but long since destroyed. See Ecl. iv. 4.

442. *Divinos lacus.* The lakes of Avernus and Lucrinus are here called divine, probably on account of their nearness to the cave of the Sibyl. The lake *Avernus*, (plu. *Averna*,) was formerly surrounded with high woods, which occasioned a very noxious atmosphere; so that it is said no bird could fly over it without being suffocated. Hence it derived its name. From the noxious quality of its waters, the poets feigned it to be the mouth of hell. See Æn. vi. 126.

443. *Insanam vatem:* the inspired prophetess.

444. *Canit:* here, in the sense of *explicat*, vel *aperit. Mandat:* in the sense of *inscribit. Notas:* her characters. *Nomina:* words—prophecies.

Varro informs us, that the prophecies of the Sibyl were written on the leaves of the palm-tree.

445. *Carmina. Carmen* properly signifies a verse or song. But because the responses were delivered in poetic numbers, *carmen* came to signify, as here, a prophecy, or prediction. *Descripsit:* in the sense of *inscripsit.*

446. *Digerit in numerum:* she places in measure—she arranges in poetic numbers. *Seclusa:* a part. of *secludor:* laid by themselves in her cave.

449. *Janua:* the door being open, hath deranged. *Saxo:* for *antro.*

451. *Revocare:* in the sense of *restituere.*

452. *Inconsulti:* without receiving advice—unadvised. *Homines* is understood.

453. *Ne qua dispendia moræ:* let no expense of delay be to you of so much value, (importance,) but that you go to the prophetess, &c.

455. *Secundos sinus:* prosperous sails—full sails. *Sinus* is properly the middle, or belly of the sail; here put for the whole sail. The expression implies that the wind be fair for prosecuting their voyage. It would be better to read this and the preceding line as a parenthesis. *Vi:* in the sense of *vehementer.*

Quin adeas vatem, precibusque oracula poscas
Ipsa canat, vocemque volens atque ora resolvat.
Illa tibi Italiæ populos, venturaque bella,
Et quo quemque modo fugiasque ferasque laborem,
Expediet; cursusque dabit venerata secundos.
Hæc sunt, quæ nostrâ liceat te voce moneri.
Vade, age, et ingentem factis fer ad æthera Trojam.
   Quæ postquàm vates sic ore effatus amico est,
Dona dehinc auro gravia sectoque elephanto
Imperat ad naves ferri, stipatque carinis
Ingens argentum, Dodonæosque lebetas,
Loricam consertam hamis, auroque trilicem,
Et conum insignis galeæ, cristasque comantes,
Arma Neoptolemi: sunt et sua dona parenti.
Addit equos, additque duces;
Remigium supplet: socios simul instruit armis.
   Intereà classem velis aptare jubebat
Anchises, fieret vento mora ne qua ferenti.
Quem Phœbi interpres multo compellat honore.
Conjugio Anchisa Veneris dignate superbo,
Cura Deûm, bis Pergameis erepte ruinis,
Ecce tibi Ausoniæ tellus: hanc arripe velis.
Et tamen hanc pelago præterlabare necesse est.
Ausoniæ pars illa procul, quam pandit Apollo

456. Poscasque precibus *ut* ipsa canat oracula, volensque resolvat vocem

458. Illa expediet tibi populos Italiæ

460. *Illa* venerata dabit

478. Necesse est *ut* præterlabare hanc *proximam partem Italiæ* pelago

479. Illa pars Ausoniæ *est* procul, quam Apollo pandit *tibi*

NOTES.

457. *Canat:* reveal—disclose—declare.

460. *Expediet:* in the sense of *explicabit.*

463. *Postquàm:* in the sense of *cùm.*

464. *Dehinc:* in the sense of *deinde. Gravia auro:* heavy with gold and ivory. Ivory is the tooth of the elephant, cut and polished.

465. *Stipat:* stows, or crowds in his ships a great mass of silver. *Carinis:* properly, the keels; here taken for the ships, by synec.

466. *Dodonæos lebetas:* Dodonean kettles—kettles made of Dodonean brass. Dodona was a city of Epirus, whose brass was much celebrated. Here Jupiter had a very celebrated temple. The manner of delivering the oracles in this temple, we are told, was by a certain number of brass kettles suspended, so as to touch each other; and any motion communicated to any one of them, would be given to the rest. From the sounds thus emitted, the meaning of the oracle was gathered by the priests.

467. *Loricam.* The Lorica was a coat of armour, which covered the body down as far as the waist. It was at first made of leathern thongs, whence it derived its name. It was afterwards made of thin plates (*laminæ*) of iron, linked together with hooks or rings. These plates were sometimes single, sometimes double, and triple. The one here mentioned was of the latter form. *Hamis auroque:* for *aureis hamis*, by hend. The meaning is, that this coat of armour was of triple fold, or consisting of three plates (*trilicem*) of iron, fastened (*consertam*) together with gold rings, or hooks.

468. *Conum.* Whatever has the form of the fruit of the pine may be called *conus*, a cone. This form is round, and diminishing to the top. Hence it is taken for that part of the helmet, which rises at the top, and supports the crest, or plume. All these accusatives are governed by the verb *stipat.*

469. *Sua dona:* there are also for my father his own gifts—gifts suitable to his dignity. *Arma Neoptolemi.* The coat of mail, the helmet, and the crest, had belonged to Pyrrhus; at whose death, they fell to Helenus, as his successor. *Sua:* in the sense of *propria* vel *apta.*

470. *Duces:* pilots to direct their course.

471. *Remigium:* in the sense of *remiges.*

473. *Ferenti:* blowing fair. Ruæus says, *faventi. Interpres:* in the sense of *vates.*

475. *Anchisa:* O Anchises, honored with the exalted bed (embrace) of Venus, the care, &c.

476. *Erepte:* agreeing with *Anchisa.* He was twice saved from the ruins of Troy: first when it was taken by Hercules, and a second time, when destroyed by the Greeks.

477. *Arripe hanc:* take possession of it with your ships—direct your course to it. *Velis:* in the sense of *navibus;* so says Ruæus.

478. *Præterlabare:* in the sense of *naviges ultrà.*

479. *Pandit:* in the sense of *ostendit.*

Vade, ait, ô felix nati pietate : quid ultrà
Provehor, et fando surgentes demoror Austros ?
Nec minùs Andromache, digressu mœsta supremo,
Fert picturatas auri subtemine vestes,
Et Phrygiam Ascanio chlamydem ; nec cedit honori :
Textilibusque onerat donis, ac talia fatur.
Accipe et hæc, manuum tibi quæ monumenta mearum
Sint, puer, et longum Andromachæ testentur amorem,
Conjugis Hectoreæ. Cape dona extrema tuorum,
O mihi sola mei super Astyanactis imago !
Sic oculos, sic ille manus, sic ora ferebat ;
Et nunc æquali tecum pubesceret ævo.
Hos ego digrediens lachrymis affabar obortis :
Vivite felices, quibus est fortuna peracta
Jam sua : nos alia ex aliis in fata vocamur.
Vobis parta quies ; nullum maris æquor arandum ;
Arva neque Ausoniæ semper cedentia retrò

489. O *tu qui es* sola imago mei Astyanactis super mihi

493. Vivite felices, *vos* quibus

494. Vocamur ex aliis *fatis* in alia fata. Quies parta *est* vobis

NOTES.

481. *Provehor:* in the sense of *procedo. Austros* here is taken for wind in general, the *species* for the *genus.*

482. *Nec minùs:* likewise Andromache, sad at our departure, brings garments wrought (embroidered) with a thread of gold.

Heyne conjectures these vestments were wrought with the needle; and accordingly takes *subtemine auri*, for a thread of gold. He also takes *picturatas* in the sense of *pictas.* Her presents of the loom *textilibus donis*, are mentioned, verse 485, and are different from these.

484. *Chlamydem.* The Chlamys was properly a military garment, a cassock, which the general wore over his corslet. It was embroidered with needlework, of which the Phrygians were the inventors. *Nec cedit honori:* nor does she fall below her dignity. *Nec malè respondet ejus dignitati*, says Ruæus. Scaurus explains the word thus: *non cedit Heleno liberalitate et munificentia*, taking *honori* for *honore* in the abl. Servius says, *Tanta dat munera, quanta merebatur Ascanius:* nor is her bounty disproportionate to the merit and quality of its object.

485. *Onerat textilibus donis:* and she loads him with woven presents—presents, the production of her loom. It was usual for women of the highest rank to be engaged in the works of the loom, as appears from the story of Penelope, the wife of Ulysses.

486. *Puer, accipe et hæc:* O boy, take even these, which, &c. *Monumenta:* memorials. *Et*, here is plainly in the sense of *etiam*, aut *quoque.*

487. *Longum:* lasting—continuing long.

489. *O sola imago:* O thou, the only image of my Astyanax, remaining to me! *Super*, here is plainly in the sense of *superstes*, vel *supervivens* Ruæus says, *Quæ restat.* Heyne, *quæ superes*, in the 2d pers.

Astyanax was the son of Hector and Andromache. His name is compounded of two Greek words, and signifies the king of a city. After the destruction of Troy, the Greeks were delayed for some time from returning home by contrary winds. In the mean time, Chalcas, their augur and prophet, declared that Astyanax must be put to death. For if he lived, he would prove a greater hero than his father, and would avenge his country. Whereupon Ulysses, having discovered where his mother had hid him, killed him, by throwing him from the wall.

490. *Sic ille ferebat:* just so he moved his eyes, just so his hands, just so his countenance: he had just such eyes—just such hands, &c. This reflection of Andromache is extremely delicate and moving. It is the voice of nature. She immediately adds: *Et nunc*, &c. This suggests the delight she would have felt to have seen Iülus, and Astyanax together, engaged in friendship, and fond of the same pursuits.

It may be observed, that while Helenus gives presents to Anchises and Æneas, Andromache is entirely taken up with Ascanius, and the recollection of her lost *Astyanax.* She confines her gifts to him alone.

491. *Et nunc pubesceret:* and now he would be of equal age with thee, if he had lived.

492. *Obortis:* gushing from my eyes.

494. *Nos vocamur ex aliis in:* we are called from one series of calamities to another.

496. *Cedentia:* a part. agreeing with *arva:* retreating, or fleeing backward. It implies an impatience on the part of Æneas to arrive at, and take possession of his des-

Quærenda: effigiem Xanthi, Trojamque videtis,
Quam vestræ fecêre manus, melioribus, opto,
Auspiciis, et quæ fuerit minùs obvia Graiis.
Si quando Tybrim vicinaque Tybridis arva
Intrâro gentique meæ data mœnia cernam:
Cognatasque urbes olim, populosque propinquos
Epiro, Hesperiâ, quibus idem Dardanus auctor,
Atque idem casus, unam faciemus utramque
Trojam animis: maneat nostros ea cura nepotes.
  Provehimur pelago vicina Ceraunia juxta:
Unde iter Italiam, cursusque brevissimus undis.
Sol ruit intereà, et montes umbrantur opaci.
Sternimur optatæ gremio telluris ad undam,
Sortiti remos; passimque in litore sicco
Corpora curamus: fessos sopor irrigat artus.
Necdum orbem medium nox horis acta subibat:
Haud segnis strato surgit Palinurus, et omnes
Explorat ventos, atque auribus aëra captat.
Sidera cuncta notat tacito labentia cœlo,
Arcturum, pluviasque Hyadas, geminosque Triones,

502. Faciemus olim cognatasque urbes, propinquosque populos, *tuos in* Epiro, *meos in* Hesperia, quibus idem Dardanus *fuit* auctor, atque *quibus fuit* idem casus, *faciemus, inquam,* utramque Trojam *esse* unam animis

516. Circumspicit Arcturum, pluviasque

NOTES.

tined country. And, although he had been several years in pursuit of it, it was still at a great distance. The verb *sunt* is to be supplied with *quærenda.*

497. *Effigiem Xanthi:* the image or representation of Xanthus. It appears that Andromache gave the name of Xanthus to some river of Epirus, and also the name of Troy to some town. Xanthus was a river of Troy, the same as *Scamander.* Homer says its first name was given by the gods, but the latter by men.

499. *Melioribus auspiciis:* for better fortune. *Obvia:* in the sense of *exposita.*

501. *Data:* in the sense of *destinata.*

502. *Olim.* This word refers to time past, and also to time to come. This last is the meaning here—*hereafter.*

504. *Faciemus olim cognatas:* we will make hereafter the kindred cities, and resembling people (yours) in Epirus, (and mine) in Italy, &c. Buthrotus, the city of Helenus, bore some resemblance, perhaps, to old Troy; or this may be the city which he called by the name of Troy. Æneas, when he arrived in Italy, intended to build a city, and call it Troy; each of which cities, *utranque Trojam,* he designed should be one in affection and good will. The distance of the Tiber from Epirus is too great to justify the taking of *propinquos* in the sense of *vicinos,* as Ruæus has it. Mr. Davidson renders it by *allied,* (near of kin;) but this is mere tautology. That relation is sufficiently expressed by *cognatas.* It appears the better to understand it, of the people resembling each other in manners, customs, and habits; both having descended from the same stock, Dardanus being the parent (*auctor*) and founder of both. *Casus.* fortune—calamity.

506. *Ceraunia:* neu. plu. These were exceeding high mountains on the north of Epirus, so called from their being much exposed to thunder. They are sometimes called *Acroceraunia.* They lie over against the promontory of *Iäpygium.* Here the distance between Italy and Epirus is the shortest; it is said about 50 miles. The prep. *in* or *ad* is understood to govern *Italiam.*

508. *Ruit:* in the sense of *occidit.*

509. *Sternimur:* in the sense of the middle voice of the Greeks: we throw ourselves down upon the bosom of the wished for land.

510. *Sortiti remos:* having distributed the oars by lot—having cast lots for the oars, to see who should perform the duty of oarsmen. This they did before they retired to rest, that they might start the following day without hindrance or delay. *Ad undam* refers to *sternimur,* and not to *sortiti,* as in some copies.

511. *Curamus:* we refresh our bodies. *Irrigat:* invigorates. This is a beautiful metaphor. It is taken from the effect and influence which gentle showers, or percolating streams, have upon the thirsty land, and parched herbs.

512. *Acta:* in the sense of *provecta. Necdum,* &c. This is a fine circumlocution to denote that it was not yet midnight.

516. *Arcturum.* Arcturus, a star near the tail of the Great Bear: it rises about the beginning of October. See Geor. i. 68. *Hyadas:* they are said to have been the daughters of *Atlas,* king of Mauritania, in Africa;

Armatumque auro circumspicit Oriona.
Postquàm cuncta videt cœlo constare sereno,
Dat clarum è puppi signum; nos castra movemus,
Tentamusque viam, et velorum pandimus alas.
Jamque rubescebat stellis Aurora fugatis,
Cùm procul obscuros colles, humilemque videmus
Italiam. Italiam primus conclamat Achates;
Italiam læto socii clamore salutant.
Tum pater Anchises magnum cratera coronâ
Induit, implevitque mero, Divosque vocavit,
Stans celsâ in puppi:
Dî, maris et terræ tempestatumque potentes,
Ferte viam vento facilem, et spirate secundi.
Crebrescunt optatæ auræ, portusque patescit
Jam propior, templumque apparet in arce Minervæ.
Vela legunt socii, et proras ad litora torquent.
Portus ab Eoo fluctu curvatur in arcum;
Objectæ salsâ spumant aspergine cautes:
Ipse latet: gemino demittunt brachia muro
Turriti scopuli, refugitque à litore templum.

528. *O Dî, inquit,* potentes maris

535. *Portus* ipse latet

NOTES.

who, grieving immoderately for the death of their brother *Hyas*, who had been killed by a wild boar, pined away, and died. They were five in number. After their death they were transferred to the heavens, and made stars near the constellation *Taurus.* The ancients supposed their rising and setting to be always attended with much rain. Their name is derived from a Greek word signifying *to rain. Triones:* the greater and lesser bear, two constellations near the north pole.

517. *Oriona:* a Greek acc. Orion is a constellation near the feet of the bull. It rises about the first of March, and rains and storms were supposed to attend it. Hence Virgil gave it the epithets *nimbosus*, and *aquosus.* Æn. i. 535. and iv. 52. Orion was a celebrated hunter, and companion of Diana. Being bit by a serpent, he lost his life. The gods, taking pity on him, translated him to the heavens. His constellation is very lucid, consisting of many very bright stars, particularly in his belt or girdle, in which his sword hangs. He is here said to be *armed with gold*, on account of his many lucid stars.

518. *Videt cuncta constare:* he sees all things to indicate fair weather—all the signs to agree in indicating fair weather. *Postquam videt cœlum habere omnia, quæ significant serenitatem*, says Servius.

519. *Movemus castra.* This was a military expression, denoting the commencement of march, from the place of encampment.

520. *Tentamus:* in the sense of *incipimus.*

522. *Humilem.* Ruæus thinks Italy is here called *low*, either because in that part, there are no mountains, because the highest parts appear low when seen at a distance—or because the sea every where appears higher than the land. He interprets it by *planam.*

525. *Induit magnum:* he crowned a large bowl with a garland. *Coronare poculum*, sometimes, signifies no more than simply to fill it up to the brim. But, in the present case, it is taken literally, *to adorn the bow with flowers:* otherwise what follows will be mere tautology. *Mero.* Merum, here, is taken for wine in general; the *species* for the *genus. Induit:* in the sense of *cinxit.*

528. *Potentes:* in the sense of *præsides* vel *rectores.* Minelius beautifully illustrates the design of this libation: *Maris*, quod navigo; *terræ*, quam peto; *tempestatum*, quas timemus.

529. *Ferte:* in the sense of *date. Spirate secundi:* and blow propitious upon us.

531. *Templum Minervæ.* Strabo mentions a temple of Minerva, on the promontory of *Iäpygium*, which is the one most probably meant. *Legunt:* in the sense of *colligunt. Arce:* for *monte.*

533. *Portus curvatur:* the port is curved into (the form of) a bow by the eastern waves, and the cliffs opposite each other foam with salt spray, occasioned by the dashing of the waves against them. These two projecting cliffs formed the mouth of the harbor. *Eoö:* the adj. *Eoüs* is derived from a Greek word signifying the morning—also, the East. This part of Italy is washed on the east by the Ionian sea. Heyne reads *Euroo*, from the sub. *Eurus.*

536. *Scopuli.* Scopulus is properly a high sharp rock. Those here mentioned resem

Quatuor hìc, primum omen, equos in gramine vidi
Tondentes campum latè, candore nivali.
Et pater Anchises: Bellum, ô terra hospita, portas:
Bello armantur equi: bellum hæc armenta minantur:
Sed tamen idem olim curru succedere sueti
Quadrupedes, et fræna jugo concordia ferre:
Spes est pacis, ait. Tum numina sancta precamur
Palladis armisonæ, quæ prima accepit ovantes:
Et capita ante aras Phrygio velamur amictu;
Præceptisque Heleni, dederat quæ maxima, ritè
Junoni Argivæ jussos adolemus honores.
  Haud mora: continuò, perfectis ordine votis,
Cornua velatarum obvertimus antennarum,
Grajugenûmque domos, suspectaque linquimus arva.
  Hinc sinus Herculei, si vera est fama, Tarenti
Cernitur. Attollit se Diva Lacinia contrà,
Caulonisque arces, et navifragum Scylacæum.
Tum procul è fluctu Trinacria cernitur Ætna:

537. Hìc vidi in gramine primum omen, *nempe*, quatuor equos è nivali candore, tondentes

539. Et pater Anchises *inquit*

545. Et velamur *quoad* capita Phrygio amictu ante *ejus* aras; *exque* præceptis Heleni,

548 Haud mora *est*

NOTES.

bled towers, and stretched forth on both sides in the form of arms, making a double wall. *Refugit.* While they were at a distance, the temple appeared near the shore; but, as they approached, the distance between it and the port seemed to increase. It receded, or fled, from the shore.

537. *Hìc vidi:* here I saw the first omen. It was a custom among the ancients carefully to observe the first objects which presented at landing in a country where they designed to form settlements: and hence to draw prognostics of their future good or bad fortune. *Tondentes:* in the sense of *carpentes*. *Gramine:* in the sense of *pratis*.

539. *Hospita.* This Ruæus interprets by *hospitalis;* but that illy agrees with *portas bellum.* Mr. Davidson renders it, *foreign:* to which we are strangers.

541. *Curru:* for *currui*, the dat. . See Ecl. v. 29. *Concordia fræna:* the gentle reins. This implies perfect submission to the will of the driver. *Jugo.* Jugum properly signifies the yoke which passes over the necks of the horses, and holds up the tongue or pole of the carriage. Here, perhaps, the harness in general. *Olim:* in the sense of *diu*.

543. *Numina:* in the sense of *divinitatem*.

544. *Armisonæ:* sounding in arms. This is an epithet of *Pallas*, or Minerva, as goddess of war. *Ovantes:* in the sense of *lætos*. *Nos* is understood.

547. *Adolemus jussos honores.* Ruæus interprets these words by, *offerimus præscripta sacrificia.* *Jussos:* ordered, or appointed by Helenus. See 435. *supra, et sequens.*

548. *Continuò:* immediately—forthwith. Ruæus considers it an adj. agreeing with *ordine* *Perfectis:* in the sense of *persolutis.*

549. *Velatarum antennarum.* The *antennæ* were spars or yards which crossed the mast, to which the sails were fastened and suspended. The extremities of them were called *cornua.* By shifting or turning his sails, he would naturally alter his course. He now sails southward; and, as he passes along, he gives us a very particular description of the country. He takes his departure from the promontory of *Iäpygium.*

551. *Tarenti.* Tarentum was a famous city and port at the northern extremity of the *Sinus Tarentinus*, founded by *Taras*, the son of Neptune, according to Straba. The same author informs us that Hercules had here a colossus of brass, made by *Lysippus*, which *Fabius Maximus* carried to Rome. Not only the city, but also the adjacent country, was famous for the actions of that hero. Hence the poet gives it the epithet, *Herculean.*

552. *Contrà:* on the other side (of the bay) the goddess *Lacinia* raises herself. *Diva Lacinia* is here put for the temple of the goddess, by meton. Lacinia as an epithet of *Juno*, taken from the promontory *Lacinium*, on which the temple stood.

553. *Arces Coulonis:* the towers of Caulon, or Caulonia. Caulon was a city farther south, at first called *Aulonia*, from a valley, which was in sight. It was founded by the Greeks. *Scylacæum.* This was a city situated near the southern extremity of a bay of that name, founded by a colony of Athenians, according to Strabo. The navigation on this coast was dangerous.—Hence it is called *navifragum.*

554. *Ætna:* a well known mountain and volcano on the island of Sicily. It is said to be sixty miles in circumference at its

Et gemitum ingentem pelagi, pulsataque saxa
Audimus longè, fractasque ad litora voces;
Exultantque vada, atque æstu miscentur arenæ.
Et pater Anchises: Nimirùm hæc illa Charybdis:
Hos Helenus scopulos, hæc saxa horrenda canebat.
Eripite, ô socii, pariterque insurgite remis.
  Haud minùs ac jussi faciunt: primusque rudentem
Contorsit lævas proram Palinurus ad undas:
Lævam cuncta cohors remis ventisque petivit.
Tollimur in cœlum curvato gurgite, et îdem
Subductâ ad Manes imos descendimus undâ.
Ter scopuli clamorem inter cava saxa dedêre:
Ter spumam elisam et rorantia vidimus astra.
Intereà fessos ventus cum Sole reliquit:
Ignarique viæ, Cyclopum allabimur oris.
  Portus ab accessu ventorum immotus, et ingens

560. Eripite *vos hinc*, ô socii

561. *Illi* faciunt haud minùs ac jussi *facere*

563. Lævam *partem* remis

568. *Nos* fessos cum sole

570. Portus *est* immotus ab accessu

NOTES.

base. *Fluctu:* in the sense of *mari.* The meaning is: while they were a great distance at sea.

555. *Pulsata:* beaten, or lashed by the waves. *Voces:* in the sense of *sonitus. Gemitum:* in the sense of *fremitum.*

557. *Vada exultant:* the shallows boil, and the sands are mingled with the tide. The sea breaks and foams upon the shallows, and the sand is tossed up by the whirling eddies.

559. *Scopulos—saxa. Scopulus* properly signifies a high sharp rock; *saxum,* any rock—rocks in general. *Canebat:* for *prædicebat.*

560. *Pariter:* equally—all as one.

561. *Minùs:* in the sense of *aliter. Ac:* in the sense of *quàm.*

562. *Palinurus primus:* Palinurus first turned the creaking prow to the left waters. Some read *rudente,* for *rudentem,* a sub. instead of the part. By this they would understand a rope fastened to the side of the ship, by the help of which the helmsman turned the ship which way he pleased. Ruæus interprets it by *stridentem:* creaking as it plunged into the waves.

563. *Cuncta cohors:* in the sense of *omnes socii.*

564. *Gurgite:* in the sense of *fluctu.*

565. *Manes.* These properly were that part of the dead, which the ancients supposed to be below—the shade, or ghost. Sometimes it is used for the place of the dead, and sometimes for the infernal gods. The plain meaning is: that when they were on the top of a surge, or wave, they were elevated very high; and when they were in a hollow between two waves, they descended very low; in other words, the sea here was very rough.

566. *Clamorem:* in the sense of *sonitum.*

567. *Rorantia ast a:* the stars bedewed, or besprinkled. This is an extravagant hyperbole. Catrou, and some others, would understand this of the dewy drops, which thrown up by the dashing of the waters against the rocks, sparkled like stars in the sun-beams. This appears to be the opinion of Heyne.

568. *Ventus cum sole.* These circumstances have a happy effect in preparing the reader for the following description of mount Ætna. The winds are hushed, that the bellowings of the mountain might be more distinctly heard; and night is brought on that in the dusky sky the flames might appear more conspicious.

569. *Cyclopum.* It is said the Cyclops were the first inhabitants of Sicily, especially about mount Ætna. They are said to have been of gigantic stature, and of a nature savage, cruel, and inhospitable. Hence the poets took occasion to represent them of a monstrous form, having only one eye, and that in their forehead, and as being cannibals. From their vicinity to Ætna, it is said, they were employed by Vulcan in forging the thunderbolts of Jupiter.

The port, where Æneas landed, was near the place where the city *Catanea* now stands, near the foot of mount Ætna. The Cyclops were supposed to be the sons of Cœlus and Terra. They took their name from the circumstance of their having but one eye. This tradition originated from their custom of their wearing small bucklers of steel, which covered their faces. These had a small aperture in the middle, which corresponded exactly to the eye. They were reckoned among the gods, and had a temple dedicated to them at Corinth. Ætna is now called mount Gibel, and stands not far from the eastern shore of Sicily. Its modern name implies, the mount of mounts.

570. *Ingens:* in the sense of *capax.*

Ipse; sed horrificis juxtà tonat Ætna ruinis:
Interdumque atram prorumpit ad æthera nubem,
Turbine fumantem piceo et candente favillâ:
Attollitque globos flammarum, et sidera lambit
Interdum scopulos avulsaque viscera montis
Erigit eructans, liquefactaque saxa sub auras
Cum gemitu glomerat, fundoque exæstuat imo.
Fama est, Enceladi semiustum fulmine corpus
Urgeri mole hâc, ingentemque insuper Ætnam
Impositam, ruptis flammam expirare caminis:
Et, fessum quoties mutat latus, intremere omnem
Murmure Trinacriam, et cœlum subtexere fumo.
Noctem illam tecti sylvis immania monstra
Perferimus; nec, quæ sonitum dèt causa, videmus.
Nam neque erant astrorum ignes, nec lucidus æthrâ
Sidereâ polus; obscuro sed nubila cœlo,
Et Lunam in nimbo nox intempesta tenebat.
  Postera jamque dies primo surgebat Eoo,
Humentemque Aurora polo dimoverat umbram;
Cùm subitò è sylvis, macie confecta supremâ,
Ignoti nova forma viri, miserandaque cultu,
Procedit, supplexque manus ad litora tendit.
Respicimus. Dira illuvies, immissaque barba,
Consertum tegmen spinis: at cætera Graius,
Et quondam patriis ad Trojam missus in armis.
Isque ubi Dardanios habitus et Troïa vidit

580. Impositam insuper *eum*

583. *Nos* tecti *in* sylvis perferimus

590. Nova forma viri ignoti *nobis*, confecta supremâ macie, miserandaque cultu, procedit è sylvis,

593. Dira illuvies *erat ei*

594. At *quoad* cætera *erat*

NOTES.

572. *Prorumpit:* in the sense of *emittit.*

573. *Candente favillâ:* with hot, or burning embers.

574. *Lambit:* in the sense of *tangit.*

576. *Eructans:* in the sense of *evomens. Avulsa:* torn loose.

577. *Glomerat:* and whirls about melted rocks into the air.

578. *Fama est:* there is a report, that the body of Enceladus, half consumed by lightning, is pressed under this mass of matter; and that ponderous Ætna being placed upon him, casts up flames from its burst furnaces; and as often as he, &c.

Virgil here gives us the fabulous account of the origin of this burning mountain, and the cause of its eruptions. Enceladus was the chief of the Giants, and the son of Titan and Terra. In the war of the Giants against the gods, he was struck with the thunderbolt of Jupiter, and placed under mount Ætna, by way of punishment: and, as often as he turns his weary side, an eruption follows. Ovid places Typhœus, another of the Giants, under the same mountain. *Insuper:* in the sense of *super.*

580. *Expirare:* in the sense of *emittere.*

583. *Immania monstra:* in the sense of *infanda prodigia. Illam noctem:* in the sense of *per illam noctem.*

584. *Perferimus:* we endure or suffer. The cause of this eruption was unknown to them—the appearances were new and unexpected. Hence they may be called with propriety, *immania monstra.*

585. *Ignes:* lights of the stars. *Polus lucidus:* nor the heaven bright in the starry firmament. *Polus,* by synec. put for the whole heaven.

587. *Intempesta nox:* profound darkness. It properly signifies the darkest time of night—midnight. Here it denotes the quality of that night in particular, when one face of thick darkness prevailed through the whole night, like that which prevailed at the midnight hour. *Nimbo:* in the sense of *nebuloso aëre.*

588. *Primo Eoo:* with the first dawn. *Eous,* the star Venus. When it rises before the sun, it is called Lucifer; when setting after him, Hesperus: here put for the dawn of day. *Aurora.* See Geor. i. 249.

590. *Confecta supremâ:* wasted away with extreme leanness. *Confecta* agrees with *forma.*

591. *Nova forma viri ignoti:* simply, a man unknown to us.

594. *Tegmen consertum:* his covering sewed, or fastened together with thorns. It probably consisted of the leaves of trees. Ruæus says, *vestis contexta spinis. At cætera:* but as to other things—his stature, gait, language, &c. he was a Greek.

596. *Habitus:* in the sense of *vestes.*

Arma procul, paulùm aspectu conterritus hæsit,
Continuitque gradum: mox sese ad litora præceps
Cum fletu precibusque tulit: Per sidera testor,
Per Superos, atque hoc cœli spirabile lumen,
Tollite me, Teucri; quascunque abducite terras:
Hoc sat erit. Scio me Danais è classibus unum,
Et bello Iliacos fateor petiise Penates.
Pro quo, si sceleris tanta est injuria nostri,
Spargite me in fluctus, vastoque immergite ponto.
Si pereo, manibus hominum periise juvabit.
Dixerat: et genua amplexus, genibusque volutans
Hærebat. Qui sit, fari, quo sanguine cretus,
Hortamur; quæ deinde agitet fortuna, fateri.
Ipse pater dextram Anchises, haud multa moratus,
Dat juveni, atque animum præsenti pignore firmat.
Ille hæc, depositâ tandem formidine, fatur:
Sum patriâ ex Ithacâ, comes infelicis Ulyssei,
Nomen Achemenides: Trojam, genitore Adamasto
Paupere, mansissetque utinam fortuna! profectus.
Hìc me, dum trepidi crudelia limina linquunt,
Immemores socii vasto Cyclopis in antro

600. O Teucri, *inquit*, testor *vos* per sidera, per Superos

602. Scio me *esse* unum

608. Hortamur *eum* fari, qui sit, *et ex* quo sanguine cretus *est;* deinde fateri, quæ

614. Achemenides *est* nomen *mihi:* profectus *sum* Trojam

616. Hìc socii immemores *mei* deseruêre me in vasto antro Cyclopis, dum

NOTES.

597. *Hæsit:* hesitated—paused.

599. *Testor:* in the sense of *precor*.

600. *Hoc spirabile lumen:* by this vital light of heaven—by this light (air) of heaven, which we breathe, and by which we live. *Lumen:* in the sense of *aër*, vel *aura*.

603. *Iliacos Penates.* The *Penates* properly were the household gods—the gods of one's country. Hence the word came to signify, one's house and country, and whatever a person held most dear, by meton. See Æn. ii. 717.

604. *Pro quo:* for which—for his being a Greek, and having taken part in the war against Troy. *Sceleris injuria.* Ruæus says, *iniquitas criminis. Si scelus meum tantum est*, says Heyne.

605. *Spargite:* in the sense of *projicite:* tear me in pieces, and cast me into the sea.

606. *Si pereo*, &c. Dr. Wharton makes the following reflections upon this passage. Nothing, says he, can more forcibly strike the imagination, than these circumstances of the wandering Trojans, sheltered in a wood, upon an unknown coast, and hearing strange and terrible noises during a dark and moonless night; and not knowing whence the dreadful sounds proceeded, or by what they might be occasioned. At daybreak, how sudden and great the surprise, to see the ghastly figure of a man, who first runs towards them with great precipitation, as if to beg some assistance; but suddenly starts back at the sight of Trojan habits and arms. At last, recovering himself a little, he resolves to fling himself into their hands, whatever might be the consequence. Received into a vessel, he gives them the dreadful narration of Polyphemus, informs them that this was the island of the Cyclops, begs them to leave it instantly, and concludes most pathetically, that if he must die, it would be some comfort to him to perish by the hands of men, and not by monsters.

607. *Amplexus:* embracing our knees, and falling upon his own knees, he clung to us. Servius observes, that the several members of the body were consecrated to particular deities: the ear, to memory; the knees, to mercy; the right hand, to faith. Suppliants were accustomed to throw, or cast themselves upon their knees, and embrace those of the person of whom they asked or begged any thing.

608. *Cretus:* in the sense of *ortus*.

610. *Haud multa moratus:* delayed not a moment.

611. *Præsenti pignore.* The right hand among all nations is considered a pledge of friendship. *Præsens* here signifies, ready—propitious. So *adsum*, I am present, signifies also, to favor—to be propitious.

613. *Ithacâ:* an island in the Ionian sea. It formed a part of the dominion of Ulysses. *Hodie, Isola del Compare.*

614. *Adamasto:* Adamastus my father being a poor man. He mentions his poverty as an excuse for his going to the war; it was not his choice. Sinon pleads the same excuse. See Æn. ii. 87. *Utinam:* I wish the same state of poverty had remained to me!

617. *Cyclopis.* Polyphemus is here meant. It is said he was the son of Neptune and Thoosa, the daughter of Phorcys. It is said that Ulysses, on his return from Troy

618. Ejus domus intus *est* opaca, ingens, *et plena* sanie

Deseruere. Domus sanie dapibusque cruentis,
Intus opaca, ingens: ipse arduus, altaque pulsat
Sidera; Dî, talem terris avertite pestem!
Nec visu facilis, nec dictu affabilis ulli.
Visceribus miserorum, et sanguine vescitur atro.

623 Egomet vidi, cùm *ille* resupinus in medio antro frangeret duo corpora de nostro numero, prensa magnâ manû, ad saxum

Vidi egomet, duo de numero cùm corpora nostro
Prensa manu magnâ, medio resupinus in antro,
Frangeret ad saxum, sanieque aspersa natarent
Limina: vidi, atro cùm membra fluentia tabo
Manderet, et tepidi tremerent sub dentibus artus.

628. *Fecit id* quidem haud impunè: nec Ulysses passus *est* talia

Haud impunè quidem: nec talia passus Ulysses,
Oblitusve sui est Ithacus discrimine tanto.
Nam simul expletus dapibus, vinoque sepultus
Cervicem inflexam posuit, jacuitque per antrum
Immensus, saniem eructans ac frustra cruento
Per somnum commixta mero; nos, magna precati
Numina, sortitique vices, unà undique circùm
Fundimur, et telo lumen terebramus acuto
Ingens, quod torvâ solum sub fronte latebat,

NOTES.

visited Sicily, and the straits of Messina. He lost a part of his fleet in the whirlpool of Charybdis. This was a dangerous place to all who attempted to pass the straits. It gave rise to this proverb: *Incidit in Scyllam, qui vult vitare Charybdim*, implying that in avoiding one evil, we frequently fall into a greater. But no whirlpool is now to be found, sufficiently large to answer to the description given by the poets and other ancient writers. It is probable some change has been effected in this part of the sea in the course of time.

621. *Nec facilis visu:* nor is he easy to be looked upon, nor easy to be spoken to by any one. His terrific aspect fills you with dread, and deprives you of the power of speech. Servius says: *Cujus possit etiam aspectus ferre formidinem;* and Stephens: *Cujus ne aspectum quidem facile quis sustineat.*

625. *Limina aspera. Limen* properly signifies the threshold of the door; also the door itself, by meton. If it be taken in this sense here, then *limina aspersa sanie natarent* may mean: the door being bespattered with the blood, trickled or ran down. Ruæus says, *porta.* It may be taken either way.

627. *Manderet:* in the sense of *devoraret.*

629. *Ithacus:* a name of Ulysses, from *Ithaca*, his native island. *Tanto discrimine:* in so important a crisis—in so great danger.

631. *Inflexam:* bent, or reclined. Persons in a complete state of intoxication are unable to hold their heads erect. They recline them either upon their shoulders or breast. This was the case with Polyphemus. His head was reclined before he lay down to sleep.

632. *Immensus.* Some read *immensum*, to agree with *antrum.* But *immensus* is preferable, referring to the dimensions of Polyphemus. *Frusta commixta:* pieces (of human bodies) mingled with bloody wine. *Per somnum* is to be connected with *eructans.*

634. *Sortiti vices:* having drawn by lot our parts to act, all at once, we surround him from all quarters, and dig out, &c. Donatus thinks it should be *tenebramus*, instead of *terebramus:* we darken, or extinguish the light of his eye: which would express, as he thinks, the quickness and celerity of their action. But Homer, whom Virgil here follows, expressly mentions the circumstance of the boring out of the monster's eye; and compares the action of Ulysses and his companions to a carpenter boring a piece of timber. *Circùmfundimur*, is probably here used in the sense of the middle voice of the Greeks.

636. *Latebat* lay concealed; because his eye was shut in sleep. *Quod solum*, &c. The Cyclops are represented as having only one eye, and that one in their forehead. This is doubtless a fiction. No such people ever existed. Eustathius explains the fable thus: that in violent passion, men see only one single object, as that passion directs; in other words, see with one eye only: and further, that passion transports men into savages, and renders them brutal and sanguinary, like Polyphemus; and he, who by reason extinguishes that passion, may be said to put out that eye. Others explain it by alleging that Polyphemus was a man of uncommon wisdom and penetration, who is therefore represented as having only one eye, and that

Argolici clypei aut Phœbeæ lampadis instar :
Et tandem læti sociorum ulciscimur umbras.
Sed fugite, ô miseri, fugite, atque ab litore funem
Rumpite.
Nam, qualis quantusque cavo Polyphemus in antro
Lanigeras claudit pecudes, atque ubera pressat ;
Centum alii curva hæc habitant ad litora vulgò
Infandi Cyclopes, et altis montibus errant.
Tèrtia jam Lunæ se cornua lumine complent,
Cùm vitam in sylvis, inter deserta ferarum
Lustra domosque traho, vastosque ab rupe Cyclopas
Prospicio, sonitumque pedum vocemque tremisco.
Victum infelicem, baccas, lapidosaque corna
Dant rami, et vulsis pascunt radicibus herbæ.
Omnia collustrans, hanc primùm ad litora classem
Conspexi venientem : huic me, quæcunque fuisset,
Addixi : satìs est gentem effugisse nefandam.
Vos animam hanc potiùs quocunque absumite leto.
Vix ea fatus erat, summo cùm monte videmus
Ipsum inter pecudes vastâ se mole moventem
Pastorem Polyphemum, et litora nota petentem :
Monstrum horrendum, informe, ingens, cui lumen ademptum.
Trunca manum pinus regit, et vestigia firmat.
Lanigeræ comitantur oves : ea sola voluptas,
Solamenque mali : *de collo fistula pendet.*

653. Satìs est *mihi*, effugisse

655. Cûm videmus summo monte, pastorem Polyphemum ipsum, moventem se

660. Comitantur *eum* ea *est* sola voluptas *ipse*

NOTES.

near his brain, to denote his superior wisdom and sagacity; but that Ulysses outwitted him, and was said, for that reason, to put out his eye.

637. *Phœbeæ lampadis :* the lamp of Phœbus—the orb of the Sun. The Grecian shield was large enough to cover the whole man: and as that was of an oval form, the comparison denotes both the figure and magnitude of this eye.

639. *Miseri.* He calls them miserable, or unfortunate, in having come to this coast, and being exposed to such danger. *Sed fugite.* This interruption in his speech is extremely beautiful. The fear of the Cyclops, and the recollection of the dangers, which he had escaped, rush upon his mind, and stop him for a moment, to give the Trojans advice to flee immediately. He then resumes the subject.

He informs them that there were on the island a hundred other *infandi Cyclopes*, horrid Cyclops, such, and as huge as Polyphemus.

645. *Tertia cornua Lunæ*, &c. By this we are to understand that it had been about three lunar months since he had been in that unhappy situation : *cùm traho vitam*, &c.

647. *Deserta lustra :* the deserted dens, or haunts.

649. *Infelicem :* poor—scanty. *Corna :* the fruit of the corneil tree. It is round, and protected by a hard shell.

650. *Pascunt :* in the sense of *nutriunt. Dant :* in the sense of *præbent.*

651. *Collustrans :* in the sense of *circumspiciens.*

652. *Addixi me huic :* I have surrendered myself to it, whatever it may be—I have given myself up into your hands; do with me as you please.

654. *Vos potiùs absumite :* take away this life of mine by any death, rather than leave me behind to die by the hands of these monsters of rapacity. *Absumite :* in the sense of *perdite.*

658. *Cui lumen :* whose eye had been taken out. *Cui :* in the sense of *cujus.* The dat. is frequently used by the poets in the sense of the gen. *Est* is to be supplied with *ademptum.*

659. *Trunca pinus :* a cut pine guides his hand. From this we may form some idea of his stature. His staff is the trunk of a pine. Heyne reads *manu :* in his hand.

661. *Mali :* in the sense of *miseriæ* vel *doloris. Fistula pendet de collo.* These words are probably spurious. They are left out in some editions. Heinsius, Donatus, and Heyne reject them. Nor does Homer mention any such circumstance;

Postquàm altos tetigit fluctus, et ad æquora venit,
Luminis effossi fluidum lavit inde cruorem,
Dentibus infrendens gemitu: graditurque per æquor
Jam medium, necdum fluctus latera ardua tinxit.
Nos procul inde fugam trepidi celerare, recepto
Supplice sic merito, tacitique incidere funem
Verrimus et proni certantibus æquora remis.
Sensit, et ad sonitum vocis vestigia torsit.
Verùm ubi nulla datur dextrâ affectare potestas,
Nec potis Ionios fluctus æquare sequendo;
Clamorem immensum tollit, quo pontus et omnes
Intremuere undæ, penitùsque exterrita tellus
Italæ, curvisque immugiit Ætna cavernis.
At genus è sylvis Cyclopum et montibus altis
Excitum ruit ad portus, et litora complent.
Cernimus adstantes nequicquam lumine torvo
Ætnæos fratres, cœlo capita alta ferentes,
Concilium horrendum: quales cùm vertice celso
Aëriæ quercus aut coniferæ cyparissi
Constiterunt, sylva alta Jovis, lucusve Dianæ.
Præcipites metus acer agit quòcunque rudentes
Excutere, et ventis intendere vela secundis.

666. Nos trepidi *cœpimus* celerare fugam procul inde, supplice, sic merito, recepto *à nobis*

669. *Polyphemus* sensit *hoc*, et torsit

670. Nulla potestas datur *illi* affectare *nos* dextrâ; nec potis *est*

673. Exterrita *fuit* penitùs

679. *Tales* quales cùm aëriæ quercus, aut coniferæ

682. Acer metus agit *socios* præcipites excutere

NOTES.

whom Virgil here imitates. *Ea sola voluptas*, &c. probably refers to his sheep.

663. *Inde:* in the sense of *deinde*. Or, perhaps it may be considered merely expletive.

665. *Fluctus:* in the sense of *aqua*.

668. *Certantibus:* in the sense of *laborantibus*.

669. *Sonitum vocis.* This may refer to the sound of *their voices*. For though it is said they went off silently; this can only mean, they did it with as little noise as possible. There must have been some, to give the necessary orders. But more probably to the sound of their oars; for *vox* sometimes signifies any sound whatever.

670. *Affectare dextrâ:* to grasp or seize with his right hand.

The common reading is *dextram*, but this is more difficult. Heyne reads *dextra;* which is approved by Valpy, although he retains *dextram*. Davidson observes some ancient copies have *dextrâ attrectare*.

671. *Fluctus:* in the sense of *mare*. He could not equal the depth of the sea.

673. *Undæ intremuere.* Dr. Trapp says, this is a most noble hyperbole. Some there are, who think it too bold. But they not only forget the prerogative of poetry, but the real nature of fear; which always swells and heightens its object. *Penitùs:* in the sense of *intimè*.

674. *Immugiit.* in the sense of *remugiit*.

675. *Genus:* in the sense of *gens*. Some copies read *gens*.

677. *Lumine:* in the sense of *oculo*. *Nequicquam:* in vain; because we were out of their reach.

679. *Concilium:* in the sense of *turbam*.

680. *Coniferæ cyparissi:* such as when the aërial oaks, or cone bearing cypresses stand together with their lofty tops, &c. The cypress tree bears a fruit resembling the figure of the cone; hence called *conifera*. The *quercus* was sacred to Jove; hence *alta sylva Jovis:* and the cypress was sacred to *Proserpina* or *Diana;* hence *lucus Dianæ*.

682. *Præcipites:* in the sense of *celeres*. *Quocunque:* for *quocunque modo*, in any direction or way whatever.

683. *Excutere rudentes. Rudentes* may be taken for those ropes, which seamen call the sheets. By the help of these, they draw in the sail when they wish to go near the wind; or let it out when they sail before it, or with a fair wind. It is usually fastened to the extremity of the sail, or to the boom or yard which extends the sail. That it does not here mean the *cables*, will appear, when we consider that they had already cut their cables, *incidere funem*, verse 667 supra, and were out at sea. *Excutere rudentes*, therefore, will be, *to let out*, *to loose* or *extend the sheets*, so as to sail before the wind. This is more fully expressed by *intendere vela secundis ventis*, to spread the sails to the favorable winds. It was not so much the object of Æneas, in this juncture, to proceed on his direct course, as to sail in

Contra, jussa monent Heleni Scyllam atque Charybdim :
Inter utramque viam, leti discrimine parvo,
Ni teneant cursus ; certum est dare lintea retrò.
Ecce autem Boreas angustâ à sede Pelori
Missus adest : vivo prætervehor ostia saxo
Pantagiæ, Megarosque sinus, Tapsumque jacentem.
Talia monstrabat relegens errata retrorsùm
Litora Achemenides, comes infelicis Ulyssei.
  Sicanio prætenta sinu jacet insula contra
Plemmyrium undosum : nomen dixere priores
Ortygiam. Alpheum fama est huc, Elidis amnem,

690. Relegens retrorsùm litora errata *jam antè à se*

694. Fama est Alpheum amnem Elidis egisse *sibi* occultas vias huc subter mare; qui *amnis exiens è* tuo ore, O Arethusa, nunc

NOTES.

any direction, so as to escape the hands of the Cyclops. Heyne says, *explicare, intendere, evolvere rudentes.* See 267. supra.

684. *Contrà jussa Heleni:* on the other hand, the commands of Helenus warn (my companions) of Scylla and Charybdis. That they may not hold their course in either way, in so great danger (small a distance) of death, it is determined to sail backward. That we may not pass near Scylla and Charybdis, nor near the monster Polyphemus, and his associates; in either way, we should be in imminent danger of death, we determine to spread our sails backward. The usual explication of this passage refers *utramque viam*, to *Scylla* and *Charybdis:* implying that the passage between the rock Scylla and the whirlpool Charybdis was dangerous, and *parùm à morte distare.* The explanation, referring *utramque viam* both to the straits of *Messina*, and the *Cyclops*, appears the easiest. In order to shun the dangers of each, they determined to sail back into the open sea, or from whence they came. The wind probably at that moment blew from the south, and prevented them from pursuing their direct course. But shifting to the north, they changed their purpose, and sailed down the eastern shore of Sicily. This, and the two following lines, Heyne conjectures are an interpolation.

685. *Discrimine:* in the sense of *spatio*, vel *distantia:* also, of *periculo.*

686. *Ni:* in the sense of *ne. Lintea:* in the sense of *vela.*

687. *Pelori.* Pelorus is the northern promontory of Sicily, forming, with Italy, the *straits of Messina*, so called from a city of that name on the Sicilian shore. These straits are about one mile and a half wide. The wind blowing from them, was fair for him to sail down the eastern shore of Sicily, according to the direction of Helenus. It is here called *Boreas*, because it came from the north. Æneas speaks of this wind as a person *sent*, or commissioned by Heaven to aid and assist him: *Missus adest. Angusta sede.* Ruæus says: *angusto freto.*

689. *Pantagiæ ostia.* Pantagia was a small river, whose mouth (*ostia*) was enclosed on each side with a steep rock. The prep. *è*, vel *ex*, is understood before *vivo saxo. Megaros Sinus:* the bay of Megara. This bay lies between the river Terias and Syracuse. In this bay was Tapsus, a peninsula, which lay low, and almost level with the sea.

690. *Monstrabat:* Achemenides pointed out to us these things, as he was sailing back along the shores, along which he had wandered before.

Virgil here follows the opinions of those who make Ulysses to have sailed from the country of the *Lotophagi* in Africa, to the southern part of Sicily; and turning the promontory of *Pachynum*, sailed along the eastern shore, and visited Ætna, and the country of the Cyclops. The course of Æneas being to the south, was the reverse of that of Ulysses. Achemenides, therefore, might be said to *sail back again*, with the greatest propriety. Dr. Wharton observes, that Virgil is an exact observer of probability. If it should be objected by any one, that Æneas was a perfect stranger to this coast, and could not be supposed acquainted with the several places, which he passed; an answer is at hand: Achemenides, who had lately passed along the same shores, pointed them out to him.

691. *Infelicis:* unfortunate. This may refer in general to the disasters he suffered in his return from Troy; and particularly the loss of a part of his fleet in the straits of Messina. The return of Ulysses from Troy, is the subject of the Odyssey.

692. *Insula prætenta:* an island lies in front of the Sicilian bay, over against boisterous *Plemmyrium.* This was a promontory near Syracuse, against which the waves from the sea beat. Hence the epithet *undosum.* Between this promontory and Syracuse lay the island of *Ortygia.*

693. *Priores:* in the sense of *majores.*

694. *Alpheum.* Alpheus, a celebrated river of the Peloponnesus, rising from the mountain *Stymphalus*, running in a westerly direction, passing through a part of Arcadia and Elis, falls into the *Sinus Cyparissæus.*

Occultas egisse vias subter mare; qui nunc
Ore, Arethusa, tuo Siculis confunditur undis.
697. *Ut eramus* jussi *Heleno*, veneramur
Jussi numina magna loci veneramur: et inde
Exsupero præpingue solum stagnantis Helori.
Hinc altas cautes projectaque saxa Pachyni
Radimus; et fatis nunquam concessa moveri
Apparet Camarina procul, campique Geloi,
Immanisque Gela, fluvii cognomine dicta.
Arduus inde Agragas ostentat maxima longè
Mœnia, magnanimûm quondam generator equorum
Teque datis linquo ventis, palmosa Selinus:
Et vada dura lego saxis Lilybeïa cæcis.
Hinc Drepani me portus et illætabilis ora
Accipit. Hìc, pelagi tot tempestatibus actus,
Heu! genitorem, omnis curæ casûsque levamen,
710. Hìc, O optime pater, deseris me fessum
Amitto Anchisen: hìc me, pater optime, fessum
Deseris, heu! tantis nequicquam erepte perîclis.

NOTES.

696. *Arethusa.* This was a fountain on the west side of the island of Ortygia. The poets feigned that Alpheus, the river-god, being in love with the nymph Arethusa, rolled his stream from Elis under ground, pasing through the sea, without intermingling with it, and arose up in this fountain, mingling his waters with those of the nymph. What makes this fable the more absurd, is, that the distance between the Peloponnesus and Sicily is not less than 450 miles. *Egisse:* in the sense of *fecisse. Ore:* in the sense of *fonte. Undis:* in the sense of *aquis.*

698. *Exsupero:* in the sense of *prætereo.* It is sometimes written, *exupero. Helori.* Helorus, or Elorus, was a river falling into the sea, a little to the north of the promontory *Pachynum.* It overflowed its banks like the Nile of Egypt, and rendered the country fertile, through which it passed. Hence the epithet *stagnans*, overflowing—stagnating.

699. *Pachyni.* The southern promontory of Sicily was called *Pachynum. Hodie, Capo Passaro.*

701. *Camarina.* The name of a lake at the southern part of Sicily, near a city of the same name, built by the people of Syracuse. In the time of a plague, which the inhabitants imagined originated from its stagnant waters, they consulted the oracle of Apollo concerning the expediency of draining it. The oracle advised them to let it remain, alleging it would be better to endure its noxious vapors, than to remove it. This explains the words: *nunquam concessa moveri fatis;* never permitted by the fates to be removed. However, the people made the experiment, and they found the words of the oracle true. For the enemy entered on the ground where the lake stood, and took the city. *Hodie, Lago di Camarina. Campi Geloi:* the plains of *Gelas. Geloi:* an adj. of *Gelas*, or *Gela*, a river not far from Camarina, near the mouth of which stood *Gela*, once a large (*immanis*) and respectable city, founded by the Rhodians and Cretans. It was destroyed by the *Agrigentini.*

702. *Dicta cognomine:* called after the name of the river.

703. *Agragas:* a city situated at the mouth of a river of the same name. It was built on the summit of a hill, or mountain: hence called *arduus*, high. It was one of the largest cities of Sicily. Its horses were celebrated for their performance at the Olympic games. Hence, *quondam*, &c. *once the breeder of generous horses.*

705. *Selinus:* a city whose plains abounded in palm-trees. Hence the epithet *palmosa. Datis:* in the sense of *faventibus.*

706. *Lilybeïa:* an adj. from *Lilybeum*, the western promontory of Sicily. The water here is said to be shoal to the distance of three miles from the land, and the bottom rocky. Hence *lego:* I coast along the Lilybean shallows, dangerous (*dura*) with latent rocks. Ruæus interprets *dura* by *aspera.* In this sense it will allude to the roughness of the sea, occasioned by the rocks lying on the bottom.

707. *Portus Drepani.* Drepanum (*hodie, Trepani*) a city and harbor a few miles to the north of the promontory just mentioned. Here Æneas lost his father. He therefore calls it *illætabilis ora:* an unjoyous coast. It is said the inhabitants still show his tomb.

708. *Actus:* in the sense of *jactatus.*

709. *Levamen:* in the sense of *solatium.*

710. *Fessum:* weary—worn out with toils and misfortunes.

711. *Erepte:* voc. agreeing with *optime pater.* In placing the death of Anchises here, Virgil differs from Strabo, who represents Æneas as arriving in Italy with his father, and his son Ascanius.

Nec vates Helenus, cùm multa horrenda moneret,
Hos mihi prædixit luctus; non dira Celæno.
Hic labor extremus, longarum hæc meta viarum.
Hinc me digressum vestris Deus appulit oris.
Sic pater Æneas, intentis omnibus, unus
Fata renarrabat Divûm, cursusque docebat:
Conticuit tandem, factoque hìc fine quievit.

713. Dira Celæno non prædixit

714. Hic *fuit* extremus labor

718. Fine *narrationis*

NOTES.

712. *Moneret:* in the sense of *prædiceret.*

714. *Hic extremus:* this line may be taken in two senses either to mean the end of Anchises' labor, and the termination of his long voyage, or that the death of his father was to Æneas the greatest of all his afflictions, and the end of his voyage toward the Italian coast. Ruæus takes it in the former sense; Mr. Davidson in the latter.

715. *Deus appulit:* a god directed me, departing hence (from the coast and port of Drepanum) to your shores.

717. *Unus renarrabat:* he alone related the purposes (decrees) of the gods (toward him,) and declared his wanderings. *Unus*. in the sense of *solus.*

718. *Quievit:* he rested—he went to rest. Segrais observes that the second and third books may be recited in two hours. The story did not appear long to Dido and the guests: for he ceased, *intentis omnibus*, and at midnight too, nor will they appear long to any reader of taste and judgment.

QUESTIONS.

How did Æneas employ his time during his residence at Antandros?

How many ships had he when he set sail?

At what time of the year did he set sail?

How long probably after the capture of the city?

To what place did he direct his course?

What city did he found in Thrace?

What did he call the name of it?

What did he call his followers from this circumstance?

Did he soon abandon the idea of remaining in Thrace?

Why did he thus abandon it?

Who was Polydorus?

How came he by his death?

From Thrace, to what place did Æneas direct his course?

Where is Delos situated?

Of what cluster of islands is it one?

How was he here received?

Who was at that time king of the island?

For what is this island famous?

What is the fable or story respecting it?

From what Greek word is the name derived?

What is the signification of that word?

Did he consult the oracle of Apollo at this place concerning the land destined to him?

What answer did he receive?

How did his father Anchises interpret that answer?

From Delos, to what place did he sail?

What prevented him from making a settlement in Crete?

What did he call the city, which he there founded?

Why did Æneas go to Crete?

Who were the founders of the Trojan race?

Of what country were they natives?

From Crete, to what country was he directed to sail?

How did he receive this instruction?

What befel him soon after he set sail?

What land did he first make?

In what sea are the Strophades?

By whom were these islands inhabited?

Who was the chief of the Harpies?

Did she give to Æneas any intimation of suffering and want, before he should find a permanent settlement?

How was this prediction accomplished?

From these islands, which way did he direct his course?

At what places did he land?

What games did he celebrate?

For what was this coast celebrated?

Between whom was the battle fought?

From Actium, to what part of Epirus did he proceed?

What surprising news did he hear on entering the port?

Was the meeting of his friends very interesting as well as unexpected?

What does Dr. Trapp observe of it?

How was Andromache employed at that time?

What effect had the sight of Æneas and the Trojans upon her?

Leaving Epirus, what sea did he first pass over?

How many miles is Italy from Epirus in that place?

What was the name of the promontory, where he landed?

What course did he then take?

Why did he not pass through the strait of Messina?

Where does this strait lie?

What is the navigation of it—safe or dangerous?

What renders it dangerous?

Why is Sicily sometimes called *Trinacria?*

What are the names of its three promontories?

Where did Æneas first land on this island?

What famous mountain was near?

How long did he remain?

Was there an eruption at that time?

What effect had it upon the Trojans?

What is the fabulous account of the cause of an eruption?

Is this very far from the true cause?

Who were the inhabitants of that part of Sicily?

Who was at that time their king?

From what circumstance were they called *Cyclops?*

How large was their eye said to be?

What was their employment according to the poets?

Who had been upon this coast a short time before the arrival of Æneas?

To what place was Ulysses bound?

What misfortune befel him in the strait of Messina?

What did he do to Polyphemus?

Why did he thus punish him?

From whom did Æneas receive this account of the Cyclops?

How many of these giants were there then on the island?

Who was Achemenides?

On what part of Sicily did Æneas afterward land?

What is the name of the port?

What loss befel him here?

Does this close the account, which Æneas gave to Dido at her request?

When does the poem open?

Where was Æneas at that time?

LIBER QUARTUS.

This book opens with the love of Dido for Æneas, and her conference with her sister Anna upon the subject. Juno perceiving her passion, conceived the plan of forming a connexion between them. To effect this the easier, she endeavors to draw Venus over to her views. In the mean time, Æneas and Dido prepare to go on a party of hunting; and while in the chase, Juno raises a violent tempest. The thunder rends the skies, and torrents of rain fall. The party seek shelter wherever they can. Through a device of Juno, Æneas and Dido repair to the same cave, where the goddess consecrates their nuptials. Fame immediately spread the news abroad; and it reached the ears of Iarbas, king of the Getuli, the reputed son of Jupiter Ammon. He had formerly proposed a match with Dido, who rejected his offers. As soon as he heard that she was married to a stranger, he was transported to rage, mingled with grief. In this state of mind he made complaint to his father, who, taking pity on him, sends Mercury to dissolve the match, and to order Æneas to prepare to leave Carthage for Italy. In obedience to his commands, he privately makes the necessary preparations for setting sail. Dido perceiving his movements, endeavors to dissuade him from his purpose, in the tenderest and most affectionate strain; but it had no influence over him. Being warned a second time, he weighs anchor in haste, and the love-sick Queen beholds him leaving her coast. The sight wrung her soul, and drew from her lips the most severe reproofs and bitter imprecations. She enjoins it upon her people to revenge the injury done to her, and to pursue his descendants with irreconcilable hatred. Having ordered a funeral pile to be erected, she ascends it, and with her own hand puts an end to her existence. (The nature of the subject renders this book highly interesting; and it is considered one of the finest in the Æneid.)

At regina, gravi jamdudum saucia cura,

NOTES.

. *Regina.* Dido sometimes called Eliza, was a Tyrian princess. Josephus informs us her father's name was *Melginus.* He obtained his information from the records of the Tyrians: and Theophilus of Antioch calls him *Melten.* Her grandfather was *Badezorus,* and her great grandfather was Ithobalus, called in Scripture *Ethbaal,* whose daughter Jezebel was married to Ahab, king of Israel. Virgil, however, makes the name

Vulnus alit venis, et cæco carpitur igni.
Multa viri virtus animo, multusque recursat
Gentis honos: hærent infixi pectore vultus,
Verbaque: nec placidam membris dat cura quietem.
Postera Phœbeâ lustrabat lampade terras,
Humentemque Aurora polo dimoverat umbram

6. Postera Aurora lustrabat terras Phœbeâ lampade

NOTES.

of her father to be *Belus*. Æn. i. 625. Marollius has given a list of the kings of Tyre, and makes *Belus* an abbreviation of *Ithobalus*, the father of Pygmalion and Dido; but he follows fabulous and traditionary accounts, which should always be received with caution. Among other things, what renders his account doubtful, is, that he brings Dido upon the stage of action more than a hundred years before the destruction of Troy.

After the death of his father, Pygmalion ascended the throne. He was an avaricious prince, and stopped at nothing by which he could increase his riches. He conceived the plan of murdering *Acerbas*, or *Sicharbas*, the beloved husband of his sister. Virgil calls him *Sichæus*, softening the name to make it flow more easily into his verse. *Sichæus* was the richest of all the Tyrians. Pygmalion coveted his treasures; but there was no way to possess them while he was living. He therefore formed the purpose of taking away his life. He came upon him unexpectedly, and slew him while he was performing his devotions before the altar. This atrocious deed, the base prince had the address to conceal, for some time, from his sister. At length the whole matter was laid open to Dido by the ghost of her deceased husband, and she was admonished to flee her country. Having collected what treasure she could on so sudden an emergency, and seizing some vessels that were then ready for sea, she set sail, accompanied by many of her countrymen: and, after a long and tedious voyage, she arrived in Africa. It appears to have been her purpose to join her countrymen, who, many years before, under Xorus and Carchedon, had formed a settlement, to which they gave the name of *Utica*, about 15 miles from the place where *Tunis* now stands. This place was afterward rendered famous by the death of the second *Cato*, who was hence called *Cato*, *Uticensis*. Dido met with a welcome reception, and was desired to build a city on the spot where she landed. For this purpose, she purchased a tract of country of the natives, many of whom joined her, together with some from Utica. She called her city *Catharda* or *Carthage*, which, in the *Phœnician* and *Hebrew* languages, signifies a *new city*. It stood about 700 years, and was destroyed by the Romans under *Scipio*, in the year of Rome 603, and before Christ 145. See Rollin's An. His. lib. ii. ch. 1.

There are some who say that Dido, on her arrival in Africa, found Carthage already built, and that she only fortified it, and added a tower or citadel, which she called *Byrsa*. This word is evidently from the Hebrew *Bosra*, which means a fortification, or fortified place. The Greeks, mistaking the meaning, or overlooking it, supposed, from the similarity of the words, that it was the same with their *Byrsa*, which means a bull's hide. Virgil followed the received opinion. See Æn. i. 367. It has been the general opinion that Virgil, in making Æneas and Dido cotemporary, is guilty of an anachronism. Bochart is positive of this, and says that all the ancient chronologers of any credit, place the destruction of Troy, at least 60 years before the reign of Saul, king of Israel; and the time of Dido's building *Byrsa*, the fortress of Carthage, at least 200 years after it, making 260 years to intervene between the destruction of Troy, and the building of *Byrsa*. In this case, the destruction of Troy will be 1160 years before the Christian era. Sir Isaac Newton, however, in his chronology, has brought it down nearly 300 years; and thus makes Æneas and Dido cotemporary. However the case may be, it was undoubtedly a received opinion among the Romans, that they were cotemporary, and this was sufficient for the poet; and even if he knew otherwise, he acted prudently in following the general opinion, since it contributed so much to the embellishment of his poem.

Jamdudum: a long while. Servius explains it by *nimiùm*, or *vehementiùs*. Though it were only a short time since Æneas came to Carthage, yet, with respect to Dido's passion, and the impatience of her love, it might be said to be *a long time*. *Cura:* Ruæus says, *solicitudine*.

2. *Alit vulnus:* she nourishes a wound in her veins, and is consumed by the secret fire of love. This is said in allusion to Cupid's arrow and torch; the former to wound, and the latter to inflame. *Cæco igni.* Valpy says, "a concealed passion."

3. *Multa viri virtus:* the many virtues of the hero, and the many honors of his race, recur to her mind. By his father, Æneas descended from the royal family of Troy; and, by *Venus* his mother, from Jove himself.

6. *Phœbeâ Lampade:* with the lamp of Phœbus, that is, with the sun. By *Tapinosis*. *Polo:* in the sense of *cœlo*.

Cùm sic unanimem alloquitur malè sana sororem
Anna soror, quæ me suspensam insomnia terrent!
Quis novus hic nostris successit sedibus hospes!
Quem sese ore ferens! quàm forti pectore et armis!
Credo equidem, nec vana fides, genus esse Deorum.
Degeneres animos timor arguit. Heu, quibus ille
Jactatus fatis! quæ bella exhausta canebat!
Si mihi non animo fixum immotumque sederet,
Ne cui me vinclo vellem sociare jugali,
Postquàm primus amor deceptam morte fefellit;
Si non pertæsum thalami tædæque fuisset;
Huic uni forsan potui succumbere culpæ.
Anna, fatebor enim, miseri post fata Sichæi
Conjugis, et sparsos fraternâ cæde penates,
Solus hic inflexit sensus, animumque labantem
Impulit: agnosco veteris vestigia flammæ.
Sed mihi vel tellus optem priùs ima dehiscat,
Vel pater omnipotens adigat me fulmine ad umbras,

8. Malè sana *regina* alloquitur

10. Quis novus hospes hic successit

12. *Eum* esse genus Deorum

16. Ne vellem sociare me cui *in* jugali vinclo, postquàm *meus* primus amor fefellit *me*

24. Sed optem vel ima tellus dehiscat mihi, vel pater omnipotens adigat me fulmine ad umbras, pallentes umbras Erebi, profundamque noctem, priùsquàm, *O* pudor, *ego* violo te

NOTES.

8. *Malè sana:* the love-sick queen addressed her concordant sister. *Unanimem*, here, is very emphatical. It implies that there was such a harmony and agreement subsisting between them, that they both seemed to be animated with the same soul: (of *unus* and *animus.*) *Malè sana: Malè*, here, has the force of *non.* The queen was so in love with Æneas, that she disregarded the sober dictates of reason, and her better judgment. Valpy says, "with disturbed mind." *Insomnia:* dreams. *Suspensam:* in the sense of *solicitam.*

11. *Quem sese ferens ore:* what an illustrious person, showing himself (to be) by his countenance! of how great fortitude and prowess!

The *Quàm forti pectore et armis*, is an elliptical expression. It is thus filled: *Quàm forti pectore est ille; et quàm fortibus armis.* The preposition *è*, or *ex*, being still understood, governing the ablative cases. By the *forti pectore*, we are to understand his fortitude in undergoing hardships, and supporting misfortunes: and by the *armis*, his courage and prowess in arms.

13. *Timor arguit:* fear shows a base and ignoble mind. As fear argues a base and ignoble mind, so courage and valor bespeak a noble and divine original. The poet has filled the speech of *Dido* with these abrupt half sentences, and made her speak incoherently, on purpose to show the confusion and perturbation of her mind.

14. *Exhausta:* drawn out—endured to the last. Not only begun, but accomplished, and with resolution brought to an end. Here is plainly an allusion to the draining of some bitter cup to the very last dregs. A participle from *exhaurio. Fatis.* The word *fatum* signifies, sometimes, as in this place—distress—misfortunes—calamities.

14. *Canebat:* in the sense of *narrabat.*

15. *Sederet:* in the sense of *maneret.*

16. *Sociare:* to connect myself in marriage with any one.

17. *Primus amor:* after my first love deceived me, disappointed by the death of my husband. She had pictured to herself an uninterrupted course of conjugal felicity, of which she was disappointed by the death of her husband. This led her to enter into the resolution of never forming a second connexion.

18. *Si non pertæsum fuisset:* if I had not been weary (displeased) with the marriage bed, and nuptial torch, perhaps, &c. *Tædæ.* It was a custom among the Romans to carry a torch before the newly married wife, when she was conducted to the house of her husband. Hence it is often put for the nuptials themselves.

19. *Potui:* I might yield to this one fault. *Potui:* in the sense of *potuissem.*

Second marriages were considered disreputable among the Roman women, as showing a want of respect for the memory of the deceased, and as conveying a suspicion of incontinency.

But *culpa* is sometimes taken simply for the indulgence of the passion of love, however innocent.

21. *Fraternâ cæde.* Sichæus was murdered, by her brother, at the altar. Hence the murder is called *fraternal. Fata:* in the sense of *mortem.* See note 1. supra.

22. *Inflexit sensus:* he alone hath changed my inclinations, and made an impression upon my wavering mind.

Pallentes umbras Erebi, noctemque profundam,
Antè, pudor, quàm te violo, aut tua jura resolvo.
Ille meos, primus qui me sibi junxit, amores
Abstulit; ille habeat secum, servetque sepulchro.
Sic effata, sinum lachrymis implevit obortis.
Anna refert: O luce magìs dilecta sorori,
Solane perpetuâ mœrens carpêre juventâ?
Nec dulces natos, Veneris nec præmia nôris?
Id cinerem, aut Manes credis curare sepultos?
Esto: ægram nulli quondam flexere mariti,
Non Libyæ, non antè Tyro: despectus Iarbas,
Ductoresque alii, quos Africa terra triumphis
Dives alit: placitone etiam pugnabis amori?
Nec venit in mentem, quorum consederis arvis?
Hinc Getulæ urbes, genus insuperabile bello,
Et Numidæ infræni cingunt, et inhospita Syrtis:
Hinc deserta siti regio, latèque furentes

28. Ille *Sichæus* **abstulit meos amores, qui**

31. O *tu*, magìs dilecta sorori lucê, **sola-ne** mœrens carpêre *in* **perpetuâ** juventâ?

34. Credis **cinerem** *Sichæi*, aut sepultos

36. *Esto:* Iarbas **despectus** *est*, aliique **ductores**

NOTES.

26. *Erebi:* the place of the dead—the infernal regions.

27. *Antè.* The *antè* here is plainly expletive. *Priùs* goes before it, and is to be connected with *quàm.* Some copies have *violem* and *resolvam.* *Pudor:* in the sense of *pudicitia.*

30. *Implevit sinum:* she filled her bosom with flowing tears. Servius and Turnebus take *sinum*, here, for the cavity of the eye. But the common import of the word is much more expressive, as it shows her tears to be much more copious, and paints her passion as more violent. *Refert:* in the sense of *respondet.* *Luce:* in the sense of *vita.*

32. *Sola-ne carpêre:* will you fade and wither away, mourning alone as a widow through all your youth, &c. Ruæus says, *an sola consumeris dolens per totam juventutem.* But *carpêre* may be used in the sense of the Greek middle voice. The meaning is obvious.

35. *Nulli mariti:* no suitors moved you sorrowing—while your loss was fresh in your memory, and your grief unabated. *Mariti:* in the sense of *proci.* *Ægram:* in the sense of *dolentem.* *Te* is understood.

36. *Iarbas.* Among the many who made suit to *Dido*, was Iarbas, a rich and powerful prince of Africa, and reputed son of *Jupiter Ammon.* But Justin gives a very different account of the matter from the one given here by the poet. He says, *Iarbas*, having gotten ten of the principal Carthaginians, demanded of them *Dido* in marriage; and, in case of a refusal, he threatened to declare war against them. Fearing to deliver the message to the queen, they said the king demanded a person who might teach him and his people the arts of civilized life; but that no one could be found who was willing to leave his relations and friends to undertake the business; upon this the queen rebuked them, and declared that if the safety of his country required it, any one should be willing to give up even his life. They then opened the whole matter, saying, the very thing she had enjoined on others, she had to perform herself, if she would consult the good of the city. Being taken by this device, after much lamentations, and many invocations of her husband, she declared that she would obey the call of her country. Having passed three months in this manner, she caused a funeral pile to be erected in one part of the city, as if to appease the *Manes* of her departed husband, and to offer sacrifices for him before her nuptials. She ascended the pile, and taking a sword in her hand, said to her people, that she would go to her husband as they required, and, with her own hand, put an end to her existence. While Carthage remained, she was worshipped as a goddess.

37. *Terra dives triumphis.* It appears from *Servius*, that the Africans were the inventors of triumphal shows. Some say they never triumphed. But *Justin* tells us that *Asdrubal*, in particular, was honored with four triumphs. *Placito:* in the sense of *grato* *Ne* is interrogative.

40. *Getulæ urbes.* The Getuli were a brave and warlike people, to the south of Carthage. *Hinc*, when it has its correspondent *hinc*, the former is rendered, *on the one side;* and the latter, *on the other side.*

41. *Numidæ.* The Numidians, again, were a people fierce and uncivilized, lying to the westward. *Inhospita Syrtis.* Both the greater and the less *Syrtis* lay in the *Sinus Libycus*, to the north and east of Carthage and rendered the navigation dangerous.

42. *Deserta siti* rendered desert by drought.

Barcæi. Quid bella Tyro surgentia dicam,
Germanique minas ?

45. *Ego* equidem reor Iliacas carinas tenuisse cursum huc vento, Dîs auspicibus, et Junone secundâ.

Dîs equidem auspicibus reor, et Junone secundâ,
Huc cursum Iliacas vento tenuisse carinas.
Quam tu urbem, soror, hanc cernes ! quæ surgere regna
Conjugio tali ! Teucrûm comitantibus armis,
Punica se quantis attollet gloria rebus !
Tu modò posce Deos veniam, sacrisque litatis,
Indulge hospitio, causasque innecte morandi ;
Dum pelago desævit hyems, et aquosus Orion ;
Quassatæque rates, et non tractabile cœlum.

54. Animum *jam* incensum amore

His dictis incensum animum inflammavit amore,
Spemque dedit dubiæ menti, solvitque pudorem.
Principio delubra adeunt, pacemque per aras
Exquirunt : mactant lectas de more bidentes
Legiferæ Cereri, Phœboque, patrique Lyæo

59. *Sed* Junoni ante omnes, cui jugalia vincla *sunt* curæ.

60. Pulcherrima Dido ipsa tenens pateram dextrâ fundit *vinum* inter media cornua candentis vaccæ :

Junoni ante omnes, cui vincla jugalia curæ.
Ipsa tenens dextrâ pateram pulcherrima Dido,
Candentis vaccæ media inter cornua fundit :
Aut ante ora Deûm pingues spatiatur ad aras,

NOTES.

43. *Barcæi.* These were a people to the east, inhabiting a dry and barren country.

Quid dicam : why shall I mention the wars arising from Tyre, and the threats of your brother ? Justin says, when Pygmalion understood that Dido had fled her country, and taken with her much treasure, he determined to pursue her ; but was dissuaded from his purpose by his mother, and the threats of the gods.

45. *Junone secunda.* Juno is here particularly named, because she presided over marriage, and because Carthage was under her peculiar protection. *Auspicibus :* in the sense of *fautoribus*, vel *auctoribus. Secunda :* in the sense of *propitia.*

49. *Quantis rebus :* by what noble deeds will the Carthaginian glory exalt itself, the arms of the Trojans accompanying yours ?

50. *Sacris litatis :* sacrifices being offered. The proper signification of *litare*, is, to propitiate by sacrifice. *Sacris :* in the sense of *victimis.*

51. *Innecte :* devise causes for detaining him.

52. *Desævit.* Ruæus takes this in the sense of *desæviet*, the present for the future.

53. *Non tractabile :* in the sense of *procellosum*, vel *sævum. Cœlum :* the air or weather. Æneas arrived in Africa, it is probable, in the latter part of autumn, some time before the approach of winter. It appears to be the plan of Anna to detain him during the pleasant part of the season, until the navigation should become dangerous, and when it would be imprudent to set sail ; in the hope that having passed so long a time with them, he might be persuaded finally to settle at Carthage, and give over his intended purpose of settling in Italy.

54. *Incensum :* burning, or inflamed with love.

55. *Dubiæ :* wavering. *Solvit pudorem.* removed her scruples in regard to disrespect to the memory of her late husband. Valpy.

57. *Exquirunt pacem per aras :* they seek peace by the altars. This refers to the way of prying into the entrails of the victims, in order to know the will of the gods. *Bidentes lectas de more.* It was a regulation that no victims should be offered to the gods, but such as were without blemish. *Bidentes :* properly sheep of two years old.

58. *Legiferæ Cereri.* Ceres was the daughter of Saturn and Ops, and the goddess of husbandry. It is said, she was the first institutor of laws, especially those of marriage. See Ecl. v. 79. *Phœbo.* Dido offers sacrifices to Phœbus, as the god who presided over futurity, that he might send her favorable omens. See Ecl. iv. 10. To father Bacchus, as the god of mirth and jollity, that he might crown the match with joy. See Ecl. v. 69. And especially (*ante omnes*) to Juno, as the goddess who presided over nuptials. *Cui vincla jugalia curæ :* to whom the marriage knot is for a care. See Æn. i. 4.

61. *Fundit*, &c. This was according to the manner of the Romans performing sacrifice. After the *immolatio*, which consisted in throwing corn and frankincense, together with the *mola*, (which was made of bran or meal mixed with salt and water,) upon the head of the victim, the priest sprinkled wine between the horns.

62. *Spatiatur :* she walks before the images (*ora*) of the gods, &c. It was a custom among the Romans for matrons to walk on holy days, in a grave and solemn

Instauratque diem donis, pecudumque reclusis
Pectoribus inhians, spirantia consulit exta.
Heu, vatum ignaræ mentes! quid vota furentem,
Quid delubra juvant? est mollis flamma medullas
Intereà, et tacitum vivit sub pectore vulnus.
Uritur infelix Dido, totâque vagatur
Urbe furens: qualis conjectâ cerva sagittâ,
Quam procul incautam nemora inter Cressia fixit
Pastor agens telis, liquitque volatile ferrum
Nescius: illa fugâ sylvas saltusque peragrat
Dictæos: hæret lateri lethalis arundo.
Nunc media Æneam secum per mœnia ducit;
Sidoniasque ostentat opes, urbemque paratam.
Incipit effari, mediâque in voce resistit.
Nunc eadem, labente die, convivia quærit;
Iliacosque iterum demens audire labores
Exposcit, pendetque iterum narrantis ab ore.
Pòst, ubi digressi, lumenque obscura vicissim
Luna premit, suadentque cadentia sidera somnos;
Sola domo mœret vacuâ, stratisque relictis
Incubat: illum absens absentem auditque videtque:
Aut gremio Ascanium, genitoris imagine capta,
Detinet, infandum si fallere possit amorem.
Non cœptæ assurgunt turres, non arma juventus
Exercet, portusve, aut propugnacula bello
Tuta parant: pendent opera interrupta, minæque
Murorum ingentes, æquataque machina cœlo.

65. ***Eam*** **furentem**

69. ***Talis*****, qualis cerva, sagittâ conjecta, quam pastor agens telis fixit incautam procul inter Cressia nemora, liquitque volatile ferrum** ***in vulnere*****, nescius** ***facti***

74. Nunc ***Dido*** **ducit Æneam secum**

79. Ore ***Æneæ*** **narrantis**

80. Ubi ***omnes*** **digressi** ***sunt ad quietem***

83. ***Illa*** **absens auditque videtque**

NOTES.

manner, before the altars, with torches in their hands. *Ora:* in the sense of *statuas*, vel *imagines*.

63. *Instaurat:* she passes the day in offerings. Ruæus says, *renovat sacrificia per diem*.

64. *Inhians:* prying into—exploring attentively. *Spirantia:* throbbing—palpitating. *Exta:* properly the part which we call the lungs, including the heart, liver, &c.

65. *Vatum:* in the sense of *extispicum*.

66. *Mollis flamma est:* a gentle flame consumes. *Est:* in the sense of *edit*. *Furentem:* in the sense of *amantem*. *Tacitum:* concealed.

69. *Qualis cerva.* This is a very proper comparison, and agrees almost in every circumstance. There is a peculiar beauty in the *hærit lateri lethalis arundo*, which strongly images the fast hold that the arrows of Cupid had gotten of Dido's heart. *Cressia:* an adj. Cretan.

71. *Ferrum:* in the sense of *arundinem*.

74. *Mœnia:* properly the fortifications of a city. Ruæus says, *munimenta*.

77. *Eadem:* the same entertainment she had received the preceding night.

81 *Luna obscura vicissim:* the moon, in turn obscure, withdraws her light. This shows the approach of day. When the stars disappear in the superior light of the sun, they are said to set; so when the sun disappears, and withdraws his light, they become visible, and are said to rise. The same may be said of the moon. *Vicissim:* after having given light in her course.

82. *Relictis stratis.* The couch on which Æneas had been sitting, and which he had just left to retire to rest.

84. *Capta:* taken, or captivated with the resemblance of his father, she hugs, &c.

88. *Pendent:* stand, or remain. *Interrupta:* in the sense of *imperfecta*. *Ingentes minæ murorum.* Heyne takes this simply for the high walls, (*alti muri*,) which by their altitude, presented a threatening aspect. Valpy is of the same opinion: but most interpreters take *minæ murorum* to be the fortifications built upon the walls, which presented a threatening appearance to an enemy. Hortensius and Ruæus are of opinion, they were huge and unfinished parts of the wall, which seemed to threaten a ruin, and presented a terrific appearance.

89. *Machina.* By this we are most probably to understand the engines used in raising stones, beams, and timber generally, for carrying on the building. Heyne says, *moles—ædificium*, referring to the buildings themselves.

90. Quam (*Didonem*) simul ac Saturnia, chara conjux Jovis, persensit teneri tali peste, nec famam obstare *ejus* furori, aggreditur Venerem talibus dictis: verò tuque tuusque puer refertis egregiam laudem et ampla spolia, magnum et memorabile numen; si una fœmina victa est dolo duorum Divûm. Nec adeò fallit me, te, veritam nostra mœnia habuisse domos altæ Carthaginis suspectas.

98. Modus *nostræ contentionis*

103. Liceat *Didoni* servire

107. Contrà Venus ingressa est *respondere* olli sic; enim sensit *eam* locutam *esse* simulatâ mente, quò averteret

Quam simul ac tali persensit peste teneri
Chara Jovis conjux, nec famam obstare furori,
Talibus aggreditur Venerem Saturnia dictis:
Egregiam verò laudem, et spolia ampla refertis
Tuque puerque tuus, magnum et memorabile numen:
Una dolo Divûm si fœmina victa duorum est:
Nec me adeò fallit, veritam te mœnia nostra,
Suspectas habuisse domos Carthaginis altæ.
Sed quis erit modus? aut quò nunc certamina tanta?
Quin potiùs pacem æternam pactosque hymenæos
Exercemus? habes, totâ quod mente petîsti:
Ardet amans Dido, traxitque per ossa furorem.
Communem hunc ergò populum, paribusque regamus
Auspiciis: liceat Phrygio servire marito,
Dotalesque tuæ Tyrios permittere dextræ.
Olli, sensit enim simulata mente locutam,
Quò regnum Italiæ Libycas averteret oras,
Sic contrà est ingressa Venus: Quis talia demens
Abnuat, aut tecum malit contendere bello?
Si modò, quod memoras, factum fortuna sequatur.
Sed fatis incerta feror, si Jupiter unam
Esse velit Tyriis urbem, Trojâque profectis;

NOTES.

90. *Peste:* in the sense of *amore.* Ruæus says, *veneno.*

93. *Spolia:* in the sense of *victoriam.*

94. *Numen.* This is the reading of Heyne, after Pierius, Heinsius, and Burmannus. It is also approved by Valpy, though he retains the common reading, *nomen.* In a note upon this passage, he has *numen*, and observes that *vestrum* is understood. "Your divine power will be nobly employed," says he. Heyne makes this turn to the words: *Magnum verò et memorabile erit numen vestrum, si vos duo Dei circumveneritis unam fœminam.* He takes *numen* in the sense of *potestas*, vel *potentia. Nomen* is the common reading. This part of Juno's speech is extremely satirical. *Tuus puer:* Cupid. He was the son of Jupiter and Venus.

98. *Aut quò nunc:* or, for what purpose now are so great contentions? Juno and Venus took opposite sides in the affairs of Æneas and the Trojans. The former is always represented their bitterest enemy, and the latter their warmest friend. The whole of Juno's speech is artful, and the plan deep laid. She now proposes to lay down their arms, to conclude a lasting peace —to form a match between Æneas and Dido, and by these means unite the Trojans with the Carthaginians into one people. This plan, could she have brought it about, would have been to her a complete victory over her antagonist. The common reading is *certamine tanto.* Heyne reads *certamina tanta*, which is much easier, and he says, is he true reading.

99. *Hymenæos:* match.

102. *Regamus hunc populum.* The meaning plainly is: Let us rule this people (*communem*) composed of Trojans and Carthaginians, with equal authority and power. Let them be both equally under our protection and auspicious influence. *Auspiciis* in the sense of *potestate.*

103. *Phrygio.* Servius, and some others, say, that *Phrygio*, here, is a word of contempt, and implies that Æneas was in exile and in slavery, as the *Phrygians* then were. But Virgil uses the words *Phrygius* and *Trojanus* promiscuously. Beside, Juno plays the hypocrite, and would, therefore, industriously avoid every expression that might be offensive, or render her suspected. The expression *servire marito* is in allusion to one of the three ways of contracting marriage among the Romans, (viz.) *Coemptio:* when the parties solemnly bound themselves to each other by the ceremony of giving and taking a piece of money. By this the woman gave herself over into the power of the man, and entered into a state of liberal servitude, or subjection to him.

104. *Dotales:* as a dowry. *Dos* is properly the patrimony of the wife—any thing given to the husband with the wife. *Tyrios* nempe, *regnum Carthaginis.*

105. *Olli:* for *illi*, by *antithesis.*

110. *Feror incerta fatis, si:* I am rendered uncertain by the decrees of the gods, whether, &c

Misceri ve probet populos, aut fœdera jungi.
Tu conjux: tibi fas animum tentare precando.
Perge; sequar. Tum sic excepit regia Juno:
Mecum erit iste labor: nunc quâ ratione, quod instat,
Confieri possit, paucis, adverte, docebo.
Venatum Æneas, unàque miserrima Dido,
In nemus ire parant, ubi primos crastinus ortus
Extulerit Titan, radiisque retexerit orbem.
His ego nigrantem commixtâ grandine nimbum,
Dum trepidant alæ, saltusque indagine cingunt,
Desuper infundam, et tonitru cœlum omne ciebo.
Diffugient comites, et nocte tegentur opacâ.
Speluncam Dido dux et Trojanus eandem
Devenient. Adero, et, tua si mihi certa voluntas,
Connubio jungam stabili, propriamque dicabo.
Hic Hymenæus erit. Non adversata, petenti
Annuit, atque dolis risit Cytherea repertis.
  Oceanum intereà surgens Aurora reliquit.
It portis, jubare exorto, delecta juventus
Retia rara, plagæ, lato venabula ferro,
Massylique ruunt equites, et odora canum vis.
Reginam thalamo cunctantem ad limina primi
Pœnorum expectant: ostroque insignis et auro
Stat sonipes, ac fræna ferox spumantia mandit.
Tandem progreditur, magnâ stipante catervâ,

regnum Italiæ *ad* Libycas oras

113. Tu *es ejus* conjux: fas *est* tibi tentare

115. Nunc, adverte *tu*, docebo paucis *verbis*, qua ratione, *id*, quod instat, possit confieri.

121. Dum alæ trepidant, cinguntque saltus indagine, ego desuper infundam his nigrantem nimbum, grandine commixta, et ciebo omne cœlum tonitru.

125. Si tua voluntas *sit* certa mihi

128. Cytherea non adversata annuit *ei* petenti, atque risit dolis repertis

NOTES.

114. *Excepit:* replied—answered.

117. *Venatum:* a sup. in *um*, of the verb *venor*, put after the verb *ire*. Dido is here called *miserrima*, most unhappy, on account of the issue of her love.

119. *Titan:* in the sense of *Sol.* See Ecl. iv. 6. and Geor. iii. 48. *Radiisque:* and shall have disclosed the world by his beams. The poets pretended that light sunk into the ocean every night, and was every morning brought from hence by the returning sun. Hence the propriety of the verb *extulerit.*

121. *Dum alæ.* By *alæ*, Servius understands the horsemen, or riding hunters, who are termed *alæ*, *wings*, because they covered the foot as the cavalry of an army. Or *alæ* may signify the horsemen in general spread over the ground, like stretched out wings. *Trepidant* very strongly expresses the hurry and bustle of a company of horsemen, flying and scampering over the ground in quest of their prey. *Indagine.* By this some understand the arranging of the hounds, and the placing of them in proper places for taking the game: but *Ruæus*, and most commentators, take it for the *nets* and *toils* in which the game was taken. For *alæ*, Ruæus has *equites.*

126. *Jungam* I will join them in firm wedlock, and will consecrate her to be his own. I will give her over to be his peculiar property.

127. *Hic Hymenæus erit:* this shall be a marriage. Some take the meaning to be that *Hymen* should be present. But this would be unnecessary, since the nuptials were to be performed by *Juno*, without the assistance of any other. See Geor. iii. 60. *Cytherea*, a name of Venus. See Æn. i. 229.

130. *Jubare:* in the sense of *luce* vel *diluculo.*

131. *Retia rara:* the wide nets, the toils, the spears of broad point, and the Massilian horsemen, &c. rush forth.

132. *Odora vis canum. Vis* is here used in the sense of *copia*, or *multitudo.* And *odora*, in the sense of *odororum*, by *antiptosis:* a multitude of strong scented dogs. *Massyli.* They were a people of Africa, placed by Virgil to the westward of *Carthage.* Little is known concerning them.

133. *Primi:* in the sense of *primores.*

135. *Stat sonipes insignis:* her horse stands ready, richly decked in purple and gold. *Stat:* in the sense of *adest.* To take it literally would ill agree with the fine image of the courser here given; *ferox mandit spumantia fræna. Insignis:* in the sense of *ornatus.*

137. *Circumdata Sidoniam:* covered with a Tyrian cloak. The *chlamys* was both a military and hunting dress. It was a loose upper garment, which covered the breastplate, and folded about the left arm to de-

Sidoniam picto chlamydem circumdata limbo.
Cui pharetra ex auro; crines nodantur in aurum;
Aurea purpuream subnectit fibula vestem
Necnon et Phrygii comites, et lætus Iülus,
Incedunt: ipse ante alios pulcherrimus omnes
Infert se socium Æneas, atque agmina jungit:
Qualis, ubi hybernam Lyciam Xanthique fluenta
Deserit, ac Delum maternam invisit Apollo,
Instauratque choros, mixtique altaria circum
Cretesque Dryopesque fremunt, pictique Agathyrsi
Ipse jugis Cynthi graditur, mollique fluentem
Fronde premit crinem fingens, atque implicat auro
Tela sonant humeris. Haud illo segnior ibat
Æneas; tantum egregio decus enitet ore.
 Postquam altos ventum in montes, atque invia lustra,
Ecce feræ saxi dejectæ vertice capræ
Decurrêre jugis: aliâ de parte patentes
Transmittunt cursu campos, atque agmina cervi
Pulverulenta fugâ glomerant, montesque relinquunt.
At puer Ascanius mediis in vallibus acri
Gaudet equo: jamque hos cursu, jam præterit illos:
Spumantemque dari pecora inter inertia votis
Optat aprum, aut fulvum descendere monte leonem.
 Intereà magno misceri murmure cœlum
Incipit: insequitur commixtâ grandine nimbus.
Et Tyrii comites passim, et Trojana juventus,
Dardaniusque nepos Veneris, diversa per agros
Tecta metu petiere; ruunt de montibus amnes.
Speluncam Dido dux et Trojanus, eandem
Deveniunt: prima et Tellus et pronuba Juno

138. Cui *est* pharetra ex auro

142. Æneas ipse pulcherrimus ante omnes alios infert se socium.

143. *Talis*, qualis *est* Apollo, ubi deserit hybernam Lyciam, fluentaque Xanthi, ac invisit maternam Delum

148. Implicat *cum* auro

151. Postquam ventum *est* in altos montes, atque invia lustra; ecce feræ capræ dejectæ vertice saxi decurrêre jugis

153. De aliâ parte cervi transmittunt

159. Optatque votis spumantem aprum dari *sibi* inter inertia pecora

NOTES.

fend them from the wild beasts. The construction is a Grecism.

143. *Qualis.* The poet (Æn. i. 498.) compared Dido to Diana: here he compares Æneas to Apollo, her brother. It was a common opinion that, at certain times of the year, the gods changed the place of their residence. Servius says, it was believed that *Apollo* gave out oracles at *Patara*, a city of Lycia, a country of Asia Minor, during the six months of the winter; and at *Delos*, the remaining six months of the year. Hence he was called both *Patareus* and *Delius*. *Fluenta:* in the sense of *fluvium.*

144. *Maternam Delum.* See Æn. iii. 75.

146. *Cretesque: the Cretans, Dryopes, and painted Agathyrsi, mingled together, express their joy (fremunt) around the altars.* When Apollo came, or was thought to come to *Delos*, the several people that came to consult his oracle, celebrated his arrival with hymns and dances. *Dryopes.* These were a people who dwelt at the foot of mount Parnassus. *Agathyrsi.* These were a people of Scythia, who used to paint their bodies with various colors. The nations here mentioned seemed to be selected for *Apollo's* retinue, on account of their skill in archery.

148. *Premit:* binds up. *Fingens:* adjusting it. *Molli fronde:* with a soft wreath of leaves. Ruæus says, *tenera coronâ.* *Auro:* in the sense of *aurea vitta.*

149. *Haud segnior:* he moved not less graceful than he—than Apollo himself.

150. *Ore:* in the sense of *vultu.*

152. *Dejectæ:* dislodged—routed. *Jugis:* the sides of the rocks, or mountains.

154. *Transmittunt:* in the sense of *percurrunt.*

155. *Glomerant fugâ:* in their flight, they crowd together the dusty herds, &c. Ruæus says, *colligunt se in greges pulverulentos.*

159. *Optat votis:* he wishes with vows—he greatly wishes, that a foaming boar, &c.

163. *Dardanius nepos Veneris:* the Trojan grandson of Venus—*Ascanius.* *Tecta;* tectum signifies any covered place. Here shelters, or retreat from the storm.

166. *Tellus et pronuba.* Pronuba, a title of *Juno*, from her being the goddess of marriage: compounded of *pro* and *nubo.*

Dant signum: fulsere ignes, et conscius æther
Connubiis; summoque ululârunt vertice Nymphæ.
Ille dies primus lethi, primusque malorum
Causa fuit: neque enim specie famâve movetur,
Nec jam furtivum Dido meditatur amorem:
Conjugium vocat: hoc prætexit nomine culpam.
Extemplò Libyæ magnas it Fama per urbes:
Fama, malum, quo non aliud velocius ullum:
Mobilitate viget, viresque acquirit eundo:
Parva metu primò: mox sese attollit in auras,
Ingrediturque solo, et caput inter nubila condit.
Illam Terra parens, irâ irritata Deorum,
Extremam, ut perhibent, Cœo Enceladoque sororem
Progenuit, pedibus celerem et pernicibus alis:
Monstrum horrendum, ingens: cui quot sunt corpore plumæ,
Tot vigiles oculi subter, mirabile dictu!
Tot linguæ, totidem ora sonant, tot subrigit aures.
Nocte volat cœli medio terræque per umbram
Stridens, nec dulci declinat lumina somno.
Luce sedet custos, aut summi culmine tecti,
Turribus aut altis, et magnas territat urbes:
Tam ficti pravique tenax, quàm nuntia veri.
Hæc tum multiplici populos sermone replebat
Gaudens, et pariter facta atque infecta canebat:
Venisse Æneam, Trojano à sanguine cretum,
Cui se pulchra viro dignetur jungere Dido:
Nunc hyemem inter se luxu, quàm longa, fovere,

167. Conscius connubiis *fulsit*

169. Ille dies primus fuit causa lethi *Didoni*, primusque *fuit causa* malorum

178. Parens terra irritata irâ Deorum progenuit illam, ut *homines* perhibent, extremam sororem Cœo Enceladoque, celerem pedibus, et pernicibus alis

181. Monstrum horrendum, ingens; cui *sunt* tot vigiles oculi subter, mirabile dictu! tot linguæ, totidem ora sonant, subrigit tot aures, quot sunt plumæ *in* corpore.

191. *Canebat* Æneam venisse, cretum à Trojano sanguine, cui viro pulchra Dido dignetur jungere se: nunc luxu fovere inter se hyemem, quàm longa *est*,

NOTES

Its primitive meaning is *bride-maid*. Some rank *Tellus* among the Divinities that presided over marriage. She gave signs of disapprobation by an earthquake, or some motion of the earth. *Servius* says, there was no omen more inauspicious to nuptials than this. *Juno* also gave her sign against the match, by rain and storms of hail. Flashes of lightning supplied the place of the nuptial torch; and the only song was the howling of the mountain nymphs. These were all sad presages of the future.

169. *Ille dies primus fuit causa: that day, the first* (in an especial manner,) *was the cause of death to Dido; and the beginning* (*primus*) *of her woes.*

170. *Specie fama-ve.* By the *species* we are to understand the appearance and deformity of the action, as it passed in review before her own mind; and by *fama*, the scandal and infamy of it, in the eyes of the world.

172. *Prætexit:* palliates or covers. *Culpam:* in the sense of *crimen.*

174. *Fama malum quo: Fame, a fiend, than which there is not another more swift,* &c. In this account of fame, the Poet imitates *Homer's* description of discord. A judicious critic is of opinion that this description of fame is one of the greatest ornaments of the Æneid. It has not, however, escaped censure. *Malum:* in the sense of *pestis* vel *monstrum.*

179. *Cœo Enceladoque.* These were two Giants, who took the lead in the war against the gods. They were the sons of *Titan* and *Tellus.* Their object in the war was to restore their father Titan to the throne, from which Jupiter had driven him. They attempted to attack Heaven, by putting mount *Ossa* upon *Pelion;* but in the attempt they were chastised by Jupiter, in an exemplary manner. At this vengeance (*ira*) of the gods, *Tellus* was irritated; and by way of revenge, produced *fame*, their youngest sister, swift on the foot, and on the nimble wing.

184. *Medio:* in the middle of heaven and earth—between heaven and earth. *Umbram:* in the sense of *tenebras.*

186. *Luce:* in the sense of *die.* *Custos:* a spy.

188. *Tam tenax:* as tenacious of falsehood and wickedness, as a messenger of truth.

189. *Sermone:* in the sense of *rumore.*

190. *Canebat:* she equally proclaimed facts and fictions.

193. *Nunc fovere luxu:* that now in luxury they caress one another during the winter, as long as it may be. *Hyemem quàm longa:* in the sense of *longam hye-*

Regnorum immemores, turpique cupidine captos
Hæc passim Dea fœda virûm diffundit in ora.
Protinùs ad regem cursus detorquet Iarbam ;
Incenditque animum dictis, atque aggerat iras.
Hic Ammone satus, raptâ Garamantide Nymphâ,
Templa Jovi centum latis immania regnis,
Centum aras posuit ; vigilemque sacraverat ignem,
Excubias Divûm æternas, pecudumque cruore
Pingue solum, et variis florentia limina sertis.
Isque amens animi, et rumore accensus amaro,
Dicitur ante aras, media inter numina Divûm,
Multa Jovem manibus supplex orâsse supinis :
Jupiter omnipotens, cui nunc Maurusia pictis
Gens epulata toris Lenæum libat honorem,
Aspicis hæc ? an te, genitor, cùm fulmina torques,
Nequicquam horremus ? cæcique in nubibus ignes
Terrificant animos, et inania murmura miscent ?
Fœmina, quæ nostris errans in finibus urbem
Exiguam pretio posuit, cui litus arandum,
Cuique loci leges dedimus, connubia nostra
Reppulit, ac dominum Ænean in regna recepit

198. Hic satus Ammone, Nymphâ Garamantide raptâ, posuit Jovi centum immania templa *in* latis regnis, *posuit* centum aras ; sacraveratque

203. Isque amens animi, et accensus amaro rumore, dicitur supplex orâsse Jovem multa supinis manibus, *stans* ante aras, inter media numina Divûm.

212. Cui *dedimus* litus

NOTES.

mem. Ruæus says, *traducere hyemem inter se luxu.*

194. *Cupidine:* by cupido, Servius informs us that the ancients understood an ungovernable and irregular passion of love—lust. *Captos:* enslaved.

198. *Hic Ammone satus: this man, sprung from Ammon, had built to Jove,* &c. Jupiter Ammon had a celebrated temple and oracle in Libya, on a spot of ground watered by a fountain, and enclosed by a pleasant grove. This temple is said to have been built by Bacchus, or Hercules. This *Ammon* some will have to be the same with *Ham*, the son of Noah. Sir Isaac Newton thinks him to have been the father of *Sesostris*, and cotemporary with Solomon, king of Israel. Iarbus was the son of this Jupiter Ammon, by the nymph *Garamantis. Aggerat:* in the sense of *auget.*

200. *Vigilem ignem.* Plutarch informs us that in this temple there was a lamp continually burning. This was also a custom common to many nations. *Posuit:* in the sense of *ædificavit.*

201. *Excubias æternas Divûm:* a perpetual watch of the gods—sacred to the service of the gods. *Solum:* a tract of ground enriched by the blood of victims.

202. *Limina florentia:* an entrance (into the temples) adorned with various garlands. *Amens animi:* distracted in mind ; of *à*, privitivum, and *mens.*

204. *Numina:* the shrines or statues, which represented the gods. *Supinis.* Ruæus says, *elatis:* properly, with the palm upwards.

206. *Qui nunc:* to whom the Moorish nation, feasting on painted couches, &c. The *Maurusii*, vel *Mauri*, were inhabitants of Mauritania, an extensive country in Africa, bounded on the west by the Atlantic ocean, on the north by the Mediterranean sea, and on the east by Numidia and Carthage. It seems this news reached Iarbas, while he and his people were feasting upon the remains of the victims which had been offered to *Ammon.* At such banquets, it was usual to pour forth wine by way of libation to the gods—an offering of wine.

207. *Lenæum honorem:* simply, wine—the liquor of Bacchus. *Lenæus*, a name of Bacchus, used as an adj. derived from a Greek word, signifying a wine-press. *Epulata:* feasting, or having feasted.

209. *Cæci:* undirected—fortuitous. *Ignes:* lightnings. *Inania murmura:* vain, or empty sounds.

212. *Posuit:* in the sense of *condidit. Litus arandum:* the shore to be ploughed. The province or territory of Carthage is here called *litus*, because it lay along the sea coast—a tract of country to cultivate. *Pretio.* This alludes to the price paid, or stipulated to be paid, for her territory, or tract of country. See the following note.

213. *Cuique dedimus:* and on whom we imposed the laws of the place. We are told that Dido engaged to pay the Africans an annual tribute for the tract of country which she purchased for her colony. This, however, the Carthaginians afterwards refused to do, and was the cause of the first war in which they were engaged. Excepting this tribute, Carthage, from the first, was an independent sovereignty.

Et nunc ille Paris, cum semiviro comitatu,
Mæoniâ mentum mitrâ crinemque madentem
Subnexus, rapto potitur: nos munera templis
Quippe tuis ferimus, famamque fovemus inanem.
Talibus orantem dictis, arasque tenentem
Audiit omnipotens: oculosque ad mœnia torsit
Regia, et oblitos famæ melioris amantes.
Tunc sic Mercurium alloquitur, ac talia mandat:
Vade, age, nate, voca Zephyros, et labere pennis:
Dardaniumque ducem, Tyriâ Carthagine qui nunc
Expectat, fatisque datas non respicit urbes,
Alloquere, et celeres defer mea dicta per auras.
Non illum nobis genitrix pulcherrima talem
Promisit, Graiûmque ideò bis vindicat armis:
Sed fore qui gravidam imperiis, belloque frementem
Italiam regeret, genus alto à sanguine Teucri
Proderet, ac totum sub leges mitteret orbem.
Si nulla accendit tantarum gloria rerum,

217. Subnexus ***quoad*** **mentum madentemque crinem Mœonia mitrâ, potitur rapto**

220. Omnipotens audiit ***eum*** **orantem** ***in*** **talibus dictis, tenentemque aras, torsitque** ***ejus*** **oculos ad regia mœnia, et** ***ad*** **amantes oblitos melioris famæ.**

226. Alloquereque Dardanium ducem, qui nunc expectat ***in*** **Tyria Carthagine, nonque respicit urbes datas** ***et*** **fatis**

227. ***Ejus*** **pulcherrima genitrix non promisit**

NOTES.

215. *Et nunc ille Paris.* Here Iarbas calls Æneas, Paris, to denote him effeminate, and a ravisher, who had carried off a princess whom he considered his own. In allusion to this, he says, *potitur rapto:* he possesses the ravished prize. *Semiviro comitatu:* with his effeminate train. This is said in allusion to the Phrygians, who were great worshippers of the goddess *Cybele*, whose priests were eunuchs.

216. *Mæoniâ mitrâ:* a Mæonian, or Lydian mitre. This was a kind of bonnet worn by the Lydian and Phrygian women. It was a part of dress unbecoming in men, more especially when it had the fillets or strings with which it was tied under the chin. Iarbas mentions it as a mark of infamy and badge of reproach. *Mæonia:* an extensive country in the Lesser Asia. It is here used as an adj. Its more modern name is *Lydia*, from *Lydus*, one of its kings, as Strabo tells us. That part bordering upon Ionia and Caria, still retains its ancient name. Athenæus observes, that Homer attributes the use of unguents to none of his characters in the Iliad, besides Paris. These were chiefly for the hair. The use of them was considered a mark of effeminacy. Iarbas therefore says of Æneas, that his hair was moistened or besmeared with unguents—*crinem madentem.*

217. *Subnexus:* in the sense of *subligatus.*

218. *Quippe nos ferimus:* we to be sure bring offerings to thy temples, and cherish the vain report of being thy offspring.

Iarbas speaks by way of complaint. The offerings which we present unto thee are of no avail, and the report of thy being our father is vain and without foundation, or else thou wouldst not have suffered this evil to fall upon me. Heyne observes, that the words of Iarbas, *quippe*, &c. are extremely ironical. *Ironia acerba vocabulo, quippe, inest*, says he. Both Ruæus and Heyne take *quippe* in the sense of *scilicet.* But *quippe* may be taken perhaps in the sense of *dum:* while we are presenting offerings unto thee, &c. Æneas is enjoying the ravished prize.

219. *Tenentem aras.* holding the altars. It was a custom in the more solemn acts of religion, to embrace the altars. It was especially so for suppliants.

221. *Amantes:* lovers—Æneas and Dido.

223. *Pennis:* in the sense of *alis.* Mercury was represented as having winged shoes, on which he was borne through the air. They were called *talaria.*

225. *Expectat:* in the sense of *moratur.*

228. *Bis vindicat:* preserved him twice, &c. Æneas was twice saved by Venus from impending death: once in a contest with Diomede, when he was struck to the ground by the stroke of a huge stone, and would have been slain, had not Venus cast her veil over him, and carried him off from the fight; and a second time, when under her own conduct, he passed unhurt through the flames of Troy, and the midst of his enemies, during the sack of that city.

229. *Gravidam imperiis.* Ruæus says, *plenam regnis.* Servius says, *parituram imperia, vel unde multi imperatores possunt creari.* Heyne says, *quæ proferet multos potentes, et latè imperantes populos.* It appears to be in the sense of *paritura magnum imperium, populumque latè dominantem.* In which a mighty empire is about to be established, says Valpy.

231. *Proderet genus:* should evince or prove his descent, &c.

Nec super ipse suâ molitur laude laborem ·
Ascanio-ne pater Romanas invidet arces?
Quid struit? aut quâ spe inimicâ in gente moratur?
Nec prolem Ausoniam et Lavinia respicit arva?
Naviget. Hæc summa est: hic nostri nuntius esto
 Dixerat. Ille patris magni parere parabat
Imperio: et primùm pedibus talaria nectit
Aurea; quæ sublimem alis, sive æquora supra,
Seu terram, rapido pariter cum flamine portant.
Tum virgam capit: hâc animas ille evocat Orco
Pallentes; alias sub tristia Tartara mittit:
Dat somnos adimitque, et lumina morte resignat.
Illâ fretus agit ventos, et turbida tranat
Nubila. Jamque volans apicem et latera ardua cernit
Atlantis duri, cœlum qui vertice fulcit:
Atlantis, cinctum assiduè cui nubibus atris
Piniferum caput et vento pulsatur et imbri:
Nix humeros infusa tegit: tum flumina mento
Præcipitant senis, et glacie riget horrida barba.
Hìc primùm paribus nitens Cyllenius alis
Constitit: hinc toto præceps se corpore ad undas
Misit: avi similis, quæ circum litora, circum
Piscosos scopulos, humilis volat æquora juxta.
Haud aliter, terras inter cœlumque, volabat

nobis illum *fore* talem, ideòque bis vindicat *illum ab* armis Graiûm: sed *promisit illum* fore *unum*, qui regeret Italiam gravidam imperiis, frementemque bello; *qui* proderet

237. Hic esto *illi* nuntius nostri

248. Atlantis, cui piniferum caput assiduè cinctum atris nubibus pulsatur et vento et imbri: nix infusa

256. Haud aliter Cyl-

NOTES.

233. *Molitur laborem:* undertakes the enterprise for his own glory.

235. *In gente inimicâ:* in a hostile nation. This is said by anticipation, because of the enmity which subsisted between Rome and Carthage in after times. *Struit:* in the sense of *parat.*

236. *Lavinia arva.* See Æn. i. 2.

239. *Talaria.* These were a kind of winged shoes, which the poets say the messengers of the gods wore—sandals.

241. *Flamine:* in the sense of *vento.*

242. *Virgam.* This was the celebrated rod, or Caduceus, presented to Mercury by Apollo, in return for his lyre. Mercury, in his way to Arcadia, observing two serpents going to fight, appeased them by casting down his rod between them. Hence a rod wreathed round with two serpents, became a symbol of peace. *Orco:* the place of the dead.

243. *Tartara:* the lowest part of hell—the place of the damned.

244. *Lumina morte resignat:* he opens eyes in death. This is the sense given to *resigno* by Turnebus, Davidson, and others. They think the poet alludes to a Roman custom of opening the eyes on the funeral pile, though shut all the time the corpse lay in the house. But Servius takes *resigno* in the sense of *claudo:* he closes, or shuts eyes in death. Ruæus says, *aperit oculos ex morte,* id est, *revocat corpora è morte.* This seems to be the opinion of Heyne.

247. *Atlantis duri.* Atlas is a very high mountain, or rather range of mountains, commencing at the Atlantic ocean, to which it gives name, and running in an easterly direction, dividing Mauritania from Libya Interior. It is fabled that Atlas, king of Mauritania, was transformed into this mountain by Perseus, at the sight of his Gorgon's head, because he refused to treat him with hospitality. Virgil describes the mountain as retaining the form and shape of a man. Atlas was a very skilful astronomer and astrologer: this probably gave rise to the fable. His supporting heaven on his shoulder is explained, from the circumstance of the top of the mountain being lost in the clouds. Its top, or summit, was covered with perpetual snow. Hence, *nix infusa tegit humeros.*

248. *Cui:* in the sense of *cujus.*

250. *Mento senis:* from the chin of the old man.

252. *Cyllenius:* Cyllenius moving (*nitens*) on equal or balanced wings, stopped. This was a name of Mercury, from *Cyllene,* in Arcadia, the place of his birth. He was the son of Maia, the daughter of Atlas, by Jupiter.

254. *Similis avi.* The whole of this passage is in imitation of Homer, Odys. Lib. v. 43. The bird here alluded to, is supposed to be the coot, or cormorant.

256. *Volabat.* This and the two following lines, Heyne marks as spurious. They were probably left in an unfinished state. Bentley would alter *volabat* to *legebat*, which

Litus arenosum Libyæ, ventosque secabat,
Materno veniens ab avo Cyllenia proles.
  Ut primùm alatis tetigit magalia plantis,
Æneam fundantem arces, ac tecta novantem
Conspicit: atque illi stellatus iaspide fulvâ
Ensis erat, Tyrioque ardebat murice læna
Demissa ex humeris: dives quæ munera Dido
Fecerat, et tenui telas discreverat auro.
Continuò invadit: Tu nunc Carthaginis altæ
Fundamenta locas, pulchramque uxorius urbem
Extruis! heu, regni rerumque oblite tuarum!
Ipse Deûm tibi me claro demittit Olympo
Regnator, cœlum et terras qui numine torquet:
Ipse hæc ferre jubet celeres mandata per auras:
Quid struis? aut quâ spe Libycis teris otia terris?
Si te nulla movet tantarum gloria rerum,
Nec super ipse tuâ moliris laude laborem;
Ascanium surgentem et spes hæredis Iüli
Respice: cui regnum Italiæ Romanaque tellus
Debentur. Tali Cyllenius ore locutus,
Mortales visus medio sermone reliquit,
Et procul in tenuem ex oculis evanuit auram.
  At verò Æneas aspectû obmutuit amens;
Arrectæque horrore comæ; et vox faucibus hæsit.
Ardet abire fugâ, dulcesque relinquere terras,
Attonitus tanto monitu imperioque Deorum.
Heu! quid agat? quo nunc reginam ambire furentem
Audeat affatu? quæ prima exordia sumat?
Atque animum nunc huc celerem, nunc dividit illuc;
In partesque rapit varias, perque omnia versat.

lenia proles veniens ab materno avo volabat arenosum litus Libyæ, inter terras cœlumque, secabatque ventos

280. Comæ *sunt* arrectæ

NOTES.

is the reading of Davidson; but without sufficient authority. Between heaven and earth, he flew along the sandy shore, and cut the winds.

258. *Ab materno avo.* Mercury was the son of Maia, the daughter of Atlas, which made him his grandfather on his mother's side. *Cyllenia proles:* simply, Mercury.

259. *Magalia:* neu. plu. either the huts of the African shepherds, mentioned Geor. iii. 340, or the towers and buildings of Carthage erected on the spot where the *magalia* once stood.

261. *Ensis erat illi stellatus:* there was to him a sword studded with yellow jasper. The hilt and scabbard were studded with gems, sparkling like stars, particularly with jaspers. Servius informs us it was a received opinion that there was a virtue in the jasper-stone, to assist orators in their pleadings, and that Gracchus wore one of them for that purpose.

262. *Læna.* This was a thick double garment—a cassock. *Ardebat:* in the sense of *fulgebat.*

264. *Discreverat telas:* had distinguished the web with a small thread of gold. Ruæus says, *distinxerat.*

265. *Invadit:* in the sense of *alloquitur.*

266. *Uxorius:* a slave to your wife. It refers to the pron. *tu*, understood.

267. *Oblite:* the voc. of *oblitus*, agreeing with *Æneas*, understood.

271. *Teris otia:* you waste your time. *Struis:* in the sense of *facis*, vel *paras.*

276. *Tali ore:* in the sense of *talibus verbis.*

277. *Reliquit:* in the sense of *mutavit.* Mercury had assumed a human form, *mortales visus*, in his conference with Æneas; but as soon as he had ended his speech, *in medio sermone*, and before Æneas had time to make any reply, he left, changed, or put it off, and vanished from his eyes. *Sermo* is properly a conference between two or more persons, and, when one only has spoken, it is not complete or finished.

279. *Amens:* in the sense of *attonitus* vel *stupefactus.*

283. *Quo affatu:* in what words—by what address. *Ambire:* to speak to—to address.

285. *Dividit:* in the sense of *vertit.*

Hæc alternanti potior sententia visa est.
Mnesthea Sergestumque vocat, fortemque Cloanthum:

289. *Jubet ut* taciti aptent classem.

Classem aptent taciti, sociosque ad litora cogant,
Arma parent; et, quæ sit rebus causa novandis,
Dissimulent: sese intereà, quando optima Dido
Nesciat, et tantos rumpi non speret amores,

293. Intereà *statuit* sese tentaturum aditus, et quæ *sint* mollissima tempora fandi; quis modus *sit* dexter rebus *conficiendis*

Tentaturum aditus, et quæ mollissima fandi
Tempora; quis rebus dexter modus. Ocyùs omnes
Imperio læti parent, ac jussa facessunt.
At regina dolos (quis fallere possit amantem?)
Præsensit, motusque excepit prima futuros,
Omnia tuta timens. Eadem impia Fama furenti
Detulit armari classem, cursumque parari.
Sævit inops animi, totamque incensa per urbem

301. *Talis* qualis Thyas, excita

Bacchatur: qualis commotis excita sacris
Thyas, ubi audito stimulant trieterica Baccho
Orgia, nocturnusque vocat clamore Cithæron.
Tandem his Æneam compellat vocibus ultrò:

305. O perfide *homo*, sperâsti te posse

Dissimulare etiam sperâsti, perfide, tantum
Posse nefas, tacitusque meâ decedere terra?
Nec te noster amor, nec te data dextera quondam,
Nec moritura tenet crudeli funere Dido?
Quin etiam hyberno moliris sidere classem,
Et mediis properas Aquilonibus ire per altum,

311. O crudelis *hospes!* Quid? si *tu* non peteres

Crudelis! Quid? si non arva aliena domosque
Ignotas peteres, et Troja antiqua maneret;
Troja per undosum peteretur classibus æquor?

NOTES.

287. *Hæc alternanti:* this plan seemed the better to him, wavering in mind, and examining what had best be done in his present situation. Ruæus says *consilium*, for *sententia*.

293. *Aditus:* the avenues or passages to her heart. *Quæ:* what might be the fittest or softest moments of addressing her, to obtain her consent. *Rebus:* for effecting his purposes.

298. *Excepit:* heard—found out. *Timens omnia tuta:* fearing all things when even safe—fearing danger when all things are safe. *Furenti:* in the sense of *ad aures furentis*, sive *amantis*. *Impia:* in the sense of *sæva*, says Heyne. *Detulit:* in the sense of *nuntiavit*.

300. *Inops animi:* devoid of reason.

301. *Qualis Thyas:* as a bacchanal roused at the moving of the sacred symbols, &c. *Servius* informs us that *commovere sacra* was a phrase used by the Romans to signify the opening of the solemnities of particular divinities, on their high festival days; when their sacred symbols were removed from their temples, in order to be carried about in pompous procession. This was particularly the case in celebrating the *Orgia*, or mysteries of Bacchus, when the statues of that god were removed from his temples, and carried about in procession by his frantic votaries. The mysteries of Bacchus were celebrated every third year: hence they are called *trieterica*.

302. *Thyas:* a bacchanal; from a Greek word signifying to roar about in wild and frantic disorder.

303. *Nocturnus Cithæron.* Cithæron was a mountain in Beotia sacred to Bacchus. Here his mysteries were celebrated in the most distinguished manner by his infatuated followers. They were, for the most part, celebrated in the night. Hence *nocturnus Cithæron. Eam* is understood after *vocat.*

307. *Dextera quondam data:* thy right hand once given. This alludes to their marriage. Supra, 172. *Tenet* is to be supplied, or repeated, with each of the preceding nominatives.

309. *Moliris classem:* do you prepare your fleet in the winter season. The north winds were directly against Æneas in sailing from Africa to Italy. This speech of Dido is tender and persuasive. And since it appeared his purpose to sail to Italy, she endeavors to dissuade him from it, until the winter and contrary winds were over, in the hope that, by repeated instances of her affection and regard, he might be induced to

Mene fugis? per ego has lacrymas dextramque tuam, te,
Quando aliud mihi jam miseræ nihil ipsa reliqui,
Per connubia nostra, per inceptos Hymenæos;
Si benè quid de te merui, fuit aut tibi quicquam
Dulce meum; miserere domûs labentis, et istam,
Oro, si quis adhuc precibus locus, exue mentem.
Te propter Libycæ gentes, Nomadumque tyranni
Odere, infensi Tyrii: te propter eundem
Extinctus pudor, et, quâ solâ sidera adibam,
Fama prior. Cui me moribundam deseris, hospes?
Hoc solum nomen quoniam de conjuge restat.
Quid moror? an mea Pygmalion dum mœnia frater
Destruat? aut captam ducat Getulus Iarbas?
Saltem si qua mihi de te suscepta fuisset
Ante fugam soboles; si quis mihi parvulus aulâ
Luderet Æneas, qui te tantùm ore referret;
Non equidem omninò capta aut deserta viderer.
Dixerat. Ille Jovis monitis immota tenebat
Lumina, et obnixus curam sub corde premebat.
Tandem pauca refert: Ego te, quæ plurima fando
Enumerare vales nunquam, regina, negabo
Promeritam: nec me meminisse pigebit Elisæ;
Dum memor ipse mei, dum spiritus hos reget artus.
Pro re pauca loquar. Nec ego hanc abscondere furto
Speravi, ne finge, fugam; nec conjugis unquam

314. Ego oro te per has lacrymas, tuamque dextram (quando ipsa jam reliqui nihil aliud mihi miseræ) per nostra

317. Aut *si* quicquam meum fuit dulce tibi, miserere

321. Odere me, *et* Tyrii infensi *sunt mihi:* propter te eundem, *meus* pudor extinctus *est*, et *mea* prior fama

327. Siqua soboles saltem suscepta fuisset mihi de te ante fugam; si quis parvulus Æneas

334. O Regina, ego nunquam negabo te promeritam *esse* plurima *de me*, quæ *tu* vales enumerare fando

336. Dum *ego* ipse *ero* memor mei, dum

NOTES.

give over the idea of it altogether. *Sidere:* in the sense of *tempore.*

316. *Hymenæos:* in the sense of *amores. Qui novitate sunt dulces,* says Servius.

319. *Mentem:* purpose—design of leaving me.

320. *Tyranni Nomadum:* the kings of the Numidians. The ancient Romans used the words *tyrannus* and *rex* promiscuously.

321. *Tyrii infensi.* She here alludes to the purpose of her brother to pursue her, as already mentioned.

322. *Pudor extinctus:* my chastity is gone, and my former fame, by which alone I reached the stars.

324. *Quoniam hoc nomen:* since this name alone remains of the husband. It is to be observed that Dido does not address him by the endearing name of husband, but by that of stranger or guest, *hospes:* and she can look upon him in no other light, since he is going to leave her.

325. *Quid moror?* what do I wait for?

328. *Siquis parvulus:* if any little Æneas could play to me in my hall, who only might resemble you in form, I should not, &c. Some ancient copies read *tamen,* instead of *tantùm:* who nevertheless should resemble thee, &c. Some explain the words, *qui te tantùm referret ore;* as if Dido did not wish her son to resemble Æneas in his mind, cruelty and hardness of heart, but only in person and features. But this sentiment does not very well agree with the present strain of her discourse; which is full of tenderness, soft address, and moving expostulation.

Since she could not enjoy his person, it would have been some alleviation of her distress, if she had a son by him, who might only set the image of the father before her eyes, if he could do nothing more. Heyne reads *tamen.* Ruæus says, *qui repræsentarit te tantùm modò vultu.*

330. *Capta.* Ruæus interprets this by *decepta,* which is very harsh, and cannot be the meaning of the speaker. *Capta* refers to what she had said just before, 326 supra, *aut captam ducat Getulus Iarbas.*

In order to paint her distress to Æneas in the liveliest colors, she represents him as the only person, on whom she could depend for protection; and now he was going to abandon her, considers herself forlorn, deserted, and left a prey to her enemies, who had already, as it were, made her their captive. This is the dreary image that haunts her disturbed fancy by day, and her dreams by night. See verse 466. infra.

333. *Refert:* in the sense of *respondet.*

337. *Loquar pauca pro re:* I will speak a few things to the point in question. *Nec ego speravi:* nor did I hope to conceal my departure, &c. This is a reply to Dido's

Prætendi tædas, aut hæc in fœdera veni.
Me si fata meis paterentur ducere vitam
Auspiciis, et sponte meâ componere curas;
Urbem Trojanam primùm dulcesque meorum
Relliquias colerem; Priami tecta alta manerent;
Et recidiva manu posuissem Pergama victis.
Sed nunc Italiam magnam Grynæus Apollo;
Italiam Lyciæ jussêre capessere sortes.
Hic amor, hæc patria est. Si te Carthaginis arces
Phœnissam, Libycæque aspectus detinet urbis:
Quæ tandem Ausoniâ Teucros considere terrâ
Invidia est? et nos fas extera quærere regna.
Me patris Anchisæ, quoties humentibus umbris
Nox operit terras, quoties astra ignea surgunt,
Admonet in somnis et turbida terret imago:
Me puer Ascanius, capitisque injuria chari,
Quem regno Hesperiæ fraudo et fatalibus arvis.
Nunc etiam interpres Divûm, Jove missus ab ipso,
(Testor utrumque caput) celeres mandata per auras

345. Grynæus Apollo *jussit me capessere* magnam Italiam, Lyciæ sortes jussêre *me*

350. Fas *sit* et nos quærere

353. Turbida imago patris Anchisæ admonet et terret me in somnis, quoties

354. Puer Ascanius, injuriaque *ejus* chari capitis, quem fraudo regno Hesperiæ, et fatalibus arvis, *admonet* me.

NOTES.

accusation, *dissimulare etiam*, &c. Verse 305, supra.

339. *Prætendi.* Ruæus takes this in the sense of *Prætexui*, in allusion to verse 172, where it is said of Dido, *prætexit culpam hoc nomine:* nor did I ever cover over our marriage with the name of husband, or come into the bands of Hymen.

Some take *prætendi* in the sense of *prætuli:* nor did I ever bear before me the nuptial torch: in allusion to a Roman custom of carrying lighted torches before the new married couple. In either case, the plain meaning is: I had no part in our nuptials—I consented not to them; nor did I enter into any contract of that nature. This answers Dido's charge against him: *Nec te noster amor*, &c. Verse 305, supra.

340. *Si fata paterentur:* if the destinies had permitted me to lead my life, &c.

This passage furnishes the critics with a pretext to condemn Æneas of ingratitude and insensibility. Was it not enough, say they, for him to let Dido know that he was forced by the Destinies elsewhere, without insulting her with an open declaration, that he preferred other objects to her? But we shall not think Æneas so much to blame, if we consider the true meaning of his words. Dido had urged him to stay; he answers, it is not in his power, because the Destinies opposed it: in proof of it, he assures her that if they had left him to his own choice, he would never have left his native country: he would have rebuilt Troy, which now lay in ashes. This is not saying; if I were at liberty, I would forsake you and return, and rebuild Troy; but I would never have formed any other design than that of repairing the desolation of my country. What makes the objection appear the more specious is, that Virgil uses *colerem* for *coluissem;* but there are many instances where the imperfect of the sub. has the same signification with the plup., and it is plain that it has in the present instance, both from the sense, and the use of *posuissem* in the following line, with which the preceding verbs are connected. *Auspiciis:* in the sense of *voluntate. Curas:* in the sense of *negotia*, says Heyne.

344. *Recidiva:* rebuilt—raised up after a fall. *Posuissem:* in the sense of *restituissem*.

345. *Grynæus Apollo.* The epithet *Grynæus* was given to Apollo from *Gryna*, a city of *Æolia*, near which was a grove called *Grynæum*, where Apollo had an oracle of great antiquity, and also a splendid temple.

346. *Lyciæ sortes. Lycia*, a maritime country of *Asia Minor*, in which was the city *Patara*, where Apollo had a famous temple and oracle. This and some other *Oracles* were called *Sortes*, because they determined the fate of the person by casting or drawing lots, throwing dice, or by some such method, which was thought to be under the immediate direction of the god.

350. *Fas.* This word properly signifies a divine law—what is right or lawful—also a duty towards God. *Et*, often, as here, hath the sense of *etiam*, vel *quoque*.

355. *Fatalibus arvis:* fields destined to him by fate.

Æneas had all along been directed to go to Italy, under the assurance of a peaceful settlement. This country the gods had destined to him.

357. *Testor utrumque caput:* I call to witness each god, viz. Mercury and Jove.

Detulit. Ipse Deum manifesto in lumine vidi
Intrantem muros, vocemque his auribus hausi.
Desine meque tuis incendere, teque querelis:
Italiam non sponte sequor
  Talia dicentem jamdudum aversa tuetur,
Huc illuc volvens oculos, totumque pererrat
Luminibus tacitis, et sic accensa profatur:
Nec tibi Diva parens, generis nec Dardanus auctor,
Perfide, sed duris genuit te cautibus horrens
Caucasus, Hyrcanæque admôrunt ubera tigres.
Nam quid dissimulo ? aut quæ me ad majora reservo ?
Num fletu ingemuit nostro ? num lumina flexit ? [est ?
Num lachrymas victus dedit ? aut miseratus amantem
Quæ quibus anteferam ? jam jam nec maxima Juno,
Nec Saturnius hæc oculis pater aspicit æquis.
Nusquam tuta fides. Ejectum litore, egentem
Excepi, et regni demens in parte locavi:
Amissam classem, socios à morte reduxi.
Heu! furiis incensa feror. Nunc augur Apollo,
Nunc Lyciæ sortes, nunc et Jove missus ab ipso
Interpres Divûm fert horrida jussa per auras.
Scilicet is Superis labor est, ea cura quietos
Sollicitat. Neque te teneo, neque dicta refello.
I, sequere Italiam ventis; pete regna per undas.

362. *Dido* jamdudum aversa tuetur *illum* dicentem

374. Excepi *eum* ejectum litore, egentem *omnium;* et demens locavi *eum* in parte regni

NOTES.

Caput, by synec. is here put for the whole body, or person: so also in line 354. Valpy understands it of Dido and Æneas. But he is singular in this. Ruæus says, *utrumque Deum.*

359. *Hausi his auribus:* I drew his voice into these ears—I heard his voice. This is a pleonasmus common to most languages. It adds strength to the affirmation.

360. *Incendere:* to trouble—afflict.

362. *Aversa:* in the sense of *infensa.*

363. *Pererrat:* surveys him all over.

364. *Tacitis:* steady—fixed.

365. *Nec tibi Diva*, &c. Dido, finding Æneas deaf to all her entreaties, after recalling all the fine things she had said of him, verse 12 *et sequens*, breaks forth into the most bitter invectives: Nor is a goddess your parent—nor Dardanus the founder of your race; but frightful Caucasus brought you forth among its hard rocks, and the Hyrcanian tigers gave you suck.

Caucasus: a very inhospitable mountain, which divides Scythia from India. It lies between the Caspian and Euxine seas. *Hyrcaniæ tigres:* Hyrcania, a country in Asia, anciently a part of Parthia, lying between *Media* on the west, and *Margiana* on the east; and having the Caspian sea on the north. It is subject to the Persians. *Hodie, Tabarestan.* This country was infested with the most savage beasts. *Admôrunt:* they moved their teats to you.

368. *Majora:* in the sense of *majores injurias.*

369. *Num ingemuit nostro:* did he sigh at my tears? did he move his eyes, &c. This refers to 331 supra: *Ille Jovis monitis immota tenebat lumina.*

371. *Quæ quibus anteferam:* what things can I mention before these? Ruæus says: *Inter quæ omnia signa immanitatis, quænam aliis majora dicam.* Valpy says: how shal. I express myself? to which feeling shall I first give utterance? But the words will bear another meaning: before whom can I carry these things? viz. my complaints. To this we are led from considering what follows; as if Dido had said: to whom can I apply for redress? since neither powerful Juno, nor father Jove regards my sufferings with equal eyes. There is justice neither in heaven nor earth.

373. *Ejectum:* shipwrecked.

375. *Reduxi:* in the sense of *servavi.* See Æn. vii. 431. *Amissam:* in the sense of *quassatam.*

376. *Nunc augur Apollo.* She here alludes to what Æneas had said before, verse 345, et sequens. *Feror:* in the sense of *rapior.*

381 *I, sequere Italiam ventis*, &c. This Quintilian gives as an instance of the ironical style. Nothing is more in character of an injured lover, than to order him to do the very thing, which was contrary to her

382. Spero equidem te hausurum supplicia *in* mediis scopulis, et sæpe vocaturum Dido nomine, si pia numina possunt *efficere* quid

387. Hæc fama *tuarum pœnarum* veniet mihi sub imos

390. Linquens *eum* cunctantem metû, et

395. Labefactus *quoad* animum magno amore, tamen exsequitur jussa

401. Cernas *Trojanos* migrantes, ruentesque

402. Ac veluti cùm formicæ memores hyemis populant ingentem acervum farris, reponuntque *in* tecto

Spero equidem mediis, si quid pia numina possunt,
Supplicia hausurum scopulis, et nomine Dido
Sæpe vocaturum. Sequar atris ignibus absens
Et, cùm frigida mors animâ seduxerit artus,
Omnibus umbra locis adero. Dabis, improbe, pœnas:
Audiam, et hæc Manes veniet mihi fama sub imos.
His medium dictis sermonem abrumpit, et auras
Ægra fugit, seque ex oculis avertit et aufert,
Linquens multa metu cunctantem et multa parantem
Dicere. Suscipiunt famulæ, collapsaque membra
Marmoreo referunt thalamo, stratisque reponunt.
At pius Æneas, quanquam lenire dolentem
Solando cupit, et dictis avertere curas;
Multa gemens, magnoque animum labefactus amore.
Jussa tamen Divûm exsequitur, classemque revisit.
Tum verò Teucri incumbunt, et litore celsas
Deducunt toto naves: natat uncta carina;
Frondentesque ferunt remos, et robora sylvis
Infabricata, fugæ studio.
Migrantes cernas, totâque ex urbe ruentes.
Ac veluti ingentem formicæ farris acervum
Cùm populant, hyemis memores, tectoque reponunt:
It nigrum campis agmen, prædamque per herbas

NOTES.

inclinations. Servius observes too, that Dido commands in a way that implies dissuasion, by mentioning the winds and the waves, which served to remind him of his danger; and by using the word *sequere*, as if Italy fled from him.

382. *Spero equidem:* I hope indeed you will suffer punishment among the intervening rocks, &c. *Hausurum:* part. fut. of *haurio:* to drink. This seems to be used in allusion to the death which she hoped he would die, that is, by drowning. This was reckoned the peculiar punishment reserved by Heaven for perfidious lovers. *Dido:* a Greek acc. of the contracted nouns.

384. *Absens sequar*, &c. The meaning is: that the remembrance of Dido, whom he had abandoned, though absent, would still haunt his guilty mind, like a grim fury. This satisfaction she should have in life; and when death should separate her soul and body, and her ghost, *umbra*, should be at liberty to range over the universe, it should also haunt him wherever he went. *Atris ignibus* refers probably to the representation of the furies, armed with torches; which Cicero explains of the stings and torments of a guilty conscience.

386. *Umbra adero:* I, a shade, or ghost, will be present with you, &c.

387. *Hæc fama veniet:* this news shall come to me under the lowest shades. The ancients observed a threefold distinction in the immortal part of man, viz.: the *Umbra*, phantom or shade, which commonly frequented the place where the body was buried; or haunted those abodes to which it had been accustomed in life: the *Manes*, which were confined to the lower regions; and the *Spiritus*, which returned to heaven, its original abode. *Manes* is frequently taken for the place of the dead, by meton. which is the meaning here.

388. *Auras:* in the sense of *lucem.*

389. *Ægra fugit auras:* faint, she fled the light—she withdrew from further conference with Æneas, into her private apartment. Here, quite overcome, she fainted, as we may suppose, when her servants came to her aid, and placed her upon her bed. "She withdrew from the light to her apartment," says Valpy. Some think she fainted quite away, and ceased to breathe; but this is not consistent with what follows: *avertit et aufert*, &c.

390. *Multa.* The *multa* in the preceding part of the line, appears entirely expletive.

393. *Dolentem:* referring to Dido. Some copies have *dolorem*, as Heyne informs us.

398. *Deducunt:* launch the lofty ships along the whole shore.

399. *Ferunt remos:* they bring from the woods green (unwrought) oars, and rough timber; such was their hurry and impatience to be gone. *Frondentes:* covered with leaves—not even stripped of their leaves.

403. *Tecto:* in their cells, or holes

Convectant calle angusto: pars grandia trudunt
Obnixæ frumenta humeris: pars agmina cogunt,
Castigantque moras: opere omnis semita fervet.
Quis tibi tunc, Dido, cernenti talia sensus?
Quosve dabas gemitus, cùm litora fervere latè
Prospiceres arce ex summa, totumque videres
Misceri ante oculos tantis clamoribus æquor?
Improbe amor, quid non mortalia pectora cogis!
Ire iterum in lachrymas, iterum tentare precando
Cogitur, et supplex animos submittere amori;
Ne quid inexpertum, frustrà moritura, relinquat.
Anna, vides toto properari litore: circùm
Undique convenêre: vocat jam carbasus auras,
Puppibus et læti nautæ imposuêre coronas.
Hunc ego si potui tantum sperare dolorem—
Et perferre, soror, potero. Miseræ hoc tamen unum
Exsequere, Anna, mihi: solam nam perfidus ille
Te colere, arcanos etiam tibi credere sensus;
Sola viri molles aditus et tempora nôras.
I, soror, atque hostem supplex affare superbum:

408. Quis sensus *erat* tunc tibi

410. Videresque totum æquor misceri

412. Quid non cogis mortalia pectora *perpetrare*

419. O soror, si ego potui sperare hunc tantum dolorem, *potui perferre;* et potero perferre *eum.*

421. Nam ille perfidus *homo solebat* colere te solam, etiam credere arcanos sensus tibi: *tu* sola nôras molles aditus

NOTES.

405. *Convectant:* they carry often. By using this verb, the poet represents those animals marching backward and forward, and returning frequently to their cells, full laden with their booty, like soldiers reaping the spoils of an enemy. *Pars obnixæ:* a part, shoving with their shoulders, push along the large grains.

406. *Moras:* in the sense of *morantes:* those that delay. Frequent allusions have been made by poets of all ages to the ants, as examples of industry, wisdom, and foresight. "Go to the ant, thou sluggard, consider her ways, and be wise," says Solomon. Modern observation has not discovered in them any such instances of industry. On certain days they carry out of their cells, and expose to the warmth of the sun, their eggs; but we find no store of provisions laid up against approaching want. For during the cold season of the year, they lie in a torpid state, and require no food.

409. *Fervere:* to be all in a bustle—to be busily occupied.

412. *Improbe:* in the sense of *crudelis*, vel *vehemens.*

414. *Cogitur ire iterum:* she is forced again to go into tears, again to try him by supplication, &c. As the poet had used *cogis* just before, so here he repeats the same word, and shows the constraining power of love in Dido's conduct—she is forced, in spite of her pride, her resentment, her resolutions, and her imprecations.

Animos. Animus, in the plu. properly signifies the affections or passions of the mind. The meaning of the passage is: she is forced again to have recourse to tears, again to try him with prayers, and to submit her passions, her resentment, her pride, and her indignation, to love—to give up all to the superior power and efficacy of her love.

415. *Moritura frustrà.* Commentators are not agreed upon the meaning of the word *frustrà* in this place. Servius connects it with *inexpertum.* The meaning then will be: that she might not leave any thing unattempted, though in vain; since she was resolved to die. But it is more like a lover to entertain some glimmering hope as long as the dear object is within reach. The better meaning is: lest by leaving any thing unattempted, or untried, she should die in vain—she should seem to throw away her life.

416. *Properari:* there is a hastening, stir, or bustle around on the whole shore. This verb is used impersonally.

418. *Nautæ imposuere:* the joyous mariners have placed garlands on the sterns. It was a custom among sailors to deck the sterns of the ship, both at sailing and landing. The reason for this was, that on the sterns was a chapel in honor of the gods *Petæci*, who were considered the patrons and protectors of the ship.

419. *Si ego potui sperare*, &c. Ruæus obscures this, and the following line, by connecting them closely together. It is plain there is an ellipsis of the words *potui perferre*, which must be supplied This sudden and abrupt transition is perfectly agreeable to the temper of Dido's mind, and shows the propriety of *potero* being in the future: which otherwise cannot be justified on any principles of language.

421. *Exsequere:* do—perform.

422. *Colere:* in the sense of *amare.*

424. *Hostem.* This word sometimes was used by the ancients in the sense of *hospes*

425. Ego non juravi Aulide cum Danais exscindere Trojanam urbem, misi-ve

Non ego cum Danais Trojanam exscindere gentem
Aulide juravi, classemve ad Pergama misi:
Nec patris Anchisæ cineres Manesve revelli.
Cur mea dicta negat duras demittere in aures?
Quò ruit? extremum hoc miseræ det munus amanti:
Expectet facilemque fugam, ventosque ferentes.
Non jam conjugium antiquum, quod prodidit, oro;
Nec pulchro ut Latio careat, regnumque relinquat
Tempus inane peto, requiem spatiumque furori;
Dum mea me victam doceat fortuna dolere.
Extremam hanc oro veniam: miserere sororis!
Quam mihi cùm dederit, cumulatum morte remittam.

NOTES.

a guest or stranger. Cicero says: *Apud majores nostros, is dicebatur hostis, quem nunc peregrinus dicemus.*

426. *Aulide:* abl. of *Aulis*, a town upon the strait, which separates Eubœa from Beotia, nearly opposite Chalcis. Here the Greeks, on their way to the siege of Troy, took an oath never to return to their country, till they had destroyed that city.

427. *Revelli:* in the sense of *violavi.*

428. *Demittere:* to admit—receive.

430. *Ferentes:* in the sense of *secundos. Munus:* benefit—favor.

431. *Non jam oro:* I do not now plead our former marriage, which he hath violated. *Antiquus* sometimes signifies, honorable. This is the sense Mr. Davidson gives to the word in this place.

433. *Peto inane tempus:* I ask a little time as a respite, and a space for (allaying) my love. *Ad extinguendum amorem*, says Ruæus.

435. *Veniam:* request—favor.

436. *Quam mihi cùm.* This verse has very much perplexed commentators, and divided their opinions. The readings, also, are various. Ruæus' reading is most generally approved. He makes the following comment upon the passage: *Cùm contulerit mihi hoc beneficium paulò longioris moræ, hanc extremam gratiam, remittam illum, sinam abire, et adjiciam meam mortem, quasi cumulum votis ejus.*

The meaning of this much disputed passage will in a great measure depend upon the reading either of *cumulatum* or *cumulatam.* Servius reads: *Quam mihi cùm dederis, cumulatam morte relinquam*, referring to her sister Anna. *Morte relinquam*, he takes in the sense of *sola morte relinquam te.* Here *cumulatam* is made to agree with the pron. *te.* But of this it is difficult to make any sense. Nor will it be easier, if we refer the *cumulatam* to *veniam*, as some commentators have done. Heyne reads: *Quam mihi cùm dederis, cumulatam morte remittam*, referring likewise to Anna. *Cumulatam remittam*, he takes in the sense of *cumulatè referam*, and *morte* in the sense of *antequam moriar*, vel *grata ero per totam vitam usque ad mortem.* This must appear to the most superficial reader a forced and unwarranted exposition; and nothing but the difficulty attending the reading could have led that learned commentator into it. Valpy observes of this exposition of Heyne, that "though stated by him with considerable confidence, it appears forced and improbable."

If we consider the passage as referring to Æneas, it will be rendered easier. In this case, we must read *cumulatum.* Ruæus considers it in this view, but appears to have mistaken the sense of *cumulatum*, and thereby given to the words, *cumulatum morte remittam*, a turn which they will hardly bear. *Adjiciam meam mortem, quasi cumulum votis ejus*, says he. By *adjiciam meam mortem*, we are to understand that Dido informed her sister of her resolution to kill herself, and that she makes a direct declaration to that effect. But from the subsequent part of the story, it appears to have been her anxious solicitude to conceal from her that desperate resolution. And, by *cumulum votis ejus*, we are given to understand that her death was an object of desire to Æneas—that it would afford him pleasure, and be a source of gratification to him. But this is altogether inconsistent with those feelings which he manifested towards her, verse 393 supra, et sequens; and also with those tender expressions of his in the sixth book, when he met her in the regions below. See verse 450, et sequens.

Hortensius reads *cumulatum*, and takes it in the sense of *abundè pensatum:* abundantly, or fully compensated, or requited.

Dido had besought Æneas to stay a short time longer with her, till the weather should be more favorable for his departure, since he was resolved to leave her; and till she should bring her mind the better to bear his loss. This was the *extremam veniam*, the last, the only favor she asked of him; and if granted to her, she would dismiss him, or

Talibus orabat, talesque miserrima fletus
Fertque refertque soror: sed nullis ille movetur
Fletibus, aut voces ullas tractabilis audit.
Fata obstant; placidasque viri Deus obstruit aures.
Ac velut annoso validam cùm robore quercum
Alpini Boreæ, nunc hinc, nunc flatibus illinc
Eruere inter se certant; it stridor, et altè
Consternunt terram concusso stipite frondes:
Ipsa hæret scopulis: et quantùm vertice ad auras
Æthereas, tantùm radice in Tartara tendit.
Haud secùs assiduis hinc atque hinc vocibus heros
Tunditur, et magno persentit pectore curas:
Mens immota manet; lachrymæ volvuntur inanes.
Tum verò infelix fatis exterrita Dido
Mortem orat: tædet cœli convexa tueri.
Quò magis inceptum peragat, lucemque relinquat;
Vidit, thuricremis cùm dona imponeret aris,
Horrendum dictu! latices nigrescere sacros;

441. Ac velut cum Alpini Boreæ nunc hinc, nunc illinc certant inter se flatibus eruere quercum validam annoso robore.

445. Tendit tantùm radice ad Tartara, quantùm vertice *tendit* ad æthereas auras.

453. Cùm imponeret dona thuricremis aris, vidit sacros latices.

NOTES.

consent to his departure, fully compensated or requited for the favor and indulgence, by her death.

Dido here conforms to the usual language of disappointed lovers, who suppose they confer the greatest possible favor upon those they love, by dying for their sake. See Ecl. viii. verses 59 and 60. The most weighty objection to this interpretation is, that it includes a declaration of her death; but it does not necessarily imply, that it would be by her own hand. Her grief, sorrow, and affliction, in consequence of his loss, might become insupportable, and bring her to the grave.

But, after all the ingenuity displayed by commentators, *cumulatum*, perhaps, is to be taken in its usual acceptation. *Cumulatum morte remittam:* I will dismiss him loaded, or oppressed, with my death—with the reflection and consciousness of being the cause of my death, by leaving me in this cruel manner.

This appears the least objectionable of any solution that has been proposed. Nor does it necessarily include the idea of suicide. Dido may be supposed to declare, that though he should comply with her request, and tarry with her till the weather became favorable for his departure, yet that she should eventually be unable to support his loss, and that grief and disappointment would be the cause of her death.

For this suggestion, I acknowledge my obligations to a distinguished classical scholar of our own country.

438. *Miserrima soror:* her sister, most distressed, carries, and again carries, such tears—such piteous messages. *Preces cum lachrymis*, says Heyne.

439. *Tractabilis:* in the sense of *exorabilis.*

442. *Boreæ.* The north wind is here called Alpine, from the circumstance of the Alps lying north of Mantua, and a great part of Italy. And the poet would give us to understand that the north wind had its seat among those mountains, and from thence descended in storms, and mighty blasts.

446. *Tantùm radice.* This is said according to the opinion of those naturalists, who suppose the roots of the tree equal to the body. *Tartara:* neu. plu. properly the lowest part of hell—that place which the poets assign for the punishment of offenders. *In Tartara:* toward Tartarus—downward. It is opposed to *ad æthereas auras:* toward heaven—upward.

448. *Curas:* in the sense of *dolores.*

449. *Inanes:* his tears are useless—unavailing, both with respect to himself and Dido; as they produced not the effect which she desired, and altered not his steadfast resolution.

451. *Tædet:* it irketh her to behold the canopy of heaven. *Convexa*, neu. plu. of *convexus*, taken as a substantive. It appears, hence, that *convexus* in Latin, has a different meaning from *convex* in English. The convex face of heaven to us is invisible. It is the vaulted arch, or canopy alone, which we can behold—the *cava cœli convexitas*, as Dr. Clark explains it. So, also: *in convexo nemorum*, in the bosom, or under the shelter of the bending groves. And Justin, speaking of the actions of Xerxes, says: *montes in planum ducebat, et convexa vallium æquabat.*

Fusaque in obscœnum se vertere vina cruorem.
Hoc visum nulli, non ipsi effata sorori.
Prætereà, fuit in tectis de marmore templum
Conjugis antiqui, miro quod honore colebat,
Velleribus niveis et festâ fronde revinctum.
Hinc exaudiri voces et verba vocantis
Visa viri, nox cùm terras obscura teneret:
Solaque culminibus ferali carmine bubo
Sæpe queri, et longas in fletum ducere voces.
Multaque præthereà vatum prædicta piorum
Terribili monitu horrificant. Agit ipse furentem
In somnis ferus Æneas: semperque relinqui
Sola sibi, semper longam incomitata videtur
Ire viam, et Tyrios desertâ quærere terrâ.
Eumenidum veluti demens videt agmina Pentheus,
Et solem geminum, et duplices se ostendere Thebas:
Aut Agamemnonius scenis agitatus Orestes,
Armatam facibus matrem et serpentibus atris
Cùm fugit; ultricesque sedent in limine Diræ.
  Ergò ubi concepit furias, evicta dolore,
Decrevitque mori; tempus secum ipsa modumque

456. Effata *est* hoc visum nulli, non *etiam*

460. Hinc voces, et verba viri vocantis *eam* visa *sunt* exaudiri, cùm obscura nox teneret terras: solaque bubo sæpe *visa est* queri ferali carmine *super* culminibus, et ducere

466. Æneas ipse ferus agit *eam* furentem in somnis; semperque videtur sibi relinqui sola, semper incomitata ire longam viam, et quærere

NOTES.

455. *Obscœnum cruorem.* Servius explains *obscœnum*, by *mali ominis*, of bad omen. So says Heyne. *Vina fusa:* the wine poured out upon the altar, to turn, &c.

457. *Fuit in tectis:* there was in the palace a marble chapel of her former husband. By *templum*, some understand the sepulchre of Sichæus, which Dido had caused to be built in her palace, and which she had consecrated to his memory. Others think it to have been a *chapel*, or *shrine*, sacred to his memory. Others again take it to be an image or statue sacred to his memory. Servius thinks Virgil had reference to the custom of the Romans, of the bride, when she came to the door of her husband's house, which was garnished with flowers and leaves, binding about the posts woollen fillets, and washing them over with melted tallow to keep out enchantments and sorcery. According to him, Dido, in building this temple to Sichæus, had devoted herself to him forever, by performing the same nuptial rites towards him as if he had been living; and thereby signified her resolution never to marry again. But this appears a refinement. It is much easier to consider it a reference to the general custom of adorning the door-posts of temples with fillets of wool, especially on holy-days.

461. *Viri:* of her husband calling her.

462. *Bubo:* the owl. *Ferali carmine:* in a mournful strain—cry. *Sola:* some copies have *sera*, in reference to the time of her singing; which is generally *late* at night. *Voces:* notes.

464. *Piorum.* Some copies have *priorum:* but *piorum* is the best. It is a proper epithet of prophets. Heyne reads *piorum*.

469. *Eumenidum:* as crazy Pentheus sees bands of furies, and a double sun, and Thebes to show itself double. The poet here compares the fury of Dido with that of the frantic *Pentheus* and *Orestes*. Pentheus was king of Thebes in Beotia, son of Echion, and grandson of Cadmus. He prevented his subjects from worshipping Bacchus, and commanded that god to be put in prison; for which he was deprived of his senses by the god. After this, he went to mount Citheron, where the bacchanals were celebrating their orgies. As soon as they saw him, they set upon him, and tore him in pieces. See Ovid Met. 3. 700. Virgil here speaks of the furies as being an army (*agmina*) whereas they were only three in number. See Geor. i. 278.

470. *Et solem.* This line is taken from Euripedes.

471. *Orestes.* He was the son of Agamemnon. He is said to have been haunted by the ghost of his mother, *Clytemnestra*, whom he had slain, and by the furies. He went to the oracle of Apollo, at Delphi, to consult in the business, and was informed that he had been acquitted by the court of *Areopagus*, at Athens. Whereupon the furies blocked up the door, so that he could not get out. He, however, made his escape. Hence the expression, *sedent limine:* they sit in the door. See Æn. iii. 331. *Agitatus:* acted, or exhibited on the stage.

474. *Concepit:* received or admitted.

Exigit; et, mœstam dictis aggressa sororem,
Consilium vultu tegit, ac spem fronte serenat;
Inveni, germana, viam, gratare sorori,
Quæ mihi reddat eum, vel eo me solvat amantem.
Oceani finem juxta Solemque cadentem,
Ultimus Æthiopum locus est: ubi maximus Atlas
Axem humero torquet, stellis ardentibus aptum.
Hinc mihi Massylæ gentis monstrata sacerdos,
Hesperidum templi custos, epulasque draconi
Quæ dabat, et sacros servabat in arbore ramos,
Spargens humida mella, soporiferumque papaver.
Hæc se carminibus promittit solvere mentes,
Quas velit; ast aliis duras immittere curas;
Sistere aquam fluviis, et vertere sidera retrò:
Nocturnosque ciet Manes. Mugire videbis
Sub pedibus terram, et descendere montibus ornos.
Testor, chara, Deos et te, germana, tuumque
Dulce caput, magicas invitam accingier artes.
Tu secreta pyram tecto interiore sub auras

487. **Hæc promittit se** ***posse*** **solvere** ***illas*** **mentes,** quas velit; **ast immittere** duras curas aliis

492. *O* chara germana, testor Deos et te, tuumque dulce caput, *me* invitam accingier *ad has*

494. Tu secreta erige pyram *in* interiore tecto sub auras; et superimponas arma viri

NOTES.

476. *Exigit:* she concludes—fixes upon. *Aggressa:* in the sense of *compellans.*

477. *Serenat spem fronte: she brightens,* (or clears up) *hope on her countenance.* She shows it on her countenance. *Vultu:* visage—looks.

481. *Æthiopum.* Æthiopia is properly a country of Africa, now called *Abyssinia.* But the name was frequently applied by the ancients to any country lying in a warm climate. *Æthiops* is compounded of two Greek words, and means a person of a tawny complexion—one scorched by the heat of the sun.

482. *Aptum:* fitted—adorned—bespangled with refulgent stars. See 247, supra. *Axem:* for *cœlum.*

483. *Massylæ gentis.* The *Massyli* or *Masæsyli* were a people between the rivers *Malva* and *Mulucha,* both of which fall into the Mediterranean. Hence the adj. *Massylus. Sacerdos:* in the sense of *saga. Monstrata:* was shown to me. *Est* is understood.

484. *Custos templi Hesperidum.* The gardens of the *Hesperides,* Virgil places in Mauritania, near the shore of the Atlantic, and not far from the town of *Lixus.* There are, however, various opinions respecting their situation. The Hesperides were the fabled daughters of Atlas, or of *Hesperus,* his brother, and the nymph *Hesperis.* Their father gave them gardens, in which were trees producing golden apples. Hercules, at the command of Eurystheus, king of *Mycenæ,* stole the apples, having slain the dragon that kept them. These apples were sacred to Venus.

The truth of the matter is this: the *Hesperides* were shepherdesses of noble birth, whose flocks produced wool of a reddish color, somewhat resembling gold, which Hercules plundered, having slain their keeper, whose name was *Draco.* The Greek word for sheep, signifying also apples, made the poets feign that Hercules stole the apples of the Hesperides: and their keeper's name being *Draco,* led them to pretend they were kept by a dragon. See Ecl. vi. 61.

486. *Soporiferum papaver.* As the dragon was always to be awake, a question arises, how the priestess came to feed him with poppy. To solve this there are several conjectures. Some will have it that poppies mixed with honey, was his food, and had no effect to lay him asleep. Others say it was to procure sleep for him at certain intervals. *Servius* thinks that the poppy, which procures sleep to men, has a contrary effect upon dragons, and keeps them awake. Others again, to avoid this difficulty, make a full stop after *ramos,* connecting this line with the following one. Some again think it is only mentioned to show the skill of the Sorceress, that she was even able to lay the wakeful dragon asleep. But as this animal had a hundred heads, we may suppose that they kept awake and slept by turns. She is said to be the keeper, *custos,* of the temple, because she gave food to the dragon, and supported him.

487. *Solvere mentes:* to free minds from love by her magic rites (*carminibus*) or charms.

493. *Accingier invitam:* that I was unwilling to betake myself to these magic arts. *Accingier:* by paragoge, for *accingi.* The verb here is used in the sense of the Greek middle voice. It has a reflux signification

Erige: et arma viri, thalamo quæ fixa reliquit
Impius, exuviasque omnes, lectumque jugalem,
Quo perii, superimponas. Abolere nefandi
Cuncta viri monumenta jubet monstratque sacerdos.
Hæc effata silet: pallor simul occupat ora.
Non tamen Anna novis prætexere funera sacris
Germanam credit: nec tantos mente furores
Concipit; aut graviora timet, quàm morte Sichæi.
Ergò jussa parat.
At regina, pyrâ penetrali in sede sub auras
Erectâ ingenti, tædis atque ilice sectâ,
Intenditque locum sertis, et fronde coronat
Funereâ: super exuvias, ensemque relictum,
Effigiemque toro locat, haud ignara futuri.
Stant aræ circùm: et crines effusa sacerdos,
Tercentum tonat ore Deos, Erebumque, Chaosque,
Tergeminamque Hecaten, tria virginis ora Dianæ.
Sparserat et latices simulatos fontis Averni;
Falcibus et messæ ad Lunam quæruntur ahenis
Pubentes herbæ, nigri cum lacte veneni.

501. Nec concipit tantos furores *esse in ejus* mente; aut timet graviora quàm *quæ evenerant* morte Sichæi. Ergò parat *quæ* jussa *erant*

504. Ingenti pyrâ erectâ in penetrali sede sub auras, è tædis atque secta ilice

509. Effusa *quoad* crines

NOTES.

495. *Arma viri.* The sword which Æneas left hanging in Dido's bedchamber.

498. *Jubet:* the priestess orders and directs me to burn all the memorials of the cursed man. These she had just mentioned—his sword—his clothes—the bridal bed, &c.

500. *Prætexere:* in the sense of *celare.*

504. *Penetrali sede:* in the inner court—middle of the palace.

505. *Tædis.* The *tæda* or *teda* was a tree of a resinous nature, of which torches were made. The *ilex* was a species of oak called the holm. Of these two kinds of wood the funeral pile was constructed.

506. *Intendit:* in the sense of *cingit.*

508. *Effigiem:* she places his image on the bed upon his clothes and sword.

One of the rites of magic was to prepare an image of the person against whom the enchantment was designed, either of wax or wool, and use it in the same manner as they would have used the person himself if he had been present. Or, *super* may be taken in the sense of *insuper* (moreover;) or *super-locat* may be considered a compound word in the sense of *superimponit.* The meaning will then be, that the image, the clothes, and sword, were placed upon the bed without any reference to their situation.

510. *Tonat ore:* she thunders out with her voice three hundred gods. Servius informs us, that in the sacred rites of *Hecate* in particular, they used to imitate thunder; which gives a reason for the use of the word *tonat. Hortensius* would read *sonat.* We are not to suppose that the priestess invoked the precise number of three hundred gods—that definite number is used for an indefinite number. *Erebum.* Erebus was the son of *Chaos* and *Nox.* For aiding the Titans in their war against the gods, he was changed into a river, and placed in the lowest part of hell. He is one of the infernal gods. *Chaos.* He was the most ancient of the gods, and the father of them all, according to Hesiod. Geor. iv. 347.

511. *Hecaten.* Hecate is called *tergeminam* from the circumstance of her having three names. In heaven she is called *Luna;* on the earth *Diana;* in hell *Proserpina.* Hecate was not so properly her name, as an epithet given her to denote her hundred various qualities; or because she was appeased by a hundred victims. From a Greek word signifying a hundred. The goddess was painted with three heads, one of a *horse,* another of a *dog,* and another of a *man.* Hence *tria ora virginis:* the triple form of the virgin.

512. *Sparserat:* she had sprinkled the fictitious (or substituted) waters of the lake Avernus. In performing magic rites, those materials requisite to the occasion, that could not be conveniently procured, were allowed to be emblematically represented, as in the present case. *Averni.* Avernus, a lake in Campania, fabled to be the entrance of hell. Its waters were of a very noxious quality, which occasioned an unwholesome atmosphere; insomuch so, that it was shunned by birds of every kind. Its name is of Greek origin. See Geor. iv. 493.

514. *Pubentes herbæ* full blown herbs, cut by moonlight, are sought for. The

Quæritur et nascentis equi de fronte revulsus,
Et matri præreptus amor.
Ipsa molâ manibusque piis, altaria juxta,
Unum exuta pedem vinclis, in veste recinctâ,
Testatur moritura Deos, et conscia fati
Sidera: tum, si quod non æquo fœdere amantes
Curæ numen habet justumque memorque, precatur
 Nox erat, et placidum carpebant fessa soporem
Corpora per terras, sylvæque et sæva quiêrant
Æquora: cùm medio volvuntur sidera lapsu:
Cùm tacet omnis ager, pecudes, pictæque volucres,
Quæque lacus latè liquidos, quæque aspera dumis
Rura tenent, somno positæ sub nocte silenti
Lenibant curas, et corda oblita laborum.
At non infelix animi Phœnissa: neque unquam
Solvitur in somnos, oculisve aut pectore noctem
Accipit. Ingeminant curæ, rursusque resurgens
Sævit amor, magnoque irarum fluctuat æstu.
 Sic adeò insistit, secumque ita corde volutat:
En! quid ago? rursusne procos irrisa priores

515. Et amor *equæ* revulsus de fronte nascentis equi, et præreptus matri

517. *Dido* ipsa moritura, exuta *quoad* unum pedem vinclis, in recincta veste, *stans* justa altaria, molâ piisque manibus, testatur Deos, et sidera conscia fati. Tum precatur numen, si quod justumque memorque habet amantes *junctos* non æquo fœdere curæ *sibi*.

526. Quæque latè tenent liquidos lacus, quæque *tenent* rura aspera dumis, *omnes* positæ sub silenti nocte lenibant curas somno; et corda oblita *sunt* laborum.

NOTES.

dews, which were thought to distil from the moon upon herbs, were reckoned favorable for magic. Those herbs, however, were to be cut with brazen sickles, *ahenis falcibus*. *Lacte:* in the sense of *succo*.

516. *Et amor revulsus:* and the love (of the mare) torn from the forehead of a newly foaled colt. The poet here means what is called the *hippomanes;* of which there are two kinds. See Geor. iii. 280. *et sequens.* The one here meant is very different from the one there described. According to the account given of it by the ancients, it was a lump of flesh growing on the forehead of the foal just brought forth, which the mare presently devours, or else she loses all affection for her young, and denies it suck. Its being so greedily sought after by the mother, is the reason of its being called her *love.* The circumstance just mentioned gave rise to the vulgar opinion of its efficacy in philtres, love potions, and magic rites.

518. *Exuta pedem.* It appears from this passage that Dido put herself in the habit of a sorceress. According to Ovid, it was their custom to strip bare one of their feet, and to be clad in a loose flowing robe. Ruæus takes *recincta*, in the sense of *succincta;* but in this he differs from most commentators. Heyne takes it in the sense of *soluta.*

520. *Non æquo fœdere:* by this we are to understand *an inequality* in the love and affection of the parties—in an unequal match: where love is not reciprocated.

522. *Nox erat.* The whole of this description is a most beautiful, and, at the same time, perfect image of nature. Dr. Trapp objects to it as imperfect. But it is to be observed that the poet did not design it as a description of night in general; but only of a calm and serene one, in order that he might set off to greater advantage the opposite image of Dido's anxiety and disquietude. And indeed nothing could give us a more lively idea of her restless situation, than thus to set it forth in opposition to the universal quiet and repose which reigned over all nature beside. She is so far from partaking of the blessings of sleep with the rest of the world, that the silence and solitude of the night, which dispose others to rest, only feed her care, and swell the tumult of her passion.

524. *Lapsu:* in the sense of *cursu.*

527. *Tenent:* in the sense of *incolunt.*

528. *Lenibant curas*, &c. This beautiful line Heyne marks as spurious, and concludes the sentence at *silenti.* It is not found in some ancient MSS.

529. *Phœnissa.* Dido is so called, because she was a native of *Phœnicia*, a country lying on the eastern shore of the Mediterranean; within the boundaries of which was the kingdom of Tyre. The words *leniebat curas* are to be supplied.

530. *Noctem:* in the sense of *quietem.*

532. *Irarum:* passions—affections. *Amor sævit.* Here love is represented as a mighty sea, which had been for some time calm and still; but now begins to rise in furious waves, and rack her soul with a variety of tumultuous passions. *Volutat:* in the sense of *cogitat.*

534. *Rursus-ne irrisa*, &c. Ruæus and Servius take *rursus* in the sense of *vicissim:* shall I in turn have, &c. Dido had rejected the match of Iarbas and others; and shall she now pay court to them, as they had

Experiar? Nomadumque petam connubia supplex,
Quos ego sum toties jam dedignata maritos?
Iliacas igitur classes, atque ultima Teucrûm
Jussa sequar? quiane auxilio juvat antè levatos,
Et benè apud memores veteris stat gratia facti?
Quis me autem, fac velle, sinet? ratibusque superbis
Invisam accipiet? nescis heu, perdita, necdum
Laomedonteæ sentis perjuria gentis?
Quid tum? sola fugâ nautas comitabor ovantes?
An Tyriis, omnique manu stipata meorum,
Insequar? et quos Sidoniâ vix urbe revelli,
Rursus agam pelago, et ventis dare vela jubebo?
Quin morere, ut merita es, ferroque averte dolorem.
Tu lachrymis evicta meis, tu prima furentem
His, germana, malis oneras, atque objicis hosti.
Non licuit thalami expertem sinè crimine vitam
Degere more feræ, tales nec tangere curas?
Non servata fides cineri promissa Sichæo.
Tantos illa suo rumpebat pectore questus.
Æneas celsâ in puppi, jam certus eundi,
Carpebat somnos, rebus jam ritè paratis.
Huic se forma Dei, vultu redeuntis eodem,
Obtulit in somnis, rursusque ita visa monere est;
Omnia Mercurio similis, vocemque, coloremque,

538. Quiane juvat *me eos* antè levatos *fuisse meo* auxilio; et gratia veteris facti stat apud *eos* benè memores *ejus?*

540. Autem fac *me* velle *sequi eos*, quis

543. Quid tum *agendum est? ego-ne* sola fugâ comitabor

544. An stipata Tyriis, omnique manu meorum *civium* insequar *eos*

552. Fides promissa Sichæo cineri non servata *est.*

556. Forma Dei redeuntis eodem vultu obtulit se huic in somnis, visaque est rursus ita monere *eum:* similis Mercurio *quoad* omnia,

NOTES.

formerly done to her? *Irrisa:* mocked—despised. Ruæus says, *contemnenda.*

536. *Dedignata sum:* disdained as husbands.

537. *Ultima:* the lowest—basest.

538. *Quia-ne juvat:* because it *delighted* me formerly, that they should be relieved by my assistance; and the grateful remembrance of my former deed remains with them, duly mindful of it? Dido here speaks ironically. Some copies have *exilio*, in allusion to the friendly retreat which Dido gave to Æneas and his followers: but *auxilio* is the most approved reading.

541. *Invisam:* hated—an object of their aversion. Some copies have *irrisam.* This is the reading of Ruæus. Heyne reads, *invisam*, and assures us it is the best.

542. *Necdum sentis*, &c. Here Dido alludes to the well known story of Laomedon, who defrauded the gods, Neptune and Apollo, of their hire for building the walls of Troy. See Geor. i. 502. *Laomedonteæ:* an adj. in the sense of *Trojanæ.*

543. *Ovantes:* in the sense of *lætantes*, vel *triumphantes.* It is applicable to mariners in general, who usually set out with acclamations of joy: but here it is to be considered in that particular, in which Dido viewed them as triumphing over her in their departure. *Insequar.* Some copies have *inferar.* This is the reading of Heyne, and Valpy after him.

544. *Stipata:* in the sense of *comitata.*

546. *Rursus agam:* shall I again conduct on the sea, those whom with difficulty I forced from the Sidonian city? *Sidonia:* an adj. from *Sidon*, which formed a part of the kingdom of Tyre: here in the sense of *Tyria. Revelli:* this expresses the difficulty of her former enterprise.

248. *Tu, Germana, evicta:* thou, O sister overcome by my tears, thou first, &c. *Furentem:* in the sense of *amantem.* Dido here alludes to the speech of her sister. See verse 32. supra, and following. Anna could not bear to see her pine away in mournful widowhood, and therefore dissuaded her from it, and encouraged a love for Æneas.

550. *Non licuit:* was it not lawful for me, without blame, to lead a life free from the marriage bed, &c. Some copies have *expertam vitam:* a life having experienced the marriage bed. But the other is evidently the most approved reading.

Though Dido here seemingly approves of a single life; by representing it as the life of a savage beast, she in fact condemns it; and insinuates that marriage is the most perfect society, and distinguishes the life of man from that of brute animals.

551. *Tangere:* to know, or experience.

558. *Similis Mercurio omnia:* like Mercury in all things. All the commentators make this god to be Mercury himself, except *Catrou.* He thinks it to be some other god, who assumed the likeness of Mercury.

Et crines flavos, et membra decora juventæ:
Nate Deâ, potes hoc sub casu ducere somnos?
Nec, quæ circumstent te deinde pericula, cernis?
Demens! nec Zephyros audis spirare secundos?
Illa dolos dirumque nefas in pectore versat,
Certa mori, varioque irarum fluctuat æstu.
Non fugis hinc præceps, dum præcipitare potestas?
Jam mare turbari trabibus, sævasque videbis
Collucere faces; jam fervere litora flammis;
Si te his attigerit terris Aurora morantem.
Eia age, rumpe moras: varium et mutabile semper
Fœmina. Sic fatus nocti se immiscuit atræ.
Tum verò Æneas, subitis exterritus umbris,
Corripit è somno corpus, sociosque fatigat:
Præcipites vigilate, viri, et considite transtris:
Solvite vela citi. Deus æthere missus ab alto,
Festinare fugam, tortosque incidere funes,
Ecce iterum stimulat. Sequimur te, sancte Deorum,
Quisquis es, imperioque iterum paremus ovantes.
Adsis, ô, placidusque juves, et sidera cœlo
Dextra feras! Dixit: vaginâque eripit ensem
Fulmineum, strictoque ferit retinacula ferro.
Idem omnes simul ardor habet: rapiuntque, ruuntque·
Litora deseruere: latet sub classibus æquor.
Adnixi torquent spumas, et cœrula verrunt.
Et jam prima novo spargebat lumine terras
Tithoni croceum linquens Aurora cubile:

563. Illa *Dido* certa mori versat dolos

566. Dum potestas *est tibi* præcipitare

576. Ecce Deus missus ab alto æthere iterum stimulat *me* festinare fugam, incidereque tortos funes.

583. Cœrula *maria*

NOTES.

560. *Sub hoc casu:* in this juncture or crisis of affairs.

561. *Deinde:* this appears to be in this place entirely *expletive. Videtur otiosum esse*, says Heyne.

563. *Versat:* in the sense of *meditatur.*

566. *Turbari trabibus:* to be in commotion with ships. Heyne says, *impleri navibus Carthaginiensium:* and Ruæus, *agitari remis.*

567. *Fervere:* to glitter—to shine with flames. The meaning is, that as soon as the morning shall return, Dido will pursue you with her ships, with torches and with flames. You must weigh anchor and be gone.

570. *Fœmina:* a woman is something always variable, and subject to change. This is a singular construction. Mercury here insinuates that hatred may succeed to Dido's love for him; which might induce her to seek revenge. *Umbris:* apparition.

572. *Fatigat:* arouses his companions.

573. *Vigilate:* wake quick—in haste. *Transtris:* the seats or benches on which the rowers sat.

575. *Tortos funes:* the ropes, or cables, by which the ships were moored. Dr. Bentley thinks the *anchors* are intended; but how *tortos* can be applied to them, I see not.

576. *Sancte Deorum:* O holy one of the gods, whoever thou art, &c. This mode of expression is in imitation of the Greeks.

578. *O adsis:* O may thou be propitious.

579. *Dextra sidera:* favorable, or propitious stars in the heavens. *Feras:* give—grant.

580. *Ferit:* in the sense of *secat. Fulmineum:* shining, glittering. Ruæus says, *coruscantem.*

582. *Deseruere litora.* This change of the tense adds much to the description. They *hale off*, and *hurry away;* and no sooner have they done this, than they *have left the shore*, and are completely out to sea.

585. *Et jam Aurora:* and now Aurora, leaving the saffron bed of Tithonus, first spreads the earth over with early light. Tithonus was either the son or brother of Laomedon, king of Troy. On account of his beauty and gracefulness, Aurora fell in love with him, and endued him with immortality; but not thinking to bestow on him perpetual youth and beauty, he grew so weak and exhausted by old age, that he wished for mortality. But the goddess not being able to restore it to him, in pity to his case, changed him into a grasshopper. See Geor. iii. 48. This is a most beautiful circumlocution to denote the early dawn, when the earth becomes first enlightened by the beams of the sun.

Regina è speculis, ut primùm albescere lucem
Vidit, et æquatis classem procedere velis;
Litoraque et vacuos sensit sinè remige portus:
Terque quaterque manu pectus percussa decorum,
Flaventesque abscissa comas: Proh Jupiter! ibit
Hic, ait, et nostris illuserit advena regnis?
Non arma expedient, totâque ex urbe sequentur?
Diripientque rates alii navalibus? ite,
Ferte citi flammas, date vela, impellite remos.
Quid loquor? aut ubi sum? quæ mentem insania mutat?
Infelix Dido! nunc te facta impia tangunt.
Tum decuit, cùm sceptra dabas. En dextra, fidesque!
Quem secum patrios aiunt portare Penates!
Quem subiisse humeris confectum ætate parentem!
Non potui abreptum divellere corpus, et undis
Spargere? non socios, non ipsum absumere ferro
Ascanium, patriisque epulandum apponere mensis?
Verùm anceps pugnæ fuerat fortuna: fuisset.
Quem metui moritura? faces in castra tulissem.
Implêssemque foros flammis: natumque patremque
Cum genere extinxêm: memet super ipsa dedissem.
Sol, qui terrarum flammis opera omnia lustras;
Tuque, harum interpres curarum et conscia, Juno,
Nocturnisque, Hecate, triviis ululata per urbes,

589. Percussa *quoad* decorum pectus manu, abscissaque *quoad* flaventes comas, ait: Proh

593. *Non-ne* alii diripient

597. Decuit *te* tum *cogitare de his*, cùm dabas sceptra *tua perfido homini.* En dextra, fidesque *illius*, quem aiunt

601. Non *potui* absumere socios, non *potui absumere* Ascanium ipsum ferro, apponereque *eum*,

606. *Ego* ipsa dedissem memet super *eos.*

NOTES.

587. *Velis æquatis:* the sails were equally distended on each side of the mast. This shows that the wind blew fair, and directly after them: in nautical phrase, wing and wing.

593. *Diripient alii:* will not others tear my ships from the docks, and go in pursuit of him?

596. *Nunc impia facta.* Mr. Davidson observes that this is the reading of the Cambridge edition, founded on the authority of Probus and the *Codex Mediceus;* and it makes the sense obvious. By *impia facta*, we are to understand the violation of her faith to Sichæus, and her amours with Æneas; by which she brought on herself infamy and disgrace. Now she feels the weight of those actions, and the punishment due to her deeds. Ruæus and others, who read *fata*, take *impia* in the sense of *crudelia. Nunc ultima fata, dura sors, suprema dies instant tibi*, says Ruæus. Heyne and Davidson read *facta.*

599. *Subiisse:* to have carried, or borne upon his shoulders.

600. *Divellere.* There is here an allusion to the manner in which the Bacchanals tore the bodies of Orpheus and Pentheus in pieces.

602. *Apponere:* served him up to be feasted upon at his father's table Reference is here had to the story of Progne, who, to be revenged upon Tereus, for his cruel treatment of her sister Philomela, served up his son Itys for him at a banquet. See Ecl. vi. 78.

603. *Fortuna:* in the sense of *eventus.*

604. *Moritura:* in the sense of *cùm decreverim mori. Castra:* in the sense of *classem.*

605. *Foros:* the decks or hatches of his ships. *Extinxêm:* by syn. for *extinxissem:* in the sense of *interfecissem.*

607. *Sol.* Dido invokes the sun, either because he is the supporter of life in general, or because, surveying all things here below, could be a witness of her wrongs; Juno, because she was the goddess of marriage; and Hecate, because she presided over magic rites; the Furies, because they were the avengers of wrongs. *Flammis:* in the sense of *luce.*

608. *Interpres:* interpreter of these my cares (sorrows) and conscious of my wrongs. Servius takes *interpres* to mean, witness, judge, or arbitress. Ruæus interprets *curarum* by *nuptialium negotiorum.*

609. *Hecate ululata:* Hecate invoked, or called upon, &c. When Pluto ravished Proserpine, or Hecate, her mother Ceres traversed the earth in search of her with lighted torches, stopping at those places where two or three ways met, to invoke her name, which she did with a doleful outcry. Hence it became a custom in her sacred rites, for the matrons, on certain days, to go about the streets and crossways filling the

Et Diræ ultrices, et Dî morientis Elisæ,
Accipite hæc, meritumque malis advertite numen,
Et nostras audite preces. Si tangere portus
Infandum caput, ac terris adnare necesse est;
Et sic fata Jovis poscunt: hic terminus hæret:
At bello audacis populi vexatus et armis,
Finibus extorris, complexu avulsus Iüli,
Auxilium imploret, videatque indigna suorum
Funera: nec, cùm se sub leges pacis iniquæ
Tradiderit, regno aut optatâ luce fruatur;
Sed cadat ante diem, mediâque inhumatus arenâ.
Hæc precor: hanc vocem extremam cum sanguine fundo.
Tum vos, ô Tyrii, stirpem et genus omne futurum
Exercete odiis: cinerique hæc mittite nostro
Munera: nullus amor populis, nec fœdera sunto.
Exoriare aliquis nostris ex ossibus ultor;
Qui face Dardanios ferroque sequare colonos,
Nunc, olim, quocunque dabunt se tempore vires.
Litora litoribus contraria, fluctibus undas
Imprecor, arma armis: pugnent ipsique nepotes.

612. Si necesse est infandum caput tangere portus, ac

615. At vexatus bello et armis audacis populi extorris, *suis* finibus, avulsus complexû Iüli

624. *Esto* nullus amor *his* populis, nec sunto

628. Imprecor litora contraria litoribus, undas *contrarias* fluctibus, arma *contraria* armis

NOTES.

air with shrieks and howlings. *Nocturnis triviis.* The epithet *nocturnis* is used, because the rites of Hecate were celebrated in the night, and in a place where three ways met. See 511, supra.

611. *Advertite:* turn a due regard to my misfortunes. Ruæus and others understand by *malis*, the wicked, to wit, the Trojans. But this seems not to agree with the tenor of the subject. Ruæus says: *applicate numen meritum à sceleratis huc.* Heyne, on the other hand, says: *advertite vestrum numen* (*vim et potestatem*) *contra improbos et impios Trojanos.* Davidson renders the words: turn your divine regard to my wrongs.

613. *Caput:* properly, the head; by synec. the whole body—here, Æneas.

614. *Hæret:* in the sense of *fixus sit.*

615. *At bello vexatus.* It was a prevailing opinion among the ancients, that the prayers of the dying were generally heard, and their last words prophetic. Thus Virgil makes Dido imprecate upon Æneas a series of misfortunes, which actually had their accomplishment in his own person, or in his posterity. After his arrival in Italy, he was engaged in a war with Turnus, a bold and warlike prince. He was torn from the embrace of his son, and as it were an exile, forced to go to Etruria, to implore the assistance of Evander. See Æn. viii. 80. He saw his friends slain, and lie dead before his eyes. It is said he submitted to the terms of a disadvantageous peace with king Latinus, among which it was stipulated that the Trojans should abandon their native language, drop their appellation, and adopt that of the Latins. In the third year after this treaty, in a war with the Tuscans, he was himself slain (*ut plerique tradunt*) by Mezentius their king, on the banks of the river Numicus, where his body was left unburied, and finally carried off by its waters, and never more seen. The Romans and Carthaginians were bitter enemies to each other: no league, no religious obligations, could bind them in peace; and after Hannibal arose, he proved himself Dido's avenger. He entered Italy with fire and sword; the Roman armies fled before him; and Rome itself was providentially saved from his conquering arms.

617. *Indigna:* cruel—undeserved.

620. *Cadat ante diem:* let him fall before his time—let him die an untimely death.

621. *Vocem:* in the sense of *verba.*

623. *Mittite hæc:* present these offerings to my ashes. This is said in allusion to the sacrifices that were offered to the dead. They were usually poured upon the tomb, and consisted of milk, wine, and blood. *Exercete:* in the sense of *persequimini.*

625. *Exoriare aliquis ultor:* arise some avenger from my bones. This is much more forcible, and shows more fully the state of her mind, than if she had used the third person. Allusion is here made to Hannibal. *Dardanios colonos:* simply, the Trojans. *Dardanios:* an adj. from *Dardanus*, one of the founders of Troy.

627. *Olim.* This word signifies the future, as well as the past time: now, hereafter, whenever power shall present itself.

628. *Contraria:* in the sense of *hostilia* vel *infesta.*

Hæc ait: et partes animum versaba. in omnes,
Invisam quærens quàm primùm abrumpere lucem
Tum breviter Barcen nutricem affata Sichæi,
Namque suam patriâ antiquâ cinis ater habebat:
Annam, chara, mihi, nutrix, huc siste sororem:
Dic corpus properet fluviali spargere lymphâ,
Et pecudes secum et monstrata piacula ducat.
Sic veniat: tuque ipsa piâ tege tempora vittâ.
Sacra Jovi Stygio quæ ritè incepta paravi,
Perficere est animus, finemque imponere curis;
Dardaniique rogum capitis permittere flammæ.
Sic ait. Illa gradum studio celerabat anili.
At trepida, et cœptis immanibus effera Dido,
Sanguineam volvens aciem, maculisque trementes
Interfusa genas, et pallida morte futurâ,
Interiora domûs irrumpit limina, et altos
Conscendit furibunda rogos, ensemque recludit
Dardanium, non hos quæsitum munus in usus.
Hìc postquam Iliacas vestes notumque cubile
Conspexit, paulùm lachrymis et mente morata,
Incubuitque toro, dixitque novissima verba:
Dulces exuviæ, dum fata Deusque sinebant,
Accipite hanc animam, meque his exsolvite curis.
Vixi, et, quem dederat cursum fortuna, peregi;
Et nunc magna mei sub terras ibit imago.

632. Affata *est* Barcen

634. O chara nutrix, siste sororem Annam huc mihi: dic *ut* properet

639. Animus est *mihi* perficere sacra ritè incepta, quæ paravi Stygio Jovi, imponereque

644. Interfusa *quoad* trementes genas maculis, et pallida

NOTES.

635. *Spargere fluviali lymphâ:* to sprinkle her body with river water. It was a custom of the Greeks and Romans to wash their bodies before they performed sacrifice. See Æn. ii. 719. But this was only observed in regard to the superior gods. They sprinkled themselves only, when they were to offer sacrifice to the infernal gods, as in the present case.

636. *Pecudes:* in the sense of *victimas. Monstrata:* in the sense of *jussa*, vel *designata.*

638. *Stygio Jovi:* Pluto. He was the brother of Jupiter, and in the division of the world, the infernal regions fell to him by lot. The epithet *Stygius* is added, from *Styx*, a well known fabulous river of hell.

640. *Permittere:* to commit the funeral pile of the Trojan (Æneas) to the flames. *Capitis:* by synec. for the body, or whole man—here, the Trojan, to wit, Æneas.

641. *Studio:* zeal—officiousness.

642. *Immanibus:* awful—horrid. *Effera:* in the sense of *efferata.*

644. *Interfusa:* spotted—streaked.

645. *Irrumpit:* she rushed into the inner apartment of the palace. It is plain that *limen* signifies any part of the house, as well as the threshold. The funeral pile was erected *in penetrali side*, in the inner apartment. See 504, supra.

646. *Rogos.* The funeral pile was called *rogus*, before it was set on fire: while burning, it was called *pyra;* and after it was consumed, *bustum:* all of which are derived from the Greek.

647. *Munus non quæsitum:* a present not designed, or gotten for such a use—for being the instrument of her death. From this, some infer that Æneas had made Dido this present of a Trojan sword—*Dardanium ensem.* But it is more probable that it was a present from Dido to Æneas; and that in his hurry to be gone, he had left it with some other things, in her bedchamber. *Quæsitum.* Ruæus says, *comparatum.*—Heyne, *paratum, acceptum, datum.*

652. *Curis:* troubles—sorrows.

654. *Et nunc:* and now my ghost (*imago*) shall descend illustrious to the shades below. *Mei:* in the sense of *mea*, agreeing with *imago.*

Turnebus thinks the epithet *magna* is used, because ghosts make their appearance at night, when to the affrighted imagination of the spectators, the object appears larger than life. But this is a very singular opinion. Dido is speaking in the language of majesty, and setting forth her illustrious deeds. She had built a flourishing city and laid the foundation of a powerful king dom—she had punished her brother for the death of her husband—she had reigned in glory—in a word, she had been happy in every instance, till the Trojan fleet visited her coast. In this situation of mind, nothing

Urbem præclaram statui: mea mœnia vidi;
Ulta virum, pœnas inimico à fratre recepi:
Felix, heu nimiùm felix! si litora tantùm
Nunquam Dardaniæ tetigissent nostra carinæ.
Dixit: et, os impressa toro, moriemur inultæ!
Sed moriamur, ait: sic, sic juvat ire sub umbras.
Hauriat hunc oculis ignem crudelis ab alto
Dardanus, et nostræ secum ferat omina mortis
Dixerat: atque illam media inter talia ferro
Collapsam aspiciunt comites, ensemque cruore
Spumantem, sparsasque manus. It clamor ad alta
Atria: concussam bacchatur fama per urbem:
Lamentis, gemituque, et fœmineo ululatu
Tecta fremunt: resonat magnis plangoribus æther.
Non aliter quàm si immissis ruat hostibus omnis
Carthago, aut antiqua Tyros; flammæque furentes
Culmina perque hominum volvantur perque Deorum.
Audiit exanimis, trepidoque exterrita cursu,
Unguibus ora soror fœdans et pectora pugnis,
Per medios ruit, ac morientem nomine clamat:
Hoc illud, germana, fuit? me fraude petebas?
Hoc rogus iste mihi, hoc ignes aræque parabant?
Quid primùm deserta querar? comitemne sororem
Sprevisti moriens? eadem me ad fata vocâsses,
Idem ambas ferro dolor, atque eadem hora tulisset.
His etiam struxi manibus, patriosque vocavi
Voce Deos; sic te ut positâ crudelis abessem?
Extinxstî me teque, soror, populumque, patresque

661. Crudelis **Dardanus** hauriat hunc **ignem** *suis* oculis ab alto, et

664.* Comites aspiciunt illam collapsam ferro inter media talia *verba*, ensemque spumantem, manusque *ejus* sparsas cruore

671. Perque *culmina* Deorum

672. Soror exanimis audiit *hæc*, exterritaque trepido cursu, fœdans ora unguibus, et pectora pugnis, ruit per medios, et clamat morientem *sororem* nomine

676. Iste rogus *parabat* hoc mihi; *isti* ignes, aræque parabant hoc *mihi?*

680. Struxi *rogum* etiam his manibus, vocavique patrios Deos voce, ut crudelis abessem te sic positâ? *O* soror, extinxstî me teque

NOTES.

can be more natural than for her to conceive her ghost to be of great and illustrious rank, and distinguished even in the other world above others, as she had been herself distinguished in this.

656. *Recepi pœnas.* She had recovered from her brother her own wealth, and the treasure for which he murdered her husband. It is with great propriety, therefore, she uses the word *recepi*, when speaking of the revenge she had taken of Pygmalion.

659. *Moriemur inultæ:* shall I die unrevenged? but let me die. Thus, thus, it delights me to descend to the shades below. *Inultæ:* unrevenged of Æneas and the Trojans. The fatal moment having arrived, the poet represents her to us in the very act of stabbing herself, by the turn of his verse. The repetition of the *sic* sets her before us, plunging the instrument in her breast, and thrusting it home with a kind of desperate complacency. *Impressa os toro:* having kissed the bed, she said, &c.

666. *Bacchatur:* in the sense of *discurrit. Concussam:* in the sense of *commotam*, vel *attonitam*

668. *Fremunt:* in the sense of *resonant.*

669. *Ruat:* falls. Ruæus says, *subvertatur*

670. *Furentes:* the furious flames were rolling through the houses of men, and the (temples) of the gods. *Culmen* is properly the ridge of the house; by synec. put for the whole house.

675. *Hoc illud fuit:* O sister, was this your design—was this the object you had in view, in erecting this funeral pile?

677. *Deserta:* being thus abandoned, of what shall I first complain?

678. *Fata:* in the sense of *mortem.*

679. *Dolor:* pain—ache—anguish. Heyne says, *vulnus.*

681. *Sic positâ:* thus lying dead.

682. *Extinxstî:* thou hast destroyed me and thyself, &c. Some copies have *exstinxi*, in the first person. By this Anna turns the reproach from Dido to herself. But most commentators prefer the second person. *Sidonios patres.* By these we are to understand probably the Carthaginian senators, or the legislative branch of the government. It is plain that they are distinguished from the body of the people. *Extinxstî:* by syn. for *extinxisti. Date:* in the sense of *ferte. Lymphis:* in the sense of *aquâ.* This was a rite performed towards the bodies of the dead by their nearest relations. Hence the mother of Euryalus regrets that

683. Date *aquam ut* abluam vulnera

Sidonios, urbemque tuam. Date, vulnera lymphis
Abluam, et, extremus si quis super halitus errat,
Ore legam. Sic fata, gradus evaserat altos,
Semianimemque sinu germanam amplexa fovebat
Cum gemitu, atque atros siccabat veste cruores.
Illa, graves oculos conata attollere, rursus
Deficit: infixum stridet sub pectore vulnus.
Ter sese attollens cubitoque innixa levavit,
Ter revoluta toro est: oculisque errantibus, alto

692. Ingemuitque, *ea* repertâ.

Quæsivit cœlo lucem, ingemuitque repertâ.
Tum Juno omnipotens longum miserata dolorem,
Difficilesque obitus, Irim demisit Olympo,
Quæ luctantem animam nexosque resolveret artus.

696. Nam Proserpina nondum abstulerat illi flavum crinem vertice, damnaveratque caput Stygio Orco, quia

Nam, quia nec fato, meritâ nec morte peribat,
Sed misera ante diem, subitoque accensa furore;
Nondum illi flavum Proserpina vertice crinem
Abstulerat, Stygioque caput damnaverat Orco.
Ergò Iris croceis per cœlum roscida pennis,

702. Ego jussa fero hunc *crinem* sacrum Diti; solvoque te *ab* isto corpore.

705. Omnis calor dilapsus *est*.

Mille trahens varios adverso Sole colores,
Devolat, et supra caput adstitit: hunc ego Diti
Sacrum jussa fero, teque isto corpore solvo.
Sic ait: et dextrâ crinem secat. Omnis et unà
Dilapsus calor, atque in ventos vita recessit.

NOTES.

she had not shut his eyes, nor washed his wounds. Æn. ix. 485.

684. *Siquis extremus:* if any last breath remain, that I may catch it with my mouth. Virgil is here thought to allude to a ceremony among the Greeks and Romans: when a person was just expiring, the nearest relation put his mouth to his that he might catch the last breath. Ruæus interprets *super* by *adhuc*. *Super-errat* is evidently used in the sense of *superesset*. The substitution of *esset* for *errat* makes the reading easy. Some copies have *esset*.

688. *Conata:* agreeing with Dido.

689. *Vulnus stridet:* the wound hisses, occasioned by the gushing out of the blood. *Infixum:* made.

693. *Dolorem:* pain. *Obitus:* departure—death.

695. *Resolveret animam:* might separate her soul and body. *Nexos artus:* compacted or united limbs.

696. *Quia nec fato.* The ancients divided death into three kinds: *natural*, *merited* or *deserved*, and *accidental*. The natural death was when a person accomplished the ordinary term of human life, or that space allotted to him in the councils of the gods. The merited or deserved death was, when a person was deprived of life by the immediate interposition of the gods for the punishment of atrocious conduct. The *casual*, or *accidental*, was, when a person took away his own life in some way or other: such an one was said to die before his time. This was the case with Dido.

697. *Furore:* passion. *Diem:* in the sense of *tempus*.

698. *Nondum illi:* Proserpine had not yet plucked for her the yellow lock, &c. The ancients had a notion that none could die till Proserpine, either in person, or by *Atropos*, had cut a lock of hair from the crown of their head. This was considered a kind of first-fruits to Pluto. This custom took its rise from sacrifices: when they used to pluck some of the hairs from the front of the victim, and cast them into the fire.

699. *Orco:* dat. of Orcus, a name of Pluto.

700. *Iris ergò:* dewy Iris flies through heaven. Iris was the messenger of the goddesses, especially of Juno. She is said to be the daughter of Thaumas and Electra. Servius observes that *Iris* is, for the most part, employed in matters of mischief, and contention. See Æn. v. 606. and ix. 803. *Iris:* the rainbow. This interesting appearance is occasioned by the rays of the sun, reflected by the vapors or drops of rain. It can only take place, or be seen, when the sun and cloud are opposite to each other, in regard to the spectator.

QUESTIONS.

What is the subject of this book?
What is its nature, and character?
How does it commence?
What plan did Juno propose to effect her purpose of averting the Trojans from Italy?
Did she effect a union between Dido and Æneas?
Was that union dissolved?
By whom was it dissolved?
By whom was Æneas commanded to leave Carthage?
How did Dido receive the information that he was ordered to leave her?
What effect had it upon her?
What course did she pursue in order to divert him from his purpose?
As soon as the match was concluded between Dido and Æneas, was the news of that event spread abroad?
By whom was it spread?
Whom does Virgil imitate in the description of Fame?
Who was Iarbas?
What had he previously proposed to Dido?
How was that proposition received?
What effect had the news of Dido's marriage upon that prince?
How was he occupied at that time?
Who was said to be his father?
Who was Jupiter Ammon?
Had he any celebrated temple?
Where was it situated?
Whom does Sir Isaac Newton make this Ammon to have been?
Does Justin the historian give a different account of this matter?
What does he say of it?
What was the issue of it as related by him?
In what character was Dido considered afterward by her countrymen?
Who was Dido?
What is the meaning of that word?
By what other name was she sometimes called?
What was the name of her father, according to Josephus?
What does Virgil call him?
What does Marollius call him?
Is Belus, probably, an abbreviation of *Ithobalus?*
To whom was she married at Tyre?
Who was Sichæus?
What office did he hold?
What was the character of Pygmalion, her brother?
What atrocious deed did he perform?
What was his conduct afterward?
How was Dido informed of the cruel deed?
What advice did the ghost of her husband give her?
What did she do in consequence of that?
Did many of her countrymen accompany her?
What appears to have been her original purpose in leaving Tyre?
Had a colony of Tyrians previously settled in Africa?
Who were the leaders of that colony?
Where did they settle?
What did they call their settlement?
How was Dido received by her countrymen?
What did they desire her to do?
What did she call her city?
What is the meaning of that word in the Phœnician language?
But do not some give a different account?
What do those historians say?
What did she call the town or citadel?
What is the meaning of *Byrsa* in the Greek language?
To what mistake did that lead?
How have some attempted to explain that story?
What does Rollin say of it in his history of Carthage?
Did Dido purchase any tract of country for her city?
What was the nature of the contract?
Did the Carthaginians perform it?
What was the consequence of their refusal?
Is it supposed by some that Virgil is guilty of an anachronism in making Dido and Æneas cotemporary?
What does Bochart say of it?
Upon what does he found his conclusions?
Does Sir Isaac Newton make a different calculation?
How much later has he brought down the destruction of Troy?
Is it a fair conclusion that it was a general received opinion, they were cotemporary?
Was this sufficient ground for the poet to assume it as a fact?
Does the introduction of Dido into the Æneid add much to its embellishment?
How long did Carthage continue?
What was the character of its inhabitants?
Were the Carthaginians a powerful nation?
Who was the most distinguished commander and general among them?
By whom was Carthage finally destroyed?
In what year of Rome was that effected?
Finding she could not prevail upon Æneas to remain at Carthage, what desperate resolution did Dido make?
Under what pretence did she order the altar to be erected?
What effect had the departure of the Trojans from her coast upon her?
Did she make any imprecation against Æneas and the Trojans?

Was it realized with regard to Æneas, if we may believe history?

Was it realized in regard to the Romans, his descendants?

Was there always a jealousy subsisting between the two nations?

How many celebrated wars were waged between them?

How does the book conclude?

How did Dido put an end to her life?

LIBER QUINTUS.

This book opens with the departure of Æneas from Carthage. He had not been long at sea before a violent storm arose, which forced him to turn his course to Sicily. He entered the port of *Drepanum*. Here he is received with great cordiality and affection by king Acestes. After offering sacrifice, and celebrating the anniversary of his father's death, Æneas institutes four kinds of games in honor of him. These occupy from verse 114 to 602. In the mean time, the Trojan women, at the instigation of *Iris*, who was sent by Juno for that purpose, set fire to the ships, in the hope, by these means, to put an end to the voyage of which they were weary. At the intreaty of Æneas, Jupiter sent a heavy shower of rain, which extinguished the flames. Four of the fleet, however, were lost. Upon this Nautes advises Æneas, since he had lost part of his fleet, to leave in Sicily the aged, and all who were weary of the voyage. This advice was confirmed the following night by the ghost of Anchises, which appeared to him in a vision. It also directed him to go to the Sibyl of *Cumæ*, who would conduct him to the infernal regions, where he should receive a fuller account of his own fortune, and of that of his race.

The hero followed the advice; and having founded a city, which he called *Acestes*, after his venerable friend, he set sail for Italy.

He had not long been at sea, before he lost Palinurus, the pilot of his ship, who fell overboard in sleep; after which Æneas took upon himself the duty and business of pilot.

This book is of a gay and lively nature, and very properly comes after the tragical account of Dido's unhappy end. The games are imitated from the 23d book of the *Iliad*, where Achilles is represented as instituting games in honor of his friend *Patroclus*.

INTEREA medium Æneas jam classe tenebat
Certus iter, fluctusque atros Aquilone secabat:
Mœnia respiciens, quæ jam infelicis Elisæ
Collucent flammis: quæ tantum accenderit ignem,
Causa latet: duri magno sed amore dolores
Polluto, notumque, furens quid fœmina possit,
Triste per augurium Teucrorum pectora ducunt.
Ut pelagus tenuere rates, nec jam ampliùs ulla
Occurrit tellus, cœlum undique, et undique pontus,
Olli cœruleus supra caput adstitit imber,
Noctem hyememque ferens: et inhorruit unda tenebris

5. Sed duri labores *ex* magno amore polluto, *noti;* quidque furens fœmina possit *facere*, notum, ducunt

9. *Sed* undique cœlum, et undique pontus *apparet*

NOTES.

1. *Medium iter.* This is literally the middle of his course. But this, strictly speaking, cannot be; for he beheld the flames of Dido's funeral pile. Ruæus and Davidson take *medium* in the sense of *profundum;* and understand the phrase to mean, that Æneas had gotten into the *full* or *deep sea.* If we could read *mare* instead of *iter*, then there would be no difficulty in this interpretation.

2. *Certus:* determined on going. *Fluctus atros Aquilone:* he cut the waves blackened by the wind; or he cut the blackened waves before the wind. *Aquilo:* the north wind, put for wind in general; the *species* for the *genus. Mœnia:* in the sense of *urbem.*

6. *Polluto:* in the sense of *læso*, vel *violato.*

7. *Per triste augurium:* through gloomy presages or conjectures.

8. *Ut:* in the sense of *quando.*

10. *Imber:* in the sense of *nubes* vel *nimbus. Olli* for *illi*, by antithesis.

Ipse gubernator puppi Palinurus ab altâ :
Heu! quianam tanti cinxerunt æthera nimbi ?
Quidve, pater Neptune, paras ? sic deinde locutus,
Colligere arma jubet, validisque incumbere remis ;
Obliquatque sinus in ventum, ac talia fatur:
Magnanime Ænea, non, si mihi Jupiter auctor
Spondeat, hoc sperem Italiam contingere cœlo.
Mutati transversà fremunt, et vespere ab atro
Consurgunt venti : atque in nubem cogitur aër
Nec nos obniti contrà, nec tendere tantùm
Sufficimus : superat quoniam fortuna, sequamur.
Quòque vocat, vertamus iter. Nec litora longè
Fida reor fraterna Erycis, portusque Sicanos
Si modò ritè memor servata remetior astra.
Tum pius Æneas : Equidem sic poscere ven.
Jamdudum, et frustrà cerno te tendere contrà
Flecte viam velis. An sit mihi gratior ulla,
Quòque magis fessas optem demittere naves
Quàm quæ Dardanium tellus mihi servat Ac n,

12. Palinurus ipse gubernator *exclamat* ab altâ puppi: heu! quianam

21. Nos sufficimus nec tendere contrà, nec tantùm obniti

24. Nec reor fida fraterna litora Erycis, Sicanosque portus *es* longè.

28. An ulla tellus s gratior mihi, quòque ma gis optem demittere fe sas naves, quàm qu servat mihi Dardanu Acesten, et *quæ* con plectitur ossa patris An chisæ *in ejus* gremio?

NOTES

13. *Quianam:* in the sense of *cur.*

14. *Quidve, pater Neptune, paras?* This apostrophe to Neptune gives us a very lively idea of his wonder and astonishment.

15. *Arma:* properly signifies any kind of instruments whatever—here the tackling of the ship—the sails, spars and rigging of every description. Davidson confines it to the sails. But this is not necessary. It was proper that all things should be stowed away, as well as the sails reefed, that the ship might the better weather the storm.

16. *Obliquat sinus:* he turns the sail into the wind—he brings the vessel more into the wind—he lies, in nautical language, nearer the wind.

17. *Auctor:* the founder of our race.

18. *Cœlo:* in this weather. *Vespere:* in the sense of *occidente.*

19. *Transversà:* an adj. neu. plu. taken as an adverb in imitation of the Greeks.

21. *Nec nos sufficimus:* nor are we able to proceed against it, nor so much as to hold our own—to bear up against the storm —to contend against it.

24. *Reor fida:* I think the faithful fraternal shores of Eryx, &c. Eryx was the son of *Butes* and *Venus*, according to common report. Some say, his mother was *Lycaste*, a Sicilian courtezan, who, on account of her extraordinary beauty, was called Venus. Virgil, following tradition, calls him the brother of Æneas, both being reputed to be the sons of Venus. His grandfather was *Amycus*, who was slain by Pollux in a contest with the gauntlet: upon which *Butes* fled into Sicily, and founded a city. *Eryx*, in like manner, was slain by Hercules. He gave his name to a mountain and city not far from the *Promontorium Lilybœum.*

25. *Si modò ritè:* if now, remembering ri , I measure over again the stars ol s before. From the relative situatio se stars which he had observed upo ast of Sicily, and from their corre p ice with his present observations, h judg himself to be on that coast again.

27. *Tendere:* strove—contended.

28. *Viam:* in the sense of *cursum.* Turn your course before the wind. The southwest wind was favorable for them to go to Sicily.

29. *Demittere:* in the sense of *dirigere:*

30. *Acesten.* What is said of the origin of Acestes, is so incorporated with fable that little dependence can be placed upon it. The account, which Dionysius Halicarnassus gives, is probably the most correct. It appears that Laomedon, king of Troy, being offended at some Trojan nobleman, caused him and his sons to be put to death. Lycophron calls him *Phœnodamus:* but *Servius* and *Pomponius* call him *Hippotes.* But thinking his daughters, who were three in number, less deserving his displeasure, the king sold them to some Sicilian merchants, on condition that they should transport them to some foreign country. A person of some distinction being on board, by the name of *Crinisus*, *Crimisus*, or *Crimissus*, fell in love with one of them, whose name was *Egesta*, and married her. Soon after she bore a son, whom Virgil calls *Acestes*, but others *Egestes*, or *Ægestes.* Upon the death of Laomedon, he obtained permission of Priam to return to Troy; where he was during the siege and destruction of that city, when he contracted a friendship with Æneas. He afterward returned to Sicily. The river *Crinisus* being afterward called by his name, gave rise to the fabulous account of his birth.

Et patris Anchisæ gremio complectitur ossa?
Hæc ubi dicta, petunt portus, et vela secundi
Intendunt Zephyri: fertur cita gurgite classis:
Et tandem læti notæ advertuntur arenæ.
At procul excelso miratus vertice montis
Adventum, sociasque rates, occurrit Acestes,
Horridus in jaculis et pelle Libystidis ursæ:
Troïa Crimiso conceptum flumine mater
Quem genuit. Veterum non immemor ille parentum,
Gratatur reduces, et gazâ lætus agresti
Excipit, ac fessos opibus solatur amicis.
Postera cùm primo stellas oriente fugârat
Clara die; socios in cœtum litore ab omni
Advocat Æneas, tumulique ex aggere fatur:
Dardan magni, genus alto à sanguine Divûm,
Annuu xactis completur mensibus orbis;
Ex quo lliquias divinique ossa parentis
Condidi terrâ, mœstasque sacravimus aras.
Jamque s, ni fallor, adest; quem semper acerbum,
Semper h oratum, sic Dî voluistis, habebo.
Hunc ego ætulis agerem si syrtibus exul,
Argolicov ri deprensus, et urbe Mycenæ:
Annua vot nen, solemnesque ordine pompas
Exsequere rueremque suis altaria donis.
Nunc ultr cineres ipsius et ossa parentis,
Haud equ em sinè mente, reor, sinè numine Divûm,

32. Ubi hæc dicta *sunt*

35. At Acestes *ex* excelso vertice montis procul miratus adventum, sociasque rates, occurrit *nobis*, horridus

39. Quem Troïa mater genuit conceptum Crimiso flumine.

42. Cùm postera clara dies fugârat stellas primo oriente, Æneas

45. *Quorum* genus *est*

50. O Dî, *vos*, sic voluistis.

51. Ego agerem hunc *diem*, si *essem* exul *in* Gætulis syrtibus, deprensus-ve

55. Nunc ultrò adsumus ad cineres et ossa ipsius parentis, equidem reor haud sinè numine Divûm

NOTES.

33. *Gurgite:* in the sense of *mari.*

34. *Læti: socii* is understood: my joyous companions.

35. *Miratus:* observing—wondering at. Our arrival was unexpected, and a matter of wonder to him.

37. *Horridus in jaculis:* rough with javelins, and the hide of an African bear. The word *horridus* is very applicable to the dress and equipage of a hunter, bearing his darts and javelins in his hands, and guarded against the savages of the mountains. In which character Acestes is here represented. *Libystidis:* an adj. from *Libystis*, and that from the noun *Libys.* Pliny says there were no bears in Africa, on account of its great heat. But there are many good authorities against him. *Solinus* says the Numidian bears excel all others in beauty and form: which is probably the reason that Virgil dresses *Acestes* in one of their skins.

39. *Genuit.* in the sense of *peperit.*

40. *Agresti gazâ:* with his homely fare. *Gaza* is a word of Persian origin, and signifies any kind of sumptuous expense, either in provision or furniture. *Nos* is to be connected with *reduces.*

44. *Aggere: summitate*, says Ruæus.

46. *Annuus orbis:* the annual circle (to wit, a year) is completed.

49. *Acerbum:* afflictive—sorrowful.

50. *Habebo:* I shall consider. *Agerem.* I would observe, or keep.

53. *Solemnes pompas.* This is peculiarly proper in this place. *Pompa* properly signifies a funeral or other procession; and, *exsequerer: I would perform the exsequiæ*, or funeral obsequies; the principal of which was the following of the corpse to the grave, or funeral pile. Hence *exsequiæ* came to signify the whole funeral rites: from *sequor*, I follow.

54. *Struerem altaria:* I would cover the altars with his own proper gifts. These were milk, wine, honey, and blood, poured upon the tomb. Upon these it was thought the *Umbra*, or shade of the deceased, fed, and especially upon the blood. Valpy says, fit offerings.

56. *Haud sinè mente.* Æneas here attributes their arrival in Sicily to the interposition of the gods, as if they designed it to afford him an opportunity of paying divine honors to his father. *Mente:* design. Ruæus says, *consilio.*

58. *Lætum honorem:* the joyous festival. Ruæus interprets *honorem* by *sacrificium.* But it is plain that *honorem* includes every part of the rites and ceremonies which were performed upon that occasion, as well as the offerings or sacrifices.

Adsumus; et portus delati intramus amicos.
Ergò agite, et lætum cuncti celebremus honorem:
Poscamus ventos, atque hæc me sacra quotannis
Urbe velit positâ templis sibi ferre dicatis.
Bina boum vobis Trojâ generatus Acestes
Dat numero capita in naves: adhibete Penates
Et patrios epulis, et quos colit hospes Acestes.
Prætereà, si nona diem mortalibus almum
Aurora extulerit, radiisque retexerit orbem,
Prima citæ Teucris ponam certamina classis
Quique pedum cursu valet, et qui viribus audax,
Aut jaculo incedit melior, levibusve sagittis;
Seu crudo fidit pugnam committere cæstu;
Cuncti adsint, meritæque expectent præmia palmæ
Ore favete, omnes, et cingite tempora ramis.
  Sic fatus, velat maternâ tempora myrto:
Hoc Elymus facit, hoc ævi maturus Acestes,
Hoc puer Ascanius: sequitur quos cætera pubes.
Ille è concilio multis cum millibus ibat
Ad tumulum, magnâ medius comitante catervâ.
Hìc duo ritè mero libans carchesia Baccho
Fundit humi, duo lacte novo, duo sanguine sacro;
Purpureosque jacit flores, ac talia fatur:
Salve, sancte parens: iterum salvete, recepti

58. Et *nos* delati *huc* instramus

59. Poscamus ventos *ab eo*, atque *ut* velit me, urbe positâ, quotannis ferre hæc sacra *in* templis dicatis sibi

62. In *singulas* naves

67. Et qui incedit audax viribus

75. Ille ibat medius *e* concilio cum multis millibus ad

NOTES.

60. *Positâ urbe:* a city being built—that is, after they had founded a city and erected temples in it dedicated to him.

61. *Acestes generatus.* Acestes sprung from Troy, gives, &c. *Bina capita boum:* simply, *two oxen.*

62. *Adhibete Penates,* &c. Servius is of opinion that the poet here alludes to the Roman custom called *Lectisternia*, or sacred banquets, prepared at the solemn games for the gods, whose images were placed on couches, and set down at the most honorable part of the table, as principal guests.

64. *Si:* in the sense of *cum.*

66. *Ponam:* in the sense of *instituam.* Æneas here institutes four kinds of games or sports—a rowing match—a foot race—a shooting match, and a gauntlet fight; and proposes suitable rewards for the victors in each.

67. *Valet:* in the sense of *præstat. Incedit:* in the sense of *est.*

69. *Fidit:* in the sense of *audet.*

70. *Præmia meritæ palmæ:* rewards of meritorious victory—or rewards worthy of victory. *Palmæ:* in the sense of *victoriæ:* by moton.

71. *Favete omnes ore: favete ore,* vel *favete linguis*, was the phrase made use of by the public criers before the celebration of solemn games or sacrifices. The import seems to be: Favor us with your religious attention—pronounce no words of bad omen that may profane the sacred ceremonies: or, let us have the concurrence of your prayers to render the gods favorable to us: or, lastly, aid us by your applause and joyful acclamations.

72. *Velat tempora.* The poet here alludes to a practice among the Romans, of persons of every age and condition, who appeared at these solemn games, to wear a garland upon their heads. The myrtle was sacred to Venus; hence the propriety of the expression, *materna myrto.*

73. *Maturus ævi:* a Grecism. In the sense of *provectus ætate*, vel *annis.*

77. *Hic duo ritè:* here in due form offering, he pours on the ground, &c. *Carchesia:* large bowls without handles: plu. of *carchesium. Libans:* pouring out—offering. *Baccho:* for *vino. Mero:* pure—unmixed.

80. *Iterum salvete:* Ye ashes revisited in vain, and soul and shade of my father, again hail.—*Cineres recepti nequicquam.* By these words Servius understands Anchises himself, whom Æneas rescued from the flames of Troy in vain; since he lost him before his arrival in Italy. But the sense given above is easier. Æneas lost his father a year before on his way to Italy; but, meeting with a storm, he was obliged to go to Africa. Now on his return he visits his tomb, and in a manner receives him again, but in vain, since it was not permitted that he should take him with him to Italy. *Animæque um-*

82. Non licuit *mihi tecum* quærere Italos fines

85. Cùm ingens lubricus anguis traxit septem gyros

87. Cui terga cœruleæ notæ *incendebant*, et *cujus* squamam fulgor

90. Tandem ille serpens longo agmine inter

Nequicquam cineres, animæque umbræque paternæ.
Non licuit fines Italos, fataliaque arva,
Nec tecum Ausonium, quicunque est, quærere Tybrim.
Dixerat hæc : adytis cùm lubricus anguis ab imis
Septem ingens gyros, septena volumina traxit,
Amplexus placidè tumulum, lapsusque per aras :
Cœruleæ cui terga notæ, maculosus et auro
Squamam incendebat fulgor : ceu nubibus arcus
Mille trahit varios adverso Sole colores.
Obstupuit visu Æneas : ille agmine longo
Tandem inter pateras et levia pocula serpens,
Libavitque dapes, rursusque innoxius imo
Successit tumulo, et depasta altaria liquit.
Hôc magìs inceptos genitori instaurat honores :
Incertus, Geniumne loci, famulumne parentis
Esse putet : cædit quinas de more bidentes,
Totque sues, totidem nigrantes terga juvencos :
Vinaque fundebat pateris, animamque vocabat
Anchisæ magni, Manesque Acheronte remissos,
Necnon et socii, quæ cuique est copia, læti
Dona ferunt : onerant aras, mactantque juvencos
Ordine ahena locant alii : fusique per herbam
Subjiciunt verubus prunas, et viscera torrent
   Expectata dies aderat, nonamque serenâ
Auroram Phaëthontis equi jam luce vehebant.

NOTES.

bræque. Some consider these as genitives connected with and governed by *cineres.* Servius explains it upon the principles of Plato and Aristotle; who gave to man a fourfold soul—the *intellectual*, the *sensual*, the *vital*, and the *vegetative.* To each of these they assigned a shade or ghost. It is most probable the poet here, as elsewhere, uses the plural for the singular, in order to aggrandize his subject: that is, *animæ* for *anima*, and *umbræ* for *umbra*, in the voc. sing. This is the opinion of Ruæus and Heyne.

84. *Adytis.* The tomb of Anchises here is spoken of as a temple—a shrine.

87. *Cui:* in the sense of *cujus.* *Terga:* acc. plu. governed by *incendebant*, or some other verb of like import, understood.

88. *Fulgor maculosus:* a brightness variegated with gold—with a golden hue. *Incendebat:* made or rendered resplendent.

91. *Serpens:* a part. of the verb *serpo*, agreeing with *ille* in the preceding line.

92. *Libavit dapes:* tasted the banquet, and again, &c. The *dapes* was the offer ing to the shade of Anchises, spoken of 54, supra.

93. *Depasta:* fed upon—just tasted.

94. *Instaurat:* in the sense of *renovat.* *Honores:* in the sense of *sacrificia.*

95. *Incertus-ne:* uncertain whether he should consider him (the serpent) to be, &c. The ancients had a notion that there were *Genii* appointed, some the protectors of countries and cities, and others the guardians of particular persons, who never left them even after death.

98. *Vocabat.* Æneas here not merely called upon his ghost to partake of the repast he had prepared, but invoked him as a god to be propitious to him, thereby deifying him.

99. *Manes remissos Acheronte:* the shade or ghost sent back from the dead to partake of the banquet. *Acheron:* a fabulous river of hell—often put for hell itself: or the place of the dead, as here.

100. *Quæ copia est cuique:* in the sense of *secundùm copiam quæ est unicuique.*

101. *Onerant:* some copies have *onerantque.* Heinsius, Pierius, and Heyne omit the *que.*

103. *Viscere:* by this we are to understand the meat in general.

105. *Equi Phaëthontis:* the horses of the sun brought the ninth, &c. *Phæton*, was the son of *Phœbus* and *Clymene.* He obtained from his father the management of his chariot for one day; but unable to govern the fiery steeds, he was precipitated into the Po. See Ovid. Met. 2. Here put for the Sun himself. The poets represented the sun as drawn in a chariot by four horses, whose names were *Pyroïs*, *Eoüs*, *Æthon*, and *Phlegon*, all of Greek origin.

Famaque finitimos et clari nomen Acestæ
Excierat: læto complêrant litora cœtu,
Visuri Æneadas, pars et certare parati.
Munera principio ante oculos, circoque locantur
In medio, sacri tripodes, viridesque coronæ,
Et palmæ, pretium victoribus; armaque, et ostro
Perfusæ vestes, argenti aurique talenta:
Et tuba commissos medio canit aggere ludos.
Prima pares ineunt gravibus certamina remis
Quatuor, ex omni delectæ classe, carinæ.
Velocem Mnestheus agit acri remige Pristin,
Mox Italus Mnestheus, genus à quo nomine Memmî:
Ingentemque Gyas ingenti mole Chimæram,
Urbis opus, triplici pubes quam Dardana versu
Impellunt: terno consurgunt ordine remi.
Sergestusque, domus tenet à quo Sergia nomen,
Centauro invehitur magnâ; Scyllâque Cloanthus
Cœruleâ, genus unde tibi, Romane Cluenti.
Est procul in pelago saxum, spumantia contra
Litora; quod tumidis submersum tunditur olim
Fluctibus, hyberni condunt ubi sidera Cori:
Tranquillo silet, immotâque attollitur undâ
Campus, et apricis statio gratissima mergis.
Hìc viridem Æneas frondenti ex ilice metam
Constituit, signum nautis, pater: unde reverti
Scirent, et longos ubi circumflectere cursus.

108. *Pars* visuri Æneadas, et pars parati certare.

111. Pretium *destinatum* victoribus

113. Tuba canit *è* medio aggere ludos commissos *esse*.

115. Quatuor carinæ delectæ ex omni classe, pares gravibus remis

117. A quo nomine *oritur* genus

118. Gyas *agit* ingentem Chimæram *ex* ingenti mole

121. Sergestusque, à quo Sergia domus tenet nomen, invehitur magna Centauro; Cloanthusque *invehitur* cœruleâ Scylla; unde genus *est* tibi

127. Silet *in* tranquillo *cœlo*, attolliturque *ex* immotâ unda, *tanquam* campus

129. Hic pater Æneas constituit viridem metam ex frondenti ilice, *tanquam* signum nautis unde.

NOTES.

108. *Æneadas:* in the sense of *Trojanos.*

110. *Sacri tripodes.* The tripod was properly a kind of three-footed stool or table, on which were placed the sacred bowls and other vessels for the libation. It is called *sacred* on account of its various uses in the ceremonies of religion. We learn from Homer that the Greeks used to make presents of tripods to their heroes and great men.

111. *Palmæ.* The palm was the ordinary prize of every conqueror at the games. Plutarch gives this reason for it; because the palm is a fit emblem of fortitude, as it is not crushed, nor borne down by any weight; but still maintains its growth, and rises superior to opposition. *Perfusæ* dyed, or colored. *Talenta:* one talent of each.

116. *Agit:* in the sense of *regit* vel *gubernat.* *Acri remige:* with a valiant band of rowers.

117. *A quo nomine:* from whose name is the family of *Memmius.* In order to recommend himself to the noble families at Rome, Virgil derives their origin from Trojans of distinction. *Genus:* in the sense of *familia.*

118. *Opus urbis:* in the sense of *instar urbis.*

119. *Triplici versu:* with a triple row of oars. What Virgil says of the nature of these boats, is an anticipation; but it was not necessary that he should conform exactly to chronological fact. The galley, it is well known, was not invented till long after, and was of various sizes. Some had two, some three, and others four banks, or rows of rowers: and, accordingly, they were called *Biremis, Triremis, quadriremis,* &c. Their banks of rowers were raised, slopingly one above another, so that those of the second bench rested their feet where those of the first were seated, &c. *Remi consurgunt terno ordine.* By this we are to understand that the oars rose together, and, as it were, kept time throughout the three rows. Ruæus makes a distinction between *versus* and *ordo.* The first, according to him, signifies the series of oars reckoned horizontally from stem to stern. The *ordines* he makes to be the same oars reckoned vertically, or as they rose obliquely above one another.

121. *Domus:* properly the house, by meton. the family—race.

123. *Genus:* race—family.

125. *Olim:* continually—usually.

126. *Condunt:* cover over—hide them in clouds.

127. *Tranquillo.* In calm weather this rock was visible; but in storms it was covered with waves, and resounded with the dashing of the waters. It rose above the surface like a plain.

132. Ipsi ductores longè effulgent in puppibus, decori auro ostroque.

135. Perfusa *quoad* nudatos humeros oleo nitescit.

145. Currus non tam præcipites corripuere campum

151. Gyas effugit ante alios: primusque elabitur undis inter turbam fremitumque.

Tum loca sorte legunt: ipsique in puppibus auro
Ductores longè effulgent ostroque decori:
Cætera populeâ velatur fronde juventus,
Nudatosque humeros oleo perfusa nitescit.
Considunt transtris, intentaque brachia remis:
Intenti expectant signum: exultantiaque haurit
Cordă pavor pulsans, laudumque arrecta cupido.
Inde, ubi clara dedit sonitum tuba, finibus omnes,
Haud mora, prosiluere suis: ferit æthera clamor
Nauticus; adductis spumant freta versa lacertis.
Infindunt pariter sulcos: totumque dehiscit
Convulsum remis rostrisque tridentibus æquor.
Non tam præcipites bijugo certamine campum
Corripuere, ruuntque effusi carcere, currus:
Nec sic immissis aurigæ undantia lora
Concussere jugis, pronique in verbera pendent.
Tum plausu fremituque virûm, studiisque faventûm
Consonat omne nemus, vocemque inclusa volutant
Litora; pulsati colles clamore resultant.
Effugit ante alios, primusque elabitur undis
Turbam inter fremitumque Gyas: quem deinde Cloanthus
Consequitur, melior remis; sed pondere pinus

NOTES.

134. *Populea fronde.* Servius observes, the reason of their wearing garlands of the poplar tree, was, that they were celebrating funeral games. Hercules, it is said, brought that tree from the infernal regions.

136. *Brachia intenta remis:* their arms are stretched to the oars. Ruæus has no stop after *remis*, but connects it with the following words. This, however, is not so easy: and, beside, it takes from the solemnity of the description. The verb *sunt* is understood.

138. *Pulsans pavor:* throbbing fear, and an eager desire of praise, draws their beating hearts. This is very expressive. It raises such palpitations in their breasts, as if it would draw their hearts out of their bodies. *Pulsans* is a very proper epithet to *pavor*, beating—palpitating.

139. *Finibus. Finis*, here, means the line, place, or bound, from which they start—the mark. *Sonitum:* the signal.

141. *Lacertis adductis.* Dr. Trapp observes, by this we are to understand the motions of the rowers, when, in pulling at the oar, they draw the arms close to the body. This they do, especially when they row with all their strength.

142. *Infindunt pariter sulcos:* they cleave furrows in the sea at the same time—they start all at once.

143. *Æquor convulsum:* the whole surface of the sea convulsed, &c. Some editions have *stridentibus*. But this violates the measure of the verse; the first syllable of *stridentibus* being always long. Ancient medals explain the matter; on some of which there is plainly seen a *rostrum*, or beak of a ship with three teeth. *Tridens*, of *tres* and *dens*.

144. *Præcipites:* in the sense of *celeres*. *Certamine:* the chariot race. *Bijugo* signifies or implies that two horses were yoked or harnessed in the chariot. Macrobius observes that Virgil here excels Homer. Indeed nothing can be more finely imagined, or represented more to the life. *Carcer:* the mark, or starting place; *meta*, the goal or turning place. *Currus*, by meton. for *equi*.

146. *Nec aurigæ sic:* nor have the charioteers so shook, &c. *Jugis:* the yoke, by meton. put for the horses harnessed in it. *Immissis jugis:* the horses flying with loosened reins—at full speed.

148. *Studiis:* in the sense of *acclamationibus*.

149. *Litora inclusa*, &c. Ruæus observes that this is, by a figure called *commutatio*, for *volutant inclusam vocem.* Or perhaps *inclusa* may be taken here in the sense of *curva*.

151. *Primus.* Davidson has *primis*, agreeing with *undis*. He glides away on the nearest waves. *Primus* is however the easier, and conveys the same idea. It is the reading of Ruæus and others. *Resultant:* echo it back.

153. *Pinus:* the timber of the pine tree, put by meton. for the ship or galley made of it.

Tarda tenet. Post hos, æquo discrimine, Pristis
Centaurusque locum tendunt superare priorem.
Et nunc Pristis habet; nunc victam præterit ingens
Centaurus; nunc unà ambæ junctisque feruntur
Frontibus, et longâ sulcant vada salsa carinâ.
Jamque propinquabant scopulo, metamque tenebant;
Cùm princeps, medioque Gyas in gurgite victor,
Rectorem navis compellat voce Menœten:
Quò tantùm mihi dexter abis? huc dirige cursum,
Litus ama, et lævas stringat, sine, palmula cautes:
Altum alii teneant. Dixit: sed cæca Menœtes
Saxa timens, proram pelagi detorquet ad undas.
Quò diversus abis? iterum; Pete saxa, Menœte,
Cum clamore Gyas revocabat: et ecce Cloanthum
Respicit instantem tergo, et propiora tenentem.
Ille inter navemque Gyæ scopulosque sonantes
Radit iter lævum interior, subitusque priorem
Præterit; et metis tenet æquora tuta relictis.
Tum verò exarsit juveni dolor ossibus ingens,
Nec lachrymis caruere genæ: segnemque Menœten,
Oblitus decorisque sui, sociûmque salutis,
In mare præcipitem puppi deturbat ab altâ.
Ipse gubernâclo rector subit, ipse magister:
Hortaturque viros, clavumque ad litora torquet.
At gravis ut fundo vix tandem redditus imo est
Jam senior, madidâque fluens in veste, Menœtes,
Summa petit scopuli, siccâque in rupe resedit.
Illum et labentem Teucri, et risere natantem:
Et salsos rident revomentem pectore fluctus.
Hìc læta extremis spes est accensa duobus,
Sergesto Mnestheoque, Gyam superare morantem.
Sergestus capit antè locum, scopuloque propinquat:

163. Et sine *ut* palmula stringat lævas cautes

174. Oblitusque sui decoris, salutisque sociûm, deturbat segnem Menœten, præcipitem

178. At ut Menœtes senior *et* gravis *undis* jam tandem vix redditus est imo fundo: fluensque in madida veste, petit summa scopuli, reseditque

NOTES.

154. *Discrimine:* in the sense of *intervallo*. *Superare:* in the sense of *occupare*, vel *obtinere*.

156. *Habet.* This is the reading of Heinsius, Heyne, Davidson, and others. Ruæus has *abit*.

157. *Junctis frontibus.* They moved on together head and head. Neither one gaining of the other. It is of the same import with *æquatis rostris*.

158. *Salsa vada:* the briny sea.

160. *Princeps:* in the sense of *primus*. *Gurgite:* in the sense of *mari*.

161. *Rectorem:* the helmsman—steersman.

162. *Mihi.* Ruæus conjectures that *mihi* here is merely expletive, as in many other places. *Ama litus:* keep close to or hug the rock.

166. *Diversus:* contrary—a different way.

170. *Ille radit interior*, &c. In the races it was customary to keep the *meta*, or goal, on the left hand. This will serve to explain the present case. Cloanthus on the inside (*interior*) and nearer the meta than Gyas, cut along the left way (*iter lævum*) and suddenly passed Gyas, who just before had been ahead of him; *præterit Gyam modò priorem.* Both in the naval and chariot race the great art lay in turning as near the goal as possible. For the nearer they kept to it, the shorter circumference they had to make, and the less distance to run. This was a great advantage to be gained, but it was attended with danger. *Subitus.* Some copies have *subitò*. The sense is the same with either. Heyne has *subitò*, on the authority of Burmannus; but observes that the other is the more poetical.

172. *Juveni:* the dat. in the sense of the gen

174. *Decoris:* in the sense of *dignitatis*.

176. *Rector ipse.* Gyas hitherto had only acted as pilot. He now discharges the office both of pilot and helmsman.

177. *Litora:* to the rock or goal.

178. *Redditus est:* issued or rose from with difficulty.

183. *Accensa est:* was kindled—arose

184. *Superare:* in the sense of *præterire*.

186. Nec tamen ille *est* prior, tota carinâ præeunte; *una* parte *est* prior; Æmula Pristis premit *aliam* partem rostro.

Nec totâ tamen ille prior præeunte carinâ:
Parte prior, partem rostro premit æmula Pristis.
At mediâ socios incedens nave per ipsos
Hortatur Mnestheus: Nunc, nunc insurgite remis,
Hectorei socii, Trojæ quos sorte supremâ
Delegi comites: nunc illas promite vires,
Nunc animos; quibus in Gætulis syrtibus usi,
Ionioque mari, Maleæque sequacibus undis.

194. *Ego* Mnestheus non peto prima *loca*

196 O *utinam possem*

Non jam prima peto Mnestheus, neque vincere certo
Quanquam ô! sed superent, quibus hoc, Neptune, dedisti
Extremos pudeat rediisse: hoc vincite, cives,
Et prohibete nefas. Olli certamine summo
Procumbunt: vastis tremit ictibus ærea puppis,
Subtrahiturque solum: tum creber anhelitus artus
Aridaque ora quatit: sudor fluit undique rivis.
Attulit ipse viris optatum casus honorem.

202. Namque dum Sergestus furens animi suburget proram

Namque furens animi dum proram ad saxa suburget
Interior, spatioque subit Sergestus iniquo;
Infelix saxis in procurrentibus hæsit.
Concussæ cautes, et acuto in murice remi
Obnixi crepuere; illisaque prora dependit.

NOTES.

187. *Prior parte.* The meaning is, that Sergestus was ahead, but not by the whole length of his galley; only by a part of it.

190. *Hectorei socii:* my brave companions, whom I chose, &c. In order to animate them the more, he calls them *Hectorei*, as brave and valiant as Hector. Nothing can be more expressive. *Sorte:* in the sense of *ruinâ*, vel *exitio.*

192. *Gætulis:* African. The *Gætuli* were a people of Africa, not far from Carthage. The word is here used as an adj. *Syrtibus:* see Æn. i. 111. *Usi: sunt* is to be supplied.

193. *Ionio mari.* That part of the Mediterranean lying between Epirus, Italy, and Sicily, was called the Ionian sea. Through or over this sea Æneas passed with his fleet. *Maleæ.* Maleæ, a promontory of the Peloponnesus between the *Sinus Argolicus* and the *Sinus Laconicus*, extending about five miles into the sea. It was *dangerous* sailing near it. It gave rise to the proverb, *Maleam legens, obliviscere, quæ sunt domi.* The epithet *sequacibus*, given to the waves of that coast, represents them as so many fierce and devouring monsters, that pursued ships in order to overwhelm them.

195. *Quanquam, ô!* This is an instance where Virgil is eloquent even in silence. This abrupt exclamation is more expressive of the mind of *Mnestheus* than any words could have been, especially to those who saw the looks and gestures that would accompany his voice. Having observed that he did not strive with an expectation of conquering, he turns upon himself: *O that I could!* but let them conquer, to whom, O Neptune, thou hast given that honor.

197. *Nefas:* disgrace—ignominy, of being the last to come out. *Olli:* by antithesis for *illi*, they. *Procumbunt:* they ply their oars with the greatest earnestness—they spring upon them with all their strength.

199. *Solum subtrahitur:* the surface is drawn from under them. Whatever is spread under any thing as its support and foundation is called in Latin *solum*, as the *sea* is to a ship; the *air* to a fowl on the wing. So rapidly did the galley move that the surface of the sea seemed to withdraw from under her.

201. *Casus ipse:* chance itself—mere chance.

202. *Suburget proram:* while he presses the prow to the rock on the inside, &c. *Interior*, between Mnestheus and the goal, taking a nearer course to it. But he had not left to himself sufficient room, and was therefore forced to run his galley upon that part of the rock which projected farther than the other points of the same rock. Ruæus reads *prorâ* in the abl. Heyne, Davidson, and Valpy, read *proram.*

203. *Iniquo:* in the sense of *angusto.*

205. *Cautes concussæ:* the rocks were struck. In other words, the galley received a violent shock; for action and reaction are equal. *Murice. Murex* properly signifies the shell-fish, of the liquor of which, it was thought, purple color was made. Hence it is taken for the prominence of a rock, which tapers into a sharp point like the shell of that fish.

206. *Crepuere:* in the sense of *fracti sunt.* The prow ran or slid up upon the rock, and in that elevated situation stuck fast

Consurgunt nautæ, et magno clamore morantur:
Ferratasque sudes, et acutâ cuspide contos
Expediunt, fractosque legunt in gurgite remos.
At lætus Mnestheus successuque acrior ipso,
Agmine remorum celeri, ventisque vocatis,
Prona petit maria, et pelago decurrit aperto.
Qualis speluncâ subitò commota columba,
Cui domus et dulces latebroso in pumice nidi,
Fertur in arva volans, plausumque exterrita pennis
Dat tecto ingentem: mox aëre lapsa quieto,
Radit iter liquidum, celeres neque commovet alas:
Sic Mnestheus, sic ipsa fugâ secat ultima Pristis
Æquora; sic illam fert impetus ipse volantem.
Et primùm in scopulo luctantem deserit alto
Sergestum, brevibusque vadis; frustràque vocantem
Auxilia, et fractis discentem currere remis.
Inde Gyan, ipsamque ingenti mole Chimæram
Consequitur; cedit, quoniam spoliata magistro est.
Solus jamque ipso superest in fine Cloanthus:
Quem petit, et summis adnixus viribus urget.
Tum verò ingeminat clamor; cunctique sequentem
Instigant studiis: resonatque fragoribus æther.
Hi proprium decus, et partum indignantur honorem,
Ni teneant; vitamque volunt pro laude pacisci.
Hos successus alit: possunt, quia posse videntur.
Et fors æquatis cepissent præmia rostris;
Ni palmas ponto tendens utrasque Cloanthus
Fudissetque preces, Divosque in vota vocâsset:
Dî, quibus imperium est pelagi, quorum æquora curro;
Vobis lætus ego hoc candentem in litore taurum

213. *Talis* qualis columba; cui domus et dulces nidi *sunt* in latebroso pumice, subitò commota *è* speluncâ, volans fertur in arva; exterritaque dat ingentem plausum tecto pennis

229. Hi indignantur ni teneant proprium decus et honorem *jam* partum; voluntque pacisci

NOTES.

207. *Clamore:* noise—bustle—confusion. *Morantur:* are delayed—stopped.

208. *Sudes.* This was a pole used by boatmen, and usually prefixed with iron. Hence the epithet *ferratas*. Heyne reads *trudes*.

211. *Celeri agmine:* by or with the quick motion of the oars. *Acrior: ardentior*, says Ruæus.

212. *Petit prona:* he seeks the easy waters, &c. *Pronus* here is easy—unobstructed, as appears from the words which follow, *pelago decurrit aperto:* he runs on the open sea.

214. *Dulces nidi:* the nests are here put for the young ones in them, by meton. *Cui:* in the sense of *cujus*.

216. *Dat ingentem:* the pigeon gives the stroke to her nest (*tecto*) with her wings when she first leaves it, and commences her flight.

217. *Liquidum:* in the sense of *aëreum*.

218. *Ultima æquora:* by this we are to understand the last part of the race—that part of it which lay beyond the *meta*, or goal.

220. *Deserit:* in the sense of *præterit*. *Brevibus vadis:* simply, shallows. Here the rock on which his galley stuck.

222. *Discentem:* in the sense of *tentantem*.

224. *Cedit:* she yields—falls behind.

225. *Cloanthus superest*, &c. Mnestheus had gotten ahead of Sergestus and Gyas, and Cloanthus remained alone to contest the prize with him. Him he pursues, and presses closely, straining every nerve. The prize was not to be given to him, who first arrived at the goal, but to him who returned first to the port, or place from whence they set out.

228. *Fragoribus.* Some ancient manuscripts have *clamoribus*, but this makes false quantity. The other is doubtless the true reading. *Studiis:* huzzas—acclamations.

229. *Hi indignantur:* these consider it a disgrace, unless, &c. *Hi:* these, meaning the crew of Cloanthus. *Hos*, in verse 231 infra, the crew of Mnestheus.

231. *Alit:* in the sense of *animat*.

232. *Et fors cepissent:* they would have gotten to the shore together; so that it could not have been determined who was the victor, and both received equal prizes, had not Cloanthus, &c. *Fors:* in the sense of *fortasse*.

Constituam ante aras voti reus, extaque salsos
Porriciam in fluctus, et vina liquentia fundam.
Dixit: eumque imis sub fluctibus audiit omnis
Nereïdum Phorcique chorus, Panopeaque virgo;
Et pater ipse manu magnâ Portunus euntem
Impulit. Illa Noto citiùs volucrique sagittâ
Ad terram fugit, et portu se condidit alto.
 Tum satus Anchisâ, cunctis ex more vocatis,
Victorem magnâ præconis voce Cloanthum
Declarat, viridique advelat tempora lauro:
Muneraque in naves, ternos optare juvencos,
Vinaque, et argenti magnum dat ferre talentum.
Ipsis præcipuos ductoribus addit honores:
Victori chlamydem auratam, quam plurima circùm
Purpura Mæandro duplici Melibœa cucurrit;
Intextusque puer frondosâ regius Idâ
Veloces jaculo cervos cursuque fatigat,
Acer, anhelanti similis: quem præpes ab Idâ
Sublimem pedibus rapuit Jovis armiger uncis.
Longævi palmas nequicquam ad sidera tendunt
Custodes, sævitque canum latratus in auras.
At, qui deinde locum tenuit virtute secundum,
Levibus huic hamis consertam auroque trilicem
Loricam, quam Demoleo detraxerat ipse

248. Dat *ei* optare ternos juvencos vinaque, et ferre magnum talentum argenti; *quæ erant* munera in naves.

250. Victori *Cloantho dat* auratam

NOTES.

237. *Reus voti.* When a person has taken upon himself a vow on a certain condition, he is said to be *Reus voti*, exposed to, or liable for his vow. When the condition is granted on the part of the gods, he is said to be *damnatus voti* or *damnatus votis:* bound to the performance of his vow. See Ecl. v. 80.

238. *Porriciam:* in the sense of *projiciam.* This verb properly signifies to place an offering to the gods upon an altar or otherwise. *Liquentia:* in the sense of *pura.*

240. *Omnis chorus:* all the choir of the Nereïds, &c. The Nereïds were the fabulous daughters of Nereus and Doris. See Ecl. 6. 35. *Phorci.* Phorcus or Phorcys was a marine god, the son of Neptune and Terra, and father of the Gorgons. *Panopea*, one of the Nereïds. Servius says she is here mentioned by name, because she was the only virgin among them.

241. *Pater Portunus ipse:* father Portunus himself, &c. Portunus, one of the marine gods, whose name is derived from *portus*, because he presided over ports and harbors. *Euntem* may agree either with *eum*, (to wit,) *Cloanthum*, understood, or with *navem.* The sense is the same in either case.

It may be observed, that Virgil omits no opportunity to instruct, as well as to please. He keeps to strict decorum in this first game. He gives the palm of victory to him who had invoked the gods. He shows us, also, the rashness of youth punished in the case of Gyas, whose fool-hardiness makes him lose the victory, of which he had the fairest prospects at the first. He sets forth the equity and liberality of Æneas in rewarding Sergestus for saving his galley, since he could not give him a prize as a conqueror.

242. *Illa:* to wit, *navis. Noto:* the south wind, put for wind in general—the *species* for the *genus.*

250. *Circùm quam plurima:* around which very much Melibœan purple run in a double maze. *Mæander* was a river in the Lesser Asia, running between Caria and Ionia into the Ægean sea. It was so full of windings and turnings, that the word came to be used for any turning or windings whatever. For *mæandro*, Ruæus says *flexu. Melibœa* was a city in Thessaly, at the foot of Mount Ossa, famous for dying purple. Here used as an adj.

252. *Regius puer intextus:* the royal boy interwoven in it, (the *chlamys*,) pursues with his javelin, and with speed, &c. The boy here meant is *Ganymede.* He was taken up from Mount Ida by Jove in the form of an eagle, and made cupbearer to the gods in the place of *Hebe.* See Æn. i. 28. *Fatigat* in the sense of *sequitur.*

255. *Præpes armiger Jovis:* the swift-winged armour-bearer of Jove—the eagle. Pliny observes that the eagle is proof against thunder; and this is the reason of its being selected for Jove's armour-bearer.

260. *Loricam consertam,* &c. The coat

Victor apud rapidum Simoënta sub Ilio alto,
Donat habere viro, decus et tutamen in armis.
Vix illam famuli Phegeus Sagarisque ferebant
Multiplicem, connixi humeris: indutus at olim
Demoleus, cursu palantes Troas agebat.
Tertia dona facit geminos ex ære lebetas,
Cymbiaque argento perfecta, atque aspera signis.
  Jamque adeò donati omnes, opibusque superbi,
Puniceis ibant evincti tempora tænîs:
Cùm sævo è scopulo multâ vix arte revulsus,
Amissis remis, atque ordine debilis uno,
Irrisam sinè honore ratem Sergestus agebat.
Qualis sæpe viæ deprensus in aggere serpens,
Ærea quem obliquum rota transiit, aut gravis ictu
Seminecem liquit saxo lacerumque viator:
Nequicquam longos fugiens dat corpore tortus;
Parte ferox, ardensque oculis, et sibila colla
Arduus attollens; pars vulnere clauda retentat
Nexantem nodos, seque in sua membra plicantem.
Tali remigio navis se tarda movebat:
Vela facit tamen, et plenis subit ostia velis.
Sergestum Æneas promisso munere donat,
Servatam ob navem lætus, sociosque reductos.
Olli serva datur, operum haud ignara Minervæ,
Cressa genus, Pholoë, geminique sub ubere nati.
  Hoc, pius Æneas, misso certamine, tendit
Gramineum in campum, quem collibus undique curvis
Cingebant sylvæ: mediâque in valle theatri
Circus erat; quò se multis cum millibus heros

269. Evincti *quoad* tempora

270. Cùm Sergestus agebat irrisam ratem sinè honore, vix revulsus è sævo scopulo multâ artê, remis amissis, atque debilis uno ordine.

275. Aut viator gravis ictu liquit seminecem, lacerumque saxo;

278. *Altera* pars clauda

235. Cressa *quoad* genus, *nomine* Pholoe, geminique

NOTES.

of mail usually consisted of several thin plates of iron or brass, which were fastened together with hooks or rings. Hence *consertam hamis.* See Æn. iii. 467. and vii. 639.

264. *Multiplicem. Multiplex*, any thing consisting of many folds, or thicknesses. Of *multum* et *plico.*

265. *Agebat palantes Troas.* The poet here pays to Æneas a very high compliment in an indirect manner. For if Damoleus was able to drive before him whole troops of Trojans, flying in confusion and dismay: how great a hero must he be, who slew this mighty champion!

266. *Facit:* in the sense of *dat.* This present was given to Gyas, who came in the third victor. *Signis:* with figures—with carved work.

268. *Donati:* were rewarded. The verb *sunt* is to be supplied.

270. *Revulsus.* Some copies have *revulsam*, agreeing with *ratem* vel *navem.* But *revulsus*, referring to Sergestus, is the most approved reading. If *revulsam* be read, then we must read *debilem*, instead of *debilis.*

271. *Debilis uno ordine:* disabled in one bank or tier of oars. Dr. Trapp thinks this means all the oars on one side. But this cannot be, since the galley had three banks or tiers of oars on a side.

273. *Aggere viæ. Agger viæ* is properly the eminence or the highest part of the road; which is raised or cast up in the middle for the purpose of carrying off the rain.

276. *Dat:* in the sense of *movet* vel *format. Tortus:* in the sense of *flexus.*

278. *Retentat:* in the sense of *moratur. Nexantem nodos:* in the sense of *torquentem se in nodos.* Heyne reads, *nodis.*

284. *Serva datur.* The games here are imitated from Homer. In that barbarous age, that one of the prizes should be a female, is no matter of wonder. *Haud ignara:* not unskilled in the works of Minerva; that is, in manufactures. The Cretans were very skilful in manufactures and the works of the loom.

286. *Certamine:* in the sense of *ludo Misso:* in the sense of *finito*, vel *dimisso.*

289. *Erat circus theatri.* The *theatrum* was the place at Rome appropriated for scenical representations. See Geor. ii. 381 The *circus* was destined for the celebration of the Roman games, especially horse-races It was built by *Tarquinius Priscus*, between

Consessu medium tulit, extructoque resedit.
Hìc, qui fortè velint rapido contendere cursu,
Invitat pretiis animos, et præmia ponit.
Undique conveniunt Teucri, mixtique Sicani:
Nisus et Euryalus, primi.
Euryalus formâ insignis, viridique juventâ;
Nisus, amore pio pueri: quos deinde secutus
Regius egregiâ Priami de stirpe Diores.
Hunc Salius, simul et Patron; quorum alter Acarnan:
Alter ab Arcadiâ, Tegeææ sanguine gentis.
Tum duo Trinacrii juvenes, Elymus Panopesque,
Assueti sylvis, comites senioris Acestæ.
Multi prætereà, quos fama obscura recondit.
Æneas quibus in mediis sic deinde locutus:
Accipite hæc animis, lætasque advertite mentes:
Nemo ex hoc numero mihi non donatus abibit.
Gnossia bina dabo lævato lucida ferro
Spicula, cœlatamque argento ferre bipennem:
Omnibus hic erit unus honos. Tres præmia primi
Accipient, flavâque caput nectentur olivâ.
Primus equum phaleris insignem victor habeto.
Alter Amazoniam pharetram, plenamque sagittis

291. Hìc pretiis invitat animos *eorum*, qui fortè velint

298. Salius, simul et Patron *secutus est* hunc

300. Tum *secuti sunt* duo Trinacrii

302. Prætereà multi *secuti sunt;* quos obscura

306. Dabo *iis* ferre bina Gnossia spicula lucida lævato ferro,

311. Alter *victor habeto*

NOTES.

the mountains *Aventinus* and *Palatinus*, for the celebration of games in imitation of the Olympic games. This Sicilian valley, having some resemblance to it, is therefore called *circus theatri*, the circuit of a theatre. See Geor. ii. 381.

290. *Resedit*, &c. The meaning probably is, that Æneas sat down upon an eminence that had been erected for the occasion. In this case, *loco* is to be understood with *extructo:* on a place built up. Ruæus seems to think otherwise: he says, *in composito cœtu resedit*. By connecting *consessu* with *extructo*, he implies that the company or assembly sat down on an elevated place. And it is no way improbable that Æneas, with some of the chief men, was seated in the centre of the whole assembly on an elevated place, that they might be the more conspicuous.

There seems to be here an allusion to the custom, in the Roman camp, of the general to address his soldiers from the *agger*, or *suggestus*.

292. *Pretiis*. By *pretium* we may understand the value of the rewards; and, by *præmia*, the rewards themselves.

296. *Pio amore*. *Pius amor* signifies a generous, tender, and disinterested love, such as that of parents to children. An account of the love of *Euryalus* for *Nisus*, we have in the 9th book, verse 176, and following. Nothing can more forcibly set forth his love for the lad, than that tender expostulation in his favor, verse 427 et seq. *quod vide.*

298. *Salius*. The names here mentioned are not of the poet's invention. Varro says that Salius came into Italy with Evander, and there instituted the Salian dance; which was performed by persons clad in armour, in honor of Mars. *Acarnan*, a native of *Acarnania:* a region of Epirus.

299. *Tegeææ gentis.* Tegea was a city of Arcadia, sacred to Pan. Patron was a native of this city, and Salius was of Epirus. Heyne reads *Arcadio*, an adj. agreeing with *sanguine:* of Arcadian blood. But Arcadia is the common reading.

302. *Quos fama:* whose names, fame obscure by length of time, hath concealed from us.

304. *Mentes:* thoughts—attention.

306. *Gnossia spicula:* Gnossian darts. *Gnossius*, an adj. from *Gnossus*, a city of Crete, whose darts and missive weapons were very much celebrated. The *spiculum* was about five feet long, tipped with steel of a triangular form: hence *lucida lævato ferro:* shining with polished steel. It was the same with the *pilum*, a military weapon, used by footmen; which in a charge, they darted against the enemy.

309. *Nectentur:* they shall be bound, as to the head, with yellow olive. This alludes to the conquerors at the Olympic games, who were crowned with garlands of olive leaves, which are of a yellow color. The olive was sacred to Minerva.

311. *Amazoniam:* an Amazonian quiver; one of the same form with those that the Amazons used. They were said to have

Threïciis; lato quam circùmplectitur auro
Balteus, et tereti subnectit fibula gemmâ.
Tertius Argolicâ hâc galeâ contentus abito.
Hæc ubi dicta, locum capiunt, signoque repentè
Corripiunt spatia audito, limenque relinquunt
Effusi, nimbo similes: simul ultima signant.
Primus abit, longèque ante omnia corpora Nisus
Emicat, et ventis et fulminis ocyor alis.
Proximus huic, longo sed proximus intervallo,
Insequitur Salius. Spatio pòst deinde relicto,
Tertius Euryalus.
Euryalumque Elymus sequitur. Quo deinde sub ipso
Ecce volat, calcemque terit jam calce Diores,
Incumbens humero: spatia et si plura supersint,
Transeat elapsus prior, ambiguumve relinquat.
Jamque ferè spatio extremo fessique sub ipsum
Finem adventabant: levi cùm sanguine Nisus
Labitur infelix, cæsis ut fortè juvencis
Fusus humum viridesque super madefecerat herbas.
Hìc juvenis, jam victor ovans, vestigia presso
Haud tenuit titubata solo: sed pronus in ipso
Concidit immundoque fimo, sacroque cruore.
Non tamen Euryali, non ille oblitus amorum:
Nam sese opposuit Salio per lubrica surgens;
Ille autem spissâ jacuit revolutus arenâ.
Emicat Euryalus, et munere victor amici
Prima tenet, plausuque volat fremituque secundo.
Pôst Elymus subit; et nunc tertia palma Diores.
Hic totum caveæ consessum ingentis, et ora

312. **Balteus** *è* **lato auro**

315. Ubi hæc *sunt* dicta, *omnes*

321. Deinde, spatio relicto pòst *Salium*, Euryalus *sequitur* tertius

323. Sub quo ipso ecce Diores deinde volat

326. *Certamen* ambiguum

329. Ut fortè *ex* juvencis cæsis fusus *erat* super humum, madefeceratque virides herbas.

334. Ille non *oblitus est* Euryali, non oblitus *est* amorum

335. Lubrica *loca*

336. Ille *Salius* jacuit

338. Tenet prima *spatia*, volatque

NOTES.

been a nation of females inhabiting a part of Thrace. Much is said of them among the ancients, the greater part of which is doubtless fable. *Alter:* in the sense of *secundus.*

312. *Circumplectitur.* The common reading is *circùm amplectitur.* Heyne reads, *circumplectitur*, and observes that the best copies do the same. *Balteus lato auro.* Ruæus says, *latus balteus ex auro.*

316. *Relinquunt limen:* they leave the mark, rushing forth like a tempest. *Corripiunt spatia:* they seize the first ground—they start. *Limen.* In the Roman circus, when at the height of its magnificence, the racers started from under a kind of portico; over whose threshold they leaped. Hence *limen* came to signify the starting place. In a temporary *circus*, such as the one here mentioned, a line drawn in the sand served as the barrier, or starting place. *Spatium* we may suppose to be the whole ground lying between the *carcer* and *meta.* The race was twice that distance, or divided in the middle by the *meta*, or turning place. Hence the propriety of the plu. *spatia*, as applied to the race ground.

317. *Signant*, &c. *Notant oculis, animoque designant metam*, says Heyne. They fix their eyes steadfastly upon the goal. *Ultima: spatia* is understood.

318. *Omnia corpora:* all the rest. Nisus is to be taken with *primus.* He gets the start of all the others.

323. *Sub quo ipso:* close up to whom—to Elymus.

325. *Si plura spatia supersint:* if there had been more distance to run, he would have overtaken Elymus and gotten ahead of him; or at least left the victory doubtful.

332. *Haud tenuit:* did not hold firm his tottering steps, &c.

337. *Munere:* in the sense of *beneficio.*

339. *Pòst Elymus subit:* afterward Elymus comes out; and now Diores (comes out) the third victor. *Palma:* the prize, or victory itself, put by meton. for the victor or conqueror.

340. *Ingentis caveæ.* The middle part or area of the Roman theatre was called *cavea*, because it was considerably lower than the other parts of it. Here the common people had their seats. It was capable of containing 80,000 men. By synec. put, for the whole theatre.

Prima patrum magnis Salius clamoribus implet;
Ereptumque dolo reddi sibi poscit honorem.
Tutatur favor Euryalum, lachrymæque decoræ,
Gratior et pulchro veniens in corpore virtus.

345. Diores adjuvat *Euryalum*

Adjuvat, et magnâ proclamat voce, Diores,
Qui subiit palmæ: frustràque ad præmia venit
Ultima, si primi Salio redduntur honores.
Tum pater Æneas, Vestra, inquit, munera vobis
Certa manent, pueri, et palmam movet ordine nemo.
Me liceat casûs misereri insontis amici.
Sic fatus, tergum Gætuli immane leonis
Dat Salio, villis onerosum atque unguibus aureis.
Hìc Nisus, Si tanta, inquit, sunt præmia victis,
Et te lapsorum miseret; quæ munera Niso
Digna dabis, primam merui qui laude coronam

356. Ni *eadem* inimica fortuna tulisset me, quæ *tulit* Salium

Ni me, quæ Salium, fortuna inimica tulisset?
Et simul his dictis faciem ostentabat, et udo
Turpia membra fimo. Risit pater optimus olli,
Et clypeum efferri jussit, Didymaonis artes,
Neptuni sacro Danais de poste refixum.
Hoc juvenem egregium præstanti munere donat.

362. Pòst, ubi cursus confecti *sunt*, et peregit dona, *Æneas inquit:* Nunc, si *sit* cui virtus, animusque præsens in pectore, *ille* adsit, et attollat brachia evinctis palmis

Pòst, ubi confecti cursus, et dona peregit:
Nunc, si cui virtus animusque in pectore præsens,
Adsit, et evinctis attollat brachia palmis.
Sic ait, et geminum pugnæ proponit honorem:

NOTES.

341. *Salius implet prima ora:* Salius fills the whole assembly of the huge pit, and the foremost seats of the fathers, &c. Virgil here applies a verb to two nouns, though in strict propriety it suits only one of them. *Implet concessum* is very proper, but *implet prima ora* can only be used in poetry. The *patres* and principal men sat in the first or foremost seats; hence the epithet *prima.* The meaning appears to be this: that *Salius* standing before, or in front of the *patres* or principal men, demanded the palm of victory in loud and vociferous language, which filled the ears of the whole assembly. *Prima ora patrum:* in the sense of *priores ordines, quibus seniores sedebant.*

344. *Veniens:* in the sense of *existens*, vel *apparens.*

346. *Venit ad ultima præmia.* The three first, by the condition of the race, were to have a prize. And Diores, who was next to Elymus, was entitled to the third or last, provided Salius was set aside, and Euryalus allowed to have the first prize.

351. *Tergum:* in the sense of *pellem.*

352. *Onerosum villis:* heavy with shag and golden claws. The fur of lions and other wild beasts were worn in ancient times by persons of distinction, and their claws were often gilt for ornament and show. Africa was infested with lions and other wild beasts of prey, especially *Gætulia,* whose lions are said to have been the largest, and the most savage.

355. *Laude:* in the sense of *virtute in cursu. Coronam:* honor—reward. *Merui.* in the sense of *meruissem.*

356. *Tulisset.* This verb here has a peculiar signification: to bear down, to overpower, or get the better of. Some explain it by Hypallage: for *tulissem inimicam fortunam;* but this is hardly allowable. Ruæus takes *tulisset* in the sense of *obstitisset.*

359. *Artes:* the workmanship of Didymaon. This is a fictitious name, signifying a skilful or ingenious workman.

360. *Refixum Danais:* torn down by the Greeks from the sacred post of Neptune's temple. Servius thinks that this was a buckler or shield, which Pyrrhus had taken from Neptune's temple in the sacking of Troy; and that after his death it fell into the hands of Helenus, who presented it to Æneas at his departure from Epirus. It was usual to fix up arms won from the enemy on the door posts of the temples, as consecrated offerings to the gods.

363. *Virtus.* This, for the most part, signifies military bravery, skill, and prowess. These the ancients considered the most valuable qualities and the first virtues.

364. *Palmis:* with his hands bound with the gauntlet.

Victori velatum auro vittisque juvencum ;
Ensem, atque insignem galeam, solatia victo.
Nec mora : continuò vastis cum viribus effert
Ora Dares, magnoque virûm se murmure tollit :
Solus qui Paridem solitus contendere contra :
Idemque ad tumulum, quo maximus occubat Hector,
Victorem Buten immani corpore, qui se
Bebryciâ veniens Amyci de gente ferebat,
Perculit, et fulvâ moribundum extendit arenâ.
Talis prima Dares caput altum in prælia tollit,
Ostenditque humeros latos, alternaque jactat
Brachia protendens, et verberat ictibus auras.
Quæritur huic alius : nec quisquam ex agmine tanto
Audet adire virum, manibusque inducere cæstus.
Ergò alacris, cunctosque putans excedere palmâ,
Æneæ stetit ante pedes : nec plura moratus,
Tum lævâ taurum cornu tenet, atque ita fatur :
Nate Deâ, si nemo audet se credere pugnæ,
Quæ finis standi ? quò me decet usque teneri ?
Ducere dona jube. Cuncti simul ore fremebant
Dardanidæ, reddique viro promissa jubebant.
Hìc gravis Entellum dictis castigat Acestes,
Proximus ut viridante toro consederat herbæ :
Entelle, heroum quondam fortissime frustrà,

367. Victo ensem atque insignem galeam *quæ sint* solatia *ejus*.

371. Idemque *Dares* ad tumulum, quo maximus Hector occubat, perculit victorem Buten immani corpore, qui ferebat se, *utpote* veniens de Bebryciâ gente Amyci, et extendit *eum* moribundum *in* flava arenâ.

384. Quòusque decet me teneri

386. Promissa *præmia* reddi

NOTES.

366. *Velatum auro vittisque :* ornamented with gold and fillets—simply, golden fillets, by *hendiadis.* It was customary to adorn the oxen with fillets, and gild their horns, both when they were designed for sacrifice, and also when they were to be given away as rewards of merit.

370. *Paridem.* Paris, the son of Priam, though dissolute and effeminate in his morals, was naturally strong and valiant, as appears from Homer, and always behaved himself well in arms. He is said to have been superior to Hector in the gauntlet fight. *Murmure :* applause—shouts of applause.

371. *Quo maximus Hector.* It is said, upon the death of Hector there was a truce of two months between the Greeks and Trojans, during which games were celebrated by the latter at Hector's tomb on the promontory of Sigeum; where Dares distinguished himself.

372. *Buten perculit :* he smote victorious Butes, of huge body, who boasted that he sprung from the Bebrycian race of Amycus, &c. The Butes here mentioned was not the son of Amycus and father of Eryx, for he must have been dead long before; but of another of the same name, who lived in the time of the Trojan wars, and boasted to be of the same race as the other.

373. *Bebryciâ.* This was the original name of Bythinia, a province of Asia Minor. Here Amycus reigned. He is said to have received no person into his dominions, only on the condition that they would try the gauntlet with him. He was at last vanquished and slain by Pollux, one of the Argonauts.

379. *Audet adire virum :* dares engage the man, and draw the gauntlets on his hands. It is not easy to say what was the exact nature of the cæstus. Some take it to be a kind of club or bludgeon, with lead at the end. It is more probable, however, it was a sort of leathern guard for the hands and arms, composed of thongs, and filled with lead to add force and weight to the blow. It was bound about the hands and arms, as high as the elbows, both as a guard, and to keep them from slipping off. This explains *evinctis palmis*, 364, supra.

To this, the account which Virgil here gives of the weapon best agrees. The word *cæstus* most probably is derived from the word *cædo.* The gauntlet fight was so cruel and bloody that the celebrated *Lycurgus* made a law forbidding the Spartans to practise it.

380. *Excedere palmâ :* to decline or leave the prize—to depart from it.

381. *Plura moratus.* Ruæus says, *diutius tardans. Plura* here, properly an adj. neu. plu. is taken adverbially in imitation of the Greeks.

384. *Standi :* in the sense of *expectandi.*

385. *Fremebant ore :* they all expressed approbation with their mouths

390. Tam-ne patiens sines tanta dona tolli

391. Ubi nunc *est* Eryx, ille Deus nobis, nequicquam memoratus *tuus* magister? Ubi *est tua* fama *inclyta*

397. Si, si nunc illa juventa foret mihi, quæ quondam fuerat

404. Animi *spectatorum* obstupuere: septem ingentia terga tantorum boum rigebant plumbo ferroque insuto.

413. Cernis *ea* adhuc infecta

414. Ego suetus *sum pugnare* his, dum melior sanguis dabat vires *mihi*, necdum æmula senectus sparsa canebat

Tantane tam patiens nullo certamine tolli
Dona sines? ubi nunc nobis Deus ille, magister
Nequicquam memoratus, Eryx? ubi fama per omnem
Trinacriam, et spolia illa tuis pendentia tectis?
Ille sub hæc: Non laudis amor, nec gloria cessit
Pulsa metu: sed enim gelidus tardante senectâ
Sanguis hebet, frigentque effœtæ in corpore vires.
Si mihi, quæ quondam fuerat, quâque improbus iste
Exultat fidens, si nunc foret illa juventa;
Haud equidem pretio inductus pulchroque juvenco
Venissem: nec dona moror. Sic deinde locutus,
In medium geminos immani pondere cæstus
Projecit: quibus acer Eryx in prælia suetus
Ferre manum, duroque intendere brachia tergo.
Obstupuere animi: tantorum ingentia septem
Terga boum plumbo insuto ferroque rigebant.
Ante omnes stupet ipse Dares, longèque recusat:
Magnanimusque Anchisiades, et pondus, et ipsa
Huc illuc vinclorum immensa volumina versat.
Tum senior tales referebat pectore voces:
Quid si quis cæstus ipsius et Herculis arma
Vidisset, tristemque hoc ipso in litore pugnam?
Hæc germanus Eryx quondam tuus arma gerebat.
Sanguine cernis adhuc fractoque infecta cerebro.
His magnum Alciden contra stetit: his ego suetus,
Dum melior vires sanguis dabat, æmula necdum
Temporibus geminis canebat sparsa senectus.
Sed, si nostra Dares hæc Troïus arma recusat,

NOTES.

394. *Sub:* in the sense of *ad. Inquit*, or a verb of the same import, is understood. *Non:* in the sense of *nec.*

395. *Enim:* in the sense of *equidem. Hebet:* is chilled. *Tardante:* enfeebling old age.

396. *Frigent:* fail. In the sense of *torpent.*

400. *Moror:* value—regard. *Præmium non curo*, says Heyne.

403. *Tergo:* properly the back; by *meton.* the hide or skin. *Ferre manum in prælia:* to engage in fight; a phrase. *Intendere:* in the sense of *cingere.*

406. *Longè:* in the sense of *valde* vel *vehementer. Recusat:* declines the fight.

407. *Anchisiades:* the son of Anchises—Æneas. A patronymic noun.

408. *Vinclorum:* by syn. for *vinculorum:* the *cæstus* or gauntlets with which their hands and arms were bound.

409. *Senior:* namely, Entellus.

411. *Tristem pugnam.* The fight is called *tristem*, sad or woful; because Eryx was slain. The occasion of the combat is said to have been this: Hercules having slain *Geryon*, king of Spain, was returning with his booty, which was a herd of fine oxen. In his way having visited Sicily, he received a challenge from Eryx to fight him with the gauntlet. If the victory fell to Eryx, he was to have the oxen; and if he were vanquished, the island of Sicily was to fall to Hercules. Some say one of the oxen passed over into Sicily and was taken by Eryx, who refused to give it up, which occasioned the combat.

412. *Tuus germanus Eryx:* your brother Eryx. See verse 24, supra.

413. *Fracto.* This is the reading of Heyne, on the authority of Heinsius, Burmannus, and others, as he informs us. The common reading is *sparso.* The sense is the same with either.

414. *Alciden:* Hercules, who, though the reputed son of Jupiter and Alcmene, was also called *Amphitryoniades*, from *Amphitryo*, the husband of *Alcmene;* and *Alcides*, from *Alcæus* the father of *Amphitryo.* See Æn. vi. 801.

415. *Æmula senectus:* envious age, not yet spread over my temples, &c. The meaning is: while old age had not yet covered his head with gray hairs. Some say, old age is here called (*æmula*) *envious*, because it is apt to envy the strength and vigor of youth, and emulate their feats in vain. But it may be called *envious* on account of the many evils and infirmities which it

Idque pio sedet Æneæ, probat auctor Acestes;
Æquemus pugnas. Erycis tibi terga remitto;
Solve metus: et tu Trojanos exue cæstus.
Hæc fatus, duplicem ex humeris dejecit amictum:
Et magnos membrorum artus, magna ossa, lacertosque
Exuit; atque ingens mediâ consistit arenâ.
Tum satus Anchisâ cæstus pater extulit æquos,
Et paribus palmas amborum innexuit armis.
Constitit in digitos extemplò arrectus uterque,
Brachiaque ad superas interritus extulit auras.
Abduxere retro longè capita ardua ab ictu:
Immiscentque manus manibus, pugnamque lacessunt.
Ille, pedum melior motu, fretusque juventâ;
Hic, membris et mole valens: sed tarda trementi
Genua labant: vastos quatit æger anhelitus artus.
Multa viri nequicquam inter se vulnera jactant;
Multa cavo lateri ingeminant; et pectore vastos
Dant sonitus: erratque aures et tempora circum
Crebra manus: duro crepitant sub vulnere malæ.
Stat gravis Entellus, nisuque immotus eodem:
Corpore tela modò atque oculis vigilantibus exit.
Ille, velut celsam oppugnat qui molibus urbem,
Aut montana sedet circum castella sub armis;
Nunc hos, nunc illos aditus, omnemque pererrat
Arte locum, et variis assultibus irritus urget.
Ostendit dextram insurgens Entellus, et altè
Extulit: ille ictum venientem à vertice velox
Prævidit, celerique elapsus corpore cessit.
Entellus vires in ventum effudit, et ultrò
Ipse gravis, graviterque ad terram pondere vasto
Concidit: ut quondam cava concidit aut Erymantho,

424. Tum pater *Æneas* satus Anchisâ extulit

439. Ille, velut qui oppugnat molibus celsam urbem, aut sedet sub armis circum montana castella, nunc pererrat hos, nunc illos aditus, omnemque locum arte.

448. Ut quondam cava pinus eruta radicibus, concidit aut

NOTES.

brings along with it, and the little comfort it yields, as if it envied man the enjoyment of life. *Æmula:* in the sense of *invida.*

418. *Sedet:* in the sense of *placet* vel *probatur. Auctor:* the author or adviser of the combat.

419. *Terga:* the gauntlets of Eryx.

423. *Exuit:* in the sense of *nudavit.*

425. *Innexuit:* bound the hands, &c.

426. *In digitos:* upon their toes. Each stood tiptoe that the blow might fall with the more force.

430. *Ille, melior motu:* the former (Dares) is more active in the movements of his feet, and relying upon his youth; the latter (Entellus) excelling, &c.

431. *Membris et mole:* simply, the size of his limbs, by hend.

432. *Tarda janua labant:* his feeble knees totter under him trembling. Hard breathing, &c.

433. *Nequicquam:* in vain, because they were without effect. *Vulnera:* in the sense of *ictus.*

434. *Ingeminant:* they repeat.

435. *Errat:* moves, or passes around, &c.

437. *Gravis:* in the sense of *firmus.*

438. *Modò exit:* he only with his body and watchful eyes avoids the blows. *Exit:* in the sense of *evitat* vel *eludit. Tela:* for *ictus.*

439. *Molibus:* with batteries: engines.

441. *Pererrat:* in the sense of *exquirit.*

442. *Irritus:* being foiled—disappointed—baffled.

445. *Elapsus cessit:* simply for *elabitur.*

447. *Et ipse gravis, graviterque:* and heavy he fell heavily to the ground with his vast weight. The *graviterque* appears to be merely expletive. The sense is complete without it. Entellus had raised himself with the intention of giving a heavier blow to Dares, who, having observed it, slipt from the stroke. By these means his own natural weight, and the impetus he gave to himself, brought him to the ground. Or the *gravis* may refer to his unwieldy size and bulk, while the *graviter* refers to the violence of the shock he gave himself in missing the blow aimed at Dares. But this is rather a refinement.

448. *Erymantho:* Erymanthus was a fa-

Aut Idâ in magnâ, radicibus eruta pinus.

450. *Diversis* studiis

Consurgunt studiis Teucri et Trinacria pubes:
It clamor cœlo: primusque accurrit Acestes,
Æquævumque ab humo miserans attollit amicum
At non tardatus casu, neque territus heros:
Acrior ad pugnam redit, ac vim suscitat ira:
Tum pudor incendit vires, et conscia virtus:
Præcipitemque Daren ardens agit æquore toto;
Nunc dextrâ ingeminans ictus, nunc ille sinistrâ.
Nec mora, nec requies: quàm multâ grandine nimbi
Culminibus crepitant; sic densis ictibus heros
Creber utrâque manu pulsat versatque Dareta.

461. Pater Æneas haud passus *est* iras

Tum pater Æneas, procedere longiùs iras,
Et sævire animis Entellum haud passus acerbis:
Sed finem imposuit pugnæ; fessumque Dareta
Eripuit, mulcens dictis, ac talia fatur:
Infelix! quæ tanta animum dementia cepit?
Non vires alias, conversaque numina sentis?
Cede Deo. Dixitque, et prælia voce diremit.

468. Ast fidi æquales ducunt illum ad naves, trahentemque ægra genua

Ast illum fidi æquales, genua ægra trahentem,
Jactantemque utroque caput, crassumque cruorem
Ore ejectantem mixtosque in sanguine dentes,
Ducunt ad naves: galeamque ensemque vocati
Accipiunt: palmam Entello taurumque relinquunt.
Hìc victor, superans animis, tauroque superbus,
Nate Deâ, vosque hæc, inquit, cognoscite, Teucri,
Et mihi quæ fuerint juvenili in corpore vires,

476. Et à qua morte servetis

Et quâ servetis revocatum à morte Dareta.
Dixit: et adversi contra stetit ora juvenci,

480. Arduusque, dextrâ reducta, libravit duros cæstus inter media cornua, illisitque *eos* in ossa, cerebro effracto,

Qui donum adstabat pugnæ: durosque reductâ
Libravit dextrâ media inter cornua cæstus
Arduus, effractoque illisit in ossa cerebro.
Sternitur, exanimisque tremens procumbit humi, bos

NOTES.

mous wood and mountain in Arcadia, where Hercules slew the celebrated boar.

453. *At heros non tardatus:* but the hero not disabled, nor terrified by the fall, &c. By the rules of the combat, if one fell, the other was not to take the advantage of it, but allow him time to rise and return to the fight.

459. *Sic:* in the sense of *tam*, corresponding with *quàm* in the preceding line. *Nimbi:* storms.

463. *Eripuit fessum Dareta:* he rescued weary Dares. Virgil follows Homer throughout these games, but has varied from him in the issue of the combat, with judgment, and with an improvement of the moral. He gives his readers the pleasure of seeing an arrogant boaster humbled by an infirm old man, roused by his courage to engage in an unequal contest. Whereas in Homer, the younger and the stronger vanquishes the more feeble, which contributes nothing to the surprise or pleasure of the reader.

466. *Non sentis alias vires:* do you not perceive other strength, and the gods to be changed? *Alias vires:* other or foreign strength—that which you did not expect to be exerted against you, and therefore it is in vain to contend. *Cede Deo.* By the god here mentioned we are to understand the one by whom Entellus was aided; perhaps *Eryx*, whom the Sicilians had deified.

470. *Ejectantem:* some copies have *rejectantem.* Pierius prefers this. Heyne reads *ejectantem;* so also Heinsius and Davidson.

473. *Superans:* in the sense of *lætans.*

476. *Revocatum:* rescued—freed—delivered.

478. *Donum:* in the sense of *præmium.*

481. *Sternitur:* the ox falls, and trembling, &c. This verse *Servius* thinks a very bad one, because it ends with a monosyllable. Mr. Davidson thinks it is to be admired for that very reason. This abrupt ending of the verse, says he, is like a rub in a person's

Ille super tales effudit pectore voces:
Hanc tibi, Eryx, meliorem animam pro morte Daretis
Persolvo: hìc victor cæstus artemque repono.
Protinùs Æneas celeri certare sagittâ
Invitat, qui fortè velint, et præmia ponit:
Ingentique manu malum de nave Seresti
Erigit; et volucrem trajecto in fune columbam,
Quò tendant ferrum, malo suspendit ab alto.
Convenere viri: dejectamque ærea sortem
Accepit galea: et primus clamore secundo
Hyrtacidæ ante omnes exit locus Hippocoöntis·
Quem modò navali Mnestheus certamine victor
Consequitur, viridi Mnestheus evinctus olivâ.
Tertius Eurytion, tuus, ô clarissime, frater,
Pandare: qui quondam, jussus confundere fœdus,
In medios telum torsisti primus Achivos.
Extremus galeâque imâ subsedit Acestes,
Ausus et ipse manu juvenum tentare laborem.
Tum validis flexos incurvant viribus arcus,
Pro se quisque, viri, et depromunt tela pharetris:
Primaque per cœlum nervo stridente sagitta
Hyrtacidæ juvenis volucres diverberat auras,
Et venit, adversique infigitur arbore mali.
Intremuit malus, timuitque exterrita pennis
Ales, et ingenti sonuerunt omnia plausu.
Pòst acer Mnestheus adducto constitit arcu

482. Super *bove*

488. Et suspendit ab alto malo volucrem columbam

492. Locus Hippocoöntis Hyrtacidæ exit primus ante omnes

495. Eurytion *est* tertius, tuus

501. Tum viri, quisque pro se, incurvant flexos arcus

506. Omnia *loca*

NOTES.

way; it forces him to stop and dwell upon the object with attention.

483. *Meliorem:* either, because brute victims were more acceptable to the gods than human victims; or it alludes to the second victims, which, when the first escaped, were substituted in their room, and were called *meliores*, better. *Animam:* in the sense of *victimam.*

484. *Repono*, &c. This is an allusion to the gladiators in after times, who, when their age exempted them from practising the art, hung up the arms of their profession on the doorposts of the temple of Hercules. *Persolvo:* in the sense of *immolo.*

487. *Ingentique manu:* Æneas may not do it with his own hand; for men are often said to do what they order to be done by others. Heyne says, *magna multitudine.*

488. *In fune trajecto:* by a rope put through the mast; *trajecto per malum. Volucrem:* fluttering. *Ferrum:* for *sagittam.*

491. *Ærea galea accepit*, &c. In war, and among soldiers, a helmet supplied the place of an urn to receive the lots.

492. *Hippocoöntis.* Hippocoön, the son of Hyrtacus. Homer says he was cousin to Rhesus, who was slain by Ulysses and Diomede in the first night after his arrival on the Trojan shore. See Æn. i. 469. *Locus:* in the sense of *sors*

496. *Pandare.* Pandarus was the son of Lycaon. Homer makes him to have broken the truce (*confundere fœdus*) between the Greeks and Trojans, when they had agreed to put the decision of the war upon the issue of a single combat between Paris and Menelaus. Paris was rescued by Venus, when he was nearly overcome. Juno, unwilling that the disaster of Troy should so soon be terminated, urged Jupiter to bring about a violation of the truce. He employed Minerva as his agent in the business. By her persuasion, Pandarus shot an arrow among the Greeks at Menelaus, which rekindled the war. The epithet *clarissime*, is given to him as being a distinguished archer. Homer equals him to Apollo. He was at last killed by Diomede.

498. *Acestes subsedit.* Acestes remained the last in the bottom of the helmet: that is, the lot of Acestes.

501. *Tela:* in the sense of *sagittæ.*

502. *Sagitta juvenis Hyrtacidæ:* the arrow of the youth Hippocoön first, &c. *Stridente nervo:* from the whizzing string.

503. *Volucres auras:* the light air.

504. *Arbore mali:* in the wood of the mast.

505. *Timuit:* fluttered with her wings—expressed signs of fear.

506. *Ingenti plausu:* with loud shouts, or acclamations of the spectators.

Alta petens, pariterque oculos telumque tetendit:
Ast ipsam miserandus avem contingere ferro
Non valuit: nodos et vincula linea rupit,
Queis innexa pedem malo pendebat ab alto.
Illa Notos atque atra volans in nubila fugit.
Tum rapidus jamdudum arcu contenta parato
Tela tenens, fratrem Eurytion in vota vocavit:
Jam vacuo lætam cœlo speculatus, et alis
Plaudentem nigrâ figit sub nube columbam
Decidit exanimis, vitamque reliquit in astris
Aëriis, fixamque refert delapsa sagittam.
Amissâ solus palmâ superabat Acestes:
Qui tamen æthereas telum contorsit in auras,
Ostentans artem pariter arcumque sonantem.
Hìc oculis subitò objicitur magnoque futurum
Augurio monstrum: docuit pòst exitus ingens,
Seraque terrifici cecinerunt omina vates.
Namque volans liquidis in nubibus arsit arundo,
Signavitque viam flammis, tenuesque recessit
Consumpta in ventos: cœlo ceu sæpe refixa
Transcurrunt, crinemque volantia sidera ducunt.
Attonitis hæsêre animis, Superosque precati
Trinacrii Teucrique viri: nec maximus omen
Abnuit Æneas: sed lætum amplexus Acesten
Muneribus cumulat magnis, ac talia fatur:

515. Jam speculatus columbam lætum in vacuo cœlo, et plaudentem alis, figit *eam* sub

523. Ingens exitus docuit *hoc* pòst

527. Ceu sæpe sidera refixa *è* cœlo transcurrunt, volantiaque

NOTES.

510. *Nodos et linea vincula rupit:* he cut the knots, and the hempen cords, with which, being tied by the foot, &c. Mr. Pope, in comparing the games of Homer and Virgil, owns that Virgil has outdone his master by the addition of two circumstances that make a beautiful gradation. In Homer, the first archer cuts the string that held the bird, and the other shoots him as he is mounting. In Virgil, the first only hits the mark, the second cuts the string, the third shoots him, and the fourth, to show the strength of his arm, directs his arrow up to heaven, where it kindles into a flame, and makes a prodigy.

512. *Fugit in notos: Notus* is properly the south wind. Sometimes it is put for any wind. Here it seems to be used for the air simply; wind being only air put in motion. *In nubes ac cœlum evolavit*, says Heyne.

513. *Tum rapidus Eurytion:* then intrepid Eurytion, a long time holding the arrow extended on his ready bow, &c. Servius says that *Pandarus* was worshipped as a hero among the Lycians. This explains the conduct of Eurytion in invoking him, in this critical moment, to direct his arrow.

520. *Contorsit:* the reading of Heyne is *contendit.*

523. *Monstrum:* here a prodigy, and about to be of great import, is suddenly presented to our eyes. *Monstrum* signifies any thing that is, or happens, contrary to the ordinary course of events. It is from *monstro;* because prodigies were thought to be sent from heaven to signify some remarkable future event. This one presaged the burning of the fleet of Æneas. *Subitò.* This is the common reading. Heyne, after Heinsius, reads *subitum.*

524. *Cecinerunt:* they interpreted the omens late.

Servius explains *sera* by *gravia*, others by *futura*, and Cerdanus by *tarda.* The common aceptation of the word is the easiest, implying that the soothsayers could make nothing of the omen, till the event took place; and then, when it was too late to avert it, and the ships on fire, they agreed that this must have been the thing signified by the prodigy.

528. *Crinem:* a train of light.

529. *Hæsêre attonitis:* they stood with astonished minds. Ruæus says: *steterunt stupefacti animo.*

531. *Æneas abnuit:* nor did great Æneas reject the omen; but embracing joyful Acestes, &c. He accepted it, considering it to be propitious or favorable to him. He was probably led to this from its resemblance to that which shone from the head of *Ascanius*, his son. See Æn. ii. 680. It appears from this that the soothsayers had not yet interpreted the omen; otherwise Æneas would not have received it with joy.

Sume, pater; nam te voluit rex magnus Olympi
Talibus auspiciis exsortem ducere honorem.
Ipsius Anchisæ longævi hoc munus habebis:
Cratera impressum signis, quem Thracius olim
Anchisæ genitori, in magno munere, Cisseus
Ferre sui dederat monumentum et pignus amoris.
Sic fatus, cingit viridanti tempora lauro,
Et primum ante omnes victorem appellat Acesten
Nec bonus Eurytion prælato invidit honori,
Quamvis solus avem cœlo dejecit ab alto.
Proximus ingreditur donis, qui vincula rupit:
Extremus, volucri qui fixit arundine malum.
  At pater Æneas, nondum certamine misso,
Custodem ad sese comitemque impubis Iüli
Epytiden vocat, et fidam sic fatur ad aurem:
Vade, age, et, Ascanio, si jam puerile paratum
Agmen habet secum, cursusque instruxit equorum,
Ducat avo turmas, et sese ostendat in armis,
Dic, ait. Ipse omnem longo decedere circo
Infusum populum, et campos jubet esse patentes.
Incedunt pueri, pariterque ante ora parentum
Frænatis lucent in equis: quos omnis euntes
Trinacriæ mirata fremit Trojæque juventus.
Omnibus in morem tonsâ coma pressa coronâ.
Cornea bina ferunt præfixa hastilia ferro,
Pars leves humero pharetras: it pectore summo
Flexilis obtorti per collum circulus auri.

533. Sume *hæc, O* pater

536. Quem Thracius Cisseus olim dederat Anchisæ genitori ferre in magno munere, *quasi* monumentum et pignus sui amoris.

544. *Ille ingreditur* extremus, qui fixit

545. At pater Æneas. certamine nondum misso, vocat Epytiden ad sese

548. Vade, age, ait, et dic Ascanio, si jam habet puerile agmen paratum secum, instruxitque cursus equorum, *ut* ducat turmas avo, et

556. Coma pressa *est* omnibus tonsâ coronâ in morem.

558. Pars *fert* leves pharetras humero.

NOTES.

534. *Exsortem:* compounded of *ex* and *sors.* An allusion is here had to a custom among the Greeks, who used, before the booty was divided among the soldiers, to give those who had distinguished themselves, some of the choicest articles, not by lot, but as they judged meet and right. By *exsortem honorem,* we are, therefore, to understand *the first* or *choicest honor.* Davidson renders it, *an honor out of course.* Heyne reads, *exsortem honores,* referring the *exsortem* to the pron. *te.* Valpy reads the same. Ruæus says, *extraordinarium honorem.* The common reading is *exsortem honorem.*

Talibus auspiciis: by such signs, tokens, or omens.

536. *Signis:* in the sense of *figuris.*

537. *Cisseus.* He was king of Thrace, and the father of Hecuba, the first wife of Priam.

541. *Prælato.* Heyne takes this in the sense of *prærepto.* He does not envy the honor taken from him, and given to Acestes. But *prælato* may retain its usual signification, if we give the passage this gloss: he does not envy the honor to Acestes preferred before him. This is the sense of Markland.

543. *Ingreditur:* he enters next for the prizes, who, &c. Both *ingreditur,* and *incedit* are military terms, and imply stateliness, and an air of dignity and pride.

546. *Custodem:* either the guardian of his education, or his tutor in the military art.

547. *Epytiden:* a patronymic noun; the son of *Epytus,* the herald of Anchises. His name was *Periphas,* or *Periphantes.*

549. *Agmen:* troop—battalion. *Instruxit cursus:* hath arranged the movements, march, &c.

551. *Circo:* ring—course. *Infusum:* in the sense of *diffusum,* vel *sparsum.*

553. *Pueri incedunt:* the boys march forward, and shine equally, &c. This game, commonly known by the name of *lusus Trojæ,* is wholly of the poet's invention. He had no hint of it from Homer. He substituted this in the room of three in Homer. (viz.) *the wrestling, the single combat, and the discus;* and it is worth them all. Virgil added this game to please *Augustus,* who, at that time, renewed the same.

554. *Fremit:* in the sense of *plaudit,* vel *laudat.*

556. *Tonsa corona.* This crown consisted of green boughs, bent into a circular form, resembling a crown. It was probably placed upon their helmets.

559. *Flexilis circulus obtorti auri.* This is a circumlocution to express *a golden chain.*

563. *Est* una acies juvenum, quam ovantem parvus Priamus

566. Vestigia primi pedis *sunt*

568. Alter *dux est* Atys.

570. Extremus *dux est* Iülus, pulcher ante omnes formâ, invectus Sidonio equo

578. *Illis* paratis

582. Infesta tela *in se invicem.*

Tres equitum numero turmæ, ternique vagantur
Ductores: pueri bis seni quemque secuti,
Agmine partito fulgent, paribusque magistris
Una acies juvenum, ducit quam parvus ovantem
Nomen avi referens Priamus, tua clara, Polite,
Progenies, auctura Italos: quem Thracius albis
Portat equus bicolor maculis: vestigia primi
Alba pedis, frontemque ostentans arduus albam.
Alter Atys, genus unde Attî duxere Latini;
Parvus Atys, pueroque puer dilectus Iülo.
Extremus, formâque ante omnes pulcher, Iülus
Sidonio est invectus equo; quem candida Dido
Esse sui dederat monumentum et pignus amoris.
Cætera Trinacriis pubes senioris Acestæ
Fertur equis.
  Excipiunt plausu pavidos, gaudentque tuentes
Dardanidæ; veterumque agnoscunt ora parentum.
Postquam omnem læti consessum oculosque suorum
Lustravêre in equis: signum clamore paratis
Epytides longè dedit, insonuitque flagello.
Olli discurrêre pares, atque agmina terni
Diductis solvêre choris; rursùsque vocati
Convertêre vias, infestaque tela tulere.
Inde alios ineunt cursus, aliosque recursus,

NOTES.

goes over the neck, down to the upper part of the breast.

560. *Vagantur:* march along. *Oberrant*, says Ruæus.

562. *Magistris:* in the sense of *ducibus.*

564. *Polite.* Polites was the son of Priam, and slain by Pyrrhus in the presence of his father. See Æn. ii. 526. He is said, however, to have accompanied Æneas into Italy, and to have founded the city *Politorium*, which was afterward destroyed by Ancus, a king of the Romans. Virgil seems to attribute the building of the city to his son here mentioned. *Auctura Italos:* either to increase the Italians by founding a city, or by conferring honor and dignity upon them.

566. *Vestigia:* the fetlocks of his fore feet. Cerdanus explains this of his right foot alone. But *vestigia* is here evidently used out of its ordinary sense.

568. *Unde genus:* whence the Latin *Atti*, &c. Virgil mentions this in compliment to his prince, whose mother's name was *Attia.* Attius Balbus married Julia, the sister of Julius Cæsar, and had by her a daughter, who married Octavius, the father of Augustus. The poet signalizes *Iülus*, and *Atys*, the founders of his prince's family, both on his father's and mother's side: and by making so close a friendship to subsist between the two, he alludes to the affinity between the Julian and Attian families, now united in the person of Augustus. Some say however, that he was the son of Julia, the sister of Cæsar, and his lawful heir.

576. *Dardanidæ excipiunt:* the Trojans with applause receive them, anxious and solicitous for praise and victory; and, beholding them, they rejoice, and know the features of their aged parents. They trace the resemblance between the children and parents, and know the former by the latter For *pavidos*, Ruæus says, *solicitos de gloria.*

577. *Postquam læti:* after they joyous went round the whole assembly, and the eyes of their parents, &c. The *oculos suorum*, if duly considered, will appear very beautiful and emphatic. They made the circuit of the spectators', and their parents' eyes; as much as to say, their parents were all eyes, and all attention to their motions and whole deportment.

580. *Pares.* This may imply that they moved or marched abreast—head and head in the sense of *pariter.* Or it may mean that they marched in a double file, that is, two abreast. This is the sense given to *pares*, by Davidson. *Terni:* some copies have *ternis*, which makes the sense easier. The meaning of the passage is: after they had marched round the company in order to be reviewed, upon a signal given, they (the three leaders, *terni*) divided (*solvêre*) the troops into three separate companies, (*di ductis choris*) and marched over the plain each company performing its exercises on different grounds.

581. *Choris:* in the sense of *turmis.*

583. *Cursus:* a going forward—advance *Recursus:* a retreat—a going backward.

Adversis spatiis; alternosque orbibus orbes
Impediunt, pugnæque cient simulacra sub armis.
Et nunc terga fugâ nudant, nunc spicula vertunt
Infensi, factâ pariter nunc pace feruntur.
Ut quondam Cretâ fertur Labyrinthus in altâ
Parietibus textum cæcis iter, ancipitemque
Mille viis habuisse dolum, quà signa sequendi
Falleret indeprensus et irremeabilis error.
Haud aliter Teucrûm nati vestigia cursu
Impediunt, texuntque fugas et prælia ludo:
Delphinum similes, qui per maria humida nando
Carpathium Libycumque secant, luduntque per undas.
Hunc morem cursûs, atque hæc certamina primus
Ascanius, longam muris cùm cingeret Albam,
Rettulit, et priscos docuit celebrare Latinos;
Quo puer ipse modo, secum quo Troïa pubes:
Albani docuere suos: hinc maxima porrò
Accepit Roma, et patrium servavit honorem:
Trojaque nunc pueri, Trojanum dicitur agmen.
  Hàc celebrata tenus sancto certamina patri.
Hìc primùm fortuna fidem mutata novavit.
Dum variis tumulo referunt solemnia ludis,
Irim de cœlo misit Saturnia Juno
Iliacam ad classem: ventosque aspirat eunti,
Multa movens, necdum antiquum saturata dolorem.
Illa viam celerans per mille coloribus arcum,

586. **Nunc** *quasi* **infensi** vertunt spicula *in se invicem*

588. **Ut Labyrinthus** in alta Cretâ **fertur** quondam habuisse iter textum cæcis parietibus, dolumque ancipitem mille viis, quà

597. Ascanius primus rettulit hunc morem cursûs, atque hæc certamina, cùm

599. Quo modo puer ipse *celebravit ea*, quo *modo* Troïa pubes secum; *eodem modo* Albani docuere suos *posteros*. hinc porrò maxima Roma accepit

602. Nuncque pueri *et* Trojanum agmen dicitur Troja

603. Hàctenus certamina celebrata *sunt* sancto patri

609. Illa virgo *Iris* celerans viam

NOTES.

Alios appears to be merely expletive in both places. *Ineunt:* they advance and retreat from opposite grounds, or in front of each other.

584. *Alternos orbes:* alternate circles, or circles in turn, one after another. Heyne reads *alternis*, agreeing with *orbibus*. *Impediunt:* in the sense of *implicant* vel *miscent*. *Cient:* in the sense of *exhibent*.

587. *Feruntur:* in the sense of *incedunt*.

589. *Cæcis:* obscure—dark. *Ancipitem dolum:* a maze, intricate, and perplexed by a thousand passages. The Labyrinth was an edifice full of cells, which communicated with one another; and was perplexed with winding avenues, disposed in such manner as to lead backward and forward in a maze; and so bewildered those who entered it, that they could not trace their way out. The original one was in Egypt, carried on at the expense of many kings, and at last finished by *Psammetichus*. After this model, Dædalus built one in Crete, but much smaller, in which the *Minotaur* was confined.

590. *Quà signa sequendi:* where error undiscoverable, and inextricable, deceived the signs of going forward. The nature of the labyrinth was to perplex and bewilder the visitant, while he discovered, or knew nothing of it; and when he supposed he was coming out, to carry him backward.

594. *Similes delphinum:* like dolphins. *Similes* has sometimes the genitive after it; but most commonly the dative.

595. *Carpathium:* an adj. That part of the Mediterranean between Crete and the island of Rhodes, was called the Carpathian sea, from the island *Carpathus*. *Libycum:* an adj. from *Libya*, a part of Africa lying over against Crete. *Mare* is understood.

595. *Hunc morem cursûs.* Heyne reads, *hunc morem, hos cursus.*

604. *Mutata novavit:* simply for *mutavit*, says Heyne. Fortune is here represented as a friend, on whom Æneas had depended for favor and protection. She now changes sides, breaks her faith, and becomes treacherous. *Referunt:* they pay—perform.

606. *Irim misit.* Servius observes, that as Mercury is mostly sent on messages of peace, so Iris is generally sent on mesages of mischief and contention. She is chiefly employed by Juno, but sometimes carries messages for the other deities.

607. *Aspirat ventos:* Ruæus says, *adjuvat eam euntem ventis.*

608. *Movens multa:* revolving much mischief in her mind—plotting, &c. *Saturata* may be taken as a Grecism. Here is an allusion to the decision of Paris. See Æn. i. 4.

Nulli visa cito decurrit tramite virgo.
Conspicit ingentem concursum; et litora lustrat,
Desertosque videt portus, classemque relictam.
At procul in solâ secretæ Troades actâ
Amissum Anchisen flebant, cunctæque profundum
Pontum aspectabant flentes: heu, tot vada fessis,
Et tantum superesse maris! vox omnibus una.
Urbem orant: tædet pelagi perferre laborem.
Ergò inter medias sese haud ignara nocendi
Conjicit, et faciemque Deæ vestemque reponit.
Fit Beroë, Ismarii conjux longæva Dorycli,
Cui genus, et quondam nomen, natique fuissent.
Ac sic Dardanidûm mediam se matribus infert:
O miseræ, quas non manus, inquit, Achaïca bello
Traxerit ad letum, patriæ sub mœnibus! ô gens
Infelix! cui te exitio fortuna reservat?
Septima post Trojæ excidium jam vertitur æstas;
Cùm freta, cùm terras omnes, tot inhospita saxa,
Sideraque emensæ ferimur; dum per mare magnum
Italiam sequimur fugientem, et volvimur undis.
Hìc Erycis fines fraterni, atque hospes Acestes:
Quis prohibet muros jacere, et dare civibus urbem?
O patria, et rapti nequicquam ex hoste Penates!
Nullane jam Trojæ dicentur mœnia? nusquam

611. Concursum *ad ludos vel certamina.*

615. Heu! tot vada et tantum maris superesse *nobis* fessis! *erat* una vox omnibus.

618. Ergò *Iris* haud ignara *artis* nocendi conjicit sese inter

623. O miseræ *vos*, inquit, quas Achaïca manus non traxerit ad letum *in* bello sub

630. Hìc *sunt* fraterni fines Erycis, atque *hic est*

633. Nulla-ne mœnia dicentur *mœnia* Trojæ?

NOTES.

611. *Lustrat.* Ruæus reads, *lustrans*—Heyne, *lustrat.* Davidson, also, reads, *lustrat.*

613. *At Troades*, &c. It was reckoned an indecency among the Greeks and Romans, for women to be present at the public games. Virgil, who all along has a view to the Roman customs, represents the matrons as apart by themselves on the lonely shore, deploring the death of Anchises.

620. *Beroë—Dorycli:* these are fictitious names. *Ismarii:* an adj. from *Ismarus*, a mountain in Thrace.

621. *Cui quondam:* to whom there was a noble descent, and once renown, and illustrious offspring. *Genus* here is used in the sense of *nobilitas;* Valpy says, rank. *Nomen:* in the sense of *fama.*

623. *Achaïca manus:* the Grecian troops.

628. *Ferimur:* in the sense of *vagamur* vel *erramus. Emensæ:* having measured out—having passed over so many seas, &c. *Ferimur emensæ:* in the sense of *emensæ sumus*, says Heyne. *Sidera:* climes--regions. To account for Æneas's having spent seven years in his voyage, a French critic (says Davidson) has the following computation. He finds from history that Troy was taken in the month of May or June. He allows Æneas ten months for fitting out his fleet at Artandros, and makes him set out in the month of March in the following year. From this to his arrival in Epirus he computes four years and some months which time he spent in building cities in Thrace and in Crete. Having spent some time in Epirus, he set out from thence in the end of autumn in the fifth year, and having made a compass almost round Sicily, arrived at *Drepanum* in the beginning of the following year. Here he lost his father in the beginning of February, and, according to the custom of the ancients, devoted ten months to grief and retirement. According to his calculation, Æneas did not sail from Sicily till the month of November, and here the action of the Æneid begins. Æn. i. 34. *Vix è conspectu.* Soon after this he was driven by a storm on the coast of Carthage, about the middle of the seventh year of his voyage, where he spent three months of winter, and from thence set out for Italy in the end of January following, and arrived again in Sicily in the month of February, about the end of the seventh year, where he spent one month in celebrating his father's anniversary, and about the beginning of the eighth year arrived in Italy, in the end of March or beginning of April, when the spring was in bloom.

629. *Sequimur Italiam:* while over the mighty deep we pursue Italy fleeing from us. This is highly poetical. Servius takes *magnum* to mean stormy—swelling high Heyne says, *vastum—immensum. Volvimur* in the sense of *jactamur.*

630. *Fraterni.* For the reasons that *Eryx* is here called the brother of Æneas, see 24, supra.

Hectoreos amnes, Xanthum et Simoënta videbo?
Quin agite, et mecum infaustas exurite puppes.
Nam mihi Cassandræ per somnum vatis imago
Ardentes dare visa faces: hìc quærite Trojam;
Hìc domus est, inquit, vobis: jam tempus agit res.
Nec tantis mora prodigiis: en quatuor aræ
Neptuno! Deus ipse faces animumque ministrat.
Hæc memorans, prima infensum vi corripit ignem
Sublatâque procul dextrâ connixa coruscat,
Et jacit. Arrectæ mentes, stupefactaque corda
Iliadum. Hìc una è multis, quæ maxima natu,
Pyrgo, tot Priami natorum regia nutrix:
Non Beroë vobis; non hæc Rhœteïa, matres,
Est Dorycli conjux: divini signa decoris,
Ardentesque notate oculos: qui spiritus illi,
Qui vultus, vocisve sonus, vel gressus eunti.
Ipsa egomet dudùm Beroën digressa reliqui
Ægram, indignantem, tali quòd sola careret
Munere, nec meritos Anchisæ inferret honores.
Hæc effata.
  At matres primò ancipites, oculisque malignis
Ambiguæ, spectare rates, miserum inter amorem
Præsentis terræ fatisque vocantia regna:
Cùm Dea se paribus per cœlum sustulit alis,
Ingentemque fugâ secuit sub nubibus arcum.
Tum verò attonitæ monstris, actæque furore,
Conclamant, rapiuntque focis penetralibus ignem:
Pars spoliant aras, frondem ac virgulta facesque
Conjiciunt: furit immissis Vulcanus habenis
Transtra per, et remos, et pictas abiete puppes.

636. Nam imago vatis Cassandræ per somnum visa *est* dare

639. Nec *sit* mora tantis

643. Mentes Iliadum *sunt* arrectæ

644. Hìc una è multis, quæ *erat* maxima natu, Pyrgo *nomine*, regia nutrix tot natorum Priami, *inquit*: *hæc* non *est* Beroë vobis.

653. *Illa* effata *est* hæc. Et matres primò *cœperunt* spectare rates malignis oculis, ancipites, ambiguæque inter miserum amorem præsentis terræ regnaque

NOTES.

634. *Hectoreos amnes:* the Trojan streams.

638. *Tempus agit res:* now the time demands the thing. Some read *tempus agi res:* it is time the things be done. But Pierius found the former in the *Codex Romanus* and *Mediceus*, and in some others. Heyne reads, *agi res*. Ruæus prefers the former; *Occasio ipsa urget rem*, says he.

639. *En quatuor aræ*, &c. It is not said by whom these altars were erected. Ruæus conjectures they were built by Cloanthus for his naval victory. See 234, *supra*. Or by the Trojans generally, for mention is made of their offering sacrifice. See 100, *supra*. The verb *sunt* is understood.

642. *Sublatâque:* and exerting her strength, her right hand being raised, she waved the torch (*infensum ignem*) and threw it at a distance. *Infensum:* in the sense of *inimicum*.

645. *Pyrgo*. This is a fictitious name. The tendency of her speech was not to dissuade the Trojan matrons from executing the purposes of Juno, but rather to incite them to it, by showing them that the person who appeared to them in the form of Beroë was really a goddess. *Rhœteïa:* an adj. from *Rhœtium*, a promontory of Troas

648. *Ardentes oculos*. Here are mentioned four distinguished marks or signs of a divine person: 1. Beauty, radiant eyes, &c., *qui vultus:* 2. A fragrant breath which perfumed the air around, *qui spiritus:* 3. An easy and majestic motion, *qui gressus:* 4. A sound, tone, or accent of voice which distinguished them from mortals, *qui sonus vocis*.

651. *Careret:* that she should be deprived of such an employment—of celebrating the anniversary of Anchises. *Indignantem:* in the sense of *dolentem*.

655. *Ambiguæ:* in the sense of *dubiæ*. *Ancipites:* in the sense of *infestæ*.

660. *Focis penetralibus:* from the inmost hearths. Davidson renders it, *from the hallowed hearths*. Ruæus says, *intimis aris*.

662. *Vulcanus:* the god of fire, put by meton. for fire itself. *Immissis habenis:* without restraint—with violence.

663. *Pictas abiete:* either the sterns, by synec. for the whole ships, on which was carved work of the fir tree; or *pictas* must be taken in the sense of *constructas*, built or made. Ruæus says, *structas ex abiete pictas puppes*. Valpy says, constructed of fir.

Nuntius Anchisæ ad tumulum, cuneosque theatri,
Incensas perfert naves Eumelus: et ipsi
Respiciunt atram in nimbo volitare favillam.
Primus et Ascanius, cursus ut lætus equestres
Ducebat, sic acer equo turbata petivit
Castra: nec exanimes possunt retinere magistri.
Quis furor iste novus? quò nunc, quò tenditis, inquit,
Heu miseræ cives! non hostem, inimicaque castra
Argivûm, vestras spes, uritis. En ego vester
Ascanius! Galeam ante pedes projecit inanem,
Quâ ludo indutus belli simulacra ciebat.
Accelerat simul Æneas, simul agmina Teucrûm.
Ast illæ diversa metu per litora passim
Diffugiunt, sylvasque, et sicubi concava furtim
Saxa petunt: piget incepti, lucisque: suosque
Mutatæ agnoscunt: excussaque pectore Juno est.
Sed non idcircò flammæ atque incendia vires
Indomitas posuere: udo sub robore vivit
Stuppa, vomens tardum fumum: lentusque carinas
Est vapor, et toto descendit corpore pestis:
Nec vires heroum, infusaque flumina prosunt.
Tum pius Æneas humeris abscindere vestem,
Auxilioque vocare Deos, et tendere palmas:
Jupiter omnipotens, si nondum exosus ad unum
Trojanos, si quid pietas antiqua labores
Respicit humanos; da flammam evadere classi
Nunc, pater, et tenues Teucrûm res eripe leto:
Vel tu, quod superest, infesto fulmine morti,
Si mereor, demitte; tuâque hìc obrue dextrâ.
Vix hæc ediderat, cùm effusis imbribus atra
Tempestas sinè more furit: tonitruque tremiscunt
Ardua terrarum, et campi: ruit æthere toto
Turbidus imber aquâ; densisque nigerrimus Austris

665. Eumelus nuntius ad tumulum Anchisæ perfert naves incensas esse

672. *Sed uritis* vestras spes

677. Petuntque furtim sylvas, et sicubi *sint* concava saxa

685. Pius Æneas *cœpit*

687. Si nondum *tu* exosus *es* Trojanos ad unum; si *tua* antiqua pietas respicit humanos labores quid, nunc, *O* pater, da classi

692. Vel tu demitte *me* morti *cum* infesto

695. Arduaque *loca terrarum*, et campi tremiscunt tonitru.

NOTES.

664. *Cuneos.* These were seats in the Roman theatre for the common people, so called because they were in the form of a wedge, the narrowest part toward the stage. Reference is here made to the *theatre* mentioned or spoken of 288, supra.

668. *Sic acer equo:* the meaning is that Ascanius rode up to the confused camp quick on his horse, just in the same habit as he led the cavalcade, *equestres cursus.*

669. *Magistri:* either *Priamus* and *Atys*, commanders of the cavalcade, or *Epytides* and the other guardians and instructors of the youth.

670. *Quò nunc tenditis:* what now do you aim at?—what do you intend by thus burning your ships? The repetition of the *quò* is emphatical.

679. *Juno excussa est pectore:* Juno is driven from their breast—the fury with which she had inspired them. This is an allusion to the frantic Bacchanals, who returned to themselves after the god, with whom they pretended to be possessed was driven out of them.

682. *Stuppa:* this was a kind of coarse flax or hemp driven into the seams and chinks, and then overlaid with pitch to keep out the water and render the vessel tight—oakum. *Vivit:* lives—continues to burn. *Lentus vapor:* a slow fire. *Est:* in the sense of *edit.* *Pestis:* in the sense of *flammæ.*

684. *Flumina:* in the sense of *aqua.*

685. *Pius Æneas abscindere*, &c. Tearing their hair and garment was reckoned a sign of extreme distress both by Jews, Egyptians, and Greeks.

688. *Pietas:* pity—compassion—clemency.

693. *Effusis imbribus:* with falling rains—with floods of rain. *Imbribus:* in the sense of *pluviis.*

696. *Imber turbidus:* the cloud, thick with water, and black with the heavy south winds, pours down from the whole heaven. The south winds were more impregnated with

Implenturque supèr puppes: semusta madescunt
Robora, restinctus donec vapor omnis; et omnes,
Quatuor amissis, servatæ à peste carinæ.
At pater Æneas casu concussus acerbo,
Nunc huc ingentes, nunc illuc, pectore curas
Mutabat; versans, Siculisne resideret arvis
Oblitus fatorum, Italasne capesseret oras.
Tum senior Nautes, unum Tritonia Pallas
Quem docuit, multâque insignem reddidit arte,
Hæc responsa dabat; vel quæ portenderet ira
Magna Deûm, vel quæ fatorum posceret ordo.
Isque his Æneam solatus vocibus infit:
Nate Deâ, quò fata trahunt retrahuntque, sequamur.
Quicquid erit, superanda omnis fortuna ferendo est.
Est tibi Dardanius divinæ stirpis Acestes:
Hunc cape consiliis socium, et conjunge volentem.
Huic trade, amissis superant qui navibus; et quos
Pertæsum magni incepti rerumque tuarum est;
Longævosque senes, ac fessas æquore matres;
Et quicquid tecum invalidum, metuensque perîcli est,
Delige; et his habeant terris, sine, mœnia fessi.
Urbem appellabunt permisso nomine Acestam.
Talibus incensus dictis senioris amici:
Tum verò in curas animus diducitur omnes.
Et nox atra polum bigis subvecta tenebat.
Visa dehinc cœlo facies delapsa parentis
Anchisæ, subitò tales effundere voces:
Nate, mihi vitâ quondam, dum vita manebat,
Chare magìs; nate Iliacis exercite fatis,
Imperio Jovis huc venio, qui classibus ignem
Depulit, et cœlo tandem miseratus ab alto est.
Consiliis pare, quæ nunc pulcherrima Nautes

712. Cape hunc socium *tibi in tuis* consiliis

713. Trade huic *eos*, qui superant

715. Deligeque longævos senes, ac matres fessas

717. Et sine *ut* illi fessi habeant mœnia

719. *Æneas* incensus *est*

722. Dehinc facies parentis Anchisæ delapsa cœlo visa *est* subitò effundere tales voces: Nate, quondam magìs chare mihi vitâ *ipsa*, dum

NOTES.

vapor than any other, which, meeting with the cold northern air, was condensed into clouds and rain. Hence the epithet, *densis*. *Imber* is, properly, a shower or fall of rain. It may, by meton. be taken for the cloud containing the vapor. In this sense the meaning is plain and easy.

697. *Semusta:* for *semiusta*, by syn. This contraction is necessary for the sake of the verse. *Supèr:* in the sense of *desuper*.

702. *Mutabat:* in the sense of *volvebat*. *Versans:* in the sense of *deliberans*.

704. *Unum:* in the sense of *solum;* or we may take it in the sense of *unicum*, vel *præcipuum*.

705. *Arte:* knowledge. Ruæus says, *multis vaticiniis*.

713. *Qui superant.* Nautes advises to deliver to Acestes the crews of those ships that had been burnt—those who were weary of the enterprise—the old men and women, &c. and to found a city for them in Sicily, to be called after the name of their friend, Acestes. This city was on the western side, about five miles from the shore. It was also called *Egesta*, *Ægesta*, and *Sergesta*.

716. *Perîcli:* by syn. for *periculi*.

718. *Permisso nomine:* by a permitted name. Acestes agreed that it might be so called.

720. *Animus.* Davidson and Heyne read *animum*, in the acc. Valpy and Ruæus have *animus*, which is the easier.

721. *Atra nox:* dark night, wafted in her two-horse chariot, possessed the heavens. As the chariot of the sun is represented as drawn by four horses, so that of the moon and the night by two, and those of a black or sable color. *Polum:* by synec. the whole heavens.

722. *Facies delapsa*, &c. The ancients distinguished between the soul and the shade or phantom. The former, they believed, went to heaven, while the other had its residence in the infernal regions. Thus Anchises descends from heaven in regard to his soul, while at the same time his shade was in the regions below, as appears from verse 733.

725. *Fatis:* in the sense of *casibus*.

727. *Pulcherrima:* in the sense of *optima*.

Dat senior: lectos juvenes, fortissima corda,
Defer in Italiam: gens dura, atque aspera cultu,
Debellanda tibi Latio est. Ditis tamen antè
Infernas accede dómos, et Averna per alta
Congressus pete, nate, meos. Non me impia namque
Tartara habent tristesque umbræ; sed amœna piorum
Concilia, Elysiumque colo. Huc casta Sibylla
Nigrantûm multo pecudum te sanguine ducet.
Tum genus omne tuum, et, quæ dentur mœnia, disces.
Jamque vale: torquet medios nox humida cursus,
Et me sævus equis Oriens afflavit anhelis.
Dixerat: et tenues fugit, ceu fumus, in auras.
Æneas, Quò deinde ruis? quò proripis? inquit:
Quem fugis? aut quis te nostris complexibus arcet?
Hæc memorans, cinerem et sopitos suscitat ignes;
Pergameumque Larem, et canæ penetralia Vestæ
Farre pio, et plenâ supplex veneratur acerrâ.
  Extemplò socios, primumque arcessit Acesten,
Et Jovis imperium, et chari præcepta parentis
Edocet; et quæ nunc animo sententia constet.
Haud mora consiliis; nec jussa recusat Acestes.
Transcribunt urbi matres, populumque volentem

744. Supplexque veneratur Pergameum Larem, et penetralia canæ Vestæ pio farre

NOTES.

730. *Cultu:* in the sense of *moribus.*

731. *Tamen antè accede,* &c. This apparition of Anchises, and the direction he gives his son to descend to the regions below, are a proper preparation for the following book. The art of the poet is admirable in thus making one event rise out of another and preparing the reader beforehand. This raises that pleasing suspense, which is the principal thing that charms in an epic poem. *Ditis:* gen. of *Dis*, a name of Pluto.

735. *Elysium.* This was the name of the place assigned for the residence of the happy. Here they placed their heroes and other distinguished characters. *Casta Sibylla:* the Sibyl hath the epithet *casta*, because those prophetesses were virgins. *Concilia:* in the sense of *sedes.*

736. *Multo sanguine:* with much blood of black victims; that is, after having offered many black victims in sacrifice. Victims of a black color were sacrificed to the infernal deities.

738. *Humida nox;* humid night turns its middle course. This is a metaphor taken from the chariot-races, when they wheeled about at the *meta* or goal, and returned to the *carcer* or starting place. So here night was on her return, having passed her farthest point, the hour of midnight, which divides her course in the middle.

739. *Sævus Oriens:* the cruel morning (the approaching sun) had breathed on me with his panting steeds. The morning is here called *sævus*, because it broke off his conversation, and forced him to retire. It was a prevailing opinion that ghosts and apparitions were only allowed to appear in the darkness of night, and were chased away by the dawn of day.

743. *Suscitat cinerem:* he opens the ashes and kindles up the dormant fire. This is one of those passages where Virgil uses the same verb with two nouns, when it can be properly applied only to one of them. *Sopitos:* buried up—covered over.

744. *Veneratur:* he worships the Trojan *Lares*, and the shrine of hoary Vesta, &c. The *Lares* were the images consecrated to the souls of their departed ancestors, which the ancients worshipped at their own houses by oblations of incense and cakes of fine flour, called *far;* see Geor. iii. 344. The *Lares*, like the *Penates*, were *household gods. Penetralia Vestæ:* this shrine, or sanctuary of *Vesta*, was commonly the hearth or fireplace in the apartment where they lodged. Here was kept a fire always burning, in honor of that goddess. See Æn. i. 292. Æneas is said to have introduced into Italy the worship of the *Penates*, the *Lares*, and of *Vesta* or the unextinguished fire. Heyne takes *penetralia Vestæ* for Vesta herself, because, says he, the goddess had her residence in the inmost part of the house, remote from the view of men. She is called *cana*, either on account of the antiquity of her worship, or because the vestal virgins were clad in *white* robes.

748. *Constet:* in the sense of *sedet.*

750. *Transcribunt.* This word was applied to those whose names were enrolled in order to be transported to some new colony; and those thus enrolled were called

Deponunt, animos nil magnæ laudis egentes.
Ipsi transtra novant, flammisque ambesa reponunt
Robora navigiis: aptant remosque rudentesque:
Exigui numero, sed bello vivida virtus.
Intereà Æneas urbem designat aratro,
Sortiturque domos: hoc, Ilium, et hæc loca, Trojam
Esse jubet; gaudet regno Trojanus Acestes,
Indicitque forum, et patribus dat jura vocatis.
Tum vicina astris Erycino in vertice sedes
Fundatur Veneri Idaliæ: tumuloque sacerdos
Et lucus latè sacer additur Anchisæo.
Jamque dies epulata novem gens omnis, et aris
Factus honos; placidi straverunt æquora venti:
Creber et aspirans rursus vocat Auster in altum.
Exoritur procurva ingens per litora fletus:
Complexi inter se noctemque diemque morantur.
Ipsæ jam matres; ipsi, quibus aspera quondam
Visa maris facies, et non tolerabile numen,
Ire volunt, omnemque fugæ perferre laborem.
Quos bonus Æneas dictis solatur amicis,
Et consanguineo lachrymans commendat Acestæ.

754. Exigui *in* numero, sed *eorum* virtus *erat* vivida bello.

757. Jubet hoc *spatium esse* Ilium, et hæc loca esse Trojam.

767. Jam matres ipsæ; *et* ipsi *homines*, quibus quondam facies

NOTES.

transcripti; hence the word came to signify to transfer, designate, or appoint.

751. *Deponunt:* they leave—set apart. *Egentes:* in the sense of *cupidos.*

755. *Designat urbem.* This refers to a custom of the Romans, who, when they were about to build a city, first marked out the boundary of it by drawing a furrow with a plough, which they lifted over those spaces where they intended to have the gates. Hence *porta* (from *porto*, to carry) came to signify a gate.

756. *Hoc, Ilium:* history mentions no city in Sicily by the name of *Ilium.* Æneas may have called it so at first, but agreed that Acestes should change its name afterward. Or *Ilium* may be the tower of the city *Acesta* or *Segesta*, and here taken for the whole city by synec. as *Pergamus*, the tower or citadel of Troy, is often put for the city itself. This is the opinion of Ruæus. Strabo mentions two rivers near the city *Segesta*, by the names of *Xanthus* and *Simoïs*, and that they were so called by Æneas.

758. *Indicit forum:* he appoints courts of justice, and gives laws to his assembled senators. The Roman senators were called *Patres*, either on account of their age, or to remind them that they were the fathers of the people.

759. *Erycino:* an adj. from *Eryx*, a mountain in Sicily, in height next to Ætna; from *Eryx*, king of that island, who was slain by Hercules. See 411, supra. Æneas built a temple to his mother Venus on the top of this mountain. Some say it was founded by *Eryx*, and only decorated by Æneas. *Venus* is called *Idalian*, from *Idalium* or *Idalia*, a town and grove on the island of Cyprus. This whole island was sacred to *Venus. Sedes:* in the sense of *templum.*

761. *Lucus additur.* A priest and grove, sacred far around, is added to the tomb of Anchises. It appears hence that he was buried on Mount *Eryx.* Some say that he arrived in Italy along with his son: others that he died before he arrived in Sicily.

762. *Gens:* in the sense of *populus.* The verb *fuerat* is to be connected with *epulata. Honos factus:* in the sense of *sacrificium factum erat.* All his people had kept the anniversary festival of his father for nine days, and performed the usual offerings, when the weather became favorable; and having repaired the damages occasioned by the fire, they make ready for their departure. Here a most interesting scene ensued. A day and a night they pass in embracing each other before their final separation. Those who before were weary of the voyage, now summon up courage, and are willing again to encounter the danger of the sea. The interesting scene brought tears from the hero's eyes.

768. *Numen.* This is the usual reading. The sense is, *that the divinity*, or divine power, *of the sea, seemed to them insupportable*—more than they could endure after all their fatigues. But Heyne, upon the authority of Heinsius, reads *nomen.* The sense in this case will be: and the name of sea seemed insupportable to them. They could not bear to hear its name mentioned. *Nomen maris*, says he, *auditu, et dictu intolerabile visum.* He observes of *numen: Explicationem commodam non habet.* The reader will judge for himself.

771. *Consanguineo.* Acestes was in truth

Tres Eryci vitulos, et tempestatibus agnam
Cædere deinde jubet, solvique ex ordine funes.
Ipse caput tonsæ foliis evinctus olivæ,
Stans procul in prorâ, pateram tenet, extaque salsos
Porricit in fluctus, ac vina liquentia fundit.
Prosequitur surgens à puppi ventus euntes:
Certatim socii feriunt mare, et æquora verrunt.
At Venus intereà Neptunum exercita curis
Alloquitur, talesque effundit pectore questus:
Junonis gravis ira et inexsaturabile pectus
Cogunt me, Neptune, preces descendere in omnes:
Quam nec longa dies, pietas nec mitigat ulla;
Nec Jovis imperio fatisve infracta quiescit.
Non mediâ de gente Phrygum exedisse nefandis
Urbem odiis satis est, pœnam traxisse per omnem
Relliquias: Trojæ cineres atque ossa peremptæ
Insequitur. Causas tanti sciat illa furoris.
Ipse mihi nuper Libycis tu testis in undis
Quam molem subitò excierit. Maria omnia cœlo
Miscuit, Æoliis nequicquam freta procellis:
In regnis hoc ausa tuis.
Proh scelus! ecce etiam Trojanis matribus actis,
Exussit fœdè puppes; et classe subegit
Amissâ socios ignotæ linquere terræ.
Quod superest: oro, liceat dare tuta per undas
Vela tibi: liceat Laurentem attingere Tybrim.

774. Ipse evinctus *quoad* caput foliis tonsæ olivæ, stans

783. Quam, *nempe Junonem.*

784. Nec quiescit infracta imperio Jovis fatisve. Non satis est *ei* nefandis odiis exedisse urbem de media gente Phrygum, *et* traxisse *ejus* relliquias per omnem pœnam:

789. Tu ipse *fuisti* testis mihi, quam molem subitò excierit nuper in Libycis undis.

792. Ausa *est* hoc in tuis regnis.

795. Et, classe amissâ, subegit socios linquere *eas mulieres* ignotæ terræ.

796. Oro *ut* liceat *Trojanis* dare tibi vela tuta per undas; *ut* liceat *iis*

NOTES.

no way related to Æneas. See 30, supra. *Consanguineus* is properly a relation by blood; *agnatus*, one by the father's side; *cognatus*, by the mother's side; and *affinis*, by marriage.

772. *Tempestatibus.* Storms and tempests were deified by the Romans, and goats and *lambs* were offered to them in sacrifice.

773. *Cædere:* in the sense of *immolare. Funes:* the cables. Some copies have *funem.* This is the reading of Heyne, after Pierius and Heinsius. The sense is the same either way.

775. *Stans procul:* standing at a distance on the prow, he holds the bowl and scatters the entrails upon the briny waves. *Procul* implies that he stood as far as he could from the shore on the extremity of the head of the vessel toward the sea. *Porricit*, from *porro* and *jacio: to throw at a distance.* It was a custom among the Romans to present offerings to the marine gods before sailing, which consisted principally in casting the entrails of the victims upon the sea. Sometimes, however, they offered libations also, as in the present instance.

781. *Gravis ira Junonis:* the heavy anger of Juno, &c. An allusion is here made to the decision of Paris in the case of the prize of beauty, which ever after made her a bitter enemy to the Trojan race. *Pectus* in the sense of *animus.*

784. *Infracta:* overcome—made to desist from her purpose. *Dies:* in the sense of *tempus.* Juno persisted in her opposition to Æneas, in spite of the authority of Jove, and the decrees of the gods, which directed him to Italy.

787. *Cineres et ossa:* the ashes and bones of ruined Troy. By these we are to understand Æneas and his company, who were on their way to Italy—the only remains or survivors of that once flourishing city.

788. *Illa sciat:* she may know, &c. Venus here insinuates that there was no cause for her resentment. She may perhaps know; as for me, I do not.

790. *Quam molem:* what a tempest she raised, &c. *Molem:* for *tempestatem.*

791. *Nequicquam freta:* relying in vain, &c. Because she had not accomplished her purposes; she and Æolus being controlled by Neptune. See Æn. i. 86, *et sequens.*

793. *Proh scelus.* Heyne and some others read *per scelus* taking *per* in the sense of *in*, vel *ad.* *Trojanis matribus actis in vel ad scelus.* The common reading appears the easiest, which takes *Proh scelus* as an exclamation or interjection. Oh horrid crime! —Oh wickedness! Juno burned the Trojan ships, by impelling their matrons to do it.

797. *Tibi:* by thee—under thy care and protection. *Si:* in the sense of *siquidem.*

Si concessa peto; si dant ea mœnia Parcæ.
Tum Saturnius hæc domitor maris edidit alti;
Fas omne est, Cytherea, meis te fidere regnis,
Unde genus ducis; merui quoque. Sæpe furores
Compressi, et rabiem tantam cœlique marisque;
Nec minor in terris, Xanthum Simoëntaque testor,
Æneæ mihi cura tui. Cùm Troïa Achilles
Exanimata sequens impingeret agmina muris,
Millia multa daret leto, gemerentque repleti
Amnes, nec reperire viam atque evolvere posset
In mare se Xanthus; Pelidæ tunc ego forti
Congressum Æneam, nec Dîs, nec viribus æquis,
Nube cavâ eripui; cuperem cùm vertere ab imo
Structa meis manibus perjuræ mœnia Trojæ.
Nunc quoque mens eadem perstat mihi: pelle timorem.
Tutus, quos optas, portus accedet Averni.
Unus erit tantùm, amissum quem gurgite quæret;
Unum pro multis dabitur caput.
His ubi læta Deæ permulsit pectora dictis,
Jungit equos auro Genitor, spumantiaque addit
Fræna feris, manibusque omnes effundit habenas.
Cœruleo per summa levis volat æquora curru:
Subsidunt undæ, tumidumque sub axe tonanti
Sternitur æquor aquis: fugiunt vasto æthere nimbi.

800. Fas est te fidere omne meis regnis, unde ducis genus; merui quoque *ut fidas*

803. Nec minor cura *fuit* mihi tui Æneæ in terris

808. Tunc ego eripui cavâ nube Æneam congressum forti

816. Ubi Genitor permulsit læta pectora Deæ

NOTES.

799. *Tum Saturnius domitor.* Mr. Davidson observes there is a grandeur and boldness in this line, suitable to the majesty of him whose speech it introduces, which make it worthy the attention of the reader. *Neptune* was the son of *Saturn*, and in the division of the world the sea fell to him by lot. Hence the adj. *Saturnius*, and also the propriety of *Domitor alti maris*. *Edidit:* in the sense of *dixit*.

801. *Unde genus.* This alludes to the fabulous account of her springing from the foam of the sea.

805. *Exanimata:* may mean that the Trojans were weary and out of breath, or were affrighted and struck with dismay. *Impengeret:* drove—forced.

810. *Eripui cava nube:* I snatched away in a hollow cloud Æneas engaging, &c. This encounter Homer gives us in the twentieth book of the Iliad. But the great slaughter which Achilles made among the Trojan troops, so as to choak the rivers *Xanthus* and *Simoïs* with their dead bodies, is given us in the following book. *Cùm cuperem:* though I wished to overturn from the foundation the walls, &c. See Geor. i. 502, and Æn. ii. 610.

812. *Eadem mens:* the same disposition.

813. *Averni:* Avernus, a lake in Campania, the fabulous descent to hell. See Æn. iv. 512.

817. *Auro:* his golden car. The common reading is *curru*, but Pierius observes that all the ancient manuscripts have *auro* instead of *curru*. It has more dignity, and saves the disagreeable repetition of *curru*, which occurs in the next line but one. Beside, nothing is more common than to put, by meton. the metal for the instrument made or composed of it, as *ferrum*, for a sword, axe, or knife; *auro*, for a golden bowl, &c. Davidson has *auro*. Heyne reads *auro* also: in the sense of *aureo curru*.

818. *Effundit:* in the sense of *laxat*. *Feris:* in the sense of *equis*.

823. *Glauci.* Glaucus, according to Servius, was a famous fisherman of Anthedon in Beotia, who, having laid some fishes on the grass that he had just caught, perceived them to recover their life and motion, and to leap into the sea. He supposed there was some virtue in those herbs that produced this effect: whereupon he tasted them, and was immediately transformed into a *sea-god*. *Inoüs:* an adj. from *Ino*, the daughter of Cadmus. See Geor. i. 437. *Senior chorus Glauci:* by *commutatio*, for *chorus senioris Glauci*. These were the *nymphs* and the *tritons*. *Palæmon.* He is supposed by some to be the god whom the Latins worshipped under the name of *Portunus*. He was so called from *portus*, because he was supposed to preside over ports and harbors. It was thought that mariners were under his special care and protection. See 241, supra

822. Tum variæ facies comitum *apparent;* immania cete

825. Læva *spatia maris*

Tum variæ comitum facies: immania cete,
Et senior Glauci chorus Inousque Palæmon,
Tritonesque citi, Phorcique exercitus omnis.
Læva tenent Thetis et Melite, Panopeaque virgo,
Nesæe, Spioque, Thaliaque, Cymodoceque.
Hic patris Æneæ suspensam blanda vicissim
Gaudia pertentant mentem: jubet ocyùs omnes
Attolli malos, intendi brachia velis.
Unà omnes fecere pedem: pariterque sinistros,
Nunc dextros solvêre sinus: unà ardua torquent
Cornua detorquentque: ferunt sua flamina classem.
Princeps ante omnes densum Palinurus agebat
Agmen: ad hunc alii cursum contendere jussi.
Jamque ferè mediam cœli nox humida metam
Contigerat: placidâ laxârant membra quiete

837. Nautæ fusi per dura sedilia sub remis axârant

Sub remis fusi per dura sedilia nautæ:
Cùm levis æthereis delapsus Somnus ab astris
Aëra dimovit tenebrosum, et dispulit umbras,
Te, Palinure, petens, tibi tristia somnia portans
Insonti: puppique Deus consedit in altâ,

NOTES.

824. *Omnis exercitus:* the whole army of Phorcus—all the Nereïds, whom Phorcus was wont to collect. He was the son of *Pontus* and *Terra*, and father of the *Gorgons. Tritones.* Triton was the son of Neptune and Amphitrite. His upper part was like a man, and his lower part like a fish. He was said to be Neptune's trumpeter. He used the *concha*, or shell, in room of a trumpet.

826. *Thetis et Melite*, &c. These are the names of some of the sea-nymphs: all of Greek derivation. Of all the nymphs, it is said that *Panopea* was the only virgin.

827. *Vicissim:* in turn—in the room of the anxiety which he had before felt on account of the burning of his ships: now soothing (pleasant) joys, &c.

829. *Intendi brachia velis.* When they arrived in port, it was usual for mariners to take down the masts; and, when they departed, to raise them up again. The *intendi brachia velis*, is the same in import as *intendi vela brachiis:* to stretch the sails to the yards. The *brachia* were those parts of the *antennæ*, or sail yards, which were near the mast, here put for the whole yards. The extremities of the *antennæ* were called *cornua.* It may be observed, however, that the old Roman copy has *intendi brachia remis:* he orders their arms to be stretched to the oars; which is easier, and in Virgil's style. The *antennæ* were long spars, extending across the mast at right angles; and to which the sails were fastened. Here called *brachia*, from their resemblance to the extended arms of a man

830. *Fecere pedem:* they worked the sheet—they lengthened or shortened it, and shifted it from one side of the ship to the other as occasion required. *Pedem.* The *pes* was a rope, halser, or sheet, fastened to the lower corners of the sail, and also to the sides of the ship, when she was under sail. And, as these were lengthened or shortened, the sail would be turned accordingly, more or less to the wind. *Solvêre:* they spread—expand, or let out. The perf. here is used in its appropriate sense. It continues the past action up to the time in which it is mentioned. *Sinus:* in the sense of *vela. Unà—pariterque.* These words imply that they all worked together with equal eagerness, and with uniform motions. *Sinistros:* they turned the sails sometimes to the right, and sometimes to the left, as the wind veered or shifted. In nautical language, they shifted their tacks as, &c.

832. *Sua:* in the sense of *prospera* vel *secunda:* prosperous gales—favorable winds.

833. *Princeps:* in the sense of *primus.* Palinurus was the pilot of the ship of Æneas. He fell overboard, and was drowned: the only one lost in the whole fleet.

834. *Agmen:* in the sense of *classem. Contendere.* Palinurus led the fleet, and all the other ships were ordered to follow him—to direct their course after him.

835. *Humida nox:* humid night had almost reached the middle point of heaven. It was almost midnight. This is a metaphor taken from the races. It had almost reached the turning point.

840. *Tristia somnia:* in the sense of *tristem* vel *lethalem somnum.*

Phorbanti similis, funditque has ore loquelas:
Iaside Palinure, ferunt ipsa æquora classem,
Æquatæ spirant auræ, datur hora quieti.
Pone caput, fessosque oculos furare labori.
Ipse ego paulisper pro te tua munera inibo.
Cui vix attollens Palinurus lumina fatur:
Mene salis placidi vultum fluctusque quietos
ignorare jubes? mene huic confidere monstro?
Ænean credam quid enim fallacibus Austris,
Et cœli toties deceptus fraude sereni?
Talia dicta dabat: clavumque affixus et hærens
Nusquam amittebat, oculosque sub astra tenebat
Ecce Deus ramum Lethæo rore madentem,
Viique soporatum Stygiâ, super utraque quassat
Tempora; cunctantique natantia lumina solvit.
Vix primos inopina quies laxaverat artus,
Et super incumbens, cum puppis parte revulsâ,
Cumque gubernâclo, liquidas projecit in undas
Præcipitem, ac socios nequicquam sæpe vocantem.
Ipse volans tenues se sustulit ales in auras.
Currit iter tutum non seciùs æquore classis,
Promissisque patris Neptuni interrita fertur.
Jamque adeò scopulos Sirenum advecta subibat,

849. *Jubes*-ne me

854. Ecce Deus quassat ramum madentem Lethæo rore, soporatumque Stygia vi, super utraque tempora

862. Classis currit iter *in* æquore non seciùs tutum, ferturque interrita

NOTES.

842. *Phorbanti.* Phorbas was one of the sons of Priam.

843. *Iaside.* Iasius was some Trojan, the father or grandfather of Palinurus.

844. *Æquatæ:* steady—fair. So that they spread the sails, in nautical language, *wing and wing.*

846. *Inibo:* I will discharge your offices, &c.

848. *Me-ne jubes:* do you bid me to disregard the face of the calm sea, and the waves at rest? do you bid me to trust to that appearance? As if he had said: though the face of the sea be smooth, and its waves at rest, I am not so ignorant of sailing, as to trust to that circumstance; the winds may suddenly rise, and things be materially changed. *Salis:* in the sense of *maris.*

851. *Et:* in the sense of *etiam:* even I so often deceived, &c.

854. *Rore:* in the sense of *aqua.*

855. *Soporatum vi:* impregnated with a Stygian quality. By this, Servius understands a mortal or deadly quality; such as effected his death.

856. *Cunctanti:* to him struggling against it, and endeavoring to keep awake. *Solvit:* in the sense of *claudit.*

857. *Primos artus.* Sleep is here represented as creeping, or diffusing itself over the several members of the body, and *relaxing* them one after another. The *primos artus* may mean the extremities of the body, which are apt to be first affected with sleep.

858. *Et super-incumbens:* when (the god) leaning against him, threw him headlong, &c. The *et* here must have the force of *cùm*, as Mr. Davidson very justly observes. The part of the ship which Palinurus carried with him into the sea, enabled him to float three days. See Æn. vi. 350.

860. *Nequicquam:* in vain; because his companions were asleep, and could afford him no assistance.

861. *Ales:* in the sense of *celer.* *Ipse,* nempe *Deus somnus.*

862. *Non seciùs tutum:* in the sense of *non minùs tutum.* *Interrita:* safe, without fear of danger. *Secura*, says Ruæus.

864. *Scopulos Sirenum:* the rocks of the Sirenes. *Subibat:* was approaching—was coming to. *Classis* is understood. The *Sirenes* are said to have been three beautiful women, who inhabited steep rocks on the sea-coast, whither they allured passengers by the sweetness of their music, and then put them to death. They are fabled to have been the daughters of *Acheloüs*, and *Calliope.* One sung, one played on the flute, and one on the lyre. The poets say, it was decreed that they should live till some person should be able to resist their charms. Ulysses being informed of this by Circe, escaped the fatal snare by stopping the ears of his companions with wax, and fastening himself to the mast of his ship. Upon which they threw themselves into the sea in despair, and were transformed into fishes from the waist downward. The truth of the fable is this: they were lewd women, who, by their

868. Cùm pater *Æneas* sensit ratem errare fluitantem, magistro amisso, et

870. O Palinure, *inquit*, nimiùm confise sereno cœlo et pelago, nudus jacebis in ignota arenâ.

Difficiles quondam, multorumque ossibus albos;
Tum rauca assiduo longè sale saxa sonabant:
Cùm pater amisso fluitantem errare magistro
Sensit, et ipse ratem nocturnis rexit in undis,
Multa gemens, casuque animum concussus amici:
O nimiùm cœlo et pelago confise sereno,
Nudus in ignotâ, Palinure, jacebis arenâ.

NOTES.

charms, enticed men to debauchery. The place of their residence was in the three islands called *Sirenusæ*, in the *Sinus Pæstanus*, in the Tyrrhene, or Tuscan sea. Their names were *Leucosia*, *Ligea*, and *Parthenope*.

865. *Difficiles:* dangerous on account of the rocks and shoals. *Albos ossibus:* white with the bones of ship-wrecked mariners.

867. *Assiduo sale:* with a constant dashing of the waves against the rocks.

868. *Errare fluitantem:* to stray, or go adrift—to be carried here and there at the pleasure of the winds and waves.

870. *O nimiùm confise:* O Palinurus, trusting too much, &c. Æneas had been asleep; and he speaks only by conjecture as to the cause of his misfortune, not knowing that a god had thrown him overboard. The truth of the case is this: Palinurus was overcome by sleep in spite of his efforts to keep awake; and, in that situation, fell overboard. Some say he was not drowned; but swam to the Italian coast, and was there killed by the inhabitants. See Æn. vi. 387.

QUESTIONS.

How does this book open?
What is its nature and character?
What happened to Æneas soon after he was out to sea?
To what place was he forced to direct his course?
At what place in Sicily did he land?
How was he received by his friend Acestes?
What did Æneas do soon after his arrival?
How long had Anchises been dead?
Did he institute games in honor of him?
How many kinds of games?
From whom were they imitated?
In honor of whom were Homer's games instituted?
By whom were they instituted?
In what book of the Iliad is the account of them given?
What do you understand by *carcer*, when applied to races in general?
What by *meta*?
Why is the word *limen* sometimes used for the starting place?
What was the first game?
How many ships or galleys contended for the prize?
Who was the first conqueror?
To what circumstance does the poet attribute his victory?
Who was the second victor?
Did Mnestheus make any animated address to his oarsmen?
What did he call them?
What effect had this address upon them?
What was the second game?
Who entered the list for the prizes?
Who took the first prize?
How did it happen that Euryalus came out the first?
What befel Nisus?
Who was next to him?
And why did not Salius obtain the prize?
What was the third game?
What is the nature of the gauntlet fight?
Can it be practised in an improved state of society?
What did Lycurgus in regard to this kind of exercise?
Who entered the list on the part of the Trojans in this game?
Had Dares distinguished himself in this fight before?
Whom had he slain on the plains of Troy?
With whom was he accustomed to contend at Troy?
Was Paris said to be superior to Hector at the gauntlet?
Who was the antagonist of Dares?
Who was Entellus?
What was his age?
What was the issue of the contest?
What was the fourth game?
Where was the bird suspended?
Whose arrow cut the cord by which the bird was bound?
Whose arrow pierced her?
Where was the bird at that moment?
Whose brother was Eurytion?
What is Pandarus said to have done during the Trojan war?
Was he a distinguished archer?
Is it said that he received divine honors
Who last shot his arrow?
What happened to it as it passed through the air?
In what light was this considered by Æneas?

Could the soothsayers interpret the omen, or prodigy, in a satisfactory manner?

What was it afterward understood to point out?

What was the fifth game?

Can you give me an account of this cavalcade?

Who were the leaders?

How many *turmæ*, or companies, were there?

At whose instigation was the fleet of Æneas set on fire?

Who was *Iris?*

On what kind of business was she usually employed?

How many ships were destroyed?

How was the fire finally extinguished?

What was the design of the Trojan women in burning their ships?

Were they weary of their long voyage?

What effect had the loss of these ships upon the mind of Æneas?

What course was he advised to pursue by Nautes?

Did he found a city for those who were willing to remain in Sicily?

What did he call it?

In the mean time, did the ghost of his father appear to him in a vision?

What direction did it give him?

Having repaired his fleet, to what place did he direct his course?

In his voyage, did he lose his pilot overboard?

How was that effected, and by whom?

Who were the *Sirenes?*

How many in number were there?

What were they said to do?

How did Ulysses escape when he approached their shores?

What islands did they inhabit?

What were they supposed to be?

What became of them at last?

After his arrival in Italy, did Æneas follow the direction of his father?

Who conducted him to the regions below?

Who was this Sibyl?

Where did she reside?

What was the place whence she delivered her predictions?

By what god was she inspired?

LIBER SEXTUS.

This is one of those books which Virgil read in the presence of Augustus and Octavia. The subject is the descent of Æneas to the infernal regions. After his arrival in Italy, he repaired immediately to the cave of the Sibyl, where he learned the difficulties that awaited him before his peaceful settlement. He then consults her about his intended descent. She informed him of the danger of the enterprise, and that he must, in the first place, obtain a golden bough from a certain tree which was sacred to Hecate. She then informs him that one of his friends lay dead on the shore, and directs him to perform his funeral rites, and afterward come and offer sacrifice. He returned to his companions, and found *Misenus* dead. Having found the golden bough, he goes to the Sibyl, who conducts him down to hell. She describes to him the various scenes of those regions as they pass along, and shows him the several apartments; in one of which he sees Dido. He attempts to address her, but she turns from him in proud disdain. He then proceeds till he comes to the residence of his father; who explains to him the nature of transmigration according to the notion of Pythagoras, and shows him the illustrious race of heroes that should descend from him. After which he returns to the upper regions, through the ivory gate, and revisits his companions.

This book is entirely episodical, and interrupts the thread of the story. It is probable that Virgil took the hint of conducting his hero to the regions of the dead, from Hercules, Orpheus, Ulysses, and others, who had visited them before. This gave him an opportunity of elucidating the economy of those regions according to the doctrines of Pythagoras, Plato, and other philosophers; of inculcating, in the most forcible manner principles of morality and religion; of developing the leading incidents of Roman history, and of flattering the vanity of his countrymen, and his prince.

Bishop Warburton considers this book as an allegorical representation of the *Eleusinian Mysteries*, at one time very much celebrated through Greece. But there is a difficulty in this interpretation. A considerable portion of the book cannot be considered in that light: for it contains a biographical sketch of the principal characters, from Æneas down to the time of Augustus, and embraces the most important events connected with the Roman government. Besides, it is not certain that Virgil was ever initiated into those mysteries; and, if it were, it is doing injustice to his character to suppose he would divulge them; when every one that was admitted, bound himself; in the most solemn manner, to keep them secret, and from the knowledge of the vulgar. Heyne observes there is some resemblance between the mysteries and the machinery of the poet; but to consider the book as an allegory, destroys the force and beauty of the whole. *Perit tandem omnis epica vis et poëtica suavitas, si res à poëta narrata ad allegoriam revocetur,* says he.

Those who would see the substance of the arguments on both sides, may consult M'Knight on the Epistles—introduction to the epistle to the Ephesians.

SIC fatur lachrymans, classique immittit habenas:
Et tandem Euboïcis Cumarum allabitur oris.
Obvertunt pelago proras: tum dente tenaci
Anchora fundabat naves, et litora curvæ
Prætexunt puppes: juvenum manus emicat ardens
Litus in Hesperium: quærit pars semina flammæ,
Abstrusa in venis silicis; pars densa ferarum
Tecta rapit sylvas, inventaque flumina monstrat.
At pius Æneas arces, quibus altus Apollo
Præsidet, horrendæque procul secreta Sibyllæ,
Antrum immane, petit: magnam cui mentem animumque
Delius inspirat vates, aperitque futura.
Jam subeunt Triviæ lucos, atque aurea tecta.
Dædalus, ut fama est, fugiens Minoïa regna,
Præpetibus pennis ausus se credere cœlo,
Insuetum per iter gelidas enavit ad Arctos,

7. Pars rapit sylvas, densa tecta ferarum, monstratque

10. Immaneque antrum, secreta Sibyllæ horrendæ procul; cui Delius vates inspirat

NOTES.

1. *Sic fatur.* This refers to what he said in the two last lines of the preceding book. *O nemiùm confise,* &c. *Immittit:* he gives full reins to his fleet. It implies that the wind was fair, and that the ships were under full sail.

This is a common metaphor, taken from the horse and his rider.

2. *Euboïcis:* an adj. of *Eubœa,* an island in the Ægean sea, lying to the east of Achaia; hodie, *Negropont.* From hence *Megasthenes,* of the city of Chalcis, transplanted a colony into Italy, and built *Cumæ,* a town in Campania. Hence, *Euboïcis oris Cumarum.*

4. *Anchora fundabat:* the anchor moored the ships. *Fundabat:* in the sense of *tenebat.*

5. *Puppes:* here used in its appropriate sense—the sterns of the ships.

6. *Semina:* the seeds—the sparks of fire.

8. *Rapit:* plunders the wood; for the purpose of collecting fuel. Ruæus says, *colligit ligna arborum. Densa tecta,* &c. is put in apposition with *sylvas.*

9. *Arces:* in the sense of *templum.* We are informed that a temple was built to Apollo in this place, in the form of a cave, that seemed to be hollowed out of a rock. In the inmost part of this temple, was the grotto, or cell, of the Sibyl.

40. *Horrendæ procul.* The avenues and approaches to her cell were *awful* and *gloomy,* for a considerable distance. It is the peculiar characteristic of this Sibyl, that she keeps her consultors at an awful distance, and fences the approaches to her cave with *Procul, O procul este, profani!*

11. *Cui magnam:* whose great mind and soul Apollo inspires. *Cui* has the sense of *cujus. Mens* properly signifies the understanding—*animus,* the soul. *Delius vates:* Apollo. He is called *Delian* from *Delos,* the place of his birth.

13. *Triviæ.* Trivia, a name of Diana. *Aurea tecta.* This was the temple built to Apollo by Dædalus.

14. *Dædalus.* An Athenian artist, who, having put to death *Perdix,* his sister's son, for rivalling him in his art, fled to *Crete:* where he soon incurred the displeasure of *Minos,* then king of that island, for assisting his wife *Pasiphaë,* in carrying on her amours with *Taurus:* and, on that account, was confined with his son *Icarus* in a tower. He escaped, however, by the help of wings. He flew into Sicily, according to *Pausanias* and *Diodorus;* but, according to Virgil and others, to *Cumæ,* where he built this temple to Apollo, for conducting him safe in his flight through the airy element.

16. *Enavit.* There is such a similitude between sailing or swimming, and flying, that the terms which properly belong to the one, are indiscriminately applied to the other. A ship is said to *fly* through the liquid element, and Mercury is said to *swim* through the air. Æn. iv. 245. And Dædalus, on wings, *swam* to the cold north, and consecrated *remigium alarum,* those wings

Chalcidicâque levis tandem superadstitit arce.
Redditus his primùm terris, tibi, Phœbe, sacravit
Remigium alarum; posuitque immania templa.
In foribus, letum Androgeï: tum pendere pœnas
Cecropidæ jussi, miserum! septena quotannis
Corpora natorum: stat ductis sortibus urna.
Contrà elata mari respondet Gnossia tellus.
Hic crudelis amor tauri, suppôstaque furto
Pasiphaë, mixtumque genus, prolesque biformis
Minotaurus inest, Veneris monumenta nefandæ
Hic labor ille domûs, et inextricabilis error.
Magnum reginæ sed enim miseratus amorem
Dædalus, ipse dolos tecti ambagesque resolvit,
Cæca regens filo vestigia. Tu quoque magnam
Partem opere in tanto, sineret dolor, Icare, haberes.

20. In foribus lethum Androgei *sculptum erat:* tum Cecropidæ jussi quotannis pendere pœnas, O miserum! *nempe, bis* septena corpora *suorum* natorum

24. Hic inest crudelis amor tauri, Pasiphaëque suppôsta furto, Minotaurusque mixtum genus, biformisque proles, monumenta nefandæ Veneris.

31. *Si* dolor *patris*

NOTES.

on which he had cut his way through the air, as oars divide the water. But what gives a greater propriety to these phrases, is, that Dædalus was the inventor of navigation by the use of sails; and that his wings were nothing else than the sails of the ship, in which he escaped from Crete. *Enavit*: in the sense of *advolavit.*

17. *Chalcidica:* an adj. from *Chalcis*, a city of Eubœa. See 2. supra. *Chalcidica arce:* the city of *Cumæ*. Here Dædalus first landed in Italy; and built the temple to Apollo, which Æneas is about to enter. It is said that he first went to Sardania, and from thence to Italy. *Redditus:* having arrived.

20. *Androgeï:* gen. of *Androgeus.* He was the son of Minos; and frequenting the public games at Athens, contracted a friendship with the sons of Pallas, brother to Ægeus, king of Athens. Not having as yet acknowledged *Theseus* to be his son; and suspecting *Androgeus* to have entered into a conspiracy with his nephew to dethrone him, *Ægeus* employed assassins to take away his life. To revenge this atrocious deed, Minos made war upon him, and forced him to sue for peace. This was granted on the condition that he should every year, or, as others say, every third, or ninth year, pay a tax of seven of their young men, and as many virgins, who were chosen by lot as victims, for the preservation of their country. Some say that Androgeus having been repeatedly victorious at the public games of Greece, excited the envy and jealousy of some persons, who procured his death. However the case may be, his death brought upon the Athenians a war with Minos, his father, then king of Crete.

The death of Androgeus was represented on the gates or doors of the temple, the Athenian youth sent as an expiation for the barbarous deed, and the urn from which the fatal lots were drawn. On the opposite side arose the island of Crete—Pasaphaë, the wife of Minos—the Minotaur—the Labyrinth, and the ingenious workmen (Dædalus) explaining its mysteries to Theseus; all these were in carved work. *Posuit:* in the sense of *ædificavit. Pendere pœnas:* to make retribution or satisfaction for the crime.

21. *Cecropidæ:* the Athenians so called from *Cecrops*, their first king. He built the city of Athens, and called it *Cecropia.*

23. *Gnossia tellus:* Crete. *Gnossia:* an adj. from *Gnossus*, a city of that island.

24. *Amor tauri.* Pasiphaë, the wife of Minos, and daughter of the Sun, was fabled to have fallen in love with a beautiful bull, and to have gratified her passion by a contrivance of Dædalus, who shut her up in a wooden cow. From this unnatural connexion sprang the *Minotaur*, a monster half man and half bull, that fed on human flesh; and devoured the Athenian youth, whom Minos shut up in the Labyrinth. The truth of the story is this: *Pasiphaë* fell in love with a nobleman of the court, whose name was *Taurus;* and made Dædalus her confidant, who kept it concealed, and even lent his house to the lovers. *Supposita furto.* This refers to Pasiphaë's being shut up in the wooden cow that she might receive the embrace of the bull—substituted through artifice or contrivance in the room of a cow.

26. *Inest:* in the sense of *sculptus est Veneris nefandæ:* of execrable lust.

27. *Labor domûs*, &c. By these we are to understand the Labyrinth. See Æn. v. 588.

28. *Miseratus magnum:* Dædalus, pitying the great love of the queen, discovers (to Theseus) the deception and intricacies of the structure, &c. Theseus, the son of Ægeus, king of Athens, proposed to go to Crete, along with the victims, to fight the Minotaur in the Labyrinth. Ariadne, the daughter of *Minos* and *Pasiphaë*, whom

Bis conatus erat casus effingere in auro ;
Bis patriæ cecidêre manus. Quin protinùs omnia
Perlegerent oculis ; ni jam præmissus Achates
Afforet ; atque unà Phœbi Triviæque sacerdos,
Deïphobe Glauci, fatur quæ talia regi :
Non hoc ista sibi tempus spectacula poscit
Nunc grege de intacto septem mactare juvencos
Præstiterit, totidem lectas de more bidentes.
Talibus affata Æneam, nec sacra morantur
Jussa viri, Teucros vocat alta in templa sacerdos.
Excisum Euboïcæ latus ingens rupis in antrum ;
Quò lati ducunt aditus centum, ostia centum ;
Unde ruunt totidem voces, responsa Sibyllæ.
Ventum erat ad limen, cùm virgo, Poscere fata
Tempus, ait : Deus, ecce, Deus ! Cui talia fanti
Ante fores, subitò non vultus, non color unus,
Non comptæ mansêre comæ : sed pectus anhelum,
Et rabie fera corda tument ; majorque videri,
Nec mortale sonans : afflata est numine quando
Jam propiore Dei. Cessas in vota precesque,
Tros, ait, Ænea ? cessas ? neque enim antè dehiscent
Attonitæ magna ora domûs. Et talia fata,
Conticuit. Gelidus Teucris per dura cucurrit
Ossa tremor ; fuditque preces rex pectore ab imo :
Phœbe, graves Trojæ semper miserate labores,

34. Ni Achates præmissus *ad Sibyllam ab Ænea*, jam afforet, atque unà Deïphobe *filia* Glauci, sacerdos.

40. Sacerdos affata Æneam talibus *verbis* vocat Teucros

41. Ingens latus Euboïcæ rupis excisum *est* in

46. Cui fanti talia ante fores, subitò non *est unus* vultus, non unus color ; comæ non mansêre comptæ ; sed pectus anhelum *est*, et *ejus* fera corda tument rabie : *cœpit*que videri major *vitâ*, nec *vox ejus est* sonans mortale.

52. Antè *quàm emiseris vota precesque.*

NOTES.

Virgil here calls *regina*, fell in love with Theseus, and taught him how to vanquish the *Minotaur*, and also gave him a clew, which she had received from Dædalus, whereby he could extricate himself from the Labyrinth. It was agreed as a condition of the combat, that if Theseus killed the Minotaur, the Athenian youths should be released, and his country freed from that humiliating condition. Theseus was victorious. By the clew we are to understand the plan and contrivance of the Labyrinth. *Enim :* in the sense of *equidem.*

29. *Resolvit :* in the sense of *explicuit.*

30. *Cæca :* in the sense of *incerta.*

31. *Icare.* Icarus, as the fable goes, was the son and associate of Dædalus. He attempted to make his escape from Crete by the help of wings, but being unable to manage them with dexterity, he wandered from his way, and fell into the Ægean sea, and was drowned. He gave name to *Icarus*, an island between *Samos* and *Mycene.*

33. *Patriæ manus cecidêre.* Dædalus attempted to represent the calamity (*casus*) of Icarus, but his grief and sorrow prevented him. He attempted it twice, and twice his hands failed ; otherwise *Icarus* would have made a distinguished figure in the carved work.

34. *Perlegerent omnia :* the Trojans would have examined all the carved work and curious sculpture of the temple, had not Achates, &c. *Protinùs :* in the sense of *in ordine. Perlegerent :* in the sense of *perlegissent.*

35. *Afforet :* in the sense of *redivisset.*

38. *Intacto :* untouched by the yoke.

39. *Bidentes :* in the sense of *oves.*

40. *Nec viri morantur :* nor do the men (the Trojans) delay to perform her sacred commands concerning offering sacrifice. *Sacerdos.* The daughter of Glaucus. She was the priestess, attendant upon the Sibyl, who was at this time in her cell or cave. *Antrum.* This is the same with *alta templa* in the preceding line. By this we are not to understand the temple of Apollo already mentioned, but the residence of the Sibyl—her cave, here called *templum.*

45. *Ventum erat :* they had come to the entrance of the cave, when, &c. *Fata :* in the sense of *oracula. Est* is understood with *tempus.*

46. *Ecce, Deus :* behold, the god, the god is here—Apollo.

47. *Subitò non vultus :* suddenly her countenance changes, and her color comes and goes

50. *Quando jam afflata est :* when now she is inspired with a nearer influence of the god Apollo. *Cessas :* dost thou delay to go into vows and prayers ? *Neque :* in the sense of *non.*

57. *Qui dirêxti Dardana tela :* who didst direct the Trojan darts, and the hands of

Dardana qui Paridis dirêxti tela manusque
Corpus in Æacidæ: magnas obeuntia terras
Tot maria intravi, duce te, penitùsque repôstas
Massylûm gentes, prætentaque Syrtibus arva:
Jam tandem Italiæ fugientis prendimus oras.
Hàc Trojana tenus fuerit fortuna secuta.
Vos quoque Pergameæ jam fas est parcere genti,
Dîque Deæque omnes, quibus obstitit Ilium, et ingens
Gloria Dardaniæ. Tuque, ô sanctissima vates,
Præscia venturi, da, non indebita posco
Regna meis fatis, Latio considere Teucros,
Errantesque Deos, agitataque numina Trojæ.
Tum Phœbo et Triviæ solido de marmore templa
Instituam, festosque dies de nomine Phœbi.
Te quoque magna manent regnis penetralia nostris.
Hìc ego namque tuas sortes, arcanaque fata
Dicta meæ genti ponam; lectosque sacrabo,
Alma, viros: foliis tantùm ne carmina manda,
Ne turbata volent rapidis ludibria ventis:
Ipsa canas, oro. Finem dedit ore loquendi.
At, Phœbi nondum patiens immanis in antro

59. Te duce, intravi tot maria obeuntia magnas terras, gentesque Massylûm penitùs repôstas

66. Da Teucros, errantesque Deos, agitataque numina Trojæ considere *in* Latio, non posco.

75. Ne turbata volent *tanquam* ludibria rapidis ventis: oro *ut tu* ipsa canas *ea ex ore.*

NOTES.

Paris, against the body of Achilles. It is said that Achilles was killed by Paris in the temple of Apollo, at Troy.

57. *Dirêxti:* for *direxisti*, by syncope.

59. *Penitùs repôstas:* far remote.

60. *Massylûm.* The *Massyli*, a people of Africa, put for the Africans in general, or for the Carthaginians in particular. See Æn. iv. 483. *Prætenta:* lying before. *Arva:* the lands—country.

61. *Italiæ fugientis:* the nearer they approached to Italy, new obstructions arose, which seemed to prevent access to it, as if it *fled* from them.

62. *Hactenus:* hitherto—thus far. It is separated by *tmesis*, for the sake of the verse. *Trojano fortuna:* id est, *adversa fortuna.*

64. *Dîque Deæque omnes, quibus:* ye gods and goddesses all, to whom Ilium and the great glory of Troy was offensive, it is just that you too, &c. The deities here meant were Juno, Minerva, and Neptune. *Obstitit: invisa sunt*, says Heyne.

68. *Agitata numina:* persecuted deities of Troy.

70. *Instituam Phœbo:* I will build to Phœbus and Diana temples of solid marble, and institute festival days, &c. Here is an allusion to the *Ludi Apollinares*, which were instituted in the first Punic war, and to the building of a temple to Apollo by Augustus, after his victory over Anthony and Cleopatra, at Actium. Heyne reads *templum*, after Heinsius. The common reading is *templa.* Virgil here uses the verb *instituam* with two nouns, when in strict propriety it can apply to one of them only. We can say, *institute festivals*, but it is quite another thing to say, *institute a house or temple.* Our language will not admit of this liberty and freedom of expression. See Æn. vii. 431, and Æn. viii. 410. Some copies have *constituam.*

71. *Te quoque magna:* a spacious sanctuary too awaits thee in our realms. This alludes to the shrine or sanctuary in the temple of *Jupiter Capitolinus*, where the Sibylline books were kept in a stone chest under ground. Fifteen persons, called *Quindecemviri*, were appointed to take care of them, and to consult them in the affairs of state. They were chosen from the *Patricians*, and had great influence in public affairs. It was a very easy matter to make these Sibylline books speak what language they pleased.

72. *Sortes:* in the sense of *oracula. Dicta:* in the sense of *declarata.*

74. *Ne manda:* do not commit, &c. It was the custom of this Sibyl to write her prophetic responses upon the leaves of the palm tree. Before the invention of parchment and paper, there was no better material for writing than the leaves and bark of trees. *Alma:* O holy prophetess.

77. *Nondum patiens*, &c. The meaning is this: the Sibyl was not docile and submissive (*patiens*) to Phœbus, and would not utter oracles according to his will, but resisted him until he had subdued her ferocious temper and formed her to his purposes by force and restraint. *Excussisse:* the perf. in the sense of the pres. The terms here used are taken from the horse and the rider. The Sibyl is compared to the former; and Apollo, breaking her and rendering her submissive and obedient to him, to the latter

78. *Tentans*, si possit excussisse

83. O *tu* tandem defuncte magnis perîclis pelagi! sed graviora *pericula*

86. Sed et volent *se* non venisse *eò*.

89. Alius Achilles partus *est tibi*

91. Cùm in egenis rebus, quas gentes Italûm, aut quas urbes, non tu supplex oraveris? Conjux hospita iterum *erit* causa tanti mali Teucris; externique thalami iterum *erunt causa.*

Bacchatur vates, magnum si pectore possit
Excussisse Deum: tantò magìs ille fatigat
Os rabidum, fera corda domans, fingitque premendo
Ostia jamque domûs patuere ingentia centum
Sponte suâ, vatisque ferunt responsa per auras:
O tandem magnis pelagi defuncte perîclis!
Sed terrâ graviora manent. In regna Lavinî
Dardanidæ venient, mitte hanc de pectore curam:
Sed non et venisse volent. Bella, horrida bella,
Et Tybrim multo spumantem sanguine cerno.
Non Simoïs tibi, nec Xanthus, nec Dorica castra
Defuerint: alius Latio jam partus Achilles,
Natus et ipse Deâ: nec Teucris addita Juno
Usquam aberit. Cùm tu supplex in rebus egenis,
Quas gentes Italûm, aut quas non oraveris urbes?
Causa mali tanti conjux iterum hospita Teucris;
Externique iterum thalami.
Tu ne cede malis; sed contrà audentior ito,
Quà tua te fortuna sinet. Via prima salutis,
Quod minimè reris, Graiâ pandetur ab urbe.
  Talibus ex adyto dictis Cumæa Sibylla

NOTES.

The verb *excutio* is applied to the horse when he throws his rider. *Immanis:* in the sense of *immaniter* vel *vehementer.* An adjective closely connected in construction with a verb, is better rendered by its corresponding adverb. *Bacchatur: furit in more Baccharum*, says Ruæus.

80. *Fatigat rabidum os:* he curbs—holds in, &c. This alludes to the manner of breaking and taming horses when they are unruly and impatient of the bit. The rider curbs or holds them in by pulling up the reins. *Fingitque:* and forms and prepares her for the delivery of his oracles.

82. *Ferunt:* in the sense of *emittunt.*

83. *Defuncte:* voc. O thou, having passed through—escaped. Ruæus says, *Qui evasisti. Perîclis:* by syn. for *periculis.*

84. *Lavinî:* by apocope for *Lavinii*, gen. of *Lavinium*, a country to the east of the Tyber, so called from the city *Lavinium*, which Æneas built. See Æn. i. 2. Some read, *regna Latini*, which perhaps is the best reading: the kingdom of Latinus. He received Æneas, on his arrival, with hospitality, gave him his daughter in marriage, and was succeeded by him in his kingdom. Heyne prefers *Lavinî*, and observes that it is more in the language of prophecy than *Latini.*

88. *Non Simoïs tibi:* neither Simoïs, nor Xanthus, nor the Grecian camp, shall be wanting to you, &c. Here the prophetess, to prepare the mind of Æneas to meet the worst, or rather the poet to do honor to his hero in overcoming such powerful opposition, gives a terrible representation of the war in which he was to be engaged in Italy, comparing it with the Trojan war, both as to its similitude of characters, places, and causes. Xanthus and Simoïs are the Tyber and Numicus; Turnus is Achilles; Lavinia, the daughter of Latinus, is a second Helen.

90. *Natus Deâ:* Turnus, a brave and warlike prince, the son of the nymph *Venilia.* *Addita:* in the sense of *inimica.* Ruæus says *infesta; et quasi lateri semper affixa.*

91. *Cùm:* in the sense of *tum*, says Heyne. Ruæus reads *quem*, but gives no authority for it; the best copies have *cùm.* *Rebus egenis:* in your distress—difficulty.

93. *Conjux hospita.* As the rape of Helen by Paris, whom she entertained in her palace at Sparta, was the cause of the Trojan war, so shall Lavinia, the daughter of Latinus, who shall receive Æneas under his hospitable roof, be the cause of a second war, by espousing Æneas after she had been promised to Turnus. *Thalami:* in the sense of *nuptiæ.*

96. *Quà:* the common reading is *quàm*, but of this it is difficult to make sense. It is not probable that the Sibyl could advise Æneas to proceed with more courage or boldness than prudence dictated, or his fortune permitted. To preserve the reading of *quàm*, Mr. Davidson renders the words *quàm tua*, &c., "The more that fortune shall oppose you;" giving to the verb *sinet* a turn which it will by no means bear. Heyne reads *quà*, taking it in the sense of *qua via et ratione*, vel *quantùm per fatum licebit.* Heinsius and Burmannus read *quàm*, which they take in the sense of *quantum.*

97. *Graiâ urbe:* this was the city Pallanteum, where Evander reigned. See Lib. 8.

Horrendas canit ambages, antroque remugit,
Obscuris vera involvens: ea fræna furenti
Concutit, et stimulos sub pectore vertit Apollo
 Ut primùm cessit furor, et rabida ora quiêrunt:
Incipit Æneas heros: Non ulla laborum,
O virgo, nova mî facies inopinave surgit:
Omnia præcepi, atque animo mecum antè peregi.
Unum oro: quando hìc inferni janua regis
Dicitur, et tenebrosa palus Acheronte refuso;
Ire ad conspectum chari genitoris, et ora
Contingat; doceas iter, et sacra ostia pandas.
Illum ego per flammas et mille sequentia tela
Eripui his humeris, medioque ex hoste recepi:
Ille meum comitatus iter, maria omnia mecum,
Atque omnes pelagique minas cœlique ferebat
Invalidus, vires ultra sortemque senectæ.
Quin, ut te supplex peterem, et tua limina adirem,
Idem orans mandata dabat. Natique patrisque,
Alma, precor, miserere: potes namque omnia; nec te
Nequicquam lucis Hecate præfecit Avernis.
Si potuit Manes arcessere conjugis Orpheus,
Threïciâ fretus citharâ fidibusque canoris:
Si fratrem Pollux alternâ morte redemit,
Itque reditque viam toties. quid Thesea, magnum
Quid memorem Alciden? et mî genus ab Jove summo
 Talibus orabat dictis, arasque tenebat.

106. Dicitur *esse* hìc, et tenebrosa palus *surgens ex* Acheronte

109. *Ut* contingat *mihi* ire ad

112. Ille comitatus *est* meum iter; *et* invalidus ferebat omnia maria mecum, atque omnes minas pelagique cœlique, ultra

115. Quin, idem *Anchises* orans dabat mandata *mihi*, ut

122. Quid *memorem* Thesea

123. *Est* mî et genus ab

NOTES.

99. *Canit horrendas:* she delivers her awful predictions. *Ambages:* (*ex ambi*, et *ago*) mysteries, says Valpy.

100. *Ea fræna furenti:* Apollo shakes those reins over her, raging, (inspired,) and turns his spurs under her breast. The metaphor of the horse and the rider, is still continued.

104. *Mî:* by apocope for *mihi.* Æneas speaks like a man long accustomed to the calamities and misfortunes (*laborum*) of life, and so well fortified in his mind to meet every vicissitude of things, that no form of toil and suffering could arise, new and unexpected.

195. *Præcepi:* I have anticipated all things—I have received information of all those difficulties before.

107. *Tenebrosa palus:* the gloomy lake, (arising) from the overflowing of Acheron. The lake here is *Avernus*, which was fabled to arise from the overflowing of the river Acheron, a fabulous river of the infernal regions. See Geor. iv. 4.

111. *Eripui:* in the sense of *sustuli.*

114. *Sortem:* state—condition.

119. *Si Orpheus potuit:* if Orpheus could call back the ghost of his wife, relying upon, &c. See the story of his descent to hell. Geor. iv. 454.

121. *Si Pollux redemit:* if Pollux redeemed his brother by an alternate death, &c. Castor and Pollux were twin brothers of Leda, the wife of Tyndarus, king of Sparta. Jupiter being the father of *Pollux*, he was immortal, while *Castor*, being only the son of Tyndarus, was subject to mortality. Upon the death of *Castor*, his brother, out of the great love he bore to him, obtained of Jupiter leave to share with him his immortality; whereupon they lived, by turns, one day in heaven and one in hell.

122. *Thesea:* a Greek acc. He was the son of *Ægeus*, king of Athens. He and Pirithoüs are fabled to have made a descent to hell for the purpose of liberating Proserpina, but were seized by Pluto, who gave Pirithoüs to *Cerberus* to be devoured, while Theseus he bound in chains, where he remained till he was set at liberty by Hercules. See 28, supra.

123. *Alciden:* Hercules, so called from *Alceus*, his grandfather. He was the son of Jupiter and Alcmene. He is said to have descended to the infernal regions, and to have carried off Cerberus in spite of Pluto himself. *Mî:* for *mihi*, by apocope, and in the sense of *meum. Mî genus:* my descent also is from Jove supreme. Æneas descended from *Dardanus*, the son of Jove He was also the son of *Venus*, the daughter of the same god. *Et:* in the sense of *etiam*

Tunc sic orsa loqui vates: Sate sanguine Divûm,
Tros Anchisiade, facilis descensus Averni:
Noctes atque dies patet atri janua Ditis:
Sed revocare gradum, superasque evadere ad auras,
Hoc opus, hic labor est. Pauci, quos æquus amavit
Jupiter, aut ardens evexit ad æthera virtus,
Dîs geniti, potuere. Tenent media omnia sylvæ,
Cocytusque sinu labens circumfluit atro.
Quòd si tantus amor menti, si tanta cupido est,
Bis Stygios innare lacus, bis nigra videre
Tartara; et insano juvat indulgere labori:
Accipe quæ peragenda priùs. Latet arbore opacâ,
Aureus et foliis et lento vimine ramus,
Junoni infernæ dictus sacer: hunc tegit omnis
Lucus, et obscuris claudunt convallibus umbræ.
Sed non antè datur telluris operta subire,
Auricomos quàm quis decerpserit arbore fœtus.
Hoc sibi pulchra suum ferri Proserpina munus
Instituit. Primo avulso, non deficit alter
Aureus; et simili frondescit virga metallo.
Ergò altè vestiga oculis, et ritè repertum
Carpe manu: namque ipse volens facilisque sequetur,
Si te fata vocant; aliter non viribus ullis
Vincere, nec duro poteris convellere ferro.
Præterea jacet exanimum tibi corpus amici,
Heu nescis! totamque incestat funere classem;
Dum consulta petis, nostroque in limine pendes.
Sedibus hunc refer antè suis, et conde sepulchro
Duc nigras pecudes: ea prima piacula sunto
Sic demùm lucos Stygios, regna invia vivis

131. Geniti Dîs, potuere *efficere id*

136. Accipe *ea*, quæ *sunt* peragenda *tibi* priùs.

140. Non datur subire operta *loca* telluris antè quàm quis

145. Ergò vestiga *ramum* oculis altè, et manu ritè carpe *eum* repertum

147. Vocant te *ad inferos.*

153. *Deinde* duc *ad aram* nigras

NOTES.

128. *Revocare gradum:* to return—to retrace your steps; a phrase. *Superas auras:* to this upper world—the upper regions of light; they are so called in reference to the regions below.

132. *Cocytusque:* and Cocytus gliding along with its gloomy stream, flows around them. *Cocytus*, a river in Campania in Italy, but by the poets feigned to be a river in hell. *Sinu:* in the sense of *flexu*.

134. *Innare:* in the sense of *navigare. Insano:* vast—mighty. Ruæus says, *vano.*

135. *Accipe:* in the sense of *audi*, vel *disce.*

137. *Ramus aureus:* a bough, golden both in its leaves and limber twig, &c. lies concealed in a shady tree. This is considered by some a mere fiction of the poet, but probably it is founded on some historical fact, or refers to some fabulous tradition, which it is not easy to find out. Servius thinks it alludes to a tree in the midst of the sacred grove of *Diana*, not far from Aritia, a city of Latium, where, if a fugitive came for sanctuary, and could pluck a branch from the tree, he was permitted to fight a single combat with the priest of her temple, and if he overcame him, to take his place.

138. *Junoni:* Proserpine. She is here called *Infernal Juno;* as Pluto is sometimes called *Stygius Jupiter.*

141. *Auricomos fœtus:* the golden bough. *Fœtus:* the young of any thing animate or inanimate. Here, a bough, shoot, or scion

142. *Suum:* in the sense of *charum.*

143. *Instituit:* in the sense of *jussit. Primo avulso: ramo* is understood. For *primo*, Ruæus says, *uno.*

144. *Frondescit:* in the sense of *pullulat. Virga:* in the sense of *ramus.* When one bough was plucked, another immediately shot forth of the same form, shape, and color.

146. *Sequetur:* will follow—will yield to you, if, &c.

148. *Avellere:* in the sense of *amputare* vel *cædere.*

150. *Incestat:* defiles. *Funere:* in the sense of *cadavere. Consulta:* advice—counsel.

151. *Pendes:* in the sense of *hæres.*

152. *Suis sedibus:* to his own proper place—to the earth.

Aspicies Dixit; pressoque obmutuit ore.
  Æneas mœsto defixus lumina vultu
Ingreditur, linquens antrum, cæcosque volutat
Eventus animo secum: cui fidus Achates
It comes, et paribus curis vestigia figit.
Multa inter sese vario sermone serebant,
Quem socium exanimem vates, quod corpus humandum
Diceret. Atque illi Misenum in litore sicco,
Ut venêre, vident indignâ morte peremptum;
Misenum Æoliden, quo non præstantior alter
Ære ciere viros, Martemque accendere cantu.
Hectoris hic magni fuerat comes. Hectora circum
Et lituo pugnas insignis obibat et hastâ.
Postquam illum victor vitâ spoliavit Achilles,
Dardanio Æneæ sese fortissimus heros
Addiderat socium, non inferiora secutus.
Sed tum, fortè cavâ dum personat æquora conchâ,
Demens, et cantu vocat in certamina Divos,
Æmulus exceptum Triton, si credere dignum est,
Inter saxa virum spumosâ immerserat undâ.
Ergò omnes magno circùm clamore fremebant;
Præcipuè pius Æneas. Tum jussa Sibyllæ,
Haud mora, festinant flentes: aramque sepulchri
Congerere arboribus, cœloque educere certant.
  Itur in antiquam sylvam, stabula alta ferarum:
Procumbunt piceæ: sonat icta securibus ilex:
Fraxineæque trabes, cuneis et fissile robur
Scinditur: advolvunt ingentes montibus ornos.
Necnon Æneas opera inter talia primus
Hortatur socios, paribusque accingitur armis.
  Atque hæc ipse suo tristi cum corde volutat,
Aspectans sylvam immensam, et sic ore precatur:

161. Quem socium vates diceret *esse* exanimem, quod corpus humandum *esse*

167. Et obibat pugnas circum Hectora, insignis lituo et hastâ.

175. Circùm *illum*

177. Tum flentes festinant *exsequi* jussa Sibyllæ

NOTES.

156. *Defixus lumina:* a Grecism. Or, in the sense of *figens oculos in terram*, says Ruæus.

160. *Serebant multa:* they made many conjectures—they talked much, &c.

164. *Æoliden.* Misenus is here called the son of *Æolus*, the fabulous god of the winds; because he excelled in blowing upon wind instruments. *Præstantior:* more expert. The verb *erat* is understood.

165. *Martemque accendere cantu.* This hemistich Virgil is said to have added in the mere heat of fancy, while he was reciting the book before Augustus; having left the line imperfect at first. *Ære:* with his brazen trumpet. Any thing made of brass may be called *æs*.

167. *Lituo.* The *lituus* was a trumpet not so straight as the *tuba*, nor so crooked as the *cornua*. It was used, for the most part, by the cavalry. *Obibat pugnas:* simply, he fought.

170. *Inferiora:* in the sense of *inferiorem ducem*.

171. *Personat æquora:* he makes the sea resound, &c. *Conchâ.* Shell trumpets were in use at first; before those instruments came to be made of brass.

172. *Vocat:* he challenges the gods to a trial of music.

173. *Triton æmulus:* Triton envious (jealous of his fame) drowned in the foaming waves the man taken by surprise among the rocks. Triton was the son of Neptune and Amphitrite. He was half man and half fish; and was Neptune's trumpeter.

175. *Fremebant:* in the sense of *lamentabantur*.

177. *Aramque sepulchri:* the funeral pile, so called because built in the form of an altar. *Ingentem pyram*, says Heyne.

180. *Sonat:* in the sense of *procumbit*. *Trabes:* for *arbores*. *Fissile robur:* the fissile oak.

183. *Primus:* chief in command—captain of the company.

184. *Accingiturque,* &c.: and is arrayed with equal arms. By *armis*, we are to understand the axes, and other implements for cutting and preparing wood for the funeral pile of *Misenus*.

186. *Ore.* This is the common reading

Si nunc se nobis ille aureus arbore ramus
Ostendat nemore in tanto! quando omnia ver*

189. Nimium *verè*

Heu! nimiùm de te vates, Misene, locuta est.
Vix ea fatus erat, geminæ cùm fortè columbæ
Ipsa sub ora viri cœlo venêre volantes,
Et viridi sedêre solo. Tum maximus heros
Maternas agnoscit aves, lætusque precatur:

195. O *vos*, este duces mihi, siqua

Este duces, ô, siqua via est; cursumque per auras
Dirigite in lucos, ubi pinguem dives opacat
Ramus humum: tuque, ô, dubiis ne defice rebus,
Diva parens. Sic effatus. vestigia pressit,
Observans quæ signa ferant, quò tendere pergant.

199. Illæ pascentes *cœperunt* prodire volantes tantùm

Pascentes illæ tantùm prodire volando,
Quantùm acie possent oculi servare sequentûm.
Inde, ubi venêre ad fauces graveolentis Averni;
Tollunt se celeres; liquidumque per aëra lapsæ,
Sedibus optatis geminæ super arbore sidunt,
Discolor unde auri per ramos aura refulsit.

205. Quale viscum, quod sua arbos non seminat, solet *in* sylvis virere novâ fronde *in* brumali frigore

Quale solet sylvis brumali frigore viscum
Fronde virere novâ, quod non sua seminat arbos,
Et croceo fœtu teretes circumdare truncos.
Talis erat species auri frondentis opacâ
Ilice: sic leni crepitabat bractea vento.

210. Corripit *ramum*

Corripit extemplò Æneas, avidusque refringit
Cunctantem, et vatis portat sub tecta Sibyllæ.

213. Ferebant suprema *officia.*

Nec minùs intereà Misenum in litore Teucri
Flebant, et cineri ingrato suprema ferebant.

NOTES.

but Heyne and others have *voce.* The sense is the same either way.

187. *Si:* in the sense of *utinam.*

189. *Vates:* the prophetess.

193. *Maternas aves.* Pigeons were sacred to Venus, it is said, on account of their fecundity.

196. *Dubiis rebus:* perplexity—difficulty. *Defice:* in the sense of *desere.*

197. *Pressit vestigia:* he stopt his pace—he stood still.

198. *Ferant:* in the sense of *dent* vel *præbant. Pergant:* proceed to go. *Tendere:* in the sense of *ire* vel *prodire.*

198. *Illæ pascentes,* &c.: they flew, and then alighted to feed. And this they did by turns, so that they just kept within sight of the followers, *sequentûm.*

200. *Acie:* with the sight. Ruæus says, *acutissimo visu.*

201. *Fauces:* in the sense of *os.* The junction of the lakes *Avernus* and *Lucrinus. Graveolentis:* noxious—pestiferous.

203. *Optatis sedibus:* they both alight on the tree near the place whence the golden bough shone through the branches of the tree.

204. *Discolor aura:* the variegated gleam of gold shone through the boughs. It varied its color according to the different shades of light in which it was seen. The leaves mingling their green shade with the lustre of the gold, produced that variegated color. *Aura:* in the sense of *splendor.*

205. *Viscum.* This is a kind of shrub of a glutinous nature, called *misletoe.* It grows on trees principally of the oak kind. The winter is the proper season for its production; and it is of a color resembling gold. It was thought to grow out of the excrements of birds, that alighted on those trees: to which the poet alludes in these words: *quod non sua seminat arbos:* which its own tree does not produce: but this opinion is incorrect. The ancient Druids made great use of this in their religious ceremonies.

206. *Seminat:* in the sense of *producit. Fœtu:* see 141. supra.

208. *Frondentis auri:* of the golden bough—the verdant gold. Ruæus says, *pullulantis auri.*

209. *Bractea:* the golden leaves rustled in the gentle wind. *Bractea,* properly, thin *laminæ,* or leaves of gold; taken here in the sense of *auræ frondes.*

211. *Cunctantem:* in the sense of *tardè sequentem.*

213. *Ferebant suprema:* they were performing the last offices. *Ingrato:* being insensible of the honors conferred upon it, and therefore ungrateful for them. Or it may

Principio pinguem tædis et robore secto
Ingentem struxere pyram: cui frondibus atris
Intexunt latera, et ferales antè cupressos
Constituunt, decorantque supèr fulgentibus armis
Pars calidos latices et ahena undantia flammis
Expediunt; corpusque lavant frigentis et unguunt
Fit gemitus: tum membra toro defleta reponunt,
Purpureasque supèr vestes, velamina nota,
Conjiciunt. Pars ingenti subiere feretro,
Triste ministerium! et subjectam more parentum
Aversi tenuere facem. Congesta cremantur
Thurea dona, dapes, fuso crateres olivo.
Postquam collapsi cineres, et flamma quievit,
Relliquias vino et bibulam lavêre favillam:
Ossaque lecta cado texit Chorinæus aheno.
Idem ter socios purâ circumtulit undâ,
Spargens rore levi et ramo felicis olivæ;
Lustravitque viros, dixitque novissima verba.
At pius Æneas ingenti mole sepulchrum

215. Struxere ingentem pyram, pinguem e tædis et robore secto

226. Collapsi *sunt*.

NOTES.

be understood as causing sorrow to all—being an object or spectacle no way pleasant or agreeable. In this sense, *ingrato* may be rendered mournful—unjoyous. *Cineri:* in the sense of *cadaveri. Ingrato: nec sentienti nec referenti gratiam*, says Heyne.

Virgil here gives us most of the ceremonies used among the Romans in burying the dead.

214. *Tædis.* The *tæda*, or pine, is a fat and unctuous wood. Hence the epithet *pinguem. Secto robore:* in the sense of *fisso robore.*

215. *Pyram.* The funeral pile was called *pyra* when it was set on fire, *rogus* before it was set on fire, and *bustum* after it was consumed. The higher it was raised, the more honorable it was considered; and therefore they endeavored to raise it to heaven: *certant educere cœlo*, 178. supra. *Cui frondibus atris:* whose sides they interweave with black boughs. The boughs of the yew, pine, and such like trees, are of a sable color, and were therefore used in funeral obsequies. *Cui:* in the sense of *cujus.*

216. *Cupressos:* the cypress is here called mournful; and used on the occasion, either because its strong smell prevented any thing disagreeable from the corpse; or rather as it was a fit emblem of death; for when it is once cut, it never grows up again. *Antè:* before—in front: an adv.

217. *Supèr* above—on the top.

218. *Latices:* in the sense of *aquam.*

221. *Nota velamina:* the garments of Misenus. Or it is said in allusion to a Roman custom of placing a purple covering over the corps of distinguished persons on the funeral pile

222. *Pars subiere:* a part supported (went under) the huge bier, a mournful office! and turned (*aversi*) away with their faces, held a torch under it, &c. They turned away their faces to show how unwilling they were to part with him, and that their grief would not allow them to look upon his pale and lifeless body; which was now about to be reduced to ashes.

225. *Dapes.* By this we are to understand the fat and other parts of the victims that were consecrated to the gods. *Crateres:* goblets of oil poured out upon the pile. Whole goblets were offered to the infernal gods; but to the celestial gods only libations. *Thurea dona:* gifts of frankincense. There is an allusion here to the custom of placing frankincense, oil, and other unctuous substances upon the funeral pile, to accelerate its burning.

227. *Relliquias*, &c. After the body was consumed, they extinguished (*lavêre*) the coals and embers with *wine*, that the ashes might the more easily be collected. *Bibulam:* in the sense of *siccam.*

228. *Cado:* in the sense of *urna. Texit:* in the sense of *inclusit.*

229. *Idem ter circumtulit:* the same thrice went around his companions with holy water, sprinkling them, &c. The ordo of construction is, *circum socios*, &c. which means, to go round them three times: but because the priest used to sprinkle them, at the same time, with the *aqua lustralis*, or holy water, it came to signify, *to purify.*

230. *Levi rore:* with a dew or spray. He sprinkled the water with a bough of olive.

231. *Lustravit:* he purified the men. *Novissima verba.* These were *vale, vale, vale*, when they all departed.

Imponit, suaque arma viro, remumque, tubamque,
Monte sub aërio, qui nunc Misenus ab illo
Dicitur, æternumque tenet per sæcula nomen.
His actis, properè exsequitur præcepta Sibyllæ.
Spelunca alta fuit, vastoque immanis hiatu,
Scrupea, tuta lacu nigro nemorumque tenebris;

239. Super quam haud ullæ volantes.

Quam super haud ullæ poterant impunè volantes
Tendere iter pennis: talis sese halitus atris
Faucibus effundens supera ad convexa ferebat;
Unde locum Graii dixerunt nomine Avernum.

243. Hic sacerdos constituit quatuor juvencos nigrantes *quoad* terga

Quatuor hìc primùm nigrantes terga juvencos
Constituit, frontique invergit vina sacerdos;
Et summas carpens media inter cornua setas,

246. Imponit *eas*, *quasi* prima libamina

Ignibus imponit sacris libamina prima,
Voce vocans Hecaten, cœloque Ereboque potentem
Supponunt alii cultros, tepidumque cruorem
Suscipiunt pateris. Ipse atri velleris agnam

250. Æneas ipse ferit ense agnam atri velleris matri

Æneas matri Eumenidum magnæque sorori
Ense ferit; sterilemque tibi, Proserpina, vaccam
Tum Stygio regi nocturnas inchoat aras,

254. Superfundens que pingue

Et solida imponit taurorum viscera flammis,
Pingue supèrque oleum fundens ardentibus extis.

256. Solum *cœpit* mugire sub pedibus, et juga sylvarum cœpta *sunt* moveri, canesque visæ *sunt*

Ecce autem, primi sub lumina Solis et ortus,
Sub pedibus mugire solum, et juga cœpta moveri
Sylvarum; visæque canes ululare per umbram,
Adventante Deâ. Procul, ô, procul este, profani

NOTES.

233. *Imponit*, &c. The poet here uses the verb *imponit* with two nouns, when, in strict propriety it can agree with one of them only. He builds a tomb, and places upon it (*imponit*) his arms, &c. He orders to be carved upon it his arms, to denote that he was a warrior—an oar, to show that he perished in a naval expedition—and a trumpet, to denote his office.

234. *Monte sub aërio, qui.* The mountain here meant is the promontory *Misenus*, which forms the western shore of the *Sinus Puteolanus*, or *Neapolitanus. Hodie, Capo Miseno.* Not far from it was the *Portus Misenus*, where Augustus kept a part of his fleet.

238. *Tuta:* in the sense of *defensa. Volantes:* in the sense of *aves.*

240. *Halitus:* vapor—stench. *Supera convexa:* the high canopy of heaven. *Effundens:* in the sense of *erumpens.*

242. *Avernum.* See Geor. iv. 493.

243. *Hic primùm*, &c. The lake Avernus appears to have been chosen as the place of this sacrifice, because, by it, it was thought an easier access was had to the infernal deities, particularly Hecate. Having prepared her victims, the Sibyl poured wine between their horns; afterward cut a lock of the topmost hair, and cast it upon the fire as the first offering, to show that the sacrifice was then begun, and that the victims were then devoted to the gods.

247. *Vocans Hecaten.* Servius informs us, that Hecate was usually invoked not by words, but by certain mystic and inarticulate sounds.

248. *Alii supponunt:* others apply the knives (i. e. slay the victims) and catch, &c. *Suscipiunt:* in the sense of *excipiunt.*

250. *Matri Eumenidum:* to the mother of the furies, that is, *Nox.* See Geor. i. 278. Night is said to have brought forth the furies to *Acheron;* which, in the language of poetry, signifies that night or darkness is the mother of horrid shapes, visionary forms, and apparitions. *Magnæ sorori:* to her great sister, that is, to the earth, *Tellus:* for night is only the shadow of the earth, or the absence of light.

252. *Aras:* by meton. for the sacrifices offered upon them. They were offered in the night: hence the epithet *nocturna.* For *aras*, Ruæus says *sacrificia.*

253. *Solida viscera.* By these we are to understand the whole or entire carcases of the victims; so that this sacrifice was properly what was called a *holocaust*, or whole burnt-offering. *Totam victimam*, says Heyne.

256. *Solum:* in the sense of *terra.*

258. *Procul! O procul!* be at a distance—at a distance, O ye profane! This was

Conclamat vates, totoque absistite luco.
Tuque invade viam, vaginâque eripe ferrum:
Nunc animis opus, Ænea, nunc pectore firmo.
Tantum effata, furens antro se immisit aperto:
Ille ducem haud timidis vadentem passibus æquat.
Dî, quibus imperium est animarum, umbræque silentes,
Et Chaos, et Phlegethon, loca nocte silentia latè,
Sit mihi fas audita loqui: sit numine vestro
Pandere res altâ terrâ et caligine mersas.
Ibant obscuri solâ sub nocte per umbram,
Perque domos Ditis vacuas, et inania regna.
Quale per incertam Lunam sub luce malignâ
Est iter in sylvis; ubi cœlum condidit umbrâ
Jupiter, et rebus nox abstulit atra colorem.
Vestibulum ante ipsum primisque in faucibus Orci,
Luctus et ultrices posuere cubilia Curæ:
Pallentesque habitant Morbi, tristisque Senectus,
Et metus, et malesuada Fames, et turpis Egestas,
Terribiles visu formæ! Letumque, Laborque:
Tum consanguineus Leti Sopor, et mala mentis
Gaudia, mortiferumque adverso in limine Bellum,
Ferreique Eumenidum thalami, et Discordia demens

261. Nunc opus *est* animis, *O Ænea,*

263. Ille æquat ducem vadentem, haud timidis

624. *Vos*que silentes umbræ, et

266. *Fas* sit *mihi* vestro numine, pandere res mersas

270. *Tale* quale *est* iter in sylvis per incertam Lunam

275. *Hic quoque* pallentesque morbi

278. Tum in adverso limine *sunt* Sopor

NOTES.

the usual preamble with which the sacred mysteries were ushered in. Those who were not initiated, were called *scelesti*, *inexpiati*, and *profani;* and were prevented from access to such holy rites. *Dea adventante.* By *Dea*, we are to understand *Hecate*, accompanied by her dogs. Heyne observes that the furies are sometimes called *canes*. But they are not so to be taken in this place. *Sunt canes Hecaten comitantes, et passim memorati in sacris magicis.*

259. *Absistite:* in the sense of *recedite.*

260. *Eripe ferrum:* draw the sword from the sheath. This indicated danger, and the hazard of the enterprise.

262. *Tantum:* so much—this only.

263. *Vadentem:* in the sense of *euntem*, vel *ingredientem.*

265. *Chaos:* properly, a confused and indigested mass of matter, out of which it is supposed all things were made.—One of the most ancient gods of the Heathens; or rather the parent of them all. *Phlegethon:* the name of one of the infernal rivers, of Greek derivation. According to the poets, there were five rivers of hell, *Acheron*, *Cocytus*, *Styx*, *Phlegethon*, and *Lethe*, all of Greek derivation. *Silentia:* this is the common reading; but Heyne, on the authority of Heinsius, has *tacentia.*

267. *Mersas:* in the sense of *tectas* vel *occultas.*

268. *Obscuri solâ nocte:* by hypallage, for *soli obscura nocte.*

270. *Per incertam lunam.* By this, some understand the new moon soon after its change, when it shines with a feeble or glimmering light. Others, the moon occasionally hid and obscured by clouds. *Malignâ luce:* envious light—that which shines so faintly, as if it grudged one the happiness of enjoying it. *Condidit:* hath hid, or covered.

273. *Vestibulum.* This was the space or area contained between the house and highway. In this *vestibulum* of hell, the poet describes the various calamities of human life, as having their residence: all of which he clothes with a kind of airy body.

274. *Curæ:* in the sense of *conscientia*, says Heyne.

276. *Fames malesuada:* hunger persuading to evil. *Quæ suadet rapinas sceleraque*, says Heyne. *Non tantùm inopia victûs; sed etiam avaritia, et auri sacra fames*, says Ruæus. That avarice and thirst for gold, which persuades and hurries men to the perpetration of crimes, and is the fruitful source of evils.

278. *Sopor:* sleep, the brother of death. The poets tell us that *Somnus* and *Mors* were children of *Nox*. Or, in the language of poetry, *sleep* and *death* may be called brothers, on account of their resemblance. *Mala gaudia mentis:* the criminal joys of the mind. *Tum:* then—in the next place.

280. *Ferrei thalami*, &c. By the iron beds of the furies, we are to understand the racking torments of a guilty conscience, the consequence of a course of vice and sensuality: and, by frantic discord, bound as to its viperous locks with bloody fillets, we are to understand all those base and turbulent passions, which unhinge the mind, and over-

Vipereum crinem vittis innexa cruentis.
In medio ramos annosaque brachia pandit
Ulmus opaca, ingens: quam sedem Somnia vulgò
Vana tenere ferunt; foliisque sub omnibus hærent.
Multaque prætereà variarum monstra ferarum,
Centauri in foribus stabulant, Scyllæque biformes,
Et centum geminus Briareus, ac bellua Lernæ
Horrendùm stridens, flammisque armata Chimæra;
Gorgones, Harpyiæque; et forma tricorporis umbræ.
Corripit hìc subitâ trepidus formidine ferrum
Æneas, strictamque aciem venientibus offert.
Et, ni docta cŏmes tenues sinè corpore vitas
Admoneat volitare cavâ sub imagine formæ,
Irruat, et frustrà ferro diverberet umbras.
Hinc via, Tartarei quæ fert Acherontis ad undas.
Turbidus hìc cœno vastâque voragine gurges
Æstuat, atque omnem Cocyto eructat arenam.
Portitor has horrendus aquas et flumina servat
Terribili squalore Charon: cui plurima mento
Canities inculta jacet: stant lumina flamma:
Sordidus ex humeris nodo dependet amictus.
Ipse ratem conto subigit, velisque ministrat,
Et ferrugineâ subvectat corpora cymbâ

285. Multa monstra variarum ferarum stabulant in foribus *Orci*, *nempe*, Centauri

292. Et irruat, et frustrà diverberat umbras ferro, ni docta comes admoneat *eum illas* tenues vitas volitare sinè corpore

295. Hinc *est* via, quæ

296. Hìc gurges turbidus cœno

298. Portitor Charon horrendus terribili squalore servat

NOTES.

turn the peace of society. These, with great propriety, are placed in the opposite threshold, confronting the criminal joys of the mind.

Thalami: not the marriage bed; for the furies were never married; but rather the place where they were begotten, or where they resided.

284. *Hærent.* Dreams are here represented as only perching upon the leaves, perhaps on account of their light wandering nature. *Ferunt:* they report—say. *Tenere:* in the sense of *occupare.*

285. *Multa monstra:* many forms or spectres of savage beasts.

286. *Centauri:* these were fabled to have been monsters, half man and half horse. They may, therefore, properly be said to *be stabled.* The truth is, they were a people of Thessaly, who first broke horses, and made use of them in war *Scyllæ biformes.* See Ecl. vi. 74.

287. *Briareus:* one of the giants, said to have had a hundred hands. *Bellua Lernæ:* the beast of Lerna—the snake which was bred in the lake of Lerna, and destroyed by Hercules. It had seven heads, and some say fifty; and as soon as any one of them was cut off, another sprang up in its place. *Stridens:* hissing horribly.

288. *Chimæra:* a monster said to vomit flames. Its head was that of a lion, its breast and middle parts resembled a goat, and its tail a serpent. He was slain by Bellerophon on the horse Pegasus. The truth of the fable is this: *Chimæra* was the name of a mountain in Lycia, in Asia Minor, whose top was infested with lions, and its bottom with serpents, while its middle parts and sides abounded with goats. Bellerophon rendered it habitable, and was therefore said to have slain the monster.

289. *Forma tricorporis umbræ:* the form of the three-bodied ghost *Geryon.* He was fabled to have had three bodies, because he reigned over three islands, *Minorca, Majorca,* and *Urica.* He was a king of Spain.

291. *Offert:* presents. *Vitas:* in the sense of *umbras.*

293. *Formæ:* in the sense of *figuræ* vel *corporis.*

296. *Gurges:* the river *Styx* or *Acheron. Eructat:* in the sense of *immittit. Cocyto:* in the sense of *in Cocytum.*

298. *Horrendus terribili squalore:* frightful with horrid filthiness.

299. *Cui plurima mento:* on whose chin a very large hoary beard lies neglected and undressed. *Cui:* in the sense of *cujus.*

300. *Lumina:* in the sense of *oculi. Flamma.* This is the common reading, but the Roman, Medicean, and some other copies, have *flammæ* in the plu. Davidson reads *flammæ* Heyne reads *flamma,* but takes it in the sense of *flammea,* and *stant,* in the sense of *sunt: Lumina sunt flammea.* Some copies have *lumine stant flammæ,* taking *lumine* for *oculis,* which makes the reading easy. Ruæus says, *oculi sunt pleni igne.* Valpy reads, *flammâ,* in the abl.

303. *Corpora:* in the sense of *umbras,* vel *inania corpora. Ferrugineâ:* dark-colored —of an iron hue.

Jam senior: sed cruda Deo viridisque senectus.
Huc omnis turba ad ripas effusa ruebat;
Matres, atque viri, defunctaque corpora vitâ
Magnanimûm heroum, pueri innuptæque puellæ,
Impositique rogis juvenes ante ora parentum:
Quàm multa in sylvis autumni frigore primo
Lapsa cadunt folia, aut ad terram gurgite ab alto
Quàm multæ glomerantur aves, ubi frigidus annus
Trans pontum fugat, et terris immittit apricis.
Stabant orantes, primi transmittere cursum,
Tendebantque manus ripæ ulterioris amore.
Navita sed tristis nunc hos, nunc accipit illos:
Ast alios longè submotos arcet arenâ.
  Æneas, miratus enim motusque tumultu,
Dic, ait, ô virgo, quid vult concursus ad amnem?
Quidve petunt animæ? vel quo discrimine ripas
Hæ linquunt, illæ remis vada livida verrunt?
Olli sic breviter fata est longæva sacerdos:
Anchisâ generate, Deûm certissima proles,
Cocyti stagna alta vides, Stygiamque paludem,
Dî cujus jurare timent et fallere numen:
Hæc omnis, quam cernis, inops inhumataque turba est:
Portitor ille Charon: hi, quos vehit unda, sepulti.
Nec ripas datur horrendas, nec rauca fluenta
Transportare priùs, quàm sedibus ossa quiêrunt.
Centum errant annos, volitantque hæc litora circum:
Tum demum admissi stagna exoptata revisunt.
  Constitit Anchisâ satus, et vestigia pressit,
Multa putans, sortemque animo miseratus iniquam.
Cernit ibi mœstos, et mortis honore carentes,

304. Cruda viridisque senectus *est illi utpote* Deo

309. *Tam multi*, quam multa folia lapsa cadunt in sylvis primo frigore autumni; aut quàm multæ aves glomerantur

327. Nec datur *eis* transportare *eos* horrendas ripas, nec rauca

NOTES.

306. *Defuncta:* in the sense of *privata.*

310. *Gurgite:* in the sense of *mari. Glomerantur:* in the sense of *congregant. Frigidus annus:* the cold season of the year—the approach of winter.

315. *Tristis:* inexorable. Ruæus says, *asper.*

316. *Ast arcet alios:* but drives others removed far from the shore. Those that were unburied were not permitted to pass over, until such time as they had received the rites of burial.

318. *Quid vult:* what means this concourse, &c.

319. *Quo discrimine:* by what distinction; or by what reason.

320. *Vada:* in the sense of *aquas*, vel *amnem.*

321. *Longæva sacerdos.* Servius tells us that Apollo, out of affection for the Sibyl, promised her whatever she should ask; upon which she took up a handful of sand, and desired to have her life prolonged to a length of years equal to the number of the sands the mass contained. Her request was granted, on condition she should remove from *Erythræ* to *Cumæ*, and there spend the remainder of her days. She lived so long that she was so completely emaciated that she retained nothing but her voice.

323. *Alta stagna:* the deep waters.

324. *Cujus numen Dî:* by whose divinity the gods fear to swear and to deceive. The river *Styx* was held in such veneration by the gods that they used to swear by it, and if they violated their oath they were deprived of their divinity, and were excluded from *nectar* and *ambrosia* for nine years; some say for a hundred years. The reason assigned for their conferring this honor upon *Styx* is, that her offspring, Victory and Strength, had given the gods such signal assistance in the war against the *Titans. Per cujus numen Dii*, &c.

325. *Inops:* poor—unable to pay their fare, which was an *obolus.* Or, unable to pay the expenses of burial, and so remained *inhumata*, unburied.

327. *Datur:* in the sense of *permittitur.*

328. *Sedibus:* in their graves.

330. *Admissi:* in the sense of *recepti. Revisunt:* in the sense of *transeunt.*

331. *Pressit vestigia:* in the sense of *continuit gressum* vel *pedem;* a phrase.

333. *Honore mortis:* burial. *Privatos honore sepulturæ*, says Ruæus.

Leucaspim, et Lyciæ ductorem classis Orontem:
Quos simul à Trojâ ventosa per æquora vectos
Obruit Auster, aquâ involvens navemque virosque
   Ecce gubernator sese Palinurus agebat:
Qui Libyco nuper cursu, dum sidera servat,
Exciderat puppi, mediis effusus in undis.
Hunc ubi vix multâ mœstum cognovit in umbrâ,
Sic prior alloquitur: Quis te, Palinure, Deorum
Eripuit nobis, medioque sub æquore mersit?
Dic, age.. Namque mihi fallax haud antè repertus,
Hoc uno responso animum delusit Apollo;
Qui fore te ponto incolumem, finesque canebat
Venturum Ausonios: en! hæc promissa fides est?
Ille autem: Neque te Phœbi cortina fefellit,
Dux Anchisiade; nec me Deus æquore mersit.
Namque gubernâclum multâ vi fortè revulsum,
Cui datus hærebam custos, cursusque regebam,
Præcipitans traxi mecum. Maria aspera juro,
Non ullum pro me tantum cepisse timorem;
Quàm tua ne, spoliata armis, excussa magistro,
Deficeret tantis navis surgentibus undis.
Tres Notus hybernas immensa per æquora noctes
Vexit me violentus aquâ: vix lumine quarto
Prospexi Italiam, summâ sublimis ab undâ
Paulatim adnabam terræ, et jam tuta tenebam,
Ni gens crudelis madidâ cum veste gravatum,
Prensantemque uncis manibus capita aspera montis,
Ferro invasisset, prædamque ignara putâsset.
Nunc me fluctus habet, versantque in litore venti

343. Namque Apollo, haud antè repertus mihi fallax, delusit animum hoc uno responso; qui canebat

349. Namque præcipitans traxi mecum gubernâclum fortè revulsum

351. Juro *per* aspera maria *me* non cepisse ullum

358. Tuta *loca*, ni crudelis gens ferro invasisset *me*

NOTES.

336. *Obruit:* drowned—sunk.

337. *Agebat sese:* in the sense of *ferebat sese.*

338. *Libyco cursu.* Palinurus was not drowned in the Libyan, but in the Tuscan sea, after he set sail from Sicily. The voyage was commenced from Africa, or Libya, which is the reason of its being called a Libyan course, or voyage. *Effusus:* in the sense of *lapsus* vel *præcipitatus.*

347. *Cortina:* the table or tripod on which the statue of Apollo was placed, whence responses were given; by meton. the oracle itself. *Neque te.* In this and the following line some imagine a difficulty; to remove which, they make a point after the pronoun *me*, reading it thus: *Nor hath the oracle of Apollo deceived you, nor me;* a god plunged me into the sea. For the poet had informed us, Lib. v. 841, that Palinurus was actually thrown overboard by the god *Somnus.* Others connect the *me* with *mersit*, and say, though it was a god, yet Palinurus believed it to be Phorbas, one of the sons of Priam. But there is no need of this refinement.

348. *Nec mersit:* nor hath a god drowned me in the sea. Although Palinurus was thrown overboard by Somnus, he was not drowned. He arrived safe to the shores of Italy, and therefore the promise of Apollo was not false and deceptive. *Mersit:* in the sense of *submersit.*

350. *Cui hærebam:* to which I clung, being the appointed helmsman. With the part of the ship which he carried with him, Palinurus kept himself above the water, and was enabled to swim to the land.

353. *Ne tua navis, spoliata:* lest your ship being deprived of its rudder and destitute of a pilot, &c. *Arma* signifies, when applied to navigation, the whole tackling or equipments of a ship, whether for use, steerage, ornament, or defence. *Excussa:* in the sense of *privata.* *Armis:* for *gubernaculo.*

357. *Sublimis:* raised high on the top of a wave, I saw Italy. *Lumine:* in the sense of *die.*

358. *Paulatim:* at my ease—slowly. There are several instances in Virgil where the indicative appears to be used instead of the subjunctive, or where the sense evidently requires the sub. *Jam tuta tenebam:* I should have now been safe on land, had not, &c.

359. *Ni:* in the sense of *sed*, vel *autem.*

361. *Putâsset:* by syn. for *putavisset.* They ignorant thought me a prize.

362. *Versant:* toss my dead body on the shore.

Quòd te per cœli jucundum lumen et auras,
Per genitorem oro, per spes surgentis Iüli;
Eripe me his, invicte, malis: aut tu mihi terram
Injice, namque potes; portusque require Velinos:
Aut tu, si qua via est, si quam tibi Diva creatrix
Ostendit (neque enim, credo, sinè numine Divûm
Flumina tanta paras Stygiamque innare paludem)
Da dextram misero, et tecum me tolle per undas,
Sedibus ut saltem placidis in morte quiescam.
Talia fatus erat: cœpit cùm talia vates:
Unde hæc, ô Palinure, tibi tam dira cupido?
Tu Stygias inhumatus aquas, amnemque severum
Eumenidum aspicies? ripamve injussus adibis?
Desine fata Deûm flecti sperare precando.
Sed cape dicta memor, duri solatia casûs.
Nam tua finitimi, longè latèque per urbes
Prodigiis acti cœlestibus, ossa piabunt;
Et statuent tumulum, et tumulo solemnia mittent:
Æternumque locus Palinuri nomen habebit.
His dictis curæ emotæ, pulsusque parumper
Corde dolor tristi: gaudet cognomine terrâ.
Ergò iter inceptum peragunt, fluvioque propinquant:
Navita quos jam inde ut Stygiâ prospexit ab undâ
Per tacitum nemus ire, pedemque advertere ripæ;
Sic prior aggreditur dictis, atque increpat ultro:
Quisquis es, armatus qui nostra ad flumina tendis,
Fare, age, quid venias: jam istinc et comprime gressum.
Umbrarum hic locus est, Somni, Noctisque soporæ:
Corpora viva nefas Stygiâ vectare carinâ.
Nec verò Alciden me sum lætatus euntem

373. Unde *est* hæc tam dira

375. *Alteram* ripam

377. Sed memor cape *mea* dicta, *tanquam* solatia *tui* duri casûs. Nam finitimi acti cœlestibus prodigiis piabunt tua ossa

382. Curæ emotæ *sunt*, dolorque parumper pulsus *est ejus*

385. Quos, ut navita jam inde ab Stygiâ undâ prospexit, ire per

391. Nefas *est* vectare

NOTES.

365. *Eripe me:* rescue me from these evils, invincible hero. While he remained unburied he could not pass over to the peaceful abodes of heroes; not until the expiration of a hundred years. This was the evil here complained of.

366. *Portus Velinos. Velinos*, an adj. from *Velia*, a city on the shore of *Lucania*, between the promontories of *Palinurus* and *Posidium*, founded by Servius Tullius, more than six hundred years after Æneas. The poet mentions this by way of anticipation.

367. *Creatrix:* in the sense of *mater.*

369. *Innare:* in the sense of *transire.*

371. *Quiescam:* that at least in death I may rest in peaceful seats. Palinurus' life had been full of labor and toil: and, therefore, there is a peculiar emphasis in his begging for rest in the regions of the dead.

376. *Fata:* decrees—purposes. *Flecti:* to be changed, or turned from the fixed order of things.

379. *Piabunt ossa.* We are told by Servius that the inhabitants of Lucania, as a punishment for the inhuman murder of Palinurus, were visited with a plague. They consulted an oracle upon the subject, and were directed to appease his *Manes.* They dedicated to him a grove, and built him a tomb to the south of *Velia*, upon the promontory, which from that time was called after his name.

380. *Mittent solemnia:* they shall make anniversary offerings upon the tomb. *Ferent inferias*, says Heyne. *Ferent munera*, says Ruæus.

383. *Gaudet cognomine terrâ:* he delights in the land called after his name. *Cognomine:* an adj. agreeing with *terrâ.* Vide *cognominis.*

385. *Navita:* Charon.

387. *Ultrò:* of his own accord—first—before being spoken to.

389. *Jam istinc:* and now stop your progress there—from this moment proceed not a step farther. *Quid:* in the sense of *cur.* Or, *ob quid venias.*

392. *Nec lætatus sum:* nor indeed was I pleased that I took over the lake Hercules, coming hither, &c. The poets tell us that when Hercules descended to hell, Charon was terrified at his appearance, and immediately took him into his boat, for which

Accepisse lacu; nec Thesea, Pirithoümque;
Dîs quanquam geniti, atque invicti viribus essent.
Tartareum ille manu custodem in vincla petivit,
Ipsius à solio regis traxitque trementem:
Hi dominam Ditis thalamo deducere adorti.
  Quæ contra breviter fata est Amphrysia vates
Nullæ hìc insidiæ tales; absiste moveri;

400. *Nostra* tela ferunt vim: *per nos* licet *vt*

Nec vim tela ferunt: licet ingens janitor antro
Æternùm latrans exsangues terreat umbras;
Casta licet patrui servet Proserpina limen.
Troïus Æneas, pietate insignis et armis,
Ad genitorem, imas Erebi descendit ad umbras.
Si te nulla movet tantæ pietatis imago,
At ramum hunc (aperit ramum, qui veste latebat)

407. Corda *Charonis* residunt ex tumidâ irâ. Nec plura his *dicta sunt.*

Agnoscas. Tumidâ ex irâ tum corda residunt.
Nec plura his. Ille admirans venerabile donum
Fatalis virgæ, longo pòst tempore visum,
Cœruleam advertit puppim, ripæque propinquat.
Inde alias animas, quæ per juga longa sedebant,
Deturbat, laxatque foros: simul accipit alveo
Ingentem Æneam. Gemuit sub pondere cymba
Sutilis, et multam accepit rimosa paludem.

415. Tandem *Charon* exponit vatemque virumque incolumes

Tandem trans fluvium incolumes vatemque virumque
Informi limo glaucâque exponit in ulva.
  Cerberus hæc ingens latratu regna trifauci
Personat, adverso recubans immanis in antro.
Cui vates, horrere videns jam colla colubris,
Melle soporatam et medicatis frugibus offam

NOTES.

Pluto bound him in chains for a whole year. To this he here alludes.

394. *Quanquam geniti:* although they were the sons of the gods, and invincible in strength. *Hercules* was the son of Jupiter; *Theseus*, of Neptune; and *Pirithoüs*, according to Homer, was the son of *Dia*, the wife of *Ixion*, by Jove.

395. *Tartareum custodem:* the Tartarean keeper—the dog Cerberus. His proper place was at the entrance of the infernal regions. *Ille:* Hercules. He drew Cerberus from the throne of his master, whither he had fled for shelter. Or, by the *throne* of Pluto we may understand his dominions in general. *Petivit:* seized—bound him in chains.

397. *Hi adorti:* Theseus and Pirithoüs. These attempted to carry off Proserpine from the bed of Pluto: both daring attempts.

398. *Amphrysia vates:* the prophetess of Apollo. *Amphrysia:* an adj. from *Amphrysus*, a river of Thessaly, where Apollo kept the flocks of Admetus, when banished by Jove from heaven for killing the Cyclops, who forged his thunderbolts. Here taken as a name of Apollo. *Contra quæ:* in answer to which—in reply to which.

402. *Patrui* gen. of *patruus*. Pluto was both uncle and husband of Proserpine. She was the daughter of Ceres and Jove, the brother of Pluto.

406. *Aperit:* in the sense of *ostendit*.

409. *Fatalis virgæ*. By this we are to understand the bough or branch, which was the pledge or evidence that the person who bore it was authorized and licensed by *fate* to be admitted into the infernal regions. This appears to have been presented to Charon for a similar purpose, at a former time: perhaps by Theseus or Pirithoüs.

412. *Deturbat alias animas:* he drives out other souls, that sat on the long benches (*juga*) and clears the deck. Or, *Laxat foros* may be rendered, *opens the hatches*. Valpy says, "empties the hold."

414. *Sutilis—rimosa:* patched—leaky *Paludem:* for *aquam*.

416. *Exponit:* lands.

417. *Cerberus*. He was represented as having three separate heads. Hence the epithet *trifauci*.

418. *Personat hæc regna:* the same as *sonat per hæc regna*.

420. *Objicit offam:* she throws a cake, soaked in honey and medicinal fruits. By *frugibus* we are to understand the seeds of

Objicit. Ille fame rabidâ tria guttura pandens,
Corripit objectam, atque immania terga resolvit
Fusus humi, totoque ingens extenditur antro.
Occupat Æneas aditum, custode sepulto,
Evaditque celer ripam irremeabilis undæ.
Continuò auditæ voces, vagitus et ingens,
Infantumque animæ flentes in limine primo:
Quos dulcis vitæ exsortes, et ab ubere raptos
Abstulit atra dies, et funere mersit acerbo.
Hos juxta, falso damnati crimine mortis.
Nec verò hæ sinè sorte datæ, sinè judice, sedes.
Quæsitor Minos urnam movet: ille silentûm
Conciliumque vocat, vitasque et crimina discit.
Proxima deinde tenent mœsti loca, qui sibi letum
Insontes peperêre manu, lucemque perosi
Projecêre animas. Quàm vellent æthere in alto
Nunc et pauperiem et duros perferre labores!
Fata obstant, tristique palus inamabilis undâ
Alligat, et novies Styx interfusa coërcet.

422. Corripit *eam* objectam, atque *fusus* humi

428. Quos exsortes dulcis vitæ, et raptos ab ubere atra dies abstulit

430. *Sunt illi* damnati mortis *sub*

432. Silentûm *umbrarum.*

434. Deinde mœsti, qui insontes peperêre letum sibi *sua* manu, perosique lucem projecêre animas, tenent proxima loca

NOTES.

the poppy, and other soporiferous ingredients.

422. *Resolvit:* relaxes. *Terga:* in the sense of *artus*, vel *corpus.*

424. *Sepulto:* buried in sleep. *Somno* being understood.

425. *Evadit:* he ascends—or mounts the bank of the impassable stream. *Unde non reditur*, says Ruæus.

427. *Infantumque animæ.* The wailings of those infant ghosts or shades, considered only in a poetical light, are very properly disposed of in the entrance of Pluto's kingdom, as they cast a melancholy gloom over the scene, and excite such tender passions in the mind of the reader, as prepare him for relishing the beauties of so grave and solemn a representation. But then their lamentation and weeping we are not to consider as the effect of punishment, so much as an expression of their grief and sorrow at being taken away by an untimely death.

428. *Exsortes dulcis vitæ:* deprived of sweet life, and snatched from the breast, &c. Ruæus says, *privatos.*

429. *Funere:* in the sense of *morte.* Davidson says, "an untimely grave."

430. *Damnati mortis.* That they should be punished who suffer death under a *false charge or accusation*, may at first view appear unjust. Though they were innocent of the crime for which they were condemned, it does not follow that they were wholly free from fault, and innocent in their lives. And according to the doctrine of the Platonic philosophy, none could have access to the Elysian fields till their stains and pollutions were purged away. It became necessary, therefore, that they should under go a degree of punishment, proportioned to their actual sins.

431. *Sorte.* Servius takes *sorte* to imply sentence, appointment, or destination. *Judice.* The judges of hell, according to the poets, were three: *Minos*, *Rhadamanthus*, and *Æacus.* Minos was a king of Crete, celebrated for the equity of his administration, and the justice of his laws; hence feigned to be the first judge of hell. *Rhadamanthus* was his brother and prime minister; both were sons of *Jove* and *Europa.* *Æacus* was the son of Jove and Ægina, the father of *Peleus*, king of Thessaly, and grandfather of Achilles.

The several apartments of the infernal regions were appointed or assigned to the several shades, according to the decision of the judges appointed to sit in judgment upon their lives and actions.

432. *Movet urnam:* he shakes the urn which contains each one's sentence. In other words, he determines every one's doom, and assigns their proper stations. This is an allusion to the custom among the Greeks, who used two urns, into the one or other of which the judges cast their *calculi sortes*, or suffrages, according as they were inclined to condemn or absolve. *Silentûm:* of the shades.

434. *Mœsti:* the sad—melancholy.

435. *Insontes:* innocent, in other respects.

436. *Quàm vellent:* how willing they now are to bear, &c. *Alto æthere:* in the upper world—in the regions of light.

438. *Fata.* This is the common reading. Heyne reads *Fas*, and informs us that Heinsius, Servius, and Donatus, do the same. *Inamabilis:* hateful—odious.

439. *Styx:* it was said to flow nine times

Nec procul hinc, partem fusi monstrantur in omnem
Lugentes campi: sic illos nomine dicunt.
Hìc, quos durus amor crudeli tabe peredit,
Secreti celant calles, et myrtea circùm
Sylva tegit: curæ non ipsâ in morte relinquunt.
His Phædram Procrinque locis, mœstamque Eriphylen
Crudelis nati monstrantem vulnera cernit,
Evadnenque, et Pasiphaën. His Laodamia
It comes; et, juvenis quondam, nunc fœmina, Cæneus,
Rursùs et in veterem fato revoluta figuram.
Inter quas Phœnissa recens à vulnere Dido
Errabat sylvâ in magnâ: quam Troïus heros
Ut primùm juxta stetit, agnovitque per umbram
Obscuram; qualem primo qui surgere mense
Aut videt, aut vidisse putat, per nubila lunam;
Demisit lachrymas, dulcique affatus amore est:
Infelix Dido! verus mihi nuntius ergò
Venerat, extinctam, ferroque extrema secutam?
Funeris heu tibi causa fui! per sidera juro,
Per Superos, et, si qua fides tellure sub imâ est,
Invitus, regina, tuo de litore cessi.
Sed me jussa Deûm, quæ nunc has ire per umbras,
Per loca senta situ cogunt, noctemque profundam,

442. Hìc secreti calles celant, et myrtea sylva circùm-tegit *eos*, quos durus

446. *Æneas* cernit Phædram

451. Juxta quam, ut primùm Troïus heros stetit,

453. *Talem* qualem, qui aut videt

456. Ergò verus nuntius venerat mihi *te esse* extinctam, secutamque extrema ferro?

459. *Et per fidem*, si qua fides

NOTES.

around the realms of Pluto. *Fusi:* spread—extending in every direction.

445. *Phædram.* She was the daughter of Minos, and wife of Theseus. She fell in love with her step-son Hippolytus, who refused to comply with her request. Whereupon, she accused him to her husband of offering violence to her. Upon this he slew him with his own hand. As soon as she heard of this, she was so stung with remorse that she finally hung herself *Procrin. Procris* was the daughter of Erechtheus, king of Athens, and wife of *Cephalus.* She lost her life through jealousy of her husband. She watched him one day in the woods, where he was wont to go a hunting, and overheard him, in the heat of the day, invoking the cool breeze, and repeating to himself, *aura veni.* She imagined he was calling his mistress; and, coming from the place of her concealment to make the discovery, she made the bushes move; which Cephalus observing, and taking her for some beast of prey, slew her with a javelin. *Eriphylen.* She was the wife of *Amphiaraus*, the prophet of *Argos.* Foreseeing that he should die if he went to the Theban war against *Eteocles*, he sought to conceal himself; but was discovered by his wife, who was bribed by Polynices, the brother of Eteocles, with a golden necklace. He was forced to the war, and perished by an earthquake as he was fighting valiantly. His son *Alcmæon* revenged his death by killing *Eriphyle*, his mother.

447. *Evadnen.* She was the daughter of Mars, and wife of *Capaneus.* Her husband being slain in battle; while she was performing his funeral rites, she threw herself on the pile, and was consumed with him. *Laodamia.* She was the daughter of Acastus, and wife of *Protesilaus*, who was the first of the Greeks slain in the Trojan war. When she heard the news of her husband's death, nothing would satisfy her, but the sight of his ghost, which the gods granted to her: she breathed out her soul in the fond embraces of the phantom. *Pasiphaën.* See 24. supra. *Extrema:* in the sense of *mortem. Secutam: esse* is understood. To have brought death upon yourself, &c.

448. *Cæneus. Cænis*, the daughter of Elatheus, one of the *Lapithæ.* By subjecting herself to the embrace of Neptune, she obtained from him the change of her sex; and that she should never be wounded by an arrow. After the change had been effected, Cæneus distinguished himself in the wars against the Centaurs, and became so much elated with pride, that he despised the gods themselves. Whereupon, they determined he should return to his former sex, that is, become a woman again. Hence, *revoluta fato:* changed by fate.

453. *Primo mense:* in the first of her monthly course—soon after her change, when her light is feeble.

462. *Senta:* in the sense of *sparsa* vel *plena.* A metaphor taken from lands in a

Imperiis egêre suis: nec credere quivi,
Hunc tantum tibi me discessu ferre dolorem.
Siste gradum, teque aspectu ne subtrahe nostro.
Quem fugis? extremum fato quod te alloquor hoc est.
Talibus Æneas ardentem et torva tuentem
Lenibat dictis animum, lachrymasque ciebat.
Illa solo fixos oculos aversa tenebat:
Nec magìs incepto vultum sermone movetur,
Quàm si dura silex, aut stet Marpesia cautes.
Tandem corripuit sese, atque inimica refugit
In nemus umbriferum; conjux ubi pristinus illi
Respondet curis, æquatque Sichæus amorem.
Nec minùs Æneas casu percussus iniquo,
Prosequitur lachrymans longè, et miseratur euntem.
  Inde datum molitur iter. Jamque arva tenebant
Ultima, quæ bello clari secreta frequentant.
Hìc illi occurrit Tydeus, hìc inclytus armis
Parthenopæus, et Adrasti pallentis imago.
Hìc multùm fleti ad superos, belloque caduci
Dardanidæ: quos ille omnes longo ordine cernens,
Ingemuit: Glaucumque, Medontaque, Thersilochumque,
Tres Antenoridas: Cererique sacrum Polybœten,
Idæumque, etiam currus, etiam arma tenentem.
Circumstant animæ dextrâ lævâque frequentes.
Nec vidisse semel satìs est: juvat usque morari,

466. Hoc est extremum *tempus permissum* fato, quod alloquor te. Talibus dictis Æneas lenibat *ejus* animum ardentem, et tuentem torva

478. Quæ secreta viri clari bello frequentant.

487. Nec satìs est *iis* vidisse *eum* semel:

NOTES.

state of neglect—covered with weeds and filthiness.

463. *Quivi:* in the sense of *potui.*

466. *Quod.* If he could read *quo*, in the abl. the passage would be easier. Ruæus takes it in that sense: *quo tecum loquor*, says he.

467. *Talibus dictis Æneas:* in such words Æneas was soothing her soul, &c. *Torva:* an adj. of the neu. plu. of *torvus*, taken as an adverb in imitation of the Greeks, the same as *torvè.*

469. *Aversa:* turned from him. Ruæus says, *infensa;* but that idea is expressed by *inimica*, infra.

470. *Movetur vultum:* moved with regard to her countenance: a Grecism. This interview of Æneas and Dido, is in imitation of the Odyssey, where the poet brings Ulysses and Ajax together in the infernal regions. The conduct of Dido is copied from that of Ajax. Longinus observes that the silence of Ajax is more sublime than any words could have been.

471. *Marpesia:* an adj. from *Marpesus*, a mountain on the island of *Paros*, one of the Cyclades, famous for its white marble.

472. *Inimica:* hating—detesting him.

475. *Iniquo casu:* in the sense of *acerba morte. Nec minùs:* nevertheless.

477. *Molitur:* in the sense of *prosequitur.*

479. *Tydeus.* Tydeus was one of those generals who commanded at the Theban war, about thirty years before the siege of Troy. He was the father of the famous Diomede, and was slain by *Menalippus* the Theban, at the siege of Thebes. *Parthenopæus* was the son of Meleager and Atalanta. He went to the Theban war when very young. It is said he afterward died at the siege of Troy. *Adrasti.* Adrastus was father-in-law both to Tydeus and Polynices. Having lost a numerous army before *Thebes*, he was forced to raise the siege of that city, and retreat precipitately to his own country. His ghost, or shade, is called *pale*, because paleness is a companion of flight and fear.

481. *Superos:* those above—the upper world—the living. *Multùm:* in the sense of *valdè.*

483. *Glaucum.* Glaucus was the son of Hippolochus, and grandson of the famous Bellerophon. He, with Sarpedon, commanded the Lycian troops in the Trojan war. *Thersilochus.* He was of Macedonia, in the confines of Thrace. He was slain by Achilles. *Tres Antenoridas:* the three sons of Antenor. Homer calls them, *Polybus*, *Agenor*, and *Acamus. Idæum.* He was the charioteer of Priam.

484. *Sacrum:* in the sense of *sacerdotem.* Homer makes no mention of *Polybœtes* among the Trojans. He mentions him among the Greeks, under the name of *Polypœtes*, the son of *Pirithoüs*

Et conferre gradum, et veniendi discere causas.
At Danaûm proceres, Agamemnoniæque phalanges,
Ut vidêre virum, fulgentiaque arma per umbras,
Ingenti trepidare metu: pars vertere terga,
Ceu quondam petiêre rates: pars tollere vocem
Exiguam: inceptus clamor frustratur hiantes.
Atque hìc Priamiden laniatum corpore toto
Deïphobum vidit, lacerum crudeliter ora;
Ora, manusque ambas, populataque tempora raptis
Auribus, et truncas inhonesto vulnere nares.
Vix adeò agnovit pavitantem, et dira tegentem
Supplicia: et notis compellat vocibus ultrò:
Deïphobe armipotens, genus alto à sanguine Teucri,
Quis tam crudeles optavit sumere pœnas?
Cui tantum de te licuit? Mihi fama supremâ
Nocte tulit, fessum vastâ te cæde Pelasgûm
Procubuisse super confusæ stragis acervum.
Tunc egomet tumulum Rhœteo in litore inanem
Constitui, et magnâ Manes ter voce vocavi.
Nomen et arma locum servant. Te, amice, nequivi
Conspicere, et patriâ decedens ponere terrâ.
Ad quæ Priamides: Nihil ô tibi, amice, relictum est.
Omnia Deïphobo solvisti, et funeris umbris:
Sed me fata mea et scelus exitiale Lacænæ
His mersere malis: illa hæc monumenta reliquit.
Namque, ut supremam falsa inter guadia noctem
Egerimus, nôsti; et nimiùm meminisse necesse est:

491. *Cœperunt* trepidare ingenti metu: pars *cœpit* vertere.

495. Lacerum crudeliter *quoad* ora, ora, ambasque manus, temporaque populata

501. Quis optavit sumere *de te* tam crudeles pœnas? Cui licuit *sumere* tantum *supplicii* de te?

508. Et decedens ponere *te sepultum* patriâ terrâ

509. Priamides *ait:* Nihil, ô amice, relictum *est*

511. Hæc *vulnera tanquam* monumenta *ejus amoris*

513. Namque nôsti, ut egerimus

NOTES.

488. *Conferre gradum:* to meet him—to come in close conference with him: a phrase. *Usque:* in the sense of *diu.*

489. *Phalanges:* in the sense of *turmæ.*

492. *Ceu quondam,* &c. The account of the fight to which the poet here alludes, is given, Iliad 15. The Trojans under Hector drove the Greeks, forced their entrenchments, pursued them to their ships, and set them on fire.

493. *Clamor inceptus:* the cry begun, frustrates them, gaping and opening their throats. They were so terrified at the sight of Æneas, as to be unable to finish the scream which they had begun. It perished in their throats. Ruæus takes *frustratur* in the sense of *fallit.*

495. *Deïphobum.* Deïphobus was the son of Priam, and married Helen after the death of Paris. What is here said of his being cruelly mangled, is agreeable to the account given by *Dictys Cretensis.* He was slain by Menelaus. This representation of *Deïphobus'* mangled shade or ghost, is according to the philosophy of Plato, who taught that the dead retain the same marks and blemishes in their bodies, which they had when alive.

496 *Populata:* in the sense of *privata* vel *spoliata.* *Raptis:* in the sense of *sectis.* When the concluding word of a preceding line is repeated in the beginning of the following line, the figure is called anadiplosis. It is usually emphatical, as in the present instance. *Truncas:* cut—gashed.

499. *Supplicia:* in the sense of *vulnera* vel *plagas.* *Notis:* familiar. Or it may have reference to their speaking the same language. This is the sense in which Ruæus takes it: *cognita voce,* says he.

500. *Genus:* offspring. It is placed in apposition with *Deïphobe.*

504. *Confusæ stragis:* of mingled carcases.

507. *Nomen et arma:* by *commutatio,* for *locus servat nomen et arma:* the place preserves your name and arms.

509. *Ad quæ.* Ruæus, and some others read *atque hìc.* Heyne and Valpy read, *ad quæ.* Heinsius and Burmannus read, *ad quæ hæc.*

510. *Funeris:* the corpse, or dead body itself.

511. *Lacænæ:* of Helen—of the *Lacedæmonian.*

512. *Illa reliquit:* she hath left those scars and wounds, which you see, as monuments of her love.

Cùm fatalis equus saltu super ardua venit
Pergama, et armatum peditem gravis attulit alvo.
Illa chorum simulans, evantes orgia circùm
Ducebat Phrygias: flammam media ipsa tenebat
Ingentem, et summâ Danaos ex arce vocabat.
Tum me confectum curis, somnoque gravatum
Infelix habuit thalamus, pressitque jacentem
Dulcis et alta quies, placidæque simillima morti.
Egregia intereà conjux arma omnia tectis
Emovet, et fidum capiti subduxerat ensem.
Intra tecta vocat Menelaum, et limina pandit.
Scilicet id magnum sperans fore munus amanti,
Et famam exstingui veterum sic posse malorum.
Quid moror? irrumpunt thalamo; comes additur unà
Hortator scelerum Æolides. Dî, talia Graiis
Instaurate; pio si pœnas ore reposco.
Sed te qui vivum casus, age, fare vicissim,
Attulerint: pelagine venis erroribus actus?
An monitu Divûm? an quæ te fortuna fatigat,
Ut tristes sinè sole domos, loca turbida, adires?
Hâc vice sermonum roseis Aurora quadrigis

518. Ducebat Phrygias *fœminas*, evantes circùm orgia

526. Sperans id fore magnum munus amanti, et famam

532. Venis-ne *huc* actus erroribus

NOTES.

515. *Cùm fatalis*, &c. See Æn. ii. 234. *et sequens.*

517. *Evantes:* shouting in praise of Bacchus. The word is of Greek derivation; and is applied to the bacchanals, or devotees of the god Bacchus. *Evantes orgia: ex more orgiorum*, says Heyne.

519. *Vocabat.* Helen made signals from the walls to the Greeks, that all things were ready for the assault. Her leading the Phrygian women around the city, as if in honor of Bacchus, the giver of joy, on account of the departure of their enemies, was mere pretence—mere deception to cover her plans.

521. *Infelix:* unhappy; because he was slain in it, and thereby prevented from joining his comrades in arms, and avenging their falling country. *Pressit.* His sleep was so sound, that it seemed to press him down like a great weight, lying upon him.

523. *Egregia conjux:* precious wife. This is spoken ironically. The meaning is, *odious*—abominable.

524. *Subduxerat:* and had withdrawn my faithful sword from my head. It was a custom among the warriors to lay their swords under their heads when they slept.

525. *Vocat Menelaum:* she called Menelaus into the house, &c. After the death of Paris, Helen married Deïphobus, his brother. It is said she endeavored to be reconciled to her first husband, by aiding the Grecian arms. Here she calls to him, and opens the door. That Deiphobus might fall an easy prey, she had previously removed all the arms from the house, and his sword from under his head. What befell Helen after the capture of Troy is not certain. Some say she returned to Sparta, and passed her days with Menelaus; and was buried with him in the same tomb. Others say, after his death, being banished from Sparta, she fled to Rhodes, where she died. Homer informs us, Odys. iv. 277, that Helen went three times round the wooden horse, calling each of the Greeks by name. To this the poet alludes, 517. supra.

526. *Amanti:* to her husband—viz. Menelaus. *Munus:* favor—gift.

527. *Et famam:* and that the infamy of her former crimes might in this way be blotted out. *Famam:* in the sense of *infamiam.*

529. *Æolides.* This is a reproachful name given to *Ulysses.* It insinuates that he was not the son of *Laërtes*, but of Sisyphus, the son of Æolus, with whom his mother Anticlea is said to have been familiar.

530. *Instaurate:* in the sense of *reddite.*

532. *Erroribus:* dangers. Davidson renders it *casualties.*

533. *Quæ fortuna:* what (adverse) fortune forces or impels you, that, &c.

534. *Turbida:* in the sense of *obscura*, vel *tenebrosa.*

535. *Hâc vice sermonum:* during the course (or change) of conversation, the sun in his rosy chariot had now passed, &c. By *Aurora*, here, we are undoubtedly to understand the sun. *Quadrigis:* properly, a chariot drawn by four horses. Ruæus thinks the middle of the day is here meant by *medium axem;* and not the middle of the

537. Per talia *colloquia*

541. Dextera *est via*, quæ tendit

542. Hàc *via* est iter *nobis* ad Elysium: àt læva *pars* exercet

552. *Est* porta adversa

553. Ut nulla vis virûm *valet*, non

557. Gemitus *cœperunt* exaudiri hinc

558. Tum stridor ferri, tractæque catenæ *cœperunt exudiri*

560. O virgo, *inquit*, effare, quæ facies scelerum *sunt illic*

Jam medium æthereo cursu trajecerat axem,
Et fors omne datum traherent per talia tempus;
Sed comes admonuit, breviterque affata Sibylla est:
Nox ruit, Ænea: nos flendo ducimus horas.
Hìc locus est, partes ubi se via findit in ambas.
Dextera, quæ Ditis magni sub mœnia tendit·
Hâc iter Elysium nobis: at læva malorum
Exercet pœnas, et ad impia Tartara mittit.
Deïphobus contrà: Ne sævi, magna sacerdos.
Discedam; explebo numerum, reddarque tenebris.
I decus, i, nostrum: melioribus utere fatis.
Tantum effatus, et in verbo vestigia torsit.
  Respicit Æneas subitò; et sub rupe sinistrâ
Mœnia lata videt, triplici circumdata muro:
Quæ rapidus flammis ambit torrentibus amnis
Tartareus Phlegethon, torquetque sonantia saxa.
Porta adversa, ingens, solidoque adamante columnæ.
Vis ut nulla virûm, non ipsi exscindere ferro
Cœlicolæ valeant. Stat ferrea turris ad auras:
Tisiphoneque sedens, pallâ succincta cruentâ,
Vestibulum insomnis servat noctesque diesque.
Hinc exaudiri gemitus, et sæva sonare
Verbera: tum stridor ferri, tractæque catenæ.
Constitit Æneas, strepitumque exterritus hausit:
Quæ scelerum facies, ô virgo, effare, quibusve
Urgentur pœnis? quis tantus plangor ad auras?

NOTES.

night, as Servius, and most interpreters suppose. The time appointed for performing the preliminary rites, and visiting the infernal regions, here called *tempus datum*, was a day and two nights, as we learn from Plutarch's treatise concerning the genius of Socrates. Now Æneas had passed the whole of the first night in offering the prescribed sacrifices, verse 255. He commenced his descent the next morning about sunrise. *Medium axem* must therefore mean the meridian, which the sun had passed, and was hastening to the western horizon. The intervening time Æneas may be supposed to have passed in going through so many apartments. The remaining part of the day and following night, he visits his father, and the Elysian fields; and returns the following morning to his companions.

537. *Fors:* in the sense of *fortasse.*

542. *Læva exercet*, &c. The meaning of this passage is, that they had now arrived at the place where the way separated into two: the right led to the city of Pluto, and the left ed to the place where the impious are punished. *Tendit:* in the sense of *ducit. Mittit*, also, in the sense of *ducit.*

545. *Discedam; explebo numerum*, &c. The meaning of this line has not been settled by commentators. There are three opinions which seem to prevail. 1. *Discedam et implebo numerum turbæ, ex qua discessi ut te alloquerer:* I will depart, and fill up the number of the multitude which I left, that I might converse with you. This is the opinion of Heyne and Davidson. According to Plato's notion of transmigration, the souls of the deceased passed a certain number of years in purification, before they assumed other bodies; therefore, 2d. *Discedam, impleturus numerum annorum purgationis, quæ fit in his tenebris:* I will depart to fill up the number of the years of purification, which is done in this darkness. 3. *Discedam; modo, sine ut expleam numerum, et periodum orationis meæ, quam incepi:* I will depart; only let me fill up the number and period of the discourse which I have begun. Only let me finish what I have begun to say. This last Ruæus prefers.

546. *I decus, i, nostrum:* pass on, pass on thou glory of our nation: experience fates more propitious. The repetition of the *I* is emphatical.

549. *Mœnia:* in the sense of *urbem.*

551. *Phlegethon:* the name of one of the five rivers of hell: from a Greek word signifying, *to burn*, or to be on fire.

558. *Verbera:* scourges—lashes. *Stridor ferri:* a grating, or din of iron.

559. *Hausit strepitum:* he heard the tumult—confused noise.

560. *Facies:* forms—kinds.

561. *Urgentur:* in the sense of *cruciantur.*

Tum vates sic orsa loqui: Dux inclyte Teucrûm,
Nulli fas casto sceleratum insistere limen:
Sed, me cùm lucis Hecate præfecit Avernis,
Ipsa Deûm pœnas docuit, perque omnia duxit.
Gnossius hæc Rhadamanthus habet durissima regna,
Castigatque, auditque dolos: subigitque fateri,
Quæ quis apud superos, furto lætatus inani,
Distulit in seram commissa piacula mortem.
Continuò sontes ultrix accincta flagello
Tisiphone quatit insultans; torvosque sinistrâ
Intentans angues, vocat agmina sæva sororum.
Tum demum horrisono stridentes cardine sacræ
Panduntur portæ. Cernis, custodia qualis
Vestibulo sedeat? facies quæ limina servet?
Quinquaginta atris immanis hiatibus hydra
Sævior intus habet sedem. Tum Tartarus ipse
Bis patet in præceps tantùm, tenditque sub umbras,
Quantus ad æthereum cœli suspectus Olympum.
Hìc genus antiquum Terræ, Titania pubes,
Fulmine dejecti, fundo volvuntur in imo.
Hìc et Aloïdas geminos, immania vidi
Corpora; qui manibus magnum rescindere cœlum
Aggressi, superisque Jovem detrudere regnis.
Vidi et crudeles dantem Salmonea pœnas,
Dum flammas Jovis et sonitus imitatur Olympi.
Quatuor hic invectus equis, et lampada quassans,

563. Fas *est* nulli casto insistere

567. Subigitque *eos* fateri quæ piacula commissa apud superos, quis distulit

571. Tisiphone ultrix, accinta flagello, quatit sontes insultans; sinistraque *manû*

574. *Sibylla inquit:* cernis-*ne* qualis

577. Sævior Hydra, immanis quinquaginta atris hiatibus

579. Quantus *est*

NOTES.

tur. Plangor: shrieking—outcry. The verb *surgit*, is understood.

568. *Apud superos:* with the living—in the upper world. *Furto:* privacy—concealment. *Inani:* vain or unprofitable, because however great the privacy might have been, in which crimes were committed: they were, nevertheless, all known to the gods. Ruæus says, *vana simulatiòne.*

569. *Piacula:* in the sense of *crimina*, vel *scelera.*

571. *Quatit:* strikes. *Verberat*, says Ruæus.

572. *Sæva agmina sororum.* The furies were reckoned three in number. Their names are *Tisiphone*, *Alecto*, and *Megara.* They may be called *agmina*, bands or troops, on account of their complicated rage; or these may be only the principal ones, and might have others under their command. *Intentans:* shaking or brandishing.

573. *Sacræ:* in the sense of *sceleratæ.*

576. *Hiatibus:* mouths.

579. *Suspectus:* height—distance. *Æthereum Olympum:* the ethereal vault of heaven—the highest pinnacle—the seat of the gods.

580. *Titania pubes:* the giants, the sons of *Titan* and *Terra.* They attempted to scale heaven, and dethrone Jupiter; but he crushed them with his thunder. Their object, in the attempt, was to restore their father to his throne, from which he had been driven by Jupiter. *Volvuntur:* in the sense of *premuntur.*

582. *Aloïdas.* These were the giants *Otus* and *Ephialtes*, the sons of Neptune by Iphimedia, the wife of *Aloëus.* Homer makes them nine cubits broad, and nine ells high, in the ninth year of their age. Odyss. xi. 304.

585. *Salmonea:* a Greek acc. of Salmoneus. He was the son of *Æolus*, a king of Elis. He made a bridge of brass, over which he drove his chariot, boasting that by the rattling of his wheels, and the prancing of his horses, he imitated the thunder of Jove; who was highly honored at Elis. At the same time, to counterfeit his lightning, he hurled flaming torches at his subjects, and ordered every one to be put to death, at whom he threw his torch. He was struck by the thunderbolt of Jove, for his impiety and cruelty. *Pœnas. Pœna* properly signifies a recompense or satisfaction. Hence the phrase *dare pœnam* vel *pœnas*, to be punished—that is, to make retribution or satisfaction.

586. *Flammas:* lightning. *Sonitus:* thunder.

Per Graiûm populos, mediæque per Elidis urbem
Ibat ovans, Divûmque sibi poscebat honorem:
Demens! qui nimbos, et non imitabile fulmen
Ære et cornipedum cursu simularet equorum.

592 Ille *Jupiter* non *contorsit* faces, nec lumina fumea *è* tædis, *ut Salmoneus fecit*

At pater omnipotens densa inter nubila telum
Contorsit (non ille faces, nec fumea tædis
Lumina) præcipitemque immani turbine adegit.
Nec non et Tityon, Terræ omniparentis alumnum,

596. *Licitum* erat cernere Tityon

Cernere erat: per tota novem cui jugera corpus
Porrigitur; rostroque immanis vultur obunco
Immortale jecur tundens, fœcundaque pœnis
Viscera, rimaturque epulis, habitatque sub alto
Pectore: nec fibris requies datur ulla renatis.
Quid memorem Lapithas, Ixiona, Pirithoümque?
Quos super atra silex jamjam lapsura, cadentique
Imminet assimilis. Lucent genialibus altis

604. Epulæ paratæ *sunt* ante *eorum* ora, *cum*

Aurea fulcra toris, epulæque ante ora paratæ
Regifico luxu: Furiarum maxima juxtà
Accubat, et manibus prohibet contingere mensas;
Exsurgitque facem attollens, atque intonat ore.

608. Hìc *sunt illi*, quibus fratres *erant* invisi

Hìc, quibus invisi fratres, dum vita manebat,
Pulsatusve parens, et fraus innexa clienti;
Aut qui divitiis soli incubuêre repertis,
Nec partem posuere suis; quæ maxima turba est
Quique ob adulterium cæsi; quique arma secuti

NOTES.

588. *Urbem mediæ Elidis.* For *mediam urbem Elidis:* through the middle of the city of Elis. Heyne observes that some copies read *mediam*, which is the easier.

590. *Nimbos:* storms—tempests.

591. *Simularet.* This is the reading of Heyne. Most copies have *simulârat*, the plu. perf. of the ind.

592 *Telum:* thunderbolt.

595. *Tityon.* Tityus was the son of Jupiter and Elara, the daughter of Orchomenus. When Jupiter found her with child, he shut her up in the earth for fear of Juno; where *Tityus* issuing forth in a gigantic form, was thought to be the son of the earth. Virgil, therefore, calls him *alumnus*, &c: *the foster-child of all-bearing earth.* He was slain by Apollo for offering violence to Latona. He was punished by a huge vulture, that continually preyed upon his liver and vitals; which, as they were devoured, always grew afresh. Hence *immortale jecur:* his immortal liver; because it never was consumed. *Rimatur epulis:* rummages them for his meal. *Renatis:* springing up anew.

596. *Cui:* in the sense of *cujus.*

598. *Tundens:* beating—tearing. This is the common reading. But Heyne reads *condens. Fœcunda pœnis:* fertile in punishment. This is said, because as soon as any part was torn away, and consumed by the vulture, its place was immediately supplied. His punishment would therefore be perpetual.

601. *Lapithas:* the *Lapithæ* were a people of Thessaly of dissolute manners. *Ixiona.* Ixion, the son of Phlegyas, was their king. He was admitted to an intimacy with Jupiter, which he forfeited by designing an intimacy with Juno. Jupiter knowing his purpose, substituted a cloud for the goddess; and was content at first only to remove him from heaven; but finding that he boasted of having been honored with Juno's bed, he hurled him down to Tartarus, and ordered Mercury to bind him to a wheel, hung round with serpents, which he was doomed to turn without any intermission. *Pirithoüm.* He was the son of Ixion. See 122, supra.

609. *Pulsus-ve parens:* the crime of parricide is so horrid and unnatural, that he passes it by, not supposing any of the human race could be guilty of it. He puts the case only of one who had *beaten a parent. Fraus innexa clienti:* fraud practised upon a client. The claim of the client to the faith and protection of his patron was considered sacred among the Romans; like that of a child to the protection of the parent. Among the laws of the twelve tables it is said: "if any patron shall defraud his client, let him be accursed."

611. *Nec partem:* nor have distributed a part to their own. *Arma:* in the sense of *bella*

Impia; nec veriti dominorum fallere dextras;
Inclusi pœnam expectant. Ne quære doceri
Quam pœnam, aut quæ forma viros fortunave mersit.
Saxum ingens volvunt alii, radiisque rotarum
Districti pendent. Sedet, æternùmque sedebit
Infelix Theseus: Phlegyasque miserrimus omnes
Admonet, et magnâ testatur voce per umbras
Discite justitiam moniti, et non temnere Divos.
Vendidit hic auro patriam, dominumque potentem
Imposuit: fixit leges pretio atque refixit.
Hic thalamum invasit natæ, vetitosque hymenæos.
Ausi omnes immane nefas, ausoque potiti.
Non, mihi si linguæ centum sint, oraque centum,
Ferrea vox, omnes scelerum comprêndere formas,
Omnia pœnarum percurrere nomina possim.
Hæc ubi dicta dedit Phœbi longæva sacerdos:
Sed jam age, carpe viam, et susceptum perfice munus:
Acceleremus, ait. Cyclopum educta caminis
Mœnia conspicio, atque adverso fornice portas,
Hæc ubi nos præcepta jubent deponere dona.

614. *Hi omnes inclusi hic* expectant

615. Quam pœnam *pendent*, aut quæ forma

624. Hi omnes *ausi sunt* immane nefas, et potiti *sunt* auso

626. Non possim comprêndere omnes formas

632. Ubi *Dî* jubent r . s

NOTES.

613. *Fallere dextras dominorum:* to violate the faith of their masters—pledged to their masters. *Dextra:* in the sense of *fides.*

615. *Forma—fortuna.* By *forma*, Servius understands the *form* or rule of justice: and by *fortuna*, Dr. Trapp understands the *sentence* of the judge. What punishment they undergo, or in what form or state of misery they are overwhelmed or involved. This is plainly the meaning of the passage.—Heyne says, *Quæ forma pœnæ, quod-ve miseriæ genus mersit, vel manet viros.*

616. *Ingens saxum.* This refers to the case of *Sisyphus*, the son of Æolus, a notorious robber. He was sentenced to hell, and compelled to roll a great stone to the top of a hill; which, before he reached the top, returned to the bottom again. Thus his labor became perpetual. *Districti radiis:* bound to the spokes of wheels, they hang. This alludes to the case of *Ixion.* See 601, supra.

617. *Æternùm sedebit.* This may be explained by referring it to the shade or ghost of Theseus after death: for he was set at liberty by Hercules, after he had been bound by Pluto, and returned to the intercourse of men. See 122, supra.

618. *Phlegyas.* He was the father of *Ixion*, and king of the *Lapithæ.* His daughter *Coronis*, being ravished by Apollo, in revenge for the injury, he burnt his temple; for which he was thrust down to Tartarus. He is represented as calling aloud to the shades, and admonishing all to take warning by him, not to despise the gods, nor commit acts of impiety.

620. *Moniti discite justitiam:* ye being admonished by my example, learn justice. This is the great moral of all those infernal punishments, that the example of them might deter from vice, and stimulate to virtue. *Moniti meo exemplo*, says Heyne.

622. *Fixit leges:* he made and unmade laws for a price. This is said in reference to the Roman custom of engraving their laws upon tables of brass, and *fixing* them up in public places, to the view of the people; and when those laws were abrogated or repealed, they were said to be *refigi*, to be unfixed, or taken down. *Hymenæos:* in the sense of *nuptias.*

624. *Potiti auso:* accomplished their bold undertaking. Dr. Trapp thinks *auso* may be used for *præmio usi*, they now have their reward, by way of sarcasm. But the sense commonly given is easier, and contains this moral, that however successful men are in wickedness, they are not the less odious to God, and will hereafter receive their due reward.

629. *Perfice susceptum munus:* finish the undertaken offering. This refers to the golden bough, which Æneas promised to deposit in the palace of Proserpine.

630. *Cyclopum.* The Cyclops were the first inhabitants of Sicily. To them is attributed the invention of forging iron, and of fortifying cities. The expression here denotes that these walls were made of iron, and strongly fortified. *Educta:* drawn out, or wrought in the forges of the Cyclops. See Geor. i. 471.

631. *Portas fornice adverso:* the gates, with their arch directly opposite to us, or in front of us.

632. *Hæc præcepta dona:* these command-

Dixerat: et pariter gressi per opaca viarum,
Corripiunt spatium medium, foribusque propinquant
Occupat Æneas aditum, corpusque recenti
Spargit aquâ, ramumque adverso in limine figit.
His demum exactis, perfecto munere Divæ,
Devenêre locos lætos, et amœna vireta
Fortunatorum nemorum, sedesque beatas.
Largior hìc campos æther, et lumine vestit
Purpureo: solemque suum, sua sidera nôrunt. — 641 *Incolæ* nôrunt
Pars in gramineis exercent membra palæstris,
Contendunt ludo, et fulvâ luctantur arenâ:
Pars pedibus plaudunt choreas, et carmina dicunt.
Necnon Threïcius longâ cum veste sacerdos
Obloquitur numeris septem discrimina vocum:
Jamque eadem digitis, jam pectine pulsat eburno.
Hìc genus antiquum Teucri, pulcherrima proles, — 648. Hîc *est* antiquum genus
Magnanimi heroës, nati melioribus annis:
Ilusque, Assaracusque, et Trojæ Dardanus auctor
Arma procul, currusque virûm miratur inanes.
Stant terrâ defixæ hastæ, passimque soluti
Per campos pascuntur equi. Quæ gratia currûm
Armorumque fuit vivis; quæ cura nitentes
Pascere equos; eadem sequitur tellure repôstos. — 655. Eadem *cura* sequitur *eos* repóstos tellure.
Conspicit ecce alios dextrâ lævâque per herbam
Vescentes, lætumque choro pæana canentes,

NOTES.

ed gifts. This refers to the golden bough, which was sacred to Proserpine, and which Æneas was directed to deliver to her. Ruæus says, *munera decerpta ex arbore*.

633. *Opaca viarum:* the dark places of the way, or simply, the dark way. *Spatia* vel *loca* may be understood.

634. *Spatium:* ground—way.

636. *Spargit corpus:* he sprinkles his body with fresh water; either because he was polluted by the sight of Tartarus, or because he presented an offering to Proserpine. *Spargit aquâ*, &c. In the entrance of the heathen temples, *aqua lustralis*, or holy water, was placed, to sprinkle the devout on their entrance. This custom of sprinkling with holy water in the Roman church, La Cerda admits was borrowed from this practice of the heathen.

637. *Divæ:* Proserpine. *Perfecto:* finished—presented to her.

638. *Devenêre:* they came to.

639. *Fortunatorum:* in the sense of *felicium*. *Amœna viriditate herbarum arborumque*, says Ruæus.

640. *Vestit:* in the sense of *circumdat*.

641. *Purpureo:* clear—resplendent.

642. *Palæstris:* in the sense of *locis*. *Palæstra*, both the place of exercise, and the exercise itself.

644. *Dicunt:* in the sense of *canunt*.

645. *Threïcius sacerdos:* the Thracian poet warbles the seven distinctions of sound (the seven different notes) in music. Orpheus is here represented clothed in a long robe, that being anciently the garb both of a priest and musician; in which character he is here represented.

646. *Septem*, &c. Allusion is here had to the harp or lyre, which at first had only seven chords or strings. Two were afterwards added to make the number nine, in honor of the muses. *Pectine*. The *pecten* or *plectrum*, was a kind of instrument which the musician struck the strings of the harp or lyre with, called *a quill*.

647. *Eadem*. Markland conjectures this should be changed to *fidem*, the strings or chords of the lyre. The present reading refers to *discrimina*. The same (*discrimina*) he at one time strikes with his fingers, at another, &c.

650. *Ilusque*. For the genealogy of these, see Geor. iii. 35.

653. *Gratia:* in the sense of *amor*. *Vivis:* *iis* is understood: in the sense of *dum illi vixerunt*.

657. *Pæana*. Pæan was a sacred hymns or song of praise. It was sometimes sung in honor of Mars, especially before battle. It was sung in honor of Apollo, after a victory; and it was sometimes sung in honor of all the gods. It is derived from a Greek word, signifying to wound or pierce. It was first sung in honor of Apollo after he killed the *Python*. *Inter:* simply, for *in*.

Inter odoratum lauri nemus: unde supernè
Plurimus Eridani per sylvam volvitur amnis.
Hìc manus, ob patriam pugnando vulnera passi:
Quique sacerdotes casti, dum vita manebat:
Quique pii vates, et Phœbo digna locuti:
Inventas aut qui vitam excoluêre per artes:
Quique suî memores alios fecêre merendo:
Omnibus his niveâ cinguntur tempora vittâ.
Quos circumfusos sic est affata Sibylla,
Musæum ante omnes: medium nam plurima turba
Hunc habet, atque humeris exstantem suspicit altis:
Dicite, felices animæ, tuque, optime vates;
Quæ regio Anchisen, quis habet locus? illius ergo
Venimus, et magnos Erebi tranavimus amnes.
Atque huic responsum paucis ita reddidit heros:
Nulli certa domus: lucis habitamus opacis,
Riparumque toros, et prata recentia rivis
Incolimus: sed vos, si fert ita corde voluntas,
Hoc superate jugum, et facili jam tramite sistam.
Dixit: et ante tulit gressum, camposque nitentes
Desuper ostentat: dehinc summa cacumina linquunt.
At pater Anchises penitùs convalle virenti
Inclusas animas, superumque ad lumen ituras,

660. Hìc *est* manus *eorum, qui* passi *sunt* vulnera pugnando

661. Quique fuerant casti

662. *Fuerant* pii vates, et locuti

672. *Paucis* verbis

673. *Est* certa domus nulli *nostrum.*

677. Tulit gressum ante *eos*

679. Pater Anchises lustrabat animas penitùs inclusas *in* virenti convalle, iturasque ad superum lumen, recolens *eas* studio

NOTES.

658. *Unde supernè.* Interpreters are not agreed as to the meaning of this passage. Some make it to be this: *unde magna pars Eridani è superis præcipitat ad inferos.* This interpretation is founded on what we are told by Pliny, that the Po, soon after its rise, passes under ground and flows out again in a part of Piedmont. Others: *unde magnus Eridanus fluit ad superiores incolas terræ.* This seems to be the opinion of Ruæus. This appears to be founded upon the general received opinion that the great source of rivers is in the body of the earth. Mr. Davidson differs from both of these interpretations. He takes *supernè* in its common acceptation, denoting from an eminence or rising ground. *Unde:* whence (that is, from the Elysian fields,) from an eminence, or rising ground, the great river Eridanus rolls or flows. This is the easiest and most natural meaning.

662. *Quique pii vates. Vates* signifies either a poet or a prophet. Poets were originally the only persons who taught a knowledge of the divine nature, and declared the sublime doctrines of religion. *Locuti digna Phœbo:* and spoke things worthy of Phœbus; such doctrines of religion and morality as were worthy of the inspiration of that God.

663. *Excoluêre:* improved human life.

664. *Quique fecêre alios:* and those who had made others mindful of them by their merit. These included all patriots and public spirited men—all who had distinguished themselves in the arts and sciences, and all the benefactors of mankind.

665. *His omnibus:* the dat. in the sense of the gen. *horum omnium.*

666. *Circumfusos:* in the sense of *circumstantes.*

667. *Musæum.* Musæus was the disciple of Orpheus. He was an Athenian by birth, and flourished under Cecrops the second, a considerable time before the destruction of Troy. He was an heroic poet. There are said to be some fragments of verses which go under his name, but probably they are the production of a later poet. Some have censured Virgil for preferring Musæus to Homer as a poet. But it is to be remembered that Homer did not live till some time after this descent of Æneas, and therefore to have mentioned him, would have been wholly out of place.

668. *Exstantem:* rising above the rest by his head and lofty shoulders. *Suspicit:* in the sense of *admiratur.* Æneas is understood.

670. *Ergo illius:* on account of him we have come. *Ergo* is here used in the sense of *causâ.*

674. *Toros riparum:* Ruæus says, *herbosas ripas. Recentia rivis:* verdant or green on account of its streams or rivers. *Virentia propter vicinas aquas*, says Heyne. *Fert:* inclines you.

676. *Jugum:* in the sense of *collem.*

678. *Antè tulit gressum;* he (Musæus) went before them; a phrase.

680. *Superum lumen:* the upper world—the regions of light. Here is an allusion to

684. Vidit Ænean tendentem *cursum* adversum *ei* per gramina

686. Lachrymæ effusæ *sunt* genis

688. Tuaque pietas spectata *mihi* parenti vicit durum

692. *Per* quas terras, et per quanta æquora accipio te *esse* vectum!

700. Collo *patris*

Lustrabat studio recolens: omnemque suorum
Fortè recensebat numerum, charosque nepotes,
Fataque, fortunasque virûm, moresque, manusque.
Isque ubi tendentem adversùm per gramina vidit
Ænean; alacris palmas utrasque tetendit,
Effusæque genis lachrymæ, et vox excidit ore:
Venisti tandem, tuaque spectata parenti
Vicit iter durum pietas! datur ora tueri,
Nate, tua; et notas audire et reddere voces!
Sic equidem ducebam animo rebarque futurum,
Tempora dinumerans: nec me mea cura fefellit.
Quas ego te terras, et quanta per æquora vectum,
Accipio! quantis jactatum, nate, perîclis!
Quàm metui, ne quid Libyæ tibi regna nocerent!
Ille autem: Tua me, genitor, tua tristis imago
Sæpiùs occurrens, hæc limina tendere adegit.
Stant sale Tyrrheno classes. Da jungere dextram,
Da genitor: teque amplexu ne subtrahe nostro.
Sic memorans, largo fletu simul ora rigabat.
Ter conatus ibi collo dare brachia circùm;
Ter frustrà comprênsa manus effugit imago,
Par levibus ventis, volucrique simillima somno
 Intereà videt Æneas in valle reductâ
Seclusum nemus, et virgulta sonantia sylvis,
Lethæumque, domos placidas qui prænatat, amnem.
Hunc circum innumeræ gentes populique volabant
Ac veluti in pratis, ubi apes æstate serenâ
Floribus insidunt variis, et candida circum
Lilia funduntur: strepit omnis murmure campus.
Horrescit visu subito, causasque requirit
Inscius Æneas: quæ sint ea flumina porrò,
Quive viri tanto complêrint agmine ripas.
Tum pater Anchises: Animæ, quibus altera fato

NOTES.

the doctrine of transmigration, maintained by Pythagoras and his followers.

683. *Manus:* achievements—noble deeds. *Tendentem:* in the sense of *venientem ad se.*

687. *Spectata.* This is the reading of Heyne, and is easier than *expectata,* which is the common reading. Ruæus seems to approve of it, although he has *expectata. Doctissimi legunt spectata, id est, cognita, perspecta, probata,* says he.

688. *Datur:* in the sense of *permittitur. Mihi* is understood.

690. *Sic equidem ducebam:* indeed I was concluding in my mind, and thinking it would be so; computing and reckoning the time for you to arrive. The ghost of Anchises had directed Æneas to repair to the regions below. See lib. v. 731.

693. *Accipio:* in the sense of *audio.*

697. *Tyrrheno sale.* That part of the Mediterranean lying to the south of Italy, and having Sicily on the east and Sardinia and Corsica on the west, was called the *Tuscan sea. Sale:* in the sense of *mari,* by meton.

699. *Largo fletu:* in the sense of *multis lachrymis.*

700. *Circumdare:* they are separated by *tmesis* for the sake of the verse. *Conatus* sum, &c.

704. *Seclusum:* in the sense of *separatum. Virgulta sonantia sylvis.* Heyne takes these words in the sense of *virgulta sylvarum sonantia;* and this again for *sylvæ sonantes. Sonantia:* sounding—rustling with the wind.

705. *Prænatat:* in the sense of *præterfluit.*

709. *Funduntur:* in the sense of *volant.*

713. *Animæ quibus:* the souls, for which other bodies are destined by fate, drink, &c. There were some who were exempt from transmigration. Such were those, who, for their exalted virtue, had been admitted into the society of the gods. Among this number was Anchises. What Æneas here converses with under the appearance of his

Corpora debentur, Lethæi ad fluminis undam
Securos latices et longa oblivia potant.
Has equidem memorare tibi, atque ostendere coràm,
Jampridem hanc prolem cupio enumerare meorum :
Quò magis Italiâ mecum lætere repertâ.
O pater, anne aliquas ad cœlum hinc ire putandum est
Sublimes animas ? iterumque ad tarda reverti
Corpora ? quæ lucis miseris tam dira cupido ?
Dicam equidem, nec te suspensum, nate, tenebo ;
Suscipit Anchises, atque ordine singula pandit.
  Principio cœlum, ac terras, camposque liquentes,
Lucentemque globum Lunæ, Titaniaque astra
Spiritus intus alit ; totamque infusa per artus
Mens agitat molem, et magno se corpore miscet.
Inde hominum pecudumque genus, vitæque volantûm,
Et quæ marmoreo fert monstra sub æquore pontus.
Igneus est ollis vigor, et cœlestis origo
Seminibus ; quantùm non noxia corpora tardant,
Terrenique hebetant artus, moribundaque membra.
Hinc metuunt cupiuntque, dolent gaudentque : neque au- [ras
Respiciunt, clausæ tenebris et carcere cæco.
Quin et supremo cùm lumine vita reliquit ;
Non tamen omne malum miseris, nec funditùs omnes
Corporeæ excedunt pestes ; penitùsque necesse est
Multa diu concreta modis inolescere miris.
Ergò exercentur pœnis, veterumque malorum

716. Equidem jampridem cupio memorare tibi, atque ostendere has *animas* coràm, *et* enumerare hanc prolem meorum; quò

728. Unde *oritur* genus hominum

729. Et monstra, quæ pontus fert

732. Terrenique artus, moribundaque membra *non* hebetant *illum vigorem*

733. Hinc *animæ* metuunt

738. Multa *vitia* diu concreta penitùs inolescere *iis*

NOTES.

father, was only his image, his *Idolum* or *Simulacrum*, which the poets feigned to reside in the infernal regions, while the soul was in heaven among the gods. *Latices securos:* draughts expelling care—producing a peaceful and quiet mind.

719. *Cœlum:* this means here the upper world—the regions of light: *ad superas auras—ad vitam.*

720. *Sublimes:* in the sense of *illustres. Lucis:* in the sense of *vitæ.*

724. *Principio spiritus:* in the first place a spirit within supports the heaven, &c. Here Anchises explains to Æneas the system or economy of the world, on the principles of the Pythagorean, and Platonic philosophy. The same is explained in other words, Geor. iv. 221, et seq. The doctrine here inculcated is, that God is intimately united with every part of the universe, and that his spirit sustains the whole, the heavens, the earth, and the starry lamps; that a mind, or intelligence, diffused through every part of matter, actuates and gives life and motion to the whole. And from this active principle sprang the various kinds of animals. *Liquentes campos:* elegantly put for the sea, or watery element.

725. *Titania astra.* By these we are to understand the sun and stars, since they all equally shine by their own light *Titania:* an adj. from *Titan*, a name given to the sun, of Greek origin. Also, the son of Cœlus and Vesta, and the father of the *Titans.* These were all distinguished astronomers, as we are told by Diodorus and Pausanias, especially Hyperion. This might lead the poets to feign them transformed into the bodies of the sun and stars after their death.

726. *Agitat:* in the sense of *movet. Artus:* in the sense of *omnes partes.*

728. *Volantum:* in the sense of *avium.*

730. *Ollis:* for *illis*, by antithesis.

731. *Non tardant:* do not clog it.

733. *Hinc metuunt.* The passions are generally ranked under these four heads: fear and grief; joy and desire. The two first have for their object present or future evil; the two last, present or future good. *Auras:* in the sense of *cœlum.*

735. *Quin et cum:* but when life hath left them, even in the last glimmering light, &c.

737. *Pestes:* stains—pollutions.

738. *Diu concreta:* a long time habitual. Ruæus says, *conglutinata. Mala* is understood in the sense of *pestes*, as above. *Inolescere:* in the sense of *adhærescere.*

739. *Ergò exercentur pœnis.* These punishments were of three kinds, according to the nature of the stains with which the soul was infected. Those, whose stains or pol-

Supplicia expendunt. Aliæ panduntur inanes
Suspensæ ad ventos: aliis sub gurgite vasto
Infectum eluitur scelus, aut exuritur igni.
Quisque suos patimur Manes. Exinde per amplum
Mittimur Elysium, et pauci læta arva tenemus:
Donec longa dies, perfecto temporis orbe,
Concretam exemit labem, purumque reliquit
Æthereum sensum, atque auraï simplicis ignem.
Has omnes, ubi mille rotam volvêre per annos,

748. Deus evocat omnes has *animas*

NOTES.

lutions were the slightest, were suspended and exposed to the winds; others were washed away; others again, whose pollutions were of the deepest dye, were burnt in the fire. The elements, air, water, and fire, are of a purifying nature, and have been figuratively used by all writers as emblems of moral purification.

740. *Expendunt:* suffer—undergo. *Inanes:* in the sense of *leves.*

743. *Quisque patimur:* we all suffer every one his own *Manes.* This passage hath very much perplexed commentators. It is not certain in what sense we are to take *Manes.* The ghosts, or Manes of the dead, were supposed to haunt and disturb the living, from whom they had received any great injury. Hence the word *Manes* may signify the fiends, furies, or tormenting demons of the lower world. According to Plato, every person at his birth hath assigned him a *genium* or *demon,* that guards him through life, and after death accompanies him to the shades below, and becomes a minister of purification. By *Manes* we may understand these *Platonic demons.* Some understand by *Manes* the stings and fierce upbraidings of a guilty conscience. These every offender carries about with him, and by these means becomes his own tormentor. *Patimur Manes* is the same with *patimur supplicium per Manes.* The above is the usual acceptation of the words. In the present instance Heyne differs from the current of interpreters. He confesses it a perplexed and intricate passage, and conjectures it was left in an unfinished state by the poet. That part of the dead which the ancients called *Manes* they placed in the infernal regions, while the *umbra* remained upon earth and the soul ascended to heaven. He takes *Quisque suos patimur Manes,* in the sense of *nostrum omnium Manes patiuntur:* vel, *ista supplicia patienda omnibus Manibus.* His *ordo* of construction is: *nos Manes patimur quisque quoad suos.* According to the notion of Plato and others, all must undergo purification before they could be admitted to *Elysium,* to the *læta arva.* Now as the *Manes* alone descended to the shades below, they alone could suffer: *Hi sunt, qui purgantur: qui patiuntur: qui subeunt illas purgationes, pro sua cujusque parte.* This is the substance of his reasoning.

745. *Donec longa dies,* &c. It is the general opinion of commentators that the ordo is here inverted, and that this line should immediately follow *Quisque suos patimur Manes;* and that *exinde,* &c. should follow after *auraï simplicis ignem.* This is the only way in which the common meaning of *donec* can be retained: we suffer every one his own Manes, till length of time, the period of time being completed, hath taken away the inherent stains, and left the ethereal sense pure, &c. then, after that, we are sent: *exinde mittimur,* &c. Ruæus takes *donec* in the sense of *quando,* and it is the only sense it will bear in the present ordo of construction. *Exinde,* &c.: then we are sent—when length of time, &c.

746. *Labem.* The poet hath found no less than five different words to express the stains or pollutions of sin: *malum, corporeæ pestes, vetera mala, infectum seclus,* and *labes. Concretam:* inherent—contracted—habitual.

747. *Ignem simplicis auraï.* By this we are to understand the soul. The Platonists supposed the soul to be of a fiery quality. This may have led the poet to call it emphatically *the fire,* or flame *of simple brightness. Simplicis:* simple—uncorrupted—uncompounded. *Auraï:* for *auræ.* Nouns of this declension sometimes formed the gen. sing. in *aï.*

748. *Has omnes.* The meaning is, that after these *animæ,* or souls, had passed a thousand years in Elysium, the god calls them to the river Lethe, where, by drinking copiously of its water, they might forget the happiness of those peaceful abodes, and be prepared and willing to return again to life, and to visit this upper world. This notion of the transmigration of souls, as little as it is founded in truth, was generally received among the ancients. There were some exceptions to this transmigration. Those who had been admitted into the society of the gods, such as deified heroes, were exempted. Their *anima* or soul resided in heaven, while their *Idolum,* vel *simulachrum,* always remained in Elysium, to enjoy its pleasures and delights. So we are to understand of Anchises. His *Idolum* conversed with

Lethæum ad fluvium Deus evocat agmine magno:
Scilicet immemores supera ut convexa revisant,
Rursùs et incipiant in corpora velle reverti.
Dixerat Anchises: natumque, unàque Sibyllam,
Conventus trahit in medios, turbamque sonantem:
Et tumulum capit, unde omnes longo ordine possit
Adversos legere, et venientûm discere vultus.
Nunc age, Dardaniam prolem quæ deinde sequatur
Gloria, qui maneant Italâ de gente nepotes,
Illustres animas, nostrumque in nomen ituras,
Expediam dictis, et te tua fata docebo.
Ille, vides, purâ juvenis qui nititur hastâ,
Proxima sorte tenet lucis loca; primus ad auras
Æthereas Italo commixtus sanguine surget,
Sylvius, Albanum nomen, tua postuma proles:
Quem tibi longævo serum Lavinia conjux
Educet sylvis regem, regumque parentem:
Unde genus Longâ nostrum dominabitur Albâ.
Proximus ille, Procas, Trojanæ gloria gentis;
Et Capys, et Numitor; et, qui te nomine reddet,
Sylvius Æneas; pariter pietate vel armis
Egregius, si unquam regnandam acceperit Albam.
Qui juvenes quantas ostentant, aspice, vires!
At, qui umbrata gerunt civili tempora quercu:
Hi tibi Nomentum, et Gabios, urbemque Fidenam;

750. Scilicet ut immemores *præteritorum* revisant

756. Nunc age, expediam dictis, quæ gloria deinde sequatur Dardaniam prolem, qui nepotes maneant *te* de Itala gente

760. Ille juvenis, qui nititur

763. *Dictus* Sylvius.

764. Quem serum conjux Lavinia *in* sylvis educet tibi longævo *futurum* regem

767. Ille proximus *est*

768. *Deinde sunt* et Capys, et Numitor; et Sylvius Æneas, qui

772. Hi *imponent* Nomentum

NOTES.

Æneas, while his *anima* enjoyed the converse of the gods. *Rotam volvĕre:* in the sense of *traduxerunt tempus.* It is a metaphor taken from the rolling or turning of a wheel.

749. *Deus.* Some take the god here mentioned to be Mercury. But Heyne thinks *deus* is here used indefinitely for any *dæmon* or *genium*, in allusion to the notions of Plato, which the poet here hath in his view. Perhaps it is better to suppose that each shade is called by its own special *dæmon* to the waters of Lethe, to prepare for a return to life. This makes the sense easier, and is in perfect accordance with the principles of that philosophy, here inculcated and explained.

750. *Supera convexa:* in the sense of *superas auras;* or simply, *vitam.*

753. *Sonantem:* in the sense of *strepentem.*

755. *Legere:* in the sense of *recensere*, vel *cognoscere.*

763. *Sylvius.* Dionysius Halicarnassus informs us that Lavinia, at the death of Æneas, was pregnant, and for fear of Ascanius fled into the woods to a Tuscan shepherd, where she was delivered of a son, whom, from that circumstance, she called *Sylvius.* But Ascanius, moved with compassion toward her, named him his successor in the kingdom of *Alba Longa.* From him, the kings of Alba took the common name of *Sylvii.* Livy, however, makes him the son of Ascanius. In order to make the historian and the poet agree some would understand by *longævo*, in the following line, *advanced to the gods*, *immortal*, relying upon Æschylus, who calls the gods *longævi.* *Postuma proles.* The meaning of *postuma* here will, in a good degree, depend upon the sense given to *longævo.* If it be taken as abovementioned, to denote one advanced to the life of the gods, then *postuma proles* will mean *posthumous child*, one born after the death of the father. But if we take *longævo* in its ordinary acceptation, to denote an old man, or one advanced in age, then *postuma* must be taken in the sense of *postrema:* last—your last child, whom late your wife Lavinia brought to you advanced in age.

765. *Educet:* in the sense of *pariet.*

767. *Proximus.* Not the one who should succeed Sylvius in the throne of *Alba*, for Procas was the thirteenth king; but the one who stood next to him in the Elysian fields.

772. *At, qui gerunt:* but who bear their temples shaded with the civic crown. This was made of oak, because the fruit of that tree supported man at the first. It was conferred upon the man who had saved the life of a Roman citizen in battle. *Quercu:* the oak; by meton. the crown made of it.

773. *Hi Nomentum:* these shall found Nomentum, &c. This was a town of the Sabines, situated upon the river *Allia*, about

Hi Collatinas imponent montibus arces,
Pometios, Castrumque Inuï, Bolamque, Coramque.
Hæc tum nomina erunt, nunc sunt sinè nomine terræ.
Quin et avo comitem sese Mavortius addet
Romulus, Assaraci quem sanguinis Ilia mater
Educet. Viden' ut geminæ stant vertice cristæ,
Et pater ipse suo Superûm jam signat honore?
En hujus, nate, auspiciis illa inclyta Roma
Imperium terris, animos æquabit Olympo,
Septemque una sibi muro circumdabit arces,
Felix prole virûm: qualis Berecynthia mater
Invehitur curru Phrygias turrita per urbes,
Læta Deûm partu, centum complexa nepotes,
787. Omnes tenentes supera *et* alta *loca* — Omnes cœlicolas, omnes supera alta tenentes.
Huc geminas huc flecte acies: hanc aspice gentem,
789. Hic *est* Cæsar, et omnis — Romanosque tuos. Hic Cæsar, et omnis Iüli
Progenies, magnum cœli ventura sub axem.
791. Quem sæpius audis promitti tibi, *nempe* — Hic vir, hic est, tibi quem promitti sæpiùs audis,
Augustus Cæsar, Divi genus; aurea condet
Sæcula qui rursùs Latio, regnata per arva
Saturno quondam: super et Garamantas et Indos

NOTES.

twelve miles from Rome, on the east. *Gabii:* a town about ten miles from Rome, also toward the east. *Fidena:* a town situated on the Tyber, about five miles north of Rome. *Collatiæ:* a town not far from *Fidena*, to the east. *Pometia*, or *Pometii:* a town of the *Volsci*, situate to the north of the *Pomptinæ paludes*. *Castrum Inuï:* a maritime town of the *Rutuli*. It was dedicated to that god whom the Greeks called *Pan*, but the Latins called *Inuus* or *Incubus*. *Bolæ* vel *Bola:* a town of the *Æqui* near *Præneste*, to the east. *Cora:* a town of the *Volsci* not far from *Pometia*, to the north. These towns were not all in *Latium*, properly so called, as the poet would insinuate. They were built after their respective people were incorporated among the Romans, and their lands made a part of the Roman state.

774. *Imponent:* in the sense of *condent*. *Collatinas arces:* the town or city *Collatiæ*.

777. *Comitem avo.* *Comes* here is an assistant or helper. Numitor, the son of *Procas*, was driven from his throne by his brother *Amulius*. Romulus being informed of this, collected a company of men, joined the party of Numitor, and restored him to his throne. Romulus was the reputed son of *Mars* and *Ilia*, the daughter of Numitor, who was therefore his grandfather. *Mavortius:* an adj. from *Mavors*, a name of Mars, agreeing with Romulus, who is said to have been the son of that god.

779. *Educet:* in the sense of *pariet*.

780. *Pater Superûm:* Jupiter, who is styled the father of the gods, and king of men. Some understand *Mars*, the father of Romulus.

781. *Auspiciis:* conduct—government.

782. *Animos:* courage—valor.

783. *Unaque circumdabit:* and it alone shall surround for itself seven hills.

784. *Berecynthia mater:* as the Berecynthian mother, crowned with turrets, is wafted in her car, &c. Cybele is here meant, who was said to be the mother of most of the gods. Hence *læta Deûm partu:* rejoicing in a race or progeny of gods. The epithet *Berecynthia* is added to her from *Berecynthium*, a castle of *Phrygia*, on the river Sagaris, or from a mountain of that name, where she was worshipped in a distinguished manner. Cybele is often put, by meton. for the *earth;* for which reason she is represented as wearing a *turreted crown*. *Prole virûm:* in a race of heroes.

788. *Gentem:* race—progeny.

792. *Genus Divi:* the offspring of a god, This the poet says to flatter the vanity of Augustus, who, from the time that he deified *Julius Cæsar*, his father by adoption, assumed the title of the son of a god, *filius Divi*, as appears from ancient inscriptions. Or his divine descent might be traced from Dardanus, the founder of the Trojan race, the reputed son of Jove. Some copies have *Divûm*. Heyne reads *Divi*. *Aurea sæcula condet:* who again shall establish the golden age in Latium, through the country, &c. See Ecl. iv. 6.

793. *Augustus.* This is the first time that Virgil called his prince *Augustus*. This title was decreed to him by the senate, in the year of Rome 727.

Proferet imperium: jacet extra sidera tellus,
Extra anni solisque vias, ubi cœlifer Atlas
Axem humero torquet stellis ardentibus aptum.
Hujus in adventu jam nunc et Caspia regna
Responsis horrent Divûm, et Mæotica tellus,
Et septemgemini turbant trepida ostia Nili.
Nec verò Alcides tantum telluris obivit;
Fixerit æripedem cervam licèt, aut Erymanthi
Pacârit nemora, et Lernam tremefecerit arcu.
Nec, qui pampineis victor juga flectit habenis
Liber, agens celso Nysæ de vertice tigres.
Et dubitamus adhuc virtutem extendere factis?
Aut metus Ausoniâ prohibet consistere terrâ?
Quis procul ille autem, ramis insignis olivæ,
Sacra ferens? nosco crines incanaque menta

804. Nec Liber *obivit tantum telluris*, qui victor flectit juga pampineis habenis, agens

808. Autem quis *est* ille procul, insignis ramis

NOTES.

795. *Proferet imperium super:* he shall extend his empire over, &c. The Garamantes were a people inhabiting the interior of Africa. *Indos.* Suetonius informs us that the kings of India, properly so called, being moved at the fame of Augustus, sought his friendship. But it is well known that he did not extend his empire over them. Most probably the people here mentioned under the name of *Indos* were the Æthiopians, or some nation of Africa. Besides, any country lying in a hot climate, or within the tropics, was anciently called *India*, and its inhabitants *Indi*, as might be shown by abundant testimony.

795. *Tellus jacet:* their land lies, &c. *Sidera*, here, does not mean the stars and constellations in general; but the particular signs of the zodiac, as appears from the following words: *extra vias annui solis.* This description agrees very well to Africa, which extends beyond the tropic of Cancer to the north, and, also, beyond the tropic of Capricorn to the south.

797. *Axem:* by synec. for *cœlum.*

798. *Caspia regna.* By this we are to understand the kingdoms bordering upon the Caspian sea. To the north were the Sarmatians and Scythians; to the south, the Parthians; to the west, the Arminians. This sea has no visible outlet or communication with any other waters. It is said to be about 630 miles long, and 260 broad. The Wolga, the largest river in Europe, empties into it. *Mæotica tellus.* By this we are to understand the northern nations of Europe, bordering on the *Palus Mæotis*, or sea of Azoff, on the north of the Euxine, or black sea. *Horrent:* tremble at the responses of the gods.

800. *Trepida ostia:* the astonished mouths of the seven-fold Nile are troubled. *Turbant* has, in this place, the signification of *turbantur*, vel *trepidant.* Ruæus says, *commoventur.* The Nile is the largest river of Africa, and falls into the Mediterranean sea by seven mouths. It annually overflows its banks, and occasions the fertility of Egypt. The Egyptians worshipped it as a divinity.

801. *Alcides:* a name of Hercules, from *Alcæus*, his grandfather. He is sometimes called *Amphitryoniades*, from *Amphitryon*, the husband of *Alcmene*, of whom Jupiter begat him. He travelled over many parts of the world, performing feats of valor. He was in the Argonautic expedition. In Egypt he slew *Busiris;* in Spain, *Geryon;* in Sicily, *Eryx;* in Thrace, *Diomede;* in Africa he destroyed the gardens of the Hesperides. The poet here mentions three instances of his valor: 1. His piercing the brazen-footed hind. *Fixerit æripedem*, &c. This hind inhabited the mountain *Mænalus*, in Arcadia. Servius, in order to reconcile Virgil with mythology, takes *fixerit*, in the sense of *statuerit*, stopped, out-run, took, &c. because, being sacred to *Diana*, it would have been impious to put her to death. Heyne takes *fixerit* in the sense of *ceperit.* 2. His subduing the groves of Erymanthus: *pacârit nemora;* that is, subdued the wild boar that infested them. He took him alive, and carried him to Eurystheus, king of *Mycenæ.* 3. His making Lerna tremble with his bow: *Lernam tremefecerit;* that is, the fens of Lerna, between Argos and *Mycenæ*, where he slew the Hydra with fifty heads.

804. *Juga:* the yoke, by meton. for the carriage. The car of Bacchus was drawn by *tigers.*

805. *Nysæ.* There were several mountains by this name, all sacred to Bacchus. *Agens tigres:* driving the tigers from, &c. Tigers are said to be transported with fury at the sound of tabrets and drums; which perhaps, is the reason of their being given to Bacchus, the god of fury and enthusiastic rage.

Regis Romani; primus qui legibus urbem
Fundabit, Curibus parvis et paupere terrâ
Missus in imperium magnum. Cui deinde subibit,
Otia qui rumpet patriæ, residesque movebit
Tullus in arma viros, et jam desueta triumphis
Agmina. Quem juxtà sequitur jactantior Ancus,
Nunc quoque jam nimiùm gaudens popularibus auris.
Vis et Tarquinios reges, animamque superbam
Ultoris Bruti, fascesque videre receptos?
Consulis imperium hic primus, sævasque secures

812. Cui deinde Tullus subibit, qui rumpet otia patriæ, movebitque

817. Vis-*ne* videre et Tarquinios

NOTES.

810. *Romani regis.* The person here spoken of is *Numa Pompilius*, the second king of Rome. He was a Sabine by birth. After the death of Romulus, a dispute arose between the Romans and Sabines upon the choice of his successor. They finally agreed that the Romans should choose, but the choice must fall upon a Sabine. It accordingly fell upon Numa. He proved to be a peaceful monarch. He is, therefore, here represented as bearing an olive branch, the badge of peace. He reigned forty-three years, and died at the age of eighty. This justifies the *incana menta;* his white chin—beard. The prep. *in*, in composition, sometimes changes the signification of the primitive, at others, increases it. This last is the case here. Hitherto the Romans had been little better than a band of robbers, associated together for the purpose of extending their rapine more widely. It was Numa's first care to establish the influence of religion over the minds of his subjects, and to enact a code of laws for their civil government. He is therefore represented bearing sacred utensils. See nom. prop. under *Numa.* Hence it is said, *fundabit urbem legibus:* he shall found the city by laws.

811. *Curibus: Cures* was a small city of the Sabines. *Paupere terra:* from a poor or humble estate.

814. *Tullus.* Tullus Hostilius, the third king of the Romans. He was a descendant neither of Numa, nor Romulus. The government of Rome was then an elective monarchy, though great deference was paid to the will of the last king, and sometimes it very much influenced the choice. Tullus broke the peace with the Albans, and a bloody war ensued. *Viros resides movebit et agmina:* he shall rouse his inactive men to arms, and his troops long unaccustomed to triumphs. *Otia:* in the sense of *pacem.*

815. *Ancus.* This was Ancus Martius, the fourth king of Rome. He courted the favor of the people: hence it is said of him, *gaudens popularibus auris.* Nor was he inferior to his predecessor in the arts of peace and war. He was the grandson of Numa by his daughter. Being indignant that Tullus should possess the throne in preference to himself, he sought means to procure his death, and that of his family. No mention is here made of Servius Tullius, the sixth king of Rome.

816. *Auris: aura*, applause—favor.

818. *Ultoris Bruti.* Tarquin, surnamed the proud, the seventh and last king of Rome, had rendered himself odious to the people. His son *Sextus*, enamored with the beautiful *Lucretia*, the wife of Collatinus, offered violence to her. Unable to survive the disgrace, she killed herself with her own hand. This caused a general sensation. Brutus, a leading member of the Senate, roused that body to assert their rights against the tyrant, and procured a decree to banish Tarquin and his family for ever. For this reason, he is called *ultor*, the avenger. The government was changed from *regal*, to *consular;* and Brutus and Collatinus were chosen the first consuls. These officers were chosen annually. *Fasces receptos:* these words may mean, *the authority and power recovered*, and restored to the people, from whom they had been taken by usurpation and tyranny. Heyne says, *regiam dignitatem, et imperium translatum à regibus in consules.* This is also the opinion of Dr. Trapp. But this is going too far. It is better to understand it of the power recovered and restored to the people, from whom it had been taken. In confirmation of this, history informs us, that the consuls were obliged to bow their *fasces* to the assembly of the people, as an acknowledgment that the sovereign power was theirs. *Fascis:* properly, a bundle of rods bound together with an axe in the middle, carried before the consuls and chief magistrates, to denote that they had the power to scourge and to put to death—the rods to scourge, and the axe (*securis*) to put to death. Hence by meton. it came to signify the power itself—the ensigns of authority and royalty—also power and authority in general. *Securis* is properly an axe. But being used as an instrument of executing the sentence of the law against offenders, it came to signify *the sentence itself.* And as the sentence of the law is to be considered *just*, it is taken also for *justice* in a general sense. *Sævus*

Accipiet; natosque pater, nova bella moventes,
Ad pœnam pulchrâ pro libertate vocabit
Infelix. Utcunque ferent ea facta minores,
Vincet amor patriæ, laudumque immensa cupido
Quin Decios, Drusosque procul, sævumque securi
Aspice Torquatum, et referentem signa Camillum.
Illæ autem, paribus quas fulgere cernis in armis,
Concordes animæ nunc, et dum nocte premuntur,
Heu! quantum inter se bellum, si lumina vitæ
Attigerint, quantas acies stragemque ciebunt!
Aggeribus socer Alpinis, atque arce Monœci
Descendens; gener adversis instructus Eois.
Ne, pueri, ne tanta animis assuescite bella:
Neu patriæ validas in viscera vertite vires.
Tuque prior, tu parce, genus qui ducis Olympo
Projice tela manu, sanguis meus!
Ille triumphatâ Capitolia ad alta Corintho

820. Infelix pater vocabit natos, moventes

826. Autem illæ animæ, quas cernis fulgere in paribus armis concordes nunc, et dum premuntur nocte, heu!

835. *Tu qui es* meus sanguis

NOTES.

securi: rigid, stern, or impartial justice—the sword of justice. Perhaps the poet here alludes to the sentence passed upon the sons of Brutus, for being among the number of conspirators to restore the Tarquins, which was rigidly enforced by their father. They were beheaded with the *axe.*

820. *Natos.* The two sons of Brutus, Titus and Tiberius, conspired with other noble youths of Rome, to recall Tarquin. But being discovered, their father commanded them to be put to death; and stood by, and saw the sentence put in execution. The epithet *infelix*, connected with *pater*, is very just, as well as expressive. Some copies connect *infelix* with *utcunque minores.* However posterity shall regard that action, love of country will prevail and justify the father.

824. *Decios aspice:* but see the Decii, &c. They were a noble family at Rome. Three of them devoted their lives for their country. *Drusos:* Drusus was the surname of the Livian family, from *Drusus*, a general of the Gauls, slain by one of that family. Of this family was *Livia Drusilla*, the wife of Augustus.

825. *Torquatum.* Titus Manlius, surnamed *Torquatus*, from a golden chain or collar (*torques*) which he took from a general of the Gauls, whom he slew, *anno urbis*, 393. It became afterward the common name of the family. He was three times consul, and as often dictator. He ordered his son to be slain for fighting the enemy against his order, although he gained the victory. In allusion to this, he is called *sævum securi. Camillum:* a Roman of noble birth. He was banished from Rome for envy of his talents and military renown. While he was in exile, the Gauls made an incursion into Italy, and took Rome. This roused Camillus. He forgot the injury done to him; and, collecting a body of men, fell upon them unawares, and cut them in pieces. He was five times dictator, and four times he triumphed.

828. *Heu! quantum:* alas! how great a war, &c. Here is an allusion to the civil war between Cæsar and Pompey. Pompey married Julia, the daughter of Cæsar. The troops that composed the army of Cæsar (*socer*, the father-in-law) were chiefly Gauls and Germans from the west. Hence he is said to come from the Alpine hills, and the tower of *Monœcus.* This was a town and port on the coast of Liguria, where the Alps begin to rise. The place was well fortified. The troops of Pompey (*gener*, the son-in-law,) were from the eastern part of the empire, *adversis Eois:* from the opposite east. *Populis* vel *militibus* is understood.

832. *Ne assuescite tanta bella animis:* by commutatio, for *ne assuescite animos tantis bellis.*

833. *Neu patriæ.* This verse, in a very remarkable manner, conveys to the ear the sound of tearing and rending, which it is designed to express.

835. *Meus sanguis.* Julius Cæsar is here meant, who, according to Virgil, descended from *Venus*, through *Iülus*, the son of Æneas. The poet here very artfully expresses his abhorrence of the civil war which placed the Cæsars on the imperial throne; but he does it so artfully as leaves to Augustus no room for taking offence.

836. *Corintho triumphatâ:* Corinth being triumphed over. This was a famous city of Greece, situated on the isthmus which connects the Peloponnesus with the main land. This city privately formed an alliance with the principal Grecian states; which gave offence to the Romans. Upon this, they sent ambassadors to dissolve this alliance or council of the states, as it was called; who were treated with violence and abuse.

Victor aget currum, cæsis insignis Achivis.
Eruet ille Argos, Agamemnoniasque Mycenas,
Ipsumque Æaciden, genus armipotentis Achillei;
Ultus avos Trojæ, templa et temerata Minervæ.
Quis te, magne Cato, tacitum; aut te, Cosse, relinquat?
Quis Gracchi genus? aut geminos, duo fulmina belli,
Scipiadas, cladem Libyæ? parvoque potentem
Fabricium? vel te sulco, Serrane, serentem?

842. Quis *relinquat* genus Gracchi *tacitum?* aut

NOTES.

Rome instantly declared war, which ended in the destruction of Corinth, and the subjugation of its allies. This was completed by the consul Mummius, in the year of Rome 609. *Ille victor.* This refers to Mummius. He was honored by a triumph. *Capitolia:* neu. plu. a famous temple of Jupiter at Rome, commenced by Tarquinius Priscus upon the hill called *Tarpeius*, but afterward *Capitolinus*, from the circumstance of a human head (*caput*) being found when they were laying the foundation of that edifice. Hitherto the victors used to be drawn in a car to place their laurels in the lap of Jove.

838. *Ille eruet Argos:* he shall overthrow Argos, &c. Virgil is here supposed by *Hyginus* to confound two events which took place at different periods—the war of *Achaia*, which ended in the destruction of Corinth, and the war with *Pyrrhus*, king of Epirus. The former was conducted by the consul *Mummius*, to whom the *ille*, in the preceding line, refers; but it is not certain to whom the *ille* here refers; whether to *Quinctius Flaminius*, *Paulus Æmilius*, *Cæcilius Metellus*, or *M. Curius*, each of whom acted a distinguished part in the war with Greece and Epirus. By *Argos—Mycenæ*, the best interpreters understand the power of Greece in general. And by *Æaciden*, not Pyrrhus, but the power—the government of Epirus. This was not destroyed during the reign of that monarch. It was, however, completed in the reign of *Perses* or *Perseus*, king of Macedonia, the last of the descendants of Achilles, whom Paulus Æmilius led in triumph. He may be called *Æacides*, as being descended from *Achilles*, the grandson of *Æacus*, by *Olympias*, the daughter of *Pyrrhus*, king of Epirus. He united the interests of northern Greece.

840. *Ultus avos Trojæ:* having avenged his ancestors of Troy. *Temerata templa:* the violated temple of Minerva. This alludes to the violence offered to it by Diomede and Ulysses, in taking away the *Palladium.*

841. *Cato.* There were two distinguished persons of this name. The one here spoken of is the *Cato Major*, sometimes called *Cato Censorius*, from his great gravity and strictness in the censorship. He lived to a very great age. He sprang from an obscure family; and, on account of his wisdom and prudence, was called *Cato*, from *catus*, wise or prudent. The other Cato was his great grandson, and called *Minor* He arrived at the prætorship. He subjugated Sardinia; and, in the year of Rome 560, obtained a triumph in Spain, where he acted as proconsul. He took part against Cæsar, and, when he saw the republic was lost, slew himself. *Cosse:* Cornelius Cossus. He slew the king of the *Veientes*, and consecrated his spoils to *Jupiter Feretrius.* These were the second *spolia opima*, since the building of Rome. He was afterward nominated dictator, and triumphed over the *Volsci.*

842. *Genus Gracchi.* Tiberius Sempronius Gracchus was the most distinguished of his family. He was appointed prætor, and triumphed over the *Celtiberi* in Spain, destroying three hundred of their towns, in the year of Rome 576. He was twice consul, and once censor. He married *Cornelia*, the daughter of Scipio Africanus. By her, among other children, he had the two famous brothers *Tiberius* and *Caius.* They were both appointed tribunes of the people at different times, and were the sincere advocates of their rights. This excited the jealousy of the senate, who raised a tumult, in which they both perished. The former in the year of Rome 621, and the latter in the year 633.

843. *Scipiadas.* There were two Scipios, Cornelius Scipio major, and Cornelius Scipio minor. They were both surnamed *Africanus.* The latter was grandson of the former, and was adopted by *Paulus Æmilius*, and to distinguish him from the former, he was called also *Æmilianus.* They were both distinguished men. At the age of twenty-four, *Scipio Major* was appointed to command in Spain against the Carthaginians, whom he expelled from that country He was afterward, *anno urbis* 549, made consul. He passed over into Africa, where he defeated them again, and terminated the second Punic war, much to the advantage of the Romans. He obtained a triumph, *anno urbis* 553. Hence he was called *Africanus. Scipio Minor* was appointed consul in 607. He took the department of Africa in the third Punic war, and entirely erased Carthage. He triumphed in 608. Hence also called *Africanus. Duo fulmina belli:* two thunderbolts of war. They were so called by *Lucretius* and *Cicero.*

Quò fessum rapitis, Fabii? Tu Maximus ille es,
Unus qui nobis cunctando restituis rem.
Excudent alii spirantia molliùs æra,
Credo equidem: vivos ducent de marmore vultus;
Orabunt causas meliùs; cœlique meatus
Describent radio, et surgentia sidera dicent:
Tu regere imperio populos, Romane, memento:
Hæ tibi erunt artes; pacisque imponere morem,
Parcere subjectis, et debellare superbos.
Sic pater Anchises: atque hæc mirantibus addit:
Aspice, ut insignis spoliis Marcellus opimis
Ingreditur, victorque viros supereminet omnes.
Hic rem Romanam, magno turbante tumultu,
Sistet eques: sternet Pœnos, Gallumque rebellem;
Tertiaque arma patri suspendet capta Quirino.
Atque hìc Æneas; unà namque ire videbat

845. Fabii, quò rapitis *me* fessum?

854. Pater Anchises *dixit:* atque

857. Hic eques sistet Romanam rem, magno tumultu turbante *eam*

860. Hìc Æneas *ait:* O pater quis *est* ille, qui sic comitatur virum euntem? namque videbat

NOTES.

844. *Fabricium.* Fabricius was raised from a low estate to the command of the Roman army. The Samnites and Pyrrhus both attempted to corrupt him with money; but he gave them to understand that Rome was not ambitious of gold, but gloried in commanding those who possessed it. He was twice consul, and twice he triumphed. *Serrane:* Quinctius Cincinnatus. He was twice dictator. At the age of eighty he was taken from his farm of four acres only, which he ploughed and sowed with his own hand. Whence he is called *Serranus,* from the verb *sero.* Florus calls him *dictator ab aratro.*

845. *Fabii.* These were a noble family at Rome, of whom *Quintius Fabius* was the most distinguished. In the second Punic war Annibal reduced the Roman state to the brink of ruin by two signal victories obtained over them, one at *Trebia,* the other at *Trasimenus.* In this state of things, Fabius was appointed dictator, and took the command of the army against the conqueror. By delaying to give him battle, by degrees he broke his power and compelled him to leave Italy. *Cunctando restituis rem:* by delaying you restore the state. He was honored with the surname of *Maximus.* He was five times consul, twice dictator, once censor, and twice he triumphed.

846. *Rem:* the state—the republic. Most copies have *restituis,* in the present; some *restitues,* in the future.

847. *Alii excudent:* others shall form with more delicacy the animated brass, &c. The Corinthians were famed for statuary; the Athenians for eloquence, and the Chaldeans and Egyptians for astronomy. These are the arts or sciences here alluded to. The Romans are advised to neglect them, or consider them of inferior importance to the art of war, to ruling the nations, and dictating the conditions of peace. It is well known that for a long time the Romans paid little attention to the arts of civilized life; not until they had made themselves masters of Greece. *Vivos:* to the life. *Æra: statuas ex ære.*

849. *Meatus cœli:* nempe, *cursus siderum. Radio:* the *radius* was a stick or wand, used by the geomitricians to mark or describe their figures in the sand. *Dicent:* shall explain—treat of.

852. *Morem:* in the sense of *legem,* vel *conditiones.*

855. *Marcellus ingreditur:* Marcellus moves along, distinguished by triumphal spoils, &c. The *spolia opima* were those spoils which a Roman general took from the general of the enemy, whom he had slain with his own hand on the field of battle. Such spoils Marcellus won from *Viridomarus,* the general of the Gauls. *Tumultu.* By *tumultus* here we are to understand a Gallic war, which broke out and threatened the peace of Italy. A civil war, or intestine commotion, was properly called *tumultus. Majores nostri tumultum Italicum, quod erat domesticus; tumultum Gallicum, quòd erat Italiæ finitimus; prœterea nullum tumultum nominabant,* says Cicero. Marcellus was appointed to the command of the army, and wishing to attack the Gauls by surprise, or before they were prepared to receive him, he left his infantry behind, and proceeded with his cavalry, or horse, alone, because they could march with speed. Hence he is called here *eques. Sistet:* in the sense of *firmabit.*

859. *Suspendetque tertia arma.* The first *spolia opima* were offered to Jupiter Feretrius by Romulus, taken from Acron, king of the *Caninenses.* The second were offered by *Cornelius Cossus,* mentioned 841, supra. The third were taken by Marcellus from Viridomarus. It is not certain who

Egregium formâ juvenem, et fulgentibus armis;
Sed frons læta parùm, et dejecto lumina vultu:
Quis, pater, ille virum qui sic comitatur euntem?
Filius? anne aliquis magnâ de stirpe nepotum?
Quis strepitus circà comitum! quantum instar in ipso est
Sed nox atra caput tristi circumvolat umbrâ.
Tum pater Anchises lachrymis ingressus obortis:
O nate, ingentem luctum ne quære tuorum:
Ostendent terris hunc tantùm fata, neque ultrà
Esse sinent. Nimiùm vobis Romana propago
Visa potens, Superi, propria hæc si dona fuissent.
Quantos ille virûm magnam Mavortis ad urbem
Campus aget gemitus! vel quæ, Tyberine, videbis
Funera, cùm tumulum præterlabêre recentem!
Nec puer Iliacâ quisquam de gente Latinos
In tantùm spe tollet avos: nec Romula quondam
Ullo se tantùm tellus jactabit alumno.
Heu pietas! heu prisca fides! invictaque bello
Dextera! non illi quisquam se impunè tulisset
Obvius armato: seu cùm pedes iret in hostem,
Seu spumantis equi foderet calcaribus armos.

865. Quis strepitus comitum *est* circa *eum!* quantum instar *Marcelli* est in ipso!

869. Neque sinent *eum* esse ultrà. Romana propago visa *esset* vobis, O Superi, *esse* nimiùm potens, si

872. Quantos gemitus virûm ille campus ad magnam urbem

879. Non quisquam obvius tulisset se illi armato impunè, seu

NOTES.

we are to understand by *Patri Quirino*, to whom these spoils were to be suspended and offered. Nascimbænus explains *Quirino* by *Marte*, vel *bello*. He suspends to father Jove the spoils taken (*capta*) in battle. Servius, by *Quirino* understands Romulus. He suspends to father Romulus, &c. and produces a law of Numa which ordered the first *spolia opima* to be offered to Jupiter, the second to Mars, and the third to Romulus. But this law regarded those who might repeat the *spolia opima*. Ruæus understands by *Patri Quirino*, Jupiter Feretrius, in the same manner as Janus is called *Quirinus* by Suetonius; because he presided over war, and because his temple was built by *Romulus Quirinus*. He thinks *Jupiter Feretrius* may be called *Quirinus*. *Suspendet*, &c.: he shall suspend to father Jove the third triumphal spoils taken from the enemy. Marcellus was of a plebeian family, and was advanced to the consulship five times. In his third, he was sent to Sicily, where he distinguished himself in the defeat of Hannibal. He laid siege to Syracuse, and took it after he had been before it three years. It was nobly defended by the celebrated mathematician Archimedes, who repeatedly destroyed the fleet of the assailants by his machines and burning glasses. It was at last taken by stratagem, and Archimedes slain.

862. *Parùm læta:* in the sense of *tristis*.

863. *Virum:* M. Marcellus, the consul.

867. *Ingressus:* in the sense of *cœpit*. *Obortis:* gushing from his eyes.

869. *Fata ostendent:* the fates will only show him to the earth, &c. This is *Marcus Marcellus*, the son of Caius Marcellus and Octavia, the sister of Augustus. He designed him for his daughter Julia. When a boy, he adopted him as a son, and intended him for his successor in the empire. He died about the age of twenty years, at *Baïas*. His body was carried to Rome, and consumed to ashes in the *campus Martius*. The Romans were much affected at his loss, and made great lamentation over him. He was interred near the banks of the Tiber with great pomp. *Propago:* race—stock—offspring.

871. *Propria:* lasting—permanent; that is, if Marcellus had been permitted to live.

872. *Quantos gemitus ille:* how great groans of men shall that Campus Martius send forth! *Mavortis*, gen. of *Mavors*, a name of Mars. Rome was sacred to *Mars*, as being the father both of Romulus and Remus. *Aget:* in the sense of *emittet*. *Ad:* in the sense of *prope*.

876. *Tantùm spe.* Some read, *in tantam spem:* others, *in tanta spe.* Heyne reads *in tantùm spe;* so also Ruæus. But *spe* may be for *spei*, the gen. (as *die* is put for *diei*, Geor. i. 208.) governed by *tantùm*. This last I prefer.

878. *Heu pietas! heu prisca fides!* The poet here deplores the loss which virtue, integrity, and valor, sustained in him. Both *Velleius* and *Seneca* give young Marcellus a most excellent character.

880. *Seu cùm pedes.* The meaning is: whether, as a footman, he should rush against the foe, or whether he should spur on his foaming steed to the attack.

881. *Armos:* in the sense of *latera*.

Heu, miserande puer! si quà fata aspera rumpas,
Tu Marcellus eris. Manibus date lilia plenis:
Purpureos spargam flores, animamque nepotis
His saltem accumulem donis, et fungar inani
Munere. Sic totâ passim regione vagantur
Aëris in campis latis, atque omnia lustrant.
Quæ postquam Anchises natum per singula duxit,
Incenditque animum famæ venientis amore:
Exin bella viro memorat quæ deinde gerenda;
Laurentesque docet populos, urbemque Latini;
Et quo quemque modo fugiatque feratque laborem.
  Sunt geminæ Somni portæ: quarum altera fertur
Cornea, quâ veris facilis datur exitus umbris:
Altera, candenti perfecta nitens elephanto:
Sed falsa ad cœlum mittunt insomnia Manes.
His ubi tum natum Anchises unàque Sibyllam
Prosequitur dictis, portâque emittit eburnâ.
Ille viam secat ad naves, sociosque revisit.
Tum se ad Caïetæ recto fert litore portum.
Anchora de prorâ jacitur: stant litore puppes.

888. Per quæ singula, postquam Anchises duxit natum

895. Altera nitens perfecta *est è* candenti elephanto; sed *per hanc* Manes mittunt

NOTES.

882. *Aspera:* in the sense of *dura*, vel *crudelia*. *Plenis manibus:* in full hands.

883. *Marcellus eris.* On hearing this line, it is said, Octavia fainted. The encomium which the poet passes upon this noble youth is esteemed one of the finest passages of the Æneid. Augustus was so much pleased with it when he heard Virgil read it, that he ordered a present to be given him of ten *sestertia* for every line, which is about seventy-eight pounds sterling.

886. *Munere:* Ruæus says *officio*.

887. *Latis campis aëris.* By this we are to understand the Elysian fields, so called; *quia vacuum, et inanibus umbris habitatum; vel quia situm in aëreis pratis*, says Ruæus. Heyne takes the words simply in the sense of *locis caliginosis*.

888. *Per quæ:* through all which things. *Singula:* properly, all taken separately and singly—all one by one. *Venientis:* in the sense of *futuræ*.

890. *Viro:* Æneas. *Exin:* (for *exinde*:) in the sense of *tunc*.

891. *Laurentes.* See Æn. vii. 63.

893. *Geminæ portæ.* This fiction is borrowed from the Odyss. lib. 19. The most probable conjecture why true dreams are said to pass through the horn gate, and false ones through the ivory gate, is, that horn is a fit emblem of truth, as being transparent and pervious to the sight, whereas ivory is impervious and impenetrable to it.

894. *Umbris.* Heyne takes this in the sense of *somniis*. Ruæus says *figuris*.

895. *Perfecta:* in the sense of *facta est*.

896. *Manes:* here the infernal gods. *Ad cœlum:* in the sense of *ad homines*, vel *ad superas auras*.

897. *Ubi.* This is the common reading. Some copies have *ibi*. The sense is the same with either.

898. *Prosequitur Anchises:* Anchises accompanies Æneas and the Sibyl through the various parts of the infernal regions, and *discourses with them* as they pass along, till they arrive at the ivory gate, through which he dismisses them. Servius thinks that Virgil, by telling us that Æneas passed through the ivory gate, would have us believe all he had been here saying was fiction. But it is hardly to be imagined that so judicious a poet, by one dash of his pen would destroy the many fine compliments he had paid his prince and the whole Roman people, by informing them the whole was false. Mr. Davidson conjectures that Virgil had in view the Platonic philosophy. By emitting his hero through the ivory gate, through which lying dreams ascend to the earth, he might mean that thus far he had been admitted to see the naked truth—had the true system of nature laid open to his view, and the secrets of futurity unveiled; but henceforth he was returning to his former state of darkness, ignorance, and error; and therefore he is sent forth from those regions of light and truth by the ivory gate, in company with lying dreams and mere shadows, which are to attend him through life. But, on the whole, as the poet hath concealed from us the reason of his hero's passing through the ivory gate, after all our conjectures on the subject, we may be as far as ever from the truth. *Prosequitur:* in the sense of *alloquitur*.

900. *Fert se ad portum:* he takes himself along the shore direct to the port, &c. *Caïeta*

was a promontory and town of the *Ausones* (*hodie*, *Gaëta*) a name derived from the nurse of Æneas, who died there. Some derive it from a Greek word, which signifies *to burn*, because the fleet of Æneas was here burnt by the Trojan women, as some authors say. *Litore:* this is the common reading, but Heyne reads *limite* in the sense of *via*, vel *itinere*.

QUESTIONS.

Is this one of the books which Virgil read in the presence of Augustus and Octavia?

What is the subject of it?

What is the nature of it?

What, probably, suggested to the poet this fine episode?

Can you mention any others who, according to the poets, visited those regions?

What, probably, was the object of the poet in conducting his hero thither?

In what light does bishop Warburton consider this book?

Were these mysteries in great repute at one time in Greece?

Is there no difficulty in this interpretation?

What are the principal difficulties?

Is it certain that Virgil was ever initiated into those mysteries?

If he had been acquainted with them, is it probable he would have divulged them?

What does Heyne say upon this subject?

At what place in Italy did Æneas land?

Who founded the city of *Cumæ?*

What celebrated temple was there?

By whom was it built?

Who was Dædalus?

What is said of him?

Was there any curiously carved work upon the doors of this temple?

What was this sculpture designed to represent?

What was the residence of the Sibyl?

By whose inspiration did she give prophetic responses?

What direction did she give Æneas in regard to his descent to the regions below?

Where was this golden bough to be found?

In what way did he find it?

To whom was the bough considered sacred?

Where does the poet represent the entrance to those regions?

What did Æneas and his guide do immediately preceding their descent?

What is the lake *Avernus* properly?

Why was that thought to give admission to the regions of the dead?

From what circumstance did it receive the name of *Avernus?*

What is its Greek name?

According to the poets, how many rivers watered the realms of Pluto?

What were their names?

Which one was said to flow around them nine times?

Why did the gods swear by the river Styx?

If they violated their oath, what was the penalty?

Who was Charon?

What was his employment?

From what historical fact is this fable supposed to be derived?

On the approach of Æneas, what did the ferryman do?

What effect had the sight of the golden bough upon him?

What punishment had he received for carrying over Hercules?

Who was said to be the door keeper of Pluto's realms?

How many heads had Cerberus?

What did Hercules do to him?

What did the Sibyl do that he might permit them to pass?

How many were represented as judges of the dead?

What were their names?

Who was Minos?

Who Radamanthus?

Who Æacus?

Why were they made judges of the dead?

How was Minos employed, when Æneas visited his court?

As he passed along, and viewed the various apartments, did he see Dido?

What effect had the sight of her upon him?

What is the nature of his address to her?

What effect had it upon her?

Did Dido leave him abruptly?

Where did she go?

What passage of the Odyssey had Virgil here in view?

What was the conduct of Ajax?

What does Longinus say of his silence?

After this, to what place did he go?

What was his object in visiting the court of Pluto?

Where did he see the place of punishment?

What was the name of that place?

What river surrounded it?

What is the meaning of the word *Phlegethon?*

From what language is it derived?

From the palace of Pluto, where then did Æneas and the Sibyl go?

Whom did they meet in the way?

What was the employment of Orpheus?

What poet was distinguished above all the rest?

Why was no mention made of Homer?

Who was Musæus?

When did he flourish?

Are there any fragments of his poems extant?

What information did Musæus give them?
Where did they find Anchises?
In what part of the regions below?
How was Anchises engaged at that time?
Was he expecting the arrival of his son?
What was the nature of their meeting?
Anchises explained to Æneas the system of the world upon the Pythagorean and Platonic philosophy: what were some of the leading points of that philosophy?
Had this philosophy many advocates?
Who was the inventor of the doctrine of transmigration?
What were some of its leading principles?
According to the principles of that philosophy, Anchises points out to his son a list of distinguished men who were to descend from him: can you mention some of their names?
Whom does he specially mention?
Was Augustus highly pleased with any part of this book?
What part was that?
Is it said that Octavia fainted at the mention of Marcellus?
Who was this Marcellus?
What did Augustus order to be given Virgil for each line of that *eulogium?*
To how much would that amount in sterling money?
What leading doctrine of religion and morality does the poet here inculcate?
Are the punishments here inflicted in proportion to the offence?
Is that a principle founded in reason and justice?
How long was the time assigned for a visit to the regions below?
Through which gate did Æneas ascend to the upper regions?
How many gates were there?
What is the most probable reason that can be given for his ascent through the ivory gate?

LIBER SEPTIMUS.

FROM Caïata, or Cajeta, Æneas pursues his course westward, and arrives in the Tiber, in the kingdom of *Latium;* where he was kindly entertained by Latinus, then advanced in age. He had an only daughter, the heiress of his crown, then young and beautiful. Many of the neighboring princes sought her in marriage; among whom was Turnus, king of the *Rutuli*, every way worthy of her; and whose addresses were pleasing to her mother Amata. For several reasons, however, her father was opposed to the match; particularly, on account of the responses of the oracle of *Faunus.* From this he learned that a foreigner was destined to be his son-in-law. He conceived Æneas to be the person pointed out by the oracle, and accordingly proposed to him a match with his daughter. In the mean time, Juno, displeased at the friendly reception of the Trojans, and especially at the proposal of the king, set about to frustrate it. For this purpose, she called Alecto from below. Through her means Turnus is roused to arms, and a skirmish brought about between some Latin shepherds and rustics on one side, and the Trojans on the other; in which Almon, the eldest son of Tyrrhus, the royal herdsman, was slain. This kindles the war. Both Turnus and the Latins repair to the palace of the king, and urge him to an immediate declaration of war. The aged monarch resists their importunity. In this state, things remain, till Juno descends from above, and opens the brazen doors. The report is soon spread abroad that war is begun. The neighboring nations join Turnus, and make a common cause of the war. The poet concludes by giving us an account of the auxiliaries, and their respective leaders. Throughout the whole, he has displayed a great degree of taste and judgment. In these six last books, the poet has imitated the Iliad of Homer.

A celebrated critic, Valpy observes, accuses Virgil of losing, instead of increasing, in interest, in these books. The Trojan and Greek heroes, whose names have been familiar with us from infancy, disappear; and we are introduced to personages of whom we have not before heard; and whose names do not appear elsewhere either in fable or history. But he does not consider, in making his charge, that the poet wrote for his own countrymen, and not for us. The adventures of Æneas in Italy, little as we may be interested in them, relate to the supposed ancestors of the Romans, to their domestic history, and to the foundation of their empire. The narration must, therefore, have then excited emotions in which we do not partake; and caused an interest in them, to which we, as we are situated, and at this distance of time, are strangers.

TU quoque litoribus nostris, Æneïa nutrix,
Æternam moriens famam, Caïeta, dedisti:
Et nunc servat honos sedem tuus; ossaque nomen
Hesperiâ in magnâ, si qua est ea gloria, signat.
At pius exsequiis Æneas ritè solutis,
Aggere composito tumuli, postquam alta quiêrunt
Æquora, tendit iter velis, portumque relinquit.
Aspirant auræ in noctem: nec candida cursum
Luna negat: splendet tremulo sub lumine pontus.
Proxima Circææ raduntur litora terræ;
Dives inaccessos ubi Solis filia lucos
Assiduo resonat cantu, tectisque superbis
Urit odoratam nocturna in lumina cedrum,
Arguto tenues percurrens pectine telas.
Hinc exaudiri gemitus, iræque leonum
Vincla recusantûm, et serâ sub nocte rudentûm:
Setigerique sues, atque in præsepibus ursi
Sævire, ac formæ magnorum ululare luporum:
Quos hominum ex facie Dea sæva potentibus herbis
Induerat Circe in vultus ac terga ferarum.
Quæ ne monstra pii paterentur talia Troës
Delati in portus, neu litora dira subirent,

3. Nomen tuum signat ossa in magna

15. Hinc gemitus *cœperunt* exaudiri

17. Setigerique sues, atque ursi *auditi* sævire

19. Quos sæva Dea Circe induerat

NOTES.

1. *Tu quoque.* This refers to what he had told us in the preceding book, verse 232, *et sequens*, of the monument erected to the memory of *Misenus*, on the Italian coast. Thou, also, O Cajeta, didst give, &c.

3. *Tuus honos.* Some consider this an hypallage, for *sedes servat tuum honorem:* the place preserves thy honor. But perhaps her name may be considered a kind of guardian to the place. In this sense, there is no need of any figure. The words may be taken as they stand: thy honor, or fame, protects the place. This is the better and more poetical. *Sedem:* in the sense of *locum. Ossa:* in the sense of *sepulchrum.* There is a promontory and city in this part of Italy, by the name of Cajeta, or *Gaëta.*

6. *Aggere tumuli composito:* a tomb being erected. The earth heaped up over the corpse or ashes of the dead, was called *agger tumuli.*

8. *Auræ aspirant.* Dr. Trapp observes that, down to the 18th line, is, beyond expression, elegant and affecting. A funeral had been just performed. They sail in the still night by the light of the moon. They pass along an enchanted coast, whence they hear the roaring of lions, and other beasts of prey. Upon the four last lines he passes the highest encomium. *Candida.* As the sun, from his flaming brightness, is called *aureus*, golden; so the moon, from her paler light, is called *candida*, white or silvered.

10. *Circææ:* an adj. from *Circe*, a celebrated sorceress, the daughter of *Sol*, and the nymph *Perse.* She was the sister of Æetes, king of Colchis, the father of the famous *Medea.* Some say she was the sister of Medea. She was called *Ææa*, from *Æa*, an island and city of Colchis, near the mouth of the river Phasis. It is said she married a king of the Sarmatians, whom she killed with her poisons; after which she fled to Italy to the promontory and mountain which, from her, is called *Circæus: hodie*, *Circello.*

12. *Resonat inaccessos lucos:* she makes the inaccessible groves resound with her continual song. Not absolutely inaccessible; for Ulysses and his company landed here-- but difficult of access.

14. *Arguto pectine:* the shrill sounding shuttle.

15. *Iræ:* the rage—fury.

18. *Formæ magnorum luporum:* simply, the great wolves.

19. *Quos ex facie hominum:* whom the cruel goddess Circe had changed from the shape of men, into the apperance and form (*terga*) of wild beasts, &c. *Induerat* is evidently to be taken in the sense of *mutaverat. Terga:* the backs, by synec. for the whole bodies.

The fable of Circe is taken from the Odyssey, lib. 10. where Homer informs us that the followers of Ulysses were changed into swine. He alone was preserved by the aid of Mercury, and the eating of the herb *moly.* At his request, however, they were restored to their former shapes. Beside poisonous herbs, she made use of a magical wand, with which she touched them.

21. *Quæ talia monstra:* any such monstrous changes—shapes—forms.

Neptunus ventis implevit vela secundis,
Atque fugam dedit, et præter vada fervida vexit.
Jamque rubescebat radiis mare, et æthere ab alto
Aurora in roseis fulgebat lutea bigis:
Cùm venti posuere, omnisque repentè resedit
Flatus, et in lento luctantur marmore tonsæ.
Atque hìc Æneas ingentem ex æquore lucum
Prospicit: hunc inter fluvio Tiberinus amœno,
Vorticibus rapidis et multâ flavus arenâ,
In mare prorumpit. Variæ circùmque supràque
Assuetæ ripis volucres et fluminis alveo,
Æthera mulcebant cantu, lucoque volabant.
Flectere iter sociis, terræque advertere proras
Imperat: et lætus fluvio succedit opaco.
Nunc age, qui reges, Erato, quæ tempora, rerum
Quis Latio antiquo fuerit status, advena classem
Cùm primùm Ausoniis exercitus appulit oris,
Expediam: et primæ revocabo exordia pugnæ.
Tu vatem, tu, Diva, mone. Dicam horrida bella,
Dicam acies, actosque animis in funera reges,
Tyrrhenamque manum, totamque sub arma coactam
Hesperiam. Major rerum mihi nascitur ordo:
Majus opus moveo. Rex arva Latinus et urbes
Jam senior longâ placidas in pace regebat.
Hunc Fauno et Nymphâ genitum Laurente Maricâ

37. Nunc age, O Erato expediam qui reges, quæ tempora, quis status rerum fuerit

47. Accipimus hunc genitum *esse* Fauno, et Maricâ Laurente Nymphâ.. Picus *erat* pater

NOTES.

26. *Bigis.* Aurora is represented by the poets as drawn in a chariot of two horses. *Lutea:* an adj. from *lutum*, an herb with which yellow or saffron color is dyed. The poet, here, has given a charming description of the morning.

27. *Posuere:* in the sense of *quieverunt.*

28. *Tonsæ:* the oars labor in the smooth surface of the sea. *Tonsa*, properly, the blade of the oar. Dr. Trapp takes *lento*, to denote here yielding or giving way to the oar. *Marmore:* the sea unruffled by the wind.

30. *Tiberinus inter hunc:* through this grove, with its pleasant streams and rapid course, (whirls,) yellow with much sand, &c. Some take Tiberinus, not for the river itself, but for the god of the river. In this case it may be rendered Tiberinus, god of the pleasant river, in rapid whirls, &c. The prep. *è*, or *ex*, being understood. The Tiber is, next to the Po, the largest river in Italy. It rises in the Appennines, and running in a southern direction, dividing Latium from Etruria or Tuscany, falls into the sea by two mouths. Its original name, we are told, was *Albula.* It took its present name from a Tuscan king, who was killed near it. But Livy says it took its name from *Tiberinus*, a king of the Albans, who was drowned in it.

34. *Mulcebant æthera:* they charmed the air with their song. This is highly poetical. The air, calm and still, is represented as listening to the music of the birds that were flying in all directions about the river, and being charmed with their melody. Indeed the whole is extremely beautiful, and cannot be too much admired. It would appear from this, that Æneas arrived in the Tiber about the middle of the spring, when the birds are most lively and musical.

37. *Erato:* the muse that presides over love affairs. She is invoked because the following wars were in consequence of the love of Turnus and Æneas for Lavinia. It is derived from the Greek. *Rerum.* Most commentators connect *rerum* with *tempora;* but it is evident its place is after *status:* what state of things there was in Latium, when first a foreign army arrived on the Italian shores. Heyne connects it with *tempora:* Davidson with *status.*

42. *Animis:* in the sense of *ira.*

43. *Manum:* troops—forces.

45. *Latinus.* Virgil places Latinus only three generations from Saturn. *Faunus*, *Picus*, then *Saturn.* Others place him at the distance of nine. His origin is much obscured. Dionysius of Halicarnassus, agrees with Virgil, that, when Æneas arrived in Italy, Latinus reigned in *Latium*—that he had no male issue; but an only daughter, whom Æneas married. *Arva:* the country *Placidas:* in the sense of *quietas.*

Accipimus. Fauno Picus pater : ipse parentem
Te, Saturne, refert : tu sanguinis ultimus auctor.

50. Fuit *nullus* filius huic *Latino* fato Deorum, nulla virilis proles: *quæque* oriens

Filius huic, fato Divûm, prolesque virilis
Nulla fuit : primâque oriens erepta juventâ est.
Sola domum et tantas servabat filia sedes ;
Jam matura viro, jam plenis nubilis annis.
Multi illam magno è Latio totâque petebant
Ausoniâ. Petit ante alios pulcherrimus omnes

56. Quem regia conjux *Amata* properabat miro amore adjungi generum *sibi*

Turnus, avis atavisque potens : quem regia conjux
Adjungi generum miro properabat amore
Sed variis portenta Deûm terroribus obstant.
Laurus erat tecti medio, in penetralibus altis,
Sacra comam, multosque metu servata per annos :

61. Quam inventam, pater Latinus ipse ferebatur sacrâsse Phœbo, cum

64. Densæ apes, vectæ ingenti stridore trans liquidum æthera obsedêre summum apicem hujus *arboris.*

Quam pater inventam, primas cùm conderet arces,
Ipse ferebatur Phœbo sacrâsse Latinus ;
Laurentisque ab eâ nomen posuisse colonis.
Hujus apes summum densæ, mirabile dictu !
Stridore ingenti liquidum trans æthera vectæ,
Obsedêre apicem : et, pedibus per mutua nexis,
Examen subitum ramo frondente pependit.
Continuò vates, Externum cernimus, inquit,
Adventare virum, et partes petere agmen easdem
Partibus ex îsdem, et summâ dominarier arce.

NOTES.

48. *Accipimus:* in the sense of *audimus.*

49. *Ultimus auctor :* the first or remotest founder of our race. *Ultimus*, ascending, is the same with *primus*, descending. *Refert:* in the sense of *habet.*

50. *Filius huic.* It is evident that Latinus had, in the course of his life, male issue ; but at that time he had none. It is not said whether he had one, two, or more sons; and we have a right to suppose either. I have supposed that he had, in the course of his life, several, and accordingly have inserted the word *quæque*, before *oriens : quæque oriens:* every one growing up was snatched away in early life.

52. *Filia sola servabat.* By this we are to understand, that his daughter *alone* preserved his family from extinction, and his kingdom from passing into the hands of others: or that she alone was the heiress of his crown and kingdom—*tantas sedes. Totam regionem*, says Ruæus.

56. *Potens avis atavisque :* powerful (in grandfathers and great grandfathers) in his ancestors. The queen was taken with such an illustrious match for her daughter; and accordingly urged, with great importunity, that Turnus should be received into the family as their son-in-law. *Amore :* Ruæus says, *studio.*

59. *Penetralibus.* The interior of a house or palace, though not roofed, may be called *penetrale.* Such must have been the palace of Latinus; otherwise a stately laurel could not have grown in that place.

60. *Servata metu :* preserved with religious awe and veneration. *Sacra comam :* a Grecism.

63. *Laurentis colonis.* The name *Laurens* was originally given to a grove of laurel, near the shore of the Tuscan sea, extending to the east of the Tiber. Hence the neighboring country was called *Laurens.* Also, the nymph *Marica*, the wife of *Faunus*, and mother of *Latinus*, was called *Laurens.* Turnus, too, is called *Laurens*, from the circumstance of this grove bordering upon his dominions. It appears that Latinus only raised fortifications, and embellished the city, which must have been built before; for we are told that his father Picus had erected here a noble palace ; see 171. The city, after the time of Latinus, was called *Laurentum*, from a very large laurel growing on the spot where he founded the tower. This however, was the common name of the whole neighboring country, from the grove above mentioned. The inhabitants were called *Laurentes—Laurentini—Laurentii et Laurenti.*

64. *Densæ apes :* a thick swarm of bees.

66. *Per mutua :* taken adverbially. Their feet being mutually joined or linked together.

68. *Cernimus :* we see a foreigner approach, and an army seek those parts, which the bees sought, from the same parts from which they came.

70. *Dominarier :* by paragoge, for *dominari :* to rule—bear sway.

Prætereà castis adolet dum altaria tædis;
Ut juxta genitorem adstat Lavinia virgo,
Visa, nefas! longis comprêndere crinibus ignem,
Atque omnem ornatum flammâ crepitante cremari:
Regalesque accensa comas, accensa coronam
Insignem gemmis: tum fumida lumine fulvo
Involvi, ac totis Vulcanum spargere tectis.
Id verò horrendum ac visu mirabile ferri.
Namque fore illustrem famâ fatisque canebant
Ipsam, sed populo magnum portendere bellum.
At rex sollicitus monstris, oracula Fauni
Fatidici genitoris, adit; lucosque sub altâ
Consulit Albuneâ; nemorum quæ maxima sacro
Fonte sonat, sævamque exhalat opaca mephitim.
Hinc Italæ gentes, omnisque Œnotria tellus
In dubiis responsa petunt: huc dona sacerdos
Cùm tulit, et cæsarum ovium sub nocte silenti
Pellibus incubuit stratis, somnosque petivit:
Multa modis simulacra videt volitantia miris,
Et varias audit voces, fruiturque Deorum
Colloquio, atque imis Acheronta affatur Avernis.
Hìc et tum pater ipse petens responsa Latinus;
Centum lanigeras mactabat ritè bidentes;
Atque harum effultus tergo stratisque jacebat
Velleribus. Subita ex alto vox reddita luco est:
Ne pete connubiis natam sociare Latinis,
O mea progenies: thalamis neu crede paratis.
Externi veniunt generi, qui sanguine nostrum
Nomen in astra ferent; quorumque à stirpe nepotes,

73. Visa *est*, O nefas! comprêndere ignem longis crinibus

75. *Visa est* accensa *quoad* regales comas, accensa *quoad*

76. Tum fumida *visa est* involvi

79. Namque *vates* canebant *Laviniam* ipsam fore

NOTES.

71. *Dum adolet altaria:* while he kindles the altar with holy torches, &c. Some connect *adolet* with Lavinia, and understand her to have set fire to the altars. But it is evidently better to understand this of the father, his daughter standing near him. *Castis:* in the sense of *puris* vel *sacris*.

72. *Ut: et* is the common reading.—Heyne reads *ut*, which makes the sense easier.

76. *Fulvo.* Ruæus takes this in the sense of *rutilanti*.

77. *Vulcanum:* in the sense of *flammam* vel *ignem*.

78. *Id verò*, &c. This line is capable of a double meaning, according to the sense given to *ferri*. If it be taken in its usual sense, it will be: this terrible thing, and wonderful to the sight, (began) to be spread abroad. If it be taken in the sense of *haberi*, it will be: this thing (began) to be considered terrible and wonderful to the sight. This is the sense given both by Ruæus and Davidson. Dr. Trapp favors the former.

79. *Fatis. Fatum*, here, is in the sense of *fortuna*. *Canebant:* in the sense of *prædicebant*.

81. *Monstris:* at the prodigies, or wonderful signs. *Monstrum*, any thing that is contrary to the ordinary course of nature. *Fatidici:* prophetic.

82. *Consulit:* he consults the grove under lofty Albuna. This was a fountain from which flowed the river *Albula*. Its waters were very deeply impregnated with sulphur. It was surrounded with a very gross and putrid atmosphere, which the poet calls *sævam mephitim*. Here was a grove sacred to Faunus.

85. *Œnotria tellus:* Italy. See Æn. i. 530.

91. *Affatur Acheronta:* converses with the infernal powers in deep Avernus. *Acheronta:* acc. sing. of Greek formation. *Acheron*, by the poets, is made one of the rivers of hell. Here it is evidently used for the infernal gods.

94. *Atque jacebat:* and lay, supported by their skins and outspread fleeces—he lay down upon them.

97. *Paratis.* This alludes to the contemplated match with Turnus. *Thalamis:* in the sense of *nuptiis*.

99. *Quorumque stirpe:* descending from

Omnia sub pedibus, quà Sol utrumque recurrens
Aspicit Oceanum, vertique regique videbunt.
Hæc responsa patris Fauni, monitusque silenti
Nocte datos, non ipse suo premit ore Latinus ;
Sed circùm latè volitans jam fama per urbes
Ausonias tulerat ; cùm Laomedontia pubes
Gramineo ripæ religavit ab aggere classem.
  Æneas, primique duces, et pulcher Iülus,
Corpora sub ramis deponunt arboris altæ :
Instituuntque dapes, et adorea liba per herbam
Subjiciunt epulis (sic Jupiter ille monebat)
Et Cereale solum pomis agrestibus augent.
Consumptis hìc fortè aliis, ut vertere morsus
Exiguam in Cererem penuria adegit edendi ;
Et violare manu, malisque audacibus orbem
Fatalis crusti, patulis nec parcere quadris :
Heus ! etiam mensas consumimus, inquit Iülus.
Nec plura, alludens. Ea vox audita laborum
Prima tulit finem : primamque loquentis ab ore
Eripuit pater, ac stupefactus numine pressit.
Continuò, Salve, fatis mihi debita tellus ;
Vosque, ait, ô fidi Trojæ, salvete Penates.
Hìc domus, hæc patria est. Genitor mihi talia, namque
Nunc repeto, Anchises fatorum arcana reliquit :
Cùm te, nate, fames ignota ad litora vectum
Accisis coget dapibus consumere mensas ;

103. Latinus ipse non premit suo ore hæc responsa

112. Hìc fortè aliis *cibis* consumptis, ut penuria edendi

117. Nec *dixit* plura *verba*

119. Paterque eripuit *eam* primam ab ore *filii* loquentis

124. *Dicens*, *O* nate, cùm fames coget te vectum

NOTES.

whose stock, our posterity shall see all things reduced, &c. This alludes to the extent of the Roman empire, which, in the height of its greatness, embraced the greater part of the then known world. It ruled the subject nations with a rod of iron.

105. *Laomedontia pubes :* the Trojan youth ; so called from Laomedon, one of the kings of Troy. *Tulerat :* spread them abroad.

106. *Religavit :* moored.

110. *Subjiciunt :* they place along the grass wheaten cakes under their meat. They use them in the room of plates or trenchers.

111. *Solum :* any thing placed under another to support it, may be called *solum. Cereale solum*, therefore, must be those wheaten cakes which they used on this occasion as plates. *Augent :* they load them with, &c.

112. *Morsus :* in the sense of *dentes.*

113. *Ut penuria edendi :* when want of other provisions forced them to turn their teeth upon the small cake, &c. *Edendi :* in the sense of *cibi.*

114. *Violare.* The eating tables among the ancients were considered sacred. They were a kind of altar, on which libations were made to the gods, both before and after meals. To destroy them was considered a kind of sacrilege or violence. *Orbem fatalis crusti.* By this we are to understand the cake or trencher—*the orb of the ominous cake. Fatalis* is not to be understood in the sense of *fatal* in English, but rather as importing some great event, or something destined and ordered by fate. *Patulis quadris :* the broad or large quadrants. These cakes were divided by two lines, crossing each other in the centre, and dividing each cake into four equal parts, called quadrants. *Audacibus malis :* with greedy or hungry jaws.

117. *Alludens :* joking—smiling.

119. *Stupefactus numine pressit.* The prophetic Celæno (Æn. iii. 257.) had foretold that the Trojans should be reduced to such extremity as to consume their tables before they could expect an end to their wanderings. By *numine* we are to understand the solution or fulfilment of this prophecy, or divine purpose. *Pressit* does not refer to the words of Ascanius, as Servius supposes, but to Æneas. The prophecy had been wrapped up in mystery till the present moment. The solution of it was a matter of surprise and joy. It excited a degree of wonder and admiration, and caused him to pause a while upon the subject. *Pressit :* he kept silence. *Vocem* is understood.

123. *Repeto :* I recollect—I call to memory. *Memoriam* is understood.

125. *Dapibus accisis :* your provisions having failed—being consumed

Tum sperare domos defessus, ibique memento
Prima locare manu, molirique aggere tecta.
Hæc erat illa fames: hæc nos suprema manebant,
Exitiis positura modum.
Quare agite, et primo læti cum lumine solis,
Quæ loca, quive habeant homines, ubi mœnia gentis,
Vestigemus; et à portu diversa petamus
Nunc pateras libate Jovi, precibusque vocate
Anchisen genitorem, et vina reponite mensis.
Sic deinde effatus, frondenti tempora ramo
Implicat, et, Geniumque loci, primamque Deorum
Tellurem, Nymphasque, et adhuc ignota precatur
Flumina: tum Noctem, noctisque orientia signa,
Idæumque Jovem, Phrygiamque ex ordine matrem
Invocat; et duplices cœloque Ereboque parentes.
Hìc pater omnipotens ter cœlo clarus ab alto
Intonuit, radiisque ardentem lucis et auro
Ipse manu quatiens ostendit ab æthere nubem.
Diditur hìc subitò Trojana per agmina rumor,
Advenisse diem, quo debita mœnia condant.
Certatim instaurant epulas, atque omine magno
Crateras læti statuunt, et vina coronant.
Postera cùm primâ lustrabat lampade terras
Orta dies; urbem, et fines, et litora gentis
Diversi explorant: hæc fontis stagna Numici,
Hunc Tybrim fluvium, hìc fortes habitare Latinos.
Tum satus Anchisâ delectos ordine ab omni
Centum oratores augusta ad mœnia regis
Ire jubet, ramis velatos Palladis omnes:
Donaque ferre viro, pacemque exposcere Teucris.
Haud mora: festinant jussi, rapidisque feruntur
Passibus. Ipse humili designat mœnia fossâ,

130. *Nos* læti vestigemus, quæ *sint hæc* loca, qui-ve homines habeant *ea;* ubi *sint* mœnia gentis; et petamus diversa *loca* à portu.

142. Ipseque ostendit ab æthere nubem ardentem radiis lucis et auro, quatiens *eam* manu.

150. *Discunt* hæc *esse* stagna fontis Numici, hunc *esse*

152. Jubet centum oratores delectos ab omni ordine ire

NOTES.

129. *Modum:* bounds—end. *Exitiis:* to our woes—calamities.

133. *Pateras:* the bowls, by meton. put for the wine in them.

136. *Primam Deorum.* According to Hesiod, *Tellus*, or Terra, was reckoned the first of the gods except *Chaos. Implicat:* in the sense of *cingit.*

138. *Noctem.* This goddess sprang from Chaos, according to Hesiod. Æneas *invokes* her, fearing, perhaps, during the darkness, some mischief from the natives.

139. *Idæum:* an adj. from *Ida*, a mountain in Crete, where Jupiter was brought up. *Phrygiam matrem:* Cybele.

140. *Duplices parentes:* both his parents, *Venus* and *Anchises;* the former in heaven, the latter in Elysium; at least his *idolum*, or *simulacrum.*

141. *Clarus:* may mean loud—shrill; or perhaps it may imply that the sky was clear, which was considered a good omen.

142. *Radiis lucis et auro.* This is for *aureis radiis lucis*, by hend. the golden beams of light.

144. *Diditur:* is spread abroad.

145. *Debita:* in the sense of *destinata.*

148. *Lampade:* in the sense of *luce.*

150. *Stagna fontis:* the streams of the fountain *Numicus.* This was a small river, or stream, flowing between Laurentum and Ardea. *Diversi:* they in different directions.

154. *Ramis Palladis:* with the boughs of Pallas—with the olive. The olive was sacred to Minerva, and the badge of peace. *Velatos: coronatos*, says Ruæus.

157. *Ipse designat:* he himself, in the mean time, marks out his city with a low furrow, and prepares the place for building. This city of Æneas was situated on the east bank of the Tiber, a little above the sea. He called the name of it Troy. In after times, Ancus Martius, a king of the Romans, founded here a city, which he called *Ostia*, from its vicinity to the *mouth* of the Tiber. See Æn. v. 755.

158. Cingitque primas sedes in litore pennis atque aggere
160. Jamque juvines emensi iter cernebant

169. Medius suorum civium.

174. Hoc templum *erat* illis curia; hæ sedes *destinatæ erant* sacris epulis.
177. Effigies veterum avorum e cedro antiqua adstabant vestibulo, *positæ* ex ordine

Moliturque locum; primasque in litore sedes,
Castrorum in morem, pinnis atque aggere cingit
Jamque iter emensi, turres ac tecta Latinorum
Ardua cernebant juvenes, muroque subibant.
Ante urbem pueri, et primævo flore juventus
Exercentur equis, domitantque in pulvere currus.
Aut acres tendunt arcus, aut lenta lacertis
Spicula contorquent, cursuque ictuque lacessunt.
Cùm prævectus equo longævi regis ad aures
Nuntius ingentes ignotâ in veste reportat
Advenisse viros. Ille intra tecta vocari
Imperat, et solio medius consedit avito.
Tectum augustum, ingens, centum sublime columnis,
Urbe fuit summâ, Laurentis regia Pici,
Horrendum sylvis et religione parentum.
Hinc sceptra accipere, et primos attollere fasces
Regibus omen erat: hoc illis curia templum,
Hæ sacris sedes epulis: hìc ariete cæso
Perpetuis soliti patres considere mensis.
Quin etiam veterum effigies ex ordine avorum

NOTES.

159. *Cingitque primas:* and he incloses his first settlement on the shore with a rampart, and a mound, &c. The *pinnæ* originally were the tufts or crests on the soldier's helmet. Hence they came to be applied to the turrets and battlements in fortifications.

160. *Emensi iter:* having completed their journey to the city of Latinus.

163. *Domitant:* they break the harnessed steeds in the dusty plain. *Currus* is properly a chariot: by meton. the horses harnessed in it.

164. *Acres arcus:* elastic bows. *Lenta:* tough—rigid—not easily bent.

165. *Lacessunt:* they challenge one another at the race, and missive weapon. La Cerda understands by *cursu* the throwing of the javelin as they ran forward: and by *ictu*, the shooting of the arrow. But it is better to take *cursu* for the races and other exercises on horseback and in the chariot, and *ictu* for the shooting of the arrow and throwing of the javelin.

167. *Nuntius prævectus:* a messenger on horseback relates, &c.

169. *Avito solio:* on the throne of his ancestors.

170. *Tectum augustum:* a building, &c. put in apposition with *regia*.

171. *Regia Laurentis Pici.* This magnificent palace was erected by Picus, the father of Latinus. It was situated on the highest ground or part of the city, and supported by a hundred columns. *Horrendum:* awful by its sacred groves, and the religion of their ancestors. By *religione*, Mr. Davidson understands the religious monuments, images, groves, &c. that had been consecrated by the founders of the family; some of which are mentioned. *Sublime:* high—raised high upon, &c.

173. *Primos fasces:* the first badges of authority—the first ensigns of power: by meton. the first power.

174. *Omen erat regibus.* Ruæus and Dr. Trapp take *omen* in the sense of *initium*. Davidson takes *omen* in the sense of *mos*, a custom or practice; but one on which they laid a religious stress, and on which they imagined the prosperity of their kings, in a degree, to depend; and had they been consecrated in any other place, they would have considered it deficient and imperfect. Valpy is of the same opinion with Davidson. *Hoc templum.* In this noble structure, it appears there was one part for religious purposes, another for the senate, and a third for sacred banquets.

175. *Ariete cæso:* in the sense of *victimâ cæsa:* sacrifice being offered.

176. *Considere perpetuis.* The most ancient posture at table was sitting; afterward luxury introduced that of reclining on couches. *Perpetuæ mensæ*, were tables that extended from one end of the hall to the other.

177. *Quin etiam effigies:* moreover the statues of their ancestors of ancient cedar stood in the vestibule arranged in order, &c Ruæus and Heyne connect *Vitisator* with *pater Sabinus*, which appears incorrect; for the planting of the vine in Italy is ascribed to Saturn by most authors; and the scythe was the well known symbol of that god. La Cerda makes a full stop after *Sabinus*, which is unnecessary and improper.

Antiquâ è cedro, Italusque, paterque Sabinus,
Vitisator, curvam servans sub imagine falcem,
Saturnusque senex, Janique bifrontis imago,
Vestibulo adstabant: aliique ab origine reges,
Martia qui ob patriam pugnando vulnera passi.
Multaque præterea sacris in postibus arma,
Captivi pendent currus, curvæque secures,
Et cristæ capitum, et portarum ingentia claustra,
Spiculaque, clypeique, ereptaque rostra carinis.
Ipse Quirinali lituo parvâque sedebat
Succinctus trabeâ, lævâque ancile gerebat
Picus, equûm domitor; quem capta cupidine conjux
Aureâ percussum virgâ, versumque venenis,
Fecit avem Circe, sparsitque coloribus alas.
Tali intus templo Divûm, patriâque Latinus
Sede, sedens, Teucros ad sese in tecta vocavit:
Atque hæc ingressis placido prior edidit ore:
Dicite, Dardanidæ; neque enim nescimus et urbem,
Et genus, auditique advertitis æquore cursum;
Quid petitis? quæ causa rates, aut cujus egentes,
Litus ad Ausonium tot per vada cœrula vexit?
Sive errore viæ, seu tempestatibus acti,
(Qualia multa mari nautæ patiuntur in alto)
Fluminis intrâstis ripas, portuque sedetis:
Ne fugite hospitium; neve ignorate Latinos
Saturni gentem, haud vinclo nec legibus æquam,
Sponte suâ, veterisque Dei se more tenentem.
Atque equidem memini (fama est obscurior annis)

181. Aliique reges ab origine *gentis*, qui passi *sunt*.

187. Picus ipse, domitor equûm sedebat *cum* Quirinali lituo, succinctusque

189. Quem percussum aurea virgâ, versumque venenis conjux Circe, capta cupidine *ejus*, fecit avem

194. *Illis* ingressis

196. *Vos*que auditi advertitis cursum *huc* æquore.

197. Quæ causa vexit rates *vestras* ad Ausonium litus per tot cærula vada, aut egentes cujus *rei advenistis huc*? sive acti errore viæ

204. *Sed* suâ sponte.

NOTES.

178. *Antiqua:* may here mean durable—lasting. It is the quality of cedar not to decay. *Italus:* a king of Sicily, who extended his conquests into Italy, then called *Œnotria*, to which he gave the name of *Italia*. *Sabinus.* He was the second king of Italy, and the founder of the Sabines, to whom he gave name.

179. *Sub imagine.* Servius explains this by *sub oculis.* The meaning is, that the scythe hung down in his hand, and the statue was in a stooping posture over it, and looking upon it.

180. *Janique bifrontis:* double-faced Janus. See 610, infra.

187. *Quirinali lituo:* the augural wand. The *lituus* was a wand or rod used by the augurs. It was crooked toward the extremity. It is here called *Quirinalis*, from *Quirinus*, a name of Romulus, who, we are informed, was very expert at augury.

188. *Trabea.* This was a robe worn by augurs, and sometimes by kings and other officers of state. Broad trimmings of purple ran across it like beams, from which it took its name. *Ancile.* This was a small oval shield worn chiefly by the priests of Mars.

191 *Circe:* a famous sorceress. *Conjux*, here, is plainly used in the sense of *amatrix*. a lover. She desired to become his wife. *Sparsit alas:* she spread or covered his wings with colors. These were purple and yellow. The bird into which *Picus* was changed, is the pie or woodpecker. See Ovid. Met. lib xiv. 320.

194. *Edidit:* in the sense of *dixit*.

196. *Auditi;* heard of—being known.

198. *Vada. Vadum*, properly, signifies *shallows*, places in the sea, or rivers, where one may walk, from *vadere*. Here it is put for the sea in general.

200. *Multa qualia:* many such things.

202. *Neve ignorate:* in the sense of *noscite.*

203. *Æquam:* just, not by restraint, nor by laws. *Vinculum* is any thing that binds or fastens. Reference may here be made to the golden age, when Saturn reigned. Latinus calls his people the nation of Saturn, either because he reigned in *Latium* over the same people; or because they governed themselves by the principles of justice and equity, and walked in the steps of that god.

205. *Fama est obscurior annis:* the tradition is rather obscure through years. Scaliger would understand it, as being more obscure than might be expected, consider-

Auruncos ita ferre senes: his ortus ut agris
Dardanus Idæas Phrygiæ penetravit ad urbes,
Threïciamque Samum, quæ nunc Samothracia fertur.
Hinc illum Corythi Tyrrhenâ ab sede profectum
Aurea nunc solio stellantis regia cœli
Accipit, et numerum Divorum altaribus auget.
Dixerat. Et dicta Ilioneus sic voce secutus:
Rex, genus egregium Fauni, nec fluctibus actos
Atra subegit hyems vestris succedere terris;
Nec sidus regione viæ, litusve fefellit.
Consilio hanc omnes animisque volentibus urbem
Afferimur; pulsi regnis, quæ maxima quondam
Extremo veniens Sol aspiciebat Olympo.
Ab Jove principium generis: Jove Dardana pubes
Gaudet avo. Rex ipse, Jovis de gente supremâ,
Troius Æneas tua nos ad limina misit.
Quanta per Idæos sævis effusa Mycenis
Tempestas ierit campos; quibus actus uterque
Europæ atque Asiæ fatis concurrerit orbis,
Audiit; et si quem tellus extrema refuso
Submovet Oceano, et si quem extenta plagarum
Quatuor in medio dirimit plaga solis iniqui.
Diluvio ex illo tot vasta per æquora vecti,
Dîs sedem exiguam patriis, litusque rogamus
Innocuum, et cunctis undamque auramque patentem

212. Et Ilioneus secutus *est* dicta *regis*

216. *Nos* omnes afferimur consilio

220. *Noster* rex ipse *ortus* de suprema gente Jovis, Troïus Æneas *nomine*, misit

222. *Quisque* audiit quanta tempestas *belli* effusa

225. Et si extrema tellus submovet quem refuso Oceano; et si plaga iniqui Solis extenta in medio quatuor plagarum dirimit quem *ab cæteris hominibus*, *ille audivit.*

NOTES.

ing how few years had elapsed since. But this is a gloss which the passage will hardly bear. Virgil mentions the fact as having taken place long before; and handed down from the ancient *Aurunci*. These were the first inhabitants of Italy. And as several kings had reigned in Troy after *Dardanus*, it is plain his departure from Italy was ancient, the tradition or report of it obscure, and the memory of it almost lost.

206. *Ferre:* in the sense of *narrare*, vel *dicere*.

208. *Samum.* Samus was an island in the Ægean sea, not far to the south of the mouth of the Hebrus. There were two others of the same name: one in the Ionian sea, to the west of the *Sinus Corinthiacus;* the other in the Icarian sea, not far from the ancient city of Ephesus, in *Asia Minor.*

209. *Corythi.* Corythus was a mountain and city of Tuscany, where Dardanus resided; *hodie, Cortona.* After his death, Dardanus was deified; which the poet beautifully expresses: *nunc aurea regia stellantis, &c.*

215. *Nec sidus:* neither star nor shore hath misled (*fefellit*) us from the direct course of our voyage.

217. *Pulsi regnis.* The greatest part of Asia Minor was subject to Priam. This justifies Ilioneus in saying they were expelled from the greatest kingdom the sun surveyed in his diurnal course. *Afferimur:* we are all brought to your city by design, &c.

222. *Quanta tempestas:* how great a tempest of war issuing from cruel Mycenæ overran the Trojan plains, &c. This is beautiful and highly poetical. *Quibus fatis:* by what fates each world of Europe and Asia impelled, engaged in arms.

225. *Extrema tellus.* The ancients supposed the frigid zones were not habitable on account of the extreme cold; as, also, the torrid or burning zone, on account of its extreme heat. Experience, however, has proved their opinion incorrect. By *extrema tellus*, we are to understand the frigid zone; and by *plaga iniqui solis*, the torrid zone. Dr. Trapp takes *refuso* in the sense of *refluens*, refluent, ebbing and flowing. Davidson takes it in the sense of wide, expanded, which certainly is sometimes the meaning of the word. This last I prefer. In this sense Valpy takes it.

228. *Diluvio.* The poet had represented the war under the figure of a tempest, rising out of Greece; and he continues the idea. The effect of this tempest was a *deluge*, which swept away the Trojan state, and the wealth of Asia.

230. *Innocuum:* safe—secure—that will be offensive to none. *Undam:* in the sense of *aquam*. *Patentem:* in the sense of *communem.*

Non erimus regno indecores: nec vestra feretur
Fama levis, tantive abolescet gratia facti:
Nec Trojam Ausonios gremio excepisse pigebit.
Fata per Æneæ juro, dextramque potentem,
Sive fide, seu quis bello est expertus et armis:
Multi nos populi, multæ (ne temne, quòd ultrò
Præferimus manibus vittas ac verba precantia)
Et petiêre sibi et voluêre adjungere gentes.
Sed nos fata Deûm vestras exquirere terras
Imperiis egêre suis. Hinc Dardanus ortus,
Huc repetit: jussisque ingentibus urget Apollo
Tyrrhenum ad Tybrim, et fontis vada sacra Numici.
Dat tibi præthereà fortunæ parva prioris
Munera, relliquias Trojâ ex ardente receptas.
Hoc pater Anchises auro libabat ad aras:
Hoc Priami gestamen erat, cùm jura vocatis
More daret populis; sceptrumque, sacerque tiaras,
Iliadumque labor, vestes.
Talibus Ilionei dictis, defixa Latinus
Obtutu tenet ora, soloque immobilis hæret,
Intentos volvens oculos. Nec purpura regem
Picta movet, nec sceptra movent Priameïa tantùm,
Quantùm in connubio natæ thalamoque moratur;
Et veteris Fauni volvit sub pectore sortem:
Hunc illum fatis externâ à sede profectum
Portendi generum, paribusque in regna vocari
Auspiciis: hinc progeniem virtute futuram
Egregiam, et totum quæ viribus occupet orbem.
Tandem lætus ait: Dî nostra incepta secundent,
Auguriumque suum. Dabitur, Trojane, quod optas:

234. *Perque ejus* potentem dextram, sive quis expertus est *eam* fide

236. Multi populi, multæ gentes, et petiêre, et voluêre adjungere nos sibi

243. Præthereà *noster rex* dat tibi parva munera

255. Hunc illum profectum à sede externa portendi generum

257. Hinc progeniem futuram *esse*

NOTES.

231. *Feretur:* in the sense of *habebitur. Levis:* small—light.

232. *Abolescet:* be effaced from our minds.

237. *Præferimus.* It was a custom among the ancients for suppliants to carry in their hands a bough of olive, bound about with woollen fillets. The fillets here are only mentioned. *Precantia:* Ruæus reads, *precantûm.*

239. *Fata:* decrees—declaration. Ruæus says, *voluntas.*

240. *Dardanus.* Dardanus, sprung from hence, calls us hither. This is the sense given by Davidson. This seems to be the opinion of Valpy, who connects *repetit* with *Dardanus ortus.* Ruæus interprets *repetit* by *revertitur.* This represents Dardanus as coming in person to claim, and take possession of Italy, his native country. This is the more poetical. Heyne seems to consider Apollo the nominative to *repetit.* He says, *Dardanus ortus hinc; huc repetit jussisque ingentibus urget Apollo.* If we take Apollo for the nom. to *repetit*, there should be a colon after *ortus*, or at least a semicolon. It was principally under the directions of this god, that Æneas came to Italy.

242. *Vada:* properly, the shallow, or shoal part of the river. Here the water of the river. *Fontis:* in the sense of *rivi* vel *fluminis.*

244. *Receptas:* saved from, &c.

245. *Hoc auro:* in this golden bowl, father Anchises, &c.

246. *Gestamen:* the garment—robe.

250. *Obtutu:* in a steady, attentive posture.

252. *Picta purpura:* the embroidered purple robe. Embroidery was invented among the Phrygians.

253. *Moratur:* reflects upon—dwells or meditates upon.

254. *Sortem:* in the sense of *oraculum* vel *responsum oraculi.*

255. *Hunc illum:* that this very person come, &c. *Portendi:* in the sense of *designari.*

257. *Auspiciis:* in the sense of *potestate. Progeniem:* an issue—race—offspring.—*Hinc:* from the union of the Trojans and Latins in the persons of Æneas and Lavinia.

260. *Augurium:* this refers to the response of the oracle of *Faunus*, concerning the marriage of *Lavinia.* See 96, supra.

Munera nec sperno. Non vobis, rege Latino,
Divitis uber agri, Trojæve opulentia deerit.
Ipse modò Æneas, nostri si tanta cupido est,
Si jungi hospitio properat, sociusque vocari,
Adveniat; vultus neve exhorrescat amicos.
Pars mihi pacis erit dextram tetigisse tyranni.
Vos contrà regi mea nunc mandata referte
Est mihi nata, viro gentis quam jungere nostræ,
Non patrio ex adyto sortes, non plurima cœlo
Monstra sinunt: generos externis affore ab oris,
Hoc Latio restare canunt, qui sanguine nostrum
Nomen in astra ferant. Hunc illum poscere fata
Et reor, et, si quid veri mens augurat, opto.
 Hæc effatus, equos numero pater eligit omni.
Stabant tercentum nitidi in præsepibus altis.
Omnibus extemplò Teucris jubet ordine duci
Instratos ostro alipedes pictisque tapetis.
Aurea pectoribus demissa monilia pendent:
Tecti auro fulvum mandunt sub dentibus aurum.
Absenti Æneæ currum geminosque jugales,
Semine ab æthereo, spirantes naribus ignem:
Illorum de gente, patri quos Dædala Circe
Suppositâ de matre nothos furata creavit.
Talibus Æneadæ donis dictisque Latini
Sublimes in equis redeunt, pacemque reportant.
 Ecce autem Inachiis sese referebat ab Argis
Sæva Jovis conjux, aurasque invecta tenebat.
Et lætum Æneam, classemque ex æthere longè
Dardaniam Siculo prospexit ab usque Pachyno.

268. Est mihi nata, quam sortes ex patrio adyto *non sinunt*, plurima monstra *de* cœlo non sinunt, jungere viro

271. Canunt hoc restare Latio, generos affore

276. Extemplò jubet alipedes instratos ostro pictisque tapetis duci

280. *Jubet* currum, geminosque jugales *equos* ab æthereo semine, spirantes ignem naribus *duci* absenti Æneæ; *equos* de gente illorum, quos Dædala Circe, furata patri *Soli*, creavit nothos de supposita matre.

288. Et ex æthere longê usque ab Siculo Pachyno

NOTES.

262. *Uber divitis agri:* the fruitfulness of a rich soil, &c. *Deerit.* In scanning, the two first vowels make one syllable.

266. *Pars erit pacis:* it will be part of a treaty of amity and friendship, to have touched the right hand of your king. It will be a considerable step toward it. *Pars:* in the sense of *pignus*, says Heyne.

269. *Sortes.* The responses of some oracles were given by drawing or casting lots. Hence *sors* came to signify an oracle, or the *response* of the oracle. *Ex patrio adyto:* from his father's oracle. See 97, supra. *Adytum:* the most sacred place of the temple, particularly the place where the oracle stood. Hence the oracle itself, by meton. *Plurima monstra:* very many prodigies from heaven, &c. some of which were mentioned 59, supra, et seq.

277. *Alipedes. Alipes*, properly, an adj.: swift of foot. Here it is used as a sub.: swift horses. *Pictis tapetis:* with embroidered trappings.

279. *Mandunt:* they champ the golden bit under their teeth. *Aurum*, properly, gold—any thing made of gold: also, a golden or yellow color.

282. *De gente illorum.* Circe, as the fable goes, stole, by some means, one of the fiery steeds of her father Phœbus. By *substituting a mare* of common breed, she was enabled to procure what is called, in common language, a half blood. This production, or mixed breed, the poet calls *nothos.* Of this race, or stock, descending from the celestial breed, were the horses that Latinus presented to Æneas. *Dædala:* an adj. of *Dædalus*, an ingenious artificer of Athens. He built a labyrinth at Crete, in imitation of the one in Egypt. It is said he escaped from Crete on artificial wings. *Dædala:* cunning—artful.

285. *Sublimes.* This may mean simply: high, elevated upon their horses. Or it may be taken in the sense of *læti.*

286. *Argis:* a city of the Peloponnesus, dear to Juno. It is called *Inachian*, from Inachus, one of its kings; or from the river Inachus, which flowed near it.

288. *Longè ex æthere usque:* and from the heavens afar off, even from Sicilian Pachynus, she beheld joyous Æneas, &c. *Pachynus:* the southern promontory of Sicily *Hodie*, *Capo Passaro.* For *longè*, Heyne reads *longo*, agreeing with *æthere:* but *longè* is the common reading, and is the easier.

Moliri jam tecta videt, jam fidere terræ,
Deseruisse rates. Stetit acri fixa dolore:
Tum, quassans caput, hæc effudit pectore dicta:
Heu stirpem invisam, et fatis contraria nostris
Fata Phrygum! num Sigeïs occumbere campis?
Num capti potuêre capi? num incensa cremavit
Troja viros? medias acies, mediosque per ignes
Invenêre viam. At, credo, mea numina tandem
Fessa jacent: odiis aut exsaturata quievi.
Quin etiam patriâ excussos infesta per undas
Ausa sequi, et profugis toto me opponere ponto.
Absumptæ in Teucros vires cœlique marisque.
Quid Syrtes, aut Scylla mihi, quid vasta Charybdis
Profuit? optato conduntur Tybridis alveo,
Securi pelagi atque mei. Mars perdere gentem
Immanem Lapithûm valuit: concessit in iras
Ipse Deûm antiquam genitor Calydona Dianæ:
Quod scelus, aut Lapithas tantum, aut Calydona merentem?

294 Num *potuêre* occumbere Sigeïs campis num capti potuêre capi?

299. Infesta ausa *sum* sequi *eos* excussos patriâ per undas

307. Quod tantum scelus aut Lapithas *merentes*, aut Calydona merentem?

NOTES.

290. *Moliri:* to build--to lay the foundations of their houses. The word *Trojanos* is to be supplied, governed by *videt*. *Fidere:* to trust to the land. Davidson reads *sidere:* to settle on the land. He informs us that Pierius found *sidere* in the most of the ancient MSS. The sense is the same with either.

291. *Stetit:*-she stops pierced with, &c.

294. *Num Sigeïs:* could they fall upon the Sigean plains? could the captives be taken? &c. Juno here speaks as if nothing less than the protection of the gods, that were opposed to her, could have saved them amidst such havoc and desolation of fire and sword. She had done her best to destroy them.

Fata Phrygum. This may mean the success or fortune of the Trojans, in escaping all the dangers, and surmounting all the difficulties in their way to Italy. And *fatis nostris*, may mean the power, will, or inclination of Juno. It was her earnest desire to destroy them all, and she exerted her utmost power to effect it; but she was baffled in all her attempts. Their success, or fortune, prevailed against her. Or, by *fata Phrygum*, we may understand the decrees and purposes of the gods in their favor, opposed to the will and inclinations of Juno, and baffling all her power.

298. *Aut odiis.* This is capable of a twofold version: I, satiated with resentment, have ceased: or, satiated, I have ceased from my resentment. The sense is the same either way.

299. *Excussos:* expelled or cast from their country. It is a metaphor taken from a person's being tost or thrown out of a chariot.

304. *Mars valuit.* Pirithoüs, king of the *Lapithæ*, invited all the gods to his nuptials with Hippodame, except Mars. This indignity the god revenged upon his subjects. The *Lapithæ* were a people of Thessaly, inhabiting mount Pindus. *Immanem:* savage—barbarous: or great, large, in reference to their size and stature. This last seems to suit the design of the speech the best; which was to magnify the power of Mars, in destroying such an enemy. *Securi:* regardless of—safe from.

305. *In iras:* in the sense of *ad pœnam et vindictam*, says Heyne.

306. *Calydona:* acc. sing. of Greek formation, from *Calydon*, the chief city of *Ætolia*, near the river Evenus. Æneas, its king, paid homage to all the gods, except Diana. The goddess being provoked at this neglect, sent a wild boar that laid waste his whole country, till he was slain by his son Meleager.

307. *Quod tantum scelus.* Ruæus and Davidson have *Lapithis, Calydone merente:* the meaning will then be: what so great punishment did the Lapithæ or Calydon deserve? *Scelus* is here in the sense of *pœna* vel *supplicium:* the punishment for crimes or wicked actions. Heyne, and others, read *Lapithas*, and *Calydona merentem*, governed by the verb *concessit* understood. In this case, the words may be rendered: deserving what so great punishment did he give up either the Lapithæ to Mars, or Calydon to Diana. If the Lapithæ deserved such signal punishment for neglect shown to Mars; and if Calydon deserved it for contempt of Diana, what do not these Trojans deserve for contempt of me, the wife of Jove, and queen of the gods? Thus she reasoned. For the cause of Juno's resentment against the Trojans, see Æn. 1. 4, and 28.

Ast ego, magna Jovis conjux, nil linquere inausum
Quæ potui infelix, quæ memet in omnia verti;
Vincor ab Æneâ. Quòd si mea numina non sunt

311 Quod *numen* est usquam

Magna satis, dubitem haud equidem implorare quod usquam est.
Flectere si nequeo Superos, Acheronta movebo.

313. Esto, non dabitur *mihi* prohibere *Trojanos* Latinis regnis

Non dabitur regnis, esto, prohibere Latinis,
Atque immota manet fatis Lavinia conjux;
At trahere, atque moras tantis licet addere rebus;
At licet amborum populos exscindere regum.
Hâc gener atque socer coëant mercede suorum.
Sanguine Trojano et Rutulo dotabere, virgo:
Et Bellona manet te pronuba. Nec face tantùm
Cisseïs prægnans ignes enixa jugales:
Quin idem Veneri partus suus, et Paris alter,
Funestæque iterum recidiva in Pergama tædæ.
Hæc ubi dicta dedit, terras horrenda petivit.
Luctificam Alecto dirarum ab sede sororum,
Infernisque ciet tenebris: cui tristia bella,
Iræque, insidiæque, et crimina noxia cordi.
Odit et ipse pater Pluton, odere sorores
Tartareæ monstrum: tot sese vertit in ora,

329. Tam sævæ facies *sunt illi; illa* atra pullulat tot colubris.

Tam sævæ facies, tot pullulat atra colubris.
Quam Juno his acuit verbis, ac talia fatur:

NOTES.

308. *Quæ potui:* who could leave nothing untried—who had power to try every thing.

309. *Infelix:* unsuccessful—not having accomplished my purpose. *Verti memet in omnia:* I have had recourse to all expedients—I have tried all the means in my power.

312. *Acheronta:* acc. sing. of *Acheron:* properly, a river of hell. Here put for the infernal gods.

314. *Immota:* certain—fixed—determined.

315. *Trahere:* in the sense of *differre.*

317. *Hâc mercede:* at this cost, or price of their people, let them unite. *Merces* sometimes signifies a *condition.* In this sense it will be: let them unite upon this condition, viz. the destruction of both their people, the Trojans and Latins, mentioned in the line above. Heyne takes *mercede* in the sense of *malo et pernicie.*

318. *Virgo, dotabere:* O virgin, thou shalt be dowered with Trojan and Rutulian blood—thou shalt receive thy dowry in Trojan, &c.

319. *Bellona manet:* and Bellona awaits thee as a bride-maid. Bellona, the goddess presiding over war. She was the sister of Mars, and prepared his chariot for him, when he went out to war. *Pronubæ* were the women who managed those things that pertained to nuptials, and placed the bride in her bed. It is used in the singular for the goddess of marriage. What gives emphasis to the expression here, is, that Juno herself was the *Pronuba*, as being the goddess who presided over marriage.

320. *Cisseïs.* Hecuba, the wife of Priam, is so called, from *Cisseüs*, her father. Before she was delivered of Paris, she dreamed she had a torch in her womb. *Enixa jugales ignes:* she brought forth a nuptial fire-brand, to wit, Paris; who was the cause of the Trojan war, and the destruction of his country. Any thing belonging to or connected with marriage, or the marriage state, may be called *jugalis.*

321. *Quin suus partus;* but her own son shall be the same to Venus, even another Paris. The meaning is, that Æneas should prove the same to Venus his mother, that Paris did to his. He should kindle the flames of another war, which should end in the destruction of Troy, rising again from ruins. It is evident that this must be the meaning of *recidiva.* Æneas had just founded a city which he called Troy. It was rising from the ruins of old Troy. Ruæus takes *recidiva*, in the sense of *iterum cadentia.*

322. *Tædæque funestæ:* and a torch or fire-brand, again fatal, &c.

324. *Luctificam:* doleful—causing sorrow. See Geor. i. 278.

326. *Cordi:* dat. of *cor*, for a pleasure or delight. The verb *sunt* is to be supplied.

327. *Pluton.* The *n* is added on account of the following word, beginning with the vowel *o.*

Hunc mihi da proprium, virgo sata nocte, laborem,
Hanc operam; ne noster honos, infractave cedat
Fama loco; neu connubiis ambire Latinum
Æneadæ possint, Italosve obsidere fines.
Tu potes unanimes armare in prælia fratres,
Atque odiis versare domos: tu verbera tectis
Funereasque inferre faces: tibi nomina mille,
Mille nocendi artes: fœcundum concute pectus,
Disjice compositam pacem, sere crimina belli:
Arma velit, poscatque simul, rapiatque juventus.
Exin Gorgoneis Alecto infecta venenis
Principio Latium et Laurentis tecta tyranni
Celsa petit, tacitumque obsedit limen Amatæ:
Quam super adventu Teucrûm, Turnique hymenæis,
Fœmineæ ardentem curæque iræque coquebant.
Huic Dea cœruleis unum de crinibus anguem
Conjicit, inque sinum præcordia ad intima subdit:
Quo furibunda domum monstro permisceat omnem.
Ille inter vestes et levia pectora lapsus
Volvitur attactu nullo, fallitque furentem,
Vipeream inspirans animam: fit tortile collo
Aurum ingens coluber, fit longæ tænia vittæ,
Innectitque comas, et membris lubricus errat.
Ac dum prima lues udo sublapsa veneno
Pertentat sensus, atque ossibus implicat ignem,
Necdum animus toto percepit pectore flammam;

331. *O virgo* sata nocte, da mihi

336. Tu *potes* inferre verbera

340. *Fac ut* Juventus velit, simulque poscat

344. Quam *Amatam* ardentem super adventu Teucrûm hymenæisque Turni, fœmineæque

349. Ille *anguis* lapsus inter vestes

352. Ingens coluber fit tortile

NOTES.

331. *Hunc proprium laborem:* this peculiar task—this task or business which properly belongs to you.

332. *Infracta:* declining—broken. Of *in* and *fracta.* Ruæus says, *victa.*

333. *Ambire:* in the sense of *circumvenire.*

336. *Domos:* in the sense of *familias.*

337. *Mille nomina:* there are to you a thousand pretences, a thousand ways of doing hurt, or mischief. *Verbera:* blows—scourges. *Inferre:* in the sense of *immittere.*

339. *Disjice.* This is the common reading. Heyne reads *dissice.* Pierius says he found *dissice* in all the ancient MSS. *Crimina belli:* the causes of war. *Compositam pacem:* the treaty to which Latinus had agreed, or the match of Lavinia with Æneas.

341. *Gorgoneis venenis infecta:* infected with Gorgonian poisons—with such poisons as the serpents had, with which the head of the Gorgon, *Medusa,* was encircled. According to fable, *Perseus* cut off her head, and took it with him in his travels into Africa. The drops falling from it, sprung up immediately into venomous reptiles. The Gorgons were the daughters of *Phorcys* and *Ceto.* They were three in number, *Stheno, Medusa,* and *Euryale.* See Ovid. Met. lib. iv. *Exin:* forthwith. She stays not to make reply. She is so bent on mischief, that she obeys as soon as desired. See nom. prop. under *Gorgon.*

345. *Fœmineæ curæ:* female cares and angry passions tortured her, inflamed at, &c. The *curæ* may refer to the match with Turnus, which she was very anxious to bring about; and the *iræ,* to the arrival of the Trojans.

346. *Cœruleis crinibus:* from her serpentine locks. *Cœruleis.* This is said of serpents, because they are streaked with bluish spots. Instead of hair, the heads of the Gorgons were attired with serpents. *Huic:* to *Amata.*

348. *Quo monstro:* by which serpent, rendered furious, (or driven to fury,) she might embroil the whole family.

350. *Nullo attactu:* without any perceptible touch.

352. *Tortile aurum collo:* wreathed gold for the neck—a chain of wreathed gold—a necklace.

354. *Prima lues sublapsa:* and while the first infection, gliding gently downward, with its humid poison, penetrates the senses, &c. Most interpreters connect *sublapsa udo veneno* together, and consider the infection as gliding under the humid poison. Davidson thinks, *udo veneno* should be connected

357. *Regina* locuta est molliùs, et de solito more matrum, lachrymans multa

361. Nec miseret *te* matris; quam *iste* perfidus prædo relinquet primo Aquilone

365. Quid *erit* tua sancta fides

369. Equidem reor omnem terram *esse* externam, quæ libera *à* nostris sceptris dissidet *à nobis;* et *reor* Divos dicere sic. Et, si prima origo *ejus* domûs repetatur, Inachus, Acrisiusque *reperientur* patres Turno; Mycenæque mediæ *Greciæ, ejus patria.*

Molliùs, et solito matrum de more, locuta est,
Multa super natâ lachrymans, Phrygiisque hymenæis
Exulibusne datur ducenda Lavinia Teucris,
O genitor! nec te miseret natæque tuique?
Nec matris miseret; quam primo Aquilone relinquet
Perfidus, alta petens, abductâ virgine, prædo?
At non sic Phrygius penetrat Lacedæmona pastor,
Ledæamque Helenam Trojanas vexit ad urbes?
Quid tua sancta fides, quid cura antiqua tuorum,
Et consanguineo toties data dextera Turno?
Si gener externâ petitur de gente Latinis,
Idque sedet, Faunique premunt te jussa parentis:
Omnem equidem sceptris terram quæ libera nostris
Dissidet, externam reor; et sic dicere Divos.
Et Turno, si prima domûs repetatur origo,
Inachus Acrisiusque patres, mediæque Mycenæ.
His ubi nequicquam dictis experta, Latinum
Contrà stare videt; penitùsque in viscera lapsum
Serpentis furiale malum, totamque pererrat:
Tum verò infelix, ingentibus excita monstris,
Immensam sinè more furit lymphata per urbem:
Ceu quondam torto volitans sub verbere turbo,

NOTES.

with *pertentat sensus.* He observes that serpents leave a humidity, a kind of infectious poison or slime, where they pass along; and as the motion of this serpent was downward, *sublapsa* is very properly used.

360. *Genitor.* The whole of this speech of the queen is very artful, and very well calculated to produce the intended effect. She applies to him not the title of king, nor the name of husband; but the tender appellation of father. Thus making her address to his parental affections, that if he had any compassion, it might be moved in behalf of his only daughter, the support of his family, and the heiress of his kingdom. She puts him in mind of the conduct of Paris at the court of Menelaus; and intimates that Æneas, like a *perfidious robber,* would carry off his daughter the first opportunity.

363. *At non.* This is the common reading. Mr. Davidson reads *an non. Phrygius pastor:* Paris. *Penetrat:* in the sense of *intravit.*

366. *Turno.* His mother's name was *Venilia,* the sister of Amata, the wife of Latinus. He was therefore connected with the royal family of *Latium. Consanguineo:* properly, a relation by blood.

368. *Sedet:* is resolved upon. *Statutum est,* says Ruæus.

370. *Dissidet:* in the sense of *separatur.*

372. *Inachus.* He was one of the first kings of Argos, and gave his name to the river near that city. *Acrisius* was one of his descendants, and the last king of Argos. He, or his grandson *Perseus,* removed the seat of government to *Mycenæ.* He ordered his daughter *Danaë* to be shut up in a wooden chest, and cast into the sea. Here it is said she was impregnated by Jupiter, and had Perseus. She was wafted to the coast of Italy, where she was taken up by Polydectes. Afterward, she married Pilumnus, who was one of the ancestors of Turnus. She founded the city *Ardea,* in the country of the *Rutuli. Mycenæ* was situated on the river Inachus, which flows into the *Sinus Argolicus,* on the eastern side of the Peloponnesus. It is here said to be the middle of Greece. But this is more from its being the chief city, or capital of Greece than from its local situation.

373. *Experta:* having tried—addressed him.

374. *Stare contrà:* in the sense of *resistere.*

375. *Furiale malum:* the infuriate poison. *Pererrat:* in the sense of *penetrat.*

376. *Excita ingentibus:* roused by the mighty monsters. The effect of the poison upon her imagination made her see a thousand monsters, which affrighted and distracted her.

377. *Lymphata:* frantic,—furious. This is thought, by most interpreters, to express that kind of fury with which persons are seized who have been bitten by a mad dog; and whose madness, when it comes to the height, is accompanied with a dread of water. From *lympha,* water. *Sinè more:* beyond bounds—immoderately.

378. *Ceu quondam:* as when a top whirl

Quem pueri magno in gyro vacua atria circum
Intenti ludo exercent. Ille actus habenâ
Curvatis fertur spatiis: stupet inscia turba,
Impubesque manus, mirata volubile buxum:
Dant animos plagæ. Non cursu segnior illo
Per medias urbes agitur, populosque feroces.
Quin etiam in sylvas, simulato numine Bacchi,
Majus adorsa nefas, majoremque orsa furorem,
Evolat; et natam frondosis montibus abdit,
Quò thalamum eripiat Teucris, tædasque moretur:
Evoë Bacche, fremens; solum te virgine dignum
Vociferans, etenim molles tibi sumere thyrsos,
Te lustrare choro, sacrum tibi pascere crinem.
  Fama volat: furiisque accensas pectore matres
Idem omnes simul ardor agit, nova quærere tecta.
Deseruere domos: ventis dant colla comasque.
Ast aliæ tremulis ululatibus æthera complent,
Pampineasque gerunt incinctæ pellibus hastas.
Ipsa inter medias flagrantem fervida pinum
Sustinet, ac natæ Turnique canit hymenæos,
Sanguineam torquens aciem: torvùmque repentè
Clamat: Io matres, audite, ubi quæque, Latinæ:
Si qua piis animis manet infelicis Amatæ
Gratia, si juris materni cura remordet;

384. *Regina* agitur non segnior illo cursu per

389. Vociferans te *Bacche*, solum *esse* dignum virgine; *eam* sumere molles thyrsos tibi, lustrare te

397. *Regina* ipsa fervida sustinet

400. Io Latinæ matres, audite, ubi quæque *estis:* si qua gratia infelicis Amatæ manet

NOTES.

ing under the twisted lash, which boys, intent on their sport, &c. Dr. Trapp observes, this simile is the perfection of elegance. Nothing can be more finely described.

380. *Exercent:* in the sense of *agitant. Habenâ:* with the string.

382. *Buxum:* the box wood, of which tops were made—the top itself, by meton.

383. *Dant animos plagæ.* This is capable of two meanings, according as *plagæ* is taken for the nom. plu. or the dat. sing. Dr. Trapp insists on the former, and renders it: the lashes give (it) life; taking *animos* in the sense of *vitam;* and this again for *rapidum motum.* Davidson objects to this, and prefers the latter: they give their souls to the stroke. This is the more elegant, and poetical. Dryden renders it thus: "and lend their little souls to every stroke." Valpy takes *animos* in the same sense with Dr. Trapp. Heyne says, *concitatiorem motum. Non segnior:* not less impetuous is the queen driven in her course through, &c.

386. *Orsa:* part. from *ordior,* I begin or enter upon. *Numine Bacchi:* the influence of Bacchus being pretended. She pretended to be under the influence or impulse of that god. Ruæus takes *numen* in the sense of *religio,* making the queen to feign a zeal for the service or worship of Bacchus. Valpy says, under a pretence of celebrating the orgies of Bacchus. *Adorsa:* attempting. *Nefas:* in the sense of *crimen* vel *scelus.*

388. *Thalamum:* in the sense of *conjugium. Tædas:* in the sense of *nuptias.*

390. *Etenim.* In some editions, there is a full stop after *vociferans.* This perplexes the whole passage: whereas, if we make *vociferans* to govern the following infinitives, all will be plain and easy. Ruæus, and Dr. Trapp, think they are governed by *fama volat.* The *etenim,* here, appears to be expletive. *Thyrsos.* The *thyrsus* was a kind of spear wrapped about with vine and ivy leaves, which Bacchus and his retinue used to wear.

391. *Choro.* Some copies have *choris,* others *choros.* The sense is, however, the same with either. The bacchanals used to dance round the image of Bacchus. *Sacrum tibi.* It was a custom among the Romans and Greeks, for maidens to consecrate their hair to some god or goddess; and never to cut it off till just before they were married, when they suspended it in the temple of that deity, in honor of whom they had preserved it. *Lustrare:* in the sense of *circumire. Pascere:* in the sense of *servare.*

393. *Tecta:* abodes, to wit, the woods.

399. *Torvùm:* an adj. neu. taken as an adverb; in imitation of the Greeks. In the sense of *torvè.*

400. *Latinæ matres:* ye Latin matrons hear, wherever any of you be. The verb *estis* is understood. *Ubi:* in the sense of *ubicunque.*

Solvite crinales vittas, capite orgia mecum.

404. Alecto agit Reginam talem stimulis Bacchi undique

Talem inter sylvas, inter deserta ferarum,
Reginam Alecto stimulis agit undique Bacchi.

408. Postquam *Alecto* visa *est sibi* acuisse primos furores *Amatæ*

Postquam visa satìs primos acuisse furores,
Consiliumque omnemque domum vertisse Latini
Protinùs hinc fuscis tristis Dea tollitur alis
Audacis Rutuli ad muros: quam dicitur urbem
Acrisioneïs Danaë fundâsse colonis,
Præcipiti delata Noto: locus Ardua quondam
Dictus avis, et nunc magnum manet Ardea nomen
Sed fortuna fuit. Tectis hìc Turnus in altis
Jam mediam nigrâ carpebat nocte quietem.
Alecto torvam faciem et furialia membra
Exuit: in vultus sese transformat aniles,
Et frontem obscœnam rugis arat: induit albos
Cum vittâ crines: tum ramum innectit olivæ.
Fit Calybe, Junonis anus, templique sacerdos

420. Et offert se juveni ante oculos cum his verbis

Et juveni ante oculos his se cum vocibus offert:
Turne, tot incassùm fusos patiere labores,
Et tua Dardaniis transcribi sceptra colonis?
Rex tibi conjugium, et quæsitas sanguine dotes
Abnegat; externusque in regnum quæritur hæres.
I nunc, ingratis offer te, irrise, perîclis:
Tyrrhenas, i, sterne acies: tege pace Latinos

427. Adeò omnipotens Saturnia ipsa jussit me fari hæc palam tibi, cùm

Hæc adeò tibi me, placidâ cùm nocte jaceres,
Ipsa palam fari omnipotens Saturnia jussit.
Quare age, et armari pubem, portisque moveri
Lætus in arma para: et Phrygios, qui flumine pulchro
Consedêre, duces pictasque exure carinas.

NOTES.

407. *Vertisse:* in the sense of *turbavisse.*

410. *Fundâsse,* &c. Danaë founded a city, which she called *Ardea* or *Ardua,* most probably from its high and elevated situation. *Acrisioneïs colonis:* for her Grecian colony. *Acrisioneïs:* an adj. from *Acrisius,* the name of her father. See 372, supra.

411. *Præcipiti noto:* by a violent wind wafted to Italy. *Noto:* the south wind, put for wind in general.

412. *Avis:* in the sense of *majoribus. Magnum:* great—illustrious.

413. *Sed fortuna fuit.* Most interpreters take this to mean no more than *fortè,* or *ita evenit:* so it was, or so it happened; and connect it with what follows. It happened so that Turnus, &c. Ruæus says, *casus ita tulit.* But this is very flat, and makes the conjunction *sed* a mere expletive. It is better to refer it to *Ardea* just mentioned; which, though illustrious and flourishing, was now doomed to be destroyed by Æneas; taking *fortuna fuit* in the sense of Æn. ii. 325. where *fuimus Troes, fuit Ilium,* imports: we Trojans once were, Ilium once was; but is now no more.

417 *Obscœnam:* filthy—deformed. *Arat:* in the sense of *sulcat.*

421. *Fusos:* part. of *fundor:* to be lost—to be thrown away, in vain. *Esse* is understood.

422. *Transcribi:* to be transferred to a Trojan colony. This word was generally applied to those persons, whose names were enrolled in order to be transplanted into some new colony. Such persons were called *transcripti.* Hence the verb came to signify *to transfer.*

423. *Conjugium:* in the sense of *Laviniam,* vel *nuptias Laviniæ.*

426. *Tege:* defend—protect. The Latins, in their wars with the Tuscans, received aid from Turnus, and by his means obtained peace. To this circumstance, here is an allusion.

430. *Para:* in the sense of *jube. Arma:* in the sense of *bellum.*

431. *Exure Phrygios,* &c. The poets sometimes connect two words together in the same sentence to be governed by a verb: when strictly it can agree with one of them only. Thus, in the present case, *exure* agrees with the *pictas carinas;* but it does not suit *Phrygios duces.* The meaning is: destroy the Trojan leaders, and burn their painted ships.

Cœlestûm vis magna jubet. Rex ipse Latinus,
Ni dare conjugium, et dicto parere fatetur,
Sentiat, et tandem Turnum experiatur in armis.
Hìc juvenis vatem irridens, sic orsa vicissim
Ore refert: Classes invectas Tybridis alveo,
Non, ut rere, meas effugit nuntius aures:
Ne tantos mihi finge metus: nec regia Juno
Immemor est nostrî.
Sed te victa situ, verique effœta senectus,
O mater, curis nequicquam exercet; et arma
Regum inter, falsâ vatem formidine ludit.
Cura tibi, Divûm effigies et templa tueri:
Bella viri pacemque gerant, queis bella gerenda.
Talibus Alecto dictis exarsit in iras.
At juveni oranti subitus tremor occupat artus
Diriguere oculi: tot Erinnys sibilat hydris,
Tantaque se facies aperit. Tum flammea torquens
Lumina, cunctantem et quærentem dicere plura
Reppulit, et geminos erexit crinibus angues,
Verberaque insonuit, rabidoque hæc addidit ore:
En! ego victa situ, quam veri effœta senectus
Arma inter regum falsâ formidine ludit.
Respice ad hæc: adsum dirarum à sede sororum;
Bella manu, letumque gero.
Sic effata facem juveni conjecit, et atro
Lumine fumantes fixit sub pectore tædas.
Olli somnum ingens rupit pavor: ossaque et artus
Perfudit toto proruptus corpore sudor.
Arma amens fremit; arma toro tectisque requirit.
Sævit amor ferri, et scelerata insania belli,
Ira supèr. Magno veluti cùm flamma sonore
Virgea suggeritur costis undantis aheni,
Exsultantque æstu latices: furit intus aquæ vis,

435. Hìc juvenis *Turnus* irridens vatem, sic vicissim refert *hæc* orsa *ex* ore: nuntius non effugit meas aures, ut *tu* rere

440. Sed, O mater, senectus victa situ, effœtaque veri

443. *Sit* tibi cura tueri effigies

449. Reppulit *cum* cunctantem

452. En! ego *sum illa* victa situ

461. Amor ferri, et scelerata insania belli, supèr ira sævit. Veluti cùm virgea flamma

NOTES.

432. *Vis:* in the sense of *potentia.*

433. *Ni fatetur:* unless he consent to ratify the match, and abide by his word, &c.

435. *Orsa:* in the sense of *verba;* from the verb *ordior.*

440. *Situ. Situs* properly signifies the squalor or mustiness that grows upon old walls and dark places. Here put for the hoariness, (gray hairs,) deformity, or rust of old age. Ruæus interprets it by *annis,* and it may be used very well for years, or old age, by meton. *Effœta* is said of a woman who is past child-bearing. *Effœta veri,* will then mean, *barren of truth*—one who has ceased to speak the truth. Dr. Trapp renders it, impotent of truth. *Victa:* enfeebled—overcome.

442. *Ludit:* in the sense of *decipit. Vatem* a priestess. *Te* is understood. *Inter arma regum.* Ruæus says, *super bellis regum.*

446. *Oranti:* in the sense of *loquenti,* vel *dicenti.*

448. *Tanta facies:* so horrid an appearance of her disclosed itself to his view. She displayed so terrific an appearance to the astonished youth, that a sudden trembling seized his limbs, &c.

450. *Reppulit:* prevented—repelled.—*Erexit:* in the sense of *extulit.*

451. *Verbera:* her lash—whip.

457. *Fumantes atro lumine:* smoking with gloomy light. Servius interprets *atro* by *furiali—inferno.*

459. *Proruptus:* gushing—bursting from his whole body, drenched—wet, &c.

460. *Fremit:* he raves for his arms. Ruæus says, *fervet.*

462. *Super.* This is used here in the sense of *insuper:* furthermore—beside. It may seem a strange climax, says Dr. Trapp, to mention anger after madness. The former relates to the hurry of his thoughts about war in general, and the latter to his own resentment and jealousy. *Veluti cùm:* as when a fire of twigs, with a great roaring

Fumidus atque altè spumis exuberat amnis:
Nec jam se capit unda; volat vapor ater ad auras

467 Ergò *Turnus* indicit primis juvenum iter ad regem

Ergo iter ad regem, pollutâ pace, Latinum
Indicit primis juvenum: et jubet arma parari,
Tutari Italiam, detrudere finibus hostem:

470. *Ait* se venire satìs ambobus

Se satìs ambobus Teucrisque venire Latinisque.
Hæc ubi dicta dedit, Divosque in vota vocavit,
Certatim sese Rutuli exhortantur in arma.

473. Egregium decus formæ atque juventæ *sui regis* movet hunc: reges *ejus* atavi *movent* hunc: dextera *inclyta* claris factis *movet* hunc

Hunc decus egregium formæ movet atque juventæ;
Hunc atavi reges; hunc claris dextera factis.
Dum Turnus Rutulos animis audacibus implet,
Alecto in Teucros Stygiis se concitat alis:
Arte novâ speculata locum, quo litore pulcher
Insidiis cursuque feras agitabat Iülus.
Hìc subitam canibus rabiem Cocytia virgo
Objicit, et noto nares contingit odore,
Ut cervum ardentes agerent: quæ prima laborum
Causa fuit, belloque animos accendit agrestes.
Cervus erat formâ præstanti, et cornibus ingens

484. Quem raptum ab ubere matris pueri Tyrrheidæ nutribant

486. *Cui* custodia campi latè *erat* credita. Sylvia soror *eorum* ornabat *eum* assuetum

Tyrrheidæ pueri quem matris ab ubere raptum
Nutribant, Tyrrheusque pater, cui regia parent
Armenta, et latè custodia credita campi.
Assuetum imperiis soror omni Sylvia curâ
Mollibus intexens ornabat cornua sertis.
Pectebatque ferum, puroque in fonte lavabat.
Ille manum patiens, mensæque assuetus herili,
Errabat sylvis: rursùsque ad limina nota

NOTES.

is placed under the sides of a boiling chaldron, &c.

464. *Latices:* in the sense of *aqua*. *Exultant:* boil up. *Aquæ vis:* the force or power of the water. Heyne reads *Aquaï:* the old gen. of *aqua*, and connects it with *fumidus amnis*. The common reading is *aquæ vis*.

465. *Fumidus amnis:* the steam or vapor. *Exuberat:* abounds—overflows. Nothing can give us a greater and more terrible idea of human rage and fierceness, than the boiling of water in a chaldron. Dr. Trapp thinks with Pierius, that the force of eloquence is here wonderfully displayed in the variety of words to express the same thing.

467. *Pace pollutâ.* A league or treaty of peace was considered sacred, and ratified by solemn rites of religion; and the violation of it was considered an act of pollution and profaneness.

470. *Satìs venire:* that he is a match for both, &c. *Venire:* in the sense of *esse*.

472. *Certatim:* eagerly—with emulation. *In arma:* in the sense of *ad bellum*.

473. *Hunc:* one—this one.

474. *Atavi:* in the sense of *majores*. The poet here enumerates the different incitements to the war. One is induced to take up arms from the grace and dignity of his king; a second, from a consideration of his long line of royal ancestors; and a third, from his noble achievements and feats in arms.

Atavi reges. These words are here used in the sense of *regales majores:* his royal ancestors.

477. *Speculata:* having observed the place, on what shore beautiful Iülus, &c. *Nova arte:* with a new purpose, design, or object in view—with a design different from her visit to Latinus or Turnus, that she might actually kindle the war.

478. *Insidiis:* snares—traps.

479. *Cocytia:* hellish or infernal; an adj. from *Cocytus*, a fabulous river of hell.

480. *Noto odore:* the known scent of the stag.

481. *Ardentes:* eager—fierce.

484. *Tyrrheidæ:* the sons of Tyrrheus—a patronymic noun. Tyrrheus kept the herds of Latinus.

487. *Imperiis:* authority—commands. Ruæus takes *assuetum*, in the sense of *docilem*.

489. *Ferum.* Ferus properly signifies a wild or savage animal. Here, and in some other places of Virgil, it signifies a tame one.

Ipse domum serâ quamvis se nocte ferebat.
Hunc procul errantem rabidæ venantis Iüli
Commovêre canes: fluvio cùm fortè secundo
Deflueret, ripâque æstus viridante levaret.
Ipse etiam eximiæ laudis succensus amore
Ascanius curvo direxit spicula cornu:
Nec dextræ erranti Deus abfuit, actaque multo
Perque uterum sonitu, perque ilia venit arundo
Saucius at quadrupes nota intrà tecta refugit,
Successitque gemens stabulis; questuque cruentus
Atque imploranti similis, tectum omne replevit.
Sylvia prima soror, palmis percussa lacertos,
Auxilium vocat, et duros conclamat agrestes.
Olli, pestis enim tacitis latet aspera sylvis,
Improvisi adsunt: hic torre armatus obusto,
Stipitis hic gravidi nodis: quod cuique repertum
Rimanti, telum ira facit. Vocat agmina Tyrrheus,
Quadrifidam quercum cuneis ut fortè coactis
Scindebat, raptâ spirans immanè securi.
At sæva è speculis tempus Dea nacta nocendi,
Ardua tecta petit stabuli, et de culmine summo
Pastorale canit signum, cornuque recurvo
Tartaream intendit vocem: quâ protinùs omne
Contremuit nemus, et sylvæ intonuêre profundæ.
Audiit et Triviæ longè lacus, audiit amnis
Sulfureâ Nar albus aquâ, fontesque Velini:

501. Cruentusque, atque similis imploranti *opem*, *cervus* replevit

505. Aspera pestis *Alecto* latet

507. Hic *armatus* nodis gravidi stipitis *adest*: ira facit *id* telum, quod *est* repertum cuique rimanti. Tyrrheus spirans immanè, securi raptâ, vocat agmina, ut fortè

NOTES.

493. *Rabidæ:* in the sense of *furiosæ.*

494. *Deflueret secundo:* when by chance he was swimming down the stream—along with the current. *Commovêre:* roused up as he was roving at large.

495. *Levaret:* allaying—assuaging the heat.

497. *Curvo cornu:* from his bent, or elastic bow.

498. *Deus.* Alecto is here meant. *Deus* is of both genders. *Erranti:* Dr. Trapp observes, there is an elegancy in this. He erred even by hitting the animal, considering the consequences. But he thinks by *Deus*, we are to understand any god, or fortune. Most commentators, however, take *erranti* in its common acceptation. His hand was erring in itself, and would have erred, had it not been guided by the goddess. *Acta:* in the sense of *immissa*, vel *impulsa.*

499. *Sonitu:* in the sense of *stridore.* It made a whizzing noise as it cut the air.

505. *Aspera pestis:* the odious fiend lurks, &c. But La Cerda understands it of the fury which seized the rustics. This is not so natural and easy, though the sense be the same.

509. *Cuneis coactis:* with wedges driven into it.

510. *Spirans immanè.* Davidson understands this of the passion into which Tyrrheus was thrown, on hearing of the death of the stag: breathing fury—panting for vengeance. Dr. Trapp understands it of his puffing and blowing in felling and splitting timber. Valpy is of the same opinion with Davidson.

514. *Intendit:* she swells her infernal voice through the crooked horn. By means of the horn, the sound was greatly increased.

515. *Profundæ sylvæ:* either the woods in deep valleys, or the inmost and thickest part of the woods.

516. *Lacus Triviæ:* the lake of Diana. This was near the city *Aricia*, about three leagues from Laurentum to the north. *Hodie*, *Lago di Nemo.*

517. *Nar.* This river rises in the Apennines, and running in a south-western direction, separating *Umbria* from the country of the Sabines, falls into the Tiber. Its surface is whitened for a considerable distance by the foam, occasioned by the dashing of the water against the rocks that lie in its bed. Its name is of Sabine origin, and signifies *sulphur*, with which the water is impregnated. *Hodie*, *Nera. Fontes Velini:* the river Velinus. This river rises in the country of the Sabines, and flows into the Nar

Et trepidæ matres pressêre ad pectora natos.
Tum verò ad vocem celeres, quà buccina signum
Dira dedit, raptis concurrunt undique telis
Indomiti agricolæ: necnon et Troïa pubes
Ascanio auxilium castris effundit apertis.
Direxere acies: non jam certamine agresti,
Stipitibus duris agitur, sudibusve præustis;
Sed ferro ancipiti decernunt, atraque latè
Horrescit strictis seges ensibus, æraque fulgent
Sole lacessita, et lucem sub nubila jactant.
Fluctus uti primo cœpit cùm albescere vento;
Paulatim sese tollit mare, et altiùs undas
Erigit, inde imo consurgit ad æthera fundo.
  Hìc juvenis primam ante aciem stridente sagittâ,
Natorum Tyrrhei fuerat qui maximus, Almon
Sternitur: hæsit enim sub gutture vulnus, et udæ
Vocis iter, tenuemque inclusit sanguine vitam.
Corpora multa virûm circà: seniorque Galæsus,
Dum paci medium se offert, justissimus unus
Qui fuit, Ausoniisque olim ditissimus arvis.
Quinque greges illi balantûm, quina redibant
Armenta, et terram centum vertebat aratris.
  Atque, ea per campos æquo dum Marte geruntur,
Promissi Dea facta potens, ubi sanguine bellum
Imbuit, et primæ commisit funera pugnæ;
Deserit Hesperiam, et cœli convexa per auras,
Junonem victrix affatur voce superbâ:
En perfecta tibi bello discordia tristi!
Dic, in amicitiam coëant, et fœdera jungant,
Quandoquidem Ausonio respersi sanguine Teucros.
Hoc etiam his addam, tua si mihi certa voluntas:

519. Tum verò indomiti agricolæ celeres concurrunt undique, telis raptis, ad vocem, quà dira

531. Hìc juvenis Almon, qui fuit maximus natorum Tyrrhei, sternitur, ante

535. Multa corpora virûm *sternuntur* circà *illum:* seniorque Galæsus *sternitur quoque*

545. En discordia perfecta *est* tibi

547. Dic *illis*, *sit* coëant

NOTES.

520. *Indomiti:* rude, unpolished, countrymen, &c.

522. *Effundit:* in the sense of *mittit.*

523 *Direxere acies:* they arranged the lines. They drew up their respective forces in order of battle. *Non agitur agresti:* they do not now engage in rustic fight, with, &c. *Agitur:* in the sense of *pugnatur.*

525. *Ancipiti ferro:* with the two-edged sword. Ruæus says, *dubiis gladiis*, alluding to the issue of the contest. *Atra seges:* a direful field (crop) of drawn swords waves afar, &c. The prep. *è* is understood before *strictis ensibus.*

526. *Æra:* brazen armor; plu. of *æs:* brass. Any thing made of brass may be called *æs*, vel *æra.*

533. *Vulnus:* the wound; here put, by meton. for the wounding instrument—the arrow. *Udæ Vocis.* The voice is here called humid, because it passes through a moist or humid passage. The same as *udum iter vocis.*

534. *Inclusit:* in the sense of *obstruxit.*

536. *Medium paci:* a mediator of peace.

538. *Redibant:* returned home to him from pasture. He had five flocks of sheep, and five herds of cattle.

540. *Æquo Marte.* This cannot mean that the loss was equal on both sides, for the slain was on the part of the Latins only. Donatus explains it by *aperto Marte;* and Ascensius, by *æquo et plano campo;* meaning, that the field of battle was a plain and level spot of ground. Ruæus takes it to refer to the fight itself; when the issue was as yet equal; or it was uncertain, on which side the victory would turn.

541. *Dea facta potens:* the goddess having accomplished her promise. *Potens:* in the sense of *compos. Bellum.* Davidson renders it, by field of war; which evidently is its meaning in this place. When she stained the field of battle with blood, she had then fulfilled her engagement with Juno.

542. *Funera:* in the sense of *cædem. Commissit:* in the sense of *incepit.*

543. *Convexa:* in the sense of *vecta.*

544. *Victrix:* victorious—having effected her object.

Finitimas in bella feram rumoribus urbes,
Accendamque animos insani Martis amore,
Undique ut auxilio veniant: spargam arma per agros.
Tum contrâ Juno: Terrorum et fraudis abundè est:
Stant belli causæ: pugnatur cominùs armis.
Quæ fors prima dedit, sanguis novus imbuit arma.
Talia connubia et tales celebrent hymenæos
Egregium Veneris genus, et rex ipse Latinus.
Te super æthereas errare licentiùs auras
Haud pater ipse velit summi regnator Olympi.
Cede locis. Ego, si qua super fortuna laborum est,
Ipsa regam. Tales dederat Saturnia voces:
Illa autem attollit stridentes anguibus alas,
Cocytique petit sedem, supera ardua linquens.
Est locus, Italiæ in medio sub montibus alti
Nobilis, et famâ multis memoratus in oris,
Amsancti valles: densis hunc frondibus atrum
Urget utrinque latus nemoris, medioque fragosus
Dat sonitum saxis et torto vortice torrens.
Hìc specus horrendum, et sævi spiracula Ditis
Monstrantur: ruptoque ingens Acheronte vorago,
Pestiferas aperit fauces: queis condita Erinnys,
Invisum numen, terras cœlumque levabat.
Nec minùs intereà extremam Saturnia bello
Imponit regina manum. Ruit omnis in urbem
Pastorum ex acie numerus: cæsosque reportant,

556. *Æneas*, egregium genus Veneris, et rex Latinus ipse celebrent

558. Pater *Jupiter* ipse regnator summi Olympi haud velit te errare

565. *Nempe* valles amsancti. Latus nemoris, atrum densis frondibus urget hunc *locum* utrinque, medioque *ejus*

570. *In* queis Erinnys, invisum numen, condita

NOTES.

550. *Amore insani.* Ruæus takes this for *insano amore Martis*, by hypallage. But *insanus* is an epithet highly applicable, and proper for Mars, or war; where nothing but havoc and mad fury reign.

551. *Arma:* in the sense of *bella.*

554. *Novus sanguis:* new (or recent) blood hath stained the arms, which, &c. The *novus*, alludes to the blood which had been shed in the recent or late encounter. *Fors:* chance—fortune. *Dedit:* offered—presented.

559. *Cede locis:* depart from the places of this upper world. The earth is called the celestial or ethereal regions, in opposition to the infernal regions, or regions of darkness. *Superest.* The parts of the verb are separated by *tmesis. Fortuna laborum:* Ruæus says, *discrimen in hoc negotio.*

560. *Voces:* in the sense of *verba.*

561. *Attollit:* in the sense of *explicat.* She (Alecto) spreads her wings hissing, &c.

562. *Supera ardua:* the lofty places of this upper world. *Loca* being understood.

565. *Valles Amsancti.* Commentators are not agreed about the situation of this place. Mr. Addison is of opinion that the *Velinus*, mentioned 517, is the place which the poet had in his view. The river, says he, is extremely rapid before its fall, and rushes down a precipice a hundred yards high. It throws itself into the hollow rock, which has probably been worn by such a constant fall of water. It is impossible to see the bottom, on which it breaks, for the thickness of the mist that rises from it; which looks at a distance like clouds of smoke, ascending from some vast furnace; and distils in perpetual rains on all the places near it. He observes, that this was the most proper place in the world for a fury to make her exit, after she had filled a nation with distractions and alarms; and, I believe, continues he, that every reader's imagination is pleased, when he sees the angry goddess, thus sinking as it were in a tempest, and plunging herself into hell amidst such a scene of horror and confusion. This cascade is near the middle of Italy. *Amsanctus:* of the old *amphi*, and *sacer vel sanctus.*

567. *Torto vortice:* with its whirling eddy *Fragosus:* roaring among the rocks.

568. *Spiracula:* in the sense of *ostia.*

569. *Ingens vorago:* a vast gulf issuing from overflowing Acheron—from Acheron, having burst its barriers. *Acheron*, a river of hell: also hell itself—the infernal deities. Davidson takes it absolutely with *rupto.*

570. *Condita:* being hid—sunk. *Levabat:* relieved them from her presence, by disappearing from these upper regions. Heyne says, *linquebat.*

572. *Saturnia regina:* Juno, the daughter of Saturn, and wife of Jove. Hence sometimes styled the queen of the gods.

Almonem puerum, fœdatique ora Galæsi,
Implorantque Deos, obtestanturque Latinum.
Turnus adest, medioque in crimine cædis et ignis,
Terrorem ingeminat: Teucrosque in regna vocari;
Stirpem admisceri Phrygiam; se limine pelli.
Tum, quorum attonitæ Baccho nemora avia matres
Insultant thiasis, neque enim leve nomen Amatæ
Undique collecti coëunt, Martemque fatigant
Ilicèt infandum cuncti contra omina bellum,
Contra fata Deûm, perverso numine poscunt.
Certatim regis circumstant tecta Latini.
Ille, velut pelagi rupes immota, resistit:
Ut pelagi rupes, magno veniente fragore,
Quæ sese, multis circumlatrantibus undis,
Mole tenet: scopuli nequicquam et spumea circùm
Saxa fremunt, laterique illisa refunditur alga.
Verùm ubi nulla datur cæcum exsuperare potestas
Consilium, et sævæ nutu Junonis eunt res:
Multa Deos, aurasque pater testatus inanes,
Frangimur heu fatis, inquit, ferimurque procellâ!
Ipsi has sacrilego pendetis sanguine pœnas,
O miseri! Te, Turne, nefas, te triste manebit
Supplicium; votisque Deos venerabere seris.
Nam mihi parta quies, omnisque in limine portus,

578. *Queritur* Teucros vocari
579. Admisceri *Latinis*
580. Tum *illi*, quorum matres attonitæ Baccho insultant thiasis *per*
588. Quæ tenet sese *sua* mole, magno fragore *procellæ* veniente
595. O miseri! *vos* ipsi pendetis has

NOTES.

575. *Ora:* in the sense of *caput;* and *fœdati*, in the sense of *occisi:* or *ora fœdati Galæsi*, may mean simply the body of Galæsus, mangled and disfigured with wounds.

577. *Medio crimine*, &c. By *crimen* here we are undoubtedly to understand the charge or accusation, which the rustics brought against the Trojans, for the death of Almon and Galæsus. While they are making the accusation, *in medio crimine*, Turnus comes up, and increases the alarm. Dr. Trapp takes it for the crime of murder simply; and Ruæus interprets it by *in medio cadaverum.*

580. *Attonitæ:* inspired—under the influence of. Ruæus says, *percitæ.*

581. *Insultant thiasis:* leap and dance in choirs through the pathless groves. For *thiasis*, Ruæus says *choreis*. *Nomen:* influence—authority.

582. *Fatigant:* in the sense of *poscunt*. *Martem:* war.

583. *Omina.* These were the flight of bees and fiery appearance about Lavinia. See 64, supra et sequens.

584. *Fata:* these were the responses of the Oracle of Faunus. *Perverso numine.* Ruæus takes this in the sense of *contra voluntatem Deorum:* the will of the gods being against it. Heyne is of the same opinion. *Perverso:* in the sense of *adverso.*

587. *Fragore:* in the sense of *tempestate.*

588. *Circumlatrantibus:* in the sense of *circumsonantibus.*

589. *Scopuli:* properly high sharp rocks. *Saxa:* any rocks—rocks in general.

590. *Alga illisa:* the sea-weed dashed against its sides is repelled, or washed off.

591. *Cæcum:* in the sense of *insanum.*

593. *Testatus multa:* having often besought the gods and skies—having called them to witness. *Multa:* a Grecism, for *multùm, vel sæpe. Inanes auras: vacuum aërem*, says Ruæus. *Auras:* the skies or heavens, as the word frequently signifies. Dr. Trapp thinks it should be read *aras*, and, accordingly, he connects *inanes* with it: the vain or useless altars; because of the league which had been made in due form, but now was broken. But Davidson reads *inanis*, agreeing with *pater*, in the sense of *inaniter*: in vain—to no purpose; and he observes it is the reading of some ancient copies. Heyne reads *inanes* agreeing with *auras*. Valpy and La Cerda do the same. Pierius connects *inanes* with *frangimur.*

595. *Sacrilego sanguine.* Latinus calls their blood sacrilegious, because they had compelled him to the war against the will of the gods.

596. *Nefas:* an impious or wicked person. As Æn. ii. 585. Or it may be taken in the sense of *infandum*, agreeing with *supplicium*. Ruæus interprets it by *crimen.* Davidson renders it: "the impious promoter of this war," in apposition with *Turne.*

598. *Nam quies:* for rest is prepared for

Funere felici spolior. Nec plura locutus,
Sepsit se tectis, rerumque reliquit habenas.
  Mos erat Hesperio in Latio, quem protinùs urbes
Albanæ coluêre sacrum, nunc maxima rerum
Roma colit, cùm prima movent in prælia Martem
Sive Getis inferre manu lachrymabile bellum,
Hyrcanisve, Arabisve parant; seu tendere ad Indos,
Auroramque sequi, Parthosque reposcere signa.
Sunt geminæ belli portæ, sic nomine dicunt,
Relligione sacræ, et sævi formidine Martis:
Centum ærei claudunt vectes, æternaque ferri
Robora; nec custos absistit limine Janus.
Has, ubi certa sedet patribus sententia pugnæ;
Ipse, Quirinali trabeâ cinctuque Gabino
Insignis, reserat stridentia limina consul;
Ipse vocat pugnas: sequitur tum cætera pubes,
Æreaque assensu conspirant cornua rauco.
Hoc et tum Æneadis indicere bella Latinus
More jubebatur, tristesque recludere portas.

604. Sive parant manu inferre

611. Ubi certa sententia pugnæ sedet patribus, consul ipse insignis Quirinali trabeâ, Gabinoque cinctu reserat has *portas*, (i. e.) stridentia limina

NOTES.

me, and my whole haven is at the door. This is a fine metaphor. The weather-beaten mariner enters the haven with joy. It is a place of rest and quiet, from the dangers of the ocean. So the aged monarch views death at the door, as the end of his toils, and as a rest from his cares and labors. All he loses is the satisfaction of leaving his people in peace and prosperity.

600. *Habenas rerum;* the reins of government. A metaphor, taken from the management of horses, with bit and reins. *Sepsit:* in the sense of *clausit.*

601. *Mos erat.* This custom was instituted in the time of Numa, as we are told by Livy; but, for the sake of embellishment, the poet refers the origin of it to the earliest ages of his country. *Protinùs:* constantly. Ruæus says, *perpetuò.*

602. *Coluêre:* in the sense of *servaverunt. Rerum:* the world.

603. *Movent Martem.* We are told that the Romans used, upon the declaration of war, to enter the temple of Mars, where the sacred bucklers were suspended, and strike upon them, with the words: *Mars vigila,* Mars awake. Hence the expression, *movent Martem:* in the sense of *excitant Martem.*

604. *Getis.* The Getæ were a people of Dacia, near the mouth of the Danube. The proconsul L. Crassus triumphed over them, just before the time of Virgil.

605. *Hyrcanis.* Hyrcania was formerly a part of Parthia. Against them, as a distinct people, the Romans did not declare war. In the year of Rome 730, Augustus attempted the subjugation of the Arabians, but he failed in it. *Indos.* It is well known that the Romans made no conquests in India, properly so called But Dion informs us that, overawed by the fame of Augustus, they made peace with him, and presented him with rich gifts, while he tarried at *Samos,* in Asia, about the year 734. *Tendere ad:* to march against the Indians, and to penetrate the remotest parts of the east, *sequi auroram.*

606. *Parthos reposcere:* to demand back the standards from the Parthians.

608. *Relligione:* religious veneration.

609. *Vectes æternaque:* a hundred brazen bars, and eternal strength of iron, shut them.

610. *Janus.* This is said because the statue of Janus was in the threshold; or because he presided over all doors, which, from him, were called *januæ.* Janus was the most ancient king of Italy. Some suppose him to have been Japhet, the son of Noah. See Ecl. iv. 6. He was represented with two faces.

611 *Pugnæ:* in the sense of *belli. Sententia:* determination; and *sedet:* in the sense of *hæret. Has.* This must refer to *portas* understood. But it would seem quite unnecessary. The idea is sufficiently conveyed by *limina stridentia,* which is to be placed in this case, in apposition with *has portas.* Ruæus takes *limina* in the sense of *cardines,* but this seems a refinement unnecessary. He says, *has* (portas) *et earum stridentes cardines.* Heyne and Valpy take them as meaning the same thing—the doors of the temple of Janus.

612. *Quirinali trabeâ:* with his augural robe. So called, because worn by Romulus, who was also called *Quirinus.* See 187, supra. *Gabino cinctu.* This dress Servius derives from Gabii, a city of Latium. See Lex. under *cinctus.*

617. *Recludere:* to open the direful doors

620. Tum Saturnia regina Deûm, delapsa, cœlo, ipsa

629. Adeò quinque magnæ urbes

Abstinuit tactu pater, aversusque refugit
Fœda ministeria, et cæcis se condidit umbris.
Tum regina Deûm, cœlo delapsa, morantes
Impulit ipsa manu portas, et, cardine verso,
Belli ferratos rupit Saturnia postes.
Ardet inexcita Ausonia atque immobilis antè:
Pars pedes ire parat campis; pars arduus altis
Pulverulentus equis furit: omnes arma requirunt
Pars leves clypeos et spicula lucida tergunt
Arvinâ pingui, subiguntque in cote secures:
Signaque ferre juvat, sonitusque audire tubarum.
Quinque adeò magnæ positis incudibus urbes
Tela novant: Atina potens, Tiburque superbum,
Ardea, Crustumerique, et turrigeræ Antemnæ.
Tegmina tuta cavant capitum, flectuntque salignas
Umbonum crates: alii thoracas ahenos,
Aut leves ocreas lento ducunt argento.
Vomeris huc et falcis honos, huc omnis aratri
Cessit amor; recoquunt patrios fornacibus enses.
Classica jamque sonant: it bello tessera signum
Hic galeam tectis trepidus rapit: ille frementes

NOTES.

The doors of the temple of Janus were open in time of war, but shut in time of peace. Immediately on the declaration of war, the consul, with much parade and solemnity, opened them. What is said here on the subject, is by anticipation. *Jubebatur:* is urged—importuned.

622. *Postes. Postis*, properly, the door-post, or that part of the frame to which the door is hung. Also, the door itself, by meton.

624. *Pars arduus:* a part raised on lofty steeds, involved in clouds of dust, rage for war. The meaning of the passage is: a part prepare to take the field as infantry, (*pedites*,) a part as cavalry.

627. *Arvinâ:* tallow—any fat.

629. *Urbes:* the cities; by meton. the inhabitants. *Incudibus positis:* on their erected anvils, or their anvils being erected.

630. *Novant tela:* they repair their weapons. *Atina:* a city of the *Volsci*. *Tibur:* this was a city in the northern part of Latium, near the cataract of the river *Anien.* It was situated near the top of a mountain. Hence the epithet *superbum. Hodie, Trivoli.*

631. *Ardea.* This was the capital of the Rutuli. See 372, and 410, supra. *Crustumeri:* this was a city situated not far from the place where Rome was afterward built. Little, however, is known of it. *Antemnæ:* a city near the confluence of the rivers *Anien* and *Tiber.*

633. *Crates umbonum.* These were the supporters or frames of the shields, made of osiers, or small pieces of wood, and afterward covered with the hides of beasts *Umbo:* the farthest projecting point of the shield; by synec. put for the whole shield. These frames were made of willow.

634. *Ducunt:* in the sense of *excudunt*. *Leves ocreas:* smooth greaves of ductile silver. These were armor for the legs and thighs.

635. *Honos vomeris:* the honor (regard) of the ploughshare and of the pruning knife gives place (*huc*) to the preparations for war; and all the love of the plough yields to them They are so intent upon war, that they disregard the business of agriculture.

636. *Recoquunt:* they form anew—they make over again.

637. *Tessera signum:* the *tessera*, the signal for war, goes forth. This was a square figure like a dice, on which was inscribed the watchword or private signal, by which they could distinguish friends from foes in battle. Or, according to others, it contained the order and regulations of the march This was distributed among the soldiers. Hence the phrase: *it tessera.* It was afterward given *viva você*. *Classica:* the trumpets. The *tuba* was a straight trumpet: the *cornua*, a crooked trumpet, resembling a horn. They were also called *buccina.* The *lituus* was a trumpet not so straight as the *tuba*, nor so crooked as the *cornu*. *Classicum*, properly, the sound of the trumpet: the trumpet itself, by meton.

639. *Trilicem auro.* The coat of mail was composed of plates of iron linked together by rings. Some of them were fringed or bordered in the lower extremity with gold tissue of two or three textures, and were accordingly called *bilix*, *trilix*, &c. *Ad Juga*

Ad juga cogit equos ; clypeumque, auroque trilicem
Loricam induitur, fidoque accingitur ense.
  Pandite nunc Helicona, Deæ, cantusque movete :
Qui bello exciti reges : quæ quemque secutæ
Complêrint campos acies : quibus Itala jam tum
Floruerit terra alma viris, quibus arserit armis.
Et meministis enim, Divæ, et memorare potestis :
Ad nos vix tenuis famæ perlabitur aura.
  Primus init bellum Tyrrhenis asper ab oris
Contemptor Divûm Mezentius, agminaque armat.
Filius huic juxtà Lausus ; quo pulchrior alter
Non fuit, excepto Laurentis corpore Turni :
Lausus equûm domitor, debellatorque ferarum,
Ducit Agyllinâ nequicquam ex urbe secutos
Mille viros ; dignus patriis qui lætior esset
Imperiis, et cui pater haud Mezentius esset.
  Post hos, insignem palmâ per gramina currum,
Victoresque ostentat equos, satus Hercule pulchro
Pulcher Aventinus ; clypeoque insigne paternum,
Centum angues, cinctamque gerit serpentibus hydram :
Collis Aventini sylvâ quem Rhea sacerdos
Furtivum partu sub luminis edidit oras,
Mixta Deo mulier : postquam Laurentia victor,
Geryone extincto, Tirynthius attigit arva,

639. Induiturque clypeum, loricamque trilicem auro

641. O Deæ *Musæ*, pandite

642. Qui reges exciti *fuerint;* quæ acies

643. Quibus viris jam tum Itala, alma terra

648. Asper Mezentius, contemptor Divûm, primus init

649. Huic filius Lausus *sequitur* juxtà, quo

652. Ducit mille viros secutos *eum* nequicquam

655. Post hos pulcher Aventinus, satus pulchro Hercule, ostentat currum insignem palmâ

657. Clypeoque gerit paternum insigne, *nempe*

659. Quem Rhea sacerdos, mulier mixta Deo, partu edidit furtivum sub oras luminis

NOTES.

to the chariots. Chariots were anciently used in war by all distinguished persons.

640. *Induitur:* in the sense of *induit.*

641. *Helicona:* a Greek acc.: a mountain in Bœotia sacred to the muses. The poet here imitates the Iliad. lib. ii. both in this invocation, and in the enumeration of the forces of the Italian princes. But, in several particulars, he has improved upon his model.

646. *Tenuis aura:* a small breath of fame, &c.—scarcely a slender thread of tradition hath extended down to us.

647. *Asper:* fierce—cruel.

648. *Mezentius.* We are told that he commanded his subjects to pay him a tax of the first fruits, and the firstlings of their flocks; which before were given to the gods. On this account, he was considered an atheist, *contemptor divûm.* The poet here gives us a list of the troops engaged on the part of Turnus.

649. *Huic.* The dative of the personal pronouns is often used in the sense of the genitive. *Huic:* in the sense of *hujus.*

650. *Corpore Turni:* a Grecism, for Turnus himself.

652. *Argyllina:* an adj. from *Argylla,* a city of Tuscany, near the confines of Latium. It was founded by a colony of Thessalians. *Nequicquam:* in vain, because he was to be slain in the war with his troops: or, because he could not prevent thereby the purposes of the gods concerning the Trojan

653. *Dignus,* &c. This line is somewhat perplexed. The usual ordo is, *dignus qui esset lætior,* &c. It would be easier by transposition thus: *qui esset dignus (fuisse) lætior,* &c.: who was worthy to have been happier in his father's authority. It was in obedience to his father that he came to the war. If he had not been constrained, he would have tarried at home, shunned the toils and dangers of the war, and by that means have saved his life. He was worthy to have lived. Ruæus interprets *imperiis* by *regno,* implying that he deserved to be happier in his father's kingdom—to have remained at home, and, by that means, saved his life *Cui:* to whom Mezentius ought not to have been a father; who could have imposed such commands upon a son.

657. *Pulcher.* Dr. Trapp thinks this cannot here mean beautiful; but rather stout, illustrious, renowned; as the same word is applied to Hercules, his father. *Paternum insigne:* his father's ensign, or impress. This was the figure of the conquered hydra, shooting up into a hundred heads.

660. *Edidit partu:* brought forth at a birth into life, &c.

661. *Mixta:* uniting—mingling with—having intercourse with. Hercules, after he had slain Geryon, the king of Spain, and taken his herds, returned with them through Italy. It was at this time, that the priestess Rhea conceived Aventinus, and afterward bore him to that hero.

662. *Tirynthius:* a name of Hercules.

Tyrrhenoque boves in flumine lavit Iberas.
Pila manu, sævosque gerunt in bella dolones:
Et tereti pugnant mucrone, veruque Sabello.
Ipse pedes, tegmen torquens immane leonis,
Terribili impexum setâ, cum dentibus albis,
Indutus capiti: sic regia tecta subibat
Horridus, Hèrculeoque humeros innexus amictu.
Tum gemini fratres Tiburtia mœnia linquunt,
Fratris Tiburti dictam cognomine gentem,
Catillusque, acerque Coras, Argiva juventus:
Et primam ante aciem densa inter tela feruntur.
Ceu duo nubigenæ cùm vertice montis ab alto
Descendunt Centauri, Omolen Othrynque nivalem
Linquentes cursu rapido: dat euntibus ingens
Sylva locum, et magno cedunt virgulta fragore.
Nec Prænestinæ fundator defuit urbis;
Vulcano genitum pecora inter agrestia regèm,
Inventumque focis, omnis quem credidit ætas,
Cæculus. Hunc legio latè comitatur agrestis:
Quique altum Præneste viri, quique arva Gabinæ
Junonis, gelidumque Anienem, et roscida rivis
Hernica saxa colunt: quos, dives Anagnia, pascis,
Quos, Amasene pater. Non illis omnibus arma,
Nec clypei currusve sonant: pars maxima glandes

664. *Ejus milites* gerunt.

670. Tum gemini fratres, Catillusque, acerque Coras, Argiva juventus linquunt

678. Nec Cæculus fundator Prænestinæ urbis defuit; quem regem omnis ætas credidit genitum *esse*

682. Quique viri colunt altum Præneste, quique *colunt*,

685. Quos *tu pascis*, O pater Amasene. Arma non *sunt* omnibus

NOTES.

from *Tyrins*, a city near Argos, where he was brought up.

663. *Tyrrheno flumine:* the river Tiber, which divided Tuscany or Etruria from Latium. *Iberas boves:* his Spanish herds. *Iberas:* an adj. from *Iberus*, a river of Spain. *Hodie*, *Ebro*.

664. *Dolones*. These were long poles or battoons, with bayonets enclosed at the end, which were hardly to be observed. Hence they were called *dolones*, from *dolus*, being a kind of deceitful weapon.

665. *Veru*. This was a kind of dart used by the Sabines and Samnites. Hence the epithet *Sabello*, that is, *Sabino* vel *Samnitico*.

668. *Indutus capiti:* he put it (the shaggy lion skin) upon his head. *Cinctus circa caput*, says Ruæus.

669. *Innexus:* covered, as to his shoulders, with the garment of Hercules, his father. This was the hide of the Nemæan lion

673. *Feruntur:* in the sense of *incedunt*. *Ante primam:* before the first line—in the front of the battle.

674. *Nubigenæ:* cloud-born sons. These were the Centaurs, whom Ixion begat, it is said, upon a cloud. They were a people of Thessaly, and celebrated for horsemanship. Ixion was their king.

675. *Omolen—Othryn*. These were mountains of Thessaly, where the Centaurs resided.

678. *Fundator* &c Cæculus, we are told, had very small eyes, as his name implies. He was very ambitious, and was the founder of a colony. He pretended that he was the son of Vulcan, and that the brightness of his father's fire had injured his sight. He built the city *Præneste*, situated on a mountain. Hence called *altum Præneste*, about 24 miles from Rome.

680. *Inventum focis:* found upon the hearth. He was therefore reputed the son of Vulcan. The verb *esse* vel *fuisse* is understood.

682. *Gabinæ Junonis. Gabinæ:* an adj. from *Gabii*, a town of the Volsci, between Rome and Præneste. Here Juno had a splendid temple. Hence she is called Gabinian Juno.

683. *Gelidum Anienem:* the river Anien, which empties into the Tiber from the north-east. Its water was very cold. Hence the epithet *gelidum*.

684. *Hernica saxa:* the towns of the Hernici. They were a people between the Æqui, the Marsi, and the Volsci. Their country was very mountainous. Hence their towns were called *saxa*, being built amongst rocks. Their chief town was *Anagnia*. *Roscida rivis:* watered with rills or streams.

685. *Amasene*. The river Amasenus, which watered the country about *Anagnia*. The epithet *pater* is common to all the river gods. *Hodie*, *Toppia*.

686. *Glandes plumbi:* balls of lead. *Spargit:* throws.

Liventis plumbi spargit, pars spicula gestat
Bina manu, fulvosque lupi de pelle galeros
Tegmen habet capiti: vestigia nuda sinistri
Instituêre pedis; crudus tegit altera pero.
At Messapus equûm domitor, Neptunia proles,
Quem neque fas igni cuiquam nec sternere ferro,
Jampridem resides populos, desuetaque bello
Agmina, in arma vocat subitò, ferrumque retractat.
Hi Fescenninas acies, æquosque Faliscos;
Hi Soractis habent arces, Flaviniaque arva,
Et Cimini cum monte lacum, lucosque Capenos.
Ibant æquati numero, regemque canebant:
Ceu quondam nivei liquida inter nubila cycni
Cùm sese è pastu referunt, et longa canoros
Dant per colla modos: sonat amnis, et Asia longè
Pulsa palus.
Nec quisquam æratas acies ex agmine tanto
Misceri putet, aëriam sed gurgite ab alto

692. Quem neque *erat* fas cuique sternere

695. Hi *ducunt* Fescenninas

NOTES.

688. *Fulvos galeros:* tawny caps of the wolf's skin, &c.

689. *Vestigia nuda:* they formed the prints or tracks of the left foot naked—their left foot was naked. *Crudus pero:* unwrought leather covers the other. *Vestigia* is understood. The *pero* was a kind of high shoe, made of raw hide, and worn by rustics principally. *Instituêre:* in the sense of *posuêre.*

691. *Messapus.* By birth he was a Greek. After his arrival in Italy, he occupied the eastern part, which was from him called *Messapia,* afterward Calabria. He was a skilful navigator; and hence called *Neptunia proles:* the offspring of Neptune. Virgil places his dominions in the eastern part of Etruria, not far from the place where Rome was afterward built.

693. *Populos jampridem:* his people, a long time inactive, and disengaged from the pursuits of war.

695. *Fescenninas acies:* the Fescennine troops. These were from the city Fescennia, or Fescennium, a town of Etruria, a little below the confluence of the Nar and Tiber. *Acies,* properly, an army drawn up in order of battle. Here, troops in general. *Æquosque Faliscos.* These were a people situated a little below *Fescennium.* Their city was *Faliscum.* Servius says, they were called *Æquos,* because the Romans borrowed from them their *jura fecialia,* or laws of arms: also, a supplement to the laws of the twelve tables. Others make *Æqui* the name of a people, called, also, Æquicolæ, and read, *Æquosque Faliscosque.* The *hi* in this and the following line, appears to refer to Messapus, within whose territories all these cities and people were, here mentioned; and, consequently, he was their commander in chief. The plu. may be used for the sing. by way of aggrandizement, as is common to all languages. Or the *hi* must refer to the subordinate officers and commanders of Messapus. This seems to be the opinion of Ruæus, who has: *hi duces Messapi.*

696. *Soractis.* Soracte was the name of a mountain in the country of the *Falisci.* *Arces:* the towers or strong places built upon it. *Flavinia arva.* Little is known of this place, nor is its situation exactly ascertained.

697. *Cimini.* Ciminus was a mountain in the western part of Etruria. It had a lake and a grove. *Capenos:* an adj. of *Capena,* a city on the banks of the Tiber. Here was a grove and temple. All these followed Messapus to the war.

698. *Ibant æquati:* they marched with equal steps, and uniform motion. By *numero,* we are to understand a kind of harmony and keeping time with their music. Or, rather, the order of their march—rank and file.

699. *Ceu quondam,* &c. This simile is taken from the *Iliad,* lib. ii. and is very finely expressed.

701. *Amnis et Asia:* the river and the Asian lake, struck from afar, resound. The *Amnis* is the *Caÿstrus.* See Geor. i. 383. *Modos:* in the sense of *voces.*

702. *Nec quisquam putet:* nor would any one (who heard their music only) have thought them armed troops of so great numbers, united and joined together; but an aërial cloud of sonorous fowls, &c. The words, *who heard their music only,* are necessary to make the sense complete. For the poet could not intend that those who saw them, would have taken them for a flock of birds.

Urgeri volucrum raucarum ad litora nubem.
Ecce, Sabinorum prisco de sanguine, magnum
Agmen agens Clausus, magnique ipse agminis instar,
Claudia nunc à quo diffunditur et tribus et gens
Per Latium, postquam in partem data Roma Sabinis.
Unà ingens Amiterna cohors, priscique Quirites,
Ereti manus omnis, oliviferæque Mutuscæ:
Qui Nomentum urbem, qui rosea rura Velini:
Qui Tetricæ horrentes rupes, montemque Severum,
Casperiamque colunt, Forulosque et flumen Himellæ.
Qui Tybrim Fabarimque bibunt: quos frigida misit
Nursia; et Hortinæ classes, populique Latini:
Quosque secans infaustum interluit Allia nomen.
Quàm multi Libyco volvuntur marmore fluctus,
Sævus ubi Orion hybernis conditur undis:
Vel quàm Sole novo densæ torrentur aristæ,
Aut Hermi campo, aut Lyciæ flaventibus arvis.

710. Unà *cum eo ibant* ingens Amiterna cohors, priscique

712. *Illi quoque ibant* qui *colunt* urbem Nomentum, qui *colunt* rosea rura Velini; qui colunt

715 *Illi ibant quoque*, quos frigida Nursia misit

717. *Illi* que, quos Allia, infaustum nomen, secans interluit, *ibant unà cum eo.*

NOTES.

707. *Clausus.* After the expulsion of the kings, *Atta Clausus* removed with his family, and about five thousand clients and friends, from Regillum, a city of the Sabines, to Rome. After which he took the name of Appius. He was admitted into the patrician order. The poet makes the *Clausus* here named, to have been one of his ancestors. *Instar agminis:* himself like a mighty army—a match for.

708. *Diffunditur:* in the sense of *propagatur*, vel *spargitur.*

709. *In partem Sabinis.* The poet here alludes to the union of the Sabines and Romans, which put an end to the wars between the two nations. These were the conditions of the compact. The Sabines were to remove to Rome, which was to retain its name. The citizens were to take the name of *Quirites*, from *Cures*, a city of the Sabines; and the government was to be jointly administered by Tatius and Romulus.

710. *Amiterna cohors.* The poet here enumerates various places, all belonging to the Sabines. *Amiterna:* an adj. from *Amiternum*, a town situated among the Apennines. *Quirites* were the inhabitants of *Cures*, whence the Romans were afterward sometimes called *Quirites. Eretum* was a village near the confluence of the rivers Allia and Tiber. *Hodie, Monte Rotundo. Mutuscæ:* a village beyond the Palus Reatina, to the north. *Hodie, Monte Leone. Nomentum*, was a town near *Eretum* on the east. *Hodie, Nomentano.*

712. *Rosea rura.* Part of the country of Reatina, according to Pliny, was called *rosea*, from *ros*, dew; which, falling copiously, fertilized that part of the country. Mr. Addison observes, that the river Velinus is shaded by a green forest made up of several kinds of trees, which preserve their verdure all the year. The neighboring mountains are covered with them; and, by reason of their height, are more exposed to dews and drizzling rains than the adjacent parts. Some copies have *roscida.* Dr. Trapp prefers *rosea*, and takes it for a patronymic adjective; and observes it should be written with a capital R. Heyne writes it with a capital. *Tetricæ—Severum.* The names of two mountains, so called from their wild aspect and barrenness. Their situation is uncertain.

714. *Casperiam.* Casperia was a town not far from *Cures. Hodie, Aspera. Forulos.* Foruli was a town in the neighborhood of Amiternum. *Himellæ.* This was a small river falling into the Tiber, a little below *Cures. Hodie, Aia.*

716. *Nursia.* This city was situated among the Apennines, and much exposed to frost. Hence the epithet, *frigida. Hodie, Norcia. Hortinæ:* an adj. from Hortanum or Horta, a city at the confluence of the *Nar* and *Tiber. Classes.* It is plain that *classes* here means land forces, or troops in general. Heyne says, *copiæ.*

717. *Allia.* A river that runs into the Tiber a little below *Eretum.* Here the Romans were completely defeated by the *Galli Senones*, under Brennus, their king: on which account, Virgil calls it *infaustum nomen:* an inauspicious name. *Secans:* in the sense of *dividens.*

719. *Orion:* a constellation much dreaded by mariners; hence called *sævus:* stormy.

720. *Novo sole.* By this interpreters understand the sun in the beginning of the summer. But perhaps the sun is called *new*, not in respect of the year; but of the *aristæ*, the ears of corn. *Hermi.* Hermus was a river of Lydia, a most fertile country *Lyciæ.* This was a country on the south of

Scuta sonant, pulsuque pedum tremit excita tellus
Hinc Agamemnonius, Trojani nominis hostis,
Curru jungit Halesus equos, Turnoque feroces
Mille rapit populos. Vertunt felicia Baccho
Massica qui rastris: et quos de collibus altis
Aurunci misêre patres, Sidicinaque juxta
Æquora: quique Cales linquunt; amnisque vadosi
Accola Vulturni; pariterque Saticulus asper,
Oscorumque manus. Teretes sunt aclides illis
Tela; sed hæc lento mos est aptare flagello:
Lævas cetra tegit: falcati cominùs enses.
Nec tu carminibus nostris indictus abibis,
Œbale; quem generâsse Telon Sebethide Nymphâ
Fertur, Teleboûm Capreas cùm regna teneret
Jam senior: patriis sed non et filius arvis
Contentus, latè jam tum ditione premebat
Sarrastes populos, et quæ rigat æquora Sarnus:
Quique Rufas, Batulumque tenent, atque arva Celennæ:
Et quos maliferæ despectant mœnia Abellæ:

725. Rapit mille feroces populos *in auxilium* Turno. *Illi veniunt* qui vertunt rastris Massica *arva* felicia Baccho; et *illi veniunt* quos Aurunci patres, Sidicinaque juxta æquora misêre

732. Cetra tegit lævas *manus;* falcati enses *sunt illis ad pugnandum* cominùs. Nec tu, *O pater* Œbale, abibis indictus

739. *Veniunt*que, qui tenent

740. Et *illi* quos mœnia

NOTES.

Asia Minor, abounding in corn. *Torrentur:* dried—ripened.

722. *Excita:* in the sense of *commota.*

723. *Hinc:* in the next place, Halesus, &c.

724. *Halesus.* Either the natural son of Agamemnon, or an illegitimate one. Or perhaps by *Agamemnonius,* we are to understand simply his being a Greek by birth. *Curru:* for *currui.*

726. *Massica.* The poet here mentions several nations and places in Campania. *Massica:* an adj. agreeing with *arva* understood. Massicus was a mountain in Campania near the sea, in the confines of Latium, very fertile in vines. *Aurunci patres.* The *Aurunci,* or *Ausones,* were the most ancient inhabitants of Italy, and therefore styled *Patres.* They were between Campania and the Volsci. *Sidicina:* plu. of *Sidicinum,* a tract of country to the eastward of the *Aurunci,* bordering upon the sea. *Cales:* plu. a town built upon the mountain *Massicus. Hodie, Calvi.*

729. *Accola:* the inhabitants of the fordable river *Vulturnus*—those who live near the river, &c. came also to the war. Mr. Davidson observes that *vadosus* must be used here metaphorically, to signify dangerous; or it must refer to those parts of the river near the mouth, where it spreads and runs with a gentle course, and consequently is shoal. The *Vulturnus* is a river of Campania, noted for its rapidity. *Vadosus:* from *vadum,* a shoal or sand-bank. This river takes its rise in the Apennines, and after a very circuitous course falls into the sea not far from the ancient Cumæ. *Saticulus:* an inhabitant of *Saticula,* or *Satricula,* a town to the east of Vulturnus, and Capuæ. *Manus Oscorum.* The *Osci,* were a people descended from the ancient *Ausones,* and inhabited the city Capua. All these troops were under the command of Halesus.

730. *Teretes aclides.* The *aclis* was a kind of missive weapon, with a sharp point at each end. It had a string fastened to it, by which the owner drew it back after a throw. These in close fight were formidable weapons. It is probable they bound them about the wrist with a cord, (*flagello,*) or string, by way of security.

732. *Falcati:* in the sense of *curvi.*

733. *Indictus:* unsung—unmentioned.

734. *Telon:* acc. of Greek ending. *Sebethide:* the nymph *Sebethis.*

735. *Capreas:* Caprea, an island over against the *Surrentinum Promontorium.* The *Teleboi,* a colony from Epirus, possessed it. *Hodie, Capri.*

737. *Premebat ditione:* held in bondage—in subjection.

738. *Sarnus.* A river flowing through Campania, into the *Sinus Neapolitanus. Sarrastes.* These were the inhabitants of the promontory *Surrentinum,* in that part of Italy called Campania. *Æquora:* in the sense of *campi* vel *arva. Æquor,* properly signifies any plane, or level surface, whether land or water

739. *Rufas:* Rufæ, or Rufræ, was a city farther to the east. *Hodie, Rufo.* The situation of *Batulum* and *Celennæ* is unknown.

740. *Abella:* Abella a town to the north of *Sarnus,* in the confines of Campania and the Harpini. It was celebrated for that sort of nuts, called *nuces avellanæ,* or filbert-nuts, *Hodie Avella.* It was built on an elevated

Teutonico ritu soliti torquere cateias;
Tegmina queis capitum raptus de subere cortex,
Æratæque micant peltæ, micat æreus ensis.
Et te montosæ misêre in prælia Nursæ,
Ufens, insignem famâ et felicibus armis:
Horrida præcipuè cui gens, assuetaque multo
Venatu nemorum, duris Æquicola glebis.
Armati terram exercent; semperque recentes
Convectare juvat prædas, et vivere rapto.
Quin et Marrubiâ venit de gente sacerdos,
Fronde super galeam et felici comptus olivâ,
Archippi regis missu, fortissimus Umbro:
Vipereo generi et graviter spirantibus hydris
Spargere qui somnos cantuque manuque solebat,
Mulcebatque iras, et morsus arte levabat.
Sed non Dardaniæ medicari cuspidis ictum
Evaluit: neque eum juvêre in vulnera cantus
Somniferi, et Marsis quæsitæ in montibus herbæ
Te nemus Angitiæ, vitreâ te Fucinus undâ,
Te liquidi flevêre lacus.
Ibat et Hippolyti proles pulcherrima bello,

742. Queis tegmina capitum *sunt* cortex

746. Cui præcipuè Æquicola *in* duris glebis, horrida gens, assuetaque multo venatu nemorum, *paret*

750. Quin et fortissimus Umbro venit missu regis Archippi, sacerdos de Marrubiâ gente

754. Qui solebat spargere somnos vipereo

759. Nemus Angitiæ *flevit* te, Fucinus vitreâ undâ *flevit* te

NOTES.

situation. Hence it is said to look, *despectant*, down upon the inhabitants below. *Maliferæ:* fruit-bearing.

741. *Cateias.* The *cateia* was a kind of halbert or dart, used by the Germans, and Gauls. All the nations just mentioned were subject to *Œbelus*, and followed him to the war. *Ritu:* after the Teutonic manner, they used, &c. *Soliti: sunt* is understood. The *Teutones* were a people of Germany, near the *Chersonesus Cimbrica. Hodie*, Denmark.

742. *Tegmina:* coverings for the head—helmets. Ruæus says, *galeæ. Queis:* the dat. in the sense of *quorum.*

744. *Nursæ:* the situation of this place is not known, probably it was among the Apennines.

745. *Insignem famâ:* illustrious by fame, and successful arms. This is equivalent to *insignem famâ felicium armorum.*

748. *Exercent:* in the sense of *colunt.*

749. *Vivere rapto:* to live upon plunder. This is agreeable to what Livy says of those nations: *Fortuna Volscis Æquisque prædonum potiùs mentem quàm hostium dedit.* The *Æquicoli* or *Æqui* were a people to the east of Latium, not far from the source of the river *Anien.* Their country was hard and mountainous. Virgil calls it, *Æquicola duris glebis:* Æquicola of hard soil. These were under the command of Ufens, and followed him to the war.

750. *Marrubiâ.* an adj. of *Marrubium* or *Marruvium*, a city of the Marsi, to the east of the Æqui, on the river Liris.

751. *Comptus super:* decked upon his helmet with leaves, and the auspicious olive—having his helmet adorned with the leaves of the happy olive. *Fronde et felici oliva*, by hend. for *fronde felicis olivæ.*

752. *Missu:* by the command, or order.

754. *Spargere somnos:* to diffuse sleep over the viperous race, &c. *Cantu:* by his charms, or incantations.

755. *Levabat:* he healed—cured.

756. *Ictum:* in the sense of *vulnus.* The wounds inflicted by the weapons of the Trojans.

757. *Juvêre:* helped—aided. Ruæus says, *profuerunt.*

758. *Somniferi cantus:* soporific charms. *Herbæ:* herbs gathered in the mountains of the *Marsi.* These people were skilled in enchantments, particularly in charming serpents. This they learned from *Marsus*, the son of Circe, the founder of their race.

759. *Angitiæ.* Angitia was the sister of Circe, and came with her into Italy. She occupied the country in the neighborhood of the lake *Fucinus.* The town she built is now called *Luco*, situated to the westward of the said lake. *Hodie, Lago Fucino. Vitrea:* clear—pellucid.

760. *Liquidi:* in the sense of *puri.*

761. *Hippolyti:* Hippolytus was the son of Theseus king of Athens. Refusing the overtures of his step-mother *Phædra*, he was accused by her to his father, who condemned him to death. As he was driving his chariot along the shore, his horses were affrighted by sea-monsters, tore his chariot in pieces and killed him. Diana pitying his hard fate, by the help of Æsculapius,

Virbius; insignem quem mater Aricia misit,
Eductum Egeriæ lucis, humentia circum
Litora, pinguis ubi et placabilis ara Dianæ.
Namque ferunt famâ Hippolytum, postquam arte novercæ
Occiderit, patriasque explêrit sanguine pœnas,
Turbatis distractus equis, ad sidera rursus
Ætherea, et superas cœli venisse sub auras,
Pæoniis revocatum herbis, et amore Dianæ.
Tum pater omnipotens, aliquem indignatus ab umbris
Mortalem infernis ad lumina surgere vitæ,
Ipse repertorem medicinæ talis et artis
Fulmine Phœbigenam Stygias detrusit ad undas.
At Trivia Hippolytum secretis alma recondit
Sedibus, et Nymphæ Egeriæ nemorique relegat:
Solus ubi in sylvis Italis ignobilis ævum
Exigeret, versoque ubi nomine Virbius esset.
Unde etiam Triviæ templo lucisque sacratis
Cornipedes arceantur equi, quòd litore currum
Et juvenem monstris pavidi effudêre marinis.
Filius ardentes haud seciùs æquore campi
Exercebat equos, curruque in bella ruebat.
Ipse inter primos præstanti corpore Turnus
Vertitur, arma tenens, et toto vertice supra est.
Cui triplici crinita jubâ galea alta Chimæram
Sustinet, Ætnæos efflantem faucibus ignes:
Tam magìs illa fremens, et tristibus effera flammis,

765. Hippolytum *Virbium*, postquam occiderit arte novercæ, distractusque turbatis equis, explêrit patrias pœnas, venisse rursus

772. Fulmine detrusit Phœbigenam, repertorem

781. Filius *hujus Virbii* haud seciùs exercebat

784. Et est supra *omnes* toto vertice

787. Illa *est* tam magìs fremens, et effera tristibus flammis,

NOTES.

restored him to life, and commended him to the care of *Egeria*, the nymph of the Aricinean grove. Here he was worshipped as a demi-god and called *Virbius;* from the words *vir* and *bis.* Virgil makes him the son of Hippolytus and the nymph Aricia. By *mater*, we are to understand his mother.

762. *Aricia.* This was a city of ancient Latium, not far from the mouth of the Tiber. It might be so called from the nymph Aricia. Servius understands by *mater* this city, which was the birth-place of the mother of Augustus, and the parent of an illustrious family. But it is better to take it as above. In its neighborhood was a grove sacred to Egeria. With this nymph, Numa Pompilius pretended to be intimate, and to receive instructions in religion.

763. *Humentia litora:* the shores of the lake Aricinus.

764. *Pinguis:* this is said of the altar, in reference to the number of victims offered upon it. *Placabilis:* easy to be appeased. The verb *est* is understood.

766. *Explêrit:* had satisfied—filled up. *Turbatis:* affrighted.

768. *Sub superas auras cœli:* to the upper regions of light—this upper world.

769. *Pæoniis herbis:* such herbs as were used by *Pæan*, the physician of the gods: by Apollo, his father, who is also styled *Pæan*—medicinal herbs.

773. *Phœbigenam:* Æsculapius, the son of Phœbus and Coronis, the daughter of a king of the Lapithæ. He is esteemed the father of physic. It is said he raised several from the dead.

775. *Relegat:* she consigns him to the nymph, &c. *Triviæ:* a name of Diana, from *tres* et *via.*

776. *Ignobilis:* unknown—retired from the world.

778. *Unde:* hence—from that circumstance—to wit, their being affrighted at the monsters.

780. *Pavidi:* affrighted at the sea-monsters, they overturned—ran away with the chariot, &c.

781. *Filius haud:* the son, not less intrepidly than the father, managed the fiery steeds, &c.

784. *Vertitur inter primos:* he marches in the foremost ranks. *Vertitur:* in the sense of *incedit.*

785. *Galea crinita:* his lofty helmet waving with a triple crest, &c. The figure of the Chimæra was represented on his helmet. See Æn. vi. 288.

787. *Effera:* fierce—dreadful. *Tristibus:* horrid—awful.

Quàm magis effuso crudescunt sanguine pugnæ.

789. At) *ex* auro sublatis cornibus, insignibat levem clypeum *Turni*

At levem clypeum sublatis cornibus Io
Auro insignibat, jam setis obsita, jam bos,
Argumentum ingens! et custos virginis Argus,
Cœlatâque amnem fundens pater Inachus urnâ
Insequitur nimbus peditum, clypeataque totis
Agmina densantur campis, Argivaque pubes,
Auruncæque manus, Rutuli, veteresque Sicani,

796. Labici picti *quoad* scuta: qui arant tuos saltus, *O* Tiberine

Et Sacranæ acies, et picti scuta Labici:
Qui saltus, Tiberine, tuos, sacrumque Numici
Litus arant: Rutulosque exercent vomere colles,
Circæumque jugum: queis Jupiter Anxurus arvis
Præsidet, et viridi gaudens Feronia luco:

801. Gelidusque Ufens quærit iter per

Quà Saturæ jacet atra palus; gelidusque per imas
Quærit iter valles, atque in mare conditur Ufens.
Hos super advenit Volscâ de gente Camilla,

805. Illa non assueta *est* fœmineas manus colo

Agmen agens equitum et florentes ære catervas,
Bellatrix: non illa colo calathisve Minervæ

NOTES.

788. *Crudescunt:* rage—grow more and more fierce and bloody.

789. *Io.* The poets say she was the daughter of the river-god *Inachus.* Jove had an amour with her; and likely to be discovered by Juno, he changed her into a heifer. Juno suspecting the trick, desired the heifer to be given to her. Having obtained her request, she gave her into the custody of the shepherd Argus, fabled to have had a hundred eyes. He was slain by Mercury; and Juno placed his eyes in the tail of her peacock. After this she drove the heifer into Egypt, where she was restored to her former shape by Jove. Here she married Osiris, king of Egypt; and after her death, was worshipped as a goddess, under the name of Isis. This fable was represented on the shield of Turnus. He was descended from Inachus, king of Argos. See 372, supra.—*sublatis:* high—wide—spreading.

790. *Obsita:* covered with hairs. *Bos:* in the sense of *vacca.*

791. *Argumentum:* subject—device. *Ingens:* noble—illustrious.

792. *Pater,* here refers to the father of *Io. Cœlata urna:* from his embossed urn.

794. *Argivaque pubes.* The poet now enumerates the nations that followed Turnus. The Argive troops, most probably came from *Ardea.* See 372, supra.

795. *Auruncæ manus.* These were the descendants of the old Aurunci, or Ausones, the first people of Italy. *Sicani.* These were the inhabitants of some part of Latium; or the remains of the *Siculi,* whom Cluverius thinks to have been among the first inhabitants of Italy; but, being expelled their country, fled to Sicily, to which island they gave their name.

796. *Sacranæ:* an adject. from *Sacrani.* These were a people made up of the aborigines and the Pelasgi: who, after their expulsion of the Siculi, were themselves driven by the Sabines beyond the river *Anien,* and settled near the place where Rome was afterward built. *Labici.* Their city *Labicum,* was in the northern part of *Latium.*

798. *Exercent:* in the sense of *excindunt* vel *vertunt.*

799. *Circæum jugum.* This was the hill and promontory which bounded old Latium on the east. Here was the residence of the celebrated Circe. *Hodie,* mount *Circello. Anxurus:* an epithet of Jupiter, from *Anxur,* or *Anxurus,* a town of the Volsci, where he was particularly worshipped.

800. *Feronia:* Feronia rejoicing in a verdant grove. This was situated between *Mons Circæus,* and Terracina or Anxur. It is not certain what goddess is meant by *Feronia.* Most interpreters take her to be the same with Juno. But La Cerda thinks her to be the same with *Flora,* relying on the authority of Dionysius.

801. *Atra palus Saturæ:* the dismal lake of Satura. By this we are to understand the *palus pontina,* or pontine lake, which extended along the maritime coast of the Volsci. It gave rise to many foul and unwholesome streams. Here fitly called *atra palus. Ufens.* This river flows in deep winding vales, to which the sun can hardly have access. Hence the epithet, *gelidus.*

803. *Super hos:* beside these—in addition to the troops already mentioned, Camilla brings her squadrons of horse and foot.

804. *Florentes ære:* glittering, or gleaming in brazen armor. The Volsci, her people, were brave and warlike; and had the

Fœmineas assueta manus; sed prælia virgo
Dura pati, cursuque pedum prævertere ventos.
Illa vel intactæ segetis per summa volaret
Gramina, nec teneras cursu læsisset aristas:
Vel mare per medium, fluctu suspensa tumenti,
Ferret iter, celeres nec tingeret æquore plantas
Illam omnis tectis agrisque effusa juventus,
Turbaque miratur matrum, et prospectat euntem,
Attonitis inhians animis; ut regius ostro
Velet honos leves humeros; ut fibula crinem
Auro internectat; Lyciam ut gerat ipsa pharetram,
Et pastoralem præfixâ cuspide myrtum.

808. Sed virgo *assueta est* pati dura prælia

810. Suspensa tumenti fluctu, vel ferret iter per medium mare

814. *Videns* ut regius

NOTES.

Latins on the west, the Aurunci and Campani on the east, and the Hernici and Æqui on the north.

806. *Assueta:* she had not accustomed her female hands to the distaff, &c. *Calathis Minervæ. Calathus* is a basket for women to put their sewing and other work into. Hence, by meton. the work itself. Then will *calathis Minervæ* mean, light and easy female employments in general. She had not accustomed her hands to these; but to endure the fatigue and hardships of war.

808. *Illa vel volaret:* she could even fly along the topmost stalks of the corn untouched, &c. *Gramina:* the stalks or blades of corn. We may observe that the poet here does not say she actually flew over the fields of corn; but, by an hyperbole, to denote her swiftness, she could even do it, nor touch them in her course.

812. *Omnis juventus effusa:* all the youth issuing from city and country, and the crowd of matrons, wonder at her, &c. *Tectis* and *agris* are plainly opposed to each other; the one put for the city, and the other for the country.

814. *Inhians:* gazing upon her.

815. *Regius honos:* how the regal ornaments, &c.

816. *Ut ipsa gerat:* how she bears the Lycian quiver, &c. The poet gives her this quiver, because the Lycians were famed for skill in archery.

817. *Myrtum.* The myrtle was a suitable wood for spears. Hence, by meton. the spear itself. It is called *pastoral*, because she had lived among shepherds with her father Metabus. *Cuspide:* this is put for the point of the spear, which was tipped with steel. Ruæus says, *armatam cuspide;* meaning *myrtum*, the spear or javelin.

QUESTIONS.

From Cajeta to what place did Æneas direct his course?

What time of the day did he set sail?

What does Dr. Trapp observe of the opening of this book?

After his arrival in the Tiber, what were the first measures which he adopted?

How were his ambassadors received by *Latinus?*

Who was Latinus?

How many generations was he from Saturn?

Why was his kingdom called *Latium?*

Had he any children?

What was the name of his daughter?

In the course of his life, had he any sons?

What was the age of his daughter at that time?

Had any of the Italian princes sought her in marriage?

Who was the most distinguished of her suitors?

Had she been promised in marriage to Turnus?

Who was Turnus?

Of what country were his ancestors?

What was the character of Turnus?

Was Latinus in favor of this connexion?

What was the reason of his opposing it?

What particularly influenced his mind upon this subject?

What was the response of the oracle of *Faunus?*

Did he consider Æneas to be the person alluded to by the oracle as his son-in-law?

Did he propose to the Trojan ambassadors a connexion between him and his daughter?

Was this connexion opposed by Turnus?

What was the consequence of this?

How was the mother of Lavinia affected toward Turnus?

What was her name?

Did she endeavor to persuade her husband to consent to the match?

Did she make any speech to him upon the subject?

What is the character of that address?

How was she affected with the determination of *Latinus?*

Æneas had been told that his followers should be reduced to the necessity of consuming their trenchers, before they should find a permanent settlement: how was that prediction fulfilled?

Who made this prophetic declaration to Æneas?

How was the accomplishment received by him and his associates?

How was Juno affected with this kind reception of the Trojans?

What does the poet represent her as doing to kindle the war?

What course does Alecto pursue?

While these things are going on, what do the Trojans?

While in the chase, what does Ascanius?

To whom did this beautiful stag belong?

Whither did the wounded animal flee?

What effect had this upon the minds of the rustics?

Who was killed in this skirmish?

Who was Almon?

Who was Tyrrheus?

What was his employment?

Was there any other person slain?

Did the Trojans suffer any loss?

What was the next measure adopted?

What course did Latinus pursue?

Did Turnus also urge the aged monarch to declare war against the intruders?

How was the war finally declared?

What was the manner or form of declaring war?

In time of peace, what was the state of the temple of Janus?

What in time of war?

After the war had been thus declared what effect had it upon the neighboring nations?

Which side did they join?

Who may be considered the commander-in-chief?

How does the book conclude?

Who was the first who joined the confederacy?

Who was Mezentius?

Over what people was he king?

What was his character?

Why did the people expel him from his throne?

Had he any son?

What was his name?

What does the poet say of him?

Who is mentioned as a distinguished horseman?

What troops had he under his command?

Among the commanders, was there any distinguished female? What was her name?

Of what people was she queen?

For what was she especially distinguished?

What does the poet say of her speed, and the rapidity of her course?

Do these last books excite in us an interest equal to the first books of the Æneid?

Has the poet been censured on this account?

Is this censure justly founded?

Why is it not justly founded?

LIBER OCTAVUS.

WAR being determined upon, Turnus sends to Diomede to engage him in his interest; and Æneas, at the direction of the god of the Tiber, ascends that river to Evander to obtain supplies. He finds the aged monarch engaged in the sacred rites of Hercules. He receives him very kindly, informs him of their relationship, and of his former acquaintance with Priam and Anchises, who visited Arcadia, his native country. He then proceeds to give him an account of the victory of Hercules over the monster Cacus, a noted robber: in memory of which, the rites, in which he was then engaged, were instituted. He also recounts to him the antiquities of that part of Italy, and mentions, particularly, the rock or hill on which the Capitol at Rome was afterward built. While these things are going on, Venus repairs to Vulcan, and engages him to make armor for Æneas. He immediately repairs to the Æolian Islands, where he had his forges, and sets about the business with all haste.

Evander furnishes two hundred horse, and sends Pallas, his son, with as many more. At this time the Tuscans are in arms to avenge the barbarities of Mezentius, their king who had fled to Turnus for safety. These gladly join Æneas in the war. The book concludes with a description of the armor of Æneas, brought to him by Venus through the air. The scene is here changed from the country of Latinus to that of Evander This book is chiefly *episodical*, and abounds in matter of the most interesting kind. Dr. Trapp thinks, on the whole, it is one of the noblest, most elegant, and most entertaining of the whole Æneid.

UT belli signum Laurenti Turnus ab arce
Extulit, et rauco strepuerunt cornua cantu ;
Utque acres concussit equos, utque impulit arma
Extemplò turbati animi : simul omne tumultu
Conjurat trepido Latium, sævitque juventus
Effera. Ductores primi, Messapus, et Ufens,
Contemptorque Deûm Mezentius, undique cogunt
Auxilia, et latos vastant cultoribus agros.
Mittitur et magni Venulus Diomedis ad urbem,
Qui petat auxilium, et Latio consistere Teucros,
Advectum Æneam classi, victosque Penates
Inferre, et fatis regem se dicere posci,
Edoceat ; multasque viro se adjungere gentes
Dardanio, et latè Latio increbrescere nomen.
Quid struat his cœptis, quem, si fortuna sequatur,
Eventum pugnæ cupiat, manifestiùs ipsi,
Quàm Turno regi, aut regi apparere Latino.
Talia per Latium : quæ Laomedontius heros
Cuncta videns, magno curarum fluctuat æstu ;
Atque animum nunc huc celerem, nunc dividit illuc,
In partesque rapit varias, perque omnia versat.
Sicut aquæ tremulum labris ubi lumen ahenis
Sole repercussum, aut radiantis imagine Lunæ,
Omnia pervolitat latè loca ; jamque sub auras
Erigitur, summique ferit laquearia tecti.
Nox erat, et terras animalia fessa per omnes
Alituum pecudumque genus sopor altus habebat :
Cùm pater in ripâ gelidique sub ætheris axe
Æneas, tristi turbatus pectora bello,
Procubuit, seramque dedit per membra quietem.
Huic deus ipse loci, fluvio Tiberinus amœno,
Populeas inter senior se attollere frondes
Visus. Eum tenuis glauco velabat amictu

4. Extemplò animi turbati *sunt*

10. Et edoceat *eum* Teucros consistere Latio ; Æneam advectum *esse* classi,

15. *Et addat,* quid *Æneas* struat his cœptis ; quem eventum pugnæ cupiat, si fortuna sequatur *eum*, apparere manifestiùs ipsi *Diomedi* quàm

18. Talia *fiunt* per Latium ; quæ cuncta

28. Cùm pater Æneas, turbatus *quoad* pectora, procubuit

NOTES.

1. *Signum.* The poet here alludes to the custom among the Romans, of hanging out the sign or signal of war from the Capitol.

2. *Cornua:* trumpets. See Æn. vii. 637. *Concussit equos:* roused the active horses. This he did by the sound of the trumpets, the clashing of their arms, &c. *Impulit arma.* Some understand by this the throwing of the spear into the enemy's country, which was a practice among the Romans. This was a declaration of war. Servius understands it of the rattling of the arms in the temple of Mars. But it is easier to understand it of his striking on his shield as a sign and prelude to the war.

8. *Vastant:* in the sense of *spoliunt. Cultoribus:* the farmers—inhabitants.

9. *Urbem Diomedis:* the city of Diomede, Arpos or Argyripa, a city built by him in Apulia, after the destruction of Troy. See Æn. xi. 243, et seq.

12. *Posci fatis:* that he was demanded by the fates or destinies as a king over the Latins.

14. *Nomen:* the name of Æneas—his fame—renown, had spread widely.

18. *Talia:* the verb *fiunt*, or another of the like import, is understood.

22. *Sicut aquæ:* as when the tremulous light in brazen vats of water, reflected from the sun, or the image of the radiant moon, flies through, &c. This simile Dr. Trapp observes is of the low kind; but extremely elegant and beautiful. By *sole*, we are to understand the *image* of the sun.

24. *Sub auras:* simply, on high.

27. *Alituum:* in the sense of *volucrum.*

28. *Sub axe:* under the canopy of the cold sky.

31. *Senior Tiberinus, Deus loci:* old Tiberinus, the god of the place, seemed to him to raise himself from the pleasant stream among, &c. This is a most beautiful description.

35. Tum *cœpit* affari *cum* sic

39. Hìc *erit* certa domus tibi; *hìc erunt* certi Penates *tibi:* ne absiste *ab incepto*

44. Jăcebit recubans solo, *ipsa* alba, et *ejus* nati albi circum ubera

49. Nunc adverte, docebo *te* paucis *verbis*, quâ ratione *tu* victor

51. Arcades, genus profectum a Pallante, qui comites *secuti sunt* regem Evandrum, qui secuti *sunt ejus* signa, delegêre

Carbasus, et crines umbrosa tegebat arundo.
Tum sic affari, et curas his demere dictis:
O sate gente Deûm, Trojanam ex hostibus urbem
Qui revehis nobis, æternaque Pergama servas,
Expectate solo Laurenti, arvisque Latinis:
Hìc tibi certa domus; certi, ne absiste, Penates
Neu belli terrere minis. Tumor omnis et iræ
Concessêre Deûm.
Jamque tibi, ne vana putes hæc fingere somnum,
Litoreis ingens inventa sub ilicibus sus,
Triginta capitum fœtus enixa, jacebit,
Alba, solo recubans, albi circum ubera nati.
Hic locus urbis erit, requies ea certa laborum:
Ex quo ter denis urbem redeuntibus annis
Ascanius clari condet cognominis Albam.
Haud incerta cano. Nunc, quâ ratione, quod instat,
Expedias victor, paucis, adverte, docebo.
Arcades his oris, genus à Pallante profectum,
Qui regem Evandrum comites, qui signa secuti,
Delegêre locum, et posuêre in montibus urbem

NOTES.

34. *Tenuis carbasus:* fine lawn—a robe of lawn. In this habit, river-gods were commonly represented on medals and ancient monuments.

36. *Gente:* of the family—race—stock. Æneas sprang from Jove both by Dardanus and Venus.

37. *Revehis:* who bringest back to us the Trojan city, &c. *Æterna Pergama:* and Pergamus to continue forever—to be eternal. Here is an allusion to the opinion of the Romans, of the eternal duration of their empire. Dardanus, the founder of the Trojan race, was a native of Italy.

38. *Expectate:* welcome—looked for: a part. adj. agreeing with *sate* in the voc. *Solo:* in the sense of *terra.*

39. *Penates:* properly household gods; by meton. a house or dwelling. *Certi Penatis:* a certain or fixed abode.

41. *Concessêre.* It is evident that Juno was still the enemy of the Trojans. To save Virgil from a seeming inconsistency, Servius makes the sense, as well as the line, abrupt; and observes that some have filled it up thus: *Concessêre Deûm profugis nova Mœnia Teucris.* La Cerda observes, that Virgil does not say *all the gods*, and thinks that it is sufficient for the poet's purpose, that Jupiter and Neptune, who took part with the Greeks, were now reconciled to the Trojans. *Iræ:* the anger of the gods has ceased—subsided.

44. *Fœtus enixa:* having brought forth a litter of thirty head, &c. Helenus informed Æneas, (lib. iii. 389.) that when he should find a white sow under the holms on the side of the river, with a litter of thirty white pigs around her, he might be assured that was the place destined to him by the gods. Tiberinus here repeats the same, lifts the curtain of futurity, and gives him some directions in his critical affairs.

45. *Jacebit recubans:* shall he prostrate, or stretched on the ground, &c. I think *recubans* should be taken in the sense of *strata*, or *prostrata*, and connected with *jacebit.* To take *recubans* in its usual sense and meaning, would be mere tautology. But in the sense of *strata*, it gives this additional idea, that the animal was lying flat, or at full length, in the attitude of giving suck to her pigs.

47. *Ex quo:* from which time, thirty years having rolled away, Ascanius shall, &c. The thirty years here spoken of, are not to be reckoned from the discovery of the sow, for that would not agree with history; but from the death of Æneas, who sat on the throne of Lavinium three years. Ascanius succeeded him, who, in the thirtieth year of his reign, built *Alba Longa*, and made it the seat of his government.

49. *Cano:* in the sense of *dico*, vel *prædico.*

50. *Expedias:* you may accomplish, or effect.

51. *Arcades:* plu. of *Arcas*, a native of Arcadia, a country of the Peloponnesus. This was the birth-place of Evander. He migrated into Italy, and settled on the banks of the Tiber, upon a mount, which he called *Palantium*, *Pallanteum*, or *Palatium*, from his native city Pallantium: or from Pallas, king of Arcadia, his great grandfather. On the same spot Rome was afterward built.

53. *Posuêre:* in the sense of *condiderunt.*

Pallantis proavi de nomine, Pallanteum.
Hi bellum assiduè ducunt cum gente Latinâ:
Hos castris adhibe socios, et fœdera junge,
Ipse ego te ripis et recto flumine ducam,
Adversum remis superes subvectus ut amnem.
Surge, age, nate Deâ; primisque cadentibus astris
Junoni fer ritè preces, iramque minasque
Supplicibus supera votis. Mihi victor honorem
Persolves. Ego sum, pleno quem flumine cernis
Stringentem ripas, et pinguia culta secantem,
Cœruleus Tybris, cœlo gratissimus amnis.
Hic mihi magna domus; celsis caput urbibus exit.
Dixit: deinde lacu fluvius se condidit alto
Ima petens: nox Æneam somnusque reliquit.
Surgit, et ætherii spectans orientia Solis
Lumina, ritè cavis undam de flumine palmis
Sustulit, ac tales effudit ad æthera voces;
Nymphæ, Laurentes Nymphæ, genus amnibus unde est;
Tuque, ô Tybri tuo genitor cum flumine sancto,
Accipite Ænean, et tandem arcete periclis.
Quo te cunque lacus miserantem incommoda nostra
Fonte tenet, quocunque solo pulcherrimus exis;
Semper honore meo, semper celebrabere donis:
Corniger Hesperidum fluvius regnator aquarum,

62. Ego sum *ille*, quem cernis

72. Tuque, O genitor Tybri, cum tuo sancto flumine

75. Quocunque solo *tu* exis pulcherrimus *amnis; tu* celebrabere semper meo honore, semper *meis* donis: O corniger fluvius

NOTES.

54 *Pallanteum:* the name of the city.

56. *Junge fœdera:* make—ratify a treaty with them.

57. *Recto flumine.* This does not mean that the river was straight, or in a direct line; but that it would lead him to the place of his destination—to the residence of Evander, in a direct or unerring course. *Absque errore*, says Ruæus.

58. *Adversum amnem.* By this we are to understand the current of the river, which was against him as he ascended it. *Ut subvectus:* that borne along, you may overcome, &c.

59. *Primis astris cadentibus:* the first stars setting. By this we are to understand the early dawn. The stars are said to set, when they disappear at the approach of the sun.

63. *Stringentem ripas:* touching lightly, or rolling gently along the banks with my full stream. *Secantem:* in the sense of *dividentem*.

65. *Caput exit*, &c. There are some commentators who take these words in a prophetic or oracular sense, that here *should be the head to lofty cities*—Rome, the empress of the world. The chief difficulty in this is the word *exit*, the present for the future: Dr. Trapp thinks this not very material, especially in a prophetic or oracular sentence. Others take them in a literal sense. Here is my palace; my source or head rises near, or flows from lofty cities. The former is the best idea. But it is probable, Virgil intended to include both: and, therefore, expressed himself ambiguously. Davidson renders the passage thus: "here is my spacious mansion; near lofty cities my fountain springs."

66. *Alto lacu:* the deepest part of the stream—the bed of the river.

68. *Spectans orientia*, &c. It was a custom of the ancients, in prayer, to turn their faces toward the east. It was also a custom to wash their hands before they performed any acts of religion. Æneas for that purpose takes water (*undam*) from the river, and turns his face toward the rising sun.

74. *Quocunque fonte:* in whatever place thy lake holds, or contains thee pitying, &c. It was the opinion of some philosophers, that rivers took their rise from great *lakes*, or reservoirs of water under ground. Æneas here promises to worship the god Tiber, in whatever place he found his residence to be; whether in his primary reservoir, in his fountain, or in the course of the river. *Fonte* appears to be used here in the sense of *loco*.

76. *Celebrabere.* Some manuscripts have *venerabere:* thou shalt be worshipped. *Honore:* worship—veneration.

77. *Corniger fluvius.* Horns are an emblem of power, and are therefore, applicable to the Tiber, here called the ruler of the Italian rivers. But it is common with the poets to ascribe to rivers the form of the

Adsis ô tantùm, et propiùs tua numina firmes!
Sic memorat: geminasque legit de classe biremes,
Remigioque aptat: socios simul instruit armis.
Ecce autem subitum atque oculis mirabile monstrum!
Candida per sylvam cum fœtu concolor albo
Procubuit, viridique in litore conspicitur sus:
Quam pius Æneas, tibi enim, tibi, maxima Juno,
Mactat, sacra ferens, et cum grege sistit ad aram.
Tybris eâ fluvium, quàm longa est, nocte tumentem
Leniit; et tacitâ refluens ita substitit undâ,
Mitis ut in morem stagni placidæque paludis
Sterneret æquor aquis, remo ut luctamen abesset.
Ergò iter inceptum celerant rumore secundo.
Labitur uncta vadis abies: mirantur et undæ,
Miratur nemus insuetum, fulgentia longè
Scuta virûm, fluvio pictasque innare carinas.
Olli remigio noctemque diemque fatigant,
Et longos superant flexus, variisque teguntur
Arboribus, viridesque secant placido æquore sylvas
Sol medium cœli conscenderat igneus orbem,
Cùm muros, arcemque procul, et rara domorum
Tecta vident, quæ nunc Romana potentia cœlo

81. Autem ecce monstrum subitum atque mirabile *offert sese* oculis, candida sus, concolor, cum albo fœtu procubuit per sylvam

84. Quam pius Æneas mactat tibi, (enim tibi *jussus est*) O maxima Juno, ferens sacra, et sistit *eam*

88. Ut sterneret æquor aquis in morem mitis stagni

92. Nemus insuetum *his spectaculis* miratur scuta virûm, fulgentia longè

95. Longos flexus *fluvii*

NOTES.

bull. The reason of this is, that the roaring noise of rivers resembles the bellowing of that animal. See Geor. IV. 372. The Tiber could not be called the king of Italian rivers from its magnitude; that belongs to the *Eridanus* or Po, called the king of rivers. Geor. I. 482. There must be some other reason for it; the future magnitude and glory of Rome, built on its banks; or Æneas may be supposed to speak from his own knowledge, supposing the *Tiber* to be the largest river. *Fluvius*, here, is plainly in the vocative case.

78. *Numina:* oracles—prophetic declarations.

84. *Enim tibi.* Mr. Dryden says the word *enim* was of such necessity among the Romans, that a sacrifice could not be performed without it. But this appears a notion entirely his own. Servius says, it is merely expletive and ornamental. It is plain there is an ellipsis, which, to make sense, must be filled. Æneas had just been ordered by Tiberinus to offer prayers and supplications to Juno, and to overcome her resentment by vows and offerings. He sacrifices (*mactat*) to thee, O supreme Juno; for to thee he was commanded, &c. As Jupiter is called *Maximus*, so Juno, his consort and queen, is called *Maxima*. For the same reason, she is sometimes called *omnipotens*.

85 *Grege:* her pigs—litter of pigs.

86. *Eâ nocte:* in that night. *Tumentem lenuit:* it smoothed (lowered) its swelling current.

89. *Ut sterneret:* that it might level the surface of its waters in the manner, &c. *Aquis:* the dat. in the sense of the gen.

90. *Secundo rumore.* By this we are, most probably, to understand the shouts and acclamations with which they animated each other, under the assurance of a prosperous issue. This assurance they had from the omen of the white sow. They understood by this that they should succeed to their wishes.

91. *Uncta abies labitur:* the ship glides easily along on the water, as if it were moving down the current. *Abies:* properly the fir-tree; by meton. a ship, because ships were made of that wood. This is the sense given by Ruæus and Davidson. Heyne connects *secundo rumore* with *uncta abies.*, understanding by it the noise made in the water by the oars and the keel as they moved along. Valpy is of the same opinion. It appears to be an unnecessary refinement.

92. *Insuetum:* unaccustomed to such sights. *His spectaculis*, says Ruæus.

94. *Fatigant:* in the sense of *traducunt*. *Remigio:* in rowing.

95. *Flexus:* the windings and flexures of the river.

96. *Secant virides:* they cut the verdant trees in the smooth surface—the shades of the trees, which appeared in the water of the river, by meton.

97. *Medium orbem.* This is a fine circumlocution for the middle of the day. The sun had ascended the middle of his course

Æquavit. tum res inopes Evandrus habebat
Ocyùs advertunt proras, urbique propinquant.
  Fortè die solemnem illo rex Arcas honorem
Amphitryoniadæ magno Divisque ferebat,
Ante urbem, in luco. Pallas huic filius unà,
Unà omnes juvenum primi, pauperque senatus,
Thura dabant: tepidusque cruor fumabat ad aras.
Ut celsas vidêre rates, atque inter opacum
Allabi nemus, et tacitis incumbere remis;
Terrentur visu subito, cunctique relictis
Consurgunt mensis: audax quos rumpere Pallas
Sacra vetat, raptoque volat telo obvius ipse,
Et procul è tumulo, Juvenes, quæ causa subegit
Ignotas tentare vias? quò tenditis? inquit.
Qui genus? unde domo? pacemne huc fertis, an arma?
Tum pater Æneas puppi sic fatur ab altâ,
Paciferæque manu ramum prætendit olivæ:
Trojugenas ac tela vides inimica Latinis,
Quos illi bello profugos egêre superbo.
Evandrum petimus: ferte hæc, et dicite lectos
Dardaniæ venisse duces, socia arma rogantes.
  Obstupuit, tanto percùlsus nomine, Pallas:
Egredere, ô quicunque es, ait, coràmque parentem
Alloquere, ac nostris succede penatibus hospes.
Accepitque manu, dextramque amplexus inhæsit.
Progressi subeunt luco, fluviumque relinquunt.
Tum regem Æneas dictis affatur amicis:
Optime Grajugenûm, cui me fortuna precari,
Et vittâ comptos voluit prætendere ramos:
Non equidem extimui, Danaûm quòd ductor et Arcas,

106. Dabant thura huic *Deo*

107. Atque *viros* allabi inter

111. Ipseque, telo rapto, volat obvius *iis*, et procul è tumulo inquit

114. Qui *estis quoad* genus? Unde *venistis* domo?

124. Accepit *Æneam* manu

127. Cui fortuna voluit me precari, et prætendere

129. Equidem non extimui *facere id*, quòd *fores* ductor Danaûm, et Arcas, quòdque

NOTES.

of circuit. The next day after their departure, they arrived at the city of Evander; it was small, and its inhabitants poor.

102. *Arcas rex.* Evander is called *Arcas*, an Arcadian, because he was a native of that country. *Honorem:* in the sense of *sacrificium.*

103. *Amphitryoniadæ magno:* to great Hercules. A patronymic noun, from Amphitryon, the husband of Alcmene, the mother of Hercules, by Jove. See Æn. VI. 801.

106. *Dabant:* in the sense of *offerebant.*

108. *Tacitis:* silent—not moving. The *impetus*, which the galleys had already received, was carrying them forward, without the assistance of the oars, which consequently were still. The oarsmen were resting upon their oars at the same time, *incumbere*, &c.

113. *Quò tenditis:* whither are you going?

114. *Arma:* in the sense of *bellum.*

118 *Profugos.* Most probably we are to understand by this, the Trojans driven from their native country, and wandering from place to place without any habitation. The same term he used, Æn. I. 2. in reference to his leaving his own country, &c. As Pallas had proposed his questions in a brief manner, so Æneas is as brief in his answers. *Trojugenas profugos* answers to the question: *Qui genus, et unde domo?* The olive-branch is a sufficient reply to *Pacem-ne huc fertis, an arma?* To remove any suspicion arising from their arms, he informs him they were *Inimica Latinis.* Having been made satisfied of their friendly intention, Pallas immediately invites them on shore.

122. *Egredere:* come on shore—land, whoever thou art—whatever be thy name. Æneas had informed him they were Trojans, but had not as yet told his name.

126. *Regem:* Evander.

128. *Ramos comptos vittâ:* to hold out boughs adorned with the fillet. Olive boughs wrapped around with wreaths of white wool, hanging down over the hands of the suppliant, were emblems of peace, and denoted that the persons came with a friendly intention.

Quòdque à stirpe fores geminis conjunctus Atridis,
Sed mea me virtus, et sancta oracula Divûm,
Cognatique patres, tua terris didita fama,
Conjunxere tibi, et fatis egêre volentem.
Dardanus, Iliacæ primus pater urbis et auctor,
Electrâ, ut Graii perhibent, Atlantide cretus,
Advehitur Teucros: Electram maximus Atlas
Edidit, æthereos humero qui sustinet orbes.
Vobis Mercurius pater est, quem candida Maia
Cyllenes gelido conceptum vertice fudit.
At Maiam, auditis si quicquam credimus, Atlas,
Idem Atlas generat, cœli qui sidera tollit.
Sic genus amborum scindit se sanguine ab uno.
His fretus; non legatos, neque prima per artem
Tentamenta tui pepigi; memet ipse, meumque
Objeci caput, et supplex ad limina veni.
Gens eadem, quæ te, crudeli Daunia bello
Insequitur: nos si pellant, nihil abfore credunt,
Quin omnem Hesperiam penitùs sua sub juga mittant
Et mare, quod suprà, teneant, quodque alluit infrà.
Accipe, daque fidem. Sunt nobis fortia bello
Pectora, sunt animi, et rebus spectata juventus.
Dixerat Æneas: ille os oculosque loquentis
Jamdudum, et totum lustrabat lumine corpus.
Tunc sic pauca refert: Ut te, fortissime Teucrûm,

138. **Quem conceptum candida Maia fudit**

142. Sic genus amborum *nostrûm* scindit se

143. *Ego* fretus his *reus* non pepigi

146. Eadem Daunia gens, quæ insequitur te crudeli bello, *insequitur nos quoque*

149. Et teneant mare, quod alluit *eam* suprà, quodque *alluit eam* infrà

152. Ille *Evander* jamdudum lustrabat os oculosque *Æneæ* loquentis

NOTES.

130. *A stirpe fores conjunctus*, &c. It appears that Evander was related to the sons of Atreus, Agamemnon and Menelaus, the bitter enemies of the Trojans. Atlas was their common ancestor. He had seven daughters; of one of them Jove begat Tantalus, the grandfather of Atreus. Of another (Maia) he begat Mercury, the reputed father of Evander. *Stirpe:* in the sense of *origine.*

131. *Oracula:* these were the answers or responses of the Sibyl. See Æn. VI. 96. *Didita:* diffused—spread.

132. *Cognati patres.* Electra, the daughter of Atlas, was the mother of Dardanus, by Jove; so that Æneas and Evander had the same common origin—Atlas and Jove. Their ancestors were relations.

133. *Fatis:* by their power—authority; they forced or impelled me hither by their authority. Yet he came willingly—their commands and directions concurred with his own inclinations.

135. *Cretus:* sprung from Electra, the daughter of Atlas. Here the poet traces the line of relationship between Æneas and Evander.

137. *Edidit:* in the sense of *genuit.*

139. *Fudit:* in the sense of *peperit*, vel *edidit.*

140. *Si credimus quicquam:* if we give any credit to things heard—to tradition. Atlas. See Æn. IV. 247. and Geor. I. 138. *Cyllenes:* gen. of *Cyllene:* a mountain in Arcadia, where Mercury was born; whence he is sometimes called *Cyllenus.*

143. *Genus:* in the sense of *gens*, vel *familia.*

144. *Non pepigi prima:* I did not make the first trial of your inclinations in this matter by ambassadors, nor by art; but I have come in person—I have exposed myself and my life to the consequences. *Pepigi:* the perf. of *pango.* Heyne says, *non priùs te sentavi per legatos, et callida consilia*, which is evidently the sense of the passage.

146. *Daunia:* an adj. from Daunus, the father of Turnus.—Rutulian or Italian.

149. *Et mare, quod:* should they be able to expel us, they hope to be able to subject all Italy, from the Adriatic sea on the north, to the Tuscan or lower sea on the south.

151. *Spectata rebus:* tried or exercised in action. *Animi:* courage.

153. *Lustrabat lumine:* surveyed with an attentive eye. *Lumine:* in the sense of *oculis.*

157. *Hesiones:* Hesione was the daughter of Laomedon, king of Troy. She married Telamon, king of the island of Salamis, in the *Sinus Saronicus. Hesiones:* gen. of *Hesione;* put in apposition with *sororis.*

159. *Protinùs.* Dr. Trapp renders this *in his way.* But Arcadia lies to the west of Salamis. It must mean, *at the same time—continuing his journey forward.* Priam, being

Accipio, agnoscoque libens! ut verba parentis
Et vocem Anchisæ magni vultumque recordor!
Nam memini Hesiones visentem regna sororis
Laomedontiadem Priamum, Salamina petentem,
Protinùs Arcadiæ gelidos invisere fines.
Tum mihi prima genas vestibat flore juventa:
Mirabarque duces Teucros, mirabar et ipsum
Laomedontiaden: sed cunctis altior ibat
Anchises. Mihi mens juvenili ardebat amore
Compellare virum, et dextræ conjungere dextram.
Accessi, et cupidus Phenei sub mœnia duxi.
Ille mihi insignem pharetram, Lyciasque sagittas
Discedens, chlamydemque auro dedit intertextam,
Frænaque bina, meus quæ nunc habet aurea Pallas.
Ergò et, quam petitis, juncta est mihi fœdere dextra:
Et, lux, cùm primùm terris se crastina reddet,
Auxilio lætos dimittam, opibusque juvabo.
Intereà sacra hæc, quando huc venistis amici,
Annua, quæ differre nefas, celebrate faventes
Nobiscum, et jam nunc sociorum assuescite mensis.
  Hæc ubi dicta, dapes jubet et sublata reponi
Pocula, gramineoque viros locat ipse sedili:
Præcipuumque toro et villosi pelle leonis
Accipit Æneam, solioque invitat acerno.
Tum lecti juvenes certatim aræque sacerdos
Viscera tosta ferunt taurorum, onerantque canistris
Dona laboratæ Cereris, Bacchumque ministrant.
Vescitur Æneas, simul et Trojana juventus,
Perpetui tergo bovis, et lustralibus extis.

166. Ille discedens dedit mihi

172. Interea, quando vos venistis huc *tanquam* amici, faventes celebrate nobiscum hæc annua sacra, quæ *est* nefas differre

175. Ubi hæc dicta *sunt*, jubet

NOTES.

on a visit to his sister at Salamis, proceeded with his company and attendants to visit the cool borders of Arcadia. Anchises accompanied him, with whom Evander, then a youth, contracted an acquaintance and friendship.

160. *Flore.* *Flos* here may mean the down on his cheeks, before he had properly a beard. Ruæus says, *lanugine.* *Vestibat:* by syn. for *vestiebat.*

165. *Phenei.* Pheneum or Pheneus, was a city in Arcadia, near mount Cyllene. *Duxi:* I led Anchises, &c.

166. *Lycias:* an adj. from Lycia, a country of Asia Minor, whose inhabitants were famed for their skill in archery. Here Apollo, the god of the bow, had a famous temple.

169. *Mihi:* in the sense of *mea*, agreeing with *dextra.*

171. *Auxilio.* This may refer to the men, whom Evander sent with him to the war, and *opibus*, to the provisions, and other necessaries, with which he furnished him.

172. *Intereà hæc sacra.* This is an episode of the finest kind, and adds much to the excellence of this book. The story in brief is this: Cacus, a monster, the son of Vulcan, half man and half beast, had his residence in an inaccessible mountain, whence he used to make excursions into the plain, and plunder and lay waste the country. Hercules on his return from Spain, happened to pass this way; and having discovered the monster, by the lowing of one of his heifers, which he had stolen, came upon him and slew him. For this act, the inhabitants considered him their benefactor, and paid him divine honors.

175. *Reponi:* to be replaced—brought back. They had finished their repast, and the dishes had been removed.

178. *Acerno:* maple—made of the wood of the maple-tree.

179. *Sacerdos aræ.* The feast at the end of the ceremony was always considered as a part of the sacrifice. The priest, therefore, does nothing out of character in serving at this entertainment.

180. *Tosta viscera:* the roasted flesh, &c.

181. *Dona laboratæ Cereris:* a circumlocution for bread. *Bacchum:* for *vinum.*

183. *Tergo perpetui bovis:* they feast upon the chine of an entire ox, and the hallowed entrails. At some of their entertainments, it is evident from Homer, that the ancients used to roast, and serve up whole oxen. Homer assigns the chine to his heroes, and that whole and unbroken.

Postquam exempta fames, et amor compressus edendi,
Rex Evandrus ait: Non hæc solemnia nobis,
Has ex more dapes, hanc tanti numinis aram,
Vana superstitio veterumve ignara Deorum
Imposuit: sævis, hospes Trojane, perîclis
Servati facimus, meritosque novamus honores.
Jam primùm saxis suspensam hanc aspice rupem:
Disjectæ procul ut moles, desertaque montis
Stat domus, et scopuli ingentem traxêre ruinam.
Hìc spelunca fuit vasto submota recessu,
Semihominis Caci facies quam dira tenebat,
Solis inaccessam radiis; semperque recenti
Cæde tepebat humus; foribusque affixa superbis
Ora virûm tristi pendebant pallida tabo.
Huic monstro Vulcanus erat pater: illius atros
Ore vomens ignes, magnâ se mole ferebat.
Attulit et nobis aliquando optantibus ætas
Auxilium adventumque Dei: nam maximus ultor,
Tergemini nece Geryonis spoliisque superbus,
Alcides aderat: taurosque hàc victor agebat
Ingentes: vallemque boves amnemque tenebant.
At furiis Caci mens effera, ne quid inausum
Aut intractatum scelerisve dolive fuisset,
Quatuor à stabulis præstanti corpore tauros
Avertit, totidem formâ superante juvencas.
Atque hos, ne qua forent pedibus vestigia rectis,
Caudâ in speluncam tractos, versisque viarum
Indiciis raptos, saxo occultabat opaco.

191. Ut moles disjectæ *sunt* procul

193. Hìc fuit spelunca submota vasto recessu, quam inaccessam radiis solis, dira facies

199. *Ille* vomens atros ignes illius *patris ex* ore ferebat se

201. Nam Alcides aderat, maximus ultor *criminum*, superbus nece, spoliisque

209. Atque occultabat hos opaco saxo, tractos in speluncam caudâ, raptosque versis indiciis viarum, ne qua vestigia forent *ex* pedibus rectis

NOTES.

184. *Compressus:* was allayed. The verb *est* is understood.

186. *Hanc aram:* this sacrifice in honor of so great a god. *Ara*, by meton. for the sacrifice offered upon it.

187. *Non superstitio:* not superstition, vain and ignorant of the old gods, hath imposed on us these solemn rites, these, &c. Superstition here is opposed to religion. The former was the worship of modern gods, to the neglect of the old ones; while the latter was adhering to the established worship of the old gods exclusively. The religion of Evander was not a false superstition, disregarding the ancient gods, and the established order of their worship. It was founded in gratitude to Hercules, for a great deliverance from a most cruel monster.

189. *Meritos honores:* Ruæus says, *meritum cultum*. *Novamus:* we repeat.

191. *Ut:* in the sense of *quomodo*.

194. *Dira facies Caci*, &c. Dr. Trapp observes, it is a peculiar elegancy in poetry, to put a person's most remarkable quality in a substantive, as an epithet to him in an adjective. Thus: *sapientia Lœli*, for wise Lælius. *Vis Herculis*, for powerful Hercules. *Dira facies Casi*, for direful-looking Cacus. See supra. 172.

197. *Ora:* in the sense of *capita.*

199. *Magnâ mole:* of vast size or magnitude.

200. *Ætas aliquando:* time at length brought also aid, and the presence of a god to us wishing it—greatly desiring it. *Et:* also. It brought aid, &c. to us, as it had done to many others, whose grievances Hercules had redressed.

202. *Geryonis:* Geryon was said to have three bodies, because he reigned over the three islands, Majorca, Minorca, and Ivica, on the Spanish coast of the Mediterranean. See Æn. vi. 289.

204. *Amnem:* this must mean the banks of the river, and not the river itself. *Effera:* in the sense of *concitata*. *Mens Caci:* the mind of Cacus, by meton. for Cacus himself.

208. *Avertit:* in the sense of *abducit*. *Superante:* in the sense of *eximia*, vel *pulchra*. The prep. *è* is understood, to govern *formâ*. It also governs *corpore*, in the preceding line.

209. *Ne qua vestigia forent*, &c. The meaning is: that Cacus drew the cattle backward to his cave, that their tracks might seem to proceed from it; and might lead the searcher for them the other way; and by that means prevent discovery.

211. *Saxo opaco.* By this we may understand his cave, which was in a rocky mountain. Or by *saxum*, the stone which shut the mouth or entrance of his cave. He hid

Quærentem nulla ad speluncam signa ferebant.
Intereà cùm jam stabulis saturata moveret
Amphitryoniades armenta, abitumque pararet,
Discessu mugire boves, atque omne querelis
Impleri nemus, et colles clamore relinqui.
Reddidit una boum vocem, vastoque sub antro
Mugiit, et Caci spem custodita fefellit.
Hìc verò Alcidæ furiis exarserat atro
Felle dolor: rapit arma manu, nodisque gravatum
Robur, et aërii cursu petit ardua montis.
Tum primùm nostri Cacum vidêre timentem,
Turbatumque oculis. Fugit ilicèt ocyor Euro,
Speluncamque petit: pedibus timor addidit alas.
Ut sese inclusit, ruptisque immane catenis
Dejecit saxum, ferro quod et arte paternâ
Pendebat; fultosque emuniit objice postes;
Ecce furens animis aderat Tirynthius, omnemque
Accessum lustrans, huc ora ferebat et illuc,
Dentibus infrendens. Ter totum fervidus irâ
Lustrat Aventini montem; ter saxea tentat
Limina nequicquam; ter fessus valle resedit.
Stabat acuta silex, præcisis undique saxis,
Speluncæ dorso insurgens, altissima visu,
Dirarum nidis domus opportuna volucrum.
Hanc, ut prona jugo lævum incumbebat ad amnem,
Dexter in adversum nitens concussit, et imis

212. Nulla signa ferebant *heroa* quærentem *boves*

215. Boves *cœperunt* mugire discessu, atque omne nemus *cœpit* impleri querelis. et colles *cœperunt* relinqui clamore

221. Ardua *juga* aërii montis

222. Nostri *homines*

236. *Hercules* dexter nitens in adversum concussit hanc *silicem*, ut prona incumbebat jugo ad lævum amnem, et solvit *eam* avulsam

NOTES.

them in his cave, by shutting the entrance upon them. *Indiciis:* in the sense of *signis.*

212. *Quærentem:* Hercules searching for his cattle. *Ferebant:* in the sense of *ducebunt.*

214. *Abitum:* a sup. in *um*, of *abeo;* to depart.

215. *Discessu:* in their departure—as he was driving them off. This bellowing of his cattle was in consequence of the loss of those that had been stolen by Cacus. At this moment one of those shut up in the cave, hearing the bellowing of her mates, answered, and by that means, led to a discovery.

216. *Relinqui:* the hills were left by the cattle, to proceed on their way; and consequently, they would cease to resound with the lowings of the herd.

219. *Furiis:* in the sense of *in furias.*

220. *Dolor atro felle:* then indeed rage from the black gall of Hercules, flamed into fury. *Alcidæ:* gen. of *Alcides*, a name of Hercules. The poet here supposes the gall to be the seat of the angry passions.

221. *Robur:* the club was the principal weapon of Hercules.

223. *Oculis.* By this is evidently meant the sight of Hercules. On seeing the hero approach. Cacus was filled with fear and consternation. Dr. Trapp and Mr. Davidson both give a very singular turn to this. They think that Cacus by his eyes expressed his fear and dismay. Ruæus says *visu.*

226. *Paterna arte:* by his father's art. The Cyclops, the servants of Vulcan, are said to have invented the art of fortifying cities.

227. *Postes:* properly the door-posts. By meton. the door or entrance. *Objice:* from *obex*, a bolt or bar—any thing that shutteth in or out, and preventeth passage. *Fultos:* secured.

228. *Tirynthius.* A name of Hercules, from *Tirynthus*, a town of Argolis, in the Peloponnesus, where he passed the greater part of his youth.

229. *Ferebat ora:* he cast his eyes—he looked on every side.

233. *Acuta silex stabat*, &c. The meaning of the passage is this: on the side of the cave, stood a large flinty rock, and projecting with its top over the river on the left. This the hero observing, he took his stand opposite to it on the right; and exerting his strength, started it from its bed, and pulled it over. By this means, an aperture was made into the cave of the monster. This cave was on Mount *Aventinus*, on the east of the Tiber. *Saxis præcisis undique:* the rock being sharpened or tapered all around toward the top. This rock was a suitable place for the haunts of inauspicious birds.

Avulsam solvit radicibus: inde repentè
Impulit, impulsu quo maximus insonat æther.
Dissultant ripæ, refluitque exterritus amnis.
At specus, et Caci detecta apparuit ingens
Regia, et umbrosæ penitùs patuere cavernæ.

243. Non secùs ac siquâ vi terra dehiscens penitùs reseret infernas sedes

Non secùs ac siquâ penitùs vi terra dehiscens
Infernas reseret sedes, et regna recludat
Pallida, Dîs invisa; supèrque immane barathrum
Cernatur, trepidentque immisso lumine Manes

247. Ergo Alcides premit *eum* telis desuper, repentè deprensum in insperata luce

Ergò insperatâ deprensum in luce repentè,
Inclusumque cavo saxo, atque insueta rudentem,
Desuper Alcides telis premit, omniaque arma
Advocat, et ramis vastisque molaribus instat.
Ille autem, neque enim fuga jam super ulla pericli est,
Faucibus ingentem fumum, mirabile dictu!
Evomit; involvitque domum caligine cæcâ,
Prospectum eripiens oculis: glomeratque sub antro
Fumiferam noctem, commixtis igne tenebris.

256. Alcides *ardens* animis non tulit *hoc;* ipseque jecit

Non tulit Alcides animis; seque ipse per ignem
Præcipiti jecit saltu, quà plurimus undam
Fumus agit, nebulâque ingens specus æstuat atrâ.
Hìc Cacum in tenebris incendia vana vomentem

260. Complexus *eum* in nodum

Corripit, in nodum complexus; et angit inhærens
Elisos oculos, et siccum sanguine guttur.
Panditur extemplò foribus domus atra revulsis:
Abstractæque boves, abjuratæque rapinæ

265. *Nostra* corda nequeunt,

Cœlo ostenduntur; pedibusque informe cadaver
Protrahitur. Nequeunt expleri corda tuendo

NOTES.

236. *Jugo:* in the sense of *vertice.*

238. *Solvit:* loosened it.

239. *Quo impulsu:* by the fall of which.

240. *Ripæ dissultant.* Mr. Davidson thinks this is to be taken in a literal sense; the banks leap different ways. The tumbling rock shatters the bank, and makes it fly in pieces. These shattered fragments, together with the splinters of the rock, falling into the river, drive back its current. This plain natural effect, the poet describes in animated style: *Dissultant ripæ*, &c.

241. *Detecta:* uncovered.

242. *Umbrosæ:* in the sense of *tenebrosæ. Penitùs:* widely—deeply.

244. *Reseret:* in the sense of *aperiat.*

245. *Invisa Dîs:* abhorred—hated by the gods. Ruæus interprets *invisa*, by *inaspecta:* unseen—invisible. Dr. Trapp thinks this to be one of the finest *similes* that ever was written. The idea is taken from Homer. Iliad, Lib. 20. *Super:* in the sense of *desuper.*

248. *Rudentem insuetà:* roaring hugely *Insueta:* an adj. neu. plu. taken as an adv. in imitation of the Greeks.

250. *Ramis.* Here the boughs are taken for the trees that bore them, by synec.; for the boughs would have been too feeble weapons. *Molare* is properly a mill-stone—here any stone. *Advocat:* calls to his aid every kind of weapon, &c.

251. *Fuga:* escape. *Super est.* The parts of the verb are separated by tmesis.

253. *Involvit:* in the sense of *implet.*

254. *Oculis:* from the eyes of Hercules. *Glomerat:* whirls around in his cave, &c.

256. *Animis:* in the sense of *irâ.*

257. *Quà fumus:* where the smoke ascends thickest in wavy columns; and where the capacious den waves in black clouds of smoke.

260. *Inhærens angit:* holding him fast, he squeezes his eyes started from their sockets, and his throat destitute of blood. He held him so fast about the neck, that his eyes started from their sockets. It also prevented the circulation of the blood; the consequence of which was death.

263. *Abstractæ boves:* these were the stolen or filched heifers of Hercules. *Abjuratæ rapinæ:* abjured plunder. Most probably these were things which Cacus had denied upon oath to have been in his possession.

264. *Cœlo:* in the sense of *luci.*

265. *Corda:* in the sense of *animi*, vel *oculi.*

Terribiles oculos, vultum, villosaque setis
Pectora semiferi, atque extinctos faucibus ignes.
Ex illo celebratus honos, lætique minores
Servavere diem; primusque Potitius auctor,
Et domus Herculei custos Pinaria sacri,
Hanc aram luco statuit; quæ maxima semper
Dicetur nobis, et erit quæ maxima semper.
Quare agite, ô juvenes, tantarum in munere laudum,
Cingite fronde comas, et pocula pôrgite dextris;
Communemque vocate Deum, et date vina volentes.
Dixerat. Herculeâ bicolor cùm populus umbrâ
Velavitque comas, foliisque innexa pependit;
Et sacer implevit dextram scyphus. Ocyùs omnes
In mensam læti libant, Divosque precantur.
Devexo intereà propior fit vesper Olympo:
Jamque sacerdotes, primusque Potitius, ibant,
Pellibus in morem cincti, flammasque ferebant.
Instaurant epulas, et mensæ grata secundæ
Dona ferunt, cumulantque oneratis lancibus aras.
Tum Salii ad cantus, incensa altaria circum

267. Pectora semiferi *Caci* villosa

268. Ex illo *tempore* honos *Herculis* celebratus *est*

270. Et Pinaria domus, custos Herculei sacri

275. *Herculem* communem Deum.

285 Tum Salii evincti *quoad* tempora populeis ramis adsunt

NOTES.

269. *Auctor:* institutor—founder.

270. *Domus:* in the sense of *familia*. *Sacri:* in the sense of *sacrificii*, says Ruæus. *Custos:* keeper—preserver. Ruæus interprets it by *ministra;* which implies that this family performed the offerings and sacrifices to Hercules themselves. Davidson renders it: "the depository of this institution sacred to Hercules."

271. *Quæ dicetur:* which shall always be called the greatest by us, &c. Dionysius informs us that this was the altar on which Hercules offered the tenth of his spoils. On that account it became the object of their chief veneration; and was therefore called *maxima*, to distinguish it from the numerous altars, which that hero had in Italy.

273. *Munere tantarum:* in the celebration of so great virtue, &c. *Laudum:* praiseworthy deeds. *Munus*, says Donatus, *dicitur cura cujusque rei perficiendæ imposita cum necessitate faciendi.*

275. *Communem Deum.* Those gods were called *communes*, or common, who were worshipped on account of their general good, or utility. Such were Mars and Mercury. Hercules was one of them. The Arcadians, Trojans, and Italians, equally worshipped them.

276. *Populus bicolor*, &c. The poplar tree was sacred to Hercules, because, in his descent to hell, he made himself a crown of the leaves of that tree. The part next his head retained its color, while the outer part became black with the smoke of the infernal regions. Hence it is called *bicolor:* double-colored. *Herculeâ umbra:* with its Herculean shade.

277. *Innexa:* in the sense of *implicata*.

278. *Scyphus:* a large vessel or cup used by Hercules, and sacred to that god. It is of Greek origin.

280. *Vesper fit:* the evening becomes nearer, the heaven being set—the day being closed. This is said according to the notion of those philosophers, who taught that the whole heavens revolve about the earth in the space of twenty-four hours. As the hemisphere of day sets, that of the night arises. *Devexo Olympo:* the day drawing toward a close. This is the better version. For night had not yet arrived. It was only fast approaching—it was coming near.

282. *Cincti:* clad in skins according to custom. This custom was founded on the habit of Hercules, which was the skin of a lion.

284. *Cumulant aras:* they heap the altars with full chargers. La Cerda understands this of the incense, which, on solemn occasions, used to be offered on broad plates. This seems to agree best with the following words: *circum incensa altaria:* around the altars burning with incense. Others refer it to the *dona secundæ mensæ;* the fruits and other delicacies which used to be served up in the second course; and, in the sacred banquets, were first presented on the altar by way of consecration. The ancients divided their feasts into one, two, and sometimes three courses, or tables: the first course consisted of meats, which being removed, a second course was brought on, consisting of fruits, deserts, wine, &c. They were denominated *prima mensa*, *secunda mensa*, &c.

285. *Salii.* These were a choir of twelve men of patrician order, first instituted by

Populeis adsunt evincti tempora ramis.
Hic juvenum chorus, ille senum; qui carmine laudes
Herculeas et facta ferunt: ut prima novercæ
Monstra manu, geminosque premens eliserit angues,
Ut bello egregias idem disjecerit urbes,
Trojamque, Œchaliamque; ut duros mille labores
Rege sub Eurystheo, fatis Junonis iniquæ,
Pertulerit. Tu nubigenas, invicte, bimembres,
Hylæumque, Pholumque manu; tu Cressia mactas
Prodigia, et vastum Nemeæ sub rupe leonem
Te Stygii tremuere lacus: te janitor Orci,
Ossa super recubans antro semesa cruento.
Nec te ullæ facies, non terruit ipse Typhœus
Arduus, arma tenens: non te rationis egentem
Lernæus turbâ capitum circumstetit anguis.
Salve, vera Jovis proles, decus addite Divis;
Et nos, et tua dexter adi pede sacra secundo.

287. Hic *est* chorus juvenum, ille *est chorus* senum; qui

288. Ut premens manu eliserit prima monstra novercæ *Junonis*, geminosque angues:

293. Tu, *O* invicte *heros, mactas* bimembres nubigenas

296. *Cerberus* janitor Orci, recubans cruento antro super semesa ossa, *tremuit* te: nec ulla facies *terruerunt* te

300. Lernæus anguis *cum* turba capitum circumstetit te non egentem rationis.

302. *Tu* dexter adi et nos et tua sacra

NOTES.

Numa in honor of Mars. Virgil supposes that Evander was the founder of it in honor of Hercules, so called from *salio*. Evander divided his band into two choirs; the one consisting of youths, the other of old men.

286. *Adsunt:* in the sense of *accedunt* vel *saltant*. *Cantus:* music—song. Ruæus says, *inter cantus*.

288. *Ferunt carmine:* they celebrate in song the praises of Hercules, and his heroic deeds. The chief of these are ten, which are denominated *labors*. 1. When in his cradle, he killed the two serpents that Juno sent to devour him; 2. He took Troy in the reign of Laomedon, because he refused to pay the promised reward for delivering his daughter *Hesione* from a whale; 3. He destroyed the city of *Œchalia*, in Thessaly, because Eurytus, its king, refused to give him his daughter after he had promised her to him; 4. The servitude imposed upon him by Eurystheus, king of Mycenæ; 5. His victory over the centaurs, a people of Thessaly; 6. His victory over the bull that ravaged Crete. This bull vomited or breathed flames. Some say he killed him, others that he carried him to Eurystheus; 7. His victory over the lion in the Nemæan grove; 8. His descent into hell; 9. He assisted the gods in the war against the giants; 10. He killed the hydra of a hundred heads in the lake of Lerna. It is said he built a funeral pile on mount *Œta*, in Thessaly, on which he threw himself; and having become purified from all mortal pollution, he ascended to heaven, and took a seat among the gods. See Lex. under Hercules. *Ferunt:* in the sense of *memorant* vel *celebrant*.

289. *Premens:* grasping in his hand, he killed the first monsters, &c. *Ut:* how.

292. *Eurystheo.* Eurystheus was king of Mycenæ, to whom Hercules was made subject by the fates for a term of years. He imposed on him the severest labors, at the instance of Juno, with an intention to destroy him. Juno was the bitter enemy of her stepson. Hence she is called *iniquæ Junonis*. *Fatis:* by the order—destination. *Per potestatem Junonis*, says Ruæus.

293. *Nubigenas:* the cloud-born sons.—They were fabled to have been the sons of *Ixion* and *Nubes*. Their upper part was human, their lower part a horse. Hence they are called *bimembres:* double membered. The truth of the fable is this: Mount Pelion was infested by a species of wild cattle or bulls, that proved very troublesome to the inhabitants of the adjacent country. Ixion, king of Thessaly, offered a great reward to any who should destroy them. Whereupon, the young men of a village called *Nephele* undertook it. For this purpose they mounted on horseback, and attacked them with such success, that, in a short time, they were utterly destroyed. Hence the fable of their being begotten by Ixion on a cloud, *Nephele* being the Greek word for a cloud. They were called *Centauri*, from the circumstance of their killing these bulls. *Tu, invicte.* This is a beautiful transition from the third person to the second. This figure, properly used, renders composition animated and lively.

294. *Cressia prodigia:* the bull that breathed fire, and the hind with brazen feet. *Prodigia:* monsters.

296. *Tremuēre:* in the sense of *timuerunt*.

299. *Egentem rationis:* wanting presence of mind—reason. *Circumstetit:* surrounded—assaulted on every side.

301. *Addite:* added to the gods as an honor to their assembly. *Addite:* a part. agreeing with *vera proles*, in the voc.

302. *Dexter:* favorable—propitious. *Adi:* approach—visit. Ruæus says, *veni*. *Secundo pede:* with favorable omens—signs.

Talia carminibus celebrant; super omnia Caci
Speluncam adjiciunt, spirantemque ignibus ipsum.
Consonat omne nemus strepitu, collesque resultant.
Exin se cuncti divinis rebus ad urbem
Perfectis referunt. Ibat rex obsitus ævo;
Et comitem Æneam juxtà natumque tenebat
Ingrediens, varioque viam sermone levabat.
Miratur, facilesque oculos fert omnia circum
Æneas, capiturque locis; et singula lætus
Exquiritque auditque virûm monumenta priorum.
Tum rex Evandrus, Romanæ conditor arcis:
Hæc nemora indigenæ Fauni Nymphæque tenebant,
Gensque virûm truncis et duro robore nata:
Queis neque mos, neque cultus erat; nec jungere tauros,
Aut componere opes norânt, aut parcere parto;
Sed rami, atque asper victu venatus alebat.
Primus ab æthereo venit Saturnus Olympo,
Arma Jovis fugiens, et regnis exul ademptis.
Is genus indocile ac dispersum montibus altis
Composuit, legesque dedit: Latiumque vocari
Maluit, his quoniam latuisset tutus in oris.
Aurea, quæ perhibent, illo sub rege fuerunt
Sæcula; sic placidâ populos in pace regebat.
Deterior donec paulatim ac decolor ætas,
Et belli rabies, et amor successit habendi.
Tum manus Ausoniæ, et gentes venêre Sicanæ:
Sæpiùs et nomen posuit Saturnia tellus.
Tum reges, asperque immani corpore Tybris;
A quo pòst Itali fluvium cognomine Tybrim
Diximus: amisit verum vetus Albula nomen.

313. Conditor Romanæ arcis *inquit:* Fauni, Nymphæque indigenæ, gensque virûm nata

322. Maluitque *regionem* vocari Latium, quonia

330. Tum reges *venerunt;* asperque Tybris *ex* immani corpore *venit,* à quo *nos* Itali pòst

NOTES.

303. *Super omnia:* above all—in addition to all other things.

307. *Obsitus ævo:* sown thick with age—with gray hairs, and other marks of age. This is a metaphor taken from a field of corn.

310. *Faciles oculos:* his rolling eyes—his eyes eager to observe the various scenes that presented to his view.

311. *Capitur:* is captivated—charmed.

312. *Singula:* all—every one. This word signifies all taken singly—one by one.

313. *Conditor Romanæ arcis.* Evander's city Pallanteum was built upon the hill, afterward called *mons Palatinus;* where Romulus laid the foundation of Rome.

314. *Indigenæ:* properly, a sub. here used as an adj.: born in the place—native of the country—not foreign.

315. *Gens virûm nata:* a race of men sprung from the trunks of trees and hard oak. At first men inhabited the deserts and forests. Hence they were thought to have sprung from trees. *Mos:* in the sense of *leges. Cultus:* civil institutions.

317. *Aut parcere parto:* or to use frugal- in what they had acquired. This description of the state of the spot where Rome was afterward built, and its comparison with its state when the poet wrote, must have been highly gratifying to his countrymen.

318. *Asper:* in the sense of *durus.*

320. *Regnis ademptis:* his possessions (kingdom) being taken from him—banished from his throne and kingdom.

322. *Composuit:* he united together—he formed into society a race, &c.

326. *Donec deterior:* till, by little and little, a depraved and corrupt age, and a rage for war, &c. Here is an allusion to the silver, brass, and iron ages. See Ecl. iv. 6.

327. *Habendi:* of possessing—getting wealth.

329. *Posuit nomen:* changed its name—laid it down.

330. *Tybris.* He was a king of the Tuscans, and, being slain near the river, gave his name to it. Its original name was Albula. Some derive its name from *Tiberinus,* king of the Albans, who was drowned in it. *Asper:* fierce.

332. *Diximus:* called. *Apellavimus,* says Ruæus.

Me pulsum patriâ, pelagique extrema sequentem,
Fortuna omnipotens et ineluctabile fatum
His posuere locis: matrisque egêre tremenda
Carmentis Nymphæ monita, et Deus auctor Apollo.
Vix ea dicta, dehinc progressus, monstrat et aram,
Et Carmentalem Romano nomine portam,
Quam memorant Nymphæ priscum Carmentis honorem
Vatis fatidicæ; cecinit quæ prima futuros
Æneadas magnos, et nobile Pallanteum.
Hinc lucum ingentem, quem Romulus acer asylum
Rettulit, et gelidâ monstrat sub rupe Lupercal,
Parrhasio dictum Panos de more Lycæi.
Necnon et sacri monstrat nemus Argileti:
Testaturque locum, et letum docet hospitis Argi.
Hinc ad Tarpeiam sedem et Capitolia ducit,
Aurea nunc, olim sylvestribus horrida dumis
Jam tum relligio pavidos terrebat agrestes
Dira loci; jam tum sylvam saxumque tremebant.
Hoc nemus, hunc, inquit, frondoso vertice collem,
Quis Deus, incertum est, habitat Deus. Arcades ipsum

336. Tremendaque monita Carmentis Nymphæ *meæ* matris, et Deus Apollo auctor egêre *me huc.*

337. Vix ea dicta *fuerunt*, dehinc *Evander* progressus monstrat

339. Quam *homines* memorant *fuisse* priscum honorem Nymphæ Carmentis

342. Hinc *monstrat* ingentem

347. Hinc ducit *Ænean* ad

351. *Evander* inquit: Deus (*sed* quis Deus, est incertum,) habitat hoc nemus, *et* hunc

NOTES.

333. *Sequentem:* experiencing the dangers of the sea. Ruæus says, *quærentem ultima spatia maris.* Heyne takes *extrema pelagi*, in the sense of *ultimum mare.*

336. *Auctor.* By this Servius understands the author of oracles. Ruæus takes it in the sense of *suasor:* persuader, or adviser. This is the sense given to the word by Davidson.

337. *Dehinc:* in the sense of *cùm.*

340. *Fatidicæ vatis:* a prophetic prophetess. *Cecinit:* in the sense of *prædixit.*

342. *Quem asylum:* which Romulus rendered an asylum—reduced or turned into an asylum. This was a place of safety to all criminals who should take refuge in it. Multitudes fled thither from the neighboring nations. By this means, Romulus increased the number of his subjects; which was the object he had in view. But then they were desperate and abandoned characters generally. *Hinc:* in the sense of *deinde.*

343. *Lupercal.* This was a place at the foot of Mount *Palatine*, where the Arcadians under Evander built a temple to *Pan*, the god of *Arcadia;* where he was worshipped as the protector of their flocks from wolves. *Lupercal*, from *lupus*, a wolf. Here the young men performed their annual plays naked, and were called *Luperci.* Some suppose Romulus to have instituted these sports, because, in that place, he was nourished by *Lupa.*

344. *Dictum de:* so called from the Arcadian manner of Lycæan Pan. *Parrhasio* an adj. from *Parrhasia*, a district and city of Arcadia. *Lycæi:* an adj. from *Lycæus*, a mountain in Arcadia, where Pan was particularly worshipped.

345. *Argileti.* Argiletum was a place between mount *Aventinus* and *Capitolinus*, so called because it belonged to *Argus;* or because he here hospitably entertained Evander on his arrival in Italy; or, lastly, because he was buried there. For some cause or other, *Argus* was killed by the new comers, without the knowledge of Evander, who gave him a sumptuous burial.

346. *Testatur locum:* he calls the place to witness, &c. On seeing the place, the remembrance of his friend and host sensibly affected him. He began immediately to make protestations of his innocence, and call the place to witness that he was clean from the foul deed. *Docet:* he relates—he informs Æneas of the death of his host.

347. *Tarpeiam sedem:* the Tarpeian rock. This is so called by anticipation. It was not given to the place till the time of Romulus. It was first called *Saturnium*, from a city built by Janus, in memory of his friendship and union with Saturn. Afterwards called by Romulus *Tarpeium*, and lastly *Capitolinum*, because the head of a man (*caput*) was found there, when the foundations of the capitol were laid.

349. *Dira relligio:* even then the awfu sanctity of the place terrified the fearful rustics. Dr. Trapp observes, there is something wonderfully grand and awful in this image, both as it is in itself, and as it is connected with what follows; the capitol is to be built upon it. A god had already chosen it for his residence. Ruæus says, *horrida sanctitas.*

350. *Tremebant:* they feared even then the grove, &c.

Credunt se vidisse Jovem ; cùm sæpe nigrantem
Ægida concuteret dextrâ, nimbosque cieret.
Hæc duo prætereà disjectis oppida muris,
Reliquias veterumque vides monumenta virorum.
Hanc Janus pater, hanc Saturnus condidit urbem :
Janiculum huic, illi fuerat Saturnia nomen.
  Talibus inter se dictis ad tecta subibant
Pauperis Evandri ; passimque armenta videbant
Romanoque foro et lautis mugire Carinis.
Ut ventum ad sedes : Hæc, inquit, limina victor
Alcides subiit ; hæc illum regia cepit.
Aude, hospes, contemnere opes, et te quoque dignum
Finge Deo, rebusque veni non asper egenis.
Dixit : et angusti subter fastigia tecti
Ingentem Ænean duxit ; stratisque locavit,
Effultum foliis et pelle Libystidis ursæ.
  Nox ruit, et fuscis tellurem amplectitur alis.
At Venus haud animo nequicquam exterrita mater,
Laurentûmque minis et duro mota tumultu,
Vulcanum alloquitur ; thalamoque hæc conjugis aureo
Incipit, et dictis divinum aspirat amorem :
Dum bello Argolici vastabant Pergama reges
Debita, casurasque inimicis ignibus arces ;
Non ullum auxilium miseris, non arma rogavi
Artis opisque tuæ : nec te, charissime conjux,
Incassùmve tuos volui exercere labores ;
Quamvis et Priami deberem plurima natis,
Et durum Æneæ flevissem sæpè laborem ;
Nunc Jovis imperiis Rutulorum constitit oris :
Ergò eadem supplex venio, et sanctum mihi numen

355. Prætereà vides hæc duo oppida

358. Janiculum fuerat nomen huic Saturnia fuerat nomen illi.

361. Mugire *in loco, deinde dicto* que Romano foro, et lautis Carinis.

367. Locavitque *eum* stratis, effultum foliis

370. At Venus mater *Æneæ* haud nequicquam exterrita animo, motaque

372. Incipitque hæc *verba* in aureo

376. Non rogavi ullum auxilium miseris *Trojanis*, non *rogavi ulla* arma tuæ artis opisque

NOTES.

354. *Ægida :* acc. sing. of *ægis*, a shield made of goat skin, from a Greek word signifying a goat. *Nimbos : nimbus* properly signifies those deep and black clouds, which brew storms, thunder, and lightning —the tempest itself.

355. *Muris disjectis :* their walls being demolished—thrown down.

361. *Carinis. Carinæ* was the name of a magnificent street in Rome, where Pompey had his house.

362. *Ad sedes :* to the palace of Evander. *Ventum : est* is understood : in the sense of *venerunt.*

364. *Aude :* be not afraid to despise. Davidson says, "have greatness of mind to undervalue magnificence," &c.

365. *Finge te quoque :* manifest yourself worthy of a god. By *Deo*, some understand Hercules, whom Evander would have Æneas to imitate. But the *quoque* seems to determine it to be taken in a general sense : as Hercules acted worthy of a god, so do you. *Veni non asper :* come not displeased with our poverty. *Finge :* Ruæus says, *ostende. Asper :* for *offensus.*

370. *At Venus* This is a fine episode. It consists, properly, of three parts : the conversation between Venus and her husband —the casting and forging of the arms by the Cyclops, with a description of the place —the sculpture upon the shield of Æneas, &c. The whole is in imitation of the Iliad, lib. 18. where Thetis entreats Vulcan to make arms for her son. But Virgil is superior to Homer in dignity of sentiment.

373. *Aspirat.* Some copies have *inspirat.* The sense is the same in either case. She inspires into her husband a divine love, by her endearing words.

375. *Debita :* destined—doomed to destruction, in consequence of the perjury of Laomedon. After which, Neptune and Apollo became the enemies of Troy. See Geor. i. 502.

379. *Deberem :* I owed very much to the sons of Priam.

382. *Eadem venio :* I, the same affectionate wife, who have always been so tender of your honor, and so loth to give you trouble, come to you a suppliant, and ask of your divinity, sacred to me, arms a

383. *Thetis* filia Nerei *potuit flectere* te, *et* Tithonia conjux potuit flectere te *suis* lachrymis

388. Fovet *Deum* cunctantem *molli* amplexu.

393 Conjux *ejus* læta dolis, et conscia formæ *suæ* sensit *id*

401. Quicquid curæ *est* in mea arte possum promittere *tibi*.

403. Quantùm ignes animæque valent, *promitto id:*

Arma rogo, genitrix nato. Te filia Nerei,
Te potuit lachrymis Tithonia flectere conjux.
Aspice, qui coëant populi, quæ mœnia clausis
Ferrum acuant portis, in me excidiumque meorum.
Dixerat: et niveis hinc atque hinc Diva lacertis
Cunctantem amplexu molli fovet: ille repentè
Accepit solitam flammam; notusque medullas
Intravit calor, et labefacta per ossa cucurrit:
Non secùs atque olim tonitru cùm rupta corusco
Ignea rima micans percurrit lumine nimbos.
Sensit læta dolis, et formæ conscia conjux.
  Tum pater æterno fatur devinctus amore:
Quid causas petis ex alto? fiducia cessit
Quò tibi, Diva, mei? similis si cura fuisset,
Tum quoque fas nobis Teucros armare fuisset.
Nec pater omnipotens Trojam, nec fata vetabant
Stare, decemque alios Priamum superesse per annos.
Et nunc, si bellare paras, atque hæc tibi mens est:
Quicquid in arte meâ possum promittere curæ,
Quod fieri ferro, liquidove potest electro,
Quantùm ignes animæque valent: absiste precando
Viribus indubitare tuis. Ea verba locutus,
Optatos dedit amplexus: placidumque petivit
Conjugis infusus gremio per membra soporem.
  Inde, ubi prima quies medio jam noctis abactæ

NOTES.

mother for a son. Verbs of asking, &c. govern two accusatives.

383. *Filia Nerei:* the daughter of Nereus—Thetis, the reputed mother of Achilles. See Ecl. iv. 37.

384. *Tithonia conjux:* Aurora.

385. *Mœnia:* cities—fortified towns. Here put for the inhabitants, by meton. *Acuant:* sharpen—prepare.

386. *In me:* against me. Venus here identifies herself with Æneas and the Trojans.

388. *Cunctantem:* hesitating—loth to undertake the business.

391. *Atque:* in the sense of *quàm. Olim:* sometimes. This word signifies time past, future, and indefinite. This last is the meaning here.

392. *Ignea rima.* Ruæus says, *flammeus hiatus, apertus fulgenti fulmine. Nimbos:* in the sense of *nubes.* Servius, whom Dr. Trapp follows, takes *corusco*, for darted or brandished. Ruæus interprets it by *fulgenti*, shining. The former is the best, inasmuch as thunder does not shine; it is the lightning alone that becomes visible. There may be reference here to the darting of the thunderbolt of Jove. It pierces the cloud, and disengages the lightning, which, let loose, runs across the heavens, in forked light. *Ignea rima*, very beautifully expresses a stream of fire, bursting through a rived cloud—lightning.

394. *Pater:* Vulcan is meant.

395. *Quid causas petis:* why do you seek reasons from far? Instead of coming to the point at once, you have recourse to far-fetched arguments.

398. *Nec pater.* It hath been observed by commentators, upon this and similar passages of Virgil, that though the fates could not be changed, they might be deferred. But Mr. Dryden hath made it appear, that this very deferring is in consequence of a decree. In this sense, these words of Vulcan are to be understood. Troy did fall at such a time; but it was not necessary it should. The fates would have permitted me to defer its doom for ten years longer; and I would have done it, if you had desired it: but I could have done it no longer—it being then destined to be destroyed.

401. *Curæ:* skill.

402. *Liquido electro.* A composition of gold and silver is called *electrum.* Pliny makes the proportion to be four fifths of silver, and one fifth of gold. Here put for metals in general: the *species* for the *genus.*

403. *Animæ:* the wind or breath of the bellows. *Absiste:* cease to distrust your power at entreaty.

406. *Infusus gremio:* and resting on the bosom of his spouse, he sought soft sleep, &c. Ruæus says, *jacens.*

407. *Medio curriculo noctis jam:* in the middle course of night, now being past. This marks the time to be just after mid-

Curriculo expulerat somnum; cùm fœmina, primum
Cui tolerare colo vitam tenuique Minervâ,
Impositum cinerem et sopitos suscitat ignes,
Noctem addens operi, famulasque ad lumina longo
Exercet penso; castum ut servare cubile
Conjugis, et possit parvos educere natos.
Haud secùs ignipotens, nec tempore segnior illo,
Mollibus è stratis opera ad fabrilia surgit.
Insula Sicanium juxta latus, Æoliamque
Erigitur Liparen, fumantibus ardua saxis;
Quam subter specus, et Cyclopum exesa caminis
Antra Ætnæa tonant, validique incudibus ictus
Auditi referunt gemitum, striduntque cavernis
Stricturæ Chalybum, et fornacibus ignis anhelat;
Vulcani domus, et Vulcania nomine tellus.
Huc tunc ignipotens cœlo descendit ab alto.
Ferrum exercebant vasto Cyclopes in antro,
Brontesque, Steropesque, et nudus membra Pyracmon.
His informatum manibus jam parte politâ
Fulmen erat; toto genitor quæ plurima cœlo
Dejicit in terras; pars imperfecta manebat.
Tres imbris torti radios, tres nubis aquosæ

408. Cùm fœmina, cui *est* primum *officium* tolerare vitam colo

418. Subter quam specus, et Ætnæa antra exesa caminis Cyclopum tonant.

422. *Hæc est* domus Vulcani, et tellus *dicta est* Vulcania, *ejus* nomine.

426. Erat his *in* manibus fulmen informatum *ex illis*, quæ plurima genitor *Deorum* dejicit toto cœlo in terras, parte jam politâ

NOTES.

night. Rest is here said to expel sleep, because, when we have taken rest, sleep becomes unnecessary. *Curriculo:* circle—course. Ruæus says, *spatio.*

409. *Tenui Minerva.* This may mean handycraft in general, or spinstry in particular. Or, perhaps, it is better to understand it of the works of the loom.

410. *Suscitat impositum,* &c. Virgil here connects the same verb with two substantives, when it can properly be used with one of them only. This is frequent with him, and is a beauty which our language will not admit. *Cinerem impositum* is, doubtless, the ashes that cover the fire, which she first removes; and then she kindles or awakes the dormant fire (*sopitos ignes*) into a flame. See Æn. vii. 431.

411. *Addens noctem:* adding the night to her work—working in the night, before the approach of day.

412. *Castum:* chaste—undefiled. Here the poet gives us a fine description of domestic industry, on the part of the mistress of the house.

414. *Ignipotens:* a name of Vulcan. *Nec segnior:* nor less active--*industrious* than she.

415. *Ad fabrilia opera:* to his mechanic labors.

416. *Insula erigitur,* &c. Between Sicily and the Italian coast there are seven islands, called *Æolidæ,* from Æolus, who reigned there; and *Vulcaniæ,* from Vulcanus, whose forge was fabled to have been in one of them. This is imitated from Homer. He, however, places Vulcan's forge in heaven; Virgil, with more propriety, places it on the earth. As the eruptions of Ætna are matters of fact, the poet, with much judgment, places the forge of the Cyclops in the neighborhood of that mountain. The whole description is of the noblest kind. *Brontes, Steropes,* and *Pyracmon,* were his principal assistants. All of Greek derivation.

418. *Exesa:* excavated—hollowed out by the forges of the Cyclops.

421. *Stricturæ:* bars of iron or steel. *Chalybum.* The *Chalybes* were a people of Spain; or, according to some, of Pontus, celebrated for their iron works. Here, by meton. put for iron and steel.

426. *Informatum:* unfinished. A part only was polished, the rest remaining in an imperfect state.

429. *Tres radios torti imbris.* By the *torti imbris,* the wreathed shower, commentators understand hail. The *torti* expresses the violence with which hail in a storm is hurled or darted. *Radios.* These are the forks or spikes with which lightning is painted or described. The form of thunder, to which Virgil here seems to allude, is known from medals. It consisted of twelve wreathed spikes or darts, extended like the *radii* of a circle, three and three together, with wings spread out in the middle. The wings denote the lightning's rapid motion, and the spikes or darts, its penetrating quality. By the four different kinds of spikes, Servius understands the four seasons of the year. According to him, the *tres imbris torti radios,* or the three spikes of hail, denote the winter season, when hail-storms abound. The *tres nubis aquosæ radios,* or the three

Addiderant, rutili tres ignis et alitis Austri.
Fulgores nunc terrificos, sonitumque, metumque
Miscebant operi, flammisque sequacibus iras.
Parte aliâ Marti currumque rotasque volucres
Instabant, quibus ille viros, quibus excitat urbes:
Ægidaque horriferam, turbatæ Palladis arma,
Certatim squamis serpentum auroque polîbant;
Connexosque angues, ipsamque in pectore Divæ
Gorgona, desecto vertentem lumina collo.
Tollite cuncta, inquit, cœptosque auferte labores,
Ætnæi Cyclopes, et huc advertite mentem.
Arma acri facienda viro: nunc viribus usus,
Nunc manibus rapidis, omni nunc arte magistrâ:
Præcipitate moras. Nec plura effatus. At illi
Ocyùs incubuêre omnes, pariterque laborem
Sortiti. Fluit æs rivis, aurique metallum;
Vulnificusque chalybs vastâ fornace liquescit.
Ingentem clypeum informant, unum omnia contra
Tela Latinorum; septenosque orbibus orbes
Impediunt. Alii ventosis follibus auras
Accipiunt redduntque; alii stridentia tingunt
Æra lacu: gemit impositis incudibus antrum.
Illi inter sese multâ vi brachia tollunt
In numerum, versantque tenaci forcipe massam.
Hæc pater Æoliis properat dum Lemnius oris,
Evandrum ex humili tecto lux suscitat alma,
Et matutini volucrum sub culmine cantus.
Consurgit senior, tunicâque inducitur artus,
Et Tyrrhena pedum circumdat vincula plantis.

434. Quibus ille excitat viros, quibus *excitat* urbes *ad arma:*

436. Certatimque polîbant horriferam Ægida, arma turbatæ Palladis squamis

438. Gorgonaque ipsam in pectore Divæ vertentem

439. *Vulcanus* inquit, *Vos, O* Ætnæi Cyclopes, tollite cuncta *hæc*

441. Nunc *est* usus viribus

447. Unum *sufficientem* contra

454. Dum Lemnius pater *Vulcanus* properat

456. Matutini cantus volucrum sub culmine *suscitant* Evandrum ex humili tecto, alma lux *suscitat eum.*

NOTES.

spikes of a watery cloud, denote the spring season, which is called *imbriferum ver*, because rain then abounds. The *tres rutuli ignis radios*, or the three spikes of sparkling fire, denote the summer season, when lightning is most frequent. The *tres alitis Austri radios*, or the three spikes of winged wind, denote the autumnal season, when storms of wind are frequent and violent.

430. *Addiderant.* This part they had completed; therefore he uses the plu. perf. tense: they had done with it. But in the following line, he says, *nunc miscebant:* they were now mingling with the work, the terrific lightning, &c. This distinction of tense is worthy of notice.

432. *Sequacibus:* persecuting—avenging.

435. *Horriferam.* Pierius informs us that this is the true reading of all the ancient manuscripts. Heyne reads, *horriferum.* Davidson reads the same. Valpy and Ruæus have *horrificam.* *Turbatæ:* in the sense of *iratæ.*

436. *Squamis serpentum auroque:* with the scales of serpents and gold; by hend. for *aureis squamis serpentum.* *Polîbant:* in the sense of *ornabant.*

438. *Gorgona:* acc. sing. of *Gorgon.* See Æn. ii. 616. *Desecto collo:* her neck being cut off.

444. *Incubuêre:* they applied vigorously—they set about it in earnest.

445. *Sortiti:* having distributed by lot—having assigned to each one his part.

446. *Chalybs:* steel. See 421, supra.—also, Geor. i. 58. *Unum: alone* sufficient.

449. *Impediunt:* they involve or infold seven orbs in orbs. Ruæus says, *connectunt.* *Alii accipiunt:* simply, some blow the bellows, others put, &c.

451. *Lacu:* the trough.

452. *Illi tollunt brachia.* In the very turn of the verse, we see them lifting up, and letting fall their hammers alternately, and keeping time with one another. *In numerum:* in regular motion—keeping stroke with one another.

454. *Lemnius pater:* Vulcan. He was banished from heaven to *Lemnos*, an island in the Ægean sea, not far from the Hellespont. See Geor. i. 295.

457. *Inducitur:* in the sense of *induit* vel *vestit.*

458. *Tyrrhena vincula:* he binds his Tuscan sandals to the bottom of his feet. These sandals were of wood, about four inches

Tum lateri atque humeris Tegeæum subligat ensem,
Demissa ab lævâ pantheræ terga retorquens.
Necnon et gemini custodes limine ab alto
Procedunt, gressumque canes comitantur herilem.
Hospitis Æneæ sedem et secreta petebat,
Sermonum memor et promissi muneris, heros.
Nec minùs Æneas se matutinus agebat.
Filius huic Pallas, olli comes ibat Achates.
Congressi jungunt dextras, mediisque residunt
Ædibus, et licito tandem sermone fruuntur.
Rex prior hæc.
Maxime Teucrorum ductor, quo sospite, nunquam
Res equidem Trojæ victas aut regna fatebor.
Nobis ad belli auxilium pro nomine tanto
Exiguæ vires. Hinc Tusco claudimur amni;
Hinc Rutulus premit, et murum circumsonat armis.
Sed tibi ego ingentes populos, opulentaque regnis
Jungere castra paro, quam fors inopina salutem
Ostentat: fatis huc te poscentibus affers.
Haud procul hinc saxo colitur fundata vetusto
Urbis Agyllinæ sedes: ubi Lydia quondam
Gens, bello præclara, jugis insedit Etruscis.
Hanc multos florentem annos rex deinde superbo
Imperio et sævis tenuit Mezentius armis.
Quid memorem imandas cædes? quid facta tyranni
Effera? Dî capiti ipsius generique reservent!
Mortua quin etiam jungebat corpora vivis,
Componens manibusque manus atque oribus ora,

460. Retorquens *in dextram* terga pantheræ

466. Pallas filius *ibat comes* huic *Evandro;* Achates ibat comes olli *Æneæ.*

471. Nunquam equidem fatebor res Trojæ victas *esse*, aut regna *eversa esse.* *Sunt* nobis exiguæ

474. Premit *nos*, et circumsonat *nostrum* murum armis.

481. Deinde rex Mezentius tenuit hanc *urbem* florentem multos annos

484. Dî reservent *talia* capiti ipsius, generique.

NOTES.

broad, and fastened to the feet with gilded thongs. The poet here makes a very happy transition from the smoke, fire, and noise of Vulcan's cavern, to the sweet air of the morning, and the charming music of birds.

459. *Tegeæum:* an adj. from Tegea, a city of Arcadia, where Pan was especially worshipped: Arcadian.

460. *Retorquens terga*, &c. This panther's skin was cast or thrown back over the right shoulder, passed around, and hung down over the left. *Terga:* in the sense of *pellem.*

461. *Gemini canes*, &c. These two dogs, that are all the guard Evander has, gives us a lively image of the poverty and simplicity of that good monarch.

463. *Secreta:* private apartments, which Æneas occupied.

464. *Muneris:* aid—assistance.

465. *Agebat:* in the sense of *movebat.*

468. *Licito:* free—unrestrained.

471. *Res Trojæ:* the power of Troy.

472. *Pro tanto nomine:* for, or in proportion to, the greatness of the Trojan name; or the greatness of the cause in which he was about to engage.

473. *Exiguæ vires:* small ability, or means to support, &c. *Tusco amni:* the Tiber, which bounded his territory on the west, and divided it from the Tuscans.

476. *Paro:* Ruæus says, *meditor.*

478. *Fundata: structa antiquis lapidibus*, says Ruæus.

479. *Agyllinæ:* an adj. from *Agylla*, a city of Etruria or Tuscany. It was planted by a Lydian colony. It was afterward called *Cerè.* *Hodie, Cerveteri.* *Lydia:* an extensive country of Asia Minor: here used as an adjective. Part of it was called *Mæonia.*

480. *Etruscis jugis:* on the Tuscan mountains.

482. *Mezentius tenuit*, &c. This story is of importance to the subject, and very properly introduced in this place. For, without the auxiliary forces of the Tuscans, Æneas could not have carried on the war. The tyranny of Mezentius gives an air of probability to the whole.

485. *Quin etiam jungebat* moreover he joined dead bodies to the living, putting, &c. The invention of this cruel kind of punishment, is ascribed, by Cicero and others, to the Tuscans. Virgil takes occasion hence to form a character of uncommon barbarity in one of his personages.

487. *Genus tormenti!* et sic necabat *homines* fluentes sanie taboque, in *hoc* misero

491. Jactant ignem ad fastigia *ejus regiæ.*

493. *Capit* confugere et defendier armis

498. Retinet *eos: dicens,* O delecta juventus,

501. Et *quos* Mezentius accendit merita irâ; *est* fas nulli Italo

505. Tarchon ipse misit oratores

507. *Rogans ut* succedam

509. Viresque *jam nimis* seræ ad fortia *facta invident mihi.* Exhortarer *meum* natum *facere id,* ni

515. Adjungam hunc *meum filium* Pallanta tibi, spes, et solatia nostri; *ut* sub te magistro

Tormenti genus! **et sanie taboque fluentes,**
Complexu in misero, **longâ sic morte necabat.**
At fessi tandem cives infandâ furentem
Armati circumsistunt, ipsumque, domumque:
Obtruncant socios, ignem ad fastigia jactant.
Ille inter cædes Rutulorum elapsus in agros
Confugere, et Turni defendier hospitis armis.
Ergò omnis furiis surrexit Etruria justis,
Regem ad supplicium præsenti Marte reposcunt.
His ego te, Ænea, ductorem millibus addam.
Toto namque fremunt condensæ litore puppes,
Signaque ferre jubent. Retinet longævus aruspex,
Fata canens: O Mæoniæ delecta juventus,
Flos veterum virtusque virûm; quos justus in hostem
Fert dolor, et meritâ accendit Mezentius irâ:
Nulli fas Italo tantam subjungere gentem:
Externos optate duces. Tum Etrusca resedit
Hoc acies campo, monitis exterrita Divûm.
Ipse oratores ad me regnique coronam
Cum sceptro misit, mandatque insignia, Tarchon:
Succedam castris, Tyrrhenaque regna capessam.
Sed mihi tarda gelu, sæclisque effœta, senectus
Invidet imperium, seræque ad fortia vires.
Natum exhortarer, ni, mixtus matre Sabellâ
Hinc partem patriæ traheret. Tu, cujus et annis
Et generi fatum indulget, quem numina poscunt,
Ingredere, ô Teucrûm atque Italûm fortissime ductor
Hunc tibi prætereà, spes et solatia nostrî,
Pallanta adjungam. Sub te tolerare magistro
Militiam, et grave Martis opus, tua cernere facta

NOTES.

487. *Genus tormenti:* O horrid kind of torture! This is the sense of Ruæus and Valpy. But Heyne and Davidson take them not as an exclamation. *Fluentes:* wasting—pining away.

489. *Infandà:* an adj. neu. plu. taken as an adverb, in imitation of the Greeks: in the sense of *immaniter.*

490. *Circumsistunt:* in the sense of *obsident.*

491. *Socios:* his friends—those who adhered to the king. Their houses were covered with straw, even the palaces of kings; which was the reason of their throwing fire on the roof of Mezentius's palace.

493. *Defendier:* by paragoge, for *defendi.*

497. *Puppes:* the ships, by meton. for the troops in them. *Fremunt:* impatient for the war.

498. *Ferre signa:* to bear forward the standards—to march. A military phrase.

499. *Mœonia.* Mæonia is a country of Lydia, in Asia Minor, whence a colony removed to Tuscany, and settled. They built the city Agylla. *Lydia* and *Mœonia* are used, however, sometimes indiscriminately for the same country.

501. *Dolor:* in the sense of *indignatio*. *Fert:* in the sense of *impellit.*

502. *Subjungere:* to subdue.

503. *Resedit:* sat down. *Acies:* troops in general. *Optate:* choose ye.

504. *Monitis:* admonitions—prophetic declarations. Ruæus says, *oraculo.* The same with *fata*, verse 499.

506. *Mandatque:* and commits the ensigns (or badges) of royalty to me. These were the crown and sceptre just mentioned.

508. *Tarda gelu:* benumbed by the frost of age. This is highly metaphorical. *Sæclis. Sæculum* properly signifies the space of thirty years; in which the old actors are already gone off the stage, and new ones have arisen in their room. Thus Nestor is said to have lived three ages, or ninety years, as Plutarch explains it. *Sæclis:* by syn. for *sæculis:* here used in the sense o *annis.* *Effœta:* worn out—enfeebled.

510. *Sabellâ matre:* his Sabine mother By her, he became heir to a part of her native country. It was therefore inconsistent with his duty to his people, to accept of the Tuscan crown.

Assuescat; primis et te miretur ab annis.
Arcadas huic equites bis centum, robora pubis
Lecta, dabo; totidemque suo tibi nomine Pallas
 Vix ea fatus erat, defixique ora tenebant
Æneas Anchisiades et fidus Achates,
Multaque dura suo tristi cum corde putabant,
Ni signum cœlo Cytherea dedisset aperto.
Namque improvisò vibratus ab æthere fulgor
Cum sonitu venit, et ruere omnia visa repentè,
Tyrrhenusque tubæ mugire per æthera clangor.
Suspiciunt: iterum atque iterum fragor intonat ingens.
Arma inter nubem, cœli in regione serenâ,
Per sudum rutilare vident, et pulsa tonare.
Obstupuere animis alii: sed Troïus heros
Agnovit sonitum, et Divæ promissa parentis.
Tum memorat: Ne verò, hospes, ne quære profectò
Quem casum portenta ferant: ego poscor Olympo.
Hoc signum cecinit missuram Diva creatrix,
Si bellum ingrueret; Vulcaniaque arma per auras
Laturam auxilio.
Heu quantæ miseris cædes Laurentibus instant!
Quas pœnas mihi, Turne, dabis! quàm multa sub undas
Scuta virûm, galeasque, et fortia corpora volves,
Tybri pater! Poscant acies, et fœdera rumpant.
 Hæc ubi dicta dedit, solio se tollit ab alto:
Et primùm Herculeis sopitas ignibus aras
Excitat: hesternumque Larem, parvosque Penates

525. Et omnia visa *sunt* ruere repentè

533. Ego poscor Olympo *ad bellum.*

535. *Se*que laturam Vulcania arma per auras *pro* auxilio *mihi*

NOTES.

517. *Primis annis:* from his first and earliest years for bearing arms; which, among the Romans, was about the age of seventeen.

522. *Putabant:* they were just entering into a train of perplexing thoughts, as to the present crisis of affairs: and would have pursued them, had not Venus interposed. They were revolving in their minds many difficulties that might arise, &c.

524. *Fulgor vibratus:* a flash of lightning darting across the sky, &c.

526. *Tyrrhenus clangor:* a Tuscan sound of the trumpet began, &c. The sound of the trumpet is called Tuscan, because it is said they were the inventors of that instrument. It was understood to indicate that Æneas was invited to the throne of the Tuscans.

529. *Pulsa tonare.* This seems to imply that the thunder was the effect of the clashing of the arms that appeared in the air. Being struck (*pulsa*) they seemed to thunder. *Rutilare:* to flash—shine through the clear air or sky. *Visa sunt* is understood.

532. *Ne verò, hospes, ne:* do not indeed, do not indeed, inquire what event these prodigies portend. This repetition is very emphatical. Some copies repeat the *quære* thus: *ne quære verò, ne quære profectò.*

534. *Cecinit:* in the sense of *prædixit.* *Missuram* that she would send, &c.

537. *Instant:* in the sense of *imminent.*

540. *Poscant acies:* let them demand war—let them break their treaties. This is spoken ironically. Ruæus says, *petant bellum.* Latinus had proposed Æneas for a son-in-law; and entered into an alliance or treaty of friendship with him. To that circumstance this is an allusion.

542. *Sopitas aras,* &c. Most commentators take this for, *sopitos ignes in Herculeis aris,* by hypallage: the dormant fires on the altar of Hercules. But it does not appear that Æneas returned to the grove, where the sacred rites had been performed the day before to Hercules. The *altar* here mentioned may have been Evander's domestic altar, to which the remains of the hallowed fire, from the altar of Hercules, might have been conveyed. If we suppose this, there will be no need of an hypallage. *Excitat:* he kindles up the dormant altars with the Herculean fire—the fire taken from the altar of Hercules as supposed. This seems to be the opinion of Ruæus and Davidson.

543. *Hesternum Larem.* By this some understand the hallowed hearth, on which the sacrifices have been offered the day before But it may be Evander's *Lar,* or guardian god, to whom Æneas had sacrificed the day before; and with whom he had then become acquainted. *Parvos Penates.* The

Lætus adit: mactant lectas de more bidentes
Evandrus pariter, pariter Trojana juventus
Pòst hinc ad naves graditur, sociosque revisit:
Quorum de numero, qui sese in bella sequantur,
Præstantes virtute legit; pars cætera pronâ
Fertur aquâ, segnisque secundo defluit amni,
Nuntia ventura Ascanio rerumque patrisque.
Dantur equi Teucris Tyrrhena petentibus arva
Ducunt exsortem Æneæ, quem fulva leonis
Pellis obit totum, præfulgens unguibus aureis.
   Fama volat parvam subitò vulgata per urbem,
Ocyùs ire equites Tyrrheni ad limina regis.
Vota metu duplicant matres; propiùsque perîclo
It timor, et major Martis jam apparet imago.
Tum pater Evandrus dextram complexus euntis
Hæret, inexpletum lachrymans, ac talia fatur:
O mihi præteritos referat si Jupiter annos!
Qualis eram, cùm primam aciem Præneste sub ipsâ
Stravi, scutorumque incendi victor acervos:
Et regem hâc Herilum dextrâ sub Tartara misi:
Nascenti cui tres animas Feronia mater,
Horrendum dictu! dederat; terna arma movenda;
Ter leto sternendus erat: cui tunc tamen omnes
Abstulit hæc animas dextra, et totidem exuit armis.
Non ego nunc dulci amplexu divellerer usquam,

547. De numero quorum legit *eos* præstantes

552. Ducunt *unum* exsortem *equum* Æneæ

558. Complexus dextram *filii* euntis hæret *illi*

561. *Et faciat me talem*, qualis eram, cùm stravi primam aciem

567. Et exuit *eum* totidem armis. Nunc ego non divellerer usquam

NOTES.

Penates were tutelary deities, either for families, or for cities and provinces. The former were the *Parvi Penates*, sometimes called *Lares:* the latter, the *Magni Penates.*

544. *Bidentes:* properly sheep of two years old, of *bis* and *dens.*

549. *Fertur pronâ aqua:* borne down the descending stream. *Segnis defluit*: without labor, float down the current—at their ease, float, &c. Ruæus says, *lenta descendit.*

550. *Ventura nuntia:* to be messengers to Ascanius, of his father, and of the state of his affairs—to bear tidings to Ascanius, &c.

551. *Petentibus Tyrrhena:* to the Trojans going to the Tuscan territory.

552. *Exsortem:* in the sense of *insignem:* a distinguished horse.

553. *Aureis unguibus.* The claws of the skin were overlaid with gold, for the sake of ornament. *Obit:* in the sense of *tegit.*

557. *Timor it propiùs*, &c. This passage, has puzzled commentators very much. Davidson supposes the word *major*, is to be supplied with *timor:* their fear grows greater, the nearer they are to danger. Ruæus takes *propiùs* in the sense of *prope:* near—approaching to. He makes the meaning to be: their fear comes near to danger. They are so much impressed with the idea of danger, that it becomes to them almost a reality. *It:* in the sense of *est* vel *fit.* Most copies have *jam* immediately after *Martis.* But Pierius informs us, that in most of the ancient *MSS.* which he consulted, it was wanting. Heyne reads *jam.*

559. *Inexpletum:* an adj. neu. gen. used as an adverb: immoderately—beyond measure.

560. *O mihi*, &c. This is one of the finest parts of the Æneid. We see an aged father, delivering his farewell address to his only son, the hope and solace of his old age, while he holds him close in his embrace, and is full of anxious apprehension of never seeing him again. The relation of those exploits, which he performed when he was in the vigor of manhood, is very natural, and the conclusion is extremely pathetic.

561. *Præneste.* The founder of this city was Cæculus, who took part with Turnus. See Æn. vii. 678. How then could Herilus have been its king so long before? He might have laid its foundations, and Cæculus added its fortifications, &c. Hence he might be called its founder.

562. *Scutorumque*, &c. It was a custom among the Romans, to gather up the armor that lay scattered on the field of battle, and burn it as an offering to one of their deities.

564. *Feronia mater:* to whom, at his birth, his mother had given three lives, and three sets of armor to be wielded. See Æn. vii. 800.

568. *Non ego nunc:* I would not now be torn from thy sweet embrace. This is a

Nate, tuo: neque finitimus Mezentius unquam,
Huic capiti insultans, tot ferro sæva dedisset
Funera, tam multis viduâsset civibus urbem
At vos, ô Superi, et Divûm tu maxime rector
Jupiter, Arcadii, quæso, miserescite regis,
Et patrias audite preces. Si numina vestra
Incolumem Pallanta mihi, si fata reservant;
Si visurus eum vivo, et venturus in unum;
Vitam oro: patiar quemvis durare laborem.
Sin aliquem infandum casum, Fortuna, minaris;
Nunc, ô, nunc liceat crudelem abrumpere vitam,
Dum curæ ambiguæ, dum spes incerta futuri;
Dum te, chare puer, mea sera et sola voluptas,
Complexu teneo; gravior ne nuntius aures
Vulneret. Hæc genitor digressu dicta supremo
Fundebat: famuli collapsum in tecta ferebant.
  Jamque adeò exierat portis equitatus apertis:
Æneas inter primos et fidus Achates;
Inde alii Trojæ proceres: ipse agmine Pallas
In medio. chlamyde et pictis conspectus in armis.
Qualis ubi Oceani perfusus Lucifer undâ,
Quem Venus ante alios astrorum diligit ignes,
Extulit os sacrum cœlo, tenebrasque resolvit.
Stant pavidæ in muris matres, oculisque sequuntur
Pulveream nubem, et fulgentes ære catervas.
Olli per dumos, quà proxima meta viarum,
Armati tendunt. It clamor; et, agmine facto,
Quadrupedante putrem sonitu quatit ungula campum.
  Est ingens gelidum lucus prope Cæritis amnem,
Relligione patrum latè sacer: undique colles

576. Et venturus in unum *locum cum illo*, oro

580. Dum *meæ curæ sunt* ambiguæ, dum spes futuri *est* incerta

589. *Talis* qualis Lucifer *est*, quem Venus diligit ante alios ignes astrorum, ubi perfusus unda Oceani extulit

594. Quà meta viarum *est* proxima

596. Ungula *equorum* quatit putrem

NOTES.

most tender line, and paints the paternal affections in the deepest colors.

571. *Viduâsset:* in the sense of *privâsset.*

574. *Numina:* power—will.

576. *Venturus in unum:* to meet him again.

577. *Patiar:* I will consent—agree to.

578. *Sin Fortuna minaris:* but if, O Fortune, thou threatenest any dire calamity to him. *Infandum:* properly is that which may not be spoken, or expressed—which I dare not name.

579. *Nunc, ô, nunc,* &c. This is much of the nature of Æn. ii. 644. *Sic, O sic,* &c. There is so much force and emphasis in the repetition of the *sic,* that if we remove it, we destroy the chief beauty and energy of the line. So also with the *nunc,* in the present instance.

580. *Dum curæ:* while my sorrows be doubtful, &c. While it be yet uncertain, whether I shall see my dear son again.

583. *Supremo digressu:* at his final departure.

588. *Conspectus:* conspicuous—distinguished.

589. *Qualis ubi,* &c. This is a beautiful simile, and said to have been greatly admired by Scaliger. *Perfusus:* wet, dipped.

590. *Ante alios ignes astrorum:* above other orbs of the stars—above other starry orbs.

591. *Resolvit:* in the sense of *dissipat.*

594. *Meta viarum:* the boundary of the way. Simply, the way.—*Via,* says Heyne. *Proxima:* the nearest. *Olli:* for *illi,* by antithesis.

595. *Agmine. Agmen* properly signifies a moving body or multitude—an army of men on the march. *Tendunt:* in the sense of *incedunt,* vel *progrediuntur.* *It:* in the sense of *surgit.*

596. *Quadrupedante sonitu:* with a prancing sound. Every ear perceives, that the numbers of the verse imitate the prancing of the horses. There are no less than five dactyls in it, which give it a quick and galloping motion. *Quatit:* strikes.

597. *Cæritis prope gelidum:* near the cold river of Cæris. *Cæris:* a town of Tuscany, whose inhabitants were called *Cærites.* In the neighborhood was a small river with a grove. Hence the epithet, *gelidus.*

598. *Relligione:* religious veneration—regard.

Inclusêre cavi, et nigrâ nemus abiete cingunt.
Sylvano fama est veteres sacrâsse Pelasgos,
Arvorum pecorisque Deo, lucumque diemque,
Qui primi fines aliquando habuere Latinos.
Haud procul hinc Tarcho et Tyrrheni tuta tenebant
Castra locis: celsoque omnis de colle videri
Jam poterat legio, et latis tendebat in arvis.
Huc pater Æneas et bello lecta juventus
Succedunt, fessique et equos et corpora curant.
At Venus, æthereos inter Dea candida nimbos,
Dona ferens aderat: natumque in valle reductâ
Ut procul egelido secretum flumine vidit;
Talibus affata est dictis, seque obtulit ultrò:
En perfecta mei promissâ conjugis arte
Munera! ne mox, aut Laurentes, nate, superbos,
Aut acrem dubites in prœlia poscere Turnum.
Dixit: et amplexus nati Cytherea petivit:
Arma sub adversâ posuit radiantia quercu.
Ille, Deæ donis et tanto et lætus honore,
Expleri nequit, atque oculos per singula volvit;
Miraturque; interque manus et brachia versat
Terribilem cristis galeam, flammasque vomentem,
Fatiferumque ensem, loricam ex ære rigentem,
Sanguineam, ingentem: qualis cùm cœrula nubes
Solis inardescit radiis, longèque refulget:
Tum leves ocreas electro auroque recocto,
Hastamque, et clypei non enarrabile textum.
Illìc res Italas, Romanorumque triumphos,
Haud vatum ignarus, venturique inscius ævi,

600. Fama est veteres Pelasgos, qui primi aliquando habuere Latinos fines sacrâsse lucumque, diemque Sylvano

610. Utque vidit natum secretum procul

612. En munera perfecta promissâ

622. *Talem*, qualis *est* cœrulea nubes, cùm inardescit

624. Tum *versat* ocreas leves *ex* electro.

626. Ignipotens, haud ignarus vatum, insciusque venturi ævi fecerat illìc

NOTES.

599. *Cavi:* in the sense of *curvi:* winding hills.

600. *Pelasgos.* These were a colony from Æmonia, the ancient name of Thessaly. They expelled the *Etrusci*, and settled in their country. They, in turn, were expelled by the *Tyrrheni*, a colony from Lydia, or Mæonia in the lesser Asia.

605. *Tendebat:* pitched their tents in the open fields. *Legio:* troops in general.

607. *Curant:* rest—refresh. Ruæus says, *reficiunt.*

608. *Nimbos:* in the sense of *nubes.*

610. *Flumine:* near the cool river—on the banks of the cold stream. *Secretum:* retired—remote.

612. *Perfecta:* made—finished.

613. *Mox ne dubites:* clad in this armor, my son, you may not hesitate to challenge either the proud, &c. The epithet *superbos*, refers to the outrage, which they had offered to Æneas and his followers, mentioned 118. supra.

618. *Expleri:* to be satisfied in looking upon them.

619. *Versat interque:* he turns and shifts his armor every way, the less in his hands, the larger in his arms—between his hands and his arms. *Miratur:* he wonders at them. Ruæus says, *stupet.*

620. *Galeam:* the helmet vomiting out flames. He means only that the crest or plume was of a fiery red color, and seemed to rise out of his helmet like flames.

621. *Fatiferum:* mortal—causing death.

622. *Cœrula nubes:* an azure cloud; such an one as receives the tincture, and reflects the various colors of the rainbow.

624. *Leves:* smooth—polished. *Recocto:* doubly purified. Ruæus says, *repurgato.*

625. *Non enarrabile textum:* the inexpressible texture of the shield.

626. *Italas res:* the Italian history.

627. *Haud ignarus*, &c. We now come to the conclusion of the book; and, certainly, there never was a book more nobly finished. Having given us the particulars of the arms and armor, the poet proceeds to the description of the sculptures upon the shield. And by way of prophecy, he gives us a very important piece of history in these engravings, and by that means, makes them one of the most important parts of the poem. It is imitated from Homer; but greatly improved. *Vatum:* in the sense of *vaticiniorum* vel *prædictionum.* Valpy says, "Of

Fecerat Ignipotens: illìc genus omne futuræ
Stirpis ab Ascanio, pugnataque in ordine bella.
 Fecerat et viridi fœtam Mavortis in antro
Procubuisse lupam: geminos huic ubera circum
Ludere pendentes pueros, et lambere matrem
Impavidos: illam tereti cervice reflexam
Mulcere alternos, et corpora fingere linguâ.
Nec procul hinc Romam, et raptas sinè more Sabinas
Concessu caveæ, magnis Circensibus actis,
Addiderat: subitòque novum consurgere bellum
Romulidis, Tatioque seni, Curibusque severis.
Pòst ìdem, inter se posito certamine, reges
Armati, Jovis ante aras paterasque tenentes
Stabant; et cæsâ jungebant fœdera porcâ.
 Haud procul inde citæ Metium in diversa quadrigæ
Distulerant; at tu dictis, Albane, maneres!
Raptabatque viri mendacis viscera Tullus
Per sylvam; et sparsi rorabant sanguine vepres.
 Nec non Tarquinium ejectum Porsenna jubebat
Accipere, ingentique urbem obsidione premebat.

628. Illìc *expresserat* omne genus

635. Nec procul hinc addiderat Romam, et Sabinas *virgines* raptas sinè more

636. Circensibus *ludis* actis.

645. Et vepres sparsi sanguine rorabant. Nec non Porsenna jubebat *Romanos* accipere

NOTES.

what had been foretold," by preceding prophets. Davidson says of Vulcan: "A prophet not unskilful," taking *ignarus vatum* in the sense of *ignarus vates* vel *propheta.*

628. *Ignipotens:* a name of Vulcan; of *ignis* and *potens. Fecerat:* in the sense of *expresserat.*

630. *Fœtam:* not pregnant, but in the sense of *enixam:* having just brought forth her young. This description is thought to have been taken from a statue of Romulus and Remus sucking the wolf, that was in the capitol in Virgil's time. See Æn. i. 274.

635. *Sabinas raptas.* After Romulus had founded his city, he became sensible that a body of men could not long be kept together, without some common bond; nor could his state continue long without women. He therefore proposed alliances with his neighbors, for the purpose of obtaining wives for his subjects; but they refused any connexion with a band of ruffians. He then conceived the plan of taking them by violence. For this purpose he instituted sports, which were then called *Consuales,* afterward *Circenses.* In these he invited his neighbors, especially the Sabines, from the city *Cures,* and upon a signal given, the Romans were to rush upon the women, and convey them to their own homes. This they did, in violation of good faith, and every principle of justice. War immediately ensued between the two states, which however was settled between Tatius king of the Sabines, and Romulus, upon these conditions: the Sabines should migrate to Rome; the government should be administered jointly by the two kings; that Rome should retain its name; but that the citizens should be called *Curites,* or *Quirites,* from *Cures. Sinè more:* without regard to law or right. Servius says, *absque exemplo,* whom Ruæus follows: without precedent, or example. Davidson thinks it should be taken in the sense of *malo more:* wickedly—atrociously. For, says he: Romulus, *solatus earum mœstitiam, docuit, non injuriâ sed connubii causâ, ipsas raptas esse; et demonstravit morem istum et Græcum et antiquum esse. Ex Dionysio.*

636. *Concessu caveæ:* in the crowded circus—in the assembly of the circus: when the great Circensian games were celebrated. For *caveæ,* see Geor. ii. 381.

638. *Romulidis:* dat. of *Romulidæ,* the Romans, so called from Romulus. *Curibus severis. Cures,* was a city of the Sabines: by meton. put for the inhabitants. These are again put by synec. for the Sabines in general. They were a people remarkable for their integrity and rigid virtue. Hence the epithet *severis.*

640. *Tenentes pateras:* holding goblets ready to offer *libations* on the altar.

642. *Metium distulerant.* The poet, sensible that the story of Metius might shock the humanity of his reader, is careful to remind him of the cause, for which the Roman king was so terribly severe, both in his apostrophe to the traitor, and in giving him the epithet of *mendax,* false or treacherous. See nom. prop. under *Metius.*

645. *Rorabant:* in the sense of *distillabant.*

646. *Porsenna.* He was king of the *Etrusci,* and took part with Tarquin after his expulsion, and endeavored to restore him to his throne. And he came near effecting it. He took possession of *Janiculum,* on the western bank of the Tiber,

Æneadæ in ferrum pro libertate ruebant.
Illum indignanti similem, similemque minanti
Aspiceres, pontem auderet quòd vellere Cocles,
Et fluvium vinclis innaret Clœlia ruptis.

652. In summo *clypeo* Manlius, custos

In summo custos Tarpeiæ Manlius arcis
Stabat pro templo, et Capitolia celsa tenebat:
Romuleoque recens horrebat regia culmo.
Atque hìc auratis volitans argenteus anser
Porticibus, Gallos in limine adesse canebat:
Galli per dumos aderant, arcemque tenebant,
Defensi tenebris, et dono noctis opacæ.

659. *Erat* ollis aurea

Aurea cæsaries ollis, atque aurea vestis;
Virgatis lucent sagulis: tum lactea colla
Auro innectuntur; duo quisque Alpina coruscant

662. Protecti *quoad* corpora

Gæsa manu, scutis protecti corpora longis.

663. Hìc extuderat exsultantes Salios

Hìc exsultantes Salios, nudosque Lupercos,
Lanigerosque apices, et lapsa ancilia cœlo,

NOTES.

over which a bridge was built to connect it with the main city. This bridge was defended on the western end by *Cocles*, against the Etruscan army, as they attempted to pass it, until the Romans on the eastern shore broke it down. After which he cast himself into the river, and swam to his friends. By this means the city was saved. See nom. prop. under *Tarquinius*.

648. *Æneadæ:* the Romans, so called from *Æneas*.

649. *Illum:* Porsenna.

651. *Clœlia.* One of the conditions of peace exacted by Porsenna of the Romans, was the surrender of their virgins to him as hostages. Among these hostages was Clœlia. Under the pretence of bathing herself, she eluded her guards, and with some others mounted their horses, and swam over the Tiber. Porsenna demanded her, and she was restored. But he set her at liberty with such other of the hostages, as she thought proper to name. The Romans presented her with an equestrian statue.

652. *Manlius.* In the year of Rome 364, the Gauls, under Brennus, routed the Roman army at the river Allium, and proceeded to Rome and took it. Marcus Manlius collected a body of men, threw himself into the capitol, and defended it. By this means the city was saved. See 347. supra.

654. *Regia horrebat:* the palace appeared rough, and newly repaired with Romulian straw. This thatched palace of Romulus, which was built on mount *Capitolinus*, was repaired from time to time, as it fell to decay. Virgil here represents it as standing in the time of Manlius, 327 years after the death of Romulus. It was held in great veneration, as a monument of their ancient frugality.

655. *Argenteus anser.* It is said that at the time the Gauls held possession of Rome, an attempt was made to seize upon the capitol in the dead of the night. The only access was by a narrow passage. The Gauls had succeeded in eluding the guards; and an alarm was given by the noise of a flock of geese, which was near this private passage: and by that means the capitol was saved. The goose afterward was held in high estimation. To this circumstance the poet here alludes.

656. *Canebat:* in the sense of *monebat*, vel *indicabat*.

658. *Dono:* by the favor—assistance.

659. *Aurea cæsaries*, &c. Here we have a description of the Gauls, and an account of their armor. They are said by Livy and others to have had long yellow hair, and a remarkable white neck. Their hair, therefore, the poet calls *aurea*, golden, and their necks *lactea*, milk-white.

660. *Sagulis.* The *sagulum* was a cloak or upper garment worn by the ancient Gauls. It was streaked or striped with different colors. Hence the epithet *virgatis*.

661. *Auro:* in the sense of *aureis monilibus*.

662. *Gæsa.* The *gæsum* was a long, but a light and slender spear, so that two of them could easily be carried in one's hand. They are here called *Alpina*, because peculiar to the Gauls, who inhabited about the Alps.

663. *Salios.* See 285. supra. *Lupercos.* See 343. supra.

664. *Lanigeros apices:* woollen caps. *Ancilia.* The *ancile* was a kind of oval shield, worn only by the priests of Mars on certain days. One of them is said to have fallen from heaven in the reign of Numa; and to have portended that the city of Rome

Extuderat: castæ ducebant sacra per urbem
Pilentis matres in mollibus. Hinc procul addit
Tartareas etiam sedes, alta ostia Ditis:
Et scelerum pœnas: et te, Catilina, minaci
Pendentem scopulo, Furiarumque ora trementem:
Secretosque pios: his dantem jura Catonem.
  Hæc inter tumidi latè maris ibat imago
Aurea, sed fluctu spumabant cœrula cano;
Et circûm argento clari delphines in orbem
Æquora verrebant caudis, æstumque secabant.
In medio classes æratas, Actia bella,
Cernere erat: totumque instructo Marte videres
Fervere Leucaten, auroque effulgere fluctus
Hinc Augustus agens Italos in prœlia Cæsar,
Cum patribus, populoque, Penatibus, et magnis Dîs,
Stans celsâ in puppi: geminas cui tempora flammas

670. Piosque secretos *ab impiis: et* Catonem

672. Sed cœrula *æquora* spumabant cano fluctu

675. In medio *mare* erat cernere

NOTES.

should become most powerful, and be rendered invinsible, so long as that remained in it.

665. *Extuderat:* had represented. Ruæus says, *sculpserat.*

666. *Pilentis*, &c. In the war with the Veientes, Camillus vowed an offering of gold to Apollo of Delphi; and not having it in his power to perform it, the women of distinction brought together their jewels, and presented them to him. Whereupon they received the honor of being carried at the public shows, and other exhibitions, in light coaches (*pilentis mollibus*) at the public expense.

668. *Catilina.* L. Sergius Catiline was of patrician rank, but of a very abandoned character. He twice sought the consulate, and was as often disappointed; which so enraged him, that he entered into a conspiracy with some others to murder the consuls and burn the city. The whole plot was discovered by the vigilance of Cicero, and Catiline expelled from Rome. He afterward perished on the field of battle, about the middle of December, 58 years before the Christian era. His associates also perished, many of them miserably, by the hand of the public executioner. Sallust has given a full account of this most daring conspiracy, written in purely classic style.

670. *Catonem.* Some understand *Cato the Censor;* but others, with more reason, perhaps, *Cato Uticensis* La Cerda here censures Virgil very much in making Cato give laws in hell to gratify Augustus. But, it is to be observed, that Cato does not sustain that character in the place of the condemned; but in the abodes of the blessed. Beside, it could not be a dishonor to Cato to be ranked with Minos and Rhadamanthus, those distinguished legislators. A question may here arise: what is the use of giving laws to those in *Elysium*, who are established in perfection and virtue? Perhaps by *jura*, we are to understand their rights or just rewards. This Cato was distinguished for his integrity and rigid virtue.

671. *Inter hæc*, &c. The poet now proceeds to the ever memorable victory which Augustus obtained over Antony and Cleopatra on the shores of Epirus, near *Actium*, in the year of Rome 723. Upon this, the poet exerts all the energy of his mind, with a view to immortalize the name of his prince. The previous description of the sea is a painting which nothing can surpass. *Imago ibat:* the surface of the wide-swelling sea was golden. *Ibat:* in the sense of *erat* vel *apparebat.*

672. *Cœrula. Maria* is understood. Th expresses the waters in general, without any particular reference to color in this place. *Cano fluctu:* with white silvered waves.

673. *Clari:* shining in silver.

674. *Æstum:* in the sense of *fluctus* vel *mare.*

675. *Actia bella:* the Actic fight. *Actia:* an adj. from *Actium*, a promontory of Epirus, where Augustus gained a complete victory over Antony and Cleopatra, in the year of Rome 723. This victory placed Augustus securely on the imperial throne. *Æratas:* brazen beaked.

676. *Instructo marte:* with the marshalled fight. *Leucaten.* See Æn. iii. 274.

678. *Hinc Augustus*, &c. Here the poet arranges the respective armies. On the one side, Augustus, with his Italian forces, the fathers of his country, and its guardian gods. On the other side, Antony, with his foreign forces, and the gods of Egypt. Every line is beyond expression admirable.

680. *Cui læta tempora:* whose joyous temples, &c. *Cui:* in the sense of *cujus. Geminas flammas.* Some refer this to his

Læta vomunt, patriumque aperitur vertice sidus
Parte aliâ, ventis et Dîs Agrippa secundis,
Arduus, agmen agens: cui, belli insigne superbum,
Tempora navali fulgent rostrata coronâ.
Hinc ope barbaricâ variisque Antonius armis
Victor, ab Auroræ populis et litore rubro
Ægyptum, viresque Orientis, et ultima secum
Bactra vehit: sequiturque, nefas! Ægyptia conjux.
Unà omnes ruere, ac totum spumare reductis
Convulsum remis rostrisque tridentibus æquor.
Alta petunt: pelago credas innare revulsas
Cycladas, aut montes concurrere montibus altos:
Tantâ mole viri turritis puppibus instant.
Stuppea flamma manu, telisque volatile ferrum

682. *In* alia parte *erat* Agrippa

683. Cui tempora fulgent. rostrata navali coronâ

685. Hinc victor Antonius, barbaricâ ope, variisque armis, vehit Ægyptum, viresque Orientis, et ultima Bactra secum, *usque* ab populis

689. Omnes *videntur* ruere unà, ac totum æquor

NOTES.

helmet, the cone or tuft of which had red fiery plumes. Others, to his diadem, which was set with sparkling gems.

681. *Patrium sidus.* This alludes to the manner in which he used to be represented in the Roman sculpture, having over his head the star into which his adopted father Julius Cæsar was supposed to have been changed. *Vomunt flammas.* The poet here imitates Homer in his description of the helmet of Diomede.

682. *Agrippa:* a noble Roman, and highly honored by his prince. To his skill and conduct, the victory at *Actium* was chiefly owing. He was the son-in-law of Augustus, and also his adopted son. He died in the year of the city 742. *Secundis:* in the sense of *propitiis.*

684. *Rostrata:* adorned with the naval crown. This crown was bestowed on such as signalized themselves in an engagement at sea. It was set around with figures like the beaks of ships.

685. *Antonius.* Marcus Antonius was the companion of Julius Cæsar in all his expeditions, and was *magister equitum* during his dictatorship. After the death of Cæsar, he was *triumvir* with Octavius (afterward Augustus) and Lepidus. He overthrew the army of Brutus and Cassius, and with them the hopes of the republicans, on the plains of Philippi. He performed many noble deeds for his country, and triumphed over the Parthians in the year of Rome 716. He put away his wife for the sake of Octavia, the sister of Augustus. He put her away in turn, and married Cleopatra, queen of Egypt; whereupon he was declared an enemy by the Senate. War was immediately declared against him. The two armies, or rather fleets, engaged at Actium, a promontory of Epirus. Antony was vanquished, and fled to Alexandria in Egypt, which was soon besieged; and was taken the following year. He killed himself, to prevent falling into the hands of his enemies. The same was the end of Cleopatra, who died by the bite of asps, which she kept for that purpose. The army of Antony was made up chiefly of Asiatics. Hence *populis Auroræ:* from the nations of the morning—of the east. *Variis armis:* with various arms—with arms of various kingdoms and nations.

686. *Rubro litore:* from the coast of the *Red sea.* This sea separates Egypt from Arabia. *Victor.* This is mentioned with reference to his victory and triumph over the Parthians. It is added to do honor to Augustus in conquering so formidable an enemy.

688. *Bactra:* neu. plu.: a principal city of Bactriana, a country lying to the southeast of the Caspian sea, put, by synec. for the whole country. The Romans, like the Greeks before them, called all other nations *barbarians.* So here the forces of Antony are called, *barbarica opes.* *Ultima:* the farthest, or most remote part of the empire. *Ægyptia conjux:* Cleopatra.

690. *Reductis remis:* with laboring oars. *Reductis,* shows the men laboring at the oar, and with all their might pulling home every stroke. *Tridentibus rostris:* with trident beaks. See Æn. v. 143.

692. *Cycladas.* The Cyclades were a cluster of islands in the Ægean sea. Delos, one of them, was the birth-place of *Apollo* and *Diana.* The poet likens the ships, on account of their magnitude, to these islands floating on the sea, and to mountains engaging with one another. The comparison is of the noblest kind.

693. *Turritis puppibus.* These were ships that had turrets or towers erected on their decks; from which the soldiers threw all manner of weapons, as if they had been on dry land; and so engaged with the greatest fury imaginable. Of so great size or bulk: *tantâ mole.*

694. *Stuppea flamma.* These were bundles of tow or hemp set on fire, and cast on

Spargitur: arva novâ Neptunia cæde rubescunt.
Regina in mediis patrio vocat agmina sistro;
Necdum etiam geminos à tergo respicit angues.
Omnigenûmque Deûm monstra, et latrator Anubis,
Contra Neptunum et Venerem, contraque Minervam
Tela tenent. Sævit medio in certamine Mavors
Cœlatus ferro, tristesque ex æthere Diræ;
Et scissâ gaudens vadit Discordia pallâ,
Quam cum sanguineo sequitur Bellona flagello.
Actius hæc cernens arcum intendebat Apollo
Desuper: omnis eo terrore Ægyptus, et Indi,
Omnis Arabs, omnes vertebant terga Sabæi.
Ipsa videbatur ventis regina vocatis
Vela dare, et laxos jam jamque immittere funes.
Illam inter cædes, pallentem morte futurâ,
Fecerat Ignipotens undis et Iapyge ferri:
Contrà autem magno mœrentem corpore Nilum,
Pandentemque sinus, et totâ veste vocantem
Cœruleum in gremium, latebrosaque flumina victos.

696. In mediis partibus clypei regina Cleopatra vocat

701. Tristesque Diræ sæviunt ex æthere.

710. Ignipotens fecerat illam inter cædes, pallentem futura morte ferri

711. Autem contra cælaverat Nilum magno corpore mœrentem, pandentemque suos sinus, et tota veste expassâ vocantem victos

NOTES.

board the enemy. *Stuppea:* an adj. from *stuppa. Telis volatile ferrum.* It is not easy to come at the meaning of these words. If we could take *telis* in the sense of *machinis*, the engines with which the weapons were thrown, there would be no difficulty. Heyne thinks this can hardly be done. He suggests the reading of *teli* in the gen. The volatile steel of the dart is thrown. The dat. is frequently used in the sense of the gen. If it be in the present case, the meaning will be: The volatile steel of (to) the darts is thrown; that is, the darts and missive weapons themselves. *Ferrum:* the point or barb of the dart, by synec. the whole dart.

695. *Neptunia arva:* a most beautiful expression for the sea. *Nova cæde:* with great—unusual slaughter.

696. *Sistro.* The *sistrum* was a kind of timbrel peculiar to the Egyptians, and used by them in the worship of *Isis.* The epithet *patrio* is therefore very proper.

697. *Geminos angues.* This is supposed to allude to the manner of her death. As she was to die by the bite of asps, it is supposed that Vulcan engraved them behind her, to show what was to be her destiny, though she was not then apprehensive of it.

698. *Omnigenûm*, &c. The Egyptians were notorious for consecrating as gods the several kinds of animals. Cicero says of them: *omne ferè genus bestiarum Ægyptii consecrârunt.* The deities, however, most honored, were *Osiris*, one of their kings, and *Isis* his wife. Also, *Anubis.* He was most probably their servant, and, for his fidelity, was consecrated. He was represented with a dog's head, in allusion to his fidelity; the dog being the most faithful of animals. Virgil calls him *latrator.*

702. *Gaudens scissâ pallâ:* discord rejoicing in her rent mantle. By the rent mantle, the poet very forcibly expresses the effect of discord in dividing the minds of men, and destroying the peace of society.

704. *Actius.* Apollo is here called Actius, from Actium, a promontory on the coast of Epirus, where he had a famous temple. The whole coast was sacred to him. The word *Actium* is derived from a Greek word which signifies the shore, or *litus.*

705. *Indi:* either the Bactrians, or the Æthiopians. These composed a part of the forces of Antony. The inhabitants of any warm climate were sometimes called *Indi*, indiscriminately. *Sabæi:* the inhabitants of *Arabia Felix.* These, also, were with Antony. *Eo terrore:* with the fear of that, &c.

708. *Immittere laxos funes:* to give loose ropes—to let go the ropes that contracted the sails. This is a metaphor taken from loosening the reins of a horse, to let him go at full speed.

710. *Iapyge.* This wind blew from Apulia, the most eastern part of Italy, and consequently toward Egypt. It is called *Iapyx*, from the ancient name of Apulia. *Fecerat:* had engraved—represented.

711. *Nilum.* This personification of the river Nile is extremely fine. The Nile is the largest river of Africa. Rising in the mountains of Abyssinia, and running a northerly course, fertilizing the country through which it passes, it falls into the Mediterranean sea by seven mouths. Its inundations are occasioned by the periodical rains, which fall within the tropics. *Mœrentem:* in the sense of *dolentem.*

713. *Latebrosa:* winding—affording a safe and secure retreat.

At Cæsar, triplici invectus Romana triumpho
Mœnia, Dîs Italis votum immortale sacrabat,
Maxima ter centum totam delubra per urbem.
Lætitiâ, ludisque viæ plausuque fremebant:
Omnibus in templis matrum chorus; omnibus aræ
Ante aras terram cæsi stravêre juvenci.
Ipse, sedens niveo candentis limine Phœbi,
Dona recognoscit populorum, aptatque superbis
Postibus. Incedunt victæ longo ordine gentes,
Quàm variæ linguis, habitu tam vestis et armis.
Hìc Nomadum genus, et discinctos Mulciber Afros,
Hìc Lelegas, Carasque, sagittiferosque Gelonos
Finxerat. Euphrates ibat jam mollior undis,
Extremique hominum Morini, Rhenusque bicornis,
Indomitique Dahæ, et pontem indignatus Araxes.
Talia, per clypeum Vulcani, dona parentis
Miratur: rerumque ignarus imagine gaudet,
Attollens humero famamque et fata nepotum

716. *Nempe* tercentum maxima delubra

718. *Erat* chorus matrum *in* omnibus templis; *erant* aræ

720. *Augustus* ipse, sedens *in* niveo limine candentis *templi*

724. Hìc Mulciber finxerat genus

729. *Æneas* miratur talia dona parentis *Veneris*

730. Gaudetque imagine rerum, *quarum est adhuc* ignarus

NOTES.

714. *Triplici triumpho.* Augustus obtained three victories: one over the Illyrians, another over Antony and Cleopatra, and a third over Egypt, which was reduced to a Roman province. This was effected by the capture of Alexandria in the year of Rome 724, and in the month *Sextilis;* which afterward was called *Augustus.* Soon after this, the year was begun on the first day of January.

716. *Ter centum,* &c. A definite number is here used for an indefinite number. We are informed that Augustus built several sumptuous temples at Rome, among which was one to Julius Cæsar, his adopted father. This was built on mount *Palatine,* of *white* Parian marble. Hence the epithet *candentis,* verse 720, infra. *Viæ:* the streets of the city. *Fremebant:* in the sense of *resonabant.*

723. *Linguis:* language. *Habitu:* manner, or form of their apparel.

724. *Nomadum.* The *Nomadæ* vel *Numadæ* were a people of Africa, situated to the west of Carthage. Their capital city was *Cirta.* They derived their name from a Greek word which signifies *pasture;* pasturage being their chief business. *Discinctos:* the Africans are so called from the looseness of their apparel, or from their general inactivity and aversion to labor. *Mulciber:* a name of Vulcan.

725. *Lelegas.* The *Lelegæ* were a people of Asia Minor. Homer places them about the bay of *Adramyttium.* By some they are confounded with the *Cares.* These were a people to the south of *Ionia,* and to the north of *Doris.* *Gelonos.* These were a people of Scythia, or Thrace, skilful in throwing the arrow.

726. *Finxerat:* in the sense of *sculpserat.*

727. *Morini.* These were a people inhabiting the northern parts of Gaul over against Britain; which the Romans considered the boundary of the world to the westward. Hence they are called *extremi hominum:* the most remote of men. Their capital was *Tarvanna.* Caius Carinus triumphed over them, on the same day that Augustus obtained his first triumph. *Rhenus:* the Rhine, a well-known river. It arises in the Alps, and taking a northerly direction, unites with the *Main* from the east. Hence it is called *bicornis,* two horned. It falls into the German sea by several mouths.

728. *Dahæ.* Where these people were situated is uncertain. Stephanius thinks they were a nation of Scythia. Others place them in Asia, near the river Oxus, which falls into the Caspian sea, from the south-east, separating Bactriana from Sogdiana. If this be correct, they were allies of Antony. *Araxes.* This is a river, rising in Armenia, taking an easterly direction, and falling into the Caspian sea. It carried away the bridge which Alexander built over it. Hence it is said: *indignatus pontem:* it disdained a bridge.

730. *Ignarus,* &c. Although Æneas was delighted with these figures and representations upon his shield, he knew not what they were designed to represent and foreshow.

QUESTIONS.

What is the subject of this book?

At whose direction did Æneas go to the court of Evander?

Where was his city situated?

What was the name of it?

Why was it called *Pallanteum?*

How was he received by the aged monarch?

Of what country was he a native?

What was he doing at the time of the arrival of Æneas?

Were Æneas and Evander in any way related to each other?

How was that relationship deduced?

Who was their common ancestor?

Had Evander any acquaintance with Anchises?

On what occasion had he seen him?

Where is the island of Salamis situated?

How came Priam to visit that island?

What other places did he visit at the same time?

On what account were those sacred rites instituted in honor of Hercules, in which Evander was then engaged?

Who was Hercules?

What other names had he?

On what occasion did he visit Evander?

Who was Cacus?

Where had he his residence?

What had he done to bring the vengeance of Hercules upon him?

In what way did he take these heifers to his cave?

What was his object in doing this?

How was a discovery finally made?

Where was the cave of Cacus situated?

On the approach of Hercules, what did Cacus do?

How did the hero find admission into his den?

What resistance did he make?

How did Hercules kill the monster?

Did Hercules perform any other distinguished actions?

What are some of them?

To whom was he made subject by Juno?

How many actions did he perform at the command of that king?

What are they called by way of distinction and eminence?

What was the object of Æneas in going to the court of Evander?

Did he furnish him with men and supplies for the war?

What was the character of Evander as a soldier?

Had he performed, in his youth, any feats of valor?

What are some of them?

How many men did he send with Æneas?

Who commanded them?

What was the age of Pallas at that time?

What was the state of the Tuscans?

Where were they situated in respect to the Tiber?

What was the cause of their being in arms?

Was the throne of Tuscany at that time vacant?

Had they made any offer of the crown to Evander?

Why did he decline it?

Who commanded the Tuscan troops?

What was the object of Æneas in visiting the Tuscan camp?

Did the Tuscans willingly place themselves under his command?

Had there been any prophetic declarations upon this subject?

What prince does Turnus endeavor to bring over to his interest?

In what part of Italy were his possessions?

What was the name of his city?

Who was Diomede?

What did Venus in the mean time?

Where were the forges of Vulcan?

Who were his workmen?

What were the names of the chief of them?

What were they doing at that time?

On the shield of Æneas was there any carved work?

Were there any events of the Roman history there represented?

What were some of those events?

How did Æneas receive this impenetrable shield?

Where was he at the time?

Was this a very unexpected event to him?

In what light may this book be considered?

Where is the scene laid?

What does Dr. Trapp observe of this book?

What part, in particular, is the finest and most noble?

In what description does the poet appear to have exerted all the powers of his mind?

Where was that battle fought?

What was the consequence of that victory to Augustus?

What was the end of Antony?

What was the end of Cleopatra?

In what manner did she die?

How does the book conclude?

LIBER NONUS.

In this book the war commences. Turnus, taking the advantage of the absence of Æneas, assaults the Trojan camp; and attempts to set fire to their ships, when they are changed into sea-nymphs. In a state of consternation, they send Nisus and Euryalus to recall Æneas. This introduces the episode of their friendship, generosity, and the conclusion of their adventures: which extends from the 176th line to the 502d, and is one of the finest pieces of the Æneid. The next morning, Turnus renews the assault, and performs prodigies of valor. At length, being informed that the Trojans had opened the gates, he repairs thither; when a most desperate conflict ensues. The Trojans take refuge within their gates. The hero enters along with them, and the gates are closed upon him. Juno assists him, and a great slaughter ensues. The Trojans flee in all directions before him. At last, however, they are rallied by Mnestheus and Sergestus, and renew the fight. Turnus retires before them, escapes from their entrenchments, and returns in safety to his camp.

This book is distinguished from the rest by the total absence of Æneas. It contains more fighting than any of the other. Dr. Trapp considers the transformation of the ships into nymphs of the sea, as a blemish to the book.

ATQUE ea diversâ penitùs dum parte geruntur,
Irim de cœlo misit Saturnia Juno
Audacem ad Turnum. Luco tum fortè parentis
Pilumni Turnus sacratâ valle sedebat:
Ad quem sic roseo Thaumantias ore locuta est:
Turne, quod optanti Divûm promittere nemo
Auderet, volvenda dies en attulit ultrò!
Æneas, urbe, et sociis, et classe relictâ,
Sceptra Palatini sedemque petivit Evandri.

10. Nec *est hoc* satìs; penetravit

Nec satìs: extremas Corythi penetravit ad urbes:
Lydorumque manum, collectos armat agrestes.

12. Nunc *est* tempus *poscere* equos

Quid dubitas? nunc tempus equos, nunc poscere currus.
Rumpe moras omnes, et turbata arripe castra.
Dixit: et in cœlum paribus se sustulit alis;
Ingentemque fugâ secuit sub nubibus arcum.

NOTES.

1. *Geruntur.* This refers to what has been related in the preceding book—the transactions at the court of Evander.

3. *Parentis.* Pilumnus was not the immediate parent of Turnus, but one of his ancestors; either his grandfather or great grandfather. Servius says *Pilumnus* was the common name of the family.

5. *Thaumantias.* Iris, the daughter of Thaumas and Electra. See Æn. iv. 700.

6. *Optanti:* to you wishing so favorable an opportunity.

7. *Dies volvenda:* the time (that was) to be revolved—the time destined by the fates. *Dies:* in the sense of *tempus.*

8. *Urbe.* This city of Æneas is sometimes called a camp. It was a camp, fortified in the form of a city, with turrets, ramparts, and gates.

9. *Evandri.* Evander is here called *Palatine*, because he dwelt on mount Palatine, or *Palitinus*, where Romulus afterward dwelt; and, also, the Roman emperors, down from Augustus. *Sceptra:* the realms. Ruæus says, *regna.* *Sedem:* palace—city.

10. *Corythi.* Corythus, a city of Tuscany founded by Corytus, a Tuscan king, and called by his name.

11. *Lydorum.* The Tuscans are called Lydians, because they were a colony from Lydia in *Asia Minor.*

15. *Secuit arcum:* she cut the mighty bow, &c. The rainbow was reckoned the chariot of *Iris;* so that the meaning is: she cut

Agnovit juvenis, duplicesque ad sidera palmas
Sustulit, ac tali fugientem est voce secutus:
Iri, decus cœli, quis te mihi nubibus actam
Detulit in terras? unde hæc tam clara repentè
Tempestas? medium video discedere cœlum,
Palantesque polo stellas. Sequar omina tanta,
Quisquis in arma vocas. Et sic effatus, ad undam
Processit, summoque hausit de gurgite lymphas,
Multa Deos orans: oneravitque æthera votis.
 Jamque omnis campis exercitus ibat apertis,
Dives equûm, dives pictaï vestis, et auri.
Messapus primas acies, postrema coërcent
Tyrrheidæ juvenes: medio dux agmine Turnus
Vertitur arma tenens, et toto vertice suprà est.
Ceu septem surgens sedatis amnibus altus
Per tacitum Ganges; aut pingui flumine Nilus,
Cùm refluit campis, et jam se condidit alveo.
 Hìc subitam nigro glomerari pulvere nubem
Prospiciunt Teucri, ac tenebras insurgere campis.
Primus ab adversâ conclamat mole Caïcus:

16. Juvenis *Turnus* agnovit *eam*

22. Quisquis *Deorum* vocas *me* in arma. Et sic effatus processit ad undam *Tibris*

27. Messapus *coërcet* primas acies

29. Et est supra *omnes alios* toto vertice

31. Aut *ceu* Nilus pingui flumine *fluit*, cùm

NOTES.

her way through it, to mount up again into heaven in that vehicle.

16. *Palmas:* properly, the palm of the hand: by synec. the whole hand.

19. *Unde hæc tam:* whence this so glaring brightness, all on a sudden? *Tempestas* evidently means, in this place, serenity, brightness, or brilliancy. *Detulit:* in the sense of *demisit. Tempestas tam clara.* Ruæus says, *facies cœli tam splendida.*

20. *Video medium:* I see heaven open in the midst, and stars shooting across the sky. When the lightning bursts through the clouds, the skies seem at times to be rent asunder. We are to understand by *stellas,* the meteors, and other electric appearances, that shoot across the skies like stars. Servius understands it of the stars themselves. That they should ever appear in the daytime is very extraordinary, but that they should appear in the additional light brought by *Iris,* was much more so. This, therefore, confirmed *Turnus* in the opinion that it was something preternatural and divine. *Sequar tanta omina,* was therefore his immediate determination.

23. *Lymphas:* in the sense of *aquam. Summo gurgite:* from the surface of the stream.

24. *Æthera:* in the sense of *cœlum.*

26. *Pictaï* the old genitive for *pictæ:* variegated—embroidered.

27. *Coërcent:* in the sense of *inferant.* Ruæus says, *regunt. Postrema:* the rear. *Agmina* is understood.

28. *Tyrrheidæ:* the sons of *Tyrrheus,* a patronymic noun. Tyrrheus was the shepherd of Latinus, whose eldest son was killed in the first skirmish. See Æn. vii.

29. *Vertitur:* in the sense of *incedit.* This line is marked by Heyne as an interpolation.

30. *Ceu altus Ganges:* as the deep Ganges, rising silently from seven still streams, flows on its course silent and still, so moves the army of Turnus. This is a beautiful simile, and is intended to express the majestic slowness and silence of their march: also, their order, after having been scattered and dispersed; as those rivers glide within their channels, after having overflowed the country. An ellipsis here is necessary in order to make the sense clear, which I have filled. The Ganges is the largest river of Asia, and divides India into two parts. After a course of about 2,000 miles, in which it recieves the waters of a number of considerable streams, it falls into the bay of Bengal by several mouths. Like the Nile, it overflows its banks. By *septem sedatis amnibus,* we are to understand the several rivers which flow into the Ganges, and augment its waters. Hence the propriety of *surgens.* The natives worship the river as a god.

31. *Per tacitum:* taken adverbially, in the sense of *tacitè.*

32. *Cùm refluit:* when it hath retired, or flowed back from the plains, and confined itself to its channel. *Pingui flumine:* with its fertilizing waters. The fertility of Egypt is wholly owing to the overflowing of the Nile. See Geor. iv. 293. and Æn. viii. 711.

33. *Glomerari:* to be formed—to ascend in wreathy columns, like clouds of smoke.

35. *Mole:* rampart—tower

Quis globus, ô cives, caligine volvitur atrâ?
Ferte citi ferrum, date tela, scandite muros
Hostis adest, eja. Ingenti clamore pèr omnes
Condunt se Teucri portas, et mœnia complent.
Namque ita discedens præceperat optimus armis
Æneas: si qua intereà fortuna fuisset;
Ne struere auderent aciem, neu credere campo.
Castra modò, et tutos servarent aggere muros.
Ergò, etsi conferre manum pudor iraque monstrat,
Objiciunt portas tamen, et præcepta facessunt;
Armatique cavis exspectant turribus hostem.
  Turnus, ut antevolans tardum præcesserat agmen,
Viginti lectis equitum comitatus, et urbi
Improvisus adest: maculis quem Thracius albis
Portat equus, cristâque tegit galea aurea rubrâ.
Ecquis erit mecum, juvenes, qui primus in hostem?
En, ait; et jaculum intorquens emittit in auras,
Principium pugnæ; et campo sese arduus infert.
Clamore excipiunt socii, fremituque sequuntur
Horrisono. Teucrûm mirantur inertia corda:
Non æquo dare se campo, non obvia ferre
Arma viros; sed castra fovere. Huc turbidus atque huc
Lustrat equo muros, aditumque per avia quærit.
Ac veluti pleno lupus insidiatus ovili,
Cùm fremit ad caulas, ventos perpessus et imbres,
Nocte super mediâ: tuti sub matribus agni
Balatum exercent: ille asper et improbus irâ
Sævit in absentes: collecta fatigat edendi
Ex longo rabies, et siccæ sanguine fauces

39. Omnes Teucri condunt se ingenti clamore per portas

41. Intereà siqua *dura* fortuna fuisset

51. O juvenes, ecquis *vestrum* erit, qui primus *irruet* in hostem mecum!

56. Viros non dare se æquo campo, non ferre arma obvia

57. *Turnus* turbidus lustrat

64. Rabies edendi collecta ex longo *tempore* fatigat *eum*, et fauces siccæ sanguine *fatigant eum*

NOTES.

36. *Globus:* a troop, or multitude of soldiers. *Quis:* in the sense of *quantus. Volvitur:* is approaching. Ruæus says, *accedit ad nos.* But *volvitur* may be taken perhaps in the sense of *involvitur:* is involved, or concealed from us, in that thick cloud of dust.

37. *Ferrum:* here, must mean arms in general.

38. *Per:* in the sense of *intra.*

40. *Optimus armis:* most skilful in the art of war—most valiant in arms.

41. *Siqua fortuna:* if there should be any danger or hazard during his absence, he directed that they should not, &c. If war should break out while, &c.

43. *Modò:* only—they should attempt nothing more. *Aggere:* in the sense of *munimentis.*

44. *Monstrat conferre:* urges them to engage hand to hand—in close quarters, and on equal terms, yet, &c.

45. *Equitum:* gen. plu. for *equitibus*, to agree with *lectis.*

49. *Albis maculis:* of white spots. The prep. *è* vel *ex* is understood.

52. *Intorquens jaculum:* brandishing his javelin, he threw it into the air, as the beginning, &c. This is an allusion to the Roman ceremony of throwing a javelin into the enemy's territory, as a signal of war. *Principium:* in the sense of *initium.*

54. *Horrisono fremitu:* with terrific shouts. *Excipiunt:* they answer with acclamation—they second, &c.

55. *Inertia:* cowardly—fearful.

56. *Obvia:* in the sense of *adversa.*

57. *Fovere castra:* to cherish or hug their camp—keep close to it. This is an opprobrious expression. It is a metaphor taken from timorous mothers, who hug their children, and keep them close to their bosoms. when apprehensive of their being in danger. *Turbidus:* in the sense of *iratus.*

58. *Per avia:* in the sense of *per inaccessa loca. Avia:* of *a* priv. and *via.*

60. *Cùm fremit:* growls around the sheepcotes. *Perpessus:* enduring—suffering.

61. *Super:* until—as far as. Ruæus says, *sub mediam noctem.*

62. *Ille asper:* he fierce and outrageous with anger, &c. *Absentes:* the lambs shut up in the fold, and out of his reach. *Exercent:* in the sense of *emittunt.*

63. *Sævit:* in the sense of *furit. Eos* is understood.

64. *Rabies edendi:* a rage for eating—

Haud aliter Rutulo muros et castra tuenti
Ignescunt iræ: et duris dolor ossibus ardet;
Quâ tentet ratione aditus; et quâ via clausos
Excutiat Teucros vallo, atque effundat in æquor.
Classem, quæ lateri castrorum adjuncta latebat,
Aggeribus septam circùm et fluvialibus undis,
Invadit; sociosque incendia poscit ovantes,
Atque manum pinu flagranti fervidus implet.
Tum verò incumbunt: urget præsentia Turni,
Atque omnis facibus pubes accingitur atris.
Diripuêre focos: piceum fert fumida lumen
Tæda, et commixtam Vulcanus ad astra favillam.
Quis Deus, ô Musæ, tam sæva incendia Teucris
Avertit? tantos ratibus quis depulit ignes?
Dicite. Prisca fides facto, sed fama perennis.
Tempore, quo primùm Phrygiâ formabat in Idâ
Æneas classem, et pelagi petere alta parabat;
Ipsa Deûm fertur genitrix Berecynthia magnum

76 Et Vulcanus *feri* commixtam favillam ad astra.

79. *Est* prisca fides facto, sed fama *ejus est* perennis.

82. Berecynthia ipsa genitrix Deûm fertur affata *esse* magnum Jovem

NOTES.

hunger. *Edendi:* in the sense of *cibi. Fatigat:* urges him on. Ruæus says, *vexat. Siccæ:* dry—thirsting for blood.

65. *Rutulo:* to the Rutulian—to Turnus.

66. *Dolor:* indignation—anguish.

67. *Qua ratione:* in what way he may obtain access; and in what way he may dislodge the Trojans, shut up in their intrenchments, &c. It is much better to take *via* in the abl. than the nominative to the verb *excutiat*, with Heyne and Valpy. This obscures the sense, while the former renders it obvious. Ruæus and Davidson read *quâ via.* Heyne, *quæ via.*

69. *Adjuncta:* adjoining—near to. Ruæus says, *admota.*

70. *Circùm septam:* protected around. Ruæus says, *defensam. Fluvialibus undis:* by the waters of the river—simply, by the river Tiber.

71. *Poscit incendia:* he demands flames of his joyous companions. He orders them to take fire, and assist him in burning the ships. Verbs of commanding, &c. govern two accusatives.

73. *Incumbunt:* they exert all their strength—they spring to it earnestly.

75. *Diripuere:* they strip—plunder the hearths. *Fert:* in the sense of *emittit.*

76. *Vulcanus:* the god of fire, by meton. put for fire itself. *Tæda:* a firebrand—torch. *Favillam:* the sparks.

78. *Depulit:* in the sense of *avertit.*

79. *Prisca fides*, &c. There have been various conjectures upon the sense of this passage. Servius takes *prisca* in the sense of obsolete. It was once believed, but now is not; yet the report continues, and is likely to be immortal. This Dr. Trapp approves. Some take *prisca fides facto*, simply for *priscum factum*, with the addition of its being believed. But to put *fides facto* for *factum*, though with the addition of belief, is harsh and singular. Heyne takes *facto*, in the sense of *facti*, which makes the sense easier. The belief of the fact was ancient, but the report or tradition will always continue. Davidson renders the words: "ancient is the testimony of the fact, but immortal is its fame." Valpy says, "the fact was at first credited on good authority, but the tradition has been constant."

80. *Tempore, quo*, &c. By some critics, Virgil has been censured for this *metamorphosis* of the ships of Æneas into sea-nymphs. Dr. Trapp has considered this matter at some length in a note upon this place. In conclusion he says: Virgil we know was not the first who wrote of the coming of Æneas into Italy: and, among other traditions of his country, it is probable he found the story coined to his hand, and could not omit it without disobliging those whom it was his business to please. This appears probable, if we consider the judgment of this great poet, (who is not likely to be the inventor of a story which exceeds all Ovid's in improbability,) and also the hints which he gives of his own disapprobation of it. However, he does all he can to cover its absurdity, and deludes us as much as possible. He invokes the muses afresh; introduces it as a thing scarcely credible: it is done by the greatest of the gods at the request of his mother. The story is short and elegant. But when all is said, the faulty image is not covered. Upon the whole, I am satisfied that Virgil was forced to insert it contrary to his judgment; or that he would have erased it, had he lived to perfect the poem. *Alta: spatia* is understood.

82. *Berecynthia:* a name of Cybele, who

Vocibus his affata Jovem: Da, nate, petenti,
Quod tua chara parens domito te poscit Olympo.
Pinea sylva mihi multos dilecta per annos,
Lucus in arce fuit summa, quò sacra ferebant,
Nigranti piceâ trabibusque obscurus acernis.
Has ego Dardanio juveni, cùm classis egeret,
Læta dedi: nunc solicitam timor anxius urget.
Solve metus, atque hoc precibus sine posse parentem,
Ne cursu quassatæ ullo, neu turbine venti
Vincantur. Prosit nostris in montibus ortas.
Filius huic contrà, torquet qui sidera mundi:
O genitrix, quò fata vocas? aut quid petis istis?
Mortaline manu factæ immortale carinæ
Fas habeant! certusque incerta pericula lustret
Æneas? cui tanta Deo permissa potestas?
Imò, ubi defunctæ finem, portusque tenebunt
Ausonios; olim quæcunque evaserit undis,
Dardaniumque ducem Laurentia vexerit arva;
Mortalem eripiam formam, magnique jubebo
Æquoris esse Deas: qualis Nereïa Doto
Et Galatea secant spumantem pectore pontum.
Dixerat: idque ratum, Stygii per flumina fratris,
Per pice torrentes atrâque voragine ripas,
Annuit: et totum nutu tremefecit Olympum.
Ergò aderat promissa dies, et tempora Parcæ
Debita complêrant; cùm Turni injuria matrem

85. Fuit in summâ arce pinea sylva dilecta mihi per multos annos, *nempe*, lucus

88. Ego læta dedi has *arbores*

91. *Ut illæ naves* ne vincantur quassatæ ullo cursu, neu *ullo* turbine venti: prosit *iis eas* ortas *esse* in

98. Ubi defunctæ *periculis maris* tenebunt

101. Eripiam *huic* mortalem

104. Annuitque id ratum *esse* per flumina

108. Cùm injuria Turni admonuit matrem *Cybelen* depellere tædas

NOTES.

is said to have been the mother of the gods. See Æn. vi. 784.

84. *Olympo domito.* Jupiter had dethroned his father Saturn, and reduced all the gods to his obedience. The mention of this circumstance is emphatical. For kings are most likely to grant favors on their first accession to their thrones. And besides, it was peculiarly proper to be mentioned by her; for it was by her means that he was so advanced. He had been preserved by her from Saturn; and for the undisturbed possession of Olympus, he was indebted to his mother. Jove could not therefore refuse her prayer.

86. *Lucus:* put, in apposition with *pinea sylva. Ferebant:* in the sense of *offerebant. Sacra:* sacrifices.

87. *Obscurus:* darkened—shaded; agreeing with *lucus. Arce summa:* mount Ida, where Cybele was peculiarly worshipped. This mountain was sacred to her. *Trabibus acernis:* ash-trees. *Trabs:* the trunk, put by synec. for the whole tree.

88. *Classis:* gen. governed by *egeret.*

89. *Urget:* this is the common reading. Davidson reads *angit.*

90. *Solve metus:* dismiss my fears. Fear may be considered as a yoke in which a person is bound. Ruæus says, *expelle. Posse hoc:* to obtain this by intreaties—to have sufficient influence with you to obtain, &c.

91. *Ullo cursu:* in any voyage—course. *Turbine venti:* a storm, or gale of wind.

94. *Vocas:* in the sense of *vertis. Fata:* the course—order of things. *Istis:* for those ships. *Navibus* is understood.

96. *Immortale fas:* an immortal privilege, or right. *Lustret:* surmount—pass through. *Certus:* safe—secure from harm. For *lustret*, Ruæus says *adibit.*

100. *Laurentia arva:* It ly—the land of Laurentum. The prep. *ad* is understood.

102. *Doto—Galatea:* the names of two nymphs of the sea, the daughters of Nereus and Doris. See Ecl. ii. 46.

104. *Annuitque id ratum:* he assented it should be granted—he bowed his head as a sign that it was granted to her. The gods were wont to swear by the infernal rivers, particularly by Styx; and if they did not perform, they lost their divinity for an hundred years. See Geor. iii. 551.

105. *Torrentes:* in the sense of *fluentes.* Cybele had requested of Jove, that the ships of Æneas should not, under any circumstance, be overcome or destroyed. He intimates this to be a singular request. Could ships built by mortal hands, enjoy the privilege of immortality? was it certain, that Æneas would escape the dangers of his long and perilous voyage? what she demanded was out of his power to grant unconditionally. But if any of them should

Admonuit sacris ratibus depellere tædas.
Hic primùm nova lux oculis effulsit, et ingens
Visus ab Aurorâ cœlum transcurrere nimbus,
Idæique chori: tum vox horrenda per auras
Excidit, et Troüm Rutulorumque agmina complet:
Ne trepidate meas, Teucri, defendere naves,
Neve armate manus: maria antè exurere Turno
Quàm sacras dabitur pinus. Vos ite solutæ,
Ite, Deæ pelagi: genitrix jubet. Et sua quæque
Continuò puppes abrumpunt vincula ripis;
Delphinumque modo demersis æquora rostris
Ima petunt. Hinc virgineæ, mirabile monstrum!
Reddunt se totidem facies, pontoque feruntur,
Quot priùs æratæ steterant ad litora proræ.
Obstupuere animis Rutuli: conterritus ipse
Turbatis Messapus equis: cunctatur et amnis
Rauca sonans; revocatque pedem Tiberinus ab alto.
At non audaci cessit fiducia Turno.
Ultrò animos tollit dictis, atque increpat ultrò:
Trojanos hæc monstra petunt: his Jupiter ipse
Auxilium solitum eripuit: non tela, nec ignes
Expectant Rutulos. Ergò maria invia Teucris,
Nec spes ulla fugæ: rerum pars altera adempta est:
Terra autem in manibus nostris: tot millia gentes
Arma ferunt Italæ. Nil me fatalia terrent,
Si qua Phryges præ se jactant, responsa Deorum
Sat fatis Venerique datum, tetigere quòd arva
Fertilis Ausoniæ Troës. Sunt et mea contrà

112. Idæique chori *simul*: tum

115. Dabitur Turno exurere maria antequàm *has* sacras pinus

116. Genitrix *Deorum* jubet *id*.

120. Hinc totidem virgineæ facies

130. Ergo maria *sunt* invia

133. Fatalia responsa Deorum, si qua Phryges jactant præ se

136. Et sunt mihi mea fata contrà *illa*, *nempe* exscindere

NOTES.

escape the dangers of the sea, and arrive safe in Italy, he would grant to such, to become nymphs of the sea. This he promises in the most solemn manner, and ratifies it by the usual oath.

109. *Tædas:* in the sense of *flammas.*

110. *Hic primùm,* &c. This implies, that Cybele had before been unknown in Italy: and now made her first appearance in that country, in favor of the Trojans. *Oculis:* in the sense of *visui.*

111. *Nimbus:* a bright cloud, or cloud of glory, the vehicle of the goddess. *Aurora:* the east.

112. *Idæique chori:* her Idæan choir. These were the priests of Cybele, the *Corybantes*, *Curetes*, or *Dactyli.* They made a sound about the goddess on their brazen cymbals, as she passed through the sky. *Horrenda:* awful—inspiring dread.

113. *Excidit:* in the sense of *emittitur.*

114. *Trepidate:* in the sense of *properate.*

116. *Vos ite solutæ:* go, ye, free, go, goddesses of the sea.

119. *Modo:* in the sense of *more. Demersis:* sunk—immerged. Like dolphins, they dive with their prows or beaks to the bottom of the sea.

121. *Reddunt se*, &c. The meaning is: after they had gone to the bottom, each one came up with a virgin face, and floated down the stream into the sea.

124. *Turbatis:* affrighted--alarmed. *Cunctatur:* stopt—delayed.

125. *Raucà:* an adj. neu. plu., taken as an adv. *Revocat pedem:* recalls his current from the deep.

127. *Tollit animos:* he rouses the courage of his men (*militum*) by his words, and rebukes their fears.

128. *Petunt.* in the sense of *spectant.*

130. *Expectant: naves Trojanæ* is understood.

131. *Altera pars rerum:* one part of the world is taken from them, now their ships have left them; namely, the sea: and the land is in our possession. There is no way for them to escape.

133. *Arma:* by meton. for the men who bear them. *Ferunt:* bring to our aid. *Terrent nil*, &c. This whole speech of Turnus, bespeaks him the soldier and intrepid commander. And to turn those very prodigies, which encouraged and animated his enemies, against them, marks his undaunted spirit. He calls them Phrygians by way of contempt.

Fata mihi, ferro sceleratam exscindere gentem,
Conjuge præreptâ. Nec solos tangit Atridas
Iste dolor; solisque licet capere arma Mycenis.
Sed periisse semel satìs est: peccare fuisset
Antè satìs, penitùs modò non genus omne perosos
Fœmineum. Quibus hæc medii fiducia valli,
Fossarumque moræ, leti discrimina parva,
Dant animos. At non viderunt mœnia Trojæ,
Neptuni fabricata manu, considere in ignes?
Sed vos, ô lecti, ferro quis scindere vallum,
Apparat, et mecum invadit trepidantia castra?
Non armis mihi Vulcani, non mille carinis
Est opus in Teucros: addant se protinùs omnes
Etrusci socios: tenebras et inertia furta
Palladii, cæsis summæ custodibus arcis,
Ne timeant: nec equi cæcâ condemur in alvo
Luce palam certum est igni circumdare muros.
Haud sibi cum Danais rem, faxò, et pube Pelasgâ
Esse putent, decimum quos distulit Hector in annum.
Nunc adeò, melior quoniam pars acta diei;
Quod superest; læti benè gestis corpora rebus

140. Sed dicetur, est satìs eos periisse semel: fuisset satìs eos peccare antè, penitùs perosos *esse* non modò omne

146. Sed vos, O lecti viri, quis *vestrum* apparat

150. Ne timeant tenebras

154. Faxo *ut* haud putent esse rem sibi cum Danais

NOTES.

138. *Conjuge præreptâ.* Lavinia had been promised to Turnus in marriage: and he already considered her as his wife. She was taken (*prærepta*) from him, and transferred to Æneas.

139. *Licetque Mycenis:* nor is it lawful for Greece alone to take up arms. It is lawful for us too, in a similar cause. It is plain that the negation is to be continued, in this last member of the sentence.

140. *Sed periisse semel,* &c. This is a difficult passage; and it is so rendered by its conciseness. To make the sense, something must be supplied. There is a note in the *Variorum* edition upon this place, in these words: *Verùm dicent Trojani se luisse jam Helenæ raptum. Respondet: desiissent ergò peccare: dedicissent odisse potiùs fœminas omnes, quàm vel unam rapere: quod quia in Lavinia faciunt, iterum pereant. Ex quo colligitur, quoties peccaverint, toties eos perire debere.* Upon the words *penitùs modo non,* Dr. Trapp observes, the *penitùs* should be connected with *perosos:* and the *modo non,* he takes in the sense of *propemodum,* and joins them with *omne genus,* &c. That they should utterly hate almost the whole female sex. They could not hate all women; their mothers, sisters, and relations, must be excepted. Ruæus makes the first clause an interrogation: which is incorrect. It is a supposed objection, to which *peccare fuisset,* &c. is the answer.

142. *Quibus hæc fiducia:* to whom this confidence of an intervening rampart, &c. give courage. The meaning of the passage is this: let them not presume on their fortifications and ramparts, that these will save them from death, since their former treachery was punished, when they were guarded by much stronger munitions, even those walls which were built by the hand of Neptune. *Parva discrimina lethi:* a small space, or feeble partition between them and death. *Medii:* intervening—between them and us.

144. *At:* this is the reading of Heyne, and Valpy. The common reading is *an.*

147. *Trepidantia castra:* trembling—in terror and consternation, now their leader is absent.

148. *Non armis opus est:* either that he needed not arms made by Vulcan, such as Achilles had; or that he would not use his own sword, which was also the workmanship of the god of fire. See Æn. xii. 90.

151. *Palladii,* &c. Here is an allusion to the exploit of Diomede and Ulysses, who privately entered the temple of Minerva in Troy, and stole the Palladium, having slain the guards. Hence, *inertia furta:* such cowardly and unmanly conduct, Turnus disdains.

153. *Luce palàm:* I am resolved to surround, &c. Turnus promises the Trojans fair play, that he will not have recourse to those stratagems and arts, which the Greeks employed when before Troy. This bespeaks a manly and dignified spirit; one, truly becoming the hero. *Luce palàm:* openly—in the day.

154. *Faxo:* I will do or cause that, &c.

157. *Rebus benè gestis.* These words are to be taken absolutely. Things being favorably begun. This is the sense given by

Procurate, viri; et pugnam sperate parati.
  Intereà vigilum excubiis obsidere portas,
Cura datur Messapo, et mœnia cingere flammis.
Bis septem Rutuli, muros qui milite servent,
Delecti: ast illos centeni quemque sequuntu ,
Purpurei cristis juvenes, auroque corusci.
Discurrunt, variantque vices, fusique per herbam
Indulgent vino, et vertunt crateras ahenos.
Collucent ignes: noctem custodia ducit
Insomnem ludo.
Hæc supèr è vallo prospectant Troës, et armis
Alta tenent; nec non trepidi formidine portas
Explorant, pontesque et propugnacula jungunt:
Tela gerunt. Instant Mnestheus acerque Serestus:
Quos pater Æneas, si quando adversa vocarent,
Rectores juvenum, et rerum dedit esse magistros.
Omnis per muros legio sortita perîclum
Excubat, exercetque vices, quod cuique tuendum est.
  Nisus erat portæ custos, acerrimus armis,
Hyrtacides; comitem Æneæ quem miserat Ida
Venatrix, jaculo celerem levibusque sagittis:
Et juxtà comes Euryalus, quo pulchrior alter
Non fuit Æneadûm, Trojana nec induit arma;
Ora puer primâ signans intonsa juventâ.
His amor unus erat, pariterque in bella ruebant:
Tunc quoque communi portam statione tenebant.
Nisus ait: Dî-ne hunc ardorem mentibus addunt,

158. O viri, læti procurate corpora

162. Ast centeni juvenes purpurei cristis

172. Quos pater Æneas dedit esse rectores juvenum, et magistros rerum

175. Exercetque vices *quoad id*, quod est cuique tuendum.

179. Et juxta *eum* comes Euryalus, quo

NOTES.

Davidson and Ruæu . Or the meaning may be: prepare yourselves for noble exploits, on the morrow.

158. *Procurate:* refresh—invigorate. *Sperate:* in the sense of *expectate.*

159. *Excubiis vigilum:* simply, with sentinels or guards. *Obsidere:* to besiege the gates of the Trojan camp—to block up, &c.

160. *Cingere mœnia:* to encompass their walls with fires to give them light in the night, lest the enemy should sally out upon them unobserved; or in despair, leave their city.

162. *Sequuntur illos quemque:* follow them every one. *Quisque* is a distributive pronoun. *Delecti:* fourteen Rutulians were chosen to superintend the watch, and see that due attention was paid, and each one performed his duty. *Milite:* with soldiers; the same as *militibus.* The guard amounted then to fourteen hundred men.

164. *Variant vices:* they shift, or change their tours of duty. They stand guard by turns.

169. *Alta:* the high places of the walls. *Loca* or *spatia* is understood.

170. *Jungunt,* &c. The same as *jungunt propugnacula cum pontibus.* They laid bridges from one bulwark or tower to another for the purpose o ready and easy communication. They connected their towers or ramparts together by means of bridges.

172. *Adversa:* in the sense of *res adversæ. Vocarent:* should require—demand.

173. *Dedit:* appointed.

175. *Exercet vices:* they perform their watch in turns. *Exercet:* in the sense of *variat. Tuendum:* to be attended to—performed—done.

176. *Nisus erat,* &c. Here the poet begins his celebrated episode of the friendship of Nisus and Euryalus. He had in the fourth book considered the force of love. Here he gives us a specimen of his skill in the power of friendship; and never was any thing more artfully disposed, more noble, more moving, and pathetic, than this piece. It is introduced without any formal introduction. He was speaking of the several posts that were to be defended; and among the rest, was one committed to the care of these two friends.

177. *Ida:* either the mother of Nisus: or mount Ida, which is sometimes called *venatrix,* because it abounded in game, and was frequented by hunters. *Hyrtacides:* a noun patronymic, from Hyrtacus, the father of Nisus.

181. *Intonsa ora:* his beardless face—unshaven face.

182. *Bella:* in the sense of *pugnam.*

185. An sua dira cupido fit Deus cuique?

196. Videor *mihi* posse reperire viam sub illo tumulo ad

199. Nise, fugisne adjungere me socium *tibi in* summis rebus?

201. *Meus* genitor Opheltes assuetus bellis non sic erudiit me sublatum

205. Hìc est, *hìc* est animus, contemptor lucis, et qui credat istum honorem, quo tendis, benè emi vitâ *ipsa*.

209. Quicunque *Deus* aspicit

Euryale? an sua cuique Deus fit dira cupido?
Aut pugnam, aut aliquid jamdudum invadere magnum
Mens agitat mihi; nec placidâ contenta quiete est.
Cernis, quæ Rutulos habeat fiducia rerum:
Lumina rara micant: somno vinoque soluti
Procubuêre: silent latè loca. Percipe porrò,
Quid dubitem, et quæ nunc animo sententia surgat.
Æneam acciri omnes, populusque, patresque,
Exposcunt; mittique viros, qui certa reportent.
Si tibi, quæ posco, promittunt; nam mihi facti
Fama sat est; tumulo videor reperire sub illo
Posse viam ad muros et mœnia Pallantea.
  Obstupuit magno laudum perculsus amore
Euryalus, simul his ardentem affatur amicum:
Me-ne igitur socium summis adjungere rebus,
Nise, fugis? solum te in tanta pericula mittam?
Non ita me genitor, bellis assuetus Opheltes
Argolicum terrorem inter Trojæque labores
Sublatum erudiit: nec tecum talia gessi,
Magnanimum Ænean et fata extrema secutus.
Est hìc, est animus, lucis contemptor; et istum
Qui vitâ benè credat emi, quò tendis, honorem.
Nisus ad hæc: Equidem de te nil tale verebar;
Nec fas: non. Ita me referat tibi magnus ovantem
Jupiter, aut quicunque oculis hæc aspicit æquis.
Sed si quis (quæ multa vides discrimine tali)
Si quis in adversum rapiat casusve Deusve,
Te superesse velim: tua vitâ dignior ætas.

NOTES.

185. *Dira:* great, vehement, or ardent. Ruæus says, *ardens.*

187. *Agitat:* urges—impels. *Mihi:* in the sense of *mea.*

189. *Rara:* here and there—few. *Micant:* in the sense of *splendent.*

190. *Percipe quid dubitem:* hear what I am meditating, and what, &c. This first speech is noble and disinterested. Nisus communicates his purposes to his friend; who is struck with the proposal, and takes it ill, that he should think of excluding him from a share of the danger and glory of the enterprise. *Dubitem:* in the sense of *mediter.*

193. *Certa:* the truth—true things.

195. *Fama:* the glory of the deed, &c.

196. *Mœnia Pallantea:* the city of Evander.

197. *Laudum:* in the sense of *gloriæ.*

199. *Rebus:* enterprises—undertakings.

200. *Fugis:* refuse—reject.

202. *Inter labores Trojæ.* This intimates that he was about seventeen years of age. For Æneas' wanderings had continued seven years, and the Trojan war ten years. This made him just the age when youth among the Romans began to bear arms. It also agrees with what is said verse 181, supra, of his just beginning to have a beard.

203. *Sublatum.* This alludes to the Roman custom of laying down the child naked upon the ground as soon as born, that the father might *take it up*, in token of his owning it for his own child. Heyne says, *natum et educatum. Nec gessi:* nor have I performed such actions in your company, that you should now refuse me as your companion and partner in your hazardous enterprise; nor have I acted so cowardly, &c.

205. *Est hìc,* &c. These two lines are extremely fine. Nisus replies to them in a speech extremely pathetic. He declines the company of Euryalus, chiefly on account of the dangers of the undertaking, his youth and inexperience; and his being more worthy of a long life. The whole is greatly heightened by the mention of his aged mother *Hìc est, est animus:* here is, here is a soul, a despiser of life; and which, &c. *Lucis:* in the sense of *vitæ.*

206. *Quò tendis:* whither—to which you aspire, or aim at.

210. *Tali discrimine:* in such a hazardous enterprise, as he had in contemplation.

211. *Adversum:* a sub. in the sense of *periculum. Rapiat me:* hurry me—carry me, &c

Sit, qui me raptum pugnâ, pretiove redemptum,
Mandet humo solitâ; aut, si qua id fortuna vetabit,
Absenti ferat inferias, decoretque sepulchro.
Neu matri miseræ tanti sim causa doloris:
Quæ te sola, puer, multis è matribus ausa,
Persequitur; magni nec mœnia curat Acestæ.
Ille autem: Causas nequicquam nectis inanes;
Nec mea jam mutata loco sententia cedit.
Acceleremus, ait. Vigiles simul excitat: illi
Succedunt, servantque vices: statione relictâ,
Ipse comes Niso graditur, regemque requirunt.
Cætera per terras omnes animalia somno
Laxabant curas, et corda oblita laborum.
Ductores Teucrûm primi, et delecta juventus,
Consilium summis regni de rebus habebant:
Quid facerent, quisve Æneæ jam nuntius esset.
Stant longis adnixi hastis, et scuta tenentes,
Castrorum et campi medio. Tum Nisus, et unà
Euryalus, confestim alacres admittier orant:
Rem magnam, pretiumque moræ fore. Primus Iülus
Accepit trepidos, ac Nisum dicere jussit.
Tunc sic Hyrtacides: Audite, ô, mentibus æquis,
Æneadæ; neve hæc nostris spectentur ab annis,
Quæ ferimus. Rutuli somno vinoque sepulti
Conticuere: locum insidiis conspeximus ipsi,
Qui patet in bivio portæ, quæ proxima ponto.
Interrupti ignes, aterque ad sidera fumus
Erigitur. Si fortunâ permittitis uti,

213. Sit *aliquis*, qui mandet me solitâ humô

219. Autem ille *Euryalus respondet.*

232. *Dicunt* rem *esse* magnam

NOTES.

213. *Sit qui mandet:* may there be some one who will commit me to the solitary earth, snatched from the field of battle, or redeemed with money, &c.

215. *Ferat:* or may perform the funeral rites to me absent, and honor me with an empty tomb. It was usual among the Romans, when the corpse could not be obtained, to perform the same funeral rites, as if it were present. The tomb was said to be empty, because the corpse was not there. Of such a burial, Nisus here speaks.

217. *Ausa:* having courage—daring. Ruæus says, *audax.*

218. *Mœnia Acestæ.* This was the city which Æneas founded in Sicily, and called after the name of his friend Acestes. Here he left the aged and infirm, and all who were not willing to accompany him into Italy. The mother of Euryalus was among those who braved the dangers of the voyage, and accompanied him, the poet intimates, for the sake of her son.

219. *Causas:* pretexts—excuses.

221. *Excitat vigiles:* at the same time, he wakes the watch—those who were to keep watch in turn.

223. *Regem:* Ascanius here is intended, as being a prince and heir to the crown.

224. *Cætera animalia,* &c. This is very expressive, and greatly heightens the image. At this time, when all nature was silent, and enjoying repose, the Trojan chiefs were assembled in council upon the state of their affairs. At this moment, they are surprised by Nisus and Euryalus, who demand to be admitted.

227. *Regni:* government—state.

231. *Admittier:* by paragoge, for *admitti.*

232. *Pretium moræ.* He observes that the subject he wished to propose, was of great importance, and would sufficiently compensate for the interruption of their deliberations.

235. *Spectentur:* in the sense of *æstimentur.* *Ferimus:* in the sense of *proponimus.*

237. *Insidiis locum:* we have observed a place for our purpose—one fit for the execution of our design. Nos *ipsi:* we our selves.

238. *In bivio portæ:* in the forked ways of the gate—where the way before the gate divides into two paths.

239. *Ignes interrupti:* the fires are dying away; or, only here and there one is burning, the rest having gone out.

240. *Uti fortunâ:* to embrace this opportunity.

241. Si permittitis *nos uti hâc* fortuna, *vos* cernetis Ænean quæsitum *a nobis* ad mœnia Pallantea, mox affore hìc

Quæsitum Ænean ad mœnia Pallantea,
Mox hìc cum spoliis, ingenti cæde peractâ,
Affore cernetis. Nec nos via fallit euntes:
Vidimus obscuris primam sub vallibus urbem
Venatu assiduo, et totum cognovimus amnem.
Hìc annis gravis, atque animi maturus Alethes:
Dì patrii, quorum semper sub numine Troja est,
Non tamen omnino Teucros delere paratis,
Cùm tales animos juvenum, et tam certa tulistis
Pectora. Sic memorans, humeros dextrasque tenebat
Amborum, et vultum lachrymis atque ora rigabat.

252. Quæ, quæ digna præmia rear posse solvi vobis, O viri, pro

Quæ vobis, quæ digna, viri, pro talibus ausis
Præmia posse rear solvi? pulcherrima primùm
Dî, moresque dabunt vestri: tum cætera reddet
Actutùm pius Æneas, atque integer ævi

256. Non unquam *futurus* immemor tanti meriti

257. Ascanius, cui sola salus *est in* genitore reducto, excipit; immò ego obtestor vos, O Nise

Ascanius, meriti tanti non immemor unquam.
Immò ego vos, cui sola salus genitore reducto,
Excipit Ascanius, per magnos, Nise, Penates,
Assaracique Larem, et canæ penetralia Vestæ,
Obtestor; quæcunque mihi fortuna fidesque est,
In vestris pono gremiis; revocate parentem,

262. Nihil *erit* triste *nobis* illo recepto.

Reddite conspectum: nihil illo triste recepto.
Bina dabo argento perfecta, atque aspera signis
Pocula, devictâ genitor quæ cepit Arisbâ;
Et tripodas geminos, auri duo magna talenta;
Cratera antiquum, quem dat Sidonia Dido.
Si verò capere Italiam, sceptrisque potiri,

268. Si verò contigerit *mihi* victori

Contigerit victori, et prædæ ducere sortem
Vidisti quo Turnus equo, quibus ibat in armis,
Aureus? ipsum illum clypeum cristasque rubentes
Excipiam sorti: jam nunc tua præmia, Nise.

NOTES.

242. *Peractâ:* made—done.

244. *Primam urbem:* the front of the houses, or the skirts of the city Pallanteum. Perhaps, simply, the suburbs of the city.

246. *Animi:* understanding—judgment.

247. *Numine:* in the sense of *potestate.*

248. *Non tamen,* &c. The word *tamen* shows that there is an ellipsis here of *licet ad tempus irascamini,* or of some others of the like importance were angry with us for a time, yet ye determine not to destroy, &c.

249. *Tulistis:* ye have produced or granted. *Pectora:* courage—resolution.

252. *Talibus ausis:* for such an enterprise, or bold undertaking. Heyne reads, *istis laudibus;* and Valpy after him. The common reading is *talibus ausis.*

253. *Pulcherrima:* in the sense of *optima.*

254. *Mores vestri:* your virtues. *Cætera: præmia* is understood.

255. *Integer ævi.* Dr. Trapp thinks this refers to the future manhood of Ascanius. This, too, is the opinion of the *Variorum* edition. Others take it for the present state of his youth—mature in age.

258. *Excipit:* in the sense of *incipit.*

259. *Larem Assaraci.* This was the tutelar deity or guardian god of Assaracus and his family. *Vesta* was the goddess that presided over the inextinguishable fire. She was called *cana,* hoary, or aged, because she was the most ancient of all the goddesses, and deemed the mother of all the living.

263. *Signis:* figures—carved work.

264. *Arisbâ devictâ.* Most interpreters understand by this that Arisba was taken by the Trojans. But Catrou thinks it was one of those cities taken by the Greeks in the first nine years of the war; and that these cups were saved by Æneas from the hands of the Greeks, when they plundered the town. Pliny informs us that Arisba was a city of Troas, and part of the kingdom of Priam.

267. *Sceptris:* in the sense of *imperio* vel *regno,* by meton.

268. *Ducere sortem:* to draw lots for the booty—to divide the booty by lot.

271. *Excipiam:* I will exempt from the lot—I will reserve.

Prætereà bis sex genitor lectissima matrum
Corpora, captivosque dabit, suaque omnibus arma:
Insuper his, campi quod rex habet ipse Latinus.
Te verò, mea quem spatiis propioribus ætas
Insequitur, venerande puer, jam pectore toto
Accipio, et comitem casus complector in omnes.
Nulla meis sinè te quæretur gloria rebus:
Seu pacem, seu bella geram, tibi maxima rerum
Verborumque fides. Contra quem talia fatur
Euryalus: Me nulla dies tam fortibus ausis
Dissimilem arguerit; tantùm fortuna secunda,
Haud adversa cadat. Sed te super omnia dona
Unum oro: genitrix Priami de gente vetustâ
Est mihi, quam miseram tenuit non Ilia tellus
Mecum excedentem, non mœnia regis Acestæ.
Hanc ego nunc ignaram hujus quodcunque perîcli est,
Inque salutatam linquo: nox, et tua testis
Dextera, quòd nequeam lachrymas perferre parentis.
At tu, oro, solare inopem, et succurre relictæ.
Hanc sine me spem ferre tui: audentior ibo
In casus omnes. Percussâ mente dederunt
Dardanidæ lachrymas; ante omnes pulcher Iülus;
Atque animum patriæ strinxit pietatis imago.
Tum sic effatur:
Spondeo digna tuis ingentibus omnia cœptis.
Namque erit ista mihi genitrix, nomenque Creüsæ
Solum defuerit: nec partum gratia talem

274. Insuper his, *genitor dabit id* campi quod

275. Verò accipio te, venerande puer,

285. Quam miseram excedentem mecum non Ilia tellus

288. Nox, et tua dextra *sunt* testis, quòd

NOTES.

272. *Bis sex lectissima corpora:* twelve most choice matrons, and as many captives of men, &c. *Sua:* in the sense of *propria:* it should be taken after *arma.* The arms peculiar to (that belonged to) them all. *Corpora matrum:* simply, matrons—women.

274. *Insuper his:* in addition to these—beside these. Some copies have *insuper, id campi quod,* &c. The sense will be the same either way. We are not to understand the kingdom of Latinus; but his own private lands and possessions.

275. *Propioribus spatiis.* By this we are to understand that Ascanius and Euryalus were nearly of the same age. Davidson renders the words: "in the nearer stages of life."

280. *Contra:* in the sense of *ad.*

282. *Arguerit:* shall show me unequal to. Ruæus says, *ostendet degenerem. Tantùm fortuna secunda:* only let fortune fall prosperous, and not adverse. This is the reading of Heinsius, Ruæus, and Davidson.—Heyne reads, *tantum: fortuna, secunda aut adversa, cadat,* which scarcely makes sense. The pointing, too, tends to obscure it. Valpy who follows Heyne, sensible of the difficulty attending this reading, conjectures the passage was left by the poet in an unfinished state.

283. *Super:* above—more than.

284. *Genitrix,* &c. The meaning is, that neither the land of Troy, nor the city of Acestes, could prevent or induce his mother from following the fortunes of her son through all dangers. This reply of Euryalus is very pathetic. It speaks a dutiful and affectionate son.

286. *Excedentem:* from going with me—from accompanying me in all our dangers.

288. *Inque salutatam:* this is for *insalutatamque,* by tmesis: not bidden farewell. *Nox et tua dextera,* &c. This picture of filial piety is admirably drawn.

290. *Relictæ:* bereaved—disconsolate.

292. *Dederunt:* in the sense of *effuderunt. Percussâ.* This is the reading of Heyne. Some copies have *perculsa,* from the verb *percello.* The sense is the same with either.

294. *Imago patriæ pietatis,* &c. The Trojans were moved at this image, or pattern of piety toward a parent; but in an especial manner it touched the heart of young Ascanius; who consoles the anxious youth, assuring him that his mother should not want a friend while he had life—that he would immediately take her for his mother, and load her with honors.

299. *Manet:* awaits--is due. *Partum*

Parva manet. Casus factum quicunque sequetur
Per caput hoc juro, per quod pater antè solebat
Quæ tibi polliceor reduci, rebusque secundis,
Hæc eadem matrique tuæ generique manebunt.
Sic ait illachrymans: humero simul exuit ensem
Auratum, mirâ quem fecerat arte Lycaon
Gnossius, atque habilem vaginâ aptârat eburnâ.
Dat Niso Mnestheus pellem horrentisque leonis
Exuvias: galeam fidus permutat Alethes.

308. Quos euntes omnis manus primorum, juvenumque senumque prosequitur

Protinùs armati incedunt; quos omnis euntes
Primorum manus ad portas juvenumque senumque
Prosequitur votis: necnon et pulcher Iülus,
Ante annos animumque gerens curamque virilem,
Multa patri portanda dabat mandata: sed auræ
Omnia discerpunt, et nubibus irrita donant.
Egressi superant fossas, noctisque per umbram
Castra inimica petunt; multis tamen antè futuri
Exitio. Passim vino somnoque per herbam
Corpora fusa vident; arrectos litore currus;
Inter lora rotasque viros, simul arma, jacere,
Vina simul. Prior Hyrtacides sic ore locutus:
Euryale, audendum dextrâ; nunc ipsa vocat res.

320. *Aliquid* audendum *est* dextrâ

Hâc iter est: tu, ne qua manus se attollere nobis
A tergo possit, custodi, et consule longè.
Hæc ego vasta dabo, et lato te limite ducam.

323. Ego dabo hæc *loca* vasta, et

Sic memorat, vocemque premit: simul ense superbum
Rhamnetem aggreditur; qui, fortè tapetibus altis
Extructus, toto proflabat pectore somnum;
Rex idem, et regi Turno gratissimus augur;
Sed non augurio potuit depellere pestem.

329. Juxta *eum* premit tres famulos jacentes

Tres juxtà famulos temerè inter tela jacentes,
Armigerumque Remi premit, aurigamque sub ipsis
Nactus equis; ferroque secat pendentia colla.

NOTES.

the bringing forth such a son—bearing such a son. Ruæus says: *nec levis favor debetur ipsi, quòd peperit talem filium.*

300. *Juro per hoc caput*, &c. The head was considered by the ancients as something sacred, and they were wont to swear by it. Ascanius, therefore, swears by his head: which Æneas had done on several occasions before.

301. *Rebusque secundis:* and the enterprise being successful; namely, his journey to Æneas.

302. *Generi:* Ruæus says, *familiæ.*

303. *Illachrymans:* weeping abundantly. Of *in*, intensivum, and *lachrymans.*

304. *Lycaon.* He was a famous artificer of *Gnossus*, a city of Crete, where arms were curiously made. *Arte:* art—skill.

305. *Aptârat habilem:* had fitted it exact with, &c.

306. *Horrentis:* rough—shaggy.

309. *Primorum:* gen. of *primores:* nobles—chief men.

311. *Ante annos:* above his years—more than could be expected considering his age.

313. *Sed auræ:* but the winds disperse them all, and give them unavailing to the clouds. This is a beautiful metaphor. By this the poet intimates they were to die before they reached Æneas, and be lost entirely. *Discerpunt:* in the sense of *dissipant.*

315. *Antè:* not before they reached the camp of the enemy, but before they were slain themselves. *Futuri:* to be for a destruction to many, before they were slain.

317. *Currus arrectos:* their chariots turned up, as when laid aside from use. Their poles or tongues were standing erect.

318. *Vina:* wine; by meton. for the vessels containing it.

322. *Tu custodi, et:* watch thou, and observe at a distance, that no hand, &c. *Hæc vasta: arva* vel *loca* is understood: those fields laid waste.

328. *Pestem:* in the sense of *mortem.*

330. *Premit:* he kills three servants, &c

Tum caput ipsi aufert domino, truncumque relinquit
Sanguine singultantem : atro tepefacta cruore
Terra torique madent. Nec non Lamyrumque Lamumque
Et juvenem Serranum ; illâ qui plurima nocte
Luserat, insignis facie, multoque jacebat
Membra Deo victus : felix, si protinùs illum
Æquâsset nocti ludum, in lucemque tulisset.
Impastus ceu plena leo per ovilia turbans,
Suadet enim vesana fames, manditque trahitque
Molle pecus, mutumque metu : fremit ore cruento.
Nec minor Euryali cædes : incensus et ipse
Perfurit ; ac multam in medio sinè nomine plebem,
Fadumque Hebesumque subit, Rhœtumque Abarimque
Ignaros ; Rhœtum vigilantem, et cuncta videntem ;
Sed magnum metuens se post cratera tegebat :
Pectore in adverso totum cui cominùs ensem
Condidit assurgenti ; et multâ morte recepit
Purpureum : vomit ille animam, et cum sanguine mixta
Vina refert moriens. Hic furto fervidus instat.
Jamque ad Messapi socios tendebat, ubi ignem
Deficere extremum, et religatos ritè videbat
Carpere gramen equos : breviter cùm talia Nisus,
(Sensit enim nimiâ cæde atque cupidine ferri)
Absistamus, ait : nam lux inimica propinquat.
Pœnarum exhaustum satìs est : via facta per hostes.
Multa virûm solido argento perfecta relinquunt

334. Nec non *occidit* Lamyrumque

336. Jacebatque victus *quoad* membra

343. Ac subit multam plebem sinè nomine in medio, Fadumque

345. Ignaros *periculi*

347. Cui assurgenti condidit totum ensem cominùs

353. Enim sensit *se et socium* ferri nimiâ cæde atque cupidine

NOTES.

Temerè : carelessly—at random. *Promiscuè*, says Ruæus.

332. *Domino :* their master Remus.

333. *Singultantem*, &c. Dr. Trapp renders this, *weltering in blood ;* but this is not the meaning of *singulto*, which denotes the sound that a liquid makes when poured out of a bottle, or some vessel of a narrow neck.

335. *Plurima :* neu. plu. taken as an adv. in imitation of the Greeks : very much.

337. *Deo multo :* by much wine. See Æn. i. 636. By *Deo*, we are to understand Bacchus, the god of wine, put by meton. for wine itself. *Felix si protinùs :* happy if he had, without intermission, equalled that sport with the night—if he had continued it all the night.

338. *Tulisset :* in the sense of *produxisset.*

339. *Per ovilia turbans :* Dr. Trapp thinks with Servius, that this is for *pertùrbans*, by tmesis. *Ceu :* as a hungry lion raging among a full fold of sheep, &c. Ruæus says, *tumultuans in plenis ovilibus.*

340. *Vesana :* in the sense of *immoderata* vel *vehemens. Trahit :* in the sense of *lacerat. Suadet :* in the sense of *impellit.*

344. *Subit :* he comes to—he assaults—attacks. Ruæus says, *aggreditur. Multam plebem :* a promiscuous throng—a great number.

348. *Recepit purpureum :* he drew back the sword red, or bathed in blood, having effected a mortal wound. Heyne says, *retraxit ensem purpureum cum multo sanguine.* This also is the sense of Ruæus : he says, *retraxit eum (ensem) post certam mortem.*

Dr. Trapp renders *recipit :* he receives him (Rhœtus) with certain death. Rhœtus was rising up toward Euryalus, and as it were meeting him half-way. He buried the sword in his breast, and received him with certain death, meaning the full and fair stroke which he had at his breast. This he insists upon as the true interpretation. Davidson renders the words : "he receives him with copious death." Heyne reads *purpureum* connected with *ensem.* The common reading is *purpuream*, agreeing with *animam :* but of that it is not easy to make sense. Valpy, Ruæus, and Davidson, read *purpuream.*

350. *Furto :* in the sense of *cædi* vel *stragi :* any thing done in a private or secret manner, may be called *furtum.*

352. *Religatos :* in the sense of *solutos.*

354. *Nimiâ cæde atque cupidine :* the same as *nimia cupidine cædis :* with too great a desire of slaughter.

356. *Satìs pœnarum :* enough of vengeance or punishment has been taken. *Exhaustum :* in the sense of *sumptum.*

357. *Perfecta :* in the sense of *ornata* vel *facta.*

Armaque, craterasque simul, pulchrosque tapetas.
Euryalus phaleras Rhamnetis, et aurea bullis
Cingula : Tiburti Remulo ditissimus olim
Quæ mittit dona, hospitio cùm jungeret absens,
Cædicus : ille suo moriens dat habere nepoti :
Post mortem bello Rutuli pugnâque potiti :
Hæc rapit, atque humeris nequicquam fortibus aptat.
Tum galeam Messapi habilem cristisque decoram
Induit. Excedunt castris, et tuta capessunt.
Intereà præmissi equites ex urbe Latinâ,
Cætera dum legio campis instructa moratur,
Ibant, et Turno regi responsa ferebant,
Tercentum, scutati omnes, Volscente magistro.
Jamque propinquabant castris, muroque subibant;
Cùm procul hos lævo flectentes limite cernunt :
Et galea Euryalum sublustri noctis in umbrâ
Prodidit immemorem, radiisque adversa refulsit.
Haud temerè est visum : conclamat ab agmine Volscens,
State, viri : quæ causa viæ ? quive estis in armis ?
Quòve tenetis iter ? Nihil illi tendere contrà ;
Sed celerare fugam in sylvas, et fidere nocti.
Objiciunt equites sese ad divortia nota
Hinc atque hinc, omnemque aditum custode coronant.
Sylva fuit, latè dumis atque ilice nigrâ
Horrida, quam densi complêrant undique sentes :
Rara per occultos ducebat semita calles.

359. Euryalus *rapit* phaleras

361. Quæ dona ditissimus Cædicus mittit olim Tiburti Remulo, cùm absens jungeret *se* illi

367. Intereà tercentum equites omnes scutati, Volscente magistro, ibant, et ferebant responsa regi Turno, præmissi ex Latinâ urbe, dum

372. Hos *duos juvenes*

374. Adversa radiis *Lunæ* refulsit

377. Illi *voluerunt* tendere nihil contrà ; sed *cœperunt*

383. Rara semita ducebat *ad eam sylvam*

NOTES.

359. *Phaleras.* These were certain ornaments worn by persons of distinction among the Romans. Dr. Trapp and some others, explain this of the ornaments of Rhamnes' horse. But they, doubtless, belonged to his own person: for Euryalus put them on. *Bullis:* the *bullæ* were studs or bosses upon girdles, something like the head of a nail, and usually of gold. *Cingula aurea bullis:* a girdle or belt with golden bosses.

363. *Post mortem:* after the death of Remulus, &c. This is one of the thirteen passages of Virgil, which Servius considers inexplicable. The common editions have *pugnâque;* but the Roman manuscript has *prædaque.* The meaning appears to be this: that in a war between the Tiburtines and the Rutulians, in which the grandson of Remulus, who commanded the former, was slain, the Rutulians took from him those spoils, with the rest of the booty. Davidson reads *præda.* Heyne and Ruæus read *pugna. Potiti:* gained the battle—the victory; and consequently the booty fell into their hands. The verb *sunt* is understood.

364. *Aptat nequicquam:* he fits them to his shoulders in vain—in vain, because he was so soon to be slain, and lose them.

366. *Capessunt:* in the sense of *petunt. Loca* is understood with *tuta.*

368. *Cætera legio.* These were the foot. A Roman legion consisted of four thousand foot, and three hundred horse. These troops were furnished by Latinus, or rather Amata, his queen. The horse, as being light troops and more expeditious in their movements, advanced, and arrived in the camp, while the infantry were on the plain advancing more slowly.

372. *Lævo limite:* the left-hand way, or path. See 238. supra.

373. *Galea:* this was the helmet of Messapus, which he had put on. *Immemorem:* heedless—unmindful of the danger he incurred by so doing.

374. *Adversa:* opposite to. That part of the helmet struck by the rays of light, reflected them to a distant object—it shone.

375. *Haud temerè visum est.* Ruæus takes these words in the sense of *non falsò visum est nobis*, referring them to Volscens. Heyne says, *res animadversa est haud in vanum—res non neglecta est.* He makes a full stop after *visum.* Davidson renders the words; "Scarcely was the object seen, when Volscens," &c. "This passed not unobserved," says Valpy.

377. *Tendere:* in the sense of *respondere.*

379. *Divortia:* passes—passages.

380. *Coronant:* in the sense of *circumdant*, vel *obsident.* Heyne reads *abitum.* The common reading is *aditum.*

383. *Rara:* few—dispersed here and there *Occultos calles:* secret or private ways.

Euryalum tenebræ ramorum onerosaque præda
Impediunt, fallitque timor regione viarum.
Nisus abit: jamque imprudens evaserat hostes,
Atque lacus, qui pòst Albæ de nomine dicti
Albani: tum rex stabula alta Latinus habebat.
Ut stetit, et frustra absentem respexit amicum:
Euryale infelix, quâ te regione reliqui?
Quàve sequar? Rursùs perplexum iter omne revolvens
Fallacis sylvæ, simul et vestigia retrò
Observata legit, dumisque silentibus errat:
Audit equos, audit strepitus, et signa sequentûm.
Nec longum in medio tempus, cùm clamor ad aures
Pervenit, ac videt Euryalum; quem jam manus omnis,
Fraude loci et noctis, subito turbante tumultu,
Oppressum rapit, et conantem plurima frustrà.
Quid faciat? quâ vi juvenem, quibus audeat armis
Eripere? an sese medios moriturus in hostes
Inferat, et pulchram properet per vulnera mortem?
Ocyùs adducto torquens hastile lacerto,
Suspiciens altam Lunam, sic voce precatur:
Tu, Dea, tu præsens nostro succurre labori,
Astrorum decus, et nemorum Latonia custos:
Si qua tuis unquam pro me pater Hyrtacus aris
Dona tulit; si qua ipse meis venatibus auxi,
Suspendi-ve tholo, aut sacra ad fastigia fixi:
Hunc sine me turbare globum, et rege tela per auras.
Dixerat: et toto connixus corpore ferrum
Conjicit. Hasta volans noctis diverberat umbras,
Et venit adversi in tergum Sulmonis; ibique

385. Fallit *eum à recta* regione

388. Alta stabula *illic*.

395. Nec longum tempus *intervenit* in medio

404. Tu, *O* Latonia Dea, tu præsens succurre nostro labori, *tu* decus

408. Suspendi-ve *aliqua dona* tholo

NOTES.

384. *Onerosa:* in the sense of *gravis.*

386. *Imprudens:* regardless of his friend -not aware of his being behind.

387. *Lacus.* This is the reading of Heyne and Davidson. But Ruæus reads *locos*, and thinks it to be the true reading. For, says he, the lake Albanus was at least four leagues distant. Beside, it was about the middle of the night, when Nisus and his friend left the Trojan camp. He could not have had time to do so much, to go that distance, and return in search of his friend: and all this in the space of half a summer's night. For this reason, he prefers *locos*, and explains it of the Alban territory, which might extend as far as the place where he then was.

391. *Revolvens:* in the sense of *remetiens.*

393. *Legit vestigia:* he follows, or traces his steps, &c.

397. *Fraude loci et noctis:* through the treachery of the place, and of the night. The poet represents the place and night as two traitors, to whom Euryalus had committed his safety, and they betrayed him. *Subito tumultu turbante:* in a sudden tumultuous bustle—there being a sudden, &c.

398. *Oppressum:* in the sense of *interceptum*, vel *traditum.*

400. *Eripere:* rescue—free.

403. *Altam Lunam.* Diana on the earth, is Luna in heaven, and Hecate in hell. She is called *Latonia* from *Latona*, the name of her mother.

404. *Succurre:* in the sense of *fave.*

407. *Si qua: dona* is to be supplied. *Auxi:* have increased—added any offering to those made by my father.

408. *Tholo: tholus* was the middle, and highest part of the arched roof of the temple, from which the spoils of war used to be suspended.

409. *Hunc globum:* this company of men.

412. *Adversi. Adversus* signifies right against, or opposite, without regarding whether the face or back be turned to the object. This passage, Servius reckons among his thirteen *inexplicables.* The meaning is plainly this: the spear entered his back and reached to his breast, which it might very well do, though it were broken (*frangitur*) from the wood. *Adversi.* This is the common reading. Heyne reads *aversi.* Ruæus says, *oppositi.*

Frangitur, ac fisso transit præcordia ligno.
Volvitur ille, vomens calidum de pectore flumen,
Frigidus, et longis singultibus ilia pulsat.

416. Ecce idem acrior hoc *successu*

Diversi circumspiciunt. Hoc acrior idem
Ecce aliud summâ telum librabat ab aure;
Dum trepidant. Iit hasta Tago per tempus utrumque
Stridens, trajectoque hæsit tepefacta cerebro.
Sævit atrox Volscens, nec teli conspicit usquam
Auctorem; nec quò se ardens immittere possit.
Tu tamen intereà calido mihi sanguine pœnas
Persolves amborum, inquit. Simul ense recluso
Ibat in Euryalum. Tunc verò exterritus, amens
Conclamat Nisus; nec se celare tenebris
Ampliùs, aut tantum potuit perferre dolorem:

427. Me, me *occidite:* adsum qui feci *id:* O Rutuli, convertite ferrum in me: omnis fraus *est* mea. Iste *fecit* nihil, nec ausus *est;* nec potuit *facere.*

Me, me; adsum, qui feci; in me convertite ferrum,
O Rutuli! mea fraus omnis. Nihil iste, nec ausus;
Nec potuit; cœlum hoc, et conscia sidera testor:
Tantùm infelicem nimiùm dilexit amicum.
Talia dicta dabat: sed viribus ensis adactus
Transabiit costas, et candida pectora rumpit.
Volvitur Euryalus leto, pulchrosque per artus
It cruor, inque humeros cervix collapsa recumbit.
Purpureus veluti cùm flos, succisus aratro,
Languescit moriens; lassove papavera collo
Demisêre caput, pluviâ cùm fortè gravantur
At Nisus ruit in medios, solumque per omnes
Volscentem petit: in solo Volscente moratur;
Quem circùm glomerati hostes hinc cominùs atque hinc
Proturbant. Instat non segniùs, ac rotat ensem
Fulmineum, donec Rutuli clamantis in ore
Condidit adverso, et moriens animam abstulit hosti.
Tum super exanimem sese projecit amicum
Confossus, placidâque ibi demùm morte quievit.

NOTES.

413. *Fisso ligno. Fissus* here must be taken in the sense of *fractus;* unless we suppose the wood might be broken, and split and shattered withal; and this split and shattered part to pass through his *præcordia.* This appears to be the opinion of Dr. Trapp.

414. *Volvitur:* in the sense of *cadit. Flumen:* for *sanguinem.*

416. *Diversi:* they look about them in different directions. *Idem:* namely, Nisus.

418. *Tago:* to Tagus. The dat. is frequently used in the sense of the gen., especially among the poets. The spear pierced both his temples.

419. *Tepefacta:* warmed by its rapid motion through the air.

421. *Auctorem:* the owner of the weapon—the one who threw it.

424. *Ibat:* in the sense of *irruebat.*

427. *Me, me,* &c. This abrupt exclamation admirably marks the perturbation and disorder of his mind He calls them Rutulians, although they were Latins. The former were the principals in the war.

431. *Dabat:* in the sense of *dixit. Ensis:* the sword of Volscens.

432. *Rumpit:* pierces—lays open.

435. *It:* in the sense of *fluit.*

437. *Languescit:* withers. This is a most beautiful comparison.

439. *Moratur.* Ruæus says, *defigit oculos in,* &c. "Persists in his attack upon Volscens," says Valpy.

440. *Circum quem,* &c. The enemy gathered around Nisus to keep him off, and prevent him from doing any mischief to them, wishing to take him a prisoner, rather than kill him.

441. *Segniùs.* Heyne reads *seciùs.* The common reading is *segniùs.*

442. *Fulmineum.* This is very expressive. It denotes the rapid motion of the sword, and the force with which it was driven, as well as its glittering. *Rotat:* brandishes

Fortunati ambo! si quid mea carmina possunt,
Nulla dies unquam memori vos eximet ævo:
Dum domus Æneæ Capitolî immobile saxum
Accolet, imperiumque pater Romanus habebit.
Victores prædâ Rutuli spoliisque potiti,
Volscentem exanimem flentes in castra ferebant.
Nec minor in castris luctus, Rhamnete reperto
Exsangui, et primis unâ tot cæde peremptis,
Serranoque, Numâque. Ingens concursus ad ipsa
Corpora, seminecesque viros, tepidâque recentem
Cæde locum, et plenos spumanti sanguine rivos.
Agnoscunt spolia inter se, galeamque nitentem
Messapi, et multo phaleras sudore receptas.
Et jam prima novo spargebat lumine terras
Tithoni croceum linquens Aurora cubile:
Jam Sole infuso, jam rebus luce retectis,
Turnus in arma viros, armis circumdatus ipse,
Suscitat; æratasque acies in prælia cogit
Quisque suas, variisque acuunt rumoribus iras.
Quin ipsa arrectis, visu miserabile! in hastis
Præfigunt capita, et multo clamore sequuntur,
Euryali et Nisi.

452. Nec *fuit* minor luctus in castris *Rutulorum*

459. Et jam prima Aurora, linquens croceum cubile

464. Quisque *dux* cogit suas

465. Quin præfigunt ipsa capita Euryali et Nisi in arrectis hastis

NOTES.

447. *Nulla dies:* no length of time shall ever erase you from mindful posterity. This is the meaning of *memori ævo.*

448. *Immobile saxum.* This implies that the foundation of the Roman empire was to be as fixed and lasting as the Capitoline mount, on which the city was built. After the time of Tarquinius Priscus, the Romans were of opinion that their empire would become universal, and have no end. Some explain *domus Æneæ*, of the family of Augustus; which Virgil deduces from Æneas. But it may with propriety be taken for the Romans in general. Heyne says, *Julia gens:* the Julian family.

449. *Pater Romanus.* Ruæus thinks Romulus is meant, he being the founder of Rome. Davidson thinks *Pater* here means prince, as kings are often called the fathers of their people. *Pater Romanus*, then will mean a Roman prince, or sovereign. Heyne understands, by *Pater Romanus*, Jupiter Capitolinus; to whom a famous temple was built upon the Capitoline mount. This story of Nisus and Euryalus makes a very considerable part of this book, and a very interesting part too. It is nevertheless liable to objection on the ground of probability. It is difficult to conceive that a whole army should be asleep, and their sentinels among the rest, when it was their business to see that the Trojans were kept close. It is said one was awake indeed; but he gave no alarm. Besides, we might suppose that they would have considered themselves sufficiently fortunate, to be able to pass the camp of the enemy in safety, without attempting any thing. But poetry delights in the wonderful and marvellous.

453. *Primis:* chief men—nobles.

455. *Tepida cæde.* Davidson reads *tepidum*, agreeing with *locum.* Heyne reads *tepida.* So also Ruæus, and others. The Roman manuscript has *tepidum.* The sense is the same with either. Ruæus interprets the words: *ad locum tepefactum recenti strage.*

456. *Rivos plenos*, &c. Dr. Trapp thinks, that no more is meant than streams of blood upon the ground: *rivos spumantis sanguinis.* It is difficult to imagine that two men, in so short a space, could spill so much blood as to justify the hyperbole, that the rivers were filled and foamed with blood. Beside, there was only one river, and that one not very near. Heyne is of the same opinion with Dr. Trapp.

458. *Sudore:* in the sense of *labore. Phaleras.* These were taken from *Rhamnes* See 359, supra.

461. *Sole jam infuso:* the sun now being ushered into the world—the sun having already arisen. *Rebus:* objects—things. *Retectis:* brought to view—uncovered. The world and all things therein had been wrapt up in the mantle of night. They are now disclosed and brought to view, by the rays of light.

463. *Acies:* troops in general. *Æratas:* armed with brass—clad in brazen armor.

464. *Rumoribus:* Heyne takes this in the sense of *hortationibus* vel *vocibus. Iras* in the sense of *furorem.*

471. Præfixa *hastis*, nimis nota miseris *sociis*

478. Scissa *quoad* comam, amens

480. Illa non *erat* memor virûm, illa non *erat memor* perîcli

481. Tu-ne *es* ille *futurus* sera

483. Nec copia data *est* miseræ matri affari te

486. Nec *ego* mater produxi te *ad* tua funera

488. Tegens *tuum cadaver* veste, quam *ego* festina

Æneadæ duri murorum in parte sinistrâ
Opposuêre aciem; nam dextera cingitur amni;
Ingentesque tenent fossas, et turribus altis
Stant mœsti; simul ora virûm præfixa videbant,
Nota nimìs miseris, atroque fluentia tabo.
  Intereà pavidam volitans pennata per urbem
Nuntia Fama ruit, matrisque allabitur aures
Euryali: at subitus miseræ calor ossa reliquit
Excussi manibus radii, revolutaque pensa.
Evolat infelix; et, fœmineo ululatu,
Scissa comam, muros amens atque agmina cursu
Prima petit: non illa virûm, non illa perîcli,
Telorumque memor: cœlum dehinc questibus implet:
Hunc ego te, Euryale, aspicio? tu-ne illa senectæ
Sera meæ requies? potuisti linquere solam,
Crudelis? nec te, sub tanta pericula missum,
Affari extremùm miseræ data copia matri?
Heu! terrâ ignotâ, canibus data præda Latinis
Alitibusque, jaces! nec te tua funera mater
Produxi, pressive oculos, aut vulnera lavi,
Veste tegens; tibi quam noctes festina diesque
Urgebam, et telâ curas solabar aniles.
Quò sequar? aut quæ nunc artus avulsaque membra,
Et funus lacerum tellus habet? hoc mihi de te,

NOTES.

469. *Aciem:* the army of Turnus. *Cingitur:* protected—defended.

474. *Nuntia:* as a messenger—herald.

475. *Subitus:* in the sense of *subitò*. *At:* this is the reading of Heyne.

476. *Radii excussi:* the shuttle fell from her hands, as she was weaving. Or, by the *radii*, we may understand a machine with spokes something like a wheel, which the women held in their hands, and on which they wound or reeled the yarn from the spindles, on which it was put, as it was spun.

What is properly called the episode of Nisus and Euryalus, ended with the 449th verse. The lamentation of the mother of Euryalus most agreeably brings us back to the subject again, when we imagined we had done with it. Whether it be considered a part of, or a sequel to, that episode, is not material. It certainly equals, if not exceeds, any part of it; and we are much indebted to the poet for the picture, which he has given us of maternal grief and sorrow. Scaliger was enraptured with it. *Pensa:* her work—labor.

481. *Aspicio hunc te:* do I see that you? —Is that one I see you, O, Euryalus? These broken half sentences she uttered, while she beheld his head suspended upon the spears of the Rutulians, as she stood upon the ramparts.

482. *Sera requies:* in the sense of *serum solatium*.

484. *Copia:* leave—opportunity. *Extremùm.* This alludes to the custom of the Romans, when they retired from the tomb, of repeating the word *vale* three times.

487. *Produxi te tua*, &c. Servius takes *tua funera*, for the nom. agreeing with *mater*, and tells us that the near relations of the dead assisted at burial, and were called *Funeræ*. But it is better to adhere to the usual acceptation of the word. And this we may do, if we supply the prep. *ad* before it. *Produxi* may signify the laying out of the corpse for burial, or walking before it to the place of interment. This is considered an intricate passage: and various have been the conjectures upon the proper construction. Heyne proposes *funere*, for *funera:* and Ruæus informs us that *proluxi* has been proposed for *produxi*. He seems to take *funera*, with Servius and Scaliger in the nom. He says, *nec ego mater protuli te ante ædes, ut curatrix tui funeris*. The construction proposed above appears the easiest. Davidson renders the words, "Nor I, thy mother, laid thee out for thy funeral obsequies." Valpy observes, that though no variation from this reading has been discovered in any of the ancient MSS., there is probably some error.

489. *Solabar:* I was consoling my aged cares with the loom—with weaving and preparing garments for you.

490. *Sequar:* in the sense of *ibo*.

491. *Funus:* in the sense of *cadaver*. *Quæ tellus nunc*, &c.

Nate, refers? hoc sum terrâque marique secuta:
Figite me, si qua est pietas; in me omnia tela
Conjicite, ô Rutuli; me primam absumite ferro:
Aut tu, magne pater Divûm, miserere, tuoque
Invisum hoc detrude caput sub Tartara telo;
Quando aliter nequeo crudelem abrumpere vitam.
Hoc fletu concussi animi, mœstusque per omnes
It gemitus: torpent infractæ ad prœlia vires.
Illam incendentem luctus Idæus et Actor,
Ilionei monitu et multùm lachrymantis Iüli,
Corripiunt, interque manus sub tecta reponunt.
At tuba terribilem sonitum procul ære canoro
Increpuit: sequitur clamor, cœlumque remugit.
Accelerant actâ pariter testudine Volsci,
Et fossas implere parant, ac vellere vallum.
Quærunt pars aditum, et scalis ascendere muros;
Quâ rara est acies, interlucetque corona
Non tam spissa viris. Telorum effundere contrà
Omne genus Teucri, ac duris detrudere contis,
Assueti longo muros defendere bello.
Saxa quoque infesto volvebant pondere, si quà
Possent tectam aciem perrumpere: cùm tamen omnes
Ferre juvat subter densâ testudine casus.
Nec jam sufficiunt: nam, quâ globus imminet ingens,
Immanem Teucri molem volvuntque ruuntque,
Quæ stravit Rutulos latè, armorumque resolvit

492. O nate, refers hoc *caput solum* mihi de te

495. Miserere *mei*, detrudeque hoc *meum* caput invisum *tibi*

498. Animi *Trojanorum* concussi *sunt*

500. Idæus et Actor, monitu Ilionei et Iüli

509. Contrà Teucri *cœperunt*

514. Cùm tamen juvat *Rutulis* ferre omnes casus

515. Nam quâ ingens globus *hostium*

NOTES.

492. *Secuta sum:* have I followed this (*caput*) over sea and land? Have I followed thee over sea and land for this—to come to this?

493. *Pietas.* Here *pietas*, doubtless, means pity, or compassion. If there be any pity in you, O Rutulians, &c.

494. *Me primam.* We are to suppose her speaking from the rampart, where none, as yet, had been slain.

497. *Aliter.* Dr. Trapp observes, that what is here said cannot be true, unless *aliter* be taken in a limited sense. Being full of grief, and referring every thing to that, he thinks she refers this, also; as if she had said: since my grief will not end my wretched life as I would have it, I desire either the enemy or the gods to do it. Mr. Davidson thinks she only talks somewhat inconsistently, as might be expected in her state of mind; and observes that it is not improbable she had attempted to lay violent hands upon herself, and was hindered by those about her.

The crime of self-murder is of so horrid a nature, that the poet might well suppose no one could be guilty of it. She wished for death, since her son, the support and solace of her declining years, was taken from her. But where can she find it? Not from her friends. She had called upon the enemy; and now she appeals to Jove, and entreats him to end her miserable existence; for otherwise she could not break the cords of life.

499. *Infractæ:* in the sense of *fractæ. Torpent:* fail.

505. *Testudine actâ:* the testudo being formed. See Æn. ii. 441.

508. *Quâ acies est rara.* The meaning is: they seek to attack the walls and fortifications, where the troops are thin; and the ranks or lines not so thick with men, but they may be seen through. *Acies:* properly an army drawn up in order of battle—here troops in general. *Corona:* a body of men standing round in the form of a circle. Here, the ranks or lines of the men upon the walls, without any distinction.

510. *Detrudere:* to push down the enemy with, &c.

511. *Longo bello.* This alludes to the Trojan war, which lasted ten years.

512. *Infesto:* in the sense of *ingenti* vel *magno.* By their great weight, they became fatal to the enemy.

513. *Tectam aciem:* the protected troops—those who were covered by the *testudo*, or target defence.

516. *Molem:* any large mass of matter may be called *moles.* Ruæus says, *saxum.*

Tegmina: nec curant cæco contendere Marte
Ampliùs audaces Rutuli; sed pellere vallo
Missilibus certant.
Parte aliâ horrendus visu quassabat Etruscam
Pinum, et fumiferos infert Mezentius ignes.
At Messapus, equûm domitor, Neptunia proles,
Rescindit vallum, et scalas in mœnia poscit.
Vos, ô Calliope, precor, aspirate canenti;
Quas ibi tum ferro strages, quæ funera Turnus
Ediderit; quem quisque virum demiserit Orco:
Et mecum ingentes oras evolvite belli:
Et meministis enim, Divæ, et memorare potestis.
Turris erat vasto suspectu, et pontibus altis,
Opportuna loco; summis quam viribus omnes
Expugnare Itali, summâque evertere opum vi
Certabant: Troës contrà defendere saxis,
Perque cavas densi tela intorquere fenestras.
Princeps ardentem conjecit lampada Turnus,
Et flammam affixit lateri; quæ plurima vento
Corripuit tabulas, et postibus hæsit adesis.
Turbati trepidare intus, frustràque malorum
Velle fugam. Dum se glomerant, retròque residunt
In partem, quæ peste caret; tum pondere turris
Procubuit subitò, et cœlum tonat omne fragore
Semineces ad terram, immani mole secutâ,
Confixique suis telis, et pectora duro
Transfossi ligno, veniunt. Vix unus Helenor,
Et Lycus elapsi; quorum primævus Helenor;
Mæonio regi quem serva Lycimnia furtim

520. Sec certant pellere *Trojanos*

525. Vos, *O Musæ, præcipuè* Calliope, precor, aspirate *mihi* canenti

533. Contrà Troës densi *certabant* defendere *eam* saxis, densique

538. *Trojani* turbati *cœperunt* trepidare

542. *Trojani* semineces veniunt ad terram, immani mole *turris* secutâ

NOTES.

518. *Cæco Marte:* concealed or covered fight—covered and protected by their shields held over their heads.

522. *Pinum:* his spear or javelin made of the pine tree—*pineam hastam. Fumiferos ignes.* By this we are to understand a fire-brand—some resinous wood which Mezentius carried in one hand on fire. The poet, on every occasion, represents Mezentias as a monster in wickedness, in shape, and in appearance. He is here *horrendus visu:* horrid to the sight. *Visu:* for *visui.* See Ecl. v. 29. *Infert:* Ruæus says, *injicit.*

525. *Calliope.* She was chief of the muses, and presided over heroic poetry: for which reason, she is particularly mentioned. *Aspirate:* in the sense of *docete.*

527. *Ediderit:* in the sense of *fecerit* vel *effecerit.*

528. *Oras belli:* limits, extent, or compass of the war. *Evolvite:* in the sense of *explicate.*

530. *Pontibus altis.* The planks on which they ascended from one story to another of these towers, were called *pontes*, stages. *Vasto suspectu:* of vast height, or altitude. The prep. *e* or *ex* being understood.

531. *Loco:* in the sense of *situ.*

532. *Sūmma vi opum:* with the utmost force in their power.

534. *Fenestras:* the holes or apertures made in the tower through which to annoy the assailants.

535. *Lampada. Lampas* was a kind of flaming brand, made up of hemp, pitch, rosin, and such like materials: which being stuck around with sharp points, and hooks of iron, was flung against wooden walls, &c., where it stuck fast till it seized the boards with its flame. *Lampada:* a Greek acc.

536. *Quæ plurima vento:* which being widely spread by the wind—becoming very large, &c.

537. *Adesis postibus:* to the consumed timbers—till the timbers were consumed.

539. *Fugam malorum:* a flight—escape from the danger. *Malum:* in the sense of *periculum. Residunt:* in the sense of *recedunt.*

540. *Peste:* the devouring flame.

545. *Primævus:* born first—the elder of the two.

546. *Mæonio regi.* Mæonia was a country of Asia Minor, sometimes confounded with Lydia. Homer reckons its people

Sustulerat, vetitisque ad Trojam miserat armis;
Ense levis nudo, parmâque inglorius albâ.
Isque ubi se Turni media inter millia vidit;
Hinc acies, atque hinc acies adstare Latinas:
Ut fera, quæ densâ venantûm septa coronâ
Contra tela furit, seseque haud nescia morti
Injicit, et saltu supra venabula fertur;
Haud aliter juvenis medios moriturus in hostes
Irruit; et, quà tela videt densissima, tendit.
At pedibus longè melior Lycus, inter et hostes,
Inter et arma, fugâ muros tenet; altaque certat
Prendere tecta manu, sociûmque attingere dextras.
Quem Turnus, pariter cursu teloque secutus,
Increpat his victor: Nostrasne evadere, demens,
Sperâsti te posse manus? Simul arripit ipsum
Pendentem, et magnâ muri cum parte revellit.
Qualis ubi, aut leporem, aut candenti corpore cycnum
Sustulit alta petens pedibus Jovis armiger uncis:
Quæsitum aut matri multis balatibus agnum
Martius à stabulis rapuit lupus. Undique clamor
Tollitur. Invadunt, et fossas aggere complent:
Ardentes tædas alii ad fastigia jactant.
Ilioneus saxo, atque ingenti fragmine montis,
Lucetium, portæ subeuntem ignesque ferentem:
Emathiona Liger, Chorinæum sternit Asylas:
Hic jaculo bonus, hic longè fallente sagittâ:
Ortygium Cæneus, victorem Cænea Turnus:
Turnus Ityn, Cloniumque, Dioxippum, Promulumque,
Et Sagarim, et summis stantem pro turribus Idam:
Privernum Capys. Hunc primò levis hasta Themillæ
Strinxerat: ille manum, projecto tegmine, demens

548. *Ille erat* levis nudo ense

560. Increpat *eum* his *verbis*

561. O demens *juvenis*, sperâsti-ne te posse evadere

563. *Talis*, qualis ubi *Aquila* armiger Jovis, petens alta *cœla* sustulit uncis pedibus aut

565. Aut *talis qualis* Martius lupus, *ubi* rapuit

568. Ad fastigia *murorum*. Ilioneus *sternit* Lucetium

572. Hic *erat bonus* sagittâ fallante longè Cæneus *occidit*

576. Capys *occidit* Privernum.

NOTES.

among the auxiliaries of Priam. Helenor was an illegitimate son of the king of Mæonia, by his slave Licymnia.

547. *Vetitis armis:* in forbidden arms. Either against the will of the gods; or in allusion to a law or custom of the Romans, which forbid slaves to bear arms, unless they had been set free, except in cases of the greatest danger. In the time of Hannibal, all hands were employed in the common defence. *Sustulerat:* in the sense of *pepererat.*

548. *Levis nudo ense.* The poet here describes Helenor such, as those troops among the Romans called *Velites*, from *velocitas.* They had a small round shield or buckler, a sword, and some light missive weapons. *Alba parma.* There was no heroic device upon it. He had done nothing to distinguish him, and deserve praise. His shield was a mere blank.

551. *Corona:* a troop—company. *Septa:* surrounded—encircled.

553. *Supra venabula:* upon the hunting spears.

556. *Melior* in the sense of *celerior*

557. *Tenet:* reaches—arrives at the walls

558. *Tecta alta:* the high summits, or tops of the walls. Ruæus interprets it by *altas pinnas.*

559. *Pariter cursu:* he followed him with equal pace, and, with his dart, kept close to his heels. Or, he kept pace with the *dar* which he flung at him. This last gives us a fine idea of the quickness of his speed. It equalled the motion of his dart. Valpy takes it in this sense.

565. *Balatibus:* bleatings—much bleating.

566. *Martius.* The wolf was sacred to Mars: hence the epithet *Martius.*

567. *Aggere:* simply, with earth.

572. *Hic bonus jaculo:* the one skilful in throwing the javelin; the other, &c. *Sagittâ fallante longè.* This is a beautiful epithet of an arrow; which steals upon its object unawares, and surprises him with unseen death.

575. *Pro:* before—in front. Or, perhaps, we are to understand that he stood on the front of the towers next the enemy.

577. *Strinxerat:* in the sense of *vulnera-*

Ad vulnus tulit; ergò alis allapsa sagitta,
Et lævo infixa est lateri manus, abditaque intus
Spiramenta animæ letali vulnere rupit.
Stabat in egregiis Arcentis filius armis,
Pictus acu chlamydem, et ferrugine clarus Iberâ,
Insignis facie; genitor quem miserat Arcens,
Eductum Martis luco, Symæthia circum
Flumina, pinguis ubi et placabilis ara Palici.
Stridentem fundam, positis Mezentius armis,
Ipse ter adductâ circum caput egit habenâ:
Et media adversi liquefacto tempora plumbo
Diffidit, ac multâ porrectum extendit arenâ.
Tum primùm bello celerem intendisse sagittam
Dicitur, antè feras solitus terrere fugaces,
Ascanius, fortemque manu fudisse Numanum,
Cui Remulo cognomen erat; Turnique minorem
Germanam, nuper thalamo sociatus, habebat.
Is primam ante aciem digna atque indigna relatu
Vociferans, tumidusque novo præcordia regno
Ibat, et ingenti sese clamore ferebat:
Non pudet obsidione iterum valloque teneri,
Bis capti Phryges, et morti prætendere muros?

586. Mezentius ipse, armis positis, egit stridentem fundam

588. Et diffidit media tempora *juvenis* adversi

590. Tum primùm Ascanius dicitur

594. *Qui*que habebat minorem

596. Tumidusque *quoad* præcordia

598. *Ait*, non pudet *vos*, O Phryges, bis capti, teneri

NOTES.

rerat. Tegmine: his shield. Being wounded, he put his hand to the wound to stop the blood, and threw away his shield for that purpose. Hence he is called *demens.*

578. *Sagitta allapsa alis:* the arrow glided swiftly on its wings, &c. The arrow passed through his hand as he held it upon his wound, fixed it to his side, and then passed into his body, piercing his vitals. *Spiramenta animæ:* the lungs. This was not the arrow that first wounded him.

582. *Pictus:* embroidered as to his cloak with needle work—having an embroidered cloak. *Ibera ferrugine:* in Iberian purple. *Ferrugo* is the color of polished iron, which approaches nearly to purple. *Ibera:* an adj. from *Iberia.* Some take this for a country lying between the Euxine and Caspian seas, formerly called Iberia, now *Georgia.* A colony of these people removed to Spain, and settled near the river Iberus, to which they gave name. Others take it for Spain itself, sometimes called *Iberia.* It abounded in the best iron and steel. *Facie:* in the sense of *formâ.* *Clarus:* in the sense of *splendens.*

585. *Palici.* These were the sons of Jove and the nymph Thalia, the daughter of Vulcan. They were gods worshipped in Sicily, near the river Symethia. It is not easy to assign the reason of their altar being called *placabilis.* Some conjecture they were appeased only by human victims at first; but afterward by common victims. Perhaps their altar may be so called, because it was the altar of atonement, as distinguished from others that were altars of thanksgiving and divination. Diodorus Siculus relates that slaves, who were illy treated by their masters, fled here for safety. And their masters were not allowed to take them away until they had given security for their good treatment of them. Hence Ruæus thinks it was called *ara placabilis.* This is the most probable reason.

587. *Habenâ ter:* the string being whirled three times around his head to give the greater force to the ball.

588. *Liquefacto plumbo:* with the melted lead. This is a poetical exaggeration, to express the velocity of the ball through the air. The expression is borrowed from Lucretius. Or the poet may allude to the casting of the ball at first. Ruæus says, *calefacto plumbo.*

590. *Intendisse:* to have shot—directed.

592. *Fudisse:* in the sense of *stravisse.*

593. *Cui Remulo:* in the sense of *cui Remulus erat cognomini:* to whom Remulus was for a surname. This construction is in imitation of the Greeks.

594. *Sociatus nuper:* being lately connected with her in marriage.

595. *Relatu:* a sup. in *u*, in the sense of *dictu.*

596. *Novo regno:* with his new power, which he acquired by being connected with the royal family.

597. *Ferebat sese:* marched along—took himself along.

598. *Teneri:* in the sense of *claudi.*

599. *Prætendere:* to oppose your walls to

En qui nostra sibi bello connubia poscunt!
Quis Deus Italiam, quæ vos dementia adegit?
Non hìc Atridæ; nec fandi fictor Ulysses.
Durum à stirpe genus. Natos ad flumina primùm
Deferimus, sævoque gelu duramus et undis
Venatu invigilant pueri, sylvasque fatigant;
Flectere ludus equos, et spicula tendere cornu.
At patiens operum, parvoque assueta juventus,
Aut rastris terram domat, aut quatit oppida bello.
Omne ævum ferro teritur, versâque juvencûm
Terga fatigamus hastâ. Nec tarda senectus
Debilitat vires animi, mutatque vigorem.
Canitiem galeâ premimus; semperque recentes
Convectare juvat prædas, et vivere rapto.
Vobis picta croco et fulgenti murice vestis;
Desidiæ cordi; juvat indulgere choreis;
Et tunicæ manicas, et habent redimicula mitræ.
O verè Phrygiæ, neque enim Phryges! ite per alta
Dindyma, ubi assuetis biforem dat tibia cantum.
Tympana vos buxusque vocant Berecynthia matris
Idææ. Sinite arma viris, et cedite ferro.
 Talia jactantem dictis, ac dira canentem
Non tulit Ascanius: nervoque obversus equino

600. En *homines*, qui poscunt

606. *Eorum* ludus *est*

613. Juvat *nos*

614. *Est* vobis vestis picta

615. Desidiæ *sunt vobis* cordi:

618. *Vobis* assuetis *huic sono.*

621. Ascanius non tulit *Numanum* jactantem, ac

NOTES.

death—to screen yourselves behind your wall, and save yourselves from death. Heyne reads *Marte.* The common reading is *morti.*

600. *Nostra connubia:* our brides. This is said in allusion to the case of Lavinia.

602. *Fictor fandi:* the dissembler of speech. *Fandi:* in the sense of *verborum.*

603. *Durum genus:* but we are a hardy race from our origin.

605. *Venatu:* for *venatui.* See Ecl. v. 29. *Invigilant:* are fond of—have a special regard to. *Fatigant sylvas:* weary the woods —the beasts or game in the woods, by meton.

606. *Cornu:* from the bow. *Spicula:* in the sense of *sagittas.*

608. *Domat:* in the sense of *exercet. Quatit:* in the sense of *impugnat.*

609. *Ferro:* with the sword; that is, in war.

610. *Fatigamus terga:* we strike the backs of our oxen, &c. So constant were they in the use of their arms, that they did not even lay them aside when engaged in agriculture. They used their spears, &c. to spur, or urge on their oxen while in the plough.

611. *Mutat:* in the sense of *pellit.*

612. *Premimus,* &c. By this we are to understand that their old men had sufficient vigor and strength of nerve, to bear arms.

613. *Rapto:* the plunder.

615. *Desidiæ cordi:* sloth is to you for pleasure and delight.

616. *Tunicæ habent:* your vests have sleeves, and the ribbons of the mitre. Other nations, particularly the Romans, had their arms and necks naked, and looked upon the covering of those parts as a mark of effeminacy. This is said by way of reproach.

617. *O verè Phrygiæ,* &c. He here speaks by way of contempt, calling them not even Phrygian men, but Phrygian women. The Phrygians were noted for their effeminacy and luxury. See Æn. iv. 216.

618. *Dindyma:* neu. plu. sing. *Dindymus,* a mountain in Phrygia, sacred to Cybele. Hence she is sometimes called *Dindymine.* Its name is of Greek origin, and signifies double-topt—having two tops. *Biforem.* Some understand by this a pipe with only two stops: others, two pipes with different stops, which, being played upon together, made very indifferent harmony. *Biforem cantum:* discordant music. Ruæus says, *imparem.*

619. *Tympana:* neu. plu.. timbrels. *Berecynthia:* an adj. from *Berecynthus,* a mountain and castle in Phrygia, sacred to Cybele; who sometimes was called *Berecynthia.* *Buxus:* properly, the box-wood; by meton. a pipe made of the box-wood. This wood is supposed to have abounded on mount Berecynthus.

620. *Idææ:* an adj. from *Ida,* a mountain just back of Troy, sacred to Cybele, the mother of the gods. Hence she is called sometimes *Idææ.* *Sinite:* in the sense of *relinquite.*

621. *Canentem dira:* uttering such indignities—such reproaches. Ruæus says, *loquentem.*

622. *Equino nervo:* the string of his bow was made of horse-hair

Contendit telum, diversaque brachia ducens,
Constitit, antè Jovem supplex per vota precatus
Jupiter omnipotens, audacibus annuè cœptis.

626. *Ego* ipse feram solemnia dona tibi ad tua

Ipse tibi ad tua templa feram solemnia dona,
Et statuam ante aras auratâ fronte juvencum
Candentem, pariterque caput cum matre ferentem,
Jam cornu petat, et pedibus qui spargat arenam.

630. Genitor *Deorum* audiit

Audiit, et cœli genitor de parte serenâ
Intonuit lævùm. Sonat unà letifer arcus;
Et fugit horrendùm stridens elapsa sagitta,
Perque caput Remuli venit, et cava tempora ferro
Trajicit. I, verbis virtutem illude superbis.
Bis capti Phryges hæc Rutulis responsa remittunt.

636. Ascanius *dixit* hæc tantùm.

Hæc tantùm Ascanius. Teucri clamore sequuntur,
Lætitiâque fremunt, animosque ad sidera tollunt.
Ætherea tum fortè plagâ crinitus Apollo
Desuper Ausonias acies urbemque videbat,
Nube sedens; atque his victorem affatur Iülum:
Macte novâ virtute, puer: sic itur ad astra,

642. Omnia bella ventura fato,

Dîs genite, et geniture Deos Jure omnia bella
Gente sub Assaraci fato ventura resident:
Nec te Troja capit. Simul hæc effatus, ab alto
Æthere se mittit, spirantes dimovet auras,
Ascaniumque petit: formâ tum vertitur oris
Antiquum in Buten. Hic Dardanio Anchisæ
Armiger antè fuit, fidusque ad limina custos:

649. Tum pater *Æneas* addidit *hunc*

650. Similis longævo *quoad* omnia

Tum comitem Ascanio pater addidit. Ibat Apollo
Omnia longævo similis, vocemque, coloremque
Et crines albos, et sæva sonoribus arma·
Atque his ardentem dictis affatur Iülum.
Sit satìs, Æneada, telis impunè Numanum
Oppetiisse tuis: primam hanc tibi magnus Apollo

NOTES.

623. *Ducens brachia:* drawing his arms asunder. This is the posture of a man drawing the bow to its full stretch. *Telum:* his arrow.

624. *Antè:* in the sense of *primùm.*

628. *Cadentem:* in the sense of *candidum.*

629. *Petat:* he pushes—butts.

631. *Intonuit lævum:* the left thundered; or it thundered on the left. This was a lucky omen. See Ecl. i. 18.

632. *Stridens:* whizzing loud.

633. *Ferro: ferrum,* here, the point of the arrow, which was tipt with iron or steel—the barb.

637. *Animos:* the courage—valor of Ascanius.

638. *Plaga:* here, a part, or quarter o the sky or heaven.

641. *Macte:* go on—persevere. *Sic itur ad astra:* thus men arise to the stars, thou descendant of the gods, &c. By great and noble actions, men obtain immortality. *Ascanius* descended from Venus by Æneas his father, and from Jove, by Dardanus, the founder of the Trojan race. From Ascanius, called sometimes Iülus, descended Julius and Augustus Cæsar, according to Virgil, both of whom received divine honors.

643. *Sub gente Assaraci:* under the family of Assaracus. He was of the royal family of Troy, and one of the ancestors of Ascanius. *Jure:* by justice or equity. Here is an allusion to the universal peace which took place under Augustus, at the beginning of the Christian era.

645. *Spirantes:* blowing—whispering

646. *Oris:* in the sense of *vultûs. Formâ.* This is the reading of Valpy and Ruæus. Heyne reads, *formam.* But *forma* is the easier.

651. *Sæva:* harsh in sound—terrible in sound.

652. *Ardentem:* fierce—ardent—eager for fight.

653. *Æneada:* the voc. of the patronymic *Æneades:* the son of Æneas. *Impunè:* without injuring thyself.

654. *Oppetiisse:* in the sense of *occubuisse* vel *cecidisse.*

Concedit laudem, et paribus non invidet armis.
Cætera parce, puer, bello. Sic orsus Apollo,
Mortales medio aspectus sermone reliquit,
Et procul in tenuem ex oculis evanuit auram.
Agnovêre Deum proceres divinaque tela
Dardanidæ, pharetramque fugâ sensêre sonantem.
Ergò avidum pugnæ dictis ac numine Phœbi
Ascanium prohibent: ipsi in certamina rursùs
Succedunt, animasque in aperta pericula mittunt.
It clamor totis per propugnacula muris.
Intendunt acres arcus, amentaque torquent.
Sternitur omne solum telis: tum scuta, cavæque
Dant sonitum flictu galeæ: pugna aspera surgit.
Quantus ab occasu veniens pluvialibus hœdis
Verberat imber humum: quàm multâ grandine nimbi
In vada præcipitant, cùm Jupiter horridus Austris
Torquet aquosam hyemem, et cœlo cava nubila rumpit.
  Pandarus et Bitias, Idæo Alcanore creti,
Quos Jovis eduxit luco sylvestris Hiera,
Abietibus juvenes patriis et montibus æquos,
Portam, quæ ducis imperio commissa, recludunt,
Freti armis, ultròque invitant mœnibus hostem.
Ipsi intus, dextrâ ac lævâ, pro turribus adstant,
Armati ferro, et cristis capita alta corusci.
Quales aëriæ liquentia flumina circum,
Sive Padi ripis, Athesim seu propter amœnum,

668. Quantus imber veniens pluvialibus hœdis ab occasu *solis*

675. Quæ commissa *erat ipsis* imperio

678. Et corusci *quoad* alta capita cristis. *Tales* quales geminæ aëriæ quercus consurgunt

NOTES.

655. *Paribus armis.* Apollo, when a child, killed the serpent Python in defence of his mother, as Ascanius does here Numanus in defence of his country. Dr. Trapp thinks *paribus* is to be taken in a qualified sense: not equal skill or glory in arms, but of the like kind or sort of art in arms: for it can hardly be supposed that he would compliment a boy to the dishonor of himself.

656. *Cætera parce:* hereafter, boy, abstain from fight—as to what remains, abstain, &c. *Orsus:* having thus said: a part. of the verb *ordior. Cætera:* in the sense of *cæterùm* vel *cæterò.*

659. *Dardanidæ proceres:* the Trojan nobles, or chiefs. *Dardanidæ:* a sub. used adjectively.

663. *Mittunt animas:* they expose their lives, &c. *Succedunt:* in the sense of *redeunt.*

665. *Amenta.* These were properly a kind of thongs, tied to javelins, by which they were darted out of the hand. They served to direct the weapon with more certainty. The *armenta* here appears to be used for the darts or javelins themselves; by meton. *Acres:* elastic.

667. *Flictu:* in the sense of *conflictu.*

668. *Hœdis.* The *hœdi*, or kids, are two stars in the constellation *Auriga*, just below his shoulder. The rising and setting of which were thought to influence the weather, and render it rainy. *Veniens:* arising through the influence of the rainy kids.

670. *Jupiter:* in the sense of *aër. Horridus:* black—deeply impregnated with vapor. *In vada:* upon the sea. Ruæus says, *in mare.*

672. *Idæo:* an adj. from *Ida*, a mountain of *Phrygia.*

674. *Juvenes æquos:* youths equal to their paternal oaks and mountains. This is an hyperbole to denote their great size and strength. It is said they were brought up by Hiera. Turnebus conjectures it should be *Hyæna*, which is a beast resembling a wolf; because it is said that Romulus was brought up by a wolf. *Abietibus et montibus:* the same as *abietibus montanis*, by hend.

675. *Recludunt:* in the sense of *aperiunt.*

676. *Invitant:* they invite—challenge. They stand in the entrance of the gate, and defy the enemy.

677. *Pro turribus:* like towers—in the room or place of towers: or perhaps before the towers.

680. *Padi.* Padus or Eridanus, the Po, a well known river of Italy, of considerable magnitude. *Athesim.* This river rises in the Alps, passes through Venice, and falls into the Adriatic, not far from the mouth of the Po.

Consurgunt geminæ quercus, intonsaque cœlo
Attollunt capita, et sublimi vertice nutant
Irrumpunt, aditus Rutuli ut vidêre patentes:
Continuò Quercens, et pulcher Equicolus armis,
Et præceps animi Tmarus, et Mavortius Hæmon,

686. Totis agminibus hostium

Agminibus totis aut versi terga dedêre,
Aut ipso portæ posuere in limine vitam.
Tum magìs increscunt animis discordibus iræ:
Et jam collecti Troës glomerantur eòdem,
Et conferre manum, et procurrere longiùs audent.
Ductori Turno diversâ in parte furenti,
Turbantique viros, perfertur nuntius, hostem
Fervere cæde novâ, et portas præbere patentes.
Deserit inceptum, atque immani concitus irâ
Dardaniam ruit ad portam, fratresque superbos.

696. Et primum, jaculo conjecto, sternit Antiphaten, nothum alti Sarpedonis de Thebanâ matre, enim

Et primùm Antiphaten, is enim se primus agebat,
Thebanâ de matre nothum Sarpedonis alti,
Conjecto sternit jaculo. Volat Itala cornus
Aëra per tenuem, stomachoque infixa sub altum
Pectus abit: reddit specus atri vulneris undam
Spumantem, et fixo ferrum in pulmone tepescit.
Tum Meropem atque Erymantha manu; tum sternit Aphydnum:

703. Tum *sternit* Bitian

Tum Bitian ardentem oculis, animisque frementem,
Non jaculo; neque enim jaculo vitam ille dedisset;
Sed magnùm stridens contorta falarica venit,

NOTES.

681. *Geminæ aëriæ quercus:* as two aërial oaks rise around, &c. This is a fine simile. It is taken from Homer, Iliad xi.

685. *Præceps.* Ruæus says, *temerarius.*

688. *Tum iræ:* then rage increases more and more in the hostile minds of the Trojans. *Discordibus:* in the sense of *hostilibus.* Ruæus says, *infensis.*

690. *Conferre manum:* to engage in close combat: a phrase.

692. *Turbanti:* routing—driving before him.

693. *Fervere:* rage with uncommon slaughter. *Fervere* signifies to be hot—to be busily engaged—also, to rage. *Nova:* uncommon—unusual. Ruæus says, *recenti.* But he takes *fervere*, in the sense of *animari:* to be animated—encouraged. *Præbere:* in the sense of *offerre* vel *dare.*

694. *Deserit:* in the sense of *relinquit.*

695. *Superbos fratres:* Pandarus and Bitias, mentioned above, the sons of Alcanor.

696. *Agebat se:* presented himself—took himself along.

697. *Sarpedonis.* Sarpedon was the reputed son of Jupiter. Hence the epithet *alti*, high, or nobly born. He was king of Lycia, and assisted Priam against the Greeks. *Thebana:* an adj. from *Thebes.* There were several cities of that name; one in Egypt, one in Bœotia, and one in Thessaly. The one here alluded to was in *Asia Minor:* the sovereignty of which was long disputed between the Lydians and Mysians. *Nothum:* an illegitimate son.

698. *Cornus:* the corneil-tree—also, a javelin or dart made of the wood of that tree, by meton.

700. *Specus atri vulneris:* the cavity of the dark wound emits, &c. *Specus* is properly a den or cave, which is usually dark and gloomy. This idea the poet transfers to the wound made by the javelin of Turnus. Some copies have *sanguinis* in the room of *vulneris.* In this case, *atri sanguinis* must be governed by *undam*, and not by *specus;* which would signify the wound itself. The common reading is *vulneris.* Valpy takes *specus* for the wound itself—the gaping wound. *Undam:* a stream—tide of blood. *Reddit:* in the sense of *emittit.*

701. *Fixo:* in the sense of *transfixo.*

703. *Ardentem:* flashing fire with his eyes.

704. *Non jaculo enim*, &c. The meaning of this line is: that Turnus did not kill him with an ordinary javelin, for he would not have yielded his life to a javelin—it would have had no effect on him. The others he killed with his hand—with an ordinary weapon.

705. *Falarica.* This was an oblong kind of javelin, bound about with wild fire. It was usually shot out of an engine against

Fulminis acta modo; quam nec duo taurea terga,
Nec duplici squamâ lorica fidelis et auro
Sustinuit: collapsa ruunt immania membra.
Dat tellus gemitum, et clypeum super intonat ingens.
Qualis in Euboïco Baiarum litore quondam
Saxea pila cadit, magnis quam molibus antè
Constructam jaciunt ponto: sic illa ruinam
Prona trahit, penitusque vadis illisa recumbit.
Miscent se maria, et nigræ attolluntur arenæ.
Tum sonitu Prochyta alta tremit, durumque cubile
Inarime Jovis imperiis impôsta Typhœo.
  Hìc Mars armipotens animum viresque Latinis
Addidit, et stimulos acres sub pectore vertit:
Immisitque fugam Teucris, atrumque timorem.
Undique conveniunt, quoniam data copia pugnæ;
Bellatorque animo Deus incidit.
Pandarus, ut fuso germanum corpore cernit,
Et quo sit fortuna loco, qui casus agat res,
Portam, vi multâ converso cardine, torquet,

709. Intonat super *eum.*

711. Quam constructam antè *homines* jaciunt

712. Sic illa *cadens* prona

716. Inarimeque impôsta Typhœo *quasi* durum cubile imperiis Jovis, *tremit.*

720. *Latini* conveniunt undique, quoniam copia pugnæ data *est ipsis*

NOTES.

wooden towers for the purpose of setting them on fire. To show the prodigious strength of Turnus, the poet intimates that it was cast by him. To express the rapidity of its flight, he says, it flew like a thunder-bolt: *modo fulminis.*

706. *Acta:* driven—sent. *Modo:* in the sense of *more.*

707. *Duplici squamâ.* The plates of a coat of mail were called *squamæ*, from their resemblance to scales. *Squama et auro:* for *aurea squama*, by hend. *Fidelis:* trusty—faithful. It had hitherto protected him in danger.

708. *Ruunt:* in the sense of *cadunt. Collapsa:* failing—losing their strength.

709. *Intonat*, &c. These words may be rendered: he, falling upon his mighty shield, thunders; or, his mighty shield falling upon him, &c. *Clypeum:* the same with *clypeus.* This passage is imitated from Homer, Iliad v. 42.

710. *Euboïco litore Baiarum. Baiæ* was a place in Campania, famous for its fountains of warm water, situated in the upper part of the *Sinus Neapolitanus*, near the promontory *Misenus.* A colony from Chalcis, on the island Eubœa, *hodie, Negropont*, founded the city *Cumæ*, not far from this place. Hence the shore is called *Eubœan. Qualis*, &c. The meaning is: that Betias fell like a mass of rocks, which had been built up to a great height, and cast into the sea, for the purpose of forming a dam or barrier to the water.

711. *Molibus:* for a dam or pier.

713. *Prona:* in the sense of *cadens. Illisa:* dashing upon the water. *Penitùs:* in the sense of *profundè. Recumbit:* it sinks deep to the bottom—it rests, &c. This, to us, would be a novel way of making a dam or pier in the water.

714. *Miscent se:* in the sense of *turbantur.*

715. *Prochyta:* an island lying to the south of the promontory *Misenus*, and formerly separated from the main land, by an earthquake, according to Pliny. Its name is of Greek origin. *Hodie, Procida. Alta:* high, in reference to its surface. Or, *alta* may be taken in the sense of *altè* vel *profundè.* Ruæus says, *intima.* Heyne observes, that *alta* may be considered as an epithet proper for all islands, inasmuch as they are elevated or raised above the sea, or surface of the water: *alta, epitheton commune omnium insularum, quatenùs mari eminent.*

716. *Inarime.* This is a high and elevated island, laying to the west of Prochyta. This passage is taken from Homer, Iliad ii. 283 *Typhœo.* Typhœus was one of the giants that attempted to scale heaven, and was signally punished by Jove for the audacious attempt.

718. *Vertit acres:* he turns his sharp spurs under their breast. This is a metaphor taken from the application of the spur to the sides of the horse, to increase his speed and courage.

719. *Atrum:* in the sense of *horridum* grim—ghastly.

720. *Copia:* in the sense of *opportunitas.*

721. *Incidit:* in the sense of *subiit* vel *illabitur.*

722. *Corpore fuso:* with his body stretched on the ground. *Ut:* in the sense of *quando.*

723. *Casus:* misfortune—danger. *Agat:* attends their affairs—rules—governs. Ruæus says, *impellat.*

724. *Torquet:* he shuts the gate.

Obnixus latis humeris: multosque suorum
Mœnibus exclusos duro in certamine linquit;
Ast alios secum includit, recipitque ruentes:
Demens! qui Rutulum in medio non agmine regem
729. Incluserit eum urbi, veluti — Viderit irrumpentem, ultròque incluserit urbi:
Immanem veluti pecora inter inertia tigrim.
Continuò nova lux oculis effulsit, et arma
Horrendùm sonuêre: tremunt in vertice cristæ
Sanguineæ, clypeoque micantia fulgura mittunt.
  Agnoscunt faciem invisam atque immania membra
Turbati subitò Æneadæ. Tum Pandarus ingens
Emicat, et, mortis fraternæ fervidus irâ,
Effatur: Non hæc dotalis regia Amatæ;
Nec muris cohibet patriis media Ardea Turnum.
739. Est nulla potestas — Castra inimica vides: nulla hinc exire potestas.
Olli subridens sedato pectore Turnus:
Incipe, si qua animo virtus, et consere dextram
Hìc etiam inventum Priamo narrabis Achillem.
Dixerat. Ille rudem nodis et cortice crudo
Intorquet, summis adnixus viribus, hastam.
Excepêre auræ vulnus: Saturnia Juno
Detorsit veniens; portæque infigitur hasta.
At non hoc telum, mea quod vi dextera versat,
Effugies: neque enim is teli nec vulneris auctor.
749. Sic Turnus ait: et consurgit — Sic ait: et sublatum altè consurgit in ensem,
Et mediam ferro gemina inter tempora frontem
Dividit, impubesque immani vulnere malas.

NOTES.

726. *Duro:* in the sense of *mortifero.*

731. *Continuò nova lux,* &c. Davidson refers this to the eyes of the Trojans, and not to those of Turnus. The comeliness of his person and the brightness of his arms rendered him easy to be distinguished by the enemy. New light struck their eyes. Both Dr. Trapp and Ruæus refer it to Turnus. Ruæus says, *novum lumen emicuit ex oculis Turni.*

732. *Tremunt:* wave.

733. *Micantia:* gleaming—reflecting from his shield. *Mittunt:* in the sense of *mittunt se:* throws—darts itself at a distance. Davidson and Ruæus read *mittit,* referring to Turnus. Heyne reads *mittunt,* agreeing with *fulgura* in the nom. If we read *mittit, fulgura* will be the acc. plu. governed by that verb.

What follows of the feats of Turnus is astonishingly grand. But it may be objected, that the story is beyond probability. We are to recollect, however, that it is allowable in poetry to go beyond real life: and, beside, he is assisted in his amazing exploits by a divine power.

737. *Hæc non dotalis regia:* this is not the palace of Amata, promised as a dowry to thee. It was the purpose of Amata to bestow her daughter *Lavinia* upon Turnus, and, with her, the kingdom of *Latium.* The verb *est* is to be supplied.

738. *Ardea.* The capital city of the Rutuli. *Media:* the middle or centre of your dominions. *Cohibet:* in the sense of *tenet. Patriis:* paternal walls.

741. *Consere dextram:* engage hand to hand with me.

742. *Etiam:* also—as well as among the Greeks.

743. *Hastam rudem:* a spear rough with knots, &c.

745. *Vulnus:* in the sense of *ictum,* by meton.

746. *Detorsit:* turned it aside. *Veniens.* in the sense of *interveniens.*

748. *Enim neque auctor teli:* for neither the owner of the weapon, nor the author of the stroke, is the same. He far excels you in the strength of his body, and the nerve of his arm. *Vulneris:* in the sense of *ictûs. Is:* in the sense of *idem.*

749. *Consurgit:* he rises upon his sword. raised high. He lifts up his sword, and rises on tiptoe, to give greater force to the blow. *Altè* may be connected with *consurgit,* or *sublatum.* The sense is the same in either case.

750. *Mediam frontem:* his head in the middle between, &c.

751. *Impubes:* beardless—without beard.

Fit sonus; ingenti concussa est pondere tellus.
Collapsos artus atque arma cruenta cerebro
Sternit humi moriens: atque illi partibus æquis
Huc caput atque illuc humero ex utroque pependit.
Diffugiunt versi trepidâ formidine Troës.
Et, si continuò victorem ea cura subîsset,
Rumpere claustra manu, sociosque immittere portis,
Ultimus ille dies bello gentique fuisset.
Sed furor ardentem cædisque insana cupido
Egit in adversos.
  Principio Phalarim, et, succiso poplite, Gygen
Excipit: hinc raptas fugientibus ingerit hastas
In tergum: Juno vires animumque ministrat.
Addit Halyn comitem, et confixâ Phegea parmâ:
Ignaros deinde in muris, Martemque cientes,
Alcandrumque Haliumque Noëmonaque Prytanimque.
Lyncea tendentem contrà, sociosque vocantem,
Vibranti gladio connixus ab aggere dexter
Occupat: huic uno dejectum cominùs ictu
Cum galeâ longè jacuit caput. Inde ferarum
Vastatorem Amycum, quo non felicior alter
Ungere tela manu, ferrumque armare veneno:
Et Clytium Æoliden, et amicum Cretea Musis;
Cretea Musarum comitem: cui carmina semper
Et citharæ cordi, numerosque intendere nervis;
Semper equos, atque arma virûm, pugnasque canebat.
  Tandem ductores, auditâ cæde suorum,
Conveniunt Teucri, Mnestheus acerque Serestus;
Palantesque vident socios, hostemque receptum.
Et Mnestheus, Quò deinde fugam? quò tenditis? inquit,

754. Atque caput pependit illi *scissum in* æquis partibus huc

759. Gentique *Trojanorum.*

763. Hinc ingerit hastas raptas *ab occisis* in tergum

765. Comitem *illis in morte*, et Phegea, *ejus* parmâ confixa

766. Deinde *occidit* Alcandrumque, &c. ignaros *ejus ingressûs* in muris

769. Connixus dexter ab aggere, *Turnus* occupat Lyncea

771. Inde *occidit* Amycum

774. Et *occidit* Clytium

775. Cui carmina, et citharæ *fuerant* semper cordi

780. Receptum *in muris.* Et Mnestheus inquit: quo deinde *dirigitis* fugam?

NOTES.

754. *Illi:* in the sense of *illius.* His head hung, &c. *Sternit:* he brings to the ground. Ruæus says, *trahit.*

757. *Subîsset victorem:* had the thought come into the mind of the victor to burst, &c. *Claustra:* the bars of the gate—the gate itself.

761. *Egit in adversos:* drove him furious upon his foes. He could not resist the temptation of pursuing his revenge on his enemies, when they were full in his view.

763. *Excipit:* in the sense of *interficit.* He receives or surprises them with death. *Ingerit:* in the sense of *intorquet,* vel *jacit.*

766. *Ignaros:* ignorant of his being within their walls. Not thinking of danger, and not imagining that Turnus and death were so near them. *Cientes:* rousing the martial courage of his friends—encouraging the fight.

768. *Tendentem contrà:* meeting him—coming opposite to him.

769. *Dexter:* on the right hand: or, dexterous, skilful.

770. *Occupat:* receives—takes. *Intercipit,* says Ruæus.

771. *Caput huic.* The same as, *hujus caput:* the dat. in the sense of the gen.

772. *Felicior:* more skilful—expert.

773. *Ungere:* to anoint. *Manu:* art—skill, by meton. The practice of poisoning arrows, and other missive weapons, obtained among some nations of antiquity. It is said to be done at the present day by some tribes of Indians, and some of the barbarous nations of Africa. *Ferrum:* the point or barb.

774. *Æoliden.* He was skilful at playing on wind instruments. He is therefore called metaphorically the son of Æolus. There is a propriety, therefore, in joining him with *Creteus,* who was a distinguished musician, and consequently a friend and companion of the muses. *Cretea, Lyncea, Phegea,* are Greek accusatives.

776. *Intendere numeros:* to apply notes to the strings of the lyre—to apply verse to music. Ruæus says, *edere sonos chordis. Cordi:* for a delight. *Citharæ,* may here mean musical instruments in general.

781. *Quò deinde fugam?* where next will ye direct your flight? Servius says this

Quos alios muros, quæ jam ultrà mœnia habetis?
Unus homo, vestris, ô cives, undique septus
Aggeribus, tantas strages impunè per urbem
Ediderit? juvenum primos tot miserit Orco?
Non infelicis patriæ, veterumque Deorum,
Et magni Æneæ, segnes, miseretque pudetque?
  Talibus accensi firmantur, et agmine denso
Consistunt. Turnus paulatim excedere pugnâ,
Et fluvium petere, ac partem quæ cingitur amni.
Acriùs hôc Teucri clamore incumbere magno,
Et glomerare manum. Ceu sævum turba leonem
Cùm telis premit infensis: at territus ille
Asper, acerbà tuens, retrò redit: et neque terga
Ira dare aut virtus patitur; nec tendere contrà
Ille quidem hoc cupiens, potis est per tela virosque.
Haud aliter retrò dubius vestigia Turnus
Improperata refert; et mens exæstuat irâ.
Quin etiam, bis tum medios invaserat hostes;
Bis confusa fugâ per muros agmina vertit,
Sed manus è castris properè coit omnis in unum
Nec contrà vires audet Saturnia Juno
Sufficere: aëriam cœlo nam Jupiter Irim
Demisit, germanæ haud mollia jussa ferentem;
Ni Turnus cedat Teucrorum mœnibus altis.
Ergò nec clypeo juvenis subsistere tantum,
Nec dextrâ valet: injectis sic undique telis
Obruitur. Strepit assiduo cava tempora circum
Tinnitu galea, et saxis solida æra fatiscunt:
Discussæque jubæ capiti; nec sufficit umbo
Ictibus: ingeminant hastis et Troës, et ipse
Fulmineus Mnestheus. Tum toto corpore sudor

783. Unus homo, et *ille* septus vestris aggeribus undique

787. Non miseretque pudetque *vos*, O segnes, infelicis

789. Turnus paulatim *incipit*

791. Teucri *incipiunt* acriùs hôc

795. Nec ille est potis tendere contrà per tela virosque, quidem cupiens hoc

803. Sufficere vires et contra *Teucros.*

806. Ergò juvenis valet subsistere tantum *impetum*, nec clypeo, nec dextrâ

810. Jubæ *sunt* discussæ

NOTES.

is a bitter sarcasm. It implies that they had already fled into their camp, and shut themselves up through fear, within their intrenchments. *Tenditis:* in the sense of *ibitis.*

784. *Aggeribus:* in the sense of *muris.*

785. *Ediderit:* in the sense of *effecerit.*

787. *Segnes:* cowards. Ruæus says, *O, inertes.* It is better to consider *segnes*, as the voc. than the acc. agreeing with *vos* understood, and governed by the verbs *miseret* and *pudet.* It is more animated, and more in the spirit of address.

788. *Firmantur:* in the sense of *animantur.* By these words of Mnestheus the Trojans were encouraged, and rallied; and again returned to the attack.

790. *Partem:* the part of the walls which was bounded by the river.

791. *Hôc acriùs,* &c. This retreat of Turnus gave courage to the Trojans, who began to press upon him more closely, and to form a band about him with a view to surround him, and take him prisoner.

792. *Turba:* a company of hunters.

794. *Acerbà:* an adj. neu. plu. taken as an adverb. This is common among the poets. *Tuens*, a part. of *tueor:* looking fiercely.

795. *Tendere contrà:* to go forward.

798. *Improperata:* slow—deliberate. Of *in*, negativum, and *properatus.*

800. *Confusa:* confused—disordered. Ruæus and some others read *conversa.*

801. *In unum:* against him alone. *Coit:* unites. Of *con*, and *eo.*

805. *Ni Turnus.* A threat is intimated or implied in the words, *haud mollia mandata;* which would be put in execution, unless Turnus retired from the Trojan walls.

809. *Tinnitu:* ringing. *Strepit:* in the sense of *sonat.*

810. *Jubæ:* the plumes or feathers in his helmet. These were struck from his head. *Umbo.* The boss or extreme part of the shield, by synec. the whole shield. This is not able to withstand the blows of the missive weapons.

812. *Fulmineus:* in the sense of *ardens* The Trojans, with Mnestheus at their head,

Liquitur, et piceum, nec respirare potestas,
Flumen agit: fessos quatit æger anhelitus artus.
Tum demùm præceps saltu sese omnibus armis
In fluvium dedit. Ille suo cum gurgite flavo
Accepit venientem, ac mollibus extulit undis;
Et lætum sociis ablutâ cæde remisit.

813. Nec *est* potestas *illi* respirare

816. Ille *fluvius* accepit *eum* venientem cum suo flavo gurgite, ac extulit *eum* mollibus undis, et remisit *eum* lætum sociis, cæde ablutâ.

NOTES.

attack Turnus with such fury that he is unable to maintain his ground. His solid armor of brass is bruised and shattered by the heavy stones hurled at him; his plumes fall from his head; his trusty shield begins to give way; and the enemy to repeat their strokes with redoubled fury, with darts and spears. In this situation, worn out with fatigue, and panting for breath, he flings himself into the Tiber, and returns in safety to his camp.

814. *Agit piceum flumen:* pours a black pitchy stream. Turnus sweat so copiously that it fell from him in a stream. Mingled with dust, which would adhere to his body it became tough and clammy like pitch, and nearly of a similar color. *Æger anhelitus.* This is such a difficulty of breathing as they have, who are sickly, and asthmatic.

816. *Ille suo gurgite.* This is extremely beautiful. The poet represents the river god, expanding his gulfy bosom to receive Turnus, and bearing him off in safety upon his waves.

818. *Cæde ablutâ:* the blood being washed off. Not the blood from any wounds he had received; but from those wounds which he had inflicted.

QUESTIONS.

How is this book distinguished from all the rest?

What does Turnus in the mean time?

Does he attempt to burn the Trojan ships?

What becomes of them?

At whose particular request was this granted to them?

What does Dr. Trapp observe of this passage?

Does he consider it a blemish to the book?

By whom is Turnus roused to arms?

To what does the poet compare the marching of his troops?

Where does the Ganges empty?

What is its length?

What course does it run?

In what light is it considered by those who live near it?

Where does the Nile rise?

Where does it empty?

And by how many mouths?

What effect has it upon the fertility of Egypt?

What occasions its inundations?

Is this a fine comparison?

Having failed to burn the fleet, what course does Turnus determine to pursue?

Was there any prodigy in the heavens at this time?

What was that prodigy?

What effect had it upon the Trojans?

What effect had it upon the Rutulians?

Did Turnus make an address to his men upon the occasion?

What effect had it upon them?

What is the character of that speech?

At the conclusion, what does he recommend to his men?

When does he resolve to attack the camp of the Trojans?

What orders does he give to be observed during the night?

What is the condition of the Trojans?

What do they in the mean time?

Is there any proposition made to recall Æneas?

By whom was it made?

Who were Nisus and Euryalus?

Had any mention been made of their friendship before?

In what book?

And upon what occasion?

What is the character of this episode?

How many lines does it occupy?

In what state does the poet represent the Rutulian camp during the night?

Which of the two friends is the elder?

Do they pass peaceably through the enemy's camp?

What then did they do?

How long did they continue the slaughter?

Did they both make their escape from the camp?

What prevented Euryalus from accompanying Nisus?

By whom was he taken prisoner?

Who commanded this troop of horse?

Where was Nisus during these transactions?

When he perceived his friend to be missing, what course did he pursue?

Having found him in the hands of the enemy, what did he do?

Whom did he kill?

What effect had this upon the mind of Volscens?

By whom was Euryalus slain?

When he found he was about to be killed, did Nisus discover himself?

Did he make any appeal to the enemy upon this occasion?

What was his object in doing this?

Unable to save his life, what resolution did he take?

Whom did he kill?

Was he slain himself also?

What is the character of this episode?

Is it objectionable in any respect?

What are the principal grounds of objection?

At the return of day, what does Turnus do?

In what way did the Trojans learn of the death of Nisus and Euryalus?

What effect had the news upon the mother of Euryalus?

How was she employed at that time?

What effect had the sight of his head upon her?

In what light may her lamentation be considered?

What is the character of this sequel?

Who among the ancients is said to have greatly admired it?

By what troops was the assault commenced?

What do you mean by the *testudo*, or target defence?

On what occasion was that used?

What was the character of this assault?

Were the enemy repulsed in this attack?

What feats of valor did Turnus perform?

What effect had the burning of the tower upon the Trojans?

By whom was it set on fire?

After this, was the assault renewed?

Was any part of the Trojans, at this time, without the ramparts?

Were they able to defend themselves?

What did the sentinels at the gates do in this crisis?

Why did they open the gates?

Who were stationed as guard at the gates?

What was their stature and strength?

Did Turnus enter along with the fugitives?

Was he perceived at the time?

Was the gate closed immediately on his entrance?

What feats of valor does he here perform?

Whom does he first kill?

Are the Trojans able to stand before him?

What remark does the poet make after the admission of Turnus, and the closing of the gate?

How does the poet account for this want of thought in the hero?

By whom are the Trojans finally rallied, and brought again to the attack?

What becomes of Turnus?

How does he escape from them?

Did he receive any injury from the host of weapons sent at him?

By whom was Turnus assisted in his mighty achievements?

Did he return in safety to his troops?

LIBER DECIMUS.

Jupiter calls a council of the gods, and forbids them to assist either side. On this occasion, Venus makes a very pathetic speech in favor of the Trojans, and entreats Jupiter to interfere in their favor, and not to suffer them to be entirely destroyed. Juno replies in a strain haughty and imperious, and attributes their misfortunes to their own folly and misconduct, and particularly to the conduct of Paris in the case of Helen; and insinuates that Æneas was playing the same game at the court of Latinus. Jupiter concludes their deliberations by a speech, in which he declares he will assist neither party, that success or disaster should attend their own actions.

As soon as Æneas had concluded a treaty with the Tuscans, he hastens his return, accompanied by his allies. On his way he is met by a choir of nymphs: one of whom informs him of the transformation of his ships, of the attack of Turnus upon his camp, of the great slaughter he had made, and the distress to which his friends were reduced. When he arrives in sight of his camp, the Trojans shout for joy; and Turnus resolves to prevent their landing. Leaving a sufficient number to besiege the camp, he marches with the rest of his forces to the shore. Æneas divided his troops into three divisions, and, in that order, effected a landing. Here a general engagement commences, and Æneas performs prodigies of valor. The Arcadians were routed by the Latins. When Pallas perceives them give way, he hastens along the ranks, animates his men, and brings them again to the charge. Here he performs feats of valor. Lausus, who commanded one wing of the Latins, opposed him with equal skill and valor. Arcadian, Tuscan and Trojan, fell before him.

In the mean time, Turnus, informed of the havoc made by Pallas, determines to attack him in person. He proceeds against the youthful warrior, who, undaunted, meets him with strength and arms unequal.

After the death of Pallas, a great slaughter of the Trojans ensues. Æneas, in an other part of the line, informed of the death of Pallas and the slaughter of his troops, immediately sets out in search of Turnus. In his way he kills a great number, and puts to flight whole ranks. Venus assists the Trojans, and Juno intercedes with her husband to favor the Latins; but to no purpose. However, he permits her to bear away Turnus from the fight, and save him from the vengeance of Æneas. The goddess instantly repairing to the field of battle, assumed the shape and attire of Æneas; and, by a device of hers, conducted Turnus from the fight. As soon as he was out of danger, the phantom vanished. Discovering the deception, the hero becomes frantic with rage and disappointment.

Mezentius succeeds Turnus in command, and makes head against the Trojans. The fight is renewed with great fury, and he performs feats of valor. Victory, for a time, seems equally poised. Æneas beholds him thundering along the ranks, prostrating all who stand before him; and resolves to meet him. Mezentius throws a spear, which, glancing from the shield of Æneas, kills *Antores*, who had been the companion of Hercules. The spear of Æneas wounds him in turn, but not mortally. In this situation, Lausus succors his father, and, flinging himself between the combatants, affords him an opportunity to retire, and, in the pious duty, loses his own life. He retires to the river, and washes his wound. All his anxiety is for his son, his affectionate, his dutiful Lausus. Messenger after messenger he sends to recall him from the fight. But when he learns his death, he resolves to return to fall by the hand of Æneas, or to bear off his spoils. For this purpose, he mounts his faithful courser, arms himself, and rushes into the field, seeking the victor. The book concludes with the death of Mezentius.

PANDITUR intereà domus omnipotentis Olympi:
Conciliumque vocat Divûm pater atque hominum rex
Sideream in sedem; terras unde arduus omnes,
Castraque Dardanidûm aspectat, populosque Latinos.
Considunt tectis bipatentibus. Incipit ipse:
Cœlicolæ magni, quianam sententia vobis
Versa retrò? tantùmque animis certatis iniquis?
Abnueram bello Italiam concurrere Teucris:
Quæ contra vetitum discordia? quis metus, aut hos,
Aut hos arma sequi, ferrumque lacessere suasit?
Adveniet justum pugnæ, ne accersite, tempus,

5. *Superi* considunt tectis bipatentibus. *Jupiter* ipse incipit *sic*

9. Quæ *est hæc* discordia contra *meum* vetitum? Quis metus suasit aut hos *Italos*, aut hos *Teucros* sequi

NOTES.

1. *Olympi.* Olympus is a very high mountain in the confines of Thessaly and Macedonia, whose summit is above the clouds. Hence the poets made it the residence of Jove. Here they assigned him a sumptuous palace. The epithet *omnipotens* is added by way of eminence; that being the proper epithet of Jove, who had there his residence. The poet here imitates Homer, Iliad, lib. viii.

4. *Aspectat:* in the sense of *despicit. Arduus:* in the sense of *sublimis.*

5. *Bipatentibus:* opening both ways, to the right and left.

6. *Cœlicolæ:* in the sense of *Superi. Quianam:* in the sense of *cur.* The meaning is: why have ye changed your purpose of assisting neither party? Why do ye contend with so much animosity? and disregard my prohibition that the Italians should not oppose the Trojans?

8. *Abnueram:* I had forbidden the Italian nations, &c. This prohibition had not been mentioned by the poet before. On the contrary, Jove had declared that Æneas should carry on a great war in Italy, *bellum ingens geret Italia.* Æn. i. 263. It is probable that the poet would have corrected this passage, if he had lived to revise this part of his works.

10. *Lacessere:* in the sense of *commovere,* says Ruæus. *Suasit:* in the sense of *impulit. Arma:* by meton. for *bellum.*

11. *Adveniet justum:* the proper time for war will arrive, &c. Jove declares in council that the Italians had engaged in the war against the Trojans, contrary to his wish and inclination; that it was his desire Italy should open its bosom, and receive them in friendship and amity. But do not, ye gods, infer hence that I wish they should always escape the calamities of war. The time will come in its proper season, nor do ye hasten it, when warlike Carthage shall bring a great destruction upon the Roman towers. Then you may indulge your ani-

Cùm fera Carthago Romanis arcibus olim
Exitium magnum, atque Alpes immittet apertas.
Tum certare odiis, tum res rapuisse licebit.
Nunc sinite, et placitum læti componite fœdus.
Jupiter hæc paucis: at non Venus aurea contrà
Pauca refert:
O pater, ô hominum Divûmque æterna potestas!
(Namque aliud quid sit, quod jam implorare queamus?)
Cernis ut insultent Rutuli? Turnusque feratur
Per medios insignis equis, tumidusque secundo
Marte ruat? non clausa tegunt jam mœnia Teucros·
Quin intra portas, atque ipsis prælia miscent
Aggeribus murorum, et inundant sanguine fossæ
Æneas ignarus abest. Nunquamne levari
Obsidione sines? muris iterum imminet hostis
Nascentis Trojæ, nec non exercitus alter:
Atque iterum in Teucros Ætolis surgit ab Arpis

16. Jupiter *dixit* hæc paucis *verbis*.

19. Quid aliud *numen* sit, quod

25. Æneas ignarus *harum rerum* abest.

NOTES.

mosities, then you may foment discord; but now cultivate harmony, and practice good will toward each other. Carthage was the most powerful rival of Rome. It was a very flourishing and commercial state. The interests of the two nations soon began to interfere, and a war broke out between them. A naval battle was fought off Sicily, in which the Carthaginians were victorious; but the Romans had the advantage by land. A peace was concluded very much to the disadvantage of the former. The Carthaginians gave up all the islands between Africa and Italy, and agreed to pay 2,200 talents annually, for twenty years, to the Romans. This took place in the year of Rome 513. Twenty-four years after this, a second war broke out between the two rival powers. Hannibal was commander-in-chief of the Carthaginians. He led his army into Spain, which he subjugated as far as the Iberus. He thence passed over the Alps into Italy, where he defeated the Romans in several engagements, with great slaughter, and filled Rome itself with fear and consternation; and if he had marched directly to Rome, it would, in all probability, have fallen before his victorious arms. In this juncture of affairs, Fabius Maximus was made dictator; who, by his prudent measures, and, above all, by his declining a general engagement, and protracting the war, in some measure, recovered the Roman affairs. In the mean time, Scipio was sent into Africa to attack Carthage. Hannibal was recalled to defend his country. The Romans, however, were victorious, and Carthage became tributary. The intrepid Hannibal saved his life by fleeing his country. This war lasted seventeen years. In the third Punic war, as it was called, Carthage was utterly rased, under the younger Scipio, in the year of Rome 608.

12. *Fera:* warlike—fierce.

13. *Apertas Alpes.* Scaliger thinks *per* is to be supplied; meaning that the Carthaginians marched through or over the Alps. This to be sure is the true meaning: but the construction will not bear it. We must not throw away the *atque.* Both Dr. Trapp and Ruæus understand the people of the Alps, whom Hannibal took with him. I can hardly think this to be the meaning. The expression is highly figurative and poetical. It represents Hannibal and his army pouring through the passages of the Alps, as if the mountains themselves were moved or sent against Rome.

14. *Tum licebit,* &c. The gods are here represented as divided and split into factions and parties. To calm their dissentions, Jove tells them a time will come when they may indulge their passions, and plunder and commit acts of violence. Dr. Trapp thinks the words *licebit,* &c. refer to the Trojans and Latins, on account of whom the gods were split into factions. It is common for writers, especially the poets, to ascribe the evil actions of men to the gods, under whose influence they were supposed to act. *Res:* the Roman state. Ruæus says, *Trojanas res.*

15. *Sinite:* be quiet—permit it to be so. *Componite:* in the sense of *facite,* vel *conciliate. Placitum:* in the sense of *destinatum. Quod placet mihi,* says Ruæus.

22. *Tegunt:* protect—defend.

23. *Miscent:* in the sense of *committunt*

24. *Ipsis aggeribus:* on the very ramparts of the walls.

27. *Nec non:* in the sense of *quoque,* vel *etiam. Imminet:* presses upon—besieges. Ruæus says, *instat.*

28. *Ætolis Arpis. Arpi* was a city of Apulia. It is called Ætolian from Ætolia, the country of Diomede, who led a colony into that part of Italy, and founded *Arpi.*

Tydides. Equidem, credo, mea vulnera restant:
Et tua progenies mortalia demoror arma.
Si sinè pace tuâ, atque invito numine, Troës
Italiam petière, luant peccata; neque illos
Juveris auxilio. Sin tot responsa secuti,
Quæ Superi Manesque dabant; cur nunc tua quisquam
Flectere jussa potest? aut cur nova condere fata?
Quid repetam exustas Erycino in litore classes?
Quid tempestatum regem, ventosque furentes
Æoliâ excitos? aut actam nubibus Irim?
Nunc etiam Manes (hæc intentata manebat
Sors rerum) movet: et superis immissa repentè
Alecto, medias Italûm bacchata per urbes.
Nil super imperio moveor: speravimus ista,
Dum fortuna fuit: vincant, quos vincere mavis.
Si nulla est regio, Teucris quam det tua conjux
Dura: per eversæ, genitor, fumantia Trojæ
Excidia obtestor; liceat dimittere ab armis
Incolumem Ascanium; liceat superesse nepotem.
Æneas sanè ignotis jactetur in undis;
Et, quamcunque viam dederit fortuna, sequatur:
Hunc tegere, et diræ valeam subducere pugnæ.
Est Amathus, est celsa mihi Paphos, atque Cythera,
Idaliæque domus: positis inglorius armis
Exigat hìc ævum. Magnâ ditione jubeto

30. Et *ego* tua progenies

31. Si Troës petière Italiam sine

33. Sin *fecerunt id* secuti tot responsa *oraculorum*, quæ

35. Aut cur *quisquam potest* condere

39. Nunc etiam *Juno* movet

40. Alecto immissa *in* superis *regionibus lucis*

43. Dum fortuna fuit *propitia: illi* vincant

45. O genitor, obtestor *te* per fumantia excidia

52. *Ascanius* inglorius exigat ævum hìc, armis positis.

NOTES.

He was the son of *Tydeus*. Turnus sent to him with a view to engage him in the war, but without success, as will appear in the following book. Venus, to aggravate her case, would insinuate that a Grecian army was approaching the Trojan camp under the conduct of great Diomede. This is the *hostis*, and the *alter exercitus*, just mentioned.

29. *Mea vulnera restant:* my wounds remain. Ruæus thinks this is a reference to the wound she received from Diomede, when she rescued Æneas from the encounter with that hero. Iliad, v. 335. And she fears the same thing may happen again. This elucidates the words *demoror mortalia arma.* But Venus may speak in the name of the Trojans, considering their wounds and sufferings as her own. *Demoror:* in the sense of *expecto.*

31. *Pace:* permission or leave. *Pace:* in the sense of *venia.* *Numine:* in the sense of *voluntate.*

34. *Manesque.* This perhaps refers to the predictions and intimations, which Æneas had received from the ghosts of Hector, Anchises and Creusa. *Manes*, sometimes are taken for the infernal gods. It is here opposed to *Superi*, the gods above.

35. *Flectere:* to avert or turn aside. *Fata:* purposes—decrees. *Condere:* to make—ordain—appoint. Ruæus says, *statuere.*

36. *In Erycino litore:* on the Sicilian shore. See Æn. v. 660. Where the Trojan matrons, at the instigation of Iris, set fire to their ships. *Repetam:* in the sense of *commemorem.*

37. *Regem:* Æolus king of the winds. See Æn. i.

39. *Manes movet.* Here *Manes* plainly means the infernal powers, whom Juno roused up against the Trojans, when she called up Alecto from her dire abode. This was the first time Juno had recourse to the powers below, to assist her in the destruction of the Trojans. This will help us to understand the words: *hæc sors rerum manebat intentata.* *Sors:* in the sense of *pars.*

41. *Bacchata: est* is understood.

42. *Moveor nil:* I am not solicitous about empire—I am not moved, &c.

46. *Liceat:* may it be permitted me to remove (or take) Ascanius, &c.

50. *Valeam:* I would wish to be able—I could desire to be permitted. *Tegere:* to protect—rescue.

51. *Amathus:* gen. *amathuntis;* a city of the island of Cyprus. *Hodie, Limisso.* *Paphos* or *Paphus;* another city of the same island. *Hodie, Paffo.* *Cythera:* neu. plu. an island between the Peloponnesus and Crete. *Idalium* or *Idalia:* a city of Cyprus. All these places were sacred to Venus.

52. *Domus:* in the sense of *sedes.*

54. Nihil *ortum* inde obstabit

55. Quid juvit *Ænean* evadere

57. Totque pericula maris, vastæque terræ *fuisse* exhausta, dum

61. Miseris Teucris

70. Num *persuasimus ei credere* summam belli, num credere muros puero? *Num persuasimus ei* agitare

Carthago premat Ausoniam: nihil urbibus inde
Obstabit Tyriis. Quid pestem evadere belli
Juvit, et Argolicos medium fugisse per ignes?
Totque maris, vastæque exhausta pericula terræ,
Dum Latium Teucri, recidivaque Pergama quærunt?
Non satiùs cineres patriæ insedisse supremos,
Atque solum, quo Troja fuit? Xanthum et Simoënta
Redde, oro, miseris; iterumque revolvere casus
Da, pater, Iliacos Teucris. Tum regia Juno
Acta furore gravi: Quid me alta silentia cogis
Rumpere, et obductum verbis vulgare dolorem?
Ænean hominum quisquam Divûmque subegit
Bella sequi, aut hostem regi se inferre Latino?
Italiam petiit fatis auctoribus, esto,
Cassandræ impulsus furiis. Num linquere castra
Hortati sumus, aut vitam committere ventis?
Num puero summam belli, num credere muros?
Tyrrhenamve fidem, aut gentes agitare quietas?
Quis Deus in fraudem, quæ dura potentia nostra
Egit? ubi hìc Juno, demissave nubibus Iris?

NOTES.

54. *Inde:* hence—from Ascanius. He will not be in the way, or oppose the Tyrian city.

55. *Pestem:* destruction—ruin.

57. *Exhausta:* undergone—finished—exhausted to the very dregs. The verb *esse*, vel *fuisse*, is understood.

58. *Recidiva.* Davidson thinks *recidiva*, here, means tottering again, or threatening a fall. But it also signifies, set up again after it is fallen, or rebuilt. Dr. Trapp takes it here in this sense. Commentators are not agreed upon the true import of the word. The whole speech of Venus is extremely artful, and well calculated to produce the desired effect. It is distinguished for its sweetness, tenderness, and pathos.

59. *Non satiùs:* would it not have been better for them to have settled upon, &c. The verb *esset*, vel *fuisset*, is understood.

62. *Da, pater:* grant, O, father, that they struggle again with the Trojan disasters; rather than continue in this state of suspense. These words, or words of the like import, appear to be requisite to complete the sense, and preserve the connexion.

63. *Acta:* in the sense of *impulsa* vel *agitata*.

64. *Obductum:* in the sense of *occultum*.

67. *Italiam petiit*, &c. This speech of Juno is very different from that of Venus: the one is tender, persuasive, and pathetic; the other haughty, imperious, and sarcastic. In the beginning, she acknowledges that Æneas undertook his voyage at the direction of the gods; but she will have it, that it was particularly at the instance of *Cassandra*, the daughter of Priam, a prophetess whom nobody believed. *Auctoribus:* advisers—persuaders, or the first movers.

68. *Furiis:* this Ruæus interprets by *vaticiniis.*

70. *Summam:* the management—chief command.

71. *Fidem, aut gentes, agitare*, &c. This is a difficult passage, arising partly from the conciseness of the expression, and partly from the falsehood of the assertion. Commentators are generally agreed that *fidem* is to be taken for alliance or friendship, in the sense of *fœdus.* To connect *agitare* with it in that sense, we must take the verb in the sense of *implorare*, which it will hardly bear. But if we take *fidem* to mean the loyalty and allegiance, which the Tuscans bore to Mezentius their king; and there is no reason, why it may not; then *agitare*, in its common acceptation, to disturb, shake or unsettle, may be connected with it, as well as with *quietas gentes.* It was not true, however, that the nations to which Æneas applied for assistance were at peace. For both the Tuscans and Arcadians were at war with the Latins. Heyne takes *agitare fidem*, in the sense of *solicitare societatem et fœdus.* *Quietas:* at peace.

72. *Quæ dura nostra:* what rigid power of ours. This refers to the epithet *dura*, which Venus uses in relation to her, verse 44. Commentators generally take *fraudem* to mean detriment—damage. Ruæus interprets it by *damnum*, and it may so mean here; for Juno, all along, reflects upon the false steps and bad management of Æneas. But it may also mean fraud, alluding to the attempt to draw the Tuscans from their allegiance to their king. Heyne takes *fraudem* in the sense of *malum.* Servius, in the sense of *periculum.* Davidson renders it

Indignum est, Italos Trojam circundare flammis
Nascentem, et patriâ Turnum consistere terrâ;
Cui Pilumnus avus, cui diva Venilia mater.
Quid, face Trojanos atrâ vim ferre Latinis?
Arva aliena jugo premere, atque avertere prædas?
Quid, soceros legere, et gremiis abducere pactas?
Pacem orare manu, præfigere puppibus arma?
Tu potes Æneam manibus subducere Graiûm,
Proque viro nebulam et ventos obtendere inanes;
Et potes in totidem classem convertere Nymphas:
Nos aliquid Rutulos contrà juvisse, nefandum est.
Æneas ignarus abest: ignarus et absit.
Est Paphos, Idaliumque tibi; sunt alta Cythera:
Quid gravidam bellis urbem, et corda aspera tentas?
Nos-ne tibi fluxas Phrygiæ res vertere fundo
Conamur? nos? an miseros qui Troas Achivis
Objecit? quæ causa fuit consurgere in arma
Europamque Asiamque, et fœdera solvere furto?

77. Quid *est illud*, Trojanos

79. Quid *est illud*, legere soceros, et abducere pactas *sponsas e* gremiis *sponsorum*?

84. Nos juvisse Rutulos aliquid contrà *Trojanos*.

85. Æneas ignarus *periculi urbis*.

89. *Num*, nos, *inquam*, an *ille Paris* qui

NOTES.

by the words "guileful measures," alluding to what is said in the preceding line.

74. *Indignum est:* it is a heinous crime, to be sure, that the Italians, &c.

76. *Pilumnus:* a king of the Rutuli, and reputed son of Jove. He was one of the ancestors of Turnus, and was deified. *Venilia:* she was the sister of Amata, and mother of Turnus. She also was made a goddess.

77. *Quid, Trojanos:* what is it for the Trojans to offer violence, &c. Servius explains *atra face*, by *sævo bello*. Dr. Trapp thinks this is an allusion to the story of Paris, whose mother dreamed she should bring forth a torch or fire-brand; he being the cause of the war, which proved the ruin of Troy. *Fax*, signifies the first motives or incentives to any thing. *Fax belli*, is therefore the commencement of war. *Incendia belli*, is a war when it hath come to its height, and lays every thing waste before it, like a devouring flame. *Atrâ face:* with black or hostile torches. Ruæus says, *nigris tædis*.

78. *Premere jugo:* to subjugate. *Arva:* in the sense of *terras* vel *regiones*.

79. *Legere*. Servius renders it, by *furari*. Hence they are called *Sacrilegi, qui sacra legunt;* i. e. *furantur*. *Pactas:* betrothed spouses; *sponsas* being understood, or perhaps it is implied in *pactas*. *Legere soceros:* to steal fathers-in-law; that is, to marry their daughters without their consent, and against their wills. Heyne says, *eligere—sumere*.

80. *Orare pacem:* to implore peace with the hand, and to fix arms on the sterns of their ships. This refers to the olive boughs, which they held in their hands as a sign of peace when they visited the court of Latinus. This is an invidious reflection of Juno, and entirely groundless. If it refer to the Latins, there was no crime in suing for peace, and being at the same time prepared for war. It was the most likely way to obtain it. If it relate to the Arcadians: they had no design of war upon them. Their arms were designed only to guard them against the insults of enemies on their passage to the court of Evander.

84. *Nefandum est:* it is a horrid crime for us, &c. The following line contains a most severe sarcasm. As if Juno had said: if Æneas, the general of an army, choose to be absent in so critical a juncture, and is not careful to inform himself of their state, let him, for aught I care, remain ignorant and never return.

87. *Urbem*. The city *Laurentum*, to the government of which Æneas would arrive, by marrying Lavinia. *Gravidam*. *potentem*, says Ruæus. *Aspera:* in the sense of *bellicosa*.

88. *Tibi*. This is either redundant, or used in the sense of *tuæ*, agreeing with *Phrygiæ*. Juno here speaks in the present time, though reference is had to the Trojan war. This change of tense is often very elegant. It gives life and animation to the subject. *Fluxas res*. Ruæus says, *fragile regnum*, the frail power of thy Troy.

89. *Qui*. This refers to Paris, who was the cause of the Trojan war. *Nos:* was it I, or was it not rather that Paris, who exposed the unhappy, &c.

91. *Furto:* here adultery, treachery. *Furtum* also signifies any private, or secret act of wickedness. An allusion is here made to the rape of Helen, which was an act of the basest kind; a most perfidious crime. After this the Greeks, we may suppose, would

Me duce, Dardanus Spartam expugnavit adulter?
Aut ego tela dedi, fovi-ve cupidine bella?
94 Tuis *Trojanis*
Tunc decuit metuisse tuis; nunc sera querelis
Haud justis assurgis, et irrita jurgia jactas.
Talibus orabat Juno: cunctique fremebant
Cœlicolæ assensu vario: ceu flamina prima
Cùm deprênsa fremunt sylvis, et cæca volutant
Murmura, venturos nautis prodentia ventos.
Tum pater omnipotens, rerum cui summa potestas,
Infit. Eo dicente, Deûm domus alta silescit,
Et tremefacta solo tellus, silet arduus æther:
103. Posuêre *flatum; pontus*
Tum Zephyri posuêre; premit placida æquora pontus
Accipite ergò animis atque hæc mea figite dicta.
Quandoquidem Ausonios conjungi fœdere Teucris
Haud licitum est, nec vestra capit discordia finem:
107. Secat *sibi factis, sive* fuat Tros, Rutulusve, habebo *eos*
Quæ cuique est fortuna hodie, quam quisque secat spem,
Tros Rutulusve fuat, nullo discrimine habebo:
109. Seu castra *Trojanorum* tenentur
Seu fatis Italûm castra obsidione tenentur,
Sive errore malo Trojæ, monitisque sinistris.
Nec Rutulos solvo. Sua cuique exorsa laborem
Fortunamque ferent. Rex Jupiter omnibus idem.
113. *Ille* annuit per flumina
Fata viam invenient. Stygii per flumina fratris,
Per pice torrentes atrâque voragine ripas

NOTES.

have no further intercourse, or treaties, with the Trojans: which is the idea conveyed in *solvere fœdera.* Heyne takes *furto,* in the sense of *raptu.*

92. *Expugnavit Spartam.* History informs us that Paris did not carry off Helen in an amicable manner, but by violence and force. In her heart, however, she might not have been averse to it. This the Trojan prince effected in the absence of the Grecian king, who had entertained him in a very hospitable manner. Juno here calls him an adulterer, and represents him as an insidious enemy. *Expugnavit:* he assaulted, &c.

93. *Fovi bella:* fomented—caused wars through lust. *Cupidine:* unlawful desire, or love.

94. *Nunc:* this refers to the time of the rape of Helen. Here Juno is extremely severe.

95. *Haud justis:* in the sense of *injustis. Jurgia:* reproaches—complaints.

97. *Vario assensu:* with various assent; some approved of the speech of Venus, others of the speech of Juno.

98. *Deprênsa:* caught—pent up in the woods. *Cæca murmura.* murmurs scarcely to be heard. *Prodentia:* intimating to, &c.

101. *Infit:* in the sense of *incipit.*

102. *Solo.* Whatever supports any thing may be called *solum. Solum terræ* would be the foundation of the earth. Ruæus says, *à fundamentis.*

103. *Premit;* levels—renders smooth. Ruæus says, *stesnit.*

107. *Quam spem,* &c. Servius and some others take *secat:* in the sense of *tenet* vel *habet.* But Turnebus, in the sense of *sumit;* and Ruæus, in the sense of *assumit:* takes, or assumes to himself; as when one divides a thing into parts or portions. Heyne differs from most commentators in the sense of the verb *secat.* He takes it in the sense of *incidere,* vel *perdere:* to cut off, or destroy by their actions.

109. *Fatis Italûm,* &c. This is generally understood of the fates unkind or hostile to the Italians. Ruæus interprets *fatis,* by *damno:* loss or damage. Davidson thinks *malis* is to be supplied.

110. *Malo errore:* whether by a fatal error of Troy, and inauspicious presages—whether the Trojans shall be successful in repelling the assaults of the Italians: this is expressed in the preceding line, *seu fatis:* or whether the Italians should prove victorious over the Trojans; these having been deceived by false predictions, and led into a fatal error, in coming hither to find a permanent settlement.

111. *Sua exorsa:* their own enterprises or actions shall bring to each party disaster or success. The issue of the war shall depend upon the parties engaged—I will assist neither. *Laborem:* Ruæus says, *damnum.*

112. *Idem:* in the sense of *æquus.* The verb *erit* is understood.

113. *Stygii fratris.* Pluto. See Geor. iii. 551.

Annuit, et totum nutu tremefecit Olympum
Hic finis fandi. Solio tum Jupiter aureo
Surgit; cœlicolæ medium quem ad limina ducunt.
  Intereà Rutuli portis circùm omnibus instant
Sternere cæde viros, et mœnia cingere flammis.
At legio Æneadûm vallis obsessa tenetur;
Nec spes ulla fugæ. Miseri stant turribus altis
Nequicquam, et rarâ muros cinxêre coronâ.
Asius Imbrasides, Hicetaoniusque Thymœtes,
Assaracique duo, et senior cum Castore Tymbris,
Prima acies: hos germani Sarpedonis ambo,
Et clarus, et Hæmon, Lyciâ comitantur ab altâ.
Fert ingens toto connixus corpore saxum,
Haud partem exiguam montis, Lyrnessius Acmon,
Nec Clytio genitore minor, nec fratre Mnestheo.
Hi jaculis, illi certant defendere saxis;
Molirique ignem, nervoque aptare sagittas.
Ipse inter medios, Veneris justissima cura,
Dardanius caput ecce puer detectus honestum,
Qualis gemma, micat, fulvum quæ dividit aurum,
Aut collo decus, aut capiti: vel quale per artem
Inclusum buxo, aut Oriciâ terebintho
Lucet ebur. Fusos cervix cui lactea crines
Accipit, et molli subnectit circulus auro.
Te quoque magnanimæ viderunt, Ismare, gentes
Vulnera dirigere, et calamos armare veneno,
Mæoniâ generose domo: ubi pinguia culta
Exercentque viri, Pactolusque irrigat auro.
Affuit et Mnestheus, quem pulsi pristina Turni
Aggere murorum sublimem gloria tollit;
Et Capys: hinc nomen Campanæ ducitur urbi.

125. *Hi sunt* prima acies

128. Lyrnessius Acmon, nec minor Clytio genitore, nec fratre Mnestheo, fert

130. Hi certant defendere *urbem* jaculis; illi *certant defendere eam* saxis

132. Ecce Dardanius puer ipse, justissima cura Veneris, detectus *quoad* honestum caput, inter medios, micat, qualis gemma

135. Vel quale ebur lucet per artem

141. Pinguia culta *arva*

143. Quem pristina gloria Turni pulsi aggere

NOTES.

115. *Annuit:* he ratified or confirmed it.

117. *Cœlicolæ medium*, &c. This alludes to the Roman custom of conducting the consul from the senate house to his own dwelling, or apartment.

120. *Legio Æneadûm:* simply the Trojans. The Trojans were called *Æneadæ*, from Æneas their leader.

122. *Cinxêre muros:* they defend the walls with thin ranks. Ruæus says, *exiguo numero*.

128. *Lyrnessius:* an adj. from Lyrnessum a city of Phrygia, near the *Sinus Adramyttenus*.

130. *Hi—illi.* Davidson renders these: some—others. Valpy refers the *hi* to the Rutulians who were assaulting the ramparts; and the *illi* to the Trojans who were defending them. But when these pronouns refer to separate members of the sentence, *ille* refers to the one first mentioned or more remote; and *hic* to the latter, or last mentioned.

131. *Molirique ignem:* to throw flames.

136. *Terebintho:* the *terebinthus*, or turpentine tree. Its wood bears a resemblance to ebony. *Oricia:* an adj. from *Oricum*, a town of Macedonia in the confines of Epirus, where those trees abounded.

140. *Armare:* in the sense of *ungere*. *Calamos:* darts, or missive weapons in general. *Generose:* voc. agreeing with *Ismare*: nobly descended from a Lydian family.

142. *Pactolus irrigat:* Pactolus waters them with its gold—golden stream. This was a small river, on whose banks stood the famous city Sardes, the capital of Lydia. Here Crœsus held his court. It empties into the Hermus, one of the largest rivers of Asia Minor, and with it flows into the sea near the city of Ephesus. They were both celebrated for their golden sands. The poet here supposes the water of the Pactolus to be of a golden hue.

145. *Campanæ urbi.* Capua, the capital of Campania. Here Hannibal took up his winter quarters. But the luxury and dissipation of the place, proved the ruin of his affairs in Italy.

Illi inter sese duri certamina belli
Contulerant: mediâ Æneas freta nocte secabat.
Namque ut ab Evandro castris ingressus Etruscis
Regem adit, et regi memorat nomenque genusque;
Quidve petat, quidve ipse ferat; Mezentius arma
Quæ sibi conciliet, violentaque pectora Turni
Edocet; humanis quæ sit fiducia rebus
Admonet, immiscetque preces. Haud fit mora: Tarchon
Jungit opes, fœdusque ferit. Tum libera fatis,
Classem conscendit jussis gens Lydia Divûm,
Externo commissa duci. Æneïa puppis
Prima tenet, rostro Phrygios subjuncta leones:
Imminet Ida super, profugis gratissima Teucris.
Hìc magnus sedet Æneas, secumque volutat
Eventus belli varios: Pallasque sinistro
Affixus lateri, jam quærit sidera, opacæ
Noctis iter; jam quæ passus terrâque marique.
  Pandite nunc Helicona, Deæ, cantusque movete
Quæ manus intereà Tuscis comitetur ab oris
Ænean, armetque rates, pelagoque vehatur.
  Massicus æratâ princeps secat æquora Tigri:
Sub quo mille manus juvenum; qui mœnia Clusî,
Quique urbem liquêre Cosas: queis tela, sagittæ,
Corytique leves humeris, et letifer arcus.
Unà torvus Abas: huic totum insignibus armis
Agmen, et aurato fulgebat Apolline puppis.
Sexcentos illi dederat Populonia mater
Expertos belli juvenes: ast Ilva trecentos,

148. Namque ut *primùm digressus* ab Evandro, *et* ingressus

150. Edocet quidve

157. Tenet prima *loca*, subjuncta *quoad* Phrygios leones rostro.

162. *Jam quærit* iter opacæ noctis; jam quæ *dura Æneas* passus *est*

167. Sub quo *erat* manus mille

170. Torvus Abas *erat* unà *cum illo*: huic totum agmen *fulgebat*

NOTES.

147. *Freta:* the waters of the Tiber. *Contulerant:* they had joined—engaged in. *Inter sese:* the two armies.

149. *Regem:* in the sense of *ducem* vel *imperatorem:* the commander, or chief officer. This was Tarchon.

150. *Ferat:* in the sense of *efferat.*

151. *Pectora:* the mind or temper. *Conciliet:* procures—gains over to his interest. This alludes to a supposed alliance with Turnus and the Rutulians.

154. *Opes:* troops—means of carrying on the war—power. *Ferit:* in the sense of *sancit.*

155. *Lydia gens:* after the expulsion of Mezentius, the Tuscans were forbidden by the fates to make themselves a king, unless he were a foreigner; or to march against him, unless under the command of a foreign general. They are free from this restraint, now that Æneas had arrived, and are at liberty to enter under his banner. The Tuscans were originally a colony from Lydia. Hence they are called *Lydia gens.* It is most likely, they had a fleet already prepared for an expedition. For in the short time Æneas was with them, they could not have built or even equipped one.

157. *Subjuncta.* The ship of Æneas had Phrygian lions yoked together, and placed under its prow or beak for its ensign. The lion was sacred to Cybele, who presided over Phrygia, and particularly over mount Ida, of whose pines Æneas had built his fleet.

158. *Ida:* the name of one of the galleys, commanded by Æneas in person. *Super imminet:* rises—towers above the rest.

161. *Quærit:* inquires concerning, &c.

165. *Pelago:* in the sense of *fluvio.*

167. *Clusî.* Clusium was a city of Tuscany. *Hodie, Chiusi.*

168. *Cosas:* the acc. plu. of *Cosæ* or *Cosa,* a maritime town of Tuscany, near the promontory *Argentarium. Cosas* is put in apposition with *urbem. Queis:* whose weapons were arrows, &c. *Queis:* in the sense of *quorum.*

169. *Coryti.* Corytus is a word originally Greek, of the same import with *pharetra,* a quiver.

172. *Populonia:* an adj. from Populonium, a city on the promontory of that name. It is called *mater,* in the sense that *Italia* is called *parens. Populonia mater:* simply, the city Populonium.

173. *Ilva:* an island to the south of Popu-

Insula inexhaustis Chalybum generosa metallis
Tertius, ille hominum Divûmque interpres Asylas,
Cui pecudum fibræ, cœli cui sidera parent,
Et linguæ volucrum, et præsagi fulminis ignes:
Mille rapit densos acie, atque horrentibus hastis.
Hos parere jubent Alpheæ ab origine Pisæ,
Urbs Etrusca solo. Sequitur pulcherrimus Astur,
Astur equo fidens et versicoloribus armis.
Ter centum adjiciunt, mens omnibus una sequendi,
Qui Cærete domo, qui sunt Minionis in arvis;
Et Pyrgi veteres, intempestæque Graviscæ.
Non ego te, Ligurum ductor fortissime bello,
Transierim, Cinyra; et paucis comitate, Cupavo,
Cujus olorinæ surgunt de vertice pennæ.
Crimen amor vestrum, formæque insigne paternæ.

175. Tertius *erat* ille Asylas interpres

178. *Ille* rapit mille *viros* densos acie

183. Qui *sunt ex* domo Cærete, qui sunt in arvis Minionis

186. Et *te*, O Cupavo, comitate paucis *militibus*

NOTES.

lonium. *Hodie, Elba.* It abounded in iron mines (*metallis*) according to Strabo. Virgil here calls them inexhaustible. This island sent three hundred men. *Generosa:* abounding in. Ruæus interprets it by *inclyta.* *Expertos:* expert—skilful.

177. *Ignes:* the flashes of the ominous lightning.

178. *Densos:* in the sense of *confertos.* *Milites* is understood.

179. *Pisæ, urbs Etrusca solo:* Pisæ, a city, Tuscan in its situation, Alphean in its origin, orders these troops to obey Asylas. This city stood on the western bank of the river Arnus, in Tuscany. It was supposed to have been founded by a colony from the Peloponnesus. Hence called *Alpheæ*, from *Alpheus*, a river of that country, on whose banks stood the famous city *Olympia Pisa.* *Solo:* in the sense of *situ.*

183. *Cærete domo:* from the city *Cære.* It was subject to Mezentius. *Hodie, Cerveteri.* *Minionis.* Minio was the name of a river. *Hodie, Mugnone.*

184. *Pyrgi.* These people inhabited a maritime town, not far from Cære, or Cæretanæ. It has long since been destroyed. *Graviscæ:* the name of a town on the seacoast, unwholesome on account of the fens or marshes in the neighborhood. It took its name from *gravitas aëris.* All these different cities, with one mind, enter the war.

185. *Ligurum:* the gen. of *Ligures*, the inhabitants of Liguria, an extensive country of Italy; a part of which is now the territory of Genoa.

186. *Cinyra—Cupavo.* This passage is obscure and difficult. It has divided the opinions of commentators. *Phaëton*, the son of Phœbus and Clymene, desired of his father the government of his chariot for one day; which with difficulty was granted him. The youth being unable to guide the fiery steeds, they turned from their diurnal track, and came so near the earth that it began to burn. He was thrown headlong into the Po. His sisters sought him every where. At length, finding his tomb on the banks of that river, they pined away with grief at the fate of their brother, and were transformed either into alder or poplar trees. See Ovid. Met. 2. Cinyra, king of the Ligures, was a near relation of Phaëton, and, grieving immoderately at his misfortune, was changed into a *Cycnus*, or swan. Dr Trapp takes *Cinyra* and *Cupavo* to have been brothers, the sons of him who was transformed into a swan. In this case, the application of *vestrum* is easy and proper. But to apply it to *Cupavo* alone, as most commentators do, is not so proper. He supposes their crime to have been the honoring of their father too much, by bearing his metamorphosed figure (the swan) engraven upon their shields, and his feathers on their helmets. Their love amounted to a crime, because it was for one whom the gods had punished for an offence committed against them, in his immoderate grief for Phaëton. Ruæus thinks *vestrum crimen*, to be the crime of the family in general, who, by their immoderate grief for Phaëton, offended the gods, and were many of them changed into other forms. It may be objected to the interpretation of Dr. Trapp, that *filius* is afterward used in the singular number. But he observes, though they were brothers, the oldest might be mentioned by way of distinction and eminence. Davidson reads, *Cycnus.* See Ecl. vi. 62. and Æn. v. 105. Heyne conjectures there is here an interpolation. He differs from commentators in general in the interpretation of verse 186. He connects Cinyra with Cupavo in the same member of the sentence. *Non transierim te, Cupavo, comitate à Cinyra, et paucis aliis*, is his ordo of construction.

188. *Amor crimen:* Ruæus says, *amor est crimen vestræ familiæ, et insigne petitum ex transformatione patris.*

190. Dum canit inter populeas frondes

195. Ille *Centaurus* instat

201. Sed non *est* unum genus omnibus. Illi gens *est* triplex *in origine: sunt* quaterni populi sub gente: *Mantua* ipsa *est* caput populis: *ejus* vires *sunt* de

205. Quos Mincius *oriens ex* patre Benaco, velatus.

Namque ferunt, luctu Cycnum Phaëtontis amati,
Populeas inter frondes umbramque sororum
Dum canit, et mœstum musâ solatur amorem;
Canentem molli plumâ duxisse senectam,
Linquentem terras, et sidera voce sequentem.
Filius, æquales comitatus classe catervas,
Ingentem remis Centaurum promovet: ille
Instat aquæ, saxumque undis immane minatur
Arduus, et longâ sulcat maria alta carinâ.
Ille etiam patriis agmen ciet Ocnus ab oris,
Fatidicæ Mantûs et Tusci filius amnis,
Qui muros, matrisque dedit tibi, Mantua, nomen
Mantua, dives avis, sed non genus omnibus unum.
Gens illi triplex, populi sub gente quaterni;
Ipsa caput populis; Tusco de sanguine vires.
Hinc quoque quingentos in se Mezentius armat,
Quos, patre Benaco, velatus arundine glaucâ,
Mincius infestâ ducebat in æquora pinu.
It gravis Auletes, centenâque arbore fluctum
Verberat assurgens: spumant vada marmore verso.
Hunc vehit immanis Triton, et cœrula conchâ

NOTES.

190. *Umbram sororum:* the shade of his sisters—the shade of the trees, into which his sisters were transformed.

191. *Musâ:* with music, or song.

192. *Canentem:* growing white, or being cloathed, with the downy plumes of the swan, passed out his old age, &c.

195. *Centaurum.* The name of the ship was the Centaur, so called from having a Centaur painted, or carved upon the stem, holding a huge stone in his hand, with which he seemed to threaten the waves. The *Centauri* were fabled to be monsters, half man and half horse. See Geor. ii. 456. *Promovet:* in the sense of *impellit.*

198. *Ocnus.* He was not the founder of Mantua; but rather the fortifier and enlarger. The same as Bianor. See Ecl. ix. 60. He gave it the name of Mantua, from *Manto*, the name of his mother. *Manto:* gen. *Mantûs*, the name of a nymph. Hence the epithet *fatidicæ:* prophetic. *Ciet:* in the sense of *movet* vel *ducit.*

201. *Sed non genus*, &c. It appears that the inhabitants of the Mantuan territory were not of one common origin. We are told they were partly from *Tuscia* or *Etruria*, partly from *Venetia*, and partly from *Gallia.* This explains *gens illi triplex:* implying that the population consisted of people from those three nations. The whole territory was divided into four cities, districts or communities: *populi sub gente quaterni.* Each of which had its Lucomon, or petty king. Of these four, Mantua was the principal or chief city, *ipsa caput populis.* This territory was a part of Etruria, which was divided into twelve lucommonies, or regalities. *Gens:* in the sense of *natio.* *Genus* · lineage—descent.

203. *Vires de Tusco*, &c. By this we are to understand that the Tuscan part of the Mantuan population was the greatest.

204. *Armat in se:* Mezentius arms, &c. He furnishes a just cause for their rising in arms against him.

205. *Patre Benaco.* The Benacus is a lake in the territory of Verona. *Hodie, Lago di Garda.* The river Mincius rises out of it. Hence the epithet *patre* is added to Benacus.

206. *Mincius:* here the god of the river Mincius. He is represented as moving down his stream in hostile ships to join in the war against Mezentius. Hence the epithet *patre*, which is common to all the deities. It is here given to the lake Benacus, out of which the river Mincius rises. *Velatus:* in the sense of *coronatus*, says Ruæus. *Pinu infesta.* Ruæus says, *navibus inimicis Mezentio.* *Pinus*, by meton. for *navis* vel *naves*

207. *Centena arbore:* with an hundred oars. The oar is here called *arbor*, to denote its size and magnitude. *Marmore verso:* the surface being upturned. *Vada*, here, is plainly put for the water of the Tiber; for, on this river, the fleet of Æneas was equipped. *It:* in the sense of *ducit.* Auletes was the commander of these troops.

209. *Triton.* He was the trumpeter of Neptune, and used *a shell* instead of a trumpet. His upper part was represented as a man, his lower part as a fish. Here the name

Exterrens freta: cui laterum tenùs hispida nanti
Frons hominem præfert, in pristin desinit alvus,
Spumea semifero sub pectore murmurat unda.
Tot lecti proceres ter denis navibus ibant
Subsidio Trojæ, et campos salis ære secabant.
  Jamque dies cœlo concesserat, almaque curru
Noctivago Phœbe medium pulsabat Olympum.
Æneas (neque enim membris dat cura quietem)
Ipse sedens clavumque regit, velisque ministrat.
Atque illi medio in spatio, chorus ecce suarum
Occurrit comitum, Nymphæ, quas alma Cybele
Numen habere maris, Nymphasque è navibus esse
Jusserat: innabant pariter, fluctusque secabant,
Quot priùs æratæ steterant ad litora proræ.
Agnoscunt longè regem, lustrantque choreis.
Quarum, quæ fandi doctissima, Cymodocea,
Ponè sequens, dextrâ puppim tenet: ipsaque dorso
Eminet, ac lævâ tacitis subremigat undis.
Tum sic ignarum alloquitur: Vigilasne, Deûm gens,
Ænea? vigila, et velis immitte rudentes.
Nos sumus Idææ sacro de vertice pinus,
Nunc pelagi Nymphæ, classis tua. Perfidus ut nos
Præcipites ferro Rutulus flammâque premebat:
Rupimus invitæ tua vincula, teque per æquor
Quærimus. Hanc genitrix faciem miserata refecit,
Et dedit esse Deas, ævumque agitare sub undis.
At puer Ascanius muro fossisque tenetur
Tela inter media, atque horrentes Marte Latinos.
Jam loca jussa tenet forti permixtus Etrusco
Arcas eques. Medias illis opponere turmas,
Ne castris jungant, certa est sententia Turno.

210. Cui *Tritoni* nanti hispida frons præfert hominem tenùs

219. Ecce chorus suarum comitum occurrit illi, *nempe* Nymphæ, quas

225. Quarum Cymodocea, quæ *est* doctissima fandi

228. Tum alloquitur *eum* ignarum *harum rerum* sic

231. *Olim* tua classis

235. Dedit *nos* esse Deas *maris*

NOTES.

of a ship; or the figure prefixed to the stern, like the *Centaur* above mentioned.

210. *Tenus laterum:* down to the waist.

214. *Ære:* with their brazen prows. *Æs* signifies any thing made of brass.

215. *Concesserat:* had given way—yielded to the night. *Nocti* is understood.

216. *Pulsabat:* arrived at—touched. Ruæus says, *attingebat. Olympum:* for *cœlum. Phœbe:* the moon.

221. *Habere numen maris:* to have divinity of the sea—to become nymphs of the sea.

224. *Lustrant:* in the sense of *circumeunt.*

227. *Eminet dorso:* she rises above the surface of the water with her back. *Subremigat:* she swims—rows herself along, &c.

228. *Gens:* in the sense of *soboles.*

229. *Immitte rudentes velis:* give the sheets to the sails—spread the sails to the full length of the halsers or sheets.

230. *Vertice:* in the sense of *monte.*

232. *Præcipites:* in the sense of *periclitantes*

234. *Refecit:* in the sense of *mutavit* changed us into this form. *Genitrix:* Cybele, the mother of the gods.

237. *Horrentes:* Ruæus says, *feroces. Marte:* in the sense of *bello.*

238. *Permixtus:* in the sense of *junctus. Etrusco:* the singular for the plu.: the valiant Tuscans.

239. *Arcas eques:* the Arcadian horse. These were the cavalry furnished by Evander. It is most probable that Æneas gave direction to the Arcadians and Tuscans, his allies, to repair to some particular place by land, while he went with the fleet by water; although no such place is mentioned by the poet. Turnus being informed of what was going on in Tuscany, and that Æneas was coming on with reinforcements, like a skillful general, resolves to intercept them, to attack them on the way, and prevent them from forming a junction with the Trojans in the camp, whom he was then blockading.

240. *Jungant:* join themselves to the camp—to the troops in the camp. The pron. *sese* is understood.

Surge, age, et Aurorâ socios veniente vocari
Primus in arma jube; et clypeum cape, quem dedit ipse
Invictum Ignipotens, atque oras ambiit auro.
Crastina lux, mea si non irrita dicta putâris,
Ingentes Rutulæ spectabit cædis acervos.
Dixerat: et dextrâ discedens impulit altam,
Haud ignara modi, puppim. Fugit illa per undas,
Ocyor et jaculo et ventos æquante sagittâ.
Inde aliæ celerant cursus. Stupet inscius ipse
Tros Anchisiàdes; animos tamen omine tollit.
Tum breviter, supera aspectans convexa, precatur
Alma parens Idæa Deûm, cui Dindyma cordi,
Turrigeræque urbes, bijugique ad fræna leones;
Tu mihi nunc pugnæ princeps; tu ritè propinques
Augurium, Phrygibusque adsis pede, Diva, secundo.
Tantum effatus: et intereà revoluta ruebat
Maturâ jam luce dies, noctemque fugârat.
Principio sociis edicit, signa sequantur,
Atque animos aptent armis, pugnæque parent se.
Jamque in conspectu Teucros habet et sua castra,
Stans celsâ in puppi. Clypeum tum deinde sinistrâ
Extulit ardentem. Clamorem ad sidera tollunt
Dardanidæ è muris. Spes addita suscitat iras
Tela manu jaciunt. Quales sub nubibus atris
Strymoniæ dant signa grues, atque æthera tranant
Cum sonitu, fugiuntque Notos clamore secundo.
At Rutulo regi ducibusque ea mira videri
Ausoniis; donec versas ad litora puppes
Respiciunt, totumque allabi classibus æquor.
Ardet apex capiti, cristisque à vertice flamma
Funditur, et vastos umbo vomit aureus ignes.
Non secùs ac liquidâ si quando nocte cometæ

247. Illa *navis*

252. Idæa *Cybele*, alma parens Deorum, cui Dindyma *sunt* cordi

253. Bijugique leones *Jocales* ad fræna;

256. *Æneas* effatus *est hæc* tantùm.

267. At ea *cœperunt* videri mira

270. Apex *galeæ* ardet capiti *Æneæ*

NOTES.

242. *Dedit:* in the sense of *reddidit.*

243. *Oras:* the borders or edges of the shield.

249. *Aliæ celerant:* the other nymphs accelerate the motion of the other ships, as Cymodocëa had done that of Æneas.

250. *Tollit animos.* Dr. Trapp understands this of Æneas taking courage himself. Davidson, of his encouraging his men. "He raises the spirits of his troops."

251. *Supera convexa:* the high canopy of heaven.

252. *Dindyma:* neu. plu. *Dindymus*, in the sing.: a mountain in Phrygia, so called from its having two tops. *Cordi:* for a delight.

254. *Propinques augurium:* render the omen propitious in due form. Ruæus says, *secundes omen benè—præsens sis hoc augurio.* Here the verb *propinquo*, though properly intransitive, becomes transitive, and has the acc. after it. Of *propinques augurium ritè*, Heyne says, *fac ostentum hoc ritè eventum suum habere.* La Cerda says, *facias augurium propitium.* Valpy: "by your own presence give effect to the augury."

255. *Phrygibus adsis:* aid the Trojans with thy propitious presence, *pede secundo*

259. *Aptent:* fit—prepare. Ruæus says, *excitent.*

265. *Grues dant*, &c. This comparison is taken from Homer. The cranes are called *Strymonian*, from Strymon, a river of Macedonia, in the confines of Thrace, where cranes abounded. *Signa:* signs or signals of the approaching storm by their voices.

269. *Totum æquor:* the whole surface of the water to be covered, &c. Ruæus says, *appelli.*

270. *Apex ardet capiti.* This description of the armor of Æneas, is taken from Homer's description of that of Achilles.

271. *Vomit:* in the sense of *emittit.* *Umbo:* the middle point of the shield, by synec. taken for the whole shield.

272. *Cometæ* Comets are planets irre-

Sanguinei lugubrè rubent; aut Sirius ardor,
Ille, sitim morbosque ferens mortalibus ægris,
Nascitur, et lævo contristat lumine cœlum.
Haud tamen audaci Turno fiducia cessit
Litora præripere, et venientes pellere terrâ.
Ultrò animos tollit dictis, atque increpat ultrò:
Quod votis optâstis, adest, perfringere dextrâ:
In manibus Mars ipse, viri. Nunc conjugis esto
Quisque suæ tectique memor; nunc magna referto
Facta, patrum laudes. Ultrò occurramus ad undam,
Dum trepidi, egressisque labant vestigia prima.
Audentes fortuna juvat.
Hæc ait: et secum versat, quos ducére contrà,
Vel quibus obsessos possit concredere muros.
Intereà Æneas socios de puppibus altis
Pontibus exponit. Multi servare recursus
Languentis pelagi, et brevibus se credere saltu;
Per remos alii. Speculatus litora Tarchon,
Quà vada non spirant, nec fracta remurmurat unda,
Sed mare inoffensum crescenti allabitur æstu,
Advertit subitò proras, sociosque precatur:
Nunc, ô lecta manus, validis incumbite remis:
Tollite, ferte rates: inimicam findite rostris

278. Ultrò tollit animos *suorum his* dictis

279. Adest *vobis* perfringere *hostem* dextrâ, quod

283. Dum *sunt* trepidi, primaque vestigia labant *iis* egressis *aquâ.*

285. Quos *possit* ducere contra *Ænean*, vel quibus

290. Alii *exponunt se* per remos.

NOTES.

gular in their motions, moving in very eccentric orbits. Sometimes they approach very near the sun; when they have a projection, or tail, which has a fiery or luminous appearance. This is always directly opposite the sun as seen from the comet, and is, most probably, its dense atmosphere, illuminated by the sun, and propelled by the force of the rays of light issuing from the sun. They were formerly considered ominous, portending disaster to men. The word is derived from the Greek. *Liquida:* a clear night.

273. *Rubent lugubrè:* blaze frightfully—balefully: that is, portending disaster to the world. *Sanguinei:* fiery—red. *Sirius ardor:* the star Sirius. It is sometimes called the dog-star, from the circumstance of its being in the sign *Canis*, or the dog. Sirius is here used as an adjective. It is a star of the first magnitude.

275. *Lævo:* inauspicious.

277. *Præripere:* in the sense of *antecapere.* It was the plan of Turnus to take possession of the shore, and, if possible, to prevent the landing of the troops. By doing this, he would have an advantage over them.

278. *Increpat.* This Ruæus interprets by *adhortatur. Ultrò animos.* This line is not found in several ancient MSS. Heyne marks it as an interpolation. *Ultrò*, here, implies that Turnus, immediately on seeing the enemy advance to the shore, addressed his men, and animated them to the contest. The address is short, but it bespeaks the soldier and the commander.

279. *Perfringere dextrâ.* Servius says this is a military phrase, and imports *facere fortiter. Adest:* it is arrived—the time is come. *Tempus* is understood.

280. *Mars ipse:* the battle is in your power, O men.

281. *Nunc referto:* now let each one imitate—call to his memory. Ruæus says. *memoret.*

282. *Laudes:* the glory of his ancestors. Davidson reads, *laudesque.* Others omit the *que.*

284. *Audentes:* the bold—courageous.

285. *Versat:* in the sense of *volvit.*

288. *Multi servare:* many began to observe the retreat of the ebbing sea, &c. The landing or debarkation of the troops was effected in three divisions. The one under Æneas landed on bridges thrown from the ships upon the shore. Another sought flats and shallows, which might be overflown when the tide was full, and bare at the ebb. They leap out upon these, and, by the help of oars, get to the shore. The division under Tarchon sought an open and smooth shore, where the waves flowed on without meeting with an impediment or obstacle; and where landing would be less dangerous. The verb *cœperunt* is understood.

289. *Languentis:* ebbing—falling.

291. *Spirant.* This is the reading of Heyne. The common reading is *sperat. Quà vada:* where the bottom or shallows

299. Socii *cœperunt* consurgere tonsis

302. Sed tua puppis non *erat innocua*

309. Totam aciem *suorum*, et sistit *eos* in litore contrà *Æneam.*

317. Nec longè *hinc* dejecit leto

319. Arma Herculis *juvêre* illos nihil; *suæ* validæ manus, genitorque Melampus, comes Alcidæ usque dum terra præbuit graves labores *illi*, juvêre *eos* nil.

323. Sistit *illud* in ore *ejus* clamantis. Tu quoque, O infelix Cydon, dum sequeris Clytium, *tua* nova gaudia, flaventem *quoad* malas primâ lanuginê, miserande *juvenis*, jaceres stratus Dardania dextrâ, securus amorum juvenum, qui semper erant *cari* tibi; ni

Hanc terram, sulcumque sibi premat ipsa carina
Frangere nec tali puppim statione recuso,
Arreptâ tellure semel. Quæ talia postquam
Effatus Tarchon, socii consurgere tonsis,
Spumantesque rates arvis inferre Latinis,
Donec rostra tenent siccum; et sedêre carinæ
Omnes innocuæ; sed non puppis tua, Tarchon.
Namque inflicta vadis dorso dum pendet iniquo,
Anceps sustentata diu, fluctusque fatigat,
Solvitur, atque viros mediis exponit in undis:
Fragmina remorum quos et fluitantia transtra
Impediunt, retrahitque pedes simul unda relabens
  Nec Turnum segnis retinet mora; sed rapit acer
Totam aciem in Teucros, et contrà in litore sistit.
Signa canunt. Primus turmas invasit agrestes
Æneas, omen pugnæ: stravitque Latinos,
Occiso Therone; virûm qui maximus ultrò
Æneam petit. Huic, gladio perque ærea suta,
Per tunicam squalentem auro, latus haurit apertum.
Inde Lycam ferit, exsectum jam matre peremptâ,
Et tibi, Phœbe, sacrum; casus evadere ferri
Quòd licuit parvo. Nec longè Cissea durum,
Immanemque Gyam, sternentes agmina clavâ,
Dejecit leto. Nihil illos Herculis arma,
Nil validæ juvêre manus, genitorque Melampus,
Alcidæ comes usque, graves dum terra labores
Præbuit. Ecce Pharo, voces dum jactat inertes,
Intorquens jaculum, clamantis sistit in ore.
  Tu quoque, flaventem primâ lanugine malas
Dum sequeris Clytium infelix, nova gaudia, Cydon,
Dardaniâ stratus dextrâ, securus amorum,
Qui juvenum tibi semper erant, miserande, jaceres;

NOTES.

were not rough. *Spirant:* in the sense of *æstuant.*

292. *Inoffensum:* smooth—unobstructed. *Nec fracta:* not broken—dashed against any obstruction.

296. *Premat:* in the sense of *aperiat.*

299. *Tonsis:* properly, the blade; by synec. the whole oar. *Remis*, says Ruæus.

301. *Siccum: locum* is understood.

302. *Innocuæ:* safe. Ruæus says, *illæsæ.*

303. *Iniquo dorso:* an uneven or broken bank of sand.

304. *Sustentata diu anceps:* continuing a long time in that dangerous situation. *Fatigatque fluctus.* Servius explains this by *fluctus fatigat navem;* taking *fluctus* for the nom. But it is easier, and more poetical to say: "the ship tires the waves." They beat and dash against it so long, that they may be said poetically and elegantly to be tired or wearied out. Valpy says, "buffets the waves."

310. *Canunt signa:* they sound the signal for the fight. *Canunt* in the sense of *sonant.*

311. *Omen:* in the sense of *initium* vel *faustum auspicium.*

313. *Suta:* part. pass. of the verb *suo* taken as a sub. the seams or folds of the shield—the shield itself. *Ærea suta:* the brazen shield. Some copies have *scuta.*

314. *Haurit:* in the sense of *transfigit. Huic:* in the sense of *hujus.*

315. *Exsectum:* cut out, or extracted from his mother, when dead.

316. *Ferri. Ferrum* here is the instrument with which his mother was opened. *Casus:* the danger of that instrument upon the body of the infant. *Parvo:* to him a child, or rather infant.

320. *Nil.* Heyne reads *nec.* The common reading is *nil.*

324. *Flaventem:* yellow as to his cheek. with the first down. His beard had just begun to grow.

325. *Nova gaudia:* in the sense of *novum amicum.* Heyne says, *delicias. Is qui amatur.*

326. *Securus amorum:* regardless of the love of the youths &c. because dead.

Ni fratrum stipata cohors foret obvia, Phorci
Progenies; septem numero, septenaque tela
Conjiciunt: partim galeâ clypeoque resultant
Irrita; deflexit partim stringentia corpus
Alma Venus. Fidum Æneas affatur Achaten:
Suggere tela mihi; non ullum dextera frustrà
Torserit in Rutulos; steterunt quæ in corpore Graiûm
Iliacis campis. Tum magnam corripit hastam,
Et jacit. Illa volans clypei transverberat æra
Mæonis, et thoraca simul cum pectore rumpit.
Huic frater subit Alcanor, fratremque ruentem
Sustentat dextrâ: trajecto missa lacerto
Protinùs hasta fugit, servatque cruenta tenorem,
Dexteraque ex humero nervis moribunda pependit.
Tum Numitor, jaculo fratris de corpore rapto,
Æneam petiit: sed non et figere contrà
Est licitum, magnique femur perstrinxit Achatæ.
Hìc Curibus, fidens primævo corpore, Clausus
Advenit, et rigidâ Dryopen ferit eminùs hastâ
Sub mentum graviter pressâ, pariterque loquenti
Vocem animamque rapit, trajecto gutture: at ille
Fronte ferit terram, et crassum vomit ore cruorem.
Tres quoque Threïcios, Boreæ de gente supremâ;
Et tres, quos Idas pater, et patria Ismara mittit,
Per varios sternit casus. Occurrit Halæsus,
Auruncæque manus: subit et Neptunia proles,

331. Alma Venus deflexit partim *tantùm* stringentia corpus *Æneæ.*

339. Protinus *altera* hasta missa, lacerto *Alcanoris* trajecto, fugit

350. Per varios casus sternit tres Threicios quoque, de suprema

NOTES.

330. *Partim:* a noun partitive: some of them. *Resultant:* in the sense of *resiliunt.*

331. *Deflexit:* turns aside, so that they just touched his body.

333. *Suggere:* give to me the darts, &c.

339. *Hasta protinùs missa.* It is generally thought by commentators that the same spear which killed Mæon, also wounded Alcanor in the arm. But it is difficult to conceive that a javelin, after it had passed through a shield of brass and a breast plate, should retain so much force as to pass through the body of a man, and in its course wound another person in the arm; and, after this, that it should continue its way some distance. Some conjecture they were different weapons: and for this there is considerable ground of probability. Those who think there was only one spear, rely much upon the word *protinùs*, which they say, means, strait-way—right forward; but it also means, forthwith—immediately. Beside, Alcanor did not seize his brother till he was in the act of falling, and the dart, consequently, done its execution, and passed from the body on its way. Granting that *strait-way* is the proper meaning of *protinùs* in this place, may it not refer to the quickness of Æneas in repeating his throws, as well as to the motion of the dart? After all, the supposition of there being two darts, makes the sense easier, and does no violence to the words.

After Æneas had killed Mæon, observing his brother in the act of supporting him, and bearing him off, immediately, so that there seemed to be no interval between the two darts, hurled one at him which passed through his shoulder; and, bloody from the wound it had inflicted, continued on its course for some distance. This is the opinion of Heyne. He says, *hasta alia missa ab Ænea.*

343. *Contrà:* in the sense of *vicissim.*

345. *Curibus:* from *Cures.* This was a city of the Sabines. Of this city was *Clausus*, who commanded the Sabine troops. See Æn. vii. 707.

347. *Pressâ graviter:* driven with violence under his chin. *Pressa* agrees with *hastâ.* *Pariter:* in the sense of *simul.*

350. *Boreæ.* *Boreas*, properly, the north wind, fabled to have been the son of the river Strymon in Macedonia, or rather of the god of the river Strymon. *Suprema:* in the sense of *altâ* vel *sublimi.* Some take it in the sense of *extrema*, remote: meaning they were a remote or distant nation of the earth.

351. *Ismara:* a city of Thrace, not far from mount *Ismarus*, according to Servius.

352. *Casus:* in the sense of *modos*

Insignis Messapus equis. Expellere tendunt
Nunc hi, nunc illi. Certatur limine in ipso
Ausoniæ. Magno discordes æthere venti
Prælia ceu tollunt, animis et viribus æquis:
Non ipsi inter se, non nubila, non mare, cedunt:
Anceps pugna diu, stànt obnixa omnia contrà
Haud aliter Trojanæ acies, aciesque Latinæ
Concurrunt: hæret pede pes, densusque viro vir
  At parte ex aliâ, quâ saxa rotantia latè
Impulerat torrens, arbustaque diruta ripis,
Arcadas, insuetos acies inferre pedestres,
Ut vidit Pallas Latio dare terga sequaci:
Aspera queis natura loci dimittere quando
Suasit equos; unum quod rebus restat egenis;
Nunc prece, nunc dictis virtutem accendit amaris;
Quò fugitis socii? per vos, et fortia facta,
Per ducis Evandri nomen, devictaque bella,
Spemque meam, patriæ quæ nunc subit æmula laudis,
Fidite ne pedibus. Ferro rumpenda per hostes
Est via, quâ globus ille virûm densissimus urget:
Hâc vos, et Pallanta ducem patria alta reposcit
Numina nulla premunt; mortali urgemur ab hoste
Mortales; totidem nobis animæque manusque.
Ecce, maris magno claudit nos objice pontus:
Deest jam terra fugæ: pelagus, Trojamne petemus?
Hæc ait: et medius densos prorumpit in hostes.
  Obvius huic primùm, fatis adductus iniquis,
Fit Lagus: hunc, magno vellit dum pondere saxum,

354. Nunc hi, nunc illi tendunt expellere *alii alios è loco.*

358. Ipsi *venti* non inter se, non nubila. non mare, cedunt

364. Ut *primùm* Pallas vidit Arcadas, insuetos

368. *Ille* accendit virtutem *suorum*, nunc prece, nunc amaris dictis; quod unum

369. *Oro*, per vos, et fortia facta

374. Hâc *parte* alta patria reposcit.

375. *Nos* mortales urgemur ab mortali hoste; *sunt* nobis totidem animæque manusque, *quot sunt illis.*

NOTES.

354. *Messapus.* See Æn. vii. 691. He is there called *domitor equûm*, because the horse was sacred to Neptune, his reputed father. Hence he is called, *Neptunia proles.*

358. *Cedunt.* The common reading is *cedit* in the sing. Heyne reads *cedunt*, which is preferable.

359. *Obnixa.* Some copies have *obnixi.* But Pierius informs us that he found *obnixa* in all the ancient manuscripts which he examined. It makes the sense easier, and is probably the correct reading. All things stand struggling against one another: *venti ventis, nubes nubibus, mare mari.* Heyne reads, *obnixa.* Valpy has *obnixi.*

363. *Arbusta*: in the sense of *arbores.*

364. *Inferre pedestres acies:* to sustain a fight on foot: simply, to fight on foot.

A part of the field of battle was rough and uneven ground, occasioned by the floods of the Tiber, or some torrent from the hills. Here the Arcadians chanced to fall, and being cavalry, they could not use their horses, and were obliged to dismount, and oppose the Latins on foot. But being unaccustomed to this mode of fight, they were soon thrown into confusion, and were fleeing before the enemy. In this critical state of affairs, Pallas hastened along the ranks, the only thing that remained to be done, to rally his men, and bring them up to the charge. He puts them in mind that their only hope of safety is in victory. He mentions their valiant achievements, their battles won, the name of their venerable monarch, &c. Upon this occasion, Pallas manifested the intrepid cammander.

365. *Latio:* the country, put by meton. for the inhabitants. *Sequaci:* valiant—or pursuing them in flight.

366. *Dimittere:* to dismount—to leave their horses. *Queis:* to whom, to wit, the Arcadians.

367. *Suasit:* in the sense of *coëgit.*

370. *Ducis:* in the sense of *regis. Devicta bella:* your victorious wars. Ruæus says, *relatas victorias.*

371. *Subit:* in the sense of *surgit. Patriæ laudis:* my father's glory.

374. *Reposcit:* in the sense of *vocat.*

377. *Maris:* in the sense of *aquæ.*

378. *Petemus.* The meaning is: we must either cast ourselves into the sea, and there perish, or cut our way through the enemy to the Trojan camp. Nothing else remains for us. We have no place for flight.

382. *Discrimina costis:* division—separa-

Intorto figit telo, discrimina costis
Per medium quâ spina dedit: hastamque receptat
Ossibus hærentem. Quem non super occupat Hisbon,
Ille quidem hoc sperans: nam Pallas antè ruentem,
Dum furit, incautum, crudeli morte sodalis,
Excipit, atque ensem tumido in pulmone recondit.
Hinc Sthenelum petit, et Rhœti de gente vetustâ
Anchemolum, thalamos ausum incestare novercæ.
Vos etiam gemini, Rutulis cecidistis in arvis,
Daucia, Laride Thymberque, simillima proles,
Indiscreta suis, gratusque parentibus error:
At nunc dura dedit vobis discrimina Pallas.
Nam tibi, Thymbre, caput Evandrius abstulit ensis:
Te decisa suum, Laride, dextera quærit;
Semianimesque micant digiti, ferrumque retractant.
Arcadas accensos monitu, et præclara tuentes
Facta viri, mixtus dolor et pudor armat in hostes.
Tum Pallas bijugis fugientem Rhœtea præter
Trajicit. Hoc spatium, tantùmque moræ fuit Ilo.
Ilo namque procul validam direxerat hastam:
Quam medius Rhœteus intercipit, optime Teuthra,
Te fugiens, fratremque Tyren: curruque volutus
Cædit semianimis Rutulorum calcibus arva.
Ac velut optatò, ventis æstate coortis,
Dispersa immittit sylvis incendia pastor:
Correptis subitò mediis, extenditur unà
Horrida per latos acies Vulcania campos:
Ille sedens victor flammas despectat ovantes.
Non aliter sociûm virtus coit omnis in unum,
Teque juvat, Palla. Sed bellis acer Halæsus
Tendit in adversos, seque in sua colligit arma.

382. Figit hunc intorto telo, quà spina dedit discrimina costis per medium *dorsi*, dum

384. Quem *stantem* super *Lagum*

385. Nam Pallas excipit *eum* antè ruentem, incautum, dum

390. Vos etiam gemini *fratres*, Laride, Thymberque, cecidistis in Rutulis arvis.

399. Fugientem præter *eum* bijugis

400. Hoc fuit spatium *vitæ* tantùmque moræ *ad mortem* Ilo

407. Mediis *sylvis* subitò

412. In *hostes* adversos

NOTES.

tion—parting to the ribs. Ruæus says, *divortium costarum.*

383. *Receptat:* in the sense of *retrahit.*

384. *Occupat:* in the sense of *intercipit.*

389. *Anchemolum.* He was the son of Rhœtus, king of the *Marrubii*, a people of Italy. He had an amour with his step-mother Casperia. To escape the vengeance of his father, he fled to Turnus.

391. *Daucia proles simillima:* these sons of Daucus, Laridus, and Thymber, resembled each other so exactly—were so much alike, that they could not be distinguished from each other even by their parents. *Gratus error:* a pleasing error, or delusion.

393. *Dura discrimina:* cruel—fatal distinction. He singled those two brothers from among the rest of the enemy, as the particular objects of his vengeance.

394. *Evandrius ensis:* the sword of Pallas, the son of Evander. He cut off the head of Thymber, and the right hand of Laridus. This explains the following line: *dextera decisa:* thy right hand cut off, seeks thee its owner.

396. *Micant:* in the sense of *movent.*

400. *Hoc spatium*, &c. The circumstance of Rhœteus intercepting the dart aimed at Ilus, which would have killed him, gave him a short space or time of life, and was so much respite from death.

404. *Cædit:* in the sense of *pulsat*, vel *ferit.*

405. *Optatò:* to his wish.

406. *Dispersa:* scattered abroad.

408. *Horrida Vulcania acies:* the horrid squadrons of fire, &c. This conveys a lively idea of a devouring fire raging without control, and increasing its forces in its progress, like an army pouring troops after troops. Servius censures the poet in applying *acies*, troops, or marshalled squadrons, to fire. The expression, to be sure, is bold, but not incongruous. The word in poetry is applied to fire, spreading and raging, and destroying every thing in its way, like a desolating army. *Vulcania:* an adj. from *Vulcanus* the god of fire; by meton. fire itself.

409. *Ovantes:* exulting—victorious.

411. *Acer:* valiant—intrepid in war.

412. *Colligit se:* he stoops, and contracts

Hic mactat Ladona, Pheretaque, Demodocumque,
Strymonio dextram fulgenti diripit ense,
Elatam in jugulum: saxo ferit ora Thoantis,
Ossaque dispergit cerebro permixta cruento.
Fata canens sylvis genitor celârat Halæsum:
Ut senior leto canentia lumina solvit,
Injecêre manum Parcæ, telisque sacrârunt
Evandri: quem sic Pallas petit, antè precatus:
Da nunc, Tybri pater, ferro, quod missile libro,
Fortunam atque viam duri per pectus Halæsi:
Hæc arma exuviasque viri tua quercus habebit.
Audiit illa Deus: dum texit Imaona Halæsus,
Arcadio infelix telo dat pectus inermum.
At non, cæde viri tantâ perterrita, Lausus,
Pars ingens belli, sinit agmina. Primus Abantem
Oppositum interimit, pugnæ nodumque moramque
Sternitur Arcadiæ proles, sternuntur Etrusci:
Et vos, ô Graiis imperdita corpora, Teucri.
Agmina concurrunt, ducibusque et viribus æquis:
Extremi addensent acies; nec turba moveri
Tela manusque sinit. Hinc Pallas instat et urget;
Hinc contrà Lausus: nec multùm discrepat ætas;
Egregii formâ; sed queis fortuna negârat
In patriam reditus. Ipsos concurrere passus
Haud tamen inter se magni regnator Olympi:
Mox illos sua fata manent majore sub hoste.
Intereà soror alma monet succurrere Lauso

426. At Lausus, ingens pars belli, non sinit agmina perterrita *esse*

430. Et vos, O Teucri, *quorum* corpora *erant* imperdita Graiis, *caditis.*

434. Hinc Lausus *instat et urget* contrà

435. *Ambo erant* egregii formâ.

NOTES.

himself behind the covert of his armor, particularly his shield.

413. *Mactat:* in the sense of *interficit.*

414. *Strymonio:* the dat. in the sense of the gen. He cut off the right hand of Strymonius, raised against his throat—raised for the purpose of cutting the head from Halæsus. *Diripit:* in the sense of *abscindit.*

416. *Dispergit:* in the sense of *Diffindit.*

417. *Canens:* in the sense of *prædicens,* agreeing with *genitor.* *Fata:* in the sense of *mortem ejus.*

418. *Ut solvit:* as soon as the old man closed (loosed) his eyes in death, the fates, &c. Ruæus interprets *canentia* by *senilia.* Heyne considers the words *lumina canentia,* as referring to the gray hairs, eye brows, and beard of the old man—to his appearance in general, without a particular reference to the color of his eyes.

421. *Libro:* in the sense of *mitto.*

422. *Duri:* hardy—valiant.

425. *Inermum:* naked—unprotected by his armor. *Dat:* in the sense of *offert.*

426. *Tanta cædê viri.* Most commentators take this for *cæde tanti viri,* by hypallage: at the slaughter or death of so great a man; to wit, Halæsus. But it is easier, and more natural to understand it of the great slaughter, and havoc made by Pallas.

428. *Nodum moramque:* the strength, and support of the fight. The words imply that he, (Abas,) made a firm stand against the enemy—that he was the life and soul of the fight, and a principal obstacle to victory Ruæus interprets *nodum,* by *difficultatem.*

430. *Imperdita:* not slain—destroyed. Reference is here made to the Trojan war, which proved fatal to so many Trojans.

432. *Extremi,* &c. The meaning appears to be this: that the rear ranks pressed upon the front, who were already engaged, that they also might come into action. By this means, the men became so close that they could not move their hands, or wield their weapons. *Turba:* the crowd.

433. *Pallas—Lausus.* One would naturally suppose, that the poet would have made these two young princes, so equally matched in every respect, try the fortune of the fight. But he well knew that it would be more to their glory, to fall by the hand of a superior foe, than to kill each other. He makes a fine use of their deaths afterward. The former was slain by Turnus, the latter by Æneas.

438. *Fata:* in the sense of *mors.*

439. *Soror alma:* the nymph Juturna, the sister of Turnus. She was made a nymph by Jove, who had an amour with her, as a

Turnum, qui volucri curru medium secat agmen.
Ut vidit socios: Tempus desistere pugnæ;
Solus ego in Pallanta feror; soli mihi Pallas
Debetur: cuperem, ipse parens spectator adesset.
Hæc ait: et socii cesserunt æquore jusso.
At Rutulûm abscessu, juvenis tum jussa superba
Miratus, stupet in Turno; corpusque per ingens
Lumina volvit, obitque truci procul omnia visu;
Talibus et dictis it contra dicta tyranni:
Aut spoliis ego jam raptis laudabor opimis,
Aut leto insigni: sorti pater æquus utrique est:
Tolle minas. Fatus medium procedit in æquor.
Frigidus Arcadibus coit in præcordia sanguis.
Desiluit Turnus bijugis, pedes apparat ire
Cominùs. Utque leo, speculâ cùm vidit ab altâ
Stare procul campis meditantem prælia taurum,
Advolat; haud alia est Turni venientis imago.
Hunc ubi contiguum missæ fore credidit hastæ,
Ire prior Pallas, si quà fors adjuvet ausum,
Viribus imparibus; magnumque ita ad æthera fatur:
Per patris hospitium, et mensas, quas advena adîsti,
Te precor, Alcide, cœptis ingentibus adsis:
Cernat semineci sibi me rapere arma cruenta,
Victoremque ferant morientia lumina Turni.
Audiit Alcides juvenem, magnumque sub imo
Corde premit gemitum, lachrymasque effudit inanes.
Tum genitor natum dictis affatur amicis:
Stat sua cuique dies; breve et irreparabile tempus
Omnibus est vitæ: sed famam extendere factis,
Hoc virtutis opus. Trojæ sub mœnibus altis
Tot nati cecidere Deûm: quin occidit unà
Sarpedon, mea progenies. Etiam sua Turnum
Fata vocant, metasque dati pervenit ad ævi.

441. *Inquit:* ***est*** **tempus**

443. Cuperem *ut ejus* parens

454. Utque leo advolat, cûm ab alta specula vidit taurum stare

458. *Cœpit* ire prior, imparibus viribus, ***tentans*** si quà

460. O Alcide, precor te, per

462. *Turnus* cernat me rapere

NOTES.

compensation for her violated chastity. See Æn. xii. 138. *et sequens.*

440. *Secat:* in the sense of *dividit.*

444. *Cesserunt æquore jusso:* retired from the commanded plain—from that part of the field of battle, where Pallas was, to make room for Turnus to advance against him.

447. *Obit:* surveys. *Omnia* may refer to his armor more particularly, than to his person. That had been mentioned just before. *Truci visu:* with a stern or steady look.

448. *It:* in the sense of *dicit,* vel *respondet.*

449. *Spoliis opimis.* For the *spolia opima,* see Æn. vi. 855—859.

450. *Pater æquus.* Dryden takes *pater* here for Jupiter, who, it is true, may be considered the father of all, just and impartial. But it is better to take it for Evander, the father of Pallas. It was the same thing to him whether his son were slain, or returned victorious. He was equally prepared for either event. *Equus:* in the sense of *paratus.*

452. *Coit:* congeals. It retired from the extremities to the heart; there thickened, and ceased to circulate. Such was the fear of the Arcadians for the issue of the combat. *Apparat:* in the sense of *parat.*

457. *Contiguum:* within reach of his missive spear.

460. *Hospitium.* Hercules, on his return from Spain, was entertained by Evander, and after the death of Cacus was magnificently worshipped. See Æn. viii. 184. *et sequens.*

461. *Adsis:* may you favor—aid.

462. *Rapere:* in the sense of *auferre.*

463. *Ferant:* may the dying eyes of Turnus endure to behold me victorious.

466. *Natum:* Hercules. He was the son of Jupiter by Alcmene, the wife of Amphitryon. Hence, sometimes called Amphitryoniades.

467. *Stat:* is fixed.

472. *Ad metas dati ævi:* to the end of his appointed life.

476. Illa *hasta* volans incidit, quà summa

482. Ac cuspis *teli* transverberat medium clypeum vibranti ictu, tot terga ferri, tot æris, cùm pellis tauri circumdata toties obeat *eum*, perforatque moras

486. Ille *Pallas* frustrà

488. Arma dedêre sonitum super *eum*.

492. Remitto *filium* Pallanta *ei*

495. Et fatus talia pressit *eum* exanimem

497. Nefasque impressum *in eo*, *nempe*, manus juvenum cæsa *fuerit* fœdè

501. *O* mens hominum nescia

503. Cùm optaverit *se* emptum *esse* magno *pretio* Pallanta intactum *esse*

504. Diemque, *quò interfecit eum.*

Sic ait, atque oculos Rutulorum rejicit arvis
  At Pallas magnis emittit viribus hastam,
Vaginâque cavâ fulgentem deripit ensem.
Illa volans, humeris surgunt quà tegmina summa,
Incidit, atque viam clypei molita per oras,
Tandem etiam magno strinxit de corpore Turni.
Hìc Turnus ferro præfixum robur acuto
In Pallanta diu librans jacit, atque ita fatur:
Aspice, num magè sit nostrum penetrabile telum.
  Dixerat: at clypeum, tot ferri terga, tot æris,
Cùm pellis toties obeat circumdata tauri,
Vibranti cuspis medium transverberat ictu,
Loricæque moras, et pectus perforat ingens.
Ille rapit calidum frustrà de vulnere telum:
Unâ eâdemque viâ sanguisque animusque sequuntur
Corruit in vulnus; sonitum super arma dedêre;
Et terram hostilem moriens petit ore cruento.
Quem Turnus super assistens:
Arcades, hæc, inquit, memores mea dicta referte
Evandro: qualem meruit, Pallanta remitto.
Quisquis honos tumuli, quicquid solamen humandi est,
Largior. Haud illi stabunt Æneïa parvo
Hospitia. Et lævo pressit pede, talia fatus,
Exanimem, rapiens immania pondera baltei,
Impressumque nefas; unâ sub nocte jugali
Cæsa manus juvenum fœdè, thalamique cruenti;
Quæ bonus Eurytion multo cælaverat auro:
Quo nunc Turnus ovat spolio, gaudetque potitus.
  Nescia mens hominum fati, sortisque futuræ,
Et servare modum, rebus sublata secundis!
Turno tempus erit, magno cùm optaverit emptum
Intactum Pallanta; et cùm spolia ista diemque

NOTES.

473. *Rejicit oculos:* he turned his eyes from, &c. that he might not behold a death, which he would have prevented, but was not able. Ruæus interprets the words by *retulit oculos ad campos.* Heyne says, *jacit retrò—avertit.*

477 *Molita viam:* opening, or making a way for itself, &c. A part. agreeing with *hasta*, understood.

478. *Strinxit:* it glanced from, &c. It hit his body, but did not wound him.

479. *Robur:* a dart, or javelin. *Magè*, for *magis.*

481. *Penetrabile:* penetrating. Adjectives of this form are generally passive in their signification. There are some few instances of their being used in an active sense This is one of them.

482. *Terga:* in the sense of *laminæ:* so many plates of iron, so many, &c. The spear of Turnus passed through (*transverberat*) the middle of his shield, which was composed of so many plates, &c.

483 *Cùm* · in the sense of *quamvis.* *Obeat circumdata:* simply, for *circumdatur.* Or, *circumdata* may be taken in the sense of *complicata:* folded up—doubled.

485. *Moras:* any thing that prevents—a stop or hindrance. It is here used for the folds and texture of the coat of mail.

490. *Assistens:* in the sense of *stans.*

493. *Humandi:* a gerund in *di*, in the sense of *humationis* vel *sepulchri.*

494. *Largior:* I freely bestow, or grant it. Ruæus says, *concedo.*

497. *Sub una jugali nocte*, &c. The story of the daughters of Danaus, who murdered their husbands in the night of their marriage, is here meant. See nom. prop. under *Danaïdes.*

499. *Eurytion.* The name of some artificer. The belt of Pallas was covered or overlaid with gold; in which this horrid crime was carved or engraven. *Bonus:* skilful. *Nefas:* any great or horrid crime, also, a wicked or odious person.

502. *Modum:* moderation—bounds.

503. *Erit:* in the sense of *veniet.*

Oderit. At socii multo gemitu lachrymisque
Impositum scuto referunt Pallanta frequentes.
O, dolor, atque decus magnum, rediture, parenti!
Hæc te prima dies bello dedit, hæc eadem aufert
Cùm tamen ingentes Rutulorum linquis acervos.
Nec jam fama mali tanti, sed certior auctor
Advolat Æneæ, tenui discrimine leti
Esse suos; tempus versis succurrere Teucris.
Proxima quæque metit gladio, latumque per agmen
Ardens limitem agit ferro, te, Turne, superbum
Cæde novâ, quærens. Pallas, Evander, in ipsis
Omnia sunt oculis; mensæ, quas advena primas
Tunc adiit, dextræque datæ. Sulmone creatos
Quatuor hìc juvenes, totidem, quos educat Ufens,
Viventes rapit: inferias quos immolet umbris,
Captivoque rogi perfundat sanguine flammas.
Inde Mago procul infensam contenderat hastam:
Ille astu subit, ac tremebunda supervolat hasta:
Et genua amplectens effatur talia supplex:
Per patrios Manes, et spes surgentis Iüli,
Te precor, hanc animam serves natoque patrique.
Est domus alta: jacent penitùs defossa talenta
Cælati argenti: sunt auri pondera facti
Infectique mihi: non hìc victoria Teucrûm
Vertitur: haud anima una dabit discrimina tanta.
Dixerat: Æneas contrà cui talia reddit:
Argenti atque auri, memoras quæ, multa talenta,
Natis parce tuis: belli commercia Turnus
Sustulit ista prior, jam tum Pallante perempto.

507. O *Palla*, rediture dolor, atque magnum decus parenti!

516. *Imprimis* mensæ, quas primas *ille* tunc advena adiit,

518. Hìc rapit quatuor juvenes, creatos Sulmone; totidem, quos Ufens educat, *omnes* viventes: quos immolet *tanquam* inferias umbris *Pallantis*

525. *Ut* serves hanc animam

532. Parce tuis natis multa talenta argenti

NOTES.

506. *Referunt:* his friends gathering in crowds, (*frequentes*) carry his body from the field of battle.

507. *O dolor*, &c. This is an exclamation either of the poet, or of his companions, bearing away the dead body, with a view to the grief of Evander when he should hear of the death of his son. But his grief would be in some measure lightened by the consideration of his distinguished actions.

510. *Auctor:* in the sense of *nuntius. Certior:* in the sense of *certus. Fama:* a report or rumor.

511. *Tenui discrimine:* in a small distance—in great hazard of. *Modico interstitio mortis*, says Servius. *Parùm distare ab exitio*, says Ruæus.

512. *Suos socios* is understood. *Tempus: esse* is understood.

514. *Agit:* in the sense of *facit:* he cuts down—forces with his sword, &c.

519. *Umbris:* the plu. for *umbrâ* in the sing. as in Æn. v. 81, which see. *Inferias:* offerings to the dead. These were poured upon, or into the grave. They were milk, honey, wine, &c. Upon these, it was supposed, the *umbra* feasted.

520. *Perfundat:* might wet, or sprinkle.

521. *Contenderat:* in the sense of *mittebat*

522. *Subit:* he stoops. *Astu:* with dexterity.

524. *Per patrios manes*, &c. This address of Magus is imitated from Homer, Iliad vi where Adrastus supplicates Agamemnon But the Roman poet has much improved upon the Greek. Mr. Pope observes, that nothing could be a more artful piece of address than the first lines of this supplication, when we consider the character of Æneas, to whom it was made: *per patrios Manes*, &c.

526. *Defossa penitùs:* buried deep in the earth.

527. *Pondera:* masses: plu. of *pondus. Auri facti.* By this we are to understand, gold wrought into vases, statues, &c. *Auri infecti:* of bullion—gold unwrought. *Cælati:* of embossed silver—silver carved or wrought into vases.

529. *Tanta discrimina:* so great difference. The victory of the Trojans does not turn upon this point (*hìc.*) My life can make no great difference; beside, you shall be abundantly rewarded for your clemency in doing it.

532. *Ista commercia:* those terms or conditions. *Ista pacta belli*, says Ruæus

534. Manes patris Anchisæ sentiunt

536. Abdidit ensem tenus capulo *in corpus ejus* orantis. Nec *erat* Æmonides procul,

541. Ingentique umbrâ *mortis.*

545. *Umbro* dejecerat sinistram Anxuris ense, et totum.

552. *Æneæ* ardenti. Ille, hasta reductâ, impedit *ejus* loricam

556. Super *eum* fatur hæc

557. *Tu, hostis* metuende,

Hoc patris Anchisæ Manes, hoc sentit Iülus.
Sic fatus, galeam lævâ tenet; atque reflexâ
Cervice, orantis capulo tenus abdidit ensem.
  Nec procul Æmonides, Phœbi Triviæque sacerdos,
Infula cui sacrâ redimibat tempora vittâ,
Totus collucens veste atque insignibus armis.
Quem congressus agit campo, lapsumque superstans
Immolat, ingentique umbrâ tegit: arma Serestus
Lecta refert humeris, tibi, rex Gradive, trophæum.
Instaurant acies, Vulcani stirpe creatus
Cæculus, et veniens Marsorum montibus Umbro.
Dardanides contrà furit. Anxuris ense sinistram,
Et totum clypei ferro dejecerat orbem.
Dixerat ille aliquid magnum, vimque affore verbo
Crediderat, cœloque animum fortassè ferebat,
Canitiemque sibi, et longos promiserat annos.
  Tarquitus exsultans contrà fulgentibus armis,
Sylvicolæ Fauno Dryope quem Nympha creârat,
Obvius ardenti sese obtulit: ille reductâ
Loricam clypeique ingens onus impedit hastâ.
Tum caput orantis nequicquam, et multa parantis
Dicere, deturbat terræ: truncumque tepentem
Provolvens, super hæc inimico pectore fatur:
Istìc nunc, metuende, jace. Non te optima mater
Condet humi, patriove onerabit membra sepulchro:
Alitibus linquêre feris, aut gurgite mersum
Unda feret, piscesque impasti vulnera lambent.
  Protinùs Antæum et Lycam, prima agmina Turni,
Persequitur fortemque Numam, fulvumque Camertem,
Magnanimo Volscente satum; ditissimus agri

NOTES.

538. *Infula.* This was a sort of diadem worn by priests and illustrious persons. The *vitta* was a kind of label or fillet, that hung down from the *infula*, on each side. *Cui:* in the sense of *cujus.*

540. *Congressus:* engaging, or meeting: a part. agreeing with Æneas.

541. *Ingenti umbrâ:* with the shades of death—an everlasting shade. Ruæus says, *magnis tenebris.* Davidson says, "with the deep shades of death." Heyne thinks it refers to the shield and body of Æneas; which is a very singular interpretation. *Superstans ingenti umbrâ tegit*, says he. *Tegit:* in the sense of *opprimit.*

542. *Arma lecta:* his arms gathered up, to be a trophy to thee, O Mars, king of war. Gradivus, a name of Mars.

543. *Acies:* in the sense of *pugnam.*

545. *Dardanides:* Æneas.

546. *Dejecerat:* Umbro had cut off the left arm of Anxur just as Æneas came up. He had thrown down his left arm, and with *it* his shield fell to the ground. This, and some other embarrassed sentences, occur, particularly in this book, which plainly show that Virgil had not put the finishing hand to the Æneid. *Totum orbem clypei:* simply the whole shield.

547. *Vim:* force—efficacy. *Aliquid magnum.* He had repeated some spell or incantation, which he hoped would prove efficacious against the darts of Æneas, and therefore he made head against him. Davidson says, "some mighty spell he had pronounced." Ruæus observes: *magicis quibusdam consecrationibus et carminibus adversùs vulnera se munierat.* Germanus, and some others think *magicum* should be read in the place of *magnum.*

551. *Sylvicolæ:* the dat. agreeing with Fauno: an inhabitant of the woods. Of *sylva* and *colo.* *Creârat:* in the sense of *pepererat.*

553. *Hasta reductâ:* his spear being drawn back, that he might throw it from him with greater force. *Impedit:* he encumbers, or renders useless to him, his corslet, &c. because his spear remained fast in them.

561. *Prima agmina:* the chief or principal leaders. They were so valiant, they were a host themselves. Heyne says, *qui pugnant ante ordines vel qui in prima acie*

Qui fuit Ausonidûm, et tacitis regnavit Amyclis
Ægæon qualis, centum cui brachia dicunt,
Centenasque manus, quinquaginta oribus ignem
Pectoribusque arsisse; Jovis cùm fulmina contra
Tot paribus streperet clypeis, tot stringeret enses
Sic toto Æneas desævit in æquore victor,
Ut semel intepuit mucro. Quin ecce Nyphæi
Quadrijuges in equos, adversaque pectora tendit:
Atque illi longè gradientem et dirà frementem
Ut vidêre, metu versi, retròque ruentes,
Effunduntque ducem, rapiuntque ad litora currus.
Intereà bijugis infert se Lucagus albis
In medios, fraterque Liger: sed frater habenis
Flectit equos; strictum rotat acer Lucagus ensem.
Haud tulit Æneas tanto fervore furentes;
Irruit, adversâque ingens apparuit hastâ.
Cui Liger:
Non Diomedis equos, non currum cernis Achillis,
Aut Phrygiæ campos: nunc belli finis et ævi
His dabitur terris. Vesano talia latè
Dicta volant Ligeri: sed non et Troïus heros
Dicta parat contrà; jaculum nam torquet in hostem.
Lucagus ut pronus pendens in verbera telo
Admonuit bijugos, projecto dum pede lævo
Aptat se pûgnæ, subit oras hasta per imas
Fulgentis clypei, tum lævum perforat inguen.

565. *Talis* qualis *erat* Ægæon, cui *homines* dicunt *fuisse* centum

570. Mucro *gladii* intepuit sanguine

572. Illi *equi*, ut primùm vidêre *eum* longè

578. **Eos furentes tanto**

NOTES.

564. *Ausonidûm:* gen. plu. for *Ausonidarum*, by syn. The Ausones were among the early inhabitants of Italy. *Tacitis Amyclis. Amyclæ* was a city of Latium, near Terracina, which is said to have perished through *silence.* The city having been frequently thrown into confusion by false alarms, at length a law was made that none of its inhabitants should mention the approach of an enemy. So that, when an enemy actually advanced against the city, it was suddenly destroyed for want of timely intelligence. Servius assigns another reason for the singular epithet of *tacitæ.* He observes, they held the doctrines of Pythagoras, which forbade them to offer any violence to serpents, and enjoined, at the same time, a silence of five years. At a time, a host of serpents issued from a lake near the city; the inhabitants refusing to attack them, fell a prey to them.

565. *Ægæon:* the son of Cœlus and Terra. The same as *Briareus.*

568. *Tot paribus clypeis.* It is generally thought these words imply, that the number of his shields was equal to his arms or hands. But it is difficult to conceive how that could be. The warrior carried a shield only on his left arm; and with his right hand he wielded the sword, the javelin, &c. His shields and swords (*enses,*) doubtless, equalled together the number of his hands. But *paribus* may mean that they were all of equal size and shape. *Streperet:* in the sense of *sonabat.*

570. *Ut semel:* when once his sword, &c. *Mucro:* properly, the point of the sword, by synec. the whole sword.

571. *Adversa pectora.* By these words, we are to understand the breasts of the steeds, rather than the breast of the charioteer *Niphæus.* It gives us a higher idea of the courage of Æneas, who dared to stand against, and oppose the course of these horses.

572. *Dirà:* an adj. of the neu. plu. used as an adv. in imitation of the Greeks.

574. *Effundunt:* they throw out the driver.

575. *Bijugis: bijugi* is, properly, a pair of horses harnessed: by meton. the carriage in which they are harnessed. Of *bis* and *jugum.* Lucagus was drawn in a chariot by a pair of white horses.

578. *Fervore:* heat—violence.

582. *Ævi:* of your life.

583. *His terris:* on this spot—in this place

584. *Vesano Ligeri:* from insolent Liger. *Liger* is declined like nouns of the third declension, some of which make the abl. in *i*, as well as in *e*. *Et:* also.

587. *Admonuit:* goaded on his horses with a dart—the point of his javelin, or dart. Ruæus says, *excitavit.*

Excussus curru moribundus volvitur arvis;
Quem pius Æneas dictis affatur amaris:
Lucage, nulla tuos currus fuga segnis equorum
Prodidit, aut vanæ vertêre ex hostibus umbræ:
Ipse rotis saliens juga deseris. Hæc ita fatus,
Arripuit bijugos. Frater tendebat inermes
Infelix palmas, curru delapsus eodem:
Per te, per qui te talem genuêre parentes,
Vir Trojane, sine hanc animam, et miserere precantis
Pluribus oranti Æneas: Haud talia dudum
Dicta dabas: morere, et fratrem ne desere frater.
Tum, latebras animæ, pectus mucrone recludit.
  Talia per campos edebat funera ductor
Dardanius, torrentis aquæ vel turbinis atri
More furens. Tandem erumpunt, et castra relinquunt
Ascanius puer, et nequicquam obsessa juventus.
  Junonem intereà compellat Jupiter ultrò:
O germana, mihi atque eadem gratissima conjux!
Ut rebare, Venus, nec te sententia fallit,
Trojanas sustentat opes! non vivida bello
Dextra viris, animusque ferox, patiensque perîcli!
Cui Juno submissa: Quid, ô pulcherrime conjux,
Sollicitas ægram, et tua tristia dicta timentem?
Si mihi, quæ quondam fuerat, quamque esse decebat,
Vis in amore foret! non hoc mihi namque negares
Omnipotens; quin et pugnæ subducere Turnum,
Et Dauno possem incolumem servare parenti.
Nunc pereat, Teucrisque pio det sanguine pœnas.

593. Vertêre *eos*

594. *Tu* ipse saliens rotis

597. *Oro* per te, per parentes, qui

599. Æneas *respondit illi* oranti pluribus *verbis*

600. *Tu* frater ne desere

609. Non *est illis* viris dextra

613. Si foret mihi *eadem* vis in amore, quæ

NOTES.

590. ***Excussus:*** thrown—tost from his chariot.

591. *Pius Æneas.* Dr. Trapp observes the epithet *pius* seems a little incongruous, while he is insulting a fallen enemy. Some soldier-like epithet would seem much more proper for our hero on this occasion. But he is avenging the death of his friend *Pallas*, who had just been slain; and among the heathen, that was looked upon as an act of piety.

592. *Lucage:* Mr. Davidson observes, this is a very poor sentiment, an ill-timed affectation of wit, unworthy both of the poet and the hero. Virgil appears to have been led into it, from an over fondness for Homer. *Nulla segnis:* no slow flight of your horses, &c.

594. *Juga:* properly the yoke: here, the chariot. Sometimes, also, the horses, by meton.

598. *Sine:* spare, or save this life. In the sense of *parce.* Ruæus says, *omitte.*

601. *Latebras animæ:* the seat of life. Ruæus says, *quo latet anima. Latebras* is put in apposition with *pectus.*

607. *Conjux.* Juno was both the sister, and wife of Jove. *Conjux* is both a husband, and wife

608. *Venus, ut rebare,* &c. This is said ironically, as appears both from the turn of the sentence, and the answer of Juno, which shows that she considered it in that light. How Venus supports the Trojan strength!

609. *Opes:* in the sense of *vires.* She gives strength, or power to the Trojans, to perform such mighty deeds. *Vivida:* in the sense of *ardens.*

611. *Submissa:* humble—submissive.

612. *Ægram:* afflicted—full of grief. The pron. *me,* is understood.

613. *Si foret mihi vis:* O, that there were the same force in my love—O, that I had the same influence over thy affections, &c. but I have lost it; for otherwise, thou wouldst not deny me this.

616. *Possem:* I would be able—I could desire to have power, &c.

617. *Pereat:* now he must perish, and make retribution, &c.

This is said by Juno with a degree of indignation, that the favorite of Venus should thus prevail, and that the daughter should have more influence with Jove than the wife. Davidson renders the words *det pœnas:* "let him glut the vengeance of the Trojans with his pious blood." His blood

Ille tamen nostrâ deducit origine nomen ;
Pilumnusque illi quartus pater ; et tua largâ
Sæpe manu, multisque oneravit limina donis.
Cui rex ætherei breviter sic fatur Olympi :
Si mora præsentis leti, tempusque caduco
Oratur juveni, meque hoc ita ponere sentis ;
Tolle fugâ Turnum, atque instantibus eripe fatis.
Hactenus indulsisse vacat. Sin altior istis
Sub precibus venia ulla latet, totumque moveri
Mutarive putas bellum, spes pascis inanes.
Cui Juno illachrymans : Quid si, quod voce gravaris,
Mente dares ; atque hæc Turno rata vita maneret ?
Nunc manet insontem gravis exitus ! aut ego veri
Vana feror : quòd ut ô potiùs formidine falsâ
Ludar ; et in meliùs tua, qui potes, orsa reflectas !
Hæc ubi dicta dedit, cœlo se protinùs alto
Misit, agens hyemem nimbo succincta per auras,
Iliacamque aciem, et Laurentia castra petivit.
Tum Dea nube cavâ tenuem sinè viribus umbram,
In faciem Æneæ, visu mirabile monstrum !
Dardaniis ornat telis : clypeumque jubasque
Divini assimulat capitis ; dat inania verba :
Dat sinè mente sonum, gressusque effingit euntis.
Morte obitâ, quales fama est volitare figuras,
Aut quæ sopitos deludunt somnia sensus.
At primas læta ante acies exsultat imago,
Irritatque virum telis, et voce lacessit.
Instat cui Turnus, stridentemque eminùs hastam
Conjicit : illa dato vertit vestigia tergo.
Tum verò Ænean aversum ut cedere Turnus
Credidit, atque animo spem turbidus hausit inanem :

625. **Vacat *mihi* indulsisse *tibi***

631. **Quòd, ô *sit ita* ut potiùs**

636. **Tum Dea ornat Dardaniis telis tenuem umbram sinè viribus *è* cava nube.**

646. **Illa *imago* vertit**

NOTES.

is called pious, because Turnus was descended from the gods.

619. *Quartus pater.* Turnus was the fourth in a direct line from Pilumnus, who is, therefore, called his fourth father. He was his great-grandfather's father.

620. *Limina tua:* in the sense of *tua templa.*

622. *Mora:* a delay—respite from. *Caduco:* about to fall—doomed to fall by the hand of Æneas. *Mox casuro*, says Heyne.

623. *Ponere:* to settle, fix or determine. *Constituere*, says Heyne. *Oratur:* is asked by thee.

625. *Vacat:* in the sense of *licet. Hactenus:* so far.

626. *Venia:* in the sense of *gratia.*

628. *Gravaris:* you are loth, or unwilling to grant by words.

629. *Quid si dares.* Juno here seems to express some fear, that her husband was not sincere in granting her even this favor. *Mente:* from your heart—sincerely.

630. *Exitus:* in the sense of *mors. Vana* here has the sense of *ignara.* Or else the word *augur*, vel *aruspex*, is understood. Ruæus says, *dicor ignara veritatis.*

632. *In meliùs:* taken adverbially, for the better. *Orsa:* in the sense of *incepta. Qui potes:* who hast power. Jupiter could control the fates, by deferring, or impeding their purposes, or decrees.

634. *Nimbo:* in the sense of *nube.*

636. *Tum Dea*, &c. This is taken from Homer, Iliad v., where Apollo raises a phantom in the shape of Æneas. But Virgil has greatly improved upon the original.

638. *Ornat:* in the sense of *instruit.*

640. *Effingit:* represents. Ruæus says, *exprimit.*

641. *Morte obitâ:* after death—death being past.

642. *Sopitos sensus:* the slumbering senses—or senses buried in sleep. *Quæ:* in the sense of *qualia.*

646. *Tergo dato:* the back being turned toward Turnus, it fled from him.

647. *Cedere:* in the sense of *fugere.*

648. *Turbidus:* in the sense of *tumens—elatus arrogantiâ.*

649. *Inquit*, Ænea, quò fugis?

650. Tellus quæsita per undas dabitur *tibi* hac *mea* dextrâ.

655 Quâ *nave* rex Osinius advectus *fuerat à*

660. Rapitque navem avulsam *à litore* per revoluta.

672. Quid illa manus virûm *dicet*, qui secuti *sunt*

Quò fugis, Ænea? thalamos ne desere pactos:
Hâc dabitur dextrâ tellus quæsita per undas.
Talia vociferans sequitur, strictumque coruscat
Mucronem: nec ferre videt sua gaudia ventos
  Fortè ratis, celsi conjuncta crepidine saxi,
Expositis stabat scalis, et ponte parato,
Quâ rex Clusinis advectus Osinius oris.
Hùc sese trepida Æneæ fugientis imago
Conjicit in latebras: nec Turnus segnior instat,
Exsuperatque moras, et pontes transilit altos.
Vix proram attigerat: rumpit Saturnia funem,
Avulsamque rapit revoluta per æquora navem.
Illum autem Æneas absentem in prælia poscit:
Obvia multa virûm demittit corpora morti.
Tum levis haud ultrà latebras jam quærit imago,
Sed sublimè volans nubi se immiscuit atræ:
Cùm Turnum medio intereà fert æquore turbo.
Respicit ignarus rerum, ingratusque salutis,
Et duplices cum voce manus ad sidera tendit:
Omnipotens genitor, tanton' me crimine dignum
Duxisti? et tales voluisti expendere pœnas?
Quò feror? unde abii? quæ me fuga, quemve reducet?
Laurentes-ne iterum muros aut castra videbo?
Quid manus illa virûm, qui me meaque arma secuti?
Quosque, nefas! omnes infandâ in morte reliqui?
Et nunc palantes video, gemitumque cadentûm

NOTES.

649. *Pactos thalamos:* the promised match.

652. *Nec videt:* nor does he perceive that the winds bear off his joys. This is a proverbial expression, denoting disappointment. *Mucronem:* in the sense of *ensem.*

653. *Conjuncta:* the ship was connected with, or moored to the top of a high rock. *Crepidine*, the abl. for *crepidini*, the dat.

654. *Expositis:* extended—reaching to the shore. These ladders and bridge had been made, for the purpose of landing troops from the vessel or ship.

655. *Osinius.* It is probable he was commander of these troops, or at least some distinguished man among his citizens; for *rex* does not always imply a king: sometimes a nobleman. Massicus appears to have been the king of *Clusium.*

657. *Latebras.* This word properly signifies any hiding place—or place of concealment. Here it plainly means the hold of the ship, into which the shadow or image of Æneas concealed itself.

658. *Moras:* obstacles—hindrances.

660. *Revoluta æquora:* the rolling billows. Servius thinks *revoluta* is to be connected with *navem* by hypallage. But this is unnecessary here; for *revoluta* is a very proper epithet for the sea; whose surface is continually in motion. Valpy says, "through the ebbing tide."

666. *Ingratus:* unthankful for his safety. He considers it no favor to be rescued from the field of battle, where, if he fell, he should fall in the defence of his honor, and the glory of his country.

668. *Duxisti.* Ruæus says, *existimâti.* *Crimine:* crime—-disgrace—-base actions. Didst thou consider me deserving of such an imputation, such disgrace upon my character, as that arising from deserting my companions in battle? Throughout this address, Turnus manifests the soldier and the hero. *Tanton':* for *tanto-ne.*

669. *Expendere:* to suffer—undergo.

670. *Quemve:* or what sort of a person—how disgraced? *Qualem*, says Ruæus. *Abii:* in the sense of *discessi.*

671. *Castra.* Turnus here means his own camp; perhaps the field of battle. By *muros*, he may mean the capital of his kingdom; or his country in general.

672. *Manus virûm:* that band of men—those troops of mine. Ruæus says, *multitudo hominum. Dicet* is understood.

673. *Nefas.* This is here taken as an interjection. O, disgrace!—O, foul ingratitude! *Infanda:* in the sense of *crudeli.* *Quosque:* this is the common reading. Heyne has *quos-ne:* which he takes in the sense of *eos-ne.*

674. *Palantes:* fleeing—wandering, as being without a leader. *Cadentûm:* in the

Accipio. Quid agam? aut quæ jam satìs ima dehiscat
Terra mihi? Vos, ô potiùs miserescite, venti,
In rupes, in saxa, (volens vos Turnus adoro,)
Ferte ratem, sævisque vadis immittite syrtis;
Quò neque me Rutuli, neque conscia fama sequatur.
Hæc memorans, animo nunc huc, nunc fluctuat illuc,
An sese mucrone ob tantum dedecus amens
Induat, et crudum per costas exigat ensem;
Fluctibus an jaciat mediis, et litora nando
Curva petat; Teucrûmque iterum se reddat in arma.
Ter conatus utramque viam: ter maxima Juno
Continuit; juvenemque animi miserata repressit.
Labitur alta secans, fluctuque æstuque secundo
Et patris antiquam Dauni defertur ad urbem.
  At Jovis intereà monitis Mezentius ardens
Succedit pugnæ, Teucrosque invadit ovantes.
Concurrunt Tyrrhenæ acies, atque omnibus uni,
Uni odiisque viro telisque frequentibus instant.
Ille, velut rupes, vastum quæ prodit in æquor,
Obvia ventorum furiis, expôstaque ponto,
Vim cunctam atque minas perfert cœlique marisque,
Ipsa immota manens. Prolem Dolichaonis Hebrum
Sternit humi; cum quo Latagum, Palmumque fugacem:
Sed Latagum saxo atque ingenti fragmine montis
Occupat os faciemque adversam: poplite Palmum
Succiso volvi segnem sinit; armaque Lauso
Donat habere humeris, et vertice figere cristas.
Nec non Evantem Phrygium, Paridisque Mimanta
Æqualem comitemque: unâ quem nocte Theano

676. Vos, O venti potiùs miserescite *mei, et* ferte ratem in rupes, in saxa

679. Conscia *meæ fugæ*

685. Ter conatus *est*

686. Miserata *dolorem* animi

691. Atque instant viro uni, *illi* uni, omnibusque odiis

693. Ille *manet immotus*, velut

697. *Unà* cum quo *sternit*

699. Sed occupat Latagum *quoad* os, faciemque

701. Vertice *capitis*

Nec non *sternit*

NOTES.

sense of *morientûm*. *Accipio:* in the sense of *audio*.

675. *Dehiscat:* can open sufficiently deep for me—in proportion to my crime. *Agam*. This is the common reading. Heyne has *ago*.

677 *Adoro:* in the sense of *supplico*.

682. *Induat:* in the sense of *transfodiat*. *Crudum:* in the sense of *crudelem*, vel *nudum*. Ruæus interprets it by *durum*. Heyne observes, that the Roman copy has *microni* in the dat., which he thinks preferable to the common reading, inasmuch, as it makes the sense of *induat* easier. In this case it would have the sense of *irruat:* he rushed or fell upon the point of his sword. *Induo*, compounded of *in* and *duo* vel *do*. Valpy takes it in the sense of *transfodiat:* whether he should stab himself, &c.

685. *Utramque viam:* each expedient—way.

686. *Miserata animi:* pitying the anguish of his mind, restrained and prevented the youth from executing his purpose. *Animi:* this is the reading of Heyne. *Dolorem*, or a word of the like import, is understood as in the ordo. Ruæus and Davidson have *animo*.

687. *Secundo fluctu:* the waves and current being favorable. The motion of the waves carried the vessel forward: which is saying, in other words, that the wind was in his favor. *Labitur:* in the sense of *provehitur*. *Alta:* for *maria*.

691. *Tyrrhenæ acies*. The Tuscan troops accompanied Æneas, for the purpose of taking vengeance upon Mezentius on account of the cruelties he had done, during his reign. And now they see him entering the fight, they rush upon him from all parts, and press him with their great efforts. But they are foiled in every attack. He stands their assaults like an immovable rock. The comparison is very significant.

693. *Prodit:* projects, or extends into the sea. Ruæus says, *procurrit*.

694. *Obvia:* in the sense of *opposita Ponto:* to the sea—the rage of the sea.

696. *Prolem:* in the sense of *filium*.

699. *Occupat Latagum:* he strikes Latagus upon the mouth and face, as he stood opposite him.

700. *Volvi segnem:* to wallow, or roll on the ground—disabled and wounded. Ruæus takes *segnem*, in the sense of *jacentem*. *Sinit:* he leaves him, &c.

701. *Habere:* in the sense of *ferre*.

704 *Unâ quem nocte*, &c. The meaning

In lucum genitori Amyco ded't; et face prægnans
Cisseïs regina Parin: Paris urbe paternâ
Occubat; ignarum Laurens habet ôra Mimanta
Ac velut ille canum morsu de montibus altis
Actus aper, multos Vesulus quem pinifer annos
Defendit, multosque palus Laurentia, sylvâ
Pastus arundineâ; postquam inter retia ventum est,
Substitit, infremuitque ferox, et inhorruit armos
Nec cuiquam irasci propiùsve accedere virtus,
Sed jaculis tutisque procul clamoribus instant;
Ille autem impavidus partes cunctatur in omnes,
Dentibus infrendens, et tergo decutit hastas.
Haud aliter, justæ quibus est Mezentius iræ,
Non ulli est animus stricto concurrere ferro;
Missilibus longè, et vasto clamore lacessunt.
Venerat antiquis Corythi de finibus Acron,
Graius homo; infectos linquens profugus hymenæos
Hunc ubi miscentem longè media agmina vidit,
Purpureum pennis, et pactæ conjugis ostro:
Impastus stabula alta leo ceu sæpè peragrans,
Suadet enim vesana fames; si fortè fugacem
Conspexit capream, aut surgentem in cornua cervum;
Gaudet hians immanè, comasque arrexit, et hæret
Visceribus super incumbens: lavit improba teter
Ora cruor:
Sic ruit in densos alacer Mezentius hostes.
Sternitur infelix Acron, et calcibus atram
Tundit humum expirans, infractaque tela cruentat.

705. Paris occubat paternâ urbe: Laurens ora habet

707 Ac velut ille aper, actus de altis montibus morsu canum, pastus

709. Laurentia palus *defendit* multos *annos*

712 Nec *est* virtus cuique

716. Haud aliter, non est animus ulli *eorum*, quibus

723. Ceu impastus leo sæpè peragrans alta stabula

NOTES.

is, that in the very same night Theano bore Mimas, and Hecuba, Paris. Hence they are said to be of equal age, *æqualem*. Dr. Bentley observes, that *creat* is quite redundant: for the sentence is perfect without it. Beside, there is something incongruous in making *creat*, and *dedit*, in different tenses; and also the omission of the nom. to the verb *occubat* perplexes the sense. He, therefore, conjectures the reading, as Virgil left it, must be: ——————*unâ quem nocte Theano*

In lucem genitori Amyco dedit; et face prægnans
Cisseïs regina Parin. Paris urbe paternâ occubat.

Dedit: in the sense of *peperit*, vel *protulit*.

705. *Paris.* Heyne omits *creat*, which is the common reading, and substitutes *Paris*.

706. *Ignarum:* in the sense of *ignotum*.

707. *Morsu:* in the sense of *latratu*. *Ille aper:* a boar. Servius says the pron. *ille* is used by an idiom of the language, to ennoble or enlarge the subject.

710. *Pastus.* Servius thinks this is for *pastum*, agreeing with *quem*, by antiptosis. Dr. Bentley thinks the poet wrote *pascit* or *pavit*, whose nominative would be *Laurentia palus*. *Sylvâ pastus:* having fed upon reeds. The verb *defendit* is understood after *palus Laurentia*. *Ventum est:* in the sense of *venit*.

711. *Inhorruit armos:* he bristles up his shoulders.

712. *Irasci:* to engage him—to wreak his vengeance on him.

714. *Cunctatur.* Ruæus says, *opponit se*

716. *Justæ iræ:* for a just resentment.

720. *Profugus.* Ruæus says, *adversa* Davidson renders it, "deserted to Æneas." *Hymenæos infectos:* in the sense of *nuptias imperfectas*.

721. *Miscentem:* putting into confusion—breaking through the middle ranks. Ruæus says, *turbantem*.

722. *Purpureum:* red with plumes, and the purple of his betrothed spouse—which was given him by her.

724. *Suadet:* in the sense of *urget*, vel *impellit*. *Vesana:* excessive—immoderate *Fugacem:* timorous.

725. *Surgentem in cornua.* This expresses the stately motion of a large stag, whose branching horns, as he moves along, seem to lift him up from the ground.

726. *Comas:* in the sense of *jubam*.

727. *Incumbens.* Some copies have *accumbens*. For *lavit*, the Roman copy hath *lavat*. *Improba:* hungry—ravenous. *Visceribus:* the flanks—aiming his deadly grasp at the flanks of the victim.

731. *Infracta:* in the sense of *fracta*

Atque idem fugientem haud est dignatus Oroden
Sternere, nec jactâ cæcum dare cuspide vulnus:
Obvius adversoque occurrit, seque viro vir
Contulit; haud furto melior, sed fortibus armis.
Tum super abjectum posito pede, nixus et hastâ:
Pars belli haud temnenda, viri, jacet altus Orodes.
Conclamant socii, lætum Pæana secuti.
Ille autem expirans: Non me, quicunque es, inulto,
Victor, nec longum lætabere: te quoque fata
Prospectant paria, atque eadem mox arva tenebis.
Ad quem subridens mixtâ Mezentius irâ:
Nunc morere! Ast de me Divûm pater atque hominum rex
Viderit! Hoc dicens, eduxit corpore telum.
Olli dura quies oculos et ferreus urget
Somnus; in æternam clauduntur lumina noctem.
Cædicus Alcathoum obtruncat, Sacrator Hydaspen:
Partheniumque Rapo, et prædurum viribus Orsen:
Messapus Cloniumque, Lycaoniumque Ericeten:
Illum, infrænis equi lapsu tellure jacentem;
Hunc, peditem pedes. Et Lycius processerat Agis,
Quem tamen haud expers Valerus virtutis avitæ
Dejicit: Athronium Salius; Saliumque Nealces,
Insignis jaculo, et longè fallente sagittâ.
Jam gravis æquabat luctus et mutua Mavors
Funera: cædebant pariter, pariterque ruebant
Victores victique: neque his fuga nota, neque illis.
Dî Jovis in tectis iram miserantur inanem
Amborum, et tantos mortalibus esse labores.
Hinc Venus, hinc contrà spectat Saturnia Juno.
Pallida Tisiphone media inter millia sævit.

732. Atque idem *Mezentius* haud dignatus est

736. Super *cum* abjectum

737. *Ait*, O viri, *hic* altus Orodes jacet, pars belli

739. *Ait:* quicunque es, non *vives* victor, nec lætabere longum *tempus* me inulto

749. Messapus *obtruncat*

750. Illum, *nempe, Clonium* jacentem

751. Hunc, *nempe, Ericeten* peditem, *ipse* pedes. Et Lycius Agis processerat *in Messapum*

757. Nota *est* his

NOTES.

732. *Haud dignatus est:* he disdained to kill, &c.

733. *Cuspide:* the point, taken by synec. for the whole spear.

735. *Abjectum:* in the sense of *prostratum.* We have here the image of a hero. Mezentius disdained to take any advantage of his enemy, although the laws of war would have justified him in so doing; but he met him face to face, (*adverso*,) and gave him an opportunity to try the strength of his arm, himself not his superior in stratagem, but in deeds of valor.

738. *Secuti:* in the sense of *repetentes*, vel *canentes. Pæana:* in the sense of *cantum.*

739. *Autem ille*, &c. Here Virgil makes Orodes foretell the death of his victor. In this he follows Homer, who makes Hector foretell the death of Achilles, who was afterward slain by Paris.

740. *Fata:* in the sense of *mors.*

741. *Prospectant:* in the sense of *manent.*

745. *Olli:* for *illi* by antithesis: the dat. in the sense of the gen., to be connected with *oculos*

748. *Prædurum:* very powerful.

750. *Illum. Ille* frequently signifies the former, or first mentioned, and *hic* the latter, or last mentioned. In the present case. *illum* means *Clonius*, who had fallen from his restive horse; while *hunc* means *Ericetes*, who fought on foot. Messapus, though the commander of the horse, was now on foot, *pedes. Infrænis:* in the sense of *indomiti.*

752. *Expers:* degenerate from—destitute of. Of *ex* and *pars.* The poet here compliments the Valerian family, then very influential at Rome, to which the famous Publicola belonged. *Avitæ:* in the sense of *majorum.*

753. *Dejicit:* prostrates—kills. This verb is to be supplied with *Salius*, and *Nealces.*

754. *Longè fallente:* striking him from a distance—it was shot from a distance, and approached unperceived. *Feriente á longinquo incautum*, says Heyne.

758. *Tectis:* in the palace of Jove. This was situated on Mount Olympus. *Inanem:* useless—tending to no purpose. *Vanum*, says Ruæus.

At verò ingentem quatiens Mezentius hastam
Turbidus ingreditur campo. Quàm magnus Orion,
Cùm pedes incedit medii per maximà Nerei
Stagna viam scindens, humero supereminet undas;
Aut summis referens annosam montibus ornum,
Ingrediturque solo, et caput inter nubila condit.
Talis se vastis infert Mezentius armis.
Huic contrà Æneas, speculatus in agmine longo,
Obvius ire parat. Manet imperterritus ille,
Hostem magnanimum opperiens, et mole suâ stat:
Atque oculis spatium emensus, quantum satìs hastæ.
Dextra, mihi Deus, et telum, quod missile libro,
Nunc adsint! Voveo prædonis corpore raptis
Indutum spoliis ipsum te, Lause, trophæum
Æneæ. Dixit: stridentemque eminùs hastam
Injicit: illa volans clypeo est excussa, proculque
Egregium Antorem latus inter et ilia figit:
Herculis Antorem comitem, qui missus ab Argis
Hæserat Evandro, atque Italâ consederat urbe.
Sternitur infelix alieno vulnere, cœlumque
Aspicit, et dulces moriens reminiscitur Argos.
Tum pius Æneas hastam jacit: illa per orbem
Ære cavum triplici, per linea terga, tribusque
Transiit intextum tauris opus; imaque sedit
Inguine; sed vires haud pertulit. Ocyùs ensem
Æneas, viso Tyrrheni sanguine, lætus,
Eripit à femore, et trepidanti fervidus instat.
Ingemuit chari graviter genitoris amore,
Ut vidit, Lausus; lachrymæque per ora volutæ.
Hìc, mortis duræ casum, tuaque optima facta,

764. Cùm incedit pedes, scindens viam *sibi* per maxima stagna

769. Contrà Æneas speculatus *eum* in longo agmine, parat

772. Emensus oculis spatium, quantum *esset* satìs hastæ, *ait: hæc* dextra, *quæ est* Deus mihi, et *hoc* missile telum, quod libro, nunc adsint *mihi!*

775. O Lause, voveo te ipsum *habiturum* trophæum Æneæ, *et, fore* indutum spoliis *ejus*

783. Illa transiit per cavum orbem *clypei* triplici ære, per linea terga, opusque intextum

785. Imaque *pars sui* sedit *in*

790. Lausus, ut *primùm* vidit *genitorem vulneratum*

791. Hìc, si qua vetustas latura est fidem tanto operi, equidem non silebo casum *tuæ* duræ mortis

NOTES.

763. *Turbidus:* furious—fierce—all in a rage. It would seem from hence that Mezentius hitherto had only been in the skirts of the battle. Now he presses on amidst the thickest ranks, furious for fight. This agrees best with the following comparison. Orion is here mentioned, in regard to his magnitude among the constellations. There is a great majesty and sublimity in the figure, "Orion marching through the waves." It is taken from Homer.

764. *Nerei. Nereus*, a god of the sea, taken by meton. for the sea itself. *Stagna:* properly the deep parts of the sea, or river. *Pedes* a foot-man—on foot.

766. *Referens:* resembling. This appears better than to take it with Ruæus in the sense of *reportans*. Davidson observes, that *referens* here may mean resembling, as it does in some other places. Valpy says, "resembling."

773. *Dextra Deus.* Mezentius is all along represented as an Atheist, and a monster of impiety and cruelty. Here the only god he invokes is his right hand, and the weapons which he is about to throw. Them he invokes—*adsint nunc:* may they aid me—assist my efforts.

777. *Injicit.* This is the reading of Heyne. The common reading is *jecit*, in the perf. tense. Ruæus and Davidson have *at illa*. Heyne omits the *at*. Valpy does the same.

779. *Missus:* having come from Argos, had joined, &c. Antores had been the companion of Hercules in his travels.

781. *Alieno vulnere:* by a wound designed for another. Or, *vulnere* may be taken for the weapon inflicting the wound, by meton. By a weapon intended for another—for Æneas.

783. *Orbem. Orbis* may be taken simply for the shield. Ruæus says, *clypeum*. His shield, it appears, consisted of three plates of brass, (*triplici ære*,) and as many thicknesses of the bull's hide, (*tribus tauris*,) so wrought and interwoven as to be a protection against missive weapons. These were fastened and bound together by iron or brass nails, set thick in every part of the shield. Hence *æs* is sometimes taken for a shield. *Terga:* folds. The spear of Æneas, after making its way through the shield of Me-

Si qua fidem tanto est operi latura vetustas,
Non equidem, nec te, juvenis memorande, silebo
Ille pedem referens, et inutilis, inque ligatus
Cedebat, clypeoque inimicum hastile trahebat.
Prorupit juvenis, seseque immiscuit armis.
Jamque assurgentis dextrâ, plagamque ferentis
Æneæ subiit mucronem, ipsumque morando
Sustinuit; socii magno clamore sequuntur;
Dum genitor nati parmâ protectus abiret:
Telaque conjiciunt, proturbantque eminùs hostem
Missilibus. Furit Æneas, tectusque tenet se.
Ac velut, effusâ siquando grandine nimbi
Præcipitant, omnis campis diffugit arator,
Omnis et agricola, et tutâ latet arce viator,
Aut amnis ripis, aut alti fornice saxi,
Dum pluit in terris; ut possint, sole reducto,
Exercere diem: sic obrutus undique telis
Æneas, nubem belli, dum detonet, omnem,
Sustinet: et Lausum increpitat, Lausoque minatur:
Quò, moriture, ruis? majoraque viribus audes?
Fallit te incautum pietas tua. Nec minùs ille
Exsultat demens. Sævæ jamque altiùs iræ
Dardanio surgunt ductori, extremaque Lauso
Parcæ fila legunt. Validum namque exigit ensem,
Per medium Æneas juvenem, totumque recondit.
Transiit et parmam mucro, levia arma minacis,

793. Nec *silebo* te *ipsum*, O memorande juvenis. Ille *pater* referens pedem, et inutilis *pugnæ*

798. Subiitque mucronem Æneæ, jam assurgentis

802. Tectusque *clypeo*

811. *Ait;* quo ruis, O *juvenis*, moriture

815. Fila *vitæ* Lauso

816. Minacis *juvenis*

NOTES.

zentius, had spent its force, *haud pertulit vires;* and settled down in his groin.

792. *Latura est:* will give credit to. *Vetustas:* in the sense of *posteritas* vel *posteri.*

793. *Memorande:* in the sense of *celebrande*—worthy to be praised.

Here the poet may be supposed to express his own feelings of pity and compassion for the fall of so noble a youth. The character which he has drawn of Lausus shows the consummate skill of the poet at this species of description. And surely no one can read it without partaking of his feelings, and entertaining a regret that so brave, and at the same time so pious a youth, could not have been spared to be a blessing to his people.

794. *Inque ligatus:* by tmesis, for *que inligatus:* incumbered by the spear of Æneas. *Ille.* Mezentius.

796. *Prorupit:* he sprang forward. *Armis:* the weapons of the enemy. One description of the valiant man, is, that he mingles with the enemy.

798. *Mucronem:* the poet here has in his view a circumstance recorded in the Roman history. Scipio Africanus, when he was only seventeen years old, protected his father in this manner; nor did he retreat until he had received twenty-seven wounds. *Mucronem:* in the sense of *gladium*

799. *Sustinuit ipsum:* the meaning is, that he prevented Æneas from giving the blow, which was aimed at his father, by parrying it off, and keeping him at bay for a time, until he could recover himself, and retire from the combat. This he did under cover of the shield (*parma*) of his son. *Sequuntur:* in the sense of *adjuvant. Socii.* the companions of Lausus.

801. *Proturbant:* keep off—repel. Ruæus says, *propellunt.*

803. *Nimbi effusâ grandine:* a storm of impetuous hail rushes down. The prep. *ex* is understood, to govern *effusâ grandine.*

804. *Omnis arator:* every ploughman. *Omnis:* all, collectively or individually.

805. *Arce. Arx* here, as in some other places, signifies any place of shelter, or safe retreat. *Fornice:* under the projection or covert of a high rock.

808. *Exercere diem:* to pursue the labors of the day. *Operari per diem*, says Ruæus.

809. *Nubem:* storm of war. *Detonet:* in the sense of *furit* vel *sævit.*

811. *Audes majora:* thou attemptest things beyond thy strength—greater than.

815. *Parcæ legunt:* the destinies wind up the last thread, &c. See Ecl. iv. 47. Ruæus says, *colligunt.*

816. *Totum:* *ensem* is understood.

817. *Minacis:* boasting—bold—daring.

Et tunicam, molli mater quam neverat auro;
Implevitque sinum sanguis: tum vita per auras
Concessit mœsta ad Manes, corpusque reliquit.

821. Et ora *ejus morientis*

At verò ut vultum vidit morientis et ora,
Ora modis Anchisiades pallentia miris,
Ingemuit miserans graviter, dextramque tetendit,
Et mentem patriæ subiit pietatis imago:

825. *O* puer miserande, quid *honoris nunc dabitur* tibi pro istis

Quid tibi nunc, miserande puer, pro laudibus istis,
Quid pius Æneas tantâ dabit indole dignum?
Arma, quibus lætatus, habe tua: teque parentum
Manibus, et cineri, si qua est ea cura, remitto.

829. Tamen, *O* infelix *juvenis, tu* solabere

Hôc tamen, infelix, miseram solabere mortem:
Æneæ magni dextrâ cadis. Increpat ultrò
Cunctantes socios, et terrâ sublevat ipsum,
Sanguine turpantem comptos de more capillos.
Intereà genitor Tiberini ad fluminis undam
Vulnera siccabat lymphis, corpusque levabat,
Arboris acclinis trunco. Procul ærea ramis
Dependet galea, et prato gravia arma quiescunt.
Stant lecti circùm juvenes: ipse æger, anhelans
Colla fovet, fusus propexam in pectore barbam.
Multa super Lauso rogitat: multosque remittit,

840. Qui revocent *eum à prælio*

Qui revocent, mœstique ferant mandata parentis.
At Lausum socii exanimum super arma ferebant
Flentes, ingentem, atque ingenti vulnere victum
Agnovit longè gemitum præsaga mali mens:
Canitiem immundo deformat pulvere, et ambas

NOTES.

818. *Molli auro:* with fine threads of gold. Gold is a very ductile metal, and capable of being drawn into very fine threads, or wire.

819. *Tum vita mœsta,* &c. Dr. Trapp observes, that every incident in the death of Lausus is well chosen, especially the contrast between so pious a son, and so wicked a father; between the rash valor of the youth, and the generous care and friendly admonition of his heroic enemy. Pallas had fallen by the hand of Turnus. Lausus and Pallas were of equal valor; but there is a wide difference between the conduct and bravery of their conquerors. Turnus eagerly seeks the combat, and challenges the youthful warrior. He even wishes his father were present, to behold the death of his son. Æneas is far from seeking Lausus, and singling him out as the object of his vengeance. And even when he exposed himself for the sake of his father, he begged him to retire from the combat, assuring him that his tenderness for his father would bring on him sure destruction. Nor does he attack him until he is compelled to do it in his own defence. And after he is slain, the victor fetches a deep groan, looks upon him with an eye of pity, and the image of his filial piety touches his generous heart.

820. *Mœsta:* sad—mournful. *Concessit* in the sense of *abiit.*

822. *Anchisiades:* Æneas. A patronymic noun: the son of Anchises.

825. *Laudibus:* in the sense of *virtutibus.* Ruæus says, *meritis.*

826. *Indole:* disposition—excellence of character.

828. *Remitto:* in the sense of *reddo. Cura:* care—solicitude of thine.

831. *Ipsum:* Lausus.

832. *Genitor:* the father of Lausus.

834. *Siccabat:* staunched his wounds with water—washed them with water, which being cold, stopped the flowing of the blood. Ruæus says, *tergebat:* rinsed—cleansed. Dr. Trapp takes *siccabat* in the same sense *Lymphis:* in the sense of *aquâ.*

835. *Procul:* apart by themselves—at some distance from him. This word usually implies distance, but that distance may be very small. *Acclinis:* leaning against, or upon. It agrees with Mezentius.

837. *Æger:* faint with loss of blood. *Fovet:* eases—supports. Ruæus says, *sustentat.* He leaned his head forward upon his breast, spreading his long beard over it. *Fusus:* in the sense of *fundens:* or, it may be taken as a Grecism. Ruæus says, *deponens.*

841. *Super arma:* upon his shield.

844. *Deformat:* he throws dust upon his head. *Canitiem:* his hoary hairs.

Ad cœlum tendit palmas, et corpore inhæret:
Tanta-ne me tenuit vivendi, nate, voluptas,
Ut pro me hostili paterer succedere dextræ,
Quem genui? tua-ne hæc genitor per vulnera servor,
Morte tuâ vivens? Heu! nunc misero mihi demum
Exilium infelix! nunc altè vulnus adactum!
Idem ego, nate, tuum maculavi crimine nomen,
Pulsus ob invidiam solio sceptrisque paternis.
Debueram patriæ pœnas, odiisque meorum:
Omnes per mortes animam sontem ipse dedissem!
Nunc vivo! neque adhuc homines lucemque relinquo!
Sed linquam. Simul hæc dicens, attollit in ægrum
Se femur: et, quanquam vis alto vulnere tardat,
Haud dejectus equum duci jubet. Hoc decus illi,
Hoc solamen erat: bellis hôc victor abibat
Omnibus. Alloquitur mœrentem, et talibus infit:
Rhœbe, diu; res si qua diu mortalibus ulla est;
Viximus. Aut hodie victor spolia illa cruenta,
Et caput Æneæ referes, Lausique dolorum
Ultor eris mecum: aut, aperit si nulla viam vis,
Occumbes pariter: neque enim, fortissime, credo
Jussa aliena pati, et dominos dignabere Teucros.
Dixit: et exceptus tergo consueta locavit
Membra; manusque ambas jaculis oneravit acutis;
Ære caput fulgens, cristâque hirsutus equinâ.
Sic cursum in medios rapidus dedit. Æstuat ingens
Imo in corde pudor, mixtoque insania luctu,

845. Inhæret corpore *filii*

847. Ut paterer *te*, quem genui, succedere hostili dextræ pro me? *Ego*-ne genitor

849. Nunc demum exilium *est* infelix mihi misero

853. Meorum *subditorum*

857. Quanquam vis *doloris ex* alto vulnere tardat *eum*

860. Mœrentem *equum*, et infit talibus *verbis*

864. Aperit *mihi* viam *ad ultionem*

865. Pariter *mecum*: enim neque credo, O fortissime *equorum*, *ut tu* dignabere pati

867. Consueta *huic equo*

NOTES.

846. *Voluptas:* in the sense of *cupido.*

847. *Succedere:* to substitute himself for me to the arm of the enemy—to come up to, &c.

848. *Quem genui:* whom I begat. This speech of Mezentius over the dead body of his son is extremely pathetic. He now sees the errors of his former conduct, and the misery to which he had reduced himself now stares him in the face.

850. *Infelix:* in the sense of *durum*, vel *intolerabile.* While his son was living, he could bear up under the burden of exile from his country and throne; but now he is no more, it is become insupportable to him, reduced to a state of wretcheaness and despair. The wound (the sense of his wickedness and crimes) is now opened deep and afresh. *Adactum:* is driven deep into my heart. *Est:* is understood.

851. *Idem ego:* I, the same father who begat you, and suffered you to lose your life for him, have tarnished your good name by my crimes.

852. *Invidiam.* This may signify his own invidious measures, and cruel and tyrannical government; or the odium and resentment of his subjects against him, which drove him from his throne, and brought upon him a train of evils. The former is the most in accordance with the context, since he is now awakened to a sense of his crimes, and condemns himself for them. Servius, however, prefers the latter sense; Davidson the former. Ruæus says, *propter meam cupiditatem.*

853. *Pœnas:* satisfaction—atonement.—*Dedissem:* to the resentment of my people, I should have given up my guilty life.

856. *Ægrum:* in the sense of *saucium.*

857. *Vis:* the violence of the pain from the wound he had received.

858. *Hoc:* this; to wit, his horse.

859. *Hôc:* here, is in the abl. with this horse. *Equo* is understood.

860. *Mœrentem:* sorrowing—grieving.—*Mœstum*, says Ruæus. Davidson renders it "sympathizing."

861. *Rhœbe, diu viximus:* such apostrophes, both to the animal and vegetable world, so far from being unnatural, are among the greatest beauties of poetry, and always show high emotion of soul. Had the poet made the horse reply to his master, he could not so easily be justified. This is in imitation of Homer.

863. *Referes:* you shall bear away.

867. *Exceptus:* being received by the animal upon his back, he placed.

868. *Ornavit:* in the sense of *armavit.*

869. *Crista equina:* a crest of horse hair—made of horse hair.

871. *Imo.* In many of the ancient copies,

Et furiis agitatus amor, et conscia virtus
Atque hìc Æneam magnâ ter voce vocavit.
Æneas agnovit eum, lætusque precatur :
Sic pater ille Deûm faciat, sic altus Apollo,
Incipias conferre manum.
Tantum effatus, et infestâ subit obvius hastâ.
Ille autem : Quid me erepto, sævissime, nato
Terres ? hæc via sola fuit, quâ perdere posses.
Nec mortem horremus, nec Divûm parcimus ulli :
Desine. Jam venio moriturus ; et hæc tibi porto
Dona priùs. Dixit : telumque intorsit in hostem
Inde aliud supèr atque aliud figitque, volatque
Ingenti gyro : sed sustinet aureus umbo.
Ter circùm adstantem lævos equitavit in orbes,
Tela manu jaciens : ter secum Troïus heros
Immanem ærato circumfert tegmine sylvam.
Inde ubi tot traxisse moras, tot spicula tædet
Vellere ; et urgetur pugnâ congressus iniquâ :
Multa movens animo, jam tandem erumpit, et inter
Bellatoris equi cava tempora conjicit hastam.
Tollit se arrectum quadrupes, et calcibus auras
Verberat, effusumque equitem super ipse secutus

875. **Faciat,** *ut tu* **in-cipias**

877. *Æneas* effatus *est* tantum

878. Autem ille *Mezentius* ait:

884. Umbo *Æneæ* sustinet *illa.*

885. Circum *Ænean* adstantem

887. Immanem sylvam *jaculorum infixam* ærato

888. Tædet *Æneam* traxisse tot moras, *et* vellere tot spicula *è clypeo*

NOTES.

which Pierius consulted, he found *uno corde :* in one and the same breast. Heyne reads *uno.* The common reading is *imo. Insania :* rage—fury.

872. *Et furiis.* This verse is wanting in the ancient Roman manuscript. Heyne marks it as an interpolation.

876. *Conferre manum :* to engage with me, hand to hand. This address of Æneas to the gods is a fine contrast to the impiety of Mezentius, who acknowledges no other deity than his own arm : verse 773, *supra.* The prayer is short, but the approach of a furious enemy would not permit him to say more.

877. *Subit :* in the sense of *occurrit.*

878. *Quid me terres,* &c. Mezentius seeing Æneas coming up against him with his hostile spear, instead of discovering any signs of fear, appears hardened against the terrors of death, since his son, for whose sake he lived, was now taken from him, *nato erepto.*

880. *Parcimus ulli :* Ruæus says, *reveremur ullum numen :* I do not regard any of the gods. Some take *parco* in its usual acceptation, and understand by it that Mezentius would not have spared the gods themselves, had they appeared in the field against him : he looked on them as his enemies, and would have discharged his wrath against them. Heyne takes *parcimus* in the sense of *curo—vereor* vel *metuo.*

883. *Super.* This word here is used in the sense of *insuper,* vel *prœtereà. Figit :* in the sense of *jacit,* vel *torquet.*

885. *Equitavit in lævos orbes :* he rode about to the left, that he might reach the right side of Æneas, which was not protected by his shield ; and in this way he turned quite about, forming an orb, or circle. But Æneas wheeled at the same time, and kept the same relative situation to his antagonist, as appears from the next verse : *ter Troïus :* thrice the Trojan hero, &c.

887. *Tegmine :* in the sense of *clypeo. Immanem sylvam :* this means the spears, or darts, which Mezentius had thrown at Æneas, and which stuck in his brazen shield. These he carried around with him as he turned, following his antagonist. Ruæus says, *magnum numerum jaculorum.*

888. *Traxisse tot moras :* to spend so much time.

889. *Congressus :* being engaged in unequal fight. Mezentius being on horseback, and Æneas on foot, they were not on equal terms.

890. *Movens :* in the sense of *revolvens.*

892. *Calcibus. Calces* here doubtless is to be taken for the fore feet. The horse reared, or lifted himself upon his hind feet, and in that position buffetted the air. *Posterioribus pedibus,* says Heyne.

893. *Ipse secutus :* by the rearing and kicking of his horse, Mezentius was thrown (*effusum*) to the ground. The horse himself soon following, falls upon his rider (*equitem,*) and lays upon his shoulder, as he was thus prostrate. By these means, he was unable to rise to meet his foe, or defend himself in any manner. For *secutus* Ruæus says, *cadens.*

Implicat, ejectoque incumbit cernuus armo.
Clamore incendunt cœlum Troësque Latinique.
Advolat Æneas, vaginâque eripit ensem:
Et super hæc: Ubi nunc Mezentius acer, et illa
Effera vis animi? Contrà Tyrrhenus, ut auras
Suspiciens hausit cœlum, mentemque recepit:
Hostis amare, quid increpitas, mortemque minaris?
Nullum in cæde nefas, nec sic ad prælia veni;
Nec tecum meus hæc pepigit mihi fœdera Lausus.
Unum hoc, per, si qua est victis venia hostibus, oro;
Corpus humo patiare tegi. Scio acerba meorum
Circumstare odia: hunc, oro, defende furorem,
Et me consortem nati concede sepulchro.
Hæc loquitur, juguloque haud inscius accipit ensem,
Undantique animam diffundit in arma cruore.

894. Implicat *Mezentium* equitem

897. Et *stans* super *eum dixit* hæc: Ubi *est* nunc

901. *Est* nullum nefas in *mea* cæde; nec sic veni ad prælia, *ut parceres mihi*

903. Per *veniam*, si qua venia est victis hostibus, *ut tu* patiare *meum* corpus

906. Concede me *esse* consortem

NOTES.

894. *Implicat:* incumbers—presses him down. *Cernuus:* Ruæus says, *pronus in caput*, referring to the horse.

898. *Vis:* violence—impetuosity. *Ut:* when—as soon as. Ruæus says, *postquam.*

899. *Suspiciens auras hausit.* These words are capable of a two-fold version: as soon as looking up, he saw the light; taking *cœlum* in the sense of *lucem*, and supplying the word *oculis*. This Heyne prefers. Or, as soon as looking up, he drew in his breath; taking *cœlum* in the sense of *spiritum*. This is the sense of Ruæus and Davidson. *Auras:* the prep. *ad*, is understood.

902. *Pepigit hæc:* agreed upon these terms with you for me. *Venia:* a favor.

904. *Meorum:* of my former subjects.

905. *Defende hunc:* avert, or forbid the indulgence of their furious resentment. Ruæus says, *contine.*

906. *Concede:* grant—permit. Mezentius desired to be buried in the same grave with his son. This he begged as a favor, not that he could claim it as a right. As they had not been separated in life, he wished not to be in death. It may here be remarked, that how wicked soever a person may have been in life, at the hour of his death, he earnestly desires the reward of virtue, and that in the future life, he may be a partaker with the righteous.

908. *Diffundit:* pours out his life. *Undanti cruore:* the blood flowing, or gushing upon his armor.

It may be remarked here, that the poet differs widely from the current of historians. They say, that in a war which broke out between the Latins and Tuscans, over whom Mezentius was king, that Æneas was slain by him in a battle, fought on the banks of the river Numicus, whose waters carried his dead body into the sea, where it was never afterwards found. Hence it was believed, that he was taken to heaven and made a demi-god. This took place about three years after the building of the city *Lavinium*. See Æn. iv. 615.

QUESTIONS.

How does this book open?
Where was this council held?
What is the conclusion of their deliberations?
Were there any speeches made upon the occasion?
What is the subject of the speech of Venus?
What is the character of it?
What is the nature of Juno's reply?
What is the character of it?
What is the decision of Jove?
Whom does the poet here imitate?
What book of the Iliad?
Where is mount Olympus?
Why was it taken by the poets for heaven?
Why is it here called *omnipotens?*
Where was Æneas during the transactions of the preceding book?
Having effected his object, does he make any further delay?
What part of his allies did he send by land?
By whom is he met on his way down the Tiber?
Who was the chief speaker among those nymphs?
Did she give him any particular information?
What was that information?
How was Turnus engaged in the mean time?
On the arrival of Æneas, what course did Turnus adopt?

Would this give him any advantage over the enemy?

How did Æneas effect a landing?

Into how many divisions were his troops arranged?

Was any loss sustained in landing?

Who commanded that division of the fleet?

Did Turnus effectually prevent the landing of Æneas?

What took place after the landing?

What feats of valor did Æneas perform?

Who was the first killed by him?

What took place in the wing commanded by Pallas?

Why were the Arcadians beaten by the Latins?

What was the nature of the ground, where they were engaged?

Upon this occcasion, what did Pallas do?

What effect had his address upon his troops?

What feats of valor did he then perform?

Whom did he kill?

Who commanded the troops opposed to Pallas?

Who was Lausus?

What feats of valor did he perform?

What were the ages of these young commanders?

Why did not the poet make them engage each other?

By whom were they slain?

In what pious duty did Lausus meet his death?

After the death of Pallas, what took place?

Who was the principal agent in effecting this defeat of the Trojans?

At this crisis, what did Æneas do to restore the fight?

Why does he go in search of Turnus?

By whom are the Trojans enabled to perform such feats of valor?

What did Juno do in the mean time?

What effect had her speech upon Jove?

Does she give any assistance to the Latins?

What then is she permitted to do for Turnus?

How does she effect that object?

Where does she conduct him?

When he discovered the deception, what effect had it upon him?

What did he do?

What was the character of that address?

Is he in any way thankful for the favor of Juno?

If he must die, where did he desire to do it?

Who prevented him from killing himself in this state of distraction?

Whither was he finally carried by the winds?

Who succeeded Turnus in the command?

What feats of valor did he perform?

Who assault him with fury?

Why do the Tuscans attack him in this manner?

What effect had their assault upon him?

Whom of them did he kill?

Dare any of them engage him hand to hand?

Does he finally put them all to flight?

At this time, how stands the scale of victory?

Æneas observed Mezentius thundering through the thickest of the enemy, putting whole squadrons to flight; and what did he resolve to do?

Is Mezentius ready to meet him?

Who commences the assault?

Did his spear hit Æneas?

Whom did it kill?

Who was this Antores? Was he a valiant champion?

Had the spear of Æneas any effect upon Mezentius?

Was the wound mortal?

Who succors him in this critical moment?

How does Lausus meet the foe?

What effect had the sight of him upon Æneas?

Does he make an address to him?

Is it a source of regret to him, to kill so noble a youth?

What becomes of his father in the mean time?

Does he express any concern about his son?

What does he do?

After being informed of his death, what resolution does he take?

Having arrived on the field of battle, does he challenge the foe?

Is Æneas ready to meet him?

Who commenced the fight?

What effect had his darts upon his antagonist?

Where did Æneas direct his dart?

Did he kill the faithful courser?

What effect had the pain of the wound upon him?

Did he throw his rider? And what did he do afterwards?

Did Æneas kill Mezentius in this situation?

Was this a fair trial of strength and dexterity?

Did Mezentius beg any favor of the victor?

What was that favor?

Does the poet here agree with historians, in this particular?

Do they inform us that Mezentius was slain by Æneas?

Who then was the victor in the combat?

Where was the battle fought?

How long after his settlement in Italy, and the building of *Lavinium?*

What became of the body of Æneas?

LIBER UNDECIMUS.

THE death of Mezentius turned the scale of victory in favor of the Trojans, and their allies.

This book opens with preparations for burying the dead, and performing the funeral rites to Pallas. A thousand men accompany his corpse to the city of Evander in slow and solemn procession.

In the mean time, ambassadors arrive from Latinus, praying for a truce, for the purpose of burying their dead. Æneas grants their request.

While these things are going on in the field, fear and alarm pervade the city of Latinus. Here Turnus had arrived. Drances, an aged and influential counsellor, accuses him of being the cause of the war, and the author of their calamities; and urges him to decide the dispute by single combat. Turnus however has many friends, who recount his noble deeds of valor. At this juncture, the ambassadors, who had been sent to the court of Diomede (Lib. 8.) returned. Latinus calls a council of all his senators and nobles to receive the reply, and to consult upon the present state of affairs. Venulus, the chief of the embassy, gives a full account of the mission; of his reception by Diomede; of the opinion of that monarch concerning the war, and the reason of his declining any interference in it. Latinus gives his opinion in favor of peace, and proposes to send ambassadors with rich presents to Æneas, bearing proposals of peace and amity. Drances follows in a speech of much virulence and invective against Turnus, accusing him of flight and cowardice, and proposed, if he were the mighty champion he claimed to be, that he should decide the dispute by single combat with Æneas, and prevent further effusion of blood.

Turnus replies in a manly strain: he repels the charge of cowardice by adverting to his noble achievements, to the thousands whom he had slain, and to the dismay which he had occasioned to the whole Trojan camp. He endeavors to allay their fears, and to inspire them with the hope of success. He recounts the valor of his troops; he mentions the cause in which they were engaged—the cause of their country: nor does he omit to mention the number, and fidelity of his allies. He concludes by observing, that he would not decline to meet the conqueror, if the common good required it; nor had he been so much abandoned by victory, as to refuse an enterprise of so glorious prospect, even though his enemy should prove himself a great Achilles. The whole of Turnus' speech bespeaks the soldier and the hero.

A messenger now arrives informing of the approach of the Trojans. The council dissolves. All prepare to defend the city. Turnus gives commands to several of his officers, arms himself, and appears at the head of his troops. Here he has an interview with Camilla. He confers on her the chief command of the horse, assisted by Messapus, with direction to engage the Tuscan cavalry in close fight, while he, with a chosen body of troops, would lie in ambush in a woody vale, through which, according to his information, Æneas would, with the main body of his army, advance upon the city.

The Tuscan horse in the mean time approach the city, and the embattled squadrons are arranged in order of battle in front of each other. The Trojans commence the attack and repulse the Latins, who rally, and in turn drive the Trojans. At length a most desperate conflict takes place. Camilla displayed distinguished skill and valor. She rode among the thickest combatants, and whole squadrons fled before her. Tarchon rallies his flying Tuscans, and renews the fight. Camilla is at last slain by Aruns; who also loses his life. The Trojans gain a victory. The expiring queen sends a messenger to inform Turnus of the event of the contest. He instantly leaves his retreat, and marches into the plain. No sooner had he done this, than Æneas, with his army, entered the defile, passed it, and reached the plain.

The battle would have been renewed between the rival princes, but night approached Both armies encamp in sight of each other, and wait the coming day.

2. Æneas, victor solvebat vota Deûm primo Eöo, quanquam

7. *Quod erat* trophæum tibi, O magne

14. O viri, maxima res *est*

16. Mezentius *cæsus* est

19. Ne qua mora impediat *vos* ignaros, sententiaque tardet *vos* segnes metu, ubi primùm

OCEANUM intereà surgens Aurora reliquit.
Æneas, quanquam et sociis dare tempus humandis
Præcipitant curæ, turbataque funere mens est,
Vota Deûm primo victor solvebat Eöo.
Ingentem quercum decisis undique ramis
Constituit tumulo, fulgentiaque induit arma,
Mezentî ducis exuvias; tibi, magne, trophæum,
Bellipotens: aptat rorantes sanguine cristas,
Telaque trunca viri, et bis sex thoraca petitum
Perfossumque locis: clypeumque ex ære sinistræ
Subligat, atque ensem collo suspendit eburnum.
Tum socios, namque omnis eum stipata tegebat
Turba ducum, sic incipiens hortatur ovantes:
Maxima res effecta, viri: timor omnis abesto.
Quod superest: hæc sunt spolia, et de rege superbo
Primitiæ: manibusque meis Mezentius hìc est.
Nunc iter ad regem nobis murosque Latinos.
Arma parate, animis et spe præsumite bellum:
Ne qua mora ignaros, ubi primùm vellere signa
Annuerint Superi, pubemque educere castris,
Impediat, segnesque metu sententia tardet.
Intereà socios inhumataque corpora terræ
Mandemus: qui solus honos Acheronte sub imo est.
Ite, ait: egregias animas, quæ sanguine nobis
Hanc patriam peperêre suo, decorate supremis
Muneribus: mœstamque Evandri primus ad urbem
Mittatur Pallas, quem non virtutis egentem
Abstulit atra dies, et funere mersit acerbo.
Sic ait illachrymans, recipitque ad limina gressum

NOTES.

3. *Funere:* at the death of Pallas.

4. *Primo Eöo.* *Eoüs* here is taken as a substantive: with the first dawning light. The first business of the pious Æneas is to return thanks to the gods for his victory, although he wished to perform the last offices to his friends and companions in arms, and especially to Pallas.

6. *Tumulo:* on a rising ground. This trophy was consecrated to Mars, the god of war. It consisted of a trunk of a tree placed in the ground, with its branches cut off, and dressed in shining armor, the spoils (*exuvias*) of Mezentius, whom it was intended to represent. It had his waving plumes, his breast-plate, perforated in several places, his brazen shield bound to his left arm, and his ivory handled sword suspended from his neck.

8. *Rorantes:* besmeared with blood—dripping with blood.

9. *Petitum:* struck, or hit.

15. *Hæc sunt spolia.* By the *rex superbus* here, some understand Turnus: from him he had won the spoils in general, to which he first points; then to the trophy representing Mezentius, which he had just erected, and hung around with his arms. *Hìc est:* here is Mezentius slain by my hand.

16. *Primitiæ:* the first fruits; put in apposition with *hæc spolia.* These Æneas here dedicated to Mars, the warrior god, in the same manner as the first fruits of the earth were offered to the gods.

18. *Præsumite:* anticipate. *Bellum:* in the sense of *pugnam.*

19. *Ubi primùm Superi:* when first the gods permit us, &c. They never raised or pulled up the standards to march, without first consulting the gods.

21. *Sententia metu:* resolution—purpose accompanied by fear. The same as *dubia sententia.*

23. *Qui honos solus.* It was the received opinion, that those who were unburied could not pass over the river Styx into the peaceful abodes of the happy, till after the revolution of a hundred years; which time the shade or *umbra,* roamed at large along its banks, in anxious expectation of the appointed period. See Æn. vi. 325, *et sequens.* *Acheronte.* *Acheron* here is used for the regions below, in general.

25. *Peperêre:* gotten—obtained—procured.

29. *Recipitque gressum.* This alludes

Corpus ubi exanimi positum Pallantis Acœtes
Servabat senior, qui Parrhasio Evandro
Armiger antè fuit; sed non felicibus æquè
Tum comes auspiciis charo datus ibat alumno.
Circùm omnis famulûmque manus, Trojanaque turba,
Et mœstum Iliades crinem de more solutæ.
Ut verò Æneas foribus sese intulit altis;
Ingentem gemitum tunsis ad sidera tollunt
Pectoribus, mœstoque immugit regia luctu.
Ipse caput nivei fultum Pallantis et ora
Ut vidit, levique patens in pectore vulnus
Cuspidis Ausoniæ, lachrymis ita fatur obortis:
Te-ne, inquit miserande puer, cùm læta veniret,
Invidit fortuna mihi? ne regna videres
Nostra, neque ad sedes victor veherere paternas?
Non hæc Evandro de te promissa parenti
Discedens dederam; cùm me complexus euntem
Mitteret in magnum imperium; metuensque moneret
Acres esse viros, cum durâ prælia gente.
Et nunc ille quidem spe multùm captus inani,
Fors et vota facit, cumulatque altaria donis.
Nos juvenem exanimum, et nil jam cœlestibus ullis
Debentem, vano mœsti comitamur honore.
Infelix, nati funus crudele videbis!
Hi nostri reditus, expectatique triumphi!
Hæc mea magna fides! At non, Evandre, pudendis
Vulneribus pulsum aspicies: nec sospite dirum

32. Sed tum ibat comes datus charo alumno non æquè

34. Omnisque manus &c. *stant* circùm

35. Solutæ *quoad* mœstum

48. Moneret *me Latinos* esse acres viros, *et* prælia *esse mihi* cum

54. Hi *sunt* nostri *promissi* reditus

NOTES.

to the custom of laying out the dead in the vestibule, or entrance before the door, after it was washed, anointed, and crowned with garlands. In such a place was the dead body of Pallas laid out, and watched by his aged friend Acœtes.

31. *Parrhasio.* Evander is called *Parrhasian*, from *Parrhasia*, a country, and also a city, of Arcadia, where he was born.

33. *Comes:* guardian, or tutor. *Datus:* appointed.

35. *Iliades mœstum.* The poet here represents the Trojan matrons standing around the corpse of Pallas, in mourning attire. He had before told us, Æn. ix. 216, that Æneas left them all in Sicily, except the mother of Euryalus. Servius understands *female slaves* in this place. But they are never called *Iliades.* The poet would have, probably, altered the passage, had he lived to put the last hand to the Æneid.

39. *Nivei Pallantis.* The epithet *niveus* here may refer to the fairness of his face and countenance while living; or more probably to his countenance now white, and pale, and cold in death. *Fultum:* supported—bolstered up.

41. *Cuspidis.* *Cuspis* is here taken for the whole spear, by synec. It is the spear with which Turnus killed the noble youth: here called *Ausonian*, or *Italian.*

42. *Invidit-ne fortuna:* did fortune, when she came propitious, (*læta*,) envy thee to me, O lamented youth?

44. *Veherere:* in the sense of *reducereris.*

47. *In magnum imperium:* against a powerful empire. Or it may mean, in prospect of a mighty empire. The former best agrees with what follows. Ruæus says, *in magnum imperium Etruscorum:* which is the sense of Valpy. Heyne refers it to *Latium*, to the government of which Æneas was about to succeed. It was by the aid of Evander that he overcame the *Rutuli* and *Latini.*

50. *Fors:* in the sense of *fortasse.*

51. *Nil debentem ullis.* Commentators understand by this, his being no longer a subject of the gods above, but in the power of the gods below. But it may mean, that he was now discharged from every vow which he had made to the celestial gods—that he would never return to perform any he had made himself, or which his father was making for him. *Vano:* unavailing. *Inutili*, says Ruæus. All their pomp (*honore*) and parade were of no avail to him. "The living are subject to the gods above, the dead to those below:" Valpy.

56. *Pulsum:* in the sense of *cæsum.*

Optabis nato funus pater. Hei mihi! quantum
Præsidium, Ausonia, et quantum tu perdis, Iüle!
Hæc ubi deflevit, tolli miserabile corpus
Imperat; et toto lectos ex agmine mittit
Mille viros, qui supremum comitentur honorem,
Intersintque patris lachrymis: solatia luctûs
Exigua ingentis, misero sed debita patri.
Haud segnes alii crates et molle feretrum
Arbuteis texunt virgis, et vimine querno,
Extructosque toros obtentu frondis inumbrant.
Hìc juvenem agresti sublimem in stramine ponunt:
Qualem virgineo demessum pollice florem
Seu mollis violæ, seu languentis hyacinthi;
Cui neque fulgor adhuc, necdum sua forma recessit;
Non jam mater alit tellus, viresque ministrat.
Tum geminas vestes, auroque ostroque rigentes,
Extulit Æneas: quas illi læta laborum
Ipsa suis quondam manibus Sidonia Dido
Fecerat, et tenui telas discreverat auro.
Harum unam juveni, supremum mœstus honorem
Induit, arsurasque comas obnubit amictu.
Multaque prætereà Laurentis præmia pugnæ
Aggerat, et longo prædam jubet ordine duci.
Addit equos et tela, quibus spoliaverat hostem.
Vinxerat et post terga manus, quos mitteret umbris
Inferias, cæso sparsuros sanguine flammam;

58. *Tu*, O Ausonia, perdis, *in Pallante*
62. *Quæ sunt* exigua solatia
64. Alii haud segnes texunt crates
68. *Talem*, qualem florem seu mollis violæ, seu languentis hyacinthi, demessum
76. *Quasi* supremum
77. *Alterâque veste quasi* amictu obnubit comas
81. Manus *eorum*, quos mitteret *tanquam* inferias umbris *Pallantis*
82. Flammam *rogi*

NOTES.

Though it would be a source of grief to see his son a corpse; it would nevertheless be some mitigation of that sorrow, to find that he fell not by *dishonorable wounds*—that he fell facing his enemy, and not in flight. It was considered disgraceful to be slain, or to receive a wound in the back. *Pudendis:* in the sense of *indecoris.*

57. *Nec pater optabis:* These words are susceptible of a double meaning: the father will not imprecate a cruel death to himself, in consequence of the disgrace of his son: or, he will not imprecate a cruel death upon his son, whose life had been disgracefully preserved. This last is the sense given to the passage by Davidson. Ruæus says, *nec optabis tibi mortem acerbam, filio turpiter salvo,* taken it in the former sense. This is also the opinion of Heyne.

58. *Præsidium:* protection.

59. *Ubi deflevit:* when he said these things weeping—having spoken these things with tears.

62. *Intersint:* may be present at, or bear a part with.

64. *Segnes:* in the sense of *tardi.*

65. *Arbuteis:* of the arbute tree.

66. *Toros:* here is the bed raised, or made high upon the *fevetrum*, or bier. *Obtentu frondis.* Ruæus says, *umbraculo foliorum.* They shaded the bed by spreading (*obtentu*) leafy branches over it.

67. *Stramine agresti.* By this we are to understand the bed mentioned in the preceding line. It is called *agresti*, rural, or rustic, because it was made of the green boughs of trees, leaves, &c. *Stramen*, from *sterno*, properly signifies any thing placed, or strewed under as a bed; such as straw, leaves, &c.

68. *Qualem florem:* This is a beautiful simile. He looks fair, and still blooming like a flower, just plucked by the the virgin's hand.

69. *Languentis.* This very beautifully represents the hyacinth, just after it is plucked, beginning to fade, and droop its head.

70. *Forma:* beauty—comeliness.

74. *Quas Sidonia Dido ipsa:* which Sidonian Dido herself, pleased with the labor, had made, &c.

75. *Discreverat.* Ruæus says, *distinxerat. Tenui auro:* with a slender thread of gold.

77. *Obnubit:* he binds up, or veils.

78. *Pugnæ:* of the battle, fought upon the plains of *Laurentum.*

81. *Vinxerat manus:* he bound the hands of those, &c. This barbarous custom the poet takes from Homer. It might suit the temper of Achilles, but does not agree with that of Æneas.

82. *Cæso:* in the sense of *fuso. Inferias:* sacrifices for the dead. *Umbris:* to the

Indutosque jubet truncos hostilibus armis
Ipsos ferre duces, inimicaque nomina figi.
Ducitur infelix ævo confectus Acœtes,
Pectora nunc fœdans pugnis, nunc unguibus ora :
Sternitur et toto projectus corpore terræ.
Ducunt et Rutulo perfusos sanguine currus.
Pòst bellator equus, positis insignibus, Æthon
It lachrymans, guttisque humectat grandibus ora.
Hastam alii galeamque ferunt ; nam cætera Turnus
Victor habet. Tum mœsta phalanx, Teucrique sequun-
Tyrrhenique duces, et versis Arcades armis. [tur,
Postquam omnis longè comitum processerat ordo,
Substitit Æneas, gemituque hæc addidit alto :
Nos alias hinc ad lachrymas eadem horrida belli
Fata vocant. Salve æternùm mihi, maxime Palla,
Æternùmque vale. Nec plura effatus, ad altos
Tendebat muros, gressumque in castra ferebat.
Jamque oratores aderant ex urbe Latina,
Velati ramis oleæ, veniamque rogantes,
Corpora, per campos ferro quæ fusa jacebant,
Redderet, ac tumulo sineret succedere terræ :
Nullum cum victis certamen, et æthere cassis ;
Parceret hospitibus quondam, socerisque vocatis.

84. **Figi** ***his truncis arborum.***

103. *Ut ille* redderet *illis* corpora, quæ
104. *Esse illi* nullum certamen cum victis, et *iis* cassis æthere, *ut* parceret *iis*

NOTES.

shade of Pallas. Eight prisoners were sent as victims to be offered at the funeral pile of Pallas. The poet mentions this circumstance, without any expression of disapprobation. It is true, Achilles, in the Iliad, does the same thing at the tomb of his friend Patroclus; but he is represented as a person of a very different character from Æneas, the hero of the Æneid. And moreover, the loss which he had sustained was more severe, and his grief more poignant. But above all, he lived in a state of society very different from that in which Virgil lived. These things serve in some measure to mitigate the enormity of the deed. And yet there is one passage of Homer, which Eustathius understands as conveying a strong censure of the barbarous act.

The practice of sacrificing prisoners at the funerals of their generals, in process of time, appeared to the Romans barbarous and cruel. They therefore changed it, says Servius, for the milder shows of the gladiators! See Æn. x. 518. *et seq.*

83. *Truncos:* trunks of trees. These were considered the less trophy, and were carried in the hand. They were dressed in the spoils of the enemy.

84. *Inimica nomina:* the names of the enemies to be inscribed upon them.

87. *Sternitur terræ:* he grovels, or rolls on the ground.

89. *Æthon:* the name of the horse of Pallas. *Insignibus positis:* his trappings being laid aside, he is now dressed in mourning. *Pòst:* behind.

90. *It lachrymans:* he moves on weeping. Virgil here is indebted to Homer for this thought, Iliad. 17. Where the horses of Achilles are represented as weeping at the death of their master, and obstinately refusing to obey their driver. Both Aristotle and Pliny say, that horses often lament their masters slain in battle, and even shed tears over them.

94. *Processerat.* This is the common reading. Davidson reads *præcesserat*, upon the authority of Pierius, who assures us he found that reading in the Roman, and other manuscripts, which he consulted. Heyne reads *processerat. Ordo:* the procession.

96. *Ad alias lachrymas:* to other scenes of sorrow—to the burial of the other dead.

97. *Salve mihi.* This is after the manner of the Greeks, who used their personal pronoun in the same manner. *Salve—vale:* these were the *novissima verba*, or last words, with which they departed from the funeral. *Farewell for ever, farewell for ever, most illustrious Pallas. Fata:* state—condition.

101. *Veniam:* the favor, that he would restore to them, &c.

102. *Fusa:* in the sense of *cæsa* vel *strata.*

103. *Succedere tumulo:* to be buried, or interred in the earth.

104. *Cassis:* deprived of: a part. from *careo. Æthere:* in the sense of *luce.*

105. *Quondam:* [illegible] host—friend.

106. Quos precantes *ex quæ sunt* haud	Quos bonus Æneas, haud aspernanda precantes,
	Prosequitur veniâ, et verbis hæc insuper addit
	Quænam vos tanto fortuna indigna, Latini,
109. *Vos*, qui fugiatis nos	Implicuit bello, qui nos fugiatis amicos ?
	Pacem me exanimis, et Martis sorte peremptis
111. Concedere *pacem* et vivis	Oratis ? equidem et vivis concedere vellem.
112. Nec veni *huc*, nisi	Nec veni, nisi fata locum sedemque dedissent ;.
	Nec bellum cum gente gero. Rex nostra reliquit
	Hospitia, et Turni potiùs se credidit armis.
	Æquiùs huic Turnum fuerat se opponere morti
116. Si *ille* apparat finire	Si bellum finire manu, si pellere Teucros
	Apparat, his decuit mecum concurrere telis :
	Vixêt, cui vitam Deus aut sua dextra dedisset
	Nunc ite, et miseris supponite civibus ignem.
	Dixerat Æneas. Olli obstupuere silentes ;
	Conversique oculos inter se atque ora tenebant.
	Tum senior, semperque odiis et crimine Drances
	Infensus juveni Turno, sic ore vicissim
	Orsa refert : O famâ ingens, ingentior armis,
	Vir Trojane, quibus cœlo te laudibus æquem ?
	Justitiæ-ne priùs mirer, belli-ne laborum ?
127. Hæc *tua verba*	Nos verò hæc patriam grati referemus ad urbem
	Et te, si qua viam dederit fortuna, Latino
129. *Alia* fœdera	Jungemus regi : quærat sibi fœdera Turnus.
130. Quin juvabit *nos*, et	Quin et fatales murorum attollere moles,
	Saxaque subvectare humeris Trojana juvabit.
	Dixerat hæc : unoque omnes eadem ore fremebant
	Bis senos pepigêre dies ; et, pace sequestrâ,

NOTES.

Soceris : parents-in-law, *Latinus* and *Amata.* By marrying Lavinia, he would become related to the whole Latin nation.

107. *Prosequitur veniâ :* he follows, or accompanies them with the desired favor. He granted their request as soon as asked. It was reasonable in its nature, and consonant with the laws of war.

109. *Implicuit :* hath entangled—involved.

110. *Pacem, me.* This is the reading of Heyne, and Valpy after him. Some ancient copies have the same. The common reading is *pacem-ne. Peremptis :* for those slain by the lot of war. *Martis :* for *belli.*

112. *Veni :* in the sense of *venissem.*

115. *Æquiùs fuerat :* it had been more just that Turnus, &c. It may here be remarked, that Latinus did not take part with Turnus of his own free will and accord; but was forced into it by the importunities of his wife Amata. He was convinced that he acted against the will and purposes of the gods, in so doing.

117 *Apparat :* in the sense of *statuit. Manu :* by force, or valor.

118. *Vixêt :* by syncope, for *vixisset :* the one of us would have lived, to whom, &c. It appears here that the first proposal of ending the war by single combat was made by Æneas.

122. *Odiis et :* in hatred and crimination inimical, &c. Drances embraced every opportunity to vent his envy and hatred against Turnus, and to throw upon him all the blame of the war. It is supposed, that under the character of Drances, the poet portrays Cicero, who was no friend of Virgil. See *infra*, 336. *et seq.*

124. *Orsa :* in the sense of *verba.*

126. *Justitiæ-ne :* this is the common reading. Catrou however reads, *justitiâ-ne priùs mirer, belli-ne laborê,* which Pierius says, is the reading of the Roman, and of some other manuscripts of antiquity. Servius justifies the common reading, by making it a Grecism. *Priùs :* chiefly, or most. Shall I most admire thy justice, or thy achievements in war? Ruæus says : *Admirabor te ob justitiam, an ob opera bellica.* Heyne reads, as in the text.

130. *Moles murorum :* your walls—or the towers and fortifications built upon them. *Fatales :* destined by the fates.

133. *Sequestra :* intervening—intermediate. They had agreed upon a truce, or cessation of hostilities for twelve days, for

Per sylvas Teucri, mixtique impunè Latini,
Erravêre jugis. Ferro sonat alta bipenni
Fraxinus: evertunt actas ad sidera pinus:
Robora nec cuneis, et olentem scindere cedrum,
Nec plaustris cessant vectare gementibus ornos.
  Et jam fama volans, tanti prænuntia luctûs,
Evandrum Evandrique domos et mœnia complet;
Quæ modò victorem Latio Pallanta ferebat.
Arcades ad portas ruêre, et de more vetusto
Funereas rapuêre faces; lucet via longo
Ordine flammarum, et latè discriminat agros.
Contrà turba Phrygum veniens plangentia jungunt
Agmina. Quæ postquam matres succedere tectis
Viderunt, mœstam incendunt clamoribus urbem.
At non Evandrum potis est vis ulla tenere;
Sed venit in medios. Feretro Pallanta repôsto
Procumbit super, atque hæret lachrymansque gemensque:
Et via vix tandem voci laxata dolore est:
Non hæc, ô Palla, dederas promissa parenti,
Cautiùs ut sævo velles te credere Marti!
Haud ignarus eram, quantum nova gloria in armis,
Et prædulce decus primo certamine posset.
Primitiæ juvenis miseræ! bellique propinqui
Dura rudimenta! et nulli exaudita Deorum
Vota, precesque meæ! tuque, ô sanctissima conjux,
Felix morte tuâ, neque in hunc servata dolorem!
Contrà ego vivendo vici mea fata, superstes
Restarem ut genitor. Troûm socia arma secutum
Obruerent Rutuli telis! animam ipse dedissem;
Atque hæc pompa domum me, non Pallanta, referret!
Nec vos arguerim, Teucri, nec fœdera, nec quas

135. *Et in* jugis

137. Nec cessant scindere

141. *Eadem fama*, quæ modò ferebat Latio Pallanta *esse* victorem

146. Quæ *agmina* postquam matres

151. *Præ* dolore

156. *O* miseræ primitiæ juvenis

161. Ut *ego* genitor restarem superstes *filio*. Rutuli obruerent *me*

NOTES

the purpose of burying the dead, and other rites of sepulture. This was intermediate between the war, before and after; during which time no act of hostility could be done by either party. Hence the propriety of the word *impunè* in the following line, in safety, or without fear of injury.

135. *Ferro bipenni:* an axe with two edges, one that cuts both ways.

136. *Actas:* raised—grown up to.

139. *Prænuntia:* a forerunner, or harbinger, in apposition with *fama*.

140. *Complet.* This is the common reading. But Pierius observes that most of the ancient manuscripts have *replet.*

143. *Longo ordine:* in a long train, or succession. Ruæus says, *longa serie.*

144. *Discriminat.* This word Ruæus interprets by *dividit.* Davidson renders it "illuminates."

145. *Contrà:* in an opposite direction—meeting the mourners from the city.

147. *Incendunt:* in the sense of *concitant.* Ruæus says, *commovent.*

48. *Potis est:* the same as *potest.*

149. *Repôsto:* for *reposito.* The bier being placed on the ground.

151. *Tandem vix dolore via.* At the first sight of the corpse, he was overwhelmed with grief, which entirely prevented his speech. At length, however, recovering from it, he gives utterance to the effusions of his heart, but with difficulty. A true pathos pervades this whole speech of Evander. The various turns of passion, and the alternate addresses to the living and the dead, are the very language of sorrow.

155. *Decus:* in the sense of *honor. Posset* in the sense of *valeret.*

156. *Primitiæ:* beginnings—essays. *Propinqui:* neighboring—confederated, or allied. Evander assisted Æneas as an ally: their arms were associated in the war. Ruæus says, *vicini.*

157. *Rudimenta:* in the sense of *experimenta.*

160. *Ego vici mea fata:* I have overcome my time by living—I have outlived my time. Or, *fata* may mean the purposes and decrees of the gods; that regular and ordinary

Junximus hospitio, dextras: sors ista senectæ
Debita erat nostræ! Quòd si immatura manebat
Mors natum; cæsis Volscorum millibus antè,
Ducentem in Latium Teucros, cecidisse juvabit.
Quin ego non alio digner te funere, Palla,
Quàm pius Æneas, et quàm magni Phryges, et quàm
Tyrrhenique duces, Tyrrhenûm exercitus omnis.
Magna trophæa ferunt, quos dat tua dextera leto.
Tu quoque nunc stares immanis truncus in armis,
Esset par ætas, et idem si robur ab annis,
Turne. Sed infelix Teucros quid demoror armis?
Vadite, et hæc memores regi mandata referte:
Quòd vitam moror invisam, Pallante perempto,
Dextera causa tua est; Turnum natoque patrique
Quam debere vides meritis. Vacat hic tibi solus
Fortunæque locus. Non vitæ gaudia quæro,
Nec fas: sed nato Manes perferre sub imos.
 Aurora intereà miseris mortalibus almam
Extulerat lucem, referens opera atque labores.
Jam pater Æneas, jam curvo in litore Tarchon
Constituêre pyras: huc corpora quisque suorum
More tulere patrum: subjectisque ignibus atris
Conditur in tenebras altum caligine cœlum.
Ter circum accensos, cincti fulgentibus armis,
Decurrêre rogos: ter mœstum funeris ignem
Lustravêre in equis, ululatusque ore dedêre.
Spargitur et tellus lachrymis, sparguntur et arma.
It cœlo clamorque virûm, clangorque tubarum.
Hinc alii spolia occisis direpta Latinis
Conjiciunt igni, galeas, ensesque decoros,
Frænaque, ferventesque rotas: pars, munera nota,

171. *Dignati sunt te. Illi* ferunt magna trophæa *ex illis*, quos

174. Si esset *mihi* par ætas, et idem robur ab annis *tecum; tu*, O Turne

176. *Vestro* regi: *O Æneа*, tua dextra est causa, quòd

179. Quam *dextram* vides

181. Nec *est* fas: sed *cupio* perferre *hunc nuntium mortis Turni*

189. Rogos *suorum amicorum*

195. Pars *conjiciunt mortuis* nota munera, *nempe*, clypeos

NOTES.

course of things, which takes place in the world: which is, that the son should outlive the father. This is the sense given by Heyne. Valpy says, "I have survived my own fate —I have exceeded the natural bounds of life."

165. *Sors:* calamity.

168. *Juvabit:* it will console me that he fell leading, or preparing the way for, the Trojans, &c.

169. *Digner non:* I cannot honor thee, &c. Ruæus says, *non honorabo.*

170. *Phryges:* the Trojans. They are so called from Phrygia, a country of the lesser Asia. It was divided into the greater and the less. The less Phrygia was also called Troas, the ancient kingdom of the Trojans.

174. *Par ætas*, &c. This may refer to Pallas or Evander; neither of whom was able by inequality of age and strength to meet Turnus. Davidson refers it to the father: who, had his age permitted, would have gone to the war in person. And in this case, had he met Turnus, he would have been victorious, and brought back his trophy to grace his triumph. See 6. supra.

175. *Armis:* in the sense of *ab bello.*

179. *Quam:* which (right hand) you see, owes Turnus to the son and father deserving it. *Meritis:* a part. plu. agreeing with the nouns *nato* and *patri.* Heyne connects *meritis* with *vacat.* Ruæus and Davidson, with *nato patrique.*

180. *Hic locus vacat:* this method alone remains to thee, and thy fortune. *Modus solandi me restat tibi*, says Ruæus. For *vacat*, Heyne says *relictus est.*

187. *Caligine:* in the sense of *fumo. In tenebras.* Ruæus says, *in similitudinem noctis.*

189. *Cincti:* clad in shining armor they marched, &c. *Lustravêre in equis:* they rode around. The former has reference to that part of the ceremony performed by the infantry, or foot; the latter, to that performed by the horse, or cavalry. *Funeris.* in the sense of *pyræ.*

192. *It cœlo:* in the sense of *tollitur ad cœlum.*

193. *Hinc:* in the next place—after this.

195. *Ferventes:* in the sense of *rapidas*,

Ipsorum clypeos, et non felicia tela.
Multa boum circà mactantur corpora morti:
Setigerosque sues, raptasque ex omnibus agris
In flammam jugulant pecudes. Tum litore toto
Ardentes spectant socios, semiustaque servant
Busta: neque avelli possunt, nox humida donec
Invertit cœlum stellis fulgentibus aptum.
  Nec minùs et miseri diversâ in parte Latini
Innumeras struxêre pyras; et corpora partim
Multa virûm terræ infodiunt; avectaque partim
Finitimos tollunt in agros, urbique remittunt:
Cætera, confusæque ingentem cædis acervum,
Nec numero, nec honore cremant. Tunc undique vasti
Certatim crebris collucent ignibus agri.
Tertia lux gelidam cœlo dimoverat umbram:
Mœrentes altum cinerem et confusa ruebant
Ossa focis, tepidoque onerabant aggere terræ.
  Jam verò in tectis, prædivitis urbe Latini,
Præcipuus fragor, et longè pars maxima luctûs.
Hìc matres, miseræque nurus, hìc chara sororum
Pectora mœrentûm, puerique parentibus orbi,
Dirum execrantur bellum, Turnique hymenæos:
Ipsum armis, ipsumque jubent decernere ferro;
Qui regnum Italiæ, et primos sibi poscat honores.
Ingravat hæc sævus Drances; solumque vocari
Testatur, solum posci in certamina, Turnum.
Multa simul contrà variis sententia dictis
Pro Turno; et magnum reginæ nomen obumbrat:
Multa virum meritis sustentat fama trophæis.

210. Umbram *noctis* cœlo: *illi* mœrentes

214. *Erat* præcipuus

218. Jubent ipsum *decernere* armis

222. Contrà *est* multa sententia

NOTES.

vel *celeres*. *Nota munera:* offerings of the arms which had been theirs, and consequently known to them.

196. *Non felicia:* unsuccessful darts—those that failed to do execution, when thrown against the enemy.

197. *Morti:* to the divinity *Mors*.

199. *Jugulant:* they kill over the flame, &c. This they did, probably, that the blood of the victim might fall upon the pile.

201. *Busta*. *Bustum* properly is the funeral pile after it is consumed. *Semiusta:* of *semi* and *ustus*.

204. *Partim infodiunt*. The meaning is: that they buried a part of the slain, and a part they sent to the city of Latinus. *Partim* may be considered here, a sub. in apposition with *multa corpora*. *Virûm:* of their heroes. *Avecta:* a part. of the verb *avehor:* carried away.

208. *Numero*. *Numerus* here may be taken in its usual acceptation; but it may also mean decency, or regard. They burned all the rest, a confused heap of slain, without any particular marks of regard, or honor, by way of distinction.

211. *Ruebant*. The meaning is: that they collected together the ashes and the bones mingled on the places (*focis*) where the funeral piles had been erected. After this they covered them with a mound of earth. *Altum* implies that the ashes lay thick, or deep upon the ground. Ruæus says, *evertebant*. Heyne says, *legebant*. *Ruo*, is here taken as an active verb.

213. *In tectis urbe:* in the houses throughout the city. Davidson says, "in the courts of Latinus, and in the city."

214. *Fragor:* in the sense of *plangor*. *Præcipuus:* in the sense of *magnus*, vel *maximus*.

215. *Nurus*. *Nurus* here may mean any young married woman. *Chara pectora mœrentum:* dear hearts of sisters mourning—dear, or affectionate sisters mourning the loss of their brothers and friends.

218. *Decernere:* to decide, or settle the dispute by the sword.

220. *Sævus:* in the sense of *acerbus*, says Ruæus.

221. *Testatur:* in the sense of *dicit*.

222. *Multa:* various—manifold.

223. *Obumbrat:* in the sense of *protegit* vel *tutatur*.

224. *Multa fama*. *Multa* here is plainly

Hos inter motus, medio flagrante tumultu,
Ecce supèr mœsti magnâ Diomedis ab urbe

227. *Aiunt* nihil *esse* actum

Legati responsa ferunt: nihil omnibus actum
Tantorum impensis operum; nil dona, neque aurum,

228. Dona *valuisse* nil, nec

Nec magnas valuisse preces; alia arma Latinis
Quærenda, aut pacem Trojano ab rege petendam.
Deficit ingenti luctu rex ipse Latinus.
Fatalem Ænean manifesto numine ferri

233. Recentesque tumuli ante ora *admonent*

Admonet ira Deûm, tumulique ante ora recentes.
Ergò concilium magnum, primosque suorum
Imperio accitos, alta intra limina cogit.
Olli convenêre, fluuntque ad regia plenis
Tecta viis. Sedet in mediis, et maximus ævo,
Et primus sceptris, haud lætâ fronte, Latinus.
Atque hìc legatos Ætolâ ex urbe remissos,
Quæ referant, fari jubet; et responsa reposcit

241. Silentia facta *sunt*

Ordine cuncta suo. Tum facta silentia linguis,

242. Parens dicto *Latini*

Et Venulus dicto parens ita farier infit:
Vidimus, ô cives, Diomedem Argivaque castra,
Atque iter emensi casus superavimus omnes:
Contigimusque manum, quâ concidit Ilia tellus.

246 *Dictam* cognomine

Ille urbem Argyripam, patriæ cognomine gentis,

NOTES.

in the sense of *magna*. His great fame arose from his distinguished valor, and trophies nobly won. *Meritis:* noble—distinguished. Ruæus says, *partis.*

225. *Flagrante:* raging—fierce.

226. *Super:* in the sense of *præterea* vel *insuper:* beside—in addition to these things. Servius says, *ad cumulationem malorum.*

230. *Petendam.* Some copies have *petendum.*

232. *Fatalem:* destined, and appointed by the gods to marry Lavinia, and to rule the Latin state. *Manifesto:* by the evident power and assistance of the gods. *Admonet:* declares. Ruæus says, *ostendit.* Whatever hesitance and doubt rested on the mind of Latinus, concerning his son-in-law, it was now removed. He plainly saw in the late transactions, the immediate interposition of the gods in favor of Æneas.

235. *Imperio:* in the sense of *jussu. Primos:* the chief men—the nobles of the people. *Cogit:* in the sense of *congregat*, vel *convocat.*

236. *Fluunt:* in the sense of *ruunt* vel *currunt. Plenis:* in the sense of *stipatis.*

238. *Sceptris:* in power—authority. *Regno*, says Ruæus. *Haud læta:* sad—sorrowful.

239. *Ex Ætola urbe:* the city Arpi, built by Diomede. *Remissos:* returned.

242. *Farier:* for *fari*, by paragoge. *Infit:* in the sense of *incipit.*

243. *Diomedem.* Diomede was the son of Tydeus and Deïphyle and king of Ætolia. He was one of the most valiant captains at the siege of Troy. With Ulysses, he stole the Palladium from the temple of Minerva, at Troy, and attacked the camp of Rhesus, king of Thrace, whom they killed, and carried off his horses to the Grecian camp, before they had tasted the grass of Troy or drank the water of the Xanthus. On every occasion, he distinguished himself. He had a rencounter with Hector, and with Æneas; the latter was wounded by him, and would have been slain, if it had not been for the timely aid of Venus. During his absence from his home, his wife Ægiale had an amour with Cometes, one of her servants. Disgusted with her infidelity to him, he determined to leave his country, and came into that part of Italy called *Magna Græcia.* Here he built a city, and called it *Argyrippa.* He married a daughter of Danaus, king of the country. He died with extreme old age, or as some say, by the hands of his father-in-law. His death was greatly lamented by his companions; who, according to fable, were changed into birds resembling swans. They took their flight to some islands on the coast of Apulia, where they became remarkable for their tameness toward the Greeks, and for the horror with which they shunned all other nations. They are called the birds of Diomede. He was worshipped as a god.

244. *Emensi:* having measured out our journey—having finished our journey, &c.

245. *Ilia tellus:* in the sense of *Trojanum regnum.*

Victor Gargani condebat Iapygis arvis.
Postquam introgressi, et coram data copia fandi,
Munera præferrimus, nomen patriamque docemus,
Qui bellum intulerint, quæ causa attraxerit Arpos.
Auditis ille hæc placido sic reddidit ore:
O fortunatæ gentes, Saturnia regna,
Antiqui Ausonii; quæ vos fortuna quietos
Sollicitat, suadetque ignota lacessere bella?
Quicunque Iliacos ferro violavimus agros,
(Mitto ea, quæ muris bellando exhausta sub altis,
Quos Simoïs premat ille viros) infanda per orbem
Supplicia, et scelerum pœnas expendimus omnes,
Vel Priamo miseranda manus. Scit triste Minervæ
Sidus, et Euboïcæ cautes, ultorque Caphereus.
Militiâ ex illâ diversum ad litus adacti:
Atrides Protei Menelaus ad usque columnas
Exulat: Ætnæos vidit Cyclopas Ulysses.
Regna Neoptolemi referam, versosque Penates
Idomenei? Libyco-ne habitantes litore Locros?

250. Bellum *nobis;* quæ causa attraxerit *nos ad urbem* Arpos. *His* auditis, ille

255. Quicunque *nostrum*

256. Ea *mala,* quæ exhausta *sunt nobis*

261. Ex illa militiâ *nos* adacti *sumus*

264. *Versa* regna

NOTES.

47. *Gargani:* gen. of *Garganus*, a mountain in Apulia. *Hodie, Monte di St. Angelo.* A part of Apulia was called *Iapygia*, from *Iapyx*, the son of Dædalus, who settled in those parts. *Iapygis:* an adj. for *Iapygii*, agreeing with *Gargani—Apulian.*

248. *Copia:* leave—liberty.

253. *Fortuna:* Ruæus says, *sors.*

254. *Ignota bella:* wars to which you are unaccustomed. *Suadet:* in the sense of *impellit. Lacessere:* in the sense of *movere.*

255. *Quicunque violavimus:* whoever of us violated, &c. The expression implies that it was sacrilege to injure them.

256. *Exhausta:* sustained—endured in fighting. *Mitto:* in the sense of *omitto* vel *prætereo.*

257. *Premat:* overwhelmed—bore away. Homer informs us that the river Simoïs, was so choaked with the dead bodies of those slain in one engagement, that its waters were interrupted in their course. To this, Diomede here alludes. The present tense is here used plainly for the past.

258. *Expendimus:* have endured unspeakable hardships, and suffered every punishment of our crimes. Ruæus says, *luimus.* The war of Troy proved ruinous to the Greeks as well as Trojans. Most of the Grecian heroes suffered extreme hardships on their return. Some perished on the voyage; and others found their kingdoms in a state of revolt, and their domestic peace destroyed.

259. *Manus:* a company to be pitied, even by Priam himself. The calamities which befell them, though conquerors, were greater than those which befell the vanquished. Even Priam might pity them. *Triste:* stormy—baleful.

260. *Triste sidus:* the storm, in which Ajax the son of Oïleus was drowned, and the raging constellation Arcturus, by whose influence that storm was raised, are here ascribed to Minerva, whom that hero had offended by violating *Cassandra* in her temple. *Caphereus:* a rock on the island *Eubœa*, where Ajax was shipwrecked. Hence the epithet *ultor:* the avenger.

262. *Protei.* The visit of Menelaus to Proteus, king of Egypt, is related at large in the Odyss. lib. 4. This account of the disasters of the Grecian chiefs after the downfall of Troy forms an agreeable episode. It is very natural for the poet to make the aged hero dwell upon the misfortunes of his companions in arms. And it is pleasing to see him, who was so active and fierce in the Iliad, and the first in every enterprise, laying aside his armor, and exhorting the ambassadors to peace. Homer informs us, that Menelaus wandered eight years in the seas in the neighborhood of Egypt, and went as far as the island of *Pharos*, the boundary of the realms of Proteus. Sir Isaac Newton observes, that Proteus was not the king of Egypt, but a governor or viceroy of the king, and governed a part of lower Egypt. See Geor. iv. 388. *Columnas:* in the sense of *terminos* vel *limites regni Protei.*

263. *Exulat:* in the sense of *errat.*

264. *Referam:* shall I mention the subverted realms, &c. *Penates:* the country of Idomeneus' overthrown. Ruæus says *domus*, for *Penates.* He was king of Crete. See Æn. iii. 122.

265. *Locros:* the Locrians, on their return, it is said, were forced to the coast o-

Ipse Mycenæus magnorum ductor Achivûm
Conjugis infandæ prima intra limina dextrâ
Oppetiit: devictam Asiam subsedit adulter.
Invidisse Deos, patriis ut redditus oris
Conjugium optatum, et pulchram Calydona viderem?
Nunc etiam horribili visu portenta sequuntur:
Et socii amissi petierunt æthera pennis,
Fluminibusque vagantur aves, heu dira meorum
Supplicia! et scopulos lachrymosis vocibus implent.
Hæc adeò ex illo mihi jam speranda fuerunt
Tempore, cùm ferro cœlestia corpora demens
Appetii, et Veneris violavi vulnere dextram.
Ne verò, ne me ad tales impellite pugnas.
Nec mihi cum Teucris ullum pòst eruta bellum
Pergama; nec veterum memini, lætorve malorum.
Munera, quæ patriis ad me portâtis ab oris,
Vertite ad Æneam. Stetimus tela aspera contra,
Contulimusque manus: experto credite, quantus
In clypeum assurgat, quo turbine torqueat hastam.
Si duo prætereà tales Idæa tulisset
Terra viros; ultrò Inachias venisset ad urbes
Dardanus, et versis lugeret Græcia fatis.

268. Adulter *Ægysthus*
269. *Referam-ne* Deos invidisse *mihi*, ut *ego* redditus
273. *Facti*que aves
279. Nec *est* mihi ullum
280. Pergama eruta *sunt*: Nec memini, lætor-ve *causâ* veterum malorum *Trojanorum*.
283. Credite *mihi* experto

NOTES.

Africa, where they settled in the district called *Pentapolis*.

266. *Mycenæus ductor:* Agamemnon, who was king of *Mycenæ*, and commander in chief of the Greeks in the Trojan war. On his return home, he was slain by Ægysthus, with whom his wife Clytemnestra had an intrigue during his absence. She is therefore called *nefandæ conjugis*. *Intra prima limina* implies, that he was slain as soon as he entered his palace. Servius takes it in the sense of *primo litore*, implying, that he was murdered as soon as he arrived on the shore.

268. *Subsedit devictam:* he lay in wait for conquered Asia. By killing Agamemnon, Ægysthus hoped to succeed him in his government, and take possession of his conquests in Asia. Heyne takes *Asiam devictam*, in the sense of *victorem Trojæ* the conqueror of Troy. Ruæus says, *post Asiam devictam adulter insidiatus est ei*. Davidson renders the passage, "the adulterous assassin possessed himself of conquered Asia." Valpy takes *Asiam devictam*, with Heyne. *Oppetiit:* perished—was slain.

269. *Invidisse Deos.* Diomede, on account of the conduct of his wife, left his native country, and went into exile in Apulia. Venus is said to have sent upon him this domestic affliction, as a punishment for his wounding her in battle. To this circumstance the words *invidisse Deos* refer. *Calydona:* acc. sing. the name of his country. *Invidisse:* Ruæus says, *obstitisse*. Davidson says, "forbade."

274. *Implent scopulos.* On the coast of Apulia are several islands frequented by sea birds, into which it is said the companions of Diomede were changed.

276. *Demens.* Diomede here imputes all his misfortunes to the resentment of Venus. This gives importance to the goddess, the mother and protectress of Æneas. But he does not mention his having given Mars a wound also. From the time that he presumptuously assailed the *Cœlestials*, these evils were to have been expected. *Demens:* presumptuous—infatuated.

278. *Ne verò:* do not, do not urge me. The repetition of the *ne* is emphatic.

283. *Contulimus manus:* we engaged hand to hand. Virgil here compliments his hero, out of the mouth of Diomede. But the account which Homer gives of the rencounter is very different. He was wounded, and would have been slain, if he had not been rescued by Venus.

284. *Assurgat.* In the act of throwing the javelin, or dart, the shield was elevated on the left arm, to give full room for the action of the right arm. *Turbine:* in the sense of *impetu*.

285. *Prætereà:* beside him. Its proper place is after *tales viros*. If the Trojan land had produced, &c. *Idæa:* an adj. from *Ida*, a mountain of *Phrygia Minor*, near the city of Troy.

286. *Inachias:* Grecian: so called from Inachus, one of the early kings of Greece. *Ultrò:* of their own accord—in offensive war

237. *Dardanus.* By this we are to un-

Quidquid apud duræ cessatum est mœnia Trojæ,
Hectoris Æneæque manu victoria Graiûm
Hæsit, et in decimum vestigia retulit annum.
Ambo animis, ambo insignes præstantibus armis:
Hic pietate prior. Coëant in fœdera dextræ,
Quà datur: ast, armis concurrant arma, cavete.
Et responsa simul quæ sint, rex optime, regis
Audîsti, et quæ sit magno sententia bello.
Vix ea legati; variusque per ora cucurrit
Ausonidûm turbata fremor: ceu, saxa morantur
Cùm rapidos amnes, clauso fit gurgite murmur,
Vicinæque fremunt ripæ crepitantibus undis.
Ut primùm placati animi, et trepida ora quiêrunt,
Præfatus Divos solio rex infit ab alto:
Antè equidem summâ de re statuisse, Latini,
Et vellem, et fuerat meliùs; non tempore tali
Cogere concilium, cùm muros obsidet hostis.
Bellum importunum, cives, cum gente Deorum,
Invictisque viris, gerimus: quos nulla fatigant
Prælia, nec victi possunt absistere ferro.
Spem, si quam accitis Ætolûm habuistis in armis,
Ponite: spes sibi quisque; sed, hæc quàm angusta, videtis.
Cætera quâ rerum jaceant perculsa ruinâ,
Ante oculos interque manus sunt omnia vestras.
Nec quemquam incuso: potuit quæ plurima virtus
Esse, fuit: toto certatum est corpore regni.

288. Quidquid *temporis*

291. Ambo *erant insignes*

292. Hic *Æneas erat* prior

295. Quæ sit sententia *Diomedis de*

296. Vix legati *dixerunt* ea

300. Placati *fuerunt*

303. *Et* non cogere

308. Ponite sp m, si habuistis quam *sp*

309. Quisque *sit sua* spes: sed quàm gusta hæc *spes sit*

310. *Nostrarum* rerum

NOTES.

derstand the Trojans, who were the descendants of Dardanus, one of the founders of Troy. *Versis:* in the sense of *mutatis.* The state of things would have been changed, and Troy would have been victorious over the Grecian states.

288. *Cessatum est.* was delayed, or spent before, &c.

289. *Victoria hæsit:* the victory of the Greeks was suspended by the valor, &c. This is very complimentary to the valor of those two heroes, Hector and Æneas. *Retulit vestigia:* retreated into the tenth year —was put off—deferred till the tenth year. *Hæsit.* Heyne says, *retardata est.* Ruæus says, *substitit.*

292. *Dextræ coëant.* The aged hero advises the Latins to unite in league, or treaty, with Æneas, on any terms that might be offered; but by all means, avoid to engage in arms against such a mighty champion. *Hic prior pietate.* This comparison of Æneas with Hector, is no exaggeration of the poet in favor of his hero. Homer had done it before him. This goodness and clemency of Æneas, which followed from his piety, are reasons for the Latins to hope for peace.

293. *Quà datur:* in any way that may be given—on any practicable terms.

294. *Regis:* this is the reading of Heyne and Pierius. It is governed by *responsa,* the answer of king Diomede. The common reading is *regum,* which is not so easy.

297. *Fremor:* in the sense of *murmur.*

298. *Gurgite clauso:* in a pent up flood, or stream. *Crepitantibus:* roaring—dashing against the rocks.

300. *Trepida ora:* tumultuous mouths discordant tongues.

301. *Præfatus Divos:* having addressed the gods, the king, &c. It was the custom of orators to usher in their speeches, whenever the subject was solemn, and of public concern, with an address to the gods.

302. *Summâ re:* for the safety of the state—for the common good.

305. *Gente Deorum:* with a nation of gods—with a nation deriving their origin from the gods. *Importunum:* dangerous—difficult.

308. *Accitis:* sought after—invited.—*Ætolûm:* from Diomede, who was their king. He declined to have any thing to do with the war.

309. *Ponite spem:* lay aside the hope—cease to hope. The remainder of this line is, by some, supposed an interpolation.

310. *Quâ ruinâ:* in what ruin the rest of our affairs lie overthrown—prostrate; all things are, &c.

312. *Virtus.* valor. *Plurima:* in the sense of *maxima.*

315. Docebo *vos* paucis *verbis*

317. Occasum *solis*, usque

319. Asperrima *loca* horum *agrorum*

322. *Trojanos* socios

323. Considant *illic*, si *sit illis*

327. *Si illi* valent complere *eas*

330. Prætereà placet *mihi* centum Latinos oratores de

334. Insignia nostri regni

Nunc adeò, quæ sit dubiæ sententia menti,
Expediam; et paucis, animos adhibete, docebo.
Est antiquus ager Tusco mihi proximus amni,
Longus in occasum, fines super usque Sicanos.
Aurunci Rutulique serunt, et vomere duros
Exercent colles, atque horum asperrima pascunt.
Hæc omnis regio, et celsi plaga pinea montis
Cedat amicitiæ Teucrorum; et fœderis æquas
Dicamus leges; sociosque in regna vocemus.
Considant, si tantus amor, et mœnia condant.
Sin alios fines, aliamque capessere gentem
Est animus, poscuntque solo decedere nostro;
Bis denas Italo texamus robore naves,
Seu plures, complere valent: jacet omnis ad undam
Materies: ipsi numerumque modumque carinis
Præcipiant; nos æra, manus, navalia demus.
Præterea, qui dicta ferant et fœdera firment,
Centum oratores primâ de gente Latinos
Ire placet, pacisque manu prætendere ramos:
Munera portantes eborisque, aurique talenta,
Et sellam, regni trabeamque insignia nostri.
Consulite in medium, et rebus succurrite fessis.
Tum Drances idem infensus; quem gloria Turni

NOTES.

313. *Toto corpore:* with the whole power, or force of the kingdom.

315. *Adhibete animos:* give attention.

316. *Tusco amni:* the river Tiber. This river formed the eastern boundary of Tuscany; hence called *Tuscan. Est mihi antiquus:* This proposal of Latinus to grant a tract of land to the Trojans, is no fiction of the poet. It is mentioned by historians, and other writers. It is said, that Æneas accepted the proposal. It is generally considered to be that tract of country lying between the city Laurentum and the Tiber, including the Trojan camp, or *Nova Troja.* The extent of the tract is quite uncertain. Cato, whom Servius follows, supposes it to contain about 700 acres. Others suppose that it contained 40 *stadia* in every direction from the city *Lavinium*, forming a circle of about ten miles in diameter, Others again enlarge it to 400 *stadia* in circumference. It is called *antiquus*, because it belonged to the ancient dominion of the Latin kings.

317. *Longus:* extended—stretching even beyond. *Sicanos:* an ancient people of Italy. See Lib. vii. 795. This tract of country the *Aurunci* formerly, and then the *Rutuli*, cultivated. The most rugged parts of it, they reserved for pasturage. *Serunt:* in the sense of *colunt.*

320. *Plaga:* in the sense of *tractus.*

321. *Cedat:* in the sense of *detur.*

322. *Leges:* conditions, or terms. *Dicamus:* let us appoint—name.

324. *Gentem:* region—country.

325. *Poscunt.* This is the reading of Heyne, and of Valpy after him. Ruæus reads *possunt.*

326. *Texamus:* in the sense of *struamus.*

327. *Seu:* in the sense of *vel. Complere:* to fill, or man them. *Undam:* by the water of the Tiber.

329. *Præcipiant:* in the sense of *præscribant. Modum:* the form, or shape. *Navalia. Navale* is a dock where vessels lie; or a ship-yard, where they are built. Also, the materials of which they are built, and with which they are equipped. This last is probably the meaning here. *Æra:* the money necessary to defray the expenses of building. *Manus:* the workmen.

331. *Primâ gente:* of the first rank.

333. *Portantes munera:* bearing presents. This alludes to the Roman custom of sending such presents to kings.

334. *Sellam:* the chair of state *Trabeam;* the *trabea* was a narrow robe, worn by the kings, and the consuls.

335. *Consulite:* advise, or consult for the common good. *Fessis rebus:* distressed state, or condition.

336. *Infensus:* spiteful—bearing spite The glory of Turnus—his noble birth—his fame in war, had excited his envy; and he embraced the present opportunity to give vent to his feelings. *Idem:* reference is here made to verse 122, *supra et seq.* The same Drances, &c.

Obliquâ invidiâ stimulisque agitabat amaris;
Largus opum, et linguâ melior, sed frigida bello
Dextera, consiliis habitus non futilis auctor,
Seditione potens; genus huic materna superbum
Nobilitas dabat, incertum de patre ferebat;
Surgit, et his onerat dictis, atque aggerat iras:
Rem nulli obscuram, nostræ nec vocis egentem,
Consulis, ô bone rex. Cuncti se scire fatentur,
Quid fortuna ferat populi; sed dicere mussant.
Det libertatem fandi, flatusque remittat,
Cujus ob auspicium infaustum, moresque sinistros,
(Dicam equidem, licèt arma mihi mortemque minetur)
Lumina tot cecidisse ducum, totamque videmus
Consedisse urbem luctu: dum Troïa tentat
Castra fugæ fidens, et cœlum territat armis.
Unum etiam donis istis, quæ plurima mitti
Dardanidis dicique jubes, unum, optime regum,
Adjicias: nec te ullius violentia vincat,
Quin natam egregio genero dignisque hymenæis
Des pater, et pacem hanc æterno fœdere jungas.
Quòd si tantus habet mentes et pectora terror;
Ipsum obtestemur, veniamque oremus ab ipso;
Cedat, jus proprium regi patriæque remittat.
Quid miseros toties in aperta pericula cives
Projicis? ô Latio caput horum et causa malorum!
Nulla salus bello: pacem te poscimus omnes,

338. Sed *cujus* dextera *erat*

341. *Enim* ferebat incertum *genus* de patre

342. Onerat *Turnum*

346. *Turnus* det

352. O optime regum, adjicias unum *alterum*, etiam unum, *nempe*, *filiam* istis donis, quæ

357. Tantus terror *Turni* habet *nostras*

361. O *Turne*, caput, et causa horum

362. *Est nobis* nulla

NOTES.

337. *Obliquâ*. Dr. Trapp observes, that envy is uneasy at another's happiness, and so cannot look directly upon it. Ruæus takes it in the sense of *occulta*. The envious person sees every thing with distorted, or crooked eyes. *Oculos habens distortos*. *Agitabat:* goaded—spurred on. *Amaris stimulis:* with sharp, or pungent stings.

338. *Largus:* in the sense of *abundans*. *Melior lingua*. Ruæus says, *abundantior eloquentiâ*. Drances, with all his qualifications, his eloquence, his wisdom in council, and his noble birth, was a coward. Some have imagined, that under the character of Turnus, Mark Antony is represented; and that Cicero is shadowed by Drances. It would seem, that Virgil was no great friend to Cicero, for he makes no mention of him in any part of his works.

340. *Potens seditione:* powerful in factions—a powerful party man.

341. *Materna nobilitas:* on his mother's side, he was nobly descended—from her he had an illustrious descent, or extraction. *Ferebat:* in the sense of *habebat*.

342. *His dictis:* with these invectives—reproaches. *Iras:* the common hatred against Turnus.

344. *Consulis:* in the sense of *suades* vel *hortaris*.

345. *Quid fortuna:* what the state of the nation requires. *Populi:* in the sense of *gentis*. *Mussant:* in the sense of *verentur*. Heyne says, *non audent*.

346. *Flatus:* vaunting—pride—arrogance.

347. *Auspicium:* conduct—influence.—Drances here attributes the disasters of the state to the unfortunate influence which Turnus had in the councils of Latinus, and to his perverse and determined conduct in relation to the war.

349. *Tot lumina ducum:* so many illustrious chiefs.

351. *Territat:* in the sense of *minatur*.

352. *Unum etiam*. In addition to the many presents which the king had proposed to send to Æneas, Drances advises him to add another, namely, his daughter Lavinia as the surest means of conciliating the conqueror, and obtaining for his people a lasting peace.

356. *Jungas:* in the sense of *confirmes*.

358. *Veniam*. This favor was, that Turnus should yield, or give up to the king, his own peculiar authority and right in the disposal of his daughter; and that he should resign his claim to her, for the good of his country.

359. *Remittat:* in the sense of *relinquat*.

363. Simul *poscimus* solum — Turne, simul pacis solum inviolabile pignus.
Primus ego, invisum quem tu tibi fingis, et esse
Nil moror, en supplex venio! miserere tuorum;
Pone animos; et pulsus abi. Sat funera fusi
Vidimus, ingentes et desolavimus agros.
Aut, si fama movet, si tantum pectore robur
Concipis, et si adeò dotalis regia cordi est;
Aude, atque adversum fidens fer pectus in hostem
Scilicet, ut Turno contingat regia conjux,
Nos, animæ viles, inhumata infletaque turba,
Sternamur campis. Et jam tu, si qua tibi vis,
374. Siqua vis *est* tibi, si — Si patrii quid Martis habes, illum aspice contrà,
Qui vocat.
Talibus exarsit dictis violentia Turni:
Dat gemitum, rumpitque has imo pectore voces:
Larga quidem, Drance, tibi semper copia fandi
Tunc, cùm bella manus poscunt: patribusque vocatis,
380. *Tu* primus ades — Primus ades: sed non replenda est curia verbis,
Quæ tutò tibi magna volant; dum distinet hostem
Agger murorum, nec inundant sanguine fossæ,
383. *Quod est* solitum tibi — Proinde tona eloquio, solitum tibi; meque timoris
Argue tu, Drance, quando tot stragis acervos
Teucrorum tua dextra dedit, passimque trophæis
Insignis agros. Possit quid vivida virtus,
387. Licet *ut tu* experiare *eam* — Experiare licet: nec longè scilicet hostes
Quærendi nobis: circumstant undique muros
Imus in adversos? quid cessas? an tibi Mavors
Ventosâ in linguâ, pedibusque fugacibus istis
Semper erit?

NOTES.

363. *Pignus.* This pledge consisted in his resignation of Lavinia in favor of Æneas.

364. *Invisum:* inimical—a foe. *Nil moror:* I do not hesitate to be. *Non curo esse,* says Ruæus.

366. *Fusi:* we, beaten, or routed, have seen, &c. This alludes to their recent defeat. *Animos:* in the sense of *iras.*

369. *Adeò cordi:* for such a delight to thee. *Dotalis:* given in dowry. Any property, or inheritance, belonging to a woman at the time of her marriage, may be called *dotalis.* Lavinia was the only child of Latinus, and the heiress of his kingdom. Should Turnus marry her, he would possess the palace and throne, in right of his wife.

370. *Aude:* have courage—play the hero. *Adversum:* in front—right against. It agrees with *pectus.*

371. *Ut regia conjux:* that a royal spouse may fall to Turnus, we vulgar souls, &c. This is extremely severe, and sarcastic.

374. *Martis:* in the sense of *fortitudinis.* Drances concludes, by observing that, if Turnus was that hero represented, and if he possessed any of his country's valor, he would meet Æneas, hand to hand, who had given already the challenge. In this dispute, the poet shows himself a perfect master of artful and elegant abuse. In these speeches of Drances and Turnus, there are some fine specimens of eloquence, not excelled even by the great masters of the art. *Aspice illum:* look him in the face—meet him face to face.

376. *Violentia:* in the sense of *ira.* Valpy says, *violentia Turni,* is to be taken for Turnus himself.

378. *Larga copia fandi:* great fluency of speech—a copious profusion of words. *Manus,* here, means action, in opposition to mere words.

381. *Magna:* in great abundance—in torrents.

382. *Agger:* ramparts, or bulwarks.

383. *Tona:* thunder on.

384. *Quando tua:* since thy right hand hath made so many heaps, &c. This is keen irony. *Stragis. Strages* is properly slaughter: also the bodies of the slain. Ruæus says, *cadaverum Trojanorum.*

386. *Insignis:* you adorn, or decorate the fields, &c.

389. *Adversos:* in the sense of *hostes. Mavors:* a name of Mars: here used for courage, or valor. *Tibi:* in the sense of *tuus:*

Pulsus ego? aut quisquam meritò, fœdissime, pulsum
Arguet, Iliaco tumidum qui crescere Tybrim
Sanguine, et Evandri totam cum stirpe videbit
Procubuisse domum, atque exutos Arcadas armis?
Haud ita me experti Bitias et Pandarus ingens,
Et quos mille die victor sub Tartara misi,
Inclusus muris, hostilique aggere septus.
Nulla salus bello! capiti cane talia, demens,
Dardanio, rebusque tuis. Proinde omnia magno
Ne cessa turbare metu, atque extollere vires
Gentis bis victæ; contrà premere arma Latini.
Nunc et Myrmidonum proceres Phrygia arma tremiscunt!
Nunc et Tydides, et Larissæus Achilles!
Amnis et Hadriacas retrò fugit Aufidus undas!
Vel cùm se pavidum contra mea jurgia fingit
Artificis scelus, et formidine crimen acerbat.
Nunquam animam talem dextrâ hâc, absiste moveri,
Amittes: habitet tecum, et sit pectore in isto.
Nunc ad te, et tua, magne pater, consulta revertor.
Si nullam nostris ultrà spem ponis in armis;
Si tam deserti sumus, et, semel agmine verso,
Funditùs occidimus, neque habet fortuna regressum:

392. O fœdissime *homo*

396. Haud ita experti *sunt;* et mille *alii*, quos *in uno* die *ego* victor

402. Contrà *ne cessa*

405. Amnis Aufidus *versus* retrò

407. *Sua* formidine

NOTES.

will thy valor always consist in, &c. For *Mavors*, Ruæus says, *fortitudo.*

393. *Arguet pulsum.* Turnus here vindicates himself from the charge of being vanquished, made by Drances: Who will accuse me of being beaten, that shall see the swollen Tyber, &c. *Arguet:* in the sense of *dicet.* Ruæus says, *accusabit. Esse* vel *fuisse* is understood with *pulsum.*

394. *Totam domum:* and the whole family of Evander, with his race, to be prostrated. Pallas was the only son of Evander, and as far as we know, his only child. In his death, then, the family and race became extinct.

396. *Bitias et Pandarus.* These were two brothers of gigantic stature, whom Turnus slew, at the time of his entering the Trojan camp. See Æn. ix. 672, *et sequens.*

399. *Dardanio capiti:* to the Trojan chief: simply, to the Trojan. *Caput:* the head, by synec. is frequently put for the whole body, or person. *Cane:* proclaim—declare. Drances appears to have been at the head of the Latin party, which favored the Trojan interest in opposition to Turnus. By *tuis rebus*, we are to understand this party at Latium, or the Trojans themselves, his friends.

402. *Gentis bis victæ:* of the nation twice conquered. Turnus considers that he had already subdued the Trojans; and the Greeks had done the same thing before, on the plains of Troy. And indeed, it appears, he had greatly the advantage over them, during the absence of Æneas.

403. *Proceres:* the Grecian chiefs. Agamemnon and Menelaus may be more particularly alluded to. *Myrmidonum.* These were the troops of Achilles. By synec. put for the Greeks in general.

405. *Aufidus.* A river rising in the Apennines, and in the territories of the *Hirpini*, and passing through Apulia, Daunia, and Peucetia, falls into the Adriatic sea. This river fled back, as if affrighted at the sight of the Trojan fleet, and ceased to flow in its usual course. Such is the language of the miscreant Drances, in extolling the Trojans, and spreading the terror of their name, even when, &c. These, or some other of the same import, are requisite to connect the subject, and make sense. *Fugit:* flowed back—fled back from. *Hadriacas:* an adj. from *Hadria.*

406. *Jurgia mea:* my menaces, or threats. *Fingit:* in the sense of *simulat.*

407. *Sc[illegible]s artificis:* that base villain Such was the depravity of his character that he was baseness and wickedness itself This form of expression is common with the poet. It is usually rendered by the correspondent adjective, with which the following word is made to agree. Ruæus says, *ille scelestus accusator.* Valpy says, *artifex sceleris. Crimen:* in the sense of *accusationem.*

409. *Isto pectore:* in that bosom of thine This is said by way of contempt.

413. *Funditùs:* we are utterly ruined. For *occidimus*, Ruæus says *perimus. Regressum:* return.

Oremus pacem, et dextras tendamus inermes.
Quanquam ô! si solitæ quicquam virtutis adesset.
Ille mihi ante alios fortunatusque laborum,
Egregiusque animi, qui, ne quid tale videret,
Procubuit moriens, et humum semel ore momordit.
Sin et opes nobis, et adhuc intacta juventus,
Auxilioque urbes Italæ populique supersunt:
Sin et Trojanis cum multo gloria venit
Sanguine: sunt illis sua funera, parque per omnes
Tempestas: cur indecores in limine primo
Deficimus? cur ante tubam tremor occupat artus?
Multa dies variusque labor mutabilis ævi
Retulit in meliùs: multos alterna revisens
Lusit, et in solido rursus fortuna locavit.
Non erit auxilio nobis Ætolus, et Arpi?
At Messapus erit, felixque Tolumnius, et quos
Tot populi misêre, duces: nec parva sequetur
Gloria delectos Latio et Laurentibus agris.
Est et Volscorum egregiâ de gente Camilla,
Agmen agens equitum, et florentes ære catervas.
Quòd si me solum Teucri in certamina poscunt,
Idque placet, tantùmque bonis communibus obsto:
Non adeò has exosa manus victoria fugit,
Ut tantâ quicquam pro spe tentare recusem.
Ibo animis contrà; vel magnum præstet Achillem,
Factaque Vulcani manibus paria induat arma
Ille licèt. Vobis animam hanc, soceroque Latino,
Turnus ego, haud ulli veterum virtute secundus,
Devovi. Solum Æneas vocat? et, vocet, oro.

416. Ille *videretur* mihi ante alios
422. *Si* sunt illis sua
423. Cur *nos* indecores
424. *Nostros* artus
427. *Eos* in solido *statu*
431 *Homines* delectos è
438. Contra *Ænean;* licèt ille præstet *se* vel
439. Paria *armis Achillis*
441. Ego Turnus devovi hanc
442. *Me* solum

NOTES.

416. *Fortunatus:* happy in his toils—labors. A Greek idiom. So also *egregius animi:* illustrious—heroic in soul. Ruæus says, *præstans vertute.*

419. *Intacta:* fresh—that hath not been engaged in action.

420. *Populi:* nations.

422. *Tempestas par:* an equal storm of war on both sides. Ruæus says, *par clades.* By *per omnes*, we may understand both sides, the Trojans and Italians.

424. *Ante tubam:* before the trumpet sound.

425. *Dies:* in the sense of *tempus. Mutabilis ævi:* of changing or revolving years. *Retulit multa:* changes many things, &c. Ruæus says, *vertit. Labor:* change—vicissitude—revolution. Ruæus says, *motus.*

426. *Fortuna alterna:* fortune revisiting men alternately, hath deceived many—played an unexpected game with them, and again, &c. *Alterna:* in the sense of *alternis.*

428. *Ætolus:* the Ætolian (namely) Diomede; who was by birth an Ætolian, and at that time, reigned over the city Arpi.

429. *Tolumnius.* He was an augur, and foretold the success of the war, and thereby animated the troops. He, therefore, is called *felix.*

433. *Florentes ære:* shining—gleaming in brass.

436. *Victoria non adeò.* On many of the old coins, are to be seen persons holding victory in one hand. To this circumstance, Mr. Addison conjectures, the poet here alludes. *Exosa* here is to be taken actively. Victory, disdaining his hand so much, had not abandoned him, that he would refuse, &c. This speech of Turnus is of the noblest character, and shows him to be the real soldier. It is very different from that of the envious and cowardly Drances.

437. *Tanta spe:* in the hope of victory—or the hope of obtaining the prize of victory; a royal bride.

438. *Præstet:* in the sense of *exhibeat*, vel *repræsentet. Animis:* courage—confidence of victory.

439. *Paria arma:* arms equal to those of Achilles, and made by the hands of Vulcan. Turnus was at this time ignorant that Æneas actually possessed armor made by Vulcan.

441. *Haud secundus:* not inferior—not second to any of his illustrious ancestors in valor. *Veterum* in the sense of *majorum.*

Nec Drances potiùs, sive est hæc ira Deorum,
Morte luat; sive est virtus et gloria, tollat.
Illi hæc inter se dubiis de rebus agebant
Certantes; castra Æneas aciemque movebat.
Nuntius ingenti per regia tecta tumultu
Ecce ruit, magnisque urbem terroribus implet:
Instructos acie Tiberino à flumine Teucros,
Tyrrhenamque manum totis descendere campis.
Extemplò turbati animi, concussaque vulgi
Pectora, et arrectæ stimulis haud mollibus iræ.
Arma manu trepidi poscunt, fremit arma juventus:
Flent mœsti mussantque patres. Hìc undique clamor
Dissensu vario magnus se tollit in auras.
Haud secùs atque alto in luco cùm fortè catervæ
Consedêre avium: piscosove amne Padusæ
Dant sonitum rauci per stagna loquacia cycni.
Immò, ait, ô cives, arrepto tempore, Turnus,
Cogite concilium, et pacem laudate sedentes:
Illi armis in regna ruant. Nec plura locutus
Corripuit sese, et tectis citus extulit altis.
Tu, Voluse, armari Volscorum edice maniplis;
Duc, ait, et Rutulos: equitem Messapus in armis,
Et, cum fratre, Coras, latis diffundite campis.
Pars aditus urbis firment, turresque capessant:
Cætera, quâ jussô, mecum manus inferat arma.
Ilicet in muros totâ discurritur urbe.
Concilium ipse pater et magna incepta Latinus
Deserit; ac tristi turbatus tempore differt.
Multaque se incusa, qui non acceperit ultrò

449. *Dicens* Teucros instructos *acie*, *Tyrrhenumque*

451. Turbati *sunt*

456. Cùm fortè catervæ avium consedêre in alto luco; rauci-ve cycni dant sonitum piscoso-ve

464. Messapus et Coras cum fratre, *vos*, diffundite equitem

NOTES.

443. *Nec Drances.* The meaning of these two lines, is this: that Drances should not die; whether the vengeance of the gods required that one of them should perish; or, whether valor and glory were the result of the contest, he should not bear off the prize of victory. Mr. Dryden has expressed the same sentiment:

Drances shall rest secure, and neither share
The danger, nor divide the prize of war.

Though Turnus had somewhat recovered his temper, during the time of his addressing the king, yet he could not conclude, without giving Drances this severe stroke.

444. *Luat morte:* atone by his death: that is, lose his life. If one of them must die, Turnus chose rather to be the one himself.

445. *Agebant:* in the sense of *dicebant.*

449. *Acie:* in order of battle—in battle array.

452. *Arrectæ:* aroused. *Stimulis:* impulse,

453. *Trepidi:* quick—in haste. *Fremit:* in the sense of *flagitat.*

454. *Patres:* the senators. The council of state. *Mussant:* repine—grieve.

455. *Dissensu:* disagreement—discordance.

457. *Padusæ:* one of the mouths of the river Po. *Piscoso amne:* in the fishy stream.

458. *Stagna. Stagnum,* is, properly, the deep parts of the sea, or river. Here it is taken for the whole river, or stream. *Loquacia:* resounding—echoing.

459. *Tempore arrepto:* the occasion being taken, Turnus, &c. These words of Turnus are extremely sarcastic.

461. *Illi:* the enemy.

463. *Maniplis:* in the sense of *turmis. Edice:* in the sense of *jube,* vel *impera.*

464. *Equitem:* the cavalry—horsemen in general. This is the reading of Heyne. Ruæus says, *equites. Messapus—Coras.* These are in the nom. for the voc. after the Greek idiom.

465. *Diffundite:* lead out—draw up the cavalry in arms.

467. *Cætera manus:* let the other troops, &c. *Jusso:* for *jussero,* by syn.

470. *Deserit:* in the sense of *relinquit* vel *abrumpit.* Latinus, alarmed at the dismal crisis of his affairs, gives up his plan of conciliation, and again relies upon defensive measures.

Dardanium Æneam, generumque asciverit urbi.
Præfodiunt alii portas, aut saxa sudesque
Subvectant. Bello dat signum rauca cruentum
Buccina. Tum muros variâ cinxêre coronâ
Matronæ puerique; vocat labor ultimus omnes.
 Nec non ad templum summasque ad Palladis arces
Subvehitur magnâ matrum regina catervâ,
Dona ferens: juxtàque comes Lavinia virgo,
Causa mali tanti, atque oculos dejecta decoros.
Succedunt matres, et templum thure vaporant,
Et mœstas alto fundunt de limine voces:
Armipotens belli præses, Tritonia virgo,
Frange manu telum Phyrgii prædonis, et ipsum
Pronum sterne solo, portisque effunde sub altis.
 Cingitur ipse furens certatim in prælia Turnus.
Jamque adeò Rutulum thoraca indutus ahenis
Horrebat squamis, surasque incluserat auro,
Tempora nudus adhuc: laterique accinxerat ensem,
Fulgebatque altâ decurrens aureus arce:
Exsultatque animis, et spe jam præcipit hostem.
Qualis, ubi abruptis fugit præsepia vinclis,
Tandem liber, equus, campoque potitus aperto;
Aut ille in pastus armentaque tendit equarum;
Aut assuetus aquæ perfundi flumine noto
Emicat, arrectisque fremit cervicibus altè
Luxurians; luduntque jubæ per colla, per armos.
 Obvia cui, Volscorum acie comitante, Camilla

479. Lavinia virgo *est* comes juxta *eam; quæ est* causa

480. Dejecta *quoad* decoros

487. *Ille* indutus *quoad* Rutulum

489. *Ille* nudus adhuc *quoad*

492. *Talis* qualis equus, ubi fugit præsepia, vinclis abruptis, tandem liber

498. Cui, *nempe, Turno,* Camilla, acie

NOTES.

473. *Præfodiunt portas:* some dig trenches before the gates, with a view to keep off the enemy.

474. *Subvectant:* this is the reading of Heyne and Davidson. Ruæus reads, *subjiciunt.*

475. *Variâ coronâ:* in various companies, or troops. They manned the walls in various parts. So universal was the sense of danger, that all who were capable of making resistance, took up arms. The last struggle, the *ultimus labor*, called upon every one to unite in making what resistance they could, in aid of the regular forces. *Corona:* a company, or body of men, standing around in the form of a circle or ring, was called *corona.* Here taken for the troops in general.

481. *Vaporant:* perfume.

483. *Armipotens præses:* O! powerful patroness of war, &c. This prayer is taken from Homer, Iliad 17, where the Trojan matrons invoke the aid of Pallas against Diomede. It is almost a literal version of the Greek, which Mr. Pope hath elegantly rendered into English:

Oh, awful Goddess! ever dreadful maid,
Troy's strong defence, unconquer'd Pallas, aid;
Break thou Tydides' spear, and let him fall,
Prone on the dust, before the Trojan wall.

484. *Prædonis.* She calls Æneas a robber, in allusion to the conduct of Paris, at the court of Menelaus.

485. *Effunde:* rout him—break in pieces his power under, &c.

488. *Ahenis squamis:* in his brazen armor. *Squamæ:* the plates in a coat of mail, which in some degree resembled the scales of a fish. By meton. the corslet, or coat of mail itself: and hence, by synec. armor in general. *Horrebat:* in the sense of *lucebat horrificè. Incluserat suras:* he had bound his legs in gold. He had put on his golden sandals. Any thing made of gold may be called *aurum.*

491. *Præcipit:* in the sense of *præoccupat.*

494. *Tendit:* in the sense of *fert se.*

495. *Perfundi:* in the sense of *lavari.*

496. *Emicat:* he springs forth. Ruæus says, *exilit. Fremit:* neighs. *Altè* may be connected either with *arrectis*, or *luxurians.* This last is used in the sense of *exsultans.*

498. *Acie Volscorum:* the troops of the *Volsci* accompanying her. *Acies:* properly an army in order of battle; sometimes it is put for troops in general. Here Virgil gives an instance of the high respect, that was anciently paid to the general of an army. Camilla, though a queen, leaps from her horse, to do Turnus honor; and all her troops follow her example. This speech of

Occurrit, portisque ab equo regina sub ipsis
Desiluit; quam tota cohors imitata relictis
Ad terram defluxit equis. Tum talia fatur:
Turne, sui meritò si qua est fiducia forti,
Audeo, et Æneadûm promitto occurrere turmæ,
Solaque Tyrrhenos equites ire obvia contra.
Me sine prima manu tentare pericula belli:
Tu pedes ad muros subsiste, et mœnia serva
  Turnus ad hæc, oculos horrendâ in virgine fixus:
O, decus Italiæ, virgo, quas dicere grates,
Quasve referre parem? sed nunc, est omnia quando
Iste animus supra, mecum partire laborem.
Æneas, ut fama fidem missique reportant
Exploratores, equitum levia improbus arma
Præmisit, quaterent campos: ipse ardua montis
Per deserta jugo superans adventat ad urbem.
Furta paro belli convexo in tramite sylvæ,
Ut bivias armato obsidam milite fauces.
Tu Tyrrhenum equitem collatis excipe signis.
Tecum acer Messapus erit, turmæque Latinæ,
Tiburtique manus: ducis et tu concipe curam.
Sic ait: et paribus Messapum in prælia dictis
Hortatur, sociosque duces; et pergit in hostem.
  Est curvo anfractu vallis, accommoda fraudi,
Armorumque dolis: quam densis frondibus atrum
Urget utrinque latus: tenuis quò semita ducit,
Angustæque ferunt fauces, aditusque maligni.
Hanc super, in speculis, summoque in vertice montis
Planities ignota jacet, tutique receptus:

502. **Si qua fiducia sui *sit* forti meritò, *ego* audeo**

505. *Meâ* manu

507. Turnus, fixus *quoad* oculos in horrendâ virgine, *respondet* ad hæc

510. Quando iste *tuus* animus est supra omnia *pericula*

513. *Ut* quaterent

523. Quam *vallem* latus *sylvæ* atrum densis

NOTES.

Camilla, though short, as the time required, is full of courage, and it bespeaks the heroine.

501. *Defluxit:* leaped on the ground—dismounted after the example of their queen.

507. *Horrenda:* courageous—valiant—inspiring terror.

511. *Fidem:* assurance—certainty. It is governed by *reportant.* Heyne takes it in the sense of *nuntium.*

512. *Improbus:* wicked—infamous—with a base design. Ruæus says, *callidus. Levia arma equitum:* the light-armed cavalry. *Arma:* by meton. for those who bear them.

513. *Quaterent.* Ruæus says, *vastarent.*

514 *Superans.* This is the reading of Heyne. Ruæus and Davidson read *properans. Deserta ardua:* the high deserts of the mountains. Or, *loca* may be understood connected with *deserta. Jugo:* passing over the top, or ridge of the mountain. The poet here, probably, has in view the Alban mountains, which might extend into the territory of Laurentum. Through this mountainous tract, Turnus learned, that Æneas was about to march his army. He therefore proposes to lay in ambush.

515. *Furta:* in the sense of *insidias. Convexo:* crooked—winding.

516. *Fauces:* straits—defiles: which led through the mountains in two ways. *Obsidam:* take possession of—block up. Ruæus says, *occupem.*

517. *Collatis signis:* in close fight. *Conferre signa,* is a military term, signifying to engage in close fight.

519. *Concipe curam:* take upon yourself the charge of the general—take the chief command. Ruæus says, *sume.*

522. *Curvo anfractu:* in a mazy winding—circuit. *Fraudi:* for stratagem—ambush.

523. *Dolis:* wiles of war. *Armorum:* in the sense of *belli.* The valley through which this path led, was enclosed on each side by a thick wood. Perhaps *atrum* should be connected with *densis frondibus.*

525. *Maligni aditus:* small—scanty ways—passages. *Ferunt:* in the sense of *ducunt,* as above.

526. *In speculis:* the same as, *in summo vertice:* on the highest part—pinnacle.

527. *Ignota:* unknown to the Trojans.

528. *Occurrere pugnæ:* the same as *occurrere hostibus. Jugis:* from the top, or sides of the mountain.

Seu dextrâ lævâque velis occurrere pugnæ;
Sive instare jugis, et grandia volvere saxa.
Huc juvenis notâ fertur regione viarum,
Arripuitque locum, et sylvis insedit iniquis.
Velocem intereà superis in sedibus Opim,
Unam ex virginibus sociis, sacrâque catervâ,
Compellabat, et has tristi Latonia voces
Ore dabat: Graditur bellum ad crudele Camilla,
O virgo, et nostris nequicquam cingitur armis,
Chara mihi ante alias: neque enim novus iste Dianæ
Venit amor, subitâque animum dulcedine movit.
Pulsus ob invidiam regno, viresque superbas,
Priverno antiquâ Metabus cùm excederet urbe,
Infantem fugiens media inter prælia belli
Sustulit exilio comitem, matrisque vocavit
Nomine Casmillæ, mutatâ parte, Camillam.
Ipse sinu præ se portans juga longa petebat
Solorum nemorum: tela undique sæva premebant,
Et circumfuso volitabant milite Volsci.
Ecce, fugæ medio, summis Amasenus abundans
Spumabat ripis; tantus se nubibus imber
Ruperat. Ille, innare parens, infantis amore
Tardatur, charoque oneri timet. Omnia secum
Versanti, subitò vix hæc sententia sedit.
Telum immane, manu validâ quod fortè gerebat
Bellator, solidum nodis et robore cocto:
Huic natam, libro et sylvestri subere clausam,
Implicat, atque habilem mediæ circumligat hastæ;
Quam dextrâ ingenti librans, ita ad æthera fatur:
Alma, tibi hanc, nemorum cultrix, Latonia virgo,
Ipse pater famulam voveo: tua prima per auras

529. Saxa *in hostem*, Huc juvenis *Turnus* fertur

532. Interea, Latonia, in superis sedibus compellabat

540. Cum Metabus, pulsus regno ob.

542. Sustulit *eam* infantem, comitem exilio, vocavitquê *eam* Camillam *de* nomine *ejus* matris Casmillæ, parte *nominis* mutata

547. Medio fugæ *fluvius* Amasenus

551. Sedit *illi* versanti

552. *Erat* immane telum, quod

554. Huic *telo* implicat natam, clausam libro

556. *Quam hastam* librans

557. O virgo Latonia, alma cultrix

558. *Illa* prima *tanquam* supplex

NOTES.

529. *Jugis.* The proper place for this word appears to be after *volvere:* to tumble, or roll large rocks from the top of the mountain upon the enemy.

531. *Iniquis:* rough—uneven. Ruæus says, *asperis.*

533. *Catervâ:* retinue—band.

534. *Latonia:* a name of Diana; from *Latona*, the name of her mother. *Voces:* in the sense of *verba.*

536. *Nostris armis.* Camilla was armed like Diana and the nymphs. *O, Virgo:* meaning *Opis.*

537. *Chara:* referring to Camilla. *Alias: virgines* is understood.

539. *Invidiam, viresque superbas.* Davidson renders these words: "Invidious measures, and insolent abuse of power." His tyrannical and oppressive government excited the hatred of his subjects, who, by force of arms, drove him from his throne. *Privernum* was the name of his city.

541. *Prælia belli:* contentions—strifes of war. In the sense of *certamina belli.* Ruæus says, *pugnas belli.*

544. *Longa:* in the sense of *longè posita* vel *remota.* *Portans:* carrying his child in his bosom.

545. *Solorum:* of the lonely—solitary groves. The groves upon the distant mountains, lonely and solitary.

546. *Volitabant.* This verb expresses the rapidity, and quickness of their motions.

547. *Amasenùs:* a river of the *Volsci. Hodie, Toppia.* *Summis ripis:* over the top of its banks.

551. *Subitò hæc:* on a sudden this resolution, or purpose, was fixed upon by, &c. *Vix.* He came to this determination, desperate indeed; but nothing better presented with difficulty, in spite of all his tender fears for the safety of his child. *Sedit:* in the sense of *fixa est.*

553. *Cocto:* hardened in the fire.

555. *Circumligat:* he binds the infant easy (so as not to hurt her) to the middle of the spear: having previously enclosed the child in bark and sylvan cork, to secure her from injury. *Implicat:* Ruæus says, *alligat.*

558. *Ipse pater.* This is said, because none but the father had a right to devote

Tela tenens supplex hostem fugit: accipe, testor,
Diva, tuam, quæ nunc dubiis committitur auris
Dixit: et adducto contortum hastile lacerto
Immittit: sonuêre undæ: rapidum super amnem
Infelix fugit in jaculo stridente Camilla.
At Metabus, magnâ propiùs jam urgente catervâ,
Dat sese fluvio, atque hastam cum virgine victor
Gramineo, donum Triviæ, de cespite vellit.
Non illum tectis ullæ, non mœnibus urbes
Accepêre: neque ipse manus feritate dedisset;
Pastorum et solis exegit montibus ævum.
Hìc natam in dumis interque horrentia lustra,
Armentalis equæ mammis et lacte ferino
Nutrîbat, teneris immulgens ubera labris.
Utque pedum primis infans vestigia plantis
Institerat, jaculo palmas oneravit acuto;
Spiculaque ex humero parvæ suspendit et arcum.
Pro crinali auro, pro longæ tegmine pallæ,
Tigridis exuviæ per dorsum à vertice pendent.
Tela manu jam tum tenerâ puerilia torsit,
Et fundam tereti circum caput egit habenâ,
Strymoniamque gruem aut album dejecit olorem.
Multæ illam frustrà Tyrrhena per oppida matres
Optavêre nurum: solâ contenta Dianâ,
Æternum telorum et virginitatis amorem
Intemerata colit. Vellem haud correpta fuisset
Militiâ tali, conata lacessere Teucros!
Chara mihi, comitumque foret nunc una mearum.
Verùm age, quandoquidem fatis urgetur acerbis,
Labere, Nympha, polo, finesque invise Latinos,

573. Plantis pedum

584. *Ego* vellem *ut illa* haud

586. Foret chara mihi, unaque

587. Verùm age, O nympha

NOTES.

his children to the service of the gods. And those, who were thus devoted, were, by the Latins, called *Camilli.* I the father devote, &c.

559. *Fugit hostem:* escapes from the enemy.

560. *Auris:* in the sense of *ventis.*

563. *In jaculo:* upon the whizzing spear.

566. *Cespite:* in the sense of *ripa. Triviæ:* a name of Diana. See Ecl. iv. 10. *Donum:* the infant bound to the spear; a present or gift to Diana.

567. *Non ullæ urbes:* no cities received him, &c.

568. *Neque ipse:* nor would he have given his hand, (accepted the invitation,) on account of his savage nature, choosing rather to inhabit the mountains and woods.

569. *Ævum:* in the sense of *vitam*

571. *Mammis:* the breast, or teats of a brooding mare—of one belonging to the herd, or drove of mares kept for breeding. In this solitary retreat, did Metabus bring up his infant daughter upon the milk of a brooding mare, milking the teats into her tender lips. This is a beautiful picture of paternal care and affection. *Lacte ferino.* This is the same with the milk of the animal just mentioned. *Ferino:* an adj. from *ferus* which sometimes signifies a horse, or other domestic animal.

573. *Primis:* in the sense of *prima,* to agree with *vestigia:* or in the sense of *primùm:* and as soon as the child, &c.

575. *Parvæ:* of the child.

576. *Crinali auro.* Ruæus says, *aureo ornatu capillorum.* It may be a clasp to bind and adjust the hair, or a net-work worn over the hair to keep it in order; either of which may be considered a mark of effeminacy and luxury. Camilla was not so adorned. The skin of a tiger was the only ornament of her head.

577. *Exuviæ:* the skin of a tiger hangs, &c.

578. *Puerilia:* light, such as are suited to the strength of children.

579. *Egit fundam:* she whirled the sling.

584. *Intemerata:* she, pure and unpolluted, content with Diana alone, cherished a perpetual love, &c. She had no inclination to taste the pleasures of the conjugal state.

585. *Tali militiâ:* with the love of such a war, attempting, &c.

587. *Acerbis:* in the sense of *crudelibus,*

Tristis ubi infausto committitur omine pugna
Hæc cape, et ultricem pharetrâ deprome sagittam
Hâc, quicunque sacrum violârit vulnere corpus,
Tros Italusve, mihi pariter det sanguine pœnas.
Pòst ego nube cavâ miserandæ corpus et arma
Inspoliata feram, tumulo patriæque reponam.
Dixit: at illa leves cœli delapsa per auras
Insonuit, nigro circumdata turbine corpus.
At manus intereà muris Trojana propinquat,
Etruscique duces, equitumque exercitus omnis,
Compositi numero in turmas. Fremit æquore toto
Insultans sonipes, et pressis pugnat habenis,
Huc obversus et huc: tum latè ferreus hastis
Horret ager; campique armis sublimibus ardent.
Nec non Messapus contrà, celeresque Latini,
Et cum fratre Coras, et virginis ala Camillæ,
Adversi campo apparent: hastasque reductis
Protendunt longè dextris, et spicula vibrant:
Adventusque virûm, fremitusque ardescit equorum
Jamque intra jactum teli progressus uterque
Substiterat: subito erumpunt clamore, frementesque
Exhortantur equos: fundunt simul undique tela
Crebra, nivis ritu, cœlumque obtexitur umbrâ.
Continuò adversis Tyrrhenus et acer Aconteus

590. Cape hæc *tela*
592. *Sit-ne* Tros Italus-ve, det
593. Miserandæ *virginis*
595. At illa *Opis* delapsa
596. Circumdata *quoad* corpus
608. Uterque *exercitus* progressus

NOTES.

589. *Infausto:* inauspicious—unlucky.

590. *Cape hæc:* take these weapons. While she is thus speaking, Diana gives to Opis her quiver of arrows, and directs her to draw from it one, which should be fatal to any person that, during the engagement, might violate the sacred body of Camilla.

591. *Sacrum corpus:* the sacred body of Camilla. *Hâc:* with this arrow. *Sagitta* is understood.

593. *Miserandæ:* lamented, or unhappy virgin. *Virginis* vel *Camillæ*, is plainly to be supplied.

594. *Inspoliata:* safe—untouched by the enemy—not taken away by them. The goddess here promises to bear off the body of her favorite maid, together with her armor, entire and untouched; and restore her to her own country for burial.

This episode is finely contrived. Just as we supposed the hostile troops were to commence the work of death, the poet suspends their operations, and relates the birth and education of Camilla; who was destined to perform the most distinguished part in the military operations of the day.

597. *Manus:* in the sense of *milites* vel *agmen*.

599. *Compositi:* arranged into battalions, in order of battle.

600. *Pugnat:* he resists (struggles against) the tight drawn reigns, turning, &c. He wishes no restraint—he desires loosened reins

602. *Horret ager:* an iron field of spears. *Sublimibus:* raised high.

603. *Celeres Latini:* the light-armed Latins. These were more nimble, and their motions quicker, than those who carried heavy arms.

604. *Ala.* This word signifies the wing of our army. Also, troops in general: here the cavalry of *Camilla*. These all appeared on the plain, opposite to the Trojan and Tuscan troops.

606. *Protendunt:* they extend their spears with their hands drawn far back. They draw their arms far back, that they may give a greater force to the dart. Ruæus interprets *protendunt* by *immittunt*, which is not correct. They have not commenced the fight as yet. In this menacing manner, just ready to discharge them upon the enemy, the combatants advance to the charge.

607. *Adventus:* the advance of the men, and the neighing of the horses, grows more and more fierce. As the armies approached each other, we may suppose their ardor increased, and the neighing of the horses became louder. Mr. Davidson observes, *adventus* is a feeble word to express the movements of an army, just on the point of giving battle.

610. *Exhortantur:* in the sense of *concitant*.

611. *Ritu nivis:* after the manner of snow—thick as the flakes of snow. *Umbrâ:* with darkness. So thick was the shower of

Connixi incurrunt hastis, primique ruinam
Dant sonitu ingenti, perfractaque quadrupedantum
Pectora pectoribus rumpunt. Excussus Aconteus
Fulminis in morem, aut tormento ponderis acti,
Præcipitat longè, et vitam dispergit in auras.
Extemplò turbatæ acies; versique Latini
Rejiciunt parmas, et equos ad mœnia vertunt.
Troës agunt; princeps turmas inducit Asylas.
Jamque propinquabant portis: rursùsque Latini
Clamorem tollunt, et mollia colla reflectunt:
Hi fugiunt, penitùsque datis referuntur habenis.
Qualis ubi alterno procurrens gurgite pontus
Nunc ruit ad terras, scopulosque superjacit undam
Spumeus, extremamque sinu perfundit arenam:
Nunc rapidus retrò, atque æstu revoluta resorbens
Saxa, fugit, litusque vado labente relinquit.
Bis Tusci Rutulos egêre ad mœnia versos:
Bis rejecti armis respectant terga tegentes.
  Tertia sed postquam congressi in prælia, totas
Implicuêre inter se acies, legitque virum vir.

618. Acies *Latinorum* turbatæ *sunt*

622. Mollia colla *equorum*

623. Hi, *nempe*, Trojani fugiunt *invicem*

624. Qualis ubi pontus procurrens alterno gurgite

630. *Rutuli* bis rejecti respectant *Tuscos*

NOTES.

darts, that they intercepted the rays of the sun.

613. *Ruinam:* onset—charge. *Impetum,* says Ruæus.

614. *Perfracta:* dashed—broken. *Quadrupedantum:* in the sense of *equorum.*

615. *Rumpunt pectora:* they almost rive the breasts of their horses, dashed against each other—they rush their horses breast to breast against each other, with such impetuosity, that they almost split, or rived them. Heyne says, *perfringunt.*

616. *In morem fulminis:* Aconteus, thrown from his horse with the velocity of lightning, or of a weight thrown by an engine. This is an extravagant hyperbole. *Præcipitat:* in the sense of *præcipitatur:* is thrown, at a distance.

619. *Rejiciunt parmas:* they turned their shields behind them. This was to secure them against the missive weapons of the Trojans in their retreat. This manner of fleeing, and then facing about, was according to the rules of fighting with the cavalry, as practised by the Romans.

620. *Agunt:* in the sense of *instant* vel *sequuntur.*

622. *Mollia:* obedient—submissive to the reins.

623. *Penitùs:* fully—wholly. Ruæus says, *omninò.* It is to be connected with *datis.* The Trojans retreat (are carried back) at full speed—as fast as their horses can carry them.

624. *Procurrens alterno:* rolling forward in alternate surges. *Pontus:* in the sense of *fluctus,* says Heyne. Ruæus says *mare.* But then he takes the poet here to have reference to the ebb and flow of the tide. This, also, is the sense given to the passage by Davidson. Heyne and Valpy refer it to the moving of a wave, or surge, against the shore.

626. *Sinu perfundit:* and washes the margin (or edge) of the shore with its curling waves. Servius explains *sinu,* by *curvatione et flexu,* the curling and winding of the waves. It signifies the expanded skirts, or volumes of water, into which the flowing sea stretches itself further and further on the shore, and overspreads the beach like a garment.

627. *Atque resorbens:* and sucking in the rocks, rolled back with its tide, retreats backward. *Rapidus:* in the sense of *celer* vel *præceps.*

628. *Vado:* in the sense of *fluctu* vel *undâ.* The surge, or wave, declining, or going back, leaves the shore, until another surge succeeds. The retreat of the water from the shore is frequently so rapid, that it carries along with it stones and other substances that lie on the shore. To this the poet here alludes. But Heyne takes *saxa revoluta æstu,* &c. to imply, that the waves passed over, or through the rock, in approaching and retreating from the shore: *per quæ fluctus vel unda revolvitur,* says he.

630. *Respectant:* they see the enemy covering their backs with their shields. The plain meaning is, that the Latins put the Tuscans to flight in turn: they see them covering their backs with their shields.

631. *Tertia prælia:* the third assault—the third time they engaged.

632. *Implicuêre:* in the sense of *miscuerunt.* They engaged in close fight.

633. Gemitus morientûm *audiuntur*

Tum verò et gemitus morientûm; ėt sanguine in alto
Armaque, corporaque, et permisti cæde virorum
Semianimes volvuntur equi: pugna aspera surgit.
Orsilochus Remuli, quando ipsum horrebat adire,
Hastam intorsit equo, ferrumque sub aure reliquit.

638. Jactat crura alta, pectore

Quo sonipes ictu furit arduus, altaque jactat,
Vulneris impatiens, arrecto pectore crura.

640. Ille *Remulus* excussus *equo*

641. Catillus dejicit Iolam, Herminiumque ingentem

642. Cui *erat* fulva cæsaries in nudo vertice, humerique *erant*

Volvitur ille excussus humi. Catillus Iolam,
Ingentemque animis, ingentem corpore et armis
Dejicit Herminium: nudo cui vertice fulva
Cæsaries, nudique humeri: nec vulnera terrent:
Tantus in arma patet. Latos huic hasta per armos
Acta tremit, duplicatque virum transfixa dolore.
Funditur ater ubique cruor: dant funera ferro
Certantes: pulchramque petunt per vulnera mortem.

649. Amazon, *nempe* Camilla pharetrata exsultat, exserta *quoad*

At medias inter cædes exsultat Amazon,
Unum exserta latus pugnæ, pharetrata Camilla.
Et nunc lenta manu spargens hastilia denset,
Nunc validam dextrâ rapit indefessa bipennem.
Aureus ex humero sonat arcus, et arma Dianæ
Illa etiam, si quando in tergum pulsa recessit,
Spicula converso fugientia dirigit arcu.

655. At circum *eam, sunt* lectæ

At circùm lectæ comites, Larinaque virgo,
Tullaque, et æratam quatiens Tarpeia securim,

NOTES.

636. *Horrebat adire:* he feared to attack him. *Timeret*, says Ruæus.

638. *Jactat crura:* The meaning is, that his horse reared upon his hind feet, throwing his fore feet, and beating the air with them. In doing this, he threw his rider.

642. *Dejicit:* in the sense of *prosternit*. *Cui:* in the sense of *cujus*. So *huic:* for *hujus*, 644. *infra*. *Vertice:* in the sense of *capite*. His yellow hair waved upon his naked head.

644. *Patet tantus:* so great he stands opposed to arms. This is the sense given to the words by Davidson; who observes, that Servius, and most commentators after him, understand the words to mean: that *he stood so large a mark exposed to the darts of the enemy.* But this is so far from being a reason for his not being afraid, that it is a strong reason why he should be. *In*, may be taken in the sense of *contrà*.

645. *Acta:* in the sense of *immissa;* agreeing with *hasta*. *Transfixa:* passing through his shoulders, doubles the man with the pain of the wound. The pain inflicted by the spear was so great, that he was no longer able to maintain an erect posture. Ruæus says, *incurvat hominem.*

The reading above is that of Heyne, founded upon the *Roman*, *Medicean*, and other MSS. of antiquity, and generally adopted by modern editors. Some read *duplicatque viri transfixa dolorem.* This Turnebus approves. Others read *duplicatque, virum transfixa, dolorem.*

647. *Certantes:* a part. of the verb *certo*, taken as a sub. The combatants—the contending armies.

649. *Exserta unum latus pugnæ:* her right side was naked, and disengaged for action, (*pugnæ*,) but her left was incumbered with her bow, and half-moon shield. Such a shield the Amazons wore. Or, *pugnæ* may signify the attacks of the enemy. Then the sense will be: that she had one side (to wit, the right,) exposed to the enemy, while the other was covered with her shield; which prepares the reader for the circumstance mentioned afterwards, of her receiving her mortal wound in this part of her body. Camilla is here called an Amazon, because she was armed like one of them.

650. *Spargens:* this expresses, as well as *denset*, the rapidity with which she repeated her throws. She scattered her javelins thick on every side. *Spargit densè*, says Heyne.

652. *Arma:* in the sense of *sagittæ*.

653. *In tergum:* backward: in the sense of *retrò*.

654. *Spicula:* the winged arrows from her inverted bow. She turned her bow over her shoulder, and in that position discharged her winged arrow upon the enemy. In this manner the Parthians conducted

Italides: quas ipsa decus sibi dia Camilla
Delegit, pacisque bonas bellique ministras.
Quales Threïciæ, cùm flumina Thermodontis
Pulsant, et pictis bellantur Amazones armis;
Seu circum Hippolyten; seu cùm se Martia curru
Penthesilea refert; magnoque ululante tumultu
Fœminea exsultant lunatis agmina peltis.
Quem telo primum, quem postremum, aspera virgo,
Dejicis? aut quot humi morientia corpora fundis?
Eumenium Clytio primùm patre; cujus apertum
Adversi longâ transverberat abjete pectus.
Sanguinis ille vomens rivos cadit, atque cruentam
Mandit humum, moriensque suo se in vulnere versat.
Tum Lirin Pagasumque supèr: quorum alter, habenas
Suffosso revolutus equo dum colligit; alter
Dum subit, ac dextram labenti tendit inermem,
Præcipites pariterque ruunt. His addit Amastrum
Hippotaden: sequiturque incumbens eminùs hastâ
Tereaque, Harpalycumque, et Demophoonta, Chromimque:
Quotque emissa manu contorsit spicula virgo;
Tot Phrygii cecidêre viri. Procul Ornytus armis
Ignotis, et equo venator Iapyge fertur:
Cui pellis latos humeros erepta juvenco
Pugnatori operit; caput ingens oris hiatus,
Et malæ texêre lupi cum dentibus albis;

657. *Omnes* Italides. quas dia Camilla ipsa delegit *esse* decus sibi, ministrasque

664. O aspera virgo

666. Primùm *interficit* Eumenium *natum*

670. Tum *interficit* Lirin, Pagasumque supèr. *Illi* ruunt præcipites pariterque; quorum alter

678. Venator Ornytus fertur *in* ignotis

NOTES.

their retreat; which the poet here has in his view.

657. *Italides:* Italian nymphs.

658. *Bonas:* skilful—expert.

659. *Flumina:* the river, put by meton. for the banks of the river. They beat the banks so as to make the river resound. *Thermodontis:* gen. of *Thermodon*, a river of Thrace, the country said to have been inhabited by the Amazons.

660. *Pictis armis:* with party-colored, or variegated arms. *Bellantur:* in the sense of *pugnant.*

661. *Hippolyten.* Hippolyte was a famous queen of the Amazons. It is said she was vanquished by Hercules. *Penthesilea* was also queen of that female race. She came to the assistance of Priam during the Trojan war, and was slain by Achilles, or his son Parrhus. See Æn. i. 491.

662. *Magnoque ululante:* with a loud yelling noise.

663. *Lunatis peltis:* with their crescent shields—shields in the form of a half moon.

664. *Aspera:* in the sense of *bellicosa.*

665. *Fundis:* in the sense of *sternis.*

667. *Abjete:* for *abiete:* the fir tree—any thing made of the wood of that tree—a spear or javelin of that wood. *Adversi:* an adj. agreeing with *cujus:* right against—opposite to—in front of.

670. *Supèr:* in the sense of *prœtereà:* beside—in addition to those before mentioned.

671. *Revolutus:* falling backward from his wounded horse, while, &c.

672. *Labenti:* to him falling—to his falling friend.

673. *Pariter:* at the same time—both at once fall to the ground. *Ruunt:* in the sense of *cadunt.*

674. *Incumbens:* in the sense of *petens* vel *instans.* The simple meaning of the expression is: she killed these men as they stood at a distance from her, with her javelins, thrown at them. Virgil had an admirable talent for varying his style and expression.

678 *Ignotis armis:* arms that were strange and unusual to him. *Iapyge,* for *Iapygio:* an adj. from *Iapyx*, the son of Dædalus, who first settled in *Apulia:* Apulian.—*Fertur:* rides along—moves on.

679. *Cui:* in the sense of *cujus.* *Juvenco:* in the sense of *tauro.* This was some wild bull, killed by the hunter, in whose hide he had dressed himself. *Pugnatori:* put in apposition with *juvenco.* Heyne says, *sylvestri—cum quo pugnaverat.*

680. *Ingens hiatus:* lit. the large opening of the mouth, and the jaws of a wolf with white teeth, covered his head. His head was covered with the skin taken from the

Agrestisque manus armat sparus. ipse catervis
Vertitur in mediis, et toto vertice suprà est.
Hunc illa exceptum; neque enim labor, agmine verso;
Trajicit, et super hæc inimico pectore fatur:
Sylvis te, Tyrrhene, feras agitare putâsti?
Advenit qui vestra dies muliebribus armis
Verba redarguerit. Nomen tamen haud leve patrum
Manibus hoc referes, telo cecidisse Camillæ.
  Protinùs Orsilochum et Buten, duo maxima Teucrûm
Corpora: sed Buten adversum cuspide fixit
Loricam galeamque inter, quà colla sedentis
Lucent, et lævo dependet parma lacerto;
Orsilochum fugiens, magnumque agitata per orbem,
Eludit gyro interior, sequiturque sequentem.
Tum validam perque arma viro perque ossa securim,
Altior insurgens, oranti et multa precanti
Congeminat: vulnus calido rigat ora cerebro.
  Incidit huic, subitoque aspectu territus hæsit.
Apenninicolæ bellator filius Auni,
Haud Ligurum extremus, dum fallere fata sinebant
Isque, ubi se nullo jam cursu evadere pugnâ
Posse, neque instantem reginam avertere, cernit;
Consilio versare dolos ingressus et astu,
Incipit hæc: quid tam egregium, si fœmina forti
Fidis equo? dimitte fugam, et te cominùs æquo
Mecum crede solo, pugnæque accinge pedestri:
Jam nosces, ventosa ferat cui gloria fraudem

683. Suprà *alios* toto vertice

684. *Camilla* illa trajicit hunc exceptum; enim neque *erat* labor *ei; ejus* agmine

685. Super *eum jacentem*

687. Dies advenit, qui

690. Protinùs *interficit*

692. Quà colla *ejus* sedentis *equo*

694. *Illa* fugiens

700. Bellator filius Auni Apenninicolæ, haud extremus Ligurum, dum fata sinebant *eum* fallere, incidit huic, territusque

705. Quid *est* tam egregium, si *tu bellatrix* fœmina fidis

707. Accinge *te*

NOTES.

head of a wolf, while his shoulders were covered with the hide of a wild bull. The former the hero wore for a helmet, the latter for a corslet.

682. *Sparus:* a kind of rustic weapon.

683. *Vertitur:* in the sense of *incedit* vel *movet.*

684. *Exceptum:* in the sense of *interceptum. Verso:* routed—thrown into disorder.

688. *Redarguerit:* shall confute thy words. He had, perhaps, boasted of his valor. *Nomen:* honor—renown.

691. *Adversum:* opposite—right against her. Pierius found *aversum* in some of the best manuscripts; but the sense is in favor of *adversum:* the wound which he received was in the throat, *inter loricam, galeamque,* which could not have happened, if his back had been turned towards her. Heyne reads *aversum.*

694. *Fugiens:* the sense of this passage appears to be this: the queen, fleeing from Orsilochus, was pursued by him in a large circuit. Here she lost him in the crowd, (*eludit,*) that is, he lost sight of her, which was the object she had in view. Then turning about in a circle smaller, and on the inner side, (*gyro interior,*) she came in behind him, who was supposing he was all the time in pursuit of her, and so became the pursuer in turn. Coming up with him, rising high to give her blows more effect she drove her sturdy axe through, &c.

696. *Viro:* in the sense of *viri.*

698. *Congeminat:* Ruæus says *impingit.*

699. *Incidit huic:* met her by chance. *Hæsit:* stood amazed at the sudden and unexpected sight.

701. *Ligurum:* gen. of *Ligures.* These were a people of Italy, whose country was bounded on the north by the Apennines, and extended to the Tuscan sea on the south. Cato mentions them as notorious for their tricks and deception. To this trait of character the poet here alludes, in the words *fallere.* &c. *Pugnâ:* Heyne reads *pugnæ.*

703. *Instantem:* pressing upon him.

704. *Ingressus:* attempting to effect (put in practice) his tricks and deception, by stratagem and cunning, he says (*incipit*) these things. Ruæus says, *incipiens.*

705. *Forti:* in the sense of *celeri.*

706. *Dimitte fugam:* dismiss your flight—your horse, which enables you to flee. *Æquo solo:* on the level ground—equal terms with me.

708. *Ventosa gloria:* vain—empty boasting. *Ventosa* is used here with peculiar propriety—mere empty vaunting—light as

Dixit At illa furens, acrique accensa dolore,
Tradit equum comiti, paribusque resistit in armis,
Ense pedes nudo, purâque interrita parmâ.
At juvenis, vicisse dolo ratus, avolat ipse,
Haud mora, conversisque fugax aufertur habenis,
Quadrupedemque citum ferratâ calce fatigat.
Vane Ligur, frustràque animis elate superbis,
Nequicquam patrias tentâsti lubricus artes:
Nec fraus te incolumem fallaci perferet Auno.
Hæc fatur virgo, et pernicibus ignea plantis
Transit equum cursu: frænisque adversa prehensis
Congreditur, pœnasque inimico à sanguine sumit.
Quàm facilè accipiter saxo sacer ales ab alto
Consequitur pennis sublimem in nube columbam,
Comprênsamque tenet, pedibusque eviscerat uncis:
Tum cruor, et vulsæ labuntur ab æthere plumæ.
  At non hæc nullis hominum sator atque Deorum
Observans oculis, summo sedet altus Olympo.
Tyrrhenum genitor Tarchontem in prælia sæva
Suscitat, et stimulis haud mollibus incitat iras.
Ergò inter cædes cedentiaque agmina Tarchon
Fertur equo, variisque instigat vocibus alas,
Nomine quemque vocans; reficitque in prælia pulsos:
Quis metus, ô nunquam dolituri, ô semper inertes
Tyrrheni, quæ tanta animis ignavia venit?
Fœmina palantes agit, atque hæc agmina vertit?
Quò ferrum? quidve hæc gerimus tela irrita dextris?

712. Ratus *se vicisse eam* dolo

721. *Tam* facilè quàm accipiter, ales sacer *Marti volans* ab alto saxo

725. At *Jupiter*, sator

727. *Tum ille*, genitor

731. Quemque *hominem*

733. O Tyrrheni, nunquam dolituri, O semper inertes

735. Quò *nos gerimus* ferrum

NOTES.

the wind. *Fraudem:* this is the common reading. It is the reading of the Roman MS., and for which Servius contends. Heyne reads *laudem*, but expresses a doubt upon it. *Fraudem* is to be taken in the sense of *damnum—detrimentum* vel *pœnam*, which sometimes is the meaning of the word. If *laudem* be read, it may be taken in its usual acceptation.

709. *Acri dolore:* with keen resentment.

711. *Resistit:* this is the reading of Heyne. Ruæus and Davidson read *assistit*. The sense is the same with either. *Purâ parmâ:* with her shield which had no impress upon it. The same as *alba parma*. Lib. ix. 548. *Pedes:* a footman—on foot.

713. *Conversis habenis:* his reins being turned. Here *habenis* is plainly put for the head of his horse. He turned his horse, and left her at full speed.

714. *Ferrata calcê:* with his iron heel—with his spurs. *Fatigat:* in the sense of *impellit*.

715. *Ligus:* gen. *Liguris:* deceitful Ligurian.

716. *Lubricus:* slippery—turning every way to answer his purposes of deception.

717. *Perferet:* in the sense of *reducet*.

718. *Ignea transit:* burning with ire, she with swift foot passes his horse in his course. This action of Camilla would have been incredible, if we had not been previously prepared for something of the kind. See Lib. vii. 808. where her swiftness is described. *Ignea:* Valpy says, swift, or quick as lightning. Ruæus says, *ardens*.

719. *Adversa:* opposite—right against him, in front.

723. *Pedibus:* by this we are to understand the talons, or claws of the hawk, which are crooked, or bending: hence the propriety of *uncis*. *Eviscerat:* in the sense of *dilaniat*.

725. *Non nullis oculis:* with some attention—regard. It implies, that he was attentively regarding the scenes that were passing upon the field of battle.

730. *Alas:* the light troops. See 604, supra.

731. *Reficit pulsos:* he rallies and brings back the flying troops to the fight. Ruæus says, *revocat*.

732. *Dolituri nunquam:* never to feel resentment: a part. of the verb *doleo*.

735. *Quò ferrum:* for what intent—to what purpose do we bear the sword? *Irrita.* useless—unavailing in our hands.

Tarchon is very severe upon the Tuscans calling them stupid, and patient of insults and injuries. He alludes, perhaps, to the

736. At *vos* non *estis* segnes

At non in Venerem segnes, nocturnaque bella.
Aut, ubi curva choros indixit tibia Bacchi,
Expectare dapes, et plenæ pocula mensæ,

739. Hic *est vester* amor, hoc *est vestrum*

(Hic amor, hoc studium) dum sacra secundus aruspex
Nuntiet, ac lucos vocet hostia pinguis in altos.
Hæc effatus, equum in medios moriturus et ipse
Concitat, et Venulo adversum se turbidus infert;
Dereptumque ab equo dextrâ complectitur hostem,

744. Aufert *Venulum* ante suum

Et gremium ante suum multâ vi concitus aufert.
Tollitur in cœlum clamor, cunctique Latini
Convertêre oculos. Volat igneus æquore Tarchon
Arma virumque ferens: tum summâ ipsius ab hastâ
Defringit ferrum, et partes rimatur apertas,

749. Ille *Venulus*

Quà vulnus letale ferat. Contrà ille repugnans
Sustinet à jugulo dextram, et vim viribus exit.

751. Utque cùm fulva aquila volans altè fert

Utque volans altè raptum cùm fulva draconem
Fert aquila, implicuitque pedes, atque unguibus hæsit.
Saucius at serpens sinuosa volumina versat,
Arrectisque horret squamis, et sibilat ore,

755. Illa *aquila* haud minùs

Arduus insurgens: illa haud minùs urget adunco
Luctantem rostro; simul æthera verberat alis.
Haud aliter prædam Tiburtum ex agmine Tarchon
Portat ovans. Ducis exemplum eventumque secuti
Mœonidæ incurrunt. Tum fatis debitus Aruns
Velocem jaculo et multà prior arte Camillam

NOTES.

tameness with which they endured the tyranny of Mezentius, and patiently submitted to it till it became past endurance; and now they are not ashamed to turn their backs before a woman. *Gerimus.* This is the reading of Heyne, and is found in the best MSS. Ruæus reads *geritis.*

736. *Venerem:* in the sense of *voluptatem* vel *cupidinem.*

737. *Indixit:* proclaimed—appointed.

739. *Secundus:* favorable—propitious.—The person who predicted future events by inspecting the entrails of victims, was called *aruspex.* When the *auspices* were favorable, he was called *secundus.* After the announcement of the auspices, the feast immediately followed. *Sacra.* Ruæus says *sacrificia.* Davidson, *sacred rites.*

742. *Turbidus:* in the sense of *acer.*

743. *Complectitur:* he grasps in his right hand.

744. *Ante suum gremium:* in the sense of *ante se.*

746. *Igneus:* in the sense of *ardens.*

748. *Defringit ferrum:* he breaks off the steel from the end of his spear, so that he could do him no injury. *Rimatur:* in the sense of *quærit.* *Partes:* the exposed part of his throat.

750. *Exit:* in the sense of *avertit.* It is here used actively. *Sustinet:* in the sense of *repellit.*

752. *Hæsit:* and griped him in his talons.

755. *Urget:* the more the snake struggles, and endeavors to extricate itself, the closer does the eagle gripe it in his talons and crooked beak: just so Tarchon bears off Venulus in his tenacious grasp. *Tiburtum:* the same with *Venulum.* He was commander, and a principal man among the Tiburtines. Their city was called *Tibur,* situated, some say, about twenty miles north of the place where Rome was afterwards built. It was founded by *Tiburtus,* the son of *Amphiaraus.* See Æn. vii. 630.

759. *Mœonidæ:* the Tuscans. They are here so called, because their ancestors removed from *Mœonia,* a country of Asia Minor, and settled in Italy. *Aruns debitus fatis:* Aruns devoted to death. It is said of him, because he was to kill Camilla; and whoever killed her, forfeited his life to Diana, by a decree of that goddess. See 591, supra. *Incurrunt:* in the sense of *irruunt.* *Fatis:* in the sense of *morti.*

760. *Circuit:* he goes around Camilla, for the purpose of discovering some unprotected place, where he may give her a mortal wound. He follows her over the field of battle, and closely observes her movements; and continues unobserved by her, until the fatal moment arrived. She was in the pursuit of *Chloreus,* and intent upon his spoils, when Aruns, having observed a favorable opportunity to effect his purpose, threw his spear, and a god directed it to the naked

Circuit, et, quæ sit fortuna facillima, tentat.
Quâ se cunque furens medio tulit agmine virgo;
Hâc Aruns subit, et tacitus vestigia lustrat;
Quâ victrix redit illa, pedemque ex hoste reportat;
Hâc juvenis furtim celeres detorquet habenas.
Hos aditus, jamque hos aditus, omnemque pererrat
Undique circuitum; et certam quatit improbus hastam.
Fortè sacer Cybelæ Chloreus, olimque sacerdos,
Insignis longè Phrygiis fulgebat in armis:
Spumantemque agitabat equum; quem pellis ahenis
In plumam squamis auro conserta tegebat.
Ipse, peregrinâ ferrugine clarus et ostro,
Spicula torquebat Lycio Gortynia cornu:
Aureus ex humeris sonat arcus, et aurea vati
Cassida: tum croceam chlamdemque, sinusque cre- [pantes
Carbaseos fulvo in nodum collegerat auro,
Pictus acu tunicas, et barbara tegmina crurum.
Hunc virgo, sive ut templis præfigeret arma
Troïa, captivo sive ut se ferret in auro
Venatrix, unum ex omni certamine pugnæ
Cæca sequebatur; totumque incauta per agmen,
Fœmineo prædæ et spoliorum ardebat amore.
Telum ex insidiis cùm tandem, tempore capto,
Conjicit, et Superos Aruns sic voce precatur:
Summe Deûm, sancti custos Soractis, Apollo,
Quem primi colimus, cui pineus ardor acervo
Pascitur: et medium freti pietate per ignem

762. Quâcunque furens virgò tulit se

770. Quem *equum* pellis conserta ahenis squamis *et* auro

774. Aurea cassida *est huic* vati *in capite*

777. *Ille erat* pictus acu *quoad* tunicas

778. Virgo, sive ut præfigerat Troïa arma templis, sive ut venatrix ferret se in captivo auro, cæca sequebatur hunc unum

783. Cùm tandem Aruns, tempore capto, conjicit

785. *O* Apollo, summe

787. Et *nos tui* cultores, freti *nostra* pietate

NOTES.

breast of the virgin warrior. *Circuit:* of *circùm* and *eo.*

761. *Fortuna:* time—opportunity. Valpy says, "the most vulnerable point—where the chance of hitting seemed most favorable."

766. *Pererrat:* examines—surveys. Ruæus says, *percurrit.* *Aditus:* access—approaches.

767. *Certam:* unerring—certain. *Improbus:* with wicked design. Ruæus says, *malignus.*

771. *Conserta:* compacted, or fastened with brazen nails, and gold. *In plumam:* in the form of a plume. The nails were so placed in the skin, as to represent the figure of a plume, or plumes; and served, in some measure, as defensive armor for the horse.

772. *Peregrinâ ferrugine:* in foreign blue and purple. *Clarus:* in the sense of *splendens.*

773. *Gortynia:* an adj. from *Gortyna,* a city of Crete. *Cornu:* in the sense of *arcu.*

776. *Collegerat:* then he had collected his saffron-colored cloak, and its rustling folds of fine linen, into a knot with yellow gold.

777. *Pictus:* embroidered as to his tunic. *Barbara tegmina:* the foreign coverings of his legs. These may be called *barbara,* because they were of Phrygian fashion.

780. *Ex omni:* Ruæus says, *ex omnibus certantibus in prœlio.* Davidson, "of all the warring chiefs." In this case, *certamen* will be by meton. for *certator* vel *bellator.* The meaning is, that she singled him out of all the combatants, and pursued him over the field of battle, as being the richest prize, and affording the most valuable spoils. This idea is expressed, and assigned in the following lines, as the reason of her procedure. She was so intent upon the booty and spoils, that she forgot her perilous situation. She did not perceive Aruns, nor was she in any way apprized of his design against her.

783. *Ex insidiis:* privately—or from his concealment.

785. *Soractis.* Soractes in Soracte was a mountain of Etruria, near the Tiber, about twenty-six miles north of the place where Rome was afterward built. It was sacred to Apollo; who is thence called *Custos Soractis.*

786. *Ardor:* in the sense of *ignis.* *Cui:* for whom—in honor of whom. *Ligni* is to be supplied after *acervo.*

787. *Freti pietate premimus,* &c. This circumstance is illustrated from an historical passage in Pliny, lib. 7. *Haud procul urbe Roma, in Faliscorum agro, familiæ sunt paucæ, quæ vocantur Hirpiæ: quæ sacrificio*

Cultores multâ premimus vestigia prunâ :
Da, pater, hoc nostris aboleri dedecus armis,
Omnipotens ! Non exuvias, pulsæve trophæum
Virginis, aut spolia ulla peto. Mihi cætera laudem
Facta ferent. Hæc dira meo dum vulnere pestis
Pulsa cadat, patriam rĕmeabo inglorius urbem.
Audiit, et voti Phœbus succedere partem
Mente dedit : partem volucres dispersit in auras.
Sterneret ut subitâ turbatam morte Camillam,
Annuit oranti : reducem ut patria alta videret,
Non dedit ; inque Notos vocem vertêre procellæ.
Ergò, ut missa manu sonitum dedit hasta per auras,
Convertêre animos acres, oculosque tulere
Cuncti ad reginam Volsci. Nihil ipsa neque auræ,
Nec sonitûs memor, aut venientis ab æthere teli ;
Hasta sub exsertam donec perlata papillam
Hæsit, virgineumque altè bibit acta cruorem.
Concurrunt trepidæ comites, dominamque ruentem
Suscipiunt. Fugit ante omnes exterritus Aruns
Lætitiâ, mixtoque metu : nec jam ampliùs hastæ
Credere, nec telis occurrere virginis audet.
Ac velut ille, priùs quàm tela inimica sequantur,
Continuò in montes sese avius abdidit altos,

792. Hæc dira pestis Camilla

794. Phœbus audiit ; et dedit

797. Annuit *illi* oranti, ut

801. Ipsa *est* nihil memor

809. Ille lupus, pastore, magno-ve juvenco occiso, conscius audacis facti, continuò avius

NOTES.

annuo, quod fit ad montem Soractem Apollini, super ambustam ligni struem ambulantes non aduruntur.

788. *Multa prunâ.* It is said, so manifest was the power of Apollo here displayed, that his priests and votaries could walk through the midst of fire, and tread upon burning coals, without receiving the least injury from the flames. *Vestigia :* in the sense of *pedes.*

789. *Hoc dedecus :* this disgrace of fleeing before a woman, and falling under her victorious arm.

791. *Mihi :* in the sense of *mea.*

792. *Dum :* provided that—on condition that. *Meo vulnere :* in the sense of *mea hasta. Vulnus* is frequently put by meton. for the weapon that gives the wound. Ruæus says, *vulnere à me inflicto.*

793. *Remeabo,* &c. It was an inglorious act in Aruns to wound Camilla, in that private manner, like a coward, without daring to enter the list with her in fair combat. He was sensible of this, and that he would be looked upon as a coward. Nevertheless, he was willing to lie under that disgrace, provided he could accomplish his wishes.

795. *Mente dedit.* Phœbus heard his prayer, but gave no external indication of his purpose concerning it ; or else Aruns would have been deterred from the action : he granted it in his mind, and only a part of his prayer, not the whole.

796. *Turbatam :* confused—in a state of perturbation.

797. *Alta :* in the sense of *clara* vel *nobilis.*

798. *Procellæ :* the tempest. The word properly means a violent storm at sea. *Notos :* here taken for winds in general; properly the south wind. *Vocem :* in the sense of *verba,* the words of Aruns : (to wit) that he would return in safety to his own country.

801. *Nihil :* in the sense of *non.*

803. *Perlata :* wafted—borne. Ruæus says, *veniens. Sub :* deep into her naked breast. This word is frequently used in this sense by the poet.

805. *Ruentem :* in the sense of *cadentem.*

806. *Exterritus lætitiâ :* struck—alarmed with joy, and mingled fear above, &c. His sensation was joy mingled with fear. He rejoiced that he had wounded Camilla, and at the same time, he feared the avenging weapons of the Latins. He fled immediately. We may observe how very differently the poet represents the characters and actions of Camilla and Aruns. She appears in every respect the heroine ; both valiant in action, and fearless in danger : he, on all occasions, showing himself the coward and poltron. Our feelings are interested in her behalf : and we regret, since she was doomed to fall, that it had not been by a nobler arm.

809. *Ille lupus :* and as a wolf, &c. *Ille* is used in the same sense, Æn. x. 407. *Ac velut ille aper :* and xii. 5. *Ille leo.*

810. *Avius :* alone—in secret.

Occiso pastore, lupus, magnove juvenco,
Conscius audacis facti: caudamque remulcens
Subjecit pavitantem utero, sylvasque petivit
Haud secùs ex oculis se turbidus abstulit Aruns,
Contentusque fugâ mediis se immiscuit armis.
Illa manu moriens telum trahit: ossa sed inter
Ferreus ad costas alto stat vulnere mucro.
Labitur exsanguis; labuntur frigida leto
Lumina: purpureus quondam color ora reliquit
Tum sic exspirans, Accam, ex æqualibus unam,
Alloquitur, fida ante alias quæ sola Camillæ,
Quîcum partiri curas; atque hæc ita fatur:
Hactenus, Acca soror, potui: nunc vulnus acerbum
Conficit, et tenebris nigrescunt omnia circùm.
Effuge, et hæc Turno mandata novissima perfer:
Succedat pugnæ, Trojanosque arceat urbe.
Jamque vale. Simul his dictis linquebat habenas,
Ad terram non sponte fluens. Tum frigida toto
Paulatim exsolvit se corpore, lentaque colla
Et captum leto posuit caput, arma relinquens;
Vitaque cum gemitu fugit indignata sub umbras.
  Tum verò immensus surgens ferit aurea clamor
Sidera: dejectâ crudescit pugna Camillâ.
Incurrunt densi, simul omnis copia Teucrûm,
Tyrrhenique duces, Evandrique Arcadis alæ.
  At Triviæ custos jamdudum in montibus Opis
Alta sedet summis, spectatque interrita pugnas.
Utque procul medio juvenum in clamore furentûm
Prospexit tristi multatam morte Camillam;
Ingemuitque, deditque has imo pectore voces:

816. Illa *Camilla*

821. Quæ sola *erat* fida Camillæ ante alias, quîcum *solebat*

828. *Illa* frigida paulatim

NOTES.

813. *Subjecit caudam:* puts his trembling tail between his legs, (under his belly,) keeping it close. *Remulcens:* cherishing it —fondly taking care of it.

817. *Stat:* in the sense of *hæret*. *Mucro:* the point—barb of his spear.

818. *Labitur exsanguis:* Donatus reads, *labitur et sanguis*, seemingly, to save the appearance of contradiction in the narration: for Camilla does not fall from her horse, till some time after this, verse 827. But *labitur* does not necessarily imply that she fell to the ground; but she faints, or sinks down, being supported perhaps on her horse, by her attendants, for some minutes. Davidson.

819. *Quondam:* soon after—presently. *Ora:* in the sense of *vultum*. She became pale, and her eyes became cold in death.

822. *Quîcum:* the abl. for *quâcum:* with whom.

823. *Potui.* Servius supposes *vivere* vel *pugnare* to be understood. Ruæus and Heyne supply *pugnare*. La Cerda, Davidson, and Valpy, take it absolutely. *Hactenus potui:* hitherto I have been powerful—my strength hath availed me; now, &c. *Conficit:* in the sense of *interficit*. *Me* is understood.

828. *Fluens:* in the sense of *labens*.

829. *Lenta colla:* she reclined her drooping—lifeless neck.

830. *Captum:* overcome.

833. *Dejecta:* in the sense of *occisa* vel *interfecta*.

834. *Incurrunt:* rush in crowded ranks upon the enemy.

835. *Alæ:* in the sense of *equites*.

836. *Triviæ.* This is a name of Diana; either because she presided over *Trivia*, the crossways; or, because she was fabled to have three forms. She was called *Luna* in heaven, *Diana* on the earth, and *Hecate* in hell. *Opis:* a nymph of Diana's train. She is called, therefore, *custos* in the sense of *comes* vel *famula*. She was appointed by Diana to avenge any injury done to Camilla, upon the author of it. She, therefore, hastens to kill Aruns.

839. *Multatam:* in the sense of *interfectam*. Ruæus says, *affectam*.

840. *Dedit:* in the sense of *emisit*.

Heu! nimiùm, virgo, nimium crudele luisti
Supplicium, Teucros conata lacessere bello!
Nec tibi desertæ in dumis coluisse Dianam
Profuit, aut nostras humero gessisse pharetras.
Non tamen indecorem tua te regina relinquet
Extremâ jam in morte: neque hoc sinè nomine letum
Per gentes erit, aut famam patieris inultæ.
Nam quicunque tuum violavit vulnere corpus,
Morte luet meritâ. Fuit ingens monte sub alto
Regis Dercenni terreno ex aggere bustum
Antiqui Laurentis, opacâque ilice tectum.
Hìc Dea se primùm rapido pulcherrima nisu
Sistit, et Aruntem tumulo speculatur ab alto.
Ut vidit fulgentem armis, ac vanà tumentem:
Cur, inquit, diversus abis? huc dirige gressum:
Huc, periture, veni; capias ut digna Camillæ
Præmia. Tu-ne etiam telis moriere Dianæ?
Dixit: et auratâ volucrem Threïssa sagittam
Deprompsit pharetrâ, cornuque infensa tetendit;
Et duxit longè, donec curvata coirent
Inter se capita, et manibus jam tangeret æquis,
Lævâ aciem ferri, dextrâ nervoque papillam.
Extemplò teli stridorem aurasque sonantes
Audiit unà Aruns, hæsitque in corpore ferrum.
Illum expirantem socii atque extrema gementem
Obliti ignoto camporum in pulvere linquunt:
Opis ad æthereum pennis aufertur Olympum.
Prima fugit, dominâ amissâ, levis ala Camillæ
Turbati fugiunt Rutuli; fugit acer Atinas;

842. *Tu* O virgo, luisti nimiùm

846 Hoc *tuum* letum

849. Fuit ingens bustum Dercenni, antiqui Laurentis regis

854. Ut vidit *eum*

856. Veni huc, *tu*, periture; ut

860. Duxit *illud* longè

862. *Nempe*, lævâ *manu tangeret* aciem ferri, dextrâ *manu* nervoque *tangeret ejus* papillam.

865. Socii obliti linquunt illum

NOTES.

841. *Luisti:* thou hast suffered, &c. *Nimiùm.* The *nimiùm* is here emphatical; and is to be repeated with *crudele:* too cruel, or severe.

843. *Desertæ:* alone—by thyself.

845. *Indecorem:* in the sense of *inhonoratam.*

846. *Nomine.* renown—glory.

847. *Famam inultæ:* the infamy of one unavenged. *Famam,* here is plainly to be taken in the sense of *infamiam,* as it sometimes signifies. It was considered dishonorable to die in battle, without being avenged, and a mark of infamy.

849. *Luet:* the meaning is: he shall atone for, or expiate the crime, with, &c. *Crimen* vel *scelus,* is understood.

850. *Dercenni.* This Dercennus was probably one of the kings of the aborigines, the primitive inhabitants of Italy. *Bustum:* a tomb.

852. *Nisu:* in the sense of *motu.*

854. *Vanà:* an adj. neu. pleu., used as an adverb, in imitation of the Greeks: in the sense of *vanè.*

855. *Diversus:* in the sense of *in diversam partem.*

856. *Capias digna:* the meaning is, that thou mayest be slain—mayest receive the just reward for killing Camilla. *Morte,* or a word of the like import, is understood to govern *Camillæ.*

857. *Tu-ne moriere:* shalt thou die by the weapons of Diana? Dost thou, miscreant, deserve to die by the weapons of Diana? The words imply, that he was utterly unworthy of a death so honorable.

858. *Threïssa.* Latona, it is said, brought some nymphs from the Hyperboreans to educate her children, Diana and Apollo. Servius makes them to be the same with the Thracians; and probably *Opis* was one of them. *Threïssa: nympha* is understood The same with *Opis.*

859. *Cornu:* in the sense of *arcum. Infensa:* angry. Ruæus says, *inimica,* agreeing with *Opis.*

860. *Duxit longè:* stretched it wide asunder, until the extremities, &c. Ruæus says, *extremitates ejus inflexæ. Coirent.* come together—meet. *Æquis:* level—horizontal. She touched the barb with one hand, and her breast with the other. The bow was bent to the full length of her arms. *Aciem*

Disjectique duces, desolatique manîpli
Tuta petunt, et equis aversi ad mœnia tendunt
Nec quisquam instantes Teucros, letumque ferentes
Sustentare valet telis, aut sistere contrà :
Sed laxos referunt humeris languentibus arcus,
Quadrupedumque putrem cursu quatit ungula campum.
Volvitur ad muros caligine turbidus atrâ
Pulvis : et è speculis percussæ pectora matres
Fœmineum clamorem ad cœli sidera tollunt.
Qui cursu portas primi irrupêre patentes,
Hos inimica super mixto premit agmine turba.
Nec miseram effugiunt mortem ; sed limine in ipso,
Mœnibus in patriis, atque inter tuta domorum
Confixi, exspirant animas. Pars claudere portas:
Nec sociis aperire viam, nec mœnibus audent
Accipere orantes : oriturque miserrima cædes
Defendentûm armis aditus, inque arma ruentûm.
Exclusi, ante oculos lachrymantûmque ora parentum,
Pars in præcipites fossas, urgente ruinâ,
Volvitur ; immissis pars cæca et concita frænis
Arietat in portas, et duros objice postes.
Ipsæ de muris summo certamine matres
(Monstrat amor verus patriæ) ut vidêre Camillam,

871. Tuta *loca*

877. Matres percussæ *quoad*

880. Inimica turba premit

882. Tuta *loca* domorum

883. Pars *incipit* claudere

886. Miserrima cædes *eorum* defendentûm

887. Pars *eorum, qui* exclusi *sunt* volvitur præcipites in

892. Monstrat *viam*

NOTES.

ferri: the point of the arrow was tipped with iron, or steel, to make it enter the object more easily.

870. *Manîpli. The manipulus* was properly the standard bearer, so called from a bundle of hay tied to the end of a pole, which the first Romans used instead of an ensign. It was afterwards used for the companies, or bands of soldiers, to which a *manipulus* was attached: also, for troops in general, by meton. *Desolati:* deserted by their officers—left alone. *Disjecti:* scattered abroad—slain. Ruæus says, *dissipati.*

871. *Aversi:* in the sense of *conversi.*

873. *Sustentare:* to stop—to resist.

876. *Pulvis turbidus,* &c. The meaning is, that dust rising in clouds of thick darkness approaches the city. This was a presage of defeat to the Latins, and filled the matrons with dismay and consternation. During the engagement they had been spectators of the conflict.

877. *Speculis:* in the sense of *muris.*

880. *Mixto agmine.* This may refer either to the Trojans or Latins. If it refer to the former, it will imply that they mingled with the Latins, and slew them without regard to the order of attack : if it refer to the latter, it will imply that they fled in confusion and disorder, and in that state were pursued by the enemy. It appears that some of the foremost of the pursuers entered the gates along with the Latins, and continued the work of death within the walls, and among the very houses of the city.

886. *Defendentûm:* of those who by force of arms oppose the entrance of the flying troops, and of those, who wish to force an entrance to save themselves from the hands of the enemy.

888. *Præcipites:* headlong—quick—unexpected, denoting the manner of their fall. It will agree with *pars,* as a noun of multitude. *Fossas:* these were the large holes, or pits, which the Latins dug before the gates, to impede the approach of the enemy. See 473. supra.

889. *Frænis immissis:* at full speed—the reins being given to the horses. *Cæca:* this implies that they had lost their presence of mind, and knew not what they were doing. *Concita:* in the sense of *celeris.*

890. *Duros objice:* strengthened—made strong—secured by bars.

891. *Summo certamine:* with the greatest zeal, or earnestness. Heyne says, *extremo certamine.*

892. *Ut vidêre:* as they saw Camilla. Heyne says, *exemplo Camillæ.* They had been spectators of the battle, and beheld her noble deeds of valor; and how much patriotism and love of country were displayed in all her actions. Prompted by her example, they now arm themselves in haste, and repair to the place of danger, ready to die in their country's cause.

Tela manu trepidæ jaciunt: ac robore duro,
Stipitibus ferrum sudibusque imitantur obustis
Præcipites, primæque mori pro mœnibus ardent.
Intereà Turnum in sylvis sævissimus implet
Nuntius, et juveni ingentem fert Acca tumultum:
Deletas Volscorum acies, cecidisse Camillam,
Ingruere infensos hostes, et Marte secundo
Omnia corripuisse; metum jam ad mœnia ferri.
Ille furens, nam sæva Jovis sic numina poscunt,
Deserit obsessos colles, nemora aspera linquit.
Vix è conspectu exierat, campumque tenebat,
Cùm pater Æneas, saltus ingressus apertos,
Exsuperatque jugum, sylvâque evadit opacâ.
Sic ambo ad muros rapidi totoque feruntur
Agmine, nec longis inter se passibus absunt.
Ac simul Æneas fumantes pulvere campos
Prospexit longè, Laurentiaque agmina vidit:
Et sævum Ænean agnovit Turnus in armis,
Adventumque pedum, flatusque audivit equorum.
Continuò pugnas ineant, et prælia tentent:
Ni roseus fessos jam gurgite Phœbus Ibero
Tingat equos, noctemque, die labente, reducat
Considunt castris ante urbem, et mœnia vallant.

898. *Dicit* acies Volscrum deletas *esse*

901. Ille *Turnus*

NOTES.

893. *Trepidæ:* in haste—quick. So, also, *præcipites*, in verse 895. infra.

894. *Imitantur:* they imitate the weapons of iron, with hard oak stakes, and poles hardened at the point. With these weapons, made on the exigency of the moment, in imitation of iron weapons, they arm themselves, and are desirous of dying first in the defence of their country. *Mœnibus:* in the sense of *urbi* vel *patriæ*.

897. *Fert:* in the sense of *refert* vel *nunciat*. *Secundo:* in the sense of *favente* vel *iuvante*.

901. *Numina:* decrees—purposes. *Sæva:* in the sense of *dura*. *Nam*. this is the common reading. Heyne reads, *et*.

905. *Evadit:* escapes from the wood. This shows the danger he had been in from the ambush, which Turnus laid for him.

907. *Longis passibus*. *Longis* must be taken here in the sense of *multis*, or *passibus* in the sense of *intervallo*. Ruæus says, *longo intervallo*.

910. *Sævum:* fierce—valiant in arms.

911. *Flatus:* in the sense of *hinnitus*.

913. *Ibero gurgite:* in the western ocean. Here the poet supposed the sun to extinguish his light every evening.

915. *Mœnia:* in the sense of *castra*.

QUESTIONS.

How does this book open?

What does Æneas do with the body of Pallas?

How many chosen men accompany it?

What effect had the news of his death upon his father?

How many captives did Æneas send as victims to his *Manes?*

Whom does the poet here imitate?

Does the poet here outrage the character of his hero?

Is there any expression of Homer, which disapproves of the conduct of Achilles, in offering human victims at the tomb of Patroclus?

Is there a difference in character between the two heroes?

What are the distinguishing features of character?

When the news of the defeat reached the city, what effect did it produce upon the Latins?

Did Latinus send ambassadors to Æneas, to desire a truce, for the purpose of burying their dead?

Was this granted to them?

How long a time was agreed upon for that purpose?

Who was a principal person of this embassy?

Who was Drances?

What is his character?

Where was Turnus at this time?

On the return of the ambassadors from

Diomede, did Latinus call a council of state to receive the answer?

What was the nature of that answer?

What effect had it upon the Latins?

Who was the principal person of that embassy?

Who was Diomede?

Why did he come to Italy?

What were his reasons for declining to take part with Turnus and the Latins?

What does he say of the valor of Æneas?

What course did he advise Latinus to take?

What city did he build in Italy?

Where was it situated?

What is said of his companions in arms?

Is this a ridiculous and improbable story?

What is the conclusion of Latinus in regard to the war?

Did he make any speech upon the occasion?

What did he propose to do?

What is the character of the speech of Drances?

Of what did he accuse Turnus?

What is the character of the reply of Turnus?

What is his object in this reply?

Were there any political parties at this time among the Latins?

Who may be said to have been at the head of the party in favor of Turnus?

Who was at the head of the other party?

What did this party wish to effect?

Was any proposition made to Turnus to decide the dispute with Æneas in single combat?

Who made the proposition?

How was it received by Turnus?

Did he express any reluctance to meet Æneas?

During the deliberations of the council, what information reaches Laurentum?

What effect had this advance of the enemy upon Latinus?

What did Turnus do upon this emergency?

In how many divisions were the enemy to advance?

Under whose command were the infantry to march?

In what way were they to approach the city?

How were the cavalry to advance?

Could they come in any other way?

What was the nature of the ground over which each division was to pass?

How did Turnus receive this information?

What resolution did he take on receiving this intelligence?

Would this give him any particular advantage over Æneas?

In what would it consist?

Where does Turnus meet Camilla?

Does he confer upon her the command of the cavalry?

What direction does he give her?

Who was Camilla?

Who was her father?

What did his subjects do to him?

What was the age of Camilla at that time?

How did he save his child from the fury of his subjects?

How did he save himself?

To whom did he dedicate his daughter?

What was the manner of her education?

Was she a favorite of Diana?

Did she afterward succeed to the throne of the Volsci?

How was Camilla armed?

For what was she distinguished?

Who assisted her in command, during the action?

Who commenced the fight?

How many times did the combatants charge each other and retreat?

What took place after this?

How did Camilla distinguish herself?

What were some of her deeds of valor?

By whom was she finally killed?

What effect had her death upon the issue of the battle?

By whom was Aruns slain?

By whose orders was he slain?

And by whose arrow?

Did Aruns conduct in a cowardly manner on this occasion?

Was he sensible of it?

Finding herself mortally wounded, what did Camilla do?

Whom did she send to acquaint Turnus of the state of the battle?

What effect had the news upon him?

Did he leave his place of concealment?

What took place immediately afterward?

Was this an unlucky circumstance for Turnus?

What prevented a renewal of the fight?

When was the decisive action fought?

LIBER DUODECIMUS.

Turnus, perceiving his troops to be disheartened by their reverses, resolves to accept the proposal of deciding the dispute by single combat with Æneas. Latinus, in a tender and pathetic speech, endeavors to dissuade him from it. He advises him to relinquish his claim to Lavinia, and seek a wife among the daughters of the Italian princes. He plainly tells him, that the gods forbid him to unite his daughter to any other than a foreigner. He recounts the disastrous consequences of his opposition to the Trojans and concludes by reminding him of his aged father, and the sorrow that would fall upon him, if the issue were to prove disastrous. At this critical moment, the queen comes in, seconds her husband's entreaties, and beseeches him to relinquish his rash purpose. She declares, the safety of their family and kingdom depends upon his life; and that she is resolved to perish with him, and not to see Lavinia transferred to Æneas. But the hero is not moved from his purpose, and prefers to die rather than part with his beloved Lavinia.

The virgin heard the expostulation of her mother, and love kindled a blush upon her cheeks. This thrilled through the heart of Turnus, and all the tender emotions of his soul were roused. Forthwith he sends Idmon to the Trojan camp to proclaim, that on the following day, he would decide the dispute with Æneas.

In the mean time, he prepares his armor, and examines his steeds. At the return of day, the parties repair to the field. Latinus accompanies Turnus. Here he ratifies a league with Æneas, and calls the gods to witness. To prevent its execution, Juno sent the nymph Juturna, the sister of Turnus, to rouse the Rutulians to arms, and kindle the war. For this purpose, she caused a portentous sign in the heavens, which the augur interpreted favorably for the Italians. Forthwith he hurled a spear among the Trojans, and the two armies rushed to the combat with great impetuosity. Latinus hastens from the field. Æneas is wounded by an arrow, which caused great confusion among the Trojans. Turnus, observing this, mounts his car, and drives over the field, spreading death and desolation in his course. Wherever he directs his way, whole troops and squadrons flee before him. He performs prodigious feats of valor.

In the mean time, Æneas retires from the field, and demands the speediest relief. He is miraculously healed by Venus. This being done, the hero calls for his arms, embraces Ascanius, and goes in search of Turnus. The fight now is renewed on the part of the Trojans, and the victorious Rutulians fly. At this crisis, Juturna takes the reins of her brother's steed, and drives him victorious over the plain. Æneas pursues, and seeks by every method to meet and engage him; but Juturna baffles all his efforts. Unable to effect his purpose, he resolves to wreak his vengeance upon the Rutulians; and here he commenced a dreadful slaughter: the noblest of the Italians fall. Turnus, too, drives on with no less impetuosity, and Trojan, Tuscan, and Arcadian bite the ground.

Æneas, at the suggestion of Venus, resolves to attack the city, and by one decisive blow, either force Turnus to the combat, or overthrow the empire of Latinus. For this purpose he assembles his troops, explains his designs, and exhorts them to assault the city with vigor. They instantly mount the walls, and spread the devouring flames. At this sudden change of affairs, all hearts are filled with dismay. The queen, expecting that Turnus was slain, and his troops routed, resolved not to survive the sad catastrophe, and frantic with despair, hung herself.

In this state of things, Sages flies to Turnus, and informs him that Æneas was thundering in arms; that the city was in the hands of the enemy; that all looked to him for protection; and that, in despair, the queen, his faithful friend, had deprived herself of life. At this information the hero is struck with amazement, and turning his eyes, he beholds the very tower, which he himself had built for the defence of the city, wrapt in flames. He could not bear the sight; and leaving his sister, he sprang from his chariot, and rushed through darts and foes, calling upon the hostile armies to desist from the fight; that he was come to enter the lists with Æneas. Instantly a cessation of arms took place, and the two heroes prepare for the combat. At first they throw their javelins from a distance, and rush to close combat with great violence. They blows on blows redouble. Turnus, rising high to give his blow more effect, breaks his sword by the hilt. He now discovers a fatal mistake. When first he mounted his car, ardent for the fight, he had taken the sword of his charioteer, Mitescus, instead of his own trusty sword, which Vulcan had made for his father Daunus. He is now left defenceless, and at the mercy of his foe. He flies off swift as the wind, pursued by Æneas, and pressed on all sides by the Trojans. He calls for his heavenly-tempered sword, and chides the Rutulians. None of them dare to interfere, being prevented by the threats of Æneas. Juturna, at length, restored his sword to him, and Venus disengaged the spear of Æneas. The two heroes again prepare for the combat.

At this juncture, Jove interposes in favor of Æneas. His first care is to withdraw Juturna from the contest. For this purpose, he despatches one of the furies to the field of battle, which, assuming the form of an owl, flies backward and forward before the face of Turnus. The hero knew the portentous omen. A shivering pervaded his limbs: coldness unnerved his arm. His reason left him: his speech forsook him. As soon as Juturna heard the whizzing of the fury's wings, she recognised the direful messenger; and in all the agony of grief and distress, and uttering the tenderest expressions of affectionate attachment to her brother, she fled from his sight, and plunged herself in the deep river.

Æneas in the mean time urges on the attack, and calls upon Turnus no longer to decline the contest. He replied, "I fear not thee, nor thy boasting words: I fear the gods alone: I fear Jove, who is my enemy." At this moment, he seizes a huge stone that lay near him, and hurled it at Æneas; but it reached him not. The fury had deprived him of his wonted strength. His efforts, therefore, were unavailing. His knees sunk under him; and trembling seized his whole body. Æneas throws a javelin, which wounds him in the thigh, and caused him to fall upon his knee. In this situation, he acknowledges himself vanquished, and resigns Lavinia, the royal bride, to the victor. One favor he asked, on account of his aged father, that his body might be restored to his friends. Æneas, moved with compassion at the mention of his aged father, was about also to spare his life; when, discovering upon his shoulder the belt which Pallas wore, he became indignant, and plunged into his bosom his naked sword.

TURNUS ut infractos adverso Marte Latinos
Defecisse videt, sua nunc promissa reposci,
Se signari oculis: ultrò implacabilis ardet,
Attollitque animos. Pœnorum qualis in arvis
Saucius ille gravi venantûm vulnere pectus,
Tum demùm movet arma leo; gaudetque comantes
Excutiens cervice toros, fixumque latronis
Impavidus frangit telum, et fremit ore cruento.
Haud secùs accenso gliscit violentia Turno.
Tum sic affatur regem, atque ita turbidus infit:
Nulla mora in Turno: nihil est quód dicta retractent
Ignavi Æneadæ; nec, quæ pepigêre, recusent.
Congredior: fer sacra, pater, et concipe fœdus.
Aut hâc Dardanium dextrâ sub Tartara mittam,
Desertorem Asiæ; sedeant, spectentque Latini!
Et solus ferro crimen commune refellam:

3. Oculis *omnium*

5. Qualis ille leo in arvis Pœnorum, saucius *quoad* pectus gravi

12. Recusent *facere ea* quæ

NOTES.

1. *Infractos:* broken—disheartened. *Marte:* in the sense of *pugna* vel *bello.*

2. *Promissa:* his promises that he would meet Æneas in single combat.

3. *Ultrò.* This word implies, that Turnus was impelled by some violent, but voluntary emotion.

4. *Pœnorum:* the Carthaginians, here put for the Africans in general.

6. *Movet arma:* he moves his arms—he prepares for the attack. *Comantes toros:* the shaggy, or bushy mane. *Ille leo:* a lion, by way of eminence.

7. *Latronis:* the hunter. *Fixum:* that had pierced his breast.

9. *Gliscit:* in the sense of *crescit.*

11. *Retractent dicta:* that they should retract their words. Æneas was the first who proposed to decide the dispute in single combat with Turnus; and he had pledged himself to accept the proposition: to this reference is made verse 2, supra. *Quòd:* a conj. or in the sense of *ob quod.*

13. *Fer:* in the sense of *offer.* *Concipe:* in the sense of *sanci.*

16. *Refellam:* in the sense of *avertam* vel

17. Aut *Trojanus* habeat *nos* victos; *et* Lavinia conjux cedat *illi victori.*

20. Consulere *tibi*

24. *Innuptæ virgines*

31. Eripui *eam* promissam

32. Ex illo *tempore*, O Turne, vides

38. Si paratus sum accire *Trojanos*

39. *Eo* incolumi

41. Fors refutet *hæc mea* dicta

Aut habeat victos; cedat Lavinia conjux
Olli sedato respondit corde Latinus:
O præstans animi juvenis, quantùm ipse feroci
Virtute exsuperas, tantò me impensiùs æquum est
Consulere, atque omnes metuentem expendere casus.
Sunt tibi regna patris Dauni, sunt oppida capta
Multa manu: nec non aurumque animusque Latino est.
Sunt aliæ innuptæ Latio et Laurentibus agris,
Nec genus indecores. Sine me hæc haud mollia fatu
Sublatis aperire dolis; simul hæc animo hauri.
Me natam nulli veterum sociare procorum
Fas erat, idque omnes Divique hominesque canebant.
Victus amore tui, cognato sanguine victus,
Conjugis et mœstæ lachrymis, vincla omnia rupi;
Promissam eripui genero; arma impia sumpsi.
Ex illo qui me casus, quæ, Turne, sequantur
Bella, vides; quantos primus patiare labores
Bis magnâ victi pugnâ, vix urbe tuemur
Spes Italas: recalent nostro Tiberina fluenta
Sanguine adhuc, campique ingentes ossibus albent.
Quò referor toties? quæ mentem insania mutat?
Si, Turno exstincto, socios sum accire paratus;
Cur non, incolumi, potiùs certamina tollo?
Quid consanguinei Rutuli, quid cætera dicet
Italia, ad mortem si te; fors dicta refutet!
Prodiderim, natam et connubia nostra petentem?
Respice res bello varias; miserere parentis

NOTES.

refutabo. Crimen: either the common disgrace, by the preceding defeat and flight: or the imputation thrown upon him by Drances and others, of his wanting courage to meet Æneas. This last appears to be the sense of Ruæus.

19. *Feroci:* bold—daring. *Quantùm:* in the sense of *quantò*, corresponding with *tantò*. *Præstans animi:* excelling in courage—valor.

20. *Tantò impensiùs æquum:* by so much the more anxiously, it is just that I should consult your safety.

21. *Casus:* hazard—dangers.

23. *Nec non aurumque:* Servius takes the sense of these words to be: *Latinus satìs opulentus est, et nobilis etiam absque his nuptiis:* implying that, as Turnus was powerful and wealthy enough without contracting an alliance with Latinus, so Latinus needed not to match his daughter with him for the sake of aggrandizing himself. Though this makes sense of *aurum*, it puts a forced signification upon *animus*. Ruæus says, *sunt quoque Latino divitiæ et benevolentia.*

The expression implies, that Latinus entertained a friendly disposition towards Turnus, and desired to promote his happiness in any way that his wealth could contribute to it, but he could not bestow his daughter upon him. He advises him to seek a wife among the Italian princesses; among whom he would find some one worthy of so distinguished a prince. *Manu:* by valor.

26. *Dolis sublatis:* guile, or deceit being taken away—in plain words. *Fatu:* sup. in *u* of the verb *for:* to be spoken, or said. *Hauri:* in the sense of *audi.*

28. *Canebant:* in the sense of *prædicebant* vel *monebant.*

29. *Cognato sanguine.* Turnus was the son of Venilia, the sister of Amata, the wife of Latinus. Hence the propriety of *cognato sanguine:* kindred blood. *Vincla:* restraints—obligations.

33. *Primus:* in the sense of *princeps.*

34. *Bis victi.* They were first beaten on the banks of the Tiber, when Æneas landed his reinforcements from Etruria; and a second time vanquished under the walls of Latium, in the horse fight, when Camilla was slain. See the preceding book.

37. *Quò referor:* why am I carried so often backward?—why do I change my resolution so often, of giving my daughter to Æneas?

39. *Certamina:* disputes—contests.

41. *Fors:* fortune—the issue of the contest.

43 *Res:* state—condition.

Longævi, quem nunc mœstum patria Ardea longè
Dividit Haudquaquam dictis violentia Turni
Flectitur: exsuperat magìs, ægrescitque medendo.
Ut primùm fari potuit, sic institit ore:
Quam pro me curam geris, hanc precor, optime, pro me
Deponas, letumque sinas pro laude pacisci.
Et nos tela, pater, ferrumque haud debile dextrâ
Spargimus, et nostro sequitur de vulnere sanguis.
Longè illi Dea mater erit, quæ nube fugacem
Fœmineâ tegat, et vanis sese occulat umbris.
At regina, novâ pugnæ conterrita sorte,
Flebat, et ardentem generum moritura tenebat:
Turne, per has ego te lachrymas, per si quis Amatæ
Tangit honos animum. Spes tu nunc una senectæ,
Tu requies miseræ: decus imperiumque Latini
Te penès: in te omnis domus inclinata recumbit.
Unum oro; desiste manum committere Teucris.
Qui te cunque manent isto certamine casus,
Et me, Turne, manent. Simul hæc invisa relinquam
Lumina, nec generum Æneam captiva videbo.
Accepit vocem lachrymis Lavinia matris,
Flagrantes perfusa genas: cui plurimus ignem
Subjecit rubor, et calefacta per ora cucurrit.
Indum sanguineo veluti violaverit ostro
Si quis ebur; vel mixta rubent ubi lilia multâ
Alba rosâ: tales virgo dabat ore colores.
Illum turbat amor, figitque in virgine vultus.
Ardet in arma magìs; paucisque affatur Amatam:
Ne, quæso, ne me lachrymis, neve omine tanto
Prosequere in duri certamina Martis euntem,

44. Longè *a te*

48. O optime *regum* precor *ut* deponas hanc curam pro me, quam geris

52. *Eum* fugacem

56. O Turne, *precor* te per has lachrymas, per *honorem* Amatæ, si quis honos *ejus* tangit *tuum*

58. Tu *es sola* requies *mihi* miseræ

61. Quicunque casus

62. *Iidem* manent et me

72. O mater, quæso, ne, ne prosequere me

NOTES.

44. *Ardea:* the capital city of the Rutuli. The whole address of Latinus is tender and pathetic, and bespeaks the goodness of his heart. Among other arguments to dissuade Turnus from the combat, he mentions his aged father.

45. *Dividit:* in the sense of *separat.*

46. *Ægrescit medendo:* he grows more obstinate by being persuaded—by applying remedies. *Medendo:* a gerund. in *do,* of *medeor.* This is said by way of metaphor.

47. *Institit:* he proceeded—began to speak.

48. *Geris:* in the sense of *habes.*

49. *Paçisci:* to exchange death for glory —to obtain glory and renown in the room of death—for death.

51. *De vulnere nostro:* from the wound inflicted by us.

52. *Dea mater erit longè illi.* This is a Latin idiom. The meaning is: *his mother will be far from affording him any assistance,* as she had done on former occasions. It will not be in her power to do it.

54. *Sorte: sors* here means the terms, or conditions of the combat. These were, if Turnus were slain, that Lavinia should fall to Æneas; that the Rutuli should be his subjects, &c. Verse 17, supra.

57. *Honos:* respect—regard.

59. *Domus:* in the sense of *familia. Inclinata.:* in the sense of *prona* vel *labens*

60. *Desiste:* in the sense of *omitte. Committere manum:* to engage in close combat. Ruæus says, *conserere manum.*

63. *Lumina:* in the sense of *lucem* vel *vitam.*

64. *Accepit:* in the sense of *audiit.*

65. *Perfusa genas:* wet as to her blushing cheeks with tears. A Grecism. See Ecl. i. 55.

66. *Rubor:* modesty, by meton. *Ignem;* the glow, or blush, which her extreme modesty diffused, or spread over her cheeks *Subjecit* properly signifies, spread under the skin. *Calefacta:* red (or blushing) countenance.

67. *Violaverit:* in the sense of *tinxerit.*

70. *Turbat:* in the sense of *agitat*

72. *Tanto:* in the sense of *infausto.* The repetition of the *ne* is emphatical. *Prosequer* properly signifies, to convoy; here, to

O mater: neque enim Turno mora libera mortis
Nuntius hæc, Idmon, Phrygio mea dicta tyranno
Haud placitura refer: cùm primùm crastina cœlo
Puniceis invecta rotis Aurora rubebit;
Non Teucros agat in Rutulos: Teucrûm arma quiescant
Et Rutulûm: nostro dirimatur sanguine bellum:
Illo quæratur conjux Lavinia campo.
Hæc ubi dicta dedit, rapidusque in tecta recessit,
Poscit equos, gaudetque tuens ante ora frementes,
Pilumno quos ipsa decus dedit Orithyia;
Qui candore nives anteirent, cursibus auras.
Circumstant properi aurigæ, manibusque lacessunt
Pectora plausa cavis, et colla comantia pectunt.
Ipse dehinc auro squalentem alboque orichalco
Circumdat loricam humeris; simul aptat habendo
Ensemque, clypeumque, et rubræ cornua cristæ:
Ensem, quem Dauno ignipotens Deus ipse parenti
Fecerat, et Stygiâ candentem tinxerat undâ.
Exin, quæ mediis ingenti adnixa columnæ
Ædibus adstabat, validam vi corripit hastam,
Actoris Aurunci spolium: quassatque trementem,
Vociferans: Nunc, ô nunquam frustrata vocatus
Hasta meos, nunc tempus adest; te maximus Actor,
Te Turni nunc dextra gerit; da sternere corpus,
Loricamque manu validâ lacerare revulsam
Semiviri Phrygis, et fœdare in pulvere crines,
Vibratos calido ferro, myrrhâque madentes.
His agitur furiis, totoque ardentis ab ore

74. Mora mortis *est* libera Turno. *Tu*, O Idmon, nuntius refer

82. Tuens *eos* frementes ante *ejus* ora

84. Qui *equi*

87. Dehinc *Turnus* ipse

95. O hasta, nunquam frustrata

96. *Olim* maximus Actor *gerebat* te

98. Revulsam *ab illo* *mea* valida

101. *Ejus* ardentis

NOTES.

follow, or accompany. Her tears were an inauspicious omen, or presage of the event.

74. *Neque enim:* as if he had said: your tears will be of no avail, for I have passed my word; and, if death be the event, I cannot retract; I have no power to retard, or put off my destiny. This is the plain meaning of the passage; yet Servius considers it inexplicable. *Mora:* a putting off, or deferring.

78. *Non agat:* let him not lead his Trojans, &c.

83. *Orithyia:* the daughter of Erechtheus king of Athens, who was said to be carried away by Boreas into Thrace. She was reputed a goddess, and Virgil makes Pilumnus, the great-grandfather of Turnus, to have received these horses from her. Thrace, the place of her residence, was famous for breeding generous steeds. *Decus:* plainly in the sense of *munus* vel *donum.* Ruæus says, *ornamentum.*

84. *Anteirent:* excelled—surpassed.—*Auras:* in the sense of *ventos.*

85. *Lacessunt:* in the sense of *palpant.* Heyne takes *lacessunt plausa*, simply for *plaudunt.*

86. *Plausa cavis:* stroked, or patted with their hollow hands. *Colla:* in the sense of *jubæ.*

87. *Squalentem:* rough with gold, and pale, &c.

88. *Habendo:* for carrying—wearing. A gen. in *do* of the dat. case. The same as *ad habendum.* Ruæus says, *ut gestentur.*

89. *Cornua rubræ cristæ:* the extremities of the crimson plume. The *cristæ* were the feathers worn upon the helmet, and rising above it. The *cornua* were the ends, or extremities of these plumes, put for the whole plume or tuft, by synec.: and these again, for the helmet, by meton.

90. *Ignipotens Deus:* Vulcan.

91. *Tinxerat:* in the sense of *merserat.*

93. *Validam hastam.* This spear had been taken from Auruncian Actor, either by Turnus himself, or one of his ancestors. Hence it is called *spolium.* Actor was slain.

95. *Frustrata:* deceiving—disappointing.

98. *Lacerare:* to rend—break in pieces.

99. *Semiviri Phrygis.* What is here said of Æneas, is said by way of reproach; in allusion to some custom of the Asiatics.

100. *Vibratos:* curled, or twisted up with a hot iron. To curl the hair, and smear it with unguents, were considered marks of effeminacy.

Scintillæ absistunt: oculis micat acribus ignis.
Mugitus veluti cùm prima in prælia taurus
Terrificos ciet, atque irasci in cornua tentat,
Arboris obnixus trunco, ventosque lacessit
Ictibus, et sparsâ ad pugnam proludit arenâ
  Nec minùs intereà maternis sævus in armis
Æneas acuit Martem, et se suscitat irâ,
Oblato gaudens componi fœdere bellum.
Tum socios mœstique metum solatur Iüli,
Fata docens: regique jubet responsa Latino
Certa referre viros, et pacis dicere leges.
  Postera vix summos spargebat lumine montes
Orta dies; cùm primùm alto se gurgite tollunt
Solis equi, lucemque elatis naribus efflant.
Campum ad certamen, magnæ sub mœnibus urbis,
Dimensi Rutulique viri Teucrique parabant;
In medioque focos, et Dîs communibus aras
Gramineas. Alii fontemque ignemque ferebant
Velati lino, et verbenâ tempora vincti.
Procedit legio Ausonidûm, pilataque plenis
Agmina se fundunt portis. Hinc Troïus omnis,
Tyrrhenusque ruit variis exercitus armis;
Haud secùs instructi ferro, quàm si aspera Martis
Pugna vocet. Nec non mediis in millibus ipsi
Ductores auro volitant ostroque decori;
Et genus Assaraci Mnestheus, et fortis Asylas,
Et Messapus equûm domitor, Neptunia proles.
Utque dato signo spatia in sua quisque recessit,
Defigunt tellure hastas, et scuta reclinant.
Tum studio effusæ matres, et vulgus inermum,
Invalidique senes, turres et tecta domorum
Obsedêre: alii portis sublimibus adstant.
  At Juno è summo, qui nunc Albanus habetur;

118. In medio *parabant*

120. Vincti *quoad* tempora

124. Instruct *sunt*

125. Vocet *eos*

131. Studio *videndi certamen*

134. At Juno prospiciens è summo tumulo

NOTES.

102. *Absistunt:* fly off from. Ruæus says, *erumpunt.*

103. *Mugitus:* bellowings. *Ciet:* in the sense of *emittit.*

105. *Lacessit:* in the sense of *provocat.*

106. *Proludit.* Ruæus says, *parat.*

107. *Maternis armis:* the armor made by Vulcan, at the desire of his mother. Hence called *maternis. Nec minùs:* in the sense of *nec non:* likewise—also—in like manner.

108. *Martem:* in the sense of *pugnam. Acuit:* prepares for the combat.

109. *Oblato fœdere:* upon the conditions, or terms offered.

111. *Docens fata:* teaching them the purposes of the gods concerning him. Ruæus says, *aperiens fata illis.*

112. *Dicere:* in the sense of *proponere. Leges:* terms—conditions.

114. *Alto gurgite:* from the deep ocean.

116. *Campum:* the ground—space. *Demensi*; having measured it out.

119. *Fontem:* in the sense of *aquam.*

120. *Velati lino.* Servius says that the priests and sacred ministers among the Romans, were prohibited from wearing any thing of linen; and that Virgil designedly clothes the *feciales* or priests in linen veils on this occasion, to give us to know beforehand, that the league was to be broken; since it was ushered in with unlawful rites. Heyne reads, *limo*, which was a kind of apron worn by the priests in time of sacrifice, that reached down from the navel to the feet. The common reading is *lino.*

121. *Pilata:* armed with darts or javelins. *Agmina:* troops.

124. *Instructi ferro:* furnished, and equipped with arms.

127. *Genus:* offspring, or descendants *Assaraci.* See Geor. iii. 35.

133. *Obsedêre:* in the sense of *impleverunt. Adstant:* in the sense of *stant.*

134. *Habetur:* in the sense of *vocatur*

Tum neque nomen erat, nec honos, aut gloria monti;
Prospiciens tumulo, campum spectabat, et ambas
Laurentûm Troûmque acies, urbemque Latini.
Extemplò Turni sic est effata sororem
Diva Deam, stagnis quæ fluminibusque sonoris
Præsidet: hunc illi rex ætheris altus honorem
Jupiter ereptâ pro virginitate sacravit:
Nympha, decus fluviorum, animo gratissima nostro,
Scis, ut te cunctis unam, quæcunque Latinæ
Magnanimi Jovis ingratum ascendêre cubile,
Prætulerim, cœlique lubens in parte locârim.
Disce tuum, ne me incuses, Juturna, dolorem
Quà visa est fortuna pati, Parcæque sinebant
Cedere res Latio, Turnum et tua mœnia texi:
Nunc juvenem imparibus video concurrere fatis,
Parcarumque dies et vis inimica propinquat.
Non pugnam aspicere hanc oculis, non fœdera possum
Tu, pro germano si quid præsentiùs audes,
Perge; decet: forsan miseros meliora sequentur
Vix ea; cùm lachrymas oculis Juturna profudit,
Terque quaterque manu pectus percussit honestum.
Non lachrymis hoc tempus, ait Saturnia Juno;
Accelera, et fratrem, si quis modus, eripe morti:
Aut tu bella cie, conceptumque excute fœdus.
Auctor ego audendi. Sic exhortata reliquit
Incertam, et tristi turbatam vulnere mentis.
  Intereà reges: ingenti mole Latinus
Quadrijugo vehitur curru, cui tempora circùm

138. Diva *Juno* sic affata est sororem Turni Deam; quæ

142. Ut prætulerim te unam cunctis *virginibus*, quæcunque Latinæ *virgines*

145. *Te* in parte cœli *mecum*

148. Res cedere *prospere* Latio

152. Si tu audes *facere* quid

154. Vix *dixerat* ea

160. *Eam* incertam

161. Reges *procedunt ab urbe*

NOTES.

This mount was called Alban, from *Alba Longa*, a city built by Ascanius after he had reigned at *Lavinium* thirty years. For the reason of its name, see Æn. viii. 44.

140. *Præsidet.* Juturna is by Ovid called a *Naiad.* A fountain issuing from the foot of mount Alban, and a lake which it supplied, were sacred to her. The river flowed into the Tiber. Its water was celebrated for its purity.

141. *Sacravit:* in the sense of *donavit.* This honor Jupiter conferred upon her, in compensation of her lost virginity.

143. *Prætulerim te:* I preferred thee alone, &c.

144. *Ingratum:* the bed here is called ungrateful, to save the indecency of giving that harsh epithet to Jove. The amours of Jupiter were always displeasing to Juno. Valpy observes, that the word is to be taken in the sense of *ingrati*, agreeing with Jovis. Heyne says, *invisum mihi*, referring to Juno.

145. *In parte:* in the sense of *participem.*

147. *Quà:* as far as—as long as. Ruæus says, *quatenus.*

148. *Texi:* in the sense of *defendi.*

150. *Dies et inimica:* this is a circumlocution, denoting that the last day of the life of Turnus had arrived.

152. *Præsentiùs.* Servius takes this in the sense of *efficaciùs*, vel *vehementiùs.* But it may refer to what Juno had just before said; *non pugnam:* I cannot bear to see the combat; I can only lament his hard fate, and intercede for him at a distance: but, if you have courage (*audes*) to lend your brother some nearer aid, and assist him with your presence, then set about it immediately: it becomes you to attempt it. Ruæus says, *utiliùs.*

155. *Honestum:* in the sense of *decorum.*

158. *Cie:* in the sense of *excita.* *Conceptum:* in the sense of *inceptum.* *Excute:* in the sense of *frange.* Ruæus says, *dissipa.*

159. *Ego auctor audendi:* I am the author (adviser) of the daring attempt. The gerund is here used in the sense of *ausi.*

160. *Tristi vulnere:* with bitter agony of mind. *Vulnus*, is properly a wound; by meton. the wounding instrument; also the pain, or anguish arising from the wound. Ruæus says, *solicitudine.*

161. *Ingenti mole:* with a mighty retinue. Ruæus says, *magno apparatu.*

163. *Bis sex aurati radii:* twelve golden rays or beams represented the twelve signs of the zodiac. *Cui tempora:* around whose refulgent temples, &c.

Aurati bis sex radii fulgentia cingunt,
Solis avi specimen: bigis it Turnus in albis,
Bina manu latò crispans hastilia ferro.
Hinc pater Æneas, Romanæ stirpis origo,
Sidereo flagrans clypeo et cœlestibus armis,
Et juxtà Ascanius, magnæ spes altera Romæ,
Procedunt castris: puràque in veste sacerdos
Setigeræ fœtum suis, intonsamque bidentem
Attulit, admovitque pecus flagrantibus aris.
Illi ad surgentem conversi lumina Solem,
Dant fruges manibus salsas, et tempora ferro
Summa notant pecudum, paterisque altaria libant
Tum pius Æneas stricto sic ense precatur:
Esto nunc Sol testis, et hæc mihi terra precanti,
Quam propter tantos potui perferre labores:
Et, pater omnipotens, et tu, Saturnia Juno,
Jam melior, jam Diva, precor: tuque, inclyte Mavors,
Cuncta tuo qui bella pater sub numine torques,
Fontesque fluviosque voco; quæque ætheris alti
Relligio, et quæ cœruleo sunt numina ponto:
Cesserit Ausonio si fors victoria Turno,
Convenit, Evandri victos discedere ad urbem;
Cedet Iülus agris; nec pòst arma ulla rebelles

168. Et juxta *eum*

176. Nunc *tu*, *O* Sol, et hæc terra, propter quam potui perferre tantos labores, esto testis mihi

179. Precor *vos*

180. *O* inclyte pater Mavors, qui

184. *Trojanos* victos

NOTES.

164. *Specimen:* after the manner of his grandsire, the Sun. Latinus was the grandson of *Picus*, who took Circe the daughter of the Sun to wife, and by her had *Faunus*, the father of *Latinus*, who was, therefore, the grandson of the Sun. *Albis Bigis:* in a chariot drawn by two white steeds. *It:* in the sense of *vehitur.*

167. *Flagrans:* in the sense of *resplendens* vel *lucens.*

170. *Fœtum setigeræ suis:* the young of a bristly sow—a pig. Ruæus observes, that the ewe-lamb (*intonsam bidentem*) was offered for Æneas after the manner of the Greeks, who commonly ratified a league with the sacrifice of a sheep or lamb. The swine again is for Latinus, after the Roman or Italian manner; which, according to Livy, was of great antiquity. He gives the form of ratifying a league in the reign of *Tullus Hostilius.* Having invoked Jupiter, the *fecialis* or priest says: *Illis legibus populus non deficiet. Si prior defecerit, publico consilio, dolo malo; tu illo die, Jupiter, populum sic ferito, ut ego hunc porcum hodie feriam: tantò magis ferito, quanto magis potes pollesque.*

171. *Pecus:* in the sense of *victimas. Attulit:* in the sense of *adduxit. Admovit:* in the sense of *statuit.*

172. *Lumina:* in the sense of *oculos* vel *faciem.*

173. *Dant:* in the sense of *spargunt. Fruges:* in the sense of *molam.*

174. *Pecudum:* in the sense of *victimarum. Paterisque:* and they made libations upon the altars. This was the dropping, or sprinkling of wine, or other liquor, upon the altar, from the sacred bowls, or goblets.

179. *Melior Diva.* Juno was the implacable enemy of the Trojan race. Æneas would intimate, that now at length, she was ceasing from her resentment, and becoming more favorable to them. *Precor:* I beseech you. *Melior:* in the sense of *propitia* vel *mitis.*

180. *Torques:* in the sense of *regis* vel *tenes. Numine:* in the sense of *potestate.*

181. *Quæque relligio.* By *relligio* we are here to understand the objects of religious worship—the gods of heaven above; in opposition to the objects of religious worship on the earth. The verb *est* is to be supplied. Ruæus says, *quæcunque divinitas. Voco:* in the sense of *invoco* vel *precor.*

Æneas here makes a very solemn invocation of the gods above, and of the deities that preside over the sea, to witness the ratification of the treaty. The deities here named were those that were called *Dii communes*, or gods common to both sides or parties to the contract.

183. *Fors:* in the sense of *fortè.*

184. *Convenit:* it is agreed upon. *Ad urbem Evandri:* this was the city *Pallanteum.* See Æn. viii. 54.

Æneadæ referent, ferrove hæc regna lacessent.
Sin nostrum annuerit nobis victoria Martem,
188. Firment *spem*
(Ut potiùs reor, et potiùs Dî numina firment)
Non ego nec Teucris Italos parere jubebo,
Nec mihi regna peto. Paribus se legibus ambæ
Invictæ gentes æterna in fœdera mittant.
Sacra Deosque dabo: socer arma Latinus habeto
193. Socer *habeto* solemne
Imperium solemne socer. mihi mœnia Teucri
Constituent, urbique dabit Lavinia nomen.
Sic prior Æneas: sequitur sic deinde Latinus,
Suspiciens cœlum, tenditque ad sidera dextram:
197. *O* Ænea, juro *per* hæc eadem *numina, per* terram
Hæc eadem, Ænea, terram, mare, sidera juro,
Latonæque genus duplex, Janumque bifrontem,
Vimque Deûm infernam, et diri sacraria Ditis:
Audiat hæc genitor, qui fœdera fulmine sancit:
Tango aras; mediosque ignes et numina testor:
Nulla dies pacem hanc Italis, nec fœdera rumpet,
Quò res cunque cadent: nec me vis ulla volentem
204. Non; si *illa vis* effundat
Avertet: non, si tellurem effundat in undas
Diluvio miscens; cœlumve in Tartara solvat:
Ut sceptrum hoc (dextrâ sceptrum nam fortè gerebat)
Nunquam fronde levi fundet virgulta, nec umbras,

NOTES.

187. *Nostrum: noster* here is used in the sense of *propitium* vel *secundum*. Mars is his, or on his side, whose interest he espouses. *Annuerit:* shall prove, show, or declare Mars. Servius takes it by hypallage, for *noster Mars annuerit victoriam nobis.*

188. *Numine:* Ruæus says, *auctoritate.*

189. *Non:* this appears to be merely *expletive.*

190. *Leges:* terms—conditions. *Mittant:* in the sense of *jungant.*

192. *Socer habeto arma:* let my father-in-law have the management of peace and war: which is the same thing as being king. This is more fully expressed in the next line. *Solemne:* usual—customary. Heyne says, *legitimum:* Ruæus, *supremum. Dabo:* I will attend to religious rites, and to the gods—I will regulate the ceremonies of religion, and the worship of the gods. This alludes to the *Penates*, and *Vesta*, whose worship, it is said, Æneas introduced into Italy.

197. *Juro hæc eadem.* Latinus swears by the same gods, by whom Æneas had just sworn, besides those here enumerated. *Duplex genus:* by this we are to understand Apollo and Diana, who were twin children of Latona.

199. *Vim infernam:* by the infernal power of the gods—the power of the infernal gods. That is, the infernal gods themselves. So *vis odora canum.* Æn. iv. 132. *Sacraria:* sanctuary of direful Pluto.

200. *Genitor:* Jupiter

201. *Tango aras.* It was a custom for those who made supplication, offered sacrifice, or took an oath, to lay their hands upon the altar. This custom has descended to the present time, in administering the solemnities of an oath. The party taking the oath lays his hand on *the bible*, and calls God to witness the truth of his declaration *Medios ignes:* those fires common to both parties—in which they partook.

203. *Quòcunque:* the parts of the word are separated by tmesis, for the sake of the verse: *howsoever. Avertet:* in the sense of *abducet.*

204. *Si effundat.* Servius takes this as an hypallage for *effundat undas in tellurem:* should deluge the earth—throw the waters over the earth. Ruæus takes it to imply the sinking and dissolving of the earth itself into the waters of the ocean. Heyne appears to adopt the same opinion.

Latinus here expresses his full determination to abide by the conditions of the treaty, and declares, that no power should divert him from it with his consent, not even if the world were wrapped in a deluge, and a general dissolution of things take place. Ruæus says, *dissolvat terram in aquas, confundens eam diluvio.*

205. *Solvat.* Ruæus says, *dejiceat.* Davidson renders the words, "plunge heaven into hell." Heyne says, *misceat cœlum ac Tartarum.*

206. *Ut sceptrum.* This comparison is taken almost literally from Homer. *Fundet:* shall put forth, or produce.

Cùm semel in sylvis imo de stirpe recisum
Matre caret, posuitque comas et brachia ferro;
Olim arbos; nunc artificis manus ære decoro
Inclusit, patribusque dedit gestare Latinis.
Talibus inter se firmabant fœdera dictis,
Conspectu in medio procerum. Tum ritè sacratas
In flammam jugulant pecudes, et viscera vivis
Eripiunt, cumulantque oneratis lancibus aras
At verò Rutulis impar ea pugna videri
Jamdudum, et vario misceri pectora motu:
Tum magis, ut propiùs cernunt non viribus æquis.
Adjuvat incessu tacito progressus, et aram
Suppliciter venerans demisso lumine, Turnus,
Tabentesque genæ, et juvenili in corpore pallor.
Quem simul ac Juturna soror crebrescere vidit
Sermonem, et vulgi variare labantia corda:
In medias acies, formam assimulata Camerti,
Cui genus à proavis ingens, clarumque paternæ
Nomen erat virtutis, et ipse acerrimus armis,
In medias dat sese acies, haud nescia rerum,
Rumoresque serit varios, ac talia fatur:
Non pudet, ô Rutuli, cunctis pro talibus unam
Objectare animam? numerone, an viribus æqui
Non sumus? En, omnes et Troës et Arcades hi sunt,
Fatalisque manus, infensa Etruria Turno.
Vix hostem, alterni si congrediamur, habemus.
Ille quidem ad Superos, quorum se devovet aris,
Succedet famâ, vivusque per ora feretur:

210. Olim *erat* arbos

211. Inclusit *eam* decoro ære

214. *Iisdem* vivis

216. Ea pugna *cœpit*

218. Cernunt *duces esse* non

219. Turnus adjuvat *hanc opinionem*, progressus

222. Quem sermonem *inter Rutulos* simul

227. *Inquam*, in medias acies, haud

234. Ille *Turnus*

235. Per ora *hominum*

NOTES.

208. *Cùm semel:* since once cut in the woods from the lowest stem, it is deprived of the nourishment of its parent stock.

209. *Posuit:* hath laid aside—been stripped of.

210. *Manus:* the skill of the artist. *Manus:* the hand, by meton. art—skill.

211. *Patribus:* in the sense of *regibus.*

214. *Pecudes jugulant:* they kill the sacred victims over the flames of the altar.

215. *Cumulant:* they heap, or load the altars. See Æn. viii. 284. *Oneratis:* in the sense of *plenis.*

221. *Tabentes genæ:* lank, or fallen cheeks. Some copies read *pubentes:* but *tabentes* is confirmed by the authority of the best manuscripts, and is most agreeable to the design of the poet. Heyne says, *tabentes.*

222. *Vidit:* in the sense of *sentit.*

223. *Labantia:* in the sense of *mobilia. Variare:* in the sense of *dissentire:* to be dissatisfied at the conditions of the treaty, made between Latinus and Æneas.

224. *Assimulata:* personating the form of Camertus, she throws herself, &c. The *in medias acies* is to be taken after the same words, in line 227, infra.

225. *Genus:* origin—descent. *Cui:* in the sense of *cujus. Ingens:* great—illustrious.

226. *Nomen:* renown—fame. *Acerrimus* in the sense of *fortissimus. Erat* is to be repeated with this word, and also with *genus*, in the preceding line.

229. *Talibus.* Servius thinks we are to understand by this word that all of them were equal to Turnus in valor. Ruæus says, *omnibus iis.* Davidson renders it, "all these." *Animam unam:* the life of Turnus.

231. *Hi:* this is the reading of Heyne. The common reading is *hic.*

232. *Fatalis manus.* By these words Servius understands the Trojans, who were destined to come into Italy. But it is better to understand it of the *Tuscans*, who were directed by fate to put themselves under the conduct of Æneas, a foreign leader; and on that condition alone, they were assured of success. See Lib. viii. 501. This interpretation frees Virgil from the imputation of idle repetition. *Etruria infensa Turno:* one part of Etruria was hostile to Turnus; and another assisted him, under the command of Messapus. The *fatalis manus* is evidently the same as *Etruria infensa Turno.*

233. *Alterni:* every other one. They were double the number of the enemy.

235. *Vivusque feretur per ora.* This im-

Nos, patriâ amissâ, dominis parere superbis
Cogemur, qui nunc lenti consedimus arvis.
Talibus, incensa est juvenum sententia dictis
Jam magis atque magis: serpitque per agmina murmur

240. Mutati *sunt mentibus*

Ipsi Laurentes mutati, ipsique Latini;
Qui sibi jam requiem pugnæ, rebusque salutem
Sperabant; nunc arma volunt, fœdusque precantur
Infectum, et Turni sortem miserantur iniquam.

244. His *rebus*

His aliud majus Juturna adjungit, et alto
Dat signum cœlo: quo non præsentius ullum
Turbavit mentes Italas, monstroque fefellit.

247. Namque *aquila*, fulvus ales Jovis

Namque volans rubrâ fulvus Jovis ales in æthrâ,
Litoreas agitabat aves, turbamque sonantem
Agminis aligeri: subitò cùm lapsus ad undas
Cycnum excellentem pedibus rapit improbus uncis.
Arrexêre animos Itali; cunctæque volucres
Convertunt clamore fugam, mirabile visu!
Ætheraque obscurant pennis, hostemque per auras,

254. Donec ales victus vi, et ipso pondere *cycni*

Factâ nube, premunt: donec vi victus, et ipso
Pondere defecit, prædamque ex unguibus ales
Projecit fluvio, penitùsque in nubila fugit.
Tum verò augurium Rutuli clamore salutant,
Expediuntque manus: primusque Tolumnius augur,

259. Hoc, hoc erat *id*, quod

Hoc erat, hoc, votis, inquit, quod sæpe petivi;

260. Accipio *omen*

Accipio, agnoscoque Deos. Me, me duce, ferrum
Corripite, ô Rutuli, quos improbus advena bello

NOTES.

plies, that he should be immortal. *Succedet:* in the sense of *ascendet.*

237. *Lenti:* idle—lazy—at our ease.—Ruæus says, *otiosi.*

238. *Sententia:* resolution—mind. Heyne says, *animus.*

241. *Rebus:* to the state.

243. *Infectum:* unmade—broken.

244. *His:* to these incentives—incitements.

245. *Præsentius:* more effectual: an adj. of the comp. neu. agreeing with *portentum* vel *monstrum*, understood. It governs *quo* in the abl. *than which.* It may be rendered adverbially.

246. *Monstro:* deceived them by the prodigy. Any thing that is, or happens, contrary to the ordinary course of things, may be called *monstrum.*

247. *Rubrâ æthrâ:* in the ruddy sky. *Litoreas aves:* sea-fowls—fowls frequenting the sea shore.

248. *Turbam:* in the sense of *multitudinem. Aligeri agminis:* of the winged tribe: the same in sense with *volucrum. Sonantem:* refers to the sound made by the motion of their wings, as they passed through the air. Ruæus says, *strepitantem.*

250. *Improbus:* in the sense of *avidus.*

251. *Arrexêre:* in the sense of *sustulerunt.*

252. *Fugam:* their course.

254. *Nube factâ:* a cloud being formed—closing in thick array around him, they form a cloud, and darken the sky with their wings.

255. *Defecit:* failed in his strength.

257. *Augurium.* This word here is used in its proper sense, which is an omen or prognostic, taken from the flight, or chirping of birds. The Rutulians were right in explaining the eagle to mean Æneas, the swan, Turnus, and the other birds, to mean themselves. But they were mistaken, in taking this augury, which Juturna procured, to have been sent from the gods. To this an allusion is made in verse 246, *monstroque fefellit.* This interposition of a superior power, was necessary to account for the sudden change produced in the minds of the Rutulians and Latins.

258. *Expediunt manus.* By this, Valpy understands elevating of their hand in token that they were prepared and ready for battle. Ruæus says, *explicant manus.* Davidson renders the words, "they put their troops in array," which is the sense of Ruæus. Heyne differs from both these interpretations. He says, *expediunt manus ut arma capiunt* they prepare to take their arms. These had been laid aside, while the preparations were making, and the league was ratifying. See verse 130, supra.

Territat, invalidas ut aves; et litora vestra
Vi populat. Petet ille fugam, penitùsque profundo
Vela dabit. Vos unanimi densate catervas,
Et regem vobis pugnâ defendite raptum.
Dixit: et adversos telum contorsit in hostes
Procurrens: sonitum dat stridula cornus, et auras
Certa secat. Simul hoc; simul ingens clamor; et omnes
Turbati cunei, calefactaque corda tumultu.
Hasta volans, ut fortè novem pulcherrima fratrum
Corpora constiterant contrà, quos fida creârat
Una tot Arcadio conjux Tyrrhena Gylippo;
Horum unum ad medium, teritur quà sutilis alvo
Balteus, et laterum juncturas fibela mordet,
Egregium formâ juvenem et fulgentibus armis,
Transadigit costas, fulvâque effundit arenâ.
At fratres, animosa phalanx, accensaque luctu,
Pars gladios stringunt manibus, pars missile ferrum
Corripiunt, cæcique ruunt: quos agmina contrà
Procurrunt Laurentûm. Hìc densi rursùs inundant
Troës, Agyllinique, et pictis Arcades armis.
Sic omnes amor unus habet decernere ferro.
Diripuêre aras: it toto turbida cœlo
Tempestas telorum, ac ferreus ingruit imber:
Craterasque, focosque ferunt. Fugit ipse Latinus
Pulsatos referens, infecto fœdere, Divos.
Infrænant alii currus, aut corpora saltu
Subjiciunt in equos, et strictis ensibus adsunt.
Messapus regem, regisque insigne gerentem,

268. Simul hoc *fit*

269. Turbati *sunt*

273. Hasta volans transadigit unum horum *fratrum per* costas, juvenem egregium formâ, et fulgentibus armis, ad medium *corpus*, quâ sutilis balteus

NOTES.

262. *Invalidas aves:* this agrees with *quos*, mentioned before, and signifies the same with it: as week birds.

263 *Profundo:* in the sense of *mari*. *Penitùs:* far remote—far distant. *Longè*, says Ruæus.

264. *Densate:* thicken your ranks—in close and compact array, defend, &c. Ruæus says, *colligite agmina*.

267. *Cornus:* this was a spear (*hasta*) whose shaft was made of the corneil-tree.

268. *Simul hoc.* The meaning is, that as soon as the spear was thrown by Tolumnius, all the troops were eager to engage, and their courage was roused for battle. This they signified by a great shout.

269. *Cunei.* The *cuneus* was a company of men drawn up in the form of a wedge: hence it came to signify troops in general, as in the present case.

270. *Corpora fratrum:* simply, *fratres*.

271. *Creârat:* by syn. for *creaverat:* in the sense of *pepererat*.

272. *Conjux:* wife. *Una:* one.

273. *Quà sutilis:* where the stitched belt is worn around the belly.

274. *Mordet:* binds, or fastens. *Juncturas:* the ends or extremities of the belt.

278. *Stringunt* in the sense of *educunt*.

279. *Cæci:* blind to danger.

280. *Inundant:* deluge the plain. The word is very expressive. They move like a devouring flood. *Agyllini:* the Tuscans, so called from *Agylla*, one of their cities.

282. *Unus amor:* one mind—desire.

283. *Diripuêre:* they stripped the altars.

284. *Ingruit:* pours down upon them. *Tempestas:* a cloud—storm. *It:* covers the whole heaven. *Turbida:* thick—terrific.

285. *Focos:* in the sense of *ignes*.

287. *Infrænant currus:* they prepare their chariots—they harness their horses in them. *Subjiciunt:* with a spring, they mount, or throw themselves upon their horses. Livy uses this verb in the same sense: *pavidum regem in equum subjecit*.

288. *Adsunt:* in the sense of *instant*, vel *concurrunt*.

289. *Messapus avidus*, &c. The meaning of the passage appears to be this: Messapus desirous of breaking the league, as soon as mounted on his horse, made an attack upon *Tuscan Aulestes*, with his horse full in front. This so alarmed him, that attempting to retreat or give back, he fell from his horse among the altars, which had just been erected for the purpose of ratifying the league. In this situation, Messapus, rising

292. *In* aris oppositis à tergo
295. Altusque equo desuper graviter ferit *eum* orantem multa
296. *Ille* habet hoc *vulnus*
299. Obvius Ebuso venienti, ferentique plagam
304. Podalirius sequens nudo ense
307. *Ejus* adversi
314. Fœdus ictum *est*
315. Jus concurrere *est* mihi soli; sinite me *pugnare*
316. Ego faxo manu, *ut* fœdera *sint.*

Tyrrhenum Aulesten, avidus confundere fœdus,
Adverso proterret equo: ruit ille recedens,
Et miser oppositis à tergo involvitur aris,
In caput, inque humeros. At fervidus advolat hastâ
Messapus, teloque orantem multa trabali
Desuper altus equo graviter ferit, atque ita fatur:
Hoc habet: hæc melior magnis data victima Divis.
Concurrunt Itali, spoliantque calentia membra.
  Obvius ambustum torrem Chorinæus ab arâ
Corripit, et venienti Ebuso plagamque ferenti
Occupat os flammis. Olli ingens barba reluxit,
Nidoremque ambusta dedit. Supèr ipse secutus
Cæsariem lævâ turbati corripit hostis,
Impressoque genu nitens terræ applicat ipsum.
Sic rigido latus ense ferit. Podalirius Alsum
Pastorem, primâque acie per tela ruentem,
Ense sequens nudo superimminet: ille securi
Adversi frontem mediam mentumque reductâ
Disjicit, et sparso latè rigat arma cruore.
Olli dura quies oculos et ferreus urget
Somnus; in æternam clauduntur lumina noctem.
  At pius Æneas dextram tendebat inermem
Nudato capite, atque suos clamore vocabat:
Quò ruitis? quæve ista repens discordia surgit?
O cohibete iras! ictum jam fœdus, et omnes
Compositæ leges: mihi jus concurrere soli:
Me sinite, atque auferte metus. Ego fœdera faxo
Firma manu: Turnum jam debent hæc mihi sacra
Has inter voces, media inter talia verba,

NOTES.

high upon his steed to give the blow more effect, gives him a mortal wound; while he in the mean time is pleading for his life, without avail. *Insigne:* in the sense of *ornamentum.*

291. *Proterret:* affrights—alarms—confounds. *Ruit:* in the sense of *cadit.*

294. *Trabali:* in the sense of *ingenti.*

296. *Melior victima:* a better, or more effectual victim to appease the gods, than those that had been offered for the league on the altars, where he had fallen; to wit, a lamb or a pig. *Habet hoc.* This was an expression made by the spectators at the shows of the gladiators, when any one received a mortal wound.

297. *Spoliant:* strip his limbs yet warm. Ruæus says, *nudant.*

298. *Obvius:* in the sense of *adversus.* Ruæus says, *occurrens.*

300. *Occupat os:* he strikes him on the face with the fire-brand. This prevented the blow that was intended by Ebusus to be given to him. *Occupat os:* Ruæus says, *intercepit vultum flammis.* Heyne says, *ferit occupando.* This Chorinæus was a Trojan priest. He had been engaged in offering the sacrifices; which accounts for his being at the altars. *Reluxit:* his beard caught fire, and shone—blazed.

301. *Super:* in the sense of *insuper* vel *prætereà. Ipse:* Chorinæus.

302. *Turbati:* affrighted—confused.

303. *Impresso genu:* exerting himself with his knee being thrust hard against him, he is enabled to pull Ebusus over, and bring him to the ground. *Applicat:* Ruæus says, *sternit.*

306. *Superimminet:* in the sense of *premit* vel *urget. Securi reductâ:* his axe being drawn back to give the blow—with his axe drawn back.

308. *Disjicit:* in the sense of *scindit* vel *secat.*

309. *Olli:* for *illi*, and this again in the sense of *illius.*

311. *Inermem:* unarmed: of *in*, and *arma.*

313. *Repens:* in the sense of *subita.*

315. *Leges:* the terms or conditions of the treaty.

316. *Ego faxo:* the meaning is: I will make good my part of the treaty, and these sacred rites give me security, that Turnus will perform his part. *Faxo:* for *facero*

Ecce, viro stridens alis allapsa sagitta est·
Incertum quâ pulsa manu, quo turbine adacta;
Quis tantam Rutulis laudem, casusne, Deusne,
Attulerit. Pressa est insignis gloria facti;
Nec sese Æneæ jactavit vulnere quisquam.
Turnus, ut Æneam cedentem ex agmine vidit,
Turbatosque duces. subitâ spe fervidus ardet:
Poscit equos, atque arma simul, saltuque superbus
Emicat in currum, et manibus molitur habenas.
Multa virûm volitans dat fortia corpora leto:
Semineces volvit multos, aut agmina curru
Proterit, aut raptas fugientibus ingerit hastas.
Qualis apud gelidi cùm flumina concitus Hebri
Sanguineus Mavors clypeo increpat, atque furentes
Bella movens immittit equos: illi æquore aperto
Ante Notos Zephyrumque volant: gemit ultima pulsu
Thraca pedum: circùmque atræ Formidinis ora,
Iræque, Insidiæque, Dei comitatus, aguntur.
Talis equos alacer media inter prælia Turnus
Fumantes sudore quatit, miserabilè cæsis
Hostibus insultans: spargit rapida ungula rores
Sanguineos, mixtâque cruor calcatur arenâ.
Jamque neci Sthenelumque dedit, Thamyrimque, Pholumque,
Hunc congressus et hunc; illum eminùs: eminùs ambos
Imbrasidas, Glaucum atque Ladem; quos Imbrasus ipse

320. *Est* incertum, quâ manu pulsa *sit*

331. Qualis sanguineùs Mavors, cùm

336. Circumaguntur *eum*

339. Ungula *ejus equorum*

342. Congressus *est* hunc et hunc *cominùs;* illum, *nempe, Sthenelum* eminùs; *congressus est* eminùs ambos

NOTES.

319. *Viro:* to the hero, i. e. Æneas. *Alis:* here denotes the swiftness of the arrow. It moved on wings.

320. *Quo turbine:* by what whirling force: simply, by what force. *Quo impetu,* says Ruæus. *Pulsa:* in the sense of *missa.*

322. *Pressa est:* is concealed. No one has the glory of so illustrious a deed.

325. *Fervidus ardet:* the absence of Æneas raises the courage of Turnus, and inflames him for battle. He is once more victorious, as he had been before on the banks of the Tiber, when Æneas was absent in Etruria. This indirect method of praising his hero, Virgil had learned from Homer, who makes his victory to lean on the side of the Trojans during the absence of Achilles; so, here, the absence of Æneas makes the scales turn in favor of the Latins. The absence of Æneas was sudden and unexpected by Turnus; and as soon as he saw him withdraw from the field, he was fired with the hope of retrieving the lost fortunes of his country.

326 *Superbus:* in the sense of *animosus.*

327. *Molitur:* in the sense of *tractat.*

330. *Proterit:* he crushed. Ruæus says, *sternit.* *Agmina:* the troops—the enemy.

As Turnus drove furiously through the ranks of the enemy, the wheels of his chariot crushed some to death and others wounded and half dead they rolled and tumbled along as they lay prostrate on the field. *Ingerit* he hurled—threw. *Raptas:* in the sense of *correptas* vel *arreptas.* Ruæus says, *immittit fugientibus hastas abstractas iisdem:* which implies that Turnus took the spears from the fugitives, and then threw them at them. The word *raptas* frequently signifies no more than, snatched up—suddenly taken.

331. *Flumina Hebri:* along the streams of Hebrus—along the river Hebrus. See Ecl. x. 65.

332. *Increpat:* in the sense of *sonat.*

333. *Immittit:* lets loose—gives full reins to his furious steeds.

335. *Ora atræ formidinis:* the form or countenance of grim terror—grim terror itself.

336. *Comitatus Dei:* the retinue of the god, i. e. Mars. The word *comitatus* agrees in apposition with the preceding nominatives *Ora, Iræ, Insidiæ.*

338. *Quatit:* in the sense of *impellit.* *Miserabilè cæsis:* miserably slain.

339. *Sanguineos rores:* simply, blood.

342. *Hunc, et hunc:* the two last he engaged in close fight; the former at a distance. *Hic* sometimes signifies the latter or last mentioned; *ille,* the former, or first mentioned, as in the present case.

Nutrîerat Lyciâ, paribusque ornaverat armis,
Vel conferre manum, vel equo prævertere ventos
Parte aliâ, media Eumedes in prælia fertur,
347. *Qui erat* proles antiqui
Antiqui proles bello præclara Dolonis,
Nomine avum referens, animo manibusque parentem.
Qui quondam, castra ut Danaûm speculator adiret,
350. Ausus *est* poscere
Ausus Pelidæ pretium sibi poscere currus.
Illum Tydides alio pro talibus ausis
Affecit pretio; nec equis aspirat Achillis.
353. Hunc *Eumeden*
Hunc procul ut campo Turnus conspexit aperto,
Antè levi jaculo longum per inane secutus,
Sistit equos bijuges, et curru desilit, atque
Semianimi lapsoque supervenit: et, pede collo
Impresso, dextræ mucrónem extorquet, et alto
Fulgentem tingit jugulo, atque hæc insuper addit:
359. En, Trojane, jacens, metire agros
En, agros, et, quam bello, Trojane, petîsti,
Hesperiam metire, jacens: hæc præmia, qui me
Ferro ausi tentare, ferunt: sic mœnia condunt.
Huic comitem Buten, conjectâ cuspide, mittit
363. *Interficit* Chloreaque
Chloreaque, Sybarimque, Daretaque, Thersilochumque,
Et sternacis equi lapsum cervice Thymœten.
Ac velut Edoni Boreæ cùm spiritus alto
Insonat Ægæo, sequiturque ad litora fluctus;
Quâ venti incubuêre, fugam dant nubila cœlo:
Sic Turno, quâcunque viam secat, agmina cedunt,
Conversæque ruunt acies: fert impetus ipsum;

NOTES.

344. *Ornaverat:* and had furnished them with equal arms—with equal skill, or valor in arms. *Conferre manum:* to engage in close fight.

347. *Proles præclara bello.* This is to be understood ironically, as appears from what follows: and particularly, from the character of Dolon in Homer, Iliad, lib. 10, where he appears to have undertaken the adventure here alluded to, not from true courage, but from mere covetousness. He demanded the chariot of Achilles, as a reward for this service.

348. *Referens:* representing—bearing the name of. He bore the name of his grandfather, but was like his father in courage and valor.

349. *Qui:* this refers to the father, mentioned immediately before.

350. *Pelidæ:* gen. of *Pelides*, a name of Achilles; from his father *Peleus:* a patronymic. *Pretium:* as a reward for his deed.

352. *Affecit alio pretio.* It is here intimated that Dolon was slain by Diomede.

354. *Antè secutus:* having thrown a swift dart at him before—having pursued him with a swift javelin, &c. *Inane:* in the sense of *aërem*. *Longum:* distant—at a distance.

357. *Mucronem dextræ.* Though fallen by the spear of Turnus, and dying of his wounds, Eumedes held a dagger in his hand. This the conqueror wrenched from him, and buried deep in his throat.

358. *Tingit:* stains. Ruæus says, *immersit*. He buries his glittering sword in his throat. *Immittit in jugulum ut sanguine tingatur*, says Heyne.

359. *En agros:* after a victory, the conquerors divided the conquered lands and territory; and in the first place took the dimensions of them, in order to distribute them equally among their troops. To this custom Turnus, in this bitter sarcasm, seems to allude.

362. *Cuspide:* in the sense of *jaculo*.

364. *Sternacis equi:* either stumbling and apt to fall himself; or rearing and pitching, in order to throw his rider. *Cervice:* shoulders—back. Ruæus says, *collo*.

365. *Spiritus Edoni Boreæ:* the blast of Thracian Boreas. Boreas, the north wind, is here called Thracian, because it blew from that country. The *Edoni* were a people of Thrace: hence the adj. *Edonus*. *Alto:* in the sense of *mari*. *Spiritus:* in the sense of *flatus* vel *ventus*.

367. *Dant fugam:* in the sense of *fugiunt*. *Incubuêre:* blow—rush or press forward.

369. *Ruunt:* in the sense of *fugiunt*.

Et cristam adverso curru quatit aura volantem.
Non tulit instantem Phegeus, animisque frementem:
Objecit sese ad currum, et spumantia frænis
Ora citatorum dextrâ detorsit equorum.
Dum trahitur, pendetque jugis, hunc lata retectum
Lancea consequitur, rumpitque infixa bilicem
Loricam, et summum degustat vulnere corpus.
Ille tamen, clypeo objecto, conversus in hostem
Ibat, et auxilium ducto mucrone petebat:
Cùm rota præcipitem, et procursu concitus axis
Impulit, effuditque solo: Turnusque secutus,
Imam inter galeam summi thoracis et oras,
Abstulit ense caput, truncumque reliquit arenâ.
  Atque ea dum campis victor dat funera Turnus;
Intereà Æneam Mnestheus, et fidus Achates,
Ascaniusque comes, castris statuêre cruentum,
Alternos longâ nitentem cuspide gressus.
Sævit, et infractâ luctatur arundine telum
Eripere; auxilioque viam, quæ proxima, poscit:
Ense secent lato vulnus, telique latebram
Rescindant penitùs, seseque in bella remittant.
  Jamque aderat Phœbo ante alios dilectus Iapys
Iasides; acri quondam cui captus amore
Ipse suas artes, sua munera, lætus Apollo
Augurium, citharamque dabat, celeresque sagittas.

371. *Turnum* instantem

375. Lata lancea *Turni*

388. Quæ *est* proxima: *jubet ut medici* secent

392. Cui quondam Apollo ipse captus acri amore, lætus dabat

NOTES.

370. *Adverso curru:* in his chariot facing the wind. *Aura:* in the sense of *ventus.* *Volantem:* waving. But *curru* may be for *currui*, in the dat. The wind blowing against his chariot facing it, (*adverso*,) causes his plumes to wave. *Dum currus adversùs ventum fertur*, says Heyne.

573. *Detorsit ora:* with his right hand he turned around the heads, &c. This he did to stop them, that on more equal terms he might engage Turnus. These were the horses of Turnus. *Spumantia:* foaming at the bit. *Citatorum:* in the sense of *animosorum*, vel *celerum.*

375. *Rumpit:* in the sense of *penetrat.*

378. *Petebat:* he sought aid with his drawn sword. He hoped to succeed against Turnus by attacking him sword in hand. Ruæus says, *vocabat auxilium.* Davidson renders it, " he sought assistance from his unsheathed sword." *Mucrone:* in the sense of *gladio.*

379. *Axis:* the extremities of the axle-tree extended beyond the hub of the wheel. It was most probably this part that struck Phegeus, and threw him headlong on the ground. *Concitus:* quickened and accelerated by its rapid career. The impetus it had acquired in its course served to increase its velocity. Turnus seeing him in that situation sprang from his chariot, and took off his head between the upper part of his breast-plate, and the lower part of his helmet. *Cùm:* this is the reading of Heyne and Davidson. Ruæus reads *quem.* It appears that Phegeus had let go of the horses, and was preparing to attack Turnus, when they sprang forward, and the wheel in its rapid motion struck him.

386. *Nitentem alternos:* supporting his alternate steps, &c. *Cuspide:* in the sense of *hasta*, by synec.

387. *Arundine:* the shaft of the arrow. It is placed absolutely with *infracta.* *Telum:* the barb or point of the arrow.

388. *Auxilio:* for relief. He orders them to make a gash or incision (*vulnus*) down to the very blade of the dart or javelin, (*latebram teli*,) and extract it without delay, that he may again enter the fight, and check the career of Turnus. *Proxima:* the speediest—quickest.

390. *Rescindant:* in the sense of *aperiant.*

392. *Cui:* in the sense of *cujus:* with an ardent love of whom, Apollo, &c.

393. *Suas artes dabat:* he gave to him the choice of his arts. This appears to be the meaning from verse 396, infra, *maluit scire*, &c. The arts of Apollo were, 1. Prophecy. 2. Music: whence, he is often represented with a lyre, and considered the god of poets. 3. Skill in archery: hence, he is represented with a quiver. 4. Medicine. This last was the choice of Iapys.

Ille, ut depositi proferret fata parentis,
Scire potestates herbarum, usumque medendi
Maluit, et mutas agitare inglorius artes.
Stabat acerbà fremens, ingentem nixus in hastam
Æneas, magno juvenum, et mœrentis Iüli
Concursu, lachrymisque immobilis. Ille retorto
Pæonium in morem senior succinctus amictu,
Multa manu medicâ Phœbique potentibus herbis
Nequicquam trepidat; nequicquam spicula dextrâ
Sollicitat, prensatque tenaci forcipe ferrum.
Nulla viam fortuna regit; nihil auctor Apollo
Subvenit: et sævus campis magìs ac magìs horror
Crebrescit; propiùsque malum est. Jam pulvere cœlum
Stare vident; subeunt équites, et spicula castris
Densa cadunt mediis. It tristis ad æthera clamor
Bellantûm juvenum, et duro sub Marte cadentûm.
  Hìc Venus, indigno nati concussa dolore,
Dictamnum genitrix Cretæâ carpit ab Idâ,
Puberibus caulem foliis, et flore comantem
Purpureo. Non illa feris incognita capris
Gramina, cùm tergo volucres hæsêre sagittæ.
Hoc Venus, obscuro faciem circumdata nimbo,
Detulit: hôc fusum labris spendentibus amnem
Inficit, occultè medicans; spargitque salubres
Ambrosiæ succos, et odoriferam panaceam.

399. Immobilis magno concursu juvenum

400. Ille senior *Iapys* succinctus amictu retorto in Pæonium

414. Illa gramina *sunt* non incognita

416. Venus circumdata *quoad* faciem

NOTES.

395. *Depositi:* sick—dangerously ill. *Fata:* in the sense of *mortem*. *Proferret:* put off—defer.

396. *Medendi:* the gerund in *di*, of *medeor:* in the sense of *medicinæ*. *Potestates:* properties—qualities.

397. *Mutas artes:* silent arts—arts more useful than showy. The other arts of Apollo were more ostentatious and showy. *Agitare:* practice or exercise.

398. *Acerbà:* an adj. neu. plu., used adverbially: in the sense of *acerbè*.

399. *Mœrentis:* of grieving—afflicted. *Iülus:* Heyne connects *lachrymis* with *Iüli mœrentis*. In this construction, *Iülus* alone is represented as shedding tears. The others assemble to see the wounded hero.

401. *Pæonium:* an adj. from Pæon the physician of the gods; here put for any physician. *Retorto:* turned back after the manner of Pæon, that he might perform the operation more conveniently.

403. *Trepidat multa.* in the sense of *festinat multa:* he tries many expedients to extract the arrow, to no purpose. *Multa tentat*, says Heyne.

404. *Sollicitat:* he moves, or pulls. *Ferrum:* the blade, or barbed part of the spear. *Fortuna:* success—advantage.

406. *Subvenit:* in the sense of *adjuvat*. *Auctor:* the author of medicine. *Horror:* in the sense of *terror*, says Heyne. It may mean a din or clashing of arms; which will make the sense of *malum* easy. See Æn. ii. 301.

407. *Jam vident:* they see the air or sky stand thick with dust—to be overspread or filled with dust.

411. *Indigno:* unmerited—undeserved.

412. *Dictamnum:* the herb dittany. It is said to have grown only in Crete, whence it had its name from *Dicte*, a mountain in that island. Its stalk bears soft downy leaves; and its blossoms are not single, but grow upon almost every leaf: whence, it is said to be *comantem flore purpureo:* this last denotes the color of the flower. *Caulem:* the stem or stalk: it is here put in apposition with *dictamnum*.

415. *Gramina:* in the sense of *herba*.

416. *Hoc:* this herb dittany. The *hoc* in the following line is in the abl. with this she tinged. Ruæus says, *imbuit*. *Amnem:* in the sense of *aquam*.

417. *Labris:* the vessel in which the herbs of *Iapys* were infused.

419. *Succos ambrosiæ.* Homer makes ambrosia to be the food of the gods. It properly signifies immortality. *Panacea* a salutary herb, of which Pliny mentions three kinds. According to the etymology of the word, it should be a remedy for all diseases. *Spargit:* she diffuses in it the healing juices of ambrosia. Ruæus says, *miscet*.

Fovit eâ vulnus lymphâ longævus Iapis,
Ignorans: subitòque omnis de corpore fugit
Quippe dolor; omnis stetit imo vulnere sanguis.
Jamque secuta manum, nullo cogente, sagitta
Excidit, atque novæ rediêre in pristina vires.
Arma citi properate viro: quid statis? Iapis
Conclamat: primusque animos accendit in hostes.
Non hæc humanis opibus, non arte magistrâ
Proveniunt; neque te, Ænea, mea dextera servat:
Major agit Deus, atque opera ad majora remittit.
Ille avidus pugnæ suras incluserat auro
Hinc atque hinc; oditque moras, hastamque coruscat.
Postquam habilis lateri clypeus, loricaque tergo est;
Ascanium fusis circùm complectitur armis,
Summaque per galeam delibans oscula, fatur:
Disce, puer, virtutem ex me, verumque laborem:
Fortunam ex aliis. Nunc te mea dextera bello
Defensum dabit, et magna inter præmia ducet.
Tu facito, mox cùm matura adoleverit ætas,
Sis memor, et te animo repetentem exempla tuorum,
Et pater Æneas, et avunculus excitet Hector.
Hæc ubi dicta dedit, portis sese extulit ingens,
Telum immane manu quatiens: simul agmine denso
Anteusque Mnestheusque ruunt: omnisque relictis
Turba fluit castris. Tum cæco pulvere campus
Miscetur, pulsuque pedum tremit excita tellus.
Vidit ab adverso venientes aggere Turnus,
Vidêre Ausonii; gelidusque per ima cucurrit
Ossa tremor. Prima ante omnes Juturna Latinos
Audiit, agnovitque sonum, et tremefacta refugit.
Ille volat, campoque atrum rapit agmen aperto.
Qualis, ubi ad terras abrupto sidere nimbus

424. In pristina *officia*

425. *O viri* citi

427. *Addit prætereà* hæc non proveniunt

436. *Sed disce* fortunam

437. Ducet *te*

438. Tu facito *ut sis* memor *meæ virtutis*, cùm mox

446. *Trojanos* venientes

450. Ille *Æneas* volat

NOTES.

420. *Fovit:* in the sense of *lavit.*

421. *Ignorans:* ignorant of the virtues which had been communicated to it.

422. *Quippe:* indeed—truly. *Stetit:* ceased to flow. *Constitit*, says Ruæus.

427. *Hæc:* this cure—these things.

428. *Proveniunt:* spring—arise from.—*Magistrâ:* in the sense of *medica.*

429. *Agit:* performs the cure.

430. *Incluserat suras:* had incased his legs on each side in gold.

432. *Habilis:* in the sense of *aptus.*

433. *Complectitur:* he embraces Ascanius, with his arms spread around him. The *circùm* and *fusis* are to be united into one word.

434. *Delibans:* gently touching his lips through his helmet. We have here a most interesting instance of paternal affection, and of tender solicitude for the future welfare of his son.

435. *Laborem:* fortitude—patience under difficulties.

437. *Dabit:* in the sense of *reddet* vel *faciet. Inter:* in the sense of *ad.* Heyne takes *præmia* in the sense of *victorias.*

438. *Adoleverit:* shall have become—shall have ripened.

439. *Repetentem:* calling to your mind. Ruæus says, *revolventem animo.* The following line is repeated from Æn. iii. 343.

440. *Hector.* He was the uncle of Ascanius, his mother, Creüsa, being the daughter of Priam. It is the wish of Æneas that his own example, and the example of his uncle, may excite him to piety and virtue, and to the performance of deeds of valor.

444. *Turba:* the troops—all that were in the camp. *Fluit:* in the sense of *rumpunt* vel *ruunt. Cæco:* darkening, or obscuring the air.

445. *Excita:* in the sense of *commota.*

446. *Aggere:* in the sense of *tumulo* vel *colle.*

450. *Rapit:* in the sense of *ducit* vel *trahit. Atrum:* Ruæus says, *densum.*

451. *Sidere abrupto.* Davidson observes, that *sidere* here may be taken for a storm,

452. Ille *nimbus* dabit

453. Heu, corda miseris agricolis præscia

It mare per medium: miseris, heu, præscia longè
Horrescunt corda agricolis! dabit ille ruinas
Arboribus, stragemque satis, ruet omnia latè.
Antevolant, sonitumque ferunt ad litora venti.
Talis in adversos ductor Rhœteïus hostes
Agmen agit: densi cuneis se quisque coactis
Agglomerant. Ferit ense gravem Thymbræus Osirim
Archetium Mnestheus, Epulonem obtruncat Achates,
Ufentemque Gyas. Cadit ipse Tolumnius augur,
Primus in adversos telum qui torserat hostes.
Tollitur in cœlum clamor: versique vicissim
Pulverulenta fugâ Rutuli dant terga per agros.

464. *Eos* aversos morti

Ipse neque aversos dignatur sternere morti;
Nec pede congressos æquo, nec tela ferentes
Insequitur: solum densâ in caligine Turnum
Vestigat lustrans, solum in certamina poscit.

468. Concussa *quoad* mentem hôc

471. Ipsa subit *in ejus locum*

Hôc concussa metu mentem Juturna virago,
Aurigam Turni media inter lora Metiscum
Excutit, et longê lapsum temone relinquit.
Ipsa subit, manibusque undantes flectit habenas,
Cuncta gerens, vocemque, et corpus, et arma Metisci.
Nigra velut magnas domini cùm divitis ædes
Pervolat, et pennis alta atria lustrat hirundo,
Pabula parva legens, nidisque loquacibus escas;
Et nunc porticibus vacuis, nunc humida circùm

NOTES.

which was thought to be the effect of some furious constellation. In this sense, *abrupto sidere* will mean the same with *abrupta tempestate*, vel *abruptis procellis:* bursting storms, as in the third Georgic. Or, if *sidere* be taken in its proper sense, then *abrupto* must be taken in the sense of *cadente*, setting; the constellations being thought more furious toward the time of their setting. *Nimbus:* a black cloud, fraught with thunder and rain. This is its proper meaning. Heyne takes *sidere abrupto* in the sense of *nube abrupta:* the cloud bursting, or being burst.

452. *Præscia longè:* presaging disaster, while the storm is yet at a distance—foreseeing the danger at a distance.

453. *Agricolis miseris:* the dat. in the sense of the gen. The hearts of the, &c.

454. *Ruet* in the sense of *evertet.*

456. *Rhœteïus:* in the sense of *Trojanus*, so called from *Rhœteum*, a promontory on the coast of Troas.

457. *Cuneis coactis:* the ranks being closed: "in thick array," says Davidson. *Agglomerant se:* they crowd themselves together.

458. *Gravem:* in the sense of *fortem.*

462. *Versi:* in the sense of *fugati.* The Rutuli had been victorious, while Æneas was disabled by his wound. Now he is on the field, the scale of victory is turned, and they, in turn, are put to flight.

464. *Aversos morti.* Pierius found *aversos* in the Roman manuscript. The poet is here telling us, that Æneas disdained to fight with any of the Rutulian army but Turnus. This he does by a circumlocution, dividing the Rutulians into three divisions: 1. The *aversos morti:* those that were on the flight. 2. The *congressos æquo pede:* those who were engaged in close fight, on equal terms. 3. The *ferentes tela:* those who fought with missive weapons, at a distance. Heyne reads *aversos.*

465. *Ferentes:* in the sense of *inferentes.*

466. *Caligine:* in the sense of *pulvere*, vel *nube pulveris.*

468. *Virago:* the heroine Juturna.

470. *Excutit:* in the sense of *dejicit* vel *præcipitat.*

472. *Gerens cuncta:* assuming—taking all things, both the voice, &c.

473. *Velut cùm nigra hirundo.* The epithet *nigra*, Scaliger observes, is added to distinguish this kind of swallow from those that haunt the banks of rivers, and are of a sandy color. Petronius calls it *urbana Progne*, because it loves to frequent towers, and such stately buildings as are in cities. *Ædes:* palace. Ruæus says, *domum.*

475. *Nidis:* the nests are here put for the young in the nests, by meton. *Escas:* put in apposition with *parva pabula.*

Stagna sonat: similis medios Juturna per hostes
Fertur equis, rapidoque volans obit omnia curru:
Jamque hìc germanum, jamque hìc, ostendit ovantem:
Nec conferre manum patitur: volat avia longè.
Haud minùs Æneas tortos legit obvius orbes,
Vestigatque virum, et disjecta per agmina magnâ
Voce vocat. Quoties oculos conjecit in hostem,
Alipedumque fugam cursu tentavit equorum;
Aversos toties currus Juturna retorsit.
Heu! quid agat? vario nequicquam fluctuat æstu:
Diversæque vocant animum in contraria curæ.
Huic Messapus, utì lævâ duo fortè gerebat
Lenta, levis cursu, præfixa hastilia ferro,
Horum unum certo contorquens dirigit ictu.
Substitit Æneas, et se collegit in arma,
Poplite subsidens; apicem tamen incita summum
Hasta tulit, summasque excussit vertice cristas.
Tum verò assurgunt iræ; insidiisque subactus,
Diversos ubi sensit equos currumque referri,
Multa Jovem, et læsi testatur fœderis aras.
Jam tandem invadit medios, et Marte secundo
Terribilis, sævam nullo discrimine cædem
Suscitat, irarumque omnes effundit habenas.

477. Similis *huic avi* Juturna

480. Nec patitur *eum*

483. Vocat *Turnum* magnâ voce

488. Messapus, uti fortè levis cursu gerebat lævâ *manu* duo lenta hastilia

490. Huic *Æneæ*

495. Equos *Turni rapi* diversos

497. Medios *hostes*

NOTES.

477. *Sonat:* chirps, or chatters.

478. *Obit:* goes over, or around. Ruæus says, *percurrit.*

480. *Longè avia:* far out of the way, so as not to meet Æneas. *Avia:* an adj. from *avius*, agreeing with Juturna. *Conferre manum:* to engage in close combat, or fight with Æneas.

481. *Legit tortos orbes obvius:* traces the mazy circles and windings of Turnus, not for the purpose of overtaking him, but for the purpose of meeting him. This is the sense of *obvius.*

482. *Disjecta:* scattered—flying before him.

484. *Fugam:* the speed—swiftness. Ruæus says, *celeritatem. Alipedum:* in the sense of *celerum:* the swift, or winged horses of Turnus.

485. *Retorsit currus.* The meaning is: whenever Æneas was about to intercept her course, coming up in front, Juturna wheeled about the chariot, and drove backward, so as to prevent the meeting of the two champions. *Currus:* the chariot, by meton. the horses.

486. *Heu quid agat.* Dr. Trapp explains this of Juturna; but it is evident we are to understand it of Æneas. It is he who is disappointed, and crossed in his design of meeting Turnus. *Æstu:* with a tide of passions. *Irarum* is understood.

487. *In contraria:* in opposite directions—in different ways. Taken in the sense of *in contrarias partes.*

489. *Levis:* in the sense of *celer*, agreeing with *Messapus. Præfixa:* in the sense of *armata.*

491. *Collegit se in arma:* he contracted, or collected himself into his armor. Though the word *arma* is here mentioned in general, it must be restricted to the shield, behind which he hid himself, bending upon his knee, and contracting his body. Virgil uses the word in the same sense in other places.

492. *Subsidens:* in the sense of *cadens.* Ruæus says, *incurvans se. Incita:* in the sense of *immissa* vel *celer.*

493. *Concita hasta tulit:* the meaning is: the rapid spear just grazed the top of his head, and carried with it the tuft, or plume of his helmet. *Vertice:* in the sense of *capite.*

494. *Subactus insidiis:* baffled by the stratagems of Juturna. Ruæus says, *coactus.*

496. *Testatur.* This is the reading of most of the ancient manuscripts. It is preferable to *testatus*, which is the reading of Ruæus. Heyne reads *testatur. Multa:* in the sense of *multùm.* Ruæus says, *sæpe.*

499. *Suscitat:* in the sense of *facit. Effundit habenas:* he gives full reins to his anger. This is a metaphor taken from the chariot race. *Effundere habenas:* to give full rein to your horses—to set them at full speed. *Dare—laxare—mittere—immittere* &c.—*habenas* vel *frœna*, are phrases denoting the same thing.

500. Nunc quis, quis Deus expediat mihi carmine tot acerba *funera*

503. Placuit-ne *te*, O Jupiter

510. *Ferit* hunc *Diorem* venientem

513. Ille *Æneas* mittit Talon

516. Hic *Turnus interficit* fratres

521. *Duo* ignes immissi *è* diversis

522. *In* sonantia virgulta *è* lauro

Quis mihi nunc tot acerba Deus, quis carmine cædes
Diversas, obitumque ducum, quos æquore toto
Inque vicem nunc Turnus agit, nunc Troïus heros,
Expediat? tanton' placuit concurrere motu,
Jupiter, æternâ gentes in pace futuras?
Æneas Rutulum Sucronem, (ea prima ruentes
Pugna loco statuit Teucros,) haud multa moratus,
Excipit in latus, et, quà fata celerrima, crudum
Transadigit costas et crates pectoris ensem.
Turnus equo dejectum Amycum, fratremque Diorem,
Congressus pedes; hunc venientem cuspide longâ,
Hunc mucrone ferit; curruque abscissa duorum
Suspendit capita, et rorantia sanguine portat.
Ille Talon, Tanaïmque neci, fortemque Cethegum,
Tres uno congressu, et mœstum mittit Onyten,
Nomen Echionium, matrisque genus Peridiæ.
Hic fratres Lyciâ missos, et Apollinis agris,
Et juvenem exosum nequicquam bella Menœten
Arcada: piscosæ cui circum flumina Lernæ
Ars fuerat, pauperque domus: nec nota potentûm
Limina, conductâque pater tellure serebat.
Ac velut immissi diversis partibus ignes
Arentem in sylvam, et virgulta sonantia lauro;

NOTES.

501. *Obitum:* in the sense of *mortem.*

502. *Inque vicem:* for *invicemque*, by tmesis. *Agit:* causes, or effects.

503. *Motu:* rage—violence. *Tanton':* for *tanto-ne*, by apocope.

505. *Pugna:* attack—assault. *Statuit:* stopped. The meaning of this passage may be: that the opposition made by Sucro checked the Trojans, who were before rushing on the enemy, and raging without control. Or, this assault of Æneas upon Sucro caused him, and the Trojans, to stop their career and pursuit of Turnus, and remain in the same place. This is the sense given to it by Heyne. Ruæus proposes a third meaning to the words, to wit: that the assault of Æneas upon Sucro first caused the Trojans to rally and stand their ground, who before were fleeing, and unable to resist so great a hero.

506. *Multa:* in the sense of *multùm.* This is in imitation of the Greeks, who used adjectives of the neu. gen. as adverbs.

507. *Excipit:* in the sense of *ferit*, vel *vulnerat.* *Quà fata:* where death is easiest to be effected. *Fata:* in the sense of *mors.* The verb *sunt* is understood.

508. *Crates:* acc. plu. Ruæus says, *septum.* *Crudum:* naked—bloody. *Costas—Crates.* These are governed in the acc. by the prep. *trans*, in comp., while the verb *adigit* governs *crudum ensem.*

510. *Congressus pedes:* Turnus on foot engaging Amycus, &c. *Congredi:* signifies to engage in close combat—to fight hand to hand.

514. *Congressu:* onset—assault. Ruæus says, *impetu.* *Genus:* in the sense of *prolem* vel *filium.*

515. *Echionium:* an adj. from *Echion*, the name of the Theban, who accompanied Cadmus at the building of Thebes in Beotia. *Onytes* was an Echionian, or Theban name. Ruæus says, *Thebanum.*

516. *Lycia:* a country of Asia Minor, celebrated for the oracles of Apollo. It is here put in apposition with *agris.* See Æn. iv. 143.

517. *Exosum:* a part. agreeing with *juvenem*, and governing *bella.* *Menœtes* was an Arcadian.

519. *Ars:* business, or employment. *Cui:* in the sense of *cujus.* *Lernæ:* a lake near the city of Argos in the Peloponnesus, famous for its having been the abode of the *Hydra*, that was slain by Hercules. *Flumina:* in the sense of *aquas.*

520. *Limina potentûm:* the palaces of the great were not known to him. Ursinus assures us that *limina* is the reading of the most ancient manuscript, *Liber Colitianus vetustissimus*, and he makes no doubt of its being the true reading. Heyne and Davidson read *limina.* Ruæus and Valpy read *munera.* Of this it is difficult to make sense, whereas *limina* is easy. *Conducta:* in hired land. He had no farm of his own.

522. *Virgulta:* in the sense of *nemora.*

Aut ubi decursu rapido de montibus altis
Dant sonitum spumosi amnes, et in æquora currunt,
Quisque suum populatus iter: non segniùs ambo
Æneas Turnusque ruunt per prælia; nunc, nunc
Fluctuat ira intus rumpuntur nescia vinci
Pectora: nunc totis in vulnera viribus itur.
Murranum hic, atavos et avorum antiqua sonantem
Nomina, per regesque actum genus omne Latinos.
Præcipitem scopulo atque ingentis turbine saxi
Excutit, effunditque solo. Hunc lora et juga subter
Provolvêre rotæ; crebro supèr ungula pulsu
Incita nec domini memorum proculcat equorum.
Ille ruenti Hyllo, animisque immanè frementi.
Occurrit, telumque aurata ad tempora torquet:
Olli per galeam fixo stetit hasta cerebro.
Dextera nec tua te, Grajûm fortissime Creteu,
Eripuit Turno: nec Dî texêre Cupencum,
Æneâ veniente, sui: dedit obvia ferro
Pectora, nec misero clypei mora profuit ærei.
Te quoque Laurentes viderunt, Æole, campi,
Oppetere, et latè terram consternere tergo:
Occidis, Argivæ quem non potuere phalanges
Sternere, nec Priami regnorum eversor Achilles.
Hìc tibi mortis erant metæ: domus alta sub Idâ;
Lyrnessi domus alta; solo Laurente sepulchrum.
Totæ adeò conversæ acies, omnesque Latini,
Omnes Dardanidæ. Mnestheus acerque Serestus,
Et Messapus, equûm domitor, et fortis Asylas,
Tuscorumque phalanx, Evandrique Arcadis alæ
Pro se quisque, viri summâ nituntur opum vi.
Nec mora, nec requies: vasto certamine tendunt.

524. Aut ubi amnes spumosi rapido decursu
525. Quisque omnis

529. Hic *Æneas* scopulo, atque turbine ingentis saxi, excutit Murranum.
532. Effundit *eum* præcipitem
533. Ungula equorum, nec memorum
535. Ille *Turnus* occurrit Hyllo

544. *Tu* occidis, quem

546. *Erat tibi* alta domus sub Idâ; *erat tibi* alta domus Lyrnessi; *nunc est tibi.*
548. Conversæ *sunt in se*

552. *Omnes* viri, quisque pro se

NOTES.

523 *Decursu:* descent.

524. *Æquora:* in the sense of *mare.*

525. *Populatus:* laying waste.

527. *Nescia vinci:* knowing not to be conquered—invincible. *Rumpunter:* are burst—pant and heave as if they would burst with rage.

528. *Itur:* they go—march.

529. *Sonantem:* in the sense of *jactantem* vel *gloriantem.* *Actum:* in the sense of *deductum.*

531. *Turbine:* with the force. Heyne says, *jactu.*

532. *Excutit:* in the sense of *dejicit* vel *sternit.*

533. *Supèr:* in the sense of *insuper* vel *prætereà.*

534. *Incita:* quick—in rapid movement.

536. *Aurata tempora:* his temples decked with a gilded helmet.

537. *Fixo:* being pierced—the spear passed through his helmet.

539 *Eripuit.* Ruæus says, *servavit.*

540. *Sui:* in the sense of *propitii* vel *faventes.* Or, his own gods—those gods whose priest he was. *Cupencus,* in the Sabine language, signified a priest.

541. *Ærei.* Pierius found *æris* in all the ancient manuscripts which he examined, instead of *ærei,* as in the common editions. Heyne reads *ærei.* *Mora:* resistance.

543. *Oppetere.* This word properly signifies to die, like a hero, on the field of battle *quasi ore petere terram,* to bite the ground, as we say in English.

544. *Occidis:* thou fallest. Ruæus says, *moreris.*

546. *Metæ mortis:* for *meta vitæ.* the limit or boundary of life. This is in imitation of Homer's τέλος θανάτοιο.

547. *Lyrnessi:* Lyrnessus was a city of Phrygia, near the *Sinus Adramyttenus.*

548. *Conversæ:* Ruæus says, *permixtæ.* The verb *sunt* is understood.

551. *Alæ:* in the sense of *equites,* vel *equitatus.*

552. *Nituntur:* strive—struggle. *Opum:* this appears merely expletive. Ruæus says, *virium.*

553. *Tendunt:* in the sense of *contendunt* vel *luctantur.*

Hìc mentem Æneæ genitrix pulcherrima misit,
Iret ut ad muros, urbique adverteret agmen
Ocyùs, et subitâ turbaret clade Latinos.

557. Ille *Æneas* ut circumtulit

Ille ut vestigans diversa per agmina Turnum,
Huc atque huc acies circumtulit; aspicit urbem
Immunem tanti belli, atque impunè quietam.

560. Accendit *animum*

Continuò pugnæ accendit majoris imago:
Mnesthea, Sergestumque vocat, fortemque Serestum,
Ductores; tumulumque capit, quò cætera Teucrûm
Concurrit legio; nec scuta aut spicula densi
Deponunt. Celso medius stans aggere fatur:

565. Jupiter stat *hâc parte pro nobis*
567. Eruam urbem

Ne qua meis esto dictis mora: Jupiter hâc stat:
Neu quis ob inceptum subitum mihi segnior ito.
Urbem hodie, causam belli, regna ipsa Latini,
Ni frænum accipere et victi parere fatentur,
Eruam; et æqua solo fumantia culmina ponam.
Scilicet exspectem, libeat dum prælia Turno
Nostra pati? rursùsque velit concurrere victus?

572. Hoc *est* caput, *nempe, urbs Laurentum*
576. Scalæ *apparuerunt*

Hoc caput, ô cives, hæc belli summa nefandi.
Ferte faces properè, fœdusque reposcite flammis.
Dixerat: atque animis pariter certantibus omnes
Dant cuneum, densâque ad muros mole feruntur.
Scalæ improvisò, subitusque apparuit ignis.
Discurrunt alii ad portas, primosque trucidant:
Ferrum alii torquent, et obumbrant æthera telis.
Ipse inter primos dextram sub mœnia tendit
Æneas, magnâque incusat voce Latinum:
Testaturque Deos, iterum se ad prælia cogi;

582. Italos jam bis *esse* hostes

Bis jam Italos hostes; hæc altera fœdera rumpi.
Exoritur trepidos inter discordia cives:
Urbem alii reserare jubent, et pandere portas
Dardaniidis; ipsumque trahunt in mœnia regem.

NOTES.

554. *Mentem:* mind—design—purpose. *Misit:* in the sense of *immisit.* Heyne takes *mentem* in the sense of *consilium.*

558. *Acies:* in the sense of *oculos:* some understand it of the various parts of the army. *Immunem:* in the sense of *expertem.*

563. *Nec scuta:* this was according to the custom of the Roman soldiers, who were wont to be drawn up in arms before their general, when he harangued them. *Legio:* in the sense of *turmæ* vel *acies.* Ruæus says *exercitus.*

565. *Stat hâc.* stands here with us—favors us—is on our side, in this bold undertaking. This may be said in allusion to his being the avenger of violated faith.

568. *Fatentur:* unless they consent to receive the reins and obey. *Accipere frænum,* vel *fræna* is a military phrase, denoting unconditional submission to the conqueror.—Ruæus says, *volunt.*

569. *Æqua:* level with the ground. *Ponam:* in the sense of *prosternam.*

571. *Pati nostra prælia:* to fight with me. Ruæus says, *ferre pugnam.*

575. *Dant cuneum:* they form themselves into the military wedge, which is drawn to a point in the front, and widens toward the rear; and in this close body (*densa mole*) they rush against the city. *Dant:* in the sense of *formant* vel *faciunt.* *Feruntur:* in the sense of *irrunt.* Ruæus interprets *mole* by *multitudine.*

578. *Ferrum.* Any missive weapon tipped with iron or steel, may be called *ferrum.*

579. *Tendit:* in the sense of *protendit.* *Sub:* in the sense of *ad.*

582. *Hæc altera fœdera.* The first treaty was, when Latinus promised to Ilioneus to take Æneas for his ally, and son-in-law Æn. vii. 259. The second league or treaty was that which ratified the single combat between Turnus and Æneas, 195. supra.

585. *Trahunt:* they draw the king to the walls, that he may ratify the treaty, and so put an end to the war.

Arma ferunt alii, et pergunt defendere muros.
Inclusas ut cùm latebroso in pumice pastor
Vestigavit apes, fumoque implevit amaro:
Illæ intus trepidæ rerum per cerea castra
Discurrunt, magnisque acuunt stridoribus iras.
Volvitur ater odor tectis; tum murmure cæco
Intus saxa sonant: vacuas it fumus ad auras.
  Accidit hæc fessis etiam fortuna Latinis,
Quæ totam luctu concussit funditùs urbem.
Regina ut tectis venientem prospicit hostem,
Incessi muros, ignes ad tecta volare:
Nusquam acies contrà Rutulas, nulla agmina Turni:
Infelix pugnæ juvenem in certamine credit
Extinctum: et, subitô mentem turbata dolore,
Se causam clamat, crimenque, caputque malorum:
Multaque per mœstum demens effata furorem,
Purpureos moritura manu discindit amictus,
Et nodum informis leti trabe nectit ab altâ.
Quam cladem miseræ postquam accepêre Latinæ,
Filia prima manu flavos Lavinia crines,
Et roseas laniata genas; tum cætera circùm
Turba furit: resonant latè plangoribus ædes.
Hinc totam infelix vulgatur fama per urbem.
Demittunt mentes: it, scissâ veste, Latinus,
Conjugis attonitus fatis, urbisque ruinâ,
Canitiem immundo perfusam pulvere turpans:
Multaque se incusat, qui non acceperit antè
Dardanium Æneam, generumque adsciverit ultrò.

588. Implevit *locum*

597. Contrà *prospicit* nusquam Rutulas acies *apparere*

598. Credit juvenem *Turnum* extinctum *esse*

600. Se *esse* causam

605. Lavinia prima *furit*, laniata *quoad*

NOTES.

586. *Pergunt:* in the sense of *parant.*

587. *Pumice.* *Pumex* is properly the pumice stone: here put for any stone.

588. *Vestigavit:* hath found—discovered.

589. *Castra:* their hives. *Trepidæ rerum:* alarmed for their state—condition. *Timentes suis rebus*, says Ruæus. So *fessi rerum*, Æn. i. 178.

591. *Tectis:* this again means the hives. *Odor:* fume—vapor, or smoke. *Cæco:* smothered—obscure.

593. *Fortuna:* in the sense of *calamitas.* *Fessis:* afflicted—distressed.

594. *Concussit:* in the sense of *implevit.*

595. *Tectis.* *Tectum* here is in the sense of *urbs.* *Incessi:* the inf. of the verb *incessor:* to be assaulted. *Ut:* when—as soon as.

599. *Turbata:* in the sense of *commota.* *Mentem* is put as a Grecism.

600. *Crimen:* the criminal author.

601. *Demens:* wanting reason. Of *de*, and *mens.* *Affata:* in the sense of *dicens* vel *loquens.* *Per:* through—during.

603. *Informis:* unnatural—awful. Heyne says, *turpis.* The poet here expresses his disapprobation of suicide, by calling it *informis leti.* According to the pontifical books, such persons were deprived of the rites of burial. *Nectit:* she binds, or ties the rope. *Nodum:* in the sense of *funem*, says Heyne.

605. *Accepêre:* in the sense of *audiverunt.* *Quam cladem:* in the sense of *cujus mortem.*

606. *Lavinia laniata.* After the women had learned the tragic end of her mother, Lavinia was the first to express her grief. This she did by tearing her hair, and mangling her rosy cheeks. Servius reads *floros*, or *floreos*, instead of *flavos*, in imitation of Ennius. But there is no authority to support this reading; and there is no necessity for the alteration; for *yellow*, or *golden hair*, was the color most admired among the ancients.

609. *Demittunt:* their resolution fails—they despond. Ruæus says, *dejiciunt animos.* Davidson renders it, "their souls despond."

610. *Fatis:* in the sense of *morte.*

611. *Turpans:* defiling—tearing.

612. *Multa:* in the sense of *multùm.* This and the following line are introduced from Æn. xi. 471. In some copies they do not appear in this place.

613. *Adsciverit:* admitted, or received him as a son-in-law.

618. Commixtum cæcis terroribus

625. Occurrit huic *in* talibus dictis: hâc *parte*, O Turne

630. Numero *cæsorum*

631. Turnus *respondet*

634. Fallis *me*. Sed quis *Deorum* voluit te demissam

638. Ego ipse vidi ingentem Murranum oppetere ante meos oculos, vocantem me voce, atque victum

643. *Nostris miseris* rebus

Intereâ extremo bellator in æquore Turnus
Palantes sequitur paucos, jam segnior, atque
Jam minùs atque minùs successu lætus equorum.
Attulit hunc illi cæcis terroribus aura
Commixtum clamorem, arrectasque impulit aures
Confusæ sonus urbis, et illætabile murmur.
Hei mihi! quid tanto turbantur mœnia luctu?
Quisve ruit tantus diversâ clamor ab urbe?
Sic ait: adductisque amens subsistit habenis.
Atque huic, in faciem soror ut conversa Metisci
Aurigæ, currumque et equos et lora regebat,
Talibus occurrit dictis: Hâc, Turne, sequamur
Trojugenas, quâ prima viam victoria pandit
Sunt alii, qui tecta manu defendere possint.
Ingruit Æneas Italis, et prælia miscet:
Et nos sæva manu mittamus funera Teucris.
Nec numero inferior, pugnæ nec honore recedes.
Turnus ad hæc:
O soror, et dudum agnovi, cùm prima per artem
Fœdera turbâsti, teque hæc in bella dedisti:
Et nunc nequicquam fallis Dea. Sed quis Olympo
Demissam tantos voluit te ferre labores?
An fratris miseri letum ut crudele videres?
Nam quid ago? aut quæ jam spondet fortuna salutem?
Vidi oculos ante ipse meos, me voce vocantem
Murranum, quo non superat mihi charior alter,
Oppetere ingentem, atque ingenti vulnere victum.
Occidit infelix, ne nostrum dedecus, Ufens,
Aspiceret: Teucri potiuntur corpore et armis.
Exscindi-ne domos, id rebus defuit unum,

NOTES.

614. *Æquore:* in the sense of *campo.*

615. *Segnior.* Ruæus says, *tardior.*

616. *Successu equorum.* Servius, and most interpreters after him, take the meaning to be: that Turnus was now less pleased with his horses, because they were out of breath, and fatigued. But it seems much better to understand it of his being less pleased with the easy victory he gained, now that Æneas was retired, and only a few straggling troops left in the field. This agrees with the expressions *paucos palantes. Successu equorum:* this last intimates, that the victory he gained was now so easy, that he had only to drive the enemy before his chariot, without meeting with any resistance. Turnus might think the victory not worthy of his valor, and was therefore less pleased with it, than if it had more richly rewarded him. This better accords with the sentiments of the soldier. This is the opinion of Davidson. He renders the words; "with the cheap victory of his horses." Heyne agrees with Servius. Ruæus observes: he was less pleased with his horses, because they had carried him so far from the fight.

617. *Aura:* in the sense of *ventus. Cæcis*: unknown—uncertain. Ruæus says, *incertis.*

619. *Illætabile:* mournful—unjoyous. Of *in*, neg. and *lætabilis.*

621. *Diversâ:* in the sense of *ab diversa parte urbis.* Ruæus says, *dissita.*

625. *Occurrit:* in the sense of *respondet.*

627. *Tecta:* in the sense of *urbem.*

629. *Mittamus:* in the sense of *demus. Funera sæva:* in the sense of *crudelem mortem*, says Ruæus. "Let us spread cruel death among the Trojans." Valpy.

630. *Numero:* in the number of the slain. Turnus should equal Æneas in the number of his slain, and in the glory of the fight.

632. *Agnovi:* the pron. *te* is understood.

633. *Turbâsti:* in the sense of *rupisti.*

634. *Fallis:* Heyne says, *vis latere.*

638. *Murranum.* He was one of the Italian princes, and slain by Æneas, verse 529, supra. *Ingentem:* mighty—powerful.

641. *Ufens.* He commanded the Agricolæ. See Æn. vii. 745.

643. *Unum:* in the sense of *solum.* The only thing wanting to our complete wretchedness and misery.

Perpetiar? dextrâ nec Drancis dicta refellam?
Terga dabo? et Turnum fugientem hæc terra videbit?
Usque adeòne mori miserum est? vos ô mihi Manes
Este boni; quoniam Superis aversa voluntas.
Sancta ad vos anima, atque istius inscia culpæ,
Descendam, magnorum haud unquam indignus avorum.
Vix ea fatus erat: medios volat, ecce, per hostes
Vectus equo spumante Sages; adversa sagittâ
Saucius ora ruitque, implorans nomine Turnum:
Turne, in te suprema salus; miserere tuorum.
Fulminat Æneas armis, summasque minatur
Dejecturum arces Italûm, excidioque daturum:
Jamque faces ad tecta volant. In te ora Latini,
In te oculos referunt mussat rex ipse Latinus,
Quos generos vocet, aut quæ sese ad fœdera flectat.
Præterea regina, tui fidissima, dextrâ
Occidit ipsa suâ, lucemque exterrita fugit.
Soli pro portis Messapus et acer Atinas
Sustentant aciem Circum hos utrinque phalanges
Stant densæ, strictisque seges mucronibus horret
Ferrea: tu currum deserto in gramine versas.
Obstupuit variâ confusus imagine rerum
Turnus, et obtutu tacito stetit. Æstuat ingens
Imo in corde pudor, mixtoque insania luctu,
Et furiis agitatus amor, et conscia virtus.
Ut primùm discussæ umbræ, et lux reddita menti,
Ardentes oculorum acies ad mœnia torsit
Turbidus, èque rotis magnam respexit ad urbem.
Ecce autem, flammis inter tabulata volutus

646. Est-ne usque adeò
647. Voluntas Superis *est* aversa *mihi*

652. Saucius *quoad* adversa ora
653. *Nostra* suprema salus *est*
655. Daturum *eas* arces

663. *E* strictis mucronibus

669. *Sunt* discussæ

NOTES.

644. *Dicta Drancis.* See Æn. xi. 336, *et sequens.*

646. *Est-ne usque adeò:* is it indeed so grievous a thing to die?

647. *Superis:* in the sense of *Superorum. Boni:* propitious—kind. Turnus now plainly sees, that the gods above are against him, and that he must fall beneath the sword of Æneas. He addresses himself to the gods below, (*Manes,*) not so much with a view to obtain their assistance against the purposes of Jove, as they might give his shade, his *sancta anima*, a welcome reception; since it would descend to them covered with glory, free from any imputation of cowardice or fault, and no way degenerate from his illustrious ancestors.

648. *Inscia istius culpæ:* free from the fault or crime of deserting his friends in their distress, and difficulty. This he will not do, though he knows that it must terminate in his death. *Sancta:* pure—unpolluted.

652. *Ora:* in the sense of *vultum.* He was wounded full in the face—right in front. *Implorans:* in the sense of *vocans.*

655. *Dejecturum:* would rase.

657. *Mussat.* This word strongly marks the state of Latinus' mind. On the one hand, he was inclined to match his daughter with Æneas, and fulfil his engagements: on the other, he was overawed by Turnus, and durst not openly declare his sentiments; but faintly hinted them, like one who mutters what he is afraid to speak out. Ruæus says, *dubitat.* Heyne says, *tacitè deliberat. Referunt:* turn—cast. The verb is to be repeated before each objective case.

659. *Tui:* in the sense of *tibi.*

662. *Aciem:* in the sense of *pugnam. Phalanges:* the troops in general.

664. *Deserto gramine:* in the sense of *extremo campo.* See 614, supra.

665. *Rerum:* of distress—affliction. *Imagine:* form—image.

667. *Ingens pudor:* this, and the following line are repeated from Æn. x. 870.

668. *Insania:* distraction. Ruæus says, *amentia. Furiis.* Heyne conjectures reference is had to the nuptials of Lavinia, of which he now began to despair.

670. *Acies oculorum:* the sight of his eyes; simply, his eyes. Heyne reads, *orbes.*

671. *Rotis:* in the sense of *curru.*

672. *Vortex flammis:* a whirling volume of flame rolled, &c. The prep. *è* is under-

678. Stat *mihi* pati quicquid acerbi est *in* morte

680. Ante *mortem*

684. Velut cùm saxum ruit præceps de vertice

686. Solvit *illud è loco*

694. Fortuna *hujus pugnæ* est mea: *est* veriùs

695. Luere *violatum* fœdus

701. *Tantus* quantus *est* Athos, aut quantus *est* Eryx, aut quantus *est* pater Apenninus ipse, cùm fremit

Ad cœlum undabat vortex, turrimque tenebat;
Turrim, compactis trabibus quam eduxerat ipse,
Subdideratque rotas, pontesque instraverat altos.
Jam jam fata, soror, superant; absiste morari
Quò Deus, et quò dura vocat fortuna, sequamur.
Stat conferre manum Æneæ: stat, quicquid acerbi est
Morte pati; nec me indecorem, germana! videbis
Ampliùs. Hunc, oro, sine me furere antè furorem.
Dixit: et è curru saltum dedit ocyùs arvis:
Perque hostes, per tela ruit; mœstamque sororem
Deserit; ac rapido cursu media agmina rumpit.
Ac, veluti montis saxum de vertice præceps
Cùm ruit avulsum vento, seu turbidus imber
Proluit, aut annis solvit sublapsa vetustas;
Fertur in abruptum magno mons improbus actu,
Exsultatque solo, sylvas, armenta, virosque
Involvens secum: disjecta per agmina Turnus
Sic urbis ruit ad muros, ubi plurima fuso
Sanguine terra madet, stridentque hastilibus auræ:
Significatque manu, et magno simul incipit ore:
Parcite jam, Rutuli; et vos, tela inhibite, Latini;
Quæcunque est, fortuna mea est; me veriùs unum
Pro vobis fœdus luere, et decernere ferro.
Discessêre omnes medii, spatiumque dedêre.
At pater Æneas, audito nomine Turni,
Deserit et muros, et summas deserit arces;
Præcipitatque moras omnes: opera omnia rumpit,
Lætitiâ exsultans, horrendùmque intonat armis:
Quantus Athos, aut quantus Eryx, aut ipse coruscis

NOTES.

stood to govern *flammis*. *Tabulata:* the stages or stories of the tower.

674. *Turrim, quam ipse:* the tower which he himself had raised, &c. *Eduxerat:* in the sense of *struxerat.*

675. *Subdiderat:* had placed under it wheels.

Towers were built of wood, and commonly several stories (*tabulata*) high. They were for the purpose of defence, or assault; and were so constructed that they could be moved by means of wheels or rollers, placed under them, to the place where they were required. Sometimes several of them were connected by means of bridges (*pontes*) at the tops, made of planks and timber. By these bridges the men could pass from one to another, whenever it became necessary.

678. *Stat:* the imp. of *sto.* I am resolved —it is fixed. Ruæus says, *deliberatum est.*

680. *Furere hunc:* in the sense of *indulgere huic furori.* The construction is according to a Greek idiom. Permit me, O, sister! to rage in this manner—to indulge this passion. *Ante:* this refers to his death, or his engagement with Æneas, in which he was persuaded he should be slain: *ante mortem*, vel *antiquam moriar.*

681. *Arvis:* in the sense of *terræ.*

685. *Turbidus imber:* a violent heavy rain

686. *Proluit:* washed away—undermined it. *Vetustas:* in the sense of *tempus.* *Sublapsa:* having passed away. Ruæus says, *labente.* *Solvit:* torn it away—broken it loose.

687. *Mons fertur improbus:* the massy rock is carried violent, &c. *Mons* here evidently means the same as *saxum*, just before mentioned. *In abruptum:* down the sides of the mountain. *Improbus* implies that the rock rushed down with an irresistible force. *Actu:* in the sense of *impetu.*

689. *Involvens:* in the sense of *rapiens.* *Disjecta:* scattered—fleeing before him.

690. *Plurima:* in the sense of *plurimùm.* This implies that Turnus rushed into the hottest of the battle—where the earth was wet the most with blood.

692. *Ore:* in the sense of *voce.*

693. *Parcite:* cease, or spare your arms.

694. *Veriùs:* in the sense of *æquius.* *Pro vobis:* in your room, and stead.

698. *Deserit:* in the sense of *relinquit.*

699. *Rumpit:* in the sense of *abrumpit.*

700. *Intonat:* in the sense of *sonat.*

701. *Athos:* a mountain in Macedonia.

Cùm fremit ilicibus quantus, gaudetque nivali
Vertice, se attollens pater Apenninus ad auras.
Jam verò et Rutuli certatim, et Troës, et omnes
Convertêre oculos Itali; quique alta tenebant
Mœnia, quique imos pulsabant ariete muros;
Armaque deposuêre humeris. Stupet ipse Latinus,
Ingentes genitos diversis partibus orbis
Inter se coiïsse viros, et cernere ferro.
Atque illi, ut vacuo patuerunt æquore campi,
Procursu rapido, conjectis eminùs hastis,
Invadunt Martem clypeis atque ære sonoro.
Dat gemitum tellus: tum crebros ensibus ictus
Congeminant: fors et virtus miscentur in unum.
Ac velut, ingenti Silâ, summove Taburno,
Cùm duo conversis inimica in prælia tauri
Frontibus incurrunt; pavidi cessêre magistri;
Stat pecus omne metu mutum; mussantque juvencæ,
Quis pecori imperitet; quem tota armenta sequantur:
Illi inter sese multâ vi vulnera miscent,
Cornuaque obnixi infigunt, et sanguine largo
Colla armosque lavant: gemitu nemus omne remugit.
Haud aliter Tros Æneas et Daunius heros
Concurrunt clypeis: ingens fragor æthera complet.
Jupiter ipse duas æquato examine lances
Sustinet, et fata imponit diversa duorum;
Quem damnet labor, et quo vergat pondere letum.

708. *Duos* ingentes viros genitos *in*

710. Ut *primùm*

719. Quis *taurus*

721. Cornua *inter se invicem*

NOTES.

projecting into the Ægean sea. It is said to be sixty miles in length, and so high that it overshadows the island of Lemnos. *Hodie, Monte Santo.* It is so called from the number of monasteries upon it. *Eryx:* a mountain in Sicily, next in height to Ætna, so called from a king of that name who was slain by Hercules. It is situated near the western side of the island. *Hodie, Monte Giuliano.*

703. *Pater Apenninus:* mount Apennine is here called *pater*, either as being the parent of so many noble rivers and woods; or by way of dignity, as being the greatest mountain in Italy. The Apennines are properly a range of mountains running the whole length of Italy, and dividing it nearly in the middle.

704. *Certatim:* eagerly.

708. *Ingentes viros:* that two mighty heroes born in, &c.

709. *Coiïsse:* in the sense of *congredi. Cernere:* in the sense of *pugnare*, vel *decernere.*

710. *Campi:* the ground—the space cleared for the combatants.

712. *Invadunt Martem:* in the sense of *incipiunt pugnam.*

714. *Congeminant:* they repeat—redouble. *In unum:* into one—together.

715. *Sila:* a vast forest, or tract of hills, covered with wood, that formed part of the Apennine mountains in Calabria. *Taburno:* this was a mountain in the confines of Campania, which blocks up the famous straits of *Caudi* or *Caudium.* Here the Roman army was obliged to surrender to the Samnites, and to pass under the yoke.

717. *Magistri:* in the sense of *pastores. Cessêre:* in the sense of *fugerunt.*

718. *Mussant:* Heyne says, *tacitè expectant.* Ruæus says, *timidè, et quasi tacitè mugiunt.*

721. *Largo:* in the sense of *multo.*

722. *Lavant:* Ruæus says, *tingunt.*

723. *Daunius heros:* Turnus. He was the son of *Daunus* and *Venilia.*

725. *Æquato examine:* equal poise or balance. *Examen* is the tongue, or needle of the balance, which, being exactly in *equilibrio*, shows the scales to be equal.

727. *Quem labor damnet:* whom the combat should devote or doom to death. The fates, or destiny, were not at the disposal of Jove. He could only examine into futurity. He puts (*imponit*) the fates of the combatants into the scales of the balance, to see which end of the beam would rise. Servius, and some others, take the words in the sense of *quem felix labor damnet votis:* whom the combat shall doom to pay his vows—who shall be the successful combatant. But it is easier to consider the expression as referring to one and the same person: whom the

729. Putans *futurum* impunè *sibi*, Turnus hic emicat

Emicat hic, impunè putans, et corpore toto
Altè sublatum consurgit Turnus in ensem,
Et ferit. Exclamant Troës, trepidique Latini,
Arrectæque amborum acies. At perfidus ensis
Frangitur, in medioque ardentem deserit ictu,
Ni fuga subsidio subeat. Fugit ocyor Euro,
Ut capulum ignotum, dextramque adspexit inermem

735. Fama est, *eum* præcipitem, cùm conscendebat equos junctos in prima prælia, dum trepidat, rapuisse

Fama est, præcipitem, cùm prima in prælia junctos
Conscendebat equos, patrio mucrone relicto,
Dum trepidat, ferrum aurigæ rapuisse Metisci:
Idque diu, dum terga dabant palantia Teucri,
Suffecit: postquam arma Dei ad Vulcania ventum est,
Mortalis mucro, glacies ceu futilis, ictu
Dissiluit: fulvâ resplendent fragmina arenâ.
Ergò amens diversa fugâ petit æquora Turnus,
Et nunc huc, inde huc, incertos implicat orbes.
Undique enim densâ Teucri inclusêre coronâ:
Atque hinc vasta palus, hinc ardua mœnia cingunt.

746. Æneas insequitur, quanquam genua tardata sagittâ

748. Pedem trepidi *Turni*

749. Si quando canis venator nactus

Nec minùs Æneas, quanquam tardata sagittâ
Interdum genua impediunt, cursumque recusant,
Insequitur: trepidique pedem pede fervidus urget.
Inclusum veluti si quando flumine nactus
Cervum, aut puniceæ septum formidine pennæ,
Venator cursu canis et latratibus instat:
Ille autem, insidiis et ripâ territus altâ,
Mille fugit refugitque vias: at vividus Umber

NOTES.

combat shall devote to ruin, as above. This is the opinion of Valpy. Davidson renders the words, "whom the toilsome combat destines to victory." *Labor:* in the sense of *pugna*, says Heyne. The poet here imitates Homer, who makes Jove, in like manner, weigh the fates of Hector and Achilles. *Quo pondere:* in which scale. Death was to fall to the party, whose scale sunk or fell. Ruæus says, *mors inclinat.*

729. *Altè:* this is to be taken with *sublatum.*

730. *Ferit:* Ænean is understood. *Trepidi:* trembling—in anxious fear. *Consurgit:* in the sense of *insurgit.*

731. *Arrectæ:* in the sense of *suspensæ.* The verb *sunt* is understood.

732. *Deserit:* leaves him ardent for the fight, at the mercy of his antagonist. These last, or words of the like import, are necessary to make the sense complete. When he mounted his chariot, it was his intention to take his trusty, heavenly tempered sword—that sword made by Vulcan for his father; but in his haste and perturbation, he took the sword of Metiscus, his charioteer; which here deceived him. It is therefore, called *perfidus ensis.*

733. *Ni fuga:* had not flight come to his aid—had he not instantly and, he would have fallen under the arm of Æneas, being left in that defenceless state.

734. *Capulum:* the hilt only remained in his hand. He now discovered the fatal mistake. *Ut:* when—as soon as.

737. *Trepidat:* in the sense of *properat.*

739. *Suffecit:* in the sense of *satis fuit. Vulcania arma Dei:* in the sense of *arma Dei Vulcani*, vel *Divina arma Vulcani.* Those arms which Vulcan made for Æneas. This construction is imitated from the Greeks.

740. *Mortalis mucro:* a sword made by men—a mortal sword. *Futilis:* in the sense of *fragilis.*

741. *Dissiluit:* in the sense of *fractus est.*

742. *Diversa æquora:* different parts of the plain. *Amens:* alarmed. Of *a* priv. and *mens.*

743. *Implicat:* in the sense of *facit* vel *format.* He wheels around in his flight, forming irregular figures, or circles.

744. *Coronâ densa:* in close ranks—in a close compact body.

746. *Sagitta:* the arrow by which he was wounded in the beginning of the action. Heyne says, *vulnere.*

748. *Fervidus:* in the sense of *ardens.*

749. *Flumine:* some copies have *in flumine.* Heyne omits the *in.* This is the reading of the Roman MS. *Inclusum:* enclosed, or confined by a river.

750. *Formidine.* The *formido*, as Dr. Trapp observes, was a rope stuck thick with

Hæret hians, jam jamque tenet, similisque tenenti
Increpuit malis, morsuque elusus inani est.
Tum verò exoritur clamor: ripæque lacusque
Responsant circà, et cœlum tonat omne tumultu.
Ille simul fugiens, Rutulos simul increpat omnes,
Nomine quemque vocans; notumque efflagitat ensem.
Æneas mortem contrà, præsensque minatur
Exitium, si quisquam adeat: terretque trementes,
Excisurum urbem minitans, et saucius instat
Quinque orbes explent cursu, totidemque retexunt
Huc, illuc: nec enim levia aut ludicra petuntur
Præmia; sed Turni de vitâ et sanguine certant.
Fortè sacer Fauno foliis oleaster amaris
Hìc steterat, nautis olim venerabile lignum;
Servati ex undis ubi figere dona solebant
Laurenti Divo, et votas suspendere vestes:
Sed stirpem Teucri nullo discrimine sacrum
Sustulerant, puro ut possent concurrere campo.
Hìc hasta Æneæ stabat: huc impetus illam
Detulerat, fixam et lentâ in radice tenebat.
Incubuit, voluitque manu convellere ferrum,
Dardanides; teloque sequi, quem prendere cursu
Non poterat. Tum verò amens formidine Turnus,
Faune, precor, miserere, inquit: tuque optima ferrum
Terra tene: colui vestros si semper honores,
Quos contrà Æneadæ bello fecêre profanos.
Dixit: opemque Dei non cassa in vota vocavit.

754. Hians hæret *illi*, jam jamque tenet *eum*

758. Ille *Turnus* simul *est* fugiens

761. Adeat *Turnum*: terretque *eos* trementes, minitans *se* excisurum

768. Ubi *illi* servati ex undis

772. Impetus *ejus dextræ*

775. Sequique *Turnum* telo, quem

NOTES.

red or crimson feathers to enclose, and frighten the deer, or other animals. See Geor. iii. 371.

753. *Umber:* a dog of Umbria, in the north of Italy. *Canis* is understood. *Vividus:* quick scented.

755. *Increpuit:* Ruæus says, *insonuit.*—He shuts his jaws, as if in the act of seizing him.

761. *Si quis adeat.* Virgil here outrages the character of his hero. It is true he has the example of Homer for it. But it is to be remembered the two poets lived in very different states of society. Turnus is forced to the contest with unequal weapons. Of his sword he is deprived, and left without arms. In this situation, he is pursued by Æneas, who threatens to put the person to death, who shall give him his sword, that he may be in a condition to defend himself, and be on more equal terms with his adversary. This is a course of conduct, which no age or nation, however barbarous, can justify. Much less is it becoming in the soldier, and the hero. The putting to death of unarmed and defenceless persons may be practised, but cannot be justified. Valpy.

763. *Retexunt totidem:* they retrace, or form back again, as many more. The meaning is, that Turnus went five times around the field of combat, pursued by Æneas—*Explent:* in the sense of *conficiunt. Retexunt:* Ruæus says, *relegunt.*

764. *Enim:* in the sense of *equidem. Ludicra:* trifling—of no value.

766. *Oleaster.* The wild olive was frequently planted before temples, that the consecrated offerings might be suspended upon its boughs. It was a very durable tree, and not apt to receive any injury, though ever so many nails were driven into its wood. Its leaves were bitter.

767. *Lignum:* in the sense of *arbor. Venerabile:* in the sense of *venerandum.*

769. *Votas:* in the sense of *devotas.*

770. *Nullo discrimine:* with no regard to its sacredness. *Nullo respectu habito*, says Heyne.

771. *Puro:* in the sense of *aperto*, vel *vacuo. Sustulerant:* in the sense of *absciderant.*

773. *Lenta radice:* in the tough root. It stuck fast in the root, so that it could not be drawn out.

775. *Dardanides:* Æneas. A patronymic from Dardanus. *Incubuit:* Ruæus says, *insistit.*

776. *Amens:* Ruæus says, *exanimatus.*

778. *Colui:* I have regarded, or held sacred.

780. *Cassa:* in the sense of *inutilia.*

Namque diu luctans, lentoque in stirpe moratus'
Viribus haud ullis valuit discludere morsus
Roboris Æneas. Dum nititur acer et instat,

784. Rursùs Daunia Dea mutata in faciem

Rursùs in aurigæ faciem mutata Metisci
Procurrit, fratrique ensem Dea Daunia reddit
Quod Venus audaci Nymphæ indignata licere,
Accessit, telumque altâ ab radice revellit.
Olli sublimes, armis, animisque refecti,
Hic gladio fidens, hic acer et arduus hastâ,
Adsistunt contrà certamine Martis anheli.
Junonem intereà rex omnipotentis Olympi
Alloquitur, fulvâ pugnas de nube tuentem.
Quæ jam finis erit, conjux ? quid denique restat ?

794. *Tu* ipsa scis, et fateris *te* scire Æneam indigetem deberi

Indigetem Æneam scis ipsa, et scire fateris,
Deberi cœlo, fatisque ad sidera tolli.
Quid struis ? aut quâ spe gelidis in nubibus hæres ?
Mortalin' decuit violari vulnere Divum ?
Aut ensem (quid enim sine te Juturna valeret ?)

799. Decuit-ne *eum* Divum violari

Ereptum reddi Turno, et vim crescere victis ?
Desine jam tandem, precibusque inflectere nostris :
Nec te tantus edat tacitam dolor; et mihi curæ
Sæpe tuo dulci tristes ex ore recursent.
Ventum ad supremum est. Terris agitare vel undis

805. Domum *Latini*
806. Veto *te* tentare *quicquam*

Trojanos potuisti ; infandum accendere bellum,
Deformare domum, et luctu miscere hymenæos :
Ulteriùs tentare veto. Sic Jupiter orsus·

NOTES.

782. *Discludere morsus roboris :* to loosen, or separate the hold of the wood. The poet here represents the root of the tree (*stirpe*) as a fierce dog, or wild beast, whose tusks take so fast hold of the prey, that there is no disengaging them. *Lento:* in the sense of *tenace. Discludere:* in the sense of *solvere.*

783. *Acer:* in the sense of *ardens.* Æneas is to be supplied.

785. *Daunia Dea:* Juturna, the sister of Turnus, and daughter of *Daunus:* hence the adj. *Daunia.* See 139, supra, *et seq.*

786. *Quod:* in the sense of *hoc.* It is governed by *indignata :* indignant—angry.

788. *Refecti :* in the sense of *reparati* vel *animati.*

789. *Arduus:* in the sense of *elatus.*

790. *Contrà :* against each other—face each other. *Anheli:* Ruæus refers it to Turnus and Æneas. Heyne connects it with *Martis;* and it is a very appropriate epithet of a fight, like the present. The sense is the same in either construction.

794. *Indigetem. Indiges* is, properly, a deified hero—a demi-god. Such an one was Æneas after his death.

796. *Hæres:* in the sense of *manes.*

797. *Divum :* this is said by anticipation. Æneas was not yet a god. Or *divum* may be in the sense of *divinum;* and then it will refer to the origin of Æneas; who, on the side of his mother, was of divine descent. Valpy says, "destined to divinity."

798. *Valeret:* in the sense of *posset facere.*

799. *Ereptum.* This alludes to his trusty sword, which he forgot to take with him when he mounted his chariot at the beginning of the fight. It was taken, or snatched from him, by his forgetfulness.

800. *Inflectere:* in the sense of *movere. Edat:* consume—waste away. Ruæus says, *angat. Et.* The *et* here connects, and continues the preceding negative. The *nec* is to be repeated after the *et;* or the *et* is to be taken in the sense of *nec.* This last is the opinion of Valpy. Heyne observes, the *nec* is to be repeated. *Negativa* nec *repetenda est,* says he. *Curæ :* troubles. *Solicitudines,* says Ruæus.

804. *Accendere bellum:* to kindle horrid war. See Æn. vii. 323 ; where Juno raises Alecto from the infernal regions, who broke the league which Latinus had made with Æneas, and kindled the war.

805. *Deformare :* to afflict—trouble—disgrace. Davidson says, "dishonor." Heyne thinks reference is here made to the death of Amata, who hung herself. Disgrace and ignominy always attend suicide. *Hymenæos* the match of Lavinia and Æneas. *Miscere* in the sense of *turbare.*

806. *Orsus:* in the sense of *locutus est,* Of the verb *ordior.*

Sic Dea submisso contrà Saturnia vultu :
Ista quidem quia nota mihi tua, magne, voluntas,
Jupiter, et Turnum et terras invita reliqui.
Nec tu me aëriâ solam nunc sede videres
Digna indigna pati ; sed flammis cincta sub ipsâ
Starem acie, traheremque inimica in prælia Teucros
Juturnam misero, fateor, succurrere fratri
Suasi, et pro vitâ majora audere probavi :
Non ut tela tamen, non ut contenderet arcum.
Adjuro Stygii caput implacabile fontis,
Una superstitio superis quæ reddita Divis.
Et nunc cedo equidem, pugnasque exosa relinquo.
Illud te, nullâ fati quod lege tenetur,
Pro Latio obtestor, pro majestate tuorum :
Cùm jam connubiis pacem felicibus, esto,
Component ; cùm jam leges et fœdera jungent :
Ne vetus indigenas nomen mutare Latinos,
Neu Troas fieri jubeas, Teucrosque vocari ;
Aut vocem mutare viros, aut vertere vestes.
Sit Latium ; sint Albani per sæcula reges :
Sit Romana potens Italâ virtute propago :
Occidit, occideritque sinas cum nomine Troja.
Olli subridens hominum rerumque repertor :
Et germana Jovis, Saturnique altera proles,
Irarum tantos volvis sub pectore fluctus ?
Verùm age, et inceptum frustrà submitte furorem :

808. *O* magno Jupiter, quia quidem ista tua voluntas *est* nota

815. Tamen non *suasi, nec probavi* ut *jaceret* tela, non *suasi, nec probavi* ut

820. Obtestor te *concedere* illud pro

823. Ne jubeas Latinos indigenas mutare

825. Sit Latium *in æternùm*

828. Troja occidit, *tu*que sinas *ut*

830. *Ait : tu*, et germana

NOTES.

807. *Submisso :* in the sense of *tristi.* The verb *respondit*, or some other of the like import, is understood.

810. *Nec tu nunc :* some words appear necessary here to make the sense complete : otherwise, you would not, &c. If I had not known it to be your will, you would not now see, &c. *Aëriâ sede :* in the aerial regions. Reference is here had to verse 792, where Juno is represented as viewing the field of battle, seated on a cloud.

811. *Pati digna indigna :* to bear things, becoming and unbecoming. This is a proverbial expression, the import of which is, "to bear every thing, even the greatest insults and indignities."

812. *Inimica.* Ruæus says, *adversa.*

816. *Stygii fontis :* Styx, a fabulous river of hell. The gods were wont to swear by it ; and if they swore falsely, they were doomed to lose their divinity for a length of time. Hence it is called *implacabilis :* inexorable. *Fontis :* in the sense of *fluvii. Caput :* the head, or source ; put for the whole stream, by synec. *Adjuro caput Stygii :* simply for, *juro per Stygem*, says Heyne.

817. *Una superstitio :* the fear, or dread. Servius says, the sole, or only obligation. Heyne takes *superstitio* for *religio, et metus ex ea ortus Reddita.* Servius takes this in the sense of *data* vel *facta.* Others take it to imply, imposed or retaliated upon the gods above, by the infernal gods : as if this fear, or dread of swearing by Styx, made the gods above subject, in their turn, to the gods below, as much as these latter are to the former.

819. *Tenetur :* withheld—prohibited.

820. *Tuorum.* The Latin kings derived their descent from Saturn, the brother of Jove.

822. *Component :* in the sense of *constituent.*

823. *Indigenas :* natives—those born in the country.

825. *Vocem :* language. The meaning is : do not order the men to change their language, or their dress.

827. *Romana propago sit :* let the Roman offspring be powerful, by Italian valor : i. e. let all the future glory and grandeur of the Romans be grafted on the valor of the Latins. *Propago :* in the sense of *proles.*

829. *Repertor :* in the sense of *auctor* vel *pater.*

830. *Et germana Jovis :* Ruæus and some others read *es*, in the place of *et.* Heyne reads *et.*

831. *Volvis :* why dost thou roll such mighty, &c.

832. *Submitte :* restrain—curb.

833. Victusque *tuis precibus*

Do, quod vis; et me, victusque volensque, remitto
Sermonem Ausonii patrium moresque tenebunt:

835. Corpore *Latini populi*

Utque est, nomen erit: commixti corpore tantùm
Subsident Teucri: morem ritusque sacrorum
Adjiciam: faciamque omnes uno ore Latinos.

838. Videbis genus *ortum* hinc

Hinc genus, Ausonio mixtum quod sanguine surget,
Supra homines, supra ire Deos pietate videbis.
Nec gens ulla tuos æquè celebrabit honores.
Annuit his Juno, et mentem lætata retorsit
Intereà excedit cœlo, nubemque reliquit.

843. Genitor *Deorum* ipse

His actis, aliud genitor secum ipse volutat
Juturnamque parat fratris dimittere ab armis

845. Dicuntur *esse* geminæ

Dicuntur geminæ pestes, cognomine Diræ;
Quas, et Tartaream Nox intempesta Megæram,
Uno eodemque tulit partu; paribusque revinxit
Serpentum spiris, ventosasque addidit alas.
Hæ Jovis ad solium, sævique in limine regis
Apparent, acuuntque metum mortalibus ægris,

851. Morbusque *hominibus*

Si quando letum horrificum morbosque Deûm rex
Molitur, meritas aut bello territat urbes.
Harum unam celerem demisit ab æthere summo
Jupiter, inque omen Juturnæ occurrere jussit.
Illa volat, celerique ad terram turbine fertur,
Non secùs, ac nervo per nubem impulsa sagitta;
Armatam sævi Parthus quam felle veneni,

NOTES.

833. *Remitto me:* I surrender myself—I give myself up to your entreaties and your tears.

834. *Sermonem:* in the sense of *linguam.*

836. *Subsident:* shall settle in Latium. Valpy says, "shall take the lower places." Heyne says, *infimum locum occupent. Morem ritusque:* in the sense of *modos ceremoniasque religionis.* This alludes to the introduction of the worship of the *Penates* and of *Vesta* into Italy, by Æneas. Heyne takes *sacrorum* in the sense of *religionis.*

837. *Uno ore:* of one language. The prep. *è* is understood. I will cause both nations to be incorporated under the general name of Latins, and to use one and the same language.

839. *Ire supra Deos.* This is a most extravagant compliment to the Cæsars, from the mouth of Jove. Ruæus says, *superare Deos*, in which Heyne agrees. Davidson says, "exalted above gods."

840. *Nec ulla gens.* Juno was highly honored among the Romans, particularly by the women. A magnificent temple was built to her upon mount Aventinus, in which Scipio deposited her statue that he brought from Carthage.

841. *Retorsit:* in the sense of *convertit.* Heyne says, *inflexit* vel *mutavit.*

845. *Diræ.* The furies were three in number, *Tisiphone, Megæra,* and *Alecto.* Two of them stand before the throne of Jove, to be the ministers of his vengeance upon guilty men. *Cognomine:* in the sense of *nomine.*

846. *Nox intempesta:* dead, inactive night, unseasonable for business, and when there is nothing stirring. Ruæus says, *profunda nox.*

848. *Ventosas alas:* wings of the wind—swift as the wind.

849. *Sævi regis. Sævus* is not the habitual character of Jove. It is only what he assumes, at times. The meaning is: *when he is in wrath.*

850. *Apparent:* they appear. They give their attendance, as the ministers of his will. *Acuunt:* in the sense of *excitant. Ægris.* Ruæus says, *miseris.*

852. *Meritas:* deserving, or meriting punishment—guilty. *Molitur:* in the sense of *parat.*

854. *In omen:* for an omen, or portentous sign. *Quasi portentum,* says Ruæus.

856. *Impulsa:* in the sense of *missa. Est* is understood. *Non secùs ac:* no otherwise than—just so as—just as.

857. *Felle sævi veneni:* with the essence of strong poison. Valpy says, "with bitter poison." Davidson renders the words, "with the quintessence of malignant poison." *Armatam:* imbued—impregnated—tinged. It was usual with barbarous nations to dip the point of their arrows, and other missive weapons, into poison, in order to render their wounds incurable. The Parthians were celebrated archers The

Parthus sive Cydon, telum immedicabile torsit;
Stridens, et celeres incognita transilit umbras.
Talis se sata Nocte tulit, terrasque petivit.
Postquam acies videt Iliacas, atque agmina Turni,
Alitis in parvæ subitò collecta figuram,
Quæ quondam in bustis, aut culminibus desertis
Nocte sedens, serùm canit importuna per umbras:
Hanc versa in faciem, Turni se pestis ad ora
Fertque refertque sonans, clypeumque everberat alis.
Illi membra novus solvit formidine torpor:
Arrectæque horrore comæ, et vox faucibus hæsit.
At, procul ut Diræ stridorem agnovit et alas,
Infelix crines scindit Juturna solutos,
Unguibus ora soror fœdans, et pectora pugnis.
Quid nunc te tua, Turne, potest germana juvare?
Aut quid jam miseræ superat mihi? quâ tibi lucem
Arte morer? talin' possum me opponere monstro?
Jam jam linquo acies. Ne me terrete timentem,
Obscœnæ volucres: alarum verbera nosco,
Letalemque sonum: nec fallunt jussa superba
Magnanimi Jovis. Hæc pro virginitate reponit?
Quò vitam dedit æternam? cur mortis adempta est
Conditio? Possem tantos finire dolores
Nunc certè, et misero fratri comes ire per umbras!
Immortalis ego! Aut quicquam mihi dulce meorum
Te sine, frater, erit! O quæ satìs alta dehiscat

858. Parthus, *inquam*. sive Cydon torsit *tanquam* immedicabile telum; *illa* stridens

862. *Illa* collecta *est* in

865. *Dira* pestis versa in

868. Comæ *sunt*

870. Ut Juturna infelix soror *Turni* procul agnovit

876. O *vos*, obscœnæ volucres

878. Reponit-*ne* hæc *mihi* pro virginitate *ereptâ*

883. Quicquam meorum *bonorum* erit dulce

NOTES.

word *Parthus*, by the repetition of it, is made emphatic.

858. *Immedicabile:* inflicting an incurable wound. *Cydon:* an inhabitant of the city Cydon, or Cydonia, in Crete, founded by a colony from Samos. *Hodie*, *Canea.* The Cretans were celebrated archers.

859. *Transilit:* in the sense of *transcurrit.*

860. *Sata:* in the sense of *nata* vel *filia.*

862. *Parvæ alitis:* of a small bird: small in comparison with the size of the goddess. *Subitò.* This is the common reading.—Heyne has *subitam.* *Collecta:* in the sense of *contracta.*

863. *Bustis:* in the sense of *sepulcris.*

864. *Importuna:* in the sense of *infausta.* The bird here meant is the owl, which is the only fowl that sings in the night. *Serùm:* late—in reference to the time of her singing.

866. *Pestis fertque:* the fury flies forward and backwards before the face of Turnus, screaming horribly. *Fertque refertque se:* she advances and retreats.

867. *Novus:* unusual—new. *Solvit:* in the sense of *debilitat.*

869. *Stridorem et alas:* in the sense of *stridorem alarum:* the noise, or whizzing of her wings.

871. *Fœdans:* tearing her face, &c.

872. *Quid*: Ruæus says, *quomodo.*

874. *Morer:* can I prolong. *Lucem:* in the sense of *vitam.*

875. *Jam, jam*, &c. This is in imitation of Homer, who makes Apollo quit the field just before Hector is slain by Achilles.—*Acies:* the fight—the field of battle.

876. *Obscœnæ:* inauspicious—of ill omen. *Verbera:* the strokes—flapping of your wings.

878. *Hæc reponit.* Jove had an amour with Juturna; and as a reward for her violated virginity, he conferred upon her immortality. See verse 141, supra. *Reponit* in the sense of *reddit* vel *dat.* *Superba:* in the sense of *sæva* vel *dura.*

879. *Adempta est:* taken away from me. *Quò:* why—for what purpose. Some copies have *cur.*

880. *Possem:* I wish I could—O! that I could end, &c.

881. *Certè:* at least—surely.

882. *Immortalis:* This is the reading of Heyne. Valpy and Ruæus read *mortalis.* This will make a difference in the sense. It will strip the words of any expression of strong passion on the part of Juturna. It implies that if she were mortal, she would accompany her brother to the shades below. *Aut:* Valpy and Ruæus read *haud.* Heyne reads *aut*, with an interrogation. Ruæus and Valpy read without any.

883. *Satìs alta:* sufficiently deep

Terra mihi, Manesque Deam demittat ad imos!
Tantum effata, caput glauco contexit amictu,
Multa gemens, et se fluvio Dea condidit alto.
Æneas instat contrà, telumque coruscat
Ingens, arboreum, et sævo sic pectore fatur:
Quæ nunc deinde mora est? aut quid jam, Turne, retractas?
Non cursu, sævis certandum est cominùs armis.
Verte omnes tete in facies; et contrahe quicquid
Sive animis, sive arte, vales: opta ardua pennis
Astra sequi, clausumque cavâ te condere terrâ.
Ille, caput quassans: Non me tua fervida terrent
Dicta, ferox: Dî me terrent, et Jupiter hostis.
Nec plura effatus; saxum circumspicit ingens,
Saxum antiquum, ingens, campo quod fortè jacebat,
Limes agro positus, litem ut discerneret arvis.
Vix illud lecti bis sex cervice subirent,
Qualia nunc hominum producit corpora tellus.
Ille manu raptum trepidâ torquebat in hostem,
Altior insurgens, et cursu concitus heros.
Sed neque currentem se, nec cognoscit euntem,
Tollentemve manu, saxumque immane moventem
Genua labant: gelidus concrevit frigore sanguis.
Tum lapis ipse viri, vacuum per inane volutus,
Nec spatium evasit totum, nec pertulit ictum.
Ac velut in somnis, oculos ubi languida pressit
Nocte quies, nequicquam avidos extendere cursus

885. Dea effata tantum

892. Opta *te* sequi

894. Ille *Turnus* quassans caput, *ait: O* ferox *hostis*

899. Vix bis sex lecti *homines* subirent illud *saxum*

901. Ille heros, insurgens altior, et concitus cursu torquebat *illud*

907. Nec evasit totum spatium viri, nec

NOTES.

884. *Demittat:* send me a goddess, &c. Ruæus says, *detrudet. Arboreum:* massy as a tree—like a tree.

890. *Certandum est:* the contest is to be decided in close fight, not at running. *Sævis:* in the sense of *duris.*

891. *Facies:* in the sense of *formas. Contrahe:* in the sense of *collige.*

892. *Opta:* desire—wish to ascend to. *Sequi:* in the sense of *ascendere.*

894. *Fervida:* in the sense of *superba.*

898. *Limes agro:* placed as a limit or boundary to the land. *Discerneret:* that it might terminate (prevent) disputes about the fields. Davidson says, "to distinguish the controverted bounds of the fields."

899. *Bis sex lecti,* &c. Here the poet had two passages of Homer in his eye: Iliad v. 302, where Diomede throws a stone at Æneas, such as two men in Homer's time could hardly have wielded: and Iliad, lib. xxi. 405, where Minerva gives Mars a blow with a stone that was set for a landmark. These, and some other imitations, discover less judgment and correctness, than is to be seen in the rest of the poet's works. This stone, which our hero wields with so much ease, the poet informs us was so large that twelve men, in his time, would have scarcely been able to carry it upon their shoulders! Homer makes his heroes throw stones when they have no other weapons. Turnus has his trusty sword, but there is no mention made of it. Jove prevents him from the use of it.

903. *Sed neque cognoscit se:* so disordered in his senses, that he does not perceive himself to be running, &c. The fury had deprived him not only of his strength of body, but of the powers of his mind. Heyne says, *videt solitas vires sibi deesse.*

905. *Concrevit:* hath congealed—grown thick. *Frigore:* may mean the fear and consternation, occasioned by the fury, by meton This appears better than to take it for cold or chillness. That idea is expressed by *gelidus.*

906. *Per vacuum inane:* moved through the empty air. *Inane:* in the sense of *aërem. Viri.* Servius connects *viri* with *lapis;* but it illy suits the place. Its proper place is after *spatium,* implying that the stone, passing or thrown through the air, did not go the whole distance to Æneas, but fell short of him, and consequently did not give him a blow. Ruæus connects *totum* with *ictum;* but improperly: for that would imply that the stone gave Æneas a partial stroke; but it is plain it did not hit him at all, since it did not reach him. Heyne takes *viri* with Servius, in the sense of *Turni.* Ruæus connects it with *spatium.*

909. *Avidos cursus:* the fond races—the

Velle videmur, et in mediis conatibus ægri
Succidimus: non lingua valet, non corpore notæ
Sufficiunt vires, nec vox nec verba sequuntur
Sic Turno, quâcunque viam virtute petivit,
Successum Dea Dira negat. Tum pectore sensus
Vertuntur varii. Rutulos aspectat et urbem;
Cunctaturque metu; telumque instare tremiscit.
Nec, quò se eripiat, nec quâ vi tendat in hostem,
Nec currus usquam, videt, aurigamque sororem.
  Cunctanti telum Æneas fatale coruscat,
Sortitus fortunam oculis; et corpore toto
Eminùs intorquet. Murali concita nunquam
Tormento sic saxa fremunt, nec fulmine tanti
Dissultant crepitus. Volat atri turbinis instar
Exitium dirum hasta ferens; orasque recludit
Loricæ, et clypei extremos septemplicis orbes:
Per medium stridens transit femur. Incidit ictus
Ingens ad terram duplicato poplite Turnus.
  Consurgunt gemitu Rutuli, totusque remugit
Mons circùm, et vocem latè nemora alta remittunt.
Ille humilis supplexque oculos, dextramque precantem,
Protendens, Equidem merui, nec deprecor, inquit:
Utere sorte tuâ. Miseri te si qua parentis
Tangere cura potest, oro, (fuit et tibi talis
Anchises genitor) Dauni miserere senectæ;
Et me, seu corpus spoliatum lumine mavis,
Redde meis. Vicisti: et victum tendere palmas
Ausonii vidêre: tua est Lavinia conjux.
Ulteriùs ne tende odiis. Stetit acer in armis

917. Nec videt quo eripiat
919. *Turno sic* cunctanti
931. Nec deprecor *mortem*
932. Si qua cura miseri parentis
933. Oro *ut tu* miserere
935. Et redde me meis *amicis sive vivum, seu tu* mavis, *redde meum* corpus

NOTES.

iaces on which we are intent, and eager in the pursuit.

910. *Ægri:* weak—faint from our great exertions. *Succidimus:* in the sense of *deficimus.*

911. *Notæ:* in the sense of *solitæ.* *Corpore:* in the sense of *corpori,* the dat.

913. *Quacunque virtute:* by whatever (efforts of) valor he sought the way of attacking Æneas, or of making his escape.

914. *Sensus:* thoughts. *Vertuntur:* in the sense of *volvuntur.*

916. *Cunctatur:* he hesitates—he knows not what to do—he is at a stand.

917. *Tendat:* in the sense of *irruat.*

919. *Coruscat:* in the sense of *vibrat.*

920. *Sortitus fortunam oculis:* Servius explains these words thus: *Æneas oculis elegit hunc locum ad feriendum, quem fortuna destinaverat vulneri. Fortunam* in this sense, is of the same import with *locum vulneris.* Heyne is of the same opinion. Ruæus says, *opportunitatem.*

921. *Murali tormento:* this was an engine, or machine for battering the walls of cities, and for throwing missive weapons. *Concita:* thrown, or sent.

923. *Nec tanti crepitus:* nor do such mighty peals burst from the thunder. *Crepitus:* properly a roaring or crashing. *Dissultant:* in the sense of *eduntur* vel *excitantur.* *Instar:* like a black whirlwind—swift as a whirlwind.

924. *Recludit:* opens or penetrates the extremity of his coat of mail. *Ora:* the edge or border of any thing. *Exitium:* in the sense of *mortem.*

925. *Extremos orbes:* by this we are to understand the lower part of the shield. *Septemplicis:* having seven folds or plates of brass.

926. *Ictus:* in the sense of *percussus,* vel *vulneratus.*

927. *Duplicato poplite:* upon his bended knee. Heyne says, *inflexo genu.*

929. *Remittunt:* echo—return the sound. *Vocem:* in the sense of *sonum.*

931. *Deprecor:* nor do I entreat that you should spare me.

932. *Sorte:* in the sense of *fortuna.* *Miseri:* in the sense of *infelicis.*

935. *Redde me meis,* &c. Turnus confesses himself vanquished; and entreats Æneas to send him back to his father and friends; but if he choose rather (*mavis*) to deprive him of life, in that case, that he would send

Æneas, volvens oculos, dextramque repressit.
Et jam jamque magìs cunctantem flectere sermo
Cœperat; infelix humero cùm apparuit alto
Balteus, et notis fulserunt cingula bullis,
Pallantis pueri; victum quem vulnere Turnus
Straverat, atque humeris inimicum insigne gerebat
Ille, oculis postquam sævi monumenta doloris,
Exuviasque hausit, furiis accensus et irâ
Terribilis: Tu-ne hinc spoliis, indute, meorum
Eripiare mihi? Pallas te hoc vulnere, Pallas
Immolat, et pœnam scelerato ex sanguine sumit.
Hoc dicens, ferrum adverso sub pectore condit
Fervidus. ast illi solvuntur frigore membra,
Vitaque cum gemitu fugit indignata sub umbras.

940. Sermo *Turni* cœperat flectere *Æneam* cunctantem

947. *Ait:* Tu-ne indute spoliis meorum *amicorum*

NOTES.

his dead body to them, that it might be treated according to the rites of his country.

940. *Flectere:* to turn or change him. Ruæus says, *commovere.*

941. *Infelix:* inauspicious—unfortunate. It had proved so to Pallas, whom Turnus slew: it now proves so to Turnus, who in turn is slain by Æneas. *Alto:* this is the reading of Heyne and Davidson. Ruæus and Valpy read *ingens*, referring to the belt (*balteus*) of Pallas, which Turnus wore upon his shoulders. *Alto:* refers to Turnus. This last is the best. *Bullis:* studs or bosses. Ruæus says, *clavis.*

943. *Pueri:* in the sense of *juvenis.*

944. *Insigne:* in the sense of *ornamentum.*

945. *Hausit oculis:* he saw. *Sævi doloris:* the death of Pallas caused excessive grief to Æneas; and from the moment that he heard of his fall, he vowed vengeance on Turnus. The sight of these memorials, these spoils, of his friend, roused him into fury. He had otherwise, perhaps, spared his suppliant. *Hausit:* in the sense of *vidit.*

947. *Indute:* voc. agreeing with *tu*, from the verb *induo:* clad. *Meorum:* of my friends: namely, Pallas.

948. *Eripiare:* the passive is here used in the sense of the middle voice of the Greeks: canst thou rescue thyself from my hands?

949. *Scelerato:* devoted. Ruæus says, *impio*, in reference to his having slain Pallas. Heyne is of the same opinion. *Immolat:* sacrifices you to the gods below.

951. *Fervidus:* in the sense of *ardens. Illi:* in the sense of *illius. Frigore:* with the chill of death.

952. *Indignata cum gemitu.* Heyne takes this in the sense simply of *gemens* vel *mærens.*

Mr. Davidson observes, the conclusion of this beautiful poem is unworthy of the dignity of the subject. And if Virgil had lived to finish it to his mind, he would, in all probability, have given it a more elegant termination.

QUESTIONS.

What is the condition of the troops of Turnus at the opening of this book?

What resolution does he take in consequence of that?

Does Latinus endeavor to dissuade him from the combat?

What is the character of his address to him?

What effect had it upon Turnus?

Does he refuse to give up Lavinia to Æneas?

What is the character of the reply of Turnus?

Is it characteristic of the soldier and the patriot?

Did the queen also, endeavor to dissuade him?

What arguments did she use for that purpose?

Did Lavinia hear this conversation of her mother with Turnus?

What effect had it upon her?

Did Turnus behold this blush upon her cheek?

Did he consider it indicative of her love?

What effect had it upon the hero?

What resolution did he instantly take?

Whom did he send to acquaint Æneas of that resolution?

When was the time appointed for the combat?

What did Turnus in the mean time?

What preparations were made upon the field?

For what purpose do they erect altars?

Who were the parties to this league?

What did Juno do to prevent its execution?

To what place does Juturna repair?
Whose form does she assume?
What is her object in repairing to the field of battle?
What effectually roused the Rutulians to arms?
What was that prodigy or omen?
Who was the first to observe it?
How did Tolumnius interpret it?
Who was this Tolumnius? What effect had this upon the minds of the Italians?
Who cast the first javelin? Whom did it kill?
What immediately followed?
What became of Latinus?
What did Æneas upon this emergency?
Was he wounded? Is it known by whom that wound was inflicted?
What effect had this upon the Trojans?
At this juncture, what course did Turnus take?
What feats of valor does the hero perform?
Who were among the first that he killed?
What became of Æneas?
Who attempted to extract the arrow?
Who was this Iapis?
By whom is it said, he was instructed in the healing art?
Was he able to effect a cure?
By whom was the hero finally cured?
Where did Venus obtain the plant?
What is the name of it?
What was the state of the battle, while Æneas was in his camp?
When he returned to the fight, was the scale of victory turned?
Whom does he seek to engage?
Is he prevented from meeting with Turnus?
By whom is he prevented?
How did she accomplish it?
At this juncture, what is the state of the battle?
Finding himself baffled by Turnus, what resolution does Æneas take?
What did he do previous to the assault?
Having animated his men, did they take possession of the city?
Where was Turnus in the mean time?
What effect had this upon the queen?
What became of her?
Who brought the news to Turnus of the capture of the city, and the death of the queen?
What effect had it upon his mind?
What course did he take?
Upon the arrival of Turnus, did the Trojans instantly desist from the assault?
How did the heroes commence the combat?
After that, what did they do?
What misfortune happened to Turnus?
Had he omitted to take his own sword?
By whom was his sword made?
How did he save his life at that juncture?
Was he pursued by Æneas?
Did he call for his heavenly tempered sword?
By whom was it restored to him?
What favor did Venus do for Æneas at the same time?
Having recovered their arms; do the heroes prepare for a second assault?
At this moment, which side did Jove favor?
What course did he pursue?
Whom did he send to the field of battle?
What form did the fury assume?
What does she do?
What effect had her sound upon Juturna?
What did she instantly do?
Did she utter any tender expressions for her brother?
What effect had the fury upon Turnus?
Æneas calls upon Turnus no longer to decline the fight; and what reply does he make him?
Does he express any signs of fear for him?
Whom then does he fear?
Does Turnus forget that he has his trusty sword?
With what does he attempt to assault Æneas?
What was the size of the stone?
Did it reach his antagonist?
Why did it not?
At this moment, what did Æneas do?
Did the spear wound Turnus?
Where did it wound him?
Does he acknowledge himself conquered?
Does he relinquish his claim upon Lavinia?
What favor does he ask of the victor?
Was he about to spare his life also?
Why did he not spare it?
What does Mr. Davidson observe of the ending of this book?

PUBLII VIRGILII MARONIS OPERUM.

FINIS.

A TABLE OF REFERENCE

TO THE NOTES.

The abbreviations Ecl., Geor., and Æn., stand for *Eclogue*, *Georgic*, and *Æneid*. Thus, Ecl. iv. 32, refers to the fourth Eclogue, and note upon the thirty-second line: and Geor. iii. 7, refers to the third book of the Georgics, and note upon the seventh line: and so of the Æneid.

A.

Q.

R.

S.

Æ.

Œ.

www.ingramcontent.com/pod-product-compliance
Lightning Source LLC
LaVergne TN
LVHW021058110826
845150LV00001B/110

* 9 7 8 1 4 2 5 5 6 6 4 0 1 *